ART AND ARCHITECTURE OF LATE MEDIEVAL PILGRIMAGE IN NORTHERN EUROPE AND THE BRITISH ISLES

TEXTS

EDITED BY

SARAH BLICK AND RITA TEKIPPE

BRILL
LEIDEN · BOSTON
2005

On the cover: Friedrich Herlin, *Altarpiece of St. James* (*c.* 1480-90), St. James' Church, Rothenburg ob der Tauber. Photo: Ulrich Großmann.

Brill Academic Publishers has done its best to establish rights to use of the materials printed herein. Should any other party feel that its rights have been infringed we would be glad to take up contact with them.

This book is printed on acid-free paper.

Library of Congress Cataloging-in-Publication Data

Art and architecture of late medieval pilgrimage in Northern Europe and the British Isles / edited by Sarah Blick and Rita Tekippe.
   p. cm. — (Studies in medieval and reformation traditions, ISSN 1573-4188 ; v. 104)
   Includes bibliographical references and index.
   ISBN 90-04-12332-6 (hardback : alk. paper)
   1. Christian art and symbolism—Europe, Northern—Medieval, 500-1500. 2. Christian art and symbolism—England—Medieval, 500-1500. 3. Pilgrims and pilgrimages—Europe, Northern. 4. Pilgrims and pilgrimages—England. I. Blick, Sarah. II. Tekippe, Rita. III. Series.

N7942.A77 2004
263'.0424'0902—dc22

N
7942
.A77
2005
v.1

2004054554

ISSN 1573-4188
ISBN 90 04 12332 6

PRINTED IN THE NETHERLANDS

ART AND ARCHITECTURE OF LATE MEDIEVAL PILGRIMAGE IN NORTHERN EUROPE AND THE BRITISH ISLES

STUDIES IN MEDIEVAL AND REFORMATION TRADITIONS

History, Culture, Religion, Ideas

FOUNDED BY HEIKO A. OBERMAN †

EDITED BY

ANDREW COLIN GOW, Edmonton, Alberta

IN COOPERATION WITH

THOMAS A. BRADY, Jr., Berkeley, California
JOHANNES FRIED, Frankfurt
BRAD GREGORY, University of Notre Dame, Indiana
BERNDT HAMM, Erlangen
SUSAN C. KARANT-NUNN, Tucson, Arizona
JÜRGEN MIETHKE, Heidelberg
M. E. H. NICOLETTE MOUT, Leiden
GUSTAV HENNINGSEN, Copenhagen

VOLUME CIV

SARAH BLICK AND RITA TEKIPPE

ART AND ARCHITECTURE OF LATE MEDIEVAL PILGRIMAGE
IN NORTHERN EUROPE AND THE BRITISH ISLES

We dedicate this volume to the two wonderful people who encouraged our studies and became our models for scholarship and gracious generosity;

Brian Spencer, F.S.A. and Dr. Christine Verzár

CONTENTS

PART III

EXPERIENCE AND ICONOGRAPHY AT PILGRIMAGE
CENTERS: DISCERNING MEANING

PART IV

CONNECTIONS TO JERUSALEM AND THE HOLY
JERUSALEM THROUGH PILGRIMAGE SITES

PART V

PILGRIM SOUVENIRS: MEANING AND FUNCTION

PART VI

COMMON CAUSE FOR MEDIEVAL CHRISTIANS:
POLITICS AND PRACTICALITIES OF CULT
DEVELOPMENT

ACKNOWLEDGEMENTS

It is with enormous gratitude that we thank the following at Brill Academic Press: Julian Deahl for proposing this volume and encouraging our interests, Marcella Mulder and Irene van Rossum for kindness in fielding our many questions, and Boris van Gool for ably handling the production of this massive collection of essays. We are indebted to the International Congress of Medieval Studies at Kalamazoo, Michigan for providing avenue for our many sessions on pilgrimage and for creating the arena for us to meet with so many like-minded scholars. We would also like to thank Kenyon College for the subvention from the Faculty Development Grant fund which allowed us to considerably expand the number of pictures in the volume. And we are indeed grateful to our 25 fellow authors who generously agreed to share their myriad insights and ideas regarding pilgrimage art.

Individually, we would like to thank the people and institutions which facilitated various phases of our work on this volume.

Sarah: I would like to thank my co-editor and friend Rita Tekippe who advised, helped, and inspired me every step of the way. I would also like to thank my friends and colleagues Melissa Dabakis, Eugene Dwyer, Carmen King, Ellen Mankoff, Mary M. Pepple, and Kristen Van Ausdall who patiently listened to me go on about pilgrimage art for several years, graciously read over drafts, and suggested numerous ideas and useful criticisms. My special thanks to my husband John F. Pepple, my friend Karen M. Gerhart, and my father Boris Blick who did all of the above, supporting me with good cheer (and much patience) throughout the entire process.

Rita: I am quite thankful for having Sarah Blick as my co-editor, colleague, and friend. Our collaboration has been felicitous and productive and our efforts and talents have dovetailed rather nicely. I am grateful for support and encouragement from my current institution, the State University of West Georgia, as well as my former one, the University of Central Arkansas, both of which have funded travel and research connected with this work. I am appreciative of many forms of help and support from my chairs Bruce Bobick, Ken Burchett, and colleagues, especially Pam Loos-Noji, Dorothy Joiner,

Jeanne Nemeth, Eilis Crean, and Debrah Santini. And I am blessed with the most patient and encouraging of families, particularly Byron and Chris Tekippe, Mary and Fred Goerke, Ann and Mike Gallagher, and Jim and JoAnn Wardein.

INTRODUCTION

Scope and Focus of the Volume

In the Middle Ages, enormous numbers of people went on pilgrimage. The village of Wilsnack with a population of only 1,000 swelled when 100,000 pilgrims arrived every year. On one day in 1392, residents counted the incoming pilgrims at Munich by dropping peas into a bowl, with an ultimate total of 40,000. In 1492, Aachen welcomed 142,000 eager pilgrims into their city in a single day. Obviously pilgrimage was a significant medieval social event, which found favor among both the elite and the greater populace. We define pilgrimage as travel by to visit a holy site, over long or short distances. Even when the travel occurred in the mind alone—all modes were perceived as pilgrimage at one time or place or another, in the later Middle Ages. The idea of life itself as a pilgrimage, deriving from Christian thought, became a prominent theme in literature, popularized in such works as *Piers Plowman* and the *Pilgrimage of Life*.[1] Everyone went on pilgrimage. Rich and poor, young and old, healthy and afflicted, educated and ignorant, all took part, and pilgrimage dwelt and thrived in the popular practice and imagination (even ghosts sometimes went on such trips). Yet despite the literary legacy of this theme, actual accounts of pilgrimage are few and far between— one catches glimpses of it in cathedral financial records,[2] in lawsuits against pilgrim badge artisans,[3] and in a 1448 account of a procession in which the presence of a little-known reliquary is recounted.[4] Mention of group pilgrimage supplements the record somewhat, but

---

[1] Dee Dyas, *Pilgrimage in Medieval English Literature, 700–1500* (Woodbridge, UK, 2001).

[2] Ben Nilson, *Cathedral Shrines of Medieval England* (Woodbridge, UK, 1998).

[3] Esther Cohen, "*In haec signa*: Pilgrim-badge Trade in Southern France," *Journal of Medieval History* 2: 193–214.

[4] John Stone, *The Chronicle of John Stone*, ed. W.G. Searle, *Cambridge Antiquarian Society*, 34 (1902), p. 44. Here the reliquary of St. Fleogild is translated to the beam between the shrine of St. Thomas Becket and the corona chapel in Canterbury Cathedral.

without presenting a clear picture.[5] Thus, the burden of explaining pilgrimage and discerning how pilgrims experienced the holy can be greatly elucidated by examination of the surviving visual culture— the art and architecture created to direct and enhance the pilgrimage experience.

Was there such a thing as "pilgrimage art?" While it is true that churches were built along the pilgrimage roads which housed many fine containers fashioned for relics which were known goals of pilgrim travels, these churches also had many artistic features not directly associated with pilgrimage, and since all consecrated churches had relics, the presence of a lavish reliquary did not necessarily denote a site of pilgrimage. Rather, the ways in which objects or buildings were used and regarded allows us to designate them as "pilgrimage art." Basically, any form of visual culture that was apparently intended to enhance, transmit, or direct a pilgrim's experience at a particular sacred site allows us to identify it thusly. With such a broad definition, not surprisingly, the associated artwork is quite varied, but just as the definition of pilgrimage was elastic in the Middle Ages, so too was that of artwork created to form and respond to the event.

People participated in religious devotion in myriad ways. Some approached their religious life with devout, spiritual longing, while others were guided more by convention or compunction. In like manner, artwork answered to disparate needs and purposes. Feretory shrines tended to take on similar shape, but their individual iconography differed in response to particular cult interests. In this volume, we seek to grapple with this diversity by looking beyond the previous focus on the major shrines of Jerusalem, Santiago de Compostela, and Rome—to regional shrines, both major and minor, in northern Europe and England from the early second millennium to the era of the Reformation. These scholars examine the artwork of shrines in the larger context of political and social changes that frame the basic impulses of pilgrimage. Their studies reveal the surprising variety in material culture, spurred by the needs and desires of pilgrims and the communities where the shrine sites were kept. We have deliberately excluded the rich traditions of Italian, Middle Eastern, and Byzantine pilgrimage art, focusing on objects and buildings heretofore neglected or, for those studied previously, presenting new

---

[5] See Rita Tekippe's essay in this volume.

and different explorations here. From our own interest and work on this topic, we sought out other scholars who were working on pilgrimage art, particularly from the later Middle Ages in northern Europe and the British Isles. We organized several sessions at the International Congress on Medieval Studies in Kalamazoo, Michigan, and discovered a groundswell of research by both senior and junior scholars. We hope that the many and varied essays here reflect the beginning of sustained investigation on this fascinating topic, yielding insight into the hopes and dreams of medieval people and their devotion. Because this subject reflects the interests and practices of diverse strata and segments of the population, scholars try to understand the function and reception of artwork created for diverse audiences. But pilgrimage art is an enormous topic and although this is a large collection of essays, it only scratches the surface of this mammoth subject. Our fondest hope is to stimulate thought and to spawn further lively discussion.

Pilgrimage and Art

Previous scholars of pilgrimage have ably recounted the theoretical underpinnings and motivations for pilgrimage, so that it is not necessary to repeat their results here in detail. Most examine the influential work of Victor and Edith Turner, who asserted that pilgrims, in leaving their familiar surroundings and life, entered a *communitas* where the normally all-embracing social hierarchies were shed and, in the practice of devotion, became equals. Later scholars have either challenged this theory or found evidence to support and expand some of their premises.[6] These divergent views stem from the variety of pilgrim experiences, so any episode or example selected at random may fail to sustain generalization for long. As each pilgrimage experience and pilgrimage site encompassed a multiplicity of factors, it

---

[6] Victor Turner, *The Ritual Process: Structure and Anti-Structure* (London, 1969) and Victor and Edith Turner, *Image and Pilgrimage in Christian Culture: Anthropological Perspectives* (Oxford, 1978). For commentary on these, see (eds.) John Eade and Michael J. Sallnow *Contesting the Sacred: The Anthropology of Christian Pilgrimage* (London, 1991); (ed.) Jennie Stopford, Pilgrimage Explored (York, 1999), p. xii. There are many others, particularly in the field of anthropology, some of which are cited in essays here.

can be argued that no singular, unified pilgrimage art existed. Rather, art and architecture responded to pilgrimage needs in a multifaceted manner.

The popular view of pilgrimage suggests that a "pilgrim" would choose among the "big three"—Jerusalem, Santiago de Compostela, and Rome—but we now know that numerous pilgrim sites were found in every region and that they differed widely from one another. What might be useful or compelling at an internationally-known shrine, such as Santiago de Compostela, might be useless or confusing for a smaller regional center, such as the English shrine to St. Aethelryth in Ely Cathedral. Not only did the artwork vary from site to site, but within the life of any shrine, the art and architecture reflected the changing needs over time. Like many aspects of material culture, works of art were transformed in response to such stimuli as political machinations, swirling social changes, competition of other shrines, waxing interest in private devotion, and stylistic trends.

The great richness and diversity of this social and religious phenomenon is perhaps revealed more clearly by the examination of material culture than by the written documents. Although the latter are better understood, pilgrimage was always a largely visual experience. The relative silence of extant records about the existence of large-scale objects (such as the walkable labyrinth at Chartres) or those which became remarkably numerous (like pilgrim souvenirs) challenges scholars to look beyond written sources for additional data. The story of pilgrimage and its practice cannot be told without thoughtful consideration of the visual culture developed to enhance and propagate the cults of saints in Europe. These physical objects helped the pilgrim to experience the sacred place. Certain aspects of pilgrimage sites signaled nuances of meaning and importance to visitors. The architectural forms, shrines, altars, wall paintings, stained glass, and sculpture coalesced; dignifying and enhancing the sacred spaces, thereby eliciting appropriate responses from devotees.

Works of art were used to direct pilgrims into specific areas of the church, to tell them where to go next, and to focus their attention on various significant features. Elements of the theatrical can be seen in the art: sculptural capitals directed a pilgrim's view, canopies were lifted to reveal the sparkling feretory, or carved doorways framed a pilgrim's view of a miraculous sculpture. The movement, music and chanting, colors of the windows, paintings, hangings, and the smells of incense and beeswax burning all collaborated to make this an extraordinary event. Above all, this compelling experience was mediated by the visual.

Art and its emphasis at pilgrimage centers were likely to change, as Simon Coleman and John Elsener noted: "[T]hink of [pilgrimage] not so much as a static and constant entity but rather as a shifting constellation of features, often familiar from other contexts."[7] In this regard, what was artistically effective to direct the spiritual response in one area in one time period could change or disappear, since active cults involved a continual urge to express new ideas. Custodians of cult sites might observe what was successful at another center and try to emulate it to achieve a similar effect. Any particular artwork created at a given time might accrue different implications in other times or circumstances. For instance, the twelfth-century portal sculpture at St. Pierre in Moissac depicting Christ at the Apocalypse, was read by locals in the mid-fourteenth century as picturing Clovis and his court, with the encouragement of the monks of the Abbey who emphasized the cult of St. Clovis at this time.[8]

At times, the textual tradition informed and shaped the experience, while at others the sumptuous decoration and complicated iconography orchestrated the experience of the fascinated pilgrim. Monastic guides at Canterbury, for example, helped the pilgrims understand the images in the stained glass in Trinity Chapel by reading miracle stories to them beforehand. The windows, then, with their clearly-explained stories helped the pilgrims comprehend that the miracles had occurred in that very church and led them to see themselves as eligible for the sacred assistance of St. Thomas Becket. Similarly, the Xylographic book of St. Servatius helped pilgrims destined for his Maastricht shrine to anticipate and preview their visit, and then it assisted them in re-living their experience after their departure, as did some of the pilgrim souvenirs which replicated features of the pilgrimage center. Images made the inaccessible, accessible; they illustrated the non-visible, the ethereal, the infinite (such as the Eucharistic mystery or the heavenly court of Christ) by explaining and sometimes endlessly reproducing aspects of the material and the finite.

---

[7] Simon Coleman and John Elsener , *Pilgrimage Past and Present in the World Religions*, (Cambridge, MA, 1995), p. 205.

[8] R.N. Swanson, *Religion and Devotion in Europe, c. 1215–c. 1515* (Cambridge, 1995), p. 89.

Visual literacy was carefully cultivated among the faithful, and images themselves began to show appropriation of the power accorded to relics and saints, whose presence became more widespread as they resided not only where their relics could be found, but also where their images were displayed.[9] This was especially desirable for cults that emphasized devotion to Christ and the Virgin Mary, who ostensibly had left fewer relics to revere. Indeed, pilgrimages paid for in medieval wills were most often focused on local sites where devotion was based on an image rather than a relic.[10] The experience of the sacred could be brought to the worshiper and the worshiper to the sacred by means of envisioning those sacred images and places. Through the power of artistic imagery, in a great variety of forms, ranging from the magnificent to the most humble, Christians of every class and station could participate in the spiritual experience of pilgrimage in the proximity of the sacred locus, or from a physically-distant vantage point. Art allowed and induced greater participation by all the laity.

The overall relationship of the Church to the disenfranchised classes was complex and varied, as the institution and its representatives sometimes served as a buffer against secular power, while at other times it embodied and sustained the political structure which oppressed them. However, relic cults and pilgrimage centers reached out to the peasantry in ways that made them incredibly popular, often through works of art used to attract and nourish the fervor of devotion. The Church was, occasionally, the peasants' protector against the encroachment of their land and their freedom by the military aristocracy.[11] Even when clergy wished to spurn rustic people, the requirements of sustaining a popular pilgrimage forced their interaction. For instance, the *Book of Miracles of St. Foy* (1020) relates a story of a large group of peasant pilgrims were denied access to the church lest they disturb the dignified vigils by singing crude songs and generating a noisy tumult. Yet, thanks to the wishes of the saint

---

[9] André Vachez, *Sainthood in the Later Middle Ages* trans. Jean Birrell (Cambridge, 1997), p. 448, 452.

[10] Eamon Duffy, *The Stripping of the Altars: Traditional Religion in England, c. 1400–c. 1580* (New Haven, 1992), p. 167

[11] Pierre Bonnassie, "From One Servitude to Another: The Peasantry of the Frankish Kingdom at the Time of Hugh Capet and Robert the Pious (987–1031)" in *From Slavery to Feudalism in South-Western Europe* (Cambridge, 1991) trans. Jean Birrell, pp. 307–8.

interred there, manifested by the locked doors miraculously springing open, the peasant folk were allowed entry. The opposing forces
of educated clerics and simple peasants, was eventually reconciled
and merged at the pilgrimage site, as evidenced by the eleventh-century monk's account.[12] The appealing architecture, sculpture, and
reliquaries created for the Church of St. Foy helped make Conques
a very popular pilgrimage destination in the Middle Ages.

Another example of exclusion overcome by pilgrimage is the relationship of women to the cult of St. Cuthbert in Durham Cathedral.
Because of St. Cuthbert's reputed misogyny, a line was drawn on
the floor of the nave (beyond which stood the shrine) so that women
could not step near the most sacred part of the site.[13] Conflicting
with this stated prohibition were accounts of women pilgrims and
their gifts to the saint,[14] by which they were able to gain further
access to restricted areas of the monastic pilgrimage site. While such
disparate accounts and associated changes of practice, deplored by
some, are noted elsewhere, they were sometimes celebrated in artwork of the later Middle Ages,[15] as exemplified in the stained glass
windows of York Minster where women pilgrims are repeatedly shown
at the shrine of St. William.[16]

Saintly cults evolved and new types of devotion arose in response
to changing theological ideas and popular needs. Devotion to the
Virgin and relics associated with her flourished, as did new kinds of
piety which focused on Christ (Eucharist, Five Wounds, etc.) and on
new saints, all of which contributed to vital and flourishing religious
practice. For instance, there are almost a third as many pilgrim
badges from the fifteenth-century cult of Henry VI (which lasted fifty
years) as there are for that of Thomas Becket, spanning three and
a half centuries, from 1171–1538.[17] Such changes could originate

---

[12] Bernard of Angers, *Liber miraculorum sancte Fidis*, ed. by A. Bouillet (Paris, 1897)II,
12, pp. 120–2; Bonnaise "From One Servitude to Another, " p. 301, fn. 58. For
other examples of lay pilgrim access to monastic choirs, see Nilson, *Cathedral Shrines*,
p. 94.
[13] V. Tudor, "The Misogyny of St. Cuthbert," *Archaeologia Aeliana*, 5th series, 12
(1984): 158–64.
[14] Durham, Dean and Chapter Archive, Feretrars' Rolls, for 1397, 1401; Nilson,
Cathedral Shrines, p. 95,
[15] Burton, *Chronica Monasterii de Melsa*, vol., pp. 35–6.
[16] Thomas French, *York Minster: The St. William Window* (Oxford, 1999), figs. 11e,
16e, 17c & e, etc.
[17] Spencer, "Henry VI," p. 238; Eamon Duffy, *Stripping of the Altars*, p. 195.

within the ranks of the clergy, while at other times the Church responded to popular sentiment with images reflecting the heightened emotion of a popular cult, further stimulating devotion and pilgrimage. Images were also used to explicate the occasionally complicated notions behind certain novel forms of piety. At Wilsnack, three host wafers were found to have miraculously survived a fire and to bear spots of blood—which was further explained by the imagery found on Wilsnack pilgrim badges where tiny pictures showed Christ as tied to a scourging pillar to be whipped, then crucified, and then resurrected. These visual images intertwined with an earlier, abstract idea of the Eucharist to symbolize Christ's bodily suffering.

With the development of a prosperous pilgrimage site in one's town, which offered so much in the way of sacred protection, social prestige, and potential wealth, it behooved many churches across Europe, from parish to monastery to cathedral, to create or enhance the reputation of the powerful relics held in their treasuries or displayed on their altars. This was accomplished through the addition of sumptuous decoration of church buildings and the creation of lavish reliquaries and shrine accoutrements, by establishment of popular rites and practices, by promoting visitation through broadsides, badges and, especially, the publicizing of miracles and blessings which the saint had wrought. For example, with the rise of popular devotion to the North Marston rector John Schorne († 1315), the parish church in which he had preached was enlarged through pilgrim offerings.[18] Schorne's image survives on English rood screen paintings, stained-glass windows,[19] and pilgrim souvenirs from the fifteenth and early sixteenth centuries. In order to attract pilgrims and their pious offerings, in 1478 the Dean of Windsor successfully petitioned to have Schorne's cult moved to Windsor and placed in the St. George Chapel. A shrine was built and manuscript illuminations dedicated, evoking an enormous response that brought in funds to complete the building.[20]

---

[18] At Gateley, Cawston, Bury St. Edmunds, and Sudbury. W.H. Kelke, "Master John Schorne," *Records of Buckinghamshire* vol. 3 (1869): 60–74; W. Sparrow Simpson, "Master John Schorne," *Records of Buckinghamshire* vol. 3 (1870): 354–69.; Brian Spencer (1998), pp. 192–5

[19] J.L. Nevison and J.A. Hudson, "Sir John Schorne and his Boot" *Country Life* vol. 131, no. 3391 (March 1, 1962): 467–8.

[20] Spencer (1998), p. 193; W. H. St. John Hope, *Windsor Castle* (1913), vol. 2,

Many pilgrimages were of short duration, lasting a few weeks or even only a few days.[21] Large groups of pilgrims (*ad hoc* like those of Chaucer's pilgrims or purposefully-gathered companies of people from the same town or same guild) journeyed along well-known roads, as did many solitary travelers. Companions made the trip a more festive and less individually-focused experience. The aims of communal pilgrimage were not only support and protection on the road, but also communal prayer for their own souls and those of their townsmen, their guild fellows, and their families, commonly fulfilling shared duties in obligatory visits to cathedral or mother church. What was potent for the individual blended with what was relevant for the community in the pilgrimage experience; one could pray for one's own soul and the alleviation of punishment in Purgatory, but how much more charitable and emotional it was to join in common prayer for others in the Christian community. As the numbers of pilgrims increased exponentially in the later Middle Ages, so churches responded to these crowds and to new ideas associated with pilgrimage with enhanced forms of art and architecture to meet the physical and spiritual needs. And increasing numbers of churches sought to attract the traveling throngs by promoting locally-venerated saints with the aid of newly-commissioned imagery, architectural embellishments, and accommodations for visitors.

Annual obligations to visit the bishop's church or that of a designated surrogate, as well as well-developed allegiances to particular saints, fraternal parishes or monasteries, led certain groups of parishioners, priests, or monks to undertake processional pilgrimage on regular or occasional bases. Many such ceremonies, including more-or-less elaborate liturgical equipment, shrines, costumes, and banners, evolved into strongly impressive and influential visual display of performative art, in their own right.

---

p. 411. The dedicated book of hours is illustrated in Alan Coldwells, *St. George's Chapel Windsor Castle* (Norwich, 1993), fig. 49.

[21] Denis Bruna, "La diffusion des enseignes de pèlerinage," in *Pèlerinage et croisades: Actes du 118e Congrès de la Société Historiques et Scientifiques* (Paris, 1995): 201–14; Ronald C. Finucane, *Miracles and Pilgrims: Popular Beliefs in Medieval England* (New York, 1995), pp. 164–70.

I. *The Pilgrim's Journey: Vision and Reality*

Sometimes, artwork was designed to create and shape the hopes and beliefs of pilgrims, while at other times particular works helped to fulfill their expectations by marking the goal of the excursion and giving physical form to spiritual aims. Indeed, anticipation colored the actual pilgrimage, and visual features helped to intensify the experience. What did pilgrims foresee for their journeys? How were their expectations formed and what role did material culture play in these envisionings? Word of mouth, actual exemplars, and literature helped to mold these concepts. The works of art and other aspects of material culture also framed both the actual and the imagined encounter.

Many items of pilgrim attire, including souvenirs helped create an image of a "typical" pilgrim in artwork and in reality. How much correspondence existed between the garb of actual pilgrims and the depictions in such representations? Did costumes vary by class or gender? As Anja Grebe explains in the first essay of this volume, "Pilgrims and Fashion: The Functions of Pilgrims' Garments," (Chapter 1) the emergent concept of pilgrim garb and the evidence from surviving pilgrims' costumes sometimes diverged. She explores how a pilgrim's identity was apparent in the popular clothing of travelers of the day, known from surviving clothes and from pictures.

The notion of visualization and conceptualization as an impetus in private devotion became popular in the later Middle Ages, as exemplified in some works of pilgrimage art. Through contemplation of particular imagery, devotees hoped to conjure glimpses of God in anticipation of heaven and the beatific vision.[22] In a 599 letter, Gregory the Great stated "We do no harm in wishing to show the invisible by means of the visible."[23] Controversy about undue attention to visually-impressive expressions of devotion waxed and waned through the medieval era. Bernard of Clairvaux's complaints about

---

[22] Hans Belting, *Likeness and Presence: A History of the Image before the Era of Art* trans. Edmund Jephcott (Chicago, 1994), p. 209. The importance of visualization is cited in many works. See Colin Morris, "Introduction," in Colin Morris and Peter Roberts eds., *Pilgrimage: The English Experience from Becket to Bunyan* (Cambridge, 2002), p. 5, fn. 8 for an extensive bibliography.

[23] Gregory the Great, Lib. IX, *Epistola IX Ad Serenum Eposcopum Massiliensum* in *PL* 77, cols. 1128–9 trans. David Freedberg, *The Power of Images: Studies in the History and Theory of Response* (Chicago, 1989), p. 164.

visual frills in the monastic context are well-known,[24] but Thomas
Aquinas defended images in the church by observing that they could
"excite emotions which are more effectively aroused by things seen
than by things heard."[25] Visualizing Christ, particularly in his suffering,
was part of a strong affective and active piety. By meditating on the
sorrows one could empathize with the humanity of Christ, amplify-
ing compassion, understanding, and affection. By extension, images
of his mother and the saints who had proven their own Christian
piety in extraordinary ways could inspire the faithful, while depictions of saints and of other pilgrims stimulated real and imagined
spiritual journeys. The laity, responding to such prompts, could undertake mystical worship, and art could summon mystical pilgrimage,
through contemplation of an image and the journey it implied,
through contiguous landscapes and manipulation of space.

   Thus, a pilgrimage could be completed in the mind alone. Vida
J. Hull, in "Spiritual Pilgrimage in the Paintings of Hans Memling,"
(Chapter 2) examines this notion through the iconographic innovations which enhanced devotional function in Memling's paintings,
inviting a deep engagement of worshiper with the image, as artistic
interpretation of the late medieval devotional practice of "spiritual
pilgrimage." By representing a sequence of sacred stories within
panoramic views of the Holy Land and detailed landscape backgrounds, Memling induced the worshiper to travel spiritually in both
time and space, to participate mentally and visually in a series of
holy events. Jeanne Nuechterlein, in "Hans Memling's St. Ursula
Shrine: The Subject as Object of Pilgrimage," (Chapter 3) also probes
this artist's imagery of mental pilgrimage, where he de-emphasized
the status of the shrine as valuable physical object, focusing rather
on Ursula's journey itself, the act of moving through the landscape.
Taking viewers on a mental and visual excursion to other pilgrimage
centers across Europe, he bid the devotee to circumambulate the
shrine and follow the story in both body and soul, to look through
the object itself, and to envision and participate in the pilgrimage
that Ursula and her companions took.

---

[24] Bernard of Clairvaux, *Apologia ad Guillelmum* in *PL*, vol. CLXXXII, cols. 914–16;
Caecilia Weyer-Davis, *Early Medieval Art 300–1150, Sources and Documents* (Toronto,
1986), pp. 168–70.
[25] Thomas Aquinas, *Commentarium super libros sententiarum: Commentum in librum III*,
dist. 9, art. 2, qu. 2 trans. by Freedberg, *The Power of Images*, p. 162.

Claire Labrecque demonstrates the relationship between seeing and worshipping in "A Case Study of the Relationship between Painting and Flamboyant Architecture: The St. Espirit Chapel at Rue in Picardy," (Chapter 4) by noting that pilgrims there were bidden to mentally visit precincts and relics which were officially off-limits to most commoners. Displays were manipulated so that the visitor could gaze upon what they were not allowed to touch. The portal opening through which they viewed the Volto Sancto was decorated in the spirit of iconography and framing developed by Rogier van der Weyden, so that, in looking at the sacred image through this sculpture, pilgrims could internalize sacred moments and be transformed by the mental picture.

II. *Housing for Saints: Churches and Shrines*

Pilgrimage practice was defined not only by the physical boundaries of travel and the church building, but also by the intense visual experience induced by the fabric and decoration of the church, including frescos, stained glass windows, grand sculptural facades, tapestries, and the rich array of liturgical equipment. All combined to enhance the pilgrims' feelings of awe and respect and to teach them the legendary specifics regarding the particular shrine they had come to visit. These visual accoutrements were at the heart of pilgrimage cults. Fine appointments and rich reliquary shrines were a necessary component of appropriate respect, as many legends warned of dire consequences that occurred when a saint's relics were not properly housed, including the loss of the relics themselves. The sumptuous containers, shrines, and altarpieces told stories of the great saints, and their richness signified spiritual power. Precious metals and gems were believed to have intrinsic force which, when combined with potent imagery, became both an object for intense worship and the focus of contentious ecclesiastical and secular political struggles. Because of this, artists and their patrons found ways to interlace issues of legitimacy, identity, and nationalism with the more traditionally pious meanings of these objects. The intricate iconography of many reliquaries and shrines were designed by educated clerics who used them to explicate complicated mystical ideas: on one level the imagery spoke to educated clergy and on another level it educated neophytes about the mysteries inherent in their manifold symbolism.

Using the iconography of the reliquary, a town could claim rightful ownership of a cult or a relic that in reality they did not have, or local rulers could use the imagery to make it clear to pilgrims that they were closely associated with and blessed by saints and the Virgin Mary. Their carefully-chosen imagery emphasized portions of a hagiographic story that the church in which it resided wished to make known, while suppressing other aspects. It could, by iconographic association, make a claim of legitimacy stronger or try to erase problematical doubt as to its authenticity. The reliquary shrines' association with relics endowed these objects with authority on subjects religious or secular, as they were the main focus of the cultic practice. Thus, care for their fabric and use was a necessary custodial duty, but one which sometimes involved alteration of the original design and form of the containers. Some rather rough handling during ritual use—chasses were certainly dropped, bumped, and rubbed—caused many reliquaries to be re-done over the centuries.

Albert Lemeunier, in "The Eventful Lives of Two Mosan Châsses" (Chapter 5) examines the eventful and dramatic life of the reliquary shrines of Huy. The vicissitudes of their history is revealed in their shifting iconography, extensions, and reductions. He explores the possibilities for their original dispositions, while examining the various ways they were used over the centuries. In an essay which focuses on a particular iconographic program, Ilana Abend-David in "Architectural Representations on the Medallions of the Heribert Shrine" (Chapter 6) argues that the Heribert Shrine was ordered and produced not only for spiritual purposes, but as part of an effort to re-establish the financial strength of the abbey of Deutz. This was expressed in the use of particular architectural representations that emphasized the abbey's claim on the cult of Heribert and the local castle and fortifications which controlled the western entry into the city of Cologne. James Buglsag, in "Pilgrimage to Chartres Cathedral: The Visual Evidence," (Chapter 7) suggests that the oscillating extremes of our modern conceptions of Chartres as either a major pilgrimage site or as a center fairly devoid of pilgrimage traffic is over-simplified. By analyzing the visual evidence of the several cults at Chartres, he produces a compelling vision of a lively, but changing, pilgrimage goal focused on the Virgin, various saints, and devotion to the ancient waters.

III. *Experience and Iconography at Pilgrimage Centers: Discerning Meaning*

Church decoration not only guided movement through the site (through physical layout and emphatic visual punctuation), it also disclosed and explicated its peculiar mysteries (often subtle in persuasion that its interpretation revealed the truth). Pilgrims were invited to consider themselves as performative elements, and to see the iconographic juxtapositions which presented the theological ruminations about local issues and those which engaged the larger Christian audience. Specific pictorial programs differed widely among cult centers, even when concerned with apparently similar religious truths as were taken up at other sites. It is these distinctive visual presentations which helped the viewer to apprehend the peculiar aspects of a given saint, or the very specific message of local theology, often overlaid with local political messages.

The imagined pilgrim himself, with complex and rich implications, was depicted in traditional stories and in visual representations of bible stories, such as those which showed people on Judgment Day and on the Journey to Emmaus, where Christ joins earthly travelers in the guise of a fellow pilgrim, showing kinship in humanity. In "The Journey to Emmaus Capital at Saint-Lazare of Autun," (Chapter 8) William Travis explores the culture of travel and pilgrimage as it came to encompass Christ himself in the iconography of the Emmaus story in its depiction on the sculptural capital at Autun, serving to intensify the import of the pilgrimage message.

Reaching out to the community in which the saints resided is examined by M. Cecilia Gaposchkin in "Portals, Processions, Pilgrimage, and Piety: Saints Firmin and Honoré at Amiens." (Chapter 9) Focusing on the role of procession, she connects the imagery on the portals to popular local saints and the rites performed in their honor, as depicted with the more prominent Christian mysteries in the tympanum sculpture. She considers the implications of the exalted positions given to the saints and their rituals of veneration. Anne Harris also examines the influence of the relationship of a church and its visiting pilgrims when she proposes that the decoration and focus of the cult of Becket at Canterbury changed significantly from the elite to the popular in "Pilgrimage, Performance, and Stained Glass at Canterbury Cathedral." (Chapter 10) When pilgrims viewed the miracle windows in Trinity Chapel they saw themselves. Indeed, they were testament to all the accommodations that had been made for

popular pilgrimage: the introduction of vivid physical images in preference to the imagery of mystical metaphor; the performance of the
commemoration of the saint through re-enactments of his martyrdom; and miracles in lieu of his remembrance through typological
exploration.

IV. *Connections to Jerusalem and the Holy Jerusalem through Pilgrimage Sites*

The losses of the Holy Land in 1187 and again after 1240 had enormous repercussions politically and theologically, the most obvious of
which were embodied in the ongoing Crusades. These losses affected
access to the sacred sites directly associated with the Bible. But the
longing for contact with these places and with the holy people who
walked there was unabated. Thus, marvelous stories emerged in
which the holy people either traveled to Europe, or the Holy Land
sites were miraculously moved or replicated. For instance, we hear
that Mary Magdalene traveled in a rudderless boat to France, while
the body of St. James washed ashore in a stone boat on the coast
of Galicia. The Holy House where the Annunciation took place in
Bethlehem took flight to and landed in Loretto, Italy, and was then
replicated under the direction of the Virgin Mary (via a dream) in
Walsingham, England. A powerful and vibrant desire to link local
European sites with the Holy Land manifested itself repeatedly in
the art and architecture of late medieval northern Europe. Recollection
of the sacred sites of the Holy Land occurred in two ways: through
symbolic representations and through more-or-less faithful copies of
the original monuments or of select aspects of their physical disposition and their sense of import.

Daniel K. Connolly, in "At the Center of the World: The Labyrinth
Pavement at Chartres Cathedral," (Chapter 11) writes about the
function and meaning of the walkable labyrinth pavement as a sym-
bolic copy of the lost city of Jerusalem by examining the history of
such designs and their appearance in maps, manuscripts, and on the
floors of cathedrals in the Île-de-France. Such remembrances of
Jerusalem are also evident in the symbolic quotations found in the
French church discussed by Nora Laos in "The Architectural and
Iconographical Sources of the Church of Neuvy-Saint-Sepulcre."
(Chapter 12) The building there is an architectural palimpsest whose

changes over the years reflect wishes to conjure important Holy Land
monuments, including the Church of the Holy Sepulcher and the
Dome of the Rock.

Artisans who made reliquaries of the True Cross responded to
related impetus, but faced slightly different challenges. As Kelly
Holbert in "Relics and Reliquaries of the True Cross" (Chapter 13)
observes, these containers which enclosed a precious object from the
Holy Land, were designed to effectively glorify their relic and to tell
its story. In her essay, she explores the beginnings of the Legend of
the True Cross and how this saga influenced True Cross reliquaries
from the ninth through the fourteenth centuries. She illustrates how
shapes of True Cross reliquaries varied according to ecclesiastical
function and to the region in which they were made, all linked to
the original treasure which summoned the memory of Christ in the
Holy Land. Such reminiscence could be communicated to pilgrims in
a number of ways, including through the careful copying of the original holy object. Stephen Lamia, in "*Erit sepulcrum ejus . . . gloriosam*:
Verisimilitude and the Tomb of Christ in the Art of Twelfth-Century
Île-de-France," (Chapter 14) examines the development and function
of the images of the Holy Sepulcher, as well as how and why such
images were transmitted from the Holy Land to France. He notes
how these copies, through their careful resemblance, garnered importance because it was believed that they shared in the power of the
original Holy Sepulcher.

V. *Pilgrim Souvenirs: Meaning and Function*

Among the most popular objects of the later Middle Ages were
religious memorabilia collected by pilgrims on their journeys. Mass-
produced by the hundreds of thousands, from humble materials such
as pewter and tin, these souvenirs fulfilled many different roles. In
order to prevent the piecemeal dismantling of holy sites by eager
pilgrims, churches commissioned souvenirs in the form of ampullae,
badges, and small sculptures. Although their basic function was as
nostalgic mementos, pilgrims responded to them in varied ways.
Some of them were transformed by miracle stories into secondary
relics to cure illness, ensure salvation, and ward off evil, while others
functioned as signs of allegiance to the saint revered. For art historians,
they are an unparalleled source of information on pilgrim movements,

interactions and practices, the development of saints' cults, changes in iconography, and as records of other artistic monuments associated with many pilgrimage cults.

Marike de Kroon in "Medieval Pilgrim Badges and their Iconographic Aspect" (Chapter 15) examines the different symbolic functions pilgrim souvenirs might have had. Popular stories raised these mundane objects to the level of magical amulets, capable of saving souls as well as healing bodies. Representation on pilgrim souvenirs of features of their respective cult centers makes their iconographic record valuable to scholars seeking to discover the original appearance of monuments now-altered or utterly destroyed. Sarah Blick in "Reconstructing the Shrine of St. Thomas Becket, Canterbury Cathedral" (Chapter 16) focuses on this verisimilitude found in pilgrim souvenirs and considering them a reliable source, uses them to reconstruct St. Thomas Becket's shrine at Canterbury Cathedral. By laying out written and visual records of the famed shrine, she garners evidence from pilgrim badges to propose a shrine type that relates to other surviving shrine bases and ecclesiastical tombs.

Taking a broader view, Katja Boertjes in "Pilgrim Ampullae from Vendome: Souvenirs from a Pilgrimage to the Holy Tear of Christ" (Chapter 17) surveys the known souvenirs from the popular regional pilgrimage devoted to the Holy Tear of Christ, tracing the cult's development and its changing focus (with the addition of St. George) and the shifting visual forms that reflected the cult's healing power and devotional significance to pilgrims throughout the Middle Ages. Jennifer Lee, in her essay, "Searching for Signs: Pilgrims' Identity and Experience Made Visible in the *Miracula Sancti Thome Cantuariensism*," (Chapter 18) takes issue with the notion that one of the most important functions of pilgrim souvenirs was their healing power. Using one of the largest miracle collections from the Middle Ages, the *Miracula Sancti Thome Cantuariensism*, she notes that direct references to their healing powers is actually rare. Instead, by placing the pilgrim souvenirs in their fuller context, she posits that their main function was one of identity; that is, they became markers of the pilgrim's allegiance to the saint.

These humble objects also reflect how secular issues and images were intertwined with religion and religious art. This has often been noted in the literature, such as Geoffrey Chaucer's *Canterbury Tales* or Desiderius Erasmus' *A Religious Pilgrimage* and in the legal history of the period. For instance, The Castle (inn) at Bankside, London,

catered until 1546 to pilgrim travelers by night, but it was also a
licensed brothel during the day, illustrating how closely intertwined
these two worlds sometimes were. in 1506, the inn's owners were
criticized for not separating the night and day business sufficiently.[26]
These close connections are studied by A.M. Koldeweij in "Shameless
and Naked Images: Obscene Badges as Parodies of Popular Devotion."
(Chapter 19) By drawing attention to the obscene badges dating from
c. 1350–c. 1450—which seem to mock pilgrims and religious processions, he places their imagery in the context of literature and art
that criticized and parodied pilgrims and pilgrimages in many ways.

VI. *Common Cause for Medieval Christians: Politics & Practicalities of Cult Development*

In an atmosphere of theological exploration of the roles of esteemed
relics in salvation history, and the political exploitation of cults for
community-building efforts, Eucharistic cults exploded in popularity
in the later Middle Ages. Grappling with tricky theological notions,
the artwork associated with these cults is especially complex and
emotionally charged.

Kristen Van Ausdall explores this complexity of host cults in
"Doubt and Authority in Host-Miracle Shrines of Orvieto and
Wilsnack" (Chapter 20), where she explains the role of theological
doubt and papal authority on the fate of two significant host-miracle
shrines and how this reception affected the artwork associated with
each cult center.

In contrast, Virginia Blanton, in "Building a Presbytery for St.
Aethelryth of Ely: Bishop Hugh de Northwold and the Politics of
Cult Production in Thirteenth-Century England," (Chapter 21) discusses how the more-unified development of the cult of the early
English queen was profoundly influenced by political relations of the
bishop with Henry III when designing and promoting a cult space
for St. Aethelryth. The culmination of political involvement in a pilgrimage shrine is taken up by Laura Gelfand, in "Y Me tarde: The

---

[26] Brian Spencer, "King Henry of Windsor and the London Pilgrim," in *Collectanea
Londiniensia: Studies in London Archaeology and History Presented to Ralph Merrifield* eds.
Joanna Bird, Hugh Chapman, John Clark (London and Middlesex Archaeological
Society, Special Paper, No. 2, 1978) p. 236.

Valois, Pilgrimage, and the Chartreuse de Champmol," (Chapter 22), which shows how the royal patronage of the Valois influenced the artistic choices for decoration and furnishing of the Chartreuse de Champmol. The wish was motivated not only by piety and self-aggrandizement, but a hope that pilgrims would pray for the souls of the patrons who so generously provided them with a sumptuous pilgrimage site.

Mitchell B. Merback, in "Channels of Grace: Pilgrimage Architecture, Eucharistic Imagery, and Visions of Purgatory at the Host-Miracle Churches of Late Medieval Germany," (Chapter 23) discusses the complex nature of host relics and their relationship to communal pilgrimage; in particular, how the churches which housed these treasures focused on creating a channel of grace where the blessing of the relic's power spread upwards and downwards, leading the pilgrims to imagine the dead souls imprisoned beneath the paving stones or in the same sepulchral space where the body of Christ had once fallen, or to see them rising up, liberated, moving toward heaven along the same vertical axis that the Lord's Resurrection had followed.

VII. *Cults and Cult Practices: Evolution and Expression*

As access to the Holy Land dwindled, cults featuring local saints burgeoned in popularity. The saints became exemplars of nationalism, regional politics, ecclesiastical power, and more. Hagiographical stories and artwork emphasized certain aspects of Christian piety and sanctity and also reflected power struggles between the bishops and the papacy, rival monasteries, and lords and clergy battling it out through the power of these local saints. Pilgrimage, like the local parish and guild, functioned as a vehicle for achievement of political and social power. Patronage of the wealthy and powerful were closely interlinked with their spirituality and their need to have visitors pray for them. The evolution of iconography, the development of various cult practices, and the ways on which theology and ritual affected art at regional pilgrimage sites, all influenced the ensuing cult expression.

In "The Iconography of Rhenish-Mosan Reliquary Châsses of the Thirteenth Century," (Chapter 24), Benoit Van den Bossche surveys the changing iconography of the châsses that lay at the heart of many pilgrimages over the course of a pivotal century in cult artistry development. He questions whether the imagery of several specific châsses was, in each case, conventional or innovative—featuring true iconographic programs or merely images juxtaposed without much care for meaningful coherence, while probing the underlying rationales and positing a trend in cult evolution. The specific iconography of the Servatius cult at Maastricht in"Relics and Pilgrimage in the Xylographic Book of St. Servatius of Maastricht," (Chapter 25) is considered by Scott Montgomery. He examines how this printed book, using familiar imagery, albeit with specifically-altered iconography, could help pilgrims to visualize certain elements of their visit and then assist them in re-living the experience when they departed from the sacred site.

These reliquary shrines did not always sit loftily upon an altar or pedestal, to be worshiped from near or far, but rather they were commonly paraded around the church, the town, and the countryside in lively processions which expressed the shared devotion of cult participants. Moreover, the relics were frequently companions to parishioners and other groups as they made pilgrimage to near or distant centers to pay homage to other saints, to express fraternity and piety, and to mark a variety of occasions. Rita Tekippe, in "Pilgrimage and Procession: Correlations of Meaning, Practice and Effects," (Chapter 26) posits that the ritual travels in pilgrimage and procession were originally likely one and the same, perhaps more frequently than not. Another investigation of how ritual can elucidate the relic cult is taken up by Lisa Victoria Ciresi in "The Aachen Karlsschrein and Marienschreine," (Chapter 27). She carefully examines the religious and political functions of these magnificent reliquary shrines in the context of their iconography, their spatial placement, and the specific liturgy performed in the cathedral at Aachen, where the cults of the Virgin and Charlemagne were carefully intertwined. The practice of pilgrimage and its effect on artwork was kaleidoscopic—changing with the continually-evolving needs of the church, communities, and the individual. The essays in this volume reflect those shifting transformations, by focusing on different media and by taking different and sometimes conflicting propositions. While this approach clearly leaves vast areas unexplored, we believe it is essential to take this broad view in order to begin to understand the complex and vibrant realm of pilgrimage art.

PART I

THE PILGRIM'S JOURNEY: VISION AND REALITY

CHAPTER ONE

PILGRIMS AND FASHION:
THE FUNCTIONS OF PILGRIMS' GARMENTS

Anja Grebe

A medieval pilgrimage was a dangerous undertaking. The search for salvation and spiritual as well as physical healing could end in illness, injury, even death. Therefore, the right traveling equipment was of the utmost importance to make a journey comfortable and safe and to minimize the risks of accident and illness. Medieval pilgrims' songs refer to the importance of adequate clothing and equipment:

> If you want to know misery / you should follow me on the road to Santiago / Take two pairs of shoes / a bottle and a bowl / a broad-brimmed hat / and a coat trimmed with leather / so that neither snow nor rain nor wind can do you any harm.[1]

Such practical instructions regarding the best traveling equipment are also found in pilgrims' guidebooks and other literary sources such as letters and reports. These instructions differ in their comprehensiveness, according to their time, their social milieu, their mode of travel, itinerary, and destination of the journey. However, nearly every text includes certain basic advice regarding comfortable and weather-proof outer clothing, warm underwear, comfortable and hard-wearing shoes—ideally two pairs—and a hat to protect the traveler from the elements. The equipment is completed by a shoulder bag and a walking stick.

---

[1] *Wer das elent bawen will / der heb sich auf und sei mein gsel wol auf sant Jacobs strassen / Zwei par schuch der darf er wol / ein schüssel bei der flaschen / Ein breiten hut den sol er han / und on mantel sol er nit gan mit leder wohl besetzet / Es schnei es regn es wehe der wind / dass in die luft nicht netzet.* Verses from an old pilgrim's song quoted by Cordelia Spaemann, "Wallfahrtslieder," in *Wallfahrt kennt keine Grenzen: Themen zu einer Ausstellung,* ed. Lenz Kriss-Rettenbeck and Gerda Möhler (Munich, 1984), p. 182.

*Extant Pilgrims' Garments: The Pilgrim's Garments of Stephen III Praun
in the Germanisches Nationalmuseum*

Very few medieval pilgrims' garments have been preserved. Among
these are the clothes, staff and rosary of Stephen III Praun (1544–91),
a Nuremberg merchant's son and diplomat. (fig. 1) During his short
but adventurous life, Stephen Praun visited numerous European,
Middle Eastern, and North African countries, serving different European rulers, going on pilgrimage to Santiago de Compostela and to
Jerusalem. His last years were spent in Rome where he died of the
plague in 1591. After his death, his brothers took his belongings
back to Nuremberg, among them his Spanish pilgrim's garments.
They have since become part of the famous *Praunsche Kunstkammer*
(Praun Cabinet), the family collection in Nuremberg, put on per-
manent loan to the Germanisches Nationalmuseum in 1876. Beyond
their value in the family tradition, the artistic merit of Stephen's
Spanish pilgrim garments is suggested by their inclusion in the *Praunsche
Kunstkabinett* alongside works of art by Albrecht Dürer and Italian
Renaissance masters. Because of their more or less exotic provenance
and mixture of natural and artistic elements,[2] they represent a cat-
egory of curiosities highly appreciated by art collectors in the late
Renaissance and Baroque eras.

The Pilgrim's Coats

The most prominent piece of Stephen Praun's garments is his pilgrim's
coat.[3] Strictly speaking, this garment consists of two coats: a larger
coat made of felt and a shorter leather coat, both sharing the shape
of a cape. (fig. 2) The longer cape is made of two semi-circles of
undyed wool-felt sewn together at the back. A slit of 20 cm was left
open at the lower back, suggesting that the cape was made for a
journey on horseback. The front of the cape was fastened with eight
silk buttons with ornamental trimmings and matching loops. The

---

[2] Whereas the scallop shells are of natural origin, the turned miniature bottles
and pilgrim's signs are artistic or artificial items.

[3] Nuremberg, Germanisches Nationalmuseum, Inv. No. T 550 (on permanent
loan by the Friedrich von Praunsche Familienstiftung since 1876). See *Die Kunst des
Sammelns: Das Praunsche Kabinett. Meisterwerke von Dürer bis Carracci*, ed. Katrin Achilles-
Syndram and Rainer Schoch (Nuremberg, 1994), cat. 141, p. 311.

cape's embroidered decorations were originally light blue in color, as was the high, pointed hood which is a separate item from the cape. Its lower portion is lined with green velvet and lies loosely on the collar of the cape. It was fastened with three silk buttons and loops at the front. The hood is embroidered with a lavish, interlacing oak-leaf design, whereas the coat is decorated with parallel lines that widen at the bottom to accentuate the bell-shaped form of the cape.

The black leather cape is similarly-shaped but shorter,[4] with borders accentuated by two lines of decorative stitching. Besides its decorative seam, the most prominent decoration is the big white scallop shell attached to the left side of the cape in the place over the heart. This shell is flanked by two ivory sticks, depicting miniature pilgrim's staffs. A smaller scallop shell serves as a decorative collar button.

The Pilgrim's Hat

The scallop shell and staffs also form the principal decorations of Stephen Praun's black wool-felt pilgrim's hat.[5] (fig. 3) Its large brim is turned up at the front, and both top and brim are completely covered with scallop shells, ivory pilgrims' staffs, and small ivory pilgrims' bottles in different sizes. In addition to the shells, staffs, and bottles, there are additional pilgrims' signs, made of jet, arranged deliberately and decoratively on the hat. (fig. 4) At the top of the hat, small staffs and bottles are placed in a circle around a medallion showing St. James on horseback fighting the Moors. (fig. 5) Beneath the circle, more sticks and bottles are randomly placed. At the bottom part and on the brim, larger pilgrims' staffs are sewn either crosswise or in wide angles, with the spandrels filled with small turned ivory pieces, scallop shells, and jet pilgrims' souvenirs. All together there are five figures of St. James and one of St. Anthony of Padua, with a large scallop shell marking the turned-up brim at the front of the hat.

---

[4] Nuremberg, Germanisches Nationalmuseum, Inv. No. T 551 (on permanent loan by the Friedrich von Praunsche Familienstiftung since 1876). *Die Kunst des Sammelns*, cat. 142, p. 312.

[5] Nuremberg, Germanisches Nationalmuseum, Inv. No. T 552 (on permanent loan by the Friedrich von Praunsche Familienstiftung since 1876). *Die Kunst des Sammelns*, cat. 143, p. 312.

The Pilgrim's Accessories

The pilgrim's staff is a wooden stick with a ball-like knob which tapers slightly towards the bottom and ends in an iron point.[6] It was once completely covered with tiny mother-of-pearl plates which formed a grid of narrow pointed ovals in whose squares, small crosses were enclosed. The knob itself is plated with mother-of-pearl hexagons that are fixed with small brass tacks in the center.

Another major part of Stephen Praun's pilgrim's equipment is a rosary about 165 cm long and fashioned of wood and metal.[7] The rosary consists of seventy wooden beads including seven larger beads, all connected by metal eyelets. A pendant cross on the rosary is made of turned pieces of wood also connected by metal eyelets.

Stephen's sandals are made of hemp and can be laced up at the heels.[8] They resemble modern espadrille-style shoes, fashionable in Spain. It is not certain that Stephen Praun actually used these shoes during his pilgrimage as they bear very few marks of wear. It is more likely that he made his journey in high riding boots as we know that he certainly rode to Santiago de Compostela on horseback.

The Portrait of Stephen Praun as a Pilgrim

Stephen was obviously so proud of his pilgrimage that he commissioned a portrait of himself as a pilgrim.[9] (fig. 6) The small watercolor painting on parchment, mounted on linden wood,[10] was kept

---

[6] Nuremberg, Germanisches Nationalmuseum, Inv. No. T 554 (on permanent loan by the Friedrich von Praunsche Familienstiftung since 1876). *Die Kunst des Sammelns*, cat. 144, p. 312.

[7] Nuremberg, Germanisches Nationalmuseum, Inv. No. KG 303 (on permanent loan by the Friedrich von Praunsche Familienstiftung since 1876). *Die Kunst des Sammelns*, cat. 145, pp. 312–3.

[8] Nuremberg, Germanisches Nationalmuseum, Inv. No. T 556 (on permanent loan by the Friedrich von Praunsche Familienstiftung since 1876). *Die Kunst des Sammelns*, cat. 146, p. 313.

[9] Nuremberg, Germanisches Nationalmuseum, Inv. No. Gm 655 (on permanent loan by the Friedrich von Praunsche Familienstiftung since 1876). 51 × 36.7 cm. *Die Kunst des Sammelns*, cat. 170, pp. 341–2; Kurt Löcher, *Die Gemälde des 16. Jahrhunderts* (Stuttgart, 1997), pp. 367–8.

[10] Linden wood or limewood was the material commonly used by artists in southern Germany in the Middle Ages and early modern period. Michael Baxandall, *The Limewood Sculptors of Renaissance Germany* (New Haven, 1980), pp. 27–31.

in the *Praunsche Kunstkammer* together with his garments and is now on display in the Germanisches Nationalmuseum.[11] In the painting, Stephen is shown standing upright like a giant in a hilly landscape covering the bottom portion of the work. Although his eyes are directed to the spectator, Stephen turns slightly to the right, where he holds his walking stick as if he was making a step to begin his journey or to stabilize his position. His pose is both dynamic and domineering as if he owned the landscape he has only traversed. The authoritative and self-assured aura is underlined by the clouds which form a kind of aureole around his head. Indeed, Stephen does not quite fit the traditional image of the humble pilgrim, on the contrary, the portrait conveys the impression of a stylish young nobleman.

In the portrait, Stephen wears a short black cape decorated with pilgrims' signs with a longer white coat underneath. The black cape resembles the extant cape not only in its shape, but also in its decoration; the big scallop shell framed by two pilgrim's sticks on the left side and two smaller scallop shells fixed to either side of the collar, decorating the fastener, match that of the real cape. While the white coat looks similar to the extant felt coat, it is not identical. For instance, the braid trim along the borders of the painted cape is absent on the real coat. The hood is also missing from the portrait, but this element is removable from the extant garment. The portrait figure wears a white lace ruff, according to the fashion of the late sixteenth century, in place of the hood. It was probably attached to the linen shirt which he wore underneath the cloak, and is indicated by the fashionable lace cuff emerging from the sleeve at the right wrist. Under his two coats, Stephen wears a white jerkin fastened with closely-aligned buttons at the front. The jerkin's black braid piping matches that of the white cape. According to the fashion of the time, Stephen wears knee breeches decorated with broad black stripes. The clothing is completed by very tight black over-the-knee boots. Of all the costume accessories Stephen wears in the portrait, only the hat, the staff, and the rosary have survived in the family

---

[11] *Die Kunst des Sammelns*, p. 342. The painting first appears in the inventory of 1719: "A painting on wood showing a member of the Praun family in his pilgrim's garments. The painting measures 1 foot 8 inches in height and 1 foot 2 inches in width." ("*Ein taffel, worauf auf holz gemahlt ein Praun mit einem pilgramskleid, das gemähl 1 schuh 8 zoll hoch und 1 schuh 2 zoll breit.*")

collection. For the jerkin, shirt, trousers, and boots, no preserved counterparts are known.

At first sight, the hat in the portrait resembles the real one. The black felt is completely decorated with scallop shells in different sizes, small ivory sticks, bottles, and jet pilgrims' signs. The decorative pattern is different particularly at the bottom part of the hat, whereas the upper portion is quite similar. For instance, at the bottom of the painted brim, the decoration is formed of alternating small scallop shells and crossed pilgrims' staffs, while the small bottles sewn to the real hat have been omitted. The portrait also shows Stephen wearing the turned-up brim not at the front as expected, but on the left side, thereby exposing his left ear and his forehead. Another feature of the painted hat is the small tuft of white feathers protruding from the left side—a detail missing on the real hat. It is not clear if this stylish accessory is an invention of the painter or whether it once really adorned the hat.

The long, nearly-shoulder height walking stick is entirely clad with a mother-of-pearl decoration in form of little rhombuses and crosses, resembling Stephen Praun's actual pilgrim's stick in many details. There is one remarkable difference in that the painted staff has two knobs, whereas the extant walking stick has only one. It is possible that the upper part of the real staff was damaged or lost over the centuries. The same observation can be made about the rosary which Stephen holds in his right hand, together with the walking stick. It also closely resembles the real rosary—although its pendants are formed differently, since the real rosary has only one simple wooden cross hanging from its chain.

Although Stephen Praun is shown standing and holding a walking stick, we know that he did not walk to Santiago de Compostela, but rather traveled on horseback. It is probably he who is represented riding with the small group in the landscape at his feet. The party, reaching a cross roads, meets two additional pilgrims walking up another path. There are other groups of people at various points across the landscape. In the foreground a couple is having a picnic, while on the far right a person sits and prays before a devotional image on a stele, while a woman approaches the site. There are yet more riders and wanderers on the left side of the picture. In the background hills, a line of several buildings leads the eye from the small church or monastery on the left up to the town with its cathedral on the right—apparently the pilgrims' destination. Although the landscape and architecture look southern German, the artist gave the scene a Mediterranean touch by adding a palm tree on the left side of the picture.

According to family records, Stephen Praun did not travel alone, but in the company of a certain Johann Baptist Brock. This can be deduced from an inscription in the genealogical and heraldic book of the Praun family begun in 1615 by his younger brother Jakob I Praun (1558–1627). The manuscript contains several watercolor portraits of important family members, where Stephen Praun is depicted three times. One of the portraits shows him in his Spanish pilgrims' garments, with the inscription explaining that "he was dressed like this when he traveled to Santiago de Compostela in Galicia in 1571 in the company of John Baptist Brock."[12]

The watercolor is a simplified copy of the painting discussed above. The artist used the painting as a model, omitted the landscape background, thus bringing the drawing into line with the other portraits in the manuscript. According to Christiane Lukatis, the watercolor was not in the original manuscript, but was added at a later date.[13] Compared with the other family portraits in the book, it is painted on thinner paper and was done by a different hand. Lukatis suggested that the sheet came from a different context and was inserted in the continuous pagination of the *Genealogia* after folio 60. The portrait of Stephen Praun as a pilgrim must have achieved some fame in its time as there are two other watercolors in the collections of the Germanisches Nationalmuseum that clearly copy the painted portrait of Stephen Praun.[14] (fig. 7)

The first author of the family records, Jakob Praun, was very interested in the history of his eldest brother Stephen III because he writes an extremely detailed report of his adventurous life. His biography is illustrated by two other portraits: one showing Stephen on

---

[12] "Anno 1571 is er solcher gestallt nach Sanct Jacob zu Compostell in Gallitia, mit Jann Paptista Procks zogen." The so-called *Gedechtnus* (souvenirs) or *Genealogia und Geschlecht buch der Praun* (Genealogy of the Praun family), started by Jakob Praun in 1615, was continued until 1844. It consists of 202 folios and fourteen watercolors with portraits of family members and numerous coats of arms. Nuremberg, City archives, Archives of the Praun family, Inv. No. Rep. E 28 II, No. 11.

[13] *Die Kunst des Sammelns*, cat. 138, pp. 306–7.

[14] Nuremberg, Germanisches Nationalmuseum, Inv. No. Hz 5278, Kapsel 1532, and Inv. No. Hz 5910, Kapsel 1532 (both on permanent loan by the Friedrich von Praunsche Familienstiftung).

his pilgrimage to the Holy Land undertaken in 1585, and the other one on the occasion of his 1569 journey to Constantinople as secretary to the imperial legation, under the direction of the Hungarian nobleman Kaspar von Minkwitz, traveling by land via Hungary. Stephen noted the important events in the diary of the journey, but did not comment on his clothing.[15] Therefore it is not known from which source the portraitist drew his information, especially because no other painting of Stephen at the court of the sultan is extant.

The watercolor shows Stephen in the traditional clothes of a Hungarian nobleman. Here he appears in a costume belonging to the Hungarian and oriental tradition.[16] He wears a long ruby-red robe of unspecified material with long sleeves and with a floral pattern. Around his waist is a tied sash which holds a knife and a richly-decorated lace handkerchief. Over the robe he wears a long fur coat in the Hungarian style. Stephen's high hat is also typically Hungarian or Russian, and probably made of black velvet with a narrow brim slit at the front. According to Hungarian fashion, the hat is decorated with a red and white ostrich feather. The oriental weapons and the red leather bag in the *Praunsche Kunstkammer* were most probably purchased by Stephen on the occasion of his visit to Constantinople. Thus, for this journey, he replaced his customary garments and adopted the dressing style of the country through which he traveled. The same was true for his 1585 pilgrimage to the Holy Land.

Stephen Praun embarked in Venice and traveled via Jaffa to Jerusalem where he was dubbed Knight of the Holy Sepulcher. The watercolor in the family chronicle shows him wearing a long dark robe with long sleeves and a half-length coat with a collar. The dark felt hat has a large brim. The clothes appear to be of good quality, although there is no decoration and the gray color emphasizes the general simplicity of the garments. Around his waist, Stephen tied a cord as Capuchin monks do, and this serves to carry his knife. He is holding a prayer book in his left hand and is wearing soft shoes. It is interesting to compare the watercolor to the description Stephen Praun wrote about the garments of one of his travel com-

---

[15] The diary has been published by Friedrich von Praun in: *Mitteilungen aus dem Germanischen Nationalmuseum* 1916–7, pp. 45–62; esp. pp. 49–58.

[16] On Stephen's costume see Walter Fries, "Die Kostümsammlung des Germanischen Nationalmuseums zu Nürnberg," in *Anzeiger des Germanischen Nationalmuseums* 1924/25 (1926), pp. 6–10.

panions who died shortly after their arrival in Jerusalem: "The garment that he wore to protect himself against the dangers of the country were of Syrian style and poorly-made."[17] He then lists his companion's belongings, including a watch worn around the neck, a rosary, a sheath with a knife, a gimlet, another black robe, stockings, and shirts and finally "a dress of Arab style, half black and half white with braids" (*un vestido alla araba mezo negro e mezo biancho con liesti*).

The mention of the "dress of Arab style" is of the utmost interest. The pilgrims—at least the wealthy ones like Stephen Praun—apparently did not wear their own European clothes, but put on local costumes wherever they traveled. The decision to undertake this kind of clothing assimilation was influenced not only by different climatic conditions, but was adopted for safety reasons. Stephen Praun's note, quoted above, describes the garments of his deceased companion as "in Syrian style" and as "poor," explaining that these clothes served for the "protection against the dangers of the country." The pilgrims did not want to be immediately recognized as foreigners, so they took off their European coats and robes that would have functioned like moving advertisements inviting robbers and swindlers. They took care to look as poor as possible—not only disguising their origin, but also their noble status and wealth.

This sort of disguise was apparently common among travelers to the Holy Land. We see it again in the report by Hans Ludwig von Lichtenstein who undertook a pilgrimage to Jerusalem at about the same time as Stephen Praun, who wrote before embarking in Venice in February 1586: "As the departure of the ships was delayed we had time to buy dresses in the style of Greek merchants. The garments were made of good English cloth and mainly brown, and consisted of short dresses and long coats."[18] Like Stephen Praun and his companion, Hans von Lichtenstein tried to disguise his identity as a northern European nobleman and wealthy pilgrim by taking on the identity of a Greek merchant who could travel the Holy Land with less threat of molestation than other foreigners.

---

[17] Nuremberg, City Archives, Archives of the Praun family, Inv. No. E. 28 II, Nr. 185. Quoted from: Fries "Die Kostümsammlung . . .," p. 14. The original text is in Italian.

[18] "Weilen sich die Abfahrt der Fregatten was verlängerte, hatten wir Raum, uns auf Griechisch wie derselben Kaufleute zu kleiden, in viel Braun gut Englisch Tuch, kurze Leibröck und lange Mäntel," quoted from Fries, "Die Kostümsammlung . . .," p. 14.

The simple robe Stephen Praun wears in the watercolor in the Family Chronicle fits the ideas of assimilation and dissimulation that dominated his journey to the Holy Land. Apart from the prayer-book, there was no sign that Stephen undertook a pilgrimage. It is inscribed "June 15, 1585. He was dressed like this when he went to Jerusalem from Venice on a pilgrim's ship. He arrived in Jerusalem on August 15, and on November 30, he was made a knight on St. Andrew's Day."[19]

In viewing these two watercolors, one might expect the garments of Stephen to be more decorative. Indeed: the journey to Jerusalem was certainly the most important of all his pilgrimages for several reasons. First, it was the longest, most expensive, and most danger-ous of all his pilgrimages. Second, Jerusalem was considered the center of the Christian world, and third, it was on this occasion that Stephen was made a Knight of the Holy Sepulcher, the first in his family to receive this ennobling honor. Surprisingly, the portrait in the Chronicle does not show his knightly cross. Compared to the over-decorated garments of his earlier pilgrimage to Santiago de Compostela, this image of Stephen as a pilgrim to Jerusalem is remarkably modest. He is portrayed as a humble pilgrim who respected the laws of the country and even imitated a monk's habit. He is no longer the fashionable gallant who undertook a pilgrimage as a courtly adventure—such as his diplomatic journey to Constantinople where he was richly dressed; here he gives the impression of being an earnest pilgrim who undertook the journey, above all, for religious reasons.

This change of mind reflected by the portraits, matches the change in Stephen's biography written by his younger brother in the *Chronicle*. Stephen was considered the black sheep of the family, who, after being disinherited by his father, restlessly traveled the world seeking pleasures and adventures. It seems to have been important to his family to correct the image of the pleasure-craving globetrotter into the one of a humble pilgrim. It is this Christian image of Stephen that the family wanted to maintain after his death by transforming his pilgrim's garments and belongings into family souvenirs and later into museum pieces.

---

[19] "Anno 1585. Den 15 Juni. Ist er solcher gestallt von Venedig aus, uff dem Pellegrin Schiff nach Jerusalem gefahren uff 15 August alda ankommen uff 30 November an S. Andreas tag alda zu Ritter geschlagen worden."

The Pilgrim's Coat of Jakob VII Trapp

The main problems in researching medieval pilgrims' garments are the dearth of real clothes and equipment and the sparse written tradition. The few extant examples of pre-modern pilgrims' garments, like those of Stephen Praun, belong to the sixteenth century. Moreover, of Stephen's belongings, only the lavishly decorated garments of his pilgrimage to Santiago de Compostela have survived, the simple robe he supposedly wore on his journey through the Holy Land was apparently not retained in the family collections, although these are the clothes in which he was knighted in 1585. In the case of his contemporary, the South Tyrolean knight Jakob VII Trapp of Churburg (1529–63), it was probably the very circumstance of being dubbed a knight of the Holy Sepulcher during his 1560 pilgrimage to Jerusalem that helped the preservation of his pilgrim's coat in the family collection at Churburg Castle, after his return to Churburg at the end of November 1560.

Of all his pilgrim's garments, only the coat survived.[20] (fig. 8) It is of Tyrolean origin—made of multiple pieces of a thick, dark green felt in a simple cape-like cut. The coat is fastened at the front with four hooks and eyelets. To stabilize the hooks, their left border is trimmed with linen. The shoulders are covered with a broad felt collar which served as protection against rain. Over the broad collar is a small inner collar of black linen. On the left, over the heart, is a white silk medallion on which a red velvet Jerusalem cross is sewn. This coat is mentioned in the inventory drawn up after Jakob's death as: "Our late Lord's pilgrim's coat with the red Cross of Jerusalem." (*des seligen herrn Pillgram Manntl mit ainem Roten Jherusalemischen Chreutz*) Unlike Stephen Praun's Spanish coats, the felt coat of Jakob Trapp bears clear indications of having actually been used. Jakob was proud of his pilgrimage to the Holy Land, missing no opportunity to refer to his journey. On the back of his portrait medallion ordered in the year following his pilgrimage (1561), the Jerusalem cross was depicted next to his coat of arms, emphasizing his newly-received knightship of the Holy Sepulcher.[21]

---

[20] On Churburg castle (South Tyrol, Italy) and the history of the Trapp family see Oswald Graf Trapp, *Churburg, Kleiner Kunstführer* (Munich, 1963). See also the exhibition catalogue *Wallfahrt ohne Grenzen*, ed. Thomas Raff (Munich, 1984), cat. 83, p. 72.

[21] *Wallfahrt ohne Grenzen*, cat. 85, p. 73.

The Worcester Pilgrim

A very interesting example of a full set of pilgrim's garments was discovered during the 1986 excavations at Worcester Cathedral,[22] in the late fifteenth or early sixteenth century grave of the "Worcester Pilgrim," found at the former choir wall under the tower-crossing. The ensemble consists of two layered woolen cloth garments (with the outer portion of fine cloth over a coarse undergarment), a pair of knee-length leather boots, a 155 cm wooden staff painted brownish-purple (with a double pronged wrought-iron spike at its bottom), and finally, at the bottom of the grave, close to the top of the staff, lay a cockleshell.[23]

As burials of fully-clothed laymen were highly unusual in Britain at that time, the garments probably had a symbolic or ceremonial meaning, emphasized by the leather boots which show only slight signs of wear. The man was probably not buried in the clothes he had worn during his supposed pilgrimage, but in the ideal pilgrim's costume of his time. Helen Lubin suggested that the man—who must have been of high rank to afford a burial within the cathedral and high-quality garments—might have been a member of the pilgrim's Fraternity of St. James that existed in Worcester in the late Middle Ages.[24] Further importance of the Worcester burial derives from the idea of what people in the late Middle Ages, at least in England, considered to be the "standard" pilgrims' garments.

Of course, it is still difficult to draw any general conclusions about medieval pilgrims' garments from just these few extant examples. Among them, only the coat of Jakob Trapp was actually worn during a journey, whereas Stephen Praun's well-preserved garments seem to have been used only on ceremonial occasions. Undertaking his journey on horseback, Praun certainly never used his pilgrim's staff for walking long distances, and while his richly decorated coat and hat would have been striking, they were not very practical for a long and strenuous journey on horseback. Praun would especially have run the risk of ruining the highly artistic arrangement of pilgrims'

---

[22] Helen Lubin, *The Worcester Pilgrim* (Worcester, 1990), pp. 4–7.
[23] Lubin, *The Worcester Pilgrim*, pp. 11–5.
[24] One has to ask then why the man was not buried with a real scallop shell, but with an ordinary cockleshell.

signs on his hat or the costly mother-of-pearl inlay of his staff. The special question of Stephen's hat has been discussed by Gabriel Llompart,[25] who considered the star-like arrangement at the top with its little sticks and bottles framing the figure of St. James (fig. 5) to be a symbolic allusion to a popular interpretation of the name of the place: *campus stellae* (field of stars).[26] The complicated layout of the pilgrims' signs even suggests that Stephen may have had his hat decorated after his pilgrimage ended, asking an artist to carefully arrange all the little objects. The exact history of the hat, however, is unknown. Although it seems to have been important to Praun to prove, by several certificates, that his journey to Santiago de Compostela was made purely for religious purposes,[27] his choice of clothing and the later portrait show that he was well aware of his position as a fashionable young member of the Spanish court. It is therefore not too bold to speak of his pilgrimage as of some kind of "religious tourism."[28]

Pictorial Sources: The Iconography of the Pilgrim in Medieval Art

The pictorial representations of pilgrims in medieval art can be divided into two main groups: images of pilgrims themselves and those of pilgrim saints. Both are equally important to an iconography of the pilgrim and to the questions of pilgrims' garments. Representations of pilgrims are numerous and cover a wide range of artistic genres and materials, including sculpture, painting, manuscript illumination, and prints. As so few pilgrims' garments have survived, the search for contemporary pictorial representations of pilgrims is necessary to research. The underlying idea is that the artists tried to paint or sculpt the figure of the pilgrim in as lifelike and as unambiguous manner as possible so that the viewer would recognize the figure at once. Three points should be kept in mind when art is

---

[25] Gabriel Llompart, "El sombrero de peregrinación compostelana de Stephan Praun III (1544–1591)," *Revista de Dialectología y Tradiciones Populares* 17 (1961): 321–9.
[26] Llompart, "El sombrero . . .," p. 326.
[27] According to two pilgrimage certificates, dated March 15 and 23, 1571, Stephen Praun spent more than a week in Santiago de Compostela. *Wallfahrt ohne Grenzen*, cat. 180, pp. 130–1.
[28] Llompart, "El sombrero . . .," p. 322.

used as a source for *realia* and for the reconstruction of everyday life. First, much medieval art was highly abstract and formulaic and was not bound to reality in the modern sense of the word; second, the medieval artist was generally very conservative, sometimes using the same pictorial model over centuries; and third, even if late medieval painters appear to be extremely realistic, they still relied upon their artistic sense to choose and arrange details according to artistic principles. Thus, one should always double-check the image of the medieval pilgrim against extant objects and written sources.

Apart from some early examples where the identity of the pilgrims can only be deduced from the context, the true iconography of pilgrims emerged in the twelfth century, when their more-frequent appearance in art is related to the increased number of pilgrimages. Before that time, pilgrims were represented as average travelers wearing typical travel garments without any special signs or features. This development reflects a new interpretation of the Latin word for pilgrim, *peregrinus*, that originally meant "foreigner" in general, before being understood to specifically mean "pilgrim."

The first representations of pilgrims in art occurred in the context of the biblical Emmaus scene. One of the earliest examples is a twelfth-century Spanish ivory relief, showing Christ with his two disciples on the way to Emmaus.[29] They wear similar long robes with decorated borders and long capes in the same style, one carries a T-shaped walking stick, another a book, while Christ is shown with the characteristic accessories of a pilgrim: the bag with a cross on the flap, the staff, carried over his shoulder, with a bottle and a soft hat hanging from it.

Looking at other early representations of pilgrims one notes that their clothing is not generally different from that of the other figures. There are two features, the bag and the staff, which appear in all representations as distinguishing marks. That these alone were considered to be distinctive attributes of the pilgrim can be seen on the tympanum of the main portal of St. Lazare in Autun, where among the elect at the Last Judgment two pilgrims wait in line. (fig. 9) Although both are completely naked except for their caps, they can

---

[29] New York, The Metropolitan Museum of Art. Leonie von Wilckens, "Die Kleidung der Pilger," in *Wallfahrt kennt keine Grenzen*, p. 175, Ill. 74. *Editors' note: also see William Travis' essay in this volume.

be recognized by their distinguishing signs: each carries a walking stick over his shoulder and a big shoulder bag which hides his genitalia. One bag is decorated with a large cross (like that carried by Christ on the ivory relief), and the other pilgrim's bag has a flap decorated with a large scallop shell. The tympanum at Autun is one of the earliest examples where an iconographic distinction is made according to the destination of the pilgrimage journeys. Here, the cross stands for the pilgrimage to Jerusalem, while the scallop shell represents the pilgrimage to Santiago de Compostela. The prominent position of the *Jakobsbruder* (literally: "Jacob's Brother"—a colloquial expression for the pilgrim to Santiago de Compostela, which later became a slightly-pejorative expression for all pilgrims) is probably due to the fact that Autun was an important pilgrims' station on the way to Santiago de Compostela.

It is not without reason that the bag and staff are the only signs seen on the Autun pilgrims. Documents reveal that it was customary to go to church to acquire a special blessing before setting out on pilgrimage. From the tenth century on, the blessing included a special benediction of the bag and the walking stick.[30] The sermon *Veneranda dies* (Venerable day)[31] published in the *Liber Sancti Jacobi* [32] contains a passage explaining the symbolism of the pilgrim's stick and bag. The passage starts with a version of the benediction of the bag (scrip):

> In the name of our Lord Jesus Christ receive this scrip, the habit of thy pilgrimage that after due chastisement thou mayest be found worthy to reach in safety the Shrine of the Saints to which thou desirest to go: and after the accomplishment of thy journey thou mayst return to us in health.[33]

---

[30] Louis Carlen, *Wallfahrt und Recht im Abendland* (Freiburg, 1987). Klaus Herbers, *Der Jakobsweg. Mit einem mittelalterlichen Pilgerführer unterwegs nach Santiago de Compostela* (Tübingen, 1986), pp. 57–82, esp. pp. 64–7.

[31] This sermon, meant for the feast of the Translation of St. Jacob (December 30), not only deals with the the translation of the saint from Jerusalem to Compostela, but also gives directions for a good pilgrimage.

[32] The original manuscript, kept in the Cathedral of Santiago de Compostela, is also called *Codex Calixtinus* after Pope Calixtus II (r. 1119–24) whom the Middle Ages considered to be the author. The *Liber* contains various texts on the life of St. Jacob, especially his miracles, liturgical texts and sermons for special feasts, and finally, a pilgrim's guide giving practical advice on the journey and pilgrimage.

[33] Quoted from *Sarum Missal* by Alan Kendall, *Medieval Pilgrims* (London, 1970), pp. 36–7.

The priest continued with a similar blessing of the staff, which was likened to a third leg for the pilgrim, helping stabilize him and symbolizing his belief in the Holy Trinity. The staff also helped the wanderer to defend himself against dogs and wolves, both considered symbols of the devil.[34] The bag had a symbolic meaning as well. Its relatively-small size signified trust in God as the pilgrim was to take very few provisions with him. The bag was to be made of the skin of a dead animal because the pilgrim was to deaden his own sinful flesh and desires by suffering hunger and thirst, frost, nakedness, pain, and disgrace. The bag was not fastened, but always open at the top, being a symbol of the pilgrim who shares his goods with the poor and who is later ready to give and accept gifts and alms.[35]

The sermon *Veneranda dies* admonished the pilgrim not to take too many belongings with him. The best pilgrimage was the one done in poverty so that the pilgrim could concentrate on the spiritual aim of the journey. The sermon quoted the verses of Matthew 10.9–10 where Christ advised the apostles not to take any money with them, neither bag nor a second garment, neither shoes nor a walking stick. The pilgrim was to follow the apostolic example and to sell all his property before undertaking the pilgrimage in order to share the money with the poor and not to use it for luxurious food and lodgings during the journey. The author of the sermon disapproved of those pilgrims who traveled on horseback, following neither the example of the Lord who entered Jerusalem on a donkey nor that of the founders of the two main pilgrims' centers, St. Peter and St. James, also walked barefoot to Rome and to Spain.[36]

The stick and the bag were the *signa peregrinationis* (signs of pilgrimage) of the *habitus peregrinorum*, the juridical status of the pilgrim. Like the crusader, the pilgrim was considered to be performing a work which was pleasing to God, when taking on the risks and dangers of a long journey. Therefore, he could enjoy certain privileges

---

[34] A medieval tapestry with the legend of the Nuremberg patron saint Sebaldus (Nuremberg workshop, *c.* 1420) shows a scene where pilgrims use their sticks to defend themselves against two robber barons on horseback. Nuremberg, Germanisches Nationalmuseum, Inv. No. Gew 3710 (on permanent loan from the St. Sebald Church in Nuremberg).

[35] Herbers, "Der Jakobsweg," p. 65. *Editors' note: see also Michtell Merback's essay in this volume.

[36] Herbers, "Der Jakobsweg," pp. 68–9.

and a special status.[37] To acquire the status of a pilgrim, most people had to ask permission from an authority—the king or lord, the abbot, the husband or wife. Especially in the case of a long pilgrimage, one was asked to settle one's affairs first before starting the journey. Just before the departure, the pilgrims' Mass took place at which the priest distributed the pilgrim's documents and blessed the *signa peregrinationis*, the staff (*baculus*) and the scrip (*pera*).[38] Presumably most pilgrims, above all those traveling to distant destinations, either on horseback or by ship, actually carried more than one bag with them. The small shoulder bag that was blessed at Mass, however, had the special function as a sort of briefcase in which the pilgrim's documents were kept. The certificates attested to the pilgrim's status and later to his completed pilgrimage.[39]

Late Medieval Representations of Pilgrims

Ecclesiastical sources mention only the *baculus* and the *pera* as *signa peregrinationis*. They do not list the many other pilgrims' souvenirs that so prominently appear in medieval representations of pilgrims which are also mentioned in literary descriptions of pilgrims:

> . . . they have the habits or the signs of pilgrimage and pilgrims, which means a hat, a stick and a sign either on their head, in their hands or on their clothes.[40]

Leonie von Wilckens concluded that special pilgrim's garments did not exist, and that it was the pilgrim's souvenirs that transformed dress into a pilgrim's garment.[41] This judgment is repeated in nearly all the studies of pilgrims' garments. Kurt Köster repeatedly emphasized

---

[37] Carlen, "Wallfahrt und Recht . . .," esp. pp. 115–46.

[38] Adolph Franz, *Die kirchlichen Benediktionen im Mittelalter*, vol. 2 (Freiburg, 1909).

[39] For examples of pilgrimage certificates from Trier and Santiago de Compostela, see Louis Carlen, "Wallfahrt und Recht," in *Wallfahrt kennt keine Grenzen*, pp. 87–100, Ill. 32–3.

[40] ". . . *habentes habitum vel signum peregrinationis et peregrinorum, videlicet galerum, bordonum et signum in capite et manibus seu eorum signum super vestis.*" Cited from a Mantuan manuscript from the end of the fourteenth century (Cod. Reg. 4620, Stat. Mantuae, lib. I, cap. 63) by Charles Du Fresne Du Cange, *Glossarium mediae et infimae latinitatis*, vol. 13, ed. Pierre Carpentier (Paris, 1845), p. 200. Von Wilckens, "Die Kleidung der Pilger," p. 175.

[41] Von Wilckens, "Die Kleidung der Pilger," p. 175.

the importance of the *signa* as a sort of identity card or passport of the pilgrim on his journey. According to Köster, the signs offered a kind of protection in unsafe regions or during times of war, and helped the pilgrim to obtain food, drink, and lodging during his journey.[42] Late medieval representations of pilgrims and pilgrim saints seem to confirm these statements about the importance of the *signa*. The clothing itself does not differ much from that of a normal traveler— in general, the dress is simply cut and sparsely decorated, completed by a cape-like coat and a hat to protect the wanderer against the weather. It is the souvenirs that transform the clothes into pilgrims' garments. Accordingly, it is the signs that change an anonymous saint or apostle into a pilgrim saint such as St. James or St. Sebaldus.

German and Netherlandish art of the fifteenth and early sixteenth century includes many representations of pilgrims. The most interesting with regard to the subject of pilgrims' garments are those images made for pilgrims' churches, altars of pilgrims' saints, or for pilgrims' guidebooks. They transmit the common iconography of the pilgrim, serving as direct models for those who wanted to go on a pilgrimage or who were already on their way.

Friedrich Herlin: Scenes from the Life of St. James

The first example of this type of image is a panel from the high altar in St. James' Church in Rothenburg ob der Tauber, painted by Friedrich Herlin in the late fifteenth century.[43] (fig. 10) On the outer wings of this altarpiece, Herlin represented a scene from the legend of St. James, where a German pilgrim and his son who was hanged in a French town after having been falsely accused of robbery. The father continued his pilgrimage to Santiago de Compostela, but on his way back he stopped to see his son still hanging on the gallows. St. James miraculously revived the son and the false accuser was punished instead. Herlin not only painted the protagonists, he

---

[42] Kurt Köster, "Mittelalterliche Pilgerzeichen," *Wallfahrt kennt keine Grenzen*, p. 207.
[43] Rothenburg ob der Tauber, St. Jacob Church. On Friedrich Herlin see Ernst Buchner, "Die Werke Friedrich Herlins," *Münchner Jahrbuch der bildenden Kunst* 13 (1923), 1–51.

took the opportunity to represent a whole group of pilgrims. In the foreground, four pilgrims are shown entering a town through a gate. They all wear knee-length, tunic-style garments and cape-like coats which vary in color and detail, presenting a kind of survey of pilgrims' garments of the time. The first man, with a white beard, wears a gray garment fastened with a belt and a dark blue cape which is open at the front, revealing the white lining which matches his white stockings. The cape is decorated with a large scallop shell on the left side with a small, stylized pilgrim's staff, apparently sewn on the left side. Another large scallop shell is fixed to the tied-up front brim of his hat. He carries a rosary in his left hand and a long, pointed walking stick in his gloved, right hand. His companions wear similar hats and soft shoes and carry the same kind of lance-shaped sticks. The man in the middle of the group is quite striking in his elegant red coat. His top coat is draped over his walking stick that he has shouldered. He wears black stockings and holds a rosary in his left hand. The red coat is fastened by a belt from which a bottle and a knife in a sheath hang down. He also appears to carry a shoulder bag of which only the strap is visible. The last man in the line wears a green garment and a gray sleeveless overcoat. He has pulled his hat to the back and wears a gray hood instead. The right side of his gray coat is decorated with a scallop shell and a white pilgrim's staff. His white stockings are rolled down below his knees. Only the bust of the fourth man is visible, but one can see the same sort of hat decorated with a scallop shell, the lance-like pilgrim's staff, and the small, stylized staff he wears on his greenish coat. None of the garments look as if they have been worn during a long and strenuous journey. On the contrary, the linings of coats and stockings are shiny white. Judging from the simple, but elegant garments these are definitely not poor pilgrims such as those appearing in many other paintings, especially those in charity scenes. Instead, each pilgrim is distinguished by individual clothing features; there is no habit or "uniform."

St. Joachim and St. Anne Giving Alms to the Poor

One of the most interesting examples of pilgrims in a charity scene is the anonymous *c.* 1490 Netherlandish panel illustrating Joachim

and Anne giving alms to the poor.[44] (fig. 11) In the foreground
Joachim stands in a doorway distributing coins from his open purse
to three people who line up before the house. In the doorway, behind
Joachim, is a basket with loaves of bread. The first beggar is a cripple
with two crutches, who holds out a small bowl. Next to him stands
a middle-aged woman holding out her hands, receiving money from
Joachim. The brim of her hat is decorated with pilgrims' signs: two
scallop shells framing a small figure of a knight, whom Kurt Köster
identified as St. Adrian.[45] The woman is almost completely obscured
by a long dark overcoat and by a white veil which covers her hair
and neck, with only her face visible. She is not wearing real shoes,
but rather some kind of stockings leaving her toes bare. Behind her
a man holds out a bowl containing bread and cheese. His fur hat
is also decorated with the same arrangement of two scallop shells
framing a small pilgrims' sign showing an unidentified figure under
a late Gothic arch. An interesting genre-like element is the wooden
spoon the pilgrim has stuck under the brim of his hat according to
the custom of medieval beggars and begging pilgrims.[46] A little boy
with a small basket in his right hand waits in the distance. He might
be an orphan, known from the apocryphal gospels.[47]

   In the background, St. Anne gives money to a group of pilgrims
standing before her. They are apparently a small family with the
mother carrying the youngest child, while an older boy and the
father stand behind them. They are all poorly dressed and partly in
rags. The mother wears a long dress decorated with a pair of crossed
keys on the side of the heart. These keys of St. Peter, either sewn
or painted on the dress, were souvenirs of pilgrims to Rome. The
woman carries a shoulder bag and, on her head, she wears a simple
black hat with an open veil. The baby girl on her shoulders is also
poorly-dressed and wears no pilgrims' signs. The husband holds the

---

[44] The panel is part of the altarpiece of St. Anne now in the Historical Museum
in Frankfurt/Main, Inv. No. B 323. Kurt Köster, "Pilgerzeichen und Wallfahrtsplaketten
von St. Adrian in Geraardsbergen. Zu einer Darstellung auf einer flämischen Altartafel
des 15. Jahrhunderts im Historischen Museum zu Frankfurt am Main," *Städel Jahrbuch*,
Neue Folge, vol. 4, (1973): 103–20.

[45] Köster, "Pilgerzeichen," pp. 111–2.

[46] See the panel with the distribution of alms by St. Lucy by the Master of the
Legend of St. Lucy, *c.* 1480, Bruges, Sint Jakobs-Kerk. Jacques Lavalleye (ed.),
Primitifs Flamands Anonymes (Bruges, 1969), cat. 12, pp. 48–9.

[47] Köster, "Pilgerzeichen," p. 109.

typical long, double-knobbed walking stick and his coat is decorated with crossed pilgrim's sticks at the breast, apparently sewn or perhaps painted on the coat. Only the little boy, standing between his parents, wears the typical pilgrim's hat. It is decorated with the familiar arrangement of a badge showing a figure under an arch framed by two scallop shells. The boy carries a walking stick, adapted to his height, and a small basket. Köster suggested that this is a group of professional pilgrim-beggars, also called *fahrende Jakobsbrüder*,[48] (wandering Jacob's brothers) who were paid by wealthier people to undertake a pilgrimage in their place, although there is no visual proof of Köster's thesis.

Köster interpreted the staffs and keys as general pilgrims' emblems that were sewn on the clothes before people started the pilgrimage, whereas the figures and, to some extent, the scallop shells, belong to the category of pilgrims' souvenirs customarily purchased at the destination of the pilgrimage. Therefore, they could only be worn on the return journey, since their fabrication and sale was restricted to the place of pilgrimage itself, local producers and traders carefully guarding their privileges.[49] For instance, there is no proof that the scallop shells, however widespread their pictorial representations, could be purchased outside Santiago de Compostela and other shrines in France (Mont-St-Michel) and England (Canterbury) that borrowed the scallop shell motif fairly early.[50] One might ask if the widespread

---

[48] This is the title given to a woodcut by Jost Amman (1539–91) in Hans Sachs' *Ständebuch* (1568), a publication that offered typified portraits of different social classes and professions. The woodcut shows two savage-looking, bearded pilgrims rushing through a landscape. They are adorned with the usual attributes and their capes are covered with various signs. The critical inscription gives an idea of the restless life of these pilgrim-beggars: "We are Jacob's brothers who, with many others, have been wandering through the country, from Santiago to Rome. We are singing and begging like other poor people without feeling ashamed, and we do not complain to be reduced to beggary (literally: to hold the beggar's staff in our hands) spending our lives as idle beggars." (*Wir Jacobs brüder mit grossem hauffen/ Im Land sind hin und her gelauffen/ Von Sanct Jacob/ Ach und gen Rom/ Singen und betlen one schom/ Gleich anderen presthafften armen/ Offt thut uns der Bettel Stab erwarmen/ In Händen/ alsdenn wir es treibn/ Unser lebtag faul Bettler bleiben.*)

[49] Köster, "Mittelalterliche Pilgerzeichen," pp. 206–7. Ester Cohen, "In haec signa: Pilgrim-Badge Trade in Southern France", *Journal of Medieval History* 2 (1976): 193–214.

[50] It is important to note that these shrines adapted the scallop shell to their own iconography by adding a picture or an inscription with the name of the local saint. For examples from Canterbury see Brian Spencer, *Pilgrim Souvenirs and Secular Badges*

appearance of scallop shells in late-medieval paintings, especially in decorative arrangements, is bound to reality or at least partly to the artist's imagination. This suggests that it was art that transformed the scallop shell from the souvenir of Santiago de Compostela into the general emblem of pilgrimage in the late Middle Ages.

Women as Pilgrims

Although women pilgrims were common in the late Middle Ages, they were less frequently represented in art. A *c.* 1508 engraving by Lucas van Leyden offers the opportunity to study the garments of female pilgrims. (fig. 12) In this print, two pilgrims, a man and woman, are shown at rest,[51] while in the background another pilgrim is walking. The man who is seated on the right peeling a pear, is modeled on the common image of a pilgrim: a short tunic-like garment, already torn a bit at the border, a wide coat and fur hat with three signs attached to the front—two scallop shells flanking a *vera icon*,[52] indicating that he has been to Santiago de Compostela and to Rome.

The woman, who kneels next to her companion, wears a simple, though tidy, long dress with a wide skirt. Her hair is covered by a veil that hangs down to her shoulders. Over the veil she wears the typical pilgrims' hat with the large brim on which is sewn the same selection of pilgrims' signs as that of her husband. She also has a shoulder-bag and a long pilgrims' staff. Judging from the engraving and other representations such as the Frankfurt altarpiece, (fig. 11) special garments for female pilgrims did not exist. Women wore their everyday dresses; choosing simple and functional clothes suitable for a long journey. To characterize them as pilgrims, the artists gave them the same distinguishing marks as their male counterparts.

(London, 1998), pp. 40–3. For examples from Saint Michel see Denis Bruna, *Enseignes de pèlerinage et enseignes profanes* (Paris, 1996), pp. 184–7.

[51] Nuremberg, Germanisches Nationalmuseum, Inv. No. K 15223. Ellen S. Jacobowitz *et al.*, *The Prints of Lucas van Leyden and his Contemporaries* (Washington, 1983), Cat. 7, pp. 53–4.

[52] The *vera icon* (true image) or *sancta facie* (holy face of Christ) was considered to be the true portrait of Jesus Christ on the sudarium of St. Veronica, one of the most treasured relics of St. Peter's Cathedral in Rome. Badges showing the *vera icon* count among the most popular pilgrim souvenirs of Rome. Spencer, *Pilgrim Souvenirs*, pp. 248–52.

Accordingly, the woman in Lucas van Leyden's engraving carries the staff and the shoulder bag and wears the typical hat decorated with pilgrims' signs. Thus, the attributes of a pilgrim were added to the portrayal of women. A special or independent iconography of women pilgrims did generally not exist.

Representations of Pilgrim Saints

A study of medieval pilgrims' garments has to take into account representations of pilgrim saints, above all St. James, since he was a model for pilgrims. One should also note that the iconography of pilgrim saints was more conservative than that of typical pilgrims. According to Robert Plötz, a special iconography of St. James developed in the twelfth century, paralleling the booming pilgrimage to Santiago de Compostela and the rising interest in the saint. In the beginning, St. James was represented with a book in his hands, wearing a tunic, like other apostles. The first images of St. James with more singular attributes emerge in the twelfth century assimilating the new pilgrim's image to that of the saint.[53] Plötz locates the first extant example of that iconographic "contamination" at the south portal of the Spanish monastery of Santa Marta de Tera (Zamora), where St. James, though still wearing the garments of a priest, already appears with the attributes of the pilgrim: the bag with the scallop shell fixed onto it and the long walking stick. It is this image of St. James as prototype of a pilgrim that dominates the iconography of the saint in the late Middle Ages. On the c. 1515 Nuremberg *Haller Altarpiece*, St. James is shown in the clothes of a pilgrim,[54] wearing a simple, knee-length tunic fastened with a belt around his waist, and a long wide cape, which is open at the front. As *signa peregrinationis* he carries the shoulder bag, the double-knobbed staff and the rosary, and he wears the hat with its large brim decorated with a scallop shell and crossed pilgrims' staffs. It is this basic iconographic

---

[53] Robert Plötz, "Imago Beati Iacobi. Beiträge zur Ikonographie des Hl. Jacobus Maior im Hochmittelalter," in *Wallfahrt kennt keine Grenzen*, p. 255.

[54] Nuremberg, Germanisches Nationalmuseum, Inv. No. Gm 189. Löcher, *Die Gemälde des 16. Jahrhunderts*, pp. 360–1, Ill. p. 360. The panel is also discussed by Annette Scherer, "Mehr als nur Andenken. Spätmittelalterliche Pilgerzeichen und ihre private Verwendung," in *Spiegel der Seligkeit. Privates Bild und Frömmigkeit im Spätmittelalter*, ed. Frank Matthias Kammel (Nuremberg, 2000), p. 133.

model that dominated the image of the late-medieval pilgrim as well
as other pilgrim saints like St. Sebaldus.

St. Sebaldus

Compared to the universally-venerated St. James, the young shep-
herd/pilgrim St. Sebaldus ranks as a regional pilgrim saint.[55] Canonized
in 1425, he was the patron saint of Nuremberg, where he is said to
have wrought various miracles, including a wondrous rescue of a pilgrim to Rome who was attacked by a band of robbers—a story that
increased Sebaldus' glory as a protector of pilgrims. In a 1514 woodcut created by Nuremberg artist Hans Springinklee for a printed edition of the saint's legend, Sebaldus is represented standing in an
arched frame before a landscape, holding a model of the Nuremberg
St. Sebaldus Church in his right hand.[56] (fig. 13) He wears the typical pilgrim garments: the simple tunic-like dress and the wide cape.
He carries the shoulder bag, the double-knobbed staff, a rosary with
a small purse-like pendant to contain relics, and he wears a hat with
an extra-large brim tied up at the front in the usual way in order
to attach the pilgrims' signs.[57] As he was represented in various late-
medieval paintings and graphic works, without the church model
and the halo Sebaldus could be mistaken for a common pilgrim.

Conclusions

The analysis of extant pilgrims' garments and pictorial, as well as
textual sources, has shown that special clothes for pilgrims or a pil-

---

[55] *Der Heilige Sebald, seine Kirche, seine Stadt*, ed. Svetozar Sprusansky (Nuremberg,
1979). Arno Borst, "Die Sebaldus-Legenden in der mittelalterlichen Geschichte
Nürnbergs," *Jahrbuch für fränkische Landesforschung* 26 (1966): 19–177.
[56] Nuremberg, Germanisches Nationalmuseum, Inv. No. StN 2308. *Meister um
Albrecht Dürer*, ed. Peter Strieder (Nuremberg, 1961), cat. 350, p. 193.
[57] These are, however, not identifiable. In contrast, a slightly earlier representation of Sebaldus by a Nuremberg master from the altarpiece of St. Augustin (1487),
now in the Germanisches Nationalmuseum (Inv. No. Gm 143), shows a hat decorated by four pilgrim badges. Besides an unspecified Madonna there are pilgrim's
signs from Aachen (with a mirror), Rome (a *vera icon*) and Neuss (St. Quirinius).
Eberhard Lutze and Eberhard Wiegand, *Die Gemälde des 13. bis 16. Jahrhunderts*
(Leipzig, 1936/7), pp. 127–9, ill. 77.

grim's "uniform" did not exist in the Middle Ages. The garments were chosen individually according to the practical needs of a long and strenuous journey. The choice of the garments and equipment depended on the length of the journey, the destination and itinerary, the mode of travel (on foot, on horseback, by ship, alone or in company), the social rank and wealth of the traveler, and local dress codes. The example of Stephen Praun's pilgrimage to Jerusalem shows, for instance, that pilgrims willingly adopted the local costume for reasons of safety and also because it was better suited for the climate of southern countries.

Pilgrims were advised to prepare for their journey carefully. The majority of pilgrims surely took along more than one robe, one shirt, one undergarment, and one pair of shoes. This is certainly the case of pilgrims who, traveling on horseback or by ship, could easily stow their belongings in larger containers. The wanderer probably carried a big bag or bundle—not just the small shoulder bag depicted in medieval representations of pilgrims. The question of baggage is not the only obvious difference between textual and pictorial sources of medieval pilgrimage. In contrast to the variety of costumes known from texts and extant *realia*, the iconography of the medieval pilgrim is very conservative. The paintings and graphic works discussed in this essay have shown that the medieval artists adhered to an iconographic model of a pilgrim originating in the twelfth and thirteenth centuries. This model was used for "the pilgrim" in general, despite the era, origin, gender, or rank of the individual, and it was also taken as a formula for the representation of pilgrim saints.

The pilgrim could be recognized from these four items which appeared in nearly all pictures: the staff, the shoulder bag, the hat with its characteristic brim, and the pilgrims' signs attached to the garments. Of these items, only the pilgrims' signs can be exclusively related to pilgrimage, whereas the other three objects also belong to the equipment of the "typical" traveler in the Middle Ages. Regarding the pilgrim souvenirs, it is important to note that most of the signs could only be purchased at the destination of the pilgrimage. They were not part of the garment at the beginning of the journey, but adorned the pilgrim on the way back. Thus, the thesis of their supposed function as some kind of identity sign or "passport" cannot be maintained. As distinguishing marks, pilgrim souvenirs were only imperative in medieval art.

CHAPTER TWO

SPIRITUAL PILGRIMAGE IN THE PAINTINGS OF HANS MEMLING*

Vida J. Hull

Hans Memling's iconographic innovations enhanced the devotional function of his paintings and strengthened the interaction between worshipper and image, contributing to the artistic interpretation of the late medieval devotional practice of "spiritual pilgrimage." In a spiritual pilgrimage, the worshipper imagines himself accompanying Christ through the events in the Savior's life, just as the actual pilgrim to the Holy Land was instructed to imagine that he was present at the sacred events, praying and weeping at selected sites, as Ludolph of Saxony (d. 1378) described in his *Life of Christ*:[1]

> So it will be necessary for thee at times to make thyself present by thought . . . as though thou hadst been actually present at the time of the Passion, and so to behave thyself in thy manner of speaking, living, and grieving, as though the Lord were suffering before thy very eyes. For according as thou makest Him present with thee in thought will He be present with thee in spirit, receiving thy prayers and accepting thy works.[2]

---

* This is an expanded version of a paper presented at the 1994 College Art Association meeting in New York, chaired by Barbara Lane. See also Vida J. Hull, "Devotional Aspects of Hans Memlinc's Paintings," *Southeastern College Art Conference Review* 11 (1988): 207–13, which emphasized participatory devotion, noting the idea of spiritual pilgrimage in relation to Memling's Turin *Passion of Christ*.

[1] Ludolph was a Carthusian monk in Strasbourg, Coblenz, and Mainz. His *Vita Christi* appeared in numerous Latin manuscripts before it was first printed in 1472 in Cologne and later translated into many languages. Sister Mary Immaculate Bodenschaft, *The* Vita Christi *of Ludolphus the Carthusian* (Washington, D.C., 1944), pp. 18–20. Frank L. Cross and Elizabeth A. Livingstone, ed., "Ludolf of Saxony," in *Oxford Dictionary of the Christian Church* date the first edition to 1474 in Strasbourg and Cologne. Although Memling became a citizen of Bruges on January 30, 1465, his hometown was Seligenstadt in the diocese of Mainz. Therefore, he might have known of Ludolph's book in manuscript and certainly would have been influenced by the spiritual ambience that prompted it.

[2] Ludolph the Saxon, *The Hours of the Passion taken from* The Life of Christ *by Ludolph the Saxon*, ed. and trans. Henry James Coleridge (London, 1887), p. 2.

Wealthy pilgrims returning from the Holy Lands, such as the Adornes family of Bruges,[3] might recreate the Holy Sepulcher with architectural models or set up crosses and carvings at the proper intervals between sacred sites to preserve and simulate the experience of pilgrimage. But a worshipper did not need an architectural re-creation to walk with Christ in his imagination. Devotional treatises, such as those by Ludolph of Saxony and the Pseudo-Bonaventura,[4] instruct their readers to imagine themselves participating in the events of Christ's life and furnish step-by-step, incident-by-incident accounts of the life and suffering of Christ. The efficacy of such devotion was so esteemed that, during the fifteenth century, spiritual pilgrimages were believed to earn indulgences "as entirely as if . . . [the worshippers] were in the city of Jerusalem and visited bodily all those holy places."[5]

---

[3] Pieter Adornes (d. 1464) founded the Jerusalem church in Bruges (1427), modeled on a plan of the Holy Sepulcher that he brought back from his pilgrimage to Jerusalem with his brother Jacob Adornes (d. 1465). The church was completed by Pieter's son, Anselm (d. 1483) who, with his son Jan, also made the journey to the Holy Land in 1470–71. The Adornes connection with pilgrimage and their building of the Jerusalem Church are discussed in Jozef Penninck, *De Jerusalmkerk te Brugge* (Bruges, 1986), pp. 4–7, 10–1; Maximiliaan P.J. Martens, "New Information on Petrus Christus's Biography and the Patronage of his Brussels Lamentation," *Simiolus* 20 (1990/1991), pp. 13–5; Joseph J. Rishel, "The Philadelphia and Turin Paintings: The Literature and Controversy over Attribution," in *Jan van Eyck's Two Paintings of Saint Francis Receiving the Stigmata* (Philadelphia, 1997), pp. 5–7; André Vandewalle, *Adornes en Jeruzalem: International Levens in het 15de- en 16de-eeuwse Brugges* (Bruges, 1983).

[4] "Pseudo-Bonaventura" who wrote *Meditations on the Life of Christ* is believed to have been a thirteenth century Franciscan monk. The *Meditations* were translated and adapted into different languages; over 217 manuscripts are known. Isa Ragusa and Rosalie Green, eds., *Meditations on the Life of Christ*, trans. Isa Ragusa (Princeton, 1961), pp. xxi–xxiii, esp. fn. 2, 4. Even if it cannot be proven that Memling read this particular text (p. 5) its exhortations to the reader that ". . . if you wish to profit, you must be present at the same things that is related Christ did and said, joyfully and rightly . . ." clearly relates to the devotional practices of his time and applies generally to the naturalism of Netherlandish art and specifically to the contemplative mood established by many of Memling's paintings.

[5] Herbert Thurston, *The Stations of the Cross: An Account of Their History and Devotional Purpose* (London, 1906), pp. 162–3, quotes the title page of Heer Bethlem, *Overwegingen op het Lijden des Heeren voor degenen, die den Geest de heilige Plaatsen willen bezoeken* (Considerations on the Passion of Our Lord for those who wish to visit the Holy Places in Spirit), printed in Antwerp in 1536:

> This is the indulgence of the holy city of Calvary, which indulgence everyone can gain who follows the painful and heavy way of the cross-bearing of the naked and bleeding Jesus and this with pity on the bitter Passion in his inmost heart. This is not so to be understood as if those only gained by it who are in Jerusalem or who travel there, but all persons in what place soever they are, if they turn to God and meditate with attention and compassion on those

To aid the worshipper in this type of devotion, Memling developed a new kind of composition, seen in the multi-episodic, but compositionally unified Turin *Passion of Christ* (fig. 14) and the Munich *Joys of the Virgin*.[6] (figs. 15, 17) Tommaso Portinari (1428–1501), the representative of the Medici banking interests in Bruges, and his young wife, Maria Baroncelli commissioned the *Passion of Christ* (fig. 14) and are represented as kneeling and praying donors in the lower corners of the painting. This painting can be dated 1470, the year of the donors' marriage because their first child, Margarita, born in 1471, does not appear. Children were traditionally represented with their parents in donor portraits, as Margarita and her brothers are

---

holy places where this took place—as much as humanly they can—may gain this indulgence from the mercy of God as often as they themselves wish, and as entirely as if they were in the city of Jerusalem and visited bodily all those holy places.

Thurston, pp. 77, 177–9, cited the three printed editions of this "tiny brochure of sixteen leaves," one printed at "Aesii" (Jesi in the Marches of Ancona) by Federick de Comitibus in 1475 and two others printed in Antwerp in 1536 and 1561, and fifteenth century manuscripts in the British Museum (Add. 24937), in Göttingen (MS. Theol. 295, i) and a fragment in the Pauline Library at Münster (MS. 406). He argued that the original text was written by Bartholomew, Canon of Pola in Istria between 1471–75. Because Pope Sixtus IV is mentioned, it cannot be earlier than 1471, when he ascended to the papacy, and must have been completed before the 1475 publication date. The 1475 edition names the author, not as "Heer Bethlelem," but as "*prete bartolome, chanonicheo de puole*" (the priest Batholomew, canon of Pola).

[6] This painting is also known as "Christ, the Light of the World," by William Henry James Weale, *Hans Memling* (London, 1907), pp. 23–32; "The Seven Joys of Mary" by Max J. Friedländer, *Early Netherlandish Painting* VI a: *Hans Memling and Gerard David*, trans. Heinz Norden (New York, 1971), pp. 17, 27, cat. 33; "The Life of Christ and Mary" by Ludwig von Baldass, *Hans Memling* (Vienna, 1942), pp. 24–5, 44; "Panorama of the Epiphanies" or the "Bultync Altarpiece" by Kenneth B. McFarlane, *Hans Memling*, ed. Edgar Wind and Gerald L. Harriss (Oxford, 1971), pp. 30, 32, 71, figs. 71, 77–81; and "Scenes from the Advent and Triumph of Christ" by Dirk De Vos, *Hans Memling, the Complete Works*, trans. Ted Alkins (Antwerp, 1994), pp. 173–9. "The Seven Joys of the Virgin" has long been the traditional title, despite Weale's objection, p. 24, that the painting lacks two of the official "joys": the Visitation and the Finding of the Child in the Temple. Nor are only seven events depicted. De Vos, pp. 173–6, listed twenty-five separate scenes from Annunciation to Assumption. Still, with the exception of the Massacre of the Innocents, all the scenes are with joyous and glorious episodes from the life of Christ and his mother. Perhaps the "Bultync Altarpiece" or the "Tanners Guild Altarpiece" would be most accurate, but only Memling scholars can be expected to associate his recorded patrons with their paintings. The traditional title has the virtue of familiarity and accurately conveys the festive tone of the brightly colored panel. Therefore I have chosen to retain a non-numeric version of the traditional title, without implying that it is necessarily the most precise.

in Hugo van der Goes' *Adoration of the Shepherds (Portinari Altarpiece)*. The original location of the *Passion* is uncertain. From 1482 the painting was placed in the Portinari family chapel in the Church of St. Egidio (St. Gilles) in Florence, adjacent to the Hospital of St. Maria Nuova in Florence.[7] However, a gap of over a decade from the date of the painting to its documentation in the church indicates that this was not necessarily its intended location. Perhaps the painting was originally displayed in a private chapel within the Portinari household in Bruges,[8] and it could have been moved to his chapel in the Church of Sint Jacob (St. James) in Bruges, acquired in 1472.[9] The painting may have then been brought to Florence when Tommaso returned in 1480 and subsequently moved to the Portinari family chapel there.[10]

In any of these locations, Memling's *Passion of Christ* would have been directly associated with the patron and his family and therefore would have been available for personal devotion. The subject of the painting, the *Passion of Christ*, was appropriate for an altar at which Masses would be said for the souls of the Portinari, living and dead. According to late medieval Catholic doctrine, the Mass is an

---

[7] Elisabeth Dhanens, *Hugo van der Goes* (Antwerp, 1998), p. 261; Carlo Aru and Étienne de Geradon, *La Galerie Sabauda de Turin, Les Primitifs Flamands, Corpus de la peinture des anciens Pays-Bas méridionaux au quinzième siècle*, vol. 5 (Antwerp, 1952), p. 17. S. Egidio in Florence was a Romanesque church rebuilt by the Portinari family and dedicated in 1420. It was incorporated into Hospital of S. Maria Nuova in Florence, founded by Folco Portinari in 1275 which had grown into a major charitable foundation for the Portinari family. Shirley Nielsen Blum, *Early Netherlandish Triptychs* (Berkeley, 1969), pp. 83–4. Giorgio Vasari, *Le Vite de' Più Ecellenti Pittori, Scultori, e Architettori* (Milano, 1962) I, pp. 31–2, VII, pp. 463–4 reported that a little painting, *La passione di Cristo*, by "Ausse" (Hans), a disciple of Rogier, made for the Portinari in S. Maria Nuova, was in the Medici collection in their villa in Carreggi.

[8] The Portinari resided in the Hotel Baldelin, purchased with Medici funds and retained as a Medici property. When the financial collapse of the Medici branch in Bruges came, Lorenzo de Medici cited the expensive purchase and remodeling of this distinguished residence as one example of Portinari's fiscal irresponsibility. Raymond de Roover, *The Rise and Decline of the Medici Bank 1397–1494* (Cambridge, 1963), pp. 340, 349.

[9] Aby Warburg, "Flemish Art and the Florentine Early Renaissance (1902)" in *The Renewal of Pagan Antiquity: Contributions to the Cultural History of the European Renaissance*, trans. David Britt (Los Angeles, 1999), pp. 293, 482, cited a letter of William H. James Weale concerning records found in the archives of St.-Jacques in Bruges: "1472 Tommaso Portinari's chapel in Saint Jacques. 1475 Pew for his wife."

[10] Tommaso Portinari traveled between Florence, Milan, Bruges, and London, residing in Florence 1480–82. Blum, *Early Netherlandish Triptychs*, pp. 82–4, suggested that the *Portinari Altarpiece* by Hugo van der Goes may have been brought to Florence from its original location on the altar of the chapel of the Hospital of S. Maria Nuova in 1480. Perhaps Memling's painting accompanied it.

efficacious re-enactment of Christ's suffering and his death on the cross, with continued spiritual and saving benefits for the faithful. Like Christ's Passion, the Mass itself is a redemptive sacrifice whose merits can be applied to specific persons, living or in Purgatory.[11]

Tommaso Portinari journeyed from Milan to Florence to Bruges to London to conduct business for the Medici bank. He lent large sums of his partners' money to the Valois Dukes of Burgundy, King Edward IV of England, and Maximilian of Austria. He temporarily profited while bankrupting the Medici's Bruges branch, which was forced to close in 1485.[12] As an ambitious, worldly, and avaricious man, Portinari may have felt the need for spiritual security. The reputed indulgences attached to a spiritual pilgrimage perhaps attracted him as a investment in his immortal future, a good return for his prayers, and a pilgrimage he could take without a long absence from business. If his mind was wont to wander to temporal matters, he could focus on the details of Memling's painting and relive the suffering of the Savior who died to save his soul. The painting may also have been a comfort to his wife, Maria Baroncelli,[13] able to immerse herself in prayers and meditation when her husband took his frequent business trips or later when the family's fortunes were in dire straits. He might visit the courts of England and Burgundy, but she could venture as far as the Holy Lands in her mind's eye.

---

[11] Francis Oakley, *The Western Church in the Later Middle Ages* (Ithaca, 1979), p. 85, "each Mass came to be regarded as in some sense a repetition of Christ's original sacrifice on Calvary, a fresh sacrifice that, simply by virtue of its own individual quantum of grace, . . . priests and priests alone could offer, applying its merit . . . to petitioners or benefactors, present or absent, living or dead."

[12] Blum, *Early Netherlandish Triptychs*, p. 83; Warburg, "Flemish Art and the Florentine Early Renaissance," pp. 292–3; Richard Ehrenberg, *Capital & Finance in the Age of the Renaissance: A Study of the Fuggers and Their Connections*, trans. H.M. Lucas (London, 1928), pp. 196–7; de Roover, *The Rise and Decline of the Medici Bank*, pp. 93, 340–57. Portinari was fired and the Bruges branch of the Medici was closed in 1485. His enormous loans to royalty had left him in a precarious financial state. Although he performed diplomatic services for his patrons, according to de Roover when he died, his son refused the inheritance, fearing that the debts were greater than the assets. Margaret L. Koster, "New documentation for the Portinari altarpiece," *Burlington Magazine* 145 (March 2003), pp. 164–5, 178–9, stated that de Roover "made the chief misrepresentation of the facts of Portinari's life" and presented new documents (including Tommaso's will) proving that Franceso Portinari did accept his inheritance from his father before witnesses, a strong indication that Tommaso's financial state was not as dismal as de Roover believed.

[13] This is speculative, as we know almost nothing about Maria Baroncelli. Warburg, "Flemish Art and the Florentine Early Renaissance," p. 289, noted that she was fourteen when she wed her thirty-eight year old husband in 1470 and De Roover, *The Rise and Decline of the Medici Bank*, p. 343, stated that Maria was "still a child" of fifteen years when she married the forty-year old Tommaso.

Tommaso Portinari was an artistic patron who expressed his religious aspirations in pictorial form. Around the time of his 1470 marriage he ordered two paintings from Memling, the *Passion of Christ* and a triptych featuring portraits of himself and his wife praying to a sacred image, now lost, but presumably a half-length *Virgin Mary with the Infant Christ*,[14] rather like the triptych Memling painted for Tommaso's younger brother, Benedetto Portinari, in 1487, now divided between Berlin and Florence.[15] The patrons' images continued their constant prayer and perpetual adoration of the divine, even when the actual persons returned to worldly affairs.

A strong distinction is apparent between the huge *Adoration of the Shepherds* by Hugo van der Goes, destined for the main altar of the Hospital of St. Maria Nuova, and Memling's smaller, more intimate *Passion of Christ*.[16] The painting by Hugo is a public image, large enough so that it could be viewed easily by patients too ill to leave their beds. The recipients of Portinari charity would be reminded to offer prayers for their benefactors, the family depicted in the large side panels. By contrast, Memling's painting rewards close personal viewing and the effort of contemplation.

The same is true of Memling's *Joys of the Virgin*, except that it was intended for public view.[17] Completed in 1480, a decade after the *Passion*, it was donated by Pieter Bultync and his wife, Katelyne van Ryebeke, as the altarpiece for the Tanner's or Saddler's Guild Chapel, which was also the Lady Chapel, easternmost in the Church of Our Lady in Bruges.[18] The painting honors the Virgin Mary, appropriate for the dedication of the church and its presence in the Lady Chapel. The central scene in the foreground, the Adoration of the Magi, has liturgical implications as Mary, the *ara dei* (altar of God) or *ara coeli* (altar of heaven), holds her son, the Eucharistic bread, on her lap as the Magi, representatives of the universal church, approach. Therefore, Memling's altarpiece serves both devotional and liturgical functions.[19]

---

[14] The portraits are now in the Metropolitan Museum of Art in New York. Lorne Campbell, *Renaissance Portraits* (New Haven, 1990), pp. 16, 19–23, 176–7. De Vos, *Hans Memling*, pp. 100–3.

[15] De Vos, *Hans Memling*, pp. 284–6.

[16] Hugo van der Goes' Portinari *Adoration of the Shepherds* (249 × 137 cm, center 249 × 300 cm). Memling's Turin *Passion of Christ* (55 × 90 cm).

[17] Memling's *Joys of the Virgin* at 80 × 180 cm is twice the length of the Turin *Passion*.

[18] De Vos, *Hans Memling*, pp. 178–9.

[19] Vida Joyce Hull, *Hans Memlinc's Paintings for the Hospital of Saint John in Bruges*

Masses would have been said at the altar for the living and dead members of the guild and their families, but the sight of Memling's altarpiece would not have been limited to guild members. The openness of the Gothic architecture of the church allowed a clear view of the chapel and its altar. Memling's altarpiece would have been fully visible from the ambulatory outside the Lady Chapel, and a passerby might be attracted by the bright colors and intricate scenes to come closer and pray at the altar while contemplating the events portrayed in the painting. The decorative harnesses and saddles that adorn the Magi's mounts in the foreground might serve a further purpose of advertising the guild's products.[20]

Memling's *Passion of Christ* (fig. 14) and *Joys of the Virgin* (figs. 15, 17) were new types of compositions, created to enhance the spiritual experience of traveling through time and place with the Savior and his mother. Not that the simultaneous representation of different scenes within a single image was unprecedented,[21] but Memling

---

(New York, 1981), 113–4, discussed the liturgical aspects of Memling's Prado *Adoration of the Magi*; Hull, "Devotional Aspects of Hans Memlinc's Paintings," p. 209, concerning the the Munich *Joys of the Virgin* noted: "The central image is the Adoration of the Magi, placed close to the viewer in the immediate foreground as if to encourage the worshipper to join the representatives of the universal Church in homage to the Child." For Mary as altar, see Konrad Algermissen, ed. *Lexikon der Marienkunde* (Regensburg:, 1967), p. 154; Hippolytus Marracci. "*Polyanthea Mariana*," in *Summa Aurea de Laudibus Beatissme Virginis Mariae*, ed. Joannes Jacobus Bourassé (Paris, 1862), IX, pp. 882–4, 910 (*altare* and *ara*). Ursula Nilgen, "The Epiphany and the Eucharist," *Art Bulletin* 49 (1967): 311–6, offered an Eucharistic interpretation of paintings of the three Magi, although she does not mention the Virgin as "altar of heaven."

[20] McFarlane, *Hans Memling*, p. 30, fn. 12.

[21] James Marrow graciously provided me with a copy of his comments offered in the Memling session at the 1994 College Art Association meeting. He cited scenes from the Adoration of the Magi and Passion by the early fifteenth century Bedford Master from the *Sobieski Hours* (1420–25) in the Wallraf-Richartz Museum, Cologne, and the Schöppingen Altar, Schöppingen, Pfarrkirche (mid-fifteenth century). On the *Sobieski Hours* in Windsor Castle, Royal Library, see Eleanor P. Spencer, *The Sobieski Hours: A Manuscript in the Royal Library at Windsor Castle* (London, 1977); the Wasservass *Calvary*, Frank Günter Zehnder, *Katalog der altkölner Malerei* (Cologne, 1990), pp. 485–91, fig. 293; Birgitte Corley, *Painting and Patronage in Cologne 1300–1500* (Turnhout, 2000), pp. 110–2; Rainer Budde, *Köln unde seine Maler 1300–1500* (Cologne, 1986) pp. 59–61; Rainer Budde and Roland Krischel, *Das Wallraf-Richartz-Museum: Hundert Meisterwerke* (Cologne, 2000), pp. 56–7. For the Schöppingen Altar see Alfred Stange, *Deutsche Malerei der Gotik*, VI: *Nordwestdeutschland in der Zeit von 1450 bis 1515* (Munich, 1954), pp. 5–11, figs. 4, 7, note also a similar painting, the *Soest Altar*, formerly in the Berlin Museum, destroyed in 1945, fig. 5.

To these examples I would add two Flemish tapestries in the Museo de Tapices de la Seo in Saragossa (1410–25) that tell the story of the Passion and Resurrection

adapted and augmented his predecessors' examples, combining many
more episodes into a single composition. Memling's expansive panora-
mas of continuous, believable space offer a world view that adds
both geographic and temporal breadth to the experience of spiritual
pilgrimage.

Memling's predecessors did not provide the same comprehensive
vision of spiritual pilgrimage. Either the observer must visually skip
from image to isolated image with little sense of passage between
events [22] or the scenes are crowded together, one intermingling with
the next in chaotic confusion.[23] Of all Memling's visual predecessors,
the Bedford Master best provides a real sense of movement from
place to place.[24] Within the small confines of the manuscript pages
of the *Sobieski Hours* (1420–25), several scenes from the Hours of the
Virgin and the Hours of the Passion of Christ represent the continuity of sequential events within a single landscape.[25] Most relevant

---

of Christ in fifteen episodes and the tympanum of the *Three Kings Portal* of the
Liebfrauenkirche of Frankfurt. For the tapestries see Greet Ghyslen,"The Passion
Tapestries of the Saragossa Cathedral and Pre-Eyckian Realism," *Flanders in a European
Perspective, Manuscript Illumination around 1400 in Flanders and Aboard* eds. Maurits Smeyers
and Bert Cardon (Leuven, 1995), pp. 401–16; Eduardo Torra de Arana, Antero
Hombría Tortajada, and Tomás Domingo Pérez, *Los Tapices de La Seo de Zaragoza*
(Aragon, 1985), pp. 17–8, 20, 25, 33, 37, 61–73. For the *Three Kings Portal* refer to
Donald L. Ehresmann, "The Frankfurt Three Kings Portal, Madern Gerthener,
and the International Gothic Style on the Middle Rhine," *Art Bulletin* 50 (December
1968), pp. 301–8.

[22] The *Passion* tapestry in the Museo de la Seo Sargossa represents Jerusalem;
Torra de Arana, *Los Tapices de La Seo de Zaragoza*, p. 65; Ghyslen, "The Passion
Tapestries of the Saragossa Cathedral and Pre-Eyckian Realism," pp. 411–2, figs. 1–2.

[23] For the Sargossa *Passion* tapestry of the *Crucifixion* and *Resurrection* see Torra de
Aranal, *Los Tapices de La Seo de Zaragoza*, p. 73. For the German *Calvary* Altarpieces,
such as the *Wasservass Calvary*, the *Schöppingen Altarpiece*, and *Soest Altarpiece* by the
Master of the Schöppingen Altar see Zehnder, *Katalog der altkölner Malerei*, fig. 293;
Stange, *Deutsche Malerei der Gotik*, VI, figs. 4–5.

[24] Spencer, *The Sobieski Hours*, pp. 19–21 noted that three artistic hands can be
distinguished here: the Bedford Master, the Fastolf Master, and the Master of the
Munich *Golden Legend*. The Bedford Master created the most spatially-innovative
images, including the design and execution of the eight miniatures of the Hours of
the Virgin and the design for the eight miniatures of the Hours of the Passion,
painted by the Master of the Munich *Golden Legend*. The eight miniatures correspond to the number of canonical hours at which the divine office would be chanted.
Spencer, p. 32, pl. xxx–xxxvii (folios 24, 43, 52, 57, 61, 64v, 68, 73v), pl. xlvii–liv
(folios 168, 175, 179, 182, 186v, 191, 196, 199).

[25] Such as the *Adoration of the Magi* (folio 57), the *Massacre of the Innocents* (folio
64v), *Christ among the Doctors* (folio 68), and the *Preparations for the Crucifixion* (folio
186v), illustrated by Spencer, *The Sobieski Hours*, pl. xxxiii, xxxv, xxxvi, li, and cp.
facing p. 26. Other pages contain multiple episodes crowded into a single landscape or isolated into a myriad of scenes by architectural openings or painted frames.

for Memling's multi-episodic paintings are the illuminations of the *Adoration and Journey of the Magi* and of *Christ Carrying the Cross to Golgotha*.[26]

Although the Bedford Master centered a small scene of the *Adoration of the Magi* on folio 57 and included a smaller *Circumcision* on the left, the rest of the page is devoted to a detailed rendition of the Journey of the Magi.[27] The three kings and their retinue travel through a landscape of angular crags and diminutive trees, interspersed with imaginative dwellings. Their journey begins in the upper left corner as they approach Jerusalem and follows a reverse-*S* path curving back and forth across the page. Beneath the roofs of fanciful buildings the Magi address Herod, who in turn consults two figures, representing "all the chief priests and the scribes of the people."[28] The travelers from the East bid farewell to Herod before arriving at the rustic stable where they pay homage to the Christ Child on Mary's lap. Three episodes can be seen through open arches in the adjacent tall building: in the upper storey, the *Circumcision*, one floor down, the dream of two Magi while the third snoozes within a Capital D in the text box, and on the ground level the Magi's caravan of attendants, horses, and a camel prepare to depart through an arched gateway.

Like Memling's *Joys of the Virgin*, the Bedford Master's miniature takes us on a visual journey through time and place. Unlike Memling, the manuscript painter is limited to a single page and focuses on the particular experiences of the Magi in ancient Judea. Memling's vision is broader both spatially and temporally. If the manuscript image suggests the idea of journey and pilgrimage, Memling expands that vision to a world-view with vast distances that span over thirty years of sacred history.

The miniature depicting the *Way of the Cross* (f. 186*v*) also uses the device of the curving road. The action begins at the bottom of the page where Christ, bearing his cross, visible above a crenellated wall, is led toward the viewer's left. The procession ascends the page as

---

[26] Spencer, *The Sobieski Hours*, pp. 25–6, 32–3, cp. facing p. 26, pl. xxxiii (folio 57); pl. li (folio 186v) depicted *The Preparations for the Crucifixion*: Christ carrying his cross, stripped of his garment, and nailed to the cross.

[27] My measurements of the reproduction indicate that, allowing for the text box, approximately eighty percent of the pictorial image represents various episodes of the journey of the Magi.

[28] Matthew 2.4; *Douay-Rheims Bible* (London, 1963).

if climbing switchbacks up the side of Mount Calvary. As Christ moves to the right, he gazes over his shoulder at his grieving mother while Simon of Cyrene helps support the cross. The road leads to the top of Golgotha, where anecdotal details accompany the nailing to the cross: Christ is stripped of his garment while the thieves stand by, workmen dig a hole for the cross and bring a ladder, and an executioner pulls a rope to stretch Christ's arm on the crossbar.

The Bedford Master suggests the Journey of the Magi or Christ's painful trek to Golgotha by repeating his figures, inserting them in gateways, placing them on in curving paths that wrap around the page, and facing them back and forth to indicate direction. The crenellated wall, the figure on horseback in relation to the arched gateway,[29] the exotic cupola, and executioners stretching Christ's arms with ropes, are all elements found in Memling's more elaborate and extensive composition in Turin. But the manuscript illuminator includes only a few scenes on each page. He represents the story of the Passion of Christ from the Entry into Jerusalem to the Entombment on eight folios with multiple scenes that correspond to the canonical hours, but the illuminations lack the breathtaking vastness of Memling's unified image of city and landscape.

The closest visual precedents for Memling's *Passion* are two Flemish tapestries (1410–25) in the Museo de la Seo in Saragossa. Although their Spanish provenance makes it unlikely that Memling could have known them,[30] he might have seen others, now lost, woven from the same designs. The first tapestry represents Jerusalem with crenellated walls and buildings whose front walls open to reveal the figures within, pictorial devices also used by Memling. Unlike Memling's panel, though, the figures in the tapestry are all the same size, far too large to stand within the rooms they inhabit, and the architecture lacks spatial recession. The walls of the buildings act simply as frames

---

[29] In Memling's Turin *Passion* this equestrian is Pilate. In the *Sobieski Hours* his identity is not as clear, but he is the bearded man seen again on the hilltop, supervising the execution from horseback, although his costume and beard differ from the clean-shaven Pilate appearing repeatedly in folio 182, and those of Annas, Caiphas, and Herod in fols. 175, 179. His physiognomy (although not his dress) is closest to Joseph of Arimathea in fols. 191, 196, 199. Since Joseph's garments vary from page to page, we can only assume that the illuminator was not always consistent in his representation of characters.

[30] Ghyslen, "The Passion Tapestries of the Saragossa Cathedral and Pre-Eyckian Realism," pp. 401, 407. The tapestries were owned by Don Dalmacio de Mur, archbishop of Saragossa (d. September 12, 1456), although he was not necessarily the original owner.

to divide and isolate the scenes. Instead of moving easily between episodes, the eye skips up and down to follow the narrative.

The second tapestry includes the Way of the Cross, the Crucifixion, and three scenes from the Resurrection within a continuous landscape. It bears a remarkable resemblance to the central panel of the *Schöppingen Altar* and even more to the *Soest Altar*, both attributed to the Master of the *Schöppingen Altar*, with virtually the same arrangement of scenes.[31] All three show a crowded, turbulent Way of the Cross on the left, with figures advancing forcefully in a close-packed jumble beneath the cross. In contrast, Memling represents Jerusalem and its surrounding countryside as a unified and spatially-convincing panorama in which the final events of Christ's earthly life and his Resurrection interconnect without isolation or crowding. The eye moves from event to event, following subtle clues of gesture, tonality, and shape. The apparent reality of place and movement, of an environment through which a visual traveler may pause or traverse, enhances the sense of pilgrimage, the journey from sacred site to site, following Christ's steps.

Regarding the *Joys of the Virgin*, (fig. 15) Memling's truest predecessor may be a work of art that he actually could have seen on his way from his native Seligenstadt to Flanders: the *Three Kings Portal* of the Liebfrauenkirche of Frankfurt (1425–30).[32] (fig. 16) Attributed to Madern Gerthener, architect at St. Bartholomäus in Frankfurt,[33]

---

[31] Stange, *Deutsche Malerei der Gotik*, VI, pp. 5–11, 140, 147, figs. 4–5. Instead of the Three Marys at the Tomb and the Noli me tangere in the upper right of the Saragossa tapestry, the German retables feature the Entombment. Presumably, the post-Resurrection scenes appeared in the right wing; Stange, *Deutsche Malerei der Gotik*, VI, fig. 7. Certain details found in the Saragossa tapestry and Soest altarpiece are not seen in the *Schöppingen Calvary*: Christ's compassionate gaze over his shoulder at his mother as he bears the cross, soldiers fighting over Christ's garments, Christ prodding a recumbent devil with the staff of his banner of the Resurrection in the Harrowing of Hell. The latter two are also found in Memling's Turin *Passion*.

[32] Ehresmann, "The Frankfurt Three Kings Portal," p. 301, n. 1, dated the portal sculpture to 1425–30 on the basis of costume.

[33] Madern Gerthener was *Werkmeister* (master of work or city architect) of Frankfurt in 1409 and paid for his work on the tower of the church of St. Batholomäus (*Frankfurter Dom*) from 1410–25. Ehresmann, "The Frankfurt Three Kings Portal," p. 301, fn. 2, citing Walter K. Zülch, *Frankfurter Künstler, 1223–1700* (Frankfurt, 1935), pp. 48–53. According to Ehresmann, "The Frankfurt Three Kings Portal," pp. 301–2, the attribution of the *Three Kings Portal* to Gerthener by Josef Edler, *Die Liebfrauen-Kirche zu Frankfurt am Main und ihre Kunstwerke* (Düren,1938), p. 30f., based on similarities between the architecture of the portal and the Bartholomäus-tower, was highly-speculative because there is no documented sculpture by Gerthener.

or an assistant,[34] the carved tympanum which originally surmounted
the south portal of the church, today is enclosed within the baptismal chapel. The tympanum represents the Adoration of the Magi
in the lower foreground with the eldest Magus kneeling before the
naked Christ Child on his mother's lap. Like Memling's painting, it
includes a visual image of the Journey of the Magi to pay homage
to the Christ Child, including their three separate routes.[35] Jagged
cliffs and stylized miniature trees divide the tympanum into sections
through which the equestrian Magi and their retinue approach the
holy family separately. In the point of the tympanum's arch the
Annunciation to the Shepherds takes place. Although Memling's
vision is far more expansive, he uses rocky outcroppings, in a similar fashion, as a directional device, guiding the retinue of the Magi
on their return from Bethlehem.

Earlier Flemish and German examples of simultaneous representation lack the illusionistic virtuosity of Memling's work and his ability
to combine a multiplicity of separate events within a spacious, believable setting.[36] His figures and scenery adhere to a consistent scale,

---

[34] Ehresmann, "The Frankfurt Three Kings Portal," pp. 301–8, attributed the
tympanum to the first assistant of Gerthener based on analysis of style also seen in
the Liebfrauenkirche tympanum, sculpture at Mainz Cathedral, and a drawing of
the *Holy Grave and a Sacrament Shrine* in Berlin. Because the drawing features more
conservative architectural tracery than the complex shapes found on the Bartholomäus
tower (Gerthener's documented work), Ehresmann argued that the Three Kings
Master could not be Gerthener. The *Three Kings Portal* contains two architectural
styles: the molding and baldachin of the opening correspond to Gerthener's own
style, but the tympanum itself and the surrounding decoration was crafted by the
more conservative mason, suggesting that the *Three Kings Portal* was begun by
Gerthener and completed by his assistant after Gerthener's death.

[35] Memling shows the Three Kings meeting at the juncture of their three different
roads in the upper left, as described in Johannes von Hildesheim's *Liber Trium Regum*
(1364–75) and both Gerthener and Memling use banners to distinguish the Magi.
Ehresmann, "The Frankfurt Three Kings Portal," p. 307. The same scene appears
on folio 51 *verso* of the *Tres Riches Heures du Duc de Berry* (*c.* 1416) in which the three
roads taken by the Magi converge at a pagan monument near Jerusalem (appearing in the distance with the monuments of Paris, St. Chapelle, Notre-Dame, and
Montmartre). Millard Meiss, *French Painters in the Time of Jean de Berry: The Limbourgs
and Their Contemporaries* (New York, 1974), p. 156, pl. 571; Jean Longnon and
Raymond Cazelles, *The Très Riches Heures of Jean, Duke of Berry, Musée Condé,
Chantilly* (New York, 1969), p. 48.

[36] Charles D. Cuttler, *Northern Painting From Pucelle to Bruegel* (New York, 1968),
p. 171, wrote that "Memling here approached a problem for which there was no
precedent: the organization of numerous scenes of a narrative within a single, unified
space."

diminishing in size, but remaining perfectly readable as the panorama extends into the distance. By exercising his own particular genius for transforming numerous events into a single, unified image,[37] Memling created something new: an altarpiece that guides the devout viewer on a spiritual journey through sacred history, that reveals a unified image of the Holy Land as if the worshipper were actually present and could see the holy events not only "in thought," but in the vision created by the painter's skill.

Travelers who actually journey to the Holy Land cross not only vast territories but also go back in time. As physical pilgrims tread the land where Christ once walked and kneel at the sacred sites, they are expected to imagine themselves in the presence of Christ and his mother, of the apostles, and the saints. So the spiritual pilgrim, kneeling before Memling's paintings, sees not only the individual events, but also the detailed topography that separates and links each episode of sacred history. Memling's multi-episodic paintings provide the visual experience of travel through both time and space. Devotees become sightseers, visually wending their ways through the city of Jerusalem with its narrow streets and exotic cupolas in the Turin *Passion*. They voyage over hill and dale, across seas and over bridges, along winding roads and through rocky gorges, stopping at cities and villages in the *Joys of the Virgin*. As they mentally travel through the Holy Land, they also travel through time, witnessing the betrayal and agony of the Passion, observing the Nativity and the Resurrection.

The spiritual pilgrim meditating before Memling's *Passion of Christ* (fig. 14) travels Christ's road, passing through the city gates in triumph and moving through the streets of Jerusalem, following the road as it leaves the city and ascends to Golgotha.[38] Each event, isolated in its own space by landscape or architecture, could be a focus for meditation as the devout viewer becomes a witness to all the occurrences of Holy Week. Even subsidiary incidents appear in illusionistic detail that enhance the significance and reality of the scenes.

---

[37] Memling's life of Mary and Passion of Christ is analogous to his treatment of the Apocalypse in the *Altarpiece of the Two Saint Johns* for the Hospital of St. John in Bruges. Long-standing tradition represented each vision of St. John as a separate scene, but Memling was the first to represent the entire vision as a single unified composition. Blum, *Early Netherlandish Triptychs* (Berkeley, 1969), pp. 90–1; Hull, *Hans Memlinc's Paintings for the Hospital of Saint John*, pp. 73–80.

[38] Aru and de Geradon, *La Galerie Sabauda de Turin*, pl. XXII–XXXIX.

In the glow of light cast from the open window of the upper room where Christ shares his Last Supper with the apostles, the worshipper sees Judas Iscariot stealthily departing into the darkness of night. A carving of the Judgment of Solomon above Pilate's throne room contrasts with the Roman governor's unjust condemnation of Christ. Workman construct the cross before the building in which the Flagellation takes place.[39] As Pilate presents Christ to the crowd, a soldier and a turbaned man cross their arms to suggest the mob crying out, "Crucify him!"[40] On a distant hillside, executioners tug on ropes as they stretch Christ on the cross, as described by Pseudo-Anselm and by St. Bridget of Sweden.[41] When Christ falls, it is in the foreground, beside the praying donatrix. Christ gazes directly at the viewer, reminding him that such agony is for their sake. "Look at Him well," says the Franciscan author of the *Meditations on the Life of Christ*, "as He goes along bowed down by the cross and gasping. Feel as much compassion for Him as you can, placed in such anguish, in renewed derision."[42]

Memling has re-created not only the appearance of Jerusalem and its environs, taking the worshipper back in time to witness the sacred events, but has carefully constructed the *Passion* to correspond to the times of day in which the events of the passion took place: from the sunlight entry into Jerusalem to the darkness of the night of Holy Thursday, the evening of the Last Supper, the Agony in the Garden,

---

[39] Ghyselen,"The Passion Tapestries," pp. 405–7, discussed the theme of the Making of the Cross, derived from the Legend of the True Cross, which appears in the Sargossa *Jerusalem Tapestry* and Memling's Turin *Passion*.

[40] McFarlane, *Hans Memling*, p. 40.

[41] Frederick P. Pickering, *Literature and Art in the Middle Ages* (Coral Gables, FL, 1970), p. 237–40, cited. Pseudo-Anselm, *Dialogus S. Anselmi cum B.V. Maria*, for "the assertion that they [the enemies of Christ] pulled so violently at his limbs that the words of the Psalmist (would or should be) fulfilled: 'they counted all my bones.'" Also "by the middle of the thirteenth century, there were copies in practically every monastic library in Europe," p. 237. The motif can also be found in St. Bridget of Sweden, *Revelation of St. Bridget on the Life and Passion of Our Lord and his Blessed Mother* (Fresno, CA, 1957), pp. 60, 66. Executioners tugging on ropes to increase Christ's suffering can be found in many images of Christ nailed to the cross, including the bas-de-page of the *Tres Belles Heures*, the *Wasservass Calvary* in Cologne and the *Karlsruhe Passion* (from the Church of St. Thomas in Strasbourg). Paul Durrieu, *Les Très Belles Heures de Notre-Dame du duc Jean de Berry* (Paris, 1922), pl. XXIII; Zehnder, *Katalog der altkölner Malerei*, fig. 293 the *Wasservass Calvary*; Klaus Schrenk, ed. *Die Karlsruhe Passion, Ein Hauptwerk Straßburger Malerei der Spätgotik* (Stuttgart, 1996), p. 23, pl. 6.

[42] Isa Ragusa and Rosalie Green, eds., *Meditations on the Life of Christ*, p. 331.

and the Betrayal of Judas. Friday dawns with the crowing of the cock, marking Peter's denial. In the sunlit courtyard and palaces, Christ's torments and condemnation take place, culminating in the way of the cross and the Crucifixion on a distant Mount Golgotha. Nicodemus and Joseph of Arimathea lay Christ's body in the tomb before sunset, when the sun's rays have just begun to dim. Likewise, the Resurrection occurs early Easter morning.

Memling's painting of the Infancy and post-Resurrection epiphanies of Christ in the *Joys of the Virgin*, calls for a similar devotional participation. Memling represented the donor as physically present at the Nativity, watching through a grated window in the stable. Once again, the winding road unites the episodes and serves as a device to carry the worshipper's eye and mind from event to event.

The largest scene, prominently located in the central foreground, is the Adoration of the Magi. The Wise Men from the East are archetypical pilgrims, journeying long distances to pay homage to the actual epiphany of Christ in the flesh. In Memling's painting, much attention is paid to the Journey of the Magi: traveling with their entourage to Judea where they meet at the junction of three roads, conferring with Herod, returning by land and sea to their own countries. Memling has emphasized the Magi's role as pilgrims, perhaps to suggest the worshipper's role as a spiritual pilgrim, who meditates on these events.

Indeed, the motif of the journey features prominently in this painting. From the hillside where the angel announces the birth of Christ, the shepherds travel a winding road to the stable, emerging through an arch behind the donor, who has already arrived to offer his homage. The Flight into Egypt appears in background scenes of the upper left with the Miracle of the Date Palm and the Destruction of the Idols. (fig. 17) In a perverse inversion of the sacred pilgrimage, Herod's soldiers seek the Child in order to destroy him, but are thwarted by the Miracle of the Ripening Grain. To the right of the Magi scenes, roads traveled by the Holy Women lead to the Resurrection at the Holy Sepulcher. In the distance, along the same road, appears the Journey to Emmaus. In the left foreground, the donatrix kneels before a room sheltering the Virgin and the apostles as they experience the descent of the Holy Spirit. Although the journeys of the apostles are not shown, the knowledgeable worshipper might recall that after Pentecost the apostles departed to travel to distant lands to preach.

The donatrix's eyes do not focus on the scene, but rather gaze ahead, a device used by Jan van Eyck and others to suggest a spiritual envisioning.[43] Thus the donors exemplify ways in which the worshipper might participate in the spiritual pilgrimage. By focusing on the inner life and imagining the sacred events in heart and mind, like the donatrix, the viewer becomes "present by thought" to the scenes behind her. Memling's skillful representation of the sacred scenes provides the visualization sought by the donor and by the contemplative viewer who meditates before the painting.

By developing the use of small background scenes to expand the narrative of the foreground subjects, Memling enriched the traditional altarpiece format with the idea of spiritual pilgrimage. In the inner opening of the *Lübeck Calvary* polyptych, (fig. 18) the donor kneels in prayer while the object of his contemplation, a detailed narrative of Passion and Resurrection, unfolds behind him. Gazes, gestures, and facial expressions draw the viewer into the main scenes, while additional background events occur along the road, leading the contemplative devotee with Christ from the Agony of Gethsemane to the Ascension on Mount Olivet. The donor himself kneels at the gateway to Jerusalem as Christ passes, bearing his cross. Christ gazes directly at the viewer, as does his exotically-garbed tormentor. Such parallel eye contact creates the illusion that the worshipper is actually present in the crowd and is forced to choose between the suffering Savior and the guard. The donor, like the donatrix in the *Joys of the Virgin* or Tommaso Portinari in the *Passion*, stares straight ahead, as if he does not see Christ's torment with physical sight, but follows the Savior's path in devout contemplation.

Curving roads in the background of Memling's *Crucifixion Triptych of Jan Crabbe* suggest just such a spiritual journey.[44] In the central

---

[43] The unfocused gaze indicating spiritual vision in Jan van Eyck's paintings was first identified by James Snyder, "Jan van Eyck and the Madonna of Chancellor Nicolas Rolin," *Oud-Holland* 82 (1967): 165–6; James Snyder, "Observations on the Iconography of Jan van Eyck's "'Saint Francis Receiving the Stigmata,'" in *Jan van Eyck's Two Paintings of* Saint Francis Receiving the Stigmata, pp. 75–87, esp. pp. 82–4. Craig Harbison demonstrated that other artists used the same device. Craig Harbison, "Visions and Meditations in Early Flemish Painting," *Simiolus* 15 (1985): 100–7.

[44] De Vos, *Hans Memling*, pp. 90–3. The central panel of the Crucifixion is in the Museo Civico in Venice, the interior, donor wings in the Morgan Library in New York, and the exterior *Annunciation* in the Groeningemuseum, Bruges. Maria Corti and Giorgio T. Faggin, *L'opera Completa di Memling* (Milan, 1969), pl. LII–LIII, p. 95.

Crucifixion panel, the Carthusian donor kneels beside Mary Magdalen at the foot of the cross, yet his gaze does not focus on the sacred event. Clearly Christ's sacrificial death takes place not before his physical sight, but in his mind's eye. In the background a winding road extends from Jerusalem, past the site of the Crucifixion, and behind the donatrix on the side panel. The road is the *via crucis*, the Way of the Cross traveled by pilgrims through Jerusalem to Calvary, suggesting the spiritual journey of the praying donatrix.[45] In the opposite wing her adult son reads from his devotional text, while behind him another road leads over hillocks to the distant horizon, denoting his journey home and implying that the donors take with them the spiritual benefits of their devotional pilgrimage as they return and continue on the road of life.

Although Passion scenes may be most readily associated with spiritual pilgrimages, the device of winding roads punctuated by other sacred scenes may also encourage the devout viewer to imagine himself accompanying Christ or a saint on the road of life, meditating on each event. For example, worshippers before the Bruges *Altarpiece of the Two Saint Johns* might imagine themselves in the crowd listening to the Baptist preach or experiencing the vision of the Evangelist on Patmos.[46] Following in private devotion the meandering paths to the background scenes in Memling's intimate *Rest on the Flight into Egypt*, the pious devotee might remember with mixed sorrow and joy the travail and the miraculous escape of the Holy Family as they fled Herod's soldiers. Likewise, in the flanking and exterior panels,[47] (fig. 19) the tiny scenes along the background roads lead the spiritual pilgrim through the lives of the saints to the larger, standing

---

[45] Compare to the interpretation of the winding road behind the donor in Campin's *Entombment* in Matthew Botvinick, "The Painting as Pilgrimage: Traces of a Subtext in the Work of Campin and His Contemporaries," *Art History* 15 (March 1992): 1–6.

[46] De Vos, *Hans Memling*, pp. 150–7; Hull, *Memlinc's Paintings for the Hospital of St. John*, pp. 51–91, esp. 66–80.

[47] John the Baptist and Mary Magdalen appear on the inner wings in the Louvre. The exterior panels in the Cincinnati Art Museum show St. Stephen and St. Christopher. Nicole Reynaud, "Reconstruction d'un triptyque de Memling," *La Revue du Louvre* 24 (1974): 79–90. De Vos, *Hans Memling*, pp. 186–9; Mary Ann Scott, *Dutch, Flemish, and German Paintings in the Cincinnati Art Museum, Fifteenth through Eighteenth Centuries* (Cincinnati, 1987), pp. 88–91, 126, cp. 30–1; Micheline Comblen-Sonkes and Philippe Lorentz, *Musée du Louvre Paris II*, 2 vols. *Les Primitifs Flamands, Corpus de la peinture des anciens Pays-Bas méridionaux et de la principauté de Liège au quinzième siècle 17* (Brussels, 1995), I, pp. 194–219; II, pl. CCXX–CCXLIX. For the *Rest on the Flight into Egypt*, see Corti and Faggin, *L'opera completa di Memling*, pl. XXXIX.

images of the saints or the Virgin—living statues for veneration. Falkenberg termed these small background scenes *Andachtsbilder* and "mnemograms."[48] They serve as stops along the way in the viewer's mental journey through the life of the saint, analogous to the pauses at shrines on a physical pilgrimage.

Winding roads are leitmotifs in Memling's work, serving as compositional devices uniting pictorial elements and animating the background with graceful, curving forms. In many paintings these roads also serve an iconographic and devotional function, guiding the devout viewer through a spiritual pilgrimage. When Memling represented the pilgrimage of St. Ursula and her companions, the device of the winding road indicated the progress of the journey over land and the continuity between scenes, suggesting the activity of pilgrimage. The *Ursula Shrine* (fig. 23) emphasizes the saints as martyrs and pilgrims, appropriately for its function in a medieval hospital, whose purpose was to care for the indigent sick, to house travelers overnight, and to ensure that the souls under its care prepared to make a blessed death. All patients and transients were pilgrims through life and death. The physical presence of the relics of the saints offered the potential for a miraculous cure, but they also ensured that the martyrs could be called upon to aid those in danger of death. They could also be invoked by pilgrims to aid and protect the traveler both physically and spiritually as he continues on his way.[49]

Even without the background narrative scenes, the association of road to pilgrimage was retained. Harbison interpreted Memling's *Virgin and Child with the Family of Jakob Floreins* as a pilgrimage: "Here in the landscape . . . one can trace this family's journey as it approached the shrine."[50] The image of the Virgin is the object of their pilgrimage and the focus of their veneration, analogous to a miraculously animated cult statue.[51] Although Harbison did not specifically mention

[48] Reindert Falkenburg, *Joachim Patinir: Landscape as an Image of the Pilgrimage of Life* (Amsterdam, 1988), pp. 36–7, 41.

[49] Hull, *Memlinc's Paintings for the Hospital of St. John*, pp. 27–31, 188–92; De Vos, *Hans Memling*, pp. 296–302; Corti and Faggin, *L'opera completa di Memling*, pl. XXVIII–XXX. *Editors' note, see also Jeanne Neuchterlein's essay in this volume.

[50] Craig Harbison, *Jan van Eyck: The Play of Realism* (London, 1991), p. 180; De Vos, *Hans Memling*, pp. 310–1; Comblen-Sonkes and Lorentz, *Musée du Louvre Paris II*, I, pp. 238–62, II, pl. CLXXII–CXCIII.

[51] Miraculous statues were often the goal of pilgrimages. David Freedburg, *The Power of Images: Studies in the History and Theory of Response* (Chicago, 1989), pp. 99–121; Harbison, *Jan van Eyck*, p. 178 noted that "The cult of Mary did not need relics—

the winding roads in Memling's landscape, it is the motif of the path or pilgrimage road leading to worshippers who crowd into the shrine that conveys the idea of journey and arrival.

No donors appear in the Raleigh *Christ on the Cross*,[52] (fig. 20) where the crucified Savior appears alone before a landscape. In the middle-ground two tortuous roads meet to form a single path leading toward the mound from which the cross rises.[53] One road leads

---

only statues—new or old." Miraculous images were believed not only to cure diseases and protect the faithful, but sometimes took on the attributes of life—weeping, bleeding, lactating, and speaking.

[52] Although this small painting (45 × 28 cm) is attributed to Memling by the museum, De Vos did not include it in his monograph on Memling. Wilhelm R. Valentiner, *Catalogue of Paintings Including Three Sets of Tapestries* (Raleigh, 1956), p. 64, no. 121, noted that the painting was attributed to Memling by Friedländer and it was included in *Memling Tentoonstelling, ingericht door het stadtsbestuur in het Stedelijk Museum te Brugge (22 Juni–1 October 1939) Catalogus* (Bruges, 1939), p. 69, no. 16. It was attributed to the Master of the Legend of Saint Ursula in Friedländer, *Early Netherlandish Painting*, vol. VIb, Add. 274, pl. 255.

Stanley Ferber, "The Armorial Device in Memling's *Christ on the Cross*," *North Carolina Museum of Art Bulletin* 6 (1966), pp. 17–20, identified the coat of arms as that of Pietro Barbo, who became Pope Paul II in 1464 and suggested a date of 1462, when Pietro's brother visited France. If so, the painting would be the earliest extant work by Memling. However, the landscape has more technical sophistication and spatial development than Memling's early works, so it was likely painted later, as suggested by the museum's photo label, *c.* 1480. The same armorial device of Barbo arms surmounted by a cardinal's hat was also used by Marco Barbo, whose dates as cardinal (1467–1491) and his known piety make him a more likely owner of Memling's painting. Hans-Joachim Eberhardt (Kunsthistorisches Institut, Florence), letter of November 23, 1975, in museum files, identified both Barbo cardinals and stated that the lower coat of arms belonged to one of two Brabant families, the Berghes or the van Grimsbergen. For Marco Barbo, see *Dizionario Biografica degli Italiani* vol. 6 (Rome, 1964), pp. 249–52; Margaret L. King, *Venetian Humanism in an Age of Patrician Dominance* (Princeton, 1986), pp. 6, 32, 327–8; Melissa Merian Bullard, "Renaissance Spirituality and the Ethical Dimensions of Church Reform in the Age of Savonarola: the Dilemma of Cardinal Marco Barbo," in *The World of Savonarola, Italian Élites and Perceptions of Crisis*, ed. Stella Fletcher and Christine Shaw (Aldershot, 2000), pp. 65–89. Such a small work was not necessarily commissioned, but could have been created by the artist as a devotional image to appeal to a wide range of buyers, who could have had another artist add a coat of arms.

[53] Falkenburg, *Joachim Patinir*, p. 88, cited Bosch's *Wayfarer* paintings in the Prado and Rotterdam in which a *Y*-shaped road or tree are said to refer to the choice of two paths through life, the good and the evil. In the case of Memling's *Christ on the Cross*, the roads are not strewn with allegorical temptations, but the path on Christ's right does lead to a steep and craggy mountain, the traditional image of the arduous road of virtue, as in the drawing of *Virtutes and Voluptas* (1515/16) by Peter Vischer the Younger. Chrisian Müller *et al.*, *From Schongauer to Holbein: Master Drawings from Basel and Berlin* (Washington, 1999), pp. 269–70. Along the road to Christ's left rides a man on horseback, who might represent the worldly man who turns his back and journeys away from Christ.

toward a distant city, presumably Jerusalem, recalling the *via crucis*, the way of Christ bearing his cross to Golgotha. This image, isolated from the numerous persons of the Calvary narrative, seems to be for private devotional use. Perhaps the motif of the road served to remind the viewer that they should accompany Christ on a mental pilgrimage, supplying the details from their own imagination to relive the events that brought him to the Cross. The road may also remind them of their own journey through life, a pilgrimage that leads the devout Christian to the cross of Christ, on whose sacrifice they rely for salvation.

The motif of the curving road which appears so frequently in Memling's portraits may even suggest the subject's own pilgrimage through life,[54] a metaphor that became increasingly popular during the Middle Ages.[55] Perhaps the winding road, already identified as

---

[54] Portraits by Memling with winding roads in the background include the *Man in a Red Hat* in Frankfurt, the *Man before a Landscape* in the Frick Collection in New York, *Old Man and His Wife*, split between Berlin and Paris, the *Portrait of Willem Moreel Praying* in Brussels, the *Man with a Letter* in Florence, the *Young Man in a Loggia* the Metropolitan Museum, the *Man with a Rosary* in Copenhagen, and the *Benedetto Portinari Triptych of the Virgin and Child* divided between Berlin and Florence. De Vos, *Hans Memling*, pp. 97, 111, 116–7, 132–3, 195, 201, 257, 284–5.

[55] Jonathan Sumption, *Pilgrimage: An Image of Mediaeval Religion* (Totowa, NJ, 1975), p. 300, refers to the "pilgrimage of daily life." Botvinick, "The Painting as Pilgrimage," p. 4, noted that pilgrimage became a medieval metaphor "for life itself." Falkenburg, *Joachim Patinir*, pp. 86–7, 98, described the literature and theological history of "the wider metaphor of the 'peregrinato vitae' which all men have to make." The very theme of his book is "landscape as an image of the pilgrimage of life."

Siegfried Wenzel, "The Pilgrimage of Life as a Late Medieval Genre," *Mediaeval Studies* 35 (1973), pp. 370–88; Falkenburg, *Joachim Patinir*, pp. 86–7, discussed medieval literature likening life's journey to a pilgrimage. The motif stems from Paul's letter to the Hebrews 11:13–16 in which those who "died according to faith" confess that "they are pilgrims and strangers on the earth." In the Vulgate the relevant passage from Hebrews 11:13 reads, "confetentes quia peregrine et hospites sunt super terram." The idea that human history is a pilgrimage to the heavenly city of God was expanded by St. Augustine's *Civitas Dei* (City of God), but the direct source of the pilgrimage of life motif for medieval authors was St. Bernard's "First Parable," in which man transverses an allegorical landscape to finally be led to God by Queen Charity. This gave rise to literature in which the "pilgrimage of life" is the central metaphor, such as Guillaume de Deguileville's, *Le Pèlerinage de la vie humaine* (The Pilgrimage of Human Life) (1330–31), and Jean de Courcy's *Chemin de Valliance* (The Way of Valor) British Museum (MS. Royal 14. EW. ii, fols. 1–294; Rosamond Tuve, *Allegorical Imagery: Some Mediaeval Books and Their Posterity* (Princeton, 1966), pp. 145–218. Falkenburg, *Joachim Patinir*, pp. 87, 132–3, fn. 382–6, listed books known in the Low Lands in the fifteenth century which used the theme of the pilgrimage of life. Thomas à Kempis, *The Imitation of Christ*, trans, Richard Whitford (New York: Pocket Books, 1953), I, 1, p. 68, reminds the reader that "thou art but a stranger and a pilgrim, and never shalt thou find perfect rest till thou be fully united to God."

a reference to pilgrimage in a holy scene, might refer to the sitter's journey through life. In many cases, travelers walk or ride on horseback along these roads, suggesting passage from one place to another. Although we have no proof that the road is more than a compositional motif, a graceful shape to unite foreground and background, one indication that it may be more is found in a later painting by an artist active in Bruges, who knew Memling's work.

The landscape background of a *Portrait of a Man* by Ambrosius Benson is based on Memling's familiar landscape motifs: the thatched cottage, the arched bridge, the swan swimming in a stream.[56] (fig. 22) Behind the sitter's shoulder a man with the characteristic broad hat and staff of a pilgrim strides across the bridge, headed toward the edge of the painting as he travels forth into the world.[57] Whether this is a generalized idea of man as a pilgrim on earth as he walks the road of life or a reference to a specific pilgrimage undertaken by the sitter and memorialized in the painting is impossible to tell. However, the man does clasp his hands around a small volume. Is this a devotional text, with the traveler as an alter ego, marking him as a pilgrim of the mind?

"The pilgrimage to the altar," which Botvinick discussed in relation to Campin's paintings,[58] finds fuller expression in Memling's Prado *Adoration of the Magi*. (fig. 21) The believer who approached the altar on which this triptych was placed emulated those archetypical pilgrims, the Magi, by journeying to pay homage to the Savior, present both as the consecrated host on the altar and "envisioned" in Memling's painting as the infant seen by the Magi on the lap of the Virgin, the *ara dei* (altar of God). Memling manipulated the space to enhance the experience of worshipper. This painting should be viewed on bended knee, as the worshipper before the altar, as the

---

[56] This portrait is in the Carnegie Museum of Art in Pittsburgh. Friedländer, *Early Netherlandish Painting*, vol. XI, cat. 280, pl. 179; Georges Marlier, *Ambrosius Benson et la peinture à Bruges au temps de Charles-Quint* (Damme, 1957), cat. 129, pl. LXVIII.

[57] Sumption, *Pilgrimage*, pp. 171–2, described pilgrim dress. The traveler in the Pittsburgh portrait is recognizable as a pilgrim; Marlier, *Ambrosius Benson*, cat. 129, pl. LXVIII. Marlier, pp. 247–8, called the book a breviary and identified the cluster of walled buildings over the man's left shoulder as a monastery, but did not identify the walking figure as a pilgrim. A breviary would be read by a priest, and the sitter wears secular garments. A Book of Hours or a devotional text advising spiritual pilgrimage would be far more likely for a layman. *Editors' note: see Anja Grebe's essay in this volume.

[58] Botvinick, "The Painting as Pilgrimage," pp. 9–10.

Magi before the babe.[59] The oblique walls and columns of the architecture in the side panels press toward the center, and the apsidal
structure behind the Virgin swells back into space. As the viewer
kneels before the painting, the illusion of depth is enhanced and the
viewer feels drawn toward the central, frontal image of the Virgin
and Child.

Through his pictorial interpretations of the spiritual pilgrimage,
Memling engaged the mental and emotional participation of the
devout viewer. By representing a multitude of sacred stories within
panoramic views of the Holy Land and detailed landscape backgrounds, Memling allowed the worshipper to travel spiritually in both
time and space, to participate mentally and visually in all the holy
events. His use of the gaze informs the viewer: Christ gazes directly
at the worshipper to form an emotional link, while the unfocused
gazes of donors serve as models for the pious observer, who seeks
to make himself "present by thought" at the sacred sites. Memling's
paintings provide a focus for devotion, allowing the viewer to see
with their physical eyes the events which they should experience
emotionally and spiritually. Memling creates the very path, the winding road, to guide worshippers on their spiritual journey as they
follow holy pilgrims, such as the Three Magi or the Eleven-Thousand
Virgins of Cologne, as they approach the cross of Christ, or as they
embark on the pilgrimage of their own life. The believers follow the
example of the Magi, depicted before them, as they make their own
pilgrimage to the altar, where the saving sacrifice of Christ is re-created in the Mass. Memling's painted images sanctified the everyday
world in which both saints and ordinary people make the pilgrimage of earthly existence toward everlasting life.

---

[59] The usual way of photographing paintings does not capture the angle of vision
when a painting is seen from below by a worshipper on his or her knees before the
altar. This angle of vision enhances the perception of depth and corrects seeming
disparities between frontal figures and "tipped" background space, such as the apse
behind Mary. Memling was a very subtle artist, sensitive to small nuances of gesture and placement. I believe that he deliberately crafted backgrounds to be seen
at an oblique angle. This is also true of his *Crucifixion Triptych of Jan Crabbe*; De
Vos, *Hans Memling*, pp. 90–3. In the 1994 Memling exhibit in Bruges this altarpiece was placed on a stand that simulated the height of an altar. Viewed on
museum walls at eye level or higher, the landscape with its high horizon appears
somewhat flattened. Kneeling before the reunited *Crucifixion* triptych, one could see
the landscape from its correct point of view, extending upward and in depth.

CHAPTER THREE

HANS MEMLING'S ST. URSULA SHRINE: THE SUBJECT AS OBJECT OF PILGRIMAGE

Jeanne Nuechterlein

A number of scholars have examined the thematization of pilgrimage within early Netherlandish painting. Background landscapes with winding roads terminating in foreground scenes of the life of the Virgin or Christ (as in works by Robert Campin or Joachim Patinir) have been viewed as visual references to journeying on a real or imagined pilgrimage; panels depicting the Virgin and Child in full length (for example by Jan van Eyck) have been interpreted as portraying the experience of seeing cult statues within religious architectural settings.[1] Such images, which address aspects of pilgrimage as an idea or experience, could be said to operate on a somewhat different level than, say, an icon, or a large-scale sculpture of the Virgin and Child, which often make a visual claim to simply represent divine figures directly. This latter type appears simply to be, or to embody, while the first type can also be said to be overtly *about.* Though it would probably be a mistake to try to typologize such distinctions too starkly, I would contend that the distinction does exist nevertheless, and that it is often a deliberate quality of a work in relation to its intended function. I would further suggest that artistic works constituting the goals of pilgrimage, that is shrines or cult images, tend more towards the embodiment than the representation type. There may well be "thematizing" images around or near an object of pilgrimage: for instance the paper "The Journey to Emmaus Capital at St.-Lazare of Autun" elsewhere in this volume

---

[1] Reindert Leonard Falkenburg, *Joachim Patinir: Landscape as an Image of the Pilgrimage of Life* (Amsterdam, 1988); Matthew Botvinick, "The Painting as Pilgrimage: Traces of a Subtext in the Work of Campin and His Contemporaries," *Art History* 15, no. 1 (1992): 1–18; Craig Harbison, "Miracles Happen: Image and Experience in Jan Van Eyck's *Madonna in a Church,*" in *Iconography at the Crossroads,* ed. Brendan Cassidy (Princeton, 1993): 157–66.

by William Travis examines how the capitals helped to structure the experience of approaching and interpreting the shrine, while on the traditional type of casket-shrine which I will discuss there are often narrative plaquettes included on the châsse. But the main object of the pilgrimage, the physical thing which as a whole forms the focus of the worshiper's devotion, will primarily emphasize its own significance *as* the object of pilgrimage, rather than be an image *about* the object of pilgrimage (or about pilgrimage in a broader sense).

Around the fifteenth century the kind of contemporary art most likely to play a role in pilgrimage sites, or works that incited similar acts of direct veneration, were typically non-narrative sculpture or two-dimensional representations claiming to reproduce another miracle-working image. Examples of sculptures that became objects of pilgrimage include Claus Sluter's *Well of Moses* in the Chartreuse de Champmol near Dijon, (fig. 290) which had already acquired an indulgence by 1418, and the statue of Our Lady of Tongeren made by an unknown sculptor in 1479, which likewise became (and still remains) an object of cultic veneration.[2] There are even more examples of contemporary artists producing painted or graphic copies of venerated icons, among them Petrus Christus' lost copies after the icon of Cambrai, Israhel van Meckenham's engraving after the *Imago Pietatis* icon from St. Croce in Rome, and Albrecht Altdorfer's *Schöne Madonna* painting and woodcuts after an icon involved in the 1519 Regensburg pilgrimage.[3] Such copies were usually considered to share at least some part of the properties of the original (Israhel van Meckenham claimed in his inscription that viewers reciting the requisite prayers before his print would receive tens of thousands of years of relief from Purgatory), and consequently their emphasis on being/embody-

---

[2] Kathleen Morand, *Claus Sluter: Artist at the Court of Burgundy* (London, 1991), ch. 6; on the Tongeren statue, Harbison, "Miracles Happen," p. 159. *Editors' note: see also Laura Gelfand's essay in this volume.

[3] Jean C. Wilson, "Reflections on St. Luke's Hand: Icons and the Nature of Aura in the Burgundian Low Countries During the Fifteenth Century," in *The Sacred Image East and West*, ed. Robert Ousterhout and Leslie Brubaker (Urbana, 1995), pp. 132–46, discussed the Cambrai icon copies; Peter Parshall, "Imago Contrafacta: Images and Facts in the Northern Renaissance," *Art History* 16, no. 4 (1993), pp. 556–60 examined van Meckenham and the concept of copying more generally; the Regensburg incident has been discussed by many scholars including Hans Belting, *Likeness and Presence: A History of the Image before the Era of Art* (Chicago, 1994), pp. 453–57.

ing also informs the artist's creative role. Despite being made by contemporary artists—most of them well-known at that—these images could be seen as appropriate to their spiritual function because they appear to provide a fairly transparent visual access to the venerated entity, rather than focus on the artist's own act of making, so their style tends to be visibly archaic. Sluter's work, admittedly, is somewhat exceptional in this regard given its innovative form of realistic portrayal, though it is difficult to judge the work's full effect with most of the Crucifixion superstructure now destroyed. Judging from the surviving fragments it would seem that this crucifix, which was after all the focus of the work, was perhaps more traditional than the prophets on its base. There are also other complex works, such as Tilman Riemenschneider's *Altarpiece of the Holy Blood* in Rothenburg, an unpainted sculpture containing a Holy Blood reliquary within its micro-architectural superstructure, so that the scenes on the altarpiece "comment on" the relic above them and in some senses discourage potentially idolatrous adoration of the work itself.[4] In general, however, these images do not thematize veneration, but rather receive it as a direct embodiment of the divine.

It is hard to imagine a painting by Jan van Eyck (*c.* 1390–1441) or Rogier van der Weyden (1399/1400–64) becoming a cult image in the same sense, despite the deep admiration they clearly aroused in their viewers. They may have inspired and furthered religious devotion, but there is no indication that they were ever venerated as divine or semi-divine objects in their own right. In this paper, however, I want to examine the intriguing case of Hans Memling's (*c.* 1430/40–94) *St. Ursula Shrine*, (fig. 23) where the two different functions intersect: it is both an object of veneration, and a visual field that examines pilgrimage as a theme, a combination that, I will suggest, is highly unusual. Admittedly, even though worshipers were offered forty days indulgence for venerating the shrine on Ursula's feast day of October 21,[5] Memling's work was probably never particularly important as the objective of a religious cult. We have little

---

[4] Michael Baxandall, *The Limewood Sculptors of Renaissance Germany* (New Haven, 1980), pp. 172–90, 262. Baxandall commented that the work's unpainted and comparatively inexpensive state could have served to deflect the kind of criticisms beginning to be leveled in Franconia against images and extravagance, pp. 186–8. *Editors' note: see Mitchell Merback's essay in this volume.

[5] *Sint-Janshospitaal Brugge 1188–1976* (Bruges, 1976), cat. no. A.15.

evidence that it attracted large numbers of adorers, either from outside Bruges or even inside it, even though it did, in the next few
decades, become a sought-after *art* object; as a religious attraction it
hardly competed with Bruges' Holy Blood relic, which formed a
major focus of communal identity, particularly during the annual
Holy Blood procession still carried out each year on Ascension Day.[6]
But I will argue that the Ursula shrine's comparative parochialism
actually facilitated the kind of innovations Memling produced: for a
shrine like this, which to some degree subverts the traditional experience of veneration, could never have worked at a major pilgrimage
site. Its presentation of the subject of pilgrimage as an object of pilgrimage was possible only because it was made for a comparatively
minor chapel that attracted limited numbers of outsiders. Although
it is a beautiful and compelling work, it is no coincidence that it
remained the only one of its kind.

Memling's shrine, completed by October 1489, was made for the
chapel of the Hospital of St. John in Bruges as a new receptacle for
a number of relics owned by the hospital. As the translation charter of 1489 indicates,[7] the shrine actually contained a wide range of
varied relics, but the hospital (and shrine) chose to emphasize the
remains of Ursula's companions over the others. Ursula, as one version of the legend recounts,[8] was a fifth-century Breton princess who
was asked to marry the pagan son of the king of England. She
accepted only on the conditions that he convert and that before the
marriage she be allowed to make a lengthy pilgrimage to Rome,
with a number of companions that in the legends expanded to 11,000.
They first traveled to Cologne, where Ursula had a vision that she
would be martyred upon her return. Still, they pressed on by way
of Basel to Rome, where she so impressed the pope that he decided

---

[6] Reinhard Strohm, *Music in Late Medieval Bruges*, rev. ed. (Oxford, 1990), pp.
5–6, 76–9 on the Holy Blood procession; Dirk de Vos, *Hans Memling: The Complete
Works* (London, 1994), pp. 62–3 on the shrine as an art object: Carel van Mander
wrote that the sixteenth-century Bruges painter Pieter Pourbus went to admire it
whenever it was displayed on feast days. *Editors' note: for other Holy Blood cults
see Kristen Van Ausdall's essay in this volume.

[7] Dirk De Vos, *Hans Memling: Bruges, Groeningemuseum 12 August-15 September 1994.
Catalogue* (Antwerp, 1994), p. 146.

[8] The story was probably spread most widely through Jacobus de Voragine, *The
Golden Legend: Readings on the Saints*, trans. William Granger Ryan (Princeton, 1993),
vol. 2, pp. 256–60 ("the Eleven Thousand Virgins").

to accompany her on the return journey. Back in Cologne, they discovered the city under siege by the Huns, who killed Ursula and everyone accompanying her, after she refused the advances of their leader Attila.

By the fifteenth century, Ursula had become a very popular saint especially in northern Europe, partly because of the nature of the story itself, but also partly because the vast number of her companions meant that there were many relics to be had. In the twelfth century, these relics were supposedly discovered in Cologne, and although it is likely that the unearthed bones were actually from a forgotten burial ground, they were nevertheless authenticated in the visions of Elisabeth of Schönau (1128/9–64/5) as those of Ursula's companions[9] and their popularity quickly spread across Europe. The Hospital of St. John was one of many institutions that owned some, as did other religious houses in Bruges.[10] Memling's shrine replaced a much smaller one from c. 1380–1400, (fig. 24) of which the format was quite similar—a wooden casket whose surface is entirely painted and gilded, and which also emphasized the relics of Ursula's companions above the others that it contained. Given that the old shrine still survives at the hospital in perfectly fine condition, Memling's shrine was clearly not so much a necessity as an upgrade, a visual statement about the relics' value and about the generosity and piety of the donors.

The shape of Memling's shrine, a cross between casket and microarchitecture, follows the traditional format for reliquary shrines. Among its predecessors were the thirteenth-century shrines of Charlemagne and of the Virgin at Aachen, (figs. 342, 344) or the slightly earlier shrine of the Three Kings (c. 1190–1225) made for Cologne Cathedral, (fig. 25) where it became a major attraction for pilgrims from all over northern Europe and inspired the rebuilding of the cathedral. Created by Nicholas of Verdun (c. 1169–1205) and others, this and similar shrines were covered with silver and gold, further encrusted with precious stones, jewels, and enamel. Pictorial programs for such shrines usually combined comparatively large-scale figures

---

[9] Elisabeth of Schönau, *Elisabeth of Schönau: The Complete Works*, trans. Anne L. Clark (Mahwah, 2000), pp. 213–25.

[10] The Franciscans and the Augustinian Abbey ten Eeckhout also owned relics of Ursula's companions, Lori van Biervliet, *Ursula in Bruges: An Approach to the Memling Shrine* (Bruges, 1984), pp. 17–8.

along the main sides with abbreviated narrative scenes in smaller scale on the roof sections. On the Three Kings shrine, which Memling almost certainly knew, the decoration consists of rows of prophets surmounted by apostles, and narrative medallions (now missing) of the Apocalypse and life of Christ. The Magi whose remains were contained within the shrine make their only appearance on the narrow end in a continuation of the life of Christ cycle.[11] Thus, while narrative plays some part, the narrative scenes are supplementary to the overall meaning of the shrine rather than clearly explaining the stories of the saints contained inside. Together with the figures, they enrich the viewer's understanding of the shrine's significance by demonstrating that the Magi took their part in Christian history beginning in the Old Testament, centered on the life of Christ, furthered by the acts of his followers, and ultimately destined to end at the Last Judgment—that is, if the viewer took the time to work out exactly what the decoration represents. However, it is not really necessary to work out the iconography to appreciate the overall impression created by the materials and the exquisite craftsmanship of the figures adorning the casket.

Such immediate visual impact is often apparent in small-scale reliquaries, which also served as a visual means for viewers to access the relics contained inside, particularly following the 1215 decree by the Fourth Lateran Council that relics should never be displayed outside of their containers.[12] Although it is beyond the scope of this paper to provide a comprehensive study of reliquaries, it is worth surveying some of the most common types. While the earliest forms of reliquaries were most typically box-like containers made of precious materials such as silver or ivory, many later ones take a shape which sometimes directly reflect the objects contained within, such as crucifix-shaped reliquaries holding pieces of the true cross, (fig. 171)

---

[11] *Editors' note: see Benoit Van den Bossche's essay in this volume.

[12] Norman P. Tanner, ed., *Decrees of the Ecumenical Councils* (London, 1990), vol. 1, pp. 263–4, Canon 62: "*Cum ex eo quod quidam sanctorum reliquias exponunt venales et eas passim ostendunt, christianae religioni sit detractum saepius, ne detrahatur in posterum, praesenti decreto statuimus, ut antiquae reliquiae amodo extra capsam non ostendantur nec exponantur venales.*" (The Christian religion is frequently disparaged because certain people put saints' relics up for sale and display them indiscriminately. In order that it may not be disparaged in the future, we ordain by this present decree that henceforth ancient relics shall not be displayed outside a reliquary or be put up for sale.)

including an example from *c.* 1500 still kept in the Jerusalem Church in Bruges,[13] or the large numbers of reliquaries in the shape of arms or busts,[14] such as the Goldene Kammer of St. Ursula Church in Cologne where rows of head-shaped reliquaries, many from the thirteenth and fourteenth centuries, were arranged in the Baroque period to create a dramatic impression of saintly presence. Similarly, there are reliquaries which reflect their contents in a less literal way, like the late fifteenth or early sixteenth-century *Reliquary of the Resurrection* from Bruges that takes the shape of a statuette of Christ emerging from the tomb flanked by angels, with the relics contained in the base beneath the tomb.[15] Some later reliquaries included a crystal chamber through which the relic may be seen, while others emphasize display by taking the form of a monstrance, with intricate metalwork framing the chamber revealing the relic to view. A late fifteenth-century reliquary of the Virgin's veil in the treasury of the Church of Our Lady in Tongeren reflects its contents in a particularly interesting way by using silk embroidery decorated with pearls, pendants, and gold thread to frame the fragment.

Clearly, then, the precise relationship between a relic and the container in which it was kept could vary tremendously: in some cases the form explains or reveals what is contained inside, in others it does so only indirectly or not at all. But despite these great differences, virtually all major shrines and reliquaries, and most minor ones as well, have one key aspect in common: the material out of which they were made was both precious (or aspired to be precious) and emphasized. This serves partly to highlight the object for the benefit of viewers, since reliquaries and shrines provide the primary visual access to relics, but it is also a means of honoring them, reflecting and enhancing their worth, and this principle is further extended by the care and workmanship that went into their making. The container becomes appropriate to what it contains through its beauty, craftsmanship, and magnificence, in keeping with Abbot Suger's

---

[13] Noel Geirnaert, "Bruges and the Northern Netherlands," in *Bruges and Europe*, ed. Valentin Vermeersch (Antwerp, 1992), pp. 83–4. *Editors' note: see also Kelly Holbert's essay in this volume.

[14] Caroline Walker Bynum and Paula Gerson, "Body-Part Reliquaries and Body Parts in the Middle Ages," *Gesta* 36/1 (1997): 3–7; Barbara Drake Boehm, "Body-Part Reliquaries: the State of Research," *Gesta* 36/1 (1997): 8–19.

[15] André Vandewalle, ed., *Les marchands de la Hanse et la banque des Médicis: Bruges, marché d'échanges culturels en Europe* (Oostkamp, 2002), p. 91.

influential and long-lived conception that outward splendor both honored God and inspired viewers to a higher level of spiritual contemplation.[16] Many modern-day viewers might be tempted to think
of such value in essentially materialistic terms: expensive gold, silver,
and gems emphasized the significance of relics and demonstrated the
wealth that their patrons were willing to spend on their display. But
of course there was also a more pious dimension, since precious
materials were believed to embody spiritual beauty as well, and to
show appropriate respect. One of the two miracles that Jacob de
Voragine attributed to Ursula's Eleven Thousand Virgins in the
Golden Legend concerns the appropriateness of material display.

> A certain abbot asked the abbess of Cologne to give him the body of
> one of the virgins, which he promised to enshrine in a silver casket
> in his monastery church, but for a whole year he kept the body on
> the altar in a wooden box. Then one night, while the abbot was singing
> matins with his community, that virgin descended bodily into the sanc-
> tuary and, after bowing reverently before the altar, walked out through
> the middle of the choir while the monks looked on in astonishment.
> The abbot ran to the wooden box and found it empty, so he went to
> the place from which they had taken the body, and there it was. The
> abbot begged forgiveness and the present of that body or another,
> promising most seriously that he would have a precious casket made
> for it right away. He got nothing.[17]

The legend indicates that keeping relics in a simple wooden box was
inappropriate and even insulting.

Memling's *St. Ursula Shrine* is not, of course, just a simple wooden
box. But even so, in spite of its beautiful craftsmanship and its traditional format, it is not made out of particularly valuable materials,
and more importantly, it has been only partially designed to look as
if it is. The carved micro-architectural elements have been gilded,
thus giving the "frame" of the shrine the look of metalwork. However,
the panels that make up the four main sides are contemporary panel
paintings, with the same type of representation that might be found
on altarpieces or devotional panels. We therefore need to consider
the impact of such painting, and ask why the shrine might have
been commissioned in this form.

---

[16] Abbot Suger, *Abbot Suger on the Abbey Church of St.-Denis and Its Art Treasures*, ed.
Erwin Panofsky (Princeton, 1979), pp. 60–7.
[17] Voragine, *Golden Legend*, vol. 2, p. 259.

It may be that wooden shrines were once more widespread than the surviving evidence (and art-historical interest) indicates, and even richly decorated shrines occasionally include painted ornamentation. Such painting, however, typically took a different form than Memling's, and/or (in the case of painting on richly ornamented shrines) served a specific purpose distinct from that of the other materials. In Nuremberg, for instance, the 1438–40 shrine of the imperial regalia, whose wooden core is covered in silver plates embossed with Nuremberg's coats of arms, is painted on the underside with an image of two angels carrying the relics of the True Cross and Holy Lance against a blue background. This shrine, which contained the sacred relics from the imperial treasure transferred to Nuremberg by Emperor Sigismund in 1424, was suspended high in the air above the altar of the Church of the Helig-Geist-Spital.[18] Each year on the second Friday after Easter, the shrine's contents, together with the other imperial regalia kept above the sacristy of the church, were brought to the Schopperhaus on the main market square in order to display them to the public from a temporary platform. The annual display of the imperial regalia had been secured as a feast day in 1354 by Emperor Charles IV in Bohemia, with indulgences granted to those who attended, and many of the relics' individual mountings date from Charles' reign, such as the gold sleeve around the Holy Lance.[19] Given that the shrine's contents were not always hidden from view, then, its painted underside served as a complementary form of visual access: viewers looking up "saw," by means of the painted representation, the most important of the relics, which they could then see face to face at the annual display. While the silverwork on the main body of the shrine pointed to the *significance* of its contents—and also visually recalled the nearly identical shrine of St. Sebaldus, just a short distance away in the Sebalduskirche[20]—the

---

[18] On the shrine see *Gothic and Renaissance Art in Nuremberg 1300–1550* (Munich, 1986), pp. 14–5, cat. 47.

[19] For the history and significance of the imperial regalia see Kunsthistorisches Museum Vienna, *The Secular and Ecclesiastical Treasuries* (Vienna, 1991), pp. 119–87; the Holy Lance and True Cross in cat. 155–6.

[20] This casket (1391–97), like the imperial regalia shrine, was embossed with Nuremberg's coats of arms and incorporated into the new Sebaldus tomb created in the early sixteenth century by Peter Vischer the Elder's workshop, *Gothic and Renaissance Art*, p. 390.

painted underside revealed some of the relics' physical *forms*, with
the angels reinforcing their intrinsic worth.

In other cases, painting on shrines could serve more decorative
purposes (even on the imperial regalia shrine, whose interior is painted
blue and studded with gilded tin stars),[21] and on shrines lacking rich
materials, painting may have served as an economical alternative.
Might finances, then, have played a role in the choice of material
for Memling's shrine? While we have comparatively little information about the cost of panel painting in this period, and there are
no records of how much the hospital paid for the shrine, we can
say, in general, that panel painting was far more financially accessible than the extremely expensive media of jeweled metalwork, tapestry, or large-scale embroidery; even sculpture could be quite expensive.[22]
The Hospital of St. John held valuable property as well as mer-
cantile privileges in Bruges, but it was not excessively wealthy: institutional re-organization in 1459–63, by which the lay brothers and
sisters became subject to Augustinian rule and to the Bishop of
Cambrai while the administration remained in the jurisdiction of the
city, was related to an attempt to resolve structural financial difficulties.[23]
Panel painting might therefore have appealed as an economic choice
for its new shrine, and several members of the hospital had already
become patrons of Memling a decade earlier. Two of them commissioned personalized triptychs from him in 1479 and 1480, following his completion of the hospital chapel's large altarpiece in 1479.[24]

---

[21] *Gothic and Renaissance Art*, p. 180. Presumably this decoration was intended to
make the interior look appropriately (and respectfully) ornate, given that the large
hinged opening on the side would have afforded a clear view inside when the relics
were removed and returned.

[22] Sculpture incurred the high cost of polychroming in addition to the other
material and labor costs; Lynn F. Jacobs, *Early Netherlandish Carved Altarpieces, 1380–1550:
Medieval Tastes and Mass Marketing* (Cambridge, 1998), esp. p. 86.

[23] Maximiliaan P.J. Martens, "Patronage and Politics: Hans Memling's *St. John
Altarpiece* and 'The Process of Burgundization,'" in *Le dessin sous-jacent dans le processus de création*, ed. Hélène Verougstraete and Roger van Schoute (Louvain-la-Neuve,
1995), pp. 169–76; *Sint-Janshospitaal Brugge 1188–1976*, vol. 1.

[24] For details on these works, see de Vos, *Hans Memling: The Complete Works*, cat.
31–2, 37. The main altarpiece is likely to have been commissioned by the individual members of the community portrayed on the outer wings, as there is no
record of it in the hospital archives. One of these individuals (assuming that Weale's
identification is correct) died in 1475, so it seems likely that it was initially commissioned around 1474–75, probably in relation to the rebuilding of the chapel
apse in 1473–74.

However, panel painting, particularly on the large scale of the hospital's altarpiece, did carry prestige as one of the major forms of elite urban patronage, especially as Memling was, at the time, the most prominent painter in Bruges. The hospital clearly took pride in obtaining the finest that the city could offer. In the case of the shrine, then, was Memling's work an economical (if fashionable) imitation of a more financially valuable type of shrine? Or did it instead claim a different kind of value?

We can start to answer that question by comparing the shrine with that made about a hundred years earlier. (fig. 24) Like Memling's, it consists of painted oak panels, but done in a very different fourteenth-century style. A flatly-painted red color forms the backdrop to iconic figures of haloed saints, with Ursula as the protectress of her companions foregrounded in the center, and images of the Lamb on each narrow end. This is a comparatively simple work, with no decoration (narrative or otherwise) on the upper parts (or on the back where the hinged opening is located), although the figures ranged along the front are reminiscent of the rows of figures on more prestigious shrines like that of the Three Kings in Cologne. Unlike Memling's, the wooden frame lacks gilding, which was reserved for Ursula's crown, belt, and robe, and for the haloes and certain attributes of the other painted saints. Ursula's head and body were carved in relief, with her companions painted on the inside of her outspread cloak, giving her a three-dimensional presence that overshadowed even the Virgin and Child at the left and imitates the kind of relief found on some metalwork reliquaries. The figures on the shrine are backed by landscape, providing a minimal sense of spatial placement, but the space quickly dissolves into an undetailed field of color. The shrine openly reveals its comparatively humble status and materials—a small wooden structure, with a bit of painted relief and a few touches of gilding on one side, but at the same time its general decorative format recalls that of larger and richer shrines. The shrine's maker used paint to call attention to the object itself and the row of figures, suggesting a saintly attendance on the relics inside.

Memling's painting, on the other hand, is much more about obviating the surface and the material, presenting a fictional version of both. Along the top of the shrine, the gilded micro-architecture and the small medallions with red backgrounds were designed to imitate the look of metalwork shrines, as if refusing to acknowledge that they are, after all, merely wooden at the core. Otherwise, though,

we look *through* the shrine, to two types of "space." First, the scenes
on the two narrow ends showing Ursula with some of her companions and the Virgin and Child with two kneeling nuns[25] (fig. 26)
depict chapel-like spaces that conceptually (though not literally) mirror the setting where the shrine was and is physically located.[26] Thus
the viewer looking at the shrine in the hospital chapel seems to look
further through it to another chapel where Ursula and the Virgin
perpetually stand. In the late fifteenth century this experience would
have resonated with the actual space, for at that time the chapel
was not yet fully separated from the main hospital wards, rather it
simply lay beyond a colonnaded arcade. The chapel was walled off
in 1820, so that it is only by looking at earlier paintings of the hospital interior (fig. 27) that we can see how it originally related to
the wards. In this nineteenth-century representation, the chapel is
in the left background of the picture, showing how in the hospital
itself the inhabitants could have "looked through" the architectural
columns into the chapel, much as a viewer looks through the gilded
framework of Memling's shrine. The second type of space depicted
in the shrine, on the long sides behind the architectural framework
(which is no longer in its original form),[27] recounts in deep landscapes
the narrative of Ursula and her companions' journey. (figs. 28–9) Here
we are taken into a different world entirely, and it is interesting that
Memling reverses the figure-narrative relationship often seen on this
type of shrine—that is, he emphasizes the narrative on the main
sides, while reserving small iconic figures of Ursula, the Coronation
of the Virgin, and musician angels for the roof decoration.[28]

But the important point is not just that narrative is emphasized
here. The key to Memling's innovation lies in two other main aspects:
first, his use of naturalistic representation, quite atypical for a shrine,

---

[25] De Vos, *Hans Memling: Bruges, Groeningemuseum*, cat. 36 noted that most scholars
accept Weale's identification of these two figures as Jossine van Dudzele and Anna
van den Moortele, but de Vos believes that they are simply generic representations.

[26] There are some slight similarities between the window traceries and columns
depicted on the shrine and those in the hospital chapel and in the St. Cornelius
chapel lying just off it, but there is no direct copying.

[27] De Vos, *Hans Memling: Bruges, Groeningemuseum*, cat. 36, fn. 2 on the history of
the tracery, which on the long sides of the shrine was originally more elaborate,
but had become damaged by the nineteenth century.

[28] The execution of these medallions is generally attributed to Memling's workshop, though he probably designed them himself.

and second, his selection of narrative scenes, atypical of independent painting cycles of Ursula's legend. By using the type of highly naturalistic, "seeing-through" representation characteristic of other forms of panel painting in the fifteenth century (as exemplified by the altarpieces and devotional panels by Jan van Eyck), Memling posits to the viewer that there is no surface, no materiality beyond the gilded framing. Surely, if he or his patrons had so desired, he could have made the entire shrine look like an imitation of precious materials. One of the key features of oil paint was its potential for imitating the effects of light playing off of surfaces, and it was during the 1480s that artists developed forms of visual mimicry such as the "Ghent-Bruges" type of manuscript illumination which used *trompe-l'oeil* motifs to engage the viewer with the representation on the page.[29] In fact, upon closer inspection, one discovers that the top section of Memling's shrine, with its medallions set into gilded carving, is a well-concealed *trompe-l'oeil*, a flat board painted with patterns imitating the shrine's carved micro-architecture. This remarkably effective imitation is rarely pointed out, although perfectly visible once discovered. This eye-fooling reproduction of expensive metalwork seems an entirely appropriate strategy for making a new shrine economically, and Memling could have constructed the entire shrine in a similar fashion.

Instead, he uses a different type of naturalistic representation in the narrative panels, not one that fools the eye into thinking it is something it is not, but one that allows a "seeing-through" into another spatial world that projects a plausible independent existence. The first type of representation, the *trompe-l'oeil*—in alignment with the being/embodying emphasis I described earlier—argues visually that the painted surface actually *is* something else, a claim that remains even when the viewer knows that it is fictive. The other type of representation does not attempt to fool the eye in the same direct sense, but rather creates an alternative world that is convincing as a visual possibility. In this Memling followed the path of Jan van Eyck, who more than most artists conflated these two types of representation, since his paintings not only imitated with remarkable

[29] Otto Pächt, *The Master of Mary of Burgundy* (London, 1948); Thomas DaCosta Kaufmann, *The Mastery of Nature: Aspects of Art, Science, and Humanism in the Renaissance* (Princeton, 1993), ch. 1; Maurits Smeyers, *Flemish Miniatures from the 8th to the Mid-16th Century: The Medieval World on Parchment* (Turnhout, 1999), pp. 419–24.

vividness the particular visual effects of various surfaces and textures, but also created a plausible impression of spatial experience. Other Netherlandish artists like Rogier van der Weyden were less concerned with this kind of holistic plausibility, particularly in terms of space. Memling perhaps did not achieve the intensely jewel-like quality that Jan van Eyck created, but the unified spatial landscape depicted on this shrine followed van Eyck's example in positing a holistic visual field. Unlike Rogier's *Seven Sacraments Altarpiece*,[30] which set up a spatially-coherent church interior, but then disrupted its visual plausibility (while nevertheless maintaining emotional and symbolic coherence) by placing Christ's crucifixion right in the center, Memling did nothing to remind us that his narrative landscapes were just an artistic fiction. There is nothing in either the spatial setting or in the elements they contain that reveals any obvious disparity with what one might have seen in the late-fifteenth-century world. On the contrary, Memling took great care to observe and reproduce contemporary ships and armor, and he showed Cologne, a city with which he was well-acquainted, with topographical accuracy.

In some of his earlier works Memling developed a particular kind of *trompe-l'oeil* representation that sought to obviate the distinction between represented space and the viewer's space. This innovation occured particularly on the frames of his paintings, and in some cases in the represented space itself, such as the devotional diptych of *Martin van Nieuwenhove with the Virgin and Child*. (fig. 30) Memling tried to convince us that there is no distinction between the space in which we stand and the space within the painting. First, through the rounded mirror in the background, where the reflection implies that the frame of the diptych is actually the frame of a double window, and that in looking into the scene of Martin with the Virgin we are standing outside looking into a window. This feature borrows from the famous reflecting mirror in Jan van Eyck's Arnolfini double portrait,[31] but makes the claim much more explicit, directly linking the frame of the painting to the represented space. Second, Memling pushed this even further by painting the edge of the Virgin's

---

[30] Dirk de Vos, *Rogier Van Der Weyden: The Complete Works* (New York, 1999), cat. 11.

[31] Lorne Campbell, *National Gallery Catalogues: The Fifteenth-Century Netherlandish Schools* (London, 1998), pp. 174–211.

cloak as falling onto the right inner edge of her frame as if she were crossing over into our space; moreover, he also depicted a shadow on the gilded surface of the frame beneath the edge of the cushion on which the Christ Child sits,[32] a technique that, at a fairly short distance from the diptych, creates a very powerful impression of the cushion emerging beyond the surface of the panel.

With such techniques, combining *trompe-l'oeil* with spatial seeing-through, Memling tries to create the impression that there is no surface, no painting even, just a view into an actual place. On the Ursula shrine Memling uses the two forms of representation on different sections rather than together, *trompe-l'oeil* in the upper parts and seeing-through into another space on the lower. The small scale of the narrative scenes creates a different effect from that of the life-sized portrait diptych of Martin van Nieuwenhove, so that they would not be perceived as a continuation of the viewer's surroundings in the same literal sense. Nevertheless, Memling created a very holistic impression of a plausible scene opening out beyond the actual sur-face of the shrine, lessening the distinction between viewer's and object's space—the key point being that rather than focusing on the object of the shrine itself, viewers are encouraged to look beyond it to perceive a place which is fundamentally other than that where they stand. While on the end panels Memling depicts chapel-like set-tings conceptually reflecting the actual space of the hospital chapel, on the side panels he takes the viewer away from the hospital setting entirely.

Therefore, Memling's first innovation lies in his use of naturalistic representation drawing attention away from the shrine as an object. His second innovation was that he was also highly selective about which aspects of the story the shrine tells, so that the emphasis lies almost entirely on the journey itself, the virgins' travel through an ongoing landscape. This point can be emphasized through comparison with another contemporary depiction of Ursula's legend that Memling must have known, a set of altarpiece wings attributed to the Master of the St. Ursula Legend made for the convent of the Black Sisters in Bruges. (fig. 31) Considering the representation of the Bruges bel-fry in the third scene (first on the left in the lower row), scholars

---

[32] First-hand examination demonstrates that this "shadow" is intentional and not just a coincidental discoloring.

have argued that the work must have been completed *c.* 1475–80, at least prior to 1482, when construction began on the belfry's new extension. Thus these wings would have been in Bruges for some years prior to Memling's work on the shrine, but he seems to have paid little attention to them. The Master's narrative, which recounts the story of Ursula in eight sections, begins with three scenes showing the prince's request for Ursula's hand, her decision to accept, and her departure, thus telling the full story of Ursula's experience, setting up the reason for how and why she went on the journey in the first place.

Memling, by contrast, omits all of those preliminaries, beginning instead with the arrival of Ursula and her companions at their first major stop, Cologne, where she receives the vision of her impending martyrdom as shown in the upper right background. In the next section they arrive in Basel, where they leave the Rhine and proceed on foot over the Alps into the right background, so that in the third scene, following a continuous mountain landscape, they descend into Rome (left background), where they are received ceremoniously by the pope. Inside the church, Ursula receives the Eucharist, and her fiancé and other companions are baptized. From here, the viewer must walk around to the other side of the shrine—passing the end panel with Ursula and her companions—and the story continues with the return on foot to Basel and the re-embarkation to proceed back down the Rhine. In the last two scenes, Memling used a two-panel backdrop of the Cologne cityscape to depict a continuous narrative of the initial attack on the ships, the murder of the fiancé, and finally the impending martyrdom of Ursula herself. The shrine concentrates only on the virgins' journey, and throughout Memling has carefully composed the scenes to imply continuous movement from left to right, even when it is logically contradictory. In the first panel, the virgins would actually need to travel left out of the picture to proceed up the Rhine to Basel, but Memling has used the initial disembarkation and the vision in the background to suggest an opposite direction instead and to keep the viewer moving in the correct direction around the shrine. The next scene similarly emphasizes a left-to-right movement that does not entirely correspond to the actual spatial relationship between Basel and the Alps from the depicted viewpoint (which the virgins would have had to reach by entering from the right, if they were looking south to the Alps, which should be more to the left). Fortunately, the Cologne landscape in

the final two scenes was in the correct orientation to naturally reinforce the left to right movement.

Memling's integration of implied narrative direction with the topographical specificity of the Cologne cityscape is a particularly interesting feature of the shrine. Although it is clear that topographical
accuracy takes second place to narrative requirements, Memling nevertheless seems to have taken care with the portrayal of Cologne to
reflect its actual layout and appearance. To some degree this would
have been motivated by the already-established visual tradition in
Cologne of showing recognizable details of the city skyline. The earliest known depiction of the Cologne cityscape occurs in a canvas
painting of Ursula's martyrdom by the Master of the Small Passion,[33]
and two major Ursula cycles from the mid-fifteenth century, both
originally from Cologne's St. Ursula Church, depict well-known
Cologne buildings in the backdrop of the scenes that take place in
the city. It is apparent that Memling knew at least one of these
cycles (or a common source): his compositions of Ursula's first arrival
in Cologne and her martyrdom are both closely related to the corresponding scenes from the shorter of these cycles.[34] (fig. 32) Memling
was of German origin and particularly close to painting traditions
in Cologne,[35] so his decision to include topographical detail in the
shrine emerges naturally out of previous artistic practice, but there
also seems to be more to it than that. Dirk de Vos argued that some
of the buildings in the skyline were portrayed differently from any
earlier representations and from two specific points of view, one from
the west river bank and the other from the east, implying that
Memling went to Cologne specifically to sketch the skyline from these
viewpoints to ensure the accuracy of his representation.[36] Topographical

---

[33] Wallraf-Richartz-Museum in Cologne, WRM 51; Frank Günter Zehnder, *Katalog
der Altkölner Malerei* (Cologne, 1990), pp. 340–3.

[34] This has been noted by de Vos, *Hans Memling: Bruges, Groeningemuseum*, cat. 57
and Didier Martens, "Observations sur la châsse de Sainte Ursule de Hans Memling:
sa structure, ses commanditaires et ses sources," *Annales d'histoire de l'art et d'archéologie*
16 (1994), pp. 92–8.

[35] De Vos, *Hans Memling: The Complete Works*, pp. 355–60.

[36] De Vos, *Hans Memling: Bruges, Groeningemuseum*, p. 142. The tower of Gross
St. Martin, which in the fifth scene lies to the right of St. Maria im Kapitol and
St. Severin, obscures these churches in the first scene (other than one spire of St.
Severin), suggesting that Memling has observed the relationships between the tow-
ers from two particular points, which de Vos identified as the present-day Frankenwerft
(more or less just below the cathedral and Gross St. Martin, with a view cutting

specificity was becoming an increasingly common feature in German and Netherlandish painting and printmaking during this period, but it seems to have had a range of possible motivations: 1) to assert the importance of a particular location; 2) to authenticate a representation; 3) to facilitate vicarious travel. In order to interpret the significance of Memling's depiction of Cologne, which has some bearing on our interpretation of the shrine as a whole, we need to examine which of these motivations might have influenced him and his patrons.

From the 1470s–80s it became common in Bruges painting to depict recognizable features of the city in the backgrounds of religious scenes. For instance, the Master of the St. Lucy Legend's *St. Nicholas* in Bruges and Gerard David's *Virgin and Child* depict a number of clearly-identifiable Bruges spires and buildings behind the main figures, but not with the kind of spatial consistency seen on the Memling shrine.[37] One seemingly-obvious interpretation of this practice is that artists and patrons took pride in their city and wished to honor and commemorate it in paintings; the many foreign merchants who commissioned Netherlandish panel paintings could likewise have asked for a memento of the city to be included in works they intended to take home with them. However, Craig Harbison has argued that it is no coincidence that such visual references to Bruges became popular precisely when the city was falling into actual economic decline. A city at the height of its powers would not feel a great need to reflect upon itself so that these visual references manifest a feeling of nostalgia, at a time when Bruges was actually fading fast as the center of northern European commerce.[38] Memling himself included a detail of Bruges' cityscape in the background of the Hospital of St. John's 1479 altarpiece, where in the background of the right half

---

sharply across the city) and the Kennedyufer on the opposite bank, which allows a wider angle of view. Memling's portrayal of the left section of the wall along the river bank, shown from identical angles in both scenes, somewhat confuses the issue.

[37] On the *St. Nicholas* see Till-Holger Borchert, ed., *The Age of Van Eyck: The Mediterranean World and Early Netherlandish Painting 1430–1530* (New York, 2002), cat. 46; on Gerard David, Maryan W. Ainsworth, *Gerard David: Purity of Vision in an Age of Transition* (New York, 1998), pp. 28–31. On the practice generally, Craig Harbison, "Fact, Symbol, Ideal: Roles for Realism in Early Netherlandish Painting," in *Petrus Christus in Renaissance Bruges: An Interdisciplinary Approach*, ed. Maryan W. Ainsworth (New York, 1995), pp. 21–34.

[38] Harbison, "Fact, Symbol, Ideal," pp. 26–30. Gerard David's *Virgin and Child* contains a further nostalgic reference by imitating van Eyck's *Virgin at the Fountain*, as discussed in Ainsworth, *Gerard David*, pp. 28–31.

of the central panel one of the hospital brothers measures a barrel of wine on the Kraanplein, the square in Bruges where the cargoes of incoming barges were unloaded by a large crane (and where the hospital brothers measured wine barrels to determine the tolls due, one of their financial privileges in the city).[39] On the surface, this detail seems merely to celebrate the hospital's status and commercial rights, but given the hospital's financial difficulties in the later fifteenth century, the economic-decline theory could have some bearing on its inclusion. Similarly on the St. Ursula shrine, Memling's (or his patrons') determination to depict Cologne from specific viewpoints could also relate in some way to a nostalgic interest in actual landscapes, but there is one key difference: in these other cases, there is no direct relationship between the subject of the narrative and the place of Bruges, which is simply pasted in as a backdrop, whereas with Ursula the events of her martyrdom did actually take place in Cologne (or, more accurately, were believed to have taken place in Cologne). In addition, there is no particular reason why the hospital should have been interested in visually celebrating Cologne in its own right, unlike their own immediate surroundings of Bruges. Therefore the reason for its inclusion is already supplied by the narrative; the more pressing question is why it has been depicted with such careful specificity.

Quoting a particular location within representations often played an authenticating role, particularly for those sites which were perhaps not directly well-known to many viewers, but which were nevertheless believed to be spiritually powerful, as with the Holy Land. Most people did not have a very clear sense of Jerusalem's actual appearance, and late medieval representations of the city usually referenced it through circular buildings, which were generally associated with the area through vague knowledge of the Holy Sepulcher. Even artists such as Jan van Eyck who may have actually been to Jerusalem showed little interest in representing the city's exact appearance, keeping instead to the usual emphasis on exotic-looking circular towers (in van Eyck's case entirely in keeping with his general disinterest in reproducing specific buildings or places).[40] Memling

---

[39] Martens, "Patronage and Politics," p. 170.

[40] Jan van Eyck probably went to the Holy Land on a substitute pilgrimage for Duke Philip the Good of Burgundy in 1426. His generalized portrayals of Jerusalem

takes up this mode of representation in works such as the *c.* 1480 *Seven Joys of the Virgin,* (fig. 15) which portrays the major events of Christ's life winding through a bird's-eye view of a city made to look eastern through the proliferation of centralized architecture.[41] Such generalized portrayals provide enough of a foreign note to reinforce the general conception that the city is supposed to be Jerusalem, but accurate representation of the city was not a matter of much interest to viewers, particularly since few of them would have had any direct experience of the real city for comparison.

However, there were other representations of the Holy Land throughout the medieval period that do incorporate more literal references to the original, particularly when they had some kind of ritualistic function. After the First Crusade at the turn of the twelfth century, when people from western Europe did occasionally travel to the Holy Land (increasingly so in the later Middle Ages), they brought back various elements from their experiences, including relics and information about the buildings and cities they saw. We find imitations of the Church of the Holy Sepulcher being built in Europe from as early as the ninth century, often in association with relics brought back from the Holy Land and/or to play a major part in the liturgy performed during Holy Week.[42] This kind of reproduction, as with a relic itself, is fundamentally concerned with accessing the spiritual power of an original object, place, or person. Just as a relic provided a direct physical and spiritual link with the venerated person or place, so too could an image that directly imitated identifiable features of the original participate in its miraculous powers.[43]

---

can be seen in the background of the *Adoration of the Lamb* on the Ghent Altarpiece, or in Eyckian versions of the Crucifixion; Borchert, ed., *The Age of Van Eyck*, cat. 34, 85. Léon de Laborde, *Les Ducs de Bourgogne: études sur les lettres, les arts et l'industrie pendant le XV*ᵉ *siècle et plus particulièrement dans les Pays-Bas et le duché de Bourgogne* (Paris, 1849–52), vol. 1, p. 225.

[41] De Vos, *Hans Memling: The Complete Works*, cat. 38; de Vos prefers to call the painting *Scenes from the Advent and Triumph of Christ* as a better description of its subject. *Editors' note: see also Vida J. Hull's essay in this volume.

[42] On architectural reproductions of the Holy Sepulcher see I.Q. van Regteren Altena, "Hidden Records of the Holy Sepulchre," in *Essays in the History of Architecture Presented to Rudolph Wittkower*, ed. Douglas Fraser *et al.* (London, 1967). On the use of Holy Sepulcher imitations in German Holy Grave monuments, see Annemarie Schwarzweber, *Das Heilige Grab in der deutschen Bildnerei des Mittelalters* (Freiburg im Breisgau, 1940), pp. 1–10; Gustaf Dalmann, *Das Grab Christi in Deutschland* (Leipzig, 1922).

[43] On the role of reproduction and verisimilitude in images see Parshall, "Imago

It is a curious feature that such portrayals often claim more by partial and piecemeal referencing than through accurate visual representation: Holy Sepulcher imitations often made a point of ensuring the accuracy of the measurements (or a minimal number of other key features) without worrying so much about the architectural details, as if imitating the size would in and of itself ensure the right kind of spiritual efficacy.[44] Thus this authentication by imitation had less to do with holistic visual resemblance than with referencing and then reinterpreting the original. Bruges' Jerusalem Church, a fifteenth-century private chapel built by members of the Adornes family who had gone on pilgrimage to the Holy Land, provides an interesting example of such conceptions. It is not a literal imitation of the church of the Holy Sepulcher as a whole, but an architectural interpretation of certain aspects of the original, recombined in a new way: the octagonal tower provides the expected centrally-planned reference; the raised level of the choir refers to the upper level on which the rock of Golgotha is placed; and the slightly later niche recess in the crypt reproduces the Holy Sepulcher tomb itself.[45] This selective recombination is in a sense like Rogier van der Weyden's visual practice, picking out certain key features of real experience and then rearranging them imaginatively to create something new (and distinctively *not* real). It is clear, nevertheless, that the references to the original play a major role in creating and reinforcing the spiritual significance of the new work.

Contrafacta"; David Freedberg, *The Power of Images: Studies in the History and Theory of Response* (Chicago, 1989), ch. 9.

[44] Richard Krautheimer, "Introduction to an 'Iconography of Mediaeval Architecture,'" *Journal of the Warburg and Courtauld Institutes* 5 (1942): 1–33. Schwarzweber, *Das Heilige Grab*, pp. 3–5 discussed the cases of the Jerusalem Church founded in Busdorf by Bishop Meinwerk of Paderborn in 1036, for which he sent Abbot Wino of Helmshausen to Jerusalem to obtain the correct dimensions, and the mid-twelfth century Sepulcher in Eichstätt which imitated the size of the original so closely that when Hans Tucher traveled to Jerusalem in 1479 he described the original as the same size as Eichstätt's. Dalmann, *Das Grab Christi*, fn. 27 discussed one donated to Augsburg's St. Anna in around 1507, where the donors specified that it should be like the original in size and form, but which did not correspond very closely to descriptions given by recent pilgrims to Jerusalem.

[45] Jozef Penninck, *De Jeruzalemkerk te Brugge* (Bruges, 1986); Maximiliaan P.J. Martens, "New Information on Petrus Christus's Biography and the Patronage of His Brussels Lamentation," *Simiolus* 20/1 (1990–91): 5–23 examined the artistic patronage of the Adornes family, including the Jeruzalemkerk. The niche recess, a narrow space entered by a low doorway, was added in 1523–24, though the rest of the church was built in the 1470s.

It was not until fairly late in the Middle Ages that such conceptions were extended to more literal visual reproduction, either with
architectural imitation or with topography. As mentioned in the case
of Bruges, artists began to portray specific cities in northern European
painting in the fifteenth century, although, as with Bruges, these consisted primarily of certain key buildings strung together somewhat
haphazardly, as with the inclusion of Jerusalem and Rome in the
lower corners of Enguerrand Charanton's 1453 *Coronation of the Virgin*.
The surviving contract for this work specifies which parts of the two
cities shall be shown, with an emphasis for Rome on particular buildings and their arrangement, suggesting the patron's direct knowledge
of the city, and for Jerusalem on the biblical scenes to be shown
taking place in their appropriate locations.[46] Although the contract
does not specify *why* these locations should be shown, or on what
basis of knowledge the artist will depict them, their description suggests that the patron thought of the particularity of the locations as
a key aspect of the work, contributing to its effectiveness. Such representations reinforce the significance of the actual location, but they
also point to an underlying view that an important place can be
evoked through a few major monuments portrayed in their most recognizable form, just as a major building can be evoked through a
few key measurements or features. The earlier representations of
Cologne in Ursula cycles are at least in part inspired by this attitude, (fig. 32) where, unlike in Memling's representation, the cathedral choir (which besides the partial south tower is all that had been
completed by that time) is portrayed facing the west end, how most
people would have thought of the building, but it is entirely the
wrong angle if we are supposed to be looking at it from the river
bank.[47] Specific quotations of key features of cities may have helped
to ground the representation and make the scene appear more plausible or persuasive; they also imply that viewers were expected to
recognize them. In other words, the purpose of such features may
relate not only to beliefs about the spiritual efficacy of copying, but
the attitudes and prior knowledge of viewers.

---

[46] Wolfgang Stechow, *Northern Renaissance Art, 1400–1600; Sources and Documents*
(Englewood Cliffs, NJ, 1966), pp. 141–5.

[47] The earlier Cologne depiction by the Master of the Small Passion, interestingly, does show the cathedral from the correct direction onto the east end, but
somewhat from above to show more of the structure.

The late fifteenth century saw a further development in topography, a new interest in (more or less) accurate representations of entire cityscapes. When the wealthy Mainz canon Bernhard von Breydenbach went on pilgrimage to the Holy Land in 1483, he brought an artist with him to make drawings of the cities and buildings they saw so that his published account of the trip could be illustrated by accurate woodcut reproductions.[48] Ten years later the *Weltchronik* compiled by Hartmann Schedel and produced by Anton Koberger in Nuremberg included a large number of cityscape woodcuts by Hans Pleydenwurff and Michael Wolgemut, some of which bore little or no relation to the original place, but others which made a point of attempting to represent the cities as closely as possible, especially those that were well-known to the illustrators or which had already been reproduced elsewhere. The woodcut of Nuremberg, not surprisingly, was one of the most detailed scenes, and seems to have been created specifically for this work on the basis of direct observation, thus connecting the detailed history of the city presented in the text to the contemporary city that its readers might have known.[49] These cases suggest a further development in attitudes towards representation: the image here functioned as a form of vicarious travel or experience. Breydenbach assumed that people would want to see accurate illustrations of the places he described in his text, and the *Nuremberg Chronicle* compilers assumed that their readers would want as many recognizable representations of contemporary cities as the artists could produce. In each case, the idea of reproduction extends to an entire visual field, not just to selective aspects of an object or place—at least conceptually, as I would not claim that these depictions are entirely "truthful" in an objective sense. Rather they advance claims to greater visual accuracy in comparison with previous representations. This new focus on city topographies, which seems to emerge in late fifteenth-century German representations, points to a comparatively new conception that accurate visual appearance can—and should—encourage the viewer to relate a text to the contemporary world.

---

[48] Bernhard von Breydenbach, *Die Reise ins Heilige Land, Ein Reisebericht aus dem Jahre 1483* (Wiesbaden, 1977).

[49] Hartmann Schedel, *Chronicle of the World: The Complete and Annotated Nuremberg Chronicle of 1493* (Cologne, 2001), esp. Stephan Füssel's appendix, pp. 634–67.

For his shrine Memling made a deliberate decision to show Cologne not just as a patchwork of known architectural features, but as a particular arrangement of buildings observed from direct experience, and I would argue, therefore, that it reflects this new concern to connect depiction to contemporary experience. Whether Memling himself suggested including the Cologne cityscape as a result of his prior knowledge of German painting traditions, or whether the hospital staff themselves requested its inclusion on the shrine, in the end, the patrons must have approved the decision to depict the city with a comparatively high degree of visual accuracy. This tells us something crucial about the shrine which complements Memling's two other major innovations, his de-emphasis of its status as a valuable physical object, and his focus on Ursula's pilgrimage itself, the act of moving through a landscape. For, with a typical shrine, constructed of precious materials, making an obvious visual statement about its own importance, we would expect a sense of arrival, of having reached the destination. Memling, to the contrary, immediately takes the viewer away again, on a mental and visual pilgrimage to other pilgrimage centers across the rest of the European continent. His shrine by no means declares the observer's arrival at a particularly efficacious site: it instead asks the viewer to keep moving, to circle around the shrine and follow the story both physically and mentally, to look through the object itself and visualize the pilgrimage that Ursula and her companions took.

And that is precisely what the hospital community at Bruges would have wanted. By the late fifteenth century Bruges had passed its peak as the center of northern European commerce, and the Hospital of St. John was by no means a major pilgrimage destination; but Rome certainly was, and so was the far-closer Cologne, where the Three Kings shrine represented a particularly appropriate cult for attracting late medieval pilgrims, since the Magi themselves were in a sense the first to go on Christian pilgrimage. Cologne is known to have been a major pilgrimage destination for people from the Low Countries,[50] and the city depicted on the shrine shows not what Ursula and her companions would have experienced several centuries previously, but what a contemporary pilgrim would see. Thus the hospital nuns and monks, inmates, and visitors who saw the shrine displayed on St.

---

[50] Werner Paravicini, "Bruges and Germany," p. 123.

Ursula's day would have seen not just an immediate objective of pilgrimage, but a work whose focus on pilgrimage as a theme could help them mentally recreate the experience of pilgrimage, following in the footsteps of the saints before them. They were encouraged not only to venerate the object in front of them, but to reflect upon the meaning and significance of Ursula's pilgrimage and of pilgrimage in their own day. Memling's shrine is a remarkable artistic creation and must have fully satisfied the hospital's desire for an appropriate new housing for their relics; but by turning the subject of pilgrimage into its object, he subtly turned around both the subjective and the objective experience of veneration.

CHAPTER FOUR

A CASE STUDY OF THE RELATIONSHIP BETWEEN PAINTING AND FLAMBOYANT ARCHITECTURE: THE ST.-ESPRIT CHAPEL AT RUE, IN PICARDY

Claire Labrecque

The St.-Esprit Chapel at Rue is renowned for its elaborate decoration, leading scholars to call it the epitome of exuberance in late Gothic architecture—the archetype of the Flamboyant style, because of its abundant flame motifs, curves and counter-curves, mixed with ornamental foliage motifs.[1] (fig. 33) But, beyond its stylistic characteristics, the sculpture of the chapel has never been studied for its iconography and the semiotics of this iconography which were specifically intended for pilgrims.[2] In this article I will demonstrate how the sculpture of the St.-Esprit Chapel was meant to lead viewers on a sort of internal pilgrimage—a visionary experience—through an association of themes. Central to my discussion is the sculpture on the portal opening into the chapel from the vestibule (which also connects the chapel to a double treasury-room), (fig. 34) and the sculpture of a large niche in the lower treasury-room opposite the St.-Esprit Chapel, which contained a miraculous life-size polychromed wooden crucifix known as the *Volto Santo*.[3] (fig. 35) I will argue that the decorative elements of these particular portions of the building,

---

[1] *Architecture gothique*, Roland Recht *and al.* (Paris, 1979), p. 389; François Cali, *L'ordre flamboyant et son temps. Essai sur le style gothique du XIVe au XVIe siècle* (Paris, Arthaud, 1967); Pierre Kjellberg, "Week-end flamboyant en Picardie," *Connaissance des arts* 279 (1975), pp. 84–87.

[2] Léon Aufrère, Roger Rodière, and Pierre Dubois summarized the history of the Church of St.-Wulphy and the St.-Esprit Chapel, but none went beyond a descriptive formalist approach. Pierre Dubois, *Rue (Somme). Notice historique et guide du visiteur. La chapelle du Saint-Esprit, l'église, l'hôpital, l'hôtel de ville* (Amiens, 1909); Léon Aufrère, "Essai sur l'église Saint-Wulphy et la chapelle du Saint-Esprit de Rue," *Bulletin de la Société d'Émulation d'Abbeville* (1924/5), pp. 434–534; Roger Rodière, "Rue," *Congrès archéologique de France* (1936), pp. 268–92.

[3] The niche is visible on the left in figure 35. Unfortunately, the *Volto Santo* was almost completely destroyed during the French Revolution.

largely inspired by idealized architectural motifs created by the Flemish
painter Rogier van der Weyden, were orchestrated to create an association between the *Volto Santo* in the low-treasury-room (fig. 37) and
a piece of the True Cross which was kept in a golden reliquary
probably placed on the altar of the St.-Esprit chapel.[4]

Rue, a small city in the Ponthieu region on the coast of Picardy,
was one of many stops on the pilgrim road linking Paris to Boulogne-
sur-Mer (Pas-de-Calais). As early as the twelfth century, pilgrims were
attracted to Rue by the precious relics which enriched the treasury
of its parish church, dedicated to St. Wulphy († *c.* 643), an important local saint who became the city's patron. Jacques Malbrancq,
who transcribed the *vitae* of St. Wulphy in the early seventeenth century,[5] tells us that this saint was born near Rue at the end of the
sixth century. He grew up and married, but then renounced mari-
tal life to become the priest of Rue. When Wulphy discovered that
he could not live far from his wife for long, he began visiting her
in secret. He soon felt remorse for living in sin, so he decided to
make a pilgrimage of expiation to Jerusalem, as did so many other
saints during the sixth and seventh centuries.[6] On his return to
Picardy, he became an anchorite, living in the woods near Rue, and
accomplishing many miracles.

The twelfth-century Church of St.-Wulphy, to which the St.-Esprit
Chapel was annexed in the fifteenth century,[7] was enriched by a

---

[4] The treasury of the Church of St. Wulphy was substantial, as it existed in the
early sixteenth century. It then held eleven reliquaries (two of them containing relics
of the Passion; others containing relics of saints venerated in the region), many
crucifixes, heart-shaped urns made of precious metals containing ashes, and other
valuable objects. Many of these objects were decorated with the coat of arms of
the duke of Burgundy, Philip the Good, and with the coat of arms of Portugal,
probably associated with Philip the Good's wife, Isabeau of Portugal, who both
made many pilgrimages to Rue. For a description of the contents of this treasury
see Père Ignace (Jacques Sanson) in *L'histoire ecclésiastique de la ville d'Abbeville et de
l'archidiaconé de Ponthieu, au diocèse d'Amiens* (Paris, 1646), pp. 432–4; F. Irénée Darsy,
"Notes historiques sur la ville de Rue," *La Picardie* (1878/9), p. 33.

[5] Jacques Malbrancq, *De Morinis et Morinorum rebus*, 2/2 (Tournai, 1636/9) pp.
627–30; Abbé Jules Corblet, *Hagiographie du diocèse d'Amiens*, 4 (Paris, 1874), pp.
96–106; Père Simon Martin, *La Vie de Saint Vulphly, confesseur, patron, prestre et curé de
la ville de Rue, en Ponthieu, au diocèse d'Amiens. Avec l'histoire du crucifix miraculeux de la
mesme ville* (Paris, 1636), cited in Abbé Jules Corblet, *Hagiographie du diocèse*, p. 106.

[6] Ludivine Lalanne, *Des Pèlerinages en Terre-Sainte avant les Croisades*, cited in Malbrancq,
De Morinis, p. 97, fn. 1.

[7] Major damage caused during the Revolution resulted in the destruction of the
church of St. Wulphy, as proposed by the engineer-architect Charles Sordi in

Volto Santo, which was putatively discovered on the sea shore near Rue in 1101, and from this time on venerated by worshippers. The feet of Christ on the precious crucifix were polished by the kisses of the faithful.[8] Pilgrimage to the *Volto Santo* became part of the annual celebration of the feast of St. Wulphy and of Pentecost (June 7). This pilgrimage to Rue perhaps equaled that to Lucca in Italy where another *Volto Santo* was venerated. In fact, the legend of the *Volto Santo* of Lucca seems to have inspired the legend of the *Volto Santo* of Rue, as well as several others. According to legend, the *Volto Santo* of Rue was one of three crucifixes carved by Nicodemus, the disciple of Christ who participated in his deposition and burial. After Christ's death, Nicodemus, with the help of an angel, made the crosses in remembrance of Christ. One version of the legend has them buried for centuries in the ruins of Nicodemus' house near the Golgotha gates, then found *c.* 327 by St. Helena (*c.* 247–*c.* 327), and later re-discovered in a house in Jerusalem owned by a Syrian Christian named Gregory who kept the crucifixes until he was persuaded by the Christian community (following divine inspiration) to place them out to sea in three boats from the coast of the Holy Land.[9] Another account dates the transport of the crucifixes to the time of the First Crusade to the Holy Land.[10] Their arrival on three different shores has been recounted in at least two different versions. One suggests that one of them landed at Lucca in Italy in 782 and was transported to the Cathedral of St.-Martin, and the second landed at Dives in Normandy in 1060 and was taken by the Benedictine monks to their abbey church, while the third arrived at Rue in 1101.[11] A

February 1827. In May of the same year the church, but not the adjoining chapel, was torn down, and replaced by a new church on the same site designed by Sordi. Archives diocésaines, Amiens, no DA 837 Rue; Jacques Foucart, "L'église Saint-Wulphy de Rue édifiée par l'enfant du pays Charles Sordi (1771–1857)," *Dossiers archéologiques, historiques et culturels du Nord et du Pas-de-Calais*, no. 34 (1992), p. 23.

[8] *Pedes et argento inscrutantur, alioqui forsan frequentioribus advenarum osculis jam fuissent obtriti.* Malbrancq, in *De Morinis*, p. 629.

[9] Louis-Adrien Blier, *Histoire du Crucifix miraculeux honoré dans la chapelle du Saint-Esprit de la ville de Rue, en Picardie, Diocèse d'Amiens* (1778; repr. Amiens, 1855), pp. 8–9.

[10] Abbé A. Le Sueur, "Le Crucifix de Rue et le St. Vou de Lucques," *Bulletin de la société d'émulation d'Abbeville* (1922), p. 260.

[11] For the *Volto Santo* see: Fernand de Mely, "L'image du Christ du Sancta Sanctorum et les reliques chrétiennes apportées par les flots," *Mémoires de la Société des Antiquaires de France*, 58 (1902), pp. 113–44; Don Stephano Pedica, *Il Volto Santo. Nei documenti della Chiesa*, Ph.D. Pontificia Universita S. Tomaso d'Aquino, and

second version of the story claimed that the *Volto Santo* of Lucca landed around 1100, somewhat more plausible, in view of the distinctly Romanesque style of the crucifix.[12] The two other crucifixes would have landed at Dives and Rue a bit later, and their discovery around 1061–1100 corresponds more closely to a version of the legend in which a pilgrim in Jerusalem tried to acquire them from Gregory, but failed.

Within a few years a significant pilgrimage to Rue developed, and the church was built there to accommodate pilgrims and eventually a Lazar House erected nearby at Lannoy-lès-Rue near there. Then, in the twelfth century, a Hôtel-Dieu was built near the Church of St.-Wulphy.[13] The popularity of the *Volto Santo* at Rue aroused the envy of the people of Abbeville, who, during the thirteenth century, formally claimed the right to possess it by a request at the Parliament of Paris.[14] Their right being recognized, they planned a procession to transfer the *Volto Santo* to Abbeville, but the citizens of Rue put up strong resistance. Their outrage was matched by a heavenly sign, when the horses transporting the *Volto Santo* to Abbeville miraculously stopped in their tracks and returned to the Church of St.-Wulphy. This event was seen by the people of both Abbeville and Rue as an act of God, and consequently the crucifix stayed in Rue. Until

Pontificio Ateneo "Angelicum," (Torino, 1960); Jean-Claude Schmitt, "Cendrillon crucifiée. À propos du Volto Santo de Lucques", in *Miracles, prodiges et merveilles au Moyen Âge* (Paris, 1995), pp. 241–69; Denis Bruna, *Enseignes de pèlerinage et enseignes profanes* (Paris, 1996), pp. 64–5; Brian Spencer, *Pilgrim Souvenirs and Secular Badges*, Museum of London. Medieval Finds from Excavations in London: 7 (London, 1998), pp. 254–6; *A Contribution to Medieval Archeology. Heilig en Profaan. 1000 Laatmiddeleeuwse Insignes uit de collectie H.J.E. van Beuningen*, Rotterdam Papers VIII, edited by H.J.E. van Beuningen and A.M. Koldeweij (Cothen, 1993), pp. 137–8; *A Contribution to Medieval Archeology. Heilig en Profaan 2. 1200 Laatmiddeleeuwse Insignes uit openbare en particuliere collecties*, eds. H.J.E. van Beuningen, A.M. Koldeweij and D. Kicken (Cothen, 2001), pp. 356–7; for a study of the typology and style of the *Volto Santos*, see Reiner Haussherr, "Das Imervardkreuz und der Volto-Santo-Typ," *Zeitschrift für Kunstwissenschaft* vol. 16 (1962), pp. 129–70.

[12] Père Ignace, *L'histoire ecclésiastique*, p. 428; for the *Volto Santo* of Lucca, see Don Stephano Pedica, *Il Volto Santo*.

[13] This information came from documents in the archives of the church which were destroyed in 1789. Before this, the information from the documents was published by Père Ignace in *L'histoire ecclésiastique*, p. 430, and retranscribed in 1894 by Abbé Jules Gosselin, then priest of Rue, in *Rue et le pèlerinage du Saint-Esprit* (Abbeville, 1894), p. 36. The thirteenth-century chapel of the Hôtel-Dieu still exists, embedded in a modern hospital on a site just north-east of the St.-Esprit Chapel.

[14] Abbé A. Le Sueur, "Le Crucifix de Rue," p. 265.

the eighteenth century, Rue was recognized as a major pilgrimage site in northern Europe, with travelers coming from as far away as Spain and the Holy Land to express devotion to the *Volto Santo*. Among the many nobles who came to Rue were Philip the Good (1396–1467), the duke of Burgundy, and his wife Isabeau of Portugal (1397–1471) who stopped at Rue several times between 1435 and 1455 to venerate the *Volto Santo*, making donations to the Church of St.-Wulphy.[15] Similarly, King Louis XI (1423–83), out of a profound devotion for both the Holy Spirit and the *Volto Santo*, visited Rue many times as a pilgrim, making generous donations. It might have been in recognition of the divine nature of the *Volto Santo* at Rue that Louis XI, or perhaps one of his successors, granted the treasury of the St.-Esprit Chapel relics of the Passion, including a relic of the True Cross, a thorn from the Crown of Thorns, and a piece of the stone of the Holy Sepulcher in Jerusalem.[16] The presence of those relics at Rue, as well as those of many saints venerated in northern France, contributed to the expanding number of pilgrims, to the point where entire villages in Picardy traveled to Rue on Pentecost Sunday.[17]

Until at least the fourteenth century, the *Volto Santo* was kept in one of the radiating chapels in the Church of St.-Wulphy, but as the increasing number of pilgrims to the *Volto Santo* started to disturb the regular liturgical services, it was decided to move the *Volto*

---

[15] Charters record the donations made by the ducal couple to the Church of St.-Wulphy. Isabeau of Portugal (August 22, 1432), Lille, Archives départementales du Nord, Lille, B1946, no. 56254–5; Philip the Good (July 23, 1448), Lille, Archives départementales du Nord, B2000, f. 167r. The charter of donation by Isabeau of Portugal executed post-mortem by her son Charles the Bold (1433–77), in February 1464, was published by Comte de Brandt de Galametz, "Analyse d'une charte de Charles le Téméraire en faveur de l'église du Saint-Esprit de Rue," *Bulletin de la société d'émulation d'Abbeville* (1890), pp. 309–11.

[16] For a description of the contents of the treasury of the St.-Esprit Chapel, see Père Ignace, *L'histoire ecclésiastique*, pp. 432–4; F. Irénée Darsy, "Notes historiques," p. 33; none of these sources describe the housing of these relics.

[17] The treasury contained (among other relics those of): St. Wulphy, St. Peter, St. Paul, St. James the Less, St. Piat, St. Eligius, St. Mary Magdalen, St. Stephen, and two local saints identified as Sts. Fuscien and Gentien by Pierre-Marie Pontroué, former Conservateur Départemental des Antiquités et Objets d'Art de Picardie, in Amiens. I would like to thank Mr. Pontroué for generously sharing this information with me in a letter of November 1996. On the description of the treasury, see also Louis-Adrien Blier, *Histoire du Crucifix miraculeux*, pp. 11–2; Abbé Jules Gosselin, *Rue et le pèlerinage*, pp. 25–64.

Santo to another chapel, attached to the north aisle. In 1480 Louis
XI gave 12,000 *livres tournois* to remodel the fourteenth-century St.-
Esprit Chapel, improving and embellishing it in a manner worthy of
the precious objects and relics contained in the treasury. The king's
aim was to transform the old chapel into a prestigious devotional
space.[18]

In a first stage of construction (*c.* 1480–1500), the St.-Esprit Chapel
was not only improved and embellished, but isolated from activities
in the church, which nevertheless remained visually accessible to pilgrims. (figs. 34, 36) As the south side of the old chapel was originally open to the nave through an arcade, this arcade was apparently
walled up and a new entrance for the St.-Esprit Chapel was planned
for its west end, through a vestibule in front of the old north portal of the church, located one bay west of the old St.-Esprit Chapel.
Such a vestibule would facilitate circulation between the church and
the chapel. This plan, however, was modified sometime between
1480 and 1506, when a second building phase began.

During this second stage (1506–14),[19] a two-story treasury structure was annexed to the St.-Esprit Chapel on the west side, beyond
the vestibule, for the protection of the expanding collection of relics
and precious donations, including the *Volto Santo*. This treasury was
equipped with two stairways placed at opposite angles of the building to facilitate the circulation of pilgrims between the low treasury-
room, (fig. 35) where they could see the *Volto Santo* on the south wall
and the high treasury-room where they could see other precious
relics. The treasurer was responsible for the reception of pilgrims,
for receiving donations, and for distributing pilgrimage or indulgence
certificates. After pilgrims had attended Mass either in the Church
of St.-Wulphy or in the St.-Esprit Chapel (if so privileged), the treasurer led them from the low treasury-room to the high treasury-
room, and then down the other stairs after they had made their
devotions to the relics of the saints.[20] Finally, the pilgrims were

---

[18] The written account of the donation by Louis XI was probably destroyed in
the French Revolution, along with most of the archives of the Church of St.-Wulphy,
but Père Ignace published a complete transcription of it in *L'histoire ecclésiastique*,
p. 422.

[19] Possibly supported by Louis XII (1462–1515).

[20] See fn. 17. On the role and responsibilities of the treasurer of the St.-Esprit
Chapel, see Abbé Saguez, "La paroisse Saint-Wulphy de Rue," *Bulletin de la société
d'émulation d'Abbeville*, 7 (1908), pp. 345–54.

escorted to the vestibule, opposite the portal of the St.-Esprit Chapel containing the relics of the Passion, where their tour ended. (fig. 38)

It is not certain whether pilgrims of the lower classes had access to the St.-Esprit Chapel itself at any time before 1500, since Louis XI probably made it a private chapel, but from the vestibule pilgrims could at least look into the chapel through the portal's ironwork and the openwork screen of its tympanum, and could see the reliquaries placed on the altar. The delicate openwork portal was designed to highlight the St.-Esprit Chapel and to signal the richness of its contents from the vestibule. A single pointed archivolt frames the tracery of the tympanum, which is supported on twin door lintels covered with foliage. (fig. 34) Depicted on the voussoirs is the history of the *Volto Santo* in a series of narrative scenes placed in decorated niches. Statues of Louis XI and his wife Charlotte de Savoie (1442–83) were probably placed high on the jambs, which are articulated with a series of colonettes.[21] The eight scenes in the voussoirs constituted a narrative sequence which developed from left to right. Unfortunately, the two lowest scenes are now missing. Nevertheless, examination of the voussoirs allows one to follow the history of the miraculous crucifix: an angel finishes carving the three crucifixes while Nicodemus sleeps; the crucifixes are put to sea in boats; the *Volto Santo* comes ashore on the beach near Rue; the villagers transport the *Volto Santo* to Rue; (fig. 39) the people of Abbeville try to steal the crucifix, but the horses carrying the relic stop walking, and the crucifix is returned to Rue. The missing bottom scenes at either end likely represented Nicodemus carving the images, and probably the recognition of the miraculous crucifix by Pope Innocent VIII in 1486.[22]

From this portal, visitors would have had visual access to both the relics of the Passion placed on the altar in the chapel and the *Volto Santo* symbolically accessible just above them, as well as to a stained glass window depicting the discovery of the Holy Crucifix on the shore near Rue, which was located beside the altar in one of the north windows.[23] The pictorial and architectural structure of the

---

[21] The current statues of Louis XI and his wife, and the statue in the central niche, are nineteenth-century works. The statue in the central niche of the portal represents the priest of the Church of St.-Wulphy at the time of the restoration.

[22] Malbrancq, *De Morinis*, p. 632.

[23] All the stained glass in the chapel and the treasury room was destroyed during the French Revolution. The only surviving document relating to the stained glass is a brief description by an anonymous author who travelled in the Ponthieu

voussoirs obliged the viewer to step visually into the row of niches, and from there into the interior of the chapel to the relic of the True Cross, visually leading the pilgrim through one layer of perception to another.

In general, portal voussoirs were subordinated to a central theme elaborated in the tympanum, but here it is strikingly different. This openwork tympanum invited immediate association between the narrative voussoir scenes and what was visible through the tracery. With this arrangement, pilgrims discerned a direct symbolic association between the sacred relics of the Passion and the *Volto Santo* they had just seen in the lower treasury-room.[24] Such an association was probably reinforced by the exterior portal of the north facade (*c.* 1510–15), dedicated to the Passion. (fig. 40) There, narrative episodes of the Passion were placed on the voussoirs, recalling the arrangement on the vestibule portal, but in this case they created a sort of diaphragm complementing the scenes in the tympanum. These included further narratives with the Crucifixion in the center, arranged in a manner similar to upside down T-shaped carved wooden altarpieces, such as the *Passion Altarpiece* of the Church of St. Dymphne at Geel, by the Master of the Life of St. Gudule (*c.* 1470–1500).[25] (fig. 41) Therefore, starting at their first station before the north facade, throughout their progression through the lower and the higher treasury-rooms, and ending at the portal of the chapel in the vestibule, worshippers might experience a sort of progressive meditation through an initiatory rite in which the association of the True Cross with the *Volto Santo* was an important vector in the exaltation of their convictions.

---

in 1697, published by Roger Rodière as "Voyage héraldique dans quelques églises du Ponthieu en 1697," *Mémoires de la société d'émulation d'Abbeville* 21 (1905), pp. 18–23. Unfortunately, the author did not describe the east window just behind the altar, but it is likely that its iconography was related to the Passion or to the story of the *Volto Santo*.

[24] A similar correspondence was established in the Church in the Holy Cross Chapel in the Grote Kerk at Breda, in the Low-Countries, between the Triptych of the True Cross by Jan van Scorel (*c.* 1520–30) and a relic of the True Cross which was displayed in a monstrance enhanced by an imposing ornamental wall painting, just above the altarpiece. For more details on its installation, see Jeremy Dupertuis Bangs, *Church Art and Architecture in the Low Countries before 1566* (Kirksville, MO, 1997), p. 117, ill. 121 (wrongly identified as the St. Lawrence Altarpiece from Alkmaar). The relic of the True Cross was destroyed during the Reformation.

[25] The original sculpture of the tympanum was destroyed during the French Revolution, and replaced between 1868–70 by the Seven Sorrows of the Virgin by Louis Duthoit (1807–74), but the voussoirs were preserved and are in a perfect condition; Archives Départementales de la Somme, Amiens, no. 60T 291/29.

The decorative treatment of the vestibule portal presented the viewer with two different levels of interpretation by association: from real to imaginary, and from a physical to a symbolic reality. This process can be equated with the semiological strategies used by Rogier van der Weyden in some of his paintings, such as the *Miraflores Altarpiece*[26] and the *St. John the Baptist Altarpiece* in Berlin. (fig. 42) These two works from the 1440s, feature central scenes framed by a series of smaller scenes represented fictively as carved voussoir narratives.[27] The similarity of the St.-Esprit Chapel's portal and Rogier van der Weyden's "portal-frames" is particularly apparent when examining the engraving by Aimé Duthoit (*c.* 1833), (fig. 38) which depicts the portal stripped of its openwork tracery.[28] The current openwork tympanum is a nineteenth-century restoration incorporating the remains of the original tracery elements springing from the arch embrasures. Still, it is certain that the original took a similar openwork form.[29]

Although the framing of voussoir images on carved portals with architectural canopies became common in the twelfth and thirteenth centuries, its use was largely abandoned in the fourteenth century. Then Rogier van der Weyden gave it new life in the fifteenth century by endowing it with symbolic meaning.[30] By re-integrating architectural frames into the *Miraflores* and the *St. John the Baptist Altarpieces*, Rogier tried to combine, within one composition, two temporal realms, one finding its expression in small scenes carved on the voussoirs and the other as a central scene viewed through the archway as it actually takes place. In the *St. John the Baptist Altarpiece*, he framed the central scene with voussoir images of crucial moments from the life of the saint—the narrative scenes acting as a complement to the central representation. With such a setting Rogier not only suggested a passage towards a sacred space (the central image); he also filled the frames with subsidiary images that support the central theme by analogy, rather than distributing all the subsidiary images into the

---

[26] Erwin Panofsky, *Early Netherlandish Painting, Its Origins and Character* (Cambridge, MA, 1966), 2, pl. 180–3.

[27] Erwin Panofsky studied the relations between the central and the peripheral images in these two altarpieces, *Early Netherlandish Painting*, chap. IX.

[28] The tracery was damaged during the French Revolution.

[29] Close observation of the portal makes this apparent.

[30] On the recovery of thirteenth-century architectural forms by Rogier van der Weyden, see Karl M. Birkmeyer, "The Arch Motif in Netherlandish Painting of the Fifteenth Century," *The Art Bulletin* 43 (1961), pp. 1–20.

background, as was done in other paintings such as Rogier's *Altarpiece of the Seven Sacraments*. In the *St. John the Baptist Altarpiece*, Rogier not only includes "continuous narration," but he connects the narrative foreground scenes with those in the background through the fictive voussoirs, creating a complex and more complete narrative sequence.[31] Karl Birkmeyer discussed Rogier van der Weyden's main concern:

> As a matter of fact it seems that a great amount of Rogier's art can be understood only as an answer to the trying and demanding problem of his time: How can the timeless and spaceless truths of Christianity be preserved inviolate by an art form that is based increasingly on the recognition of properties caused by space and time? As far as individual forms and details are concerned, Rogier does not contradict the naturalistic tendency of his time, but by the use of "incongruous" settings, by inconsistencies in scale and in the correlation of volume and space, by the deliberate obviousness of symbolism, Rogier succeeds in preserving the devotional function of painting. In his religious imagery he presents—in the sense of making present—the timeless metaphysical content and he evokes with his pictorial forms a direct appeal that reaches for immediate, compassionate experience.[32]

The decorative sculpture of the vestibule portal of the St.-Esprit Chapel was conceptualized in a similar way, that is, to emphatically signify the importance of the passage to its sacred space, and to establish an analogical link with the *Volto Santo* kept in the low treasury-room.

Rogier van der Weyden's portal-frames were a new sort of conception for voussoir sculpture. To the question "Where did van der Weyden find his inspiration?" the only answer can be "Nowhere precisely." Indeed, his portal-frames opening onto interiors were idealized fifteenth-century architectural motifs rather than specific features copied from real architecture of the time in Brussels, where van der Weyden spent most of his life as official painter of the city. In a study of the architectural motifs in the painting of Rogier van der Weyden and his contemporaries, Victor G. Martiny wrote that, although architectural motifs in their works were sometimes the product of their direct experience *in situ*, (for example, Rogier van der Weyden found inspiration in buildings that were being remodelled

---

[31] Lew Andrews, "Ordering Space in Renaissance Times: Position and Meaning in Continuous Narration," *Word & Image* 10 (1994), pp. 84–94.

[32] Birkmeyer, "The Arch Motif," pp. 15–6.

in Brussels such as the Church of St.-Gudule and the Church of Notre-Dame-des-Victoires) most of the time these painted motifs were largely the product of their imaginations.[33] The mono-cylindrical columns of the Church of St.-Gudule or the south transept porch of Notre-Dame-des-Victoires may have served Rogier van der Weyden in illustrating "old style or archaic architecture,"[34] as Martiny proposed, but the voussoir frames with narrative sculpture on portals were not typical elements of Brabantine architecture, which is characterized by extremely plain rather than highly-ornamented portals.[35] So it is therefore unlikely that Rogier was directly inspired by local contemporary architecture when creating his narrative frame-portals. Nor was he influenced by fourteenth or early fifteenth-century French architecture, since from the end of the fourteenth century onward the form of voussoirs in French architecture had undergone a process of simplification.

Filling the arch moldings with animated voussoir narratives, as was practiced in the thirteenth century, as at Notre-Dame de Chartres on the right doorway of the north transept portal (c. 1215–30) or on the south transept portal of Amiens Cathedral (c. 1259–69),[36] seems to have stopped after c. 1270. Might the incompatibility between the structure of archivolts and the logic of narrative sequences explain the fact that narrative imagery gained in intensity and complexity on the tympanum, which represented a perfect surface for the display of the major themes? It seems that the development of narrative scenes in voussoirs was experimental in the thirteenth century, but the latest examples, such as the right portal of the west facade of the Cathedral of Auxerre (c. 1260) and the central portal of the west facade of Strasbourg Cathedral (c. 1280–1300), show a real mastery in the creation of narrative voussoirs. Unfortunately, the disasters which occurred in the early fourteenth century, followed by the Hundred Years War, led to an interruption of construction. On the few churches erected during the fourteenth century, portals were

---

[33] Victor-G. Martiny, "Architecture in Brussels in Van der Weyden's Time," in *Rogier van der Weyden, Rogier de le Pasture. Official Painter to the City of Brussels. Portrait Painter of the Burgundian Court* (Brussels, 1979), pp. 94–101, esp. p. 94.

[34] Martiny, "Architecture in Brussels," p. 95.

[35] After looking at a few hundred Gothic churches in Belgium, I have found no other examples of portals with narrative voussoirs.

[36] Willibald Sauerländer, *Gothic Sculpture in France, 1140–1270* (London, 1972), figs 88–91, 278–9.

decorated with rigid and simplified iconic figures in the voussoirs, as
seen on the Portail de la Calende on the Cathedral of Rouen. This
can be interpreted as an economic solution. I believe that it represents a step back, a return to a more archaic style, to a simpler formula. In the majority of churches built in France between 1370 and
the mid-fifteenth century, we can observe a general simplification of
arch molding. One of the best examples of this is the portal of the
Chartreuse de Champmol at Dijon (*c.* 1385–93), built for Philip the
Bold, duke of Burgundy (1342–1404), and his wife Marguerite of
Flanders (1350–1405). (fig. 281) The arch moldings of that portal
were left plain, and the statues of the donors presented by their
patron saints to the Virgin and Child on the trumeau form the only
figural decoration. The usual sequential row of voussoir niches no
longer has a place in the portal, which is dominated by a few human-
scale figures—a treatment reflecting the individualistic tendency of
the time.[37]

In the fifteenth century, portals once again became more ornate,[38]
but they were usually decorated with either foliage, as at Notre-
Dame de Cléry (*c.* 1482) in the Loiret, (fig. 43) or by a series of
iconic images, often biblical figures or angels, as on the west portals of Notre-Dame d'Avioth (fifteenth century), Caudebec-en-Caux
in Normandy (*c.* 1484),[39] and St.-Denis de Sérans in Oise (late fifteenth
century). (fig. 44) That is, while the decoration of portals had become
increasingly simple for some time in built architecture, Rogier and
his followers emphasized the iconographic value of portal motifs,
reviving their symbolic potential in a way that the purged arch moldings of early Flamboyant architecture could not.

Curiously, it is only between *c.* 1460 and *c.* 1520, corresponding
to a period of calm for northern France after the tumult of the
Hundred Years War, that narrative voussoirs came back into use in

---

[37] Roland Sanfaçon, *L'architecture flamboyante en France* (Québec, 1971), pp. 25–45
first raised the question of the quest for individualism in Flamboyant architecture.
He elucidated the important changes in architecture at the end of the fourteenth
century, which created a sort of rupture with the restrictive rules established in
Gothic architecture. These transformations can be seen in the staggering of axes,
the prismatic dynamism, and the sobriety of architectural elements, all of which
express a sort of individualism of the forms in architecture, comparable to the individualism observable in society.

[38] About the same time, narrative made a limited resurgence in stained glass, as
well.

[39] At Caudebec-en-Caux, angels and musicians alternate in the voussoirs.

architecture, and this happened quite forcefully. There is more to this, however, than sheer revival. First, the reappearance of narrative occurred in regions where such treatment of the voussoirs had been interrupted in its full bloom—in Burgundy and Champagne,[40] and from there it spread to Picardy, where there is an important concentration of late fifteenth-century narrative voussoirs containing, for the most part, scenes of the lives and martyrdoms of locally venerated saints. Second, the sense of narrative is intensified, resulting in a theatrical animation recalling the Passion Plays that was absent from thirteenth-century sculpture. There are many examples of this, including the portal of the collegiate Church of St.-Wulfran (c. 1488–1502),[41] (fig. 45) the central portal of the Church of St.-Gilles (early sixteenth century) both in Abbeville, the portal of the Chapel of the Hôtel-Dieu (c. 1470–80), the Church of St.-Saulve (c. 1480–1504) both in Montreuil,[42] the west facade of the Church of Missy-sur-Aisne (late fifteenth century),[43] the interior of the west facade of the Church of Mailly-Maillet (1505–19) surrounding the rose in its original setting,[44] the west facade of the abbey Church of St.-Riquier (1511–36), and the north portal of the St.-Esprit Chapel at Rue, where the theatricality is unquestionable. Unless evidence is found to the contrary, it seems that the phenomenon was specifically concentrated in these regions, with a predominance of narrative voussoirs in Picardy, and it is here that one can speculate about the impact of the architectural motifs depicted in the Flemish paintings which circulated in these regions.

The application of the Rogerian formula to real architecture in the late fifteenth century is in itself an interesting issue, but limiting this study to the St.-Esprit Chapel is justified both by its uniqueness

---

[40] In Burgundy, on the north transept portal of the cathedral of Auxerre, and on the west portal of the church of Clamecy (c. 1515); in Champagne, on the west portals of the abbey church of St. Remi in Reims (early sixteenth century), the church of St. Brice at Ay, and the church of Rethel.

[41] On St.-Vulfran d'Abbeville, see Émile Delignières, "Abbeville: église Saint-Wulfran", *La Picardie historique et monumentale*, 3 (Amiens, 1904/6), pp. 3–44; Bertrand Fournier, "Abbeville. Collégiale Saint-Vulfran," in *Picardie gothique*, eds. Jean-Charles Capponnier *et al.* (Tournai, 1995), pp. 68–9.

[42] They were both heavily restored during the nineteenth century.

[43] The voussoirs contain scenes of the life of St. Radegonde, the patron saint of the church; Dany Sandron, *Picardie gothique. Autour de Laon et Soissons: L'Architecture religieuse* (Paris, 2001), pp. 82–3.

[44] Georges Durand, "Notices sur le Canton d'Acheux. Mailly," in *La Picardie historique et monumentale*, 5 (Paris, 1912/4), pp. 85–97.

and by the close similarity that specifically links the vestibule portal with the Rogerian frames. Indeed, the particularity of the vestibule portal of the St.-Esprit Chapel lies in the fact that there appears to be no other example of an interior portal with narrative voussoir scenes opening onto an interior space (at least in France and Belgium) which further suggests a Rogerian conception.[45] Although it is impossible to prove that the portal of the St.-Esprit Chapel was directly inspired by Rogier van der Weyden's paintings, one cannot deny the influence of Rogerian models in that region, which was under Burgundian domination for most of the fifteenth century.[46] If the treatment given to this portal can be interpreted as a late evocation of the symbolic Rogerian frames, how were these idealized motifs transferred into monumental sculpture? The links between painting and sculpture, and subsequently between sculpture and architecture in the late Middle Ages were perhaps more crucial than has previously been realized. In fact, considerable production of carved wooden altarpieces in northern France and the Netherlands may have contributed in the diffusion of Rogier's ideas into sculpture, and from these portable models into architecture.

The use of portal-frames as containers for symbolic scenes complementary to the central images had a deep impact on the paintings of Rogier van der Weyden's followers, as seen in Petrus Christus' *Nativity* of *c.* 1445,[47] Dieric Bouts' *Nativity* of *c.* 1445,[48] and Vrancke van der Stockt's *Redemption Altarpiece* of *c.* 1460–70. (fig. 46) So, in the middle of the fifteenth century the Rogerian portal-frame became a widespread formula for the framing images of biblical history, and in some cases the frame was as important as the central illustration, as in Vrancke van der Stockt's paintings, where the narrative scenes are rendered in colors, suggesting a higher level of realism than the usual grisaille treatment.[49] After 1475, these portal-frames with nar-

---

[45] Though my research has concentrated on these two countries, I have also studied many other portals in England, Germany, and Spain, without finding any similar example.

[46] Lucien Lecat, *Deux siècles d'histoire en Picardie: 1300–1498* (Amiens, 1982); Victor de Beauvillé, *Recueil de documents inédits concernant la Picardie* (Paris, 1860–62).

[47] National Gallery of Art, Washington D.C. See Maryam W. Ainsworth and Maximilian P.J. Martens, *Petrus Christus. Renaissance Master of Bruges* (New York, 1994), p. 159.

[48] Prado, Madrid. Ainsworth, *Petrus Christus*, p. 158.

[49] Catheline Périer-d'Ieteren, "Rogier Van der Weyden, His Artistic Personality

rative scenes lost some popularity, and painters simplified the motif
in the same way that Flamboyant arch moldings had been simplified
a few decades before, as seen in the *Madonna and Child with Angels*
by Hans Memling (*c.* 1485).[50] However, around 1500 and even later,
the Rogerian models were then revived by Flemish sculptors and
reproduced in carved wooden altarpieces. As Lydie Hadermann-
Misguich emphasized, the range of dissemination of wooden altarpieces converges with the area where Rogier van der Weyden's
innovation was known.[51] Innovation in the broad gestures and facial
expressions, as seen in a south Netherlandish carved wooden *Lamentation*
(1460–70),[52] and elements of composition contributed in giving the
drama its particular intensity.[53] Following Hadermann-Misguich, Lynn
F. Jacobs observed the late impact of Rogier's painting on Flemish
altarpieces:

> The use of the figurated arches in sixteenth-century carved retables
> has been traced to the pictorial inventions of Rogier van der Weyden,
> specifically his development of the so-called arch motif, in which scenes
> are framed with figurated arches painted in grisaille. Rogier first intro-
> duced this motif in two altarpieces, the *Miraflores Altarpiece* and the *St.
> John Altarpiece*; though the dating of these two works is not secure, the
> entire range of proposed dates, from the late 1430s to the 1450s, falls
> well before the adoption of the arch motif, within sculpted retables.[54]

With their three scenes framed by narrative voussoirs forming three
arches, the carved wooden *Virgin Altarpiece* in the Church of St.-Géry
in Boussu-lez-Mons in Belgium (1515–20), contemporary with the
portal of the St.-Esprit Chapel at Rue,[55] and the *Passion Altarpiece* by
the Master of the Life of St. Gudule at Geel (*c.* 1470–1500), (fig. 41)
share compositional features with Rogerian models. The isolation of

---

and His Influence on Painting in the XVth Century," in *Rogier van der Weyden, Rogier
de le Pasture. Official Painter to the City of Brussels. Portrait Painter of the Burgundian Court*
(Brussels, 1979), pp. 41–5.
   [50] Andrew Mellon Collection, National Gallery of Art, Washington D.C.
   [51] Lydie Hadermann-Misguich, "Conceptual and Formal Relationships Between
the Paintings of Van der Weyden and the Sculpture of his Time," in *Rogier van der
Weyden, Rogier de le Pasture. Official Painter to the City of Brussels. Portrait Painter of the
Burgundian Court* (Brussels, 1979), pp. 85–91, esp. p. 85.
   [52] Detroit Institute of Arts, cat. No. 61.164.
   [53] Hadermann-Misguich, "Conceptual and Formal Relationships," pp. 87–8.
   [54] Lynn F. Jacobs, *Early Netherlandish Carved Altarpieces, 1380–1550. Medieval Tastes
and Mass Marketing* (Cambridge, 1998), p. 138.
   [55] Marjan Buyle and Christine Vanthillo, *Retables Flamands et Brabançons dans les
monuments belges* (Brussels, 2000), p. 137.

scenes under three different arches recalls the transverse section of a church, displaying the interior with a nave flanked by aisles. These easily transportable altarpieces were common in Belgium[56] and in Picardy,[57] the latter seen at the Church of St.-Médard at Croix-Moligneaux (early sixteenth century),[58] and the Church of Lawarde-Mauger-l'Hortoy (*c.* 1500).[59] Such altarpieces may have inspired the sculptors who, at the beginning of the sixteenth century, remodeled the vestibule portal of the St.-Esprit Chapel and the niche containing the *Volto Santo* in the lower treasury-room.

It has been recognized that small-scale works of art, such as ironwork, shrines, paintings or altarpieces, were used by architects and sculptors in their design process, and vice versa.[60] For example, to serve as a model for the narrative reliefs on the choir screen of Chartres Cathedral, the sculptor Jehan Soulas († *c.* 1542) was given images on canvas by the chapter in 1519.[61] Thus, we should consider that carved or painted altarpieces may have provided inspiration for artists of monumental sculpture. The favorite themes developed on carved wooden altarpieces were the Marian Cycle and Christ's Passion, with the Passion clearly predominant.[62] It usually had as its main subject a monumental Crucifixion, placed in the central rectangular compartment of the retable, and complementary scenes distributed on the wings which extended at a lower height to either side. The altarpieces took the form of a reversed T-shape, in which the figures in action were placed under imposing canopies contributing to the theatrical language of the representation (fig. 41). In

---

[56] Buyle, *Retables Flamands*, p. 137.

[57] Picardy, which shared its eastern frontier with Belgium during the late fourteenth and part of the fifteenth century, was considered Flemish territory.

[58] Camille Enlart, "Notices sur le canton de Ham," in *La Picardie historique et monumentale* 6 (Amiens, 1923–31), p. 147.

[59] Archives photographiques, Ministère de la Culture de France, C.N.M.H.S., photograph no MH 011170P.

[60] François Bucher, "Micro-architecture as the 'Idea' of Gothic Theory and Style," *Gesta* 15 (1976), pp. 71–89; Franz Bischoff, "Les maquettes d'architecture," in *Les bâtisseurs des cathédrales*, ed. Roland Recht (Strasbourg, 1989), pp. 287–95.

[61] Maurice Jusselin, "Introduction à l'étude du tour du choeur de la cathédrale de Chartres", *Mémoires de la société archéologique d'Eure-et-Loir* (1957–61), p. 164; my thanks to James Bugslag, for sharing his knowledge with me. He has also studied the transference of architectural motifs between media in his article "The Shrine of St. Gertrude of Nivelles and the Process of Gothic Design," *Revue d'art canadienne/Canadian Art Review* 20/1–2 (1993), pp. 16–28.

[62] Buyle, *Retables Flamands et Brabançons*, p. 53.

that perspective, until 1789 when the *Volto Santo* was removed and destroyed, the Crucifixion niche of the lower treasury-room at Rue constituted an echo of the formal devices of these Passion Altarpieces. (fig. 47) The *Volto Santo* was installed against the wall inside a large and elaborate frame. It had, at its base, a frieze that probably supported statues which completed the composition of the *Calvary*, and contributed to the three-dimensionality of the installation, similar to Rogier's *Crucifixion with St. John and the Virgin* of *c.* 1454–64.[63] (fig. 48) Below the frieze, another subsidiary space, about fifty cm high, formed a niche that probably contained other sculptures, which undoubtedly complemented the Crucifix, as did the lateral panels in wooden altarpieces. It is possible that an infrared analysis of the wall in the niche could reveal under the whitewashed surface the presence of wall paintings that may have added a touch of realism to the composition in a manner similar to the *Calvary* in the north transept of the Church of Notre-Dame de Dijon (*c.* 1472), which was related to Rogier Van der Weyden's workshop during its restoration in 1990.[64] (fig. 49) That ensemble, preceded by an altar consecrated to the Holy Cross, was a remarkable instance of the interaction of painting and sculpture until its carved Crucifix disappeared during the Revolution. At Dijon, the outline of the missing Crucifix still remains on the wall painting between the good and the bad thieves, and one can see that the artist only hesitantly suggested elements of the landscape on that hidden part of the ensemble. Similarly, a scene combining wall painting and sculpture existed in the St.-Léger Chapel in the Collegiate Church of Notre-Dame in Beaune, Burgundy (*c.* 1470–74).[65] Another example of this, even closer to Rue, occurs in the remarkable carved limestone choir screen at the Cathedral of Amiens, which is decorated with a series of scenes depicting the *Life of St. Firmin* (*c.* 1495) in a very theatrical manner. (fig. 50) The combination of sculpture and painting results in an illusionistic representation of

---

[63] On Aimé Duthoit's drawing (fig. 35) one can see statues at the base of the niche, which may have come from the *Calvary* scene.

[64] Judith Kagan, "La restauration de la grande scène du Calvaire à Notre-Dame de Dijon" *Bulletin monumental* 148/2 (1990), pp. 191–3.

[65] Three statues were placed against the wall painting represented the *Stoning of St. Stephen*, but only their socles survive; Fabienne Joubert, "Les peintures de la chapelle Saint-Léger," in *La splendeur des Rolin. Un mécénat privé à la cour de Bourgogne*, ed. Brigitte Maurice-Chabard (Paris, 1999), pp. 280–1.

the different moments of the life of the saint, which strongly recalls wooden polychromed altarpieces which still survive in the churches of Northern France and Belgium.[66]

By fitting in a clever itinerary calculated to bring the pilgrim-actors into the dramatic progression, in a manner similar to going on procession through the stages of the Via Dolorosa, the sculpture of the interior portal of the St.-Esprit Chapel and of the *Volto Santo* niche contributed visually to what Craig Harbison called a "mental pilgrimage,"[67] or a "virtual pilgrimage" as suggested by Kathryn Rudy.[68] Representing stations on the pilgrims' itinerary, the monumental didactic imagery allowed worshippers into a proximity with the sacred, an access which they did not have to the altar and its relics, since they were probably excluded from the liturgical space of the Chapel of the St.-Esprit, except during the important liturgical feasts.[69] Still, in front of these persuasive encircling compositions, worshippers could feel they played a role in the liturgical ceremony, hence stepping beyond the ecclesiastical hegemony of the liturgical function. Pilgrims could find in this sculpture a way to actualize sacred moments in their mind and to be transformed by it, just as pilgrims could be convinced of the verisimilitude of fifteenth-century carved polychrome Holy Sepulchers and Entombments which decorated many churches, and were, in a sense, stone performances giving the life-size figures a sense of physical presence.

Rue is a rare example of the application of Rogerian principles in the orchestration of a pilgrimage setting. At the beginning of the sixteenth century, the artists of Rue expressed in their creation an architectural ideal which their predecessors could not have realized because of the unfavorable sociopolitical and economical conditions which persisted during the fifteenth century, at the time when Rogier van der Weyden created his architectural idealizations. I believe that

---

[66] Buyle, *Retables Flamands et Brabançons*.

[67] Craig Harbison, "The Northern Altarpiece as a Cultural Document," in *The Altarpiece in the Renaissance*, eds. Peter Humphrey and Martin Kemp (Cambridge, 1990), pp. 49–75, esp. pp. 70–1.

[68] Kathryn M. Rudy, "A Guide to Mental Pilgrimage: Paris, Bibliothèque de l'Arsenal MS. 212", *Zeitschrift für Kunstgeschichte* 63 (2000), p. 497. *Editors' note: see also Vida J. Hull's essay in this volume.

[69] On the exclusion of the believers from the liturgical space, see Kim Woods, "The Netherlandish Carved Altarpiece c. 1500: Type and Function," in *The Altarpiece in the Renaissance*, eds. Peter Humphrey and Martin Kemp (Cambridge, 1990), p. 89.

by applying pictorial models to the sculpture of the St.-Esprit Chapel, as well as to carved wooden altarpieces, later artists paid tribute, unconsciously, to the Flemish painter's imagination. The study of the impact of Rogier van der Weyden's painting on architecture, as developed at the St.-Esprit Chapel, is worthy of further study. Indeed, the application of these ideas to the St.-Esprit Chapel shows that the design of the chapel responded to and created a powerful experience for pilgrims to Rue.

PART II

HOUSING FOR SAINTS: CHURCHES AND SHRINES

CHAPTER FIVE

THE EVENTFUL LIVES OF TWO MOSAN CHÂSSES

Albert Lemeunier

Closely bound to the fate of Huy since their creation, the four châsses from the Middle Ages, the principal jewels of the Treasury of the collegiate church Notre Dame, have acquired a remarkable historical and archaeological "density." Among these four reliquaries, the quasi-twin châsses of St. Domitianus and St. Mengoldus present us with privileged testimony. (figs. 51–2) Indeed, their preservation until our time is due to restorations deemed "total" according to the historicist mode, yet the numerous scars caused by the alterations which they have undergone over time did not deprive them of their historical authenticity. These two châsses have not, up through the nineteenth century, undergone an historicist restoration which would have specifically removed the traces of all the incidents that they had experienced during their long history. Because of this, they bear the evidence of the repairs, numerous and often maladroit interventions, which were the consequence of the wars, translations, acts of vandalism and pillage that have marked their existence.

Thus, the state of decay of the two Huy feretories was such that radical repair was urgently needed, in order to stabilize their progressive degradation. This decision dictated that, beforehand, a precise evaluation be undertaken. One aspect of this would consist of an investigation into the history of the châsses, based on all archival information, narratives, and various other sources related to the reliquaries. At the same time, they were subjected to a systematic examination of all their components, with regard to the archaeological, technical, iconographic, and stylistic aspects. If certain researchers had already tried, in the past, to draw some conclusions from them, it must be admitted that their methods were generally not concerned with the complexity of these problems.

By confronting this ensemble of data, one can present a chronicle of the châsses from their origins to our day. This "account," even with lacunae, reflects the great damage and misfortune that these objects have suffered during their eight hundred years of existence, in spite of their prestige (and undoubtedly partly because of it). In this connection, one cause appears most evocative; it is that of the processions in which the Huy châsses were carried since their creation: their number can be estimated between 1500 and 2000! How many bungling gestures, maladroit handlings, and chaotic movements accompanied these sorties, in all seasons, and in the presence of avid crowds who approached too near, to see and even to touch the reliquaries!

Had the Huy châsses suffered more than others from the ravages of time? Yes and no. Yes, if one compares them with some still-extant and which were altered relatively little during their histories including the châsse of Charlemagne, (fig. 342) that of Our Lady of Aachen, (fig. 344) St. Ode of Amay, (fig. 313) St. Heribert of Deutz, (fig. 78), and St. Remaclus of Stavelot. No, if one refers to the many others which were subject to as many repairs, now hidden in the twentieth century, or to the great majority of them which disappeared in the French Revolution. Whether the few Mosan châsses still extant appear to be a rather representative reflection of what existed at one time, what do we still know—if not through some rare *membra disjecta* or descriptions—of the state in which they were found at the end of the *Ancien Régime*—of scores of others lost to the future? What knowledge do we have, not only of their commissioners, their original iconographic programs, or of their initial execution, but also of the transformations through their lives? Undoubtedly, in the majority of cases, the history of these disappeared monuments still remains to be written.

Historical Chronicle

In view of the existing literature, abundant enough, it appears that the question of the two châsses ought to be taken up again *ab initio*. Such a step implies that one places the initial creation of the châsse in the context of the twelfth-century elevation and the translation of the relics of the two Huy saints which they contain. What is revealed in the broad outlines of this examination? On the one hand, for the châsse of St. Domitianus, on the sixth of the Ides of June 1172[1] (during the reign of the emperor Frederick Barbarossa),

---

[1] 1173, according to other sources, i.e.: *Vita Domitiani* 2, cited by Leon Van Der

Raoul of Zaehringen, bishop of Liège, transferred the remains of the holy bishop, patron of Huy, to a new coffin, decorated with gold and silver. The chronicler Gilles of Orval, at the beginning of the thirteenth century, attributes the initiative to the canons of the collegiate church, adding that the châsse had existed "already for a long time" (*iam diu fabricatum existerat*), but without specifying the exact meaning of his remark.[2]

The sources are less precise for the châsse of St. Mengoldus, especially in regard to the date of the translation of the relics of this local martyr. It could have taken place a few years later, under the same episcopate (by deduction, between 1172/73–1189.) This emerges in the later chronicle of the Jean le Prêtre of 1402. Émile Schoolmeesters situated it, without formal proof or references, on June 15, 1177.

There is the question of the two châsses (*feretra*) in the famous obituary of the Huy Abbey of Neufmoustier where, on October 25 a monk, in the second half of the twelfth century, inscribed the *commemoratio Godefridi aurificis fratris nostri* (commemoration of our brother the goldsmith Godefroid), to which an apocryphal hand, most likely that of the same Gilles of Orval, added:

> This goldsmith Godefroid, citizen of Huy, and then our fellow-member canon, a person with no equal in the art of the goldsmith, made, in various regions, several châsses for saints, vessels and utensils for the use of kings; and that then he produced two châsses, one censer, and a silver chalice in the Church of Huy. And in our church, he made a reliquary of marvelous work, in which was placed a finger of St. John the Baptist that the bishop of Sidon Amalric had given to him, in recognition of a charming vessel that he had executed for him.[3]

Essen, "Etude critique et littéraire sur les vitae des saints mérovingiens," in: *Revue d' Histoire ecclésiastique* (1907), pp. 170–1; Ionnis Chapeaville, *Gesta Pontificum Leodiensium, Liège* (1613), II, p. 126.

[2] Gilles d'Orval, *Gesta episcoporum leodiensium*, éd. J. Heller, *Monumenta Germaniae Historica*, 55, vol. 25 (1880), p. 109.

[3] *Iste Godefridus aurifaber, Civis Hoyensis, et postmodum ecclesie nostre concanonicus, vir in aurifabricatura suo tempore nulli secundus, per diversas regiones plurima Sanctorum fecit feretra et cetera regum vasa utensilia. Nam in ecclesia Hoyensi duo composuit feretra, turibulum et calicem argenteos. In nostra quoque ecclesia, capsam mirifico opere decoratam, in qua recondidit iuncturam sancti Iohannis baptiste, quam ei dominus Almaricus Sydoniensis episcopus contulerat, pro eo quod quedam vasa delectabilia fecerat.*

A passage from the chronicle of Jean d'Outremeuse (1338–1400)[4] continues this narration, while specifying and certainly inventing particular facts:

> the year 1173, there returned Godefroid, citizen of Huy, the best, most expert and subtle workman whom one has seen in the world to date, among the masters of goldsmithery, and who had traversed all the regions; he returned to Huy in the month of July; he had remained abroad a good twenty-seven years and in many areas had made various good works, châsses and other diverse works. And on his return, for the Church of Huy, he made a châsse, a censer, and a silver chalice; and for the Church of Neufmoustier, near Huy, he made and donated a morse for a cape of marvelous work, in which he enclosed fragments of a finger of St. John the Baptist that Lord Almaric, bishop of Sidon, had given him because he had made him a silver vessel. And after, the canons of Huy, because he was old and was sufficiently instructed, made him a canon in Neufmoustier at Huy; there he took the habit on the 17th of July in the year 1174. And the two châsses which he made at Notre Dame of Huy (were created) at the request and the expense of Bishop Raoul of Liège; in one was put St. Domitien, bishop of Tongres, and in the other St. Mengold, which were then transferred to the Church of Notre Dame.

Among the many miracles and translations which marked the existence of the Huy châsses, the first known fact relates to that of St. Domitianus. Gilles of Orval reported that the latter was carried to Liège by the people of Huy, in 1185, as part of the offerings given by the inhabitants of the diocese toward the rebuilding of St. Lambert Cathedral, which had been destroyed by fire in the same year. In recognition, the bishop raised May 7, the anniversary of the death of St. Domitien, to the rank of a Holy day of Obligation in the dio-

---

[4] Jean d' Outremeuse, *Li Myreur des Histors* in eds. A. Borgnet and S. Bormans (Brussels, 1864–87), vol. IV, p. 357. *"L'an XI^eLXXIII revint Godefroid, citoyen de Huy, le meilleur, le plus expert et subtil ouvrier que l'on vit au monde à ce jour parmi les maîtres de l'orfèvrerie, et qui avait parcouru toutes les régions; il revint à Huy au mois de juillet; il était resté bien 27 ans en dehors et avait fait en maintes régions divers bons ouvrages, châsses et autres ouvrages divers. Et à son retour, pour l'église de Huy, il a fait une châsse, un encensoir et un calice d'argent; et pour l'église du Neufmoustier, près de Huy, il fit et donna un mors de chape d'un merveilleux ouvrage, dans lequel il enferma des fragments de phalange de saint Jean-Baptiste que Messire Almaris, évêque de Sidon, lui avait donnés du fait qu'il lui avait fait une vaisselle d'argent. Et après, les chanoines de Huy, du fait qu'il était vieux et suffisamment instruit, le firent chanoine au Neufmoustier à Huy; il y prit l'habit le XVII des kalendes de juillet de l'an 1174. Et les deux châsses qu'il fit à Notre-Dame de Huy (furent réalisées) à la requête et aux frais de l'évêque Raoul de Liège; dans l'une fut mis saint Domitien, évêque de Tongres, et dans l'autre saint Mengold qui fut alors transféré en l'église Notre-Dame."*

cese, equal in solemnity to the feast of St. Lambert, founder of the Diocese of Liège. About the châsses' odyssey to Liège, the chronicler describes the tumult surrounding it. The Liège historian, Chapeaville, reported in a particularly vivid way that one saw the feretory *". . . estant mis et assis près de celuy dudit sainct Lambert s'eslever et se rencontrer tous deux, comme s'entresaluant et conjouissant."* (. . . being placed and installed near that of St. Lambert, each rose up and met the other, as though they greeted one another and were delighted at being together.)[5] The châsse was to return only in 1187.

The veneration of the châsses was accompanied by reports of the miracles which occurred in their vicinity, from the end of twelfth century in the *Miracula* of St. Domitianus and of St. Mengoldus, and in later chronicles. Several cures were worked by their intercession, when pilgrims came into contact with their châsses (on one occasion with some flowers), while moving beneath them or in their environs. For example, during a short stay of the châsse of St. Mengoldus in the church housing his sepulcher; an invalid was revived by the saint himself; this translation, according to the texts, had been operated by the *"anciens."*[6]

One will notice however that, apart from the processions and some miracle accounts, the sources barely touch upon the pilgrimages and the devotional practices which were addressed to the relics of the two Huy saints in the Middle Ages. There are no extant pilgrim signs, no handbills of the relics of the collegiate church. Moreover, it is true that no such document exists for St. Lambert, whereas some survive for St. Servatius of Maastricht and a pilgrim badge of St. Remaclus of Stavelot (end of twelfth or the beginning of the thirteenth century) was found on the grounds at Huy. (fig. 53)

The 1274 inventory drawn up by the canon of the collegiate church, Jean d'Aps, known from a later transcription (1685),[7] reveals that three of the four feretories of the treasury were *in choro super*

---

[5] Chapeaville, *Gesta Pontificum Leodiensium* (Liège) II, p. 126.

[6] Huy; *Archives de l'Etat*, Cures de Huy, Paroisse Saint-Mengold, 13; Philippe Geoge, "Les Miracles de saint Mengold de Huy. Témoignage privilégié d'un culte à la fin du XIIᵉ siècle," *Bulletin de la Commission royale d'Histoire*, CLII (1986), p. 45. *Editors' note: see also Rita Tekippe's essay in this volume.

[7] M. Goronne, Incunabula ecclesiae Hoyensis (Liège, 1685), ed. and trans. J. Alexandre (Liège, 1880), pp. 16–7. *"Item quatuor feretra, scilicet tria in choro super Altare magnum . . . et Quartum B. Mariae Virginis nuncupatum, habens Imagines de argento deauratus."*

Altare magnum (in the choir, above the high altar). Since the châsse of the Virgin seems to be, in the same document, localized at another site, one can conclude from this that the three châsses in question were those of St. Domitianus, St. Mengoldus, and St. Marcus.

Then, for nearly two centuries, the files remain mute. It was not until 1483 when, in his will, Johan de Lonneur, clerk and citizen of Huy, after having expressed the wish to be buried in the cemetery of the collegiate church, said to leave *pour dieu et en pure almoine alle fabrique de ladite église collégiale . . . pour covertir en reparation des fitrez saint Mengould et saint Domitiane ou à l'ung d'iceulx une bocque d'or pessant environ chincque esterlin* (. . . for God and in pure charity to the canons of said collegiate church . . . to apply to the repair of the châsses of St. Mengold and St. Domitien or to the one of them, a gold ring weighing approximately five esterlins.)[8] Accounts of the institution reveal that various work was done on the châsses in 1473, 1476, and 1486, but without specifying if they were the particular châsses that concern us here.

In 1499, the châsses escaped the fire which devastated part of collegiate church and its treasury. In 1515, some nails and locks were replaced on the châsses, and two litters (*chivieres*) were acquired to carry them. In August 1528, the accounts reveal that the goldsmith Jean Pestea, inhabitant of Liège, collected thirty-one florins, then an additional eight florins, for the execution of three "images" intended for the châsse of St. Mengoldus, weighing three marcs and five ounces of silver, with the further expense of twenty florins for their gilding. Gerard Jadet was also paid for certain repairs, while the Huy goldsmith Matthieu Durtey who had, in the previous July, carried out the weighing of the silver necessary to this repair, was also paid. The reliquaries were thus, at that time, the object of intensive care.[9]

In 1537, in the presence of Johan de Izier, a priest, Jean Frérart, chaplain of the collegiate church, acting as notary, dictated that *diex florins dicte monnoie de Huy une foy* (10 florins of Huy money, for one

---

[8] The esterlin monetary unit was also used as measures of weight in England, the Netherlands, and France. At the time it was worth approximately 1.53 grams, thus the gold band weighed 7.65 grams.

[9] Huy, Archives de l'Etat, *Huy, Oeuvres, 1480–1488, f. 56; Collégiale Notre-Dame de Huy*, 215, f. 12 r., 25 v., 67 v., 286 v.; also: 216, f. 288 v. These very laconic and brief mentions do not seem to me to be of enough interest to reproduce them here as such.

time) be allotted for their repair. Moreover, a document formerly contained in the châsse of St. Domitianus explains that in 1560, it underwent a *nova reparatio* (a new repair) and an *integra restauratio* (an integral restoration) work entrusted to the care of Jaspar de Namur and his son Henri, (fig. 54) which they completed on July 13, 1560. The price of this work was paid out of the goods left after his death by the canon Nicolas Richard. In 1604, the Town of Huy ordered its revenue officer to *faire deux draps par forme de tapisse ou gottières pour servir et être employés à la décoration des fyètres des corps saints Mengold et Domitien afin les dits fiètres êtres posés sur iceux draps aux processions* (to make two cloths in the form of a cover or "gutter" to serve and to be used for the decoration of the châsses for the bodies of Sts. Mengold and Domitien so that said châsses could be placed on these cloths for the processions).[10]

From an account of the voyage of Frenchman Dubuisson-Aubenay[11] between 1623–28, we learn then that the bodies of Sts. Domitianus and Mengoldus were still *sur le maître-autel, dans une longue quaisse à clare voye de métal doré* (on the high altar in a long case with an openwork screen of gilt metal). Further, he added that in the sacristy, *on veoit encor de leurs reliques . . ., et un fuseau épointé couvert d'un fil d'or qu'ils* [les chanoines] *disent estre le fuseau de Notre-Dame* (one still sees their relics . . . and a blunt spindle covered with a gold wire that they (the canons) assert to be the spindle of Our-Lady). Then on June 23, 1670, the chapter of collegiate church invited the master of the church property to have the two châsses inspected by experts in order to replace the "wooden figures" (*figurarum lignearum*) qui remplaçaient with silver figures—a strange and curious fact. *Eadem die domini ordinarunt . . . magistri fabrice curent visitari per expertos feretra SS. Domitiani et Mengoldi et in locum figurarum lignearum eisdem applicatorum substituantur argenteae . . ."*[12] That means that at some previous time during a particularly unfavorable economic situation, the canons did not have sufficient resources to carry out necessary repairs using a noble metal.

[10] Huy, Archives de l'Etat, *Huy, Oeuvres, 1604.*
[11] L. Halkin, "L'itinéraire de Belgique de Dubuisson-Aubenay (1623–1628)," *Revue belge d'Archéologie et d'Histoire de l'Art*, XVI (1946), pp. 74–6.
[12] Huy, *Archives de l'Etat, Collégiale Notre-Dame de Huy, Conclusions capitulaires*, June 23, 1670, reg. 24, f. 33 r.

At the beginning of 1677, the châsses were transported to Liege, in order to give them shelter from the insults of enemies of the faith (*a l'abri des insultes de ennemis de la foy*), where they found refuge in the treasury of St. Lambert Cathedral. But at the chapter meeting of April 11, 1680, the Huy canons *ne pouvans qu'à leur très grand et sensible regret veoir leur église et cette ville plus longtemps privée de la présence des Stes Relictes de la très glorieuse Vierge et des Sts corps de leur glorieux patrons* . . . (having only very great and sensitive regret to see their church and this city any longer deprived of the presence of the holy relics of the very glorious Virgin and the holy bodies of their glorious patrons . . . fixed for May 5, the day before the feast of St. Domitian, the return to Huy of the precious reliquaries, by boat, and in great solemnity). In Liège, the relics were then exposed in the nave of the cathedral *sub coronam*, that is, under the crown of light suspended there. The scholar Goronne and the canon de Posson were appointed by the chapter of Huy to handle the delivery of the châsses. We are reminded that on April 12, 1676, the collegiate church missed being destroyed at the time of the siege of the city by the French troops who assaulted the castle and blew it up before withdrawing. The building owed its safeguard, says one at the time, only to the protection of the Virgin of Sarte.[13]

The insecurity resulting from the repeated sieges to which Huy was subjected was the cause of a new exile of the châsses to Liège, ending May 10, 1698, when the vicars Colard and Duchesne accepted on behalf of the chapter two-and-a-half florins in reimbursement of expenses incurred for the decoration of the high altar and of the church in the translation of the bodies of Sts. Domitianus and Mengoldus from Liège (*in translatione corporum SS. Domitiani and Mengoldi e Leodio*). Jean Longrée was noted as being responsible for putting up greenery in the interior of the church on this occasion. Among the festivities, they also organized fireworks. Undoubtedly some restoration work was generated by these adventures. In 1697–98, the goldsmith G. Libert was paid two florins for repairs, while on August 30, 1699, the chapter discharged ten florins for work of gilding by a local female artist named Miss Delloye.

---

[13] Charles Gregoire, "Les origines et les premiers développements du culte de Notre-Dame de la Sarte (1621–1676)" in *Catalogue de l'exposition "Notre-Dame de la Sarte. Culte et trésor,"* (Huy, 1991), pp. 39–40; J.-P. Rorive, *L'enfer d'une ville au siècle de Louis XIV* (Liège, 1990). Also from this epoch is the testimony of Canon Mengoldus in M. Goronne, *Incunabula ecclesiae Hoyensis*, pp. 23–5, 56–8.

With the end of the wars of Louis XIV (1713–15), encouraged by the initiative of their deacon Isidore de Bouille, the canons resolved to refurnish their church in the taste of the day, following in that a general fashion of the Country of Liège. Among many other works carried out then by the collegiate church, the high altar received, during a 1720–21 campaign, a woodwork destined to *fermer les coffres des corps saints avec le derier du grand hotel* (sic) (enclose the châsses of the holy bodies with the back of the high altar). (fig. 55) The large sum of one hundred florins, received from the chapter by the deacon to be applied to this work, signals its importance. Probably, it was at this same time that the two châsses were cut down by a sixth of their length, with the apparent aim of aligning them with the dimensions of the châsse of Notre Dame. It was also in 1732 that Pierre-Lambert de Saumery saw them, *ornées de quantité de figures en relief, ouvrage gothique, mais remarquable par le travail et par son antiquité* (decorated with a number of figures in relief, Gothic works, but remarkable for its workmanship, and for its antiquity).[14] In 1724, the Huy ironworker Gabriel Le Vasseur was entrusted with the responsibility of replacing *une pomelette au fitre de saint Mengoldus*, (a little ball [apple] for the châsse of St. Mengold). In 1780, the reliquaries were adorned with green, red, and blue velvet.

The châsses were constantly moved, going out in procession on several occasions during the year (the day of Assumption, Easter Sunday, at the *Close-Pasque* or Low Sunday, Corpus Christi, the feast-day of the saint, during that of St. John in 1748, again, following the earthquake of 1756) and especially, since 1676, for the septennial processions. The Huy châsses constituted the focus of the procession, completed by the miraculous statue of Notre Dame of Sarte and its escort. There, in the ranks, were the two châsses of the Church of the Augustins, accompanied by the Augustin Fathers and their students; the châsses of St. Marcus and St. Odilia, (fig. 56) escorted respectively by the Cordeliers and the Croisiers, the latter carried by the guild of Febvres, and the châsse of St. Mort, carried by the young men's sodality. Then came that of St. Mengoldus and St. Domitianus: surrounded by children with lanterns and surmounted by a canopy

---

[14] Pierre-Lambert de Saumery, *Les Délices du Païs de Liege, ou description géographique, topographique et chorographique des monumems sacrés et profanes de cet évêché-principauté et de ses limites* (Liège, 1738–44, repr. Brussel, 1970), vol. 4, pp. 340, 379, 382, 454, 459.

carried by the priests; while the châsses themselves were carried either by the vicars, or the governors, or the valets of the guilds. To the governors of the Butchers was generally allocated the privilege of carrying the châsse of St. Mengoldus; to those of the Millers or to the Huy magistrate, that of St. Domitianus. The châsse of the Virgin, followed by the beneficiaries of the collegiate church, immediately preceded the miraculous statue of Notre Dame. The procession of May 7, 1758 marked the twelfth centenary of the death of St. Domitianus. In the midst of the delegations of the civil company, clergy and armed detachments, the châsses of the Sts. Domitianus and Mengoldus were again present, accompanied there by the statues of both saints.

If they were sometimes abused during their many sorties, the canons were not careless of their maintenance. They were cleaned periodically (in 1739, it is the vicar Grégoire de la Garde de Dieu and his fellow-members who discharged this duty). During the exposition of the châsses, care was taken for their safety as the two vicars mounted a guard during the night prayers for the Forty Hours devotions. The padded litters (*tresses*) intended to carry the châsses, usually arranged in *la place dessus la Trésorerie* (in the room above the Treasury) (1780) were also the object of repairs: Philippe de Jeneffe discharged some in 1738. These cautions were redoubled with the approach of the jubilee of St. Domitien, celebrated, May 7, 1758, for the 1200–year anniversary of the death of the patron saint of Huy.[15]

In the course of 1762, the reliquaries were unfortunately *gatez and ruinez par les voleurs*, (damaged and ruined by thieves) and that of St. Domitianus suffered in particular from their misdeeds. As of August 25, 1762, the canons appointed their fellow-member Jean-Nicolas Vercour and the master of the church property *pour convenir avec un ouvrier pour leur réparation et nettoyement* (to meet with a workman for their repair and cleaning); (fig. 57) 135 florins drawn from the *menues*

---

[15] There are various citations from across the files: "Paid by himself (=) for the priests who carried the feretra and the children who carried the lanternes on August 15 . . ." (1734); "Paid by Grégoire de la Garde de Dieu and his fellow-vicar for having assisted in cleaning the feretra . . ." (1739); "Paid by themselves (two vicars) to have guarded the silverware at night during the Forty Hours prayers" (1750); "Paid by Philippe de Jeneffe to have mended the straps to carry the holy bodies" (1738); "Paid by Mr. Defrehy for velour for the hangings of the feretra of St. Domitien and St. Mengold" (1758). *Archives of the State at Huy*, Collegiate Church of Notre Dame of Huy, reg. 228–9.

dismes (petty cash) for this purpose, was paid to the goldsmith Derotte, then another 197 florins. Some repairs had also been entrusted to Arnould Gritte, a coppersmith, indicated by the receipts of May 20, 1763, for more than thirty florins. June 25, 1763, the canons recovered sixty-three florins, given to them by the cantor Vercour, *pour vielles argenteries et cuivres des fittres qu'il a vendus à Franxon orfevre* (for the old silver and copper from the feretories which had been sold to the goldsmith Francson). On the occasion of this work, the châsse of St. Domitianus had been opened on March 21, 1763, in the presence of the canon Vercour and of the master of the church property Charles-François d'Andriessens, again appointed by the chapter for the achievement of these procedures. They entered into one of the collegiate church registers an official report of this opening: in the châsse, they noticed, was a second case of wood reinforced with iron, and in this one (according to its weight) another still, of lead or tin, which they did not open. These repairs or restorations could be carried out thanks to the munificence of the canons and to the contributions for church property. On March 19, 1763:

> *Mrs les très Rnds doyen et chapitre . . . assemblés ont commis et députez comme ils commettent et députent par cette Mrs leurs confrères Vercour et d'Andriesens pour faire réparer les châsses ou fitres de leure Eglise gatez et ruinez par les voleurs.* (The Very Reverend Msgr., the deacon and the chapter . . . assembled, had entrusted and appointed their fellow members Vercour and Andriesens, appointed Msgr., to have repaired the châsses or feretra from their church which had been damaged and ruined by the thieves).[16]

In 1788, it is to the coppersmith Crousse that they turned again for *nettoyement et racommodage . . . des châsses des Saints . . .* (cleaning and mending of the châsses of the Saints). A few years later, the *Ancien Régime* ended, and with it, the collegiate church institution. In their chapter of June 20, 1794, the canons authorized their fellow-member de Farsy to make the purchase of a boat and to make the adjustments necessary for the transport of the effects of their ecclesiastical church in the event that the current war required it.[17] They were well-inspired: on July 15, 1795, their fellow-member crossed the Rhine, with the treasury and its insignia reliquaries. January 5, 1798, the

---

[16] *Huy, Archives de l'Etat,* Collégiale Notre-Dame de Huy, reg. 28, f. 221 v.

[17] *"l'achat d'un batteau et faire faire les ajustements nécessairs pour le transport des effets de leur." insigne église dans le cas que la nécessité de la guerre actuelle le requierre*

specially-convened chapter—one of the last before its suppression—
appointed the canons Legros and Debouré to *conjoinctement avec leur
confrère de Farsy prendre les arrangements nécessairs relativement aux argenteries et autres effets transportés en 1794* (jointly with their fellow-member
de Farsy to make arrangements necessary with regard to the silver
wares and other effects transported in 1794). Actually, de Farsy and
his precious baggage had been in Altona since 1794, in the vicinity
of Hamburg, where the châsses found asylum in the Catholic Church
of St. Joseph and where they remained for nineteen years.

They returned to Huy only on September 20, 1813; the treasurer
and musician of the collegiate church J.H. Ansiaux reported that it
was only with the greatest difficulty that they managed to get them
back, the administration of the customs being fiercely opposed to it.
At their return, they were subject to repair, the work undertaken by
the goldsmith Gritte for an amount of forty-one francs, ninety-five.
Two of the four châsses—those of the Virgin and St. Mengoldus—
were opened on this occasion. The feretories took their places again,
as before the Revolution, behind the high altar and there they
remained until 1863, when the retable traveled to the chapel of the
St.-Berthuin College of Malonne, thus depriving the collegiate church
of Huy of one of its most remarkable examples of Baroque furniture. As for the processions, after 1963, the reliquaries were no longer
part of them. (fig. 58)

In 1854, in a monograph on the collegiate church, published by
E. Noblet in Liège, with the collaboration of the archaeologist Edouard
Lavalleye, the Huy architect Emile Vierset-Godin was the first to
describe the châsses (dated at that time to the fourteenth century)
as needing, *comme la basilique elle-même une restauration complète et immé-
diate* (like the basilica itself, a complete and immediate restoration).
The Huy architect reiterated this wish in 1862, at the time of publication of an article in the *Bulletin des Commissions royales d'Art et
d'Archéologie*, devoted to the treasury of the Huy collegiate church.
Although the Gilde de St.-Thomas et de St.-Luc made this wish its
motto in 1876, it was fortunately never fulfilled.

At the end of a "life" of eight centuries full of diverse adventures,
the châsses today present a rather chaotic aspect to us, relatively
degraded and difficult to interpret, with so many alterations. For
while a certain number of the interventions visible nowadays can be
attached to the events reported by the sources, there are many others
for which no documentation survives or whose dating is difficult to
relate to the texts.

At the stage preceding disassembly of the châsses for their "restoration," the archaeological examination made it possible however to observe three principal types of alterations required by this tumultuous course. Some examples representative of these interventions will illustrate this chapter. They show at what point, on such an *objet d'art*, the problems of chronology, style and iconography, in addition to the archaeological observations, narrowly overlap.

Amputations

Amputations are the changes which most seriously marked the existence of the châsses. Most radical was that which reduced each by a sixth of its length, depriving each one of half of a bay on each side and thus of a figure, as well as of a medallion on each side of the roof. (figs. 51–2) The original length of each feretory can thus be estimated at close to one m fifty-eight cm. While the archives do not inform us of the precise date of this mutilation, Jules Helbig and Joseph de Borchgrave d'Altena supposed it, with reason, to have been done in the eighteenth century. Two dates ought to be taken into consideration in this regard. It could have occurred in 1720–21 at the time when the châsses received new woodwork for their installation behind the new high altar of the collegiate church where, undoubtedly for technical reasons, it was agreed to re-work them to a length which did not exceed that of the Marian châsse, their neighbor (one m, thirty-two cm). It could have also have been in 1763, when the old metals coming from the châsse were sold to the goldsmith Francson. Although the amputation could have taken place about 1720–21, with the canons deciding only much later to sell the recovered metal.

What did the removed portions of the châsses comprise, from an iconographic point of view? One can suppose, according to the particular iconographic program of the châsse of St. Mengoldus, that its sides featured a kind of escort of other military saints or knights; pursuing this analysis revolves upon that issue. As to the châsse of St. Domitianus, its amputation probably removed figures of apostles, who completed the series still partially in place. Ultimately, it is also possible that the elements which disappeared at the time of these amputations were not original. For example, the images of Sts. John and Andrew from the châsse of St. Domitianus had already been replaced a little before 1500.

With regard to their roofs, visible traces leave no doubt that a fifth medallion once supplemented the current series on the slopes of each of the two châsses. (fig. 59) The lost medallion ought to have been identical to the four others on that of St. Domitianus. On that of St. Mengoldus, one doubtless saw the allegories from two of the Eight Beatitudes, presented to complement those at its opposite end. The axis of symmetry of each slope would thus have consisted of the two angels proclaiming, one the verse of Hebrews 11.33, the other that of the letter of 1 John 5.4; each one would have been surrounded by four allegories of the Beatitudes, in symmetrical attitudes: their heads turned towards the adjacent medallions with the Scriptures, (fig. 60) the head in front of those on the ends. The iconographic interpretation of this composition thus appears: one sees clearly, in the axial position of the two biblical quotations which constituted the central topic of the message, the victory by Faith, accompanied by the Beatitudes, important to the Christian the eschatological dimension which saw this discourse enriched by a moral teaching. The introduction of an internal dynamic by the alternation of the attitudes of the allegories conferred on this reading an element of considerable rhetorical conviction.

Transfers and Re-employments

The archaeological examination of the châsses revealed that many elements may have been exchanged, either within the same châsse, or perhaps between the one and the other. The image of St. Victor, (fig. 61) today on the châsse of St. Domitianus constitutes the most obvious example of this. The relief is attributed to a talented goldsmith around 1400, creator of the St. Simeon on the same chasse, (fig. 62) and of an angel in bust on the roof of its counterpart. It has been noted that the iconographic program on the long sides of the châsse of St. Mengoldus is obviously devoted to the military saints, while that of St. Domitianus, with exceptions, is devoted to the apostles. It appears that, in the case of the châsse of St. Mengoldus, the original iconographic program was respected and left alone at the time of the majority of the successive restorations, still it is evident that the image of St. Victor initially belonged to the châsse of St. Mengoldus. It was obviously necessary to adapt the plate of the bottom of the figure to a new support on the châsse of St. Domitianus, carelessly done, perhaps in the eighteenth century. This reveals that the initial iconographic program of the two châsses was by then no longer understood or respected.

It has been suggested that the pinions were exchanged between the two feretories. Within the same reliquary, the two pinions are dissimilar, and this apparent anomaly is encountered on both of the châsses. The two pinions where St. Mengoldus (fig. 63) and St. Domitianus (fig. 64), respectively, are represented are "twin" from the point of view of their decorations, made up of enamels and surmounted with rock crystals. On the other hand, those of the Virgin and of Christ are surrounded by rinceaux of *vernis brun* and surmounted by gilded rosettes. How can one explain this asymmetry? Helbig and de Borchgrave d'Altena[18] advanced the seemingly-logical assumption that the pinions were exchanged between the two reliquaries: thus the châsse of St. Mengoldus would have originally had two pinions with the enamelled decorations and the châsse of St. Domitianus two pinions decorated with *vernis brun* and occupied, one by the effigy of the Savior, the other by that of His Mother. Pushing this logic to the end, de Borchgrave recognized there the iconographic program of a former Marian châsse like that of 1260 which is also preserved in the treasury of the collegiate church at Huy: the pinions there are occupied by the figures in majesty of the Savior and the Virgin, the long sides by the series of the apostles.[19] But it was forgotten that such asymmetry was encountered elsewhere, such as on the two re-worked pinions of the old châsse of St. Ode of Amay (*c.* 1160–70), where enamels on the theophanic pinion are placed opposite the *vernis brun* on that of St. Ode. In addition, an attentive examination reveals that the figures themselves were later added in the positions that they occupy today. None of those which are currently found on the pinions of the two châsses is original.

---

[18] J. Helbig, "Les Châsses de Saint Domitien et de Saint Mengold de l'ancienne collégiale de Huy . . .," *Bulletin de l'Institut archéologique liégeois*, XIII (1877), p. 231; J. de Borchgrave d'Altena, "Les châsses de saint Domitien et de saint Mengold de la collégiale Notre-Dame, à Huy," *Bulletin de la Société d'Art et d'Histoire du diocèse de Liège*, XLII (1961), pp. 36, 42.

[19] R. Didier *et al.*, "La châsse de Notre-Dame de Huy et sa restauration. Histoire-Etude archéologique," *Bulletin de l'Institut royal du Patrimoine artistique*, XII (1970), pp. 8–54. *Editors' note: see also Lisa Victoria Ciresi's and Benoit van den Bossche's essays in this volume.

The image of St. Domitianus has been re-dated from the twelfth century to the thirteenth. (fig. 64) Examination reveals that the figure was awkwardly re-attached to the plaque at the background of its niche. The same is true for the St. Mengoldus, who has sometimes been considered as an original figure, however, the technical, heraldic, archaeological, and stylistic examination reveals that it also dates from the thirteenth century. (fig. 63) On the pinion of the châsse of St. Domitianus embellished with *vernis brun*, the character of Christ argues for a re-dating, as well, because while the effigy dates to the thirteenth century, the head was added in the sixteenth century. (fig. 65) As for the Virgin and Child occupying the corresponding pinion on the châsse of St. Mengoldus, its stylistic characteristics from the beginning of the sixteenth century also signal a re-working. The current disposition shows, in any event, concern for placing the two patron saints of Huy on an equal footing, by giving to the two châsses a certain symmetry between their pinions.

The assembly marks observed here are also included in the chapter files on the transfers of elements. One can find them by a simple examination of certain figures on the long sides. There are some on the châsse of St. Mengold, but they are scattered and difficult to interpret. On the other hand, those seen on the châsse of St. Domitian are more meaningful, as they are Roman numerals engraved either on the seats, or on the bases, or on both at the same time. The Roman I is encountered on the St. Matthew of the first face of the châsse; it is the only figure on this side to carry a mark. On the other face, one finds II on St. Simeon, (fig. 62) III on St. Bartholomew, IV on St. Jude. V could not be located, but it ought to be reproduced on St. John, next to St. Andrew who carries the VI. The original sequence, before the amputation of the eighteenth century, probably placed St. Matthew at the head on this side. As the most recent of the reliefs date to the end of the fifteenth century, one can consider that their numeration dates to that time.

Do we have to also consider as resulting from a transfer the St. John the Baptist of the sixteenth century on the châsse of St. Mengoldus? (fig. 66) To tell the truth, his original place is difficult to determine. Indeed the Precursor neither fits logically into the theory of the military saints for the châsse of St. Mengoldus, nor into that of the holy apostles for the châsse of St. Domitianus. Perhaps here one ought to interpret him as one of the first martyrs, a "precursor" to St. Mengoldus himself?

The interpretation of two other figures in the iconographic program of the châsse of St. Domitianus poses the same questions. Why
include St. Simeon (undoubtedly the old christophore, *c.* 1400) and
why a deacon saint (Stephen or Lawrence, *c.* 1500) among the apostles? (fig. 67) Their presence might be explained by the existence in
the collegiate church at Huy of relics pertaining specifically to Sts.
John the Baptist, Simeon, and Lawrence. These were known to be
housed in the châsse of the Virgin in the seventeenth century. Would
they have also previously resided in the châsses of the two patron
saints of Huy? If so, would artisans of 1400 have been tempted to
adapt part of the iconography of the sides to illustrate the contents?
However, one should also consider the opposite process, which would
have led to the introduction into the châsses of the relics of the
saints present on their sides. The two hypotheses must be considered,
especially because the same Marian châsse also contained the relics
of Sts. Maurice, Exupert, Alban, and Sebastian, knightly saints like
those still depicted on the châsse of St. Mengold, (fig. 68) and of Sts.
George and Hippolitus, whom one would think might have completed
this series. Finally, as the author of *Vita Mengoldi* (*c.* 1170) explains,
the figures of Sts. Sebastian, Maurice, and Martin are models for
the cavalier ideal with which they cloak their heroes. Was St. Martin
also included among the military saints on the châsse?

To this important chapter of analysis, it is still advisable to add,
without entering into detail, the many exchanged or re-used decorative elements. Among the most curious, let us cite the stamped
bands decorated with palmettes in arches (fig. 69) which came from
the chamfers of the panels of the same châsse, probably recovered
during the amputation mentioned above. One can also note the presence, on one of the slopes of the châsse of St. Mengoldus, of strips
of *vernis brun* coming from various embellishments of the two châsses.
In the same way, the plates with *vernis brun* decorating the eaves of
the pinion of St. Mengoldus actually constitute the two halves of a
broad band, similar to those decorating the ends of the châsse, and
divided in the middle. On various pinions, one can also see the
assembly of several types of crests. These diverse observations highlight that a significant number of elements of the revetment of the
châsse (such as those in silver or in copper) were recovered during
the amputation and then reinstated.

Last, we see as re-used the strips in *opus interrasile* today constituting
the crest of the châsse of St. Domitianus. (fig. 70) Their vegetal and

zoomorphic repertoire, and their technique of execution, narrowly connect them with the group of goldsmiths, perhaps from lower Saxony, whose work can be seen on the portable altar of Watterbach and on the lower binding of the Anhalt-Morgan Evangeliary (New York, Pierpont-Morgan Library). This connection suggests a date of the eleventh century for this crest. Would this dating serve here, for the re-use of a decoration coming from a former châsse? One would be authorized to think so.

Substitutions

An archaeological approach to the Huy châsses reveals the many prostheses and other visible patches which reflect the multiple misadventures they underwent and the repairs which ensued, more than those briefly mentioned in the chronicles. It is necessary to again evoke the case of the pinions which show all the traces (poorly- or not-at-all-camouflaged) of these re-workings. Let us return in particular to the pinion of St. Domitianus: a cutting into the plaque of the background and the awkward fixings clearly show that the current effigy was later joined to the châsse in this place. The figure itself shows traces of re-working: the miter and the left band of the cross trimming the chasuble of the figure carry a decoration of small cabochons in crimped relief, which seems to be original and which differs from that of the collar and the band from right-hand side of the cross. (fig. 63) In the enameled framing of the same pinion, the thin strip on the left is poorly connected to the ornament of the gable, perhaps also indicating a reworking. An enameled ribbon, from the twelfth century, under the effigy of the holy bishop, carries the invocation: *Scs Domitianus Hoyensium Patronus* (St. Domitianus, Patron of Huy), but it is mostly illegible because of its current placement. The whole of these observations confirms that the current St. Domitianus is no longer the original, and stylistic arguments—i.e. naturalism of drapery—plead for a dating of this figure to the first decennaries of the thirteenth century.

The figure of St. Mengoldus has obviously undergone the same fate, but its insertion in the silver and gilded copper architecture of the pinion is even more awkward: too tall in relationship to the framing, his feet spill out onto the lower chamfer! The characteristics of the costume, of the armament (analyzed by Claude Gaier)[20] and of the hairstyle suggest that this substitution would have taken place at the earliest in the last third of the thirteenth century. This dating appears to be confirmed by the heraldry for, if the three leopards decorating the coat of arms evoke the English ascendance of prince Mengold (whom local legend had made the son of King Hugh of England), they only appear in the arms in the thirteenth century. An interesting fact, raised by heraldist René Wattiez,[21] concerns the simultaneous presence of the British armorial bearings on the coat of arms, and that of the Empire on the shield held by St. Mengoldus. (fig. 63) Alone, it seems, that Richard of Cornwallis, king of the Romans and brother of Henry III, could have used these two together, and in this context it is interesting to note his passage to Huy on December 29, 1258.[22]

On the pinion opposite that of St. Domitianus, the Christ in Majesty is also a substitution: the body of the figure dates to the thirteenth century and the head to the sixteenth. While it is clearly not an original work of the twelfth century, one cannot attribute it either to the Master of the St. Mengold, or to that of the St. Domitien. Rather, the style of the drapery and certain ornamental motifs may more reasonably be compared to the Sts. Matthew, Bartholomew, and Jude (fig. 71) on the sides of the same châsse, and which date to the thirteenth century. The head of this Christ, however, seems to be from a later time, as is made evident by its crude solder. (fig. 72) Stylistically, it may be attributed to the Master of the Marian pinion of the châsse of St. Mengoldus. (fig. 73)

Various substitutions transformed the sides of the châsses: about 1400, the figures of Sts. Victor and Simeon were actually on the châsse of St. Domitianus; (figs. 61, 62) towards the end of the fifteenth century, those of Sts. John and Andrew (fig. 74) were on the same châsse; also there, at the beginning of the sixteenth century, that of

---

[20] Cl. Gaier, "Contribution à la chronologie des châsses de saint Domitien et de saint Mengold à Huy," *Annales du Cercle hutois des Sciences et Beaux-Arts* (1994), pp. 181–200.

[21] R. Wattiez, "Propos héraldiques sur la châsse de saint Mengold de Huy," *Les Amis du Musée d'Art religieux et d'Art mosan, Bulletin trimestriel* (1984), no. 12, pp. 2–7.

[22] A. Joris, "La visite à Huy de Richard de Cornouailles, roi des Romains (29 décembre 1258)," *Le Moyen Âge*, 64 (1958), pp. 271–83.

a remarkable relief of a holy deacon; (fig. 75) and later, (towards the beginning of sixteenth, judging from the military equipment, according to Gaier);[23] the Sts. Cassius and Innocent were added to the feretory of St. Mengoldus (fig. 57); about 1560, those of the two anonymous saints to the châsse of St. Domitianus (fig. 75); finally in 1762–63, those of the anonymous saint and the brass heads that were attached to the châsse of St. Mengoldus. (fig. 57) It is advisable, however, to reserve particular attention for the figure of St. Candidus, on the shrine of St. Mengold because he constitutes a key element of the archaeological interpretation of the reliquaries. (fig. 76) Indeed, if one observes that this is a pastiche of the original military saints, it presents with notable differences in the epigraphy, the clothing, and the technique. The work in repoussé of the mesh/mail of the haubert and the treatment of hair, on the other hand, reveal many similarities to the St. Mengold, which is dated to the end of the thirteenth century. Some of these characteristics, just like the epigraphy, are found on the Sts. Jude, Bartholomew, and Matthew on the châsse of St. Domitianus, making it possible by comparison to also situate the fabrication of the St. Candidus figure about this time and to propose the hypothesis that a radical reworking then occurred. (fig. 70)

The roofs of the châsses also advertise the chronology of their repairs. Around 1400, an angel in a medallion was replaced on the châsse of St. Mengoldus by the Master of the Sts. Simeon and Victor, while in 1560, the ensemble of the medallions of the roof was renewed on the châsse of St. Domitianus by Jaspar and Henry de Namur (fig. 51) as were three medallions of St. Mengoldus; in 1762–63, and in 1788, the goldsmith Derotte and coppersmith Arnold Gritte and Crousse repaired some elements of the angels on the châsse of St. Mengoldus. Then, in 1724, the ironworker Le Vasseur installed a "little apple" on the same châsse. (fig. 52)

Finally, we will evoke, only for memory, the various substitutions of decorative elements like the current crest of the châsse of St. Mengold, which does not appear to date earlier than the thirteenth century, and such engraved motifs as border the hagiophanic pinion of the same châsse, in which we still see pastiches undoubtedly carried out in the sixteenth century and inspired by original elements of the twelfth century still in place. (fig. 77)

---

[23] Cl. Gaier, "Contribution à la chronologie," pp. 181–200.

Through the events of their chronicle, the two châsses of Sts. Mengold and Domitian offer today to the historian and to the historian of art an astonishing synopsis of the principal aspects of past social and religious life. The lines of force of the Middle Ages intersect there or are reflected there, in their contrasts and their extremes, sharing in luxury and misery, power and popularity, religion and paganism, light and darkness, individuality and community. In some ways, the following centuries did not modify this tableau appreciably. From the opulence of their original execution to the mediocrity of the last interventions which were aimed at their survival, they were nevertheless preserved until our day and in spite of the serious transformations along the way, that which was their original aim, of containing, while glorifying, contents even more precious because they were eminently sacred. The traces of this destiny thus form an integral part of the history of the two reliquaries, and respect for them will dictate the "restoration" of that which was essential about them. According to what precedes, it will be agreed that it is much more a question of "conserving" than of "restoring," in the sense that one understood it until these last decades.

CHAPTER SIX

ARCHITECTURAL REPRESENTATIONS ON THE MEDALLIONS OF THE HERIBERT SHRINE*

Ilana Abend-David

In this article I will argue that the Heribert Shrine was ordered and produced as part of an effort to re-establish the financial strength of the abbey of Deutz in the third quarter of the twelfth century. (fig. 78) The shrine is a rectangular wooden box of 68 × 153 cm, surmounted by a pitched roof, with gilded silver and bronze placques, and decorated with gems, pearls, and enamels. Along each of its long sides are six gilded silver figures of apostles, enthroned in a variety of postures, and interspersed with enamel panels of standing prophets. At one end of the shrine, the Virgin and Child are enthroned under an arch, accompanied by two angels, while on the opposite end is St. Heribert enthroned, vested with his archiepiscopal pallium, receiving a crozier and a book from personified Charity and Humility. On each side of the shrine's roof are six enameled medallions[1] portraying eighteen scenes from the life of St. Heribert. (figs. 79–84) Fourteen of these are set in architectural environments. Considering the relatively small size of the medallions, the effort to depict architecture should be understood as critical to the content of the narrative. This is significant because hagiographical texts identify, but

---

* An early version of this paper was presented in the session "The Arts of Regional Pilgrimage Centers in Medieval England and Northern Europe" organized by Sarah Blick and Rita Tekippe at the 35th International Congress on Medieval Studies in Kalamazoo, MI, USA, 2000. I would like to thank Professor Robin Oggins from Binghamton University and Professor Jonathan J. Alexander from the Fine-Arts Institute for commenting on early versions of this paper. I also take the opportunity to thank my advisor, Professor Barbara Abou-El-Haj from Binghamton University, for her assistance, guidance, and encouragement.

[1] The medallions on the Heribert Shrine are of *champlevé* enamel, widely used, from around 1130 in the Meuse-Rhine region, and in Limoges and Lower Saxony. For the history of medieval enamels see: Gunter Haseloff, *Email in Frühen Mittelaltar: Frühchristliche Kunst von der Spätantike bis zum den Karolingern* (Marburg, 1990); *Enamels of Limoges 1100–1350* (New York, 1996); Neil Stratford, *Catalogue of Medieval Enamels in the British Museum* (London, 1993).

do not describe the sites of even the most important narrated events in a saint's life. The designers could have chosen how to represent buildings in a way appropriate to pictorial *vitae*, which pertained to the circumstances that motivated their production. Hence, architectural representation is one key to understanding the new version of a saint's life. As Richard Krautheimer discussed, built, painted, or carved representations of structures during the Middle Ages often showed only selected aspects of the represented building.[2] Therefore, in order to establish the artists' intention to depict a particular architectural work, I will compare the buildings pictured on the shrine with other representations of the same structures that either include an identifying inscription, or a context, which establishes an unambiguous identification.

The Abbey of Deutz

Three sources mention the foundation of an abbey at the site of the castle of Deutz: Lambert of Deutz's *Vita Heriberti* (1050), Rupert of Deutz's *Vita Heriberti* (1119), and his *De incendio* (1128).[3] All three texts state that Otto III (980–1002) approved Heribert's plan to found the monastery before he died in 1002. However, neither the emperor nor the archbishop had specified a location for the monastery until the Virgin appeared to Heribert in a dream and ordered him to build it in the castle at Deutz, an event depicted on his shrine. According to Rupert, the castle needed to be purified because demonic cults had been celebrated there, and by building a monastery dedicated to Christ, the Virgin, and all the Saints, the sin would be replaced by justice.[4] A more practical reason might have been the

---

[2] Richard Krautheimer, "Introduction to an 'Iconography of Medieval Architecture,'" in *Studies in Early Christian, Medieval and Renaissance Art* (New York, 1969), pp. 115—50, esp. 126.

[3] Marianne Gechter, "Das Kastell Deutz im Mittelalter," *Kölner Jahrbuch für Vor- und Frühgeschichte* 22 (1989), 402; Lambert von Deutz, *Vita Heriberti. Miracula Heriberti. Gedichte. Lituggische Texte*, ed. Bernhard Vogel (Hanover, 2001), pp. 138–201; Peter Dinter, *Rupert von Deutz, Vita Heriberti: Kritische Edition mit Kommentar und Untersuchungen* (Bonn, 1976), pp. 55–6; Gechter, "Das Kastell Deutz," pp. 403–8; Rupert of Deutz, *De incendio Tiutiensis*, ed. P. Jaffe, *Monumenta Germaniae Historica. Scriptores* 12 (1856), pp. 632–3.

[4] "*Ego enim sum Maria, mater Domini Surge ergo et Tuitiense castrum petens locum in eodem mundari precipe, ibique monasterium Deo michique et omnibus sanctis constitue, ut ubi quondam*

strategic situation of the castle, which enabled Heribert (or anyone else who possessed it) to control the bridge to Cologne and to regulate the entrance to the town market.[5] By commanding the castle of Deutz, Heribert controlled both the Cologne market and the Rhine as it passed by—this river being the main route of commerce for the German Empire.[6] On May 3, 1020, Heribert dedicated the abbey's church to the Virgin.[7] He died one year later and was entombed in the monastery.

The only certain date regarding the sequence of building of the abbey church is its dedication day of May 3, 1020, but this cannot be the date of completion of the church, since the building project continued during the archbishopric of Heribert's successor, Pilgrim (r. 1021–36). The construction may have began as early as 1003, but when the first church collapsed, a new one had to be built. According to Lambert of Deutz, Heribert hired two experienced architects from "foreign territories" to supervise the work,[8] probably to make sure

---

habundavit peccatum et cultus demonum, ibi iustitia regnet in multitudine sanctorum." For I am Maria Mother of the Lord. Therefore rise up and go to the fortress of Deutz, order that in the same place a space is purified and build a monastery for God and me and all the saints so that where once sin and the cult of demons were present in abundance, there justice will rule because of the multitude of saints. Dinter, *Rupert von Deutz*, p. 54.

[5] Gechter, "Das Kastell Deutz," p. 384. According to Milz's list of the abbey's property, rights and acquisitions, the abbey did not control a toll at this site. Joseph Milz, *Studien zur mittelalterlichen Wirtschaft- und Verfassungsgeschichte der Abtei Deutz* (Cologne, 1970), pp. 245–88.

[6] Until the twelfth century, the German Empire only played a secondary role in European trade. However, this situation changed in the middle of the twelfth century under the Hohenstaufen emperors. The routes along the Rhine connected Italy with cities on the shore of the North Sea, England, and Scandinavia. Horst Fuhrmann, *Germany in the High Middle Ages c. 1050–1200* (Cambridge, 1986), pp. 24–7.

[7] *Rheinisches Urkundenbuch: Ältere Urkunden bis 1100*, ed. Erich Wisplinghoff (Bonn, 1972), pp. 190–5 and Gechter, "Das Kastell Deutz im Mittelalter," pp. 384, 401–2. It is unclear whether this is an original document, or a partial or total forgery.

[8] "*Inde ad modum navalis mali in altum effossa terra fundamenta firmat in solida petra primis peritiores architectos ab externis finibus exquirens et eis disciplinam totius structure committens.*" Next after the earth had been dug up as deep as the mast of a ship he strengthened the foundations on a solid rock, first seeking out more experienced architects from foreign territories and entrusting them with the construction of the entire structure. Lambert von Deutz, *Vita Heriberti. Miracula Heriberti. Gedichte. Liturgische Texte*, ed. Bernhard Vogel, p. 170. Singelton very cautiously raises the possibility that the architects were Armenians, and even suggests the name of Trdat, who repaired the dome of the Hagia Sophia in Constantinople just before 996. Barrie Singleton, "Köln-Deutz and Romanesque Architecture," *Journal of the British Archaeological Association* 143 (1990), pp. 54–58, 74. After comparing the church ground plan with ground plans of churches from Ani, the ancient capital of Armenia, that were built around

that the second church would not meet the same fate. The monastery church was a centrally-planned building, leading some scholars to suggest that it was modeled after Charlemagne's Palace Chapel at Aachen,[9] however, Singleton propsed that it was modeled after the most famous round building in the West in the Middle Ages, Hadrian's Pantheon in Rome which had been re-dedicated to the Virgin in the seventh century.[10] It would have been an appropriate model for the Ottonian imperial court,[11] and both models would have also been appropriate to German imperial policy, since the Ottonian rulers adopted Roman, Carolingian, and Byzantine forms in order to represent themselves as heirs to the Roman and Carolingian emperors, especially Constantine and Charlemagne, while they sought recognition from the Byzantines as Roman emperors in the West.

When the church at Deutz was re-dedicated to Heribert is unclear. Van Engen suggested that it took place after his canonization in the 1030s,[12] while Schnitzler contended that the saint was canonized in 1147, the year in which Heribert's relics were elevated according to Theodericus, in the monastery's codex.[13] Yet, these ceremonies are not necessarily linked.[14] Müller claimed that Heribert was never officially canonized and the first evidence that he was treated as a saint is found in a document issued by his successor, Archbishop

the same period and are also assigned to Trdat, such as the city's cathedral (989–1001) and King Gagik's Church of St. Gregory (990–1000 or 1001–5), I think this hypothesis is worth further study. For more information on Ani, see: www.virtualani. freeserve.co.uk.

[9] Hans Erich Kubach & Albert Verbeek, *Romanische Baukunst an Rhein und Mass* (Berlin, 1976), pp. 184–6.

[10] Pope Boniface IV converted the Pantheon into a church consecrated to the Virgin Mary and all the martyrs, in 609, and changed its name to Santa Maria Rotunda. Richard Krautheimer, *Rome: Profile of a City, 312–1308* (Princeton, 1980), p. 72.

[11] Singleton, "Köln-Deutz," pp. 54–8.

[12] Van Engen did not present supporting evidence for his claim. John H. Van Engen, *Rupert of Deutz* (Los Angeles, 1983), p. 230.

[13] Hermann Schnitzler, *Der Schrein des Heiligen Heribert* (Munich, 1962), pp. 2, 5, citing Theodericus Aedituus, *Thioderici Aeditui Tuitiensis Opuscula*, ed. Oswald Holder-Egger, *Monumenta Germaniae Historica. Scriptores*, 14 (1883), pp. 560–77.

[14] Relics can be elevated more than once, frequently when churches were renovated. The monastery at Deutz was renovated by Rupert (r. 1120–29), who ordered the decoration of the vaulted ceiling above the elevated platform of the church, dedicated a new chapel to St. Lawrence, and built a new dormitory. None of the medieval sources suggest, however, that Heribert's relics were elevated during this renovation.

Pilgrim, in 1032, in which Heribert is refered to as a saint. Müller termed this as "canonization *per viam cultus*" (canonization through cultivation). According to Müller the canonization bull, discovered in 1910, was a twelfth-century forgery prepared by Abbots Gerlach and Hartbern as part of their effort to revive Heribert's cult.[15] Nonetheless, during the eleventh and twelfth centuries, bishops and archbishops continued to canonize saints.[16] Singleton claimed that the church was re-dedicated in the twelfth century, but he does not present supporting evidence.[17]

From the time of its eleventh-century foundation, Deutz was under the jurisdiction of the archbishops of Cologne, who appointed its abbots and confirmed all donations to the abbey.[18] A charter from May 3, 1020 (attributed to Heribert) stated that the monastery's endowment and privileges included control over the castle in which it was built, but it is unclear whether this is an original document, or a partial or total forgery.[19] Most of the monastery's property was endowed by Heribert and Otto III to support forty monks,[20] and probably consisted of four royal manors, three royal forests, twenty-five other manors, a small castle on the Rhine, vineyards on the Mosel, and forty parochial churches—of which twenty-five paid full tithe.[21] The abbey continued to receive support from Pilgrim, but later, the number of land donations, both from emperors and arch-bishops, declined significantly. Instead the abbey received fishing, custom, and tithe privileges,[22] whose value may not have been

---

[15] For more information on the debate regarding Heribert's canonization, see Heribert Müller, *Heribert, Kanzler Ottos III. Und Erzbischof von Köln* (Cologne, 1977), pp. 36–40, 313–5.

[16] E. Waldram Kemp, *Canonization and Authority in the Western Church* (London, 1948), pp. 53, 56–81. Although during the eleventh and twelfth centuries papal canonization became more important, it was not the sole means of canonization until the thirteenth century, when Rome established control over the process.

[17] Singleton, "Köln-Deutz," p. 57.

[18] Pope Leo IX (r. 1049–54) gave Archbishop Hermann II (r. 1036–56) a char-ter that confirmed that the abbey of St. Heribert at Deutz was under the jurisdic-tion of the archbishops of Cologne. Milz, *Studien zur mittelalterlichen Wirtschaft*, p. 30.

[19] *Rheinisches Urkundenbuch*, ed. Erich Wisplinghoff, pp. 190–5; Gechter, "Das Kastell Deutz im Mittelalter," pp. 384, 401–2. Earlier charters referring to Deutz dated to 1003 and onward can be found in the same volume.

[20] I could not find any explanation for the unusually-large community. It seems that Heribert had grandiose plans for this abbey, and the church's architectural plan attest to his ambitions.

[21] Milz, *Studien zur mittelalterlichen Wirtschaft*, pp. 23–9, 245–89.

[22] Milz, *Studien zur mittelalterlichen Wirtschaft*, pp. 30–1.

sufficient, as attested by a financial decline, beginning in the 1060s. Archbishop Sigewin (r. 1079–89), who donated six shillings for his yearly memorial and some custom privileges, was the last archbishop of Cologne to donate to the abbey, and Emperor Henry IV, who continued the yearly donation of four marks made by his father, Henry III, was the last emperor to donate to the abbey, in 1059. Throughout the rest of the eleventh and twelfth centuries, the abbey relied on donations from the laity.[23] Rupert's successor, Abbot Rudolph (r. 1129–46), was accused by Theodericus, the abbey's *custus*, of exhausting its financial resources. Although there is no clear proof for this charge, the fact that Abbot Rudolph's signature appears on documents produced at the archbishop's court as witness more often than anyone else's, while no documents regarding the abbey survived from the period of his abbacy, suggest that he may have neglected the abbey's affairs.[24]

Both abbots Gerlach (r. 1146–59) and Hartbern (r. 1161–69) tried to re-establish the abbey's financial strength. Gerlach initiated an inventory of the abbey's properties written by Theodericus, which included the castle of Deutz, and various privileges. He also introduced the earliest extant document signed by a pope, Eugenus III (1145–53), that confirms these properties and rights.[25] Another list of the abbey's property and taxation privileges was confirmed in 1161, during the abbacy of Hartbern, by anti-Pope Victor IV (1159–64).[26] Abbots Gerlach and Hartbern re-purchased some of the property and privileges that their predecessors had lost.[27] As part of their efforts to re-establish the financial strength of the abbey, they also forged charters describing property donations that the abbey claimed, including the castle of Deutz.[28]

The monastery's claim over the castle dates back to Abbot Rupert who argued that the big fire of 1128, which burned large parts of the castle, but spared the abbey church, was God's punishment for the fortification of the castle in 1114. Rupert primarily blamed

---

[23] Milz, *Studien zur mittelalterlichen Wirtschaft*, pp. 31–2.

[24] Milz, *Studien zur mittelalterlichen Wirtschaft*, p. 35; Sinderhauf, *Die Abtei Deutz ihre innere Erneuerung*, pp. 122–7.

[25] Sinderhauf, *Die Abtei Deutz ihre innere Erneuerung*, pp. 122–7.

[26] Sinderhauf, *Die Abtei Deutz ihre innere Erneuerung*, p. 238.

[27] It is unclear how the abbey lost its property and privileges. They could have been sold, paid as taxes, or confiscated by the ecclesiastical or lay lords, but they do support Theodericus's accusation that Rudolph was a poor manager at best.

[28] Van Engen, *Rupert of Deutz*, p. 230.

Archbishop Fredrick of Cologne (r. 1099–1131) for the fortifications and the fire. In order to prevent such occurrences from happening in the future, Rupert claimed that Heribert had given the entire castle to the monastery as part of his endowment. Abbot Gerlach continued Rupert's claims over the castle in order to maintain the monastery's independence.[29]

With the assistance of Theodericus, Abbot Gerlach initiated the authentication of the relics of the Eleven Thousand Virgins who had accompanied St. Ursula in order to establish their cult in the monastery and to increase the profits from pilgrimage.[30] The Heribert Shrine, created during the abbacies of Gerlach and Hartbern, was a part of the effort to revive the abbey's finances. Property and architecture thus played a large role in the dealings of the monastery and this is reflected in the architecture depicted on the Heribert Shrine.

Architectural Representations on the Heribert Shrine

Royal and Aristocratic Settings

The architecture depicted on the Heribert Shrine can be classified in two groups, royal/aristocratic and ecclesiastical, both appropriate to the life of a saintly archbishop born to an aristocratic family, whose career was linked to the German emperors Otto III and Henry II. Four of the scenes on the shrine take place in royal or aristocratic palaces, beginning with Heribert's birth on the first medallion (fig. 79) where a composite interior with an exterior roof represents the palace of Heribert's father, count Hugo. Here the architecture serves to identify an important location that defines Heribert's rank while it simultaneously frames multiple scenes of the narrative. The upper part is divided into distinct spaces by three arches. The central arch that frames the most important event, Heribert's birth, is also composed of three parts designed to allude to a sacred place, as Werckmeister

---

[29] For the dispute over the castle of Deutz see Milz, *Studien zur mittelalterlichen Wirtschaft*, pp. 12–7. For more about the fire of 1128 see Rupert of Deutz, *De incendio Tuitiensis*, pp. 624–37; Gechter, "Das Kastell Deutz im Mittelalter," pp. 387–8; Paul Strait, *Cologne in the Twelfth Century* (Gainsville, FL, 1974), pp. 29–31.

[30] Sinderhauf, *Die Abtei Deutz ihre innere Erneuerung*, pp. 145–56; Theodericus Aedituus, *Thioderici Aeditui Tuitiensis Opuscula*, pp. 569–70.

has demonstrated, transferred here onto a secular setting.[31] Accordingly, the dome, signifying the vault of heaven, is replaced by a large tower appropriate to a palace which continues to emphasize the importance of the saint's birth directly below. Similarly, the gables from the scheme that Werckmeister recognised are replaced by architectural elements that belong to castles, such as small towers and a pitched roof with crenellations. Below, the throne room of Count Hugo is framed by an architrave supported by two columns with a drapery swag. The same setting is used to depict Emperor Otto III's throne room in the lower scene of the third medallion, (fig. 80) making the two visually equivalent, establishing Heribert's rank. Both settings are adapted from ruler portraits in Carolingian and Ottonian manu-scripts, such as the depictions of Charles the Bald in the *Vivian Bible* (846), and Otto III in his Gospel Book (998–1001).[32]

The throne room of Otto III is depicted once again in the upper scene of the fourth medallion, (fig. 80) where the emperor invests Heribert with the banners of the regalia of the archdiocese of Cologne, but in a different manner. The emperor sits on his throne accom-panied by a guard, but now there are no indications of the interior space. Rather, on the emperor's right, is a standard cityscape com-posed of towers and various roof elements. The same type of urban assemblage also appears as a view of Cologne in the lower scene of the fifth medallion, (fig. 81) where the people of Cologne welcome Heribert into the city, thus underscoring the two linked events. A likely model for this scene is Christ's Entry into Jerusalem, as in the *Pericopes Book of Henry II* (1002–12), where a view of the city is com-prised of a similar variety of roofs, walls, and towers. Even closer is the scene in an Epistolary from Trier (980–90), where the boy who

---

[31] The combination of gable-dome-gable above a three-part arch was used to depict holy places since the early medieval period. Werckmeister refers to two cases: the depiction of the church councils in the Nativity church at Bethlehem and the scene of Christ and the adulteress on the golden cover of the *Codex Aureus*. Otto-Karl Werckmeister, *Der Deckel des Codex Aureus von St. Emmeram* (Baden-Baden, 1962), pp. 34–7, fig. 2a.

[32] Constantine, *Carolingian Herbal*, Kassel, Landesbibliothek, Cod. Phys. Fol. 10, fol. iv; Herbert. L. Kessler, *The Illustrated Bibles from Tours* (Princeton, 1977), ill. 212. Presentation of a Bible to Charles the Bald, *Vivian Bible*, Tours, 846, Paris, BN, Ms. lat. 1, f. 423, and Otto III Seated in Majesty, *Gospel Book of Otto III*, 998–1001, Munich, Bayerische Staatbibl. Clm. 4453, f. 24; Henry Mayr-Harting, *Ottonian Book Illumination: An Historical Study* (London, 1991), fig. 30, pl. xxi.

is usually seen sitting in a tree, is depicted on one of the city roofs, just as in the medallion,[33] where he serves as a witness. This is no random adaptation. It pertains to the liturgical typology between a bishop and Christ, but also to a specific incident, which enhanced Heribert's position in relation to the emperor.[34]

After the death of Otto III in 1002, Heribert supported Duke Hermann's unsuccessful claim to the throne against that of Duke Henry of Bavaria. The dispute between Archbishop Heribert and Emperor Henry II arose in 1002, when Heribert brought Otto III's body from Italy to Aachen. When the funeral procession reached Bavaria, Henry tried to take over the funeral and seize the royal insignia, but Heribert sent ahead the holy lance, the key symbol of rulership in the empire. In retaliation, Henry imprisoned Heribert, freeing him only after he surrendered the lance.[35] After Archbishop Heribert was released, he received the body of Emperor Otto III in Cologne on Palm Sunday of 1002 in a ceremony adopted from the Palm Sunday liturgy, which was regarded by the new emperor, Henry II, as inappropriate to the occasion.[36] Although Otto III is neither depicted in the medallion scene nor mentioned in the inscription that accompanies it, the designer evokes this ceremonial entry by the choice of an architectural model similar to those used in depictions of Christ's Entry into Jerusalem. The event recalls Heribert's alliance with Otto III, the imperial patron of the abbey. This is important because Otto III is associated with an alleged document in which he and St. Heribert, then the archbishop of Cologne, donated the entire castle of Deutz to the monastery, whose possession was in dispute at the time in which the shrine was erected.

---

[33] Christ's Entry into Jerusalem, *Pericopes Book of Henry II*, Reichenau, 1002–12, Munich, Bayerische Staatsbibl., Clm. 4452, folio 78 and *Epistolary*, Trier, *c.* 980–90, Berlin, Staatsbibl., Ms. theol. lat. fol. 34, f. 15v. Both in Mayr-Harting, *Ottonian Book Illumination*, figs. 73, 75.

[34] For the liturgy of Palm Sunday and its political uses by both emperors and bishops, see Mayr-Harting, *Ottonian Book Illumination*, pp. 119–25.

[35] Mayr-Harting, *Ottonian Book Illumination*, pp. 194–5, specifies that the holy lance was the most important symbol of rulership in the empire.

[36] Mayr-Harting, *Ottonian Book Illumination*, p. 119; Thietmar, *Thietmari Merseburgensis Episcopi Chronicon*, ed. Robert Holtzman, *Monumenta Germaniae Historica. Scriptores* 9 (1955), iv, ch. 53, pp. 192–3.

Ecclesiastical Settings

In addition to the four royal or aristocratic settings, eight scenes take place inside churches. Three are ceremonial: Heribert's ordination as a priest in the third medallion (fig. 80), his consecration as a bishop on the sixth medallion (fig. 81), and his reconciliation with Henry II on the eleventh medallion. (fig. 84) Although these depictions are accompanied by inscriptions describing the events, none identify specific locations. However, two churches can be topographically identified: the monastery church at Deutz and Cologne Cathedral. The monastery church at Deutz, marked by its unusual ribbed dome, is depicted in the seventh medallion (fig. 82) as part of Heribert's vision of it being built. A comparison with the building's appearance on Deutz's seal of 1230[37] (fig. 85) shows that the principal feature in both is the large ribbed dome surmounted by a cross on a globe, differing only in the number of similar, round windows. Thus the dome clearly signified Deutz.

Three medallions show buildings with the same dome, although Heribert's *vitae* do not state that these events took place in the abbey church at Deutz. On the upper right side of the ninth medallion, (fig. 83) depicting a procession led by Heribert which caused a miraculous rain, two men sit in a room next to a table, behind which appears a part of a ribbed dome. Another domed building appears to the left. In the tenth medallion, (fig. 83) where Heribert heals a possessed man, the space in the scene is divided into two arches. On one side Heribert sits on his throne, and on the other, people wait to be healed. In the center, in front of the column, is the possessed man. Above the two arches the designer repeated the scheme of gable-dome-gable, which although it is a widely used emblem[38] may, in this context, refer to the monastery church at Deutz because of the ribbed dome at the center, even though the event should have taken place in the cathedral. The eleventh medallion, (fig. 84) in

---

[37] Additional evidence concerning the structure and appearance of the abbey church at Deutz can be found in two other seals from the second half of the thirteenth century which depict the church before its destruction. They, too, depict the same shape as seen on the shrine. Gechter, "Das Kastell Deutz im Mittelalter," ill. 8–10.

[38] Sinderhauf, *Die Abtei Deutz ihre innere Erneuerung*, pp. 145–56; Theodericus Aedituus, *Thioderici Aeditui Tuitiensis Opuscula*, pp. 569–70.

which Heribert and Henry II reconcile, also shows a domed church surmounted by a cross on a globe, with three windows, despite the text's suggestion that the event occurred in the archbishop's palace.[39]

In contrast with the abbey church at Deutz, its episcopal superior, Cologne Cathedral, is depicted only once on a separate, smaller medallion placed between the ninth and the tenth medallions, (fig. 83) so that at first sight it does not appear to be part of the narrative. The ninth medallion illustrates a procession from Cologne Cathedral to St. Pantaleon, which brought on a miraculous rain, ending a long drought. The starting point of the procession is not depicted in the medallion, only its end point. The location of the small medallion to the right of the ninth medallion suggests that the church shown is the starting point of the procession. It is striking that the cathedral, the seat of Heribert's prelacy, is not depicted in any scene on the shrine, except in this isolated medallion.[40] Here the cathedral is depicted schematically, a two-story basilica with a semi-circular entrance and two towers at the west and a semi-circular apse at the east end, the same features also appear in a painting of the cathedral in the *Codex Hillinus* (1010–40).[41] The main difference is that on the medallion the cathedral is given an additional tower on its roof, possibly depicting the pair of towers added to the east end in a reconstruction by Archbishop Rainald of Dassel (r. 1159–67).[42] The otherwise generic cathedral type, a large basilica, is distinguished from the unusual design of the abbey church at Deutz with its octagonal, domed building. The procession arrives at a church or rather a tower that is surmounted by a large ribbed dome, once again the sign for the monastery church of Deutz, although the destination was St. Pantaleon. The depiction of the dome, therefore, seems to relocate key events of Heribert's life and cult from his cathedral and its dependencies in Cologne to the monastery he founded in order to enhance the abbey's reputation.

---

[39] Peter Dinter, *Rupert von Deutz, Vita Heriberti*, p. 73.

[40] It is possible that this medallion was added some time later.

[41] *Codex Hillinus*, Cologne, Dombibliothek, Ms. 12, Seeon/Reichenau, 1010–1040. (eds.) Hiltrud Kier and Ulrich Krings, *Köln: Die Romanischen Kirchen im Bild* (Cologne, 1984), fig. 50.

[42] Hans Erich Kubach & Albert Verbeek, *Romanische Baukunst an Rhein und Maas* (Berlin, 1976–89) vol. 1, p. 503 & vol. 4, p. 14, fig. 4; (eds.) Hiltrud Kier & Ulrich Krings, *Köln: Die Romanischen Kirchen im Bild*, p. 29, fig. 50.

This is especially important in the last scene, (fig. 84) that of Heribert's death and entombment, which does not indicate a location other than a sanctuary marked by drapery and a hanging lamp. In contrast to the *vitae* which record Heribert's death at Cologne Cathedral and his entombment at Deutz, the medallion depicts both events as if they occurred in one location, suggesting that although Heribert's rank as archbishop was prominently displayed throughout the medallions, his See at Cologne was ignored, shown only once in a marginal location, omitted from the narrative. At the same time his tomb site, in the abbey church at Deutz, is given no topographical specificity in these scenes. This is significant because the tomb usually marks the site of the cult,[43] and the monastery church at Deutz is otherwise depicted throughout the medallions. It seems that the designer created a generic setting in order to blur the distinctions between the sites of Heribert's death, the cathedral, and of his entombment, the abbey.

At the end of 1164, the same year in which Theodericus stopped writing the monastery's codex, three new relics arrived in Cologne. Archbishop Rainald of Dassel, who also served as the imperial chancellor, translated the relics of the Three Magi from Milan to the Cathedral of St. Peter in Cologne.[44] During his journey, Rainald wrote to the people of Cologne that he was bringing with him relics of the Magi seized from the city of Milan after its destruction, which were given to him by the Emperor Frederick I Barbarossa. Rainald entered the city of Cologne with the relics in triumph.[45] Although the

---

[43] Barbara Abou-El-Haj, *The Medieval Cult of Saints Formations and Transformations* (New York, 1994), pp. 49–55 for discussion of scenes of entombments in other illustrated hagiographies.

[44] Patrick J. Geary, *Living with the Dead in the Middle Ages* (Ithaca, NY, 1994), pp. 243–56; Richard C. Trexler, *The Journey of the Magi: Meaning in History of a Christian Story* (Princeton, 1997), pp. 74–5, 78–9; Peter Munz, "Frederick Barbarossa and the 'Holy Empire,'" *Journal of Religious History* 3 (1964–5), 25–33.

[45] Peter Munz, *Frederick Barbarossa: a Study in Medieval Politics* (Ithaca, NY, 1969), pp. 238–9. According to Geary, there was no cult of the Magi in Milan before 1164. The three skeletons taken by Rainald of Dassel from the church of Sant' Eustorgio were unidentified. On his way, from Milan back to Cologne, Rainald invented the history of the cult of the Magi in Milan and accordingly identified the relics as those of the Magi. The reason behind this invention was to establish the city of Cologne as the equal of Aachen, the seat of the emperor, by developing a cult equal to that of Charlemagne, and by that to secure the independence and status of the archbishops of Cologne. Geary, *Living with the Dead*, pp. 243–56.

cult of the Magi reached its height only in the thirteenth-century, when the German emperors followed their coronation in Aachen with a pilgrimage to Cologne to venerate the Magi, the introduction of the relics and the return Rainald to Cologne may have prompted the elaboration of the cult of St. Heribert at the monastery at Deutz. According to Munz, Rainald thought of the Church as a military institute "with the bishops on horseback," and was respected in his diocese for the part he took in Frederick Barbarossa's campaigns in Italy.[46] St. Heribert, who was the first archbishop of Cologne to serve as the imperial chancellor for Otto III, during the emperor's campaigns in Italy, could serve as a prototype to Rainald. This might have been the motivation behind the revival of Heribert's cult, witnessed by the creation of a new gilded and enameled shrine for his relics.

The displacement of key events in Heribert's life from Cologne Cathedral to the monastery he founded with Otto III at Deutz, by means of repeated depictions of Deutz's singular dome, suggests that the commission of the Heribert Shrine was prompted not only by spiritual concerns, but also by the need to attract an audience to participate in Heribert's cult, although there were more important relics in the vicinity. It also suggests that the abbey wished to reaffirm its possession of the castle of Deutz, as seen in the documents forged during the same years. Thus the shrine was not a product of the economic surplus of the abbey, but rather, was initiated in order to raise more funds by advancing Heribert's cult.

---

[46] Munz, "Frederick Barbarossa," p. 26.

CHAPTER SEVEN

PILGRIMAGE TO CHARTRES: THE VISUAL EVIDENCE

James Bugslag

> Where are the thousands of pilgrims who came to hail the basilica of Mary? Where are the monarchs who, after battle, bowed their victorious brows in the dust of the holy crypt? Of this glorious past, Chartres preserves scarcely a memory, if the stones of Notre-Dame have not been charged with conveying it to future generations.[1]

Eugène de Lépinois was well aware of the paucity of documentary sources for tracing the history of pilgrimage to Chartres during the late Middle Ages. Yet he, like so many others, never doubted its existence.[2] Recent estimations have challenged his belief in the popular scope of pilgrimage to Chartres. The documentary sources that chart this phenomenon are certainly not as rich as historians might like. They have, nevertheless, been increasingly exploited in recent years.[3] Yet, "the stones of Notre-Dame" remain relatively mute, and other material evidence, as well, can be marshalled towards an increased understanding of the nature and scope of pilgrimage activity at Chartres. It is the purpose of this study to begin such an undertaking.

---

[1] "Où sont les milliers de pèlerins qui venaient saluer la basilique de Marie? Où sont les monarques qui courbaient, après le combat, leurs fronts victorieux dans la poussière de la sainte crypte? De ce passé glorieux, Chartres conserverait à peine le souvenir, si les pierres de Notre-Dame ne se chargeaient de la transmettre aux générations." Eugène de Lépinois, *Histoire de Chartres*, 1 (Chartres, 1854), p. 185.

[2] During a Mass at Chartres on May 31, 1855, Monseigneur Pie, the bishop of Poitiers and a major supporter of Notre-Dame de Chartres, pronounced: "I dare to predict it: Chartres will once more become, more than ever, the center of devotion to Mary in the West; crowds will flock here, as of old, from all parts of the world." "J'ose le prédire: Chartres redeviendra, plus que jamais, le centre de la dévotion à Marie en occident; on y affluera, comme autrefois, de tous les points du monde." Cited in Yves Delaporte, *Les Trois Notre-Dame de la cathédrale de Chartres*, 2nd ed. (Chartres, 1955), p. 54.

[3] A huge amount of primary documentation was destroyed when the Bibliothèque municipale in Chartres was bombed in 1944. Much, however, was either transcribed or published in the nineteenth century.

References to Chartres Cathedral as the most important Marian shrine in Europe during the Middle Ages still abound. The historiography of this interpretation leads back to local chartrain historians of the nineteenth century, among whom Lépinois was one of the most respected. They, in turn, were simply adopting the rhetoric long used by the cathedral chapter. The claim was first made by the author of the early thirteenth-century miracle collection from Chartres, written in connection with the rebuilding of the cathedral after the 1194 fire, who stated that the Virgin had chosen Chartres Cathedral "to be her special dwelling place on earth."[4] In fact, the religious geography of Marian devotion in medieval Europe was both complex and remarkably dense, and when Chartres Cathedral is considered, not from the point of view of its own institutional aspirations, but on a comparative basis, it quickly becomes evident that these claims were highly-contested and that they changed constantly in the fluctuating devotional ecosystem of Marian shrines.

There has been increasing skepticism about this presumed predominance of Chartres as a Marian shrine and a recent tendency to characterize Chartres as a pilgrimage center of largely local importance, except among the noble classes.[5] Although welcome as a corrective interpretation, when the highly-diverse nature of Marian devotion is considered, along with the elusive evidence surviving for both local and more wide-ranging pilgrimage to Chartres, it becomes clear that its cathedral was, indeed, significant as a Marian shrine. While not on the scope of Santiago de Compostela, Rome, or Canterbury—nor even such major Marian shrines as Le Puy, Rocamadour or, from the fourteenth century, Aachen—Chartres had a substantial presence in the Marian devotion within the French realm. It is not clear, however, whether devotion always translated into pilgrimage,

---

[4] The text survives in Vatican MS Regina 339; see A. Thomas, ed., "Les Miracles de Notre Dame de Chartres. Texte latin inédit," *Bibliothèque de l'école des chartes* 42 (1881), 505–50. Cited in Benedicta Ward, *Miracles and the Medieval Mind: Theory, Record and Event 1000–1215* (Philadelphia, 1987), p. 153. In the mid-thirteenth century, a miracle collection in French verse was produced. Pierre Kunstmann, ed., Jean le Marchant, *Miracles de Notre-Dame de Chartres*, Publications Médiévales de l'Université d'Ottawa, I, and Société archéologique d'Eure-et-Loir, XXVI (Ottawa, 1973).

[5] André Chédeville, *Chartres et ses campagnes (XIᵉ–XIIIᵉ s.)* (Paris, 1973), pp. 509–10; Brigitte Kurmann-Schwarz and Peter Kurmann, *Chartres. La cathédrale*, trans. Thomas de Kayser (La Pierre-qui-vire, 2001), p. 26.

and the extent and nature of veneration there have yet to be studied systematically.

Scattered documents refer generally to Chartres as a site of pilgrimage. Guibert de Nogent in the early twelfth century, for example, claimed that the "name and relics [of the Virgin Mary] at Chartres are venerated throughout almost all the Latin world."[6] Such statements have tended to suggest a monolithic and constant condition, which must be tempered by both historiographic analysis and further studies of specialized aspects of the phenomenon of pilgrimage at Chartres. Such specialized studies are beginning to appear. Gabriela Signori has recently given new attention to the miracle collections written at Chartres.[7] Even more importantly, Margot Fassler has been engaged in a ground-breaking study of the long-ignored cathedral liturgy.[8] Another aspect of the problem that has yet to be addressed is the visual evidence for pilgrimage at Chartres, its material aspects, which take many forms and present numerous problems.[9]

---

[6] John F. Benton, ed. and trans., *Self and Society in Medieval France: The Memoirs of Abbot Guibert of Nogent (1064–c. 1125)* (Toronto, 1984), p. 85.

[7] Gabriela Signori, "Marienbilder im Vergleich: Marianische Wunderbücher zwischen Weltklerus, städtische Ständvielfalt und ländischen Subsistenzproblemen (10.–13. Jahrhundert)," in *Maria. Abbild oder Vorbild? Zur Sozialgeschichte mittelalterlicher Marienverehrung*, ed. Hedwig Röcklein, Claudia Opitz and Dieter R. Bauer (Tübingen, 1990), pp. 58–90; Gabriela Signori, *Maria zwischen Kathedrale, Kloster und Welt. Hagiographische und historiographische Annäherungen an eine hochmittelalterliche Wunderpredigt* (Sigmaringen, 1995), esp. pp. 152–201; Gabriela Signori, "La bienheureuse polysémie. Miracles et pèlerinages à la Vierge: pouvoir thaumaturgique et modèles pastoraux (X^e–XIIe siècles)," in *Marie, Le culte de la Vierge dans la société médiévale*, ed. Dominique Iogna-Prat, Éric Palazzo and Daniel Russo (Paris, 1996), pp. 591–617.

[8] Margot Fassler, *Making History: The Liturgical Framework of Time and Cult of the Virgin at Chartres* (forthcoming); Margot Fassler, "Mary's Nativity, Fulbert of Chartres, and the Stirps Jesse: Liturgical Innovation circa 1000 and Its Aftermath," *Speculum* 75 (2000), 389–434; Craig Wright, "The Palm Sunday Procession in Medieval Chartres," in *The Divine Office in the Latin Middle Ages: Methodology and Source Studies, Regional Developments, Hagiography*, ed. Margot Fassler and Rebecca A. Balzer (New York, 2000), pp. 344–71.

[9] Claudine Lautier, "Les vitraux de la cathédrale de Chartres. Reliques et images," *Bulletin monumental* 161, no. 1 (2003): 3–97, appeared too late for me to take full account of it in this study. This important study shows that 64% of the saints represented in the stained glass were also represented by relics possessed by the cathedral. Her plan of the altars in the cathedral at the beginning of the seventeenth century is also of great interest, and although her concern is with relics rather than pilgrimage *per se*, her article should be consulted in conjunction with this study. Differences of interpretation between the two might fruitfully be considered in terms of a burgeoning discourse, rather than in opposition.

The visual material presented here will focus on several bodies of evidence: the fabric of the cathedral itself, imagery in the cathedral, the shrines and other pilgrimage-related objects directed at pilgrims, and the traces left by pilgrims, both in the cathedral and at a distance from it. It will also include visual aspects of the pilgrimage experience at Chartres, in so far as they can be reconstructed. Some of these elements have been well-studied from various perspectives, but not necessarily with pilgrimage in mind. Others have yet to receive any systematic treatment. One of the central problems in analyzing this material is that much of it no longer survives, and much of what does survive has undergone modification and even substantial transformation. Moreover, the nature of pilgrimage at Chartres also changed substantially over the centuries. It will, thus, be necessary both to make use of early-modern documents related to the material traces of pilgrimage at Chartres and to consider the evidence historiographically. This is particularly true for the surviving church fabric.

Bishop Fulbert's Crypt

Chartres Cathedral is usually regarded as a typical High Gothic cathedral, yet some of its pilgrimage-related characteristics serve to make it quite distinctive. From the early eleventh century, Chartres consisted not so much of a cathedral with a crypt, but an upper and lower church both of which were important elements of the site. The crypt dates from the time of Bishop Fulbert (1006–28). Whatever the significance of Chartres Cathedral before the eleventh century, the cult of the Virgin was intensified considerably at Chartres during Fulbert's episcopacy.[10] Not only did he elaborate many liturgical

---

[10] Fassler, "Mary's Nativity...". The earliest surviving reference to the consecration of the cathedral at Chartres to the Virgin Mary, in relation to the burning of the church in 743 by Hunald, the duke of Aquitaine, dates from the end of the tenth century, in the *Annales Mettenses*; Maurice Jusselin, "Dernières recherches sur les traditions de l'église de Chartres," *Mémoires de la Société archéologique d'Eure-et-Loir* 15 (1915–22), pp. 100–1, 109. Although arguments from "negative evidence" are always dangerous to make with respect to Chartres, it is at least significant that Chartres was not included in the itinerary of King Robert the Pious (996–1031) on his extensive pilgrimage tour of 1019–20, which took him to the shrines of St. Stephen at Bourges, St. Maiolus of Cluny at Souvigny, the Virgin at Le Puy, St. Julian at Brioude, St. Gilles in Provence, St. Saturninus at Toulouse, St. Vincent

aspects of Marian devotion, but he also had her cathedral rebuilt after the disastrous fire of 1020. It was consecrated in 1037, and the form it took was that of a huge pilgrimage church.[11] Fulbert's hymns to and sermons on the Virgin became very widely disseminated throughout Europe, and his association with Chartres must have done much to construct a reputation for Chartres as a center of Marian devotion. Fulbert's huge church featured an early ambulatory with radiating chapels, presumably partially to aid in accommodating pilgrimage. The most remarkable, and the most lasting, element of Fulbert's church was its crypt. (fig. 86) It is clear that the crypt was focused on much older remains, around which an ambulatory with radiating chapels was built, exactly matching those of the church above. Although little systematic archaeological investigation has been made of the crypt, it would appear that the pre-1020 structures not only formed the starting point for laying out Fulbert's church, but were, in a sense, enshrined by it, almost as relics.[12]

The form of the crypt is highly distinctive. It primarily consists of vaulted passages under the nave aisles, eleven bays long, which are joined at the east end by an ambulatory with three radiating chapels,

---

at Castres, St. Antoninus at Saint-Antonin, St. Foy at Conques, and Gerald of Aurillac, ending at Orléans; Diana Webb, *Pilgrims and Pilgrimage in the Medieval West* (London, 2001), pp. 17–8, 256 fn. 23. The itinerary of the 1112–13 tours of relics from Laon Cathedral, which included hair of the Virgin, did include Chartres Cathedral, and it is recorded that they were placed on the high altar and produced three miracles. There is no suggestion in these accounts of rivalry with relics at Chartres. Ward, *Miracles and the Medieval Mind*, p. 136, concludes that "Possibly the Shift [i.e. Tunic] of the Virgin at Chartres was not known or only achieved its full potential as a relic after the canons' visit."

[11] Harry H. Hilberry, "The Cathedral of Chartres in 1030," *Speculum* 34 (1959), 561–72, following in a tradition begun by René Merlet and Alexandre Clerval, *Un manuscrit chartrain du XIᵉ siècle* (Chartres, 1893), bases his reconstruction of Fulbert's church too centrally on the eleventh-century illumination by André de Mici in Chartres, Bibliothèque Municipale, MS nouv. acq. 4. Besides the inherent methodological limitations of topographical accuracy to be expected of eleventh-century images, Georges Bonnebas now believes that this illumination does not represent the cathedral, but rather the abbey church of St. Père; Fassler, "Mary's Nativity . . .," 407, fn. 69.

[12] Éliane Vergnolle, *L'art roman en France: architecture, sculpture, peinture* (Paris, 1994), p. 355, fn. 80: "Fulbert's crypt was built around older constructions, undoubtedly preserved by virtue of being relics"; "La crypte de Fulbert est édifiée autour de constructions plus anciennes, conservées sans doute à titre de reliques." Pending further archaeological investigation, all attempts to reconstruct earlier churches on the site, however probable, remain speculative. See Jan van der Meulen, *Notre-Dame de Chartres: Die vorromanische Ostanlage* (Berlin, 1975); Charles Stegeman, *Les cryptes de la cathédrale de Chartres et les cathédrales depuis l'époque gallo-romaine* (Chartres, n.d.); Roger Joly, *La cathédrale de Chartres avant Fulbert* (Chartres, 1999).

and "transepts" flanking the apse ("P" on figure 86), all exactly matching the corresponding elements of the upper church.[13] At the hemicycle, the ambulatory enclosed the so-called "grand caveau" (large vault) or Chapel of St. Lubin (fig. 86, "A"), a much smaller apse-like space with a narrow ambulatory of much earlier date.[14] This apsidal space was completely unconnected with Fulbert's crypt and thus played no role in its pilgrimage function. The only access was by a stair descending from the sanctuary of the church above.[15] Just west of Fulbert's "transepts," two rectangular chapels open from the inner sides of the corridor walls. The principal access to the crypt was provided by two sets of stairs located at the western terminations of the crypt aisles.[16] Thus, Fulbert's crypt was unusual not only in directing access away from the choir or crossing of the church, where entry was usual for Romanesque crypts, but in focusing predominantly on a huge ambulatory system with no centralized focus. There were precedents for aspects of this arrangement. The crypt of the Church of St. Aignan in Orléans, consecrated in 1029, had similar long corridors under the nave aisles, for example.[17] Other crypts with ambulatories are known, as well.[18]

---

[13] The rectangular foundations flanking the choir are farther east than the current transepts and much smaller in scale. The form they took in the upper church is uncertain; they may have been small transepts or large chapels. They may also have functioned as foundations for towers. At crypt level, they formed rectangular spaces adjoining the crypt passages by a double arcade, separated by a substantial pier. Stegeman, *Les cryptes de la cathédrale de Chartres*, p. 3, Figure 2a: Plan of 1020.

[14] René Merlet, *The Cathedral of Chartres* (Paris, 1913), pp. 13–4, associates the Chapel of Saint-Lubin with the edifice erected by Bishop Gislebertus (c. 859–80) after the fire of June 12, 858. The seemingly-truncated nature of this central crypt space has led to the widely-held hypothesis that it formed the eastern termination of an earlier church, which is now mostly buried under the foundations of the upper church. The problem is complicated by the foundations installed here in 1773 to support the new Baroque altarpiece.

[15] The function of this space is very uncertain. During the 1194 fire, the principal relics were probably taken to this vault, thus surviving the fire, but it does not appear to have served any specific liturgical function. The passageway now connecting the vault with the north side of the crypt ambulatory was only cut through the solid wall separating them in 1768. The access staircase to the sanctuary was also filled in and only disengaged much later, probably in 1905. Joly, *La cathédrale de Chartres avant Fulbert*, p. 11.

[16] Stegeman, *Les cryptes de la cathédrale de Chartres*, p. 4, states that the stairs to the exterior off the north aisle, just east of the present transepts, were not part of the original plan, but constitute a later addition.

[17] Vergnolle, *L'art roman en France*, p. 60.

[18] The mid-tenth century crypt of the Cathedral of Notre-Dame at Clermont-

In the eleventh century it was common for crypts to house relics and cult images. Yet, by the twelfth century, the principal relic at Chartres, the Holy Tunic of the Virgin, seems to have occupied a place just behind the high altar of the upper church.[19] The crypt, on the other hand, contained a healing well known as the *Puits des Saints-Forts* (Well of the Strong Saints), which had acquired a reputation for miraculous curative powers.[20] It seems clear that Fulbert must have wanted the crypt to accommodate pilgrimage to the *Puits des Saints-Forts*. The huge size of this space (exceptional among Romanesque crypts) makes it likely that crowds of people were expected to use it.

The *Puits des Saints-Forts* was located near the east end of the northern crypt passage. The bodies of early Chartrain martyrs were believed to have been thrown down this well.[21] Since it was walled up and

---

Ferrand had a more primitive ambulatory than Fulbert's church, with quite limited access to a central compartment; Vergnolle, *L'art roman en France*, p. 60. The crypt of the Cathedral of St. Étienne at Auxerre was built after a fire of 1023; Vergnolle, *L'art roman en France*, p. 78. The crypt of the cathedral of Notre-Dame at Rouen was probably finished by 1037; Vergnolle, *L'art roman en France*, pp. 80–1. It consisted of an ambulatory with three radiating chapels. There was not initially a central chamber, but one was excavated later, perhaps in the second half of the eleventh century. Anne Prache "L'influence de la cathédrale de Fulbert sur l'art roman," in *Enseigner le moyen âge à partir d'un monument, la cathédrale de Chartres. Le temps de Fulbert, Actes de l'université d'été du 8 au 10 juillet 1996* (Chartres, 1996), pp. 129–33, signals the importance of the crypt of Saint-Philibert at Tournus, created after the fire of 1107–8, in the development of ambulatory-type crypts, and singles out this church and Chartres Cathedral as important among early examples of ambulatory crypts for their monumental size; she claims that the long crypt corridors under the nave aisles at Chartres were unique and apparently not copied.

[19] Alain Erlande-Brandenburg, "La cathédrale de Fulbert," in *Enseigner le moyen âge à partir d'un monument, la cathédrale de Chartres. Le temps de Fulbert, Actes de l'université d'été du 8 au 10 juillet 1996* (Chartres, 1996), p. 124, claimed that Fulbert originally intended his lower church for pilgrimage activity, while the upper church was reserved as the diocesan church, but if Fulbert's crypt originally contained the church's principal relic, that arrangement certainly changed during the course of the late eleventh or early twelfth century.

[20] René Merlet, "Le puits des Saints-Forts et l'ancienne chapelle de Notre-Dame-sous-Terre," *Congrès archéologique de France, Chartres 1900* (Paris, 1901), pp. 226–55.

[21] According to the account of Paul, the monk of St. Père, in the eleventh century, the victims of the 858 attack by the Normans on Chartres were thrown down the well, but the almost contemporary Passion of Sts. Savinien and Potentien, written by a monk of Saint-Pierre-le-Vif at Sens, described the bodies of the earliest Christian converts at Chartres in the first century, including Sts. Altin and Modiste, being thrown down the well, and this belief is also reflected, from the early twelfth century, in chartrain martyrologies and breviaries. Merlet, "Le puits des Saints-Forts," pp. 227, 231.

hidden in *c.* 1645, its exact location and arrangement in Fulbert's crypt are uncertain. In his 1901 excavations, René Merlet claimed to have found the well, half embedded in the inner corridor wall opposite the north "transept."[22] (fig. 86, "E"; fig. 87) A liturgical procession to the *locus sanctus fortis* (Place of the Strong Saints) was established by the twelfth century, by which time the locus must have achieved considerable importance and possibly featured an altar.[23]

The miraculous nature of the *Puits des Saints Forts* eventually resulted in a virtual hospital in the crypt.[24] The earliest reference to the curative powers of the *Puits des Saints-Forts*, significantly, dates from the eleventh century in an account of Paul, a monk of the abbey of Saint-Père-en-Vallée at Chartres.[25] The *Hôpital des Saint-Lieux-Forts* was founded in the early twelfth century by Bishop Geoffroy de Lèves.[26] By at least 1403, this was staffed by a permanent body of lay nurses.[27] It remains to be determined how the well functioned.

---

[22] Jan van der Meulen and Jürgen Hohmeyer, *Chartres. Biographie der Kathedrale* (Cologne, 1984), p. 192, denied that the well Merlet found is the *Puits des Saints Forts*, yet their alternate proposals appear highly speculative. Their reasoning for rejecting Merlet's well as the *Puits des Saints Forts* is that the only finds made during the excavation were Gallo-Roman pottery shards, and that no medieval materials were found. Stegeman, *Les cryptes de la cathédrale de Chartres*, pp. 13–4, has questioned this argument from negative evidence. Further undermining Van der Meulen's skepticism, there were reports that Merlet found an enamelled figure of the Virgin in the fill of the well. Jan van der Meulen, with Rüdiger Hoyer and Deborah Cole, *Chartres. Sources and Literary Interpretation: A Critical Bibliography* (Boston, 1989), pp. 58–60, nos. 21, 26, 29. The question will only be decided by further archaeological investigation.

[23] The procession was included in a manuscript of a Chartrain ordinal, written shortly after 1152, the "Veridicus" manuscript, in the Archives du Hôtel-Dieu in Châteaudun (MS C 13), which disappeared before 1975, but a hand-written transcription by Delaporte exists in the diocesan archives at Chartres. The procession is also included in the thirteenth-century ordinal (Chartres, Bibliothèque municipale, MS 1058), which was badly damaged in 1944. Yves Delaporte, *L'Ordinaire chartrain du XIII⁰ siècle* (Chartres, 1953), p. 185.

[24] Marcel Bulteau, *Monographie de la cathédrale de Chartres*, III (Chartres, 1901), pp. 344–5.

[25] The narrative history known as the *Vetus Aganon* (*c.* 1077–88), written by Paul, a monk of Saint-Père-en-Vallée was recorded in two manuscripts, Bibl. Mun., MSS 1060 and 1061, both of which were badly damaged in the 1944 bombing. The account was published previously in Benjamin Guérard, ed., *Cartulaire de l'abbaye de Saint-Père de Chartres*, 2 vols (Paris, 1840), I, pp. 3–17. I am grateful to Christopher Crockett for making this text available on his website: http://www.ariadne.org/centreChartraine.

[26] Lépinois, *Histoire de Chartres*, I, p. 225.

[27] Charles Challine, *Recherches sur Chartres, transcrites et annotées par un arrière-neveu de l'auteur* (Chartres, 1918), pp. 126–7, cites a charter of October 3, 1403, which

There are no references to pilgrims drinking water from the well and no evidence of ampullae, which were commonly used to contain holy water from pilgrimage sites.[28] Rather, the sick slept in the crypt for nine nights, in proximity to the *Puits des Saints-Forts*, in hopes of a cure.[29] It, thus, rather seems to have functioned as a thaumaturgical place of martyrdom.

The new west façade and towers begun after the 1134 fire not only provided a splendid liturgical entrance to the cathedral, but monumentalized the western entrances to the crypt.[30] (fig. 86) At this time, the windows of the crypt were also enlarged.[31] Later in the twelfth century, further access was provided when a south stairway was constructed, just east of Fulbert's south transept. Peter Kurmann has dated the stairway doorway to *c.* 1140–60.[32] It is possible that the corresponding north lateral entrance was also built at this time.[33] Thus, the importance of the crypt increased through the twelfth century.

Notre Dame de Sous Terre

Another factor that must be considered in relation to this large crypt is the image of the Virgin that was housed there, which eventually came to be known variously as *Notre-Dame de Sous Terre* and *La Vierge*

---

mentions women who take care of those who have come to seek a cure. By the later seventeenth century, after the suppression of the *Puits des Saints-Forts*, these women continued to maintain the lamps and altar cloths and lived in wooden chambers built against the walls of the northern crypt passage near its west end.

[28] Eugène Lefévre-Pontalis, *Le puits des Saints Forts et les cryptes de la cathédrale de Chartres* (Caen, 1904), pp. 5–6, cites Roulliard's statement of 1609 that the well was filled in by that date and an even older statement from *c.* 1580 that the well was stopped up.

[29] According to the *Vieille Chronique* of 1389; see Eugène de Lépinois and Lucien Merlet, eds, *Cartulaire de Notre-Dame de Chartres*, I (Chartres, 1862), p. 58.

[30] On the liturgical character of the imagery of the Royal Portal, see Margot Fassler, "Liturgy and Sacred History in the Twelfth-Century Tympana at Chartres," *Art Bulletin* 75, no. 3 (Sept. 1993), 499–520.

[31] Stegeman, *Les cryptes de la cathédrale de Chartres*, pp. 4–5, 14–15.

[32] Kurmann-Schwarz and Kurmann, *Chartres. La cathédrale*, p. 96. This doorway now forms the principal public entrance to the crypt.

[33] Stegeman, *Les cryptes de la cathédrale de Chartres*, p. 16, relates it to the windows of 1134, but Van der Meulen and Hohmeyer, *Chartres. Biographie der Kathedrale*, p. 195, claim that this north entrance was only established in the mid-seventeenth century. It has been walled up since the nineteenth century.

des Miracles.[34] Despite its destruction at the French Revolution, it is known from antiquarian drawings and descriptions and from copies.[35] (fig. 88) Ilene Forsyth made a good case for dating this polychromed wooden statue, of the type known as a Black Virgin, to the early eleventh century, probably between *c.* 1010 and 1029. In *c.* 1013, Bernard of Angers, then teaching at the cathedral school at Angers, journeyed to southern France to investigate the cult statues he had heard were there, and Forsyth argued that, since he had been a student of Fulbert at Chartres until *c.* 1010, he "could hardly have written as disparagingly as he did about the statues he saw in [the south] if a famous and honored Majesty were familiar to him already in Chartres."[36] On the other hand, she cited the documented case of a wooden statue of the Virgin and Child at Châtillon-sur-Loire, not far from Chartres, being venerated by Abbot Gauzlin prior to his death in 1029. These dates define the likely period of origin for this cult statue at Chartres, and it does not appear probable that its miraculous reputation would have been secured by the time that Fulbert rebuilt the church.

Thus, however the crypt was designed to function, it would not appear that devotion to *Notre-Dame de Sous Terre* was a factor in the planning of the crypt. Such a hypothesis is strengthened by the lack of coordination between the architectural layout of the crypt and the manner in which the cult developed there. Although not well-documented, it seems rather as if this cult image gradually became associated with the miraculous reputation of the *Puits des Saints-Forts*, to the extent that, in the mid-seventeenth century, it completely usurped the sacral focus of the crypt. In *c.* 1640–50 the cathedral chapter had the well destroyed and paved over, in order to decrease what they saw by then as superstitious practices. The present chapel of *Notre-Dame de Sous Terre* was then built at the site, completely blocking Fulbert's crypt passage, so that a curving access passageway had

---

[34] That is, "Our Lady of the Crypt" and "the Virgin of Miracles."

[35] In 1681, Alexandre Pintard made a very thorough written description, transcribed in Delaporte, *Les Trois Notre-Dame*, p. 12; Sophie Cassagnes-Brouquet, *Vierges noires* (Rodez, 2000), pp. 79–80.

[36] Ilene H. Forsyth, *The Throne of Wisdom: Wood Sculptures of the Madonna in Romanesque France* (Princeton, 1972), pp. 110–1. On Bernard of Angers, see Kathleen Ashley and Pamela Sheingorn, *Writing Faith: Text, Sign, & History in the Miracles of Sainte Foy* (Chicago, 1999).

to be cut through the foundations of Fulbert's small transept or tower base.[37] (fig. 86, "G") The statue, located above the central altar, was the prominent focus of this chapel and, by that time, the central cultic focus of the crypt. This appears to represent an attempt to cleanse the cult of the Virgin at Chartres of its ancient chthonic associations, in line with seventeenth-century reforms.

There is little indication of when the statue began to be regarded as miraculous. Images of the Virgin and Child began to proliferate in the cathedral imagery from the mid-twelfth century, and it is not unreasonable to hypothesize that *Notre-Dame de Sous Terre* had begun to attract a devotional following by that time.[38] According to canon Estienne at the end of the seventeenth century, the altar associated with the statue was formerly in front of the well, suggesting an association between the two which had by then been related to ancient, subterranean "druidic" practice. This chthonic element took a particular turn with respect to the statue at Chartres during the later Middle Ages, with the gradual construction of belief in a long-standing cult that actually pre-dated Christianity. By the early fourteenth century, it was believed that the cathedral had been founded in honor of the Virgin during her own lifetime.[39] The *Vieille Chronique* of 1389 is the earliest document to claim that a statue of a Virgin who would bear a child, the so-called *Virgo Paritura*, was worshipped

---

[37] Marcel Bulteau, *Monographie de la cathédrale de Chartres*, I (Chartres, 1887), p. 21. Stegeman, *Les cryptes de la cathédrale de Chartres*, p. 11, suggests that the statue was formerly kept in the rectangular chapel opening from the inner side of the north crypt corridor, now dedicated to SS. Savinian and Potentian.

[38] Lépinois, *Histoire de Chartres*, I, p. 224, fn. 2, citing chapter records, gives the sum of ninety-eight livres tournois, left in the "collection box of the Holy Image" during the year 1338, on the days of "Saint-Martin-d'Hiver, Saint-André et Saint-Luce," but further research would be necessary to identify which image is referred to here. Claudine Lautier, "Les vitraux de la cathédrale de Chartres. Reliques et images," pp. 23, 37, claimed that, like other such Majesty statues of the time, Notre-Dame de Sous Terre contained a cavity for relics and thus constituted a "statue-reliquary." While this is possible, it does not appear to be supported by any documentary reference.

[39] Maurice Jusselin, "Les traditions de l'église de Chartres, à propos d'une bulle du pape Léon X concernant la construction de la cloture du choeur," *Mémoires de la Société archéologique d'Eure-et-Loir* 15 (1915–22), pp. 8, 14–15. A charter of Jean, count of Dreux, dating from September 22, 1330, is the earliest of a number of charters which claim that the cathedral was founded before the Virgin's Assumption. In 1322, a series of letters from various French cathedral chapters to Pope John XXII go even further, claiming that the Virgin chose Chartres specifically as her "templum"; Jusselin "Dernières recherches," pp. 101, 110–13.

here before the birth of Christ.[40] In the early fifteenth century, French
humanists extrapolated this into a site of druidic worship. The earliest mention of a druidic statue on this site occurs in the writings
of Jean Gerson, the chancellor of the University of Paris, in c. 1420.[41]
According to this legend, the druids worshiped the statue of the
Virgo Paritura in a grotto that was later enclosed in the crypt of
Chartres Cathedral, becoming the original chapel of *Notre-Dame de
Sous Terre*, and the Black Virgin worshipped in the crypt was thought
to be the druidic statue dating to the time before Christ's birth.[42]
(fig. 89) From there, Chartres Cathedral rapidly acquired a reputa-
tion as the oldest church in the French realm, and its connections
with the cult of the Virgin were paramount in this construction.[43]
The final step in this legendary accretion was to claim that the Virgin
Mary herself was worshipped at Chartres before the birth of Christ.[44]

The Presence of the Virgin in Her Church

This historiographic overview challenges the often-presumed centrality of the *Notre-Dame de Sous Terre* statue as a cultic focus at
Chartres before the very late Middle Ages. This centrality has, in
turn, colored the analysis of the many other images of the Virgin
and Child at Chartres, which are often presumed unquestioningly
to depict this cult statue.[45] It may, in fact, be impossible to deter-

---

[40] Lépinois and Merlet, *Cartulaire de Notre-Dame de Chartres*, I, pp. 1–2, 38.

[41] Yves Delaporte, "Les druides et les traditions Chartraines," *La voix de Notre-
Dame de Chartres* (Sept. 1936), 245–5.

[42] The fully developed legend was only enunciated by the early-modern historians of Chartres, beginning with Sébastien Roulliard, *Parthenie, ou Histoire de la très-
auguste et très-dévote église de Chartres: dédiée par les vieux druides, en l'honneur de la Vierge
qui enfanteroit: Avec ce qui s'est passé de plus memorable, au faict de la Seigneurie, tant Spirituelle
que Temporelle, de ladicte Eglise, ville, & Païs chartrain* (Paris, 1609). Eventually, it was
claimed that the druids had sent a delegation to the Holy Land to consult the
Prophet Isaiah in relation to the making of the statue; Jusselin, "Les traditions de
l'église de Chartres," p. 11.

[43] Jusselin, "Les traditions de l'église de Chartres," pp. 10, 19–20, cites a letter
from King Charles VII (1422–61) to the city of Chartres, dated June 1432, which
contains the earliest known reference to Chartres Cathedral as "the oldest church
in our realm."

[44] Jusselin, "Les traditions de l'église de Chartres," pp. 11, 20–3, cites documents
of Pope Leo X (1513–21) dating as early as 1517 making this prophetic claim.

[45] Delaporte, *Les Trois Notre-Dame*, pp. 68–84, has catalogued all of the images of
the Virgin in the sculpture, stained glass, and other media in Chartres Cathedral.

mine exactly the number of statues of the Virgin and Child that accumulated in the church, but the existence of several prominent ones can be ascertained. Undoubtedly the most important of them was associated with the high altar and stood above the retable. It was a silver gilt Virgin and Child about three feet high, apparently donated in May 1220, along with two silver gilt angels, by Pierre de Bordeaux, the archdeacon of Vendôme in the cathedral chapter.[46] The relationship of this image with the *Sainte-Châsse* (see below) made it an important focus of devotion.

In 1256, Alaïde, abbess of Montreuil in Picardy, donated another silver gilt Virgin which also served as a reliquary.[47] Between 1308 and 1317, Canon Gilles de Condé donated another image of the Virgin and Child, of small size and made of alabaster, that was placed against the jubé, on the right side, and was mentioned many times during the fourteenth and fifteenth centuries.[48]

In 1404, Jean, duke of Berry, donated an enamelled gold statue of the Virgin and Child, enriched with pearls, emeralds, and rubies. The enthroned Virgin was crowned and wore a blue mantle, from which she was known as *Notre-Dame Bleue*. The Christ Child stood on her lap. The Virgin supported him with one hand, while in the other she held a bouquet composed of pearls, rubies, and enamelled foliage. It was set on a reliquary base containing hairs of the Virgin. Chapter registers demonstrate that, at least in the late fifteenth century, *Notre-Dame Bleue* was carried with great pomp in processions and was subject to great veneration. In monetary value, it appears to have been among the most precious objects in the cathedral treasury.[49]

In 1432, the English, then in control of Chartres during the Hundred Years War, donated a silver statue of the Virgin and Child, with the Virgin crowned and probably standing. This statue was

---

[46] Delaporte, *Les Trois Notre-Dame*, pp. 38–9, 58; Fernand de Mély, *Le trésor de Chartres 1310–1793* (Paris, 1886), pp. 95–6. This statue was melted down, probably in 1769, by order of the canons, to pay for the redecoration of the choir in 1766–76.

[47] Mély, *Le trésor de Chartres*, p. 9. The reliquary contained a piece of the Virgin's sepulcher and fragments of the column to which Christ was tied, Christ's manger, Christ's coffin, and Moses' staff.

[48] Delaporte, *Les Trois Notre-Dame*, p. 43. This statue was moved to the axial chevet chapel in 1741.

[49] Mély, *Le trésor de Chartres*, pp. 14–16. The gold and silver in this figure weighed thirty-five marcs. In 1416, Jehan Tarenne, a money changer on the Pont aux Changes in Paris, donated an enamelled silver gilt reliquary base for the statue.

placed on a reliquary base containing Milk of the Virgin from the
miracle of Bishop Fulbert (see below) and was known as *Notre-Dame
Blanche* (from the whiteness of the silver) or *Notre-Dame de Lacte.*[50]

From the early sixteenth century, another image of the Virgin and
Child, that became enormously important, was donated by Canon
Wastin des Feugerets, probably in *c.* 1508. This originally polychromed wooden statue of an enthroned Virgin and Child survives
and is now known as *Notre-Dame-du-Pilier.* (fig. 90) This was set up
on the left-hand side of the jubé.[51] Delaporte makes a good case for
considering it as a copy of the statue on the high altar, and according to Rouillard, it was intended to deflect popular attention away
from the services in the choir.[52] There is a great deal of evidence
for devotion to this image. It is now located in its own chapel, in
the outer choir aisle, just east of the north transept, where it currently forms the most prominent cultic focus within the church.

There may well have been other three-dimensional images of the
Virgin in Chartres Cathedral, and the treasuries contained many
two-dimensional images in a variety of precious media, as well. There
are also numerous images of the Virgin and Child in the portal
sculpture and stained glass of the cathedral, and some of these, rather
than directly depicting the holy figures themselves, demonstrably
depict cult statues of the Virgin and Child. Several examples survive in the stained glass in the cathedral.[53] At the east end of the
south nave aisle is Window 38, dedicated to the Miracles of Notre-
Dame (*c.* 1205–15), in which crowds gather before—and carts are
dragged towards—an altar on which sits a gilded statue of the Virgin

---

[50] Mély, *Le trésor de Chartres*, pp. 11–12. It was twenty-four inches high and weighed
ten and a half marcs of silver. The reliquary base was added later in 1559. The
location of *Notre-Dame Blanche* before the seventeenth century is unknown. In the
1682 inventory of Canon Estienne, it was located in the treasury fitted out by
Queen Marie de Medici (r. 1600–42) in a chamber of the choir screen flanking
the high altar.

[51] On the Chartres jubé, see Jean Mallion, *Le jubé de la cathédrale de Chartres*
(Chartres, 1964); Jacqueline Jung, "Beyond the Barrier: The Unifying Rôle of the
Choir Screen in Gothic Churches," *Art Bulletin* 82, no. 4 (2000), 622–57.

[52] Delaporte, *Les Trois Notre-Dame*, pp. 33–58.

[53] See Lautier, "Les vitraux de la cathédrale de Chartres. Reliques et images."
The window numbering used here is that of the French Committee of the Corpus
Vitrearum Medii Aevi (CVMA); Louis Grodecki, Françoise Perrot, et al., *Les vitraux du Centre et des pays de la Loire*, Inventaire général des monuments et richesses
artistiques de France, Corpus Vitrearum France, série complémentaire: recensement
des vitraux anciens de la France, II (Paris, 1981), p. 26.

and Child.[54] (fig. 91) In several other windows, images depict the donor kneeling before an altar with a statue of the Virgin and Child on it, and in most of these instances, the same type of image is depicted as in the Miracles of the Virgin window.[55] (fig. 92) Delaporte quite sensibly identified these images as representations of the high altar, with the silver-gilt statue donated by Pierre de Bordeaux.[56] Moreover, Delaporte claimed that, in order to make these images conform with the most-venerated statue in the cathedral, the representations of the statue in the Miracles of the Virgin window and in the St. Nicholas window were very selectively restored in the early fourteenth century.[57] Claudine Lautier has expressed doubt about the two images in the St. Nicholas window, but confirms an early fourteenth-century date for the image in the Miracles of Notre-Dame window which, alone of this group, was probably in place before Pierre de Bordeaux's donation.[58] While there are still uncertainties surrounding the sheer variety of images of the Virgin and Child at

---

[54] Most of this window, which was probably donated by a confraternity of butchers, was destroyed in 1816 and replaced inaccurately in 1927. The bottom quatrefoil cluster, however, is original. Yves Delaporte and Étienne Houvet, *Les vitraux de la cathédrale de Chartres. Histoire et description* (Chartres, 1926), pp. 189–94.

[55] Window 11, dedicated to St. Pantaleon, in the main radiating chapel on the north, in the Middle Ages the Martyrs Chapel, was donated by the canon and subdeacon of the cathedral chapter, Nicolas Le Sesne, in *c.* 1220–25. Delaporte and Houvet, *Les vitraux de la cathédrale de Chartres*, pp. 326–7. Window 12, dedicated to St. Remi, in the axial radiating chapel, in the Middle Ages the Confessors Chapel, was donated by an unidentified, probably secular, male, also *c.* 1220–25. Delaporte and Houvet, *Les vitraux de la cathédrale de Chartres*, pp. 267–8. The right lancet of Window 29, dedicated to a Miracle of St. Nicholas, in the north choir aisle, was donated by Etienne Chardonnel, a canon of the Cathedral of Notre-Dame, Paris, who was from a chartrain family, along with a secular man and woman, undoubtedly members of the same family, probably *c.* 1225–35. Delaporte and Houvet, *Les vitraux de la cathédrale de Chartres*, pp. 366–8. The left lancet of Window 29, dedicated to St. Germain d'Auxerre, was donated by Gaufridus Chardonnel, a canon and archdeacon of Dunois in the Chartres chapter, also probably *c.* 1225–35. Delaporte and Houvet, *Les vitraux de la cathédrale de Chartres*, pp. 370–1.

[56] Delaporte, *Les Trois Notre-Dame*, pp. 39–43.

[57] Delaporte and Houvet, *Les vitraux de la cathédrale de Chartres*, pp. 190, 192.

[58] Claudine Lautier, "Les vitraux de la cathédrale de Chartres à la lumière des restaurations anciennes," in Thomas W. Gaehtgens, ed., *Künstlerischer Austausch / Artistic Exchange. Akten des XXVIII. Internationalen Kongresses für Kunstgeschichte, Berlin, 15.–20. Juli 1992*, vol. III (Berlin, 1993), pp. 413–24. For a close-up detail of the statue in the Miracles of Notre-Dame window, see Claudine Lautier, "Les restaurations des vitraux de la cathédrale de Chartres du Moyen Age à nos jours," *La Sauvegarde de l'art français* 12 (1999), fig. 6; the Virgin holds a bouquet of roundish flowers, while the Christ Child is not making the sign of blessing or holding an orb, but rather reaches for the bouquet.

Chartres, as Delaporte suggests, this evidence seems to point to devotion towards the high altar, behind which was kept at this time the
Sainte-Châsse, containing the major relic held at Chartres, the Virgin's
Tunic (discussed below). These images, thus, appear to reflect devotion at Chartres, but since most of the identified donors were canons
of Chartres, there is ambiguity in considering them as evidence of
pilgrimage *per se*. This is less the case with the only other clear image
of a statue of the Virgin and Child in the Chartres glass, which
appears in the oculus of nave clerestory Window 129, donated by
a group of people from the city of Tours, in the neighboring diocese to the south, *c.* 1205–15.[59] It is difficult to imagine that this
image does not directly reflect an act of pilgrimage, yet it is equally
clear that a different statue is being venerated in this instance. The
Christ Child is placed centrally on the Virgin's lap, holding an orb
and making a sign of blessing. The image here, in other words,
appears rather to refer to *Notre-Dame de Sous Terre*. (fig. 88) If so, this
constitutes the earliest surviving evidence of devotion to this statue
in the crypt.

Not all images of the Virgin and Child in the stained glass and
sculpture of Chartres clearly depict or refer to cult statues, as has
sometimes been claimed. The sculpture of the Virgin and Child on
the right tympanum of the Royal Portals, dating from *c.* 1145–55,
is not necessarily a copy of *Notre-Dame de Sous Terre*, which cannot
be shown to have developed appreciably as a cultic focus until later.
Moreover, it can be shown to fit, iconographically, within a more
general interpretation as a Throne of Wisdom image, of a type then
very widespread in all the arts. Even more independent from a
process of straightforward copying is the image of *Notre-Dame-de-la-
Belle-Verrière*, a large image in stained glass of the Virgin and Child,
dating from *c.* 1180, which evidently survived the 1194 fire and was
re-set in early thirteenth-century glass in the left lancet of Window
30, in the south choir aisle.[60] The particular iconographic elements

---

[59] Delaporte and Houvet, *Les vitraux de la cathédrale de Chartres*, p. 506, pl. CCLXVI.
A secular man and woman kneel to either side of the statue, and Delaporte read
the accompanying inscription as *"viri turoni dederunt has III"*—"the people of Tours
dedicated these three [window openings]." The two lancets below, dedicated to St.
Martin of Tours, form part of the same donation.

[60] Delaporte and Houvet, *Les vitraux de la cathédrale de Chartres*, pp. 217–22; Delaporte,
Les Trois Notre-Dame, pp. 61–7; Chantal Bouchon, et al., "La 'Belle-Verrière' de
Chartres," *Revue de l'art* 46 (1979), 16–24. The oculus above this lancet contains
another image of the Virgin and Child, an early example of the nursing Virgin.

of this image argue for more distinctive visual and theological traditions than are evident in other images of the Virgin and Child at Chartres. Moreover, this image itself became an independent focus of devotion within the church: in 1324 the subcantor Geoffroi des Foucheiz founded an altar attached to the pier in front of this window.[61] The local historian Bulteau, writing in 1850, claimed that this image was formerly the object of great veneration, but by his day, only country people still came to pray and light a candle in front of it.[62]

The Focus of Devotion

The undocumented character of pilgrimage at Chartres in the late Middle Ages makes analysis of this evidence problematic, but it would appear that pilgrims to Chartres Cathedral had two principal foci for their devotional attention in the early thirteenth century: the high altar with its relic and the crypt with the *Puits des Saints Forts*. In both cases, representations of that devotion have apparently been transferred from the relic and the well to images of the Virgin.[63] In addition, there were secondary foci that attracted relatively local attention.

Before turning to the upper church and its relic of the Virgin's Tunic, it seems appropriate to consider another group of images that also prominently feature depictions of the Virgin and Child, namely the pewter pilgrims' badges from Chartres. Not only do these images provide valuable perspective on the images so far discussed, but they do so in a context which makes their relationship to pilgrimage indisputable. Scholarship on pilgrims' badges in general and knowledge

---

[61] Eugène de Lépinois and Lucien Merlet, eds, *Cartulaire de Notre-Dame de Chartres*, III (Chartres, 1865), p. 214: "fundavit quoddam altare ante vitrinam beate gloriose virginis Marie"—"he founded a certain altar before the window of the blessed glorious Virgin Mary"; Delaporte, *Les Trois Notre-Dame*, pp. 61–6. The earliest reference to the image as "la belle verrière" dates from 1482.

[62] Marcel Bulteau, *Description de la cathédrale de Chartres* (Chartres, 1850), p. 254.

[63] André Vauchez, *Sainthood in the Later Middle Ages*, trans. Jean Birrell (Cambridge, 1997), chapter 15, proposes that the transfer of devotion from relics to sacred images was fairly general in the later Middle Ages. In the Byzantine Empire, a similar relationship existed much earlier between relics and images, with icons taking precedence over relics and churches as the focus of public cult. Annemarie Weyl Carr, "The Mother of God in Public," in Maria Vassilaki, ed., *The Mother of God: Representations of the Virgin in Byzantine Art* (Milan, 2000), p. 327.

of those from Chartres have both developed rapidly in recent years. Only now is it becoming possible to put surviving Chartres badges into a proper historical context.[64] Several badges from Chartres discovered in the Seine River at Paris in 1858 have long been known.[65] More recently, examples have been found in the Netherlands[66] and along the Thames at London.[67] (fig. 93) These all feature images of the Virgin and Child, and some also depict the Holy Tunic. Two other Chartres badges, depicting St. Lubin, an important local saint, have been found at Paris and in Czechoslovakia.[68] The images of the Virgin and Child on these badges are all quite similar: they depict the Virgin crowned and enthroned, with the Christ Child supported sometimes on her left knee, sometimes on her right, but never frontally placed (image reversals, and even inscription reversals, are common on pilgrims' badges). Most of these badges depict the Virgin and Child on one side and an image of the Holy Tunic on the other.[69] They all, therefore, as with most of the images of statues in

---

[64] On the general context for pilgrims' badges, see A.M. Koldeweij, "Lifting the Veil on Pilgrim Badges," in Jennie Stopford, ed., *Pilgrimage Explored* (York, 1999), pp. 161–88; Denis Bruna, "Enseignes de pèlerinage et identité du pèlerin," in *Les pèlerinages à travers l'art et la société à l'époque préromane et romane: actes des XXXIIe journées romanes de Cuxa, Les Cahiers de Saint-Michel de Cuxa*, 31 (2000), pp. 59–63.

[65] Arthur Forgeais, *Collection de plombs historiés trouvés dans la Seine*, vol. II: *Enseignes de pèlerinage* (Paris, 1863), pp. 28–32; Adolphe Lecocq, "Recherches sur les enseignes de pèlerinages et les chemisettes de Notre-Dame-de-Chartres," *Mémoires de la Société archéologique d'Eure-et-Loir* 6 (1876), 194–242. Four of these were apparently destroyed in 1871, and two others are currently in the Musée des beaux-arts at Chartres; see Pippin Michelli, "A Gordian Knot: Notes on Chartres Pilgrim Badges," *Peregrinations* 1, no. 2 (July 2002), 2–4.

[66] Found at Nieuwlande and dated 1350–1400; H.J.E. van Beuningen and A.M. Koldeweij, *Heilig en Profaan: 1000 Laatmiddeleeuwse Insignes uit de collectie H.J.E. van Beuningen*, Rotterdam Papers VIII (Cothen, 1993), p. 218.

[67] Two badges have been found at London, one in 1990 in the Vintry cofferdam. Brian Spencer, *Pilgrim Souvenirs and Secular Badges*, Medieval Finds from Excavations in London, 7 (London, 1998), pp. 224–7. The other badge from London, quite heavily damaged, is uncontextualized; see Michael Mitchener, *Medieval Pilgrim and Secular Badges* (Sanderstead, 1986), p. 263.

[68] Denis Bruna, *Enseignes de pèlerinage et enseignes profanes*, Musée du Moyen Age, Thermes de Cluny (Paris, 1996), p. 170; Helena Koenigsmarkova, "Prace z Pra prostych kovu," *Remeslo umelècke stredoveke: ze sbirek Umelecko Prumsylového Musea v Praze* (Prague, 1980), pp. 54–71. Bruna also suggests, p. 55, that pilgrims' badges depicting St. Veronica and the Holy Face emanated from a number of French sanctuaries, including Chartres.

[69] The badge found in the Netherlands depicts the Holy Tunic below the image of the Virgin and Child. One other image is included on virtually all the badges: one of various issues of a coin minted in Chartres, all featuring a "Chartrain head," a highly stylized profile portrait that appears in various forms on Chartres coins

the stained glass, appear to make reference to the silver-gilt statue of the Virgin and Child on the high altar of the cathedral, which was associated with the *Sainte-Châsse*, containing the Holy Tunic. Once again, they point to the centrality of the high altar as a focus for pilgrimage devotion at Chartres.

The Sainte-Chemise

The principal relic held by the cathedral was the Holy Tunic, or *Sainte-Chemise*, which was commonly claimed as an 876 donation of Emperor Charles the Bald (r. 840–77) who is, indeed, known to have exhibited considerable devotion towards the Virgin. The earliest references to this donation, however, only date from the beginning of the twelfth century, in the writings of William of Malmesbury and the *Chronicle of St. Martin of Tours*.[70] It is not, however, mentioned in the act of foundation, dating from the very next year, 877, of the Abbey of the Virgin, that Charles the Bald founded at the royal palace of Compiègne, just northeast of Paris, in which the preamble cites Charlemagne as having dedicated his palace chapel at Aachen to the Virgin, from which Charles the Bald is supposed to have transferred the Holy Tunic to Chartres. Dominique Iogna-Prat claims that the political symbolism of these shifts in Marian devotion away from Aachen and towards France speaks for itself, but the whole story has yet to be told.[71] The earliest recorded miracle associated

over a considerable duration; Pippin Michelli, "Iconographical Implications of the Virgin at Chartres: The Evidence of the Pilgrim Badges," a paper read at the 37th International Congress on Medieval Studies, Kalamazoo, MI, May 2–5, 2002, dated the various coins found on the badges. These coins appear to represent Chartres in a quasi-heraldic manner: the arms of the city of Chartres eventually featured three such coins. I would like to thank Pippin Michelli, Christopher Crockett, and Sarah Blick for discussions on these badges. They do not necessarily support my conclusions, however.

[70] Yves Delaporte, *Le voile de Notre Dame* (Chartres, 1927), p. 6, fn. 1.

[71] Dominique Iogna-Prat, "Le culte de la Vierge sous le règne de Charles le Chauve," in Dominique Iogna-Prat, Éric Palazzo and Daniel Russo, eds., *Marie, Le culte de la Vierge dans la société médiévale* (Paris, 1996), pp. 65–98; Delaporte, *Le voile de Notre Dame*, p. 7, fn. 1, associates this activity with Charles the Bald's defeat by his nephew, Carloman, in 876, by which he lost control over Lorraine, after which he apparently redistributed relics from Aachen to the principal churches of the part of the empire still under his control. Lautier, "Les vitraux de la cathédrale de Chartres. Reliques et images," p. 15, wrote that the earliest reference to the 876 donation

with the Holy Tunic was thought to have taken place in 911, when it was credited with saving Chartres from attack by the Normans; the earliest documented reference to this miracle, which became widely-known throughout Europe, occurs in the eleventh-century chronicle of Dudo of St. Quentin, *De moribus et actis primorum Normanniae Ducum*.[72] The Holy Tunic was kept in a reliquary casket called the *Sainte-Châsse*, (fig. 94) which existed at least by *c.* 1000 when it is mentioned in the cathedral necrology.[73] Chartrain legend attributed its creation to a craftsman named Teudon, who was credited with repairing the cathedral, when the ninth-century church burned in 962.[74] This parallels an almost contemporary claim recorded for the mid-tenth century at Clermont-Ferrand, where Adelelmus was given credit as both an architect and as the maker of the Marian reliquary.[75] This is only one of many parallel topoi which suggest that our sources for Marian devotion at Chartres should be considered in a manner comparable to hagiographic texts.

This was hardly the only tunic of the Virgin believed to exist, and it is rather remarkable that this initiatory reference to the miraculous nature of the *Sainte-Chemise* finds a more distant, and more prestigious parallel, in the Virgin's garment in the Blachernai monastery in Constantinople, which was also credited with saving that city. In fact, the two incidents follow one another remarkably closely. In 858, for example, the Normans had previously attacked Chartres; there is no mention in this case of the *Sainte-Chemise*, and the Normans appear to have quite successfully sacked the city. Only two years later, in 860, during a Russian siege of Constantinople, the Virgin's Maphorion was carried around the walls—the first documented

---

of the Holy Tunic by Charles the Bald was made only in the early seventeenth century by Jean-Baptiste Souchet, published much later in his *Histoire du diocèse et de la ville de Chartres*, II (Chartres, 1868), p. 93.

[72] Guy Philippart, "Le récit miraculaire marial dans l'Occident médiéval," in Dominique Iogna-Prat, Éric Palazzo and Daniel Russo, eds, *Marie. Le culte de la Vierge dans la société médiévale* (Paris, 1996), p. 567, fn. 23. The earlier *vita* of St. Géran, bishop of Auxerre, mentions only the miraculous intercession of the Virgin, and not the Tunic, in repelling the Normans in 911. For the early sources for this miracle, see Delaporte, *Le voile de Notre Dame*, pp. 5–6.

[73] In the obituary of Rotelinde, mother of Bishop Odon (968–1003). Delaporte, *Les Trois Notre-Dame*, p. 7; Lépinois and Merlet, eds, *Cartulaire*, III, p. 74.

[74] See his obituary in the cathedral necrology; Lépinois and Merlet, eds, *Cartulaire*, III, p. 221.

[75] Forsyth, *The Throne of Wisdom*, p. 96.

instance of this—miraculously saving the city. Shortly thereafter, we have the legendary donation of Charles the Bald in 876, and then in 911, during another Norman siege, the Holy Tunic is processed, miraculously saving the city.[76] Marian relics were so numerous in Constantinople and Marian miracles so frequent—both recorded substantially in advance of related relics and miracles in Europe—that it would be surprising if distant echoes did not reach western Europe, and there are other interesting parallels between Byzantine Marian shrines and Chartres.[77] Indeed, the eleventh century witnessed the translation of Byzantine Marian hymns, such as the Akathistos, into Latin, and many Marian miracle accounts current in Europe had their origins, as well, in the Byzantine East.[78] The military efficacy of the Virgin in protecting against enemies was one of the earliest such miracles to penetrate the West.

The Tenor of Marian Devotion

In fact, the whole tenor of the Marian cult was in process of dramatic change at this time. As Guy Philippart has pointed out, Marian miracles were rare in western Europe during the first millennium, but rapidly became remarkably common thereafter.[79] According to Ward, the earliest collections of miracles of the Virgin only date from the early twelfth century and at that time were not associated

---

[76] For Constantinople, see Maria Vassilaki, ed., *The Mother of God: Representations of the Virgin in Byzantine Art* (Milan, 2000), including the essays by Averil Cameron, "The Early Cult of the Virgin," in Vassilaki, ed., *The Mother of God*, pp. 3–15; Carr, "The Mother of God in Public;" in Vassilaki, ed., *The Mother of God*, pp. 325–37; Cyril Mango, "Constantinople as Theotokoupolis," in Vassilaki, ed., *The Mother of God*, pp. 16–25; and Alexei Lidov, "Miracle-Working Icons of the Mother of God," in Vassilaki, ed., *The Mother of God*, pp. 47–57. On the miraculous intervention of the Holy Tunic in the Norman seige of Chartres in 911, see Signori, *Maria zwischen Kathedrale, Kloster und Welt*, pp. 178–82, esp. p. 180, where she claims that relationships between Chartres and Byzantium have been too little noticed.

[77] In the early seventeenth century, Roulliard, *Parthenie*, p. 131, compared Chartres and its Marian relic with the Blachernae church in Constantinople.

[78] Philippart, "Le récit miraculaire marial," pp. 568–69. At Chartres, the city was attacked again on August 5, 962 by Richard I, duke of Normandy, who was at war with the count of Chartres, Thibault le Tricheur. There is no mention of the Virgin's Tunic at this time, and at least parts of the city and the cathedral were damaged.

[79] Philippart, "Le récit miraculaire marial," p. 566.

with any particular sanctuary, nor did they involve relics.[80] Marian
miracles, in fact, remained distinct from those of other saints, since
it was relatively rare that they could be attributed to relics, all of
which, in any case, were fairly marginal, since the Virgin's body was
not thought to be available for dismemberment and wide distribution,
and surviving hair, milk and clothing could not compensate for this
radical and quasi-theological absence. This tended both to retard the
development of Marian miracles and to make Marian cult sites distinctive from those of other saints. There was more thaumaturgical
efficacy invested in statues of the Virgin than for other saints, and
moreover, the relative density of miraculous Marian sites also set them
apart from those of other saints. Remarkably, for example, in Aimery
Picaud's twelfth-century pilgrims' guide to Santiago de Compostela,
there is no Marian shrine mentioned, even though they were frequently located on or very near the pilgrimage roads.[81] Nevertheless,
with the growing popularity of the Virgin through the eleventh and
twelfth centuries, the cult became localized. Chartres seems to have
established itself quite early among these shrines. Lack of official
recognition of such shrines very probably signals their popular, and
populist, nature. Ward, once again, stresses that the uneducated
masses did not see the Virgin as the ubiquitous power, not limited
by time or place, who was venerated by St. Anselm and St. Bernard
and was enshrined in theological dogma. To them she was Our Lady
of Chartres, Our Lady of Soissons, etc.—a highly localized persona.[82]

By the twelfth century, there is evidence for a fairly widespread
pilgrimage to Chartres and for miraculous activity there. Abbot Suger
(r. 1122–51), for example, in his *Life of Louis the Fat*, refers to the
tunic being borne in procession to avert siege and fire in 1118.[83]
More commonly in the twelfth century, however, Marian devotion
became associated with the frequent outbreaks of ergot poisoning,
the *mal des ardents* or "holy fire," caused by eating mold-infected rye.
It struck large groups of people all over England and France during
the first half of the twelfth century, and Sumption claims that in

---

[80] Ward, *Miracles and the Medieval Mind*, pp. 132–65.
[81] Annie Shaver-Crandall and Paula Gerson, *The Pilgrim's Guide to Santiago de Compostela: A Gazeteer* (London, 1995).
[82] Ward, *Miracles and the Medieval Mind*, p. 145.
[83] Signori, *Maria zwischen Kathedrale, Kloster und Welt*, p. 179.

almost every case, these outbreaks resulted in mass pilgrimage to one of several sanctuaries of the Virgin, certainly including Chartres.[84] In 1132, for example, several hundred citizens of Beauvais suffering from ergotism made the pilgrimage to Chartres. Such pilgrimages were not at all models of devotional decorum, according to Sumption, but hysterical mass movements undertaken under extreme duress, out of desperation. Only a few years previously, in 1128, it had been Soissons Cathedral that drew the crowds, and in this case, they were rewarded by a blazing light filling the cathedral, accompanied by a loud peal, like that of thunder. So report the sources, in any case, and no one was in any doubt that this constituted an appearance of the Virgin. According to the early thirteenth-century miracle collection, a similar appearance also took place in Chartres Cathedral.[85] These were only two of the several important Marian shrines associated with cures from ergotism. The chronicler, Anselm of Gembloux, for the year 1129, noted that ergotism pervaded Chartres, Paris, Soissons, Cambrai, Arras, and many other localities, but miracles brought about by the Virgin extinguished it. In 1128, Soissons took center stage; in 1132 Chartres; in 1206 it was Notre-Dame in Paris. At Arras, the pilgrimage related to ergotism provoked the foundation of a confraternity of "des ardents," i.e. those infected with ergotism, in honor of the Virgin as early as the late eleventh century, and "la Grande Procession" at Tournai developed in 1089 in the same context.

That Chartres could hold its own in this intensely-competitive arena is suggested by Guibert de Nogent's mention that when his mother, in the diocese of Beauvais, pictured the Virgin, she saw, in particular, the Virgin of Chartres.[86] And in the early thirteenth century, Guillaume le Breton, in his poem, *La Philippide*, several times

---

[84] Jonathan Sumption, *Pilgrimage: An Image of Mediaeval Religion* (London, 1975), pp. 74–5.

[85] Thomas, ed., "Les Miracles de Notre Dame de Chartres," p. 523; Kunstmann, *Miracles de Notre-Dame de Chartres*, pp. 39–40, 149–50. According to the seventeenth-century account of Souchet, *Histoire du diocèse*, II, pp. 248–9, the reason that the High Gothic cathedral was only dedicated in 1260 (he mistakenly says 1262) was that this appearance of the Virgin in her church itself constituted a dedication, "pour la dédier et la sanctifier"—"to dedicate and sanctify it."

[86] Benton, *Self and Society in Medieval France*, pp. 84–5. This is usually assumed to refer to *Notre-Dame de Sous Terre*, but we are ill-informed of other possibilities before the 1194 fire.

evokes Chartres as the city favoured above all others by the Virgin.[87] Nevertheless, there must have been intense rivalry between all of these sites. The first account in the early thirteenth-century miracle collection from Chartres relates to a woman inflicted with ergotism who made a pilgrimage to Soissons. When, later, she was cured and resolved to make a further pilgrimage of thanksgiving to Soissons, the Virgin appeared to her and redirected her to Chartres.[88] It was at this time, as well, that a miracle relating to Bishop Fulbert began to circulate, in which he, too, had been inflicted with ergotism, when Our Lady appeared to him and cured him by squirting milk from her breast onto the affected area. This miracle is first reported in the early twelfth century by William of Malmesbury, and drops of this milk were thought to have been collected in a reliquary, which was also greatly esteemed at Chartres.

This was also the period of the building miracles, the so-called Cult of Carts, in which crowds of people converged on various church-building sites and collectively dragged carts of materials to the site, like beasts of burden, while singing hymns and engaging in various communal devotions. Even taking into account the institutional propagandizing that has been claimed of such accounts, these resembled the hysterical mass pilgrimages connected with ergotism in the twelfth century, and there seems every reason to believe that Chartres benefitted from such mass, popular movements. This, indeed, may have been a large factor in the decision to rebuild after the 1194 fire on such a grand scale, and further instances of this phenomenon are prominently included in the early thirteenth-century miracle collection and even represented in the stained glass.[89] (fig. 91)

---

[87] François-Pierre-Guillaume Guizot, ed., *La Philippide, poëme, par Guillaume le Breton*, Collection des mémoires relatifs à l'histoire de France (Paris, 1825), pp. 54–5, 121–2, 219–20. The poem was written shortly before the death of King Philip Augustus in 1223. Perhaps significantly for the widespread dissemination of such beliefs, in 1219 the author had been made a canon of Senlis Cathedral, which also claimed substantial Marian relics.

[88] Miracle collections from Saint-Pierre-sur-Dive and Rocamadour likewise mention pilgrims directed away from Chartres to these sites. Signori, *Maria zwischen Kathedrale, Kloster und Welt*, pp. 152–73; Marcus Bull, *The Miracles of Our Lady of Rocamadour* (Woodbridge, 1999), pp. 125–6.

[89] Thomas, ed., *Les Miracles de Notre Dame de Chartres*; Signori, *Maria zwischen Kathedrale, Kloster und Welt*, pp. 182–6. When, in 1198, Raoul de Manunville wanted to make a donation of land to Chartres Cathedral, he had to make it at the altar of St. Lawrence because, as the charter states, he could not get access to the altar

But it does not follow that Chartres, simply because a huge church was built there, was a consistent and homogeneous magnet of Marian devotion. Marian shrines continued to multiply.[90] Rocamadour, which eventually far eclipsed Chartres as a Marian cult center, first came to prominence in the late twelfth century.[91] From the mid-thirteenth century, Aachen, which also claimed a Tunic of the Virgin, became the goal of a pilgrimage.[92] Yet, such popular pilgrimage only formed one pole of Marian devotion at Chartres.

Other aspects of the cult focused on very different segments of the populace. There is evidence that the Crusades provoked considerable devotion at Chartres among the knightly classes, who came to the cathedral to touch their own tunics to the *Sainte-Chasse* in the hopes of obtaining thaumaturgical help in battle, for both protection and victory. Once again, one of the miracles in the early thirteenth-century miracle collection provides such an instance, and the *Vieille Chronique* of 1389 claims this as almost a mass movement in its own right. I would also contend that there is ample evidence of military and crusading interests in the imagery of the cathedral, that provides further evidence for this interest.

Certainly another context for Marian devotion at Chartres was thaumaturgical aid in conception and childbirth, a very common element of Marian devotion, which recurs at site after site throughout Europe.[93] The Chartres miracle collection relates several miracles devoted to the saving of infants, but in general, aid in conception

---

of the Virgin Mary on that day because of the crowds of people around that altar who had come to witness the miracles that were taking place there. Lépinois and Merlet, *Cartulaire*, I, p. 260. So soon after the 1194 fire, these were likely to have been temporary altars, perhaps in the crypt. No other source mentions this influx of pilgrims.

[90] Cassagnes-Brouquet, *Vierges noires*, p. 42, emphasizes that, although the most renowned sanctuaries of the Virgin are located at substantial sites like Chartres and Le Puy, the vast majority of cultic sites were situated in village churches or rural chapels.

[91] Ernest Rupin, *Roc-Amadour* (Paris, 1904); Bull, *The Miracles of Our Lady of Rocamadour*. Le Puy also continued as a major Marian pilgrimage site. Georges Paul and Pierre Paul, *Notre-Dame du Puy. Essai historique et archéologique* (Le Puy, 1926).

[92] Heinrich Schiffers, *Karls des Großen Reliquienschatz und die Anfänge der Aachenfahrt* (Aachen, 1951). See also the article in this volume by Lisa Victoria Ciresi, "The Aachen Karls- and Marienschreine."

[93] Laura Spitzer, "The Cult of the Virgin and Gothic Sculpture: Evaluating Opposition in the Chartres West Façade Capital Frieze," *Gesta* 33/2 (1994), 132–50.

is a very incompletely recorded phenomenon, and with one exception, it is difficult to measure the importance of this aspect of Marian devotion at Chartres. That exception, however, is extremely important. Through the later Middle Ages, queen after queen turned to Our Lady of Chartres for help in continuing the French royal succession. The earliest instance of this that I have been able to find is in Guillaume le Breton's *Philippide*, where the birth of King Louis VIII (b. 1187; r. 1223–26) is credited to the intervention of Notre-Dame de Chartres.[94] Thereafter, there is a remarkably dense amount of evidence for continued queenly interest, and since royalty themselves carried sacral weight in the Middle Ages, royal interest in a shrine was far more important than can be measured by mere statistics. Through the seventeenth and eighteenth centuries, the chapter was in the habit of sending out "chemises de Chartres" which had lain on the *Sainte-Châsse* to new French queens, to aid them in producing a royal heir, thereby not only currying royal favor but actively building on their own legendary identity. The 1477 inventory of the abbey of Fontevrault lists no less than four linen "chemises" from Chartres, undoubtedly donated by the noble ladies who had entered the house as nuns.[95] Small metal replicas, known as "chemisettes" were also regularly sent to important members of the court.[96] Two chemisettes were also sent by the chapter to the Jesuit missions in Canada at the end of the seventeenth century; they take the form of reliquaries, sent in the hope of aiding the conversion of native groups. (fig. 95) These chemisettes take a highly conventional "chemise" form that had been used since the fifteenth century as the arms of the cathedral chapter. The earliest such emblematic use of the Holy Tunic was on the 1450 seal of Canon Regnault de Paris. The presumably earlier representations on Chartres pilgrims' badges are much less conventionalized. (fig. 93)

---

[94] Guizot, ed., *La Philippide*, p. 387. The miraculous circumstances surrounding this conception, as his mother, Queen Elisabeth, knelt in devotion to the Virgin in Chartres Cathedral, are contained in an exhortation to Louis VIII, added to the text of the poem after the death of King Philip Augustus in 1223.

[95] Bulteau, *Monographie*, I, p. 155, fn. 1.

[96] Several such chemisettes are preserved in the Musée des beaux-arts at Chartres. *Trésors de la Cathédrale de Chartres* (Chartres, 2002), pp. 51–3.

The Upper Church

Until the early nineteenth century, the upper church continued to be identified as Bishop Fulbert's early eleventh-century basilica. This interpretation can be traced back to the *Vieille Chronique* of 1389, and there have actually been suggestions that the author of this work deliberately destroyed documents referring to the 1194 fire in order to extend the age of the fabric back to the era of Chartres' most prestigious Marian devotee.[97] The focus of cultic attention in the upper church was initially the high altar, for it was here that the *Sainte-Châsse* was displayed. (fig. 96, no. 1) In 1520, the high altar was moved slightly to the east, in order to accommodate more stalls for the canons, and it remained at this location until it was moved even further east in relation to the installation of the present marble reredos in 1767–73. There was also some sort of choir screen around the choir and sanctuary, although its form is unknown, since it was replaced by the substantial early sixteenth-century choir screen which still survives. Fragments of the jubé (dated *c.* 1220–30) which enclosed the choir at the west survive. (fig. 97) Behind the high altar, in the axial hemicycle bay, there was a raised pyramidal treasury (see below). Large transepts, considerably west of those in Fulbert's church, were added after the 1194 fire, and each of them featured a monumental sculpted entrance with an elaborate porch. The function of these entrances remains poorly understood.[98] The mid-twelfth-century western entrance, the Royal Portal, clearly remained the principal liturgical entrance of the new church.

Some of the distinctive aspects of the upper church have not been widely noted. One of the reasons that it has survived in such a relatively pure thirteenth-century state is that, unlike many other Gothic cathedrals, it did not later become filled with chapels, to accommodate

---

[97] Van der Meulen, Hoyer, and Cole, *Chartres. Sources and Literary Interpretation*, p. 213; Adolphe Lecocq, "La cathédrale de Chartres et ses Maîtres de l'œuvre," *Mémoires de la Société archéologique d'Eure-et-Loir* 6 (1876), p. 398.

[98] Peter Cornelius Claussen, *Chartres-Studien zu Vorgeschichte, Funktion und Skulptur der Vorhallen* (Wiesbaden, 1975), pp. 3–17, contains the most profound survey of evidence for how the Chartres transepts functioned, but many of Claussen's possibilities are drawn more from analogy with known use elsewhere than from documented use at Chartres.

both private devotion and illustrious burial space. According to the seventeenth-century account by Sebastien Rouillard, even the construction of the Vendôme Chapel in 1417, between two south nave buttresses, was regarded negatively by many people.[99] In fact, Chartres Cathedral is virtually unique among major medieval churches in being completely devoid of burials and, apart from this one exception, of later chapels. The survival of the labyrinth in the nave pavement can similarly be accounted for.[100] (fig. 96)

The reason for this prohibition of burials seems to focus on Marian devotion. The church was seen as being as pure and integral as the Virgin Mary herself, and thus was kept free of the pollution of burials. This was accounted the reason for the miracles that took place at Chartres. The clearest explanation for this comes from a pronouncement of 1475, by the Parlement of Paris, which states that from its first foundation, the church of Chartres has been and remains complete and uncorrupt, since nobody of any estate has been buried there for any sort of donation, and it is through the virginity of Our Lady and also of the site of her church at Chartres that so many miracles take place here.[101] Beyond the pollution of the dead, this concept of purity also appears to be related to the pollution of blood that was associated with childbirth, for which reason some canonists upheld a prohibition against holding a church funeral for women who died in childbirth.[102] The single burial allowed in Chartres

---

[99] Roulliard, *Parthenie*, p. 160–2. Undoubtedly, this was because, after the death of Louis de Bourbon in 1446, his heart was deposited in this chapel. Marcel Bulteau, *Monographie de la cathédrale de Chartres*, III (Chartres, 1901), pp. 310–13.

[100] On the general phenomenon of such walkable labyrinths, see Hermann Kern, *Through the Labyrinth: Designs and Meanings over 5,000 Years* (Munich, 2000), esp. Ch. VIII, "Church Labyrinths," pp. 142–65. On the possibility that the Chartres labyrinth formed part of the pilgrimage experience of the cathedral, referring more specifically to the cathedral's engagement with Jerusalem pilgrimage, see the chapter in this volume by Daniel Connolly, "At the Center of the World: The Labyrinth Pavement of Chartres Cathedral."

[101] This is on a parchment roll, Arch. d'Eure-et-Loir, G 624. See Jusselin, "Dernières recherches," pp. 113–15. In the early seventeenth century, Roulliard, *Parthenie*, pp. 160–1, specifically mentions the pollution occasioned by dead bodies, and claims that a comparable ban on burials also applied to the Church of the 11,000 Virgins in Cologne. See also Challine, *Recherches sur Chartres*, p. 152, written shortly before Challine's death in 1678.

[102] This is explicitly stated in Johannis Beleth, *Summa de ecclesiasticis officiis*, *PL*, vol. 202, col. 13ff. and Honorius Augustodunensis, *Gemma animae*, *PL*, vol. 172, col. 541ff., although Guillaume Durand, *Rationale diuinorum officiorum*, disagreed, claiming that if great care is taken to avoid soiling the church with blood, the dead woman's

Cathedral—at the insistence of the king—was that of the Baron de Bourdeille, who died in 1568 defending Chartres from the Huguenots. This burial was imposed over the strong protests of the chapter, who finally agreed to the burial on the condition that the ground would not be disturbed and that neither the body nor the coffin would touch the pavement of the church; the coffin was supported on an iron grille and enclosed in cut stone with neither epitaph or imagery.[103] Even with these remarkable precautions, the grave was removed in 1661, in an attempt by the chapter to purify the church. Indeed, on May 16, 1661, the doors were closed to the public for several days, and when they were re-opened, not only was the burial removed, but so were the many altars that had accrued around piers and in other areas of the church. This returned the focus of devotion in the upper church to the cult of the Virgin.[104] Slightly earlier, in *c.* 1645, the *Puits des Saints Forts* in the crypt was walled up, putatively to reduce superstition, once again focusing attention on a purified Marian cult.

Thus, the character of the church itself was in a sense modelled on that of the Virgin, and reciprocally, "the Virgin's miraculous virtue emanated from the sacred architecture; and, much more notably, this same architecture embodied a principle of individuation."[105] However difficult it might be to discern or to reconstruct the reception of Chartres Cathedral as a work of architecture during the Middle Ages, it seems clear that its distinction was inseparable from its role as a locus of Marian devotion. In the verse satire, *Disputoison de Dieu et de sa mère*, i.e. "Disputation between God and

funeral may be held in church; William Durandus, *The Symbolism of Churches and Church Ornaments: A Translation of the First Book of the Rationale Divinorum Officiorum*, trans. John Mason Neale and Benjamin Webb (London, 1893), p. 86. I am grateful to Aline Hornaday and the Medieval Religion internet discussion list (MEDIEVAL-RELIGION@JISCMAIL.AC.UK) for much of this information.

[103] Challine, *Recherches sur Chartres*, p. 161. Remarkably, even though parallels were made at the time between the siege of 1568 and the Norman siege of 911, there is no indication that the Virgin's Tunic was used, either actively or symbolically, and after the deliverance of the city, a procession was made to *Notre-Dame de Sous-Terre* in the crypt. André Sanfaçon, "Événement, mémoire et mythe: le siège de Chartres de 1568," in *Événement, identité et histoire*, ed. Claire Dolan (Sillery, Québec, 1991), pp. 187–204.

[104] Challine, *Recherches sur Chartres*, p. 152. The baron de Bourdeille was reburied without ceremony in the cemetery of St. Jerome, just east of the church.

[105] Signori, "La bienheureuse polysémie," p. 611: "de l'architecture sacrée émana la *virtus* miraculeuse de la Vierge; et, fait bien plus notable, cette même architecture tenait lieu de principe d'individuation."

His Mother," from the beginning of the fifteenth century, Christ complains that people treat his Mother better than himself, and in particular, that she has dispossessed him of the most beautiful churches, citing: Reims, Chartres, Saint-Denis, Laon, Le Puy and Rocamadour.[106] This list poses some problems of interpretation, since Saint-Denis was not, to my knowledge, noted as a Marian shrine, and since, while Rocamadour was a demonstrably famous Marian shrine, it never produced a very spectacular architecture.

Yet, it seems clear that the aesthetic value attached to these buildings was not considered separately from their Marian identity. As it was rebuilt after the fire of 1194, the upper church is perhaps not as centrally innovative a structure as architectural historians once thought. It is now considered that the design took advantage of ideas already developed in the Cathedrals of Soissons (for the elevation and form of the windows) and Laon (for the arrangement of the towers and transepts), but can it be a coincidence that, besides having up-to-date architectural models to provide, these buildings were also prominent centers of Marian pilgrimage?[107] The seven towers begun at Laon and Reims were increased to nine at Chartres. Although this feature has never been tied specifically to their Marian character, it may be significant that one of the miracles related in the mid-twelfth century at Saint-Pierre-sur-Dive involves the cure of a dumb boy who saw a vision of the Virgin Mary in the church tower.[108] Although it may be speculative to relate specific architectural elements to the Marian cult, the huge Romanesque crypt that was retained and incorporated into the High Gothic design was both highly distinctive—no other High Gothic cathedral made such active use of a crypt—and incontestibly linked with pilgrimage activity, which was also gradually assimilated to Marian devotion at Chartres.

The Changing Visibility of Relics

As has been demonstrated above, the seventeenth century saw considerable changes in the nature of the Marian presence at Chartres

---

[106] Philippart, "Le récit miraculaire marial," p. 588.

[107] For a useful overview of the place of the High Gothic cathedral of Chartres in the development of Gothic architecture, see Kurmann-Schwarz and Kurmann, *Chartres. La cathédrale*, pp. 432–9.

[108] Signori, *Maria zwischen Kathedrale, Kloster und Welt*, pp. 165–73.

Cathedral, and there may well have been good reasons for this, since the existence of the Holy Tunic was then under question. Through the seventeenth century, there are increasing references to the Virgin's veil at Chartres, and in 1712, it was decided to open the *Sainte-Châsse* for the first time in official memory, and no tunic was found—only a length of silk immediately interpreted as a veil.[109] A veil had certainly been mentioned much earlier,[110] but during the later Middle Ages, there was never any doubt expressed in the existence of the Holy Tunic, since the relic was apparently never taken out of the *Sainte-Châsse* and, thus, never officially seen.[111] This contrasts with the well-established ostension of the Virgin's Tunic at Aachen which developed from the mid-fourteenth century, but the Aachen relic was initially enclosed permanently in a reliquary shrine. Even the nature of the Aachen relics was unknown until a 1237 fire damaged the previous Marian shrine there. When the relics were removed, four cloth relics, including a whole tunic, were found, and the new reliquary shrine made to replace the old one was not initially designed to be opened. When the practice of displaying the relics every seven years began in 1349, doors were cut in the reliquary.[112] The ostension of relics was not usual before this time, and the Fourth Lateran Council of 1215 actually forbade the open veneration of relics of the saints.[113]

---

[109] For the minutes of the examination, see Lucien Merlet, *Histoire des relations des Hurons et des Abnaquis du Canada avec Notre-Dame de Chartres, suivi de documents inédits sur la Sainte Chemise* (Chartres, 1858), pp. 76–8; Delaporte, *Le voile de Notre Dame*, pp. 12–14. That may have been a low point of the Marian associations with Chartres, but they bounced back in the nineteenth century. The survival of the Virgin's veil at the time of the Revolution must have had something to do with that. Most of the other relics at Chartres were destroyed, and few other Marian relics survived in France. Subsequent efforts to re-establish pilgrimage to Chartres culminated in the writings and activities of Charles Peguy in the early twentieth century, but the most dynamic period of chartrain pilgrimage, between the eleventh and seventeenth centuries, was long over. A grand ceremony was organized in 1876 to celebrate the millenial anniversary of the donation of the Virgin's veil. Delaporte, *Le voile de Notre Dame*, pp. 23–4.

[110] It is mentioned, along with the tunic, in relation to the 911 Norman siege of Chartres in the mid-thirteenth century. Kunstmann, ed., *Miracles de Notre-Dame de Chartres*, p. 45. The veil was apparently glimpsed surreptitiously through holes in the *Sainte Châsse* by the seventeenth century, and relics even circulated (fig. 95), but the circumstances of its emergence as a recognized relic are extremely vague.

[111] Delaporte, *Le voile de Notre Dame*, p. 11; Mély, *Le trésor de Chartres*, pp. 50–1, who cites the testimony of Canon Estienne in 1682 that the shrine was never opened.

[112] Ciresi, "The Aachen Karls- and Marienschriene" in this volume.

[113] Ward, *Miracles and the Medieval Mind*, p. 227, fn. 85.

Anomalously, while the Holy Tunic was apparently invisible within
its shrine, images of it appeared quite early on pilgrims' badges, (fig.
93) and from the mid-fifteenth century, stylized images of the tunic
were adopted as heraldic charges in the arms of the chapter.
Nevertheless, it would appear that the attention of pilgrims would
have been focused visually on the *Sainte-Châsse*, and its related silver
gilt image of the Virgin and Child, rather than on the Holy Tunic
itself. This shrine seems to have been associated with the high altar
in Fulbert's church, as well as in the new cathedral, placing it in a
controllable space within the sanctuary.[114] (fig. 96) A jubé was in
place, separating the nave from the canons' choir, from at least the
early twelfth century, and another one was constructed in the new
cathedral between the two eastern-most crossing piers.[115] (figs. 96–7)
The choir stalls, in place by 1221, would have closed off the first
three bays east of the crossing, according to Félibien's 1678 plan.[116]
The arcades of the fourth bay, the last straight bay of the eastern
arm, undoubtedly provided the principal entrance to the sanctuary;[117]
two steps separated the choir from the sanctuary further east. The
necessity for separating pilgrimage activity at the high altar from ser-

---

[114] The obituary of Hildeburgis, added to the cathedral necrology between 1029
and 1130, mentions the reliquary over the altar, "scrinio super altare." Auguste
Molinier, *Obituaires de la province de Sens*, vol. II: *Diocèse de Chartres* (Paris, 1906),
p. 17. In February 1212, Gauthier de Villebéon donated a candle to burn in perpetuity on the high altar before the reliquary—"super majus altare ante sacrum
scrinium ejusdem beate Virginis;" Lépinois and Merlet, eds, *Cartulaire*, III, p. 153.

[115] Bishop Yvo (1090–1115) had a jubé built, according to his obituary in the
necrology; Lépinois and Merlet, eds, *Cartulaire*, III, p. 225. For the Gothic jubé, see
Mallion, *Le jubé*, and most recently Kurmann and Kurmann-Schwarz, *Chartres. La
cathédrale*, pp. 306–26, 458, with bibliography.

[116] Regulations, dated January 1221, concerning the use of the new stalls can
safely be taken as a *terminus ante quem* for their construction. Eugène de Lépinois
and Lucien Merlet, eds, *Cartulaire de Notre-Dame de Chartres*, II (Chartres, 1863), pp.
95–6. For reproductions of close copies of Félibien's plan, see Étienne Houvet,
Cathédrale de Chartres. Architecture (Chelles, 1919–21), pl. 1; Challine, *Recherches sur
Chartres*, pp. 134–5. On Félibien's plans, see Van der Meulen, *Chartres. Sources and
Literary Interpretation*, pp. 86, 937–9.

[117] This is the location of the remarkably small sanctuary entrance doorways of
the present, sixteenth-century choir screen. These doorways were apparently originally located in the third bay of the new choir screen but were moved one bay
further east in 1531, after the stalls were extended eastward in c.1520; Françoise
Jouanneaux, *Le tour du choeur de la cathédrale de Chartres, Eure-et-Loir*, Images du
patrimoine, Inventaire général des monuments et des richesses artistiques de la
France (Orléans, 2000), pp. 4–5, 9. These small doors were blocked entirely in the
eighteenth-century remodelling of the choir and sanctuary.

vices in the choir was a considerable factor in planning and may, in fact, account for later changes in the location of the high altar and arrangements within the sanctuary.[118] The high altar was originally located on the chord of the apse, and the sanctuary was undoubtedly enclosed by screens between the hemicycle piers, except for the axial bay, in which a treasury, the *lieu des saints corps* (place of the holy bodies), was elevated on a platform which could be accessed by spiral staircases in the adjacent bays. In the 1682 inventory of relics, the arrangement on the platform consisted of a pyramidal bank of six compartments, stacked one on two on three, with gilded doors, each holding a reliquary.[119] In front of this axial treasury was another altar *de retro*, i.e. "behind" the high altar. The earliest reference to relics in this location dates from 1310, when those of St. Piat were described as located "above the altar which is behind the high altar of the church of Chartres."[120] This arrangement was altered in the early sixteenth century, when the present choir screen was erected, providing a highly complex series of chambers within a very high and solid screen. The axial treasury was tranformed, and two further treasuries were fitted into two of these chambers (flanking the high altar) during the seventeenth century. Then, in the late eighteenth century, the retro-altar was suppressed and the high altar moved further east to accommodate the monumental reredos by the sculptor Charles-Antoine Bridan, erected between 1767 and 1773.[121]

---

[118] P.-A. Sigal, "Reliques, pèlerinage et miracles dans l'église médiévale (XIe–XIIIe siècles)," *Revue d'histoire de l'église de France* LXXVI, no. 197 (1990), 193–211. Chapter deliberations mention the disruptions of pilgrims and country folk in the church. Maurice Jusselin, "Introduction à l'étude du tour du choeur de la cathédrale de Chartres," *Mémoires de la Société archéologique d'Eure-et-Loire* 20–21 (1957–61), pp. 81–172, esp. pp. 85–6.

[119] Mély, *Le trésor de Chartres*, pp. 83–92.

[120] Lucien Merlet, *Catalogue des reliques et joyaux de Notre-Dame de Chartres* (Chartres, 1885), p. 230: "super altare quod est post majus altar ecclesie Carnotensis." Lautier, "Les vitraux de la cathédrale de Chartres. Reliques et images," pp. 34–35, noted a scene in the Charlemagne window (window 7), depicting Constantine offering relics to Charlemagne: she suggested that the three reliquaries on a base supported by columns may constitute evidence of the axial treasury in the early thirteenth century.

[121] Bulteau, *Monographie*, I, pp. 214–23. At this time the piers, choir enclosure, and other decorative elements of the east end were also altered in accordance with current tastes.

The miracle collections at Chartres invariably mention pilgrims going to the high altar to pay their devotions to the Holy Tunic, and even proceeding under the shrine, but although details are lacking, access to the shrine must have been carefully controlled by the canons.[122] The *Sainte-Châsse*, although the most important cultic focus of the upper church, was not exclusive. The axial treasury contained six other reliquaries. Like any major church, Chartres Cathedral possessed a considerable collection of relics, constantly supplemented by new donations. In 1205, for example, Countess Catherine of Chartres donated the head of Mary's mother, St. Anne, obtained from Constantinople by her husband, Count Louis (d. 1204), a participant in the Fourth Crusade. It was eventually placed on an altar set against the north side of the jubé. Similarly, Gervais, the lord of Châteauneuf, another participant in the Fourth Crusade, donated the head of St. Matthew in 1205.[123]

The cathedral relics can generally be divided into two categories. First, the Marian relics constituted by far the most important focus for pilgrimage activity. Arguably, the relic of St. Anne's head might be considered along with the Marian relics, but although it must have been quite apparent in the cathedral, no miracles appear to have accrued to it, and there is no evidence that it ever achieved more than local interest.[124] Documented interest in other relics was relatively marginal and relatively local. Thus, canonized bishops of Chartres such as St. Lubin, St. Solein, or St. Bethaire, had shrines and were invoked for propitious weather, etc., but have left little trace of pilgrimage activity, apart from the St. Lubin pilgrims' badges mentioned earlier, which undoubtedly signal peripheral interest in the context of predominantly Marian pilgrimages. More important relics, such as the heads of Sts. Theodore and Matthew, do not appear to have attracted discernible pilgrimage. Only the relics of St. Piat, which were certainly important to the cathedral chapter,

---

[122] Although the exact arrangements at Chartres are unknown, on analogy with other sites, there was probably a shrine base located immediately east of the high altar, which was high enough that pilgrims could kneel within it or pass under it. Ben Nilson, *Cathedral Shrines of Medieval England* (Woodbridge, 1998), pp. 99–100.

[123] Mély, *Le trésor de Chartres*, xviii–xix. For a fuller analysis of the cathedral relics, see Lautier, "Les vitraux de la cathédrale de Chartres. Reliques et images."

[124] New canons swore an oath concerning their legitimacy on the head of St. Anne. She is depicted holding the infant Virgin Mary on the carved trumeau of the central doorway on the north transept and above this in the stained glass in the central lancet below the north transept rose (window 121).

can be said to have provoked more widespread interest. His reliquary was opened from time to time at the request of noble pilgrims.[125]

The Traces of Pilgrims in the Cathedral

Evaluating the evidence of pilgrimage through donations of materials left in the church or commissioned for it is difficult for a number of reasons. First, much of the evidence is lost, destroyed in 1793 during the French Revolution. Documentary records were haphazard and unsystematic, and would be insufficient, even if all of the documents had survived. Evidence from the chapter registers only survives from 1298 onwards,[126] and inventories of the treasury are only in evidence from the early fourteenth century.[127] Second, what evidence has survived is strongly biased. Most relates to the wealthy, who could afford to make substantial donations to mark their devotion, and to the important, whose donations were noteworthy. Material evidence for pilgrimage among the more populous lower classes of society is scant. There is, moreover, another problem in dealing with this body of evidence. Although it seems likely that most substantial

---

[125] In the eleventh century, Canon Ragembod covered the front of St. Piat's wooden coffin with gold, and in the twelfth century Archdeacon Drogo left ten marks of silver to repair the reliquary. Mély, *Le trésor de Chartres*, p. 108. On October 1, 1310, St. Piat's venerable wooden coffin was opened, the first of many recorded examinations, and the apparently incorrupt body was considered to have worked miracles; shortly afterwards, in June 1324, the chapter decided to found a chapel dedicated to St. Piat above their newly-rising chapter house, an independent, rectangular building just east of the chevet, later connected with the ambulatory by a covered staircase. René Merlet, "Les architectes de la cathédrale de Chartres et de la construction de la chapelle Saint-Piat au XIVe siècle," *Bulletin monumental*, 7 sér., 10 (1906), 225–27. This chapel appears to have been used predominantly by the canons, and there is no evidence that the relics of St. Piat were ever translated there. James Bugslag, "Entre espace pictural et architectural. La fenêtre est de la chapelle Saint-Piat à la cathédrale de Chartres," *Représentations architecturales dans les vitraux*, Dossier de la Commission Royale des Monuments, Sites et Fouilles, 9 (Liège, 2002), pp. 85–94. A popular pilgrim print of St. Piat, dating from *c.* 1700, survives; Maurice Jusselin, *Imagiers et cartiers chartrains*, 2nd ed. (Paris, 1957), pl. II.

[126] Mély, *Le trésor de Chartres*, p. xix. Most of the chapter registers were destroyed in the 1944 bombing, but much was transcribed and/or published earlier. For the state of the originals and their copies, see van der Meulen, Hoyer, and Cole, *Chartres. Sources and Literary Interpretation*, pp. 504–5.

[127] The treasury inventories have been twice published, by Merlet, *Catalogue des reliques et joyaux*, and Mély, *Le trésor de Chartres*.

donations were made on site, this is by no means a general rule, and some donations are known to have been made independent of any sort of presence at Chartres. In addition, the records do not distinguish in kind between the donations of the canons and citizens of Chartres itself and those of individuals from elsewhere. In fact, it seems clear that distance travelled is an unreliable way of defining a pilgrim. Sometimes donations were made to specific relics, but many donation records give no indication of the donor's motivations or intentions. Nevertheless, bearing these methodological limitations in mind, it is possible to deal with several different classes of material evidence for pilgrimage to Chartres.

Perhaps the most unambiguous evidence comes from the discoveries of pilgrims' badges. (fig. 93) Until recently, only six were known, all discovered at Paris, and this low rate of survival, together with the proximity of Paris to Chartres, has been used to construct arguments for the strictly local importance of pilgrimage here. Not only have more badges been found recently, over a much wider geographical range,[128] but it is now realized that the use of "negative evidence" regarding pilgrims' badges is methodologically unsound. They have survived principally in rivers, and there are substantial areas of Europe in which no medieval pilgrims' badges have been found, for lack of propitious conditions. The sampling of badges from Chartres is far from being strictly local, but is not substantial enough to use them as evidence of massive and widespread pilgrimage to Chartres.

In any event, although pilgrims' badges were often sewn into the devotional manuscripts of the nobility, the find spots of the surviving Chartres badges undoubtedly constitute evidence for pilgrimage among the lower classes. Substantiation of pilgrimage to Chartres at this "popular" level is otherwise quite elusive. The ex-voto offerings traditional among this class of pilgrims, consisting prominently of wax or lead images of body parts, etc., signalling cures and other miraculous interventions, are almost never mentioned among the written evidence for Chartres Cathedral.[129] It is likely that they once

---

[128] See section above.

[129] This contrasts with, for example, the prominent Marian shrine at Le Puy, where there are many descriptions, as well as more material evidence, for the substantial accumulation of such ex-voto offerings. Paul and Paul, *Notre-Dame du Puy*, pp. 134–40. Many ex-votos were removed from the church at Le Puy on February

existed, since one of the miracles recounted by Jean Le Marchant in the mid-thirteenth century mentions 260 wax images placed on the altar of the cathedral by sufferers of "holy fire" who were subsequently cured.[130] Perhaps the most solid evidence for their continued existence at Chartres is a colored woodcut, dating from the late eighteenth century, depicting pilgrims, with their staffs and scrips, kneeling before *Notre-Dame du Pilier*, which is surrounded by such ex-voto offerings, including body parts, crutches, weapons, chemisettes, and hearts.[131] (fig. 98) This relatively naïve image seems intended for the popular market which it also represents.

The ex-votos, *oblationes*, and marks of devotion that made their way into the treasury were very different from such popular works and from pewter pilgrims' badges.[132] Some of them had monetary value, and it is evident that the treasury accumulated an extraordinarily rich collection of reliquaries and offerings. There was a permanent body of church wardens assigned to provide security for the treasury, and the threat of theft was so great that in 1357 the chapter ordered that they should maintain two dogs to guard the church.[133]

16, 1686, and given other developments at Chartres during the mid-seventeenth century, it is certainly possible that a similar removal took place there, too. However, Jean-Pierre Bénézet, *Pharmacie et médicament en Méditerranée occidentale (XIIIᵉ–XVIᵉ siècles)* (Paris, 1999), pp. 374–86, makes the point that body-part and animal ex-votos, largely made of wax, are more numerous in regions bordering the Mediterranean. This geographical distribution may reflect on the numerous references to such ex-votos in the late twelfth-century miracle collection from Rocamadour. Bull, *The Miracles of Our Lady of Rocamadour*, pp. 97, 107, 110, 113, 118, 123, 127, 135–36, 141, 146, 149, 155, 165–66, 170–72, 185–88, 190, 192.

[130] Kunstmann, ed. *Miracles de Notre-Dame de Chartres*, pp. 50, 238–41. This story inverts the usual votive nature of wax images, making them instrumental in the miraculous intervention rather than a gift of thanksgiving. The miracle account states that, to be effective, each image had to be worth at least three deniers.

[131] Delaporte, *Les Trois Notre-Dame*, pp. 49–51; Jusselin, *Imagiers et cartiers chartrains*, pp. 83–4, pl. V, VI.

[132] Edmond-René Labande, "'Ad limina': le pèlerin médiéval au terme de sa démarche," in Pierre Gallais and Yves-Jean Riou, eds, *Mélanges offerts à René Crozet à l'occasion de son soixante-dixième anniversaire*, 2 vols (Poitiers, 1966), I, p. 286, distinguishes between an ex-voto, which is a donation made in recognition of prayers answered, and an *oblatio*, which is a donation made in order to fulfil a vow. These could both include lands, rights and privileges, but only material objects will be considered here. It is often impossible to identify an offering clearly as either an ex-voto, an *oblatio*, or (as stated above fn. 130) a donation intended to encourage intervention.

[133] Mély, *Le trésor de Chartres*, pp. xxx–xxxi. In the chapter registers, there is a reference of December 5, 1358, to the *Sainte-Châsse* being replaced over the altar from where it had been hidden, and on May 7, 1360, it was ordered that the

There were several small chambers in the early sixteenth-century choir screen, finished in 1539, in which church wardens could sleep.[134] Another was designated as a treasury for the *Sainte-Châsse*, after repeated complaints of thefts.[135] Except for ostensions and processions, this became its permanent location, and on January 5, 1547, for the first time, the shrine was covered with a silk cloth for ostension, thus increasing its exclusivity.[136] This change in location of the *Sainte-Châsse*, which distanced the reliquary from direct access by the faithful, signalled a radical change of focus for pilgrims. The high altar ceased to be the central focus of the upper church, and it is tempting to interpret this as part of a deliberate plan of the cathedral chapter to control pilgrim traffic. In 1520, the high altar had been moved further east.[137] And the silver-gilt cult statue was moved with it. According to Delaporte, it still existed in the eighteenth century but had lost its celebrity as a cult object. Delaporte also suggested that the creation of *Notre-Dame-du-Pilier*, probably a polychrome wooden replica of the silver gilt image on the high altar, was intended to deflect pilgrims from the sanctuary towards the crossing.[138] It was set up on a pillar in front of the jubé and shortly afterwards began to attract considerable attention.[139] Lay admission to the sanctuary was also greatly reduced by the form of the new choir screen being built from *c.* 1515, in which lateral access was in all likelihood reduced from a full bay on either side of the sanctuary to a relatively small

Sainte-Châsse should be moved from where it had been hidden to be shown to Edward III, the king of England and his knights; Mély, *Le trésor de Chartres*, p. 106. The shrine was, thus, apparently hidden occasionally for special security reasons.

[134] In conversation with the author in June 2003, l'abbé Pierre Bizeau, the Diocesan Archivist, recalled that, when he was young, church wardens still slept in these chambers.

[135] Jean-Baptiste Souchet, *Histoire du diocèse et de la ville de Chartres*, III (Chartres, 1869), p. 572.

[136] Mély, *Le trésor de Chartres*, p. xxxvi.

[137] Delaporte, *Les Trois Notre-Dame*, p. 42. This was apparently related to the addition of six more stalls in the choir. Souchet, *Histoire du diocèse et de la ville de Chartres*, III, pp. 505–6.

[138] This was also the opinion of Roulliard, *Parthenie*, pp. 134–5, at the beginning of the seventeenth century.

[139] Delaporte, *Les Trois Notre-Dame*, p. 48. In 1522 or 1523 it was the object of Protestant vandalism. In 1524, a substantial ex-voto was donated to the statue by the Baron de Bueil (see my fig. 97). When the jubé was demolished on April 21, 1763, *Notre-Dame du Pilier* was moved against the northwest crossing pier, where it remained until 1791. Jusselin, *Imagiers et cartiers chartrain*, p. 83. In 1791, it was exchanged with *Notre-Dame de Sous-Terre*, which was destroyed by Revolutionaries shortly later, while *Notre-Dame du Pilier* went unnoticed in the crypt. It was moved to its present location in the north choir aisle in the early nineteenth century.

doorway, both of which were blocked up during the late eighteenth-century remodelling.

Before this time, and in a limited manner afterwards, the *Sainte-Châsse* was the material focus of noble devotion, gradually acquiring a substantial incrustation of precious oblations. (fig. 94) The earliest recorded gift consisted of two enamelled gold eagles, reputedly made by St. Eligius, donated by Rotelinde, the mother of Bishop Eudes, in the late eleventh century.[140] Among the known donors of precious materials to the *Sainte-Châsse*, noblewomen maintained a notable presence.[141] So, too, did the canons and bishops of the cathedral, and there were many local donations. Thus, while all of these precious objects signal devotion to the Holy Tunic, not all of them can unequivocally be said to constitute evidence of pilgrimage. Nevertheless, there are some high-profile objects that do signal pilgrimage activity. One of the few pieces to survive the destruction of the *Sainte-Châsse* in 1793 is a large cameo of Jupiter, which was set in gold and enriched with five balas rubies and twelve pearls.[142] This was donated by King Charles V in 1367, probably on his pilgrimage of June 30. In 1510, Queen Anne de Bretagne made a pilgrimage to Chartres and donated a very rich gold belt, encrusted with large numbers of rubies, sapphires, and pearls; it was attached around the base of the shrine.[143] Thus, even taking into account donations from a distance and political motivations for some donations, the rich holdings of the cathedral treasury can be said to measure substantial royal and noble interest in pilgrimage to Chartres Cathedral.[144]

---

[140] Mély, *Le trésor de Chartres*, pp. xvi, 28, 99.

[141] Mély, *Le trésor de Chartres*.

[142] Mély, *Le trésor de Chartres*, pp. 34–9, pl. X; Françoise Baron, et al., *Les fastes du gothique. Le siècle de Charles V* (Paris, 1981), pp. 208–9. It is now in the Cabinet des Médailles of the Bibliothèque Nationale in Paris. The rubies and pearls have been replaced by fleur-de-lys and dolphins. Several other cameos from the *Sainte-Châsse* also survive in the Cabinet des Médailles. Mély, *Le trésor de Chartres*, pl. IX, opposite p. 32.

[143] Mély, *Le trésor de Chartres*, pp. xxxvi–xxxvii, 17.

[144] Among politically motivated offerings to the cathedral treasury might be cited the rich donations made in 1384, 1404, and 1406 by Jean, the duke of Berry. Mély, *Le trésor de Chartres*, pp. xxii, xxvi, xxxii, 15–16, 33, 51–3, 108–9. They appear to have been at least partially motivated by the duke's political maneuverings. In 1407, Martin Gouge of Bourges was elected bishop of Chartres specifically on the recommendation of the duke of Berry; Souchet, *Histoire du diocèse et de la ville de Chartres*, III, p. 290. Souchet called Gouge the "créature" of the duke of Berry, and the political nature of his appointment is also signalled by his banishment from the realm in 1411; Souchet, *Histoire du diocèse et de la ville de Chartres*, III, p. 305.

As noted above, two specific contexts accounted for much of this noble and royal interest. One was military and the other had to do with childbirth. The latter is well-documented, but material evidence for it is elusive. The Jupiter cameo surviving from the *Sainte-Châsse*, given by King Charles V, has been related to a pilgrimage he made to Chartres in 1367 to invoke the Virgin's aid in providing him with an heir.[145] Many chemisettes and chemises that had been placed on the *Sainte-Châsse*, sometimes for a novena, were distributed by the chapter to noble women, particularly queens.[146] (fig. 95) The chemises were full-sized garments emulating the Holy Tunic while the chemisettes were small-scale replicas of it.[147] Challine, in the seventeenth century, stated that the manufacture of chemisettes in copper, silver, and gold by the goldsmiths of Chartres was prodigious.[148] Only some of these involved pilgrimage, with others being sent out from Chartres to distant recipients. Evidence of ex-votos is very rare, even in instances where a pilgrimage of thanksgiving is known to have been made. Moreover, most of the evidence which does survive is post-medieval. The treasury on the south side of the choir screen, for example, was fitted out by Queen Anne of Austria (r. 1615–66) specifically to thank the Virgin for the safe birth of a male child, the future Louis XIV (1638–1715), and on December 8, 1662, the queen and court made a pilgrimage of thanksgiving to Chartres, where the gift was made.[149]

---

[145] Baron, *Les fastes du gothique*, no. 168, pp. 208–9.

[146] Outside of the small collection in the Musée des Beaux-Arts at Chartres (*Trésors de la cathédrale de Chartres*, no. 2, pp. 51–3), evidence of only three chemisettes seems to have survived. For the two sent to the Jesuit missions in Québec, dated 1676 and 1679, see Marius Barbeau, *Trésor des anciens Jésuites* (Ottawa, 1957), pp. 42–9. For one apparently sent to "Marie-Anne, queen of Austria", now in the Musée historique at Orléans, see O. Raguenet de Saint-Albin, "Chemises de Chartres," *Revue de l'art chrétien* (1887), p. 95.

[147] The only physical evidence for a chemise, that is, an actual garment modelled on the Holy Tunic, consists of a drawing and description by Canon Léger-François Brillon (d. 1731) of the chemise formerly preserved in the church at Boncé, in the diocese of Chartres. Archives départementales d'Eure-et-Loir, G 440, reproduced in *Trésors de la cathédrale de Chartres*, p. 52.

[148] Challine, *Recherches sur Chartres*, p. 176.

[149] Challine, *Recherches sur Chartres*, p. 137; Challine's dates are suspicious, and he may have confused two different pilgrimages. Challine (d. 1678) would have witnessed this; he states that the queen donated 4,000 livres to build the treasury, which was finished in 1664. Earlier, Queen Marie de Medici (r. 1600–42) had similarly donated the north choir screen treasury, but her motivations were unrecorded and a pilgrimage specifically for this purpose is uncertain. She is known, however, to have gone on pilgrimage to Chartres in 1600, when the body of St. Piat was

One of the most tangible reminders of the Virgin's efficacy in providing royal heirs was a set of four silver lamps, which were believed to have miraculously lighted, without human agency, in 1186, as Queen Isabelle, or Elisabeth, de Hainaut, wife of King Philip Augustus, knelt in prayer before an image of the Virgin and for the first time felt a child stirring in her womb, the future Louis VIII (1187–1226).[150] In the 1682 inventory of canon Estienne, these four lamps surrounded the image of *Notre-Dame-du-Pilier* in front of the jubé.[151] (figs. 97–8)

A Thaumaturgical Museum

The crossing, in general, seems to have been a focus for noble ex-votos.[152] This is certainly evident with respect to those related to the Virgin's intervention in military affairs. There is much more evidence for military pilgrimage to Chartres, in documented instances of knights wearing into battle "chemises" that had touched the *Sainte-Châsse*, and in pilgrimages of thanksgiving for battles won, for miraculous protection and for release from captivity.[153] The *Vieille Chronique*

---

monstrated privately for her, and her son, Louis XIII, was born the next year. Challine, *Recherches sur Chartres*, p. 187.

[150] Souchet, *Histoire du diocèse et de la ville de Chartres*, II, p. 518. The earliest source for this miracle is the poem by Guillaume le Breton, *La Philippide*, written probably in the 1220s; it occurs in neither of the Chartres miracle collections. Guizot, ed., *La Philippide*, p. 387. Vincent Sablon, *Histoire et description de l'église cathédrale de Chartres, dédiée par les druides à une vierge qui devait enfanter, Revue et augmentée D'une description de l'Église de Sous-Terre et d'un récit de l'incendie de 1836*, ed. Lucien Merlet (1671; Chartres, 1860), p. 179, and Lépinois, *Histoire de Chartres*, I, p. 114, both mistakenly give the date as 1188. In 1682, canon Estienne appears to have believed that the lighted lamps themselves miraculously appeared to the queen.

[151] Mély, *Le trésor de Chartres*, pp. 97–8. Given the relationship between *Notre-Dame du Pilier* and the silver gilt image on the high altar during the Middle Ages, this suggests that the queen was kneeling before the high altar, but it is not known whether the image donated in 1220 replaced an older image that, perhaps, did not survive the fire of 1194.

[152] Jung, "Beyond the Barrier," p. 629, points out that this was a common location for the accumulation of votive images. See also Lenz Kriss-Rettenbeck, *Ex-voto: Zeichen, Bild und Abbild im christlichen Votivbrauchtum* (Zurich, 1972). Jung, "Beyond the Barrier," p. 634, further recalls that, among the surviving relief sculptures of the jubé, which was demolished in 1763, the Nativity features Mary dressed in a substantial garment that could not help but recall the *Sainte Chemise*.

[153] The prominence of the military saints George and Eustace in the early thirteenth-century stained glass (Windows 43, 112, 115, 133) and sculpture (the outer jamb figures of the Martyrs Portal on the south transept) of Chartres Cathedral

of 1387 mentions many instances of knights touching their "chemises" to the *Sainte-Châsse* for thaumaturgical protection. One story mentioned in the thirteenth-century miracle collections involves a knight of Aquitaine being saved from the blows of his enemies by a "chemise" he took on pilgrimage to Chartres and touched to the *Sainte-Châsse* as he passed under it,[154] and Challine claimed that a "chemise" made in imitation of that of the Virgin was worn by King Richard the Lionheart of England (r. 1189–99).[155] Several subsequent protection miracles were also attributed to "chemises" of Chartres, and two of them, at least, resulted in ex-votos, the best known of which resulted from an incident in the French siege of Milan in 1523, when the Baron du Bueil, wearing a "chemise" from Chartres, was shot, but the bullet did not injure him. On January 5, 1524, he made a pilgrimage of thanksgiving to Chartres, and attached the intact "chemise," his other garments that the bullet pierced and the bullet, as well, to the crossing pier in front of *Notre-Dame-du-Pilier*.[156] (fig. 97) In 1591, another bullet, fired during the siege of Chartres by King Henri IV (r. 1589–1610), was attached to the pier.[157] By this time, the crossing had already accumulated several other ex-votos.[158]

The most prominent ex-voto (or *oblatio*) was a full-sized polychrome wooden equestrian statue of a French king, who has variously been

---

also attests military devotion at Chartres. James Bugslag, "St. Eustace and St. George: Crusading Saints in the Sculpture and Stained Glass of Chartres Cathedral," *Zeitschrift für Kunstgeschichte* 66, no. 4 (2003) pp. 441–64. The axial chevet chapel dedicated to the Apostles was also known as the Chapelle des Chevalliers because of a foundation made in the chapel by Bureau de la Rivière and other knights, in order to give thanks for a military victory on Cyprus during the Crusades. Challine, *Recherches sur Chartres*, p. 150.

[154] Thomas, ed., "Les Miracles de Notre Dame de Chartres," pp. 526–7; Kunstmann, ed., *Miracles de Notre-Dame de Chartres*, pp. 41, 167–9. This miracle is also included as Miracle No. CXLVIII in the *Cantigas de Santa Maria; Cantigas de Santa Maria de Don Alfonso el Sabio*, 2 vols (Madrid, 1889). Both of the Chartres miracle collections also recount a miracle in which a knight loses his horse's bit during a tournament, and the Virgin miraculously restores it, after the knight invoked Our Lady of Chartres.

[155] Challine, *Recherches sur Chartres*, p. 216.

[156] Souchet, *Histoire du diocèse et de la ville de Chartres*, III, p. 517. A similar miracle apparently took place in 1558 at Calais, but there is no record of an ex-voto offering. Jean-Baptiste Souchet, *Histoire du diocèse et de la ville de Chartres*, IV (Chartres, 1873), pp. 12–13.

[157] Souchet, *Histoire du diocèse et de la ville de Chartres*, IV, pp. 208–9.

[158] Small chemisettes were also considered to have thaumaturgical power. Challine, *Recherches sur Chartres*, p. 176, in the mid-seventeenth century, claims to have sent dozens of chemisettes to the knights of Malta.

identified as Philippe le Bel (r. 1285–1314) and Philippe de Valois (r. 1328–50). Souchet, in the mid-seventeenth century, gave an eye-witness description of it, but even at that time it was falling to pieces and disappeared soon afterwards. It appears to have been placed before the northeast crossing pier.[159] Although there are no known antiquarian depictions, it must have looked somewhat like the equestrian statue in Notre-Dame, Paris, which has been attributed to the same two kings.[160] Philippe le Bel is known to have made pilgrimages of thanksgiving to Chartres and to Paris after his victory at Mons-en-Pévèle on August 18, 1304. At Chartres, he assigned an annuity of 100 livres parisis to found the service of *Notre-Dame de la Victoire* on the anniversary of the battle.[161] For his part, Philippe de Valois made pilgrimages of thanksgiving to Saint-Denis, Notre-Dame in Paris, and Chartres after his victory at the Battle of Cassel on August 23, 1328. Apparently, in both Paris and Chartres, the king, in full armor, rode through the doors and up the nave to the jubé, where he dismounted and offered his warhorse and armor to the Virgin. He subsequently ransomed them back for 1000 livres.[162] Arguments can be made for either king, but one of them certainly donated the statue, which created a highly visible memorial of royal pilgrimage at a very prominent location within the public space of the church.

This, moreover, was not the only equestrian image at Chartres during the later Middle Ages. Smaller-scale equestrian statues in precious metals were also donated to the cathedral, and although the circumstances of the donations are unclear, they may well have been

---

[159] Souchet, *Histoire du diocèse et de la ville de Chartres*, III, pp. 101–2: "contre le pillier de la chapelle Sainte Anne"—"against the pier of the chapel of St. Anne."

[160] Françoise Baron, "Le cavalier royal de Notre-Dame de Paris et le problème de la statue équestre au moyen âge," *Bulletin monumental* 127 (1968), 141–54. The statue in Notre-Dame, Paris, survived until the Revolution, and several depictions of it exist.

[161] This was a substantial sum in the early fourteenth century. Souchet, *Histoire du diocèse et de la ville de Chartres*, III, pp. 101–02. According to Lépinois, *Histoire de Chartres*, I, p. 165, the annuity charter was signed in Lille only a few days after the battle; Pintard, however, states that the king also made a pilgrimage to Chartres. The service of *Notre-Dame de la Victoire* was celebrated at Chartres on August 16–17 until the Revolution, presumably to associate it more closely with the Feast of the Assumption on August 15, the major feast day of the year at Chartres. The king founded comparable services at Saint-Denis and Paris, celebrated on August 18.

[162] Souchet, *Histoire du diocèse et de la ville de Chartres*, III, 152–54; Lépinois, *Histoire de Chartres*, I, pp. 2–3.

ex-votos.[163] As early as 1219, Gauthier "le Jeune" de Villebéon, chamberlain of King Philip Augustus, donated a silver candle holder in the form an equestian warrior, weighing thirty marcs,[164] and in the early fourteenth century, there was also a silver equestrian statue of a knight of the Harcourt family.[165] Added to these three-dimensional examples are a considerable number of images of armed equestrian knights in the stained glass of the cathedral, particularly in the choir and transept clerestory, dating from the early thirteenth century; these various images certainly signal knightly devotion, but it is currently impossible to relate any of them specifically to pilgrimage.[166]

Further royal ex-votos could also be seen in the crossing. Several pieces of royal armor survive in the cathedral treasury, and during the later Middle Ages, they were set up on the jubé.[167] (fig. 99) These consist principally of a basinet with an attached coat of chain mail and a considerably smaller "brigandine" and "jaque" in red velvet and brocade, along with several pieces of a child's armor.[168] Like the royal equestrian statue, these pieces have been variously attributed, but since they can be dated by style to the period 1370–1400, the basinet and hauberk may well signal an ex-voto of King Charles V (r. 1364–80), and the smaller items may be connected with the young Charles VI (b. 1368; r. 1380–1422). Wemaëre convincingly relates

[163] Kriss-Rettenbeck, *Ex-voto*, pp. 277–8, fig. 72–5, gives several examples of votive images of knights, including equestrian examples.

[164] Mély, *Le trésor de Chartres*, p. xviii; Lépinois and Merlet, eds, *Cartulaire*, III, p. 153. Since he also funded a candle to burn perpetually before the *Sainte-Châsse*, it seems likely that this candleholder was located at the high altar. Baron, "Le cavalier royal de Notre-Dame de Paris," pp. 151–2, following Souchet, *Histoire du diocèse et de la ville de Chartres*, III, p. 2, attributes the donation to Gaucher de Bar-sur-Seine, son of a vicomte de Chartres, dating it to 1219.

[165] Baron, "Le cavalier royal de Notre-Dame de Paris," p. 152; Mély, *Le trésor de Chartres*, pp. 100–1; this was first mentioned in the chapter registers of 1310 and appeared, as well, in the treasury inventory of 1322. In 1300 the private council of the count of Chartres included the knight, G. de Harcourt (first name unspecified); Lépinois, *Histoire de Chartres*, I, pp. 165–6.

[166] Some relation to crusading, however, does seem likely. Françoise Perrot, "Le vitrail, la croisade et la Champagne: réflexion sur les fenêtres hautes du choeur à la cathédrale de Chartres," in *Les Champenois et la croisade*, eds, Y. Bellenger and D. Quéruel (Paris, 1989), pp. 109–30.

[167] J. Wemaëre, "Les armures royales du Trésor de Chartres," *Monuments historiques de la France* (1974), 57–62; Baron, *Les fastes du gothique*, no. 343–5, pp. 403–5; *Trésors de la Cathédrale de Chartres*, pp. 63–71.

[168] There was also a gold crown on the basinet, which was melted down in 1792, along with other precious metalwork. Wemaëre, "Les armures royales du Trésor de Chartres," p. 58.

the latter with the pilgrimage of thanksgiving made by the young King Charles VI in 1383, after his victory at the Battle of Roosebeke on November 27, 1382.[169] Together with the equestrian statue and, later, the bullets and chemises that were to appear in the crossing, these military vestments signalled, in a highly public manner, the thaumaturgical aid in battle associated with Notre-Dame de Chartres.

One further *oblatio* that could also be seen in the crossing was a memorial of one of the best documented pilgrimages to Chartres from the late Middle Ages. This, too, was associated with quasi-military thaumaturgical aid, but focused on the release of a prisoner rather than with protection against arms or victory. This sort of intervention was commonly associated with the Virgin in general, and with Notre-Dame de Chartres in particular.[170] On the eve of the feast of the Ascension on May 31, 1413, Louis de Bourbon, count of Vendôme and lord of Epernon and Montdoubleau, made a pilgrimage of thanksgiving to Chartres, to fulfil a vow made during his several months' captivity by his brother.[171] After offering a candle to the image of Notre-Dame at the jubé, barefoot and dressed only in his shirt, he declared himself the vassal of Notre-Dame and financed the construction of a substantial chapel between two nave buttresses off the south aisle, (fig. 96, no. 64) providing it with generous endowments. The charter of donation was signed on June 2, 1413, and to mark the occasion, he had an effigy of himself, holding a candle, set up before the jubé image of the Virgin.[172] Thus, increasingly, the crossing of the cathedral played a significant role in pilgrimage to Chartres and it accumulated a considerable number of material

---

[169] Wemaëre, "Les armures royales du Trésor de Chartres," p. 59; Souchet, *Histoire du diocèse et de la ville de Chartres*, III, p. 248; Philip the Bold, the duke of Burgundy, with many of his knights, had already made a pilgrimage of thanksgiving to Chartres late in 1382, after the Battle of Roosebeke. Philip donated a gold lamp placed before "l'image de Nostre-Dame, qui est dans la nef"—"the statue of Notre Dame which is in the nave."

[170] After the treaty of Brétigny—signed near Chartres in 1360 and also attributed to the miraculous intervention of Notre-Dame de Chartres—King Jean le Bon was released from captivity in England and made a pilgrimage of thanksgiving on his return, to Notre-Dame de Boulogne, Saint-Denis, and Chartres. Souchet, *Histoire du diocèse et de la ville de Chartres*, III, p. 213. Notre-Dame de Chartres was also credited with saving the lives of the lord of Coucy and several of his companions who were captured at the Battle of Nicopolis in 1396; Souchet, *Histoire du diocèse et de la ville de Chartres*, III, pp. 278–81.

[171] Bulteau, *Monographie*, I, pp. 147–50; Lépinois, *Histoire de Chartres*, II, pp. 66–7.

[172] Souchet, *Histoire du diocèse et de la ville de Chartres*, III, pp. 309–13.

reminders of such visits. With all of the images and ex-votos that gradually accumulated there, it must have resembled a sort of thaumaturgical museum, right at the center of the most public space within the cathedral, in which the kings and nobles of France were highly apparent.

The Role of the Cathedral Chapter

The Vendôme Chapel (1413–17) is remarkable for being the only private chapel to have appeared in Chartres Cathedral which involved a building campaign and a separate architectural identity,[173] though quite a few other private chapels were established at altars built against piers, etc. Vincent Sablon, in the late seventeenth century, enumerated thirty-eight altars in the upper church and another thirteen in the crypt,[174] the majority of which were removed in 1661.[175] These altars deserve a separate study; at present it is difficult to estimate how many of the devotional motivations behind them were the result of pilgrimage. This, as we have seen, is a consistent problem in reconstructing pilgrimage activity at Chartres. Many altars, in fact, were founded by the canons themselves, who had institutional motivations quite apart from those of pilgrims. Chartres was known in Rome as the "grand diocèse" and had one of the largest and wealthiest chapters in France. Thus, institutional factors must always be borne in mind in considering the material generosity showered on the church and its treasury. On the other hand, nobles, in particular, often had political motivations for their material generosity, and

---

[173] There appears to have been some sort of construction between the two nave piers from the thirteenth century, which was adapted at this time. Anne Prache, "La chapelle de Vendôme à la cathédrale de Chartres et l'art flamboyant en Île-de-France," *Jahrbuch für Kunstgeschichte* 47–8 (1993–94), 569–75; Delaporte and Houvet, *Les vitraux de la cathédrale de Chartres*, pp. 176–89. Ironically, Louis de Bourbon was taken captive at the Battle of Agincourt in 1415 and not released until 1422; this did not affect the construction of his chapel at Chartres.

[174] Sablon, *Histoire et description de l'église cathédrale de Chartres*, pp. 31–7, 53–64. See the plan of altars in the upper church at the beginning of the seventeenth century in Lautier, "Les vitraux de la cathédrale de Chartres. Reliques et images," p. 20.

[175] On May 16, the doors of the cathedral were closed for several days, during which the removals took place. Challine, *Recherches sur Chartres*, p. 152. It would appear that the canons anticipated substantial opposition to this dramatic alteration and decided to carry it out under a shroud of secrecy.

it is often virtually impossible to discern the intentions behind noble donations.

Yet, however cautiously one approaches the problem, it cannot be doubted that Chartres was something substantially more than a minor pilgrimage shrine. While it may not have been able to compete in sheer numbers of pilgrims with many major shrines in Europe through the later Middle Ages, the cathedral was widely considered as an important site of Marian presence, and there would appear to have been a great deal of pilgrimage activity there during the late Middle Ages, probably beginning during the course of the eleventh century, as witnessed by Bishop Fulbert's huge, new church. Although the popular aspects of pilgrimage were perhaps greatest during the ergot epidemics of the twelfth century, the major feast days of the Virgin continued to attract crowds.[176] Nevertheless, if the material evidence for popular pilgrimage is elusive, one of the reasons appears to involve the attitude of the chapter towards the popular use of their church. They appear to have been concerned, not so much to encourage pilgrimage, as to control it. There is little evidence that the chapter encouraged pilgrimage after the appearance of the thirteenth-century miracle collections, the first of which was undoubtedly prompted by the need to raise building funds. Towards the end of the Middle Ages, their attitude appears to have changed diametrically. The displacement of the *Sainte-Châsse* from the high altar in the mid-sixteenth century and the setting up of *Notre-Dame du Pilier* on the jubé appear to have been motivated by a desire to deflect crowds from the sanctuary, and the seventeenth-century suppression of altars and demolition of the *Puits des Saints-Forts* certainly channelled the attention of pilgrims in more manageable, and more theologically acceptable directions.

There appears to have been substantial differences between the attitude of the chapter to popular pilgrimage and to noble pilgrimage.

---

[176] The four principal fairs held at Chartres coincided with the major Marian feasts of the Purification of the Virgin (February 2), the Annunciation (March 25), the Assumption of the Virgin (August 15), and the Nativity of the Virgin (September 8). Otto von Simson, *The Gothic Cathedral: Origins of Gothic Architecture and the Medieval Concept of Order* (Princeton, 1988), pp. 166–7; Chédeville, *Chartres et ses campagnes*, pp. 458–60, 480, 523. According to Chédeville, von Simson greatly overestimates the financial advantage of these fairs, and he may well have overestimated, as well, the afflux of pilgrims they regularly attracted. The fairs at Chartres need further systematic study.

While the former needed controlling, the latter was encouraged and undoubtedly dovetailed with many other institutional motivations on the part of the cathedral chapter. The difference in attitude towards popular and noble pilgrims can be seen in the description of the 1591 display of St. Piat's relics in the cathedral. On October 6, at the request of the Cardinal de Bourbon, the reliquary of St. Piat was removed from its place in the axial treasury and placed on a table in the middle of the choir, where it was opened, and then carried to the sacristy where the next day the body was examined by high-ranking ecclesiastics who found it miraculously incorrupt. The next day, it was carried to the axial chevet chapel where it was displayed until evening. Several representatives of the chapter and an armed guard were on hand to protect it from the crowds of people who came to see it. Then, it was taken to the chapter house where it stayed for three days, during which nobles could pay their devotions.[177] This constitutes clear evidence that pilgrimage was managed at Chartres on a two-tiered scheme, and that noble pilgrimage was favored over that of the masses. Moreover, noble pilgrimage left highly visible traces in the public spaces of the church.

Conclusions

Chartres Cathedral cannot simply be regarded, as is usual, as a "typical" High Gothic cathedral. It is more correct to regard it as a double church, with distinctive upper and lower levels, each of which functioned in different ways to construct a powerful and varied experience for pilgrims. That experience was hierarchical, the upper church partaking of the heavenly purity of the Virgin Mary herself, while the lower church registered chthonic elements—the grotto, the water source—that defined many medieval pilgrimage sites, and particularly Marian shrines.[178] The absorption of the eleventh-century cult statue of *Notre-Dame de Sous-Terre* into this chthonic realm by the

---

[177] Souchet, *Histoire du diocèse et de la ville de Chartres*, pp. 271–2.

[178] Cassagnes-Brouquet, *Vierges noires*, as mentioned previously. The combination of relics, images, grottoes (or crypts) and miraculous springs or wells also occurred at Marian sites within the Byzantine Empire, such as the Blachernai Church in Constantinople and the monastery of Mega Spelaion in Greece. Lidov, "Miracle-Working Icons of the Mother of God," p. 54.

creative extension of its history back beyond the time of Christ is a highly distinctive aspect of the lower church. Alphonse Dupront has stressed the individuality of Marian cult sites which, nonetheless, was manifested within a proscribed range of elements: the socialization of the site, its appropriation by ecclesiastical institutions, its spatial composition, natural or artificial features in varying combinations, the surrounding environment, a more or less secular history, and finally, and above all, the religious or mythic consciousness of the consecration of the site.[179] Chartres constitutes a combination consisting of a small but important natural element—the *Puits des Saints-Forts*, in its crypt, or "grotto"—together with a magificent built environment replete with imagery (and conditioned by the presence of a powerful ecclesiastical institution) that encouraged a distinctive pilgrimage experience. Much documentary research is still necessary to fully recover the phenomenon of pilgrimage to Chartres during the later Middle Ages, but, as I hope to have shown, the visual evidence available for such a study has considerable potential.

---

[179] Alphonse Dupront, *Du sacré. Croisades et pèlerinages. Images et langages* (Paris, 1987), pp. 33, 37–8.

PART III

EXPERIENCE AND ICONOGRAPHY AT PILGRIMAGE CENTERS:
DISCERNING MEANING

CHAPTER EIGHT

THE JOURNEY TO EMMAUS CAPITAL AT SAINT-LAZARE OF AUTUN

William J. Travis

Deep in the choir of the Romanesque pilgrimage Church of St.-Lazare at Autun in Burgundy is a remarkable capital from the early twelfth century, which is usually attributed to the sculptor Gislebertus.[1] (figs. 100–102) Its subject is the Journey to Emmaus, an extraordinary tale from Luke, where we learn that, a few days after the Crucifixion, two men meet up with the resurrected Christ on the road to Emmaus. Failing at first to recognize their traveling companion, they ask if he is a stranger and invite him to dine at Emmaus, only to discover who he really is at the precise moment when Christ breaks bread, at which point he disappears from their sight and ascends into Heaven. Focusing on the Journey, rather than the Supper, the capital portrays the encounter (main side), Emmaus (right side), and an angel (left side). If a journey is inherently sympathetic to pilgrimage, the Journey to Emmaus was especially so for medieval audiences because of the precise wording of the men's conversation with Christ. Thus their question: *tu solus peregrinus es in Hierusalem* or, "art thou only a stranger in Jerusalem?"[2] may have seemed simple enough when the Vulgate Bible first appeared in the fourth century, but as the word *peregrinus* later came to mean pilgrim, this question in the Middle Ages would have implied that Christ traveled as a

---

[1] Precise dating of Romanesque sculpture in Burgundy is still unresolved, so I have used broad chronological terms, such as early, middle, or late twelfth century, in this essay. Matters of attribution are also controversial. Linda Seidel, *Legends in Limestone: Lazarus, Gislebertus, and the Cathedral of Autun* (Chicago, 1999) argued that the name inscribed on the main lintel does not refer to the sculptor (*GISLEBERTUS HOC FECIT*, Gislebertus made this). This was earlier claimed by Raymond Oursel in "Autun," *Dictionnaire des églises de France*, Paris, 1966, vol. 2A, p. 11, but I find the evidence unconvincing. Until the matter is settled, I think it best to refer to the sculptor as Gislebertus.

[2] In Luke's original Greek: Συ μονος παροικεις Ιερουσαλημ; Luke 24.18.

pilgrim. So the Journey to Emmaus, as depicted here, was at heart
a pilgrimage story and the Church of St.-Lazare at Autun was a pilgrimage church. How these two factors—story and place—played
off one another in a single capital is the subject of this inquiry.

Beautifully carved and generally well-preserved, the capital consists of two limestone blocks, joined at a point slightly above the
principal characters' feet.[3] The Church of St.-Lazare, where the capital appears *in situ*, was consecrated in 1130 by Pope Innocent II.[4]
Intended from the start as a pilgrimage church, it housed the relics
of its patron saint in the now largely-destroyed "tomb of St. Lazarus."[5]
In 1195 the church became an "alternative cathedral" with St.-
Nazaire in the same city, a title it held until 1770, when the latter
was razed and St.-Lazare became Autun's sole cathedral.[6]

The state of research on our capital can be summarized quickly.
For the Abbé Devoucoux, earliest connoisseur of Romanesque Autun,
it represented Christ Healing the Blind, Sick, and Possessed (main
side), Rachel Bemoaning the Death of her Children (right side), and
Angels (left side).[7] Victor Terret later identified the same capital as
the Healing of the Blind Man of Jericho (main side) and the Meeting
of Jesus and Zacchaeus (right side).[8] In 1961, George Zarnecki over-
turned these interpretations by arguing that the sculpture represented
the Journey to Emmaus.[9] Since then no one has seriously challenged
its identification, although scholars have read additional meanings
into the scene, such as Hélène Setlak-Garrison, who argued that here
the Journey alludes to the Last Judgment.[10] None of these scholars

---

[3] On the the capital's state of preservation, see Denis Grivot and George Zarnecki,
Gislebertus: Sculptor of Autun (New York, 1961), pp. 63, 82, fig. 2.

[4] The ceremony took place during reign of bishop Etienne de Bâgé. For a summary of the building history, see Grivot and Zarnecki, *Gislebertus*, pp. 17–9. Perpendicular to the Cathedral of St.-Nazaire, St.-Lazare is unusual for its north-south
orientation.

[5] *Le Tombeau de Saint Lazare et la sculpture romane à Autun après Gislebertus* (Autun,
1985), with further bibliography.

[6] Charles Boëll, "Le huitième centenaire de la consécration de la cathédrale,"
Semaine religieuse d'Autun, Chalon et Mâcon, 58/18 (April 30, 1932), unpaginated.

[7] Abbé Devoucoux, *Description de l'église cathédrale d'Autun* (Autun, 1845), pp. 59–60.

[8] Victor Terret, *La sculpture bourguignonne aux XIIe et XIIIe siècles: ses origines et ses
sources d'inspiration: Autun*, vol. 2 (Autun, 1925), pp. 42–3.

[9] Grivot and Zarnecki, *Gislebertus*, pp. 63–4.

[10] Devoucoux launched the discussion, Terret speculated on broader symbolic
connections, Zarnecki corrected the iconography, and Hélène Sylvie Setlak-Garrison,
The Capitals of St.-Lazare at Autun: Their Relationship to the Last Judgment Portal (Ph.D.

explored the pilgrimage subject of the capital and its placement in a pilgrimage church at any length. I will analyze the capital in terms of this critical connection, developing four interlocking themes: the scriptural basis for the scene, the iconographic innovations, the appeal to an audience, and the idea of travel. Approached in this way, our capital may also open up new ways to think about medieval pilgrimage art, by showing how style, iconography, and physical placement collaborated in bringing the pilgrim into the work of art.[11]

Scriptural Background

With the Marys at the Sepulcher and the Appearance of Christ to Peter, the Journey to Emmaus is one of three stories Luke told about Christ's Resurrection, but unlike the Marys (who found an empty tomb) and unlike the Appearance to Peter (which we hear of second-hand), the Emmaus narrative alone provides an eyewitness account of the risen Christ.[12] The Journey is also the only Resurrection story where the encounter takes place *on the road* and where Christ appears

diss., UCLA, 1984), pp. 97–9 stressed the specificity of their message to St.-Lazare. Other scholars accepting Zarnecki's reading include: Francis Salet, "La sculpture romane en Bourgogne: à propos d'un livre récent," *Bulletin Monumental* 119 (1961), p. 334; James R. Blaettler, *Through Emmaus Eyes: Art, Liturgy, and Monastic Ideology at Santo Domingo de Silos* (Ph.D. diss., University of Chicago, 1989), pp. 12–3; Brian Young, *The Villein's Bible: Stories in Romanesque Carving* (London, 1990), pp. 117–8; and William J. Travis, "The Iconography of the Choir Capitals at Saint-Lazare at Autun and the Anagogical Way in Romanesque Sculpture," *Konsthistorisk Tidskrift*, 68/4 (1999): 220–49. Denis Grivot, *Le monde d'Autun*, 2nd ed. (La Pierre-qui-Vire: Zodiaque, 1965), pp. 89–91 followed Terret's identification.

[11] See *Contesting the Sacred: The Anthropology of Christian Pilgrimage*, eds. John Eade and Michael J. Sallnow (London, 1991) and Victor and Edith Turner, *Image and Pilgrimage in Christian Culture: Anthropological Perspectives* (New York, 1978).

[12] The Incredulity of Thomas provides another "eyewitness account," but appears only in John 20.19–29. For the Journey to Emmaus in biblical scholarship, see Arthur A. Just, Jr., *The Ongoing Feast: Table Fellowship and Eschatology at Emmaus* (Collegeville, MN, 1993); Jan Wojcik, *The Road to Emmaus: Reading Luke's Gospel* (West Lafayette, IN, 1989); Louis Dussaut, "Le triptyque des apparitions en Luc 24 (analyse structurelle)," *Revue biblique* 94 (1987): 161–213; Lucien Legrand, "Deux voyages: Lc 2, 41–50; 24, 13–33," in *À cause de l'Evangile: Etudes sur les Synoptiques et les Actes* (Paris, 1985), pp. 409–29; Joseph A. Fitzmyer, *The Gospel According to Luke (X–XXIV)*, Anchor Bible 28A (Garden City, NY, 1985), pp. 1553–72; Bernard P. Robinson, "The Place of the Emmaus Story in Luke-Acts," *New Testament Studies* 30/4 (1984): 481–497; Jacques Dupont, "Les disciples d'Emmaüs (Lc 24, 13–35)," in *La Pâque du Christ: Mystère et salut* (Paris, 1982), pp. 167–95.

as a pilgrim. No other biblical tale had as strong a claim on pilgrims. Citing the scriptural text in full will give us an opportunity to explore what it said, what it neglected to say, and how Gislebertus filled in the gap:

> And behold, two of them went, the same day, to a town which was sixty furlongs from Jerusalem, named Emmaus. [13]
>
> And they talked together of all these things which had happened. [14]
>
> And it came to pass, that while they talked and reasoned with themselves, Jesus himself also drawing near, went with them. [15]
>
> But their eyes were held, that they should not know him. [16]
>
> And he said to them: What are these discourses that you hold one with another as you walk, and are sad? [17]
>
> And the one of them, whose name was Cleophas, answering, said to him: Art thou only a stranger [*peregrinus*] in Jerusalem, and hast not known the things that have been done there in these days? [18]
>
> To whom he said: What things? And they said: Concerning Jesus of Nazareth, who was a prophet, mighty in work and word before God and all the people; [19]
>
> And how our chief priests and princes delivered him to be condemned to death, and crucified him. [20]
>
> But we hoped, that it was he that should have redeemed Israel: and now besides all this,
>
> today is the third day since these things were done. [21]
>
> Yea and certain women also of our company affrighted us, who before it was light, were at the sepulcher, [22]
>
> And not finding his body, came, saying, that they had also seen a vision of angels, who say that he is alive. [23]
>
> And some of our people went to the sepulcher, and found it so as the women had said, but him they found not. [24]
>
> Then he said to them: O foolish, and slow of heart to believe in all things which the prophets have spoken. [25]
>
> Ought not Christ to have suffered these things, and so to enter into his glory? [26]
>
> And beginning at Moses and all the prophets, he expounded to them in all the scriptures, the things that were concerning him. [27]
>
> And they drew nigh to the town, whither they were going: and he made as though he would go farther. [28]
>
> But they constrained him; saying: Stay with us, because it is towards evening, and the day is now far spent. And he went in with them. [29]
>
> And it came to pass, whilst he was at table with them, he took bread, and blessed, and brake, and gave to them. [30]
>
> And their eyes were opened, and they knew him: and he vanished out of their sight. [31]
>
> And they said one to the other: Was not our heart burning within us, whilst he spoke in the way, and opened to us the scriptures? [32]

And rising up, the same hour, they went back to Jerusalem: and they
found the eleven gathered together, and those that were with them,
[33]
Saying: The Lord is risen indeed, and hath appeared to Simon. [34]
And they told what things were done in the way; and how they knew
him in the breaking of bread. [35] Luke 24.13–35[13]

---

[13] *et ecce duo ex illis ibant ipsa die in castellum quod erat in spatio stadiorum sexaginta ab
    Hierusalem nomine Emmaus [13]*

  et ipsi loquebantur ad invicem de his omnibus quae acciderant [14]

  *et factum est dum fabularentur et secum quaererent et ipse Iesus adpropinquans ibat cum
    illis [15]*

  oculi autem illorum tenebantur ne eum agnoscerent [16]

  *et ait ad illos qui sunt hii sermones quos confertis ad invicem ambulantes et estis tristes
    [17]*

  *et respondens unus cui nomen Cleopas dixit ei tu solus peregrinus es in Hierusalem et non
    cognovisti quae facta sunt in illa his diebus [18]*

  *quibus ille dixit quae et dixerunt de Iesu Nazareno qui fuit vir propheta potens in opere et
    sermone coram Deo et omni populo [19]*

  *et quomodo eum tradiderunt summi sacerdotum et principes nostri in damnationem mortis et
    crucifixerunt eum [20]*

  *nos autem sperabamus quia ipse esset redempturus Israhel et nunc super haec omnia tertia
    dies hodie quod haec facta sunt [21]*

  *sed et mulieres quaedam ex nostris terruerunt nos quae ante lucem fuerunt ad monumentum
    [22]*

  *et non invento corpore eius venerunt dicentes se etiam visionem angelorum vidisse qui dicunt
    eum vivere [23]*

  *et abierunt quidam ex nostris ad monumentum et ita invenerunt sicut mulieres dixerunt ipsum
    vero non viderunt [24]*

  *et ipse dixit ad eos o stulti et tardi corde ad credendum in omnibus quae locuti sunt prophetae
    [25]*

  nonne haec oportuit pati Christum et ita intrare in gloriam suam [26]

  *et incipiens a Mose et omnibus prophetis interpretabatur illis in omnibus scripturis quae de
    ipso erant [27]*

  et adpropinquaverunt castello quo ibant et ipse se finxit longius ire [28]

  *et coegerunt illum dicentes mane nobiscum quoniam advesperascit et inclinata est iam dies
    et intravit cum illis [29]*

  *et factum est dum recumberet cum illis accepit panem et benedixit ac fregit et porrigebat illis
    [30]*

  et aperti sunt oculi eorum et cognoverunt eum et ipse evanuit ex oculis eorum [31]

  *et dixerunt ad invicem nonne cor nostrum ardens erat in nobis dum loqueretur in via et
    aperiret nobis scripturas [32]*

  *et surgentes eadem hora regressi sunt in Hierusalem et invenerunt congregatos undecim et eos
    qui cum ipsis erant [33]*

  dicentes quod surrexit Dominus vere et apparuit Simoni [34]

  *et ipsi narrabant quae gesta erant in via et quomodo cognoverunt eum in fractione panis
    [35]*

The Scriptural quotes in this essay are from the Vulgate Bible and the translations
from the *Douay-Rheims Bible*, the sixteenth-century English translation of the Vulgate
(Los Angeles, 1912).

On the surface, the tale is a straightforward account arranged in three parts:

1) the adventure on the road where two men tell Christ about the Crucifixion and the empty tomb and Christ expounds on Scripture (verses 13–27),
2) the episode of recognition, at Emmaus, where Christ breaks bread and disappears (verses 28–31)
3) the epilogue, at Jerusalem, where the two men tell the apostles of their encounter and hear that Simon, too, has seen Christ (verses 32–35).[14]

Building suspense from initial encounter to sudden disappearance, Luke tells a gripping story. For anyone seeking a deeper or more precise meaning of the event, however, the bare-bones account opens up gaping holes, contradictions, and multiple interpretations.[15] How long, for instance, did Christ remain on earth before his Ascension— three days as implied here, or forty days as stated in Acts 1.3? Where was Emmaus—sixty furlongs from Jerusalem (about seven miles), or 160 furlongs, as described by Near Eastern editors who knew the territory better?[16] What did the breaking of bread signify—a simple meal or the Eucharist, and, if the latter, how could two men not present at the Last Supper have known of it? Who were these men?

---

[14] The Emmaus tale also appears briefly in Mark 16.12: "And after that he appeared in another shape to two of them walking, as they were going into the country."

[15] For medieval interpretations, see Ludger Thier, "Christus Peregrinus: Christus als Pilger in der Sicht von Theologen, Predigern und Mystikern des Mittelalters," in *Ecclesia Peregrinans: Josef Lenzenweger zum 70. Geburtstag*, eds. Karl Amon *et al.* (Vienna, 1986), pp. 29–41; F.C. Gardiner, *The Pilgrimage of Desire: A Study of Theme and Genre in Medieval Literature* (Leiden, 1971).

[16] The historical Emmaus was at Amwâs, i.e., Nicopolis. Most western medieval writers identified Emmaus as Nicopolis, including Eucherius of Lyon, *Instructionum ad Salonium*, in *Patrologiae cursus completus, series Latina*, ed. Jacques-Paul Migne (Paris, 1844–64): (henceforth: *PL*) 50, col. 818 ("Emmaus, in Evangelio, nomen quondam castelli, nunc civitas Nicopolis dicitur," or "Emmaus, once the name of a fortress in the Gospel, is now called the city of Nicopolis"); Jerome, *Commentariorum in Ezechielem prophetam*, in *PL* 25, col. 488 ("Emaus, quae nunc appellatur Nicopolis," or "Emmaus, which is now called Nicopolis"); and Cassiodorus Senator, *Historia Ecclesiastica*, in *PL* 69, col. 1058 ("Est itaque civitas Palaestinae Nicopolis nomine," or "It is thus the city of Palestine called Nicopolis"). If this identification as Nicopolis is correct, how did the men, who ate with Christ 'towards evening,' return to Jerusalem so quickly? Emmaus is also mentioned in the Bible in 1 Macc. 3.40, 4.3, and 9.50. Josephus identified Emmaus as a community four miles from Jerusalem.

Their description as "two of them" (*duo ex illis*) implies that they figured among Christ's seventy-two disciples (Luke 10.1), but medieval exegetes sometimes interpreted the Cleophas named in verse 18 as the uncle of Jesus (based on another Cleophas mentioned in John 19.25), in which case the text would posit a direct bloodline to Christ.[17] Most importantly, what was the central meaning, or meanings, of the episode? Or, put another way, what readings could the Emmaus story accommodate: proof of the Resurrection, the institution of the Eucharist, hospitality, or some other precept, if not all of these? As such questions imply, the biblical narrative was anything but simple. A need to explain inhered in the very nature of the source.

The phrasing of the tale offers a valuable point of entry into its meaning, especially two word clusters relating to emotion and travel. The disciples are "sad" (verse 17) and "slow of heart" (verse 25); they "hope" (verse 21) and feel their heart "burning within" them (verse 32); women returning from the sepulcher "affright" them (verse 22); Christ "suffers" (verse 26). Interestingly, the word "heart" appears twice, first as it oppresses the spirit (verse 25) and then uplifts it (verse 32)—stark opposites which stake out the emotional progression in the text. Several words also relate to travel (our second word cluster), not unexpectedly in an account which places all of its actors on their feet. The figures "go" (verses 13 and 28) or pretend to go (verse 28), "draw near" (verses 15 and 28), "walk" (verse 17), "enter" (verse 29), "stay" (verse 29), "rise up" (verse 33), and "return" (verse 33). The men are "on the road" in verses 32 and 35, and travel many furlongs (verse 13); the holy women are remembered for their travel to the sepulcher (verse 22). The word *peregrinus* from verse 18 is of special importance. Meaning "foreign," "alien," or "stranger" in classical Latin, it began to take on new connotations after the third century, ranging from "exotic" to "rare," "cruel," "exiled," and "distant from God." The two principal meanings, however, were "stranger" and "pilgrim," meanings so intertwined in medieval usage that it is sometimes difficult to tell which sense a writer had in mind.[18] What

---

[17] John 19.25; "Now there stood by the cross of Jesus, his mother, and his mother's sister, Mary of Cleophas, and Mary Magdalen." Some interpreters identified the men as Simon/Peter, Luke, or Amaon.

[18] The *Rule of St. Benedict* (*c.* 530), the Venerable Bede (673–735), the *Liber Pontificalis* (continually modified, beginning *c.* 885), William of Tyre (*c.* 1130–*c.* 90), and Hugh

appeared at first to be a simple tale of the Resurrection turns out, on closer inspection, to admit various interpretations, based in part on ambiguities embedded in the text, in part on the shifting meaning of words. We can now turn to the visual evidence.

The Iconographic Tradition

Important as written sources are, our capital was never a simple translation of ideas from word to image. Far from rehearsing Luke's text in another medium, it re-orders the narrative and intensifies the drama. It also modifies the *dramatis personae*: where Luke mentions only two men, Christ, and the town (*castellum*), the capital adds three figures and an angel. But the transformation is more profound than the number of characters involved. The capital actually contradicts the text in key points to emphasize the ecstasy felt by the sculpted pilgrims and, presumably, their flesh-and-blood successors. A brief review of the iconographic tradition will show how Gislebertus used pictorial conventions to his own ends and, where appropriate, developed new solutions.[19] We know, for instance, that the scene, first

---

of Poitiers († 1167)—key medieval texts—are among the many sources that used *peregrinus* for "pilgrim." Christ himself became a pilgrim in a sermon by Alan of Lille (*c.* 1128–*c.* 1202). *Peregrinus* also came to mean "monk," a sense that gained currency in twelfth-century Burgundy, as passages in Bernard of Clairvaux, Julian of Vézelay, and the Cistercian Statutes attest. The *Novum glossarium mediae Latinitatis*, vol. 30 (Copenhagen, 1998), pp. 416–23 is especially useful for reconstructing this history. In liturgical drama, Christ is clearly pilgrim, as in the Saint-Benoît-sur-Loire (Fleury) manuscript of the *Peregrinus* play: *Hec his cantantibus, accedat quidam alius in similitudine domini, peram cum longa palma gestans, bene ad modum peregrini paratus . . .* (While they were discussing these things, another man appearing like the Lord came up to them, carrying a scrip with a long palm leaf, dressed in the manner of a pilgrim . . .), cited in Ernst August Schuler, *Die Musik der Osterfeiern, Osterspiele und Passionen des Mittelalters* (Basel, 1951), cat. 512b, p. 295.

[19] The iconographic tradition is discussed in Hans Feldbusch, "Emmaus," in *Lexikon der christlichen Ikonographie*, ed. Engelbert Kirschbaum, vol. 1 (Rome, 1968), cols. 622–626; Gertrud Schiller, "Die Emmausjünger," in *Ikonographie der christlichen Kunst*, vol. 3 (Gütersloh: Mohn, 1971), pp. 99–104; Wolfgang Stechow, "Emmaus," in *Reallexikon zur deutschen Kunstgeschichte*, vol. 5 (Stuttgart, 1959), pp. 228–42; Louis Réau, "Emmaüs," in *Iconographie de l'art chrétien*, vol. 2, part 2 (Paris, 1957), pp. 561–7; and Emile Mâle, *Religious Art in France: the Twelfth Century*, ed. Harry Bober, trans. Martiel Mathews (1922; repr. Princeton, 1978), pp. 140–3. Specialized studies include Victor H. Elbern, "Vier karolingische Elfenbeinkästen," *Deutscher Verein für Kunstwissenschaft* 20/1–2 (1966), pp. 8–11; Otto Pächt, *The Rise of Pictorial Narrative in Twelfth-Century England* (Oxford, 1962), pp. 33–59; Hermann Schnitzler, "Eine Metzer Emmaustafel," *Wallraf-Richartz-Jahrbuch* 20 (1958), pp. 41–54.

attested in the sixth century, usually portrayed Christ with two men, that its pilgrimage connotations were a Western (non-Byzantine) development, that liturgical drama may have influenced the iconography, and that the theme often occurred in cycles, where it appeared with the Three Marys at the Sepulcher, the Incredulity of Thomas, and other Resurrection stories. Looking at some examples drawn from the catalog of seventy-three early medieval works cited in the Appendix will allow us to better understand the evolution of the theme from the sixth century down to the Romanesque.

The scene at S. Apollinare Nuovo in Ravenna, executed for the palatine church of Theodoric before 526, occupies an exceptional position in this history as the first known representation of the Journey.[20] (fig. 103) The mosaic panel, part of a Gospel cycle, depicts three large figures against a golden sky, moving toward the miniature town (*castellum*) of Emmaus perched on a mountaintop. The artist has taken care to distinguish Christ from his companions, giving him a cross-inscribed halo, increasing his size, placing him in the center, and raising his hand. The disciples wear *paenulae* (full-length woolen mantles) over tunics which, as Deichmann observed, identifies them as Jews and underscores the idea that the New Testament has replaced the Old (recalling verse 27, "and beginning at Moses and all the prophets, he expounded to them in all the scriptures, the things that were concerning him").[21] The visual paradigm of three figures journeying on a road, hands uplifted, with a town or city-gate nearby endured for centuries, although the means of transmission remain mysterious, as the scene did not become popular until three hundred years later.[22]

Once it did, it never disappeared again from medieval art. Characteristic of the Carolingian *renovatio* that restored the scene is a ninth-century Metz ivory. (fig. 104) Part of a cycle, as at Ravenna, but much reduced to fit into an ivory bookcover, the Journey is paired with the Soldiers at the Empty Tomb and the Three Marys (above) and Christ's Appearance to his Disciples (below). Men of the

---

[20] This is consistent with the mosaics' standing as the earliest Gospel cycle to survive in Western art. Friedrich Wilhelm Deichmann, *Ravenna Hauptstadt des spätantiken Abendlandes*, vol. 2/1 (Wiesbaden, 1974), p. 179 speculated that there may have been an illustrated Bible prototype.

[21] Deichmann, *Ravenna*, vol. 1, p. 188.

[22] For a rare example of the theme during this time, see Appendix #2, Rome, S. Maria Antiqua.

book, all three figures in the Journey carry codices in their left hands, a feature which would become increasingly popular in the iconography, but has special resonance on a bookcover. The emphatic gesture of the older, bearded man suggests he is beckoning the stranger to stay the night (verse 29: "stay with us, because it is towards evening"), while the complicated pose of Christ, simultaneously advancing and returning, captures the sense of the preceding verse ("he made as though he would go farther"). As in the *Utrecht Psalter*, a celebrated Carolingian manuscript where simple poses and gestures often embody complex theological conceits, the visualization of verses 28 and 29 in the ivory may symbolize a longing or prayer to remain with Jesus, a message well-suited to the Resurrection theme of the plaque. This longing is more intense as Jesus faces his disciples instead of mingling with them, creating a hierarchical relationship between savior and saved.

The same scene in the *Gospel Book of Echternach* (*c.* 1030), carries the hierarchy further by emphasizing the separateness of Christ: he alone holds a book and he alone raises his hand in speech (verse 27: "and beginning at Moses and all the prophets, he expounded to them in all the scriptures, the things that were concerning him"). (fig. 105) The illumination distinguishes between the two disciples, giving one a beard and the other a clean-shaven face. While this convention often appears in medieval representations of the theme, the nametags, identifying the men as Cleophas and Luke, are relatively new.[23] Consistent with the didactic emphasis, each scene in this Resurrection cycle carries a succinct title.[24] For the Journey it reads: DISCIPULIS VISUS EST BINIS VT PEREGRINVS (he appeared to both disciples as a pilgrim), a gloss that turns Christ/*peregrinus* into the central feature of the story, though—in an intriguing parallel to the philological evidence—he is visually more of a "stranger" than a "pilgrim."

The critical transformation of Christ to pilgrim was yet to come. One of the earliest examples is a fresco at S. Angelo in Formis (after 1072), where the representation, still close to Ravenna compositionally, takes on a new character thanks to Christ's attire. (fig. 106) Equipped with conical hat, scrip, staff, and short dress, he has at last become

---

[23] They were also identified as such in the *Egbert Codex*, Appendix #13.
[24] These include the Three Marys at the Sepulcher, Journey, Supper, Noli me Tangere, and the Incredulity of Thomas.

a pilgrim. Once this connection was made, Romanesque art was loath to let it go, as an enamel from Cologne, a bronze door from Monreale, and many other works attest.[25] In a cloister pier at St.-Trophime of Arles all three men become pilgrims. (fig. 107) Although Arles is not the first such depiction, it belongs to an extension of pilgrim status from Christ to his companions that came to characterize Romanesque art, in images as diverse as a Geneva capital, the *Winchester Psalter*, and the early stained glass at Chartres.[26] Indeed, at Arles, the storyline no longer matters; the walking and talking of pre-Romanesque Journeys has vanished, and the three figures stand like stony icons. All that counts is their role as pilgrims; they are not even traveling to Emmaus, but rather to (or from) Santiago de Compostela as the scallop shell on the right pilgrim's hat tells us.[27] Sculpted in high relief and almost life-size, the pier is among the most monumental representations of the theme in medieval art.[28]

If the scene grew larger physically, it also grew in breadth, as the Emmaus story expanded in some cases from one or two standard episodes (Journey and/or Supper) to three or four distinct moments. Particularly notable is the *St. Albans Psalter* (*c.* 1119–23), where the tale plays out over three pages (Journey, Supper, and Disappearance).[29] (fig. 108) In the Journey, the two disciples flank Christ and all three point to, or look at, the sun in the upper right corner, an intriguing feature never mentioned by Luke (compare verse 29), but explicitly included in the dialogue of the *Peregrinus* play, a twelfth-century liturgical drama.[30]

The Journey is also known in two Burgundian sculptures roughly contemporary to Autun. At Vézelay the Emmaus story depicts the Journey, Supper, and Return to Jerusalem. (fig. 109) Appearing on

---

[25] Appendix #51, 35. *Editors' note see Anja Grebe's essay in this volume.

[26] Appendix #62, 60, 20.

[27] Other iconic representations of the theme include Rome, San Giovanni a Porta Latina (Appendix #40) and Durham (#58).

[28] Other monumental depictions include Monreale (Appendix #36) and Silos (#49). Examples that give Christ special prominence include St.-Savin (#30), the Pisa Cross (38), Rome, S. Giovanni a Porta Latina (40), and the *Bible of Ávila* (46).

[29] The text in the upper left corner abbreviates Luke 24.13–29. See Otto Pächt, C. R. Dodwell, and Francis Wormald, *The St. Albans Psalter (Albani Psalter)* (London, 1960). Other extended Emmaus cycles include the Pascal I casket, a rare early example of this iconographic expansion (Appendix #9), Monreale (#36), and the destroyed thirteenth-century mosaics at S. Marco, Venice.

[30] For the miniature's debt to liturgical drama, see Pächt, *Rise of Pictorial Narrative*, p. 43.

the north narthex portal of *c.* 1120–40, beneath an image of the Ascension(?), this is the only example I know of in early medieval art where the Journey decorates a tympanum.[31] Occupying the far left register of the lintel, the Journey depicts a cross-nimbed Christ, two disciples, and a palm tree, setting the scene in an exotic locale while drawing out its Easter message. Perhaps the disciples are "palmers" by extension, a word still used to designate pilgrims.[32] The sculptor at Vézelay—like Autun a pilgrimage church—may have imposed a pilgrimage reading on the iconography, even though the visual solutions of both works could not be more different. On the other hand, a second Burgundian work, a capital from Moutiers-St.-Jean, is so close to Autun that it must be a copy, as the encounter between Christ and the disciples on the main face, the flying angel to the left, and the crowded town to the right demonstrate.[33] (fig. 110) The Moutiers capital may also help interpret certain features of Autun. For instance, where a lightly incised cross and a hat are all that identify the Autun disciples as pilgrims, the Moutiers version clarifies the identification by giving them prominent staffs visible to any spectator.[34] The theme's migration to monumental sculpture, in Burgundy as elsewhere, is characteristic of eleventh- and twelfth-century art: eighteen of the sixty-four securely-identified Journeys from our catalogue, or almost thirty percent, are Romanesque sculptures.

Taken together, these examples allow us to flesh out the iconography of the theme. We have seen that the Journey, first surfacing in an early sixth-century Gospel cycle, became popular from the ninth century on, reaching its height in the eleventh and twelfth centuries. It extended across Western Europe and appeared in several

---

[31] Francis Salet and Jean Adhémar, *La Madeleine de Vézelay* (Melun, 1948), pp. 180–1.

[32] Some medieval Journeys replaced the pilgrims' staff with a palm branch, e.g., Appendix #60, 61. On the palm as an emblem of pilgrimage, see Jonathan Sumption, *Pilgrimage: An Image of Medieval Religion* (London, 1975), pp. 173–4.

[33] Neil Stratford, "La sculpture médiévale de Moutiers-Saint-Jean (Saint-Jean-de-Réome)," *Congrès Archéologique de France* 144 (1986), pp. 167–9; Walter Cahn and Linda Seidel, *Romanesque Sculpture in American Collections*, vol. 1 (New York, 1979), pp. 124, 132–3; Grivot and Zarnecki, *Gislebertus*, p. 63. The Moutiers capital is usually assigned to the early twelfth century; I date it to *c.* 1125–35.

[34] Whereas the Autun capital is heavily-restored in the upper right corner (main face), the Moutiers capital has come down intact, showing a figure with a (drinking?) horn in the same corner. This unusual feature, otherwise known only at St.-Austremoine in Issoire (Appendix #21), suggests that the figure at Autun may have held a horn, too.

media, particularly sculpture and illuminated manuscripts. If some features remained fairly constant over the centuries (the number of figures, usually three, and the scene's appearance in Resurrection cycles) other features evolved, such as the increasing emphasis on Christ's separateness and the "pilgrimization" of the theme. The moment depicted also varied from work to work, suggesting that medieval audiences may have seen a subtler range of meanings in the Journey than we do today. Thus Sant'Apollinare Nuovo (fig. 103) and the *Echternach Gospels* (fig. 105) emphasized verse 27, linking Old and New Testaments; the Metz ivory (fig. 104) recalled verses 28–29, reflecting Christ's decision to stay; the *St. Albans Psalter* (fig. 108) re-worked verse 29, citing liturgical drama; and St.-Trophime (fig. 107) bypassed Scripture, transforming the scene into pilgrim portraits. Such variety does not mean we should interpret these works as snapshots of a specific moment in time, illustrating now one verse, now another; more to the point, the varying emphases invite us to contemplate the different theological or symbolic nuances of each work. Giving shape to Luke's account was never a simple matter of translating an idea from one medium to another.

How did our capital build on this legacy? The three main characters, their identification as pilgrims, Christ's special prominence, and the theme's popularity in Romanesque sculpture are all familiar by now and do not surprise us at Autun. But we look in vain for a work where the scene is so charged with emotion: of the many contributions Gislebertus made to the iconography of the Journey, his psychological reading is the most extraordinary, and one which we must tackle if we seek to recover its meaning for an early twelfth-century audience.[35] The emotion-laden representation is not without foundation, as it flows directly from verses 31–32, where the evangelist describes the disciples' reaction to the sight and sound of Jesus ("And their eyes were opened, and they knew him: and he vanished out of their sight. And they said one to the other: Was not our heart burning within us, whilst he spoke in the way and opened to us the scriptures?").

---

[35] Another iconographic innovation included the number of figures: no other Journey includes so many actors, besides the capital from Moutiers-St.-Jean which evidently copied it. Perhaps the sculptor wanted to animate an otherwise dead side of the capital by giving it an anecdotal richness worthy of its place near the Tomb of St. Lazarus.

To set the visual innovation in context, let us turn back to the contemporary *St. Albans Psalter*, comparing it to our capital in terms of composition, gestural language, and facial expression. To begin with, the composition reveals telling differences in the way both artists envisioned Christ's centrality. (figs. 100, 108) The illuminator places Christ in the middle of the page, while establishing a secondary, horizontal thrust in the staff which links him directly to the sun. Playing on this dichotomy between Jesus and sun, the two major foci of the page, the disciples enact a complicated *pas-de-deux* to demonstrate their awareness of both. The older man touches Christ and points to the sun; the younger man faces Christ and looks toward the sun; Christ himself strides forward while looking back at the sun. The sculptor, by contrast, has everything point to Christ, focusing our attention on a human interaction, not on external props. In terms of gesture, the illuminator uses hands to act out speech and lead the eye in certain directions, although visually the hands barely matter compared to the same figures' extraordinary feet. The sculptor uses gesture to convey states of mind; when a disciple raises a hand to his cheek at Autun, it is *to express an emotion*, so we forget the feet, but remember the hands. Most remarkable is the physiognomic characterization. In the manuscript, coiffure carries the burden of distinguishing one figure from another; one man's hair is white where the other's is dark, one has a beard where the other has none. In the sculpture, faces have expressions; they show feeling. In sum, the manuscript externalizes the story, focusing on action over inner motivation.[36] The capital addresses the inner motivation and accentuates drama. Of course, if the miniature failed to register the figures' excitement, the artist was merely following Scripture, which separates the meeting (on the road) from the moment of recognition (at Emmaus). It is the capital that deviates from the biblical account, "incorrectly" allowing the disciples to recognize Christ on the road.[37] This is an extraordinary departure from the iconography which robs the *fractio panis* ("breaking of the bread") of its force; if

---

[36] Differences in the treatment of intervals are equally revealing. In the manuscript, figures are squashed together in easy familiarity, as they touch or overlap each other. In the sculpture, the space around Christ is inviolate.

[37] Luke was explicit on this point, writing that the disciples' eyes "were held" (literally, *tenebantur*) to prevent them from recognizing Christ (*ne eum agnoscerent*); only *after* all three men entered the town were their eyes "opened" (*aperti sunt oculi eorum*).

the disciples already recognized Christ on the road, there could be no revelation at the Supper.

Why the reversal? Or, better yet, why the conflation, as an element central to the Supper (the recognition) has seeped into the Journey? One reason must be viewer response: to focus on the effect a story has on the actors in it is to provide a model of behavior for the audience.[38] The ascriptural recognition of Christ on the road enables the viewer to enter into the drama; the devout can look *with* the disciples, not just at them, in a process which relocates sacred history to the here and now. Novel as this treatment was, the sculptor (or his patron) was not acting in a vacuum. Twelfth-century Emmaus plays are rife with the type of emotionalism we saw in the sculpture, as demonstrated by a twelfth-century work from Beauvais, whose pilgrims exclaim:

> Was not our heart burning within us *with Jesus*, whilst he spoke *to us* in the way, and opened to us the scriptures? *Alas! Miserable ones, alas! Miserable ones, alas! Miserable ones! Where was our sense? Where had our understanding gone?*[39]

> Nonne cor nostrum ardens erat in nobis *de Iesu*, dum loqueretur *nobis* in uia et aperiret nobis scripturas? *Heu! miseri, heu! miseri, heu! miseri! Ubi erat sensus noster? Quo intellectus abierat?*

The heart of their speech is lifted directly from Luke 24.32, as at Autun, but the extra-scriptural additions (in italics) give it a new urgency. The wording "alas, alas, alas" may seem weak in print, but in performance the repetition of this simple expression of grief becomes a powerful rhetorical device. Writing for a more sophisticated audience of readers about the same time, Pseudo-Bernard called the Emmaus story "a jubilation in the heart, an ecstasy for the devoted mind. From each little clause . . . a certain fire break[s] forth."[40] Our capital is about that jubilation, that ecstasy, that fire.[41] The excitement

---

[38] For an iconographic reading, see Travis, "Iconography of the Choir Capitals," pp. 224–5.

[39] Cited in Karl Young, *The Drama of the Medieval Church*, vol. 1 (Oxford, 1933), pp. 468–9. The Emmaus, or *Peregrinus*, plays were usually performed at Vespers on the Monday or Tuesday following Easter. On the dramas' emotionalism, see Gardiner, *Pilgrimage of Desire*, pp. 5f.

[40] Cited in Gardiner, *Pilgrimage of Desire*, p. 48.

[41] On the emotionalism of Luke's text, see Jacques Dupont, "Les pèlerins d'Emmaüs (Luc, XXIV, 13–35)," in *Miscellanea Biblica B. Ubach*, ed. Romualdo María Díaz

may have always lurked in the iconography, but Gislebertus made it visible. Ultimately it is this concern with emotion (or passion, to use a more medieval expression) that transformed the viewer from passive onlooker to active participant, and once we participate in the Journey, we too become pilgrims.

Style and Emotion

It is one thing to portray emotion and another to provoke it. We are now in a position to ask how our sculptor used the language of art to stimulate empathy and, more specifically, how he manipulated drapery, composition, gestures, facial expressions, and glances to involve the spectator. Drapery analysis, a traditional tool for understanding medieval style, is a good place to start. Creating animated patterns over simple bodies, the drapery sets up a series of loops— mounting, descending, or swirling—that run counter to the direction of the underlying form, as horizontal and diagonal folds drape vertical bodies. Visually, this effect enlivens the surface while uniting the three principal figures in a network of interlocking curves that comes to a climax in the artificially-windblown drapery of the lower extremities. Normally protruding areas, e.g., the hips, are slightly recessed in a medieval type of "wet drapery" that, rather than revealing anatomy, varies the body's textures and surfaces. The emphasis is on movement, variation, animation. While the conventions described here are not unique to St.-Lazare, the level of excitement is rare in our church, where closely adhering, tubular folds laid out in tightly spaced parallel lines are the norm. The heightened excitement engendered by the windblown treatment occurs in scenes of exaltation, such as the Annunciation to the Virgin or the Noli me Tangere. (fig. 111) The drapery serves as so many signposts to attract the viewers' attention; after a succession of calmer scenes, it highlights the exceptional emphasis on the story at hand.

Carbonell (Montserrat, 1953), pp. 366, 371, 373. The liturgy suggests another parallel, as seen in a Roman antiphonary from Silos which, like our capital, reversed the chronology of the Emmaus story in order to emphasize the disciples' recognition of Christ; Otto K. Werckmeister, "The Emmaus and Thomas Pillar of the Cloister of Silos," in *El románico en Silos* (Burgos, 1990), p. 151.

The composition reinforces such effects by focusing attention on the moment of maximum drama. Thus the placement of Christ and the innkeeper at opposite ends of the main face enframes the astonished pilgrims, highlighting the zone where the emotion is strongest. (fig. 100) At the same time, the piece has a well-calculated instability, as seen in the individual figures' postures. Jesus and the innkeeper lean back; disciple one (to the left) leans forward; disciple two (to the right) plunges into the scene; a figure sticks out its head; an angel flies overhead. Heads and feet do not line up. There is nowhere to rest the eye.

Gestural language adds to the emotional energy: every figure on the main side with arms to use uses them in a distinct manner calculated to express that person's understanding of the miracle. Disciple two throws his arms wide open in ecstatic recognition of Christ, while disciple one draws his arms in, lifting one hand to his cheek and raising the other. One pose is expansive and declamatory; the other is quiet and inward, as if the meaning had just dawned on the man. As a formal device, this contrast between open and closed gestures is an effective way to vary the composition and to connect both ends of the capital (Jesus and Emmaus), but equally important was the sculptor's ability to turn these devices into expressions of emotion. Just how expressive they are is clear when compared to the gestures of the little man, whose hands have nothing better to do than open a door and hold a stick.[42] Gislebertus did not need to invent these gestures; instead he brought them to a new level by transforming signs of communication into signs of feeling.

Facial expression is a subtler form of communication, better suited to convey states of mind than gesture is: if hands and arms carry messages when positioned in certain ways, the human face is expressive in and of itself. As there was no code for facial expression in the eleventh and twelfth centuries, however, any attempt to break through the veneer of physiognomic neutrality was bound to attract attention, and this is precisely an area where our artist(s) excelled, as seen time and again in the sculpture at St.-Lazare.[43] The dramatic

---

[42] Christ's pointing index finger, a well-known medieval convention for speech, suggests that he is talking; see Luke verse 27 ("and beginning at Moses and all the prophets, he expounded to them in all the scriptures, the things that were concerning him.").

[43] Willibald Sauerländer, "Gislebertus von Autun: Ein Beitrag zur Entstehung

potential of mouths, for instance, is fully exploited as jaws drop to express astonishment.[44] That these figures should open their mouths at all is remarkable, as otherwise in this church only devils have gaping maws, while saints keep a tight-lipped silence. Perhaps the grotesque visage of the innkeeper was also meant to amuse, drawing on the contrast between the disciples' elevated response and the rustic's simple ways. If so, the capital may recall the Easter laughter that priests evoked from time to time in their sermons to provide comic relief for a serious subject.[45] The eyes are another critical element of facial expression which Gislebertus used to create a hierarchy of astonishment, increasing their size from the little man to disciple two to disciple one. Even the irises have a role to play. Set with their original paste, they have a slight radiance that sets them apart from other surfaces on the capital, all the more dramatically in Christ, whose deep, glowing beads are immense.

Where the figures look is equally significant. If everyone on the main side turns his head toward Christ, *he* looks at disciple one alone. Towering over the man, Christ must bend to meet the pilgrim's astonished gaze, creating an interaction of great intensity. Perhaps this disciple's unique status explains why he has wider eyes, more internalized gestures, and more excited drapery than disciple two (to the right). This is the moment of contact with the divine; a man sees the face of God. As the traveler lifts his head, the vision flows from top to bottom, analogous to the position that we ourselves, as spectators and fellow travelers, must assume to witness the event. My main concern in this section has been to bring out the intimate connection between the style and message of the sculpture. The two belong together, as the meaning of our capital is only complete once we enter into, receive, and emulate the story. Draperies, composition, gestures, facial expression, and glances are the silent language that encourages us to do so.

---

seines künstlerischen Stils," in *Studien zur Geschichte der europäischen Plastik: Festschrift Theodor Müller*, ed. Kurt Martin (Munich, 1965), pp. 17–29.

[44] Disciple two's mouth is restored.

[45] For the *risus paschalis* in Emmaus plays, especially after the fourteenth century, see Rainer Warning, *The Ambivalences of Medieval Religious Drama*, trans. Steven Rendall (1974; repr. Stanford, 2001), pp. 100–12; Hanns Fluck, "Der risus paschalis: Ein Beitrag zur religiösen Volkskunde," *Archiv für Religionswissenschaft* 31 (1934): 188–212; Gustave Cohen, "La Scène des Pèlerins d'Emmaüs: Contribution à l'étude des origines du théâtre comique," in *Mélanges de philologie romane et d'histoire littéraire offerts à M. Maurice Wilmotte*, vol. 1 (Paris, 1910), pp. 106–9.

Travel

Any attempt to connect with a viewer in a pilgrimage church was above all an attempt to connect with a pilgrim. Given this background, it is especially meaningful that so many themes at St.-Lazare are devoted to travel, enabling pilgrims to literally see a connection between their own enterprise and the road to salvation. Scholars have had little to say about the iconography of travel here, except for Linda Seidel who argued that the sculpture at Autun maps out the Holy Land, "replicat[ing] the real relationship between the cities in question."[46] Thus Bethel, corresponding to the capital with Jacob wrestling the angel, appears to the north in the church as in fact; Bethany, corresponding to the tympanum with Lazarus's resurrection, appears to the east; and so on. Intriguing as this theory is, the sculpture argues against it, as numerous scenes contradicting the geography are passed over in silence, including the Journey to Emmaus, which would have to jump to the other side of the church.[47] What really matters, in my view, is the preoccupation with travel itself. Many of the best-known journey themes from the Bible are here—including the Flight into Egypt, the Magi before Herod, and the Adoration of the Magi—and many other symbolic travelers are pressed into service, including a man riding a bird, a three-headed bird, a siren pursuing an onocentaur, and Constantine(?) on horseback. (fig. 112) The compositions themselves rush the viewer forward: the Holy Family on the Flight into Egypt (fig. 112, capital 3); Constantine (capital 8); the man riding a bird (capital 9); and the siren and onocentaur (capital 11), all move resolutely from left to right, establishing a type of directional viewing rare in early twelfth-century art. The figures are traveling and we are invited to move with them.

Travel motifs do not occur at random throughout the church but, rather, accumulate in the choir, suggesting an intensification of the pilgrim iconography as travelers approached their ultimate goal, the shrine of St. Lazarus next to the high altar. The choir scenes also conform to a left-right division, symbols of good appearing on the dexter side of the altar and symbols of evil on the sinister side.[48]

---

[46] Seidel, *Legends*, p. 155.
[47] The Flight into Egypt would also have to move.
[48] Travis, "Iconography of the Choir Capitals," p. 244.

The Adoration of the Magi (on the dexter side), for instance, was a model to emulate, while the siren and onocentaur (on the sinister side) was one to scorn (fig. 113); or, put another way, some roads led to Heaven and others to Hell. St.-Lazare of Autun is the only Romanesque church I know of with this double thematic of good versus bad travel.

The recognition that people walk through a church and are therefore likely to perceive sculpture in ever-changing relationships may have influenced the iconographic layout. Unlike a book or essay, which fixes the sequence for a reader, the vantage point in a church is always changing. On entering St.-Lazare from the east transept portal and proceeding into the choir, visitors perceive the Emmaus and Flight into Egypt as pendants (fig. 112, capitals 1, 3); moving to the center of the choir and facing north, they see Emmaus and the First Temptation (capitals 1, 7); while moving under the Emmaus capital and looking up, they see it with Luxuria (?). (capitals 1, 2) Each new pairing brings with it a different way to think about the Journey to Emmaus, as a fulfillment of the Infancy story (Emmaus-Flight into Egypt) or as a foil to temptation (Emmaus-First Temptation). We should not turn the medieval experience of viewing art into a post-modernist romp, though, where the structure of looking becomes entirely subjective, because the sculpture itself exerts a strong directional pull, as already noted. Moving into or out of spaces, the pull establishes a roadmap for the faithful, generally leading the eye to the middle in the choir, toward the sanctuary in the east aisle, and out of the church in the west aisle. Can we read the capitals as so many clues to the circulation of pilgrims in the church? It is impossible to say, although a curious fact should be noted. As we walk into the church from the east transept, then as now the main point of entry, the first two capitals in the choir (representing the Adoration of the Magi and the Magi before Herod) push us north, their strong right to left orientation beckoning us toward the shrine of St. Lazarus.

This manipulation of the viewers' physical movements is as effective, and probably as innovative, as the sculptor's ability to move the viewer in psychological terms. The two may go hand in hand, as the emotional temperature of the sculpture seems to heat up when we enter the choir. The Luxuria(?) capital, for instance—with two demons confronting each other while one of them clutches a fretful man by the hair—is at heart a depiction of agony, brought to a feverish pitch by appearing directly opposite the scene of ecstasy in

the Emmaus capital. (fig. 114) The comparison between our capital
and the adjacent Tomb of St. Lazarus is even more striking. The
ultimate aim of the pilgrims to Autun, and dominating the interior
until its destruction in the eighteenth century, the tomb was the emotional epicenter of the church. Pilgrims venturing inside the structure found a grouping of astonishing force, where Mary wept, Martha
held her nose for the stench, and Christ with outstretched arms commanded Lazarus to "come forth."[49] Seen together, the two works—
capital and tomb—reveal their common theme of resurrection, where
one episode recalls Christ's death-defying miracle, the Raising of
Lazarus, and the other Christ's own return to life, told in a vivid
sculptural language which draws attention to the witnesses' amazed
reactions. The Journey's appearance in a Resurrection cycle is therefore consistent with the visual tradition studied above, but unlike the
chronological sequence typical of such cycles, the episode here belongs
to a sequence of journeys. The emphasis on travel is so pronounced
that it overturns the iconographic precedents for the scene. Situated
at the far end of the left aisle, our capital brings the cycle to a dramatic climax, revealing Christ to the devout traveler, just as, centuries
before, he was revealed to two men on the road to Emmaus.

The Journey to Emmaus capital at Autun is an extraordinary
document of pilgrimage art. A review of the scriptural background
demonstrated that, embedded in Luke's account, were several ambiguities that later renditions of the subject needed to solve. The iconographic tradition (amplified by the catalogue of early medieval examples
in the Appendix) traced some of these solutions over the course of
seven centuries, as the theme evolved from a sixth-century mosaic
to a larger and more complex body of Romanesque images. The
increasing emphasis on Christ and the "pilgrimization" of the theme
are two features that Gislebertus inherited from the visual tradition;
to this he added a remarkable emotionalism, interpreted here as a
strategy to directly involve the pilgrim in the disciples' vision of
Christ. Style and emotion expanded on this interpretation by suggesting how the sculptor used stylistic devices to enhance viewer participation. The section on travel reviewed the church's broader sculptural

---

[49] The figures of Mary, Martha, and Andrew (who also witnessed the event) survive. Although the Tomb postdates the capital (possibly by ten years), it had to be
planned from the outset, as the church was built to house the relics of Lazarus.

context, bringing out the idea of good versus evil travel. The accent on travel resulted in a new visual sequence around the Journey to Emmaus, while preserving a connection with the Resurrection; this sequence may in turn have opened up various readings based on the shifting visual pendants we encounter in walking through the church. Summing up, the connection between the theme—the Journey to Emmaus—and its destination—the Church of St.-Lazare at Autun—was anything but incidental. Together they worked to intensify the pilgrimage message of the capital. From a broad methodological perspective, this finding may help us think about the infinite malleability of medieval art. There is not one Journey to Emmaus, but multiple Journeys to Emmaus. At Autun we find one that wants to reach out and touch us.

APPENDIX: THE JOURNEY TO EMMAUS IN EARLY MEDIEVAL ART, 500–1200 A.D.

The catalogue that follows is, to my knowledge, the most exhaustive census of the theme in early medieval art. Ivories, metalwork, and manuscripts are listed by the works' present location; for monumental sculpture the original location is given.

Early Christian

1. Ravenna, Sant'Apollinare Nuovo: nave mosaic, south wall (before 526). Illustrated in this essay, fig. 103.
2. Rome, Santa Maria Antiqua: presbytery fresco, west wall (*c.* 705–7). Illustrated in Josef Wilpert, *Die römischen Mosaiken und Malereien der kirchlichen Bauten*, vol. 4 (Freiburg im Breisgau: Herder, 1924), pl. 153.

Carolingian

3. Aachen, Cathedral Treasury: ivory bookcover (early ninth century). Illustrated in Adolph Goldschmidt, *Die Elfenbeinkunst aus der Zeit der karolingischen und sächsischen Kaiser*, vol. 1 (Berlin: Cassirer, 1914), pl. XII (22b).
4. Darmstadt, Hessisches Landesmuseum: ivory plaque (acc. no. Kg. 54:217; *c.* 850–900). Illustrated in Adolph Goldschmidt, *Die Elfenbeinkunst aus der Zeit der karolingischen und sächsischen Kaiser*, vol. 4 (Berlin: Cassirer, 1926), pl. LXXIX (39).
5. Munich, Staatsbibliothek: Clm 23631, Cim 2, fol. 197v (*Codex Purpureus; c.* 800–25). Illustrated in Katharina Bierbrauer, *Die vorkarolingischen und karolingischen Handschriften der Bayerischen Staatsbibliothek*, vol. 1 (Wiesbaden: Reichert, 1990), p. 54 (fig. 189).
6. New York, Metropolitan Museum, Cloisters: ivory plaque from casket (acc. no. 1970.324.1; *c.* 850–900). Illustrated in *Wallraf-Richartz Jahrbuch*, 20 (1958), p. 41 (fig. 16).
7. Paris, Bibliothèque Nationale: MS lat. 9390: ivory plaque from bookcover (ninth or tenth century). Illustrated in this essay, fig. 104.

8. Paris, Bibliothèque Nationale: MS lat. 9428, fol. 61v (*Drogo Sacramentary; c.* 850–55). Illustrated Gertrud Schiller, *Ikonographie der christlichen Kunst*, vol. 3 (Gütersloh: Mohn, 1971), fig. 305.

9. Rome, Biblioteca Vaticana, Museo Cristiano: silver casket of Pascal I (*c.* 817–24). Illustrated in *Wallraf-Richartz Jahrbuch*, 20 (1958), p. 48 (fig. 24).

Ottonian

10. Mainz, Cathedral: fresco (destroyed, but known from literary sources; see Otto Lehmann Brockhaus, *Schriftquellen zur Kunstgeschichte des 11. und 12. Jahrhunderts für Deutschland, Lothringen und Italien*, vol. 1, Berlin: Deutscher Verein für Kunstwissenschaft, 1938, no. 2573).

11. New York, Pierpont Morgan Library: M.781, fol. 124r (Gospel Book; *c.* 1025–50). Illustrated in Franz Unterkircher, *La miniatura austriaca* (Milan: Electa, 1953), pl. 6.

12. Nuremberg, Germanisches Nationalmuseum, Bibliothek: MS 156142, fol. 111v (*Golden Gospels of Echternach; c.* 1030). Illustrated in this essay, fig. 105.

13. Trier, Stadtbibliothek: MS 24, fol. 88r (*Egbert Codex; c.* 977–93). Illustrated in Günther Franz and Franz Ronig, *Codex Egberti*, vol. 2 (Wiesbaden: Reichert, 1983), color fol. 88r.

Romanesque

France

14. Amiens, Bibliothèque Municipale: MS 108, fol. 195r (*Picture Bible*; 1197). Illustrated in François Bucher, *The Pamplona Bibles*, vol. 2 (New Haven: Yale University Press, 1970), pl. 439.

15. Arles, St.-Trophime: cloister pier, north gallery (mid twelfth century). Illustrated in this essay, fig. 107.

16. Autun, St.-Lazare: choir capital. Illustrated in this essay, figs. 100–102.

17. Auxerre, Cathedral Treasury: Sacramentary (from St.-Julien of Tours). Illustrated in Meyer Schapiro, *Romanesque Art: Selected Papers* (New York: Braziller, 1977), after p. 306 (fig. 3).

18. Chantilly, Musée Condé: MS 1695, fol. 30v (*Ingeborg Psalter*; sometimes attributed to England; *c.* 1200). Illustrated in Florens Deuchler, *Der Ingeborgpsalter* (Berlin: de Gruyter, 1967), fig. 34.

19. Chartres, Cathedral Notre-Dame: west façade capital (mid twelfth century). Illustrated in Peter Kidson, *Sculpture at Chartres* (London: Tiranti, 1958), fig. 46.

20. Chartres, Cathedral Notre-Dame: west façade window (mid twelfth century). Illustrated in Yves Delaporte, *Les vitraux de la cathédrale de Chartres* (Chartres: Houvet, 1926), pl. I.

21. Issoire, St.-Austremoine: ambulatory capital. Illustrated in Marcel Aubert, *L'art français à l'époque romane*, vol. 2 (Paris: Morancé, 1930), pl. 52.

22. London, Victoria and Albert Museum: enamel plaque (inv. M.209–1938; attributed to Limoges; twelfth century). Illustrated in Marie-Madeleine Gauthier, *Catalogue international de l'œuvre de Limoges*, vol. 1 (Paris: Centre national de recherche scientifique, 1987), fig. 352.

23. Moutiers-St.-Jean: capital now in Cambridge (Mass.), Fogg Museum (*c.* 1125–35). Illustrated in this essay, fig. 110.

24. Nantouillet, église paroissiale (on loan to Meaux, Musée Municipal): enamel casket (Limoges, *c.* 1180–85). Illustrated in Marie-Madeleine Gauthier, *Catalogue international de l'œuvre de Limoges*, vol. 1 (Paris: Centre national de recherche scientifique, 1987), fig. 570.

25. Narbonne, St.-Paul: capital 619–620 now in Toulouse, Musée des Augustins. Illustrated in *Gesta*, vol. 11/1 (1972), p. 36 (fig. 5b).

26. New York, Pierpont Morgan Library: M.44, fol. 13r (from St.-Martial of Limoges). Photograph at Princeton University, Index of Christian Art.

27. Romans, Saint-Barnard: west façade, portal capital. Illustrated in Arthur Kingsley Porter, *Romanesque Sculpture of the Pilgrimage Roads* (Boston: Jones, 1923), pl. 1336.

28. St.-Gilles-du-Gard, St.-Gilles: west façade frieze. Illustrated in Whitney S. Stoddard, *The Façade of Saint-Gilles-du-Gard* (Middletown, CN.: Wesleyan University Press, 1973), figs. 105–6.

29. St.-Pons-de-Thomières: capital now in Cambridge, MA, Fogg Museum (mid twelfth century). Illustrated in Walter Cahn and Linda Seidel, *Romanesque Sculpture in American Collections*, vol. 1 (New York: Franklin, 1979), figs. 149–50.

30. St.-Savin, abbey church: tribune fresco. Photograph at Princeton University, Index of Christian Art.

31. Savigny, St.-Martin: capital now in private collection. Illustrated in *Gesta*, vol. 25/1 (1986), p. 78 (fig. 5).

32. Toulouse, La Daurade: capital M.145 now in Toulouse, Musée des Augustins (*c.* 1120–30). Illustrated in Kathryn Horste, *Cloister Design and Monastic Reform in Toulouse* (Oxford: Clarendon, 1992), pl. 114.

33. Vézelay, St.-Marie-Madeleine: nave façade, north tympanum (*c.* 1120–40). Illustrated in this essay, fig. 109.

34. Vienne, Cathedral St.-Maurice: south vestibule relief. Illustrated in Lucien Bégule, *L'Eglise Saint-Maurice, ancienne cathédrale de Vienne en Dauphiné* (Paris: Laurens, 1914), figs. 156–7.

Italy

35. Monreale, Cathedral: panel from bronze door by Bonanus of Pisa (1186). Illustrated in Ursula Mende, *Die Bronzetüren des Mittelalters* (Munich: Hirmer, 1983), p. 178 (pl. 205).

36. Monreale, Cathedral: transept mosaic. Illustrated in Gertrud Schiller, *Ikonographie der christlichen Kunst*, vol. 3 (Gütersloh: Mohn, 1971), fig. 316.

37. Padua, Cathedral Treasury, Lectionary, fol. 32v (1170). Illustrated in Bruno Katterbach, *Le miniature dell'Evangelario di Padova dell'anno 1170* (Vatican City: Biblioteca Apostolica Vaticana, 1931), pl. XIII.

38. Pisa, Museo Nazionale di San Matteo: cross no. 1 (early thirteenth century). Illustrated in Evelyn S. Vavalà, *La croce dipinta italiana* (Verona: Apollo, 1929), fig. 340.

39. Pisa, Museo Nazionale di San Matteo: cross no. 2 (late twelfth century). Illustrated in Gertrud Schiller, *Ikonographie der christlichen Kunst*, vol. 3 (Gütersloh: Mohn, 1971), fig. 309.

40. Rome, S. Giovanni a Porta Latina: nave fresco (*c.* 1191–98). Illustrated in Josef Wilpert, *Die römischen Mosaiken und Malereien der kirchlichen Bauten*, vol. 4 (Freiburg im Breisgau: Herder, 1924), pl. 252–5.

41. Rossano, S. Annunziata: cross (*c.* 1200). Illustrated in Evelyn S. Vavalà, *La croce dipinta italiana* (Verona: Apollo, 1929), fig. 341.

42. S. Angelo in Formis: nave fresco (after 1072). Illustrated in this essay, fig. 106.

43. Troia, Archivio Capitolare: Exultet Roll 3 (on the road). Illustrated

in Myrtilla Avery, *The Exultet Rolls of South Italy*, vol. 2 (Princeton: Princeton University Press, 1936), pl. CLXXI.

44. Troia, Archivio Capitolare: Exultet Roll 3 (entering Emmaus). Illustrated in Myrtilla Avery, *The Exultet Rolls of South Italy*, vol. 2 (Princeton: Princeton University Press, 1936), pl. CLXXI.

Spain

45. Huesca, San Pedro el Viejo: cloister capital. Photograph at Princeton University, Index of Christian Art.

46. Madrid, Biblioteca Nacional: MS E.R. 8, fol. 324v (*Bible of Ávila*; *c.* 1150–1200). Photograph at Princeton University, Index of Christian Art.

47. New York, Metropolitan Museum: ivory plaque from a reliquary (acc. no. 17.190.47; *c.* 1115–20). Illustrated in *The Art of Medieval Spain, A.D. 500–1200* (New York: Metropolitan Museum of Art, 1993), p. 251 (fig. 115c).

48. Rome, Biblioteca Vaticana: MS lat. 5729, fol. 370r (*Ripoll* or *"Farfa" Bible; c.* 1000–50). Illustrated in Wilhelm Neuss, *Die katalanische Bibelillustration* (Bonn: Schroeder, 1922), pp. 125–7 (pl. 151).

49. Silos, S. Domingo: cloister pier. Illustrated in Gertrud Schiller, *Ikonographie der christlichen Kunst*, vol. 3 (Gütersloh: Mohn, 1971), fig. 315.

50. Soria, S. Juan de Rabanera: west façade capital. Illustrated in Juan Antonio Gaya Nuño, *El románico en la provincia de Soria* (Madrid: Consejo superior de Investigaciones científicas, 1946), figs. 177–8.

Germany/Austria/Mosan Region

51. Cologne, Cathedral Treasury: *Three Kings Shrine* (destroyed enamel plaque; *c.* 1200?). Illustrated in Paul Clemen et al., *Die Kunstdenkmäler der Stadt Köln*, vol. 1, part 3 (Düsseldorf: Schwann, 1937), fig. 270.

52. Hildesheim, Cathedral Treasury: enamel plaque. Illustrated in *Pantheon*, vol. 5 (1930), fig. 4a.

53. Munich, Staatsbibliothek: Clm 835, fol. 27v (Psalter, *c.* 1200). Illustrated in Marburg Index, #135789.

54. Salzburg, Stiftsbibliothek: Peter, a.XII.7, p. 314 (Antiphonal). Illustrated in Georg Swarzenski, *Die Salzburger Malerei*, vol. 2 (Leipzig: Hiersemann, 1913), pl. C (339).

55. Strasbourg, Bibliothèque Municipale: *Hortus Deliciarum*, fol. 160v (a partial copy of the Emmaus scene was made before the manuscript's destruction in 1870). Illustrated in Herrad of Landsberg, *Hortus Deliciarum*, ed. Rosalie Green (London: Warburg Institute, 1979), pl. 96.

56. Vienna, Kunsthistorisches Museum: paten (from Wilten, *c.* 1160–70). Illustrated in *Pantheon*, vol. 21 (1938), p. 196.

England

57. Cambridge, Pembroke College: MS 120, fol. 4v (Gospel Book; from Bury St. Edmunds? *c.* 1130s). Illustrated in Otto Pächt, *The Rise of Pictorial Narrative in Twelfth-Century England* (Oxford: Clarendon), pl. VII (24).

58. Durham, Cathedral Library: relief. Illustrated in Fritz Saxl, *English Sculptures of the Twelfth Century*, ed. Hanns Swarzenski (London: Faber and Faber, 1954), pl. LXXXVI.

59. Hildesheim, St. Godehard, Treasury: MS, fol. 35r (*St. Albans Psalter; c.* 1119–23). Illustrated in this essay, fig. 108.

60. London, British Library: MS Cotton Nero, C.IV, fol. 25r (*Winchester Psalter*; from Cathedral Priory of St. Swithun's? *c.* 1150). Illustrated in Fritz Saxl, *English Sculptures of the Twelfth Century*, ed. Hanns Swarzenski (London: Faber and Faber, 1954), fig. 47.

61. London, Victoria and Albert Museum: MS 661–1894, miniature, verso (*c.* 1155–60). Illustrated in *Walpole Society*, vol. 25 (1936–37), pl. VIII.

Other

62. Geneva, Cathedral St.-Pierre: transept capital. Illustrated Camille Martin, *Saint Pierre, ancienne cathédrale de Genève* (Geneva: Kündig, 1909–10), pl. XXXII (3).

Byzantine

63. Florence, Biblioteca Laurenziana: Plut. VI, MS 23, fol. 164r (Gospel Book; eleventh century). Illustrated in Tania Velmans, *Le Tétraévangile de la Laurentienne* (Paris: Kleinsieck, 1971), p. 48 (fig. 266)

64. Paris, Bibliothèque Nationale: MS gr. 74, fol. 162r (Gospel Book; eleventh century). Illustrated in Henri Omont, *Evangiles avec peintures Byzantines du XIe siècle* (Paris: Berthaud, 1908), pl. 141(1).

Problematic identifications

65. Cairo, Museum: Stele 8705 (seventh or eighth centuries).
66. Camus (Co. Derry): cemetery cross (Peter Harbison, *The High Crosses of Ireland: An Iconographical and Photographic Survey*, Römisch-Germanisches Zentralmuseum, Monographien 17/3, vol. 1, Bonn: Habelt, 1992, p. 31).
67. Castledermot (Co. Kildare): north cemetery cross (Harbison, *High Crosses*, p. 38).
68. Castledermot (Co. Kildare): south cemetery cross (Harbison, *High Crosses*, p. 40).
69. Cologne, St. Maria im Kapitol: panel from wooden door (Romanesque; mutilated).
70. Nuaillé-sur-Boutonne, Notre-Dame: west façade archivolt (Romanesque; mutilated).
71. Peterborough, Cathedral: choir screen (destroyed; formerly attributed to the twelfth century; Lucy Freeman Sandler, "Peterborough Abbey and the Peterborough Psalter in Brussels," *Journal of the British Archaeological Association*, 3rd ser., 33 (1970): 36–49 dated to the work to the thirteenth century).
72. Rome, S. Sabina: door (5th century; Gisela Jeremias, *Die Holztür der Basilika S. Sabina in Rom*, Bilderhefte des Deutschen Archäologischen Instituts Rom 7, Tübingen: Wasmuth 1980, pp. 77–80).
73. *Sigardus Psalter* (by twelfth century; known through its mention in London, British Lib., Egerton MS 3323, fol. 31r; see Francis Wormald, "A Medieval Description of Two Illuminated Psalters," *Scriptorium* 6, 1952, p. 24).

CHAPTER NINE

PORTALS, PROCESSIONS, PILGRIMAGE, AND PIETY: SAINTS FIRMIN AND HONORÉ AT AMIENS*

M. Cecilia Gaposchkin

In the second decade of the thirteenth century a fire left the Roma-nesque Cathedral of Amiens in ruins.[1] The new edifice, (fig. 115) begun in the 1220s, included four decorated tympana. On two of these tympana were depicted episodes drawn from the *vitae* of impor-tant local saints, Firmin (west façade) (fig. 116) and Honoré (south transept façade).[2] (fig. 117) The choice of these two saints repre-sented a strategy that commemorated local history and sacralized local identity. The inclusion of Firmin and Honoré is not in and of itself surprising since both had served as early bishops of the diocese, and important relics of each saint were housed in the cathedral. What is surprising is the deliberate focus placed in the visual nar-rative of both tympana on the image of clerics carrying their reli-quaries in procession. The procession in the tympanum of the west façade (*c.* 1225) depicts the legendary discovery and translation of Firmin's relics in the sixth or seventh century by a later bishop, St. Salve. (fig. 118) The procession on the south transept portal (*c.* 1260) shows a miraculous episode from Honoré's *vita* in which an image of the crucified Christ bowed the upper half of his body to the saint when his reliquary was processed to a neighboring church.[3] (fig. 119)

---

* I dedicate this article to Stephen Murray, in gratitude for the knowledge of and enthusiasm for Gothic buildings that he has imparted to me, and especially for his generosity in doing so.

[1] The fire that destroyed the Romanesque cathedral is traditionally dated to 1218, although no medieval text indicates its exact date. A charter of 1236 specified that a fire destroyed the earlier church, and 1218 was the plausible date chosen by seven-teenth-century authors. Stephen Murray, *Notre-Dame, Cathedral of Amiens: The Power of Change in Gothic* (Cambridge, 1996), p. 128.

[2] The other two portals on the west façade are dedicated to Christ in Judgment (central portal) and the Virgin Mary (southern portal).

[3] For Firmin's translation, *Acta sanctorum*, ed. Jean Bolland, Jean Carnandet, *et al.* (1863; repr., Paris, 1965), (hereafter AASS), January 25, cols. 34–5. For the miracle

Previous scholars have traced the textual and iconographic sources of this imagery,[4] but these sources alone do not explain why images of processions should be the central event on which the tympana schemes were based. Although the processional events were important, they were by no means the defining episodes of the saints' *vitae*, and at least in the case of Firmin, earlier cycles, now lost, did not emphasize the event.[5] Yet tympana constituted precious visual space, and because the area above and around a portal was limited in extent and highly public, and because carved image cycles were both costly and permanent, portal iconography was carefully chosen. One historian has called the church portal the "Medieval Marquee" for its capacity to present an image or a message to the church's public constituency.[6] Why, then, were the visual programs of these tympana structured around reliquary processions?

The answer lies in the importance given to such reliquary processions in local religious culture. The liturgical rite at Amiens included the procession of Firmin's and Honoré's relics on a number of occasions during the year. On certain feast days, the clergy carried the châsses in procession beyond the walls of the cathedral and to the cloister, and into the town itself, or to another church. These reliquaries were also borne in votive processions when the community sought to honor the saints or to plead for intercession, or in relic-quests conducted for fund-raising purposes. These processions, often joyful and celebratory in practice, were communal events which gave the faithful of Amiens the occasion to come into contact with their local intercessors and provided an opportunity for (and produced the expectation of) the performance of miracles.

In this essay I argue that the images of reliquary processions around which both portals were constructed drew meaning from the actual ritual processions that involved Firmin's and Honoré's reliquary châsses.[7] The imagery provided a narrative of the saintly leg-

---

of the inclined crucifix, see AASS, May 16, col. 615; Victor de Beauvillé, *Recueil de documents inédits concernant la Picardie*, vol. 3 (Paris, 1877), pp. 188–9.

[4] See fn. 32 and 37 for bibliography.

[5] See the châsse discussed below which included twelve scenes from Firmin's life; p. 239.

[6] Charles F. Altman, "The Medieval Marquee—Church Portal Sculpture as Publicity," *Journal of Popular Culture* 14/1 (1980): 37–46.

[7] For the relationship between liturgy, architectural imagery, and processional practice related to monumental decoration, see Marilyn Beaven, "A Medieval

ends to the participating faithful, thereby endowing the procession with historic (or hagiographical) meaning. At the same time, the tympana honored the saintly figures in a perennial procession of unmoving stone and promoted the saints as the objects of lay devotion. Moreover, by representing the legendary reliquary processions using contemporary (that is, thirteenth-century) details, the representations echoed actual devotional practice, collapsing the time between Amiens' sacralized history and its (medieval) present. In this way, the actual processions enacted throughout the year participated in the original legendary events depicted on the cathedral.

An exploration of the meaning and function of these images reveals the symbolic and cultural affinity between pilgrimage and reliquary processions. Saints' relics and the hope of saints' intercessions lay at the heart of both devotional practices. Both processions and pilgrimage were ritual or para-ritual processes which involved the lay faithful and entailed physical movement toward a spiritual goal. The relic-quests, in which the meaning of the regularized reliquary processions were rooted, constituted a structural inversion of pilgrimage: instead of pilgrims traveling to the shrine to venerate the saint, the reliquary shrine was transported out of the cathedral to the faithful. As with pilgrimage, the practice involved the hope for and the aura of the miraculous, the donation of funds or other alms to the saint, and the interaction of the larger devotional community with the clergy and the saints. The publicly-oriented character of the reliquary processions (comparable to the tympana imagery) served to promote the existence and power of the saints, Firmin and Honoré, who resided at the cathedral. This in turn promoted these saints, and thus, the cathedral as the object of local and individual pilgrimage.

This article begins by introducing Firmin and Honoré, summarizing their hagiographic traditions, and discussing their cults as practiced at Amiens. This is followed by a discussion of the iconography on the two tympana, which juxtaposes the emphasis of the visual cycles with those of the hagiographic traditions in which they were

Procession: Sacred Rites Commemorated in a Stained Glass Panel from Soissons Cathedral," *Bulletin of the Detroit Institute of Arts* 67/1 (1992): 30–37; Barbara Abou-El-Haj, "The Urban Setting for Late Medieval Church Building: Reims and its Cathedral between 1210 and 1240," *Art History* 11/1 (1988): 17–41; Kathleen Nolan, "Ritual and Visual Experience in the Capital Frieze at Chartres," *Gazette des Beaux-Arts*, ser. 6, 123 (1994): 53–72.

rooted and demonstrates that the iconographers highlighted the processional events. I then explain this emphasis by looking at the evidence for reliquary processions at Amiens, especially the annual processions of Firmin's and Honoré's relics in which the very reliquaries so prominently pictured in the tympana were borne by clergy and sometimes by the laity in extramural processions which may have exited through these very doorways. I conclude by suggesting that the images were designed to evoke not only the historical events narrated in the tympana's registers, but also the contemporary practice of processions which involved the entire community and served to tie local community life to its sacred and legitimizing history.

The Hagiographic and Cultic Traditions

Firmin and Honoré were early bishops of Amiens whose relics were housed in the cathedral and whose feast days were celebrated in the local liturgy. The cult of St. Firmin Martyr, the putative second-century founding bishop of Amiens, was the more popular of the two. He was the touchstone for a number of civic practices and cultural traditions that constituted a mechanism of shared identity. A treaty of 1020/21 with the city of Corbie was confirmed annually on his feast day, a group of bourgeois under episcopal jurisdiction were known as "St. Firmin's men", and the dues owed the bishop were called the "respite of St. Firmin."[8] Before the twelfth century, the cathedral was dedicated to the Virgin and Firmin, a dedication acknowledged in the church cartulary by donors who were well aware of the presence of his relics in the church.[9]

According to the hagiographic tradition, Firmin was born in Spain during the second century to recently-Christianized parents.[10] After

---

[8] Murray, *Notre-Dame*, pp. 21–2.

[9] Joseph Roux and Edmond Soyez, *Cartulaire du chapitre de la cathédrale d'Amiens*, *Mémoires de la société des antiquaires de Picardie* (Amiens, 1897–1912), v. 1, nos. 1 (847–50), 2 (1034), 5 (1069), 6 (1069–74), 8 (1080–8).

[10] On Firmin Martyr see *Bibliotheca Hagiographica Latina Antiquae et Mediae Aetatis* (Brussels,1901), 2 vols. (hereafter BHL), nos. 3002–11d. His principal feast was celebrated on September 25. The feast for the invention of his relics was January 13. For the history and cult of St. Firmin see Charles Salmon, *Histoire de Saint Firmin: martyr, premier évêque d'Amiens: patron de la Navarre et des Diocèses d'Amiens et de Pampelune* (Arras and Amiens, 1861). Salmon provides all the sources for Firmin in appen-

his investiture as bishop of Toulouse, Firmin was sent to preach the Gospel in Gaul, where he made his way northward, converting people in Anjou, Normandy, and Belgium. Ultimately he came to Amiens where he founded the church and became the city's first bishop. There he converted many pagans and proved the power of God by performing miracles. Among those in the city whom he baptized was a Roman senator, Faustinus, and his family. Hearing of Firmin's successes, the Roman governor, Sebastian, came to Amiens where pagan priests denounced the bishop for turning the town away from worship of the old gods. Sebastian ordered Firmin seized, interrogated, and ultimately beheaded. After Firmin's martyrdom, Faustinus quietly spirited the body away for burial.

The *inventio*, raising, and subsequent translation of Firmin's relics are recounted in the *vita* of one of his successors, Bishop Salve, thought to have lived in the sixth or seventh century.[11] When Salve prayed that he might find Firmin's relics, an ineffably brilliant ray of light marked the location of his tomb, a sweet odor emerged when Salve opened it, and many flowers blossomed in the field making it a "verdant delight."[12] The sweet smell reached the cities of Thérouanne, Cambrai, Noyon, and Beauvais, and hordes of clergy and townspeople arrived in order to aid in the translation. Together clergy and laity processed to Amiens with Firmin's relics, "carrying candles and palms and singing psalmody and hymns."[13] As soon as Salve and

---

dixes I–X (pp. 399–501), including the liturgical texts and the evidence of his miracles drawn from breviaries from Amiens. A number of the hagiographical texts are also treated in AASS September VII (September 25), cols. 24–57 (cols. 51–7 for texts). For the legend of and sources for Firmin's life, see Salmon, who discusses the printed and manuscript sources, pp. civ–cxxviii. Firmin Martyr should not be confused with another early bishop from Amiens, Firmin the Confessor (feast September 1). BHL nos. 3012–4. AASS Sept. I (Sept. 1), cols. 175–99 (cols. 178–81 for texts).

[11] AASS January I (January 1) col. 706; AASS September VII (September 25) cols. 34–7; the *Sermo de Inventione S. Firmini*, which Salmon believes to be the oldest account of the translation, is published in *Histoire de Saint Firmin*, pp. 423–8.

[12] "A sweet odor emerged from the tomb, as if from a great variety of pigments and spices being crushed to release their odor, and the field appeared verdant with the delight of many flowers." (*Odor quoque suavitatis illico tantus excreverat, quasi illic omnia genera pigmentorum contunderentur & aromatum, & ager virens amoenitate diversorum florum adesset.*) AASS, September 25, v. 7, col. 34, Salmon, *Saint Firmin*, p. 426.

[13] AASS, September 25, v. 7, col. 34, Salmon, *Saint Firmin*, p. 427. "But indeed, all the priests and clerics, and people of both sexes, came forth at once from those cities already mentioned, [carrying] candles and palms, and singing psalmody and

the other priests lifted the relics from the ground, the weather miraculously changed from the cold of a January winter to springtime. The bishops of Thérouanne, Cambrai, Noyon, Beauvais, and Amiens carried the relics while the crowds cast off clothing in the heat and sang: *Hosanna in excelsis! Benedictus qui venit in nomine Domini.*[14] (Hosanna in the highest! Blessed is he who comes in the name of the Lord.) Trees sprouted leaves, flowers, and fruit, and their branches reached downward, as if in homage to the saint. The miraculous change in seasons lasted three hours, during which time a number of crippled or sick devotees were cured. Firmin's relics were transferred to a reliquary of gilded wood which was placed in the cathedral's crypt, and a feast day was established to commemorate the translation. By the thirteenth century, Firmin's was the strongest of the local cults in Amiens. The cathedral's calendar listed five separate feasts honoring him, including the invention and translation of his relics (January 13), his martyrdom (September 25) and its octave (October 2), a feast celebrating his arrival in Amiens (October 10), and a commemoration of the deposition of his relics in the new reliquary (October 16). The ritual display—or uncovering (*discooperitur*)—of Firmin's relics comprised a central part of the liturgical rites on Firmin's feasts and on other liturgical occasions,[15] and his relics were integral to a number of great processions during the liturgical year.[16]

The early stages of Honoré's cult were more muted than Firmin's,[17] and he does not seem to have enjoyed Firmin's wide popularity in Amiens before the thirteenth century. His earliest known *vita*, meager by comparison with Firmin's, dates to the eleventh century.[18] The catalogues compiled by Victor Leroquais indicate that Honoré

---

hymns." (*Sed omnes quidem sacerdotes et clerici, populusque diversorum sexuum praefatarum urbium statim surrexerunt cum cereis et palmis, hymnorum psalmodiam decantantes.*)

[14] A variation of Mark 11.10 relating to Christ's (processional) entrance into Jerusalem that was incorporated as an antiphon into the Palm Sunday liturgy, which itself comprised a general procession. AASS, September 25, v. 7, col. 34; Salmon, *Saint Firmin*, p. 427.

[15] Georges Durand, ed., *Ordinaire de l'église Notre-Dame, Cathédrale d'Amiens, Mémoires: Documents inédits concernant la province 22.* (Amiens, 1934), pp. 30, 109, 462, 483, 495, 500, 504, 570, etc.

[16] See discussion of Ascension procession below; Durand, ed., *Ordinaire*, pp. lviii–lix, pp. 307–9; and, for the Octave for Epiphany, pp. 108–9.

[17] For early indications of Honoré's cult beyond Amiens, see Corblet, *Hagiographie*, 3, p. 61.

[18] Corblet, *Hagiographie*, 3, p. 47.

appears in only six surviving breviaries and missals before 1300, whereas Firmin is represented in the sanctorals of twenty-six sacramentaries and thirty-six breviaries from Amiens and elsewhere.[19] At Amiens, Honoré was honored with only two feast days (May 16 and its octave).[20] The later thirteenth century and the fourteenth century, however, witnessed the acceleration of his cult and its dispersion beyond Amiens. In 1204 a chapel in Paris[21] and in 1301 a Carthusian monastery in Abbeville were dedicated to Honoré.[22] New versions of his *vita* and a proper liturgical office for his feast at Amiens were produced after 1200,[23] and his cult was increasingly incorporated into the rites of other towns in the diocese and beyond.[24] The large portal which was erected on the south transept in the 1260s appears to reflect the magnification of his cult in the thirteenth century.

Honoré's hagiography consists mostly of miracle stories from his episcopacy and after his death.[25] He was born at Porte-le-Grand, near Ponthieu, in the early sixth century, led a pious childhood, and was acclaimed bishop at the death of his predecessor Béat. The earliest tradition names him the sixth bishop of Amiens, although a later text suggested he succeeded Firmin Martyr directly.[26] Honoré is said to have resisted the episcopal honor out of humility, but a

---

[19] Victor Leroquais, *Les bréviaires manuscrits des bibliothèques publiques de France* (Paris, 1934), 1, pp. 11, 19; Victor Leroquais, *Les sacramentaires et les missels manuscrits des bibliothèques publiques de France* (Paris, 1924), 1, pp. 137, 232, 280; 2, p. 49.

[20] Durand, *Ordinaire*, p. 9. Evidence for the celebration of the octave is on pp. 296–9.

[21] The chapel was founded by Reynaldo and his wife Sancha, who were probably from Amiens; AASS, May III (May 16), col. 612. In 1301, Guillaume of Mascon, bishop of Amiens, founded a Carthusian monastery to Honoré in Abbeville, according to the legend, the place of Honoré's birth. AASS, May III (May 16), col. 612. The files at the Index of Christian Art at Princeton have only four entries under Honoré, all from Amiens after 1250.

[22] AASS, May III (May 16), col. 612.

[23] For the new *vita*, see de Beauvillé, *Recueil de documents*, pp. 181–91 found in a manuscript of the late fourteenth century. For the liturgical office, see *Analecta Hymnica Medii Aevi* ed. Guido Dreves *et al.* (Leipzig, 1886–1922), 13, no. 65, which derived from a 1554 printed breviary from Amiens. Proper offices are attested only in manuscripts of the fourteenth century; de Beauvillé, *Recueil de documents*, p. 181, fn. 1; Durand, *Ordinaire*, p. lviii.

[24] Corblet, *Hagiographie*, 3, pp. 61–5; Leroquais, *Bréviaires*, 2, pp. 367–371, 422; 3, p. 475; 4, pp. 331, 397; Leroquais, *Sacramentaires*, 3, p. 133.

[25] For Honoré, see AASS, May 16, cols. 613–5. A good summary of the legend and cult can be found in Corblet, *Hagiographie*, 3, pp. 37–77.

[26] Corblet, *Hagiographie*, 3, pp. 38–77. For the later tradition, de Beauvillé, *Recueil de documents*, p. 182.

stream of oil came directly from heaven effecting his miraculous consecration. As bishop he was once blessed with a vision of the hand
of God while celebrating the Easter Mass. In a miracle attested to
by many, the hand of the Savior himself administered the eucharistic sacrament to the sainted bishop. One of the more important
events of Honoré's episcopacy was the discovery of the relics of late-
third or early–fourth-century martyr-saints Fuscien, Victoric, and
Gentien, although curiously not by Honoré himself, but rather by
one of his priests, Lupicin.[27] The story reports that an angel told
Lupicin of the relics' whereabouts. Upon the priest's discovery of the
saints' crypt, the sweet odor of sanctity emerged, and Lupicin sang
a hymn. Honoré, far away celebrating the Mass, heard the hymn
and hastened to the crypt. Once news of the find surfaced, King
Childebert († 558) determined to remove the relics to the Abbey at
St.-Vincent of Laon. Miraculously, the king's envoys found it impossible to transport this holy trove, and Childebert eventually presented
the relics as a gift to the cathedral. At Honoré's death in the late-
fifth or early–sixth century he was buried in a parish church in his
hometown. According to the eleventh-century *vita* he was translated
to the parish church dedicated to Sts. Peter and Paul in Amiens in
the middle of the ninth century because of the danger posed by the
Danish invasions, and soon thereafter transferred to the cathedral.[28]

Honoré's most important miracles were posthumous, including his
healing of a blind woman, a paralytic boy, and a possessed cleric.
His most famous miracle—and one to which reference is made in
the thirteenth-century portal—involves the procession of his relics.
As part of a general procession, Honoré's reliquary was carried to
the nearby church of Sts. Peter and Paul (the first home of his relics
in Amiens and later dedicated to Firmin Confessor). As the reliquary
was borne from the parish church the statue of Christ on the large
wooden crucifix which sat atop the jubé inclined its head towards
the reliquary.[29] The clergy thenceforth commemorated the miracle

---

[27] Fuscien, Victoric, and Gentien were believed to have been buried at Sains
c. 303. Corblet, *Hagiographie*, 3, p. 43.

[28] Corblet, *Hagiographie*, 3, p. 49.

[29] "For, when on a certain feast day [the relics of Honoré] were going to be
carried back to their own place from the neighboring church dedicated to the
blessed apostles Peter and Paul, an image belonging to that church, representing
the crucified Jesus, bent deeply part of himself to the side where the most saintly

on Honoré's feast day with a procession in which the transport of Honoré's relics to the neighboring church was re-enacted, and the episode was commemorated in the liturgical rites for Honoré, recalling the honor in a lauds prayer and in the prose sequence of a Mass.[30]

The Portal Imagery and the Cults of Amiens' Local Saints

Two tympana—one on the west façade, the other on the south transept portal—were given over to the roles that these two episcopal saints (and their relics) played in the devotional life of the city.[31] Both included representations of reliquary processions during which important miracles occurred. Indeed, each sequence positions images of its legendary procession prominently within the visual scheme. The Firmin portal (figs. 116, 118), built in the third decade of the thirteenth century, was the left-most entryway of the west façade's three portals.[32] The central portal, dedicated to Christ, depicts the Last Judgment, and the portal to its right shows the Coronation of the Virgin.[33] Unlike Christ and the Virgin, Firmin had, as far as we

---

body was being carried away." AASS, May 16, col. 615. (*Nam dum ab ecclesia vicina, in honorem Sanctorum Apostolorum Petri & Pauli fundata, in sedem propriam quodam die solenni referretur; praefatae ecclesiae imago, Jesum Crucifixum exprimens, se toto corpore inclinavit in partem, qua corpus sanctissimum ferebatur.*)

[30] Andrew Hughes, *Late Medieval Liturgical Offices: Texts* (Toronto, 1994). Hughes designates each office and service with a reference number. The number for this office is HO51, LE. The antiphon is also reproduced in Corblet, *Hagiographie*, 3, 54, fn. 1. Corblet, *Hagiographie*, v. 3, p. 64 reproduces the prose "according to our ancient missels" (*d'après nos anciens missels*).

[31] On portal-schemes which honor local episcopal saints, see Willibald Sauerländer, *Gothic Sculpture in France, 1140–1270* (New York, 1973) pp. 39–41.

[32] Murray, *Notre-Dame*, pp. 108–11; Carl F. Barnes, "Cross-Media Design Motifs in XIIIth-Century France: Architectural Motifs in the Psalter and Hours of Yolande de Soissons and in the Cathedral of Notre-Dame at Amiens," *Gesta* 17/2 (1978), pp. 37–40; Sauerländer, *Gothic Sculpture in France*, pp. 464–6; Karen Gould, "Illumination and Sculpture in Thirteenth-Century Amiens: The Invention of the Body of Saint Firmin in the Psalter and Hours of Yolande of Soissons," *The Art Bulletin* 59/2 (1977), pp. 161–6; Charles Salmon, "Iconographie du portail de Saint-Firmin," *Revue de l'Art Chrétien* 4 (1860), pp. 617–26; Georges Durand, *Monographie de l'église Notre-Dame, cathédrale d'Amiens, Mémoires de la Société des antiquaires de Picardie* (Paris, 1901) 1, pp. 401–15.

[33] Sauerländer, *Gothic Sculpture*, pp. 462–66; Wolfgang Medding, *Die Westportale der Kathedrale von Amiens und ihre Meister* (Augsburg, 1930); Murray, *Notre-Dame*, pp. 103–23; Marcia R. Rickard, "The Iconography of the Virgin Portal at Amiens," *Gesta* 22/2 (1983), pp. 147–57; Adolf Katzenellenbogen, "The Prophets on the West Façade: Cathedral at Amiens," *Gazette des Beaux-Arts*, ser. 6 40 (1952), pp. 241–60.

know, no long-established iconographic tradition, and the portal itself constitutes a retelling of Firmin's legend.[34] Strikingly, what is shown here is not his life, travels and preaching in Gaul, conversion of Picardy, baptism of the senator Faustinus, or arrest and execution at the hands of Sebastian, but only the final episode in his legend, the invention and translation of his relics to the cathedral, suggesting that it was the presence of Firmin's relics that was deemed most relevant to advertise to the Amienois.

The tympanum proper is divided into three registers. Below, Firmin is depicted on the trumeau, wearing his bishop's miter and holding his crozier in one hand while blessing with the other. He stands atop a crouching figure, probably the Roman governor who ordered his execution; the figure balances that of Christ (the *Beau Dieu*) in the central portal and the echo no doubt represents the bishop as a type of Christ. The bottom register depicts six mitered bishops, each in a gesture of blessing or with an attribute (such as a crozier) denoting their episcopal status. These bishops formally balance the six Old Testament prophets and priests that hold the corresponding place in the Virgin portal on the right. The episcopal figures exist independently of the Firmin narrative and were probably intended to convey an episcopal succession at Amiens rooted in Firmin's sanctity and virtue.

Specific depiction of events relating to Firmin begins in the central register. At right, we see a figure kneeling in prayer, perhaps representing the Bishop Salve praying for divine guidance in finding Firmin's remains (although the figure is un-mitered). The central episode shows Salve (mitered) and a series of followers discovering Firmin's tomb, which is displayed at an angle, with either an effigy or an incorrupt Firmin lying on top. As indicated in the translation account, a ray of light descends from the heavens, illuminating the spot. Throngs of people from four cities (Thérouanne, Cambrai, Noyon, and Beauvais) arrive from all directions at the news of the discovery. These are depicted on either side of Firmin's invention: groups of people, having been summoned by the sweet odor released upon the opening of Firmin's tomb, emerge from four architectonic symbols representing the four cities.

---

[34] On Firmin's iconography, see Gould, "Illumination and Sculpture," pp. 161–6; Barnes, "Cross-Media Design," pp. 37–40.

The top register depicts the translation of Firmin's relics. (fig. 118) Beneath the hand of God, which emerges from clouds at the tympanum's peak surrounded by four angels swinging censers, the register shows an orderly, but lively ecclesiastical procession. On the left, four clerics carry Firmin's sarcophagus on their shoulders, supported by two cross beams. To the right, the cortège continues, including a cleric who holds a richly jeweled book and another who holds an arm reliquary.[35] (fig. 121) The tradition of a miraculous change in weather that accompanied the invention is alluded to by the artist with a tree which sprouts up on the very left behind a member of the procession. The *vita* specified that throngs of people joined in, escorting the remains of the sacred martyr to their new and permanent home. At the right of the top register, three figures have climbed into leafy trees in order to watch or greet the procession in an iconography designed to directly echo that of Christ's entry into Jerusalem.[36] This detail is the visual equivalent of the hagiography's incorporation of *Hosanna in excelsis*, which reinforces and sacralizes the reference to Christomimetic procession.

The south transept portal (*c.* 1260, fig. 117) also includes the prominent display of a reliquary procession.[37] (fig. 119) The elaborate decoration of that portal stands in sharp contrast to the austere north transept because, as Stephen Murray noted, the south portal opened onto the canons' cloister, one of the town's principal thoroughfares, and was designed with its "public location" in mind.[38] The south tympanum is divided into four registers, all devoted to Honoré's miracles. It sits atop a wide lintel depicting the twelve apostles, which

---

[35] Murray, *Notre-Dame*, p. 109.

[36] This feature was almost ubiquitous in the iconography of Christ's entry into Jerusalem, including the *c.* 1300 jubé. *L'art au temps des rois maudits: Philippe le Bel et ses fils, 1285–1328* (Paris, 1998), no. 39A; Françoise Baron, "Mort et résurrection du jubé de la cathédrale d'Amiens," *Revue de l'Art* 87 (1990): 29–41.

[37] For the sculptural program of the south portal transept, see Murray, *Notre-Dame*, pp. 118–20; Sauerländer, *Gothic Sculpture*, pp. 494–5; Dieter Kimpel, "Die Skulpturenwerkstatt der Vierge Dorée am Honoratusportal der Kathedrale von Amiens," *Zeitschrift für Kunstgeschichte* 36/4 (1973): 217–265; Adolf Katzenellenbogen, "Tympanum and Archivolts on the Portal of St. Honore at Amiens," in *De artibus Opuscula XL: Essays in Honor of Erwin Panofsky*, ed. Millard Meiss (New York, 1961): 280–291; Georges Durand, *Monographie;* Louis Jourdain Antoine Théophile Duval, *Le portail Saint-Honoré, dit de la Vierge Dorée de la cathédrale d'Amiens* (Amiens, 1844); Louis Jourdain and Antoine Théophile Duval, "Le grand portail de la cathédrale d'Amiens," *Bulletin Monumental* 11 (1845–46): 145–178, 12 (1846): 96–105.

[38] Murray, *Notre-Dame*, p. 118.

Adolf Katzenellenbogen suggested represented types for the function of the bishop (and might be understood as fulfilling the same function as the six bishops in the bottom register of the Firmin portal).[39] The lowest of the registers shows Honoré's early episcopacy: at left he receives miraculous consecration from heaven as several amazed onlookers witness the event. On the far right is represented the miracle for which his episcopacy was most remembered—the discovery of the relics of Fuscien, Gentien, and Victoric. Honoré is shown just left of the invention-scene, seated under an arched baldachin, probably intended to symbolize Amiens,[40] where he was when he learned of the relics' discovery. To Honoré's right, his priest, Lupicin, is shown in a leafy grove searching for the lost tombs.

The second register portrays a number of Eucharistic miracles from Honoré's episcopacy. At left, four witnesses watch as the hand of God descends to consecrate the host while Honoré celebrates the Mass. At right, Honoré cures a woman of blindness by touching the altar cloth to her eyes. A statue rests atop the altar to Honoré's right. An infirm man led by his dog emerges from the left side of the register, also about to be healed. Emphasis is placed on the liturgical authority of the bishop and the miraculous events associated with the sacraments.[41]

The procession of Honoré's reliquary is shown in the third register. Together, the third and fourth registers depict the posthumous miracle in which the image of the Savior bowed to Honoré. In the third register the processional cortège moves from right to left, and two men bear a litter supporting the reliquary on their shoulders. Three figures, bent or kneeling, are seen under the châsse, reaching up to touch it. The tympanum culminates in the top register with a (heavily restored) image of the Crucifixion which completed the depiction of the posthumous miracle. At the same time that it represents the wooden crucifix that bowed to Honoré in the neighboring church, the image constitutes a traditional image of the historical crucifixion, including the swooning Virgin and the Evangelist on either side of the cross and two kneeling angels.

---

[39] Katzenellenbogen, "Tympanum and Archivolts," p. 281.

[40] An architectural motif is often used as a visual short-hand to refer to a city, as on the Firmin Portal where four such motifs in the middle register indicate the four cities from which people came to join in the relics' invention and translation to Amiens.

[41] Noted by Murray, *Notre-Dame*, p. 119.

Reliquary processions thus figure prominently in the representation of both visual narratives. (figs. 118–9) On the south transept portal, the procession of Honoré's relics occupies a whole register, with the châsse centered squarely beneath the figure of Christ. On the west façade, the upper register is entirely devoted to the image of the procession. In both instances, men bear on their shoulders the weight of the large sepulcher-like reliquary, supported by two cross beams, mimicking thirteenth-century processional practice.

Relics and Processions in and around Amiens Cathedral

The question, then, is why the emphasis in these images on processions, and in particular reliquary processions? Why did the planners of the iconographic schemes decide not once but twice to structure the portal iconography around the event of the reliquary procession? What was the reason for commemorating these events rather than the foundation of the church, the martyrdom of Firmin, or Honoré's ministry, or his relics' royal patronage (Childebert)? The emphasis on the image of the processed reliquary may draw its importance and meaning less from the hagiographical tradition than from the patterns of processional rituals that were an important feature of Amiénois religious culture.

Processions were a regular part of the liturgical rite at Amiens.[42] In addition to frequent processional rites within the church, clerics had occasion to process into the cloister[43] and to other churches in town.[44] The processions of particular relevance to the portal iconography are those in which the reliquary-châsses of the cathedral's saints were carried beyond the confines of the cathedral's walls through the cloister or into the city and surrounding countryside. There

---

[42] This was typical. Perhaps the processional rite best known to historians is that of Salisbury. See Terence Bailey, *The Processions of Sarum and the Western Church* (Toronto, 1971). On the medieval rites of procession in general, Sabine Felbecker, *Die Prozession: Historische und systematische Untersuchungen zu einer liturgischen Ausdruckshandlung*, Münsteraner Theologische Abhandlungen. Altenberg: 1995. *Editors' note, see Rita Tekippe's essay in this volume.

[43] For example, a solemn procession entered the canons' cloister on the feast day of John the Baptist. Durand, ed., *Ordinaire*, p. 362.

[44] The canons processed to the neighboring collegiale of St.-Firmin-the-Confessor as part of the extended Easter liturgy. Durand, ed., *Ordinaire*, p. 235.

were two types of extramural transport of reliquaries: processions prescribed by the ordinary ritual which occurred on certain feast days, and extraordinary processions, or relic-quests, in which châsses were processed outside of the city and throughout the diocese either to elicit funds (often for the rebuilding or upkeep of the church) or as votive rituals in times of drought or other catastrophe. Relic-quests seem to have occurred in northern Europe with increasing frequency after about 1050, and there is ample anecdotal evidence for the practice in Amiens before the two portals were erected.[45] Reliquary processions also occurred regularly at Amiens on an annual basis in the form of ordinary rites which were part of the regular liturgical year, as, for example, on September 1 when the canons carried the relics of St. Firmin Confessor (not Martyr) around the canons' close on the south side of the church as part of his liturgical rite,[46] or the Palm Sunday liturgy, in which the châsse of St. Denis and a great silver cross were carried in a double (split) procession that met up at the old city walls.[47]

Most intriguing with regard to the portal images are the processions involving Firmin's and Honoré's relics. The shrines were processed in both ordinary (i.e. regular) and extraordinary (i.e. relic-quest) processions. Honoré's relics were sent throughout the diocese to elicit pious contributions for the church in 1060 and then again in 1240,[48] and he was invoked repeatedly in times of plague or drought or storms.[49] The propitiary procession of 1060 around the walls of the

---

[45] On relic-quests see Pierre-André Sigal, "Le voyage de reliques au XIe et XIIe siècle," in *Voyage, quête, pélerinage dans la littérature et la civilisation médiévales: [actes du colloque organisé par le C.U.E.R. M.A. les 5, 6, 7 mars 1976]*, *Sénéfiance 2* (Aix-en-Provence and Paris, 1985): 73–104; Pierre Héliot and Marie-Laure Chastang, "Quête et voyages de reliques au profit des église française du moyen âge," *Revue d'histoire ecclésiastique* 59 (1964): 759–822, 60 (1965): 5–342. At v. 59, pp. 799–800 the authors argue that relic quests began in northern France in the mid-eleventh century. See also Rita Tekippe, *Procession, Piety, and Politics: Three Medieval Rheno-Mosan Reliquary Shrines and the Cult Communities for Bishop-Saints Servatius of Maastricht, Eleutherius of Tournai, and Remaclus of Stavelot* (Ph.D. diss: Ohio State University, 1999), pp. 248–54.

[46] Durand, ed., *Ordinaire*, p. 438.

[47] Durand, ed., *Ordinaire*, pp. 217–8. Other examples include the procession on the fourth day after Easter of the reliquary of St.-Ulphe, who was depicted as a jamb figure of the Firmin portal. Durand, ed., *Ordinaire*, p. 239.

[48] Corblet, *Hagiographie*, 3, pp. 50, 61, 66. Durand, *Ordinaire*, p. lx.

[49] "When the body of that saint is carried (*defertur*) on account of plague, or on account of too great a flood of water, or on account of drought, the fast having been established and announced by the assent of the community, all of the reliquaries of the saints are carried at the same time, just as on Rogation days. The

city to combat drought was remembered for the large number of miracles that Honoré's relics performed.[50] Votive processions of Honoré's relics into town or beyond the city walls were performed in 1220 and 1288, and periodically until 1785.[51] The entry in the cathedral's Ordinary on this matter indicates that processions were determined by the assent of the religious community.[52]

Firmin's châsse was also enlisted in time of local need. On May 3, 1137, to meet the cost of the restoration of the fire-damaged cathedral, Garin of Châtillon, bishop of Amiens (r. 1127–44), ordered the transport of Saint Firmin's relics into the surrounding towns in order to solicit alms from the faithful.[53] However, the relics miraculously refused to be transported beyond the city walls and had to be returned to the cathedral, whereupon the faithful poured into town to offer alms: "gold necklaces, silver plate, precious stones, a great quantity of coins and rings, and the elegant robes that they wore on holidays . . ."[54] In response to a drought in the twelfth century,

---

Procession having been prepared for, the precentor, in his stall, in undecorated albs, before the high altar, to which a cross is carried, and a censer with two candles, and blessed water, begins, *Antiphon: Exurge Domine*, with the Psalm *Et Gloria*, without the versicle being recited. Prayer: *Parce Domine, Per Christum Dominum nostrum*. And then, all the antiphons which are specific for a threatening storm, which are found in the troper. Those not singing should recite the seven penitential psalms with the litany and prayers. And then, in the church to which [the cortège] processes, a mass is celebrated, in which priests use green chasubles with undecorated albs. . . . These actions having been taken, the reliquary of the aforementioned saint should be put back in its proper place." Durand, *Ordinaire*, pp. 536–7. (*Quando defertur corpus alicujus sancti propter pestem, seu propter nimiam aquarum inundationem, vel propter siccitatem, de communi assensu statuto et indicto jejunio, deferuntur omnes simul reliquie sanctorum a sacerdotibus sicut in letaniis. Processione vero preparata, in albis non paratis ante majus altare, in qua defertur una crux, et unum thuribulum cum duobus cereis et aqua benedicta, incipit precentor in stallo suo Ant. Exurge Domine cum pslamo et Gloria. Absque versiculo dicitur Or. Parce Domine, Per Chrisum Dominum nostrum. Deinde canuntur ordinate omnes antiphone que proprie sunt contra tempestatem imminentem, que in tropariis inveniuntur. Qui vero non cantant dicant septem psalmos penitenciales cum letania et orationes. In ecclesia siquidem ad quam proceditur celebratur missa, in qua utuntur ministri casulis viridibus cum albis non paratis. . . . Quibus actis, capsula predicti sancti in locum suum reponatur.*)
    [50] Corblet, *Hagiographie*, 3, p. 50, 66.
    [51] Corblet, *Hagiographie*, 3, p. 58; AASS, May 16, col. 615.
    [52] Durand, *Ordinaire*, p. 536. See above, fn. 49 for the text.
    [53] ". . . truly, so that the body of blessed Firmin was carried (*portaretur*) through the boundaries of his authority (*ambitum sue potestatis*, that is, the diocese) for the honorable restoration of his church." Durand, *Monographie*, 1, p. 11, fn. 1 (*. . . videlicet ut beati Firmini corpus infra ambitum sue potestatis, ad restaurationem ecclesie sue honorifice portaretur.*) Salmon, *Histoire de Saint Firmin*, pp. 179, 202 fn. 2; Edmond Soyez, *La Procession du Saint-Sacrement et les Processions Générales à Amiens* (Amiens, 1896), p. 15.
    [54] *[I]bi videlicet in foro vel in ecclesia precioso martiri preciosa munera offerunt, aurea monilia,*

Firmin's relics were carried around town in a procession during which a crippled woman was miraculously cured and was able to join the cortège.[55] Another drought in 1478 was combated by aldermen processing Firmin's relics to the Church of St. Acheul.[56]

Perhaps of greater importance to the interpretation of the tympana, both Firmin's and Honoré's reliquaries were also involved in regular annual processions. Evidence for these yearly processions is provided by the cathedral's Ordinary, copied in 1291. Because liturgical volumes of this kind tend to represent the ritual practice of roughly the half century preceding their compilation, this Ordinary is almost certain to represent the ritual practice at work prior to and during the period of the tympana's erection. The Ordinary prescribed the extra-mural processions (weather permitting) of Firmin's relics on Ascension, and for Honoré's relics on his feast day (May 16) and again on Pentecost.[57] The processional patterns of these rites had their origins in the occasional and ultimately miraculous processions which were remembered in hagiographic lore—in Firmin's case the procession of 1137, in Honoré's the procession to the nearby Church of St. Firmin-the-Confessor during which the jubé crucifix at this church bowed his head to Honoré's relics. The Ordinary (a prescriptive source, not prone to commentary glosses) even noted that the Honoré-day rite commemorated the votive procession "on account of the miracle once performed (*propter miraculum quondam factum*)."[58]

---

vasa argentea, lapides preciosis, nummerorum etiam et anulorum copia magna datur, et ea quibus festivis diebus utebantur vestimenta . . . Durand, *Monographie*, p. 10, transcribing Amiens BM ms. 112, fol. 290; Salmon, *Histoire de Saint Firmin*, p. 181, fn. 3. The story is that on the appointed day innumerable crowds lined the roads where priests planned to carry the relics, wailing that they did not want the saint to leave the city. Miraculously, the moment at which the priests were to walk through the city gate, the reliquary became so heavy that it was impossible for the clerics to support it on their shoulders, and they could take no further steps. It lightened only when they decided to return to the cathedral.

[55] Corblet, *Hagiographie*, 3, p. 166.

[56] Salmon, *Histoire de Saint Firmin*, pp. 218–9.

[57] Durand, ed., *Ordinaire*, p. 292 (Feast of Honoré), 308 (Ascension), and 319 (Pentecost), 464.

[58] "The response *O decus ecclesie*, which is sung with the verse, with *Gloria*, is begun by the precentor and the cantor for the procession. Truly, the reliquary of Saint Honoré is carried in procession through the cloister and into the middle of the church of St.-Firmin-the-Confessor, on account of the miracle that was once performed, and, while entering, the antiphon *Ave Pastor* is sung without the verse and oration. This is followed with *Salve festa dies*, as above. When the procession enters the Church of St.-Firmin-the-Confessor, incense is burned by two. When however

The annual processions were explicitly designed to re-enact these events, and they used the original procession as a template. Thus, the Ascension procession constituted a retracing of the route to the edge of town taken by the attempted relic-quest of 1137 in which the relics had refused to leave the city. Likewise, on Pentecost and May 16, Honoré's reliquary was borne along the same path it had traveled in the eleventh century when Christ nodded in its direction. By 1295, it seems, Honoré's relics were also transported annually to the church at Moreuil, a dependant town within the diocese.[59]

These processions may have entered and exited the cathedral through the very doors on which they were represented. The prescriptions for the procession of Honoré's reliquary (May 16) and Pentecost instruct the cortège to pass through the cloister (the door for which was the south transept portal dedicated to Honoré) and to the Church of Firmin-the-Confessor, before returning to the cathedral.[60] On the eve of such a procession, the reliquary was uncovered and displayed

---

the procession enters into the principal church, the response *Sedit angelus* is sung. The verse is said by four before the choir, verse *Dicitur in nationibus*. The collect [oratio] *Solita*. The benediction is given by the bishop with the arm of St. Firmin Martyr. In returning, the antiphon *Regina caeli*, the verse, *Post partum*, the collect, *Famulorum tuorum, per eundem Dominum nostrum* [is said]. No memoria are done." Durand, ed., *Ordinaire* p. 292. (*A precentore et cantore chorum regentibus in capis viridibus incipitur ad processionem r/ [O decus ecclesie] quod canitur cum versu, cum Gloria. . . . Capsula vero sancti Honorati defertur ad processionem per claustrum et medium ecclesie Sancti Firmini confessoris propter miraculum quondam factum, et intrando canitur Ant. Ave Pastor absque versiculo et oratione. Deinde sequitur Salve festa dies, ut supra. Dum vero intrat processio in ecclesiam sancti Firmini confessoris a duobus thurificatur. Dum autem intrat processio in majori ecclesia canitur r/ Sedit angelus; versus dicitur a quatuor ante chorum v/ Dicite in nationibus. Or. Solita. Ab episcopo datur benedictio cum brachio sancti Firmini martyris. In reditu, Ant: [Regina celi], v/ Post partum. Or Famulorum tuorum. Per eundem Dominum nostrum Non fiunt alie memorie.*) The ordinary continues with a description of the Mass that follows, at the end of which there are instructions that Honoré's reliquary be replaced on the high altar. "After the hour of sext the reliquary of St. Honoré is carried back and placed on the high altar, while singing the antiphon *Confessor*, and burning incense, verse/ *Ora pro nobis.*" (*Post sextam horam refertur et reponitur capsula sancti Honorati super majus altare canendo Ant. Confessor, et thurificatur v/ Ora pro nobis.*)

[59] Corblet, *Hagiographie*, 3, p. 61.

[60] For the indications for the feast day of St. Honoré, Durand, ed., *Ordinaire*, p. 292, transcribed above, at fn. 58: The indications for Pentecost are: "While singing, [the procession] advances through the cloister and through the church of Saint-Firmin-the-Confessor, if the reliquary of Saint Honoré is carried; [the reliquary] is carried in that procession, unless it was already carried or is to be later carried. Durand, ed., *Ordinaire*, p. 319. (*Sic canendo proceditur per claustrum et per ecclesiam sancti Firmini Confessoris si deferatur capsula sancti Honorati, que ad istam processionem defertur, nisi delata fuerit vel deferenda.*)

in the church.[61] The following morning, the priests would place Honoré's reliquary on their shoulders and exit the doorway of the cathedral into the canons' close—the area south of the cathedral reserved for the canons.[62] The procession proceeded through the cloister onto which the south portal opens, and the cortège thus passed through the Honoré portal on which the very procession they were re-enacting was shown. The clergy would circle the cloister and make their way to the neighboring parish church dedicated to St.-Firmin-the-Confessor. When the procession returned to the cathedral, the relics were placed back in the chancel and the bishop blessed the attendant population with the arm-reliquary of St. Firmin.[63] The rite for Pentecost was in turn based on that of the St.-Honoré-day procession.[64]

The evidence of the Ordinary is not as explicit as one would like about which doorway was used to exit and re-enter the cathedral during the processions involving Firmin's reliquary. The Ordinary simply indicates that the Ascension procession should march "through town."[65] But the Corpus Christi procession, established in Amiens in 1322, was modeled on the Ascension procession, and on this basis, Georges Durand, a historian of the cathedral and the editor of its Ordinary, argued that the Ascension procession went down the rue Notre-Dame, the rue St.-Martin, and into the marketplace, into the rue des Chaudronniers and the rue Lin, to the Place-St.-Firmin, before the Church of Saint-Firmin-à-la-Porte (so named because of

---

[61] "The reliquary of blessed Honoré, having been made ready the evening before, is carried after Matins from the high altar by canons [and] clerics of the choir, into the middle of the church singing the response *Lux celebris*, and the verse *Ora pro nobis beate Honorate*." Durand, ed., *Ordinaire*, pp. 291–2. (*Capsula beati Honorati in vespere preparata post matutinos defertur ab altari magno a canonicis clericis chori in medio ecclesie canendo r/ [Lux celebris]. v/ Ora pro nobis beate Honorate.*)

[62] This ran along a main street, the rue du Cloître, of town and was heavily used. The Honoré portal, like the west's Firmin portal, would have been seen by all. The old Church of St.-Firmin-the-Confessor was torn down for cathedral construction and rebuilt slightly further west of the original building to accommodate the new construction, but the displacement was minimal and did not affect the route of the procession. For the history of the Saint Firmin building, see Stephen Murray, "Looking for Robert de Luzarches: The Early Work at Amiens Cathedral," *Gesta*, 29/1 (1990): 111–31.

[63] Durand, ed., *Ordinaire*, p. 292. See above fn. 58 for transcription. Some form of this processional rite was in use at the beginning of the thirteenth century, though it was elaborated in the fourteenth century; Durand, ed. *Ordinaire*, p. lviii.

[64] The instructions are for the Vespers for Pentecost, see fn. 60.

[65] "*fit per villam*." Durand, *Ordinaire*, p. 308.

the miracle of 1137), stopping at the "altar of St. Firmin," a stone altar which stood in the middle of the square.[66] (fig. 123) There the reliquary remained while the choir sung the prayers of the station (i.e. the designated stopping point) before being returned to the cathedral.[67] It seems likely that on Ascension the cortège exited through the west entrance, possibly through the very portal dedicated to Saint Firmin on which the procession's historical origins are depicted since the great central judgment portal was only opened during Lent.

These processions, often festive occasions, allowed for lay involvement in ecclesiastical rituals.[68] It has already been noted that the source processions recounted in the hagiography were described as involving the urban community. The quest of 1137 was said to include a huge crowd of faithful who bewailed the departure of Firmin's relics.[69] An early thirteenth-century account by Richard of Gerberoy, the bishop of Amiens (r. 1205–10), of a miracle that occurred during the annual St. Honoré day procession indicates that the reliquary was carried among a great throng of both clerics and laymen.[70] The Ordinary's instructions for Ascension specify that

---

[66] Durand, *Ordinaire*, p. lix. For the Ascension rite, Durand, *Ordinaire*, p. 308–9. "For the procession, which is done through town . . . The aforementioned reliquary is carried by knights out of the church, and through town by citizens. When returning, when entering the church, the response *Sedit angelus* is said . . . The blessing is given by the bishop. Then the response *Inventus* is said in the middle of the church and the reliquary is put back from where it was taken." (*Ad processionem, que fit per villam. . . . Et defertur capsula predicta a militibus extra ecclesiam, per civitatem vero a civibus. In reditu, quando intratur in ecclesiam, dicitur r/ Sedit angelus. . . . Benedictio datur ab episcopo. Deinde dicitur r/ Inventus in medio ecclesie et reponitur capsula ubi fuit sumpta.*) See also Soyez, *La Procession du Saint-Sacrement*, pp. 11–8. The instructions for the procession *pro fidelibus* are more explicit in this regard. Durand, ed., *Ordinaire*, p. 505. "And the procession marches through the principal doors of the church in procession between the Church of St.-Firmin-the-Confessor and our principal church, without any stopping, through the court of the lord bishop, toward the Church of St. Michael, in a straight path all the way to the cemetery of St.-Denis." (*Et egreditur processio per majores portas ecclesie procedendo inter ecclesiam Sancti Firmini confessoris et nostram majorem ecclesiam, absque ulla statione, per curiam domini episcopi versus ecclesiam Sancti Michaelis recto tramite usque ad cimiterium Sancti Dyonisii.*)

[67] According to Durand, *Ordinaire*, p. lix, on its return, the procession descended by the rue de Lin and went down the rue des Cocquerel, rue Saint Germain, into the market, down the rue des Orfevres and to the rue basse Notre Dame, and back into the cathedral.

[68] On reliquary processions see bibliography in fn. 45.

[69] Salmon, *Histoire de Saint Firmin*, p. 180.

[70] "Indeed, on that great day of the feast of that confessor [Honoré], on which we, with a great crowd composed equally of clergy and laymen, were accustomed to carry the body of that most saintly confessor around our cloister, after we had

Firmin's reliquary should be carried out of the cathedral by knights and into town by citizens.[71] Later documents indicate that the Ascension cortège was made up of representatives from city guilds, as well as knights and noblemen, who were reported as singing "sweet and pleasing tunes,"[72] and a 1465 document records the commune's request that its members might revive the lapsed tradition to be the ones to carry the actual reliquary.[73] By the fourteenth century (and perhaps earlier), instruments and trumpeters accompanied the procession, which, it seems, included people dressed as wild and imag-

---

returned to the cloister, [and] indeed when the clergy in the choir had undertaken to celebrate the solemn mass (; and) the reliquary of the most blessed confessor was placed upon the altar in the middle of the church, was protected by the devoted services of the assisting priests (; and) the people (*plebs*), gathered in that place in honor of the Lord and the blessed confessor, poured forth their prayers all day and were promising vows. The aforementioned [crippled] boy, approaching the reliquary of that blessed confessor, and looking at those [people] who were looking at [the reliquary], as if he was about to receive something from them; he sensed within himself a hidden miracle of divine power, which was apparent to all others in its workings. Indeed, his mother being there and insisting on prayers, the boy began to proclaim that it seemed to him to come from on high; but understanding little, he was not yet acquainted with that which divine virtue had prepared for him. The mother who was strengthened in the Lord, responded to him: 'Have faith, my son, and get up, touch the reliquary of the blessed confessor. I believe that you will be saved by the one who gives aid.' At these words the boy got up, and his feet and his arms were equally restored in their strength; we who were in the choir, [were] first in amazement, resounded in praise of the Lord and sounded the bells of the church." AASS May 16, 3, col. 615. (*In die etenim magno festivitatis praedicti Confessoris, qua nos, cum multa cleri pariter & populi frequentia, corpus sanctissimi Confessoris circa claustrum nostrum deferre consuevimus, redeuntibus nobis ad ecclesiam, cum jam clerus in chorum se recepisset missarum celebraturus solennia; & theca beatissimi Confessoris in medio ecclesiae super tabulam posita, sacerdotum assistentium devotis servaretur obsequiis; & plebs, ibidem in honore Domini & beati Confessoris collecta, orationes suas diutius funderet & vota solveret repromissa; puer praedictus ad thecam beati praediciti confessoris accedens, & intuens in eos qui eam observabant, tamquam aliquid acceptarus ab eis; sensit intra se divinae virtutis occultum miraculum, quod foris omnibus manifestum est in opere. Praesente enim matre sua & orationibus insistente, clamare coepit puer, quod videbatur ei se sursum trahi: sed parum intelligens, nondum cognoscebat quae sibi virtus divina praeparasset. Cui mater in Domino confortat, respondit: Confide, fili, surge, apprehende thecam beati Confessoris. Credo enim quod ipso opitulate salvaberis. Ad quae verba surrexit puer, & pedum pariter ac tibiarum recuperata virtute, in laudem Dei pariter conclamantes, & ecclesiae pulsantes classicu; nos qui in choro eramus prius stupore.*) On this miracle, see Corblet, *Hagiographie*, 3, pp. 54–5.

[71] See fn. 66.

[72] Soyez, *La Procession du Saint-Sacrement*, pp. 71–2, "*chansons plaisantes et gracieuses.*" According to Soyez, in the fifteenth century, younger participants refused to join the procession unless they were guaranteed good food and drink following the ceremony.

[73] The document is quoted in Salmon, *Histoire de Saint Firmin*, pp. 216–7.

inary animals, including, by the fifteenth-century, those in "serpent heads" and other fantastic costumes.[74] When the Corpus Christi procession was established, the people of Amiens based the processional route on that of the Ascension procession, retracing its route and replacing Firmin's reliquary with a Eucharistic tabernacle.[75] Indeed, the Ascension rite was an appropriate model for the Corpus Christi procession which in Amiens, as elsewhere, involved a high level of lay participation.[76]

Reliquary processions provided a public, focused opportunity for contact between the faithful and their local saints, and their popularity derived in large part from the expectation of miracles. The original events on which these re-enactments had been based were recorded and remembered precisely because of the miracles which had once occurred, and there is little doubt that the crowd hoped that repeating the procession would result in new miracles. The memory and importance of the miraculous was in a sense institutionalized by the addition of the re-enactment to the regular, yearly liturgy, and soon miracles were reported during the regularized processions as well. As noted above, a local breviary attested to the healing of a crippled woman during a votive procession of Firmin's relics around the city in the twelfth century,[77] and Honoré's *vita* recounts that during one of the bi-yearly processions of his relics through the cloister a paralytic boy was healed when he approached the reliquary.[78] This is almost certainly what is being shown beneath the reliquary procession in the Honoré portal, where the artists conflated this miracle with that of Christ's respectful nod to the saint. The image thus reinforced the notion that miracles accompanied the procession of

---

[74] The Ordinary refers to "heads in the manner of serpents" (*capita ad modum serpentum*). Durand, ed., *Ordinaire*, p. lix, fn. 2. Later evidence for Corpus Christi also indicates that fantastic costumes and animal imagery were a part of the Corpus Christi processions. Soyez, *La Procession du Saint-Sacrement*, pp. 17–8.

[75] Soyez, *La Procession du Saint-Sacrement*, pp. 12, 67–9.

[76] Miri Rubin, *Corpus Christi: the Eucharist in Late Medieval Culture* (Cambridge, 1991), pp. 243–71.

[77] Corblet, *Hagiographie*, 2, pp. 166–7; Salmon, *Histoire de Saint Firmin*, pp. 201–2.

[78] AASS May 16, 3, col. 615. This was not during the same procession as the original one. The episode comes from an early thirteenth-century text, constituting either a letter or the text of a preached sermon, which stated "during the usual custom of carrying the relics of Honoré around the cloister . . ." See also Hector Josse, *La Légende de S. Honoré, évêque d'Amiens* (Amiens, 1879), p. 16.

Honoré's relics. A relic-quest of Honoré's châsse in 1240 was also marked by a number of miraculous healings.[79]

A hopeful expectation and an aura of the miraculous imbued these processions, and, as suggested above, in some sense these reliquary processions constituted inverted pilgrimages, whereby the reliquaries were brought out to the population of the faithful instead of the other way around.[80] If, as Victor Turner suggested, pilgrimages generally began as spontaneous devotions of the laity and were increasingly brought under the control and into the regularized scheme of the ecclesiastical hierarchy, the reverse might be argued of the practice of reliquary processions at Amiens: originally ecclesiastical rituals (the Ascension and Pentecost processions) was subsequently attended by a laity who saw them as opportunities to interact with the saints, and consequently these events became increasingly festive, or "ludic."[81] The same type of curative miracles which were often the goal of the pilgrim occurred within the context of these extramural (as in, *extra muros*, that is, beyond the church's walls) processions, and the portals were, in part, designed to promote the cult of these saints to attract pilgrims to their shrines. Perhaps the detail from Firmin's *vita* depicted in the middle register of his tympanum where clerics and laymen from the four surrounding cities converge around his relics to participate in Firmin's translation—one of the prototypes for the regularized processional practice—served to acknowledge or promote this very idea.

Some Thoughts on Meaning

The actual reliquaries borne in these processions were lost in 1789 during the French Revolution. We know almost nothing of Honoré's reliquary,[82] though antiquarian descriptions provide us with suggestive

---

[79] Durand, *Ordinaire*, p. lx.

[80] On the relationship between procession and pilgrimage, see Tekippe, *Procession, Piety, and Politics*, pp. 175–9.

[81] Victor Turner, *Image and Pilgrimage in Christian Culture: Anthropological Perspectives* (New York, 1978), pp. 36–38. Ludic is the term Turner used to discuss the playful and joyful communal aspects which often accompanied organized rituals, including pilgrimage.

[82] Durand, *Monographie*, 2, p. 46.

information about the original appearance of Firmin's.[83] The golden châsse, constructed and consecrated before 1204, was shaped like a house, with two slanting roofs atop a gabled rectangular-shaped box. Twelve enamel scenes from Firmin's life were depicted on its sides— probably in roundels on slanting roof faces.[84] Inscriptions identified the different scenes, and enamel rosettes separated them. Two niches on the narrow ends housed representations of the Savior and of Firmin, holding his severed head. The châsse was topped with three golden spheres. The entire shrine measured four feet seven inches in length, one foot three inches wide and two feet one inch in height (roughly, one-hundred-and-forty cm × thirty-eight cm × sixty-four cm).[85] The specifications describe the rectangular, sepulcher-like, or house-like reliquary common in the twelfth and thirteenth centuries, examples of which include the shrine of St. Heribert (1170) (fig. 78) and that of St. Elizabeth (*c.* 1249).[86] (fig. 120) More important, the description is strongly suggestive of the shrines borne by clerics depicted in both tympana.

The sepulcher depicted in the Firmin tympanum (and by extension, in the Honoré tympanum) represented not only the sarcophagus in which the saint was originally translated after his legendary invention (or, for Honoré, the procession of 1060), but *also* the sepulcher-like châsse carried in annual processions, the châsse in which, in the thirteenth century, the relics were actually housed. That is, as the cortège passed through the church's door, the image of the live procession echoed the image of its historical foundation (and vice-versa). To make the point, a number of peculiar details included in the images were not dictated by the hagiographical precedent, but rather

---

[83] On the twelfth- or thirteenth-century reliquary of St. Firmin, see Salmon, *Histoire de Saint Firmin*, pp. 183–94; Durand, *Monographie*, 2, pp. 42–6. The present-day reliquary which holds Firmin's relics, executed in *c.* 1235, was given to the cathedral only in 1850; Joseph de Borchgrave d'Altena, "La châsse de Saint Firmin," *Bulletin Monumental* 85 (1926), pp. 153–8.

[84] Salmon, *Histoire de Saint Firmin*, pp. 183–94.

[85] Salmon, *Histoire de Saint Firmin*, p. 184.

[86] The examples have been chosen at random from the many surviving examples of this type of reliquary shrine, which tend to date from the latter half of the twelfth or early thirteenth century. Another comparandum is the shrine of St. Mengold, published in *Rhein und Maas, Kunst und Kultur, 800–1400* (Cologne, 1973) 1, p. 277. These and other examples are discussed in Tekippe, *Procession, Piety, and Politics.* *Editors' note, see Ilana Abend-David's, Lisa Victoria Ciresi's, Albert Lemeunier's, and Benoit van den Bossche's essays in this volume.

were actual features of thirteenth-century practice. First, shown at
the far left of the upper register of the Firmin tympanum is a follower
wearing a foliate crown. The image refers to the miraculous change
in weather which occurred as a result of Firmin's translation, but it
also recalls part of the thirteenth-century ceremony. Murray has associated the image with the "Green Man"—a minor church official
who would dress in green and wear a wreath upon his head during
the liturgy of Firmin's invention and who gave each of the canons
a small floral crown at the Vespers office.[87] Second, and more important, the processional cortège which precedes the sepulcher/reliquary
includes details which suggest the ritualized procession enacted in
the thirteenth century. The top register of the tympanum includes
an image of a cleric bearing an arm reliquary—an object which by
definition could not have figured in the original event of Firmin's
translation when his tomb was first uncovered, but which existed in
the thirteenth century and was used liturgically throughout the year.[88]
(compare figs. 121 and 122) A relic of Firmin's arm had at some
point in the eleventh century been separated from the rest of the
remains and was placed in an arm reliquary.[89] On certain feast
days—Easter, All Saints, the Vigil for the Assumption, the Octave
of the Epiphany, the feast of Honoré, the feasts of Firmin Martyr,
and the feast of the Invention of his relics—a procession through
the church ended with a blessing of the people performed by the
bishop with this arm reliquary.[90]

---

[87] This was celebrated on January 12. Murray, *Notre-Dame*, p. 115. For the Vespers
tradition, see Corblet, *Hagiographie*, 2, pp. 172–3. Durand, ed., *Ordinaire*, 109, for
the prescriptions for the Octave for Epiphany, which coincided with the feast of
the Invention of Firmin Martyr, during which copes were discarded to "represent
the miracle of the invention of the glorious martyr Firmin." (. . . *ad representandum
miraculum inventionis gloriosi Firmini martyris, exuuntur cape nigre in choro, spargitur edera per
sacrarium et chorum, discooperitur capsula beati Firmini martyris a duobus canonicis presbyteris
capis sericis indutis* . . .)

[88] See fns. 57, 62 for the role of the arm reliquary in the yearly rite. On such
reliquaries, see Barbara Drake Boehm, "Body-Part Reliquaries: The State of Research,"
Gesta 36/1 (1997): 8–19; Cynthia Hahn, "The Voices of Saints: Speaking Reliquaries,"
Gesta 36/1 (1997): 20–31.

[89] Salmon, *Histoire de Saint Firmin*, pp. 161, 205. According to Salmon, the relic
was alienated from the cathedral in the eleventh century, and it is not known when
it was returned to the cathedral, or even whether the arm reliquary that figures in
the thirteenth-century ritual was the identical one.

[90] Durand, ed., *Ordinaire*, pp. 47, 111, 232, 423, 464, 502, fns. 1, 551, 569. In
a section on the order for the feast day of Firmin Martyr, the formula reads "[t]he
response *Invictus* is sung in the middle of the church, the verse is said by four

In the same vein, the images of the south transept portal also echoed contemporary practice. The specificity of the liturgical instruments such as the chalice and altar functioned to contemporize the image cycle. Of the eucharistic miracle in the second register of the south transept portal, Sauerländer noted that, "as is often the case in the thirteenth century, the liturgical action is reproduced with formal and pedantic exactness, down to the detail of the bowl to receive the paten (held by the choirboy), as prescribed by the order in use at Amiens."[91] These details, all specific to contemporary practice, were designed to link the historical event depicted in the tympanum with the actual ritual procession performed by clergy and laity.

Such specific details argue for the portal as a pictorial mediation between historical event and contemporary experience. As the cortège re-entered the Cathedral of Notre Dame of Amiens, the parishioners and clerics were not only re-enacting but to an extent participating in the initial and miraculous first translation of the relics. The interrelationship of the images and processional rituals drew on the ability to map immediate experience onto earlier models, an ability which was the keystone of historical and typological thought in the Middle Ages. The notion that two events, although separated by time, participated in a shared essentiality was at the heart of typological thinking in the Middle Ages. Originally rooted in a long tradition of biblical exegesis, the idea that an earlier person or event both symbolized and prefigured a later one, and that the later was the fulfillment of the former, underlay numerous artistic programs in the Gothic period.[92]

[clergy] before the choir; the verse, *Ora pro nobis beate Firmine* by members of the choir. Collect: *Deus qui es sanctorum tuorum* by the liturgically-attired priest. The benediction is given with the arm of saint Firmin Martyr by the bishop." Durand, ed., *Ordinaire*, p. 464. (*In medio ecclesie canitur r/ Invictus; versus a quatuor dicitur ante chorum. v/ Ora pro nobis beate Firmine a choristis. Or. Deus qui es sanctorum tuorum a sacerdote revestito. Ab episcopo datur benedictio cum brachio sancti Firmini martyris.*)

[91] Sauerländer, *Gothic Sculpture*, p. 494.

[92] Given the enormous importance of typology to medieval art, surprisingly little has been written which provides an overview. Kathleen Biddick, *The Typological imaginary: Circumcision, Technology, History* (Philadelphia, 2003). Christopher G. Hughes, *Visual Typology in Early Gothic Art, 1140–1240* (Ph.D. diss., University of California at Berkeley, 2000) cautioned that typology is an admittedly modern construct and that people in the Middle Ages would have been more likely to use the language of allegory, or *figura*. On the potential of this symbolism, see Paul Rorem, *Biblical and Liturgical Symbols within the Pseudo-Dionysian Synthesis* (Toronto, 1984). On strictly biblical typology, see James Paxson, "A Theory of Biblical Typology in the Middle Ages," *Exemplaria* 3/2 (1991): 359–83. On ways in which typological thinking was

This penchant to conflate historical episodes with contemporary practice, to collapse time and represent instead what Stephen Murray
has termed "the ultratemporal," was rooted in the assumption that
there could be a single typological identity to two events.[93] It was
this that allowed the crucifixion scene which topped the south transept
portal to at the same time recount two different narratives: the
crucifixion itself, with the historically specific Virgin and Evangelist
flanking, as well as the crucifix miracle, indicated by the procession
represented below. In much the same way the Eucharist (the sacrifice
on the altar) was not only the reenactment but the re-performance
of Christ's sacrifice on the cross. The thirteenth-century reliquaries
of the living processions melded with the third-century sepulcher and
the eleventh-century shrine depicted in stone, and liturgical practice
wedded the community to the historical roots of its own foundation
and legitimate sacrality.

---

widened to envelop contemporary life, see Gabrielle Spiegel, "Political Utility in
Medieval Historiography: A Sketch," *History and Theory* 14 (1975): 314–25.
    [93] The notion of the ultratemporal refers to the relationship between things which
happen in present or historic time and those which are timeless, or belong to salvific
or eschatological time. Murray, *Notre-Dame*, p. 115. In speaking of the figures of the
apostles on the Honoré portal, he elaborated on the context: "Thus, we have recognized the potential of the apostles and saints to serve *both* as projections of the
elect of the Heavenly City *and* living models demonstrating to the pious visitor that
the battle with sin was one that could be won." See also Barbara Abou-El-Haj,
"The Urban Setting for Late Medieval Church Building: Reims and its Cathedral
between 1210 and 1240," *Art History* 11/1 (1988), p 27. Abou-El-Haj offered an
interpretation of Reims imagery which has an affinity with mine, though for which
the context suggests different conclusions. Analogous interpretations of the procession on the Parthenon frieze as representing multiple processional or festival events
at the same time have been proposed. A summary of the enormous literature on
this issue can be found in Jeffrey M. Hurwit, *The Athenian Acropolis: History, Mythology,
and Archaeology from the Neolithic Era to the Present* (Cambridge, 1999), pp. 222–8. Hurwit
concluded that the frieze refers at the same time to the first legendary Panathenaia
and the many later processions and festivals enacted on the Acropolis: "the frieze
does not represent a single event at all (mythological, historical or generic) but is
a synopsis of many events, a collection of excerpts", p. 227.

CHAPTER TEN

PILGRIMAGE, PERFORMANCE, AND STAINED GLASS AT CANTERBURY CATHEDRAL*

Anne F. Harris

In his 1173 letter to the monastic community of Canterbury Cathedral announcing his intention to canonize Thomas Becket (1118?–70), Pope Alexander III (r. 1159–81) exhorted his charges to place the now "sanctum corpus" in a setting more suitable to Becket's new status and more conducive to the powers of that status. The obliging pontiff offered several motivating suggestions: a solemn procession, an event uniting the clergy and the people, a splendid altar,—all these with no less an aspiration than "the salvation of the faithful and the peace of the universal church."[1] Despite the precision, timeliness and resolve of the call to action, it would take almost fifty years for Alexander's mission to the monks to be fulfilled and for the saint's body to be moved from a humble tomb in the crypt of the cathedral to a glorious shrine in the newly-designed space of the Trinity Chapel. Seldom has a blessed figure enjoyed such a meteoric rise to sainthood only to endure such a protracted crawl to the ritual actualization of that sainthood.[2]

---

* I would like to thank Michael Mackenzie and Donna Sadler for their steadfast support, David Guinee for his expert help with the Latin passages, Madeline Caviness and M.F. Hearn for their kind encouragement, and DePauw University for a Fisher Time-Out, which allowed me to complete the research and writing of this article. I dedicate this work to my son, Oliver Leo Mackenzie, who waited so patiently to be born until his mother could "be rid of this meddlesome [but wonderful] priest," Thomas Becket.

[1] *Materials for the History of Thomas Becket.* ed. J.C. Robertson and J.B. Sheppard. (London, 1885) VII, p. 546, hereafter *Materials.* The passages in question reads . . . *ut sanctum corpus ejus cum ea qua decet reverentia et honore condatur . . . facta solemni processione, aliquo praecipuo die, congregato clero et populo, in altari honorifice recondatis . . . pro salute fidelium et pace universalis ecclesiae.* "so that his holy body maybe buried with the honor and reverence which behooves it . . . may you gather the people and the clergy on a special day, make a solemn procession, and lay him to rest upon a newly erected altar . . . for the salvation of the faithful and the peace of the universal church." Unless otherwise noted, all Latin translations in this text are my own.

[2] Nilson, Ben. *Cathedral Shrines of Medieval England* (Rochester, 1998) p. 20. The

The historical gap between the pronouncement and performance of Becket's cult presents an opportunity to delve into the medieval process of pilgrimage construction. Far from the spontaneous event that miracle records and lives of the saint promote, pilgrimage at Canterbury—especially the visual and ritual format perfected in the Trinity Chapel—was painstakingly assembled from a panoply of artistic, liturgical, and performative elements. In the process, characterized more by fits and starts than by steady development, a remarkable transformation took place at Canterbury Cathedral. An institution that had been illustriously elite, both in its political and ecclesiastical relationships, literally reinvented itself as a site of popular pilgrimage.[3] The visual and ritual codes of popular culture were still very much being worked out in the transitional years between the monastic twelfth century and the pastoral thirteenth century, and Canterbury Cathedral provides a unique opportunity to study the shifts from the contemplative, allegorical life of a cathedral chapter to the active, performative life of high medieval pilgrims.

The stained glass windows of the Trinity Chapel had a crucial, and still largely overlooked, role to play in this transformation at Canterbury.[4] (fig. 124) Images are often perceived as the reflection of a phenomenon such as the popularity of a saint, but here I will be arguing that they were the pivotal factor in the transformation of the culture of Canterbury from elite to popular. My assertion emerges from a study of the windows' unique ability to frame the pilgrimage experience in terms of visuality, memory, and the body—all crucial elements of a popular performance that was both acti-

---

longest delay between canonization and translation in the Middle Ages was sixty years for St. Hugh of Lincoln (1135–1200).

[3] One has only to note the different foci of scholarship before and after Becket's death. The incidents leading up to his death in 1170 are the purview of legal historians, analysts of the debate between *regnum* and *sacerdotum* (Crown and Church), and historians of Church doctrine (to name a few), while events ensuing from the martyrdom are the realm of hagiographic studies, pilgrimage historians, popular culture analysts (again to name a few of the many interesting strains of scholarship). The divide is by no means absolute, but nevertheless remarkable.

[4] Madeline Caviness has provided the field with two fundamental works on the Canterbury glass and positioned the windows within a variety of contexts (biblical, architectural, historical, and others) which have inspired my own analysis. This article is greatly indebted to her careful and thorough reconstructions and analysis of the glass in *The Early Stained Glass of Canterbury Cathedral; circa 1175–1220* (Princeton, 1977) and Madeline Caviness, *The Windows of Christ Church Cathedral Canterbury, Corpus Vitrearum Great Britain*, II (London, 1981).

vated and self-perpetuating beyond the framework of elite monastic culture. How did the miracle windows establish the three terms of performance isolated above? In being so very accessible visually in the crucial space encircling the saint's shrine, they offered legibility about Becket without the precondition of literacy; in what could arguably be called the first theater of memory, they gathered together, or re-membered, a wide array of the miracles that Becket's body had effected in the crypt; and, in their overwhelming emphasis on healing and resurrection, they presented the pilgrim's own body as the ultimate evidence and inspiration for the power of Becket's cult. I will not be arguing that stained glass windows were isolated incidents in the cathedral space, however—they did not effectuate these changes alone. My study will join the windows with, among other elements, key decisions in the architectural lay-out of the eastern end of the church, sermons delivered about the saint's miraculous powers, and liturgical innovations in the emerging theology of indulgences. Using these architectural, pastoral, and liturgical contexts, I will thus seek to discern the critical role of the miracle windows in the Trinity Chapel in the transformations that effected the shift from elite to popular at Canterbury: textual to visual, typology to memory, and spirit to body. Our analysis will begin with the crisis of Thomas Becket's martyrdom on Tuesday, December 29, 1170 and culminate in the celebration of the feast day of the saint's Translation on Tuesday, July 7, 1220.

These two dramatic events framed a very convoluted series of measures that shaped Becket's cult and confronted the religious realm with political power, piety with practicality, and unforeseen circumstances with carefully crafted schemes. In order to negotiate the often-confusing multitude of crises, ranging from the near-fatal fall of an architect from vault scaffolding, to the exile of the cathedral's entire monastic company, I would like to, in a first instance, present these events chronologically, and then analyze them diachronically, that is, as they influenced each other, in my three-part analysis of the windows examining visuality, memory, and body. No major event, let alone a crisis, stood isolated of moral significance or historical consequence in the Middle Ages, and the occurrences that I am bringing forth as relevant all became part of the re-vision of Canterbury Cathedral as it newly combined ritual performance with visual display in the Trinity Chapel stained glass windows to formulate the pilgrimage experience at Canterbury Cathedral.

From Martyrdom to Translation: a Chronology of Crisis

The events leading up to Becket's martyrdom pitted the privileges
of the Church to judge its own against the Crown's insistence that
clergy be governed by secular law, aligning the clergy with all other
subjects of the king.[5] Lines were drawn in the sand with the reasser-
tion of sixteen ancient customs affirming duties and fealties owed
between Church and Crown in 1164 at Clarendon.[6] The intense
legal and political complexities of this stand-off were swept away in
the drama of Becket's martyrdom on December 29, 1170 and the
archbishop was quickly reconfigured as a heroic defender of ecclesiastical privilege in a much more general sense. This initial characterization of Becket by fellow ecclesiastics, as a politico-theological
hero and not as a miracle worker, remained the purview of
Canterbury's elite culture, and appears in multiple remembrances of
Becket by the clergy to each other. King Henry II (1133–89), Becket's
chief opponent in the Clarendon Constitutions debate,[7] also experienced the imposition of a new, simplified character upon his person
via a ritual performance in the years after Becket's martyrdom. On
July 12, 1174, Henry II traveled to Canterbury from Normandy and
dramatically submitted his body politic to powerful penance in the
form of flagellation at the hands of the Canterbury clergy before
Becket's tomb in the increasingly sacred space of the crypt.[8] The
vestiges of a thirteenth-century wall painting in the crypt may well
mark the event.[9]

---

[5] Frank Barlow, *Thomas Becket* (Berkeley, 1986). Barlow's careful account of Becket's
political and eventually politico-theological career delves into the details and repercussions of the debate over clerical immunity.

[6] Barlow, *Becket*, pp. 99–106. Raymonde Foreville, "Mort and Survie de saint
Thomas Becket," *Cahiers de Civilization Médiévale* 15 (1971), p. 23, for the Norman
precedent of the Clarendon Constitutions.

[7] Barlow, *Becket*, pp. 99–106. The Clarendon Constitutions were a document,
drawn up on 11 January 1164 reasserting sixteen ancient customs that granted the
King power over the Church. The debate began when Becket refused to apply his
seal to the document, and continued most heatedly around the issue of secular jurisdiction over criminal clergy.

[8] William Urry, "Some Notes on the Two Resting Places of St. Thomas at
Canterbury," in *Thomas Becket: Actes du Colloque International de Sédières, 19–24 août
1973* (Paris, 1975), pp. 195–209. Urry provides a dramatic account of the king's
visit in pp. 197–200, as does Barlow, *Becket*, pp. 268–70.

[9] Urry, "Two Resting Places," p. 198, describes "the outline of three monkish
figures each holding a short turned baton, looking very much like the handle of a
whip."

The confluence of events in the fall of 1174 marks the first major shifts in the history of Becket's cult: the crypt had been secured and local pilgrims were now allowed access to the tomb of the saint, Henry II had reconciled himself to the Church through his ritual penance,[10] a moment of calm reigned in the turbulent politics of England's secular realm,[11] the saint had been canonized and the canonization affirmed by Pope Alexander III with a formal invitation to develop a site worthy of veneration,[12] and, after a four-year hiatus provoked by Becket's martyrdom and internal disagreements between the Church and the chapter, the seat of the archbishop of Canterbury was finally filled by Richard of Dover (r. 1174–84), a close friend of Becket's.[13] All seemed poised for the furnishing if not the fulfillment of Becket's cult. But two scenarios prevented any advancement of Becket's cause. The first was the chapter's marked lack of enthusiasm for any such development, a resistance inherited from the difficult relationship that Becket and his monks had uneasily shared during his tenure as archbishop, and which continued to exist between the monks and his successors.[14] In addition to their own criticisms of

---

[10] Barlow, *Becket*, pp. 260–62. The July 1174 penance ritual was preceded by a formal reconciliation between Henry II and the Church, in the person of Pope Alexander III, at Avranches in 1172. The alliance between the Pope and King alarmed the Cathedral chapter which saw its own power compromised in such a partnership, but Henry II's visit to Becket's tomb temporarily soothed this anxiety. The chapter stood to benefit greatly from Henry II's penance: in isolating four elements which promoted the construction of a cult to Becket, Margaret Gibson, in "Normans and Angevins, 1070–1220," in *A History of Canterbury Cathedral*, ed. Patrick Collinson *et al.*, (Oxford, 1995), pp. 38–68, notes that "Henry II's legal responsibility for the murder [acknowledged in his penance at Becket's tomb] released quite substantial royal funds for the shrine," p. 62.

[11] Barlow, *Becket*, p. 269. Several scholars, notably Urry and Hearn, have conjectured that Henry II's political success in suppressing his sons' revolt after the performance of his penance may have fueled the king's surprisingly enthusiastic support of Becket and his cult.

[12] Barlow, *Becket*, pp. 268–70. The canonization occurred on Ash Wednesday, February 21, 1173 and was predicated largely on reports of Becket's miracles.

[13] Patrick Collinson *et al.*, eds. *A History of Canterbury Cathedral.* (Oxford, 1995), p. 563 (Appendix 1). The election/appointment of Richard of Dover greatly advanced any plans for a cult dedicated to Becket, as the new archbishop had been a close companion and friend of the martyr.

[14] M.F. Hearn, "Canterbury Cathedral and the Cult of Becket," *Art Bulletin* 76/1 (March 1994), p. 47, characterizes the atmosphere at Canterbury following Becket's martyrdom thusly: "Although the archbishop was the titular abbot, the monastery operated under the de facto leadership of the prior, whose interests were not always identical with those of the archbishop ... Not surprisingly, Christ Church was a center of contention, where jealousy, ambition, deception, arrogance, and bitter

Becket, the monks had until very recently lived under the threat of
royal representatives who had called for the arrest and punishment
of anyone caught venerating the dead archbishop.[15] The second circumstance that hampered the development of Becket's cult was the
spectacular fire of September 1174, which damaged the choir of the
church and demanded, or perhaps occasioned, the complete reconstruction of the eastern end of the church. William of Sens was
brought in from France to establish the new framework for the grand
religious mission of Canterbury Cathedral, but as we will briefly see,
his plans, too, were thwarted.

The events recounted above are all culled from the series of *Lives*
written about Becket during the mid- to late-1170s and the 1180s.[16]

---

hatred flourished alongside piety, learning, industry, humility, and charity . . . [T]he
emergence of the cult was not the result of a concerted effort on the part of the
chapter." Richard of Dover's archiepiscopal election was consecrated over the protests
of the monks who supported their Prior Odo (r. 1168–75), who had been at great
odds with Thomas Becket, for the position. The archbishops who presided between
the years 1170 and 1220 were: Richard of Dover (r. 1174–84), Baldwin of Ford
(r. 1185–90), Hubert Walter (r. 1193–1205), and Stephen Langton (r. 1207–28). All
of their tenures, save Hubert Walter's, were tinged with controversies that shifted
the course of the development of Becket's cult.

[15] Barlow, *Becket*, p. 265. These threats abated as Henry II reconciled himself to
the Church, but the memory of the uneasy tension provoked by veneration of the
archbishop must have made the monks wonder if a cult was worth all the potential political trouble. The opposition between royal representations and the clergy
had been very acrimonious in the early days of the cult. Urry, "Two Resting Places,"
p. 196, details a foiled plot by the king's noblemen to steal the body of the archbishop from its first resting place in the crypt.

[16] Edwin A. Abbott, *St. Thomas of Canterbury; His Death and Miracles* (London, 1898),
pp. 11–26. Abbott presents a very thorough background for the five eyewitnesses
(I will here only provide their dates and texts for reference): Edward Grim, completed by 1177; William Fitzstephen begun around 1177; John of Salisbury, between
1170 and 1176; William of Canterbury, began miracle compilation in May 1172–74,
gave copy of his miracle record to Henry II in 1177, incorporated into the *Quadrilogus*
in 1199; Benedict, prior of Canterbury and eventually of Peterborough, between
1171 and 1175, *Life* also incorporated into the *Quadrilogus* in 1199. Herbert of
Bosham, though not an eyewitness of the martyrdom, was Becket's teacher and
wrote his *Life* between 1184/5 and 1189. Seven other *Lives* also circulated: *Quadrilogus*
reunited four authors: Herbert of Bosham, John of Salisbury, William of Canterbury,
and Alan of Tewksbury; Anonymous I (commonly called Roger of Pontigny);
Anonymous II, a.k.a. *Lambeth Anonymous*, between 1170–74; Anonymous IV, a sermon, soon after 1173; Anonymous V, 1174–75; Anonymous X, late 1170s or 1180s;
Garnier of Pont-Saint-Maxence, between 1171 and 1175; the Iceland *Saga*, after
1199. For other (very similar) suggestions as to date and authorship of the *Lives* of
Becket see Anne Duggan, "The Cult of St. Thomas Becket in the Thirteenth
Century," in *St Thomas Cantilupe Bishop of Hereford*. ed. Meryl Jancey, (Hereford,
1982), p. 34 and Barlow, *Becket*, pp. 4–8. Barlow presents a listing of fifteen authors
and texts: he substitutes some of the following from Abbott's list: Robert of Crickdale,

No less than fifteen *Lives* and other compilations of events in Becket's life and martyrdom were recorded in this surprisingly rich textual tradition. The rapid compilation and diffusion of these texts were the first certain steps in the construction of Becket's cult. The immediacy with which they were written, most of them within the first five years after Becket's death, denotes a sense of urgency, a pressing obligation to commit the events of Becket's demise and glory to text. The importance of text in Becket's cult will be discussed in greater detail below, but it must be noted now that few cults are as formed and informed by text as that of St Thomas Becket's.[17] Several of the authors cite each other, indicating a community of texts in circulation. This fluidity of narration figures prominently in the stained glass windows of the Trinity Chapel, where the viewer can see miracles first recorded in these texts. The "translation" of these texts into images renders the viewer a kind of eyewitness to Becket's miracles.

Five of the fifteen accounts are those of contemporaries: Edward Grim, William Fitzstephen, William of Canterbury, Benedict of Peterborough, and John of Salisbury.[18] These emphatically personal and detailed accounts lend an immediacy not found in most hagiographic writing. While still using conventional canonical metaphors for Becket's goodness and sanctity, their characterization of an eyewitness, of someone who vividly experienced all the action of the martyrdom, presents a new standard in hagiographic narration. The immediacy of the eyewitness is both performative and evidentiary: performative because of the vivid bodily sensations, especially in the account of Edward Grim who was wounded during the attack of the martyrdom described in the text, and evidentiary because of the impression of incontestable proof of hearing the story from someone who was present at the crucial moment of the event.

Two texts in particular, those of Benedict of Peterborough and William of Canterbury, will hold our attention. In addition to writing *Lives* of the saint, Benedict and William also acted as authenticators

1173–74; Alan of Tewksbury, 1174–76; Landsowne Anonymous (III), before 1172; Benet of St. Albans, about 1184. Barlow also provides very specific biographical information for each text.

[17] Benedicta Ward, *Miracles and the Medieval Mind* (Philadelphia, 1987). This rich text analyzes the theory and practice of miracles and provides many comparative scenarios to Becket's, which demonstrates the unique status of Becket's cult in being constructed so very early and so very thoroughly by texts.

[18] Barlow, *Becket*, pp. 4–6 provides succinct biographies for all five authors, commenting upon their relationships to Becket.

and compilers of miracles effected by Becket in the crypt tomb. Benedict of Peterborough began recording miracles as early as 1171 and was joined the following year by William of Canterbury.[19] Both finished a first edition, as it were, of the miracles around 1174, and both added on to their collections in 1178–79.[20] The miracle records had several key roles to play in the pious politics immediately following Becket's martyrdom: they were reviewed by Pope Alexander III in his decision to grant sainthood to Becket,[21] and William's miracle record was ceremoniously presented to King Henry II in 1174.[22] The vivid importance of the miracle records for our analysis is that they are the textual source for the miracle windows of the Trinity Chapel.[23] They may well have enjoyed an oral as well as a visual diffusion, in that they were read to pilgrims in the chapter house[24] as well as re-presented in the windows surrounding Becket's shrine. The ready manipulation of these texts, and their translation into other forms of experience (oral and visual), reveals the perceived limits of text by the programmers of Becket's cult. As crucial as textual expression was in the beginning of Becket's cult, it was eventually outstripped by the possibilities of visuality and performance.

A most interesting relationship existed between text and event in the building campaigns of the eastern end of the cathedral effected in the 1170s and 1180s. Gervase of Canterbury, monk of the cathedral, provided a yearly account of construction beginning in 1174 and ending in 1184.[25] The contemporaneity of miracle record with

---

[19] Abbott, *St. Thomas of Canterbury*, pp. 14–15.

[20] Abbott, *St. Thomas of Canterbury*, pp. 14–15.

[21] Barlow, *Becket*, pp. 268–69. "Thomas's advocates [for canonization] ... rested their case on three planks: the *poena*, the punishment or martyrdom; the *causa*, the issues the martyr had died for; and the *signa*, the miracles ... Alexander ... preferred the third."

[22] Barlow, *Becket*, p. 6. Abbot, *St. Thomas of Canterbury*, p. 14, suggests the date of 1177 as that on which William offered his record to Henry.

[23] Caviness, in *The Windows of Christ Church*, has discerned which miracle came from which text, detailing overlaps between the two authors as well as isolating miracles too generic to be identified to one particular story and author. Appendix Figure 6, pp. 164–66.

[24] Fitzstephen, *Materials*, III, p. 151. This practice is mentioned in William Fitzstephen's account, a 12th-century text. By the 15th-century, if the poem of the *Tale of Beryn* is to be taken as evidence, the practice was no longer in use. There is good reason to believe that the practice was active in the 13th century, namely the pilgrim's path as suggested by M.F. Hearn, to be discussed below, although it must be acknowledged that allowing laity into the chapter house was an unusual event.

[25] Gervase of Canterbury, "Tract on the Burning and Repair of the Church of

the building report is perhaps not as disconnected as scholars' very different uses of the texts would have us believe.[26] Gervase, Benedict, and William were all engaged in the urgency of historical record and the immediacy of eyewitness. Their textuality bespeaks a self-consciousness about the construction of Becket's cult which both belies spontaneity and accentuates process and procedure. Gervase's exactitude about the building campaigns is both biographical and architectural. The first campaign, headed up by William of Sens from 1174 to 1179, seemed geared towards rebuilding the liturgical space of the eastern end. The second campaign, led by William the Englishman from 1179 to 1184, was much more concerned with the architectural accommodations of a cult to Becket.[27] The transition between the two architects is marked by one of the strange tragedies of the building campaign: William of Sens's fall from a vault scaffolding in September of 1178. Though he tried to conduct the building campaign from his sick bed, he eventually gave up his position and returned to France. William the Englishman then took over the building campaign in 1179 and was the architect in charge when the choir was once again ready for liturgical use at Easter of 1180.[28] The liturgical readiness of the choir indicated a degree of architectural completion that included the stained glass windows in the clerestory of the choir.[29] These windows are not to be confused with

Canterbury," trans. Robert Willis, *The Architectural History of Canterbury Cathedral* (London, 1845), pp. 32–62.

[26] Hagiographers overwhelmingly work with the miracle accounts and lives of Becket, while architectural historians have plumbed the depths of Gervase's text to a much greater degree.

[27] This shift is one of the many interesting claims in the thorough work presented by Hearn, "Canterbury Cathedral and the Cult of Becket," p. 9. Hearn uses both Gervase's description of the burning and building of the cathedral and "his lesser-known chronicle, covering the history of the monastic community and the archiepiscopate before, during, and after the construction," in his account. Hearn's analysis of this less-architectural and more ecclesiastical text engages him in crucial contextual issues surrounding Becket's cult, the most relevant for our analysis being the construction of cultic, and not just architectural, space.

[28] A thorough chronological analysis of the building campaigns can be found in Francis Woodman, "The Gothic Choir, 1174–1184," from *The Architectural History of Canterbury Cathedral* (London, 1981), pp. 87–130. Hearn's account adds a most interesting analysis to a well-established chronology. See also, Anthony Reader-Moore, "The Liturgical Chancel of Canterbury Cathedral," *Canterbury Cathedral Chronicle* 73 (1979), p. 36.

[29] Madeline Caviness "Canterbury Cathedral Clerestory: the Glazing Program in Relation to the Campaigns of Construction," in *Medieval Art and Architecture at Canterbury before 1220* (London, 1982), p. 52.

the miracle windows, which, as we shall see, have a much less well-documented architectural history.

We have now detailed the first decade after Becket's martyrdom. In the next forty years, the construction of Becket's cult was marked by fewer, though arguably more dramatic, events, both political and architectural. From 1188 to 1189 the monks found themselves imprisoned in their own precinct over a contest with Baldwin of Ford (r. 1185–90), the new archbishop consecrated in 1185.[30] The Cistercian archbishop, a stranger to the Cluniac-affiliated monks of Canterbury, wanted to establish a college of canons dedicated to St. Stephen and St. Thomas Becket at Hackington, near Canterbury, but not within its control. The establishment and dedication of this college would have entailed moving Becket's body to the new site, a proposal the monks vigorously resisted.[31] The monks' insistence that they maintain control of Becket's body indicates their emerging commitment to a full-fledged cult of Becket by the late 1180s. A protracted legal case ensued, the monks were imprisoned and only the call to the Third Crusade, prompted by the loss of Jerusalem to Saladin (d. 1193), diffused the situation and the monks were released. Baldwin followed Richard the Lionhearted to the Holy Land, and died there in 1190.[32] The archiepiscopal seat stood empty from 1190 to 1193, when it was filled by the relatively uncontroversial election of Hubert Walter (r. 1193–1205).[33] Throughout the power struggles of the 1180s construction was brought to a virtual standstill.

The conception and construction of the miracle windows are difficult to track amidst the turbulent politics of the cathedral chapter and indeed, they remain an historical and architectural mystery in many ways. They were positioned in the Trinity Chapel only in the late 1190s and early 1200s, long after Gervase ended his chronicle of architectural construction.[34] A document of 1199 records the

---

[30] Barrie Dobson, "The Monks of Canterbury in the Later Middle Ages, 1220–1540," in *A History of Canterbury Cathedral*, ed. Patrick Collinson (Oxford, 1995), p. 70.

[31] Phyllis Roberts. "Archbishop Stephen Langton and his Preaching on Thomas Becket in 1220," in *De Ore Domini: Preacher and Word in the Middle Ages*, ed. Thomas L. Amos, Eugene A. Green, Beverly Mayne Kienzle (Kalamazoo, 1989), p. 78.

[32] Gibson, "Normans and Angevins," p. 67.

[33] Gibson, "Normans and Angevins," pp. 67–8. "Hubert Walter's archiepiscopal seal had the martyrdom of Becket on the reverse, but he himself was also primarily the servant of the King. So the community was left to its own devices."

[34] Caviness, *The Windows of Christ Church*, 163–64.

monks accepting responsibility for the decoration of the Trinity Chapel, and glazing was probably underway by 1205.[35] The windows remain remarkable for their position and legibility: they are low enough that the first few rows of miracles are at eye-level, an unusual physical proximity of viewer to image. They also seem to have maintained some of the groupings of miracles established by Benedict and William.[36] The exact process of glazing remains a mystery, however, since the construction of the cult of Becket, and the chapter of Canterbury, endured another dramatic disruption in 1206.

The crisis arose over the election of the next archbishop of Canterbury, following the death of Archbishop Hubert Walter in July of 1205. The monastic community, the king, and the pope each had their own favored candidate and when Pope Innocent III (r. 1198–1216) impressed his will by consecrating his man, Stephen Langton (r. 1207–28), King John of England (r. 1199–1216) revolted by refusing to admit Langton to England. The Pope retaliated by putting the entire country of England under interdict, a radical act that initiated a period of disgrace and liturgical exclusion that was to last from the spring of 1208 to the late summer of 1213.[37] In retaliation for their having accepted the Pope's man, King John sent the monks of Canterbury into exile in France in 1206 where they remained until late in 1213. In their absence, King John seized many of their lands and properties, a legal tangle that took several years to undo after the return of the monks to Canterbury.[38]

In 1213, decoration of the Trinity Chapel resumed with the addition of figurative pavement stones around the shrine area.[39] Order also resumed at Canterbury and Stephen Langton rose to the occasion. After so many stops and starts, constructions and destructions, plans and dissolutions, it was Langton's plan for Becket's cult that

---

[35] Madeline Caviness, "A Lost Cycle of Canterbury Paintings of 1220," *Antiquaries Journal* 54 (1974), pp. 69–70.

[36] Caviness, "A Lost Cycle of Canterbury Paintings," p. 70.

[37] Gibson, "Normans and Angevins," p. 68.

[38] Dobson, "The Monks of Canterbury," p. 69.

[39] Elizabeth Eames, "Notes on the Decorated Stone Roundels in the Corona and Trinity Chapel in Canterbury Cathedral," in *Medieval Art and Architecture at Canterbury before 1220* (London, 1982), p. 68. The figurative roundels represented the Signs of the Zodiac, Labors of the Month, the Virtues battling the Vices, and Monsters. Caviness, "A Lost Cycle of Canterbury Paintings," p. 70, points out that the figurative roundels signaled "a changed aesthetic from the austerity and abstraction of the *opus Alexandrium*."

would be the one to come to fruition in July of 1220. If not the programmer of the final installation of art objects, Langton insured enough peace and prosperity for the completion of the shrine by Walter of Colchester and Elias of Dereham, which would hold Becket's relics,[40] and the miracle stained glass windows, which would encircle that shrine and frame the Canterbury pilgrimage experience for generations to come. As we shall see below, the shrine and the windows worked together to position the pilgrim in the closest spiritual and physical proximity to the saint possible.

Langton had learned many lessons from his predecessors, and orchestrated a spectacular event to inaugurate and perpetuate worship to St. Thomas Becket in a devotional space renovated for vivid performances: with the support of Pope Honorius III (r. 1216–27)[41] he instituted a Jubilee, complete with indulgences, in honor of the Translation of Becket's bones which occurred on Tuesday, July 7, 1220, a ceremonial transfer he presided over on the same day that he declared the Jubilee. In arranging for the translation of Becket's bones, a one-time occurrence of July 7, 1220, to be remembered as one of Becket's feast days, Langton collapsed a contemporary event with its liturgical commemoration in perpetuity, and brilliantly assured the continuity of Becket's cult. All the elements, artistic, architectural, and liturgical, were in place and the popularity of Becket's cult secured. The longevity of the cult, indeed, the keen interest surrounding Becket even today, are testaments to the devotional experience Canterbury Cathedral offered its pilgrims. (fig. 125) The power of that experience was so continuous and so strong and Becket's presence so vivid at his pilgrimage site that it presented a threat centuries later to Henry VIII in his struggle during the 1530s with the Church, which the monarch perceived as real and viable enough to warrant the dismantling of the shrine in September of 1538, the partial destruction of the Trinity Chapel miracle windows, and the trial of Becket, *in absentia*. Only against such willful aggression did Becket's cult cease.[42]

---

[40] Urry, "Two Resting Places," pp. 200–203 for a description of the shrine.

[41] Raymonde Foreville, *Le Jubilé de Saint Thomas Becket du XIIIᵉ au XVᵉ siècle (1220–1470); études et documents* (Paris, 1958), p. 8.

[42] Eamon Duffy, *The Stripping of the Altars; Traditional Religion in England 1400–1580* (New Haven, 1992): pp. 411–18. Duffy notes resistance to outlawing Becket, even in the midst of the most aggressive campaign to rid the Church of Thomas Becket,

The elements of the pilgrimage experience, however, have endured through the art, architecture and archives of Canterbury Cathedral. Having tracked the chronology of Becket's cult and identified the many protagonists and circumstances which led to its construction, we are now ready to analyze the major cultural shifts which occurred at Canterbury Cathedral under the rubric of a transformation of the site from one of elite (contemplative) to popular (performative) culture. This analysis will be diachronic rather than chronological, that is, I will be moving back and forth along the chronology just outlined, and juxtaposing past and present events in order to understand the three major shifts which culminated around the miracle windows of the Trinity Chapel: from textual to visual, from typology to memory, and from spirit to body.

From Textual to Visual: Writing Lilies and Seeing Miracles

The *Lives and Miracles* compiled about Thomas Becket played a crucial preliminary role in the construction of his cult. They established a particular discourse about the saint, however, which was eventually set aside in favor of a visual approach to Becket for the devotional public. I do not wish to draw a mutually exclusive distinction between text and image, here, but rather to point out the different mechanisms of appeal at play. I am also very interested in how the monks adjusted their elite textual culture, that is, willed it to cross over to the popular culture of a secular pilgrim class with few if any biblical referents.[43] Texts about Becket intended for diffusion to a contemplative monastic audience use metaphorical imagery that called upon the audience to imagine the saint in parallel with other entities and personas. The miracle stained glass windows—those images that encircled Becket's devotional public at the shrine—prompt the worshippers to envision the saint as present in their own space. They

---

by, for example, marking out his feast days in liturgical books by using only a faint line, thus making the books perfectly legible.

[43] Caviness, *The Windows of Christ Church*, pp. 175–214. Caviness's meticulous and extensive notation on each of the Trinity Chapel windows reveals their source as the miracle records compiled by Benedict of Peterborough and William Fitzstephen. The Bible figures prominently in other windows of the Church, but not in the Trinity Chapel surrounding Becket's shrine.

seldom represent the saint himself, rather calling upon the past miracle experiences of pilgrims in the tomb and the much-desired miracles of pilgrims in the Trinity Chapel to make Becket present. The
distinction between the operations of text and image can be summarized as those between representation in metaphor and presence
in experience.

The many *Lives* of Thomas Becket will occupy us briefly with one
type of imagery they construct for the saint. This imagery would
never engage the realm of visual representation, remaining instead
within the contemplative construct of metaphor. It is at once possibly
the most vivid imagery of the saint, and at the same time the most
removed from visual images because of its radical difference from
physical reality. Five of Becket's biographers engage in the metaphor
of his blood and brains as roses and lilies in describing Becket and
his martyrdom.[44] The metaphor has a patristic origin and exercises
a connection between these origins and works of "affective meditation on the Passion."[45] We are here deeply embedded in the referential world of elite textual culture, in which the emphasis on the
floral imagery of Becket's martyrdom is intended to help the audience envision spiritual qualities of the saint, rather than any physical sufferings. These metaphors are not without appeal to the visual
imagination; the key here is that they are never seized upon by visual
representation—they exist in the realm of the imagination rather
than that of image. The metaphor of *candidus et rubicundus* (white and
red) conjures up white lilies and red roses as metaphors for virginity and martyrdom, divinity and humanity, and the resurrection and
the passion—qualities that link Becket to Christ himself.[46] In the
most elaborate of the metaphorical extrapolations, white lilies and
red roses are used to describe the appearance of Becket at the marriage feast of the Song of Songs, "clothed with a stole whitened in
the blood of the Spouse." The metaphor continues, becoming more

---

[44] The five are Edward Grim, William Fitzstephen, Garnier de Pont-Saint-Maxence,
the Icelandic *Thomas Saga*, and Anonymous IV. Herbert of Bosham uses white and
red imagery, but in terms of body and blood, not lilies and roses. Abbot, *St. Thomas
of Canterbury*, pp. 207–209 gives consideration to these metaphors.

[45] Jennifer O'Reilly, "'Candidus et Rubicundus'—an Image of Martyrdom in the
'Lives' of Thomas Becket," *Analecta Bollandiana* 99 (1981), pp. 303–304.

[46] O'Reilly, "'Candidus et Rubicundus',", pp. 305, 307, 309. Abbot adds the
possibility of the white lilies and red roses connoting the Church as Mary, both
the Virgin and the Mother, *St. Thomas of Canterbury*, I, p. 208.

complex. Not only is Becket a guest of the feast, he also "imitates the Spouse. The saint's body, or wedding garment, is not only white but crimson, like the *Beloved* as described by the Bride of Christ."[47]

This lush metaphoric imagery asks its audience to go beyond the figure of Becket to those of the Bride, the Beloved, and Christ. They strengthen the spiritual argument of Becket's kinship to Christ, emphasizing the former's sanctity through its metaphoric relationships with the latter's divinity.[48] The imagery denies physicality: to use beautiful flowers to describe the effects of a gruesome murder reveals a disinterest in the physical nature of the event and instead an invitation to transcend that physical nature for spiritual benefit. This kind of limber spiritual gymnastics is not asked of the popular audience of Canterbury. Images of Becket's sanctity are not to be imagined through extrapolation, they are made present through the materiality of the windows. The denial of physicality that metaphor invites is resolutely set aside for a celebration of physicality in the exuberant repetition of images of healing cures seen in the windows. Thus where the metaphors of textual tradition re-presented the spirituality of the saint through distant metaphors, the materiality of visual tradition presented his physicality through immediate experience.

Despite the preponderance of *Lives* written about Becket, it was the miracle records of Benedict and William that were overwhelmingly used in arranging the Trinity Chapel stained glass windows.[49] This connection between miracle text and image may have emerged from an interest on the part of the authors in establishing a new textual tradition that might have uses outside those of elite culture. The monks Benedict and William did not know that their texts would be used as the basis for images, but I will be arguing that they purposefully made those texts available for uses outside elite culture. Several indications of the fundamental difference of these texts by the authors themselves allow me to make this claim. In the introduction

---

[47] O'Reilly, "'Candidus et Rubicundus'," p. 311.

[48] Anne Duggan, "John of Salisbury and Thomas Becket," in *The World of John of Salisbury*, ed. Michael Wilks (London, 1994), p. 427. This comparison to Christ extended beyond the *Vitae* to letters exchanged amongst ecclesiastics, such as that cited by Anne Duggan of John of Salisbury to John, bishop of Poitiers in 1171, which, for five pages, compares "[Becket's] trials and sufferings with those of Christ."

[49] Caviness, *The Windows of Christ Church*, pp. 175–6, cites two possible "Lives of Becket" windows, both of which have been lost. One panel in window n. VI still represents the seated archbishop.

to his miracle record, begun in 1171, Benedict of Peterborough cites a series of visions of Becket as the inspiration for writing down the miracles of the saint.[50] In his description of the first vision, he inserts the phrase "candidus et rubicundus," but only to describe the robes of the archbishop as he knelt before an altar to celebrate mass.[51] He then goes on to specifically point out that in his conversation with Becket, he asked questions in French while the saint replied to him in Latin: "I asked him questions in French and he replied in Latin discourse."[52] This claim to the vernacular may be a means for Benedict to humble himself as a "simple" author in typical medieval fashion, but it may also have the pragmatic function of shifting the language of miracles and visions, from the elite Latin to the popular vernacular. Benedict's vision continues with a surprising insistence on visuality—not the metaphoric play of imagining one image in place of another, but rather a basic, physical visuality that plays upon the deep desire to *see*. Becket appears before Benedict with a large lantern that he waves about so that it may be seen, but which is obscured by a dense cloud.[53] The miracles will be the wind that removes this cloud and allow the light of Becket's sanctity to be seen. Benedict thus begins his miracle text with a vision and a justification with the immediacy of both the vernacular and the visual, differentiating his text aside from the more referential realm of the *Lives*. The final point to be made concerning Benedict's popular framing of his miracle record is his emphasis on the liturgical calendar. The miracles began to be recorded by Benedict as soon as the doors of the cathedral were once again open to the public for the Easter celebration

---

[50] Benedict, *Materials*, II, p. 27.

[51] Benedict, *Materials*, II, p. 27. *Aspiciebam in visu noctis martyriis ejus, et ecce dilectus noster, candidus et rubicundus, venustus facie et aspectu desiderabilis, in vestibus et ornamentis pontificalibus introibat ad altare Dei, quasi missarum celebraturus mysteria.* "In a night vision I gazed upon his martyrdom, and behold, white and red, with his beautiful face and desirable appearance, in his robes and pontifical costume, he was coming forward towards the altar of God, as though he were about to celebrate the mystery of mass."

[52] *At ille Gallice interroganti respondit sermone Latino*, Benedict, *Materials*, II, p. 27.

[53] Benedict, *Materials*, II, p. 28. *Prolatam ergo lanternam magnam cum ardente intrinsecus candela manu dextera elevavit, et ut circumspicerem praecepit: et vidi, et ecce inane aeris tantae densitatis nebula repleverat ut etiam prope astantium oculis lucernam abscondere videretur.* "Having brought forth a great lantern with a burning candle inside it, he lifted it with his right hand, and he enjoined me to look about: and I saw that below, a could of such great density had filled that place empty of air, so that it seemed to steal the lantern away from the eyes of even those standing near."

of 1171, and the good monk continued to pay close attention to the pastoral concern of the liturgy, using the liturgical calendar as an organizational frame for the first miracles. He does not delve into any of the theology associated with a particular liturgical celebration, using it, instead, to mark time within a pastoral construct recognizable to a popular audience.

William of Canterbury joined Benedict of Peterborough in the crypt in May of 1172 when the miracles became too numerous for the latter to record. He, too, sought to distinguish his miracle text from elite textual tradition. Once again, visions and visuality, as opposed to metaphors and spiritual imagery, are presented foremost. William's primary vision is surprisingly pragmatic, detailing how overwhelmed Benedict was by the influx of miracles he was to hear and record.[54] Even before these visions, which may be the monk's method of presenting his credentials as a miracle recorder, William surprises us with another pragmatic move, dedicating the entire introductory passage to the presentation of the miracle record to King Henry II. Is this pure politics, the submission of the king to the miraculous power of the saint, or is it an attempt on the part of William to engage his miracle record in the secular world? Both purposes are served in this introduction, which invites the king, and any future reader, to listen to the miracle tales of the saint. Citing an embarrassment of riches, William dispenses with organizing the miracles according to the chronology of the liturgical calendar, and instead claims to have so many miracles to choose from that he will organize them by type.

The transcription of the miracle seems to be the final step of the ritual of successful Becket worship, as Benedict and William write down tales only after the fact. Very interestingly, they are *not* eyewitnesses to the miracles, but rather verifiers of their authenticity, and collectors of the grateful pilgrims' offerings at the tomb. The

---

[54] William, *Materials*, I, p. 138. *Cum enim vires ejus res incepta videretur excedere, et emergentia miracula frater ille solus audire non sufficeret et scribere, vediebatur huic in somnis, quod stanti sibi ad orationem cum fratribus in choro vir assitens throno domini archipraesulis dicens acclamaret, 'Opera adhibe.,' tanquam ex ipso mandatum procederet.* "For since the undertaking seemed to exceed his powers, and that one brother alone did not suffice to hear and write down the emerging miracles, it seemed in a dream, that a man taking a place in the holy seat of the archbishop, proclaimed to him standing for prayer in the choir with the brethren saying, "Let us apply ourselves to work," as if having been ordered by him himself [St. Thomas Becket] to do this."

precise structure and order of things provided the early pilgrims with
a simple ritual structure based on experience and the narration of
that experience. Devoid of any theological questioning or spiritual
delving, the miracles are recorded in a succinct manner, one well
adapted to a popular audience uninterested in theological debate,
but eager for spiritual recognition by a saint. The miracle texts mark
a ritual of authentication: the monks write down past authenticated
events, not miracles they themselves have seen. In this sense, the
miracle texts carve out a new discourse between that of the elite
textual tradition of metaphor and the popular visual tradition of
experience, but it would take their translation into the visual form
of the windows close to fifty years later to make Benedict and
William's accounts truly popular.

The miracle windows of the Trinity Chapel contain an unusual
number of inscriptions.[55] The presence of text in image may sound
difficult to reconcile with the popular appeal of the miracle windows,
one that would not require verbal literacy. But the inscriptions of
the miracle windows do not behave like literary text: they may not
have been intended for reading as texts, but rather for seeing as
shape. There is good evidence to show that the inscriptions have a
figurative, that is visual, rather than literal role to play. Let us take
the example of Henry of Fordwich, whose miracle is revealed in two
panels in the northern ambulatory window, n. IV.[56] We see a man
struggling against the fetters that bind his stumbling body, as attendants forcibly drag and beat him towards Becket's tomb where a
cowled figure awaits him. (fig. 126) The next panel shows Henry
free of the sticks that had been used to control him and which have
now been cast down below the tomb. (fig. 127) The miracle could be
understood through image alone: a broken, bent body in one image,
a peaceful, praying body in the next. The text is here superfluous
in terms of revealing the narrative. We must look for its role beyond
that of the literate experience of reading for information.

---

[55] Caviness, *The Windows of Christ Church*, p. 220. "A Note on the Epigraphy of
the Early Glass."

[56] All window numbering uses that determined by Madeline Caviness in the
Corpus Vitrearum volume. "n." denotes a window in the north of the ambulatory
and "s." one in the south ambulatory. The Roman numerals progress from east to
west. The numbering of the windows is explained, and coordinated with past num-
berings, on p. xxxviii. The Henry of Fordwich panels are figures 265 and 266 in
Caviness, *The Windows of Christ Church*, and are discussed in p. 184. The miracle
text is Benedict, Book II, Chapter xiii, in *Materials*, II, p. 66.

What, then, is the figural, rather than literal, role of text in image? First, the role of recognition: the letters which arch above both scenes are fundamentally signs denoting text as opposed to language; they are recognizable *as* text and connote the *authority* of text. Other sightings of text in an ecclesiastical setting were visible on stone inscriptions, liturgical objects and vestments, and, most notably, on large-format liturgical books held up during processions. The mere presence of text frames the image in the authority of the Holy Word. Literacy is not necessary for the recognition and association of text in the windows with other texts in the holy space of the cathedral. A second figural role for the text to play is in conjunction with the image itself. Very rarely is the inscription a simple band across the visual panel—rather, text appears in the forms of scrolls, smooth arches, broken arches, bands below the image, and bands above. It has its own place within each window panel's composition. In the case of Henry of Fordwich, the text is presented in a broken arch over the broken body of the madman and in a smooth arch over that of the healed and praying Henry. There is an arguable expressivity to the frame of the text itself.

Henry's text reads *Amens Accedit*, in the first panel and *Orat Sanus Recedit* in the second. The language is disarmingly simple: "He came insane/He prayed, he left sane." The two phrases together make up a hexameter.[57] The easy rhythm of the hexameter is rendered even more dynamic by the rhyme of the *accedit* and *recedit*. The oral performance of the text, as conducted by a literate priest or fellow pilgrim, also eschews the necessity of textual literacy for a popular audience, but grants visual literacy. The hexametric form and rhyming sound of the phrase *Amens Accedit, Orat Sanus Recedit* makes the text very easy to commit to memory. The Latin of the phrase imbues it with the power of holy language. The miracle windows of the Trinity Chapel are filled with such rhyming inscriptions of simple Latin, and avail easily memorizable holy phrases to the pilgrims.

The play of presence within the windows extends from the general presence of holiness intimated by text to the highly specific presence of the saint, Thomas Becket. Making the saint present, making him vivid and immediate and available, was, as I am arguing, one of the singular and primary roles of the windows. They worked in

---

[57] Caviness, *The Early Stained Glass*, p. 147.

conjunction with the shrine in the center of the Trinity Chapel on this goal: the shrine concealed and contained the tremendous potential power of Becket's relics, while the windows revealed and projected the splendid proven power of the saint.

What were some of the visual tactics of presence? The inscriptions, as we have seen, set a visual tone of holiness and authenticity. The image of the saint himself, rarely, but effectively positioned throughout the miracle windows, places him in direct contact with miracle recipients. Again, physicality and visuality trump metaphor and imagination: Becket is presented as a hands-on saint. In window n. IV, we see Becket leaning over an ailing figure stretched out in a bed. (fig. 128) The archbishop is fully bedecked in his archiepiscopal vestments, maintaining his hold upon his crozier while leaning forward to touch the patient upon the head. Another rhyming phrase underscores the effectiveness of Becket's miracle: *Qua Dolet Hac Planat Dolet/His Trib' et Tria Sanat*—"Where the pain is, there he smooths; the pain is in these three places and he heals the three."[58] Becket does not simply appear: he makes his presence known through vision and touch in his active role as healer. The miracle recipient has his vision of Becket far from the pilgrimage site, but, by being depicted in a window of the ambulatory, Becket was shown as appearing in the very space of the cathedral. The Cure of the Daughters of Godbold in window n. III features Becket in two of the three panels of their miracle tale.[59] The two daughters arrive at the pilgrimage site with great effort to cure their lameness. Becket again appears in full archiepiscopal garb, leaning protectively first over the older sister, then the young one.[60] The two sisters are shown asleep at the

---

[58] Caviness, *The Windows of Christ Church*, pp. 181–2, fig. 254. The transcription and translation are by Caviness. The iconography of the panel remains a matter of debate. Caviness suggests a miracle from Book IV, Chapter xxvi (pp. 340–41 of *Materials*, I) of William's collection in which Robert of Lilford, after having sustained three wounds from an attack is healed once St Thomas appears to him and, touching his wounds, recommends that he pour holy water into his wounds. A pilgrim promptly appears with a drop of the holy blood water which heals Robert's wounds. The miracle window emphasizes the physicality of the vision by representing Thomas touching Robert instead of the pilgrim applying the holy water.

[59] Caviness, *The Windows of Christ Church*, p. 189, figs. 277 and 278. The miracle story is found in Benedict's account, Book III, Chapter lxx, in *Materials*, II, pp. 170–71.

[60] The third band of text is the most legible. Caviness offers Rackham's reconstruction: *Sanat Maiore[m n]ox prima, se[cun]da minorem*: "The first night brings health to the elder, the second to the younger." Notice, again, the presence of rhyming text associated with the cure.

martyr's tomb; Becket's appearance in *his* holy space of the crypt
marks the possibility of his appearance in the holy space of the
shrine. The pilgrim and Becket share the physical space of the shrine.
In both instances, Becket appears within dream visions to heal the
bodies of the afflicted. His power is such that his spiritual appearance has physical repercussions. The Plague in the House of Jordan
Fitz-Eisulf in window n. II provides yet another role for Becket's
appearance: this time as a warning to a family cured of the plague
who has not yet performed its pilgrimage of gratitude to Canterbury.[61]
(fig. 129) Becket appears twice in the cycle; once (in the upper right-
hand petal) to an intermediary, a leper named Gimp, in order to
warn Jordan Fitz-Eisulf that his miracle must be fulfilled by his pilgrimage vow. The saint leans toward the afflicted Gimp emphatically, holding onto his crozier while gesturing rhetorically to Gimp.
The speaking gesture connotes a conversation between the humble
leper and the glorious saint, and indeed, in Benedict's miracle text
of the tale, the two engage in a long conversation about the duties
of miracle recipients.[62] Becket does not appear just to heal, but can
also appear to physically threaten his subjects: the saint's second
appearance is in the central square of the cycle where he brandishes
a sword above the heads of assembled family members mourning
their fate, and regretting their lack of vigilance in worshipping Becket.
There is no mention of the healing of Gimp and more members of
Jordan-Eisulf's household die before the master and his wife finally
make their pilgrimage. The physicality of Becket's presence was not
always benign, but it was always powerful.[63]

Thomas Becket appears one last time within the extant glass in
an oft-reproduced, but still controversial panel. This panel, at the
top of window n. III, reveals the saint emerging from his shrine elevated above an arched support and hovering above the figure of a

---

[61] Caviness, *The Windows of Christ Church*, pp. 197–99, fig. 316. The story emerges
from both Benedict's and William's record. Benedict's version (Book IV, Chapter
lxiv, *Materials*, II, pp. 229–234) is longer than William's (Book II, Chapter v, *Materials*
I, p. 160).

[62] Benedict, *Materials*, II, pp. 230–31.

[63] A similar example of a miracle recipient punished for not fulfilling his pilgrimage vow is told in the tale of William of Kellett found in William (Book III,
Chapter xv, *Materials*, I, pp. 273–74) and discussed in Caviness, *The Windows of
Christ Church*, pp. 201–202, fig. 327. The saint appears to William, recently wounded
by an axe, and explains the latter's demise as the result of a non-fulfilled pilgrimage vow. William repents, is healed, and returns to work as a forester.

sleeping monk while stretching his arm towards the monk.[64] (fig. 130)
Because the figure is a monk, it has been easy to ascribe the representation to either Benedict or William's introductory visions. The
point of debate emerges from Becket's appearance in conjunction
with his shrine in the ambulatory rather than his tomb in the crypt.
Benedict and William had their visions and their roles to play exclusively in conjunction with the tomb in the crypt—their miracle records
cease in 1179, a good thirty years before the shrine was ever a physical reality in the newly constructed ambulatory. So how to reconcile
the monastic figure indicating Benedict and William with the image
of the shrine indicating much later protagonists? Instead of looking
at the image literally, or as a document of a vision of the saint,
there is the possibility for engaging with this image as a representation of the programmers' awareness of the passage of fifty years from
martyrdom to fully-furnished cult. In one succinct image, at the apex
of a window, the programmers commemorated the temporal and
spatial gap, which at once separated and united the early miracle
chroniclers by the humble tomb from/to the saint in his splendid
shrine. The fact that this gap was bridged by the successful completion of the Trinity Chapel renders the window a celebration of
the saint's power. The transformation from tomb to shrine is, in fact,
commemorated and celebrated over and over again by the miracle
windows in their continuous representation of the tomb.[65] In the
three panels beneath that of the shrine apparition, the tomb is represented three times, underscoring both the past history of the cult
in the present space of the ambulatory and the difference of its manifestations. The superimposed spaces of the crypt and the Trinity
Chapel contained powerful historical references: the tomb was laid
in the crypt in 1174 beneath the Altar to the Holy Trinity where
Becket had celebrated his first Mass in 1162.[66] The space of the
Altar to the Holy Trinity had now, almost sixty years later, been
transformed into the Trinity Chapel. The difference was that now,

---

[64] Caviness, *The Windows of Christ Church*, p. 187, fig. 273.

[65] There is only one other representation of the shrine to be found within the
extant glass: window s. VII (Caviness, *The Windows of Christ Church*, p. 214, fig. 366,
textual source unknown) reveals a woman kneeling before the altar, which was
known to exist before the shrine.

[66] Urry, "Two Resting Places," p. 196. The crypt itself was a site of hagiographical commemoration: Urry points out that Becket's tomb was laid between
the altars of St. John (to the north) and St. Augustine (to the south), p. 195.

that is, as of July 7, 1220 (the date of the Translation of the Relics from the tomb in the crypt to the shrine in the ambulatory), this holy space of Becket could be shared by his pilgrims. The consistent contrast between the tomb in the windows and the shrine in the ritual space of the viewer marked a physical and spiritual intimacy between saint and pilgrim possible only in the space of the Trinity Chapel because of its combination of shrine and stained glass images. Indeed, the dynamic of the Trinity Chapel arguably lies in its historico-architectural relationship with the foundations of the saint's cult in the crypt below.

One last contrast between the two spaces of Becket's cult needs to be analyzed. The cult that flourished around the tomb was textual, informed by the miracle records of the two monks, Benedict and William, whereas the cult that flourished around the shrine derived its power and dynamic from visuality. No miracle records were kept at the shrine by the monks; instead, written accounts about the shrine itself flourish as of its installation in 1220. The most noted contemporaneous description is by Matthew Paris who chronicled the events of the Jubilee in his *Historia Anglorum*.[67] The names of the "incomparabiles artifices" are noted: Walter of Colchester, sacristan of St. Albans, and Elias of Dereham, canon of Salisbury,[68] and Matthew's language argues that the two artists may have been involved in the preparations for the Translation ceremony and Jubilee.[69] Walter and Elias, as visual artists, form a sharp contrast to Benedict and William, our two text chroniclers. It is not that the crypt space was devoid of visual impact, but rather that its rituals and pilgrimage experiences were guided by the structure of text. The pilgrim's behavior

---

[67] The *Historia Anglorum* are edited in the *Rolls Series*, II, pp. 241–42, cited in Urry, "Two Resting Places," p. 200, fn. 19.

[68] Urry, "Two Resting Places," p. 200 and Josiah Cox Russell and John Paul Hieronimus. *The Shorter Latin Poems of Master Henry of Avranches Relating to England.* (Cambridge, 1935), p.66. Not a great deal is known about Walter of Colchester, but Elias of Dereham had a long and illustrious career at Salisbury detailed in Josiah Cox Russell, "The Many-Sided Career of Master Elias of Dereham," *Speculum* 5 (1930), pp. 378–87.

[69] The text cited by Urry, "Two Resting Places," p. 200, is of great interest: The two masters are mentioned are those *quorum consiliis et ingeniis omnia quae ad artificium thecae et ipsius elevationis et translationis necessaria fuerunt, irreprehensibiliter parabantur.* "through whose counsel and ideas all the necessities of the elevation and translation to the designed shrine were gloriously arranged." They are cited as fully in charge of preparations for the elevation and translation of the saint's bones into the splendid shrine.

at the tomb was guided more by the demands of textual recording than by those of a visual setting.[70] The pilgrim's behavior in the Trinity Chapel was guided by the multiple visual markers which shaped their experience: the splendid shrine itself, the lively visual forms of the pavement surrounding the shrine,[71] the overarching presence of the figures in the vault paintings above,[72] and the encircling presence of the miracle stained glass windows. The overall effect of the shrine might better be presented as that of an enormous reliquary, a Sainte-Chapelle avant-la-lettre.[73]

From Typology to Memory: Remembering Becket and Mapping Martyrdom

The play between tomb and shrine in the windows is not just an indication of the shift from the textual culture of the crypt to the visual exploration of the Trinity Chapel. It also signals the transformations that took place in the process of remembering Thomas Becket. The argument here is much more concerned with spaces and their ways of promoting memory. As I configured text with biblical referent as an elite textual tradition, I would like to argue here that typology is an elite remembrance tradition, one that was manipulated and transformed by innovations made to accommodate the spatial memory arranged for a popular audience. As before, I am

---

[70] Benedict, *Materials*, II, p. xxxviii. "Beside the tomb sat a monk who received the oblations of money in a long ladle, listened to the stories of pilgrims, and endeavoured to detect any falsehoods in them." Benedict shares the tale of a woman who physically beat him when he questioned the veracity of her miracle story (Benedict, *Materials*, II, p. 140). The authenticity of the text was almost sacred, and defended as such.

[71] Eames, "Notes on the Decorated Stone Roundels," p. 68. The four groups of roundels west of the shrine represented signs of the Zodiac, labors of the months, virtues overcoming the vices, and monsters.

[72] Caviness, "A Lost Cycle of Canterbury Paintings," pp. 67–69. The paintings are now completely gone, but Caviness analyzes twelve standing figures from older drawings. There may have been as many as seventy-two figures in the original program. The inscription to King Henry [III] indicates the date of 1220 for the completion of the painting cycle, coinciding with the year of Becket's Translation and first Jubilee. The only lighting for the paintings came from the clerestory windows, providing an effect of richly imbued light and a truly magnificent visual experience.

[73] Caviness, "A Lost Cycle of Canterbury Paintings," p. 71. "Rather than a new departure, the Sainte Chapelle is the culmination of this tradition, with a number of technical refinements." Hearn, "Canterbury Cathedral and the Cult of Becket," p. 44 echoes this sentiment, "The total effect is one of unparalleled magnificence, a virtual reliquary in itself."

not seeking to make typology and memory mutually exclusive, but rather to pinpoint those differences that indicate the reconstruction of the cult of Becket for an audience with a different sense of holy presence. Where typology conjured up the greatness of the saint by aligning him with past theological figures or figurations of Christ, memory, as I will be using the term here, sought to remember the saint by having pilgrims experience Becket's *own* history in *its own* space. This process of remembering is much more personal, physical, and spatial and causes us to reconsider the cathedral as a space of re-enactment and memory. The miracle windows' careful positioning in this theater of memory and their equally careful representation of space, present the culminating moment for pilgrims in mapping Becket's martyrdom and miracles onto their own experiences.

The changes that William the Englishman effected when he took over the reconstruction campaign in 1179 were not just a reconfiguration of architecture, but of the pilgrimage experience itself. Raising the floor level of the new Trinity Chapel above that of the main altar[74] rendered the space now probably meant for the shrine of Becket the visual goal and culmination of the sweep of the nave.[75] Allowing more room for the placement of stained glass windows[76] was another step in the rededication of the eastern end of the cathedral as a para-liturgical space of pilgrimage rather than the strictly liturgical space the Romanesque choir had been.[77] As there were

---

[74] Woodman, *The Architectural History*, p. 119. Caviness, "Canterbury Cathedral Clerestory," p. 50. "It is known from Gervase that English William broke through the old foundations in order to extend the Trinity Chapel to the east in the winter of 1179–80."

[75] The years 1179–80 seem to have been a turning point in the commitment of the monks to the refurbishing of the cult of Becket. It is interesting to note that in this period of renewed commitment to Becket's cult, both Benedict and William added on to their miracle records, which had remained untouched since 1174/5, dated by Caviness, *The Early Stained Glass*, p. 143. Another clear indication of the monks' change of heart towards developing a more spectacular cult to Becket can be seen in their 1188 defiance of Baldwin of Ford's wishes to have Becket's body removed to a new church in Hackington.

[76] Hearn, "Canterbury Cathedral and the Cult of Becket," p. 44: "The relative amount of surface given over to stained glass is strikingly greater than in any normal church." Caviness, "Canterbury Cathedral Clerestory," p. 52: "The architect was, evidently, acutely concerned with fenestration because he took the trouble to lift the roof line beginning with the bay over the stairs at the entrance of the Trinity Chapel."

[77] The Trinity Chapel had its own, much looser, liturgical structure in comparison with the choir of the monks. D.H. Turner in "The Customary of the Shrine

two building campaigns for the eastern end, so, too, were there two glazing campaigns: the first, a clerestory campaign, was finished in conjunction with the completion of the choir space for the celebration of Easter Mass in 1180 and included a cycle of eighty-six of Christ's ancestors and twelve typological windows.[78] The miracle windows were introduced in a second glazing campaign which may have been underway by 1205,[79] and were completed in time for and in ritual co-existence with the first Jubilee of Thomas Becket at the celebration of the Translation of his relics in 1220. The two glazing campaigns produced two very different sets of windows one earlier and typological, the other emerging after the reconstruction of the eastern end as a pilgrimage space and newly dedicated to the process and experience of remembering Thomas Becket and his miracles.

The typological windows were begun by 1177 and were part of William of Sens's 1176 design for the eastern end. William of Sens was ordained to maintain the Romanesque integrity of the choir and not to disturb it with the pilgrimage activity surrounding Becket that was to be kept separate below in the crypt.[80] The genealogy and

---

of St. Thomas Becket," *Canterbury Cathedral Chronicle* 70 (1976), pp. 16–22, analyzes the 1428 customary by John Vyel and Edmund Kyngyston for evidence of this separate, more general liturgy. The shrine was always guarded by two guardians, one spiritual, the other temporal, who had to sleep within shrine precincts. The spiritual guardian celebrated mass in honor of Becket at the shrine's altar every day except Tuesday when it was performed by the guardian of the Corona, and was served by the temporal guardian and two secular clerks. Before the daily Mass, the temporal guardian opened doors for pilgrims and travelers and rang a bell to invite them in to the service. The liturgical activity was thus scripted for the pilgrimage audience.

[78] Caviness, *The Early Stained Glass*, pp. 107–20. This glazing campaign is well-documented in Gervase and by the archaeological evidence. Interestingly, Gervase uses very typological language in describing the loss and reconstruction of the eastern end, maintaining that "the afflictions of Canterbury were no less than those of Jerusalem of old, and their wailings were as the lamentations of Jeremiah," Woodman, *The Architectural History*, p. 91, who used Willis's translation of Gervase from *The Architectural History of Canterbury Cathedral*. Gervase goes on to compare the monks of Canterbury to the displaced children of Israel and Adam expelled from Eden. The restoration of the eastern end for liturgical services in 1180 was thus a return to Paradise.

[79] Caviness, "A Lost Cycle of Canterbury Paintings," pp. 69–70.

[80] Hearn, "Canterbury Cathedral and the Cult of Becket," pp. 39, 41. "The plan of 1175 made no new accommodations for the pilgrimage cult." Woodman, *The Architectural History*, pp. 116–67. "Such a cycle would have been worked out at an early stage, and the choice of characters dictated by the original number of windows in the first plan."

typology windows are thus part of this conservative context that sought to preserve the liturgical emphasis of the elite monastic community of the cathedral. The eighty-six ancestors of Christ are culled from the genealogies presented in Luke and Matthew[81] and, at Canterbury, have a particularly typological bent: Adam is not just the ancestor of Christ, but anticipates his mortality; the ascent of Enoch is a pre-figuration of the Ascension, and so forth for every one of the eighty-six ancestors.[82] Viewing these images, positioned high up in the clerestory of the choir, demanded extensive knowledge of biblical reference and required typological, comparative, thinking. Visually, the figures are seated in regal poses and identified by inscriptions more than attributes. The experience they represent is very far removed from that of the pilgrims and instead still caters to the spiritual associations and meditative context of the monks. The twelve typological windows beneath the ancestors were also part of this earlier, more conservative glazing campaign.[83] Their machinations are too complex to enter into here, but suffice it to say that they even more emphatically engage the viewer in the meditative mind games of associations between pasts and presents at a far remove from physical experience.[84]

In contrast, the miracle windows must be understood within the performative stage set by William the Englishman between 1179 and 1184. Encircling the space significantly raised by this second building campaign, their shimmering light drew the pilgrim forward into a place of immediate experience. In subject matter, composition, and arrangement the miracle windows called for an entirely different

---

[81] Caviness, *The Early Stained Glass*, pp. 107–115. Specifically, from Luke 3.23–38 and Matt. 1.17.

[82] Caviness, *The Early Stained Glass*, p. 111. These typological interpretations are to be found in the *Glossa Ordinaria*, an early twelfth-century text from the school of Laon. Caviness presents evidence that the *Glossa* was known at Canterbury by 1175 or 1180 and was part of library of glossed texts furnished in part by Herbert of Bosham and Benedict of Peterborough.

[83] Caviness, *The Early Stained Glass*, pp. 115–38. Three deal with the early life of Christ, six windows explore his teaching and miracles, and three windows address the Passion; a thirteenth window representing the Passion and Redemption was added in the Corona, p. 118.

[84] Caviness, *The Early Stained Glass*, p. 140. The other element present in the clerestory of the choir and eastern transept spaces was a short series of windows representing the older archbishops, Dunstan (925?–988) and Alphage (954–1012), fitted into the triforium to be seen in conjunction with their two altars which were positioned on either side of the High Altar.

mode of thinking than the typological windows.[85] As Madeline Caviness
has noted, the miracle windows could be read as "distinct units"
rather than in protracted typological associations.[86] We will analyze
just one of these units, the Cure of Mathilda of Cologne in window
n. II[87] for the information it can give us concerning the narrative
composition, enlivened style, and awareness of space in the miracle
windows. (fig. 131) The window uses multiple tactics of easy recognizability to establish its narrative pattern: the protagonist, Mathilda,
is dressed in the same vivid pink garment in each scene; she is consistently positioned to the left of the visual field while progressively,
in each panel, moving closer to the tomb of Becket to the right of
said visual field. The central of the three scenes shows the climax
of the story of her madness: we see her beaten and flailing while
the holes to Becket's tomb are barred to her by the stick of an attendant. When her miracle has been accomplished, she leans forward
on the floor in a position of prayer while the attendant monk, whose
book had been opened in the central panel, stands with his cowl
over his head and the book closed. Mathilda's entire story can be
read from the highly expressive bodily poses of the figures.[88] Her
visual format is that of virtually every miracle window: the afflicted
protagonist struggles to the left and the cure is accomplished, with
a reconciliation to the tomb or the saint, to the right of the composition. In this steady narrative repetition, the windows instill a kind
of physical memory in the viewer.

Physical memory is performed through the repetition of movements through the church space. This idea applies to both the windows and the preparatory rituals that the pilgrims experienced before

---

[85] Caviness, *The Early Stained Glass*, p. 150, comments on the distinction in style
between the typological and miracle windows. "As we have seen, the painters of
some of the Trinity Chapel windows are closely related to those working on the
north choir aisle windows, yet their style is transformed, infused with new energy
and realism."

[86] Caviness, *The Early Stained Glass*, pp. 146–50.

[87] Caviness, *The Windows of Christ Church*, pp. 196–7, figs. 306–09 and plate XIV.
The tale is found in Benedict's miracle record, Book IV, Chapter xxxvii, *Materials*
II, pp. 208–09.

[88] The accompanying text, especially the most legible inscription of the central
panel, adds its usual rhyming scheme to aid in committing the miracle to memory: *Stat Modo Iocunda/Modo Lapsa Iacet Moribunda*. "Now she stands gleefully, now
she collapses and lies as if dying." Translation by Caviness, *The Windows of Christ
Church*, p. 196.

arriving in the Trinity Chapel. These rituals took the 13th-century
pilgrims through Becket's last steps, weaving them through the consecrated spaces and places of the saint's martyrdom. (fig. 132) The
pilgrim's visit began with a reading of Becket's miracles in the chapter
house.[89] This preliminary oral performance would be fulfilled in the
visual performance of the miracles in the windows—in between these
two miraculous moments, the pilgrim retraced Becket's last steps and
visited the places where his body suffered and was first consecrated.
As of 1198, three sites dedicated to Becket's experience were well
established as stopping places along the pilgrims' path and locations
of significant offerings:[90] the place of his martyrdom in the northwest transept, marked by an altar; the site of his tomb in the crypt
(empty but still visited as of 1220); and the small chapel extending
off of the eastern end of the Trinity Chapel called the Corona because
of its precious relic of the crown of Becket's skull. As of 1220 the
altar that stood before the shrine of Becket in the Trinity Chapel

---

[89] Fitzstephen, *Materials*, III, p. 151: *Sed de miraculis ejus in Anglia, sacerdotum et bonorum virorum testimonio declaratis, et in capitulo Cantuariensis ecclesiae publice recitatis, magnus
codex conscriptus exstat.* "But about his miracles, declared by the testimony of priests
and good men throughout England and recited to the public in the chapter house
of the Church at Canterbury, a great book was written down and still exists."
Robertson, in his preface to vol. I of the *Materials* series, conjectures that the *magnus codex* in question is the miracle record compiled by William, which attests to
the testimonials of good men and priests and is then recited *publice*, to the public,
in the chapter house. Fitzstephen was writing about this practice of public reading
in 1173–74, and there is no indication that it was not continued into the Trinity
Chapel fulfillment of the cult. Indeed, one could even wonder if the reading practice may not have been an inspiration for the programmers as they were deciding
how to visually frame the space of the shrine.

[90] C. Eveleigh Woodruff, "The Financial Aspect of the Cult of St. Thomas of
Canterbury," *Archaeologica Cantiana* 44 (1932), pp. 14–16. Using Treasurers' accounts,
Woodruff records ten altars which received offerings from 1198 to 1383. Those
devoted to Becket were for the tomb in the crypt, the altar of the martyrdom in
the northwest transept, the Corona at the eastern end of the Trinity Chapel, and
the shrine of Becket (after 1220). The first three altars were already in place and
in play by the time that Becket's shrine was installed, making it the culminating
experience of a well-established pilgrims' path. Woodruff goes on to argue that
"The offerings were certainly large, but so, too, was the expenditure," p. 26, indicating that the monks were more interested in constructing pathways of devotion
than making money from the pilgrimage, Indeed, Woodruff's research into Treasurers'
accounts reveals very little profit from the pilgrims' offerings. In the pre-exile years
(1198–1213), for example, the average intake from the altar was 426 pounds, 3
shillings 7 pence per annum—309 pounds 5 shillings of which came from offerings
at the Tomb. Total earnings were 1,406 pounds while total expenditures were 1,314
pounds. See also, Nilson, *Cathedral Shrines*, pp. 107–109.

became the new culmination of the pilgrims' path. Using archaeological evidence and reconstructing the flow of pilgrims through the
cathedral space, M.F. Hearn has proposed a path that pilgrims would
have followed in order to visit all four sites without either blocking
each other or interrupting the liturgical offices of the monks in the
choir.[91] (fig. 133) Having heard the miracle stories in the chapter
house to the north of the north transept entrance,[92] pilgrims would
have first visited the altar of the martyrdom where Becket was killed.
Directly from there, they would have left the upper space of the
cathedral and plunged into the depths of the crypt to visit the site
where Becket's tomb had once resided. Here is the first re-enactment site of the miracle stories heard in the chapter house. Before
even seeing the miracles presented in the stained glass windows of
the Trinity Chapel, the pilgrims moved through the actual space
where those miracles were experienced and recorded for the very
first time. They would have then emerged from the crypt into the
south aisle of the choir and ascended into the Trinity Chapel from
its south side. The walk encircling the shrine of Becket and framed
by the miracle windows would then have begun, with another stop
halfway through the procession in the Corona Chapel. Cutting across
the Trinity Chapel from north to south on its western end, pilgrims
would have left the holy space by the southern aisle and exited
through the nave on its southern side.

These somewhat complex movements through the cathedral space
remember Becket through the physical experience of the pilgrim.
There are few, if any, outside referents, each altar and commemoration being insistently local and immediate. The careful integration
of the crypt space, even as it stood empty after 1220,[93] indicates the
prioritization of physical experience in establishing the memory of
the saint. The miracle windows are equally concerned with aware-

---

[91] Hearn, "Canterbury Cathedral and the Cult of Becket," pp. 45–6.

[92] Hearn does not include the readings in the chapter house (which was to the
northwest of the northwest transept) as part of the pilgrims' path, but their inclusion in the circuit fits in very well with his reconstructed itinerary, which begins in
the northwest transept.

[93] Woodruff, "The Financial Aspect of the Cult," continues to find offerings given
at the tomb in the crypt until the very end of the celebration of Becket's cult in
1538 (date in which King Henry VIII dismantled the shrine and forbade any further worship of the saint). See also, Urry, "Some Notes on the Two Resting Places,"
pp. 203–204.

ness of space in their consistent representation of the tomb in the crypt. They are insistently *not* a mirror image of the power of the saint at the shrine, but rather a looking glass back into the memory of the power of the saint at the tomb. This memory is not configured as history, an event of the past, but rather as something that can be constantly re-enacted through walking in the saints' footsteps and spaces. When the pilgrims saw the tomb in the miracle windows they would have just emerged from the space of the tomb in the crypt. The intensity of this movement between spaces and times sets the visual pace for the windows: over and over again, we find a kind of call and response dynamic within the windows which harkens back to the movements of the pilgrims in and out of the crypt and upper spaces of the cathedral. The quick "turnaround" of some of the miracles illustrate this point. We recognize Henry of Fordwich who "came insane, prayed and left sane" as such a miracle, as is Petronella in n. IV who "grows well who was sick,"[94] Ethelreda also in n. IV, for whom "The quartan fever departs, her strength, her figure, come back as if in health,"[95] Richard in n. II who "rises languid, comes, prays, drinks, goes away,"[96] and countless others. The rhythm of the text here is imitating that of the composition of the images: in each instance, the miracle recipient is to the left of the tomb and, in approaching it, is healed with the stunning and succinct efficacy of St. Thomas Becket. Physical proximity to the tomb became spiritual proximity to the saint, thus the rapidity and power of the cures.

The miracle windows seek to replicate this logic of a spatio-spiritual relationship to the saint for the pilgrim in the space surrounding the shrine. In their consistent representation of the miracle recipient to the left of the visual field and the tomb of the saint and his attendants and/or the saint himself to the right of the visual field, the windows make the pilgrims aware of their own bodies' relationship to the shrine in the center of the Trinity Chapel. As they encircle

---

[94] Caviness, *The Windows of Christ Church*, p. 182, figs. 256, 257. Petronella was a nun suffering from epilepsy, as detailed in William's miracle record, Book II, Chapter vi, *Materials* I, p. 163. The translation is by Caviness.

[95] Caviness, *The Windows of Christ Church*, p. 185, fig. 268. Ethelreda of Canterbury's cure from fever is described in Benedict's miracle record, Book I, Chapter xx, *Materials*, II, p. 54. The translation is by Caviness.

[96] Caviness, *The Windows of Christ Church*, p. 194, fig. 298. Richard Sunieve has six panels devoted to his miraculous cure from leprosy as recounted by Benedict, in Book IV, Chapter lxxvi, *Materials*, II, pp. 245–47. The translation is by Caviness.

the shrine their bodies replicate or rather re-enact the memory of the miracles in the crypt directly below them: at any moment, they can become the miracle recipient in a precise and powerful remembered relationship with Thomas Becket.

From Spirit to Body: Indulgences, Relics and the Performances of Presence

In this final section we come to pronouncements made about Becket as his cult was inaugurated in the Trinity Chapel. The usual liturgical rhetoric announcing spiritual benefits to pilgrims was greatly changed in the introduction of one of the earliest Jubilees with indulgences dedicated to a saint.[97] The specific language used by Stephen Langton, Archbishop of Canterbury as of 1206, actual resident of the seat since 1213, and great orchestrator of Becket's Jubilee in 1220,[98] shifted the discussion of the benefits of a saint by detailing the importance of his relics in relation to the immediacy of the remis-

---

[97] Foreville, *Le Jubilé*, p. 30. The celebration of Jubilees was not regularized by the church until the 1300 Jubilee declared in Rome. Before then, the idea of Jubilee had been worked out in highly spiritual terms by Bernard of Clairvaux (1090–1153) (inspired by the spiritual benefit that the Crusaders stood to gain) and was relatively devoid of the immediacy of indulgences, which were the very popular appeal of Jubilees at Canterbury, Rome, and eventually, other holy sites. *Ainsi, dès le milieu du XII⁰ siècle, sous l'influence de saint Bernard, suivi par les prédicateurs de croisade, la notion de Jubilé reçoit le sens anagogique d'indulgences plénière. Mais, l'intervention d'Étienne Langton dans l'institution du Jubilé de saint Thomas Becket—assorti de l'idée de remission comme nous l'avons vu—permet de remonter vers une autre source non moins certaine de l'idée de jubilee, encore qu'elle ait pu être influencée à l'origine par la mystique bernardine.* "Thus, as of the middle of the 12th century, under the influence of St. Bernard, and followed by the preachers of the Crusade, the notion of Jubilee receives the anagogical sense of plenary indulgences. But, the intervention of Stephen Langton in the institution of the Jubilee of St. Thomas Becket (furnished with the idea of remission as we have seen) allows us to consider another, no less certain, source of the Jubilee, even though this source, too, may have been influenced by the mysticism of St. Bernard." Evidence for this early granting of indulgences appears in Honorius III's letters and the writings of Henry of Avranches, Foreville, *Le Jubilé*, p. 8.

[98] Foreville, *Le Jubilé*, p. 32. Langton had secured a papal bull authorizing a feast of the Translation for Becket by 1219. There is also probable evidence that the windows and shrine were completed by then—Caviness, *The Early Stained Glass*, p. 147. Roberts, "Archbishop Stephen Langton, p. 83 points out how Langton continued to nurture the indulgences gained for the Feast of the Translation by going to Rome to, among other things, ask that "the indulgences granted earlier on the occasion of the translation be extended. To this the pope replied on December 18, 1220 that the extraordinary indulgences granted earlier be enlarged and confirmed in perpetuity."

sion of sins occasioned on a Jubilee. The power of relics was not just felt spiritually, but physically by the pilgrims, whose own bodies could be healed as their sins were remitted. The transformation that I will be tracking here is that from the spiritual concerns of pilgrimage to its physical benefits. Again, the shift does not exclude spirituality from physicality—far from it; rather, it allows us to study the precise terms through which the body of the pilgrim became part of the celebration of the saint. The miracle windows make this liturgical argument clear in the most dramatic terms.

In order to track this transformation of emphasis from spirit to body, it will be instrumental to compare two sermons presented by Stephen Langton the year of Thomas's first Jubilee, 1220. On July 7, he preached a sermon celebrating the Translation of the Relics of the martyr and inaugurating his first Jubilee. On December 29 of that same year, he was invited to come to Rome and deliver a sermon commemorating the feast day of Becket's martyrdom.[99] I would like to begin with the December 29 sermon because its clerical audience and setting reveal very directly the spiritual priorities of celebrating Becket.[100] The starting point for the sermon was pulled from the highly mystical Song of Solomon, 2.3–4: "I sat down under his shadow with great delight, and his fruit was sweet to my taste. He brought me to the banqueting house and his banner over me was love."[101] Mystic metaphors ensue in the characterization of Becket as defender of church liberties: he imitates Christ in His Passion, the Church is the banqueting-house and Becket is identified as the "spiced" wine among the wine jars that are the Church's martyrs.[102]

---

[99] This sermon is distinct from the Office of Martyrdom which was probably designed by John of Salisbury. Duggan, "The Cult of St. Thomas Becket," p. 39. The Office, however, like Langton's sermon, heavily emphasizes the role of Becket as defender of the liberties of the Church compiling multiple metaphoric images of the saint from shepherd to man of God, to confessor, to imitator of Christ, until the final declarations of the Office: "Let the virgin mother church rejoice at the victory of a new martyr; let her rejoice for her new Zachariah, sacrificed in the Temple; let her rejoice for the blood of a second Abel crying out to God on her behalf against the men of blood," Duggan, "The Cult of St. Thomas Becket," p. 34.

[100] Roberts, "Archbishop Stephen Langton," p. 76, argues that Langton was very audience and setting conscious in both sermons. The martyrdom sermon exists as a single copy in a thirteenth century anonymous book of sermons, Arras 222, fols. 13r–15r.

[101] Roberts, "Archbishop Stephen Langton," p. 83.

[102] Roberts, "Archbishop Stephen Langton," p. 84. Roberts's translation: "So does the Lord introduce the faithful soul in the Holy Church and proposes that he drink

The secondary theme of the sermon is pulled from Eccl. 50.1–8 "Behold the high priest was as the flower of roses in the days of the spring and as the lilies that are on the edge of the water," as Stephen revisits the theme of lilies and roses as spiritual metaphors for the saint which we witnessed in the 1170s and 1180s *Lives* of the saint.[103]

July 7, 1220 introduced a new feast day in the liturgical celebrations of Thomas Becket.[104] Stephen Langton inaugurated this feast day with both an Office of Translation and a sermon announcing the Translation and its first Jubilee. The orchestrator was very aware of his mixed popular and noble audience, possibly numbering in the thousands,[105] and preached his new message in French.[106] The Translation sermon invited much more of a re-enactment than the sermon of the martyrdom. It was preceded by the dramatic removal of Becket's bones from his tomb in the crypt the night before: Langton set aside a few relics for himself and those he would bring to the Pope in Rome in December; the rest he ceremoniously translated to the glorious shrine awaiting its sacred treasure in the Trinity Chapel.[107]

---

the wine of love marking St. Stephen's day (December 26); the wine of purity for the feastday of St. John the Evangelist (December 27); the wine of innocence for the feast day of the Holy Innocents (December 28); and the spiced wine marking the martyrdom of the blessed Thomas (December 20) who was a zealot in the cause of ecclesiastical liberty."

[103] Roberts, "Archbishop Stephen Langton," p. 84. Langton includes his own elaborations, such as the six leaves of the lily revealing the six years that Becket spent in exile.

[104] Foreville, *Le Jubilé*, p. 11. As of 1173, Becket's martyrdom was celebrated on December 29, and his return from exile on December 2. Duggan, "The Cult of St. Thomas Becket," p. 23, identifies the three feasts as *Regressio* (December 2), *Natalitio* (December 29), and *Translatio* (July 7). The texts of the *Natalitio* and *Translatio* can be found in the *Breviarum ad usum insignis ecclesiae Sarum*, eds. F. Proctor and C. Wordsworth, vol. III (1886), pp. 445–41 and I (1882), pp. ccxlvii–cclxi. The *Regressio* text survives in fragments in the "burnt breviary." Canterbury, Dean and Chapter Library Addit. MS 6.

[105] This number is from Henry of Avranches, an eyewitness and chronicler of the Translation festivities. Russell and Hieronimus, *The Shorter Latin Poems*, p. 68.

[106] Roberts, "Archbishop Stephen Langton," p. 79. The sermon is written in Latin but Roberts and Foreville both suggest that it was probably preached in French as was the custom for many sermons when they made the transition from written to spoken. It exists as a Latin text in a fourteenth-century Vatican manuscript (Lat. 1220, fols. 257r–262v.) and has been edited in *Patrologia Latina* ed. J.P. Migne, Paris, 1863) v. 190, pp. 409–424. As both Raymonde Foreville, *Le Jubilé*, pp. 89–95 and Roberts, p. 79, argue, the sermon and the Office of the Translation have many points in common, suggesting not just similar authorship but also the perpetuation of the sermon's message in the liturgical annual repetition of the Office.

[107] Foreville, *Le Jubilé*, p. 8. and Benedicta Ward, "Two Letters Relating to Relics

Langton addressed the physical translation of the relics and detailed its spiritual benefits claiming that the martyr's "translation, solemnly celebrated, will assure forgiveness for sins and perpetual salvation."[108] The imagery brought into play is not as mystical, but instead seeks to bring Becket into the larger company of saints.[109] One image in particular is worthy of note: Becket is compared to a lamp burning brightly: "The Lord kindled this lamp when He raised him to the head of His Church; He purified this lamp when He allowed His martyr to suffer exile and affliction by insults, abuses, and countless injuries . . . The Lord extinguished this lamp when His servant was martyred, but though He extinguished it corporally, the more does it burn spiritually as a symbol of sanctity for us all to follow."[110] The reference to the lamp conjures up Benedict's first vision of Thomas which prompted him to begin writing his miracle records almost fifty years before and in which Thomas waves a lantern about, wishing to be recognized and to let his holy light shine. The image may well have biblical referent,[111] but also carries with it an expansive resonance to the popular audience who had come to recognize Benedict's miracle record stories in the past fifty years.

The theology of the Jubilee and its particular way of initiating the remission of sins through indulgences is too complex to enter into here,[112] but we can quickly perceive on what terms Langton made

---

of St. Thomas of Canterbury," in *Intellectual Life in the Middle Ages; Essays Presented to Margaret Gibson*, ed. Lesley Smith and Benedicta Ward (London, 1992), p. 175, both provide descriptive scenes of the Translation pulled from the account of Walter of Coventry, found in *Materials*, II, p. 249.

[108] Roberts, "Archbishop Stephen Langton," p. 81.

[109] Roberts, "Archbishop Stephen Langton," p. 81. The sermon begins with a long exposé of the virtues of the saints which Becket also upholds and continues, without pausing on the martyrdom or its conflicts, to configure a comparison with Judas Maccabee, the erection of stones in the desert on the order of Josiah, and the assimilation of Becket to the stoned martyrs.

[110] Roberts, "Archbishop Stephen Langton," p. 82. Translation by Roberts.

[111] Roberts, "Archbishop Stephen Langton," fn. 34, p. 90 suggests John 5.35 as used by St. Bernard of Clairvaux for John the Baptist. In another instance of relating the Translation to events of recent memory, Langton goes on to compare Henry II to a mountain that crumbled. Roberts, "Archbishop Stephen Langton," p. 82.

[112] Foreville, *Le Jubilé*, dedicates a great part of her book to understanding the evolution of indulgences from partial to plenary within the tradition of Jubilees. "Le Jubilé de Saint Thomas Becket dans la Perspective des Indulgences Médiévales," in *Le Jubilé*, pp. 21–36. What interests her a great deal about Becket's Jubilee is that it may have been a first in terms of associating immediate and extensive (although not quite plenary) indulgences with a Jubilee. Becket's Jubilee also marks

Becket's salvific power vivid to his audience. The first reason that Becket had the power to remit sins, Langton explains, was the holiness of this Translation fifty years after his martyrdom, denoting a holy time of Jubilee. Here Langton seems to almost take advantage of the time that had lapsed between Becket's death and the full articulation of his cult—what had been fifty years of turmoil, exile, and betrayal become a mark of the passage of holy time. The second reason for Becket's power deals directly with his body: it is *because of* the Translation of his relics, because of the removal of his bones from a humble place to a glorious space, that Becket has the power to remit the sins of the assembled.[113] Becket's relics had had miraculous efficacy before, but now, installed in his glorious shrine, framed by powerful liturgy, and encircled with images that would help pilgrims perpetuate the benefits of that liturgy, Becket's power was much grander than it could have ever been in the crypt.

The Jubilee, its celebration, visual and ritual grandeur, and enthusiastic popularity enjoyed many chroniclers,[114] notably one Henry of Avranches (act. 1215–62), a lay poet who had been commissioned by Prior Walter (r. 1213–22) of the cathedral to pen verses concerning Becket's miracles, but whose enduring contribution remains his rhyming poem describing the Translation ceremony.[115] Henry has been considered one of the possible authors of the rhyming hexameters found so pervasively within the miracle windows,[116] but also

---

a very important shift from the concept of Jubilee being that of the Old Testament (Levit. 25.8–17) and firmly entrenched in the Jewish tradition to Jubilee becoming a much more Christian ideal.

[113] *Patrologia Latina*, ed. J.-P. Migne, vol. 190 (Paris, 1850), p. 422, paragraph 35: *Ex hoc salutem Dei populo provenientem sermo propheticus, quem prosecuti sumus ostendit. Speremus igitur et nos, quod martyris nostri translatio, quam solemniter celebramus, nobis in praesenti veniam peccatorum.* Emphasis mine on the term for "remission of sins." "The prophetic sermon, which we have followed, revealed forthcoming salvation for the people of God. And let us therefore hope for the present remission of sins for us, because of our translation of the martyr, which we are celebrating in a solemn manner." Langton points out the conjunction of both preaching the sermon and showing the relics as part of the power of the Translation to remit sins.

[114] D.H. Turner, "The Customary of the Shrine," pp. 19–20 notes that the celebration lasted for fifteen days, from July 7 to the 21. Preparations had begun on July 5, when all the usual coverings of the shrine had been removed and all jewels and ornaments had to be cleaned by the guardians. The monks led a procession to Becket's shrine every day of the two weeks of celebration, re-enacting the excitement of July 7.

[115] Russell and Hieronimus. *The Shorter Latin Poems*, pp. 64–78.

[116] Caviness, *The Early Stained Glass*, p. 147.

interests us for the terms in which he describes the festivities surrounding the Translation. His concern is almost entirely social: he dispenses with the liturgical proceedings in a few lines, instead providing his audience with a full description of the crowds, the shrine, and an especially detailed account of the food that was served during the festivities.[117] His description of the two spectacular banquets held during the festivities, complete with details of the menu served, the seating arrangements, and the service rendered unto all the pilgrims,[118] exists in sharp contrast with Langton's metaphorical explorations of the Song of Solomon banquet.

The thousands thus assembled for the first celebration of the Feast of Becket's Translation were offered a wide array of spiritual promises and communal festivities. The importance of presence for the Jubilee cannot be discounted: in order to receive the remission of sins, the pilgrim had to be physically present at the holy site.[119] The presence and power of Becket's relics lay not just in his bones, however. With the ampullae of Becket's Holy Water, a combination of drops of his blood spilled during the martyrdom and water, we witness another innovation in the diffusion of Becket's cult according to the body. The fragmentation of Becket's body was also the multiplication of his miraculous power.[120] Here, the ampullae of Canterbury Water

---

[117] Russell and Hieronimus, *The Shorter Latin Poems*, pp. 68–69. Woodruff, "The Financial Aspect of the Cult," pp. 17–18, in his analysis of the customary of the shrine, notes that the offerings for the Jubilee were 1,142 pounds 5 shillings, 702 pounds 11 shillings 4 pence coming from offerings left at the shrine. These offerings were not all net profit, however, as the cellarer, the individual responsible for the entertainment of pilgrims, was paid 1,154 pounds 16 shillings 5 pence up from his usual 442 pounds 8 shillings, indicating that the chapter took on much of the financial responsibility for the festivities. Russell and Hieronimus note that "The debt incurred for this occasion had hardly been paid off by the time of Archbishop Boniface (r. 1245–70), the fourth archbishop after Langton," p. 66.

[118] Russell and Hieronimus, *The Shorter Latin Poems*, pp. 71–78. The second banquet "receives more attention than any other event," p. 68, and included three kinds of wine, boar, venison, and bear as well as three different kinds of fish and goose and duck.

[119] In the case of the first Jubilee, the indulgences were significant. Walter of Coventry (edited in Stubbs, *Memorale Fratris Walteri de Conventria*, London, 1873, II, p. 246) details the indulgences available to pilgrims: "The Lord Pope had granted an indulgence of forty days to all who on this day of the translation of the blessed Thomas the Martyr should come to Canterbury for reverence's sake, or within fifteen days thereafter. Likewise the Legate granted forty days each, the three archbishops granted forty days also and each of the bishops (seventeen in all) granted twenty days. Counting up all of the days they were found to be 540." Translation by Russell and Hieronimus, *The Shorter Latin Poems*, p. 65.

[120] Caviness, *The Early Stained Glass*, p. 149 points out another populism on the

and the miracle windows hold a great and intriguing deal in common. Sarah Blick has analyzed the visual correspondences between the composition of the ampullae and that of several miracle windows, thereby establishing a visual continuity between the two for medieval pilgrims.[121] I would like to suggest that this visual continuity was also a performative one, that seeing the stained glass windows of the Trinity Chapel engaged the pilgrims in some of the same intimacies and immediacies with the saint that coming into contact with an ampulla filled with Holy Water did. As Madeline Caviness has pointed out, the miracle windows availed themselves to discrete viewing, that is, to being seen one miracle story at a time. In that sense, each quatrefoil or band arrangement projected the proof of a miracle, as an ampulla contained the possibility of a miracle. The Jubilee of Thomas Becket in 1220 proclaimed the salvific power of his relics upon the celebration of his feast day. The ampullae and the windows worked to perpetuate that power beyond the liturgical boundaries ordained by the Church. They both have undocumented, but crucial para-liturgical roles in the longevity of the cult of Becket.

Conclusion: Windows as Performance

How then did the windows continue to invite popular performance within Canterbury Cathedral? As the visual frame for the shrine of Thomas Becket, they stood as the visual goal of the physical travels and travails of the pilgrims who had come to see Becket and be seen in his resplendent light. In presenting pilgrims with the miracle stories they had heard about in the chapter house and whose space they had visited in the crypt below, they stood in a culminating position, receiving *and* projecting all past re-enactments of the miracles of Becket available to the pilgrims. The windows existed as a testament to all the accommodations that had been made for popular pilgrims: the introduction of vivid physical images in preference over the imagery of mystic metaphor; the performance of the memory

---

part of the Canterbury chapter in their making the martyr's blood available to pilgrims when the blood of the Eucharist was still reserved for the elite clergy.

[121] Sarah Blick, "Comparing Pilgrim Souvenirs and Trinity Chapel Windows at Canterbury Cathedral," *Mirator* (September 2001), pp. 1–27.

of the saint through re-enactments of his martyrdom and miracles in lieu of his remembrance through typological exploration; and, with the Jubilee and its indulgences, the crucial importance of being physically present for the reception of spiritual benefits from the saint. Because they were the testament and culmination of these transformations at Canterbury Cathedral, the miracle windows were able to perpetuate the work of visuality, memory, and the body even when the rituals that conducted these activities fell away. They encircled the shrine and provided the visual boundaries of the holy space. In doing so, they also projected the benefits of the protagonist of the holy space: Thomas Becket as he interacted with pilgrims. In their repetition of this interaction, the windows provided a visual script for pilgrims to follow, one guiding their bodies through potential miraculous relationships with the saint. The windows could provide a spiritual benefit even in the absence of a Jubilee year or a miracle reading. But when coupled with these vibrant performances, the miracles windows of Canterbury Cathedral took on a luster that remains resplendent to this day.

PART IV

CONNECTIONS TO JERUSALEM AND THE HOLY JERUSALEM
THROUGH PILGRIMAGE SITES

CHAPTER ELEVEN

AT THE CENTER OF THE WORLD:
THE LABYRINTH PAVEMENT OF CHARTRES CATHEDRAL*

Daniel K. Connolly

Introduction

Recently, the rector of Chartres Cathedral had the chairs removed from the western end of the nave in order to expose the labyrinth pavement hidden beneath them. The subsequent photography of the cathedral (fig. 134), available as a postcard for tourists, now shows the labyrinth design as an integral part of the building's fabric, as it had been in the Middle Ages. The immediate cause behind this new display of the cathedral's space seems to be the tourists' increasing requests for access to the labyrinth pavement. As modern-day, secular pilgrims, these tourists want to walk the one remaining, original cathedral labyrinth pavement from the Gothic era, doubtless in search of an experience more authentic than walking the myriad copies, which, with the rise in awareness of the benefits of measured, ambulant meditations, now proliferate in the United States and elsewhere.[1] It is no accident that the wish to visit Chartres Cathedral

---

* I wish to thank the Traveling Committee and the Lippman Foundation of the University of Chicago, whose support of my dissertation research laid the groundwork for the present study, and gratefully acknowledge the unstinting assistance and support of Prof. Linda Seidel throughout the developments of this project. I wish also to thank Jonathon Alexander, Dorothy Glass, and Marcia Kupfer for their helpful questions and comments when I presented an earlier version of this work at the Annual Meeting of the Medieval Academy of America (Washington D.C., 1999).

[1] Rev. Dr. Lauren Artress, of Grace Cathedral, San Francisco and director of *Veriditas*, the worldwide labyrinth project, is probably the most active supporter of the labyrinth and its spiritual benefits. The cathedral's web-site, www.gracecathedral. org/labyrinth, provides a wide variety of information about contemporary practices. In addition, a locator service at the website lists over 400 labyrinth pavements in the U.S. alone. Most of these are outdoors and the vast majority of them copy the layout and form of Chartres' labyrinth, including the crenellations around the periphery and the six scallops around the very center. The recent translation of Herman

and its labyrinth pavement is bound up with both the desirous motivations of pilgrimage as well as the difficulty of creating an authentic
experience in those other, more accessible copies. What visitors to
Chartres Cathedral, tourists and scholars alike, don't realize is that
the labyrinth pavement there was itself a kind of copy, the motivation for which lay in the nostalgic longing of the High Middle Ages
for the most authentic pilgrimage site for the Latin West—the holy
city of Jerusalem.

In the late twelfth and throughout the thirteenth century, those
responsible for the Gothic re-constructions of cathedrals in northern
France began to install the first large scale, walkable labyrinths into
their nave pavements.[2] Those installations occurred at Sens, Chartres,
Auxerre, Amiens, Reims and Arras.[3] The labyrinth at Chartres is
the only original pavement to survive, and was one of the earliest,
if not the earliest, to be installed. In addition to these nave pavements, several outdoor labyrinths, which likely date to the latter part
of the Middle Ages, were carved into the church yards of Southern
England—the so-called turf-mazes—or they dot the landscapes of
Sweden, Finland and northern Russia with their stone-lined pathways. Without a physical context, dating these outdoor labyrinths is
especially difficult.[4]

The pavement labyrinths were made of different colored paving
stones set in circuitous yet symmetrical patterns into the western
nave bays of their cathedrals.[5] The size and placement of these pavements are radical developments for the history of ecclesiastical archi-

---

Kern's wide-ranging study on the labyrinth, so crucial for its overview of the visual
materials, is another indication of the labyrinth's increasing popularity; see Hermann
Kern, *Through the Labyrinth: Designs and Meanings over 5,000 Years* (New York: Prestel,
2000).

[2] Responsible parties include the particular chapter's prelate, bishop and archi-
tect, with duties varying according to the given assignment. Alain Erlande-Brandenburg,
The Cathedral: The Social and Architectural Dynamics of Construction, trans. Martin Thom
(Cambridge: Cambridge University Press, 1994), pp. 230–65.

[3] Later labyrinths, dating to the fifteenth and sixteenth centuries, were located
at St. Omer and St. Quentin; see generally, Kern, *Through the Labyrinth*, pp. 142–65.

[4] W.H. Matthews, *Mazes and Labyrinths: A General Account of their History and Developments*
(1922; repr. Detroit, MI: Singing Tree, 1969), pp. 71–99 and 147–55; for more
recent discussion and bibliography, see Ivor Winton, "Labyrinths: Chapters Towards
an Historical Geography," (Ph.D. diss, University of Minnesota, 1987). See also the
section in Kern, "Turf Labyrinths," in *Through the Labyrinth*, pp. 167–77.

[5] Generally the third, fourth or fifth nave bay; the location of the Sens labyrinth
in the first nave bay is exceptional.

tecture, for which there has yet to be a full accounting.[6] The labyrinth at Chartres appears to be the earliest and it likely established, through contexts of visual analogies, associations, and uses, a constellation of meanings by which I think we ought to understand the pavements in general. However, explaining the emergence of these pavements in all of these cathedrals is beyond the scope of this essay. And yet, as we shall see, the historiography of the accepted claims about the labyrinth pavements has focused on the later labyrinths and their textual inscriptions to the exclusion of the meanings generated by the performance of their spaces. The labyrinth at Chartres, I submit, was constructed in response to the recent loss of Jerusalem to Muslim forces in 1187. And by presenting its audiences with a richly meaningful image of the city of Jerusalem—one whose centrality in the nave mimicked that city's centrality in the world and whose fundamental geometry signaled a cosmic architecture—this pavement triggered associations with the city, both in its earthly and historic instance and with its future, heavenly instantiation, and it did so as it invited its audiences to perform an imagined pilgrimage to this sacred center.[7]

In contrast to other labyrinths that decorate earlier medieval manuscripts or smaller church furniture, all of these pavement labyrinths are large-scale and were easily accessed by the public.[8] Their scale

---

[6] Most of the literature is concerned with the later thirteenth-century developments of the labyrinth pavements, their inscriptions of authorship of the buildings, or paraliturgical celebrations that occurred but once a year; the implications of the introduction of these prescribed pathways into the naves of these elegantly exotic buildings and their creation of fully embodied experiences of that pathway seem to me to extend issues of authorship to the very uses and meanings of these buildings.

[7] The centrality of Jerusalem in medieval thought is grounded, perhaps most specifically, in passages from the Old Testament, like that of Ezek. 5.5, "Thus says the Lord God: This is Jerusalem; I have set her in the center of nations, with countries round about her." On imagined pilgrimage, and for further bibliography, see Daniel K. Connolly, "Imagined Pilgrimage in Gothic Art: Maps, Manuscripts and Labyrinths," (Ph.D. Dissertation., University of Chicago, 1998), and *idem.*, "Imagined Pilgrimage in the Itinerary Maps of Matthew Paris," *Art Bulletin* 81.4 (1999): 598–622. I prefer the phrase 'imagined pilgrimage' over spiritual pilgrimage because it better conveys the active, cooperative roles of both the meditant and the artwork in the creation of the pilgrimage experience.

[8] On the manuscript labyrinths, see the relevant chapter in Kern, *Through the Labyrinth*, pp. 105–42; and Wolfgang Haubrichs, "*Error Inextricabilis*: form und funktion der labyrinthabbildung in mittelaltern handschriften," in *Text und Bild: Aspekte des Zusammenwirkens zweier Künste in Mittelalter und früher Neuzeit*, ed. C. Meier and U. Ruberg (Wiesbaden: L. Reichert, 1980), pp. 63–174.

and location in the western ends of the nave make them the first
labyrinths designed precisely so that lay and clergy alike could walk
through them. With no contemporaneous text to explain these developments, such a performance of these devices, along with their representational qualities, becomes all the more imperative to our recovery
of the meanings that attended their first appearances. Chartres's
labyrinth (fig. 134), set into the middle of its nave, remains as integral to that building's fabric and its spaces as any of its more renowned
decorative ensembles. It is, moreover, far more accessible. Like other
labyrinth pavements, it is dated by the completion date of the cathedral's nave, about 1220. Early descriptions tell us that all these
labyrinths were round and generally between about thirty and forty-
five feet wide.[9] Chartres's single winding path doubles back on itself
whenever it meets one of two perpendicular axes. These axes form
then a cross within the circle, and effectively divide the circle into
distinct quadrants. Curved or scalloped crenellations run almost
entirely around the perimeter of the labyrinth; the only point of
interruption lies at the entrance 'gate' of the labyrinth.[10] At the
center, six scallops encircle a now empty space, where a bronze or
perhaps copper plaque once lay (fig. 135).

    That plaque may have depicted a city-scape of Jerusalem or a
Minotauromachy. The earliest mention of this plaque dates some
four and half centuries after its installation, by which time it was
likely worn down beyond recognition. In the late seventeenth century, Charles Challine (1596–1678) gave contradictory accounts of
this medallion, but in the published version, he says that one could
see the figure of Theseus and the Minotaur.[11] In 1750, another historian, Janvier de Flainville, contradicts that identification, saying
that the figures are too effaced to identify anything. In 1792, the
medallion was removed.[12] The absence of reliable documentary evi-

---

[9] Kern, *Through the Labyrinth*, p. 153.

[10] Some might argue that crenellations, by definition, must be square shaped. As
we shall later see, the deformation of crenellations into curved shapes, especially as
occurs in diagrammatic renderings of the Holy City, suggests its sacrality, and ultimately, its adumbration of the Heavenly Jerusalem.

[11] Craig Wright, *The Maze and the Warrior: Symbols in Architecture, Theology and Music*
(Cambridge: Harvard University Press, 2001), p. 307, note 37. Wright notes that
there are four different manuscripts of this work in libraries in Chartres and Paris.
Wright's recent and informative study of the labyrinth pavements pays closest attention to its "heyday" in late medieval intellectual and musicological contexts.

[12] Discussion of the plaque of course continued after its removal. Raymond

dence asks us to scrutinize all the more thoroughly the materials available to us.

The width of these northern pavement labyrinths introduced a singular, new element in the tradition of labyrinth depiction—they are big enough to walk through, calling for a performative activation of their spaces. The size of these labyrinths along with their open gates quite emphatically invited the medieval visitor to enter their space and follow their course to the center.[13] Although now lost, that central plaque, which itself had been worn smooth, was held in place by bolts driven into the stone (fig. 135), and their now raised relief against the softer stone bears witness both to the later footsteps of countless visitors to this specific spot, as well as to the fixity with which the builders of Chartres meant to secure the labyrinth to the nave of their cathedral. The medieval sense of that integration with the cathedral's space is attested to by no less an authority on Gothic church architecture than Villard de Honnecourt in the copy of the labyrinth pavement that he made for his famous sketchbook (fig. 136).[14] On the verso of folio 7, amidst his characteristic mélange of 'engins,' animals, and architectural draftings, Villard reproduced the labyrinth of Chartres Cathedral, but did so in reverse, as a mirror image of the pavement. This reversal was likely the result of misremembering the orientation of the complex design, for he probably drew it after the fact, as he must have done for so many of his architectural drawings. We know that Villard was at Chartres, since he drew the Rose Window from the cathedral's west facade.[15] His copy of

Bordeaux records an image of a rider entering Jerusalem at the center of the Labyrinth, and notes that the practices of substitute pilgrimage had only abated at the end of the sixteenth century, "Proces-Verbeaux," in *Séance General Publique de Sens, SAEL-PV* 27 May, 1865 and March 1868, pp. 158–64. For this debate and citing earlier scholarship, see Jean Villete, "L'énigme du labyrinth de la cathédrale," *Notre-Dame de Chartres*, March (1984): 4–12 and *idem.*, "Quand Thésée et le Minotaure ont-ils disparu du Labyrinthe de la Cathédral de Chartres," *Mémoires de la Société archéologique* 25 (1969–72): 265–70, p. 269. Cf. Wright, *The Maze and the Warrior*, p. 41.

[13] On the relative widths of pavement labyrinths, see Kern, *Through the Labyrinth*, p. 143.

[14] (fig. 136) Paris, BN, Ms. Fr. 19093, fol. 7v. While the bibliography on Villard de Honnecourt is immense, enquiry into his copy of the labyrinth is limited to Hahnloser's supposition that Villard drew the labyrinth in reference to Daedalus and as a kind of personal emblem of his status as an architect, Hans R. Hahnloser, *Villard de Honnecourt: Kritische Gesamtausgabe des Bauhüttenbuches ms. Fr. 19093 der Pariser Nationalbibliothek* (Graz: Akademische Druck- und Verlagsanstalt, 1972, 2nd ed.) pp. 38–40.

[15] Paris, BN, Ms. Fr. 19093, fol. 15v, Hahnloser, *Villard de Honnecourt*, pl. 30.

the labyrinth pavement in his sketchbook, itself a testament to Gothic architectural designs, suggests that the labyrinth was both an integral feature of the cathedral and was significantly more important than we have heretofore entertained.

Historiography

Labyrinth pavements were located in the naves of the Gothic cathedrals that have been deemed by art history as some of the most important; these are all situated around the city of Paris: at Sens, Auxerre, and Chartres to the south, and at Reims, Amiens and Arras to the north. Interestingly, it is the later and lost labyrinths of Amiens (1288) and Reims (1289) that have received the most attention by art historians, likely because those pavements had texts and pictures inscribed in them, which have helped to determine the chronology of the building.[16] Thus early authors—Panofsky and Branner—by-passed both the performative value of these designs, as well as their earlier installation in cathedrals to the south of Paris.[17] More recently, Stephen

---

[16] The pavements at Reims and Amiens are dated by associated textual evidence. The original pavements of both were destroyed in 1778 and 1827–1829, respectively; only Amiens's was replaced (1894–1897). Amiens has an inscription running around the center of the labyrinth recording 1288 as the date for the placement of the inscription itself; Stephen Murray, *Notre-Dame, Cathedral of Amiens: The Power of Change in Gothic* (Cambridge: Cambridge University Press, 1996), pp. 129 and 170–3; additional bibliography in Kern, *Through the Labyrinth*, p. 149. Similarly, inscriptions accompanied the figures in the four corners of the labyrinth at Reims and date the labyrinth to *ca.* 1289. Auxerre is dated by the completion date of its nave—the first half of the fourteenth century. The cathedral at Arras was destroyed during the French Revolution, and the tradition of a labyrinth there is based upon some brief descriptions and scattered notices in local historical publications. Matthews reported that a sketch of an octagonal labyrinth, thirty four and a half feet wide, was discovered amidst the city's bombed out debris of World War I. The cathedral was begun in 1160, and the choir and transepts completed at about this time. Construction of the nave continued throughout the thirteenth century and the nave remained unvaulted until the fifteenth century. For this labyrinth, see Matthews, *Mazes and Labyrinths*, pp. 61–3; other reports predate this sketch, see Kern, *Through the Labyrinth*, p. 150 and Matthews's bibliography, p. 222. Haubrichs dates the labyrinth to the late thirteenth century. Haubrichs, "*Error Inextricabilis*," p. 106. For the history of Arras, see *Dictionnaire d'Histoire et de Géographie Ecclésiastiques* (Paris: Letouzey, 1914), s.v. "Arras;" and Jacques Thiebaut, "Arras (cathedral)" in *The Grove Dictionary of Art*, v. 2, pp. 496–7.

[17] On Reims, see: Erwin Panofsky, "Über die Reihenfolge der Vier Meister von Reims," in *Jahrbuch Für Kunstwissenschaft* (1925): 55–82; and Robert Branner, "The Labyrinth of Reims Cathedral," *Journal of the Society of Architectural Historians*, 21 (1961): 18–25.

Murray interpreted the labyrinth at Amiens as a kind of performance; its alternating, frustrating courses, both toward the center and away from it, builds a narrative whose resolution is the revelation of its complexity and creativity evocative of Daedalus, the Master Architect. The labyrinth then is a fitting emblem of the cathedral as a whole.[18] These later pavements, equipped with texts and images of their makers, have eclipsed discussion of the preceding labyrinths, which, with their absence of text, seem to emphasize all the more strongly the performative value of their own designs.

The tendency for later textual evidence to overshadow visual and performative evidences has also promoted the myth of Theseus's triumph over the Minotaur as the paradigm in which all subsequent interpretations have been generated.[19] Penelope Doob, Katherine Woodward, and most recently Craig Wright, each commence with that myth, which had been christianized since late Antiquity as a story of Christ's victory over the Devil, and construe the labyrinth journey as an imitation of Christ's Harrowing of Hell.[20] Wright locates

---

[18] Murray, *Notre-Dame*, pp. 170–3, and pl. 31. The story of the labyrinth, of course, signals the memory of Daedalus as the famous architect of genius, and while a self-referential dynamic may have been at play for the builders of Chartres, that meaning seems to pertain more to those later labyrinths at Reims and Amiens (and possibly at Arras, although the least is known about it). There is no evidence that the labyrinth pavements south of Paris, at Sens, Chartres or Auxerre, made any textual or graphic allusion to their builders.

[19] Hermann Kern, in his broadly sweeping catalogue, presented an exception to these more textual endeavors as he sought out performative possibilities of the labyrinths, paying closest attention to their size as an invitation to be walked. In the western end of the nave, as a precursor to arriving at the altar, walking the labyrinth was a kind of initiatory rite of passage in which the Christian's soul is purified and redirected towards God. Kern, while somewhat dismissive of substitute pilgrimage, did note, by way of cursory analogy to medieval *mappaemundi*, that the labyrinths carried connotations of the world's space. Kern, *Through the Labyrinth*, pp. 146–8. Kern had amassed a great deal of information on labyrinth imagery, from different cultures and from nearly all time periods; the book grows out of a large exhibition on the subject of the labyrinth held in Milan in 1982 and presents several different and often competing theories about their uses and meanings.

[20] Penelope Reed Doob, *The Idea of the Labyrinth: from Classical Antiquity through the Middle Ages* (Ithaca: Cornell University Press, 1990), pp. 101–44, esp. pp. 119–21; as her title suggests, she is more concerned with the 'idea' of the labyrinthine in texts than with particular graphic occurrences. The dissertation by Kathryn Woodward provides important work on the intellectual contexts of medieval labyrinths, especially as signifiers of moral exegesis. Remarkably, it makes no mention of the thesis of substitute pilgrimage: Kathryn Christi Woodward, "*Error Labyrinthi*: An Iconographic Study of Labyrinths as Symbolic of Submission and Deliverance in Manuscripts and on Pavements." (Ph.D. diss., Bryn Mawr College, 1981). See also Wright, *The Maze and the Warrior*.

this imitation most clearly in the *only* medieval text extant that deals with a labyrinth pavement. The text, which dates to 1396—some two hundred years after the installation of the first cathedral labyrinth—has become a lightening rod for explorations of the labyrinth, despite its relatively late date. It tells of a peculiar, para-liturgical ritual: on the afternoon of Easter Sunday, the Dean and cannons of the chapter of Auxerre cathedral gathered on the labyrinth pavement to dance, jump, and toss a leather ball (*pelota*) back and forth, all the while singing the *Victimae paschali laudes*.[21] Other details about the size of the ball, and the feast to which the chapter and town notables retired after the performance, as well as who paid for the accoutrements, are provided in records of the various lawsuits that arose in the later fifteenth century. Disputants, objecting to the costs, but citing the festivities' lack of propriety, relied (unsuccessfully) on the *Rationale divinorum officiorum* (*c.* 1165) by John Beleth, rector of the University of Paris, and on a work of the same title by Guillaume Durand (1230–1296). Durand, Bishop of Mende, essentially copied Beleth's earlier admonition discouraging the performance of these games, though both authors understood that such ball games were played in many of the large cathedrals.[22] What emerges from these disputes is that the litigants used sources which either predate any of the large labyrinth pavements (as in the case of Beleth) or confirm the popularity of these types of games beyond those cathedrals that contained labyrinths.[23] Thus, instead of understanding the meaning of

---

[21] The ritual also took place at Sens, and perhaps elsewhere. For a more in-depth description of the ritual and discussion of these texts, as well as further bibliography, see the chapter in Craig Wright's recent book, "The Dance of the Maze," in *The Maze and the Warrior*, pp. 129–58. In addition to imitating the Harrowing of Hell, other interpretations have been suggested—that it was a form of clerical exercise, that it provided a scene of submission and redemption appropriate to Christ's resurrection on Easter Sunday, that the ball was a symbol of the Easter sun, rising with the renewal of nature in the Spring. See respectively, E. Louis Backman, *Religious Dances in the Christian Church and in Popular Medicine* (Westport CT: Greenwood Press, 1977), p. 330; Woodward, "*Error Labyrinthi*," pp. 64–99; and Kern, *Through the Labyrinth*, pp. 146–47.

[22] Doob, *Idea of the Labyrinth*, p. 123; Wright, *The Maze and the Warrior*, p. 141; and Woodward, "*Error Labyrinthi*," pp. 64–99, who offers a more thorough discussion of the sources.

[23] Indeed, Eude Rigaud, archbishop of Rouen, issued statutes in 1245 forbidding the clergy to engage in these ball games because they led to frequent injury and so could not be played without dishonor to their positions. There is no record of a labyrinth pavement at Rouen. See Woodward, "*Error Labyrinthi*," p. 72. These ball games, in addition to being widespread in popularity, appear to have been rather boisterous.

the labyrinth pavement as intimately linked with the conduct of these para-liturgical performances, interesting though they are, it appears, rather, that these types of games or rituals had been going on for some time in the naves of a number of medieval churches, and that the later labyrinth pavements simply became a likely spot for the conduct of some of those games.[24]

The thesis that these pavements were used as a kind of substitute pilgrimage is not new, but dates back to some of the earliest scholarship on Gothic cathedrals, made perhaps most renowned by the nineteenth century monograph on Chartres Cathedral by Marcel Bulteau.[25] To open his section on the 'iconography of the Cathedral,' Bulteau provided ground plans of the Cathedral that included the labyrinth design as part of the reader's apprehension of the cathedral's architecture (fig. 137); the labyrinth is understood to be just as integral to the cathedral as any column or bay vaulting system. In addition, the volume containing that section held as a frontispiece an engraving (originally dating to 1696) that shows elegantly dressed men and women walking the labyrinth pavement (fig. 138). Illustrations in our more recent histories of these Gothic cathedrals no longer include the labyrinth pavements, either as part of their ground plans or as part of the building's decorative ensembles, which otherwise constructed the buildings' uses and meanings.[26] The embarrassing

---

[24] One might even suppose that the topographical specificity that I argue belongs to Chartres's labyrinth might have been reason to play that game on top of it.

[25] Marcel Bulteau, *Monographie de la Cathédrale de Chartres*, III (Chartres: Société Archéologique d'Eure-et-Loir, 1892), pp. 43–56; see also the earlier scholarship on Gothic cathedrals, J.-P. Schmit, *Nouveau Manuel Complet de L'Architecture des Monuments Religieux* (Paris: Librarie Encyclopédique de Roret, 1859 reprint), s.v. "le labyrinthe," D. Caumont, "Le Labyrinthe de Chartres," *Bulletin Monumental* 13 (1847): 202–3; Émile Amé, *Les Carrelages Émaillés du Moyen-Age et de la Renaissance précédés de l'histoire des anciens pavages: mosaique, labyrinths, Dalles Incrustées* (Paris: Morel and Co., 1859). Doob and Wright have specifically argued against the pilgrimage thesis, relying on the lack of a medieval text corroborative of that role, and pointing out that the claim itself dates no earlier than the eighteenth century. Doob, *Idea of the Labyrinth*, pp. 118–121, Wright, *The Maze and the Warrior*, pp. 208–216. It seems obvious, however, that the lack of a text does not disprove the positive value of the visual evidence. We should not let texts do all of our work for us; not all practices, nor the meanings that extend from them, get recorded in the convenience of contemporaneous texts. And yet, even as scholars dispense with the thesis of imagined pilgrimage, they all agree that the size of the pavements indicate that they were meant to be walked through—just what meaning this walking would have generated for their users is really the central question of this essay.

[26] Prof. Murray's reading of the labyrinth experience, while celebratory of the

realities of popular practices performed in the very center of such celebrated monuments would likely upset the seamless paradigm by which modernists themselves have constructed 'The Gothic Cathedral', helping to explain why the labyrinth has been so effectively erased, both in the scholarship on these cathedrals and from the very naves themselves.[27]

Chartres' Labyrinth and the emblemata *of Jerusalem*

Chartres's labyrinth presents a clearly ordered, geometrically designed path, the width of which invites the visitor to enter its spaces and walk its circular course to its center, coming to stand then in a representation of Jerusalem. There had been a long and quite vital tradition in medieval manuscripts of using the labyrinth (in a variety of designs) to represent ancient cities of the East, usually Jericho.[28] These depictions, however, do not include features that belong to Chartres's pavement labyrinth and which, I think, were meant to

---

physical structure of the cathedral, quite fittingly describes the meditational encounter that I propose later in this essay. Murray, *Notre-Dame*, pp. 170–3.

[27] In a provocative critique of current approaches to Gothic architectural studies, Maija Bismanis writes of modernists' overarching concern for technical developments and the inherent exclusion of the cathedrals' decorative features: "Modernism's hieratic structure dictates that architectural sculpture be analyzed independent of its site. Painting is almost completely overlooked because, since it lies on the surface and comes after the fact of building, it is understood as decoration and therefore is irrelevant. The modernist model does not allow for a holistic analysis of what it addresses; to move away from its highly structured and clearly identified boundaries is to move away from modernism itself." Maija Bismanis, "The Necessity of Discovery," *Gesta* 28.2 (1989): 115–20, quote on pp. 119–20. Clearly, the labyrinth pavements too would disrupt the modernist model.

On the erasure of these pavements, see Kern, *Through the Labyrinth*, pp. 149–65. At Auxerre Cathedral, the labyrinth pavement was destroyed just before 1690. During the French Revolution, the Cathedral at Arras, along with its labyrinth pavement, were destroyed. At Amiens (1827–29), Reims (1778), and Sens (1768), the labyrinth pavements were torn out of their naves in the late eighteenth and early nineteenth centuries' efforts to renovate cathedral interiors by lightening them of their medieval shrines, altars, stations, etc., which furnished so many ritual foci to the otherwise undifferentiated spaces of these vast buildings.

[28] The labyrinth of Crete is by far the most popular city designation in manuscripts, but of ancient eastern cities, Jericho is the most popular; often a labyrinth is labeled as the Temple of Solomon or is described as such in accompanying texts. It is significant, I think, that this manuscript tradition of the ancient eastern city dies out after the loss of Jerusalem and the subsequent introduction of the large cathedral labyrinth pavements. See Kern, *Through the Labyrinth*, pp. 126–35.

set it apart as a rendering of a different, yet specific city of the ancient East. The labyrinth at Chartres made Jerusalem present to its audience's imaginations by quoting features or *emblemata* of other, contemporaneous depictions of Jerusalem that occurred in medieval maps—especially the 'Situs Hierusalem' maps (fig. 139).[29] 'Situs Hierusalem' maps were popular vehicles to convey observed, if nonetheless idealized, details of the Holy City's layout and were often included in manuscripts describing the deeds of the Crusaders.[30] This map, and numerous others like it, accompanied the popular, anonymous paraphrase of Fulcher of Chartres' chronicle, known as the *Gesta Francorum Jerusalem expugnantium*, and dates to the late eleventh or early twelfth century. It is one of the earliest maps to be associated with the Crusades.[31]

Bianca Kühnel uses the consistent design and layout of these maps as evidence of the enduring iconography of the city of Jerusalem, both in its earthly and heavenly guises.[32] Despite interruptions of access to the city, certain signal features remained constant: a well-fortified, brick-like wall delineates the city; there persists a particular exactness in rendering the places and buildings of the city; and the inner organization revolves around the intersection of the *cardo maximus* and the *decumanus maximus*—the two organizing avenues by which a Roman town was founded. Such an emphasis on these two streets remembers Constantine the Great's rebuilding of the Holy City and the particular aura he wished to give Jerusalem as a Christian and

---

[29] One might argue that the labyrinth, as a pavement, had long been represented as a city in the ancient Roman mosaic floors, which are now found in domestic interiors, *thermae* and other public sites. But these labyrinths are smaller than those of the Gothic cathedrals, and so were likely not meant to be walked; quite often they have a Minotauromachy at their center. This ancient Roman tradition, however, does not necessarily extend to the practices of northern France in the thirteenth century. For the local audience at Chartres, what identified the labyrinth as Jerusalem, or any city, has less to do with those Roman floors made some 900 years ago and as many miles away. Rather, a viewer's identification of the labyrinth pavement as an image of Jerusalem was based upon the lived experience of the visual culture that surrounded and informed its reception at Chartres cathedral. Again, see Kern, *Through the Labyrinth*, pp. 85–103.

[30] Kenneth Nebenzahl, *Maps of the Holy Land: Images of Terra Sancta through Two Millennia* (New York: Abbeville, 1968), p. 32.

[31] The manuscript is in Brussels, Bibliothèque Royale, Ms. 9823–9824, fol. 157.

[32] Bianca Kühnel, *From the Earthly to the Heavenly Jerusalem: Representations of the Holy City in Christian Art of the First Millennium* (Freiburg: Herder, 1987), pp. 138–41, and figures 99–101.

Roman institution. His rebuilding was a refounding of Jerusalem as
the sacred center of Christendom; and that sacrality centered upon
the placement of the Holy Sepulchre, which Constantine located
near what, in the architectural tradition of a Roman city, was a
place of godly connotation: the intersection of the *cardo* and the
decumanus, understood to be the burial place of the city's founder.[33]
      Ana C. Esmeijer, in her careful study of the exegetical valences
between diagrammatic and figurative artworks, points to the enduring tradition in which the ancient and sacred city of Jerusalem is
designated by a "cosmic-architectonic quaternity" comprising, like these
Crusader maps, a square or circular ground-plan, which is then divided
orthogonally or diagonally into fours.[34] This "cosmic-architectonic
quaternity" becomes the template for the representations of both
earthly and heavenly Jerusalem, which occur in either square or circular formats and were deployed in a variety of media: in manuscripts and as wall-maps; and as architectural decoration: on floors
and ceilings—often both at once, thus uniting the entire building in
a visual-exegetical surround. In fact, Kühnel has noted that the 'Situs
Hierusalem' maps also likely drew upon a Carolingian manuscript
tradition of showing the Heavenly Jerusalem as a circle, and so share
then in this eschatological intention.[35]
      The intersecting axes of Chartres's labyrinth describe a "cosmic-
architectonic quaternity" as they recreate these two cardinal avenues
of Constantine's Jerusalem and, together with its surrounding crenellations, evoke the specific and reverend topography of the walled
city of Jerusalem.[36] The force of that evocation is witnessed as well

---

[33] Kühnel, *Earthly to the Heavenly Jerusalem*, pp. 87–8. See also Annabel Jane
Wharton, *Refiguring the Post Classical City: Dura Europos, Jerash, Jerusalem and Ravenna*
(Cambridge: Cambridge University Press, 1995), pp. 85–94. Echoes of these Roman
traditions continued to reverberate in the thirteenth century. In the 1240s, Louis
IX, King of France, founded new cities in southwestern France, with the aim of
securing his territories against both English and Toulousean claims. These cities,
known as *bastides*, were laid out according to the Roman grid pattern of urban
design and were usually walled. Aigues-Mortes, founded on flat, marshy land by
the Mediterranean, is perhaps the most famous example; in its case, however, the
city was founded as a point of embarkation for Louis's Seventh Crusade. Spiro
Kostof, *The City Shaped* (London: Thames and Hudson, 1991), pp. 108–11.
[34] Ana C. Esmeijer, *Divina Quaternitas: A Preliminary Study in the Method and Application
of Visual Exegesis* (Amsterdam: Van Gorcum, 1978), p. 73.
[35] Kühnel, *Earthly to the Heavenly Jerusalem*, pp. 123–41, esp. p. 138.
[36] For a fascinating array of manuscript representations of Jerusalem as a circular
quaternity, see Rudolf Simek, "Hierusalem civitas famosissima" *Codices Manuscripti*

by the reiteration of those very elements in the Jerusalem depicted at the center of the famous Hereford *mappamundi* (figs. 140 and 141)— a large wall map that dates to about 1280–90.[37] Both the pavement labyrinth and this larger wall map show a certain insistence on the same elements constitutive of Jerusalem's *cartographic* iconography— its crenellations and the intersecting cross pattern created by its four axial portals. Labyrinths and maps then constructed references to Jerusalem's topography, which, at the same time, carried connotations of the city's foundational origins.

Moreover, at the very center of Hereford's Jerusalem (fig. 141), inside its crenellated walls, a circle is inscribed within a series of circles, which forms a kind of lobed, rosette pattern around it. This pattern echoes the rosette formed of the six scallops, which lies at the intersection of the labyrinth's axes, encircling and defining its very center. The commonality of this feature, in both labyrinth and map, underscores its significance as particular to Jerusalem.[38] A. A. Barb has described the lobed or apsidal patterns that constitute the perimeters of common liturgical objects—patens, altar tables and portable altars—as emblems that evoked early representations of the table of the Last Supper in Jerusalem.[39] These liturgical accoutrements remember Early Christian models from Greece, Eastern Europe and the Near East. One example, (figs. 142 and 143) which comes from

---

[16] (1992): 121–53; and *The Real and Ideal Jerusalem in Jewish, Christian and Islamic Art*, ed. Bianca Kühnel, a special issue of *Jewish Art* 23/24 (1997/98).

[37] On the Hereford *Mappamundi*, see Marcia Kupfer, "Medieval World Maps: Embedded Images, Interpretive Frames." *Word & Image* 10 (1994): 262–88; P.D.A. Harvey, *Mappa Mundi: The Hereford World Map* (Toronto: Univ. of Toronto Press, 1996). Most recently see: Valerie I.J. Flint, "The Hereford Map: Its Author(s), Two Scenes and a Border," *Transactions of the Royal Historical Society* 8 (1998): 19–44, and Naomi R. Kline, *Maps of Medieval Thought: the Hereford Paradigm* (Suffolk: Boydell Press, 2001).

[38] Jerusalem is often shown as a series of concentric circles (my fig. 147, discussed below) or, as in the Hereford Map, concentric circles with an added set of smaller circles surrounding them; both of these seem to be fairly standard iconographies in thirteenth-century maps. For another example of Jerusalem depicted with a set of *surrounding* circles, see P.D.A. Harvey, "Local and Regional Cartography in Medieval Europe," in the *History of Cartography*, vol. 1, *Cartography in Prehistoric, Ancient, and Medieval Europe and the Mediterranean*, ed. J.B. Harley and D. Woodward (Chicago: University of Chicago Press, 1987), p.470. For the rosette as a signifier of "city-ness" see the labyrinth that depicts the ancient city of Jericho in Kern, *Through the Labyrinth*, p. 131, fig. 222.

[39] A.A. Barb, "*Mensa Sacra*: The Round Table and the Holy Grail," *Journal of the Warburg and Courtauld Institute*, 19 (1956): 40–67. My thanks to Linda Seidel for sharing this reference.

southern France and most likely dates to the eleventh century, is a small altar-top in the form of a half-circle. Six scallops define the shallow, hallowed out basin as the area of sacral consecration. This *mensa* design, which was thought to repeat that of the Last Supper, came also to be restated in the liturgical ware with which the mass was conducted. The motif of the scalloped design, Barb noted, was especially popular in the twelfth and thirteenth centuries and was likely occasioned by increased pilgrimage to Jerusalem, where the table of the Last Supper was shown as a precious relic; such interest, of course, peaked with the Crusades.[40] Many an example (fig. 144) show striking similarities with the centers of Jerusalem in the Hereford map and in Chartres' labyrinth pavement, suggesting a specifically sacramental quality to be associated with these representations of Jerusalem.[41] Since these lobed designs occur on liturgical furnishings— as well as manuscript representations of the Last Supper—that were spread throughout the Latin West from the early Middle Ages on, it is not necessary to posit that the makers of the Hereford *mappamundi* looked to the pavement at Chartres as a model for their depiction of Jerusalem, but we can instead suggest that both map and pavement sought association with commonly used eucharistic objects as a means to further layer their already richly textured, memorializing designs of Jerusalem with the transformative values of those sacramental objects.

Both of these curved forms—the labyrinth's surrounding crenellations and its interior rosette—act as framing markers that inclined a viewer's appreciation of Jerusalem from its earthly guise towards

---

[40] Before the ninth century, notes Barb, liturgical patens did not show these lobes or apsidal patterns, but were plain, round plates. The lobed pattern became a firmly entrenched element of their design *after* the twelfth century. On the concentration of the sacred events of Christ's life in the Church of Mount Sion, including the Last Supper and Christ's washing the feet of his disciples, see John Wilkinson et al., *Jerusalem Pilgrimage, 1099–1185* (London: The Hakluyt Society, 1988), pp. 46–9.

[41] Barb illustrates numerous examples of multi-lobed patens, from four to twenty lobes. His one example of a six-lobed paten, however, dates to the late fourteenth century (his pl. 3d). The paten I show here is one of several earlier examples that display a six-lobed pattern surrounding and defining the paten's basin. Known as the Dolgelly Paten, it dates to about 1250 and is held in the National Museum of Wales, Cardiff. See more examples in Charles Oman, *English Church Plate: 597– 1830* (London: Oxford University Press, 1957). The Dolgelly Paten is reproduced in pl. 25b. Under the foot of its accompanying chalice is an inscription: NICOL'VS ME FECIT DE HERFORDIE. Nothing is known about this Nicholas, but his association with Hereford is intriguing.

its future, heavenly instantiation.[42] That is, in contrast to the contemporary maps, which are replete with the specifically historical references of streets and buildings, this representation of Jerusalem is reduced to a schematic, ideal geometry; only these scallops and crenellations, along with the intersecting axes, act as guides in appreciating the labyrinth's meaning. Several contemporaneous examples, however, suggest that these forms foregrounded more sacred, elevated appreciations. As Wright points out, the rosette was often associated with sacrality, going back to Late Antique and Early Christian traditions that saw the eight- or six-lobed rosette as symbolic of the stellar nature of the god-head.[43] More contemporary to the labyrinth, a late eighth-century map of the world shows the location of Paradise as an island in the far eastern region of the world; an eight-lobed rosette surrounds a central circle as a kind of perfect and repeating geometry that signifies the perfect place of Paradise.[44] The depiction of Jerusalem, on the other hand, comprises square and star-shaped patterns that similarly invoke repeating geometries for its significance.[45] As for the curved crenellations of Chartres's labyrinth, one does find diagrammatic images of Jerusalem in thirteenth-century manuscripts that likewise lose their concrete, historical markers as they too seek a geometric purity; in these images, the walls of Jerusalem are often curved or scalloped, which then help form the city's famous gates.[46]

---

[42] I take as a point of departure, Esmeijer comments on the exegetical value of the diagrammatic, *Divina Quaternitas*. See also the work of Helen Rosenau, *The Ideal City: Its Architectural Evolution in Europe* (London: Methuen, 1983, first published as: *The Ideal City in its Architectural Evolution*, 1959).

[43] Wright, *Maze and the Warrior*, p. 43, though I would not describe it as carrying the connotations of an amulet, capable of warding off evil. See the brief discussion of the rosette in the plan of St. Gall, Walter Horn and Ernst Born, *The Plan of St. Gall: a study of the architecture and economy of and life in a paradigmatic Carolingian monastery*, 3 vols. *California Studies in the History of Art*, no. 19 (Berkeley: University of California Press, 1979), vol. 1, p. 12.

[44] In the Psalter Map of *c.* 1250 (B.L. Ms. Add. 28681), that separate reality of Paradise, at the very top edge of the map, is denoted in two ways. It is the only part of the image without color, and the enclosure of Paradise is defined by curving scallops that, like those of Chartres' labyrinth, point outwards. See my figure 13. I wish to thank Alessandro Scafi for sharing not only his ideas and expertise on Paradise, but his enthusiasm for the discovery of new meanings in medieval maps.

[45] Vatican Library, Ms. Vat. Lat. 6018, fols. 63v–64r. For a reproduction, see: Evelyn Edson, *Mapping Time and Space: How Medieval Mapmakers viewed their World* (London: The British Library, 1997), p. 63, fig. 4.2. That square and star pattern is itself repeated on a paten, also English, found in the grave of Bishop Gravesend, and dating to *c.* 1250. For a reproduction, see Oman, *English Church Plate*, pl. 26a.

[46] See for example, Simek, "Hierusalem civitas famosissima," abb. 10 (BL Ms.

In a manuscript of Peter of Poitiers's *Compendium historiae in geneologia Christi*, likely produced at St. Albans abbey in England (*c.* 1250), Jerusalem is depicted with just the diagrammatic structure that also characterizes the design of Chartres labyrinth (fig. 145).[47] A series of concentric circles radiate out from a central text that identifies the city and labels its gates and temple complex in accordance with the messianic vision of Ezekiel 40–48.[48] Columns support the bases of six scallops that then carry the labels for the famous portals of the city. These scallops, in fact, form broad, sweeping curves that surround and outline the city, much as the scalloped crenellations surround the labyrinth, though they are fewer in number. The gated towers between the portals, stand up from behind the design, but otherwise suggest entry into the diagram. In all these instances— maps of Jerusalem, altar-tops and liturgical patens, as well as historical diagrams of the Holy City—the reductive power of repeating geometries helped to draw associations between the historic, holy city and the ideal and heavenly city.

The Labyrinth as an image of the world

By 1200, the motif of the labyrinth had long been deployed to convey different aspects of the world—either as a sinful, time-bound enterprise or, in the later Middle Ages, as the integral totality of creation. As well, labyrinths and maps were often understood in the later

---

Harley 658, fol. 39v) and 12 (a copy of the *Liber floridus* of Lamberts of St. Omer, Leiden, Bibliotheek der Rijksuniversiteit, Cod. Loss. Lat. 31, fol. 274r).

[47] Eton College Libr. Ms. 96. The manuscript records the history of the world as a genealogy of Christ. Eton Ms. 96 has received little attention. See M. R. James, *Catalogue of Manuscripts at Eton College Library* (Cambridge: Cambridge University Press, 1895), no. 96; and Nigel Morgan, *Early Gothic Manuscripts*, vol. II, in *A Survey of Manuscripts Illuminated in the British Isles* (Oxford: Oxford University Press, 1988), entry no. 90.

[48] Peter of Poitiers' *Compendium* is a brief account of biblical history that was easily amended to include classical as well as recent, local histories. It usually takes the form of a genealogy, with excerpts of history accompanying small "portrait' medallions. Unfortunately, very little of the basic editorial work has been done on the text; its brevity, combined with its popularity and its adaptability to local circumstances, make for a vast number of idiosyncratic versions. See, most recently, Hans-Eberhard Hilpert, "Geistliche Bildung und Laienbildung: Zur Überlieferung der Schulschrift *Compendium historiae in genealogia Christi* (Compendium veteris testamenti) des Petrus von Poitiers (d. 1205) in England," *Journal of Medieval History* 11.4 (1985): 315–32.

Middle Ages as images of the world similar in their evocations of passage through the world. Labyrinths and maps, when shown together or operating in mutual support of each other, depend upon a pre-conceived equi-*valence* of their meanings; walking through the labyrinth pavements, then, would also have been understood as travel through the world. By the term equi-*valent*, I stress not equations between the two images, but the homologous relations that are revealed in their performative readings, and the meanings generated by those encounters. In medieval encyclopedias, church inscriptions that accompany labyrinths, and mythological histories, labyrinths describe the world. But the labyrinthine world is also depicted by *mappaemundi*, and so *mappaemundi* and labyrinths were often discussed and displayed as equi-*valent* images of the world.

At San Savino, Piacenza, an early twelfth-century inscription that once accompanied a now lost mosaic labyrinth uses the language of metaphor to close the gap between the labyrinth and the world as it highlights the dangers of the world's entrapments. That inscription reads:

> This labyrinth denotes this world figuratively
> For one entering, wide; but for one returning, very narrow.
> Thus captured by the world, weighted down by a mass of vices,
> Each one can scarcely return to the doctrine of life.[49]

This inscription quotes the Gospels of both Matthew and John as it equates life's passage through this world as fraught with temptations labyrinthine in their seductive ability to lead one astray.[50] If you are consumed by the desires of the flesh and the variety of mundane choices, you have essentially abandoned the straight and narrow road to Christ, seeking instead greater ensconcement in this world. Lending moral vigor to this inscription is the concrete designation of the labyrinth as a figure for the world.

---

[49] Hunc mundum tipice laberinthus denotat iste / Intranti largus, redevnti set nimis artus / Sic munduo captus viciorum mole gravatus / Vix valet ad vite doctrinam quisque redire; transcription in Kern, *Through the Labyrinthe*, p. 158. Scholars give varying translations of the passage; see K. Woodward, *"Error Labyrinthi,"* p. 100. I would like to thank members of the Latin-L listserve (LATIN-L@PSUVM.PSU.EDU), especially Prof. Paul Pascal, for generous suggestions in translating this passage; any errors, of course, remain my own.

[50] Kathryn Woodward explores the theme of the labyrinth as a symbol of the time-bound world in *"Error Labyrinthi,"* pp. 100–23.

In addition to presenting sinful aspects of the world, the labyrinth
motif also coincided with and, I believe, drew upon a newly developing tradition of medieval map-making in which the world was
shown as a set of continuous spaces. That, however, had not been
the normative view of the world in medieval maps. The preponderant tradition of mapmaking showed the world's space schematically, divided into thirds (fig. 146), with Asia above, and Europe and
Africa below, forming then a 'T' within an 'O'.[51] T-in-O maps were
produced throughout the Middle Ages, but in the twelfth and thirteenth centuries, there was an explosion in both the number and
kinds of maps produced. In new, large wall maps like the Duchy of
Cornwall fragment, the Vercelli, the Ebstorf and the Hereford maps,
there developed a more concerted effort to render the world as a
network of interconnected topographies, the proliferation of whose
texts and legends keeps one's eye constantly roving their variegated
surfaces.[52] Without constructing a narrative—the presentation of texts
is more paratactic—this kind of itinerant reading nonetheless turns
the world's spaces into a journey-able whole. That new effort in rendering the profusion of places now available to the acquisitive scrutiny
of the crusading West suggests a change in the fundamental conception of the world, seen in this shift from schematic and barely
negotiable spaces to one of more fluid, permeable boundaries that
both invite a visual itinerary even as they register increasingly commonplace physical traffic across them. In addition, the earlier medieval
mappaemundi only sometimes showed Jerusalem at their center; the
centered display of the Holy City was not a dominant tradition in
medieval cartography until the thirteenth century and was occasioned, I believe, by the recent loss of Jerusalem.[53] With these larger,

---

[51] This map is found in a late 9th century copy of Isidore of Seville's *De natura
rerum*, Bern, Burgerbibliothek, Bern Ms. 417, fol. 88v; see Nebenzahl, *Maps of the
Holy Land*, plate 3.

[52] For the numbers and kinds of maps to survive from the Middle Ages, see
Woodward, "Medieval Mappaemundi," p. 298. For reproductions of these maps,
and for further bibliography, see his pl. 14 (Duchy of Cornwall *mappamundi* fragment), fig. 18.17 (the Vercelli Map), and fig. 18.19 (the Ebstorf Map). These 'transitional' maps avoid the strict divisions of the world in favor of more empirically
precise renderings of coasts, especially the Mediterranean. Such empirical renderings are also found in portolan charts that date to the fourteenth century, but the
large wall *mappaemundi* of the thirteenth also partake of this transitional period.

[53] D. Woodward, "Medieval *mappaemundi*," pp. 340–42. Woodward notes that the
tradition of a centered Jerusalem begins in the twelfth century and becomes most

more abundant descriptions of the *oikumene* (the known, inhabited world), the act of reading itself came to be a journey across the spaces of God's creation, a creation (and reading) newly centered on Jerusalem.

This shift in the medieval 'spatial mentality', this change in emphasis from schematic to continuous spaces, is precisely and self-reflexively illustrated in a *mappamundi* from an English Psalter of about 1260, called *The Psalter Map* (fig. 147).[54] Christ holds in his left hand an orb— there is just enough shading to suggest three dimensionality. The orb is divided into the traditional tripartite schema of the T-in-O maps, which must have seemed archaic compared to the 'realization' of that space below in the form of the more elaborate *mappamundi*. The tripartite orb creates a site of difference between the new conceptions informing descriptions of the world as continuous and journey-able (with Jerusalem at their center), and the way history and tradition had created it in a schema of non-negotiable space.[55]

The labyrinth becomes a privileged motif for the suggestion of continuously perusable spaces in the Hereford *mappamundi*, (fig. 140) which itself may be read as a monument of these new characteristics of a medieval spatial mentality (i.e. a centered Jerusalem and a

popular in the thirteenth. This, he suggests, is a natural outcome of the crusades. I posit here that this tradition becomes preponderant as a response to the loss of Jerusalem in 1187.

[54] (fig. 147) London, B.L. Ms. Add. 28681, fol. 9r; for further bibliography, see: Nigel Morgan, *Early Gothic Manuscripts: 1250–1285*, vol. II, *A Survey of Manuscripts Illuminated in the British Isles*, ed. J.J.G. Alexander (Oxford: Oxford University Press, 1988), pp. 82–5, entry no. 114, and ills. 84 and 85.

In his study of Purgatory, Jacques LeGoff analyzed just such a realignment of the medieval sense of space, in this case, of a cosmic space. LeGoff considers Purgatory a creation of the twelfth and thirteenth century, when the culture as a whole underwent a shift in mentality from binary to tripartite structures; Purgatory assumed an intermediate place between Heaven and Hell. As well, argues LeGoff, new and different attitudes towards numbers and calculations become apparent in the exchange of both material goods (bookkeeping), and things immaterial (time, indulgences); scale and proportionality also became important factors in the thirteenth century's acceptance and systemization of Purgatory. See Jacques LeGoff, *The Birth of Purgatory*, trans. Arthur Goldhammer (Chicago: University of Chicago Press, 1984), pp. 220–30. The large *mappaemundi*, with the contiguous, journey-able space they offer to the viewer, I believe, should also be understood within the context of these changes.

[55] In furtherance of this difference, the verso of this folio shows an image of Christ holding that same world, in the exact same outline, now as a tripartite schematic. The three segments of the circle are filled with histories of their parts of the world. London, B.L. Ms. Add. 28681, fol. 9v.

continuous, journey-able space). The wall map designates the island of Crete, in the middle of its Mediterranean Ocean, by a labyrinth. (fig. 148) This labyrinth, I believe, may be read as a *mis-en-abîme*, in which its form mirrors the map as a whole. It becomes a reduced, highly distilled sign or emblem of the map and functions then to indicate the meanings to be sought out in that larger whole. The labyrinth is labeled as the house of Daedalus and has its opening at the bottom, or in the West. The opening to the labyrinth has its analogue in the 'opening' of the map itself; at the straits of Gibraltar the Pillars of Hercules form its own portal of entry.[56] As well, different areas of the map testify to its continuous, though disorienting, spaces. Cities and their texts are often shown sideways or upside down—as at the Nile Delta just above Crete and to the right of Jerusalem—which makes reading the map a performance of its twisting and confusing spaces. Places in the map are frequently constructed by shifting ground lines and changing vantage points, the reading of which, then, is analogous to the labyrinth's turnings and disorientations. The Hereford *mappamundi* is four feet, four inches wide and five feet, two inches tall; attending to how your body responds to these confused and disoriented spaces heightens that performative experience and is like moving through the labyrinth.[57] The use of the Cretan labyrinth in this large *mappamundi* would have triggered this performative theme and added to its medieval audiences' understanding of the equivalencies between labyrinths and maps as spaces to be journeyed; that

---

[56] The Pillars of Hercules were a result of his tenth labor, to bring back the famous cattle of Geryon from Erytheia, an island near the Ocean Stream. To accomplish the task, Hercules had to travel to the ends of Europe and Africa, and as a testament to that travel, he built across the straits these pillars. At the very 'opening' of the map then, travel is signified in this portal of entry as a predominant theme by which to access the map's meanings. For various readings of the Greek and Roman sources of the myth, see Robert Graves, *The Greek Myths* (New York: Penguin Books, 1992, combined edition), pp. 494–506.

[57] The map seems to have been originally displayed within a triptych, whose wings closed over the *mappamundi*. In the 1770s John Carter made a sketch drawing of the map in its opened case that shows the angel of the Annunciation in the left wing and, on the right, the Virgin Mary. For a summary of the map's history and for further bibliography, see Harvey, Mappa Mundi: *The Hereford World Map*, pp. 11–8. Marcia Kupfer argued, against the weight of archaeological evidence, that the map should be understood less as a spiritualizing tool of devotion, and more within a didactic tradition; see her, "Medieval World Maps". Most recently, see Scott D. Westrem, *The Hereford Map* (Turnhout: Brepols, 2001) and Kline, *Maps of Medieval Thought*.

understanding was itself informed and reinforced by an understanding of them as parallel descriptions of the world.

While labyrinths could work with and on maps to connote the continuous and journey-able spaces of the thirteenth-century world, as pavements, they did so in a space that had long been associated with the mundane and worldly—the nave of the cruciform church. A continuous tradition stretching back as far as the seventh century understood both the church as a microcosm of the universe and, within that system, the individual parts of the church as belonging to different orders of the cosmos. The Byzantine theologian Maximus the Confessor (*c.* 580–662) wrote in his *Mystagogia* that the whole of the church building is symbolically composed of and simultaneously comprises different parts of the universe: "[The church] has the holy sanctuary as heaven, but it possesses the fitting appearance of the nave as earth. So likewise, the universe is the church. For it has the heaven like a sanctuary and the ordering of the earth like a nave."[58] In the West, this 'ordering' of the church continues in the later twelfth and thirteenth centuries in the staging of medieval liturgical plays, which mapped out the spaces of the church along this same cosmological schema. John Harris sums up the strategies for staging these plays: "The center of the nave, not unnaturally, is the most important, and the action relating to the material world was usually sited there, with occasional forays towards heaven and everlasting life in the east. . . ."[59] Those parts of the play that are about the world take place in the nave; those that concern heaven, move towards the sanctuary.

At Chartres, the medieval understanding of the nave as a worldly, mundane space is registered as well in its stained glass, where images of trade and negotiation, in collaboration with miracle play performances, further marked the nave as site of 'urban' and increasingly commercial concern.[60] Along with such place-rendering liturgical performances

---

[58] As quoted in Henry Maguire, *Earth and Ocean: The Terrestrial World in Early Byzantine Art* (University Park, PA: Pennsylvania State Univ. Press, 1987), p. 26; see generally pp. 21–30. The circularity of the metaphor here is remarkable.

[59] John Wesley Harris, *Medieval Theatre in Context : an introduction* (London: Routledge, 1992), p. 39, see generally pp. 23–46.

[60] See the interesting dissertations by Anne F. Harris, "The Spectacle of Stained Glass in Modern France and Medieval Chartres: a history of practices and perceptions," (Ph.D. diss., University of Chicago, 1999), pp. 115–61, as well as Dawn Marie Hayes, "Body and Sacred Place in Medieval Europe, 100–1389: Interpreting

should be included the conduct of ritual processions. The Palm
Sunday processions at Chartres remapped the town and countryside
with the topography of the Holy Land. Sustaining that remapping
were specific associations between the Chartrain region and the Holy
Land. The hill of Saint-Chéron, because of its situation east of
Chartres, invited comparison with the Mount of Olives; likewise, the
abbey of St. Josaphat was so named because it lay between Saint-
Chéron and Chartres, and thus in the fictive valley of Cédron.[61]
These Palm Sunday processions were especially important and complex affairs; and it was this sort of one-to-one remapping that facilitated the conduct of that liturgy, thereby affirming and effecting
those transformations of space. From early in the Christian era,
Easter stational liturgies had been transforming their own spaces into
sacred topographies by invoking memories of the times and places
of Christ's passion as they processed through spaces they symbolically remapped. As Jonathon Z. Smith, a theorist of ritual, describes
it, this symbolic transformation was effected by concurrent manipu-
lations of both space and time.[62] The one-to-one matching created
a spatial identity that overcame local particularities and, along with
the invocation of the narratives of Christ's life, lent liturgies the
power to change place. More specific to the situation of the labyrinth
pavement at Chartres, when inclement weather threatened to disrupt these translocative performances, participants designated the
interior of the church as those significant sites of the Holy Land by
conducting the processions *inside* the cathedral.[63] Those who walked
the labyrinth pavement at Chartres were thus used to remapping
the spaces of their nave with the topography of the Holy Land.

  Processional remapping of nave spaces had been going on for centuries, at Chartres and in other churches.[64] And medieval audiences

the Case of Chartres Cathedral," (Ph.D. diss., New York University, 1998), esp.
pp. 11–71.
  [61] Yves Delaporte, "Introduction," *L'Ordinaire chartrain du XIIIe siècle: publié d'après
le manuscrit original*, ed. and introduction by Y. Delaporte (Chartres: Société archéolo-
qique d'Eure-et-Loir, 1953), p. 45 and note 2.
  [62] Jonathon Z. Smith, *To Take Place: Toward Theory in Ritual* (Chicago: University
of Chicago Press, 1987), pp. 74–95.
  [63] Craig Wright, "The Palm Sunday Procession in Medieval Chartres," in *The
Divine Office in the Latin Middle Ages: Methodologies and Source Studies, Regional Developments,
Hagiography*, ed., Margot E. Fassler and Rebecca A. Baltzer (Oxford: Oxford University
Press, 2000), pp. 344–71.
  [64] Wright, "The Palm Sunday Procession," note 19; these processions date well
before the Crusades and were conducted at Amiens Cathedral, among other churches.

would have been aided in this type of translocative thinking by the
many allusions to and actual depictions of the Holy City that were
installed in the very pavements of their churches. Topographical
signifiers on the floors of churches and cathedrals were relatively
common place in Romanesque and Gothic Europe. At Turin,[65]
Piacenza,[66] Otranto, and Brindisi,[67] intricately wrought floor mosaics
described medieval understandings of the geographical and cosmological orders. At Brindisi and Otranto, scenes of the Old Testament,
great personages of Classical Antiquity, and the exotic animals and
different races of the world generated geographical understandings
for the passage of history.[68] A mosaic pavement in St. Remi at Reims,
now destroyed, included personifications of 'Terra,' 'Mare,' and 'Orbis
terrae,'[69] while church pavements at Lyon and Saint-Paul-Trois-
Châteaux depicted various cities, including a depiction of Jerusalem
that participates in Esmeijer's "cosmic-architectonic quaternity".[70] In
the thirteenth century, a paving tile of about one and a half meters
square displayed a kind of map beneath the organ of the collegiate
church of Notre-Dame at St. Omer. Around its perimeter were
depicted mountains, cities, rivers, roads, animals and the name

[65] The following discussion of *mosaic* pavements draws upon the seminal work of
Ernst Kitzinger, discussed below, references in note 89.

[66] William Tronzo interpreted the central panel of the mosaic pavement from
the choir of San Savino in Piacenza as a cosmological figure, evocative of both the
ancient figure of *Annus* and of *Fortuna*. The central and encircled group of figures
is itself supported by an Atlas figure, further grounding the representation within
the tradition of geographical depictions. William L. Tronzo, "Moral Hieroglyphs:
Chess and Dice at San Savino in Piacenza," *Gesta* 16 (1977): 15–26. A labyrinth
mosaic pavement once decorated the nave at San Savino; its accompanying inscription is discussed above.

[67] Nancy Rash-Fabbri, "A Drawing in the Bibliothèque Nationale and the
Romanesque Mosaic Floor in Brindisi," *Gesta* 13 (1974): 5–14.

[68] The pavements also depict figures from more contemporary stories—the *Chanson
de Roland* and Arthurian legend. Like those pavements at Turin and Nikopolis, these
are not maps in the strictest sense, but nonetheless evoke different places of the
world and generate geographical meanings. They recall what Mary Carruthers
termed a "geographical-historical-moral *mappa mundi*." Mary Carruthers, *The Book of
Memory: A Study of Memory in the Middle Ages* (Cambridge: Cambridge University Press,
1990), p. 237.

[69] Xavier Barral I Altet, "Les Mosaïques de Pavement Médiévales de la Ville de
Reims," *Congrès Archéologique de France*, 135th session, 1977 (Paris: Société Française
d'Archéologique, 1980), pp. 79–108.

[70] Henri Stern, "Les mosaïques de la cathedral de Saint-Jean de Lyon," *Cahiers
Archéologiques* 14 (1964): 217–32, fig. 16a; and Hiltrud Kier, *Der Mittelalterliche
Schmuckfussboden* (Düsseldorf: Rhineland Verlag, 1970), pp. 68–73, and abb. 403.

'IhERVSALEm.'[71] All these examples confirm that an audience at
Chartres Cathedral would have been used to thinking of the floors
of their churches as spaces that invoked other topographies, and,
most especially, that of Jerusalem.

Losing Jerusalem, performing imagined pilgrimage

All of these large, walkable pavements, it turns out, likely *post*-date
the loss of Jerusalem in 1187. The labyrinth pavements are generally dated to the completion date of their naves, a strategy confirmed
by the inscriptions at Amiens and Reims.[72] Kern, following Haubrichs,
dates the Sens labyrinth to 1180, supposing it the earliest large-scale
pavement.[73] However, continued construction of that portion of Sens
Cathedral calls for a later date for the labyrinth and confirms an
association between its labyrinth and the Latin West's loss of Jerusalem.
The labyrinth is no longer extant, but according to a nineteenth
century account, it was placed just inside the western portal, in the
first nave bay.[74] The facade and the western towers, which adjoin
this nave bay, were under construction throughout most of the thirteenth century. As the nave of Sens was nearing completion, a fire
in 1184 interrupted work; construction of the facade and Western
towers resumed sometime between 1195 and 1200, during which the
labyrinth must have been added to the first nave bay.[75] This revised

---

[71] The church dates to the thirteenth through fifteenth centuries, and at the time
of Wallet's description, the center of the tile, which was divided into three horizontal compartments, was no longer legible; for a description of this map-like design,
see M. Wallet, "Labyrinthe de Saint-Bertin," *Bulletin Monumental* 13 (1847): 199–202.

[72] See above, note 17.

[73] Kern, *Through the Labyrinth*, p. 163; and Haubrichs, "*Error Inextricabilis*," p. 104.

[74] Kern, *Through the Labyrinth*, p. 163; and Abbé Chauveau, "Origine de la
Métropole de Sens," *Congrès Archéologiques de France* 14 (1847–48): 170–218, esp.
198–9.

[75] Jacques Henriet, "La Cathédrale Saint-Étienne de Sens: Le Parti du Premier
Maître et les Campagnes du XIIe Siècle," *Bulletin Monumental* 140 (1982): 81–174,
esp. 88–102. In addition, the system of vaulting changes with this first nave bay.
The nave is six-partite throughout, but in this first bay, the vaulting is quadripartite; see the ground plan and commentary in Robert Branner, *Burgundian Gothic
Architecture* (London: A. Zimmer, 1960), pp. 180–2. The shift from six-partite vaulting to quadripartite marks one of the key transitions in the development of Gothic
architecture. For a general account of Sens, see William W. Clark, "Sens (architecture)," in *The Grove Dictionary of Art*, v. 28, p. 413. A decorative floor pavement
would likely be one of the last additions to this cathedral nave bay.

chronology advances the date of the labyrinth to 1195, if not later, and thus after the loss of Jerusalem. Moreover, the addition of a labyrinth pavement *after* these constructions explains why the labyrinth at Sens was the only one to be placed in this first nave bay, as opposed to the more interior bays, as in all the other cathedrals.

The installation of these large labyrinth pavements in the cathedrals' naves only just after the loss of Jerusalem suggests that their design, and the performance of that design, responded specifically to this deeply felt privation.[76] The disaster at Hattin, the loss of the relic of the True Cross, and the capture of the Holy City had shocked the Latin West; Urban III was said to have died upon hearing the news. Immediately, a cry went out for a new crusade. And sustaining those efforts, new liturgical prayers and processions were established to keep the faithful keenly aware of their loss of the Holy City.[77] At Chartres, special prayers, said by the canons on their knees, were inserted into the mass, requesting God's aid in delivering Jerusalem back to Christians of the West.[78]

In the desirous wake of that loss, the labyrinth at Chartres presented in the very public space of its nave a compound image in which the labyrinth, as a metaphor of travel through world, could combine with *emblemata* of the Holy City, so allusive its earthly and heavenly instantiations. Performing such scripted spaces of the labyrinth, enacting its turning and twisting course until finally reaching the center, encouraged participants to reflect upon their perambulations as a micro-journey to the city of Jerusalem by engaging them in well known and widely practiced mechanisms of meditational exercises. The labyrinth pavements thus provided a metaphoric access to the Holy City at a time when physical availability had been dramatically curtailed. In contrast to the classical myth of the Minotaur, which describes a prison of multiple passages and horrible confusion, these labyrinths, and indeed all the labyrinths inscribed on medieval pavements, church furniture, or in manuscripts, were *uni*cursal, that is of a single path. Walking through these labyrinths then entails not a

---

[76] On contemporary concerns for the loss of Jerusalem and for the desire to recapture it, see among others, Adriaan Bredero, "Jerusalem in the West," in *Christendom and Christianity in the Middle Ages: the relations between religion, church and society*, trans. R. Bruinsma (Grand Rapids, Mich: Eerdmans, 1994), pp. 79–104.

[77] Simon Lloyd, *English Society and the Crusades, 1216–1307* (Oxford: Clarendon Press, 1988), pp. 50–1.

[78] *L'Ordinaire chartrain*, ed. Y. Delaporte, p. 197.

loss of one's *way*, but the surrender of one's self to its pattern.[79] You first enter the labyrinth, (fig. 134) moving from West to East, from the cathedral doors towards the altar. Very quickly however, the labyrinth focuses your concentration on the path, else you are likely to stray from it. The path is narrow, and the turns are small and tight, requiring attention and focus. The labyrinth is at first a challenge of some dexterity, and so it also foregrounds your sense of balance and of bodily position relative to it. At the same time, there is a loss of your sense of 'place' in the church as orientations are constantly shifting and revolving. Its movements to and fro, back and forth create a regular and somewhat wearying effect that combines with the hypnotic vision of the pavement receding beneath your alternating steps. Awareness of your surrounds diminishes as the labyrinth choreographs your body in space. Walking through the labyrinth creates then a subtle, meditative experience; the goal is always the center, but access to it is a prolonged, sometimes frustrating process. At the very end of the labyrinth, a straight line appears to lead you directly to the center, to arrive, metaphorically, at the holy city of Jerusalem.

The medieval practice of imagined pilgrimage was first suggested by Dom Jean LeClercq and later expanded upon by Giles Constable; both scholars used the phrase *peregrinatio in stabilitate* to describe the interior, meditative practices that allowed monks to make a pilgrimage with their hearts and not their feet.[80] In Cistercian monasteries, meditations often focused upon scenes of Christ's nativity or the Last Supper, or even upon the more abstract idea of the Heavenly Jeru-

---

[79] The same observation is made by Penelope Doob in her study of the labyrinthine in medieval culture; here, however, I wish to emphasize not the terrible disorientation and loss of individuality, but this same diminution of self as predicate to an imagined pilgrimage. See Doob, *The Idea of the Labyrinth*, pp. 48–63. While the textual tradition describes the Minotaur's labyrinth as comprising multiple, twisting passages, which require then choices to be made, the visual tradition quite distinctly shows the labyrinth as one continuous, redundant path. Doob suggests that the force of iconographic tradition overrode what little interest there might have been in those more confusing, choice-laden literary descriptions, even though they were a closer approximation of the myth. As this essay suggests, the particular concentric symmetry of the labyrinth pavements presents advantages, in its meditative performance, over the multicursal model.

[80] Jean LeClercq, "Monachisme et Pérégrination du IXe au XIIe Siècle," *Studia Monastica*, 3 (1961): 33–52 and Giles Constable, "Opposition to Pilgrimage in the Middle Ages," *Studia Gratiana* 19 (1976): 125–46.

salem; these meditations called for the monk to project himself into the imagined scene as he sought a mystical union with the god-head.[81]

These kinds of meditations were also encouraged by the visually articulated environments of the monastic cloister. Wayne Dynes, Linda Seidel, and Ilene Forsyth have examined the sculptural decorations of the Romanesque cloisters at Monreale and La Daurade as forms of re-mapping the sites of their viewing with the sacred topography of the Holy Land.[82] Medieval authors of the eleventh and twelfth centuries had sought to understand the cloister through comparisons with the Portico of Solomon, where the apostles had all come together of one heart and soul, and held all things in common. Such a comparison invoked the *vita apostolica*, and, at the same time, touched upon the very foundation of Christianity. With the capture of Jerusalem in 1099 and the establishment of the Crusader States, the designers of sculptural programs in cloisters recreated the settings of the Holy Land based upon specific information that was only then available to the Latin West. The capture of Jerusalem had renewed the Christian fascination with Sacred Geography, and as part of this fascination, authors of pilgrimage accounts also tried to pinpoint for their readers specific holy sites, especially those connected with the life of Christ.

One such pilgrimage account is especially instructive of their uses. In 1270, Burchard of Mount Sion identified the motivations of his readers and anticipated the uses to which they would put his detailed descriptions of the Holy Land; his implied link between interiority and vivid (laborious) descriptions is significant. Writes Burchard about those unable to go on pilgrimage:

---

[81] The popular twelfth-century *Rule of a Life for a Recluse* (*c.* 1160) by Aelred of Rievaulx or the later, thirteenth-century "Meditations on the life of Christ" (*c.* 1300) by the Pseudo-Bonaventure are exercises that asked the reader to imagine herself at Christ's Nativity or at the Final Passion. See the introduction by David Knowles to *The Works of Aelred of Rievaulx, I: Treatises, The Pastoral Prayer* (Spencer, Mass., Cistercian Publications, 1971), pp. ix–xii. For the Pseuodo-Bonaventure, see Jaime R. Vidal, "The Infancy Narrative in Pseudo-Bonaventure's 'Meditationes Vitae Christi:' A Study in Medieval Franciscan Christ-Piety (*c.* 1300)" (Ph.D. diss., Fordham University, 1984), pp. 42–107, esp. 42–53.

[82] Wayne Dynes, "Medieval Cloister as Portico of Solomon," *Gesta*, 12 (1973): 61–9; Linda Seidel, "Installation as Inspiration: The Passion Cycle from La Daurade," *Gesta*, 25 (1986): 83–92; and Ilene Forsyth, "The *Vita Apostolica* and Romanesque Sculpture: Some Preliminary Observations," *Gesta* 25 (1986): 75–82.

Seeing, however, that some are possessed by a desire *to picture to their minds those things which they are not able to behold with their eyes, and wishing to fulfill their longing,* as far as in me lieth, I have, to the best of my ability, thought about, diligently taken note of, and laboriously described that land, over which my feet have often passed.[83]

The desire to partake vicariously of the holy places motivates imagined pilgrimage, and, in the case of medieval pilgrimage guides, is the reason most often cited by their authors for the production of the writing itself. In one of the more prodigiously copied guides, Theoderich's late twelfth-century *Guide to the Holy Land,* the author again iterates his own wish to satisfy the desires of those unable to see what he has seen:

We have been careful to note down . . . everything relating to the holy places . . . This we have done in order that, according to the best of our ability, *we may satisfy the desires of those who are unable to proceed there in person* by describing those things they cannot see with their own eyes or hear with their ears.[84]

The intended result of reading and meditating on the evocative, often emotionally charged details of these 'laborious' descriptions is to satisfy the longing of those unable to go on pilgrimage. Such introductory remarks in medieval travel accounts are so common to scholars of the period that they are easily overlooked as we search the text that follows for what the author says about this or that monument. But it is in such common place rhetoric that we may discern the conduct of practices not otherwise recorded.[85]

Meditative practices that dissolved one's awareness of present circumstances and allowed the meditant to imagine him or herself in the desired scene or setting constructed imagined pilgrimages and satisfied the longing to be in the holy places.[86] In the case of walking labyrinth pavements, one's awareness of the actual setting dissolves quickly enough, but it is the desire to access the goal of Jerusalem, I believe, which was the overriding catalyst in transforming the per-

[83] Burchard of Mount Sion, *"Descriptio Terrae Sanctae"* in *Palestine Pilgrims' Text Society* 12 (1896, reprint, NY: AMS Press, 1971), p. 4, emphasis added.

[84] Theoderich, *Guide to the Holy Land,* trans. Aubrey Stewart (New York: Italica Press, 1986, 2nd ed.), p. 1, emphasis added.

[85] Jean Richard offers some brief comments on these formulas in the prefatory remarks of medieval pilgrimage accounts, see his *Les Récits de Voyages et de Pèlerinages* (Turnhout: Brepols, 1985), pp. 19–23.

[86] Connolly, "Imagined Pilgrimage in Gothic Art," pp. 1–31.

formance of that setting into an imagined pilgrimage to Jerusalem. Such a full-bodied projection into an imagined setting is clearly called for in some early fourteenth-century Italian descriptions of the church of the Holy Sepulchre. Kenneth Hyde studied these descriptions and saw them as aids to an alternative form of pilgrimage. Specific measurements of the Church's monuments and their *relative* positions provided concrete details that simultaneously evoked their location and history. For example, the Holy Sepulcher is described as nine palms long and three and a half wide and standing four palms above the ground; the Chapel of Mary Magdalene is ten paces from the Sepulchre. One set of descriptions, in the more accessible vernacular, provides a key ingredient: a heading above the text reads: "these are journeys that pilgrims ought to make . . . *and that every person can do*, staying in his own house and thinking of each place that is written below."[87] The audience of such guides imagined their body moving through the Church of the Holy Sepulcher as they incorporated these descriptions and bodily measurements to map out their own houses with the imagined topography of the Holy Land. How much richer and more available was the same performative mapping in the nave of Chartres Cathedral, where the particular design of the labyrinth readily called to mind already familiar images of the layout and topography of Jerusalem?

Conclusion

The search for meaning in the performance of floor decorations, and the decoration of church floors with topographical *emblemata* that added geographical comprehensions to their ecclesiastical space— these were exactly the themes that occupied Ernst Kitzinger in his now classic study of the floor mosaic at S. Salvatore, Turin.[88] Kitzinger

---

[87] Kenneth J. Hyde, "Italian Pilgrim Literature in the Late Middle Ages," *Bulletin of the John Rylands Library* 72 (1990): 13–33. I wish to express my appreciation for the assistance of the Special Collections Library at the University of Michigan in locating the rare publication in which this heading may be found: C. Gargiolli, *Viaggi in Terra Santa* (Florence, n.p., 1862), p. 441.

[88] Ernst Kitzinger, "World Map and Fortune's Wheel: A Medieval Mosaic Floor in Turin," *Proceedings of the American Philosophical Society*, 117 (1973): 344–73. For other, earlier examples of the depiction of geography in church pavements, see *idem*, "Mosaic Pavements in the Greek East and the Question of a 'Renaissance' under Justinian," *Actes de VIe Congrès International d'Études Byzantines*, 2 (Paris, 1951): 209–23,

sought to explain geographical representations on church pavements in light of medieval condemnations of floor decorations, particularly those of St. Bernard of Clairvaux, who had protested against images of saints being ground underfoot and the faces of angels spat upon.[89] While not maps in the strictest sense, the medieval pavements discussed by Kitzinger drew upon the *emblemata* of medieval *mappaemundi* and evoked for their audiences a sense of the world's space, equating the floor with the earth and rendering, as Kitzinger so concisely stated, "the architectural space as a whole a universe *in parvo*."[90] At the end of Kitzinger's study, the decision to represent the earth on the floor had literally put the representation of its subject matter in its place, because the world, linked as it was at Turin with the Wheel of Fortune, symbolized transitoriness and vanity, an object of contempt *to be* trodden under foot. Following St. Bernard, Kitzinger likewise chose to view these pavement decorations as images that, by their placement, necessarily led to their desecration by the feet of their users—that desecration becoming a performance of its meanings. Although I do not share his negative assessment of how floor pavements could mean in the Middle Ages, my understanding of the labyrinth pavement of Chartres Cathedral similarly articulates how pavements could formulate different topographical meanings and how those meanings gained greater impact through their particular performance.

---

and "Studies on Late Antique and Early Byzantine Floor Mosaics, I. Mosaics at Nikopolis," *Dumbarton Oaks Papers* 6 (1951): 81–122.

[89] St. Bernard of Clairvaux's *Apologia ad Guillelmum Sancti-Theodericei abbatem*, ch. 12, cited in Kitzinger, "World Map and Fortune's Wheel," p. 344, nt. 3. More contemporary to his writing, Kitzinger noted that then President of the United States, Harry Truman, had ordered that the Presidential Seal be raised from the floor of the Reception Room of the White House to a place of honor above the door, because the Seal was likewise being desecrated by people walking on it.

[90] Kitzinger provides an in-depth analysis of the hybrid representation of cosmological and geographical orders in the pavement at S. Salvatore, Turin, which shows a central figure of *Fortuna* surrounded by water, islands, and other symbols of geography (the figures of the winds, and fantastic creatures of the world that may allude to their use in maps as symbols of places).

CHAPTER TWELVE

THE ARCHITECTURE AND ICONOGRAPHICAL SOURCES OF THE CHURCH OF NEUVY-SAINT-SÉPULCRE*

Nora Laos

The Romanesque church of Neuvy-Saint-Sépulcre (hereafter referred to as "Neuvy"), or "New Holy Sepulcher," is located in a small town bearing the same name in the region of Berry in central France. The town stands along one of the minor pilgrimage roads to Santiago de Compostela, to the east of the major route from Vézelay to Puenta-la-Reina.[1] The church has two distinct parts: a multi-storied rotunda and a three-aisled, vaulted basilica, linked by openings cut through the eastern wall of the rotunda. (figs. 149–151) Both sections of the building have undergone numerous modifications and today the church is a complex, yet stunning, palimpsest—a structural parchment of masonry that has been partially erased, burnished, and rewritten, so that its composite history is revealed in the embedded fragments from which it is comprised.

Akin to its multi-layered architectural constitution, the church also had multiple functions and, over time has ministered to manifold populations that linked it to pilgrimage. From its form, dedication and contents (relics of Christ, brought to Neuvy from Jerusalem in the thirteenth century by Cardinal Eudes de Châteauroux), we can

* Portions of this essay were presented at the 37th International Congress on Medieval Studies, May 2002. I am grateful to Robert Ousterhout for initially bringing the topic to my attention and for his helpful comments and suggestions. I would also like to thank Charles Little for his advice concerning the architectural sculpture of the church. In Paris I was aided by the able staff of the *Bibliothèque et Archives du Patrimoine* and, in Châteauroux, by the staff of the *Archives Départementales de l'Indre*. Many thanks are also due to Joel Cluskey, who first traveled with me to Neuvy-St.-Sépulcre and with whom I shared my first thoughts about the church *in situ*. All foreign language translations are by the author.

[1] For the location of Neuvy-St.-Sépulcre and its relationship to the better-known routes from France to Santiago see the map, in Kenneth J. Conant, *Carolingian and Romanesque Architecture 800–1200*, rev., reprinted with corrections (New York, 1979), p. 20.

surmise that the rotunda was *oriented* to Jerusalem, welcoming worshippers who came to venerate its relics. As such, the rotunda served
as a monumental reliquary—a *remembrance* of Jerusalem. Neuvy had
a secondary dedication to St. James and the basilican portion of the
church is typologically linked to the many western pilgrimage churches
located along the routes to Santiago. Both basilica and rotunda were
endowed with galleries, added in subsequent phases of construction,
presumably to accommodate crowds of pilgrims enroute to Spain.
Thus the church was also *occidented*: by addressing pilgrims who were
traveling westwards, it can be considered a *premonition* of Santiago.

Despite its significance as an architectural and functional intersection
between East and West, the church has not been the subject of serious analysis since the early twentieth century, when its documented
history was examined and its building chronology debated by several
French authors.[2] It was then acknowledged as an important structure with extant documentation linking it to the Anastasis Rotunda
of the Complex of the Holy Sepulcher in Jerusalem. Neuvy was cited
in Richard Krautheimer's 1942 study of the iconography of medieval
architecture and it was included in Robert Ousterhout's essay about
the architectural response to pilgrimage.[3] Krautheimer noted a certain
indifference toward exact duplication of a model in the Middle Ages.
Instead, architectural elements were selectively transferred and often
rearranged so that the imitation sometimes only vaguely resembled
the original. At Neuvy, we are reasonably certain that the rotunda
was intended to invoke the structure around Christ's tomb in Jerusalem,

---

[2] François Deshoulières, "Les églises romanes du Berri," *Bulletin monumental* 73
(1909), pp. 469–92; for a discussion on the church and the town, see François
Deshoulières and Emile Chénon, "Symposium Discussion," *Bulletin de la Société nationale
des antiquaires de France* (1916), pp. 190–6, 214–29; Jean Hubert, "Le Saint-Sépulcre
de Neuvy et les pèlerinages de Terre-Sainte au XIème siècle," *Bulletin monumental*
90–91 (1931-2), pp. 91–100; R. Michel-Dansac, "Neuvy-Saint-Sépulcre," *Congrès
archéologique de France* 94 (1931), pp. 523–55; Henri Perrault-Desaix, *Recherches sur
Neuvy-Saint-Sépulcre et les monuments de plan ramassé* (Paris, 1931).

[3] Richard Krautheimer, "Introduction to an 'Iconography of Medieval Archi-
tecture,'" *Journal of the Warburg and Courtauld Institutes* 5 (1942), pp. 1–33, esp. p. 7;
Robert Ousterhout, "Loca Sancta and the Architectural Response to Pilgrimage,"
in *The Blessings of Pilgrimage*, ed. Robert Ousterhout, *Illinois Byzantine Studies* 1 (Urbana,
IL, 1990), pp. 108–24, esp. p. 111; Robert Ousterhout, "Flexible Geography and
Transportable Topography," in *The Real and Ideal Jerusalem in Jewish, Christian and
Islamic Thought*, ed. Bianca Kühnel, special issue of *Jewish Art* 23–4 (1997-8), pp.
393–404.

but drawings and photographs of the rotunda prior to its twentieth-century restoration intimate another possible source for its form. The overall profile of the upper part of the building, as well as certain architectural details are reminiscent of the Islamic Dome of the Rock, appropriated by the Christians after the conquest of Jerusalem in 1099. The rotunda, thus, may be an amalgamated copy of, not one, but two sacred buildings in Jerusalem.

In this study I will reassess the architectural history of the building—constructed and remodeled in several phases between the eleventh and early thirteenth centuries, and heavily restored in the modern period, first by Viollet-le-Duc (1847–50), and again by the *Commission des Monuments Historiques* in 1936–37. After a brief description of the architectural character of the church, its documented history will be addressed, followed by a discussion about the cumbersome relationship between the two building parts, vis-à-vis the sometimes-conflicting chronologies established by the historical evidence and the architectural analysis. The essay concludes with a discussion of Neuvy's multiple functions, iconographic sources and typological origins, as reflections of its two distinct architectural forms, its sequential construction process, and its links to Jerusalem and Santiago.

Architecture: Description

The rotunda's inner diameter measures nearly twenty meters. Eleven round piers made of bonded masonry, capped by beautifully-carved foliage and animal-motif capitals, form an inner circle, supporting an arcade of rounded arches. (fig. 152) Spatially this system divides the ground floor into two parts, creating a much taller central volume ringed by an ambulatory of eleven, irregularly-sized, groin-vaulted bays. The radial bands separating each bay rest on one side above the capitals of the freestanding arcade, and against the outer wall, are supported by engaged columns. (fig. 153) The thick exterior wall appears to have been articulated with curving niches in nine of the eleven bays. Three of these niches were opened to link the rotunda with the basilica and one was filled in (with its outline remaining visible). (fig. 153) The remaining two bays were reserved for an entrance and an adjacent circular stair tower that provided access to the gallery level, now covered by a modern, flat concrete ceiling.

The gallery zone was probably added in a second construction phase, evident from the clearly-different type of masonry employed. This level is expressed on the interior by a second arcade of fourteen, slightly-pointed arches supported by short, monolithic columns with unfinished (but for one) cubic capitals. A third zone, of eight slightly-pointed, arched openings, is located above the gallery. A masonry dome, set above this level, is presently covered by the large conical roof which conceals it from the exterior.

Like the interior, the outside of the rotunda is divided into several horizontal zones. (fig. 154) A series of masonry wall buttresses articulates the lowest zone of the coursed rubble wall, rising to the height of the floor of the interior gallery. Above the buttressed portion of the wall is a strip of rubble masonry, outlined by two cut-stone moldings. The third zone is composed of a predominantly blind arcade of engaged piers, columns, and small carved capitals that support round arches. The height of the blank strip together with this arcade corresponds to the height of the interior gallery zone.

The basilican structure to which the rotunda is awkwardly joined presents obvious evidence of numerous reconstructions. Three ribbed, groin-vaulted bays define the nave, flanked by two narrower aisles with galleries above. Initially, the nave was lower, probably covered by a banded barrel vault (or a wooden roof?), supported by simple cruciform piers still visible along the south wall of the nave. (fig. 151) At this time, the nave was flanked only by aisles, with no galleries above. In a second construction phase, apparent from a marked horizontal ledge along the nave elevation, the roof must have been raised to create open galleries, with slightly-pointed arches (which have since been blocked up). Finally, in a third remodeling, the nave was covered with groin vaults resting on added, engaged columns and corbelled colonnettes at the intersection of the nave elevation and rotunda wall. (fig. 151) The north and east exterior walls of the basilica were reconstructed between the fifteenth and nineteenth centuries.[4] If it were originally a freestanding structure, the east end of

[4] Michel-Dansac, "Neuvy-Saint-Sépulcre," pp. 523–33, 544–55; Perrault-Desaix, *Recherches sur Neuvy-Saint-Sépulcre*, pp. 48–63. There is no reason to dispute their comparable analyses (both were published in 1931 and it is likely that they shared ideas between them) of the successive building phases, which are confirmed by my own on-site observations. Although the relative chronology is reasonably clear, the absolute dating of the basilica's various parts remains conjectural and will be discussed below.

the basilica would probably have been furnished with an apse and possibly with adjoining chapels. Moreover, the arches between the nave and aisles at this end of the building are taller than the other arched openings in the nave, suggesting the possibility that a transept or crossing bay may have been incorporated into the design as well. Although the original structure was constructed somewhat haphazardly (note the cruciform piers are not always aligned across the width of the nave), its easternmost bays appear to have been noticeably larger than the others, implying that these spaces might have adjoined the sanctuary. An entry portal which would have ostensibly marked the west end of the nave is now suppressed by the rotunda. Five projecting masonry courses on the last pier in the southwest corner of the nave, as well as traces of an arch embedded in the adjacent wall of the rotunda, might be the remains of one bay of a barrel-vaulted porch or narthex.[5] (fig. 151)

Historical Documentation

The awkward relationship between the rotunda and the basilica, evident in this corner, is intriguing, and provoked numerous debates about the building's overall chronology. Furthermore, the architectural evidence does not always correspond to documented history of the site. The earliest known mention of the church is in a papal bull of June 28, 1079. Pope Gregory VII addresses Boson, a feudal lord in the nearby region of Cluis, on whose land the church was constructed and who was, in some way, threatening the *ecclesia Sancti Sepulcri*. He orders Boson to stop menacing the church, noting that it was dependent on the Holy Sepulcher in Jerusalem, to which it was required to pay a tithe.[6] A 1087 investment of the Abbot of Marmoutier by the Archbishop of Bourges, with lands given to his monastery was recorded as having taken place *apud Novum Vicum ante altare Sancti Sepulcri* (at the New Town before the altar of the Holy Sepulcher).[7] Important information can be gleaned from these two

---

[5] Michel-Dansac, "Neuvy-Saint-Sépulcre," pp. 548–9; Perrault-Desaix, *Recherches sur Neuvy-Saint-Sépulcre*, pp. 51–2, pl. IV.

[6] Cited by Deshoulières, "Symposium Discussion," p. 193.

[7] Cited by J. Hubert, "Le Saint-Sépulcre de Neuvy," p. 94; cited by Eugène Hubert, *Recueil des chartes intéressant, le département de l'Indre* (Paris, 1899), p. 214.

documents: that the church was constructed on terrain belonging to
a feudal lord; and that it was situated in the *Novus Vicus*, that is, the
New Town or New Quarter.[8] In the eleventh century, the settlement
of Neuvy-St.-Sépulcre was comprised of two sections, separated by
a river. On one side was the *bourg* or town, which was older, and
on the other side the area known as the *château*.[9] This latter side
must be the site of the church because it is known to have been
part of a larger ecclesiastical complex, including a cloister and housing for the canons of the church, all enclosed by a fortification wall
and protected by a moat.[10] This *château* was a place of refuge for
the local population in times of siege. When the English seized a
neighboring town in the second half of the fourteenth century, part
of the vaults over the north aisle of the basilica collapsed due to the
weight of the furniture and foodstuffs that had been hastily stored
in the gallery above them.[11] These vaults were never replaced, thus
inadvertently creating a clerestory zone at the west end of the basilica's north façade. (fig. 150) In 1524, when the fortified walls of the
château were breached, the church was attacked and all its archives
burned.[12] Unfortunately, no traces of the cloister or enclosure wall
remain visible, the last fragments having been destroyed when a wide
road was constructed through the city in 1849, passing very close
along the north side of the church.[13]

The two eleventh-century documents do not divulge any information about the physical characteristics of the building. However,
its foundation is mentioned in three later chronicles. The earliest
one, the Chronicle of Guillaume Godel (who was ordained a priest
in Berry prior to his 1173 death), states a 1042 building charter and
a 1045 foundation. Godel also notes that the church was constructed
ad formam Sancti Sepulcri Jerosolimitani (in the form of the Holy Sepulcher

---

[8] Neuvy is the French contraction of the Latin, *Novus Vicus*.

[9] Chenon in "*Symposium Discussion*," p. 215.

[10] Chenon in "*Symposium Discussion*," p. 227.

[11] Françoise Bercé, *Les premiers travaux de la commission des monuments historiques 1837–48: procès-verbaux et relevés d'architectes* (Paris, 1979), p. 58.

[12] Chenon, in "*Symposium Discussion*," p. 217. Other primary sources were destroyed in 1871 when a fire burned the archives of the archbishopric of Bourges. G. Bautier, "Le Saint Sépulcre de Jérusalem et l'occident médiévale" (Thesis, Ecole de Chartes, 1971), p. 765; J. Hubert, "Le Saint-Sépulcre de Neuvy," p. 91.

[13] Documented in the *Dossier: Neuvy-Saint-Sépulcre*, Archives départementales de l'Indre, Châteauroux.

of Jerusalem).[14] The Chronicles of Robert d'Auxerre (1181) and of
St.-Martin de Tours (1227) also cite the Holy Sepulcher in Jerusalem
in reference to Neuvy's architectural form, but differ slightly on the
foundation dates. Robert d'Auxerre asserts that the church was
founded between the years of 1040 and 1049, while St. Martin's
Chronicle records it more precisely as 1045 or 1046.[15] In Godel's
chronicle he adds that the church was founded in the presence of
Lord Boson of Cluis and Boson's overlord Eudes de Déols, who was
a faithful patron of numerous religious establishments in the lower
Berry region and was also a pilgrim.[16] Having traveled to Rome in
1024 and to Jerusalem in 1026–27, he was familiar with the sacred
sites, although the Holy Sepulcher complex was in ruins at that time.
Although the chronicles cannot be regarded as foolproof sources, the
evidence seems to suggest that a church, affiliated with the Holy
Sepulcher in Jerusalem, was established in Neuvy St.-Sépulcre around
the middle of the eleventh century.

Architecture and Sculpture: Analysis

However, the rotunda's architectural details and capital sculpture
point to a considerably later date. The most significant evidence for
dating comes from the finely-executed foliate capitals of the ground
floor arcade with human and animal figures at each corner and in
the centers of many faces (fig. 155)—the products of a local workshop that was active in Berry c. 1090–1110. The Neuvy capitals are
closely related to those of the ground floor chevet at St.-Benoît-sur-
Loire, where construction was begun c. 1067–80, with its consecration
in 1108. The chevet capitals at St.-Benoît were most likely executed
in the first decade of the twelfth century, and provided models for
sculptors in at least a dozen churches to the southwest and south-
east of Bourges, Neuvy amongst them.[17] The closest comparisons are

---

[14] Paris, Bibliothèque nationale de France, MS lat. 4893, fol. 62 r. Cited in
Hubert, "Le Saint-Sépulcre de Neuvy," p. 92.

[15] Nicolas Camuzat, ed., *Chronologia de Robert d'Auxerre* (Troyes, 1608); *Chronique de
Saint-Martin de Tours* in Dom Martène, *Amplissima collectio* V, p. 1000. Cited by
Chenon, in "*Symposium Discussion*," pp. 217–8.

[16] Chenon in "*Symposium Discussion*," pp. 219–21; Hubert, "Le Saint-Sépulcre de
Neuvy," p. 96.

[17] The sculpture of this region has been studied by Marilyn Low Schmitt,

in the *c.* 1100 Church of Notre-Dame de la Berthenoux, about twenty kilometers northeast of Neuvy. Many of the Neuvy capitals are almost identical to those at La Berthenoux.[18]

So, although it is unlikely that the lowest level of the rotunda, as it appears today, was a mid-eleventh-century construction, it is possible that an earlier rotunda on the site was reconstructed in the twelfth century.[19] We can hypothesize that a round church, built of coursed rubble and equipped with semicircular niches, existed in some form by 1079 (the date of Gregory VII's bull) and was transformed in several phases during the twelfth century. Although this could only be confirmed by excavating under the floor, an argument in favor of such a hypothesis is the archaic nature of the carving of the capitals of the engaged columns in the ambulatory. (fig. 156) Unlike those above the freestanding columns, the capitals and bases of the columns along the wall are more crudely and simply carved; their relief is relatively flat and their forms heavy-handed. As such, stylistically, they seem to belong to a corpus of eleventh-century, rather than twelfth-century sculpture, so they might have belonged to an earlier phase of the building on the site and then been reused in the twelfth century. In order to better understand the building chronology, a closer scrutiny of the architecture is necessary. It seems that the rotunda was originally meant to stand alone, but was, at some point during its construction, attached to the basilica which, in its earliest phase, probably already existed on the site when the rotunda was begun. It is unlikely that the two building parts were conceived of together as a single design.[20]

"Traveling Carvers in the Romanesque: The Case History of St.-Benoît-sur-Loire, Selles-sur-Cher, Méobecq," *Art Bulletin*, 63 (March, 1981), pp. 6–31 and Eliane Vergnolle, "Les chapiteaux de la Berthenoux et le chantier de Saint-Benoît-su-Loire au XIe siècle," *Gazette des beaux-arts*, 80 (November, 1972), pp. 249–60. The diffusion of the sculpture types from St. Benoît to churches in the Berry region is discussed by Eliane Vergnolle, *Saint-Benoît-sur-Loire et la sculpture du XIe siècle* (Paris, 1985), esp. pp. 258–73. In 1984, the Romanesque architecture and sculpture of Bas-Berry was the subject of the 142nd session of the *Congrès archéologique de France* (Paris, 1989). Though Neuvy was presented in a paper at the congress, the work was not included in the published volume.

[18] Examples from La Berthenoux are illustrated in Vergnolle, *Saint-Benoît-sur-Loire*, figs. 279–81.

[19] This is the hypothesis proposed by Hubert, "Le Saint-Sépulcre de Neuvy," pp. 93–4.

[20] This same conclusion was reached by Perrault-Desaix, *Recherches sur Neuvy-Saint-Sépulcre*, p. 47.

The rotunda appears to have been built in separate phases. Its nearly two-meter thick external wall of rubble masonry was articulated with curved niches of unknown function. From a structural point of view, it seems that this thick, circular wall was initially intended to support a much heavier superstructure than that which exists today (perhaps a larger masonry dome?). The wall was clearly not planned in connection with the ambulatory vaulting. Here, it seems, the first design modification took place. The positioning of the engaged columns, necessary to receive the radial bands between the groin-vaulted compartments, was dictated by the placement of the niches, resulting in the skewed alignment of the bands evident in the plan. Furthermore, these bands do not rest directly on the free-standing capitals' impost blocks, as one would expect, but rather, on added projecting corbels visible above the capitals. (fig. 155). The three openings in the peripheral wall that join the rotunda to the basilica must have been cut *after* the ambulatory was vaulted, since the placement of the jambs is prescribed by the location of the engaged columns. This is especially clear in the connection between the rotunda and the nave, where the opening is not centered, but was moved to the north side in order to accommodate one of the columns. These observations and the fact that the convex curvature of the rotunda continues inside the basilica, lead to the conclusion that, in its original design, the rotunda was meant to be a free-standing structure. Moreover, the rotunda's water table and the lower of the two moldings that define the blank strip of masonry above the external wall buttresses are both visible from the interior of the basilica (note the molding just below the painting). (fig. 151) However, the ornamental arcade in the uppermost zone of the external wall (figs. 150, 154) stops where the rotunda meets the *gallery level* of the basilica. Therefore, the wall must have been articulated with this arcade *after* the two buildings had been joined *and after* the basilica was endowed with its galleries.

The lowest zone of the wall is articulated with engaged buttresses constructed of masonry comparable to the small brown-colored sandstone blocks used on the inside for the ambulatory vaults. The buttresses rise only to the height corresponding to the apex of the vaults and, on the northern side of the rotunda, coincide with the interior placement of the engaged colonettes. On the western side of the building, the buttresses lose their structural clarity and appear to have been added to modulate the solid exterior wall or to give the impression of a rhythmic division on the interior.

The construction of an ambulatory vault indicates that the patrons of the church wanted to build a gallery above it, implying that more room was necessary in the rotunda. Moreover, the subsequent physical connection of the rotunda and basilica discloses the desire to enlarge the church as a whole, presumably to accommodate more visitors. The rotunda gallery and drum above were added in a separate construction phase, evident directly above the ambulatory vaults.[21] Four courses above the central arcade, the masonry changes color and form: a much lighter limestone is employed, cut more carefully into slightly larger blocks. (fig. 152) This material is common to the churches of Berry, built in the first half of the twelfth century.[22] The gallery arcade is also constructed in a manner different from the one below. Fourteen monolithic columns, resting on molded bases, support plain cubic capitals and slightly pointed arches, with the extrados of the arcade framed by a continuously curved molding. The uppermost architectural zone, set one stone course above the arcade, is composed of a thin masonry drum, perforated by eight slightly-pointed openings.

Modern Restorations

The dome, set above the drum, brings the discussion to the modern period, since it was added to the building only in the nineteenth century. By 1845 the church had been classified as an historic monument by the Ministry of the Interior and, in the spring of that year, the *Commission des Monuments Historiques* evidently decided to pursue its restoration. L. Dobrovielsky, working for the Historic Monuments

---

[21] All who have studied the rotunda have agreed that this is the case. Eugène Emmanuel Viollet-le-Duc was the first to publish this opinion in his *Dictionnaire raisonné de l'architecture française du XIe au XIVe siècle*, 8 (Paris, 1859), p. 288. However, Viollet-le-Duc acknowledged the differences in construction technique and style between the ground floor and gallery in a report previously written to the Minister of the Interior in 1847 when he was requested to work on the restoration of the church. His unpublished report and cost estimate for the restoration, "Rapport sur l'église circulaire de Neuvy St. Sépulchre" (12 unnumbered pages) and "Devis des travaux à exécuter à l'église ronde de Neuvy St. Sépulchre" (19 unnumbered pages), are preserved in the *Dossier Neuvy-Saint-Sépulcre*, Archives départementales, Châteauroux.

[22] For example, the church of Saint Genou or the chevet of the abbey of Fontgombault; see Jean Favière, *Berry Roman* La nuit des temps 32 (La Pierre-qui-Vire: Zodique, 1970), pls. 18, 28.

Commission, prepared a detailed description of the state of preservation of both rotunda and basilica as well as an itemized cost estimate for all the work necessary to repair and restore the church.[23] Included in his account is this description: "The drum of the Dome [meaning, the drum constructed for the support of a dome] is built of cut stones and although it is in reasonable shape, it will require some repair in case this building is completed with a Dome."[24] Thus, in 1845, the rotunda did not have a dome at all. This is confirmed by measured drawings, signed by Dobrovielsky, dated May 25, 1845 of which one, the elevation of the north side of the church, (fig. 157) shows the rotunda covered with a more shallow conical roof than the one that exists today. A second drawing, a longitudinal section, (fig. 158) depicts the wooden structure of the roof, supported by the drum and exterior wall of the rotunda, with a superimposed outline of a proposed dome.

In 1847, Viollet-le-Duc was asked to prepare an analysis of the church and an estimate for its restoration.[25] He concluded that the rotunda was never completed with its intended dome, and hypothesized that the builders in this part of France were not experienced enough in dome construction to risk such a venture.[26] In order to

---

[23] L. Dobrovielsky, "Description générale de l'Eglise de Neuvy St. Sépulchre" and "Devis et estimation des travaux à faire pour consolider et réparer l'Eglise de Neuvy St. Sépulchre," handwritten manuscripts, both dated to May 25, 1845, *Dossier Neuvy-Saint-Sépulcre*, Archives départementales, Châteauroux.

[24] Dobrovielsky, "Description générale," p. 2, par. 5. The text reads: "La tour du Dôme est construite en pierres-de-taille et quoique en assez bon état, elle exigera des reparations dans le cas où l'achèvement de cet édifice aurait lieu par la construction du Dôme."

[25] See fn. 21.

[26] On the fourth page of the "Rapport sur l'église circulaire de Neuvy St. Sépulchre" Viollet-le-Duc writes: "Ce monument ne fut jamais achevé. Le peu d'habitude que les constructeurs de XIIème siècle avaient, dans cette partie de la France, de faire des coupoles, nous fait présumer qu'une fois arrivés à la naissance de la voûte, ils auront reculés devant ce travail, ne trouvant pas leur mur assez épais pour maintenir la poussé d'une calotte de vingt quatre mètres de circonférence." Translated: "This monument was never completed. The lack of skill that builders of the twelfth century in this part of France had in constructing domes makes us presume that, having arrived at the springing point of the vault, they would have backed off from this work, finding that their wall was not thick enough to counteract the thrust of a dome of twenty-four meters in diameter." Here Viollet-le-Duc must have made an error in his writing. The exterior diameter of the rotunda measures about twenty-four meters, but the dome was surely intended to be built above the much thinner *inner* drum, pierced by openings. As the architect himself attests on page six of his report, this drum *did* exist in 1847: "Enfin, sur le mur

preserve it, he proposed numerous repairs of the rotunda's masonry, as well as the construction of a wooden roof above the gallery so the clerestory windows would be exposed. Above the drum, he recommended a dome of hollow terra cotta pots, embedded in mortar and covered in lead (... *une coupole en poteries creuses et mortier, couverte en plomb*). He admitted the anachronism of using such materials, but concluded that a wooden structure would not be easy to construct over a circular drum, and that a stone dome would result in the same obstacle faced by the medieval builders: risk of collapse.[27]

This work was completed between 1848 and 1850.[28] Early twentieth-century photographs show a church that is considerably different, especially in terms of its proportions, from what we see today. (fig. 159) The clerestory zone is exposed, as it was surely intended to be since a decorative checkerboard patterned molding at the very top of the drum was undoubtedly meant to be visible and the arched openings were meant to bring light into the interior. The masonry of the drum and the roof over the gallery continued to erode over the course of the second half of the nineteenth century[29] and, by the early 1930s, the rotunda was again in a serious state of disrepair. Architect Gabriel Brun prepared a drawing (fig. 160) for another rotunda restoration project, executed in 1936–37: the gallery roof was removed and replaced by a steep cone covering the entire structure. Contemporary materials were introduced into the building at

circulaire ébreché à son sommet, se pose un énorme toit conique qui, passant *par dessus des fênetres supérieures de la nef*, va se terminer en pointe et enveloppe tout ce pauvre monument sous un couvercle hideux, bossué [*sic*] et crevé en plusieurs endroits." Translated: "Finally, at the top of the chipped circular wall rests an enormous conical roof which, passing *above the upper windows of the nave*, terminates in a point and envelopes the entirety of this poor monument under a hideous, hunched cover which has collapsed in several places."

[27] "Rapport sur l'église circulaire," Archives départementales, Châteauroux, pp. 8–10 of unnumbered manuscript.

[28] Viollet-le-Duc mentions this himself in a letter to the Minister of Culture(?), dated September 4, 1855 (*Dossier Neuvy-Saint-Sépulcre*, Archives départementales, Châteauroux). By that date, the roof of the gallery required repairs and, evidently, he was asked to work on the building again.

[29] Two letters (June 27, 1877 and May 8, 1897) to the Minister of Public Instruction and the Fine Arts from the architects, W.L. Darcy and his son, Georges Darcy, respectively, attest to the rotunda's deterioration. Numerous repairs are proposed each time (*Dossier Neuvy-Saint-Sépulcre*, Archives départementales, Châteauroux). The *dossier* on Neuvy at the Bibliothèque et Archives du Patrimoine in Paris also contains fairly continuous correspondence about the building's problems between 1852 and 1897.

this time. The floor of the gallery was leveled and raised and a reinforced concrete ceiling was placed above the gallery and tied into the exterior wall of the rotunda and to the wooden members of the new roof. In this way a kind of compression ring (*ceinturage*) was created to encircle the entire building for structural stability. This system still exists today. Repairs in the 1990s had to address only the surface conditions of the exposed masonry. Unfortunately, this last major restoration again distorted the original architectural intent of the building. Had it been completed with a dome when it was first built, this cupola as well as the clerestory zone below would have been visible from the street. We do not know how the rotunda was shielded from the weather in the Middle Ages.

Iconographical Sources: Jerusalem

Despite all of these changes, Neuvy's iconographic link to the Anastasis Rotunda of the Holy Sepulcher is clear, via its dedication and the documentary evidence already discussed. There are several other aspects of the rotunda's form and its contents that also link it to Jerusalem. Like Neuvy, the Anastasis Rotunda and the adjacent structures were remodeled numerous times over their long history.[30] The initial complex of the Holy Sepulcher dates to the first third of the fourth century, begun during the reign of Constantine the Great. This ensemble incorporated a rotunda around the supposed rock-cut tomb of Christ and a five-aisled basilica to its east, separated from the rotunda by an open courtyard, surrounded on three sides by porticoes. The rotunda was endowed with twelve columns and three pairs of square piers placed in a circle around the tomb, creating an ambulatory on the ground level and supporting a second-story gallery and, probably, a third, clerestory level. The exterior wall of the rotunda was articulated with three semi-circular niches on the north, west, and south sides; however, we are unsure how

---

[30] The most complete architectural and archaeological study of the complex of the Holy Sepulcher is Virgilio Corbo, *Il Santo Sepolcro di Gerusalemme. Aspetti archaeologici dalle origini al periode crociato*, 3 vols. (Jerusalem, 1981–2). An extensive bibliography is provided by Shimon Gibson and Joan E. Taylor, *Beneath the Church of the Holy Sepulchre Jerusalem. The Archaeology and Early History of Traditional Golgotha, Palestine Exploration Fund Monograph Series Maior* 1 (London, 1994), pp. 93–7.

the east side was expressed since later modifications have destroyed the evidence.[31]

This fourth-century complex survived, more or less intact until the Persian raids of Jerusalem in the early seventh century, when it was attacked, but not completely destroyed. Although the Christians were forced to surrender Jerusalem to the Muslims in 638, the complex of the Holy Sepulcher continued to attract Christian pilgrims by virtue of religious tolerance prevailing between the seventh and eleventh centuries. A tenth-century fire damaged Constantine's basilica, but pilgrim accounts still record the existence of the tomb in the center of the rotunda.[32]

In 1009 the situation changed dramatically when the Muslim caliph Al-Hakim, convinced that he was led by God to abolish Christianity by ravaging holy sites in Jerusalem, destroyed the tomb aedicula, the upper levels of the rotunda and the adjacent basilica. Later, under Byzantine emperor, Constantine IX Monomachus the gallery, upper zone, and roof of the rotunda were restored (1042–48) and a replica of the tomb replaced the original in its center. The basilica was never rebuilt, but an apse, framed by paired columns, was added to the east side of the rotunda, projecting into an open triportico. By this time the Anastasis Rotunda was surrounded on its north, west, and south sides by chapels and numerous rooms used by the patri-archate.[33]

The complex changed again under the patronage of the Crusaders who, after capturing the city from the Muslims in 1099, established Jerusalem as the capital of their Latin Kingdom. The Crusaders removed the eleventh-century eastern apse of the rotunda and built the structure in the open courtyard known as the "Crusader Choir." Dedicated in 1149, this choir is composed of a transept, linked to the rotunda through three openings. The central bay of the transept

---

[31] Corbo, *Il Santo Sepolcro*, I, pp. 51–137, III, pl. 3, with an English summary, I, pp. 223–8; Gibson and Taylor, *Beneath the Church of the Holy Sepulchre*, pp. 74–7.

[32] L.-Hugues Vincent and Felix-Marie Abel, *Jérusalem: Recherches de topographie, d'archéologie et d'histoire*, II (Paris, 1914), pp. 248–9.

[33] Marius Canard, "La destruction de l'église de la Résurrection par le Calife Hakim et l'histoire de la descente du feu sacré," *Byzantion* 35 (1965), pp. 16–43; Corbo, *Il Santo Sepolcro*, I, pp. 145–81, III, pls. 4–5, with an English summary, I, pp. 229–31. This stage of the history of the complex has been studied by Robert Ousterhout "Rebuilding the Temple: Constantine Monomachus and the Holy Sepulchre," *Journal of the Society of Architectural Historians* 48 (March 1989), pp. 66–78.

was covered by a dome and enclosed on the east by a chevet, incorporating an apse, ambulatory, and three radiating chapels.[34]

Through all of these modifications the essential outline of the rotunda did not change drastically and the compact double-ended solution created by the Crusaders remains today. Only the eleventh-century cover of the rotunda was replaced, by the dome that is now visible, after an 1808 fire.[35] Several seventeenth-century engravings offer an idea of the rotunda's appearance in the late eleventh and twelfth centuries. A 1619 longitudinal section by Fratello Bernardino Amico (fig. 161) depicts three interior levels, capped by a curious structure which was probably a ribbed, wooden conical vault, with an oculus over the center of the buillding to illuminate the shrine around the tomb of Christ. Oddly enough, it appears that the uppermost zone, below the roof is blind, i.e., a wall is expressed behind what is ostensibly a clerestory level. Although one can question the accuracy of the engraving (how can the left and right sides of the section cut of the rotunda's wall possibly co-exist?), other seventeenth-century views of the interior intimate a comparable solution.[36] A 1619 elevation of the south façade by Amico (fig. 162) shows the rotunda's exterior wall as a solid, curving form, highlighted by several horizontal moldings with the conical roof visible. However, the exterior profile of the rotunda presented by Amico could not correspond to either side of his section! Taking these into account, in terms of its general architectural form, the rotunda at Neuvy appears, nevertheless, to be an architectural copy of the Anastasis Rotunda. Regarding Krautheimer's remarks about the nature of medieval copies, we see certain salient features of Jerusalem's rotunda imitated at Neuvy as it must have looked in the beginning of the twelfth century: the round form of the building, the massive nature of the exterior wall, the interior arcade and two upper levels of its elevation. The architect of the medieval copy did not necessarily intend to imitate the Anastasis Rotunda as it looked in reality; rather, he projected it

---

[34] Corbo, *Il Santo Sepolcro*, I, pp. 183–209, III, pls. 6, 7, with an English summary, I, 233–5; Robert Ousterhout, "Architecture as Relic and the Construction of Sanctity, The Stones of the Holy Sepulchre," *Journal of the Society of Architectural Historians* 62 (March 2003), pp. 4–23.

[35] Ousterhout, "Rebuilding the Temple, p. 68.

[36] For example, the interior perspective, engraved by Cornelis De Bruyn in 1681 who depicts the clerestory zone with blocked arches. Corbo, *Il Santo Sepolcro*, I, pl. III; Ousterhout, "Rebuilding the Temple," pp. 70–1.

figuratively, as a memento of the venerated site and as a symbol of promised salvation. In addition, the likeness of the Holy Sepulcher migrated to the West through abridged images on small objects: memorabilia or souvenirs like lead seals or stamped terra cotta flasks that contained oil blessed at the site.[37]

The rotunda at Neuvy was also linked to its prototype by a transfer of its contents. In 1257, the church was endowed with relics from Jerusalem by Cardinal Eudes de Châteauroux. A fragment of Christ's tomb and several drops of His blood were placed in a reliquary constructed at Neuvy in the form of the tomb aedicula imitating the one rebuilt by Constantine Monomachus in the Anastasis Rotunda.[38] In the following centuries numerous papal bulls, letters, and bishops' mandates were addressed to the chapter at Neuvy to maintain the devotion to the holy relics. The reliquary stood in the center of the rotunda until 1806 when it was dismantled after priests complained that it hid the altar.[39] A detailed description of it was given by the nineteenth-century Abbot Caillaud:

> In order to store the precious relic that was sent to it by the Cardinal Eudes, the chapter had a grotto or vault constructed in the middle of the rotunda, a sort of round tower, more than three meters in height, intended to represent the sepulcher where Nicodemus and Joseph of Arimathea had placed the body of our Lord. One entered it by descending two or three steps, through a very low, Romanesque, arched opening, [constructed] in such a way that it was necessary to bend over in order to enter. This opening was closed by an iron door whose lower part was filled in, and the upper section ornamented by an openwork design of foliage. Facing the door, one discovered in this vault a small altar and to the right of the altar a rounded stone of about one and six-tenths meters in length which occupied the entire length of the vault. On this stone was a heavy beam, to which was attached, by wide bands of iron, a coffer locked with three keys, in which were

---

[37] *The Blessings of Pilgrimage*, ed. R. Ousterhout, pp. 85–150, address the material culture of pilgrimage. *Editors' note, see Stephen Lamia's essay in this volume.

[38] The history of the tomb aedicula in Jerusalem has been studied by John Wilkinson, "The Tomb of Christ: An Outline of its Structural History," *Levant* 4 (1972), pp. 83–97. Like the architecture that contained it, the aedicula was also represented on small objects that made their way to the West with pilgrims. I.Q. van Regteren Altena, "Hidden Records of the Holy Sepulchre," in *Essays in the History of Architecture Presented to Rudolf Wittkower* (London, 1967), pp. 17–21.

[39] Hubert, "Le Saint-Sépulcre de Neuvy," pp. 97–9; Perrault-Desaix, *Recherches sur Neuvy-Saint-Sépulcre*, pp. 67–9.

placed the precious relics . . . This aedicula was surrounded by blind arcades, separated by colonnettes, all in the style of the building.[40]

Although the tomb/reliquary built at Neuvy in the thirteenth century was a late addition to the Romanesque architectural ensemble, it certainly reinforced the established link between the model in Jerusalem and its imitation in France.

However, the general outline of the building before its 1936 restoration, with the flat roof over its gallery, the exposed clerestory zone and dome bring to mind another building in Jerusalem: the Islamic Dome of the Rock. Begun or completed in 691–92 by the Umayyad caliph, Abd al-Malik, this building is located on the platform of the former Jewish Temple, to the north of the Al-Aqsa Mosque.[41] Christians appropriated both buildings after the Crusader conquest of Jerusalem in 1099. The mosque and the area around it were given over to the recently-founded monastic military order of the Knights Templars in the 1120s and the Dome of the Rock was in the hands of the Canons (priests) of the Temple. The Knights Templars were one of several religious military orders founded by the Crusaders to protect Christian pilgrims in the Holy Land. They derive their name from being stationed in the existing Muslim buildings on the Temple Mount.[42] In Christian Jerusalem the mosque was identified as the

---

[40] Abbé Caillaud, *Notice sur le Précieux Sang de Neuvy-Saint-Sépulcre* (Bourges, 1865), p. 83; cited in Perrault-Desaix, *Recherches sur Neuvy-Saint-Sépulcre*, p. 67. The French text reads: Pour déposer la précieuse relique que le cardinal Eudes lui avait envoyé, le chapitre avait fait construire au milieu de la rotonde une grotte ou caveau, espèce de tour ronde, élevée de plus de trois mètres, destinée à figurer le sépulcre où Nicodème et Joseph d'Arimathie avaient déposé le corps de Notre-Seigneur. On y pénétrait, en descendant deux ou trois degrés, par une ouverture cintrée, romane, très basse, de manière qu'il fallait se courber pour y entrer. Cette ouverture était fermée par une porte de fer dont la partie inférieure était pleine et le dessus en rinceaux de feuillages. En face de la porte, on trouvait dans ce caveau un petit autel et à droite de l'autel une pierre tumulaire d'environ un mètre soixante centimètres de longeur, qui occupait toute la longeur du caveau. Sur cette pierre était un fort madrier; à ce madrier était attaché, par de larges bandes de fer, un coffre-fort fermant à trois clefs, où étaient déposées les precieuses reliques . . . Cet édicule était entouré d'arcatures aveugles, séparés par des colonnettes, le tout dans le style de l'édifice.

[41] The Dome of the Rock has been studied in all its historic phases by Oleg Grabar, *The Shape of the Holy. Early Islamic Jerusalem* (Princeton, 1996), pp. 52–116 with a substantial bibliography, pp. 219–25.

[42] The literature on the Templars is extensive. Helen Nicholson, *The Knights Templar: A New History* (Stroud, UK, 2001); Malcolm Barber, *The New Knighthood. A History of the Order of the Temple* (Cambridge, 1994), pp. 64–114 and a comprehensive bibliography pp. 399–419.

Palace or Temple of Solomon, while the Dome of the Rock, called "The Holy of the Holies" by the Greeks, was known to the Latins as the Temple of the Lord (*Templum Domini*).[43]

This *Templum Domini* (fig. 163) is a freestanding octagonal structure with four projecting porches placed along its cardinal sides. The exterior walls are lined with pilasters and windows with a flat parapet above, today covered with colored faïence tiles added by the Sultan Suleyman in 1552. A shallow shed roof, partially hidden by the parapet, covers two interior ambulatories and meets the base of a circular drum, pierced by clerestory windows, which supports a double-shell wooden dome. Directly beneath the dome is the large rock, from which Muslims believe Mohammad ascended to heaven. Restorations to the Dome of the Rock in the 1870's uncovered an arcade beneath the tiles at the parapet level. In the original construction round-headed arches rested on short engaged columns, creating a blind arcade comparable to the one seen at Neuvy. Furthermore, the windows in the drum (now rectangular) were originally rounded at the top, again in a manner similar to the clerestory openings at Neuvy.[44] A restored image of one of its original doorways (fig. 164) depicts a rectangular opening, flanked by two columns and covered by a stone lintel, above which is an open lunette intended to be filled with an iron grill. This type of construction, with an open relieving arch, is usually found in the East, particularly in Syria, but it is also employed in the rotunda at Neuvy. (fig. 165) Here, the columns that flank the entrance did not extend to the ground, but only to the level of the water table where they were set on capitals, placed upside down and used as bases. Although carved bases *are* seen in this region of France, capitals reused in this fashion are unusual and may also reflect eastern influence. They are seen in early Islamic architecture, such as the marble wall paneling of the eastern vestibule in the Great Mosque at Damascus. (fig. 166)

In a fifteenth-century engraving, (fig. 167) published by the Dutch traveler Bernhard von Breydenbach, we see the Dome of the Rock pictured on the temple platform. The image presents salient char-

---

[43] Francis E. Peters, *Jerusalem. The Holy City in the Eyes of Chroniclers, Visitors, Pilgrims, and Prophets from the Days of Abraham to the Beginnings of Modern Times* (Princeton, 1985), pp. 314–23.
[44] The fabric of the building has been studied by Keppel A.C. Creswell, *Early Muslim Architecture* I (Oxford, 1969), pp. 65–131, 213–322.

acteristics that may link the exterior of this building to the rotunda in France. Its lowest level is modulated by pilasters. The exterior wall of the Anastasis Rotunda in Jerusalem was marked by horizontal moldings, but never articulated with pilasters.[45] We also see the arcade in the parapet zone, a clerestory level, and the exposed dome. Crusader relief sculpture (fig. 168) also depicts the Dome of the Rock. Although carved in a cursory manner, the critical features are visible: an entry portal, flanked by columns, the pilasters of the lowest zone, the blind arcade above, the clerestory, and the dome.[46]

Other examples of Templar architecture in the West may help to illuminate the issue. Templar chapels generally took one of two forms: they were either solid, rectangular structures whose exterior walls were lined with buttresses or they were round or polygonal buildings, sometimes with appended spaces. One of the most famous Templar rotundas was built in Paris and although it was slowly dismantled in the aftermath of the French Revolution, eighteenth and nineteenth-century drawings and maps show its original form with the rotunda as a freestanding structure. Its exterior was lined with pilasters and inside, six piers separated the vaulted ambulatory from the taller central section lit with clerestory windows. This mid-twelfth century rotunda acquired a Gothic choir and a square bell tower to its east in the thirteenth century, as well as a two-bay porch. The church was surrounded by other buildings belonging to the Templars and, like at Neuvy, was enclosed within a fortification wall at the northern edge of the city of Paris, just inside the fourteenth-century city wall.[47]

The Templar church in London also shows a comparable solution. Although the church was heavily restored in the nineteenth century, the rotunda, consecrated in 1185, was originally a freestanding structure, articulated with buttresses on the exterior and freestanding piers on the interior, separating the central section from an ambulatory. In 1240, a three-aisled Gothic choir was added to

---

[45] None of the archaeological studies of the Anastasis Rotunda mentions the presence of pilasters on its exterior, nor do any of the visual documents indicate their existence.

[46] This sculptural fragment, presumably carved by Crusader hands before the fall of Jerusalem in 1187, was taken as loot to Cairo in the thirteenth century. It is embedded on the right-hand side of the entrance of the Mosque–Madrasa–Mausoleum of Sultan Hasan in Cairo. K.A.C. Creswell, *Early Muslim Architecture* I, pp. 84–5.

[47] Elie Lambert, *L'Architecture des Templiers* (Paris, 1955), pp. 66–71.

its east side, part of the rotunda was demolished in order to facilitate the connection, and the church was set within a fortified enclosure, as in Paris.[48]

Pilgrims' Accounts

Unfortunately, no documentary evidence survives directly linking the
church at Neuvy with the Templars. In fact, Templar command
posts were conspicuously absent between the Loire Valley and the
line formed by the regions of Provence, Languedoc and the Pyrenees.[49]
But perhaps we should look at the Dome of the Rock from the pilgrims' point of view. Known already to the Greeks as the "Holy of
Holies," in the twelfth century the *Templum Domini* acquired a sacred
history, recounted by the pilgrims who associated numerous biblical
events that took place in the Temple with this structure.[50] In the
c. 1100 pilgrim's guide, *Qualiter*, it is stated that "In the middle of
[the Temple of the Lord] is the 'Temple made without hands,' that
is, the Tabernacle. In it are preserved, so it is believed, the rod of
Aaron, the head of Zachariah, the altar which Jacob built to the
Lord, the two tablets of the Testament, the Ark of the Covenant,
and the manna with which the children of Israel were nourished in
the desert."[51] Another pilgrim, Saewulf, writing between 1101 and
1103 adds: "there [in the Temple] our Lord Jesus Christ when he
was tired of the mockery of the Jews used to rest. There is the place
of confession where his disciples used to confess to him . . . There
the child Jesus was circumcised on the eighth day, and was named
'Jesus' . . . There the Lord Jesus was offered by his parents with the
Virgin Mother Mary on the day of her Purification, and received
by the old man Simeon . . . There the footprints of the Lord still
appear in the rock when he hid himself and left the Temple . . ."[52]
  Other pilgrims relate comparable tales and embellish the stories,
so that by the middle of the twelfth century, the site of the Dome

---

[48] Lambert, *L'Architecture des Templiers*, pp. 71–6.
[49] Barber, *The New Knighthood*, fig. 22 locates Templar preceptories and castles in
Western Europe up to 1150.
[50] John Wilkinson, *Jerusalem Pilgrimage, 1099–1185* (London, 1988), pp. 38–45;
Peters, *Jerusalem. The Holy City*, pp. 314–9.
[51] Wilkinson, *Jerusalem Pilgrimage*, pp. 6, 90–1.
[52] Wilkinson, *Jerusalem Pilgrimage*, pp. 6–7, 104–5.

of the Rock, if not the building itself, had become an important *locus sanctus*. Furthermore, after the Dome of the Rock was appropriated by the Templars, its site was included in liturgical processions, and thus gained a place in the sacred topography of Jerusalem.[53] While the Church of the Holy Sepulcher, surrounded by buildings, was difficult to visualize from the exterior, the "Christianized" Dome of the Rock, in the hands of Western pilgrims for much of the twelfth century, was always visible and could have easily served as one of the models for the exterior image of a freestanding, centrally planned pilgrimage church in the West.[54] In fact, its visibility and its dominance of Jerusalem's skyline distinguish it from the other churches and holy sites in the city.[55]

Thus Neuvy-Saint-Sépulcre may have had more than a single architectural source for its form and meaning: a Christian mausoleum and maybe a Muslim shrine, appropriated by Christian pilgrims. Or perhaps the French Holy Sepulcher acquired multiple meanings as it was changed and transformed? In the twelfth century the building complex acquired a secondary dedication to St. James, the patron saint of travelers to Santiago de Compostela.[56] The construction of galleries over the aisles of the basilica and above the ambulatory of the rotunda and the subsequent connection of the two spaces at this level created a continuous pilgrims' gallery, much like those found in more traditional French pilgrimage churches located along the roads to Santiago—for example, St. Sernin in Toulouse or St. Foy in Conques.[57] As we have seen, architecture is hardly static and perhaps

---

[53] John of Würzburg, writing *c.* 1170, recounts the annual opening, on Palm Sunday, of the Golden Gate, which faces the eastern arched entrance of the raised platform on which the Dome of the Rock was constructed. Peters, *Jerusalem. The Holy City*, pp. 316–8; Wilkinson, *Jerusalem Pilgrimage*, pp. 250–1.

[54] Unfortunately, the only documented pilgrim who traveled from Neuvy to Jerusalem is Eude de Déols, who made his trip in 1026–7. At that historical moment the Anastasis Rotunda had not yet been restored and he likely did not have access to the Temple Mount, as Christians were probably still forbidden on the platform. Wilkinson, *Jerusalem Pilgrimage*, p. 28. We can only speculate that other individuals from central France went to Jerusalem later in the eleventh century or after the Latin conquest, in the second quarter of the twelfth century.

[55] Its commanding exterior form and its perception from all sides of the city have been studied in detail through computer modeling. Grabar, *The Shape of the Holy*, pp. 104–10, figs. 56–9.

[56] Chenon, in *BantFr*, p. 217.

[57] The town of Neuvy-Saint-Sépulcre was also located on a pilgrimage route to Santiago. See fn. 1.

we should consider modifications in meaning along with modifications in form. As it stood then, in the middle of the thirteenth century, after all its medieval transformations and after the arrival of the relics from the Holy Land, Neuvy-Saint-Sépulcre was a modern, updated reappraisal and readaption of older architectural forms that together provided new meaning: reliquary, memorial shrine, architectural souvenir, and pilgrimage church, all fused into one and executed in the regional idioms of this part of Romanesque France.

CHAPTER THIRTEEN

RELICS AND RELIQUARIES OF THE TRUE CROSS

Kelly M. Holbert

Of the many relics venerated in the medieval Christian world, one of the most important was the relic of the True Cross. Small fragments of this sacred wood were brought back from the Holy Land and preserved in reliquaries in parish churches and monastic communities throughout Europe. These containers took many forms, the most elaborate being made of gold and silver and encrusted with enamels and precious stones. Over time, ranging from the ninth through fourteenth centuries, the shapes taken by True Cross reliquaries have tended to vary according to ecclesiastical function and the region in which they were made. Given that hundreds of Cross reliquaries survive from the Middle Ages, it will be more fruitful to isolate and examine a small group of seven with regard to their style and form, and in so doing gain a better understanding of pilgrimage, religious life, and changing devotional practices in medieval northern Europe.

Constantine and Helena and the Legend of the True Cross

Explanations as to how relics of the True Cross were found and preserved after the crucifixion of Christ began to emerge in the fourth century and were closely tied to the lives and deeds of Constantine the Great (*c.* 272–337) and his mother, Helena (*c.* 255–330). In the legends surrounding Constantine, the cross was seen as a symbol of military triumph and of the victory that was ensured to the army that carried the cross as a standard in battle. It was not Constantine, however, but Helena who was believed to have discovered the True Cross, and who demonstrated its importance as a physical relic of the crucifixion with the power to heal and to guarantee resurrection for all believers. These two legends are bound together not only by the mother and son relationship of Constantine

and Helena, but, also, by the vital importance to all Christians of
the precious relics and sites of the Holy Land.

For the legend of Constantine, the foundation was laid by a *Vita*
of the Emperor written around 337 and generally attributed to
Eusebius (*c.* 260–339).[1] One of the key events from the life of
Constantine, his defeat of Maxentius, was also treated by Eusebius
in his *Ecclesiastical History*, translated into Latin by Rufinus of Aquileia
(345–410) around the year 402.[2] Other sources include the anonymous *Acts of Silvester* of the fifth century, which describes Constantine's
baptism in Rome in 313 by Pope Silvester,[3] and the *Inventio Sanctae
Crucis*,[4] an anonymous, fifth-century work translated into Latin before
the beginning of the sixth century.[5] Although primarily devoted to

---

[1] Eusebius of Caesarea, *De Vita beatissimi Imperatores Constantini*, ed. Friedhelm
Winkelmann, *Die Griechischen Christlichen Shriftsteller* 1 (repr. Berlin, 1975), pp. 15–151.
For attribution and dating, see Stephan Borgehammar, *How the Holy Cross Was
Found: From Event to Medieval Legend* (Stockholm, 1991), pp. 93–122; Wilhelm Levison,
"Konstantinische Schenkung und Silvester-Legende," *Miscellanea Francesco Ehrle: Scritti
di Storia e Paleografia* 2 (Rome, 1924), p. 177; Wilhelm Pohlkamp, "Kaiser Konstantin,
der heidnische und der christliche Kult in den Actus Silvestri," *Frühmittelalterliche
Studien* 18 (1984), p. 362; Friedhelm Winkelmann, "Die älteste erhaltene griechische
hagiographische *Vita* Konstantins und Helenas (BHG Nr. 365z, 366, 366a)," in *Texte
und Textkritik: eine Aufsatzsammlung*, ed. Jürgen Drummer (Berlin, 1987), p. 625.

[2] Rufinus of Aquileia, *Historia ecclesiastica*, ed. Domenico Vallarsi, *Patrologia cursus
completus, series latina*, ed. Jacques-Paul Migne (Paris, 1844–1903), 21, pp. 461–540;
Borgehammar, *How the Holy Cross Was Found*, p. 8; Jan Willem Drijvers, *Helena
Augusta: The Mother of Constantine the Great and the Legend of Her Finding of the True Cross*
(Leiden, 1992), pp. 100–7.

[3] Borgehammar, *How the Holy Cross Was Found*, p. 71; Levison, "Konstantinische
Schenkung," pp. 211–27. The *Actus Beati Sylvestri* is included as part of the *Inventio
Sanctae Crucis* in the editions of Borgehammar, pp. 255–71, and Alfred Holder, ed.,
Inventio Sanctae Crucis, Actorum Cyriaci pars I: Latine et graece ymnus antiqus de Sancta Cruce
(Leipzig, 1889), pp. 1–2. Part of the legend is also published by Boninus Mombritius
as the *Prologus in vitam Sancti Sylvestri, papae et confessoris*, in *Sanctuarium seu Vitae Sanctorum
(1480)*, ed. A. Brunet (Paris, 1910), pp. 508–16. For the Greek origins of this legend,
see Levison, "Konstantinische Schenkung," pp. 166–247.

[4] The *Inventio Sanctae Crucis* is published in Borgehammar, *How the Holy Cross Was
Found*, pp. 255–71 and Holder, *Inventio Sanctae Crucis*, pp. 1–13. Borgehammar com-
piled an edition from twenty-one manuscripts, from the sixth to the thirteenth cen-
turies, noting that there are over 120 catalogued manuscripts of the *Inventio* in
existance, although the number is probably closer to 200, pp. 201–12. The text of
Holder's edition is taken from a single manuscript, the oldest known text of the
Inventio (Paris, Bibl. Nat., lat. 2769, fols. 15r–21r), dated to the mid-sixth century.
See also *Inventio* in the *Acta sanctorum*, eds. Johannes Bollandus and Godefridus
Henschenius (Antwerp, 1643), maii I, pp. 445–8, augusti III, p. 588.

[5] Borgehammar, *How the Holy Cross Was Found*, pp. 148, 201, wrote that the original Greek text of the *Inventio* was composed between 415–50, and translated into
Latin before 450 by an unknown author in Jerusalem. The *Inventio*, (*Acts of Judas*

the legend of Helena's discovery of the True Cross, the *Inventio* begins its narrative with an account of Constantine's vision of the cross, his subsequent victory over his enemies, and his baptism in the city of Rome.

The sources for the Helena legend concerning the discovery of the True Cross are more numerous and widely dispersed. Briefly, her deeds were described by Cyril of Jerusalem (*c.* 315–87) around 347,[6] and by John Chrysostom (*c.* 344–407) in 387.[7] A few years later, in 395, Helena's finding of the Cross was also described by Ambrose (*c.* 340–97), in his *De obitu Theodosii*.[8] Helena then appears in the Greek history of the Church by Gelasius of Caesarea (367–95),[9] and in the supplement that Rufinus added to his translation of Eusebius' *Ecclesiastical History*. Helena is naturally at the center of the *Inventio Sanctae Crucis*, and is also mentioned in the sixth-century *Liber Pontificalis*.[10]

The Legend of the True Cross and Cross Reliquaries

The key events in these legends are illustrated on a reliquary of the True Cross known today as the *Stavelot Triptych*,[11] (fig. 169)[12] dated

---

Cyriacus) was listed by Pope Gelasius (492–96) among the works to be read with caution and reserve, along with the *Acts of Silvester*, which he had condemned in 494, *PL* 59: 173–4.

[6] Cyril of Jerusalem, *Epistolae ad Constantium piissimum imperatorum*, ed. Antonii Augustini Touttée, in *Patrologia cursus completus, series graeca*, ed. Jacques-Paul Migne (Paris, 1857–1903), 33, p. 1167; Borgehammar, *How the Holy Cross Was Found*, pp. 85–92.

[7] John Chrysostom, *In Ioannem. Homilia LXXXV*, ed. Bernard de Monfaucon, *PG* 59: 461; P. Jounel, "Le Culte de la Croix dans la liturgie romaine," *La Maison Dieu* 75 (1963), p. 68.

[8] Ambrose, *De obitu Theodosii*, ed. Otto Faller, *Corpus scriptorum ecclesiasticorum latinorum*, ed. Karl Schenkl (Leipzig, 1866), 73, pp. 393–7; Drijvers, *Helena Augusta*, p. 95; Dominique Iogna-Prat, "La Croix, le moine et l'empereur: dévotion à la croix et théologie politique à Cluny autour de l'an mil," in *Haut Moyen-Age: Culture, education et société. Études offertes à Pierre Riché*, ed. Michel Sot (La Garenne-Colombes, 1990), p. 459.

[9] Gelasius of Caesarea, *Historia ecclesiastica*, eds. Gerhard Loeschcke and Margret Heinemann, *Die Griechischen Christlichen Shriftsteller* (Leipzig, 1918) 28, pp. 21–200.

[10] *Liber Pontificalis*, ed. Louis Duchesne (Paris, 1886–92), 1, p. 167

[11] Joyce Brodsky, "The Stavelot Triptych: Notes on a Mosan Work," *Gesta* 11 (1972): 19–33; Philippe Verdier, "Émaux mosans et rheno-mosans dans les collections des Étas-Unis," *Revue Belge d'archéologie et d'histoire de l'art* 44 (1975), pp. 10–11; William Voelkle, *The Stavelot Triptych: Mosan Art and the Legend of the True Cross* (New York, 1980).

[12] Now in the Pierpont Morgan Library in New York, the *Stavelot Triptych* was

1156–58,[13] although a few scholars place it more generally in the 1150s to account for stylistic similarities with other Mosan works of 1145–55.[14] The open wings of the triptych are decorated with a series of scenes in champlevé enamel. At the left, three roundels depict, from bottom to top, the Vision of Constantine, the Battle of the Milvian Bridge, and the Baptism of Constantine. On the right wing, bottom to top, we see Helena Interrogating the Jews, the Finding of the True Cross, and the Testing of the True Cross over a deceased man.

The first episode on the Constantine wing illustrates the emperor's vision, or dream, and the appearance of the sign of the cross in the night sky. The sleeping Constantine is clearly labeled, and the words spoken by the angel are enclosed in a scroll held in his left hand: I[N] HOC VINCE. According to the *Inventio*, the sign of the cross appeared to the emperor in a dream while he was preparing to do battle against a group of unnamed enemies. The angel also identified the cross as the symbol which, when placed upon Constantine's standard, would ensure victory over his enemies.[15]

The scene directly above illustrates Constantine's victory at the Milvian Bridge, a direct result of his having followed the advice of the angel. In this roundel Constantine is seen on horseback, with the partially-visible heads and upper bodies of ten soldiers who, behind him, collectively represent his army, the ROMANI. Among

---

believed to have been made for the Benedictine monastery of St. Remaclus in Stavelot in eastern Belgium; eds. Joseph Halkin and Charles-Gustav Roland, *Recueil des chartes de l'abbaye de Stavelot-Malmédy*, 1 (Brussels, 1909), 2 (Brussels, 1930).

[13] Voelkle, *The Stavelot Triptych*; Joseph de Borchgrave d'Altena, *Art mosan* (Paris, 1951), p. 25; Brodsky, "The Stavelot Triptych;" Suzanne Collon-Gevaert, *Histoire des arts du métal en Belgique* (Brussels, 1951), pp. 169–70; Josef Deér, "Die Siegel Kaiser Friedrichs I. Barbarossa und Heinrichs VI. in der Kunst und Politik ihrer Zeit," in *Festschrift Hans R. Hahnloser, zum 60. Geburtstag*, ed. Ellen J. Beer (Basel, 1961), p. 77; Nigel Morgan, "The Iconography of Twelfth-Century Mosan Enamels," in *Rhein und Maas. Kunst und Kultur 800–1400*, ed. Anton Legner (Cologne, 1972), 2, p. 266; Jacques Stiennon, "La Personalité de Wibald de Stavelot et de Corvey: une problematique," in *Wibald, Abbé de Stavelot-Malmedy et de Corvey, 1130–1158*, ed. Jacques Stiennon (Stavelot, 1982), p. 74; Neil Stratford, *Catalogue of Medieval Enamels in the British Museum. II. Northern Romanesque Enamel* (London, 1993), p. 73.

[14] Brodsky, "The Stavelot Triptych," p. 31; Marie-Madeleine Gauthier, *Émaux du moyen âge occidental* (Fribourg, 1972), pp. 126, 343. Verdier, "Emaux mosans," p. 11, dated the *Stavelot Triptych* to 1155–56, but believed its design was conceived as early as 1144–45, and that the execution was for some reason deferred or delayed.

[15] *Inventio Sanctae Crucis*, in Borgehammar, *How the Holy Cross Was Found*, p. 255; Holder, *Inventio Sanctae Crucis*, p. 1. This event is notably absent from Rufinus' supplement to the *Ecclesiastical History*, PL 21: 461–540.

them, one soldier carries a cross-topped banner out to the front, the LABARUM. Fleeing to the right are the enemy soldiers, led by Maxentius in the foreground, who turns to look back at Constantine and at the lance that is being driven into his back.[16]

One of the more distinctive features of this battle scene is the standard carried by Constantine's army.[17] The standard is not only topped by a cross, as instructed by the angel, but has attached to its staff a triple pennant or banner commonly found in scenes illustrating the crusades.[18] An almost identical banner is seen, for example, in a number of stained-glass roundels from the abbey church of St.-Denis, depicting the banner being carried by the French army at the battles of Nicaea and Ascalon in the First Crusade of 1096–99.[19] These windows may have been created during the abbacy of Suger (1122–51) in the 1140s,[20] or perhaps under his successor, Odo of Deuil (1151–62), just after the end of the Second Crusade.[21]

---

[16] Here the roundel represents a conflation of the two legends as found in Rufinus, *Historia ecclesiastica* PL 21: 461–540; *Inventio* in Borgehammar, *How the Holy Cross Was Found*, p. 255.

[17] For other examples of banners carried in battle scenes in manuscripts of the eleventh and twelfth centuries, see Stiennon, "La Personalité de Wibald de Stavelot," p. 74; Laura Hibbard Loomis, "The Oriflamme of France and the War-Cry 'Monjoie' in the Twelfth Century," in *Studies in Art and Literature for Belle da Costa Greene*, ed. Dorothy Miner (Princeton, 1954), pp. 78–81; Voelkle, *The Stavelot Triptych*, pp. 13–4.

[18] Loomis, "The Oriflamme of France," p. 67; Voelkle, *The Stavelot Triptych*, p. 14; Carl Erdmann, "Kaiserliche und päpstliche Fahnen im hohen Mittelalter," *Quellen und Forschungen aus italienischen Archiven und Bibliotheken* 25 (1933/34), pp. 33–42, for a discussion of the different types of flags and banners carried by the European armies during the First and Second Crusades.

[19] Elizabeth A.R. Brown and Michael W. Cothren, "The Twelfth-Century Crusading Window of the Abbey of Saint-Denis," *Journal of the Warburg and Courtauld Institutes* 49 (1986): 1–40; Fernand de Mély, "Notes et études archéologiques. La Croix des premiers croisés," in *Exuviae sacrae constantinopolitanae*, ed. Fernand de Mély (Paris, 1904) 3, pp. 1–11.

[20] The creation and commission of the windows are attributed to the abbacy of Suger by Collon-Gevaert, *Histoire des arts du métal*, p. 171; de Mély, "Notes et études archéologiques," p. 3; Stiennon, "La Personalité de Wibald de Stavelot," p. 74. Others, including Loomis, "The Oriflamme of France," p. 81 and Voelkle, *The Stavelot Triptych*, p. 14 are undecided on this point, but believe the windows date from the mid-twelfth century. Erwin Panofsky, *Abbot Suger on the Abbey Church of St.-Denis and its Art Treasures* (Princeton, 1979), p. 195, fn. 8, dated the windows to 1231–81 as they were not included among the works listed by Suger in his 1146–7 inventory. Two of the St.-Denis roundels are in the Glencairn Museum in Bryn Atheyn, PA; Brown and Cothren, "The Twelfth-Century Crusading Window," pp. 1–14; the rest are now lost, presumably destroyed during the French Revolution. Of these lost windows, twelve are known through a series of engravings by Benedictine monk and amateur historian, Bernard de Montfauçon, in *Les Monuments de la monarchie française* (Paris, 1729), 1, p. 389, plate L.

[21] Brown and Cothren, "The Twelfth-Century Crusading Window," pp. 28–38,

The inclusion of a cross banner in a battle scene is also closely
associated with the Holy Land in a Flemish prayer book dated to
1170–80. On the opening page of this manuscript,[22] the viewer is
presented with a schematic map of the city of Jerusalem in which
the holy places of the city, including Golgotha and the Lord's
Sepulcher, are clearly marked within the four quadrants. Below the
map, Sts. George and Demetrius, carrying shields emblazoned with
the cross, are seen charging to the right in pursuit of their enemies.
In this instance, the cross staff with the tri-partite banner is held by
St. George, who levels it at his fleeing enemy and uses its point to
pierce his back. Given that this scene illustrates a legendary vision
that occurred before the Battle of Jerusalem of 1099, the two saints
in effect represent the crusaders who, with the power of the cross,
are able to defeat their enemies and liberate the city. There are also
accounts of an actual relic of the True Cross being carried as a standard by the army that protected Jerusalem.[23]

The role of the True Cross in blessing and protecting troops was
widely accepted at this time and was particularly important in raising morale before a military action.[24] Between 1099 and 1187, a
relic of the Cross was elevated or carried into battle on no fewer
than thirty-one occasions in the Kingdom of Jerusalem.[25] In the west,
crusading expeditions included forays into Spain and eastern Europe
in which soldiers carried the cross banner and were blessed by a

---

argued for a 1158 date for the St.-Denis windows. Odo of Deuil was a likely candidate as he had accompanied King Louis VII (c. 1120–80) on the Second Crusade,
De profectione Ludovici in Orientem, ed. Virginia Gingerick Berry (New York, 1948).
   [22] Den Haag, Koninklijke Bibl., Ms. 75, F5, fol. 1r. Franz Niehoff, "Umbilicus
mundi—der Nabel der Welt. Jerusalem und das Heilige Grab im Spiegel von
Pilgerberichten und -Karten, Kreuzzügen und Reliquien," in *Ornamenta Ecclesiae.
Kunst und Künstler der Romanik*, ed. Anton Legner (Cologne, 1985), 3, pp. 53–72. This
type of cross banner also appears in a Mosan psalter fragment (Berlin, Kupferstich-
kabinett, 75 A6, fol. 1v), in a scene of Abraham Pursuing the Hostile Kings.
   [23] Anton Frolow, *La Relique de la Vraie Croix: Recherches sur le développement d'un culte*,
Archives de l'orient chrétien 7 (Paris, 1961), pp. 65–7, 75–6; Berent Schwineköper,
"Christus-Reliquien—Verehrung und Politik. Studien über die Mentalität der Menschen
des früheren Mittelalters, insbesondere über die religiöse Haltung und sakrale Stellung
der früh- und hochmittelalterlichen deutschen Kaiser und Könige," *Blätter für deutsche
Landesgeschichte* 117 (1981), pp. 197, 228, 279.
   [24] Alan V. Murray, "'Mighty Against the Enemies of Christ': The Relic of the
True Cross in the Armies of the Kingdom of Jerusalem," in *The Crusades and Their
Sources: Essays Presented to Bernard Hamilton* eds. John France and William G. Zajac
(Aldershot, UK, 1998), pp. 217–38.
   [25] Murray, "'Mighty Against the Enemies of Christ,'" Appendix, pp. 232–8.

relic of the wood.[26] In the record of the conquest of Lisbon of
1147–48, the *De expugnatione Lyxbonensi*, the Anglo-Norman and Flemish
troops first received a benediction from their priest, who instructed
them to:

> Adore Christ, the Lord, who on this wood of the saving cross spread
> out his hands and feet for your salvation and glory. Under this ban-
> ner, if only you falter not, you shall conquer.[27]

The use of the phrase "In hoc vexillo . . . vincetis" is a direct reference
to Constantine's vision of the cross in the sky, made more potent
here by the elevation of the relic above the heads of the soldiers.[28]
Abbot Suger of St.-Denis is also known to have described the cross
as a "banner of the eternal victory of Our Savior."[29]

It is Constantine's victory over Maxentius that, according to one
version of the legend, persuaded him to convert to Christianity and to
be baptized in 313, as represented in the top roundel of the triptych's
left wing.[30] According to Eusebius of Caesarea, Constantine was not
baptized until 337, when he was on his deathbed.[31] However, this is
not the version that is illustrated on the *Stavelot Triptych*, which follows
the *Inventio Sanctae Crucis*. Also according to the *Inventio*, Helena was
converted to Christianity in 315, following her son's baptism, and a
few years later was inspired to make a pilgrimage to the Holy Land
to find the True Cross.[32] Like Constantine, Helena was directed by

[26] Giles Constable, "The Second Crusade as Seen by Contemporaries," *Traditio*
9 (1953): 223–37. These crusades include those against the Slavs in eastern Europe
and against the Muslims in Spain, Portugal, and North Africa.

[27] *De Expugnatione Lyxbonensi: The Conquest of Lisbon*, ed. Charles Wendell David
(New York, 1936), pp. 154–7.

[28] Similarly, the phrase *Hoc signo vincitur inimicus* is inscribed on three jeweled
crosses (808–908) from northern Spain, discussed below. The phrase became the
motto of the Asturian kingdom. Helmut Schlunk, "The Crosses of Oviedo: A
Contribution to the History of Jewelry in Northern Spain in the Ninth and Tenth
Centuries," *Art Bulletin* 32 (1950), p. 148.

[29] Panofsky, *Abbot Suger on the Abbey Church of St.-Denis*, p. 57.

[30] Mombritius, *Prologus in vitam Sancti Silvestri*, p. 512, and the *Liber Pontificalis*,
1.174.; Samuel N.C. Lieu, "From History to Legend and Legend to History: The
Medieval and Byzantine Transformation of Constantine's *Vita*," in Samuel N.C.
Lieu and Dominic Montserrat, eds., *Constantine: History, Historiography and Legend*
(London, 1998), pp. 138–44.

[31] For a discussion of the baptism of Constantine, see Timothy Barnes, *Constantine
and Eusebius* (Cambridge, MA, 1981), pp. 259–60; Thomas George Elliott, *The
Christianity of Constantine the Great* (Scranton, 1996), p. 325.

[32] *Inventio Sanctae Crucis*, in Borgehammar, *How the Holy Cross Was Found*, pp. 257–8;
Holder, *Inventio Sanctae Crucis*, pp. 2–3; Rufinus, *Historia ecclesiastica* 1.7, *PL* 21: 475–6.

a heavenly sign, described by Rufinus as a series of visions.[33] She was by this time an elderly woman and undertook her pilgrimage around the year 326, shortly before her death.[34]

In the first of the Helena series on the *Stavelot Triptych*, the bottom roundel shows her interrogation of the Jews in an attempt to locate the burial place of the True Cross. Helena is here identified as a queen, and the banderole she holds in her left hand records her demand to be told the location of the True Cross: OSTENDITE LIGNUM. Threatened with fire, the group of Jews point to Judas as the one who knows the site (JUDAS NOVIT).[35]

The center right roundel shows Helena supervising the digging for the True Cross on Mt. Golgotha. Below the pickaxe, and presumably just revealed by it, is a green enamel cross, complete with titulus and identified as the concealed wood of the Lord: LIGNU[M] D[OMI]NI ABSCONDITU[M]. Behind Judas are two assistants, represented bust-length and holding the crosses of the two thieves, the PATIBULA DUO[RUM] LAT[RO]NU[M].[36]

In the third and final roundel, the three crosses found on Calvary are tested over the body of a man, recently deceased, who is miraculously brought back to life when touched by the genuine wood of the Cross. Behind the bishop is Helena, as S[ANCTA] rather than REGINA, wears a more elaborate, two-tiered crown. At the right, an assistant carries away the two crosses of the thieves, already tested and proven to be false.[37]

A direct link between the *Stavelot Triptych* and the sites of the Holy Land is further established by the presence on the central panel of two small Byzantine triptychs that display relics of the Holy Nail and the True Cross. Most likely made in Constantinople, these triptychs have been dated to the late eleventh or early twelfth century.[38]

---

[33] Rufinus, *Historica ecclesiastica* 1.7, *PL* 2: 475–6.

[34] Borgehammar, *How the Holy Cross Was Found*, pp. 133–9; Drijvers, *Helena Augusta*, pp. 55–72; E.D. Hunt, *Holy Land Pilgrimage in the Later Roman Empire, AD 312–460* (Oxford, 1982), pp. 29–30.

[35] The source for this scene is the *Inventio*, in Borgehammar, *How the Holy Cross Was Found*, p. 263.

[36] The sources are the *Inventio*, in Borgehammar, *How the Holy Cross Was Found*, p. 263; John Chrysostom, *In Iohannem. Homiliae*, *PG* 59: 491; Ambrose, *De obitu Theodosii*, *Corpus scriptorum ecclesiasticorum latinorum* 73, pp. 394–7.

[37] *Inventio*, in Borgehammar, *How the Holy Cross Was Found*, p. 267.

[38] Voelkle, *The Stavelot Triptych*, p. 20; Jacqueline Lafontaine-Dosogne, "L'Art

On each, the square, gold frame around the central enamel is of Mosan origin, presumably dating to the time of the larger triptych's assembly at Stavelot in the mid-twelfth century.[39] The larger of the two small triptychs, containing the visible relic of the Cross, also presents the standing figures of Constantine and Helena.

These Byzantine reliquaries, which presumably occasioned the creation of the *Stavelot Triptych*, are generally thought to have been brought back to the west by Abbot Wibald of Stavelot (1130–58).[40] Although there is no documentary evidence regarding the reliquaries themselves, Wibald is known to have undertaken two diplomatic missions to Constantinople, in 1155–56 and in 1157–58, on behalf of Frederick I Barbarossa (*c.* 1123–90) to arrange a marriage between the emperor and the niece of the Byzantine emperor, Manuel Comnenus,[41] or for Wibald to negotiate an alliance between Frederick I and Manuel against their common enemy, Roger II of Sicily.[42] In both cases, the trips show the active contact between the rulers of east and west, contact which helped to keep trade and pilgrimage routes open until the early thirteenth century.

On the *Stavelot Triptych*, the relics of the smaller of the two Byzantine triptychs are not visible, but instead are preserved in a cavity in a small pouch made out of Byzantine silk.[43] Inside the pouch is a splinter of wood, a small amount of dust, and a scrap of white silk. These items are identified by twelfth-century parchment authentifications as relics of the True Cross, earth from the Holy Land, and a piece of the robe of the Virgin.[44] The relic of the Holy Nail is partially visible on the crucifixion enamel, protruding from the base of the cross directly below Christ's feet.

---

byzantin en Belgique en relation avec les Croisades," *Revue Belge d'archéologie et d'histoire de l'art* 56 (1987), p. 17; Collon-Gevaert, *Histoire des arts du métal*, pp. 169–70.

[39] Voelkle, *The Stavelot Triptych*, p. 20; Brodsky, "The Stavelot Triptych," p. 27; Verdier, "Émaux mosans," p. 10.

[40] Brodsky, "The Stavelot Triptych," p. 31; Deér, "Die Siegel Kaiser Friedrichs I. Barbarossa," p. 75; Otto von Falke and Heinrich Frauberger, *Deutsche Schmelzarbeiten des Mittelalters und andere Kunstwerke der Kunsthistorischen Ausstellung zu Düsseldorf, 1902* (Frankfurt, 1904), p. 67; Lafontaine-Dosogne, "L'Art byzantin en Belgique," p. 16; Verdier, "Émaux mosans," p. 11; Voelkle, *The Stavelot Triptych*, pp. 10–1.

[41] Voelkle, *The Stavelot Triptych*, p. 10.

[42] Lafontaine-Dosogne, "L'Art byzantin en Belgique," p. 16; Stiennon, "La Personalité de Wibald de Stavelot," p. 49.

[43] Voelkle, *The Stavelot Triptych*, pp. 19–23.

[44] The strips of parchment with their Latin inscriptions are reproduced in Voelkle, *The Stavelot Triptych*, fig. 43, pp. 19–23.

Episodes from the legends of Constantine and Helena are also seen on other twelfth-century reliquaries, such as the rectangular 1180 *Tongres Triptych* of the True Cross.[45] Engraved on its wings are two episodes from the discovery of the Cross, the first showing Helena seated before a fire and questioning the Jews, led by Judas, while the second shows Helena directing Judas and an assistant as they dig with pickaxes and reveal the buried cross. Scenes from the legend of Helena also appear on plaques from a twelfth-century Mosan cross, now in Berlin,[46] and on a quadrilobed reliquary from Tournai.[47] Scenes from the legend of Helena are particularly appropriate for these reliquaries, created to house pieces of the Cross that had been found by the queen in the Holy Land.

Pilgrimage and Cross Reliquaries

On one Cross reliquary, a late twelfth-century casket from St.-Sernin in Toulouse,[48] (fig. 170) the successful acquisition of a relic is illustrated on its enameled sides. The location is described as (H)IER(USA)L(E)M, and on one end is a scene of Helena instructing Judas to dig for the True Cross. The front shows events that took place in the twelfth century, beginning with Abbot Jean of Josephat (near Jerusalem)

---

[45] Treasury of Notre-Dame, Tongres. Dietrich Kötzsche, "Zum Stand der Forschung der Goldschmiedekunst im Rhein-Maas-Gebiet," in *Rhein und Maas*, 2, p. 213. The *Tongres Triptych* is dated to *c.* 1170 by Hanns Swarzenski, *Monuments of Romanesque Art*, 2nd ed. (Chicago, 1974), p. 73, and by Joseph de Borchgrave d'Altena, "Le Triptyque reliquaire de la Vraie Croix de Notre-Dame à Tongres," *Chronique archéologique du Pays de Liège* (1925), pp. 43–9.

[46] Kunstgewerbemuseum, Berlin. Reproduced in *Rhein und Maas*, 2, p. 212; Stratford, *Catalogue of Medieval Enamels*, pp. 68–72.

[47] This reliquary, missing since 1882, can be seen in M.D.A. van Bastelaer, "Étude sur un reliquaire-phylactère du XIIe siècle," *Annales de l'Académie royale d'Archéologie* 6 (1880), pp. 32–52; Stratford, *Catalogue of Medieval Enamels*, p. 74.

[48] For the Toulouse reliquary, see Barbara Drake Boehm, in *Enamels of Limoges: 1100–1350*, ed. John P. O'Neill (New York, 1996), no. 40, pp. 165–7; Gauthier, *Émaux du moyen âge*, no. 62, p. 337; *Ornamenta Ecclesiae* 3, no. H15, p. 95. Boehm and Gauthier dated the reliquary to the late twelfth century, and Gauthier noted that it may originally have been intended to serve as a Eucharistic vessel. This might explain why it was not included in a treasury inventory of 1246, an omission that has led some scholars to date the casket later than the mid-thirteenth century. These scholars include Frolow, *La Relique*, no. 546, and Celestin Douais, "Deux Reliquaires de l'église Saint-Sernin à Toulouse," *Revue de l'Art chrétien* 38 (1888), p. 165.

handing a cross to a man identified as Raymond Botardelli, a monk
and scribe of the Abbey of St.-Sernin who reportedly traveled to the
Holy Land to acquire a relic of the True Cross for the monastery.
He is seen getting into a boat at the right, and on the back of the
casket he kneels before Abbot Pons (1176–98) and presents him with
a cross.

The reliquary created for this piece of the Cross would have joined
other treasures in St.-Sernin of Toulouse, itself an important stop on
the pilgrimage route from Arles to Santiago de Compostela.[49] The
growing number of pilgrims visiting the town necessitated an expansion of the church that began in the late eleventh century and was
nearly completed by 1118.[50] By 1200, the church boasted a large
number of relics for pilgrims to view,[51] among them undoubtedly
the enameled casket with the piece of the wood from Jerusalem.

Given that relics of the Cross are closely tied to the sites of the
Holy Land, it follows naturally that devout Christians living in parts
of western Europe, like the monk from Toulouse, would want to see
these sites with their own eyes and bring back, if possible, one or
more relics. Pilgrimage to Jerusalem is documented as early as the
fourth century, when the nun (or pious noblewoman) Egeria traveled
to the Holy Land and witnessed in 384 the elevation of the True
Cross as part of the Good Friday celebration.[52] As described in her
letters, some of which have survived,[53] the ceremony began with a
procession in which Bishop Cyril of Jerusalem was escorted from
Gethsemane to the gates of Jerusalem, on through the city, and up
to Golgotha. At this site, a few hours later, a chair was placed for the
bishop in front of a table upon which was set a reliquary of the Cross.
The reliquary took the form of a gold and silver box containing a

---

[49] Annie Shaver-Crandell, Paula Gerson, and Alison Stones, *The Pilgrim's Guide to Santiago de Compostela: A Gazetteer* (London, 1995), pp. 357–73; William Melczer, *The Pilgrim's Guide to Santiago de Compostela* (New York, 1993).

[50] Shaver-Crandell, *et al.*, *The Pilgrim's Guide*, pp. 360–6; Henri Pradalier, "Saint-Sernin médiévale," in *Saint-Sernin de Toulouse: trésors et métamorphoses. Deux siècles de restauration 1802–1989* (Toulouse, 1989), pp. 25–34.

[51] Shaver-Crandell, *et al.*, *The Pilgrim's Guide*, p. 360; Marcel Durliat, *Saint-Sernin de Toulouse* (Toulouse, 1986).

[52] Egeria, *Itinerarium seu peregrinatio ad loca sancta*, ed. Hélène Pétré, *Sources chréti-ennes* 21 (Paris, 1948), pp. 232–7. Egeria may have come from Aquitaine, or north-western Spain. Hunt, *Holy Land Pilgrimage*, pp. 115–24, 164; John Wilkinson, *Egeria's Travels*, 3rd ed. (Warminster, 1999), pp. 1–3.

[53] Wilkinson, *Egeria's Travels*, pp. 1–3.

piece of the wood and the titulus, which were taken out and placed in front of the bishop.[54] He then held the relic while the assembled people approached one by one to touch the wood with their foreheads and eyes and to kiss it, not touching it with their hands.

An echo of the ceremony at Jerusalem is found in the veneration of the Cross at Constantinople during the last three days of Holy Week, also witnessed by western pilgrims. One account is that of a Gallic bishop named Arculf, whose recital of his travels in the Holy Land was recorded by Abbot Adamnanus of Iona (c. 627–704) following the bishop's return in 682.[55] In his *De locis sanctis*, Adamnanus set down Arculf's description of a wooden box containing three pieces of the Cross normally kept in a large chest in the church of Hagia Sophia, which, for the last three days of the Passion week, was placed open upon a golden altar.[56] On the Thursday of the Last Supper the largest and most significant relic of the Cross was kissed and venerated by the emperor and the soldiers, and, on the following day, Good Friday, by the imperial ladies and all of the women of the city. On Easter Sunday, the relic was kissed by the bishop and the clergy, after which the chest was closed and returned to its customary place in the northern repository of the church.[57]

These ceremonies not only influenced Good Friday rituals and ceremonies in the west, but apparently fostered the desire for churches to have their own relic of the Cross. This often proved to be a difficult task, as in 614 the True Cross of Jerusalem was seized as war booty by the conquering Persians.[58] A few years later, the Byzantine emperor Heraclius (602–41) managed to defeat the Persian king, Chosroes II (590–628), and returned the relic to the city in 628 at the head of a victorious procession. This victory, though, was

---

[54] Egeria, *Itinerarium*, pp. 232–4.

[55] Adamnanus, *De locis sanctis*, ed. D. Meehan, *Scriptores Latini Hiberniae*, III (Dublin 1983), pp. 9–11. Bishop Arculf presumably made his trip to the Holy Land between 679–88. John Wilkinson, *Jerusalem Pilgrims Before the Crusades*, pp. 9–10.

[56] Adamnanus, *De locis sanctis*, pp. 108–11.

[57] By the tenth century, the True Cross relics had been moved from Hagia Sophia to the treasury of the Imperial Palace. René Bornert, "La Célébration de la Sainte Croix dans le rite byzantin," *La Maison-Dieu* 75 (1963), p. 99; Frolow, *La Relique*, p. 76. In 1148, Odo of Deuil refered to holy relics being kept in a chapel of the Imperial Palace, *De profectione Ludovici in Orientem*, ed. Virginia Gingerick Berry (New York, 1948), p. 62.

[58] Jounel, "Le Culte de la Croix," p. 76; Anton Frolow, "La Vraie Croix et les expéditions d'Héraclius en Perse," *Revue des Études byzantines* 11 (1953), pp. 93–100.

short-lived, as in 635 the relic of the True Cross had to be transferred to Constantinople for safe-keeping.[59] Two years later, Jerusalem fell again to the Persian army.

In the eleventh century, the deeds of Emperor Heraclius became connected with the crusades to the Holy Land, and by 1119 Fulcher of Chartres, in his *Historia Hierosolymitana*, was moved to compare the Franks' triumphant entry into Jerusalem carrying the recovered Cross to that of Heraclius, five centuries earlier.[60] The association of Heraclius with pilgrimage and crusading is indeed a natural one, as in the minds of the western chroniclers both accounts share the elements of military victory over the Persians and the recovery of the precious relics of the Holy Land. Heraclius is also the protagonist in Honorius of Autun's twelfth-century sermon, *De exaltatione Sanctae Crucis*, in which the triumphant return of the True Cross to Jerusalem is accompanied by many miraculous cures.[61] The acts of Heraclius were at that time depicted on several crosses and reliquaries, and on one of these, a Mosan enamel cross (1160–70),[62] the scenes include Heraclius beheading Chosroes and then carrying the Cross into Jerusalem like a humble pilgrim.

Jeweled Crosses

Heraclius and Constantine are also associated with the True Cross through the shape of the most common form of reliquary to emerge in this period, the *crux gemmata*, or jeweled cross. These crosses were often associated with royalty, like the *Lothar Cross* of Otto III (Aachen, Cathedral Treasury),[63] *c.* 1000, and the early eleventh-century crosses

---

[59] Frolow, *La Relique*, p. 66.

[60] Fulcher of Chartres, *Historia Hierosolymitana* 3.6, ed. Heinrich Hagenmeyer, in *Fulcheri Carnotensis: Historia Hierosolymitana (1095–1127)*, (Heidelberg, 1913), pp. 632–3.

[61] Honorius of Autun, *Liturgica: Speculum ecclesiae, PL* 172: 1004–6.

[62] The plaques of this cross are divided among several collections, but a reconstruction is reproduced in *Rhein und Maas* 2, fig. 23, p. 209 and in Stratford, *Catalogue of Medieval Enamel*, cat. no. 4, pp. 68–77. Heraclius also appears on the *Tongres Triptych*, and on horseback, holding aloft the cross enclosed in an initial of the *Stuttgart Passional* (Stuttgart, Landesbibliothek, Cod. 56, fol. 90v), reproduced in Albert Boeckler, *Das Stuttgarter Passionale* (Augsburg, 1923), fig. 87.

[63] Percy Ernst Schramm and Florentine Mütherich, *Denkmale der deutschen Könige und Kaiser* 1 (Munich, 1962–78), no. 106; Peter Lasko, *Ars Sacra: 800–1200* (New Haven, 1994), p. 101.

of Queen Gisela, wife of Conrad II.[64] Abbesses with royal ties also commissioned jeweled crosses, among them Abbesses Mathilde († 1101) and Theophanu († 1056) in Essen.[65] Abbot Suger of the royal monastery of St.-Denis commissioned a magnificent cross and documented his difficulties in finding enough precious stones to complete the work.[66] In the end, through the miracle of a group of monks arriving with more gems to sell, he was able to amass "a great and expensive supply of other gems and large pearls" for the cross.[67]

This type of jeweled or royal cross also served as a symbol of triumph and military victory beginning with the conversion of Constantine, when the cross became part of the royal insignia used on the emperor's shields and on the Arch of Constantine in Rome. The association of victory with a jeweled cross is made clear on the famed Imperial Cross, completed under Conrad II (c. 990–1039) and now preserved in Vienna.[68] On this cross, which is covered with precious stones, the inscription echoes Constantine's use of the cross on his army's shields: *Ecce crucem Domini/fugiat pars hostis iniqui* (Behold the cross of the Lord/flee, enemy forces).[69] Even earlier, three jeweled crosses from northern Spain were inscribed with verses that named their royal patrons and extolled the crosses' ability to defeat all enemies. The first of these is the Cross of Angels, 808, and the second the Cross of Santiago, 874 (missing since 1906), both made for Alfonso II (791–842).[70] The third, the Cross of Victory, 908, was made for Alfonso III (866–910).[71] Each of these crosses bears the inscription: *Hoc signo vincitur inimicus* (Under this sign the enemy is defeated).[72] As a group, the crosses signify both the power of Christ in heaven and the rulers' indisputable power on earth.

---

[64] Schramm and Mütherich, *Denkmale*, no. 143; Lasko, *Ars Sacra*, p. 135.

[65] Schramm and Mütherich, *Denkmale*, nos. 43–6; Lasko, *Ars Sacra*, pp. 101–2, 136–7.

[66] Panofsky, *Abbot Suger*, p. 57.

[67] Panofsky, *Abbot Suger*, p. 59.

[68] Schatzkammer, Vienna. Hermann Fillitz, *Die Schatzkammer in Wien: Symbole Abendländischen Kaisertums* (Salzburg, 1986), pp. 166–7; Schramm and Mütherich, *Denkmale*, no. 145.

[69] Hermann Fillitz, *Die Insignien und Kleinodien des Heiligen Römischen Reiches* (Vienna, 1954), pp. 21–2.

[70] Cámara Santa, Oviedo Cathedral. Schlunk, "The Crosses of Oviedo," pp. 114–8; *The Art of Medieval Spain, A.D. 500–1200*, ed. John P. O'Neill (New York, 1993), pp. 146–8.

[71] Cámara Santa, Oviedo Cathedral. Schlunk, "The Crosses of Oviedo," pp. 117–8.

[72] Schlunk, "The Crosses of Oviedo," pp. 94, 100, 102.

Jeweled crosses, including the Imperial Cross, may have been inspired by Constantine's placement of a large elaborate cross on top of Mt. Golgotha to commemorate the crucifixion. According to written accounts, a large cross, covered in gold and precious stones, was set up under a protective ciborium on the rocks of Golgotha, where it served as a station of the cross between the Anastasius and the Martyrium.[73] In the next century, Theodosius II (400–50) donated a large cross ornamented with semi-precious stones.[74] The general appearance of the cross on the hill is reflected in an early fifth-century mosaic in the apse of S. Pudenziana in Rome, in which a jeweled cross is shown upon a mound of earth in the center of the cityscape of the heavenly Jerusalem.[75]

The cross, jeweled or not, is ultimately the sign of Christ, the king of heaven and earth whose second coming will be heralded by the "sign of the Son of man" appearing in the heavens (Matthew 24, 30–1). Cyril of Jerusalem, for one, described the cross in the sky as preceding Christ just as a trophy precedes a king,[76] while Augustine of Hippo referred to the cross as a royal insignia and a triumphant banner.[77] In the ninth-century writings of Rabanus Maurus, the cross is a military standard and an incorruptible scepter held by Christ, who is a king ruling over the whole world as well as a most holy and merciful emperor.[78] In the twelfth century, perhaps in a reference to Jerusalem, Honorius of Autun described the cross as a sign of the King set up in the house of God as if it were planted in a splendid, royal city.[79]

---

[73] Philippe Verdier, "Les Staurothèques mosanes et leur iconographie du Jugement dernier," *Cahiers de civilisation médiévale, X^e–XIIIe siècles* 16/2 (1973), p. 101.

[74] Adamnanus, in his late seventh-century account of Arculf's journey, described a large silver cross of silver (*magna argentea crux*) erected upon the site of the crucifixion inside the Church of Golgotha. Adamnanus, *De libri tres de locis sanctis*, pp. 48–9. This silver cross probably replaced the golden, jeweled cross erected by Theodosius II, presumably looted by the Persians in 614. Wilkinson, *Jerusalem Pilgrims Before the Crusades*, p. 97, fn. 15.

[75] For a reproduction of this mosaic, see Andrea Augenti, ed., *Art and Archaeology of Rome: From Ancient Times to the Baroque* (New York, 2000), p. 70; Joseph Wilpert, *Die Römischen Mosaiken und Malereien der kirchlichen Bauten vom IV. bis XIII. Jahrhundert*, 2nd ed. (Freiburg im Breisgau, 1917), 3, pls. 42–4.

[76] Cyril of Jerusalem, *Catechesis. De Christo Crucifixo et Sepulto, PG* 33: 821–2.

[77] Augustine, *Sermo CLV. De Passioni Domini, VI; seu de Cruce et Latrone, PL* 39: 2051–2.

[78] Rabanus Maurus, *De Laudibus Sanctae Crucis, PL* 107: 143–4.

[79] Honorius of Autun, *Gemma animae, sive de divinis officiis* 3.135, *PL* 172: 587.

The equal significance of a jeweled cross as a symbol of Christ's triumphant resurrection is reinforced in cases where the cross also contains a relic of the wood from the crucifixion. There are dozens of examples of jeweled reliquary crosses from the eleventh and twelfth centuries, a time when the number of Cross relics brought back to the west started to increase dramatically, as shown in Anton Frolow's graph documenting the evidence up to the fourteenth century.[80] The very shape of a Byzantine relic of the wood, which usually had two transverse arms, inspired the creation in the west of a number of jeweled crosses that also had a double-transverse shape.[81]

In crosses like that of Hildesheim,[82] (fig. 171) relics of the wood are located under crystal cabochons surrounded by gold and semi-precious stones, thus uniting the elements of earthly glory with Christ's triumphant victory over death. The *Hildesheim Cross* dates to 1130–40,[83] but was formerly thought to have been commissioned earlier by Bishop Bernward (993–1022) to display three Cross relics he had received from Otto III.[84] Bernward had not made a pilgrimage to Jerusalem, nor did he after the gift was received. Instead, he went to France in 1007 to obtain more relics of the Cross, as well as those of the Virgin and twelve saints.[85] Frolow's account makes clear that relics were available in various parts of western Europe, and that the desire to obtain a relic of the True Cross did not necessitate a hazardous trip to Jerusalem.

---

[80] Frolow, *La Relique*, p. 111.

[81] Double-transverse crosses of western origin include those in Aachen (St. Johann Baptist, Aachen-Burtscheid), Tournai (Cathédrale Notre-Dame), and Limoges (Trésors de la collégiale St.-Etienne, Eymoutiers). On the Aachen and Tournai crosses, see *Ornamenta Ecclesiae*, 3, nos. H31, H35; for the Limoges cross, see Marie-Madeleine Gauthier, *Les Routes de la foi: reliques et reliquaires de Jérusalem à Compostelle* (Fribourg, 1983), pp. 74–5.

[82] Frolow, *La Relique*, nos. 154, 270; Victor Heinrich Elbern, *Dom und Domschatz in Hildesheim* (Königstein im Taunus, 1979), p. 70.

[83] Frolow, *La Relique*, nos. 154, 270; Elbern, *Dom und Domschatz in Hildesheim*, p. 70.

[84] This event is recorded in Thangmar, *Vita Bernwardi, Episcopi Hildesheimensis*, in *Monumenta Germaniae Historica, Scriptores*, ed. Georg Heinrich Pertz (Hannover, 1826), 4, p. 762; Joseph Braun, *Die Reliquiare des christlichen Kultes und ihre Entwicklung* (Freiburg im Breisgau, 1940), p. 461; Swarzenski, *Monuments of Romanesque Art*, no. 34.

[85] Frolow, *La Relique*, no. 189.

Cross Reliquaries in the Twelfth Century

By the end of the eleventh century, pilgrims' access to the Holy Land, and the liberation of Jerusalem in particular, were the main motives for the crusades, and especially for the First Crusade. On November 27, 1095, Pope Urban II preached a sermon at the Council of Clermont calling for a crusade to the East in which the liberation of Jerusalem was the main topic,[86] a theme that was reinforced in the writings of Fulcher of Chartres (*c.* 1058–1127), Raymond of Aguilers (active 1095–1102), and Guibert of Nogent (*c.* 1053–1124),[87] as well as in the anonymous *Gesta Francorum et aliorum Hierosolimitanorum* (1095–1100).[88] The freeing of Jerusalem is mentioned in the earliest pages of the *Gesta Francorum*, and noblemen are described there as being moved to sew the sign of the cross onto their clothing and to take up arms against the "pagans" and "unbelievers."[89]

The liberation of Jerusalem was again urged by Pope Eugenius III in his call for a Second Crusade on December 1, 1145.[90] On this day he issued the bull *Quantum predecessores*, which was subsequently emended and reissued in 1146, at which time it was widely distributed throughout western Europe.[91] In the bull, Eugenius III refers to his great distress over the "abandonment of the eastern Church," and calls for its liberation from the "multitude of the

---

[86] This sermon is recorded in Fulcher of Chartres, *Historia Hierosolymitana* 1.132–8; Herbert E.J. Cowdrey, "Pope Urban II's Preaching of the First Crusade," *History: Journal of the Historical Association* 55 (1970): 177–88; Louise and Jonathan Riley-Smith, *The Crusades: Idea and Reality, 1095–1274* (London, 1981), pp. 40–3.

[87] Raymond of Aguilers, *Historia Francorum qui ceperunt Jerusalem*, PL 155: 591–668; Guibert of Nogent, *Gesta Dei per Francos*, ed. Lucas d'Achery, PL 156: 679–838; Robert of Reims, *Historia Hierosolymitana*, PL 155: 667–758.

[88] *Gesta Francorum et aliorum Hierosolimitanorum. The Deeds of the Franks and Other Pilgrims to Jerusalem*, ed. Rosalind Hill (London, 1962), pp. 1–103.

[89] *Gesta Francorum*, pp. 2, 7, 31, 81.

[90] The *Quantum predecessores* is found in Eugenius III, *Epistolae et privilegia*, XLVIII, "Ad Ludovicum regem Galliarum—De expeditione in Terram Sanctam suscipienda," *PL* 180: 1064–6, Erich Caspar, "Die Kreuzigungsbullen Eugens III," *Neues Archiv* 45 (1924), pp. 302–5. See also Constable, "The Second Crusade," pp. 248–54; Louise and Jonathan Riley-Smith, *The Crusades*, pp. 57–9; John Gordon Rowe, "The Origins of the Second Crusade: Pope Eugenius III, Bernard of Clairvaux and Louis VII of France," in *The Second Crusade and the Cistercians*, ed. Michael Gervers (New York, 1992), pp. 79–89.

[91] Constable, "The Second Crusade," pp. 254, 260–1; Caspar, "Die Kreuzzugsbullen," pp. 285–301. The bull is mentioned in *Gesta abbatum Lobbiensium, MGH Scriptores*, 21: 329, under the years 1142–47.

infidels" who are rejoicing at the defeat of the Christians.[92] The fall of Edessa in 1144 is cited as well, alongside the ever-present desire to liberate the Holy Sepulcher.[93]

The cause of Eugenius III was eloquently promoted by Bernard of Clairvaux (c. 1090–1153) in the 1140s in a number of sermons and letters delivered throughout Burgundy, Flanders, and England. Bernard's preaching in Lotharingia (Belgium) is mentioned in the *Gesta abbatum* of Lobbes for 1142–47, where the call for the crusade is described as a call for pilgrimage and for "the avenging of Christianity."[94] In a letter of 1146 sent to the eastern Franks, Bernard further exhorts the people to "take the sign of the cross," as through their decision to do battle for Christ they would "obtain in equal measure remission of all the sins" which they had confessed with contrite hearts.[95] Undertaken that year, the Second Crusade was led by, among others, Louis VII of France and Conrad III of Germany, with a large number of clergy also taking part, including the bishops of Arras, Langres, Metz, and Toul.[96]

The relics of the True Cross that were brought back to the west in this period were housed in a wide variety of reliquaries, their forms no longer dominated by the jeweled altar or processional cross. In the Mosan region, these often took the shape of triptychs, like that of Stavelot, with variations in iconography and subject matter. On two triptychs in Paris (1160–70),[97] angels present the relic of the

---

[92] *Quantum predecessores, PL* 180: 1064–5.

[93] *Quantum predecessores, PL* 180: 1064; Constable, "The Second Crusade," pp. 248–9. The fall of Edessa is mentioned by Odo of Deuil, *De profectione Ludovici VII in orientem*, p. 7, as being the key theme of the Bishop of Langres' sermon at the assembly at Vézelay in 1146, which was attended by King Louis VII.

[94] *Gesta abbatum Lobbiensium, MGH Scriptores*, 21: 329, under the years 1142–47. See also Ernest Oscar Blake, "The Formation of the 'Crusade' Idea," *Journal of Ecclesiastical History* 21 (1970), pp. 28–31; Adriaan H. Bredero, "Studien zu den Kreuzzugsbriefen Bernhards von Clairvaux und seiner Reise nach Deutschland im Jahre 1146," *Mitteilungen des Instituts für Österreichische Geschichtsforschung* 66 (1958), pp. 331–3; Rowe, "The Origins of the Second Crusade," pp. 79–89.

[95] Bernard of Clairvaux, *Epistolae: Epistola CCCLXIII, PL* 182: 564–8.

[96] Otto of Freising, *Gesta Friderici I. Imperatoris, MGH, Scriptores rerum Merovingicarum* ed. Georg Waitz (Berlin, 1920), 14, pp. 88–9; Jonathan Riley-Smith, "Family Traditions and Participation in the Second Crusade," in *The Second Crusade and the Cistercians*, ed. Michael Gervers (New York, 1992), pp. 101–8.

[97] Petit Palais, Paris. These two reliquaries are known as the *Dutuit Triptychs* after a previous owner. Frolow, *La Relique*, p. 355; Gauthier, *Émaux du moyen âge*, p. 347; Verdier, "Les Staurothèques mosanes," p. 111. For later additions and alterations to the medieval objects, see Stratford, *Catalogue of Medieval Enamels*, pp. 199–210.

Cross on the central panel, with busts of apostles depicted on the wings. Two flanking angels are also present on the *Sainte-Croix Triptych* in Liège,[98] where they are identified as the personified virtues of Truth and Judgment. This reliquary may have an imperial connection, as in 1006 Henry II (973–1024) gave several relics of the Cross to Bishop Notger of Liège and his newly-founded church of Ste.-Croix, for which this triptych was later made.[99]

The role of personified virtues is expanded on the delicate, enameled *Guennol Triptych* at the Cloisters, New York,[100] where the angels flanking the cross are also identified as Truth and Judgment. These are now accompanied by the virtues of Mercy, Piety, Good Works, and Prayer, as well as by a prominent figure of Justice with her scales. The theme of just judgment is made clear on this triptych by the presence of Christ at the top, and by the scenes on the wings showing angels blowing trumpets and raising the dead from their graves. The allegorical figures here embody the highest Christian virtues that will be weighed in the balance at the time of the Last Judgment. The relic of the True Cross at the center of the composition is not only a relic from the Holy Land, but also a sign that virtuous believers will receive the rewards of salvation made possible by the sacrifice of Christ upon the cross.

Personified virtues were used to enhance other Cross reliquaries from the Mosan region, including a phylactery in the Cleveland Museum of Art[101] and an enameled cross in the Walters Art Museum,

---

[98] Musée d'Art religieux et d'Art Mosan, Liège. *Rhein und Maas*, 1, no. G5; *Ornamenta Ecclesiae*, 3, no. H36; *Trésors du Musée d'Arts réligieux et mosan de Liège*, eds. Albert Lemeunier *et al.* (Paris, 1985), no. 9; Verdier, "Les Staurothèques mosanes," pp. 105–9.

[99] The small cross containing the relics was made in the late tenth century, and is seen at the center of the twelfth-century triptych. Henry II is believed to have received the relics as a gift from the French king Robert II. Frolow, *La Relique*, no. 185; *Le Temps des Croisades*, ed. Crédit Communal (Brussels, 1996), p. 99; and Hiltrud Westermann-Angerhausen, "Das ottonische Kreuzreliquiar im Reliquientriptychon von Ste. Croix in Lüttich," *Wallraf-Richartz-Jahrbuch* 36 (1974), pp. 7–22.

[100] Anonymous Loan, The Cloisters, The Metropolitan Museum of Art, NY. Gauthier, *Émaux du moyen âge*, no. 93; William S. Monroe, "The Guennol Triptych and the Twelfth-Century Revival of Jurisprudence," in *The Cloisters: Studies in Honor of the Fiftieth Anniversary*, ed. Elizabeth C. Parker (New York, 1992), pp. 167–77; *Ornamenta Ecclesiae*, 1, p. 121; Verdier, "Les Staurothèques mosanes," pp. 115–7; Voelkle, *The Stavelot Triptych*, no. 11.

[101] *Rhein und Maas*, 2, p. 211. Other Mosan works with busts or figures of personified virtues include a gable-end *Reliquary of St. Gondulphe* in the Musées royaux, Brussels, and the cover of the *Notger Gospels* in the Musée Curtius, Liège. *Rhein und Maas*, 1,

Baltimore.[102] On the cross, (fig. 172) the figure of the crucified Christ
is at the center, with a chalice placed below to catch his blood and
the hand of God appearing above. On the four cross ends are winged,
personified virtues with their attributes (top, clockwise): Hope (SPES),
holding the Eucharistic bread and chalice; Faith (FIDES) with a baptismal font; Obedience (OBEDIENTIA) with a cross; and Innocence
(INNOCENTIA) holding a lamb. Obedience is seen here presenting a cross-shaped cavity that once held the relic of the Cross.

The association of personified virtues with the cross is first suggested by a passage in St. Paul's letter to the Ephesians, in which
the four dimensions of love are metaphorically divided into four
directions:

> That Christ may dwell by faith in your hearts; that being rooted and
> founded in charity, you may be able to comprehend, with all the saints,
> what is the breadth, and length, and height, and depth. (Ephesians 3,
> 17–8)

This passage is then interpreted by Augustine as a reference to the
four arms, or dimensions, of the cross, where the horizontal arms
represent Good Works and Perseverance, the height Hope, and the
depth Grace.[103]

The virtues associated with the arms of the cross are not fixed,
however, nor limited to the four mentioned by Augustine, but instead
vary with each individual interpretation of the biblical passage.
Rabanus Maurus, for example, associates the four directions of the
cross with the four cardinal virtues of Justice, Fortitude, Temperance,
and Prudence.[104] For Bernard of Clairvaux, the virtues of the cross
are all derived from Humility:

> Indeed, these virtues are gems which adorn the four ends of the Cross:
> at the top is Charity; at the right, Obedience; at the left, Patience;
> and, at the bottom, Humility, the root of all virtues.[105]

---

nos. G9, G19. For personified virtues in general, see Adolf Katzenellenbogen, *Allegories
of the Virtues and Vices in Medieval Art from the Early Christian Times to the Thirteenth
Century* (New York, 1964).

[102] Brodsky, "The Stavelot Triptych," pp. 113–4; Verdier, "Un Monument inédit
de l'art mosan du XIIᵉ siècle: la crucifixion symbolique de Walters Art Gallery,"
Revue belge d'archéologie et d'histoire de l'art 30 (1961): 115–75.

[103] Augustine, *Sermo LIII, Caput XV. Crucis quatuor dimensiones, PL* 38: 371–2.

[104] Rabanus Maurus, *De laudibus Sanctae Crucis, PL* 107: 174.

[105] Bernard of Clairvaux, *Sermo in die Sancto Paschae, PL* 183: 275.

While the specific virtues may vary, what remains constant is the association of the cross of the crucifixion with virtues that should be embraced by Christians, a theme that was popular in the eleventh and twelfth centuries and was especially appropriate for reliquaries of the Cross.

Cross Reliquaries in the Late Middle Ages

True Cross reliquaries presumably brought great renown to the churches for which they were made. Although there is almost no surviving documentation for the majority of these precious containers, their popularity and ability to draw great numbers of pilgrims can be inferred from the numerous building campaigns undertaken in this period.[106] In Cologne, for example, the great cathedral underwent several expansions between the tenth and thirteenth centuries, especially after each new influx of relics.[107] In France, Abbot Suger wrote of the need to expand the Church of St.-Denis due to the "crowded multitude" that came to "worship and kiss the holy relics."[108] Described as a congestion of thousands of people (at times angry and rioting), these pilgrims were particularly eager to be as near as possible to the relics of the Passion.[109]

Seeing Passion relics in western Europe would have been much simpler than making a journey to the Holy Land, as the crusades of the late twelfth century had not proved very successful. What is certain, however, is that one of the last, momentous acts to affect the relic trade was the fall of Constantinople in 1204, at the end of the Fourth Crusade.[110] There are numerous accounts of the plundering of the city by western crusaders, with chroniclers such as Nicetas Choniates and Gunther of Paris describing the large-scale theft of Passion relics that occurred at the time.[111]

---

[106] Walter Schulten, "Kölner Reliquien," in *Ornamenta Ecclesiae*, 2, pp. 61–6; Renate Kroos, "Vom Umgang mit Reliquien," in *Ornamenta Ecclesiae*, 3, pp. 25–49.

[107] Schulten, "Kölner Reliquien," pp. 64–6.

[108] Panofsky, *Abbot Suger*, p. 87.

[109] Panofsky, *Abbot Suger*, p. 89.

[110] Alfred J. Andrea, *Contemporary Sources for the Fourth Crusade* (Leiden, 2000); John Godfrey, *1204: The Unholy Crusade* (Oxford, 1980); Donald E. Queller, *The Fourth Crusade: The Conquest of Constantinople* (Philadelphia, 1997).

[111] Edward Peters, *Christian Society and the Crusades, 1198–1229: Sources in Translation Including the Capture of Damietta by Oliver of Paderborn* (Philadelphia, 1971), pp. 1–24.

Even before 1204, many relics of the Cross had been brought to Europe in their original Byzantine containers, some of which took the form of rectangular boxes called *staurothecae*. The *staurotheca* shape had been used for several western Cross reliquaries of the sixth through eleventh centuries. One of the oldest is the sixth-century painted wooden box in the Vatican that holds small stones, earth, and pieces of wood gathered by a pilgrim to the Holy Land.[112] One of the most costly, in terms of gold and semi-precious stones, was commissioned by the German emperor Henry II in the early eleventh century. Henry II's reliquary panel[113] (fig. 173) was originally made as a *staurotheca* with a sliding lid that concealed the relic of the Cross at the center. The reliquary was refashioned in the Gothic period, and again when it was restored in 1740, and now has the shape of a single panel covered by a large, rectangular piece of crystal.[114] A small rectangular box, covered with crystal, also displays the relic at the center of the *Sainte-Croix Triptych*, discussed above.

After 1204, many more Byzantine *staurothecae* reached the west and became highly treasured for their exquisite craftsmanship, fine gold, enamel, and semi-precious stones. For example, the so-called *Limburg Staurotheca*, mid-tenth century, was carried back by Heinrich von Ulmen and given in 1208 to his sister's Augustinian convent of St. Nicholas in Stuben.[115] Heinrich also acquired a second, large piece of the True Cross, which he gave to the monastery of Sts. Eucharius and Matthias, in Trier.[116] A new reliquary panel was made around 1220 for this occasion, and bears an inscription that refers to the relic's origin in the city of Constantinople.[117]

---

[112] Museo Sacro, Vatican. Herbert L. Kessler and Johanna Zacharias, *Rome 1300: On the Path of the Pilgrim* (New Haven, 2000), figs. 46–7; *Ornamenta Ecclesiae*, 3, no. H8. A tenth-century *staurotheca*, also in the Vatican (Museo Sacro della Biblioteca Apostolica), was possibly given to the pope by a Byzantine emissary. Kessler and Zacharias, *Rome 1300*, pp. 53–5; *The Glory of Byzantium: Art and Culture of the Middle Byzantine Era, A.D. 843–1261*, eds. Helen C. Evans and William D. Wixom (New York, 1997), cat. no. 35.

[113] Hermann Fillitz, "Das Kreuzreliquiar Heinrichs II. in der Schatzkammer der Münchner Residenz," *Münchner Jahrbuch* 9/10 (1958/59): 15–31; Frolow, *La Relique*, no. 183; Lasko, *Ars Sacra*, pp. 127–8; Schramm und Mütherich, *Denkmale*, no. 134.

[114] Fillitz, "Das Kreuzreliquiar Heinrichs II.," pp. 15–31.

[115] Diocesan Musem, Limburg an der Lahn. Gauthier, *Les Routes de la foi*, pp. 68–72; *Rhein und Maas*, 1, no. B1; Hermann Schnitzler, *Rheinische Schatzkammer* (Düsseldorf, 1957), 1, no. 12.

[116] Frolow, *La Relique*, no. 503, and *Ornamenta Ecclesiae*, 3, no. H41.

[117] The inscription, in *Ornamenta Ecclesiae*, 3, no. H41, reads in part: "... *lignum*

The *Floreffe Triptych* was also created to display a relic of the True Cross that had been acquired in 1204.[118] In this instance, the relic was sent by the Latin emperor Baldwin I (†1118) of Flanders to his brother, Philip the Noble, Count of Namur. Philip gave the relic to Abbot Wericus of Floreffe in that year, and a miracle occurred on the feast day of the Invention (The Finding of the Cross), when the piece of wood was seen to shed a few drops of blood.[119] The miracle happened again in 1254, prompting the creation of the elaborate triptych.

In some cases, only the relics acquired in Byzantium were valued and not the original reliquaries in which they had traveled to western Europe. *Staurothecae* tended to be taken apart and reworked into different forms, which is what happened to a twelfth-century example that was brought to Cologne after 1204 and given to the Church of Mariengraden.[120] (fig. 174) The portions of the Byzantine original include the large, double-transverse cross at the center, the decorative rosettes, and the figures of Constantine and Helena on the insides of the wings. Also Byzantine are the figures of Mary and St. John the Evangelist on the exterior of the wings. Around 1230–40, these pieces were cut out of the *staurotheca* and assembled with some additional western parts to form the triptych now seen in the Cathedral Treasury in Cologne.[121] The small silver cross suspended from the relic dates to the twelfth century, and the sculpted base or foot (*c.* 1200–30) was probably added in the fourteenth century. The cross at the top is modern.

The composite nature of the *Mariengraden Triptych* demonstrates that in the end it was the relic of the True Cross that was important, and not the reliquary in which it was contained. Concern over the legitimacy of many of these Cross relics, which after 1204 were reaching Europe in large numbers, prompted a special ruling on the subject at the Fourth Lateran Council of 1215. In canon 62, there

---

sce crucis de civitate Constantinopolitana . . ." (. . . wood of the holy cross from the city of Constantinople).

[118] Musée du Louvre, Paris. Frolow, *La Relique*, no. 454; Gauthier, *Les Routes de la foi*, pp. 149–50; Jannic Durand, *The Louvre: Objets d'Art* (London, 1995), p. 39.

[119] Frolow, *La Relique*, no. 454.

[120] Frolow, *La Relique*, no. 157; Susanne Hübener, "Das Kreuzreliquiar aus Mariengraden im Kölner Domschatz," *Kölner Domblatt* (1983), pp. 231–74; *Ornamenta Ecclesiae*, 3, no. H37.

[121] Hübener, "Das Kreuzreliquiar aus Mariengraden," pp. 264–74.

is a direct warning about the sale of relics and the possible duping of pilgrims to Constantinople and the Holy Land.[122] Prelates in particular were urged not to allow members of their congregations to purchase relics that may have false documentation, and in turn to encourage them to venerate only relics that had been authenticated by a high member of the clergy. This canon, issued in direct response to the events of the Fourth Crusade, was not the first warning of its kind, for in the twelfth century Guibert of Nogent had also warned against the trade in false relics.[123]

Canon 62 of the Fourth Lateran Council also included an injunction against the direct exposure of a relic outside its container.[124] This restriction, however, did not preclude a relic being seen inside its container, as evidenced by the large number of thirteenth- and fourteenth-century reliquaries that presented the relic behind a piece of crystal. These "display reliquaries," or monstrances, were particularly favored in the thirteenth century, and allowed the relic of the saint to be visible yet carefully protected.[125] The *Jaucourt Reliquary*,[126] made around 1340–60, cleverly reuses a much earlier Byzantine *staurotheca* (tenth or eleventh century) whose exposed relic of the Cross is supported and presented to the beholder by two kneeling, gilded angels. Thus, by the thirteenth and fourteenth centuries, True Cross reliquaries were moving away from the earlier, more traditional forms of crosses, panels, and triptychs.

One of the more unusual True Cross reliquaries to be created in this later period is the *Man of Sorrows* from an imperial workshop in Prague.[127] (fig. 175) Made of gilt silver, the standing figure of Christ

---

[122] *Sacrorum conciliorum nova et amplissima collectio*, ed. John Mansi 22 (Graz, 1960–61), canon 62, cols. 1049–50.

[123] Guibert of Nogent, *De Pignoribus sanctorum*, ed. Lucas D'Achery, *PL* 156: 657–66; Klaus Guth, *Guibert von Nogent und die hochmittelalterliche Kritik an der Reliquienverehrung* (Ottobeuren, 1970), pp. 92–110.

[124] The heading of canon 62 reads in part: "relics of the saints not to be displayed outside a container . . ." (*ne reliquiae sanctorum ostendatur extra capsam . . .*). *Sacrorum conciliorum nova et amplissima collectio*, Mansi, cols. 1049–50.

[125] Rock crystal reliquaries of this period include barrel-shaped containers in the Walters Art Museum, Baltimore, and the Schnütgen Museum, Cologne; the *Hand Reliquary of St. Attala* in the Collège St.-Etienne, Strasbourg; and the Venetian finger reliquary now in the Diözesanmuseum, Eichstatt; *Ornamenta Ecclesiae* 3, no. H51, H53, H54; Anton Legner, *Reliquien in Kunst und Kult: zwischen Antike und Aufklärung* (Darmstadt, 1995), pp. 88–119.

[126] Musée du Louvre, Paris. Durand, *The Louvre*, p. 27; Gauthier, *Les Routes de la foi*, pp. 177–8.

[127] Legner, *Reliquien in Kunst und Kultur*, pp. 78–87; *Die Parler und die Schöne Stil*,

is surrounded by the instruments of his Passion, namely the cross, the column of the flagellation, and the hammer, nails, and whips, held by two small, kneeling angels. At his feet are the dice thrown by the soldiers who cast lots for his garments, and beside them a third, even smaller angel holds a gabled niche that originally housed a relic from the Crown of Thorns. A relic of the True Cross was also once contained in the gilded cross, which swings open upon small hinges. On the corners of the reliquary's base are four heraldic shields from territories in Bohemia and Moravia that were all ruled by Emperor Charles IV in 1347–49.[128] The inscription around the edge of the base refers to the donor as John Volek, Bishop of Olmütz (1334–51), and perhaps this reliquary was intended as a gift to his brother, Charles IV.[129]

The *Man of Sorrows* belongs to a new type of devotional image that began to emerge in the early fourteenth century. It is in this period that a greater desire to identify with the suffering Christ comes to the fore, in which he is seen not just as the triumphant king of heaven but also as a man who has endured terrible agonies for the salvation of the world.[130] Alongside narrative images of Christ and the Virgin, there began to be produced isolated depictions of the Virgin sorrowing over her dead son, the *Pietà*, as well as of Christ following his deposition from the cross.[131] These images, meant to arouse the deepest pity and sympathy, took the form of painted panels and pages in prayer books that were designed to stimulate the faithful in their prayers.[132]

This desire to share in the sufferings of Christ also affected the creation of precious containers that housed relics of the Passion. As seen above, the *Man of Sorrows* reliquary at The Walters is a luxurious,

---

1350–1400, ed. Anton Legner (Cologne, 1978), 2, pp. 702–3; Philippe Verdier, "Le Reliquaire de la Sainte Epine de Jean de Streda," in *Intuition und Kunstwissenschaft. Festschrift für Hanns Swarzenski*, ed. Peter Bloch *et al.* (Berlin, 1973), pp. 319–44.

[128] Verdier, "Le Reliquaire de la Sainte Epine," pp. 329–31.

[129] The inscription reads: *Hanc monstranciam cum spina chorone Domini Dns Iohannes Olomuczensis episcopus preparari fecit* (John, Bishop of Olmütz, had this monstrance made for a thorn of the crown of the Lord).

[130] Henk van Os, *The Art of Devotion in the Late Middle Ages in Europe, 1300–1500* (Princeton, 1994), pp. 104–14. Van Os also refered to the meditations and sermons of the time, including the *Meditationes Vitae Christi* of c. 1300, written by a Franciscan friar for one of the Poor Clares.

[131] Van Os, *The Art of Devotion*, pp. 104–6, pl. 31.

[132] Roger S. Wieck, *Painted Prayers: The Book of Hours in Medieval and Renaissance Art* (New York, 1997), p. 79. The sufferings of Christ were evoked especially in the Hours of the Cross.

gilded creation, yet it nevertheless also attempts to inspire a more emotional reaction through the figure of the wounded Christ standing humbly behind the instruments of his torture. These instruments are no longer symbols of triumph, like the ones depicted next to the radiant, risen Christ on the *Guennol Triptych*, but are now symbols of compassion and suffering.[133] On a later reliquary of around 1415, the theme of the suffering Christ is combined with the triptych format, now made out of tempera painted on wood. The *Norfolk Triptych*, now in Rotterdam, has at its center a depiction the Man of Sorrows supported by two angels and surrounded by the instruments of the Passion.[134] During a 1993 conservation, it came to light that a relic of the Cross, in the form of a piece of coniferous wood, had been inserted into the oak panel, making clear the dual function of this triptych as an object of contemplation and of veneration.[135]

By the fifteenth century, fewer reliquaries were being made to preserve a piece of the True Cross. This may have been due in part to the end of western rule in Palestine and Syria in the early fourteenth century, and the final fall of Constantinople to the Turks in 1453. By this time, pilgrimage to the Holy Land had become even more difficult than it had been during the crusades. The peak in the number of Cross relics brought back to Europe occurred in the twelfth and early thirteenth centuries, and is perhaps best represented by the building of the Ste.-Chapelle in Paris. Commissioned and conceived by King Louis IX (1214–70) as one large reliquary, this glowing little chapel, 1239–48, was dedicated to the relics of the Crown of Thorns and the True Cross that Louis had acquired in 1237 in Venice, where they had been since 1204.[136]

From the eleventh through thirteenth centuries, the sanctity of the Holy Land, and especially of the imperiled sites of Jerusalem, provided the impetus for the crusades, with the underlying motivation of preserving access for western pilgrims from all walks of life. Relics of the True Cross, to be found primarily in Jerusalem and Constantinople, were of supreme importance in the western Church and

---

[133] Van Os, *The Art of Devotion*, p. 114.

[134] Museum Boymans-van Beuningen (no. 2466), Rotterdam. Van Os, *The Art of Devotion*, pp. 116–20, pl. 37.

[135] Van Os, *The Art of Devotion*, p. 120.

[136] Gauthier, *Les Routes de la foi*, pp. 160–2; Daniel Weiss, *Art and Crusade in the Age of Saint Louis* (Cambridge, 1998), pp. 1–52.

served as symbols of the sacrifice made by Christ to ensure the resurrection and eternal salvation of his followers. The creation of True
Cross reliquaries in turn led to increased pilgrimage to many churches
in western Europe, drawing the faithful to cathedrals and monasteries in France, Germany, Belgium, and the Netherlands, in particular. Each church's desire to display a relic of the True Cross led
to the commission of a variety of gilded and jeweled reliquaries,
many of which also served to commemorate the sacred events and
places of the Holy Land at a time when they were most in danger
of being destroyed.

CHAPTER FOURTEEN

ERIT SEPULCRUM EJUS . . . GLORIOSUM:
VERISIMILITUDE AND THE TOMB OF CHRIST
IN THE ART OF TWELFTH-CENTURY ÎLE-DE-FRANCE*

Stephen Lamia

Innovative Imagery: Sources and Transmission

Christ's tomb, from its first representation in medieval art, had an appearance that could best be described as emblematic. To suggest the sacred sepulcher, the image incorporated forms culled from local architecture or from objects employed in the liturgical drama *Officium sepulcri*.[1] However, during the second half of the twelfth century, in certain geographic locales, the iconography of this most revered of medieval monuments—itself a popular pilgrimage destination—acquired a novel detail that expressed intimate familiarity with the tomb as it existed in Jerusalem. Making their debut on the long side of the rectangular coffin were three round apertures, aligned in a horizontal row. The triadic disposition of these openings reflected the authentic and coeval arrangement at the site itself: a box-like outer sheathing that protected the sacred slab on which the dead body of Christ was

* For valuable suggestions I would like to thank Sarah Blick and Rita Tekippe. Additionally, I would like to thank Elizabeth Valdez del Álamo for her generosity in reading a draft of this article and for offering many constructive and provocative comments. I would also like to acknowledge the support of Dowling College's Long-Range Planning and Development Committee for granting me release time to conduct research and for subvention of funds for photographs. Finally, but by no means least, I am indebted to Humberto DeLuigi of Art Resource for his helpful and thorough pictorial research.

[1] For a discussion of the pre-twelfth century iconography of the tomb of Christ in the Latin West and related material see Stephen Lamia, "*Sepulcrum Domini*: The Iconography of the Holed Tomb of Christ in Romanesque and Gothic Art" (Ph.D. diss. University of Toronto, 1982), pp. 6–86. For bibliography on the *Officium sepulcri* see *infra*, fn. 17. For the physical structure of the tomb of Christ, the *aedicula/* shrine constructed over it, and the Church of the Holy Sepulcher from the early fourth to the late twelfth centuries see Martin Biddle, *The Tomb of Christ* (Stroud, UK, 1999).

laid to rest. The perforations in triplicate afforded pilgrims physical access for such cultic practices as viewing, touching, and kissing the holy relic inside.[2]

Images of the pierced *sepulcra Domini* occur in painted, sculpted, and architectural formats throughout the Latin West. Given the breadth of this geographic distribution, one would not expect a simple, linear development of an image communicated, but instead more diverse and complex methods of transmission.[3] There are various means of such communication: artists' knowledge of other monuments; clients' wishes; and accounts—written and oral—by pilgrims themselves returning from Jerusalem. In some instances, it is clear that an artist followed artistic conventions. In others, patrons must be acknowledged in their roles as conveyors of images, since they traveled widely, and they may have desired to recreate monuments which they saw elsewhere for their own designs. Finally, descriptions by pilgrims who had seen the actual sepulcher of Christ should also be taken into consideration for even more specific information.[4]

---

[2] For cultic and devotional practices at the site of Christ's tomb in the Church of the Holy Sepulcher see Stephen Lamia, "Souvenir, Synaesthesia, and the *sepulcrum Domini*: Sensory Stimuli as Memory Stratagems," in *Memory and the Medieval Tomb*, ed. Elizabeth Valdez del Álamo with Carol Stamatis Pendergast (Aldershot, UK, 2000), pp. 19–41.

[3] A condensed list of monuments reflective of this broad area includes: a reliquary triptych of the Holy Cross (*c.* 1165) attributed to Godefroid de Claire (Godefroid de Huy); Nicholas of Verdun's enamel of the Burial of Christ (labeled SEPVL-CRV*DNI) on the Klosterneuburg Antependium (1181); Bonanus of Pisa's Holy Women at the Tomb on the bronze doors at the Porta di San Ranieri of Pisa Cathedral (*c.* 1180); the relief of the Holy Women at the Tomb at the Tumba de Rotari at Monte Sant' Angelo (twelfth century); the conflated image of the Entombment and Lamentation on the diptych of King Andreas III of Hungary from the Veneto (1290–96); an ivory liturgical comb made in the British Isles (mid twelfth century); the architectural aedicula of the Holy Sepulcher at Eichstätt (*c.* 1160); and the relief of the Holy Women at the Tomb on the lintel of the south portal on the west façade at St.-Giles-du-Gard (*c.* mid-twelfth century). For a geographic and iconographic study of the phenomenon of the pierced *sepulcrum Domini* see Lamia, *Sepulcrum Domini* . . ., pp. 184–337; Biddle, *Tomb of Christ*, pp. 37–40, 85–88; John Crook, *The Architectural Setting of the Cult of Saints in the Early Christian West, c. 300–c. 1200* (Oxford, 2000), pp. 255–6. Biddle, *Tomb of Christ*, p. 88, refers to the apertures as "port holes" and considers them to be "a feature—perhaps the defining feature—of the medieval Edicule." It is not known who covered the tomb slab with the pierced marble revetment, though given the cultic practice at tomb shrines of saints in the Latin West, it is my contention that, during the earliest refurbishing campaign carried out by the new settlers, it was they who provided the protective, yet accessible arrangement. Biddle, *Tomb of Christ*, pp. 85–8. By the fifteenth century, written evidence for the survival of these openings at Jerusalem disappears; Biddle, *Tomb of Christ*, p. 86.

[4] A thorough compendia of documents written by pilgrims to the Holy Land

The Historical Background: "Operation Holy Sepulcher"

Because the First Crusade was such a resounding victory for the West, its aftermath witnessed the settlement of many "armed pilgrims" who sought their fortunes in the newly-established Latin Kingdom of Jerusalem.[5] The over-arching sense of optimism and security which prevailed subsequently to the European occupation and colonization of the Holy Land, albeit short-lived, provided one explanation for the delay in the incorporation of the three-holed image as the representation for Christ's tomb in the West. However, in the middle of the twelfth century, the Second Crusade proved to be much less successful.[6] As a consequence, a great reflux of dismayed westerners left Jerusalem. Their departure, with their physical possessions and the precious memories of holy places visited, provided yet another means by which the pierced sepulcher could have made its debut into the visual repertory of western European medieval art. But most written records regarding Christ's tomb are sparse concerning its description, so perhaps communication about its appearance was oral, or perhaps that description was not necessary, especially if the form of the monument was not considered unusual—shrines outfitted with apertures were common in Western Europe.

---

from the Early Christian period to beyond the Middle Ages is *Palestine Pilgrims' Text Society*; also see *Jerusalem Pilgrimage, 1099–1185*, ed. John Wilkinson *et al.* (London, 1988). For an historiographic and bibliographic study of pilgrimage to Jerusalem and the Holy Land see Linda Kay Davidson and Maryjane Dunn-Wood, *Pilgrimage in the Middle Ages: A Research Guide* (New York, 1993), pp. 80–127; Aryeh Graboïs, *Le pèlerin occidental en Terre Sainte au moyen âge* (Brussels, 1998). For pilgrimage to Jerusalem from the third to the eleventh centuries see Victor W. Turner, *Image and Pilgrimage in Christian Culture* (New York, 1978), pp. 164–6; Diana Webb, *Pilgrims and Pilgrimage in Medieval Europe* (London, 1999), pp. 26–8, 39–43, 95.

[5] There is abundant literature on the Crusades including Georges Bordonove, *Les croisades et le Royaume de Jérusalem* (Paris, 1992); Peter M. Holt, *The Age of the Crusades: The Near East from the Eleventh Century to 1517* (London, 1986); Thomas F. Madden, *A Concise History of the Crusades* (Lanham, MD, 1999); Hans Eberhard Mayer, *The Crusades*, 2nd ed., trans. John Gillingham (Oxford, 1988); Jonathan Phillips, *Defenders of the Holy Land: Relations between the Latin East and the West, 1119–1187* (Oxford, 1996); Jean Richard, *The Crusades, c. 1071–c. 1291*, trans. Jean Birrell (Cambridge, 1999); Steven Runciman, *A History of the Crusades* (Cambridge, 1951–54); Kenneth M. Setton, ed. *A History of the Crusades* (Madison, WI, 1969–89).

[6] The Second Crusade is studied by all of the scholars cited in fn. 5. See also *The Second Crusade and the Cistercians*, ed. Michael Gervers (New York, 1992); Giles Constable, "The Second Crusade as Seen by Contemporaries," *Traditio* 9 (1953), 213–79.

Indeed, the synaesthetic practices imposed by the revetment at Jerusalem—bending down and poking one's head through an opening to see, touch, or kiss the holy relic of Christ's place of burial—were not unrelated to similar arrangements at other shrines and tombs in the West, which prompted unforgettable experiences for visitors to holy sites.[7] Thus, the mnemonic, sensorial devices of sight and touch employed in rituals at the place of Christ's burial contributed to the power of remembering the actual appearance of his sepulcher; these, also, may have influenced the transmission of its unusual iconography to select European areas during the twelfth century. Such notions were corroborated in Mary Carruthers' theories on memory in the Middle Ages, which focus on retention and retrieval of information not only through written documents, but by visual means.[8] This dynamic of memory was likewise discussed by Richard Krautheimer in his essay on copies of the Church of the Holy Sepulcher, proposing that the visual elements of these structures were mementos of the venerated site.[9]

Twelfth-century monuments in the Île-de France afford a glimpse of rare, innovative, but authentic imagery of a prestigious pilgrimage site as medieval travelers to the Holy Sepulcher themselves would have seen it. The objects provide a case study of veristic imagery, where specific devices for transmission of iconography shed light on cross-cultural communication between the East and West.

In an attempt to gain support for the Second Crusade, Abbot Peter the Venerable of Cluny (r. 1122–56) delivered a sermon in Paris *c.* 1147 whose title, *In Praise of the Lord's Sepulcher*, indicates the prominent role Christ's tomb played in this military campaign.[10] His

---

[7] For pierced tombs of saints see Lamia, "*Sepulcrum Domini . . .*," pp. 338–427.

[8] Mary Carruthers, *The Book of Memory: A Study of Memory in Medieval Culture* (Cambridge, 1990), pp. 17, 60, 73, 221; Mary Carruthers, *The Craft of Thought: Meditation, Rhetoric, and the Making of Images, 400–1200* (Cambridge, 1998), pp. 42–3, refers to journals written by Early Christian pilgrims to Jerusalem who experienced the *loca sancta* themselves as places for conjuring memory images and relating them to appropriate biblical narratives; see also David Freedberg, *The Power of Images: Studies in the History and Theory of Response* (Chicago, 1989), pp. 162–3 on memory and images.

[9] Richard Krautheimer, "Introduction to an Iconography of Medieval Architecture," *Studies in Early Christian, Medieval, and Renaissance Art* (New York, 1969), pp. 115–50; esp. p. 127.

[10] Petrus Venerabilis, *In laudem sepulcri Domini*, in Jacques-Paul Migne, *Patrologiae cursus completus. Series Latina* (Paris, 1854), vol. 189, cols. 973–92.

exhortation contains the following illuminating passage that makes frequent reference to the tomb of Christ:

> Although the task undertaken by you and your forefathers through the apostolic ministry in the Christian faith is now fulfilled, nevertheless it is fulfilled to a greater degree when his glorious sepulcher has been freed by you from the lord of the infidels out of love for Christ Lord and God . . . because you have placed the Lord's sepulchre before your own lives, because you have exposed yourselves to universal misfortunes for it, because for it you were not frightened of any danger, because for it you defied horrible tortures and death itself most calmly, because you have placed his glory above all your glory and that of the world. In all these things you declared his glorious dwelling to be above all earthly dwellings, according to the words of the prophet (Isaiah 11.10) who was sent before him, "His, that is Christ's, sepulcher shall be glorious.[11]

Furthermore, the abbot singled out the *locus sanctus* of the tomb of Christ as occupying a special significance among all *loca sancta*:

> We indeed honor, as is right, the crib in which the Mother of God laid the God-child whom she had borne, but we venerate with greater glory the sepulcher in which, after he had suffered many great trials, he lay after his crucifixion and death.[12]

Peter cited the example of the First Crusaders who, like the angels and Old Testament prophets, had realized the importance of the tomb of Christ; he also alluded to its designation for God's annual earthly visit, precisely on the feast of the Resurrection, through the miracle of the sacred fire, a feat of pyrotechnics by which a streak of flames appeared to descend from the dome of the Anastasis Rotunda to illuminate a lamp suspended in the aedicula over the

---

[11] *Quod licet in fide Christiana a vobis et patribus vestris per apostolicum ministerium susceptum impletum sit, tamen multo magis impletum est, quando amore Christi Domini et Dei vestri gloriosum ejus sepulcrum per vos a perfidorum domino liberatum est . . . quia sepulcrum Domini vitae vestrae praeposuistis, quia nullo pro eo pericula expavistis, quia pro eo horrenda supplicia, ipsamque mortem constantissime contempsistis, quia omnem vestram mundique gloriam ejus gloriae subjecistis. In his sane omnibus, secundum praemissae prophetiae tenorem, quae dixerat: 'Erit sepulcrum ejus, id est Christi, gloriosum'* (Isaiah 11.10), *gloriosum illud esse super omnia terranae habitationis loca declarastis.* Ibidem, col. 985; my translation. The Latin title of this article is directly derived from a section of this passage.

[12] *Honoramus quidem ut justum est, praesepe in quo Dei mater et virgo natum Deum puerum reclinavit, sed excellentiori gloria veneramur sepulcrum in quo multis magnisque laboribus perpessis post crucem et mortem pansavit.* Ibidem, col. 974; my translation.

tomb of Christ.[13] He then explained that the sepulcher of Christ is the most prominent place of theophany because only by his death and Resurrection, which occurred at that location, was his divine ministry completed. Christ's death was a victory, his Resurrection a triumph, and his sepulcher, therefore, of pivotal importance to prove his dual nature, divine and human.[14] Indeed, with all of the emphasis on the tomb of Christ that Peter imparted in his sermon, one might be tempted to call the Second Crusade, to use contemporary parlance, "Operation Holy Sepulcher."

Peter's interest in the liberation of the Holy Land actually antedates *In laudem sepulcri Domini*. Adolf Katzenellenbogen suggested a very plausible connection between the Abbot of Cluny and the program sculpted on the central tympanum at the pilgrimage church of St. Madeleine at Vézelay dated *c.* 1120–32, for which Peter most likely suggested the iconography.[15] According to Katzenellenbogen, the representations depict the prophecies of the Old Testament, their fulfillment by the mission of the Apostles, and their renewed fulfillment by the new mission of the Crusaders—ideas which can all be found in Peter's writings. Moreover, before his installation as abbot of Cluny, he was prior of the abbey church and pilgrimage center of Vézelay. Thus, we have evidence of Peter's devotion to, and concern with, the Holy Land that predated his famous sermon by more than twenty years. This sentiment was shared by the other key individuals who spearheaded the war, Bernard of Clairvaux (1090–1153), Pope Eugenius III (r. 1145–53), and King Louis VII (r. 1137–80). Bernard preached in favor of a Second Crusade at Vézelay on Easter Sunday of 1146, just one year prior to Peter's *In laudem sepulcri Domini.*[16]

The popularity of the cult of this Christological relic is further underscored by its numerous architectural copies and the many

---

[13] Odo of Deuil, *De profectione Ludovici VII in orientem*, ed. and trans. Virginia Berry (New York, 1948), pp. 153–4. For the miracle of the sacred fire see Biddle, *Tomb of Christ*, p. 138; Lamia, "*Sepulcrum Domini . . .*," pp. 87–8.

[14] This is a summary of Petrus Venerabilis, *In laudem sepulcri Domini*, cols. 988–90.

[15] Adolf Katzenellenbogen, "The Central Tympanum at Vézelay: Its Encyclopedic Meaning and Its Relation to the First Crusade," *The Art Bulletin* 26 (1944), 141–51, esp. p. 151. Michael D. Taylor suggested a different interpretation in "The Pentecost at Vézelay," *Gesta* 19 (1980), 9–15.

[16] For the sermon by Bernard of Clairvaux see Phillips, *Defenders of the Holy Land*, pp. 76–9; James A. Brundage, *The Crusades: A Documentary Survey* (Milwaukee, 1962), p. 92. For Bernard's general theory towards the Second Crusade see Hans-Dietrich Kahl, "Crusade Eschatology as Seen by St. Bernard in the Years 1146 to 1148," in *The Second Crusade*, ed. Michael Gervers, pp. 35–47.

church dedications to the Church of the Holy Sepulcher. Moreover, the expanded versions of the liturgical mystery play, *Officium sepulcri*, re-enacted the visit of the Holy Women to Christ's grave, with such symbolic stage props as crosses (for the Lord's Passion), linen cloths (for his shroud), and the altar (for his tomb).[17]

Verisimilitude: Pilgrims' Accounts and the Twelfth-Century Monuments

Artists of the early Middle Ages in the West depicting Christ's tomb disregarded the literary evidence from both biblical descriptions and pilgrims' chronicles, the earliest of which date to the fourth century, relying instead on indigenous funerary structures and conventional burial containers.[18] They visualized the tomb as a two-storied struc-ture whose origins lay in the funerary monuments of Late Antiquity, such as that seen in a *c.* 400 ivory plaque with combined scenes of the Visit of the Holy Women and the Ascension.[19] (fig. 176) The

---

[17] Both of these phenomena appear, albeit in rudimentary form, as early as the ninth and tenth centuries. For architectural copies of the Church of the Holy Sepulchre see Robert Ousterhout, "Loca Sancta and the Architectural Response to Pilgrimage," in *The Blessings of Pilgrimage*, ed. Robert Ousterhout (Urbana, IL, 1990), pp. 108–24, p. 109: "by far the most frequently copied holy site"; Geneviève Bresc-Bautier, "Les imitations du Saint-Sépulcre de Jérusalem (IXe–XVe siècles)—archéolo-gie d'une devotion," *Revue d'histoire de la spiritualité* 50 (1974), 319–42; Sabine MacCormack, "Loca Sancta: The Organization of Sacred Topography in Late Antiquity," in *The Blessings of Pilgrimage*, pp. 7–40; esp., p. 28: "the holy place par excellence"; Krautheimer, "Introduction to an Iconography," pp. 115–50. For litur-gical mystery plays, *Officium sepulcri*, see Karl Young, *The Drama of the Medieval Church* (Oxford, 1933); O.B. Hardison, *Christian Rite and Christian Drama in the Middle Ages*, (Baltimore, 1965); Blandine Berger, *Le drame liturgique de Pâques* (Paris, 1976); Marie Dolores Moore, "The *Visitatio Sepulchri* of the Medieval Church" (Ph.D. diss., University of Rochester, Eastman School of Music, 1971). For allusions to objects employed in the *Officium sepulcri* see Hardison, *Christian Rite*, pp. 193–4. *Visitatio sepulcri* and *Officium sepulcri* are the same drama; the former term is more commonly used even though the latter is more official in nomenclature.

[18] St. Jerome, *The Pilgrimage of the Holy Paula*, trans. Aubrey Stewart, *The Library of the Palestine Pilgrims' Text Society*, vol. 1 (London, 1896); John J. Wilkinson, *Egeria's Travels to the Holy Land*, rev. ed. (Warminster, 1981).

[19] For Late Antique two-storied tombs see Axel Boëthius and John Ward Perkins, *Etruscan and Roman Architecture* (Harmondsworth, 1970), pp. 299–301, 356; for the Munich ivory Wolfgang Fritz Volbach, *Elfenbeinarbeiten der Spätantike und des frühen Mittelalters*, 3rd ed. (Mainz, 1976), no. 110; Danielle Gaborit-Chopin, *Ivoires du moyen âge* (Fribourg, 1978), no. 15. Lawrence Nees suggested that the Ascension may instead be a Resurrection scene, "On Carolingian Book Painters: The Ottoboni Gospels and Its Transfiguration Master," *The Art Bulletin* 83 (2001), pp. 209–39.

sort of image prevailed with minor modifications well into the twelfth
century. This inclination to endow the *sepulcrum Domini* with a familiar, identifiably funerary form gave the viewer a functional impression of verisimilitude, although in reality the image was vastly different
from the tomb's actual form.

Among the modified forms were the *c.* ninth-tenth century images
of a coffin for Christ's sepulcher, of which the tenth-century miniature of the Deposition and Entombment in the *Codex Egberti* is a
significant example.[20] (fig. 177) Once the sarcophagus as an archetypal image for Christ's tomb began to emerge in the eleventh and
twelfth centuries, it was treated as a rectangular field embellished
with decorative motifs including arcuations, lozenges, vegetal patterns, and strigils,[21] with widespread appeal from the British Isles to
southern Italy and from Germany to the Iberian Peninsula. Included
in this geographic circumference were various centers of artistic activity in France which also followed this convention. One example is
the image of the Entombment of Christ on the 1145–55 capital frieze
from the west façade of Chartres Cathedral.[22] (fig. 178) The sarcophagus is conceived of as a soberly-displayed oblong box with
three circular depressions on its long side. Some scholars have interpreted this motif as an ornamental pattern; indeed it is not. The
capital frieze at Chartres is, in fact, one of the first monuments to
show the tomb of Christ as a coffin furnished with round openings
on one side; and this occurs not once, but twice. The second instance
is seen on the capital of the Visit of the Holy Women to the Sepulcher
also on the frieze. (fig. 178) In both cases, the three holes are aligned
in an even, horizontal fashion.

The seemingly-spontaneous debut of this novel iconography in the

---

[20] For the *Codex Egberti* (Trier, Stadtbibliothek, cod. 24, fol. 85v) see Gunther
Franz, *Codex Egberti der Stadtbibliothek Trier* (Wiesbaden, 1984); *Codex Egberti der
Stadtbibliothek Trier*, with an Introduction by Hubert Schiel (Basel, 1960).

[21] Lamia, *Sepulcrum Domini* . . ., p. 86.

[22] For Chartres capitals consult Adelheid Heimann, "The Capital Frieze and
Pilasters of the Portail Royal, Chartres," *Journal of the Warburg and Courtauld Institutes*
31 (1968), 73–102; René Crozet, "A propos des chapiteaux de la façade occidentale de Chartres," *Cahiers de la civilisation médiévale* 14 (1971), 159–65; Rachel Dressler,
"Medieval Narrative: The Capital Frieze on the Royal Portal, Chartres Cathedral,"
(Ph.D. diss., Columbia University, 1992); Laura Spitzer, "The Cult of the Virgin
and Gothic Sculpture: Evaluating Opposition in the Chartres West Façade Capital
Frieze," *Gesta* 33 (1994), pp. 132–50. Dressler's dissertation takes into account the
connection of the imagery at Chartres with the Crusades.

Île-de-France coincides with two twelfth-century pilgrims' descriptions of the *locus sanctus* in the Holy Land; ironically and disappointingly, neither is of French origin. One is that of the Russian pilgrim, Daniel the Abbot (journeying 1106–8) who observed that:

> . . . as you enter the cave by the small door, on the right hand there is a kind of shelf cut into the rock of the cave and on this shelf lay the body of our Lord, Jesus Christ. This sacred shelf is now covered with slabs of marble. On the side three small windows have been cut in order to see the holy stone, and all Christians go there to kiss it.[23]

An identical description for the arrangement and accommodation of pilgrims is mentioned by a German priest, Theoderic, who visited the site between 1169–74:

> The mouth of the Cave cannot be entered by any one without bending his knees. But arriving there he finds the treasure for which he has longed, the Sepulchre in which our most benevolent Lord Jesus Christ rested for three days. It is wonderfully decorated with Parian marble, gold, and precious stones. In the side it has three round holes, through which travelers give the kisses they have for so long desired to give to the stone on which the Lord lay.[24]

These two accounts parallel the artistic evidence at Chartres, demonstrating that a close relationship existed between an image of the *sepulcrum* and the shrine in Jerusalem. The compelling visibility of these veristic images of Christ's tomb displayed on such a strategic area as the entranceway to the church suggests a tendency to document, commemorate, and publicize the exact arrangement found at

---

[23] Daniel the Abbot, "The Life and Journey of Daniel, Abbot of the Russian Land," in *Jerusalem Pilgrimage, 1099–1185*, pp. 120–71; esp. p. 128; Daniel the Abbot, *The Pilgrimage of the Russian Abbot Daniel in the Holy Land*, ed. and annotated by Sir Charles W. Wilson (London, 1895), pp. iii–82, esp. pp. 12–13; Avraam de Noroff, *Pélerinage en Terre Sainte de l'igoumène russe Daniel au commencement du XIIème siècle* (St. Petersburg, 1864), with a French translation of the original text.

[24] Theoderic, "The Booklet on the Holy Places as Told by Theoderic," in *Jerusalem Pilgrimage, 1099–1185*, pp. 274–314; esp. p. 279; Theoderich (*sic*) of Würzburg, *Guide to the Holy Land*, trans. Aubrey Stewart, 2nd ed., with a new Introduction by Ronald G. Musto (New York, 1986), p. 9. The concordance between Daniel the Abbot's description and that of Theoderic: "Tria in latere rotunda habet foramina, per quae ipsi lapidi, in quo Dominus jacuit, optata peregrini porriguntur oscula," is mentioned by Virgilio Corbo, *Il Santo Sepulcro di Gerusalemme: Aspetti archeologici dalle origini al periodo crociato* (Jerusalem, 1981), pp. 198–99. The tomb shrine, rebuilt in the early nineteenth century, no longer possesses this arrangement; David Kroyanker, *Jerusalem Architecture* (London, 1994), p. 38.

the sacred pilgrimage site itself, thus maintaining in perpetuity both the geographically-distant city of Jerusalem and the historically-remote events of Christ's burial and Resurrection. In other words, the images, with their pronounced degree of verisimilitude, assumed the function of a memento and a replication of the place visited—as if declaring visibly to observers that they are gazing at a macro-souvenir of a pilgrimage, a monumentally conceived pilgrim's badge, that, by its very public and visible nature, is both a commonly shared experience and a collectively shared object.[25]

What does this veristic rendition ultimately imply? The answer lies in a pilgrimage encounter that is both spatial and temporal since it encompasses the past, the present, and the future: proof of the site visited, the reinforcement of the ritualistic experiences of movement, sight, and touch, the recollection of the place visited, and the symbolic association of faith and its concomitant anticipatory dimension of salvation embedded in the image of the tomb itself. As David Freedberg noted, striving for verisimilitude marks our efforts to make the absent present; and the sacred sites of the Holy Land themselves were impressions stamped by the very presence of Christ, who walked this earth.[26] Therefore, by extension, not only did the pilgrims to Jerusalem in general and to the Holy Sepulcher in particular, vicariously recreate the Passion and Resurrection of Christ by their visitation, they also recreated the biblical narrative of the Visit of the Holy Women to Christ's tomb.[27] By emphasizing the reality, or in

---

[25] More traditional pilgrim souvenirs of the Holy Sepulcher have been studied by André Grabar, *Ampoules de Terre Sainte* (Paris, 1958) a monograph on the numerous *ampullae*, or vials, that contained holy oil brought back from lamps which burned inside the Holy Sepulcher, today preserved at Monza and Bobbio. That an active market in mementos of the *sepulcrum Domini* was in existence is proven also by *quinquets*, small lamps shaped like miniature *aediculae* or rotundas in imitation of the architectural shrine erected over Christ's tomb slab itself. These objects also contained holy oil from the same source, but were themselves functional lights; Iohann Q. van Regtern-Altena, "Hidden Records of the Holy Sepulchre," in *Essays in the History of Architecture Presented to Rudolf Wittkower* (London, 1967), pp. 17–21. For a comprehensive catalogue and in-depth discussion of pilgrims' badges and souvenirs from the twelfth century onwards see Brian Spencer, *Pilgrim Souvenirs and Secular Badges* (London, 1998). I am grateful to Sarah Blick and Rita Tekippe for providing me with this latter reference.

[26] Freedberg, *Power of Images*, p. 201; Cynthia Hahn, "Loca Sancta Souvenirs: Sealing the Pilgrims' Experience," in *The Blessings of Pilgrimage*, pp. 85–96.

[27] This is a concept I have presented elsewhere in Lamia, "Souvenir, Synaesthesia, and the *sepulcrum Domini* . . .," p. 28, corroborated by Hahn in "Loca Sancta Souvenirs . . .," p. 92.

this case more properly speaking, the verisimilitude, of the image of Christ's tomb by reproducing its actual appearance *in situ*, the form assumes the potent memento ultimately associated with the owner and occupier of the tomb itself, Christ, thereby reiterating the image's function as a macro-souvenir.

The capital frieze at Chartres, however, is not an isolated manifestation of this innovative iconography in the Île-de-France. In a capital of the Holy Women at the Tomb over the south portal at Notre-Dame, Étampes, the three-holed sepulcher appears again.[28] (fig. 179) The imitation of the Jerusalem shrine-tomb is not an intrinsic part of the theological message of either façade, but it is important that the image of the pierced sarcophagus is shared by at least two hands working nearly simultaneously in the same geographic locale around the middle of the twelfth century. It might have come to the attention of the artists/designers at Chartres and Étampes as having been employed elsewhere—perhaps in a medium other than sculpture—and then been introduced here into the dense narrative repertory of their respective programmes. Let us now consider possible modes of transmission for this astonishingly truthful image.

Material Evidence: Sigillography and Itinerant Artists

Given the political situation in the Crusader Kingdom of Jerusalem in the 1140s, the fall of the city of Edessa and imminent threats from the Muslims, Louis VII, the Capetian monarch who was one of several prominent figures to support and promote the second military campaign, was undoubtedly collecting information about conditions in the far-flung realm of Outremer. This statement does not imply that the king himself was instrumental in discovering and suggesting the motif of the pierced sarcophagus to the sculptors of Chartres and Étampes; his interests were not necessarily focused on visual details of the Jerusalem monument. Rather, the disposition of the relic may have been recorded by a careful observer dispatched on a fact-finding mission to the Holy Land shortly before any military action commenced.

---

[28] Kathleen Nolan, "Narrative in the Capital Frieze of Notre Dame at Étampes," *The Art Bulletin* 71 (1989), pp. 166–84.

At this time, frequent correspondence between secular rulers and high-ranking ecclesiastics in both the royal domains of the Île-de-France and the Latin Kingdom of Jerusalem could have imparted the image in question to the Île-de-France. Seals of two of the earliest Patriarchs of Jerusalem, Guermond (r. 1118–28) and William I of Massines (or Malines) (r. 1130–45), display it prominently in vignettes of the Visit of the Holy Women to the Tomb, accompanied by identifying inscriptions.[29] (fig. 180) In addition, the seal of the Canons of the Holy Sepulcher also bore an image of the three-holed sepulcher, although in this example, a non-narrative, iconic motif of the monument enframed by its architectural setting together with its identifying inscription is employed.[30] (fig. 181) Seals were appended to all official documents emanating from these important offices, thus constituting one method of direct transmission of representations of the holed tomb from East to West. Moreover, the Cathedral of the Patriarch of Jerusalem, the Church of the Holy Sepulcher, possessed extensive estates in Europe—sixty churches in eighteen different dioceses—and a network of communication between the mother house and her western dependencies surely must have existed.[31] Naturally, official documents dispatched to the satellites of the Patriarch would have borne his seal.

If the western European destination of seals does not provide sufficient proof for them as agents of transmission for images of the pierced tomb of Christ (although this is fairly solid evidence in and

---

[29] For seals from the Holy Land in general see Gustav Schlumberger, *Sigillographie de l'Orient latin* (Paris, 1943), esp. pp. 73–4; Jacques-Paul Migne, *Dictionnaire de numismatique et de sigillographie religieuses* (Paris, 1852), cols. 306–404, 826–9; esp. 826. Schlumberger described, but did not illustrate the seal of the Patriarch Guermond. Running around its circumference is the inscription "+SPVLCHRVM DOMINI NOSTRI IESV XP-I." (The Sepulcher of Our Lord Jesus Christ). The seal of the Patriarch William reads: "+SEPVLCRVM DOMINI NOSTRI IHV XPI." (translation: same as above).

[30] Schlumberger, *Sigillographie*, pp. 134–5. This seal was appended to a document together with the seal of the Patriarch Heraclius (1180–89/90). Its inscription reads: "+SANCTISSIMI SEPVLCHRI" From the holiest sepulcher).

[31] Mayer, *The Crusades*, p. 171. The Patriarchs of Jerusalem were active administrators in their See, mediating disputes and keeping close touch with the West. Léon de Mas Latrie, "Les patriarchs latins de Jérusalem," *Revue de l'Orient latin* 1 (1893), pp. 16–41; Jonathan Riley-Smith, *The Knights of Saint John in Jerusalem and Cyprus* (London, 1967). Less information is available concerning the canons and priors of the Holy Sepulcher; Riley-Smith *passim*. Eugene de Rozière, ed., *Cartulaire de l'église du Saint-Sépulcre de Jérusalem* (Paris, 1849) records only local and papal deeds of these latter-mentioned groups.

of itself), let us bear in mind another factor: the artists who produced these insignias. The seals were struck in Holy Land ateliers—
workshops of hybrid, international communities attracting craftsmen
from diverse areas of Europe—the Île-de-France, Burgundy, Provence,
Tuscany, and Apulia, to name only a few.[32] These artists most probably returned to their homelands, contributing to the East-to-West
migration of the iconographic motif. To summarize, direct transmission of the image may well have occurred either through the
seals, itinerant artists, pilgrims to Jerusalem, clients' wishes, or a combination of all.

Innovation on the Wane: The Later Monuments

Although an acknowledged failure for the Latin West, the crusade
is important here since it coincides with the earliest manifestations
of the image of the three-holed tomb. As during the First Crusade,
in order to promote interest in this second war, the Sepulcher of
Christ was made a focal point.[33] The sermon by Peter the Venerable,
Bernard of Clairvaux's homily at Vézelay on Easter 1146, and Odo
of Deuil's account of the Second Crusade, *De profectione Ludovici VII
in orientem*, all mention this sacred Christian shrine. We also know
from Odo's writings that Louis VII managed to reach Jerusalem in
May 1148, remaining there until early summer 1149, and visiting

---

[32] On the subject of itinerant, western European artists working in the Holy Land
refer to Moshe Barasch, *Crusader Figural Sculpture in the Holy Land* (New Brunswick,
NJ, 1971), pp. 64–65; Jaroslav Folda, *Crusader Manuscript Illumination at St.-Jean d'Acre,
1275–1291* (Princeton, 1976); Jaroslav Folda, "Reflections on Art in Crusader
Jerusalem about the Time of the Second Crusade," in *The Second Crusade*, pp. 171–82;
Jaroslav Folda, *The Art of the Crusaders in the Holy Land, 1098–1187* (Cambridge,
1995), p. 474. It is no small coincidence that some of these regions, namely Provence,
Tuscany, and Apulia also witnessed the manifestation of the iconography of the
pierced *sepulcrum Domini*—a study far too large for the limitations of this article, but
explored in Lamia, "Souvenir, Synaesthesia, and the *sepulcrum Domini* . . .," pp. 22–3.

[33] In the anonymous chronicle *Gesta Francorum et aliorum Hierosolimitanorum*, ed. and
trans. Louis Brehier (Paris, 1924), p. 18, 20, written during the First Crusade,
numerous references were made to the *iter Sancti Sepulcri* and the *via sepulcri Domini*,
such as Bohemond I of Taranto (c. 1057–1111): "Bohemond the Victorious . . . taking the route of many Frankish Christians, resolved to go to the Lord's sepulcher . . . Returning from his lands, the Lord Bohemond zealously prepared to take
the road of the Holy Sepulcher. Similar use of *iter Sancti Sepulcri* may be found
throughout this chronicle. See also *La geste des Francs: chronique anonyme de la première
Croisade*, trans. André Matignon (Paris, 1992).

the holy places of the city.[34] One cannot imagine the king omitting the important *sepulcrum Domini* from his itinerary of "must see" shrines.

Thus, it is against this historical backdrop that we may associate the narrative capitals of Chartres and Étampes with the earliest images of the holed sepulcher, and soon after, they appeared elsewhere in the vicinity. But the innovative iconographic motif soon began to be misinterpreted, as seen in another geographically-close example found on a tympanum of the west façade of the collegiate church of Notre-Dame, Mantes (*c.* 1170) depicting, yet again, the Visit of the Holy Women to the Tomb.[35] (fig. 182) This religious foundation, like Chartres and Étampes, was affiliated with the monarchy. Both Louis VII and his successor Philippe Auguste (1180–1223) were its titular abbots.[36] The date of this work places it in the reign of Louis VII, who we know went to Jerusalem. There thus exists a common link among Chartres, Étampes, and Mantes which may provide the explanation for the iconographic similarity of the *sepulcrum Domini* in all three instances with one major modification: the triple openings so pristinely and prominently displayed at Chartres and Étampes have now, at Mantes, shrunken in size and have been recast into the form of tiny trefoils—a common decorative motif in both the incipient and mature phases of Gothic style. This later version of the pierced *sepulcrum Domini* indicates a direction which other thirteenth-century monuments will follow: an inclination to perceive the apertures more as an opportunity to embellish the visible, long side of the sarcophagus with ornament as opposed to what was once a statement of verisimilitude.[37] The originally unadorned oculi have lost the purity of form, but not wholly the integrity of meaning. The image of the holed sarcophagus as a type has not been completely eschewed in the later example from Mantes (and its thirteenth-

---

[34] Mentioned by Virginia Berry in her Introduction to Odo of Deuil, *De profectione Ludovici VII*, p. xix.

[35] Willibald Sauerländer, *Gothic Sculpture in France, 1140–1270* (London, 1972), pp. 408–9; Jean Bony, *French Gothic Architecture of the 12th and 13th Centuries* (Berkeley, 1983), pp. 149–51, 153–4, 185–6; Jean Bony, "La collégiale de Mantes," *Congrès archéologique de France* 104th session (1946), pp. 163–220. See also Diane Brouillette, "Early Gothic Sculpture of Senlis" (Ph.D. diss., University of California at Berkeley, 1981) for the the stylistic relationship between the sculpture of Senlis, the north portal of St.-Denis, and Mantes.

[36] Sauerländer, *Gothic Sculpture*, p. 408.

[37] For a discussion of the thirteenth-century monuments in the Île-de-France see Lamia, "*Sepulcrum Domini* . . .," pp. 281–90.

century progeny), but has instead been modified, indicating loss of original point of reference—the shrine tomb as it existed in Jerusalem. One may refer, again, to Krautheimer and his thesis concerning the model/copy relationship: inexact, elliptical references may serve to evoke the prototype.[38] In the case of the architectural copy of the Anastasis Rotunda, a polygon often sufficed for the original circular plan. In the case of the later image of the pierced *sepulcrum*, the circular apertures are implied by trefoils. This deviation from the exemplar may prompt us to consider the role of verism in relation to the iconographic issue under consideration.

On the one hand, the similarity and exactitude which verisimilitude demands calls for restrictions on the crucial aspect of creativity inherent in artistic expression.[39] On the other hand, this modification may have been prompted by the memory and importance of events and circumstances which were rapidly slipping into the past: the late thirteenth century witnessed not only a lack of enthusiasm for the affairs of the Holy Land, but also a cynicism, pessimism, and patent disinterest in the Latin Kingdom of Jerusalem, despite the fact that the image of the three-holed tomb still existed in sigillographic form on the seal of Peter, Prior of the Holy Sepulcher from 1225–27.[40] (fig. 183) When the last of the great crusading monarchs, Louis IX, died in 1270, the lofty and noble crusading ideals perished with him.[41] Acre, the only Frankish outpost in far-off Outremer, fell in 1291 without strong reaction in the West. Not surprisingly, the popularity and understanding of the true image of the pierced *sepulcrum Domini* waned as well.

---

[38] Krautheimer, "Introduction to an Iconography," p. 119 stated that an indifference toward precise imitation prevailed throughout the copies of the Church of the Holy Sepulcher and that prototypes were not necessarily copied *in toto* (p. 125). In the most extreme situations, where a copy hardly bears any resemblance to the original, a dedication alone could suffice (p. 127).

[39] This idea is corroborated by Freedberg, *Power of Images*, p. 203.

[40] Schlumberger, *Sigillographie*, pp. 135–6. The imagery on Peter's seal is identical to that of the Canons of the Holy Sepulcher: a non-narrative, architectural form complete with the three-holed tomb. Its bears the inscription: +S': PET: PRIORIS: DNICI: SEPVLC. (Seal of Peter, Dominican Prior of the Sepulcher).

[41] Setton, *History of the Crusades*, vol. 2, pp. 508–18. For the king's relationship with politics and the visual arts, especially pertaining to the Crusades, see Daniel H. Weiss, *Art and Crusade in the Age of Saint Louis* (Cambridge, 1998).

Verisimilitude: A Study in Failure

The *sepulcrum Domini* never became a universal motif like the cross
of Christ; it never became an object of isolated veneration except,
of course, in Jerusalem. Peter the Venerable and his contemporaries
who attempted to rally support for the Second Crusade might have
come closest to promoting its cause. In addition, the image of the Holy
Women and the Angel of the Resurrection at the Tomb remained
intricately bound to a liturgical, narrative sequence; only the Entombment came to independent prominence and, at that, during the later
Middle Ages.[42] The religious and psychological factors constituting
this latter representation, however, are fundamentally different. Burial
and its attendant grief are open to human understanding. Resurrection—specifically the Resurrection of Christ implicit in the iconography of the Holy Women at the Tomb—is an abstract, intangible
mystery to which only strong, nuanced religious faith can effectively
adhere.

In a condensed summary that is not meant to oversimplify the
argument, the image of the *sepulcrum Domini* underwent three general stages. The first, as depicted in the Munich ivory, (fig. 176) is
a classicizing grave memorial. As a prototype for much more frequent
use in the early Middle Ages, it never had much resemblance to the
real structure in Jerusalem. The three Marys and the angel of the
Resurrection sufficiently identify the setting. The second phase is represented by a sarcophagus, which emphasizes the act of burial and
implied Resurrection stressing, therefore, the meaning of the occasion. Even in the starkest of environments, the event is capable of
being understood, as can be seen in the *Codex Egberti*. (fig. 177) Once
again, this image bears no resemblance to the actual place of Christ's
burial. The third type of *sepulcrum* is based on the very appearance
of the Jerusalem sepulchre, borne out by pilgrims' descriptions of
the *locus sanctus* itself. The Chartres and Étampes capitals were offered
as examples. (figs. 178–9) Finally, as the twelfth century progresses,
the image begins to metamorphose and to assume a more decorative
character as the Mantes sculpture indicates. (fig. 182) By the thirteenth
century, the motif had been so widely generalized that its reference

---

[42] William H. Forsyth, *The Entombment of Christ: French Sculptures of the Fifteenth and
Sixteenth Centuries* (Cambridge, MA, 1970).

to the original had little or no meaning. Besides other reasons, such as the slackening of interest in the Holy Land during this time, contact with the original had also become sporadic, resulting in a form that was less specific in conveying accurate visual information.

The sudden appearance of the tomb of Christ furnished with three apertures in twelfth-century art was precipitated more by historical circumstance than by purely artistic invention. Almost as spontaneously as it appears, it disappears. This article can, therefore, be considered a study in failure—the failure of a novel image to gain widespread acceptance and incorporation into the repertory of archetypes upon which most medieval artists drew. The holed *sepulcrum Domini* may be viewed as a minor incident in the general overview of medieval iconography—minor in the sense of its relatively short duration and scattered distribution. It is the product, however, of the more widely significant crusader/pilgrimage phase of medieval European history whose very focus was the Holy Sepulcher itself. Hence, a study of this phenomenon defines and sharpens our understanding of this very critical time.

PART V

PILGRIM SOUVENIRS:
MEANING AND FUNCTION

CHAPTER FIFTEEN

MEDIEVAL PILGRIM BADGES AND THEIR ICONOGRAPHIC ASPECTS

Marike de Kroon

Although pilgrim badges might look insignificant in comparison to other works of art, they are a valuable source of information for medieval iconography, because as these miniature images were produced, purchased, and dispersed in substantial numbers, they actively participated in the spread of visual language. Pilgrim badges reproduced shrines or cult objects, and thus they provide iconographic information on cult objects that have perished, or suffered losses, or have been considerably altered since the Middle Ages. But these pilgrim souvenirs were not only carriers of visual information, they were also used as propaganda, spreading ideas through images. In this essay I will explore medieval religious badges as carriers of important visual information.

Even though the badges, due to their small size, inevitably required a somewhat-simplified reproduction, they were often remarkably accurate, as seen in an Aachen badge showing the bust of Charlemagne. In essence it reproduces the still-extant reliquary bust of the venerated emperor, placed in the Aachen Cathedral treasury.[1] (fig. 184) This jeweled, gold and silver work was commissioned c. 1349 by Charles IV of Bohemia. (fig. 185) The reliquary, adorned with a royal crown, is prominently depicted on the badge. Moreover, the hair and beard, and the imperial eagle insignia on the shoulders (symbol of the town of Aachen and of the Holy Roman Empire) are copied from the reliquary bust by the badge. Although simplified,

---

[1] H.J.E. van Beuningen & A.M. Koldeweij, *Heilig en Profaan. 1000 Laatmiddeleeuwse Insignes uit de collectie H.J.E. van Beuningen*, Rotterdam Papers 8 (Cothen, 1993), p. 275, fig. 264. Denis Bruna, "Quelques images de chefs-reliquaires à travers les enseignes de pèlerinage," in D. Kicken, A.M. Koldeweij, J.R. ter Molen (eds.), *Gevonden voorwerpen. Opstellen over middeleeuwse archeologie voor H.J.E. van Beuningen*, Rotterdam Papers 11 (Rotterdam, 2000), pp. 73–4. In his essay, Bruna also studies a number of other reliquary busts reproduced on pilgrim badges.

this specific head reliquary is clearly distinguishable. This is because recognizability was always the primary concern in the production of pilgrim badges. As distinctive and siginificant signs for a pilgrimage center, seeking to distinguish itself from its numerous competitors, badges helped the shrines to advertise new features. That the Charlemagne bust was carefully reproduced on the badge, underscores these religious souvenirs as valuable visual information.

Our Lady of 's-Hertogenbosch

One example of a pilgrim badge reliably depicting the situation seen by the pilgrims at the shrine, occurs with the souvenir of Our Lady of 's-Hertogenbosch. (fig. 186) The original cult object, still preserved in the Cathedral of Saint-John at 's-Hertogenbosch, is an oak statue of the Virgin and Child, (Mosan *c.* 1280–1320). In a 1380 miracle account, an old and worn figurine of the Virgin Mary discovered at the "fabric house" of the Cathedral was taken by a friar to the church and hidden from view because it was considered ugly.[2] Subsequently, when the image of the Christ child from the statue, found among children playing on the street, was reunited with the Virgin Mary, the statue began to work miracles.[3] Various pilgrim badges from this site illustrate this miraculous statue.[4]

In addition to the miracle-working statue, badges of Our Lady of 's-Hertogenbosch feature stylized tree-motifs, the figure of St. John the Evangelist, a kneeling pilgrim, and several other ex-votos.[5] All

---

[2] The term 'fabric house' is a translation of the Dutch term *bouwloods* (German *Bauhütte*), which refers to a particular medieval form of a building firm, consisting of a collective of stonemasons, bricklayers, sculptors, carpenters and other building craftsmen, which under the direction of a master were connected to a large construction or building, mainly a church, and worked in and around a special area or workshop, often a permanent building made of stone.

[3] The story is recorded in an early seventeenth-century manuscript of an undated eleven-page chronicle in rhyme, bound together with the manuscript recordings of the miracles of Our Lady that took place between 1380 and 1603. This book is kept as *Ms Mirakelboek* in the Archives of the Cathedral Church of Saint-John at 's-Hertogenbosch.

[4] Jos Koldeweij, "Vroomheid in tin en lood. Bossche pelgrimsinsignes als historische bron," in *Brabants Heem* 50 (1998) no. 2, pp. 52–61, with illustrations of badges from 's-Hertogenbosch.

[5] Koldeweij "Vroomheid," p. 55.

these elements were part of the pilgrim experience in the late medieval period in the chapel of the Virgin Mary. The tree-motifs refer to the town of 's-Hertogenbosch (*Buscoducis*), as they are part of the city arms, the city seal, and they are shown on the seal of the fabric house of the Cathedral of St. John.[6] The figure of John, recognizable by his chalice, refers to a reliquary statue of the saint which was placed next to the statue of the Virgin Mary. (This original wooden figure was replaced by a silver one in 1495.) The kneeling pilgrim, too, is an accurate depiction of a silver statue of a pilgrim that became part of the shrine setting in 1383. It was donated as an ex-voto by two brothers, who had been captured and robbed while on pilgrimage, but returned safely after having called upon the intercession of Our Lady of 's-Hertogenbosch. The miniature ship on the badge, refers to another precious ex-voto silver model at the shrine. The miracle book of 's-Hertogenbosch mentions two such silver ships among other donations of silver ex-votos.[7] Unfortunately, the miracle book does not provide any particular information about a mail shirt also shown on the badges, but it must have been an extraordinary object to be included. For only those ex-votos and statues that were prominently placed at the shrine were depicted on the badges. In addition to the ex-votos, also pictured on some of the badges were those elements to which the statues were fixed. Moreover, the exterior of the Cathedral of St. John has been faithfully depicted—albeit rather primitively—in the church building at the top of the badges.[8] One of the towers, the highest of the three, can be identified as the still-existing Romanesque west tower, connected to the nave of the church.

As such, the badges are the earliest-known visual reference to the main structure of the Romanesque church building of the St. John and probably the only depiction of the predecessor of the present

---

[6] The coat of arms of 's-Hertogenbosch has a broad-leaf (lime?) tree.

[7] H. Hens, H. van Bavel, G.C.M. van Dijck, J.H.M. Frantzen, *Mirakelen van Onze Lieve Vrouw te 's-Hertogenbosch 1381–1603*. Bijdragen tot de geschiedenis van het Zuiden van Nederland 42 (Tilburg, 1978), pp. 454–56, miracle no. 260 concerns the silver pilgrim; nos. 33, 127, 159 concern the St. John statue; nos. 76–79 mention ex-voto's of bargemen.

[8] A.M. Koldeweij, "Onder een Sint-Jan met drie torens. Pelgrimstekens uit 's-Hertogenbosch," in Wim Denslagen (ed.) *Studies in vriendschap voor Kees Peeters* (Amsterdam, 1993), pp. 304–15. In slightly alterated form in Van Beuningen, *Heilig en Profaan*, pp. 58–62.

Gothic edifice. Remarkably, the badges show two towers flanking the choir, allowing scholars to surmise that the Romanesque precursor of the present cathedral remained standing longer than was previously believed: it had one tower in addition to that of the Gothic construction. Thus, the pilgrim badges provide valuable data on the history of the church's architecture. All the elements shown on the badges from 's-Hertogenbosch refer to the actual situation that the pilgrims came across at the shrine. The badges truthfully reproduced the most characteristic elements of the objects of the pilgrim's devotion. Using pilgrim souvenirs which, as a rule, show the most characteristic components of the devotional object, one can deduce the layout at the shrine, or even the appearance of the cult object, during the height of the cult, as the 's-Hertogenbosch souvenirs illustrate.

Holy Man Job, Wezemaal

The parish in the Belgian town of Wezemaal owed its importance to the presence of the Lord of Wezemaal, his entourage, and to the pilgrimages undertaken in honor of Job.[9] The veneration of Job took place in the Church of St. Martin, which was built over two periods, 1200–1350 and 1400–1500. Exactly when the Job cult developed is not known, but in 1410, the founding of a monastery at Wezemaal was halted because the Job pilgrimage brought about too

---

[9] Job was also venerated in other places, especially in the southern parts of the Low Countries. W.H.Th. Knippenberg, *Kultuurhistorische verkenningen in de Kempen. III Oude pelgrimages vanuit Noord-Brabant* (Oisterwijk, 1968), pp. 33–6, mentions Tienen, Herenthals, Astene and Hingene. In addition in Arendonk, Carloo-St.-Job, St.-Job-in-'t-Goor and in Schoonbroek/Retie there was a cult to Job in the fifteenth century. The church of Saint-Job in Schoonbroek still has a retable of *c.* 1540–60 from an Antwerp workshop with scenes from the life of Job; Marjan Buyle & Christine Vanthillo, *Vlaamse en Brabantse retabels in Belgische monumenten*, M&L Cahier 4 (Brussels, 2000), pp. 202–5. In the Northern-Brabant towns of Enschot, Heeze, and Helvoirt, Job was also venerated; Peter J. Margry & Charles C.M. Caspers (eds.), *Bedevaartplaatsen in Nederland. Deel 2: Provincie Noord-Brabant* (Hilversum, 1998), pp. 289–92; 381–5; 389–91. The cult object in the church of Saint Martin at Heeze was a sixteenth-century wooden statue, possibly from the old chapel of Saint Job, destroyed in 1654. A small bell remains with the inscription *Job ora pro nobis anno domini 1437* (or possibly 1467), meaning "Job pray for us, the year 1437."

much perturbation, indicating that by that year, a considerable number of pilgrims streamed towards Wezemaal.[10]

The pilgrim souvenirs, both medal type and openwork type, of St. Job Wezemaal, unlike those from 's-Hertogenbosch, do not show an actual cult statue or altarpiece. Rather they depict a crucial episode in the story of the suffering Job where he is seen naked and ulcerated, seated on his dungheap, holding a circular object in his hand. He is accompanied by two or three musicians, playing instruments (a drum, a fiddle, and a wind instrument). On a number of badges there is also a small bell above Job's head. The openwork-type badges have a banderole with the words GOD GAF GOD NAM (God giveth, God taketh away), and at the bottom an inscription reads: S. JOB VAN WESEMALE. (fig. 187) All date from the fifteenth century. Particular details, especially the musicians, perhaps refer to the situation experienced by the pilgrims at the shrine, e.g. in a tableau, but this is uncertain since the two remaining statues of Job from the Wezemaal church are both solitary figures of the seated Job. One stone statue depicts Job, seated on his dunghill, his infested body covered only by a loincloth,[11] while the other, a wooden statue shows Job seated, clothed in a long garment, and holding an open book reading *God gaf, god nam* (God giveth, God taketh away).[12]

---

[10] Van Beuningen, *Heilig en Profaan*, pp. 79, 168. The parish had a chapter of seven canons from the Abbey of Averbode. Marcel Hoc, "Médailles de S. Job vénéré à Wesemaal," in *Revue Belge de Numismatique et de Sigillographie* 89 (1937), p. 42.

[11] Dimensions 177 × 87 × 43 cm, dated to the early sixteenth century. The hat worn by the stone Job can also be seen on the badges. This type of hat with a broad furlined brim turned upwards, followed the model of the *Herzogshut* (Duke's hat), which was worn by noblemen. H.M. Zijlstra-Zweens "Heiligen in het harnas" in H.J.E. van Beuningen, A.M. Koldeweij & D. Kicken (eds.), *Heilig en Profaan 2. 1200 Laatmiddeleeuwse Insignes uit openbare en particuliere collecties*, Rotterdam Papers 12 (Cothen, 2001), p. 161. It is remarkable that Job lying on his dungheap, after losing everything he owned, still wears this headgear in art. Note the wooden statues (Leiden, 1500–10) in the Catharijneconvent Museum in Utrecht and the Antwerp Museum Mayer van den Bergh (Gelre(?), 1510–20). Pictorial examples can be found in the woodcuts and miniatures of the *Speculum Humananae Salvationis*, *Biblia Pauperum*, on the Job-altarpiece by Bernard of Orley (Brussels, Musée Royale des Beaux Arts, 1521), and in two paintings of the *Derision of Job* by anonymous followers of Jeroen Bosch (both *c.* 1550, Dieghem, private collection and Douai, Musée de la Chartreuse).

[12] Height 70 cm, dated 1400–30. The hat on this wooden Job differs from those discussed in fn. 11. The outfit Job wears resembles that of Old Testament prophets. See two statuettes of seated prophets in the Museum Alter Plastik, Liebighaus,

This earlier, wooden statue is believed to be the original miracle-
working cult statue of Wezemaal,[13] but it has little in common with
the Job figure of the badges, where he wears only a loincloth, whereas
the wooden figure wears a long garment. So if the Wezemaal badges
do not reproduce the wooden cult image, they must be modeled
after another source.

An 1472–73 annual account of the Church of St. Martin mentions that during the procession on St. Job's day (May 10) three
"pijpers van Loevenen [. . .] voir sint Job pepen," (pipers from Leuven
played before the statue of Job).[14] The account also records that on
the same day about fifty-three dozen "teekens" (636 badges) were
sold.[15] Sales of religious souvenirs outside of the feast of Job were
recorded as well, but so large an amount on that day indicates its
tremendous popularity with pilgrims.[16] It is quite possible that instead
of depicting a cult image, the scenes on the badges referred to the
playing of the musicians, the pipers, for the Job statue in the church,
perhaps an *in situ* performance of a religious play. The existence of

---

Frankfurt: Jochen Sander, *Die Entdeckung der Kunst. Niederländische Kunst des 15. und
16. Jahrhunderts in Frankfurt* (Mainz, 1995), p. 193, cat. 4, pls. 8–9.

[13] According to Hoc, "Médailles," p. 43. Erroneously he describes the statue as
standing. According to the small miracle book titled *Waerachtige mirakelen gheschiedt in
de parochiale kercke tot Wesemael, door de voor-spraeck van den heylighen belyder ende propheet
Job patroon der selve kerck, wiens mirakeleus beeldt al-daer is rustende* (Leuven, 1750), this
statue was temporarily installed at Leuven in 1588 to protect it against iconoclasm.
Later it was placed in the choir on the south side of the Church of Saint Martin
at Wezemaal. A. Erens, "De Eeredienst van Sint Job te Wezemaal," *Eigen Schoon
en de Brabander* 22 (1939), p. 3. Hoc "Médailles," p. 43, also mentions a "tableau"
hanging in the choir, showing Job on his dungheap holding a potsherd. I have not
yet been able to find other sources for this tableau, nor is there any documentation in the Royal Institute of the Patrimony of Arts in Brussels.

[14] Archives of the Abbey of Averbode, A, 4, IX: Erens "De Eeredienst," p. 7.
Other musical instruments are also reported, but without any indication where and
for what purpose they were played. There is mention of a *luyteniere* (luitplayer),
veeleere (fiddler), *sackpijpen* (bagpipes), and *bongen* (drums).

[15] Erens, "De Eeredienst," p. 5: "Item ontfaen van Jannen den Scoenmakere van
iiij onssen silveren teekenen ende van ijc ende Lxxx dosynen andere teekenen hem
gelevert byden momboren met eenen kerve ende metter ghenen dat hy der toe ontfaen heeft van allen den wasse by hem vercocht binnen den tyt van deser rekeningen."

[16] Signs, among which silver ones, were delivered and sold outside the church
during winter, because at that time there was no one present at the shrine to sell
them. Erens "De Eeredienst" p. 6: "Item ontfaen van Mattys Kynderen voer j
dosyne teekenen die hy inden winter synen gasten vercocht omme datter doen nie-
mant voer sint Job en sat."

mystery plays on the life of Job is well-known.[17] These dramas were adaptations of the apocryphal *Testament of Job* (first century B.C.), which enriched the Old Testament account of Job with elements from folk tales. The most important addition focuses on Job's love for music. For example, the French *La Pacience de Job* and the English *Life of Job*, both preserved in copies from the third quarter of the fifteenth century (but the original probably dates earlier), present musicians playing for Job seated on his dungheap to soothe him in his agony.[18] In the English play, Job rewarded the musicians, for lack of something better, with pieces of his skin, which miraculously turned into pieces of gold. From the middle of the fifteenth century on this motif was rendered in depictions of Job.[19] That Wezemaal badges depict this scene of Job rewarding the musicians, most likely reflects the pilgrims' experience on the day of the procession, when the pipers from Leuven and maybe other musicians played before the statue of Job (perhaps as part of a religious play).

That the badges reflected the actual experience of the pilgrim at the shrine site is confirmed by the presence of the bell on some badges. While it has been suggested that this bell refers to Job in his capacity of patron saint to those who suffer from the plague,[20]

---

[17] Lawrence L. Besserman, *The Legend of Job in the Middle Ages* (Cambridge, MA, 1979), esp. chap. 3.

[18] *La Pacience de Job: Mystère anonyme du XVe siècle* (Paris, Bibliothèque Nationale, ms. fr. 1774), ed. Albert Meiller (Paris, 1971). The *Life of Job* is preserved in the Henry E. Huntington Library, San Marino, CA, MS HM 140 (ff. 93b–96b). Ed. G.N. Garmonsway & R.R. Raymo, "A Middle English Metrical Life of Job," in Arthur Brown & Peter Foote (eds.), *Early English and Norse Studies Presented to Hugh Smith in honour of his Sixtieth Birthday*, (London, 1963), pp. 77–98.

[19] An early example is provided by a miniature in a French manuscript by Pierre de Nesson, *Paraphrase des neuf leçons de Job*, from the second quarter of the fifteenth century (Paris, Bibliothèque Nationale, ms. fr. 1226, fol. 40). Another example is shown by the panel with scenes from the life of Job by the so-called Master of the Legend of Saint Barbara in the Wallraf-Richartz Museum at Cologne (inv. 412). A wooden Job statue in the Antwerp Museum Mayer van den Bergh also holds a circular object in his right hand that can be interpreted as a coin. These scenes from the life of Job, including this motif of Job rewarding the musicians, can be related to medieval drama; Anke Sindermann-Lange, "Theater und Kunst im 16. Jahrhundert am Beispiel des Triptychons 'De la vertu de patience' von Bernard von Orley," *Bulletin des Musées Royaux des Beaux-Arts de Belgique, Bruxelles* 43–4 (1994–95), pp. 81–102.

[20] People suffering from the plague and lepers carried a rattle, or a small bell, in order to alert the healthy to their proximity.

it seems more logical that this bell recalls Wezemaal on the day of the procession when church bells rang (Dutch *gebeyaerd*) as stated in the church account.[21] The bell would bring back aural memories of the pilgrim's experience.[22]

Influence on the Spread of Images

An examination of pilgrim badges from 's-Hertogenbosch and Weze-maal shows how the badges prompted strong memories for pilgrims, judging from depictions of either the cult image or the ceremonies surrounding the shrine. But pilgrim souvenirs also played an important role in the spread of certain iconographic themes throughout Europe. As mass-produced, sought-after commodities, the pilgrim badges from the twelfth until the fifteenth century fulfilled a role later taken on by prints. After all, as religious souvenirs taken home by pilgrims from their often-distant travels, they had the potential to spread iconography over broad areas. For instance, in this reproductive capacity, the badges of the bust of Charlemagne helped to spread the renown of the reliquary after which they were modeled.

Pierre de Luxembourg, Avignon

A badge of Pierre de Luxembourg from Avignon, may be a literal reproduction of his tomb. Pierre de Luxembourg, b. 1369, was the sixth son of Guy de Luxembourg, count of Ligny in Lorraine. Even as a child he led a spiritual life in the monastery of the Celestines in Paris. At the age of 14, he was appointed canon by antipope Clement VII (r. 1378–94), and then bishop. Shortly after this appointment, however, he withdrew from office and retired to live an ascetic life.[23] In 1386, Clement VII called on him to join the papal court

---

[21] Erens, "De Eeredienst," p. 7.
[22] Maybe there even was a church bell dedicated to Job. Regrettably one can only speculate because the tower and with it the bells of the church of Saint-Martin at Wezemaal were devastated by fire during a siege in 1489. I thank Bart Minnen, who is preparing an edition of the church accounts of Wezemaal, for this information.
[23] First in Ligny and later in Paris.

at Avignon, where he was appointed cardinal but Pierre soon demurred for health reasons and secluded himself at Villeneuve-les-Avignon, where he died of tuberculosis on July 2, 1387 at the age of 18. In accordance with his dying wish, he was buried in the Saint-Michel cemetery for the poor in Avignon.[24]

The veneration for this saintly figure began, with miracles occurring at his grave. By 1389, a wooden chapel was devoted to him, and a number of persons of high standing made donations,[25] among them King Charles VI of France, who placed a wax ex-voto statue in the chapel.[26] Soon the chapel proved to be too small to house all ex-votos and other objects of art bestowed by the kings of France and Aragon, and other members of aristocracy, necessitating the building of a larger chapel. Clement VII requested that the Celestines of Gentilly build a monastery in 1394–5 over Pierre's tomb,[27] and by 1425 it was enlarged. Ultimately, in 1432 Pierre became the patron of Avignon, although his actual beatification did not take place until 1527.[28]

Only one badge of Pierre de Luxembourg from Avignon has been found.[29] (fig. 188) This openwork badge, with a gabled top, illustrates

---

[24] Konrad Kunze "Pietro di Lussemburgo" in Filippo Caraffa (ed.) *Biblioteca Sanctorum*, X (Rome, 1961) column 705–706; J. Cambell, *Lexikon für Theologie und Kirche*, VIII (Freiburg im Breisgau, 1957–68) col. 369; Johan Huizinga, *Herfsttij der Middeleeuwen* (Amsterdam, 1997), pp. 191–2.

[25] The first wooden chapel was founded by Marie de Bretagne, widow of Louis I of Anjou. Robert Brun, *Avignon au temps des papes* (Brionne, 1983), p. 93.

[26] ". . . ymage de cire qu'il a fait faire de notre grandeur et mettre en tabernacle devant sainct Pierre de Luxembourg à Avignon," according to a letter by Charles VI (1380–1422), Archives de l'art français, vol. V, p. 344. L. Maxe-Werly, "Médaille du bienheureux Pierre de Luxembourg du XVᵉ siècle," *Mémoires de la Société des Lettres, Sciences et Arts de Bar-le-Duc*, 3rd series, VII (1898), p. 51.

[27] Dominique Thiébaut & Michel Laclotte, *l'École d'Avignon* (Paris, 1983), cat. 66, p. 240; Konrad Kunze "Pietro di Lussemburgo," col. 706. According to Kunze, the building began in 1393; Van Beuningen & Koldeweij, *Heilig en Profaan*, p. 188, mention the same year for the foundation and attribute this to the Queen of Sicily and the funding to the French king Charles VI and his brother Louis of Orléans. Huizinga; *Herfsttij*, p. 191, states that the king of France founded the monastery and the foundation stone was laid by the Dukes of Orléans, Berry, and Burgundy.

[28] It has been suggested that Pierre de Luxembourg's veneration was instigated by the antipope Clement VII in order to add to the spiritual prestige of the Avignon papal court during the Schism. Dominique Carru & Sylvain Gagnière, "Notes sur quelques objets de dévotion populaire. Ampoules et enseignes de pèlerinage du Moyen Age tardif provenant d'Avignon," *Mémoire de l'Académie de Vaucluse*, 8th series, I (1992), p. 63.

[29] It was found in Dordrecht. Van Beuningen & Koldeweij *Heilig en Profaan*, p. 188, no. 315.

an oblique altar with a book on top and Pierre de Luxembourg kneels in prayer before it, gazing towards a crucifix that has appeared to him in a vision. Pierre is clothed in cardinal vestments and his bare head is tonsured. On the left side of the altar is Pierre's coat of arms: a lion rampant, surmounted by a cardinal's hat. Across the bottom of the badge is the inscription BEAT ' P. CARD (Blessed Cardinal Pierre).

The representation on this badge is closely related to a panel painting of the Avignon School, which previously hung in the monastic church of the Celestines in Avignon, above Pierre's tomb.[30] This panel with its gold brocade background, depicts (in side view as does the badge) the beatified figure in ecstacy, kneeling in prayer before an altar with a crucifix suspended above it. (fig. 189) Pierre wears his cardinal's vestments, and his cardinal's hat lies on the floor next to the altar, and a nimbus surrounds his tonsured head. A cloth with Pierre's coat of arms with the Luxembourg lion rampant and the cardinal's hat is hung over the altar. An open book lays on a cushion atop the altar. The panel has been dated to *c.* 1450, on the basis of the drapery,[31] and the badge is dated 1425–75, also on stylistic grounds.

That the painting hung above Pierre's grave at the Celestine monastic church, the focal point of the pilgrimage clearly connects the panel and the badge, as is evident by their shared iconography. One might question whether the badge merely replicates the standard iconography of Pierre, but it is evident that the badge refers to this particular painting when one compares it to other known images of Pierre.[32] Two circular badges dedicated to Pierre have

---

[30] Now preserved at the Musée du Petit Palais in Avignon. Greta Ring, *A Century of French Painting, 1400–1500* (London, 1949), p. 207, no. 106, pl. 59.

[31] Greta Ring, *A Century*, p. 207. Her conclusion is based on fact that the drapery in this painting corresponds to the drapery in Enguerrand Quarton's *Madone de la Miséricorde* from 1452.

[32] Other kinds of badges devoted to Pierre, appear in written sources. King René, who made a pilgrimage to Pierre de Luxembourg's tomb in 1448, paid for eighteen silver badges of "St. Pierre de Luxembourg." The text mentions nothing concerning the appearance of these "enseignes." The account book of the King mentions "pour 18 enseignez d'argent de Saint Pierre de Luxembourg baillées au dit seigneur pour les distribuer à son plaisir à raison d'un demi-gros la pièce: 2 florins et 3 gros," citation after Maxe-Werly "Médaille," p. 52. Maxe-Werly believed that he had found one of these silver badges showing the vision of Pierre de Luxembourg. Unfortunately, Maxe-Werly does not provide any information regarding the dimen-

more in common with the fifteenth-century illuminated miniatures of the Vision of Pierre de Luxembourg, where his prayer occurs at the altar in a church interior.[33] The first badge depicts the scene in mirror view with an angel hovering above Pierre, supporting his head while he looks at the crucifix. The second circular badge, struck with a coin stamp and dating to the first half of the fifteenth century, pictures the same variant image, but without the angel.[34] They differ iconographically from the panel and badge because either they omit (the portrayal of) the coat of arms or it is held by an angel hovering over Pierre in the sky.[35]

---

sions of the "médaille," nor does he reveal the whereabouts of the object. Carru & Gagnière "Notes" only mention it is in Bar-le-Duc. Maxe-Werly's use of the term *médaille* for these circular badges is somewhat confusing, because this term usually indicates double-sided souvenirs from a later period.

[33] Images showing him in the company of the Virgin Mary have been left out in this discourse. For example, an image of Pierre presenting a donor to Mary can be seen on a panel from *c.* 1400 in the Worcester Art Museum, Ring, no. 35, pl. 10. A similar picture is found in a Luxemburg book of Hours from the first half of the fifteenth century in the Russian National Library at Saint Petersburg (Rasn.O.v.I, 6, fol. 10v). TamaraVoronowa & Andrej Sterligov, *Westeuropäische Buchmalerei des 8. bis 16. Jahrhunderts in der Russischen Nationalbibliothek, Sankt Petersburg* (Augsburg, 2000), p. 126, pl. 148. Also a miniature in a fourteenth-century book of hours in the Avignon Library shows just Pierre kneeling before Mary.

[34] The medal is in the collection of the Musée Calvet in Avignon. L.H. Labande, "Notes sur deux médailles du bienheureux Pierre de Luxembourg et sur son portrait conservé au Musée Calvet," *Mémoires de l'Académie de Vaucluse,* 18 (1899), pp. 409–13, illustrates both medals.

[35] This can be seen in two books of hours, one from Avignon, *c.* 1400, (Vienna, Östr. NB, Cod. 9450, fol. 50): Otto Pächt, *Französische Schule* (Vienna, 1974–77), vol. I, pl. 264, and the other the Book of Hours of Maria Stuart, French, *c.* 1430 (St. Petersburg, Russ. Nat. Library, Lat.Q.v.I,112, fol. 167v): Voronowa & Sterligov, *Westeuropäische Buchmalerei,* p. 120, pl. 144. This miniature shows the coat of arms with the lion rampant, while in all other miniatures the coats of arms have been erased. Because of this, the authors conclude that the commisioner of this manuscript must have been a member of the Luxembourg family. However, this conclusion seems a bit precipitate, considering that the coat of arms with the Luxembourg lion rampant is the "ordinary" attribute of Pierre de Luxembourg. Another picture of Pierre's vision in a church interior can be found in a book of hours from Paris, *c.* 1450–60 (Vienna, Österreichische Nationalbibliothek, Cod. 13237, fol. 276v): Pächt, *Französische Schule,* pl. 341. This shows the altar at the left and Pierre at the right, but the crucifix is different because it has seraphim wings and is leaning over backwards instead of forwards. An angel holds the cardinal's hat and over Pierre's head there is a canopy. The coat of arms is missing. In the Walters Art Gallery there are three manuscripts with miniatures of the vision of Pierrre de Luxembourg: a book of hours from Paris, *c.* 1411 (ms. W. 232, fol. 93), Lillian Randall, *Medieval and Renaissance Manuscripts in the Walters Art Gallery, Vol. I, France 875–1420* (Baltimore, 1989), p. 233, cat. 85; a miniature in a book of hours from the Loire region, late

In view of these iconographic differences, the miniatures and circular badges, apart from the common subject matter of the Vision,
appear to have very little connection with either the panel painting
or with the openwork pilgrim badge. The badge would appear to
have been produced to propagate this very painting, which was an
important part of the devotional setting at the grave of Pierre de
Luxembourg.[36] The scene of the Vision was eminently suitable for
this purpose, because it involved a saint who was venerated for his
asceticism and his devoted attitude towards life. It was not just any
scene, but the very scene which hung above his tomb.

Our Lady of Amersfoort

The connection of pilgrim badges to devotional panels is again seen
in the example of Our Lady of Amersfoort in the Netherlands. Here
the cult arises from the miraculous discovery of a statue of the Virgin
and Child, when in 1444, a young woman came to the town of
Amersfoort to enter the Agnieten-Convent. Before passing through
the town gate, she took a plain figurine of the Virgin and Child
from her belongings and threw it in the water, because she was
embarrassed to show the humble work to the sisters at the convent.
A few weeks later, another woman, Margriet Gijsen, had three successive visions in which she was instructed to go to the canal by the
town gate to rescue the Virgin Mary from the water. When she
arrived there, the woman saw the discarded figurine lying under the
ice which covered the flowing water. She fished it out and took it
home with her. After she had told her story to the priest, the statue
was taken to the Church of Our Lady of Amersfoort. Subsequently,
various miracles attracted numerous pilgrims. Unfortunately, little is
left of the miraculous figurine, making it difficult to describe or date
it accurately. From what remains one can deduce that it was a very

---

fifteenth century (ms. W. 430, fol. 165v), Randall, *Manuscripts in the Walters Art Gallery*,
II, p. 442. cat. 192; and in a miniature in a franco-flemish book of hours, *c.* 1440
(ms. W. 211, fol. 164v), Randall, *Manuscripts in the Walters Art Gallery*, III, pp. 152–3,
cat. 234.

[36] A late fourteenth-century effigy of Pierre with a mitred head, also at Avignon,
was not characteristic enough to be reproduced on the pilgrim badge. An illustration of this effigy is in *Biblioteca Sanctorum* (fn. 24) X, cols. 706–9, ill. 703.

simple statue (10–15 cm h) made of pipe clay. Two seventeenth-century manuscripts describe it variously as a small, unvarnished statuette, being barely larger than a child's foot.[37] These kind of pipe clay figurines were fairly inexpensive, mass-produced articles, comparable to pilgrim badges.[38]

A number of circular, openwork pilgrim badges from Amersfoort have been found that convey the story of the miraculous discovery of the statue. (fig. 190) A young woman, a bucket next to her, kneels on the ice. She reaches out to take a disproportionately-large statue from the water. Above, there is usually a banderole with the inscription AMERSFOERT, sometimes with the year 1445 on it (instead of 1444, in accordance with the church calendar).

A *c.* 1525 panel painting, made for the church of Our Lady in Amersfoort,[39] (fig. 191) shows the miraculous discovery of the statuette in 1444, but the painter added a church tower, which was not finished until 1470, financed by the pilgrimage revenues.[40] The similarity between the depictions on the badge and the panel is remarkable. The main difference is that on the badges, the statue has already been taken out of the bucket and the figures of the woman and the statue are disproportionately-large. The latter occurs because of the necessity for reduction to essential elements of the miracle story for the small surface of the badge—primarily the miraculous statuette of the Virgin Mary, which was the center of devotion.[41]

---

[37] Respectively Brussels, Royal Library of Belgium, ms. 8179–8180, fols. 13r–69v and Antonius Mattheus, *Rerum Amorfortiarum. Scriptores duo inediti* (Leiden, 1693); in the second part, the *Chronicon Amorfortium incerti auctoris*, p. 172, the author describes the statue as "... si talem statuam, tam exiguam, quae infantis pedem vix aexquarat..." Both are cited by Ottie Thiers, *Bedevaart en kerkeraad. De Amersfoortse vrouwevaart van 1444 tot 1720* (Hilversum, 1994), p. 22, fn. 26.

[38] That the Virgin wished to be venerated through this small, plain statuette, which embarrassed the owner, belongs to the folk theme of the Virgin's preference for the humble: Thiers, *Bedevaart*, p. 22. Another instance is the miraculous statue of Our Lady of 's-Hertogenbosch which was also very plain and regarded as ugly at first.

[39] It measures 68.5 × 99 cm and is now in the Church of the Old-Catholic Parish of Saint-George, Amersfoort.

[40] Because the earliest type of Amersfoort badges already show three towers on top, it is unlikely that they are referring to the tower of the Church of Our Lady. Rather they are depicted here as decorative element.

[41] Unfortunately, the church archives have been destroyed, so it remains unclear whether both badges and panel follow some earlier visual source, or if the depiction on the badges was the inspiration for the painter of the panel of 1525.

Adrian of Geraardsbergen, Quirinus of Neuss and Victor of Xanten

A panel from the *c.* 1490 Flemish "*Annenaltar*" from the Church of the Carmelites at Frankfurt am Main shows Joachim and Anna giving alms to pilgrims, who are recognizable by the badges on their hats and clothes.[42] The woman standing in the center of the group next to Joachim, has pinned on her hat a badge of Adrian of Geraardsbergen.[43] (fig. 192) This type of badge, from *c.* 1425, shows Adrian wearing a suit of armor with a cloak over it and standing on a lion, symbolizing his courage. He holds a sword in his right hand and a hammer and anvil in his left, which refer to his martyrdom (his legs were crushed with a hammer on an anvil and his head was cut off by a sword). The way in which the soldier-saint is rendered on this badge conforms to the general medieval iconography of St. Adrian, but how do these badges relate to the shrine of St. Adrian at Geraardsbergen?

The Benedictine Abbey of Geraardsbergen came into possession of relics of Adrian in 1175, and in 1423 these were translated to a new shrine, after which veneration increased considerably, as is evident by the many badges of Adrian found.[44] This change in the accommodation of the relics of Adrian is reflected in the badges, because *c.* 1425 a new type of badge was produced that was probably modelled after an image of Adrian on or near the new shrine. (fig. 195) While Adrian was clothed in a long garment and a cloak on earlier badges, on this new type of badge he wears a suit of armor. He also holds his attributes in a different manner. On the

---

[42] The original appearance of the altar is not precisely understood. The middle part must have consisted of a shrine with carved wooden, gilded figures; Kurt Köster, "Pilgerzeichen und Wallfahrtsplaketten von St. Adrian in Geraardsbergen. Zu einer Darstellung auf einer flämischen Altartafel des 15. Jahrhunderts im Historischen Museum zu Frankfurt am Main," *Städel-Jahrbuch* 4 (1973), p. 105.

[43] Köster "Pilgerzeichen," p. 106, identified the badge depicted on the panel as that of Adrian of Geraardsbergen. The badge that the Flemish painter used as a model was undoubtedly presented to him by one of the many Netherlandish merchants (from the Brabant region) of the brotherhood that founded the chapel for which the *Annenaltar* was meant. The chapel in fact is also known as the *Capella Brabantinorum*.

[44] Large numbers have been found in the Netherlands. In Germany, Adrian badges have been discovered on church bells and in England, at Canterbury. Brian Spencer, "Medieval pilgrim badges found at Canterbury, England," D. Kicken, A.M. Koldeweij & J.R. ter Molen (eds.), *Gevonden voorwerpen. Opstellen over middeleeuwse archeologie voor H.J.E. van Beuningen*, Rotterdam Papers 11 (Rotterdam, 2000), p. 319.

older badges he holds them close to his body, whereas on the newer badges his arms are held out further from his torso. The older badges show fashionably scalloped sleeves, while on the later versions, the scalloped sleeve is only visible on the left arm with the right arm partly hidden by a banderole with the inscription S. ADRIANUS.[45]

Badges of this type have been found in large numbers, indicating the increased veneration of St. Adrian at Geraardsbergen. Among the numerous worshippers there were various dignitaries and crowned heads of Europe, such as King Louis XI of France and his wife, Charlotte of Savoy. Between 1461–83 they commissioned a manuscript of the legend of St. Adrian, in which the first miniature depicts the king and queen as donors, kneeling in adoration at the shrine of the saint in Geraardsbergen.[46] Adrian, standing on a lion, wears a tunic with scalloped sleeves over his armor and holds a sword, a hammer, and an anvil in his hands. He fills the center part of the retable and is flanked by the two smaller figures of St. John the Baptist and St. Louis. One could argue as to what extent the formation as depicted here represents the actual disposition of the cult objects at the shrine at Geraardsbergen at that time,[47] but the resemblance between the figure of Adrian in this miniature and on the pilgrim badges is striking. Adding to this, the earlier miniatures in the 1449 *Breviary of Geraardsbergen* picture the statue of Adrian as a solitary figure on the altar.[48] (fig. 193) All these images of Adrian might have been modelled after the original at Geraardsbergen.[49] Even on a seal of Geraardsbergen abbot, Simon de Warluzel (r. 1560+),

---

[45] Zijlstra-Zweens "Heiligen in het harnas," p. 166. Compare to the Militant Saints on the *Ghent Altarpiece* by Jan and Hubert Van Eyck, *c.* 1432, at St. Bavo-Cathedral; Zijlstra-Zweens, p. 168.

[46] Vienna, Österreichische Nationalbibliothek, Cod. Ser. n. 2619, fol. 3v. Dagmar Thoss, *Flämische Buchmalerei. Handschriftenschätze aus dem Burgunderreich*, Ausstellung der Handschriften- und Inkunabelsammlung der Österreichischen Nationalbibliothek (Graz, 1987), pl. 10.

[47] Hugo Van der Velden, *Gerard Loyet en Karel de Stoute: het votiefportret in de Bourgondische Nederlanden* (Ph.D. diss. University of Utrecht, 1997), p. 165.

[48] Maredsous, Abbey library, *Brevier van Geraardsbergen*, II. 2. J. Delforge, "Le Bréviaire de saint-Adrien de Grammont," *Scriptorium* 12 (1958), pp. 102–4. In the margin of folio 1 are two miniatures showing the altar.

[49] It became the conventional iconography of Adrian as seen in the *Book of Hours of William of Hastings* (Madrid, Fundación Lázaro-Galdiano, Ms. 15503, fol. 26v) made for Lord William of Hastings in Flanders, *c.* 1465.

[50] The seal is now in Brussels, State Archives in Belgium, Seal Department, no. 6.606.

the retable with the central statue of St. Adrian is depicted.[50] (fig. 194)
By copying this statue so meticulously since the second quarter of
the fifteenth century, the badges of saint Adrian were its first dis-
seminators and thus functioned as intermediaries of the iconography
of this saint.

In Neuss-am-Rhein, the relics of the soldier-saint Quirinus were
worshipped since 1050. According to the local legend, these remains
were a gift of Pope Leo IX (r. 1049–54) to the Benedictine convent
of Neuss, of which his sister, Gepa was abbess. The pilgrimage to
Quirinus reached its climax in the fifteenth century and Neuss pilgrim
badges were produced in the fifteenth and sixteenth centuries.[51] When
looking at the Quirinus badges, the first thing that strikes one is their
remarkable similarity to the badges of Adrian of Geraardsbergen.
(fig. 196) Quirinus is also dressed in very elegant armor, covered by
a fashionable tunic with scalloped sleeves (and in some cases a cloak),
while the saint holds in his one hand a sword, pointing down, and
in the other, a lance. At his hip he has a dagger and against his
shoulder, or sometimes against his leg, rests his shield with the coat
of arms of Neuss: the nine canonballs, that can also be discerned in
the banner on the lance.[52] Further, the badges display the coat of
arms of the diocese of Cologne, the shield with a cross, and sometimes also the new town arms that Neuss obtained from Frederic III
(1440–93),[53] who granted this privilege to the town after a siege (July
1474–June 1475) of state enemy Charles the Bold (1467–77) had
been successfully resisted. After this enormous numbers of pilgrims
flowed into the town. What makes the figures of Quirinus and Adrian
on these badges "brothers in arms," is their same pose, each with
one knee slightly bent and their almost identical heads with berets.
This likeness also inspires the question as to whether the two institutions—both of Benedictine affiliation—possibly worked with the
same badge designers?

In 's-Hertogenbosch a souvenir from a third soldier-saint was
found, which also shows an eye-catching likeness to the Quirinus
badges. This badge of Victor of Xanten, identified by the inscrip-

---

[51] Kurt Köster published a survey of Quirinus-badges, including the badges cast
on bells, "Die Pilgerzeichen der Neusser Quirinus-Wallfahrt im Spätmittelalter,"
Neusser Jahrbuch 1984, pp. 11–29.
[52] The concave form of the shield and the lance opening can also be seen on
the militant saints in the *Ghent Altarpiece*.
[53] A shield with double-headed eagle and the imperial crown on top.

tion S. VICTOR and by the coat of arms, (fig. 197) in both pose and armor is practically identical to that of Quirinus. Presumably, this badge was modelled on the Quirinus badges from nearby Neuss.[54] Again the same body position is seen, with legs apart and knee slightly bent, in the portrayal of Victor, who also wears very similar armor. Just like Quirinus, Victor wears a tunic with scalloped sleeves over his armor and he holds in his right hand a lance with banner, at the foot of which stands a coat of arms. With his left hand he supports a concave shield with the lance opening placed on the ground against his leg. He also has a dagger at his hip. The main difference is the more youthful appearance of the beardless saint. From the riches of the church treasury of the Cathedral at Xanten no single reliquary or cult statue survives that can be said to have been reproduced in this badge, although there were originally many images of Victor in the church. He was depicted on a stained glass window from the middle of the fifteenth century in the northern bay and also as one of the pillar statues on the south side of the nave, yet in both cases he is shown with fewer attributes than on the badge.[55] There also was a statue, placed against the exterior wall of the "Kellerei" or "Bannita," the chapter law court of the Cathedral complex, sculpted by master Heinrich Blankebyl in 1468.[56] Was it one of these specific representations of Victor that the pilgrims wished to remember in the form of a pewter souvenir, for in most of the other holy places a miniature version of a specific object or an image was acquired as a keepsake? Or does this case illustrate a more general devotion to Victor, resulting in a sort of "chain-reaction" in the field of the iconography of pilgrim souvenirs: badges of Adrian that influence those of Quirinus (or vice-versa), which in their turn were imitated in the pilgrim signs of Victor of Xanten?

Elisabeth of Thüringen, Marburg

Lastly, the case of the badge of Elisabeth from Marburg illustrates how a pilgrim souvenir was consciously used for propaganda

---

[54] Van Beuningen & Koldeweij, *Heilig en profaan 2*, (fn. 11), p. 306.
[55] Richard Klapheck, *Der Dom zu Xanten und seine Kunstschätze* (Berlin, 1930), pp. 54, 79.
[56] Walter Bader (ed.), *Sechzehnhundert Jahre Xantener Dom* (Cologne, 1963), ill. 57.

purposes.[57] Elisabeth of Thüringen died in 1231 at the age of twenty-four. She spent the last four years of her life in the convent of the Third Order of St. Francis in Marburg, which she entered after her husband's death in 1227. Her last years were devoted to the care of the sick in the hospital she had founded at the convent and had dedicated to St. Francis. She was buried in the Chapel of St. Francis, and almost immediately afterwards pilgrims came there to honor her. Very soon after, in 1235, she was canonized by Pope Gregory IX (r. 1227–41).

Four types of badges from Marburg have been found; two discovered in Dordrecht. One is rather primitive and the other more sophisticated in form and iconography. (fig. 198) Another badge was found in Lübeck and yet another in Lund.[58] All these badges show, with varying quality, the same image. In a pointed field crowned by two towers, are the figures of Elisabeth on the left and Francis on the right, flanking a stylized column. Above them is the half figure of Christ, recognizable by his cross nimbus, placing a crown on the head of each of the saints below him. Elisabeth is clothed in a long garment and Francis in his monk's habit. Remarkably, Elisabeth is placed on the right side of Christ, the better position of the two. With this she was put on a par with the great St. Francis, if not above him. This matched the elevated status of Elisabeth in Marburg after her canonization in 1235. The local church and the hospital were renewed and placed under the patronage of Elisabeth, who posthumously, and no doubt unwillingly, overshadowed Saint Francis. The new badges, as they were intended to be distributed widely were used in the propagation of this new status immediately after Elizabeth's canonization. In this respect they were more influential than the stained glass windows in the Church of St. Elisabeth in Marburg. The *Elizabeth Window* (1240–50) also showed the coronation of Elisabeth and Francis, but even though both saints are placed side by side, it

---

[57] A.M. Koldeweij, "Pelgrimsinsignes van Elisabeth uit Marburg" in Van Beuningen *Heilig en Profaan*, pp. 69–76, examines this propaganda-role of the Elisabeth badges from Marburg extensively. This essay was the main source used here.

[58] The badges found in Dordrecht are respectively depicted and described in Van Beuningen *Heilig en profaan 2*, no. 1123; Van Beuningen *Heilig en Profaan*, no. 193. The fragment from Lübeck was excavated (1989–91 archeological dig) from a mass grave (1317) in the graveyard of the *Heilige Geist Hospital*. For the Lund badge (Museum Kulturen, inv. KM 5876, Lund, Sweden) see Koldeweij "Pelgrimsinsignes," pp. 69–75, ill. 22.

is Francis who occupies the most important position at Christ's right side, whereas Elisabeth is crowned by Mary. It is extraordinary that those responsible for the manufacturing of badges, which were disseminated on a large scale, did not recoil from using a very flagrant representation of Elisabeth in order to consciously propagate the elevated position she, at least in their view, deserved.

Summary

Pilgrim badges have proven to be an important resource in the field of iconography. After all, as a rule they reproduce the shrine or the cult object the pilgrims came to behold and venerate. In miniature they represent the object or situation concerned as a cherished keepsake for returning or continuing pilgrims. Through this, they spread the visual language as seen on the badge of Pierre de Luxembourg. Badges also contain iconographic information concerning the original disposition at the shrine. This is crucial, especially when this shrine itself no longer exists or has been considerably altered, such as with the cult of Job from Wezemaal and Our Lady of 's-Hertogenbosch. Pilgrim badges also influenced one another, as shown by the badges of the soldier-saints Adrian, Quirinus, and Victor. Not only did they spread iconographic images, they were also used as a means of propaganda, as illustrated by the case of Elisabeth from Marburg. As a visual carrier of information and an early propagator of images, the medieval pilgrim badge is a unique source, which deserves to be explored more profoundly.

CHAPTER SIXTEEN

RECONSTRUCTING THE SHRINE OF ST. THOMAS BECKET, CANTERBURY CATHEDRAL

Sarah Blick

On August 31, 1538, Sir William Penison stood before one of most important and famous shrines in all of medieval Europe, that of St. Thomas Becket at Canterbury Cathedral. With him was the noble-woman Madame de Montreuil, who had never seen the object before. She

> ... not a litle marveilled of the greate riches thereof; saing to be innu-merable, and that if she had not seen it, all the men in the wourlde could never a made her belyve it.[1]

Nine days later, the magnificent shrine was demolished and its trea-sures carted away by order of Henry VIII.[2] Canterbury with its cult

---

[1] Penison wrote to Thomas Cromwell. (ed.) Robert Peel, *State Papers of King Henry the Eighth* I (London, 1831), p. 583.

[2] In 1538, the saint was deemed a traitor and this proclamation issued,

> His [Becket's] images and pictures through the whole realm shall be put down and avoided out of all churches, chapels and other places; and that from hence-forth the days used to be festival in his name shall not be observed, nor the service office, antiphons, collects and prayers read in his name read, but rased and put out of all the books ... upon pain of his majesty's indignation and imprisonment at his grace's pleasure.

Cotton Library, Titus B. I, f. 519; Gilbert Burnet, *The History of the Reformation of the Church of England* (Oxford, 1865), p. 220. £23 16s. was paid to laborers and the Canterbury monks.

> Item payde to the saide Mr. Writhesley by like ire and lyke commaundemet xxiii li xvis for somoch money layde oute in sonndry percells by way of his maiestes rewarde vnto sondry monkes and chief officers of Christchurch in Cantbery and also to sonndry sruntes and labourers traveling abowte the dis-garnisshinge of a shryne ...

British Library, Arundel MS. 97, p. 34; Arthur Mason, *What Became of the Bones of St. Thomas?* (Cambridge, 1920), p. 151. The weight of the plate received was "gold (including 2 3/4 ounces of fine gold coins) ... no less than 4,994 3/4 ounces; the gilt plate weighed 4,425; the parcel gilt 840; and the plain silver 5,286." Royal Office Exchequer Augmentation Official Treasury Roll, i, m. 110; Francis A. Gasquet, *Henry VIII and the English Monasteries: An Attempt to Illustrate the History of Their Suppression* (London, 1889), p. 408.

of Becket was an especially-hated target in the Dissolution of the
Monasteries, because it symbolized the superiority of ecclesiastical
power. Until its demise, the shrine continued to attract pilgrims of
the highest rank, yet there was no outcry in response to its dismantling.[3] The absence of protest may reflect the waning popularity of Canterbury as a pilgrimage center, but the silence may be
indicative of fear of speaking out against a government that did not
tolerate this kind of dissent. Still, the shrine was not forgotten, for
almost as soon as it had passed out of living memory, people began
to try to reconstruct the original edifice.[4] Since then, every scrap of
information which purports to describe it has been analyzed, but
this study has proved to be an exercise in frustration because, despite
the great amount of information available, the documents differ dramatically from one another in the data conveyed. Further, these documents are sometimes called into question because of uncertainty
regarding their reliability, their poor condition, and their ambiguous
dates. Luckily, a more accurate record survives: pilgrimage souvenir
badges. These badges, produced to commemorate the shrine, have
been recognized as significant documents which "provide us with an
important, if schematic, record of the shrine of St. Thomas in the
fourteenth century,"[5] but these objects have not been examined in
detail nor compared with other surviving visual records. This essay
will examine these records and then it will focus on the pilgrim
badges, arguing in favor of their fidelity. Using the badges, it will

---

[3] Indications of continued interest include visits by Henry VIII and Emperor
Charles V in 1520 and gifts such as William Eastfeld's (mayor of London) 1446
gift of "an *ouche* of gold set with precious stone and pearls is to be ... offered at *le
Shryne* of S. Thomas of Canterbury." Roll 175 (19) and Hugh Peyntour's 1361 will
with a bequest for someone to make a barefoot pilgrimage to Canterbury and to
leave a penny at each of the major shrines therein. Roll 96 (100). (ed.) Reginald
Sharpe, *Calendar of Wills Proved and Enrolled in the Court of Husting, London, A.D.
1258–A.D. 1688* (London, 1890), 2, pp. 106–7; 510. Still, the waning popularity
might be reflected in the drop in charitable donations to the shrine from a high
of £702 11 s. in 1220 to £13 13s 3d in 1532. Ben Nilson, *Cathedral Shrines of
Medieval England* (Woodbridge, UK, 1998), pp. 148–9, though it is uncertain as many
financial documents associated with the shrine did not survive.

[4] This is reflected in the mistaken identification by Richard Scarlett, in his heraldic
collections of 1599, British Library MS Harley 1366, 83, of the Tomb of Archbishop
Hubert Walter as the shrine base. Bernard Rackham, *The Ancient Glass of Canterbury
Cathedral* (London, 1949), pl. d.

[5] Brian Spencer, "Pilgrim Souvenirs," in eds. Jonathan Alexander and Paul Binski,
Age of Chivalry: Art in Plantagenet England 1200–1400 (London, 1987), p. 219.

reconstruct the general appearance of the shrine, placing it into the context of contemporary shrine bases and ecclesiastical tombs.

The History of the Shrine of St. Thomas Becket

Of the actual shrine, nothing remains.[6] Only worn tiles on the floor mark where it once stood, revealing that it once rose on three concentric platforms, which measured at their greatest extent 8.5 × 5.2 m and at their smallest, 4.25 × 2.75 m. Fortunately, written accounts tell us more. On July 7, 1220, amidst great celebration and a jubilee in honor of the fiftieth anniversary of Becket's martyrdom, the relics of St. Thomas were translated in an iron-covered wooden box from his tomb in the crypt to the shrine.[7] The shrine, designed by Walter of Colchester (Sacrist of St. Albans) and Elias of Dereham (Canon of Salisbury), was placed directly above the tomb in the sanctuary

---

[6] Three marble fragments have been linked to the shrine: a square base or capital, a capital with curling trefoil stiffleaves, and a chipped fragment. Their high quality carving is matched by their fine media, a variegated maroon/burgundy color marble with yellow-white veins throughout. Unfortunately, there is no evidence that these pieces were once part of the shrine, although the leaves on the capital and marble type are comparable to the capitals in the east end of Trinity Chapel and inlaid floor. They may have been part of a base from one of the other many shrines which once graced Canterbury Cathedral. William Urry, "Some Notes on the Two Resting Places of St. Thomas Becket at Canterbury" in Raymonde Foreville, *Thomas Becket, Actes du Colloque International de Sédières*, Paris, 1975, pp. 204–6; Mason, *Bones of Becket*, p. 113; Neil Stratford, Pamela Tudor-Craig, A.M. Mathesius "Archbishop Hubert Walter's Tomb and its Furnishings" in *Medieval Art and Architecture at Canterbury before 1220* (London, 1982), p. 76.

[7] The box was "a seemly wooden chest adorned for the purpose, the which was well strengthened with iron, and they fastened it carefully with iron nails." *The Polistoire*, British Library, Harleian MS 636 f. 201b, col. 2, l. 15—f. 202b trans. by Mason, *Bones of Becket*, pp. 71–3; Arthur Stanley, *Historical Memorials of Canterbury* (New York, nd), pp. 306–8. Archbishop Stephen Langton (r. 1207–28), Henry III, and other nobles bore the chest up to the shrine. Stanley, *Historical Memorials*, pp. 238–43. Matthew Paris, *Matthaei Parisiensis, Monachi Sancti Albani, Historia Anglorum, Sive, ut Vulgo Dicitur, Historia Minor. Abbreviatio Chronicorum Angliae* ed. Frederick Madden (London, 1875–83), II, pp. 241–2. A fifteen-day indulgence was purchased from Pope Honorius III for the event. Joseph B. Sheppard, *Christ Church Letters: A Volume of Medieval Letters Relating to the Priory of Christ Church Canterbury* (Westminster, 1877), pp. XLV, VI. It was believed that because of the translation, England prospered, "Translato Thoma succedunt prospera cuncta." G. Marshall, "The Shrine of St. Thomas de Cantilupe, in Hereford Cathedral" *Transactions of the Woolhope Naturalists' Field Club* 27 (1930–32), p. 43. *Editors' note see Anne Harris's essay in this volume.

of the apse, Trinity Chapel.[8] The floor was inlaid with rich marble tile, and the walls adorned with stained glass windows forming a ring of colorful pictures depicting the life and miracles of Thomas Becket. It was an ideal setting for the sumptuous shrine.

All accounts agree on one aspect: the overwhelmingly opulent nature of the shrine. When the "wooden canopy [which] cover[ed] the golden Shrine . . . [was] drawn up with ropes, inestimable treasures [we]re opened to view."[9] The lavish sheen of the gold and jewels made an indelible impression upon its viewers, for the richness of a holy shrine represented not only the wealth and power of its cult, but its sacred symbolism as well; wrote Abbot Suger, "The material—gold and precious stones—clothe the object in light, and reflect or make manifest the transcendent, invisible, and all-powerful nature of visibility."[10]

Matthew Paris (c. 1220) wrote that the "body of the shrine [was] of the purest gold of Ophir and precious stones, and of workmanship even costlier than the material."[11] Walter of Coventry, in the *Annales of Waverly* (1220), noted that the shrine was "a coffin wonderfully wrought of gold and silver, and marvellously adorned with precious gems," set upon a marble altar.[12] Henry of Avranches (1220) noted that

---

[8] Matthew Paris noted "[the artists] by whose advice and ingenuity all things needful for the artificial working of the shrine and its elevation and translation were got ready without cause for blame." ed. Madden, *Matthaei Parisiensis*, II, p. 242; A.H. Thompson, "Master Elias of Dereham and the King's Works," *Archaeological Journal* 48 (1941), pp. 6–7. Elias may have organized the shrine artists' work. John Harvey, *English Medieval Architects. A Biographical Dictionary* (Boston, 1954), p. 83.

[9] Desiderius Erasmus, *Pilgrimages to Saint Mary of Walsingham and Saint Thomas of Canterbury* ed. and trans. John Gough Nichols (Westminster, 1849), p. 55. An anonymous author, in a later continuation of the *Canterbury Tales*, tells of the pilgrims' overwhelmed response to the shrine:
> Then passid they forth boystly, goglying with hir' hedis,
> Knelid a down to-fore the shryne, & hert[i]lich hir' bedis
> They preyd to Seynt Thomas, in such wise pey couth
eds. Frederick J. Furnivall, *The Tale of Beryn, with A Prologue of the Merry Adventure of the Pardoner with a Tapster at Canterbury* (London, 1909), p. 6.

[10] L. Marin, *Des pouvoirs del'image: gloses* (Paris, 1993), p. 224. Monks guarded the rich shrines from watching chambers, such as that at St. Albans Cathedral.

[11] *Praeparaverat autem thecam ad corpus honorifice collocandum de auro obrizo purissimo et gemmis pretiosissimis, artificio materiam superante*, p. 241, trans. by Mason, *Bones of Becket*, p. 79.

[12] *Annales Monastici: Annales Monasterii de Waverleia (A.D. 1–1291)* ed. Henry Luard (London, 1865) II, p. 293; . . . *et reconditum in loculo ex auro et argento miro opere constructo, gemmisque pretiosis mirifice insignito*. British Library, Cotton MS Vespasian, A.

Near to the altar, there rises a catafalque (tomb) of sculpted marble, borne aloft on marble columns. In the midst there is a tomb made of marble, a work strong enough to deter theft, and to endure for all time, thanks to the iron bars and the marble which covers the wood; the whole is covered by a magnificent cannister, which the hand of craftsmen adorned with gems and with gold.[13]

The Polistoire (*c.* 1307–27) also described how Becket's relics, in an iron-bound wooden box, were placed "under another wooden chest very richly adorned with gold and precious stones. It was also covered all over with plate of gold and richly garnished."[14]

Friar Simon Fitzsimmons, traveling to Canterbury in 1322–4, stated

[that the] body is . . . in a case made of most pure gold and adorned with innumerable precious stones, with shining pearls like unto the gate of Jerusalem, and sparkling gems, and even crowned with a regal diadem. . . .[15]

The fourteenth-century Icelandic *Thómas Saga Erikibyskups* proposed a rationale for these riches:

The love which the people bore to St. Thomas was soon revealed, since they would hear of his shrine being made of no other metal but gold alone. . . . Now by this mighty expense and choice workmanship

---

xvi f. 111, trans. by Mason, *Bones of Becket*, p. 80. For Walter of Coventry, MS in the Library of Corpus Christi College, Cambridge in *Memoriale Fratris Walteri de Coventria* ed. William Stubbs (1873, repr. London Reprint, 1965), II, pp. 245–6.

Convenienter autem provisum fuit ut quemadmodum ipse ante martyrium pro libertate ecclesiasiae conflictus varios et ventus, die Martis saepius variata, sustinuerat, et sicut angeli in coelis gavisi sunt die Martis de ejus martyrio, ita in terris populi unique confluentes exultarent de ejus corpore die Martis in feretro collacato.

[13] Henry of Avranches, *The Shorter Latin Poems of Master Henry of Avranches Relating to England* eds. Josiah Cox Russell and John Paul Hieronimus (Cambridge, MA: The Medieval Academy of America, 1935), p. 74. I am grateful to Eugene Dwyer for his help with this translation.

Are vicina sculpto de marmore surgit machina, marmoreis sursum portatacolumpnis, in cuius medio tumulus de marmore factus est adeo fortis quod furticonficiendi materies et opus spem tollent tempus in omne, pre missis barrisferri, pre marmore lignum quod tegit; egregia velatur capside totum, qua manusartificum gemmis precellit et auro.

[14] *Ilukes de suz un autre chace de fust trerichement de oer et des peres preciouses appareylee en tote reuerence honurablement cele mistrent. Si demurt par plate de oer tote part couerte et richement garnye.* British Library, Harleian MS, f. 201b, col. 2, l. 15, trans. by Mason, *Bones of Becket*, p. 72.

[15] *Itinerarium fratrum Symonis Semeonis et Hugonis illuminatoris, ordinis fratrum Minorum professorum ad Terram Sanctam A.D. 1322*, University of Cambridge MS 2-2-2 CCCCVII, is a late fourteenth-century copy of the original manuscript. Eugene Hoade, *Western Pilgrims* (1952, repr. Jerusalem, 1970), pp. iv–vi; 3–4.

the shrine was the most excellent work of art that had ever been seen, being set all round with stones, wherever beauty and effect might thereby be best set off.[16]

In 1436, Aeneas Sylvius (later Pope Pius II) agreed when he saw "more famous than all the rest, the golden mausoleum of Thomas of Canterbury covered with diamonds, pearls, and carbuncles, where it is considered sacrilegious to offer any mineral less precious than silver."[17]

A more specific description was given in 1466 by a member of the entourage of Ambassador Leo von Rozmital of Bohemia:

> The coffin wherein St. Thomas lies is all of gold and is long and broad, large enough for a middling-sized person to lie in. It is so richly adorned with pearls and precious stones that one would think there is no richer shrine in all of Christendom. The tomb is constructed of pure gold and is so adorned with gems and splendid offerings that I do not know of its equal.[18]

Confirming this is a *c.* 1500 report to the Venetian Senate by a diplomatic mission:

> But the magnificence of the tomb of St. Thomas the martyr, Archbishop of Canterbury, is that which surpasses all belief. This, notwithstanding its great size, is entirely covered over with plates of pure gold; but the gold is scarcely visible from the variety of precious stones with which it is studded, such as sapphires, diamonds, rubies, balas-rubies and emeralds; and on every side that the eye turns, something more beautiful than the other appears. And these beauties of nature are enhanced by human skill, for the gold is carved and engraved in beautiful designs, both large and small, and agates, jaspers, and cornelians set in *relievo*, some of the cameos being of such a size, that I do not dare to mention it: but every thing is left far behind by a ruby, not larger than a man's thumb-nail, which is set to the right of the altar. The church is rather dark, and particularly so where the shrine is

---

[16] *Thómas Saga Erkibyskups* ed. and trans. Erikr. Magnússon (London, 1875–83), p. 197; I, pp. xxxiii, xxxv. Thirteenth-century documents quote the *Saga*, but the earliest manuscript dates to the fourteenth century.

[17] *The Commentaries of Pius II* trans. by Florence Gragg, *Smith College Studies in History* 22/1–2 (Oct. 1936–Jan. 1937), pp. 16–7.

[18] His travels were chronicled by his squire Schaseck, a Czech, and Gabriel Tetzel of Nuremberg. Schaseck's original account is lost, but a 1577 Latin translation remains. Tetzel's account is in the Bayerische Staatsbibliothek in Munich (Cod. Germ. 1279). Malcolm Letts, *The Travels of Leo of Rozmital through Germany, Flanders, England, France, Spain, Portugal, and Italy 1465–1467* (Cambridge, 1957), pp. 43, 50.

placed, and when we went to see it the sun was nearly gone down, and the weather was cloudy; yet I saw the ruby as well as if I had it in my hand; they say it was the gift of a king of France.[19]

Desiderius Erasmus visited Canterbury in 1512–4, and in 1526 wrote "A Pilgrimage for Religion's Sake" with a character exclaiming that "the least valuable part of it was gold. Everything shone, and sparkled, and flashed with rare jewels of extraordinary size. Some were bigger than a goose's egg."[20]

The last account by a possible eyewitness is also the most detailed. The antiquary, John Stow (1525–1605), described the shrine in his 1592 *The Annales of England*.[21] It is possible that Stow might have seen the shrine as a child, as he was thirteen years old when it was destroyed, but there is no proof that he ever visited Canterbury. In his *Annales*, he wrote that the shrine consisted of a stone base the height of a man, upon which rested

> . . . tymber worke of this shrine on the outside was couered with plates of gold, damasked with gold wire, which ground of golde was againe couered with jewels of golde, as rings, 10 or 12 cramped with golde wier, into the saide grounde of golde, many of those rings hauing stones in them, brooches, images, and angels, and other precious stones, and great pearles, &c. The spoile of which shrine, in golde and precious stone, filled two great chestes, such as 6 or 8 strong men coulde do no more then convey one of them at once out of the Church.[22]

A more complex version of this description is inscribed on a seventeenth-century drawing of the shrine by Robert Cotton. Either Cotton copied a now-lost later edition of Stow's account or both Cotton and Stow accessed an earlier authority, also lost.[23] The following

---

[19] This mission was led by Andrea Trevisano. *A Relation, or Rather a True Account, of the Island of England; with Sundry Particulars of the Customs of these People and of the Royal Revenues under the King Henry the Seventh, about the Year 1500* ed. Charlotte A. Sneyd (London, 1847), p. 30.

[20] First published in Basel by Johannes Froben; Craig R. Thompson, *The Colloquies of Erasmus* (Chicago, 1967), pp. 285–7; Mason, *Bones of Becket*, p. 92.

[21] In 1580, Ralph Newbery published Stow's, *The Chronicles of England from Brute unto the present yeare of Christ* in London. In 1592, it was published again under its familiar title *The Annales of England faithfully collected out of the most authenticall Authors, Records, and other Monuments of Antiquitie from the first inhabitation untill . . . 1592*. It was re-issued in 1605 with additions, and again re-edited and continued by Edmund Howes in 1615, and once more in 1631.

[22] Stow, *The Annales of England* (1592), p. 972.

[23] Mason, *Bones of Becket*, p. 109. The specificity of the finials 'weight, not mentioned in Stow's account, indicates that Cotton may have had access to a now-lost

inscription appears with the missing portions reconstructed in brackets from the later publication of William Dugdale.

> All above the stone works was first of wood, Jewells of gold with stone ... wrought upon with gold weir. Then agayn with jewells of gold, as broch[es images of angels and rings] 10 or 12 together, cramped with gold into the ground of gold. The [spoils which filled two] chests, such as 6 or 8 men could but convey out of the church. At [one side was a stone, with] an Angell of gold poynting thereunto, offered by a king of France: [which king Henry put] into a ring and wore it on his thombe.[24]

Visual Records of the Shrine

Medieval observers, overwhelmed by the magnificence of the shrine, cannot be relied upon for accurate descriptions, but their accounts can be supplemented by visual sources. Unfortunately, because of the Dissolution of the Monasteries, only six visual records survive which purport to depict the shrine and all present trying methodological problems. None resembles any of the others, and only one can be reconciled with a written account. Moreover, it is not even certain that they all represent the shrine, a confusion caused by the varied purposes for which these pictures were originally created. Many medieval artists were not interested in the specifics of the shrine;

source. They might depict Edward I's 1285 donation of £5 12s. 8d. "for making divers pinnacles" and for the purchase of white silver for framing (*ad imponendum* "for inserting therein"). A.J. Taylor, "Edward I and the Shrine of St. Thomas of Canterbury," *Journal of the British Archaeological Association* 132 (1979), pp. 25–6; Public Record Office C47/4/2, mm. 24d, 27d; or Prior Henry of Eastry's 1314 donation of £7 10s. for a new finials (or crest) for the shrine, perhaps depicted here. List of Works of Henry Eastry (*Nova Opera in Ecclesia et in Curia Tempore Henrici Prioris*), Canterbury Cathedral Archive, DCc/MS Reg. K, f. 220; Dom David Knowles, *The Religious Orders in England* (Cambridge, 1979), p. 323; Coldstream, "Shrine Bases," p. 29; Stanley, *Historical Memorials*, p. 333

[24] British Library, Cotton MS., Tib. E, viii. folio 269, originally in the collection of Sir Robert Cotton (1571–1631), housed in Little Dean's Yard, Westminster, was partially burnt when in 1731, destroying 1/3 of the page, but the full text and its accompanying drawing was published by Sir William Dugdale (1605–86) in *Monasticon Anglicanum, sive Pandectae Coenobiorum Benedictinorum, Cluniacensium, Cisterciensium, Carthusianorum, à primordiis ad eorum usque dissolutionem, ex MSS...* (London, 1655) i, pl. 10; *Monasticon Anglicanum: A History of the Abbies and other Monasteries, Hospitals, Frieries [sic], and Cathedral and Collegiate Churches...* (1817, repr. London, 1846) i, p. 85.

rather their goal was to the render an ideal "shrine," either because they had not actually seen it or because an accurate depiction was unimportant.[25]

The first two images associated with the shrine are windows in Trinity Chapel, where the shrine once stood. The first illustrates a miraculous vision of St. Thomas Becket emerging from a gable-roofed feretory or reliquary in full pontificals as if to celebrate mass above a sleeping monk.[26] The shrine is a reliquary box with a sloping roof covering a slab on six slender pillars, with foliate fleur-de-lys capitals flanking two shallow, open arcades. (fig. 130) In contrast to written descriptions, no jewels are apparent, although the feretory is gold. In the second image, a woman lays an offering coil of wax onto an attached altar, showing a slightly different shrine. A corner of a golden gabled feretory resting on a slab is supported by a slender column which reveals the beginning of an arch. The feretory, somewhat simpler than in the first window, is covered with abstract lozenge designs, with a plain knob at the end of the crest. Both windows reflect an early shrine type pictured in the late twelfth-century *Guthlac Roll*, where the feretory rests on slender columns.[27]

The close placement of the windows to the shrine suggests that they are accurate renditions, but this is uncertain. Iconographically, the shrine in these images is anachronistic, because the miracle stories illustrated present events from 1170–73—years before the 1220 shrine was built. Moreover, the images show a stylistically-conservative shrine, since by 1220 round arches would have likely been replaced by pointed arches. Most importantly, the windows themselves date to 1213–6.[28] Thus, the windows showed either a projected shrine or

---

[25] Richard Krautheimer, "Introduction to an 'Iconography of Medieval Architecture,'" *Journal of the Warburg and Courtauld Institute*, 5, 1942, p. 199.

[26] Although inscribed *feretro* (feretory), the iconography in Window n:III(1) is uncertain. The sleeping man may be one of the recorders of Becket's miracles; Benedict (Bk. I, Ch. 1, p. 2) or William (Book I). Madeleine Caviness, *The Windows of Christ Church Cathedral Canterbury* (London, 1981), p. 187. Following Nilson, *Cathedral Shrines*, p. 35, I use the *feretrum* to describe house-shaped reliquary chests.

[27] (ed.) George Warner, *The Guthlac Roll* (Oxford, 1928), pl. XVII. The second image of the supposed shrine is in window S:VII. Caviness, *The Windows of Christ Church*, figs. 366, 366a.

[28] Urry, "Two Resting Places," p. 201. Madeleine Caviness, *The Early Stained Glass of Canterbury Cathedral, Circa 1175–1220* (Princeton, 1977), pp. 27, 32–5, dated the miracle windows in Trinity Chapel to the late twelfth/early thirteenth centuries, with the design being set as early as 1179. Window n:III could have been completed

the shrine as it appeared in the early thirteenth century. If the shrine took this form initially, evidence suggests that it underwent later, significant refurbishment.

The third image presents an entirely different picture. A fifteenth-century window from the Nettlestead Church in Kent pictures pilgrims at the shrine of Becket accompanied by the inscription, *Hic jacet egro(rum) medecina salus miserorum* (Here lies the medicine of the sick, the salvation of the miserable).[29] (fig. 199) Random golden baubles dot the face of the gabled shrine, while quatrefoils set in a diaper pattern decorate its sloping roof.[30] Two pilgrims are seated under a structure (a stone shrine base) composed of three round-arched vaulted bays (opposed to the two-arched base in the Canterbury windows), which surround recessed niches. The niches are supported by double columns with round bases and curling foliage capitals. The stone portion reflects a later shrine base which featured three

---

by 1213–16 and Window s:VII finished by 1216, p. 97. Caviness, *Windows of Christ Church*, p. 187 suggested that "some unrecorded vision is invoked which encouraged the construction of the shrine." Chistopher Wilson, *The Shrines of St. William of York* (York, 1977), p. 23, fn. 13, noted that the glaziers were familiar with patterns for shrines rather than the actual shrine of Becket.

[29] Situated at the base of a nave window, it is mostly filled with fragments of glass. Dating 1425–39, these scenes were moved to the westernmost window ("St. Thomas" window) on the north side of the nave, where they were placed under a figure of St. Thomas. W.E. Ball, "The Stained-Glass Windows of Nettlestead Church," *Archaeologia Cantiana* 28 (1909): 157–249; T.G. Faussett, "On a Fragment of Glass in Nettlestead Church" *Archaeologia Cantiana* 6 (1864–65): 129–34. Connected to Becket because the window shows a canopy topped by a tall, square central tower resembles Canterbury, but that resembles any church with a square tower. Ball, "The Stained-Glass Windows of Nettlestead Church," p. 242; Faussett, "On a Fragment of Glass," p. 131; G.M. Livett, "Nettlestead Church: Architectural Notes" *Archaeologia Cantiana* 28 (1909), pp. 270–1. One connection might be in the use of similar rhyming phrases, such as OPTIMUS EGRORUM MEDICUS FIT TOMA BONORUM (Thomas is the best doctor of the worthy sick), from a thirteenth-century pilgrim ampullae from Canterbury. Brian Spencer, "The Ampullae from Cuckoo Lane" in eds. Colin Platt & Ronald Coleman-Smith, *Excavations in Medieval Southampton 1953–1969* (Leicester, 1975), 2, p. 246. My thanks to Carolin Hahnemann for her help with this translation.

[30] Two pilgrims kneel, one clutching a walking stick, the other close behind, presumably blind. In 1909, it featured a tall figure in blue on the left (probably a monk) whose left hand was raised in greeting to the kneeling pilgrims and whose right hand rested on the shoulder of the barefooted child dressed in red, who held out his deformed hands (which now point). After the church's 1940 bombing, it was restored and re-opened in 1950. Fragments of glass that separated the Becket scenes were removed and some portions of the scenes filled in. As it was, the shrine scene was flanked by architectural borders which were probably not original. Livett, "Nettlestead Church," p. 270.

carved prayer niches in which pilgrims knelt, so that they might be as proximate as possible to the relics contained in the feretory above. This analysis is speculative, because of the window's haphazard reconstruction after the wreckage of Reformation iconoclasm and World War II bombing. The proportions of the figures are awkward, and the basic elements of a shrine are muddled. The golden feretory shrine, instead of being on top is placed to the side as would befit an altar. Still, the feretory matches written descriptions of Becket's shrine with its bejeweled, golden surface. The three niches are similar to other shrine bases such as St. Albans, though its style appears to be much earlier. (fig. 211) Other fragments of glass illustrating architectural structures might have been part of the shrine, but ascertaining this is not possible because of its poor condition.

In contrast, the condition of the fourth image, a late fifteenth-century altarpiece dedicated to St. Thomas (the Apostle, Aquinas, and Becket) from St. Jürgen at Wismar in Mecklenburg, Germany is excellent, but it presents another set of problems.[31] (fig. 200) It pictures the 1179 visit Louis VII of France to the shrine where, in gratitude for the recovery of his son, he donated a ruby called the "regal of France,"[32] mentioned in the Venetian Senate report and the Cotton manuscript. The latter source described a sculpted angel which points to the jewel. In this painting, the angel is alive as it flies to the shrine and taps the gem with its wand. The golden-gabled feretory is surrounded by a low fleur-de-lys crested grille. Underneath, large gems adorn the stone base rather than the feretory. That the artists of the altarpiece included these specific features seems to imply the veracity of their depiction, but everything else appears to contradict this, because it conforms with the style of German wooden Gothic altarpieces rather than English stone workmanship. The sweeping ogee-arch with foliate-filled spandrels is decorated with filigree tracery resembling interlinked tree branches—all features prevalent in

---

[31] Tancred Borenius, *St. Thomas Becket in Art* (London, 1932), p. 62, pls. XXI–XXII; Tancred Borenius, "Some Further Aspects of the Iconography of St. Thomas of Canterbury," *Archaeologia* 83 (1933), pp. 178–80. This is located on the right with outer wings open and the inner wings closed.

[32] Brian Spencer, *Pilgrim Souvenirs and Secular Badges: Medieval Finds from Excavations in London* (London, 1998), p. 101. See also (ed.) Henry Luard, *Chronicon Vulgo Dictum Chronicon Thomae Wykes* in *Annales Monastici* (London, 1869), 4, pp. 38–9; (ed.) Henry Ellis, *Chronica Johannes de Oxenedes* (London, 1859), p. 68; Nilson, *Cathedral Shrines*, pp. 117, 188.

Germany during the late fifteenth and early sixteenth centuries.[33] An eyewitness might have included more features which evoked the actual shrine, but no other details bear a resemblance to anything in Canterbury Cathedral. This painting should be classified as a fanciful picture of the shrine based on a pilgrim's account rather than an actual eyewitness rendition.

The fifth image is the problematic drawing associated with Robert Cotton. (fig. 201) At the top is written, "The forme or figure of the Shrine of Tho: Becket of Canterbury," and at the bottom is a description of the shrine (quoted above). The schematic drawing is a poor rendering of a rectangular stone shrine base decorated with arched window-like openings and a featureless top portion with a gabled roof. Adorning the roof are three leafy fleur-de-lys finials, with notations reporting that these were made of silver gilt, weighing between sixty and eighty ounces. Beneath the shrine is an iron casket with Becket's relics, symbolized by four bones and a portion of his skull.[34] While the drawing initially appears to offer a great deal of information, scholars have tried in vain to reconcile its image with other evidence of the shrine.[35] Their difficulty lies in the contradiction between the drawing and its accompanying description. The blank expanse of the upper shrine and the plain stone arches of the lower base reflect nothing of the sumptuous decoration detailed in the quote on the page. Some scholars suggested that the image shows the wooden cover which protected the feretory, but the three finials emerging from the top negate this.[36]

---

[33] Michael Pacher, *St. Wolfgang Altarpiece* (1471–81), St. Wolfgang Church. Michael Baxandall, *The Limewood Sculpture of Renaissance Germany* (New Haven, 1980), pl. 13, 36.

[34] The inscription reads, "This chest of iron con[tained the] bones of Thomas Bec[et skull and] all, with the wounds [of his death] and the pece cut [out of his skull]." The brackets indicate portions recovered from Dugdale's 1655 publication.

[35] Coldstream, "Shrine Bases," p. 28, called it a "strange, burnt drawing"; Urry, "Two Resting Places," p. 204, fn. 26, stated that "the crude representation of the Shrine of St. Thomas therein, which is clearly based upon a very dim and faulty recollection of the real thing"; Letts, *The Travels of Leo of Rozmital*, pp. 43–4, wrote "there is a drawing of the shrine from a Cotton MS ... but it is not impressive"; ed. Joseph T. Fowler in *Rites of Durham Being a Description or Brief Declaration of all the Ancient Monuments ... 1593* (1903, repr., Durham, 1963), p. 196, believed the drawing is "considered to be untrustworthy, not to say imaginary"; Nichols, *Pilgrimages to St. Mary and St. Thomas*, p. 166, noted that "this drawing seems to have been copied from some former original: which, if it could be recovered, might prove to be more accurately finished, and therefore afford additional information."

[36] Stanley, *Historical Memorials*, p. 354. John Morris, *The Relics of St. Thomas of Canterbury* (Canterbury, 1888), p. 9 suggested that the drawing conveyed the shrine

Most of these issues have arisen because of the assumption that the drawing was a coeval, sixteenth-century document. Yet, in 1917 D.T. Baird Wood (keeper of manuscripts at the British Library) analyzed the handwriting and found that it was written in the seventeenth century by Robert Cotton himself and that the drawing was Cotton's attempt to draw the shrine from Stow's description, rather than the other way around.[37] Of course, one could argue that Cotton's writing might accompany a sixteenth-century drawing, but, as scholars who have tried to grapple with this drawing have found, it contradicts most everything that is known about the shrine. Moreover, the writing placed on the chest suggests that the inscription was part of the original drawing since there are clearly spaces which have been left to accommodate this writing. The rest of the writing on the page matches the writing on the chests. The text of the writing is fainter than the drawing, with the heavy outlines of the drawing in a darker color, but both share the same color and same ink indicating that they were done at the same time.[38] Still, in 1655, when William Dugdale borrowed the page from Cotton to publish in his *Monasticon*, it must have been thought that the document relevant, for he had it engraved by Wencelaus Hollar (1607–77). Hollar re-drew the image, adding perspective and three-dimensional modeling, while Dugdale translated Cotton's English inscription into Latin, perhaps each adding a kind of dignity to an unusual document. Unfortunately, Dugdale published it without comment, so how the he viewed the document is uncertain.

I believe that the Cotton drawing was never viewed as a contemporary sixteenth-century document, but rather was the first attempt at reconstructing the visual appearance of the shrine. That it reconstructs what was destroyed is evident when one looks closely at the

---

after it had been defaced, as the writing notes that the upper part was wood (where the gold and jewels would be attached) and the lower stone.

[37] "The handwriting and presumably the drawing are by Cotton himself. I have compared the hand with Cotton's letters with great care, and characteristic peculiarities confirm the first general impression." Letter to Arthur Mason from D.T. Baird Wood, Esq., Keeper of Manuscripts at the British Museum, May 31, 1917. One of the first to posit that Stow's account came from the drawing was Nichols, *Pilgrimages to St. Mary and St. Thomas*, p. 166. Mason, *Bones of Becket*, pp. 108–9 noted that because Stow published his *Chronicle* in 1580, Cotton was not born until 1571, it is much more likely that Cotton borrowed from Stow.

[38] My thanks to Michael J. Boggan of the British Library for his observations concerning this manuscript page.

inscription which describes how the treasures were carted away in trunks. The date inscribed to the left of the description is Tem H 8 (period of Henry VIII); Tem without its Latin ending does not indicate whether this is a contemporary or past reference to that time period, but the wording of Temp(ore) H 8 is a dating device widely used by nineteenth-century antiquarians (although it was used by some as early as the late sixteenth century, again indicating that this inscription was not contemporary with the shrine). Yet, the most important piece of evidence is the inscription itself which describing the destruction of the shrine, refers to a time in the past, the drawing an attempt at a reconstruction.

How accurate was this reconstruction? It appears to block out the general dimensions of the shrine with a specific rendition of niches in the base made of a particularly patterned brickwork. The brickwork is reflected in the stained glass image from Trinity Chapel, (fig. 130) but the general shape of the base is entirely different. Stylistically, the base of the shrine in the stained glass is an early type with large, open arches supporting a table for the feretory, while the Cotton drawing reflects a later style with its shallow niches penetrating a massive stone base. The finials on the drawing are also in the stained glass picture, albeit in a simpler form. Scholars have posited that the shrine was rebuilt based on this drawing and the Nettlestead window.[39]

When this refurbishment might have taken place is difficult to discern from the particular style of the shrine. Its rounded arches appear to be at odds with later shrine bases which featured elaborately-carved, pointed niches, while the massive, bulky base is inconsistent with earlier shrine bases. This is probably a reconstruction based on written records and the excellent antiquarian sense of Robert Cotton. The general parameters of the shrine, its proportions, its steps, its *opus reticulatum* decoration, and its inclusion of niches is congruent with what a shrine base would be expected to look like, even though its rendition of the feretory contradicts all written descriptions, even its own. The writer or artist might have seen the remnants of the base and tried to fill in the missing feretory from its account in Stow, but this is not known. What is missing are the precise details of an eyewitness.

---

[39] Coldstream, "Shrine Bases," pp. 16–7; Taylor, "Edward I and the Shrine," pp. 22–8 suggested the king's gifts were associated with a re-building of the shrine.

Pilgrim Badges as Record of the Shrine

None of the five images cited really describe Becket's shrine. They only vaguely agree with written accounts; they do not accord with one another; they are of the wrong date; or they are in too poor a condition to be relied upon with certainty. Moreover, none consciously sought to replicate the shrine. This lack of fidelity does not discredit their value as art objects because their function was not to display the shrine with verisimilitude; only a general notion of "shrine" was required. The only picture expressly created to reproduce the shrine that survives is that on pewter pilgrim badges mass-produced at Canterbury in the fourteenth century.[40] (fig. 202) Dozens of examples have been recovered, and it is from these numerous examples that the shrine of St. Thomas Becket at Canterbury Cathedral can be securely reconstructed.

Methodological Issues

Obviously, reconstructing a likeness from a group of badges presents numerous methodological problems. First, their relatively tiny size (seven and a half cm in height) hindered the inclusion of much detail. Second, the pilgrim badge artisans, while impressive, did not produce work comparable to the high level of craftsmanship which must have characterized the shrine; not surprisingly, they omitted many important elements. Third, though the pilgrim badges were mass produced, they were cast from many different molds, creating variants and raising the question of which details are accurate. To answer this question, one must examine the notion of artistic copying in the Middle Ages and how the pilgrim souvenir became a very special kind of copy.

---

[40] Shrine badges found in datable ceramic and dendrochronological contexts include: Baynard House, Queen Victoria Street, last quarter of the fourteenth century; Billingsgate Market truck park, fourteenth and early fifteenth centuries; Trig Lane, Upper Thames Street, *c.* 1380; Vintry House, Vinters' Place, 68 Upper Thames Street, fourteenth century. Spencer, *Pilgrim Souvenirs*, pp. 24–31. Shrine badges were probably produced at least 50 years earlier, for head reliquary badges from Canterbury, found in *c.* 1320 sites, share many stylistic similarities (such as the bosses) with the shrine badges. The belling at the elbow of the cuff of the angel's tight set-in sleeve in fig. 203 also argues for an earlier date of design, after 1340. Personal communication with Brian Spencer and Michelle Nordtorp-Madsen.

It has long been agreed that imitation in the earlier Middle Ages was done on a less precise basis than modern-day viewers expect. That is, while we look for a circle in a precise copy of a circle, during the Middle Ages an octagonal shape did the job just as well. What was emphasized in medieval discussions of imitation was not shape, but the number of elements making up the shape's parts and their measurements. Richard Krautheimer pointed out that in architecture, medieval symbolism was composed of structures connected by vague connotations to ideas, which allowed for a variety of interpretations from one copyist to another.[41] The symbolic connotations (whether in shape or number) were believed by some to be ever-present, and their physical manifestations spoke to inner convictions. Architectural imitations never copied the model *in toto*; rather, they reproduced selected elements. Sometimes the specific elements being copied were casually rearranged, or new elements added to a "copy" so the direct relationship of the model to the original is now often difficult to divine.[42] In duplication, the original was broken into single elements and redone. A few conspicuous features were all it took to identify the original. Other than those, the artisans were free to add any other element they chose. Therefore, modern researchers normally cannot apply the same strict modern standards of imitation to these loose medieval copies.

Yet, by comparing surviving medieval artwork with the pilgrimage souvenirs produced to commemorate them, it becomes evident that pilgrim souvenirs as a class of objects are an exception to this rule. For example, the pilgrim badge (1350–1400) of the 1349 *Head Reliquary of Charlemagne* (fig. 185) from the Cathedral at Aachen captures the distinguishing characteristics of the original even if it does not faithfully record every detail. (fig. 184) The three fleurons of the crown, the curling locks and wavy beard, and general outline of the costume are all copied in a schematic fashion. The small size (five cm) would have made impossible the rendition of the forty-two eagles

---

[41] Krautheimer, "Introduction to an Iconography," pp. 120, 122, 124, 129.

[42] Krautheimer, "Introduction to an Iconography," p. 125; "The common element between a church which shared with its prototype only the name or the particular manner of its dedication and an architectural copy proper was evidently the fact that both were mementoes of a venerated site. The difference is rather between a more or less elaborate reproduction ... the more elaborate ones only add some visual elements to the 'immaterial' features. ..." p. 127.

decorating the bust, but the eagles are there, though reduced to just two.[43] Although the image is simplified in the extreme, major visual similarities are recognizable despite their tremendous differences in quality. Either the pilgrim souvenir artisans did not have the skill to create high quality images, or they did not believe it worth their while to do so as the souvenirs were to be sold inexpensively. Intricate details in the original (such as cameos) were either reduced or omitted, but the artisans took care to reproduce the general aspect of the reliquaries, because its function as a commemorative souvenir demanded it.

The commemorative aspect of souvenirs determined what they looked like as souvenirs are broadly divided into two types. One type is a "metonymic sign,"[44] in which the souvenir is actually part of, or representative of, the whole. By owning a small portion, one symbolically appropriates the whole. For example, a vial of water from the River Jordan is a metonymic sign. A second type is a pictorial image, such as a picture postcard or a small image of the Eiffel Tower. This category of souvenir offers a likeness of what the pilgrim witnessed, which in some way must capture the essence of what has been seen and experienced, otherwise it cannot stir memory. One needs to keep in mind what makes a good pictorial souvenir. If you purchase a small statuette of the Eiffel Tower, you expect it to look like the Eiffel Tower not the Louvre.

The low quality of the pilgrim souvenirs did not hamper their popularity. Since the pilgrim buyer was already familiar with the original, there was no need for these mementoes to be rendered with absolute precision. The images acted in a mnemonic sense, jogging the memory rather than portraying realistic action. Indeed, the reading of images (even for the illiterate) was seen as instructive when the viewers were being reminded of what they already knew, so the low-quality rendition of the artwork associated with the cult was enough

---

[43] Denis Bruna, "Quelques Images de Chefs-Reliquaires à Travers les Enseignes de Pèlerinage" in eds. Dory Kicken *et al.*, *Gevonden Voorwerpen, Lost and Found: Essays on Medieval Archaeology for H.J.E. van Beuningen* (Rotterdam, 2000), pp. 73–9. *Editors' note see Marike de Kroon's essay in this volume.

[44] Beverley Gordon, "The Souvenir: Messenger of the Extraordinary," *Journal of Popular Culture* 20/3 (Winter, 1986), p. 139; Edmund R. Leach, *Culture and Communication: The Logic by Which Symbols are Connected* (Cambridge, 1976), p. 78.

to prompt memory of the context in which the image was originally seen.[45]

Moreover, the souvenir is a very special kind of object produced to recall and confirm a special moment. In medieval times, leaving home and traveling great distances where strange sights abounded could be an extraordinary experience. Pilgrims wanted to retain some tangible reminder of their adventure. A shell, rock, or purchased object could serve that purpose, representing the memory of a rite of passage or of a heightened experience.[46] They allowed people to momentarily grasp and perhaps relive the now-past event, a reminder that they had indeed seen and experienced the *real* thing. The souvenirs prompted memories which could be summoned again and again, recalling to mind what one actually saw.

In order to encourage sales and to distinguish their wares from competitors, pilgrim souvenir artisans often embellished the original image. For example, the pilgrim badges of the head reliquary of St. Thomas Becket at Canterbury were adorned with a myriad of elaborate frames.[47] Nonetheless, in spite of this aesthetic and symbolic license taken by these badges, the central image, that of the head reliquary, is probably a broadly faithful copy of the main features of the original sacred object. Many different production lines of the shrine badge were sold, but in essence they picture the same image repeatedly: a Decorated-Style shrine base with an effigy surmounted by an elaborate feretory. Whatever the relationship of the badges to the original shrine, it is obvious that they are copying *something* independent of themselves and this speaks to their general reliability.

Is it possible to reconstruct a large-scale sumptuous shrine from a series of small metal souvenirs? Using copies to divine the nature of originals is a long-standing art-historical tradition. The development of ancient Greek sculptural style is often defined through Roman copies, and lost paintings are customarily viewed through reproductive prints. Yet, like written descriptions, pictorial depictions need to be examined by considering who made them and why, and cannot

---

[45] Lawrence Duggan, "Was Art really the 'Book of the Illiterate'?" *Word and Image* 5 (1989): 227–51; Avril Henry, *Biblia Pauperum: A Facsimile and Edition* (Aldershot, UK, 1987), pp. 17–8; Robert N. Swanson, *Religion and Devotion in Europe, c. 1215– c. 1515* (Cambridge, 1995), p. 162.

[46] Gordon, "The Souvenir," pp. 136–7.

[47] Spencer, *Pilgrim Souvenirs*, figs. 76c, 85a, 88a–111c.

be viewed as untouched photographs from the past. The purposes for which they were created caused the artisans to change certain images to fit a smaller space, to make the point clearer, etc. Still, they cannot be dismissed as wholly unreliable, for the artisans were trying to convey something of the original—and often these pictorial copies are all that remain of major artistic monuments such as the shrine of Becket.

Initially, one needs to question whether these badges really represent the shrine of St. Thomas Becket at Canterbury, as most English shrines were of an equally sumptuous nature. The certainty of this identification is based on two features: first, within English medieval art, the iconic figure of an archbishop has commonly been recognized as Becket. Pilgrim souvenirs portraying the same figure identify him as Thomas in their inscriptions. Second, the appearance of the small angel on the feretory pointing to a gem reflects other accounts of the shrine. If the picture of the shrine in the Canterbury windows of 1213–6 shows an earlier or planned version, the pilgrim badges are a record of the shrine of St. Thomas in the fourteenth century, a shrine significantly modified both in form and decoration.[48]

Feretory

The badges reveal the shrine at its most resplendent. At the badge's summit is the gabled feretory, covered with ball-shaped, unfaceted gems. On the roof, large jewels are suspended upon a trellis pattern of with tiny jewels massed over the surface in no particular order,[49]

---

[48] Spencer, "Pilgrim Souvenirs" in *Age of Chivalry*, p. 219; Spencer, *Pilgrim Souvenirs* pp. 98–102; Brian Spencer, *Pilgrim Souvenirs and Secular Badges: Salisbury Museum Medieval Catalogue* (Salisbury, 1990), p. 23; Brian Spencer, "Pilgrim Souvenirs from the Medieval Waterfront Excavations at Trig Lane London, 1974–6," *Transactions of the London and Middlesex Archaeological Society* 33 1982, pp. 311–2; B. Spencer, "Medieval Pilgrim Badges: Some General Observations Illustrated Mainly from English Sources" in *Rotterdam Papers: A Contribution to Medieval Archaeology* ed. J.G.N. Renaud (Rotterdam, 1968), pl. 6, fn. 5; Charles T. Little, "Pilgrim's Badge Depicting the Shrine of Saint Thomas Becket at Canterbury Cathedral," *Bulletin of the Metropolitan Museum of Art* (Fall, 2001), p. 19.

[49] Spencer, *Pilgrim Souvenirs*, p. 99. In 1251, Henry III gave gold coins to be attached to the shrine. *Calendar of the Liberate Rolls Preserved in the Public Record Office, Henry III (A.D. 1240–1245)* ed. and trans. J.B.W. Chapman (London, 1930), p. 1251. Gold coins were not used as currency in England in the mid thirteenth-century, but instead were used for "prestigious alms-giving" by kings. Peter Spufford, *Money*

reflecting documents that described so many gifts studding the feretory that the underlying plate was scarcely visible.[50] The badges
illustrate how the feretory was shaped through the gradual accretion
of votive gifts rather than careful iconographic planning.[51] Unlike
surviving Continental feretories, the surface of Becket's shrine did
not feature rows of figures, or if they once existed, they were covered
over by votive gifts. Valuable gifts were attached directly to the surface or onto the crest of the feretory by goldsmiths. Sometimes votives
were placed on pedestals or beams that stood near the shrine, while
others were attached to drapes hung from the buttresses supporting
the shrine base.[52] Votive gifts from royalty and high-level clergy

---

and Its Use in Medieval Europe (Cambridge, 1988), p. 183. In 1327 Archbishop Walter
Reynolds instructed that his rings "be fixed to the shrine of the glorious martyr
aforesaid [Thomas] between the other jewels which I bought and gave over to the
same shrine in times gone by." *Sede Vacante Wills: A Calendar of Wills Proved before the
Commissary of the Prior and Chapter of Christ Church Canterbury, during Vacancies in the
Primacy* ed. C.E. Woodruff (Kent, 1855), p. 68.

[50] Spencer, *Pilgrim Souvenirs*, pp. 99, 101. Matthew Paris noted that the gold-plated
shrine at Canterbury was exceptional. Henry Luard, *Matthaei Perisiensis, Monachi Sancti
Albani, Chronica Majora* (London, 1877), 4, pp. 156–7; Nilson, *Cathedral Shrines*, p. 37.
The number of large jewels differs on each badge. Hugh Tait, "Pilgrim-signs and
Thomas, Earl of Lancaster," *British Museum Quarterly* 20 (1955), fig. XVa, depicts six
jewels, while fig. 204 here shows four.

[51] In 1244, Henry II paid £24 9s. 1/2 d. to William Hardel, keeper of the mint,
to "make a golden garland (*garlendechain*) . . . to place at the head of the shrine over
the altar-table of St. Thomas the martyr at Canterbury where there is a defect."
Roll No. 20, Chapman, *Calendar of the Liberate*, pp. 196, 212. The altar at "the head"
meant that it met with the saint's head, "since the head of a corpse was always
laid to the west." Robert Willis, *Architectural History of Some English Cathedrals: A
Collection in two parts of Papers delivered during the years 1842–1863* (Chicheley, UK,
1972), p. 100. Votives were sometimes used to raise money; in 1372, Prior Gillingham
melted down images and plate. *Item recept' per manus Ricardi prioris cli de diversis ymagi-
nibus feretri beati Thome martyris fucis venditis*, Woodruff, *Sede Vacante*, fn. 2, p. 21.

[52] Votives covered every accessible surface, attached directly to the shrine, hung
over beams and buttresses, or affixed to drapes. York Minster Library, M2/2d, lists
gifts attached to the shrines in York Minster in the early sixteenthth century, including coral beads, hearts of silver, rings, precious stones, high-value coins, model bulls,
ships of silver, and more; Robert N. Swanson, *Catholic England: Faith, Religion and
Observance Before the Reformation* (Manchester, 1993), pp. 179–81. Window n7 in York
Minster shows a beam hung with votive images of a woman's head, a leg, a hand,
and a heart, while a pilgrim offers up a wax leg to the shrine of St. William.
Wilson, "St. William," cover picture. Similarly, a woodcut of pilgrims worshipping
King Henry VI (*c.* 1490) in the Bodleian Library, Oxford, MS Bodl. 277, f.375v.,
shows a beam and a small shelf displaying wax images, chains, and ships; Brian
Spencer, "King Henry of Windsor and the London Pilgrim," *Collectanea Londiniensia:
Studies in London Archaeology and History Presented to Ralph Merrifield* (London, 1978),
fig. 1. Wax votives were found in Exeter Cathedral. U.M. Radford, "Wax Images
Found in Exeter Cathedral," *Antiquaries Journal* 29 (1949), pp. 164–8. Reliquaries

enhanced the reputation of the shrine as signs of temporal power in the service of the saint. As Erasmus wrote, "There some monks stood around with much veneration: the covering being raised, we all worshipped. The Prior with a white rod pointed out each jewel, telling its name in French, its value, and the name of its donor; for the principal of them were offerings sent by sovereign princes."[53] Such gifts received pride of place on the shrine, for the most revered votive gift, the great regal ruby, is shown on the badges as a large gem placed near the center of the feretory.[54] The comments of visitors

----

were also placed on beams. During its translation in 1448, the reliquary of St. Fleogild was carried past the shrine of Becket to the beam between the shrine and the Corona chapel. John Stone, *The Chronicle of John Stone* (ed.) W.G. Searle, Cambridge, 1902, p. 44.

Columns near shrines displayed votive sculptures, as at the shrine of St. Edward the Confessor in *The Life of St. Edward the Confessor* (c. 1255–60), Cambridge University Library, Ee. 3.5.9, f. 30; Nigel Morgan, "Life of St. Edward the Confessor," *Age of Chivalry*, pp. 216–7, fig. 125. Crests also supported votive figures, such as the armored figure donated by Henry VII. This image placed "upon and in the midst of the crest of the shrine of St. Edward King, in such place as our executors shall think most convenient and honorable." Nicolas, pp. 31–2; J. Perkins, *Westminster Abbey; Its Worship and Its Ornaments*, London, 1938, 2, p. 58.

Candles were the most popular votive offering; Nilson, *Cathedral Shrines*, p. 50. "A duty of the feretrarians (keepers of the shrine) was to maintain twelve large square candles on the beam, *Maioris et quadrate forme*," *Customary of the Shrine of St. Thomas*, British Library, Add. MS 59616, f. 2. In 1284, a clerk of exchange at Canterbury gave fifty shillings to have two candles burning continuously at the shrine "as other lights around the said shrine do." (*Videlicet quemlibet de octo libris cere ardentes ibidem sicut alii faciunt circa feretrum.*) Canterbury Cathedral Archives, Reg. E, f. 143; Nilson, *Cathedral Shrines*, 137. In addition to the twelve on the beam, there were four situated on the shrine itself, and another twelve great candles, weighing three pounds each, set nearby. These were decorated with red and green stripes and golden flowers. There was an immense candle which stretched around a drum, whose length was supposed to be equal that of the circumference of the town of Dover. D. Turner, "The Customary of the Shrine of St. Thomas Becket," *Canterbury Cathedral Chronicles*, 30, 1976, pp. 17, 19. There was so much wax to contend with that a Wax Chamber in the presbytery was used to house candles and votive images; M.F. Hearn, "Canterbury Cathedral and the Cult of Becket" *Art Bulletin* 76/1 (March, 1994), pp. 31–3.

[53] Erasmus in Nichols, *Pilgrimages to St. Mary and St. Thomas*, pp. 55–6. Only for distinguished visitors would the prior (here Thomas Goldstone II) give a personal tour. Otherwise, it was the duty of the feretrarians to present the shrine to pilgrims, such as the "goodly monk" who explained the relics to Chaucer's pilgrims described in the prologue to the *Tale of Beryn*, p. 6.

[54] The *Thómas Saga Erikibyskups*, I, pp. 475–81, II, pp. 213–23, noted that the *regal* was first discovered in Jerusalem by "some hunting folk" who sold it to Charlemagne. The gem had grown under a unicorn's horn, and when it shed its horn, the jewel was shed as well. Charlemagne had it set in gold and it was used as a coronation ring. Many years later, Becket visited Louis VII and asked for the ring. When the king hesitated, Becket stated he would have the stone, "though it

on the ruby's enormous size and brilliant color guaranteed its placement on every shrine badge.[55] To insure that the prized treasure did
not go unnoticed, a small votive statue in long robes pointed to the
jewel with a long wand.[56]

The *regal* ruby and its attendant figure were only two of the many
votives which inundated the shrine. On top of the feretory, is a large
cross, reminiscent of thirteenth-century altar crosses, with a sizable
jewel at its center and fleurons on its ends.[57] Flanking the cross are

---

may be later," I, p. 479. When the king's son became ill, Louis, remembering
Becket's request, vowed to take the stone to Canterbury. His son was instantly
cured. As time passed, the king regretted his vow and decided to offer instead double the price of the stone, which the archbishop (Richard of Dover) welcomed.
When the king prayed at the shrine, the stone was torn magnetically from his ring
and attached itself to the shrine, secured "[with a] gold-fitting enclos[ing] the edge
of the circular basis all round," II, p. 221. The king then donated the stone and
begged the monks to keep the money as well

A similar story is told by Tetzel, Letts, *Travels of Leo Rozmital*, pp. 43–4. When
Louis VII knelt at the shrine to fulfill a battlefield vow, the archbishop of the
Cathedral noticed the ring and asked the King to give it to the shrine. The King
demurred, as he believed that whatever he undertook would not miscarry so long
as he had the ring; instead, he offered 100,000 florins. Immediately the stone sprang
from the ring and embedded itself in the shrine as if placed there by a goldsmith.
The King prayed to St. Thomas that his sin might be forgiven, whereupon he presented the 100,000 florins to the shrine as well. Letts notes that this story has no
documentary confirmation and was probably the invention of a guide, p. 43, fn. 2.

[55] Schaseck noted, "Among other priceless things there is to be seen in it a car-
buncle which shines at night and which is half the size of a hen's egg." Tetzel
wrote, "No one knows what the stone is. It has a clear glistening brilliance and
burns with such a brilliant light that no one can bear to examine it closely, so as
to distinguish its color. It is said to be so precious that if a king of England were
taken prisoner one could ransom him with it, for it is said to be worth more than
the whole of England." Letts, *Travels of Leo Rozmital*, pp. 44, 50–1; Stanley, *Historical
Memorials*, Appendix II, p. 231.

[56] The badges often depict this figure or angel without wings: Spencer, *Salisbury
Museum*, p. 23; Hugh Tait, *Jewellery Through 7000 Years* (London, 1976), fig. 365b;
Spencer, *Pilgrim Souvenirs*, p. 101. Sometimes the figure kneels or is omitted entirely.
Tait, "Pilgrim-Signs," pl. XVa; Little, "Pilgrims' Badge," p. 19.

[57] In 1285, Edward I presented the shrine with four crosses, one of which is perhaps depicted on the shrine badge. He also donated golden statues of St. Edward
the Confessor, a pilgrim, St. George and his horse all placed on bases with pinnacles set over them, costing £347. British Library MS 636, f. 219d and Public
Record Office E101/372/11, m.3; Taylor, "Edward I and the Shrine," pp. 23–5;
Spencer, *Pilgrim Souvenirs*, p. 100. In 1434, John Brun, the Cathedral's plumber,
gave "to the shrine of St. Thomas the Martyr one pair of beads to the value of
£10 of purest gold that is in the southern part near the Regale of France." (*Item
optulit (Joannes Brun) ad feretrum sci Thome Martyr' unum par p'cum ad valorem xli de auro
purissimo. Vide in australi parte prope regalem francie.*) Canterbury Cathedral Archives,
Treasurers' Accounts, DCc/MA 1, f. 1; Nilson, *Cathedral Shrines*, p. 188, fn. 60. The
1434 record is written on the back of a 1286 account. Charles E. Woodruff, "The

two detailed models of ships. Model ships were common gifts, especially from those who left them "in gratitude for a safe homecoming or passage at sea," for St. Thomas was revered for bringing storm-tossed ships to safety.[58] Some model ships were used to collect alms, so were doubly-appropriate gifts to a saint's shrine.[59] The cog-type ships feature castles on the fore and stern with a main topmast in the center and yard (cross beam) ending in fleurons—the latter creating a cross on top of each ship. Ships on variant shrine badges have diverse rigging, but most show two main forestays connected to the castles, with braces emerging from the principal mast. The ships' hulls are composed of three strakes curving upward to the box-like stern and forecastle. Of all the many votives that adorned the shrine, royal gifts were most prized, thus it is likely that these ships represent the two golden votives given by Edward I.[60]

The type and number of votives displayed on each badge changed with different production lines. Fig. 203 features three shields of arms and a double portrait in addition to the *regal*. The double portrait on this badge may reflect the cameos observed in the Venetian diplomatic report of 1500, "being of such a size, that I do not dare to mention it," or it might show a large coin with double portrait heads or even a lead papal bull. The heraldic shields illustrate the arms of St. George (*argent a cross gules*) on the left, and on the right, the shaggy hind legs of a lion rampant. The center shield shows a standing figure, though its worn condition makes further identification

Financial Aspect of the Cult of St. Thomas of Canterbury as Revealed by a Study of the Monastic Records," *Archaeologia Cantiana*, 44, 1932, p. 29; Spencer, *Pilgrim Souvenirs*, p. 101.

[58] Spencer, *Salisbury Museum*, p. 23. Michael Mitchiner, *Medieval Pilgrim Badges* (London, 1986), p. 51, fig. 76, wrote that the ships allude to Becket's exile in France. Spencer, *Pilgrim Souvenirs*, p. 101, noted that even minor unofficial saints such as Richard Scrope, Archbishop of York, had 40 model ships on his tomb by the early sixteenth century; Swanson, *Catholic England*, pp. 179–81. There are also pilgrim badges of Becket in a ship; Spencer, *Pilgrim Souvenirs*, pp. 79–81.

[59] In 1331, Queen Philippa paid a goldsmith for a plan of a ship for alms. (*Pro purtracta cuiusdam navis in pergameno pro exemplari inde habendo pro quadam navis argentea pro elemosina iuxta exemplar predictum facienda*) Manchester, John Rylands University Library, MS lat. 235, f. 10: Nigel Ramsay, "Artists, Craftsmen and Design in England, 1200–1400," *Age of Chivalry*, pp. 51–2, 54, fn. 27.

[60] "He adorned [the shrine] admirably with four images and two ships of pure gold, and especially with brooches and invaluable things of gold and ornate precious stones." (*Quatuor imaginibus & duabus navibus de puro auro, ac etiam firmaculis et inestimabilibus aureis et lapidibus preciosis ornatis . . . egregie decoravit.*) British Library Lansdown MS; Woodruff, "The Financial Aspect," p. 29.

impossible. Inexact and fanciful heraldry regularly decorated pilgrim souvenirs,[61] but possibly the arms of St. George and the lion were meant to enhance the reputation of the shrine through its association with royal gifts.

Other badges display additional striking images, statues of tall, slender angels which once swung thuribles from sinuous ropes on either side of the shrine base. (figs. 204–5) Each angel balances on a cantilevered perch which extends out from the lowest register of the base, resembling the angels which once alighted on pedestals on the *Tomb of Edmund Crouchback (c.* 1296) in Westminster Abbey.[62] The right angel on the badge looks toward the shrine, while the left turns its back. Figures of angels regularly adorned shrines, symbolizing heavenly space or, when holding incense boxes, indicated the Mass of the Dead in Heaven or the Ark of the Covenant.[63]

The Shrine Base

While frequent addition of individual votives regularly changed the appearance of the feretory, the marble base probably changed more slowly. Here the badges are of inestimable help, as only one account, that of Henry of Avranches, mentions the base and only briefly. What the badges reveal is that the shrine base was almost as elaborate as the feretory it supported. Every other major shrine base in England was refurbished in the Decorated Style between 1270–1350, and the

---

[61] Personal communication with Jeanne-Marie Quevado. Spencer, *Pilgrim Souvenirs*, p. 59, noted the widespread use of pseudo-arms on pilgrim souvenirs.

[62] L.L. Gee, "'Ciborium' Tombs in England 1290–1330," *Journal of the British Archaeological Association* 132 (1979), p. 37. The angels can be seen in a drawing of Westminster Abbey in *Islip's Mortuary Roll* (after 1532), Westminster Abbey Library; Christopher Wilson, "The Medieval Monuments," in *A History of Canterbury Cathedral*, (eds.) Patrick Collinson, Nigel Ramsey, Margaret Sparks (Oxford, 1995), fig. 89.

[63] Rita Tekippe, *Procession, Piety and Politics: The Evolution of Form and Custom for Rheno-Mosan Reliqaury Shrines in Three Medieval Cult Communities, Associated with the Bishop-Saints Servatius of Maastricht, Eleutherius of Tournai, and Remaclus of Stavelot* (Ph.D. diss., The Ohio State University, 1999), p. 365; Arthur Gardner, *English Medieval Sculpture*, New York, 1973, fig. 344; Eileen Roberts, *The Hill of the Martyr: An Architectural History of St. Albans Abbey* (Bedforshire, UK, 1993), fig. 47, p. 112. Erwin Panofsky, *Tomb Sculpture*, New York, 1964, p. 61. Silver angels flanked the shrine of St. Erkenwald: "Two Inventories of the Cathedral Church of St. Paul, London, dated Respectively 1245 and 1402," ed. W.S. Simpson *Archaeologia*, 50 (1887), p. 469. Similar angels flanked head reliquary badges of Becket; Spencer, *Pilgrim Souvenirs*, fig. 85a.

badge attests that the shrine base of Becket was also transformed.

English shrine bases were crucial to the function of the feretory. Contintental feretories, which were regularly taken out of the church in processions, did not have elaborate bases, while English shrines formed impressive architectural monuments in the choirs of their chuches. Most stone shrine bases measured 2.45 m in height with the feretories placed on top to keep their jewels away from thieves. The stationary position of the shrine was emphasized by wooden or cloth covers which were winched upward on a rope attached to a pulley in the ceiling above. The shape of the shrine base evolved to facilitate the pilgrimage practice of trying to get close to the relics of the saint. In the later Middle Ages, the dividing line between relic and reliquary diminished, especially for the common pilgrims who were never permitted to handle the relics directly. For them, the visual and tactile sensations of the shrine formed their experience of the sacred. Accordingly, the shrine base needed to be functional— having architectural features which allowed pilgrims to physically interact with the shrine. The shrine base also had to be suitably symbolic, to create a context worthy of its precious load. In England, this was achieved by making the shrine bases look like churches themselves, with the micro-architectural forms on shrine bases constituting grandeur and holiness.

The badges illustrate the architectural nature of Becket's stone shrine base, with the bottom adorned by a row of quatrefoils. While individual quatrefoils were typical Gothic motifs, English shrine bases and tombs of the thirteenth and fourteenth centuries commonly featured rows of them at their base. On some shrines, hoping for the blessings of a particular saint, pilgrims would insert their limbs or heads, pushing themselves closer to the relics.[64] As the badge shows

---

[64] Similar quatrefoils appear on other Canterbury pilgrim badges: Mitchiner, *Medieval Pilgrim Badges*, p. 63, fig. 103; Spencer, *Pilgrim Souvenirs*, fig. 88b. Rows of quatrefoils decorated the shrine bases of St. Bertelin, Church of the Holy Cross, Ilam, Staffordshire (*c.* 1250), St. Frideswide's, Oxford (1289), St. Albans (*c.* 1305), and St. William's, York Minster (1371). Openwork quatrefoils framed all kinds of relics, such the Stone of Scone in the base of the *Coronation Chair* at Westminster Abbey (*c.* 1300) with its "openwork tracery beneath the seat for the display of what was, in effect, a relic of state." Paul Binski, *Westminster Abbey and the Plantagenets: Kingship and the Representation of Power 1200–1400* (New Haven, 1995), p. 136, figs. 183–4. Quatrefoils were also visual markers for tombs; Frederick Crossley, *English Church Monuments A.D. 1150–1550: An Introduction to the Study of Tombs & Effigies of the Medieval Period* (London, 1921), p. 42; *The Holy Women at the Tomb* (1216–72) shows a tomb with quatrefoils, *Age of Chivalry*, fig. 307, p. 327.

the central sections blocked off by bosses, perhaps the focus for pilgrim interaction was on the band of elaborate openwork surmounting the four quatrefoils which reflects the ornamental reticulated stone tracery found on the shrine. The tracery design, quatrefoils under ogival arches over two lancets with trefoil heads (sometimes under tiny gables), is repeated four times representing four bays. Like the single quatrefoil, this motif is part of the general artistic vocabulary of the Decorated Style, seen in small scale on *Prior Eastry's Throne* (*c.* 1300).[65] The motif's appearance on a larger scale on the ecclesiastical tombs of *Bishop Giles Bridport* (1264) in Salisbury Cathedral (fig. 206) and *Bishop Peter of Aquablanca* (1270) in Hereford Cathedral reveals its function on the shrine base at Canterbury.[66] (fig. 207) On both tombs, this graceful motif appears atop slender columns that act as a screen, behind which lies the recumbent statue of the tomb occupant. The open arcades create an interior vaulted cage containing the effigy placed on a stone sarcophagus, and pilgrim badge artisans wished to convey a similar screen-like cover.

As intricate and advanced as the mold cutting and metal casting on this series of badges were, to create a separate figure behind an openwork screen would have been extremely difficult, so the badge artisans improvised. Although the two-dimensional nature of badges tended to flatten their rendering of three-dimensional originals, the artisans used the reverse mold which created the pin of the badge

---

[65] Nicola Coldstream, *The Decorated Style: Architecture and Ornament, 1240–1360* (Toronto, 1994), fig. 90. This motif also appears in the south transept rose window at Westminster Abbey (*c.* 1250), the *Westminster Retable* (*c.* 1270–80), the *Anian (Bangor) Pontifical* (*c.* 1320–8), *Age of Chivalry*, fig. 109, 329, and on other Canterbury badges, *Age of Chivalry*, fig. 61, p. 222; Mitchiner, *Medieval Pilgrim Badges*, p. 62, fig. 99. Badge variants sometimes changed this decoration. Fig. 204 reduces the motif to a cusped trefoil under gables, while another expands the number of bays to five (covering ten arches) and transforms the quartet of the quatrefoils into six cusped quadrilobes; Spencer, *Pilgrim Souvenirs* (1998), fig. 76a, p. 100; Mitchiner, p. 52, fig. 77. Spencer wrote that this badge takes on a distinctly Perpendicular style. This might reflect a later alteration, but it might also reflect changing visual tastes.

[66] The tomb of Giles de Bridport, bishop of Salisbury (1256–62), uses the microarchitecture of metal reliquaries, featuring triforium arcades with low-pitched gables. Coldstream, *Decorated Style*, p. 91; Joan Evans, *Pattern: A Study of Ornament in Western Europe from 1180–1900* (1931, repr., New York, 1975), 1, p. 18; Marion Roberts, "The Tomb of Giles de Bridport in Salisbury Cathedral," *Art Bulletin* 65/4 (Dec. 1983), p. 304. The tomb of Peter Aquablanca has a miniature vaulted roof with three bays of traceried openings. The badge more closely resembles the lightweight nature of the columns of this tomb than the Bridport tomb which encases its arcades in heavy walls.

to cast the feretory and the lower portion of the shrine base into higher relief than the other portions of the bas-relief badge.[67] Looked at closely, these box-like projections indicate that they should be seen as standing in front of the other elements of the badge, forming a canopy over the recumbent effigy similar to the spatial surrounds of the ecclesiastical tombs.

Ecclesiastical effigies on tomb chests covered by canopies began to appear in the second half of the thirteenth century.[68] At the same time shrine bases like *St. Frideswide at Oxford* (1289), *St. Thomas of Cantilupe at Hereford* (1287), (fig. 208) and *St. Edburg of Bicester* (1294–1317) incorporated canopies, which became supporting tables for feretories when they rested on the tomb chest below, merging the forms of ecclesiastical tombs and shrine bases—seen in the *Tomb of Archbishop Walter de Gray* (1255–60), York Minster, where the effigy is covered by a gabled, pinnacled canopy resembling a feretory.[69] Screens where

---

[67] Spencer, Pilgrim Souvenirs, p. 100.

[68] Crossley, *English Church Monuments*, p. 43; Kemp, p. 26. Wilson, "Medieval Monuments," pp. 452–3, noted that these immense tombs became "a potentially serious threat to the liturgical, symbolic, and aesthetic integrity of the host churches" by crowding the space occupied by the shrine. Canterbury avoided this until the fourteenth century by keeping most tombs out of the crypt and Trinity Chapel to maintain the cult focus on Becket; (ed.) W. Stubbs, *Historical Works of Gervase of Canterbury* (London, 1879), i, pp. 22–6. Tomb canopies have been interpreted in variety of ways. Brieger, pp. 101–2; Coldstream, *Decorated Style*, p. 91, wrote that tombs were made to look like shrines when their occupants were considered as good candidates for canonization. Roberts, "The Tomb of Giles de Bridport," p. 562, argued that these tombs reflect the "general trend toward greater ostentation in sepulchral monuments," with the canopy illustrating the dignity of the tomb occupant the way the episcopal throne had while he was alive. The three surviving canopy tombs (Walter de Gray, Bridport, and Aquablanca) were not connected with individuals who were canonized or popularly beatified.

[69] Coldstream, *Decorated Style*, figs. 65, 29, 72. These tombs emulated the *elevatio* of saints' bodies. Wilson, "Medieval Monuments," p. 457. Maurice Hastings, *St. Stephen's Chapel and its Place in the Development of the Perpendicular Style In England* (Cambridge, 1955), p. 119, noted ". . . architecturally speaking, tombs of important personages and the shrines become very closely interrelated." (ed.) J. Coales, *The Earliest English Brasses: Patronage, Style and Workshops 1270–1350* (London, 1987), p. 23, stated that the earliest free-standing tombs under canopies should be placed in the context of altar ciboria. Bishops' tombs and shrines (Bridport tomb, shrine base of St. Albans) included biographical carvings. Sometimes both merged as in Bishop Grosseteste's (1253) tomb, Lincoln Cathedral, which was built as a shrine in the late 1250s. John Leland described it as a "a goodly tumbe of marble and an image of brasse over it." (ed.) Lucy T. Smith, *The Itinerary of John Leland in or about the Years 1535–1543* (Carbondale, IL, 1964), p. 122, Part XI, fol. 49. William Dugdale, *Book of Monuments* (British Library Loan MS. 38, f. 105v), noted that it was "a raised Altar-Tomb for Bishop Grist head, within three Niches on the Side but no Effigies or Arms on it, but there seems to have been some Brass inlaid on it."

the canopy partially blocks the effigy first appeared on ecclesiastical tombs in the 1250s and maintained their popularity until the introduction of *Ciborium* tombs in the late thirteenth and early fourteenth century, which subdivided this screen into three parts. Some featured a wider central space where the effigy could be seen unobscured, while others, such as the *Tomb of William de March* (1302) at Wells Cathedral, used the tripartite division to kept the sense of a screen intact.[70] Becket's shrine, as seen in the pilgrim badges, maintained the more conservative, screen-like canopy, more closely associated with shrines. The columns, too, could be those mentioned in Henry of Avranches' account.

The rich plasticity of the Decorated Style architectural canopy is referred to by some scholars as "shrine treatment."[71] When the nobility employed it over their own tombs in the late thirteenth century, the canopy itself metamorphosed into a symbol of earthly authority, surpassing its original meaning as a sign of sanctity over bishops' tombs and saints' shrines.[72] The canopy on the shrine of Becket reflected these multivalent meanings: he was a powerful saint and an archbishop. In between the columns of the arcaded canopy pilgrims could place their limbs or heads or leave offerings.[73] The canopy with its openwork of columns also afforded the pilgrims visible and tactile access to the effigy as though it was laid out on an open bier, in the manner of *Pilgrims Visiting the Shrine of St. Hedwig* (1353). (fig. 209)

The evolution to this form, the box type, from the table type of shrine base can be seen in comparing the earlier Frideswide base, which mixed both types, with that of the later Hereford base. Tombs and shrine bases became taller with the introduction of Ciborium-type tombs into England *c.* 1290. Nilson, p. 46. Shrine bases, influenced by these tombs, developed bases equipped with large niches in which pilgrims knelt. Joseph Braun, *Der Christliche Altar* (Munich, 1924), pl. 21; Coldstream, "Shrine Bases," pp. 16–8; Crossley, *English Church Monuments*, p. 44, fn. 1; R. Morris, "The Remodelling of the Hereford Aisles," *Journal of the British Archaeological Association*, 3rd s., 37 (1974), p. 21; Wilson, "St. William," fn. 13.

[70] Coldstream, *Decorated Style*, p. 91, wrote that his "shrine-like tomb" was made "when the authorities campaigned for his canonization."

[71] Jean Bony, *The English Decorated Style: Gothic Architecture Transformed 1250–1350* (Ithaca, 1979), p. 54.

[72] Coldstream, *Decorated Style*, p. 137; Gee, pp. 29–41: Paul Biver, "Tombs of the School of London at the Beginning of the Fourteenth Century," *Archaeological Journal* 67 (1910), pp. 51–65.

[73] Spencer, *Pilgrim Souvenirs*, p. 100.

Effigy

The presence of an effigy on the shrine badges is problematic because no accounts mention such a figure. Its appearance might function as an apparition of Becket's actual living presence within the shrine, as in window n:III, (fig. 130) where the martyr emerges from a shrine to heal a sick man before him,[74] but its consistent rendition on the shrine badges suggests that it did grace Becket's shrine, and as such it reveals the iconographic choices placed before the designers of shrine bases. Many important ecclesiastical tomb bore effigies, and it would be surprising if the designers of the shrine base did not accord Becket the same honor as other bishops. Yet, while effigies were common on bishops' tombs, they are rarely found on surviving shrine bases like the fourteenth-century shrine of St. Simeon of Zadar.[75] Unfortunately, nearly all surviving English shrine bases belonged to saints who were not bishops.[76] Many cults such as St.

---

[74] Spencer, *Pilgrim Souvenirs*, p. 100. In 1417, Eberhard Windecke (with Emperor Sigismund) wrote that he had seen the "body" of St. Thomas as well as the shrine. (*In Canterbury in England sah ich den Leichnam St Thomä von Canterbury und den allerköstlichsten Sarg, den, glaube ich, je ein Menschenkind gesehen hat; daselbst auch das Haupt des St Dionysius.*) Because he confused the head of St. Thomas with that of St. Denis, his account may not be reliable. Mason, *Bones of Becket*, pp. 106–7, fn. 3, p. 158.

[75] Ivo Petricioli, *St. Simeon's Shrine in Zadar* (Zagreb, 1983). Spencer, *Pilgrim Souvenirs*, p. 101 wrote "bearing in mind the relative scantiness of other evidence of the shrine, the figure, in its attitude of prayer, raises the possibility that by the fourteenth century some life-size portrayal of Becket may have been present at the shrine."

[76] Evidence for the appearance of the shrines of other bishop saints is haphazard. Shrines dedicated to Chad of Lichfield, Hugh of Lincoln, and Richard of Chichester have disappeared without a trace. Some evidence remains for the shrines of Cuthbert of Durham, Erkenwald of London, and John of Beverly. On Cuthbert, see James Raine, *St. Cuthbert: With an Account of the State in Which his Remains were Found Upon the Opening of his Tomb in Durham Cathedral, in the Year MDCCCXXVII*, Durham, 1828, p. 95; Fowler, *Rites of Durham*, pp. 3–4, 66–9. For Erkenwald, William Dugdale, *The History of Saint Paul's Cathedral in London, from its Foundation: Extracted out of Original Charters, Records, Ledger-Books, and other Manuscripts* (London, 1818), pl. facing p. 74. For John, (ed.) Arthur Leach, *Memorials of Beverly Minster: The Beverly Chapter Act Book of the Collegiate Church of S. John of Beverley A.D. 1286–1347* (Durham, 1903), pp. 299–300. It is difficult to compare these to Canterbury shrine badges because they are either too early (Cuthbert), too late (Erkenwald), or are not descriptive enough (John).

Part of the shrine base of the bishop St. Swithun of Winchester remains, indicating that it was a mid-thirteenth century tomb/shrine type, where a box with holes was fitted over (or under) the coffin containing the relics. John Crook, "The Typology of Early Medieval Shrines—A Previously Misidentified 'Tomb-Shrine' Panel from Winchester Cathedral," *The Antiquaries Journal* 70, Pt. 1 (1990), pp. 50–1; John Crook,

Swithun of Winchester and St. William of York maintained a tomb site separate from that of the main shrine. Because the shrines of these bishop saints did not serve as tombs, this may explain the absence of effigies from the records of these shrines. Canterbury also venerated a tomb site in the crypt, but as all of the relics were translated from his tomb, Becket's shrine served as his tomb, rendering the addition of an effigy necessary.

The only surviving English shrine base with a tomb effigy, the late thirteenth-century shrine of St. Thomas of Cantilupe (Bishop of Hereford Cathedral) supports the notion that a tomb was the prerequisite for an effigy. (fig. 208) Like the shrine badges, it features a tomb chest on the bottom surmounted by a canopy which supported a feretory. The tomb, with its full-length brass figure of the bishop, was constructed first and the canopy was added later when Thomas of Cantilupe began to acquire a saintly reputation; a typical bishop's tomb was transformed into a shrine.[77] The brass, now

"The Thirteenth Century Shrine and Screen at St. Swithun at Winchester," *Journal of the British Archaeological Association* 138 (1985), pp. 125–31, pl. XXIII; Pamela Tudor-Craig and Lawrence Keen, "A Recently Discovered Purbeck Marble Sculpted Screen of the Thirteenth Century and the Shrine of St. Swithun," *Medieval Art and Architecture at Winchester Cathedral* (London, 1983), pp. 63–72; pls. XVII–XIX; J.D. Le Couteur and J.H.M. Carter, "Notes on the Shrine of St. Swithun formerly in Winchester Cathedral" *Antiquaries Journal* 4 (1924), pp. 360–70. This type of shrine base has been traced to the Tomb of the Holy Sepulcher in Jerusalem. Martin Biddle, *The Tomb of Christ* (Gloucestershire, 1999), p. 85. The only shrine base of an English bishop saint to survive (besides that of Thomas Cantilupe) is St. William of York and its late date (1472) renders it useless for a comparison to the shrine of Becket as shown on the badges. Wilson, "St. William," pp. 19–20. *Editors' note see Stephen Lamia's essay in this volume.

[77] In 1285 pilgrims were granted indulgences for visiting the tomb of St. Thomas of Cantilupe (1282). (ed.) W.W. Capes, *Charters and Records of Hereford Cathedral*, Hereford, 1908, p. 153. When he became revered as a saint, a canopy was placed over his tomb to hold up a feretory, the new canopy's shafts crowded the original brass. Most scholars date this alteration to 1287, when Edward I attended a translation ceremony, and the sculptural style of the naturalistic foliage appears to confirm this. Marshall, "Shrine of St. Thomas, Cantilupe," p. 39. Nilson, *Cathedral Shrines*, p. 47, though, dated this this to 1320, when the saint was officially canonized and monies were granted in the will of John de Aquablanca, Dean of Hereford, for a new shrine. (*Item fabrice tumbe sancte memorie domini Thome de Cantilupo, quondam episcopi Herefordensis, post canonizationem ejusdem, viginti solidos do, lego.*) Capes, p. 186. 1320–21 receipts record commissions to goldsmiths and marblers for work on the feretory shrine and shrine base, Capes, p. 195. In 1337, Bishop Swinfield donated 100 marks for the construction of a feretory for St. Thomas (*pro construcionne feretri sancti Thome*) Capes, p. 220. Yet, it was not until 1349 that the relics were translated into a completely new shrine. P. Morgan, "The Effect of the Pilgrim Cult of St. Thomas Cantilupe on Hereford Cathedral," (ed.) Meryl Jancey, *St. Thomas Cantilupe, Bishop*

gone, but readable through its indent, was fundamental to the cult of St. Thomas of Cantilupe, as the miracle story tells of the saint emerging "from underneath the brass image which was set on top of the tomb of the man of God."[78]

The Canterbury badges depict Becket's effigy as an integral part of the pilgrim's experience at the shrine. (figs. 204–5) While there is a possibility that the image of the effigy may be copying a painting of the deceased lying in his tomb that was painted on a wall behind the shrine, the three-dimensional form on the badges indicates that Becket's effigy was neither painting nor a flat brass.[79] A jeweled miter crowns the top of Becket's large head as luxuriant curls hang down on either side of his face. His face is characterized by a broad forehead, arching eyebrows over almond-shaped eyes open in a rigid gaze and a slender nose and a dour mouth. His pallium falls over his thin, sloping shoulders, while his hands are clasped in prayer, causing gentle arcs of the broad-fold drapery to cascade below his chest in the center of the figure. His dalmatic splays beneath in wide folds, while the jeweled, embroidered hem reveals his pointed shoes as his right leg steps forward (causing his body to sway slightly). The graceful stance and the broad drapery folds are comparable to the *Hardingstone Queen Eleanor* (1291–2), though in Becket's case the top portion of the body does not respond to the movement below. Iconographically, the effigy veers from the popular gesture of benediction in favor of hands folded in prayer.[80] The primatial cross staff,

---

of Hereford: Essays in his Honour (Hereford, 1982), p. 150. I believe that the addition was added in 1287, but the feretory and base were updated later to coincide with the canonization. The abandonment of the original shrine base as the focus of the cult probably saved it from the targeted iconoclasm of the Reformation.

[78] John de Tregoz had a 1287 *vision de sub imagine aerea, quae fusa est super sarcofagum Viri Dei* and was cured of infirmity. N.J. Rogers, "English Episcopal Monuments, 1270–1350" in Coales, *Earliest English Brasses*, p. 30. In 1660, Silas Taylor (Harley MS 4046, British Library) noted that the brass was stolen in 1652. Marshall, "Shrine of St. Thomas, Cantilupe," p. 48; E.G. Benson, "The Lost Brass of the Cantilupe Shrine," *Transactions of the Woolhope Field Club* 33 (1949–51), p. 70.

[79] In the 1240's high relief Purbeck marble effigies were incorporated into monuments featuring canopies modeled on shrine bases. Wilson, "Medieval Monuments," p. 458. Cast metal effigies were made for the *Tomb of Peter of Aquablanca*, Bishop of Hereford (1268), the *Tomb of Bishop Jocelin* (1242) of Wells, and the *Tomb of William de Langton* (1279), Dean of York, though none survive. For a painting above a tomb, see Jeffrey Hamburger, *The Visual and the Visionary: Art and Female Spirituality in Late Medieval Germany* (New York, 1998), p. 107.

[80] Coldstream, *Decorated Style*, fig. 61. While Becket's praying hands, conveying humility and dignity, were unusual for effigies of high ecclesiastics, they were com-

crooked in his right arm, breaks through the boundaries of the feretory above and the shaft on the left side of the effigy.

This boundary is broken because the badge artisans raised the image of Becket above the arches and turned it on its side. This was necessary because it would have been extraordinarily difficult to show an effigy that lay perpendicular to the audience behind an elaborate stonework screen. This view of the effigy echoed the pilgrim's experience, who stand over the effigy seeing it flat and frontal rather than in profile. This vantage corresponds to the spatial ambiguity effigy-makers presented: the images were horizontal, but their feet were firmly placed on the ground. The position of Becket's effigy is suggested in a badge which shows the figure set at an angle of perhaps fifteen degrees, as seen in some fourteenth-century effigies, making it more accessible to viewers. Becket's perpendicular position on the badge reflects the artisans' interest in showing the entire figure of the martyr instead of copying its exact position inside the open bier.[81]

Shafts, buttresses, and pinnacles

Becket's bier was supported by tall, thin, freestanding buttresses. The flying buttresses on the badges are delicately cusped on either side, and some examples are decorated with seaweed foliage crockets that

---

monly found on effigies of lower-ranking clerics and the laity starting in the late thirteenth century. Wilson, "Medieval Monuments," p. 469, fn. 83. French episcopal effigies of the same period clasped their hands in prayer while holding their pastoral staffs under their forearms. This same gesture, where the staff is caught in the crook of the elbow allowing the hands to be free to pray, is seen on the effigy of an *Abbot at Sherborne* (*c.* 1270). Gardner, *English Medieval Sculpture*, fig. 295, p. 156.

[81] The effigy of *William de March* in Wells Cathedral is tilted up towards the viewer. M.W. Morris, "English Episcopal Monument, 1270–1350 III: A Survey of English Episcopal Monuments," in (ed.) John Coales, *The Earliest English Brasses: Patronage, Style and Workshops 1270–1350* (London, 1987), p. 51. Tilting an effigy when transposing its image from three-dimensions to two was relatively common. A drawing of the funeral of *Henry Beaufort, Bishop of Winchester* (d. 1447) made for Sir Thomas Wriothesley (d. 1534), Garter King of Arms 1505–34, British Library Add. MS 45131, f. 21, shows the body facing directly out. Wilson, "Medieval Monuments," fig. 88. Other pilgrim badges also used this conceit, such as the Shroud of Turin which reveals its front and back impression from a bird's eye perspective, as do badges St. Mathurin de Larchant whose body is carried in procession on a litter. Denis Bruna, *Enseignes de Pèlerinage et Enseignes Profanes, Musée du Moyen Age Thermes de Cluny* (Paris, 1996), pp. 61, 173.

delicately climb up the diagonal shaft.[82] (fig. 204) The pinnacles topping the buttresses furthest from the shrine end in large fleur-de-ly knops, while the inner shafts are crested by pinnacles which thicken as they reach the level of the feretory. Further down these shafts, at the bottom of the feretory, smooth cap-like capitals mark the transition from shrine base to feretory. On some badges, the capitals are composed of curling, stiff-leaf foliage adorned with miniature faces which stick out their tongues. These humorous details hint at the sculpture which once decorated Becket's shrine, as they do on other English shrine bases.

How the inner and outer buttresses were attached is puzzling. Some badges connect these by four large bosses on either side under the flyers. These curious bosses with their smooth, round centers, circumferenced by an indented design, resemble the jewels, as seen on the sumptuous feretory, but their large size and placement contradict this. As each boss is attached to the shafts by thin webs of metal, it is possible that they depict large crockets that peel off of the vertical buttresses, yet their borders and large size make this unlikely. While the placement of the bosses is part of a tradition of decorative fill composed of evenly-spaced objects (trefoils, rosettes), popular in the late thirteenth through the fourteenth century,[83] there is no exact ornamental equivalent of the bosses in contemporary architecture, sculpture, fine metalwork, or manuscript illumination. The bosses may be explained, in part, by circular cutters used to carve the stone molds. The cutters creating hollows from which the bosses and the smaller depiction of jewels were cast made it easy to carve uniform circular shapes, and its simplicity might have encouraged its common usage in pilgrim badge production generally. Yet the large bosses only appear on pilgrim badges produced for the Becket cult; perhaps these bosses were a mark of a pilgrim souvenir workshop.[84]

---

[82] In the engraving by Wenceslaus Hollar in Dugdale, *The History of St. Paul's Cathedral*, facing p. 74, flying buttresses also adorn the feretory of St. Erkenwald, which resembled a small church.

[83] Regularly-spaced rosettes frame a pax in *Age of Chivalry*, cat. 624, p. 479; evenly-spaced foilage connects the outer columns to the effigy of *Bishop Kilkenny* at Ely (1256). Gardner, *English Medieval Sculpture*, fig. 297. For a different placement of the bosses see Tait, "Pilgrim Signs," pl. XVa.

[84] Spencer, *Pilgrim Souvenirs*, pp. 100, 109; personal communication with Marianne Hansen. Bosses also appear on thirteenth-century Canterbury ampullae, where they

It is likely that these bosses were used to hold together the more fragile portions of the badge and did not allude to any specific detail of the shrine, for the bosses are the only item on the badges that are illogical. While the bosses work decoratively, they make no sense as structural units. Their appearance is inconsistent from badge to badge versus the constancy of other features such as the effigy. One badge provides a more convincing depiction of how the outer and the inner pinnacles were connected by a shaft rising in two stages: the first is a trefoil-headed arch supporting an embattled buttress. (fig. 205) Based on the evidence from other larger badge fragments, one may infer that this buttress adjoined the area right below the feretory. The second stage is a string-like remnant of another decorative structural member which is reminiscent of the buttress elements found on the *Shrine Base of St. Albans.* (fig. 210)

As each pilgrim souvenir artisan sought to make sense of the overwhelming details of the shrine, they also tried to capture the shrine's brilliant color. In fact, the shrine badges were once painted, and at least one example retains clips which attached a colorful backing to its badge.[85] That color was an intrinsic part of the shrine's appeal is evident not only in the variety of gems that adorned its surface, but also in the wide range of hues employed in the roundels on the inset floor that surrounded it. Surviving shrine bases and canopy tombs all have traces of paint, a testimony that they were once saturated with color, a hallmark of the Decorated Style.

Style and Date of the Shrine of Becket

Taking into account all of the stylistic elements described above, one sees that Becket's shrine (as depicted on the pilgrim badges) was built in the Decorated Style (1250–1350). While assigning a specific date to the shrine's refurbishment is a speculative venture, the detail of the badges makes it possible to go beyond mere induction. The shrine followed the general form of ecclesiastical canopy tombs of

alternate with pyramidal shapes; Brian Spencer, "Pilgrim Souvenirs" in P.F. Wallace (ed.) *Medieval Dublin Excavations 1962–91: Miscellanea I* (1988), p. 37. Other smaller, bosses include Becket riding a boss-dappled horse and on a ship whose boards have boss-like nails. Spencer, *Pilgrim Souvenirs,* figs. 34a, 35b, 37–49.

[85] Museum of London 84.258; Tait, "Pilgrim Signs," pl. XVa.

the mid-thirteenth century and shrine bases of the 1280s, but its particular stylistic details show that it was designed in the manner associated with the London School of the 1290s–1310s.[86] The particular
micro-architectural details on the shrine badges which are associated
with this style include the ogee arch, gabled arcades on the canopy,
tall pinnacles, finials, curvilinear flowing tracery, crockets, seaweed
foliage, diaper ornament (on the feretory), use of trefoil and quatrefoil shapes, slender flying buttresses, heraldry, and inclusion of
figure sculpture on the shrine of St. Thomas Becket. These slender,
delicate, encrusted details can be found on works of the London
School, such as the *Tomb of Edmund Crouchback, Earl of Lancaster* (1296)
at Westminster and the *Shrine Base of St. Albans* (1302–9).[87]

An examination of the *Shrine Base of St. Albans* (fig. 211) allows a
glimpse of what the Canterbury shrine base must have looked like.
The Purbeck marble edifice (two and a half m) rises in three stages:
the tomb base, the niches, and the cornice which supported the feretory. The entire structure rests on two steps. The outer step features column bases which held candles, while the inner step supports
fourteen flying buttresses which attach to the cornice.

Its visual similarity to Becket's shrine badges is considerable. St.
Albans is four bays long and two bays wide. Its tomb-like base is
adorned with quatrefoils, here cusped with lozenge-shaped openings.
These openings appear to have been modified from an original
design, so they may have been closer to the round openings (depicted

---

[86] This term is debated. According to Bony, *English Decorated Style*, p. 11 the
London School began at the Court *c.* 1285 and spread outward, particularly through
the patronage of political bishops. Roberts, "Tomb of Giles de Bridport," p. 564,
wrote that ecclesiastical tombs far from London, such as the Bridport monument,
can be compared to the court style practiced at Westminster.

[87] Coldstream, *Decorated Style*, fig. 28. Before 1259, the shrine consisted of a gabled
reliquary set atop slender pillars. Matthew Paris, *The Lives of Saints Alban and Amphibalus*,
Trinity College, Dublin MS 177, fol. 61a. Later, Abbot John de Maryns (1302–9)
"caused the *tumba* and *feretrum* of St. Alban to be moved, whilst decorating it nobly,
and expended on it, not to reckon too closely, more than a 160 marks in counted
money." (*Tumbam autem Sancti Albani, et feretrum, amovere fecit, honorifice istud decorando;
et expensas exposuit, sine multis curialitatibus, plus quam centum sexaginta marcas in pecunia
numerata*); (ed.) Henry T. Riley, *Gesta Abbatum Monaterii S. Albani A Thoma Walsingham
(A.D. 793–1401)* (London, 1867–69), 2, p. 107; trans. by Roberts, *Hill of the Martyr*,
pp. 111–2. Crossley, *English Church Monuments*, p. 62, and Hastings, *St. Stephen's Chapel*,
p. 128, dated the shrine base to 1305. Nicola Coldstream "Base of the Shrine of
St. Alban, St. Albans Cathedral" *Age of Chivalry*, pp. 207–8, noted that its base type
originated 1269 and continued into the fifteenth century.

on the badges as bosses) on Becket's shrine. Above the quatrefoils
is a cavetto molding with evenly-spaced floral bosses. On the badge,
there is a convex molding with evenly-studded bosses above the
canopied niches. On St. Albans base, canopied niches also rise, showing traces of brilliant color and gold. Blind reticulated tracery forms
the back of the niches, and the pattern of this tracery, two trefoil
lancet windows topped by cusped quatrefoils, is similar to that on
the shrine badge. The arches of the niches are cusped and recusped
and topped by gables which are decorated with seaweed foliage
crockets. These crockets can be seen on one badge over the tiny
gables and on the pinnacles. (fig. 204) The flying buttresses of St.
Alban's base are also present on the badges. The upper portion is
attached to the cornice on top of the shrine base by tiny flyers which
connect to outer shafts topped by pinnacles with foliage. (fig. 210)
The shrine badges also connect their buttresses to the base by tiny
bridges. The trefoil-headed arches connecting the lower portion of
the buttresses to the base on St. Alban's shrine are similar to those
in fig. 205.[88]

No other document attests to Becket's shrine's refurbishment. The
Canterbury treasurers' rolls from 1290–1310 show no surge in donations for refurbishment, but these accounts only reveal a portion of
the finances of the shrine. Priors' rolls, which are quite irregular,
sometimes indicate (in contrast to the treasurers' rolls) that the head
reliquary of Becket received more donations than the main shrine.
Also absent are the feretrarian accounts, with only one surviving
example (1398–9), which records considerable donations to the main
shrine mentioned nowhere else.[89] Therefore, although the only surviving evidence that indicates the shrine of St. Thomas Becket was
refurbished in the Decorated Style around 1300 is that of the pil-

---

[88] A number of differences between the shrine badges and the St. Albans shrine
base include the delicate cusping on the lower portion of the bridges on the badges,
which is absent from the latter and on the base pinnacles are part of the buttresses,
while on the badges pinnacles appear on the buttresses and the main body of the
shrine. There is no effigy at St. Albans (for he was not a bishop saint), and the
heavy cornice at the top of the shrine base is only implied on the badge by the thin
line of bosses that separates the effigy from the feretory.

[89] Money controlled by the feretrarians was not listed in the priors' accounts; the
Prior's account of 1453–54, records 60 shillings at the shrine, plus £7 "received
from the feretrarians by the hand of the chaplain for making wicks." Nilson, *Cathedral
Shrines*, p. 151; Canterbury Cathedral Archives, DCc/Prior 9.

grim badges themselves, their proof is quite impressive. Fig. 212 illustrates a reconstruction of the shrine of St. Thomas Becket based on the evidence of the pilgrim badges and written records.

The secrets of the long-destroyed shrine can be rediscovered through pilgrim souvenirs. These intrinsically worthless objects became valuable to the medieval pilgrim who endowed them with powerful associations of the memories of their visit to the holy shrine. As such, they acted as a direct link between the pilgrim and their prayers and desires. Their specificity created a tangible record of what the pilgrims had seen and felt in the presence of such an edifice. It is through their accuracy that art historians can attempt to reconstruct the major components of the shrine of St. Thomas. These components place the shrine into the stylistic and iconographic context of surviving shrine bases and ecclesiastical tombs. Through this analysis, the art historian discovers that Becket's shrine followed the traditions of the London School of the Decorated Style while grappling with the tricky iconographic needs of an archbishop saint's tomb/shrine with the addition of an effigy covered by a canopy, but more significantly, the pilgrim badges allow us to catch a glimpse of the brilliant, jewel-encrusted shrine in all of its colorful, golden glory.

* This article is based on Sarah Blick, "Reconstructing the Shrine of St. Thomas Becket, Canterbury Cathedral" *Konsthistorisk Tidskrift*, Decmber 2003, with permission. My grateful thanks for their help and advice on this essay goes to: Boris Blick, Katja Boetjes, Melissa Dabakis, Eugene Dwyer, Stephen Lamia, Carmen King, Michelle Nordtorp-Madsen, Brian North Lee, Jeanne-Marie Quevado, Brian Spencer, Rita Tekippe Kristen Van Ausdall, and especially my friend Karen M. Gerhart and my husband John F. Pepple. I also wish to thank Kenyon College for their generous support of this project with a Faculty Development Grant. This article is dedicated to Brian Spencer in fond memory for all of his generous help and inspiration.

CHAPTER SEVENTEEN

PILGRIM AMPULLAE FROM VENDÔME: SOUVENIRS FROM A PILGRIMAGE TO THE HOLY TEAR OF CHRIST

Katja Boertjes

An inscription scratched in the façade of the Church of St. Stephen in Saint-Ouen-Domprot (Marne) at the beginning of the sixteenth century, tells us that a tanner, Antoine from Metz, is buried at this spot. Antoine died on his way home from a pilgrimage to Vendôme and Mont-Saint-Michel.[1] In Vendôme he undoubtedly venerated *la Sainte Larme*, a sacred tear of Christ, which according the Gospel, Christ shed, when mourning the death of his friend Lazarus.[2]

Because Christ ascended bodily into heaven, primary relics of Christ are rare. Nonetheless, during the Middle Ages at least eight French churches claimed to house a sacred tear of Christ,[3] but the

---

[1] "Ci-gît Antoine le tanneur de cuir de la cité de Metz qui mourut au retour de la Très Sainte Larme et du Mont-Saint-Michel le 22 août 1507. Priez Dieu pour lui." (Here lies Anthony, the tanner of leather from the city of Metz, who died on his return journey from the Most Holy Tear and from Mont-Saint-Michel on August 22, 1507. Pray to God for him.)

[2] Christ was on his way to Bethany to visit Lazarus when he heard of his illness. On arriving in Bethany, he was told that his friend had been buried four days before. When Mary Magdalene, the sister of Lazarus, showed the grave to Christ, he shed a tear (John 11.1–36). According to apocryphal versions of the Gospel, an angel caught this tear in a vial and gave it to Mary Magdalene. See fn. 85.

[3] The Premonstratensian Abbey of Saint-Pierre (later Sainte Larme) at Sélincourt (Somme), Thiers (Puy-de-Dôme), Saint-Leonard at Chemillé (Maine-et-Loire), the Cistercian abbey at Fontcarmont (Seine-Maritime), Saint-Maximin (Var), Saint-Pierre-le-Puellier at Orléans (Loiret), Allouagne (Pas-de-Calais) and La Trinité at Vendôme (Loir-et-Cher). René Crozet, "Le Monument de la Sainte Larme à la Trinité de Vendôme," *Bulletin monumental* 121 (1963), 171–80, here p. 12, fn. 2. Examples of other primary relics of Christ are fragments of nails or hair (both in the Volto Santo at Lucca), a milk-tooth (abbey of Saint Médard at Soissons), and blood (preserved in many medieval churches). French examples of holy blood included Billom (Puy-de-Dôme), Boulogne (Pas-de-Calais), Fécamp (Seine-Maritime), La Rochelle (Charente-Maritime), and Neuvy-Saint-Sépulcre (Indre). Editors' note: see Nora Laos' essay in this volume.

tear of Christ in the Benedictine Abbey La Trinité (Trinity) at Vendôme was the best-known and most-frequently visited of them all. The relic became known as *la Sainte Larme, la Très Sainte Larme* or (in the vernacular) *Madame Sainte Larme*.[4] Shortly before the middle of the eleventh century, the abbey came into possession of this tear, which was enclosed in a reliquary ampulla of rock crystal inserted in a golden casing, and this sparked a flourishing cult tradition. Pilgrims flocked to the shrine, and before long their desire to possess a reminder of their visit prompted production of a wide range of souvenirs.

This essay will focus on a specific type of these Vendôme souvenirs: the small pewter receptacles called ampullae, which were popular pilgrim keepsakes sold at many pilgrimage sites throughout Europe during the High and Late Middle Ages.[5] Transported from Vendôme to other places, they were usually pinned to garments or hung round the wearer's neck on a cord. Generally speaking, such souvenirs were evidence of an often-arduous pilgrimage, not only identifying the wearer as a pilgrim, but also serving as amulets to avert disaster and bring good luck. Although produced by the thousands, only fourteen more or less complete examples and one separate ampulla half have been found whose iconography points to a Vendôme provenance. Each illustrates certain aspects of the pilgrimage cult at Vendôme, but the most important element on each of these ampullae was the highly venerated tear relic of Christ.

La Sainte Larme *and the Founding of La Trinité Abbey*

The tear relic is said to have come to Vendôme from the treasury of the Byzantine emperor Michael IV Paleologus (1034–41) in Constantinople. The emperor was reported to have presented it to Geoffrey Martel (1006–60), sixth count of Vendôme and founder of La Trinité abbey, as a reward for his 1036 victory over the Saracens.[6]

---

[4] Crozet, "Le Monument de la Sainte Larme," p. 171.

[5] For a complete survey of these places of pilgrimage and a full discussion of the ampullae, see my dissertation on the tradition of medieval pilgrim ampullae, which will be published in 2005.

[6] Achille De Rochambeau, "Voyage à la Sainte-Larme de Vendôme, étude historique et critique sur cet antique pèlerinage," *Bulletin de la Société archéologique scientifique et littéraire du Vendômois* 12 (1873), 156–212, here pp. 175–7.

A less impressive, but more probable anecdote, explains that Geoffrey received the holy tear along with several other relics in 1045 or 1046 as a gift from Henry III, son-in-law of his second wife, Agnes of Poitou (1024–77).[7] Inscriptions on the outermost container, a rectangular box supported by four animals' forequarters, seem to confirm that the relic was indeed once in the possession of that prince.[8] Depicted on one of the short sides of this box was a large, stylized eye with the inscription HEINRICVS REX NITKERVS EPISCO-PUS (King Henry, Bishop Notker) below. An inscription on the box lid reads HEINRICO NITKERS DAT (Notker gives this to Henry). This latter inscription suggests that the box was presented by Bishop Notker of Freising (r. 1039–52) to King/Emperor Henry III of Germany (r. 1039–1056), who may, in turn, have given the box to Geoffrey Martel. In 1043, Henry III had married Agnes of Poitou (daughter of William V of Aquitaine and Agnes of Poitou) and both Agnes senior and Geoffrey Martel visited the Byzantine imperial court in 1045 or 1046. On that occasion, the emperor and empress could have given them the reliquary box (relics and all).[9]

Inside this outer box were three more nested boxes; the innermost displayed the relic.[10] It was shaped as a small, hexagonal monument with a dome, crowned by a globe. Four sides were made of gold with incised depictions of the resurrection of Lazarus; the two other sides were transparent, revealing the crystal ampulla containing the *Sainte Larme*.[11] Figure 213 pictures this innermost reliquary in Geoffrey Martel's left hand.

The sacred tear was not the only important relic at Vendôme.

---

[7] Crozet, "Le Monument de la Sainte Larme," pp. 172–3; Penelope D. Johnson, *Prayer, Patronage, and Power: The Abbey of La Trinité, Vendôme, 1032–1187* (New York, 1981), p. 149.

[8] A watercolor, that belonged to the French collector Roger de Gaignières (1642–1715), shows this outer reliquary (35 × 17 cm). Now in the Bibliothèque Nationale, Cabinet des Estampes, VA 81. Topographie de la France, Loir-et-Cher, Vendôme. Reproduced as a drawing in De Rochambeau, "Voyage à la Sainte-Larme," pp. 184–6, figs. 25–9.

[9] Johnson, *Prayer, Patronage, and Power*, p. 150.

[10] A description of the four boxes is given in Jean Mabillon, "Mémoires pour servir d'éclaircissement à l'histoire de la sainte Larme de Vendôme," in Jean Mabillon and Thierri Ruinart, *Ouvrages posthumes de D. Jean Mabillon et de D. Thierri Ruinart, bénédictins de la congregation de saint Maur*, part 2 (Paris, 1724), pp. 383–94, esp. pp. 386–7; De Rochambeau, "Voyage à la Sainte-Larme," pp. 183–92.

[11] De Rochambeau, "Voyage à la Sainte-Larme," p. 191.

The royal gift also included another valuable relic: an arm of St. George. This relic was given a place of honor in the small collegiate Church of Saint-Georges, also called "the count's chapel," built by Agnes shortly before 1050 within the castle walls at Vendôme. Little is known concerning the veneration of this arm, but pilgrim signs strongly suggest that this relic played an important role in the pilgrims' devotion at Vendôme together with the *Sainte Larme*.

While the arm of St. George was displayed in the count's chapel, Geoffrey presented the tear relic to the abbey church La Trinité, which he commissioned to be built in the 1030s, following a miraculous event, later recorded in a twelfth-century chronicle. One Sunday morning Geoffrey Martel and his wife Agnes saw from their castle three stars fall in rapid succession into a well outside Vendôme.[12] Interpreting the three stars as the Trinity, the couple went straight to the Church of Saint-Martin, near the well, to sing a Mass in honor of the Holy Trinity. Geoffrey subsequently consulted several priests about the significance of the miracle he had seen. Their unanimous advice was to build a monastery on the spot where the stars had fallen and to dedicate it to the Holy Trinity, making sure that the altar was situated above the well. Since the foundation charter of the abbey was issued on May 31, 1040,[13] it can be assumed that the miracle occurred shortly after 1032, when Geoffrey and Agnes were married. The holy tear reliquary was placed in the choir of La Trinité, where it was venerated until the reliquary was lost during the French Revolution.[14]

Pilgrimage to the Holy Tear

The *Sainte Larme*, which fell from the eyes of Christ, reputedly cured maladies associated with the eye. The earliest-known healing associated with the tear relic dates from the second half of the twelfth century. John, a boy who suffered from an eye ailment, asked his

---

[12] Louis Halphen and René Poupardin, *Chroniques des comtes d'Anjou et des seigneurs d'Amboise* (Paris, 1913), pp. 150–1.

[13] Charles Métais (ed.), *Cartulaire de l'abbaye cardinale de la Trinité de Vendôme*, part 1 (Paris, 1894), pp. 55–60, no. 35.

[14] Crozet, "Le Monument de la Sainte Larme," p. 172.

father to drop charges against the monks of La Trinité in connection with the Villarvent estate. The father complied with his son's request, whereupon the boy's condition improved slightly. The entire family then visited the tear relic at Vendôme, where John's eyes were completely cured by the grace of God.[15]

During the annual procession on "the Friday of Lazarus," the week before Good Friday, the relic was carried in its container through the streets of Vendôme. For this celebration, vast numbers of pilgrims came to Vendôme to worship the tear relic. In accordance with a tradition dating to 1428, every year on this day, a prisoner was set free after walking behind the *Sainte Larme* bearing a large candle.[16] The ceremony was initiated by Louis de Bourbon (1376–1446), Count of Vendôme, who had been imprisoned in the Tower of London after the battle of Agincourt, but managed to escape shortly after making a vow to the *Sainte Larme*. On his return to Vendôme he presented the abbey church a candle weighing thirty-three pounds (one pound for each year of Christ's life on earth), to be burnt in front of the tear relic.

Various French kings and the counts of Vendôme were among the many pilgrims who came to venerate the *Sainte Larme*, overwhelming La Trinité Abbey with gifts. Louis XI gave a heavy silver lamp and in 1467 promised to place the abbey, the monks, and all their possessions under his royal protection. This initiative was then adopted by his successors.[17] Pilgrimage to Vendôme also found favor with broader populace in the *Bouc van den ambachten/Livre des Mestiers* (Book of Crafts), a mid-fourteenth century school textbook which lists fifteen places of pilgrimage including Vendôme, coming sixth after Jerusalem, the Sinai, Rome, Santiago de Compostela, and Rocamadour.[18] Vendôme's location on the pilgrimage route from the

---

[15] Charles Métais (ed.), *Cartulaire de l'abbaye cardinale de la Trinité de Vendôme*, part 2 (Paris, 1894), p. 450, no. 580.

[16] Arthur Forgeais, *Collection de plombs historiés trouvés dans la Seine et recueillis par Arthur Forgeais, Tome IV: Imagerie religieuse* (Paris, 1865), pp. 66–7; De Rochambeau, "Voyage à la Sainte-Larme," pp. 197–9.

[17] De Rochambeau, "Voyage à la Sainte-Larme," p. 199.

[18] Fol. 23. The original manuscript, compiled in Middle-Dutch and Middle-French by an anonymous schoolmaster of Bruges, is in Paris, Bibliothèque Nationale de France, MS Néerl. 16. The text is published in Jan Gessler (ed.), *Het Brugsche Livre des Mestiers en zijn navolgingen: vier aloude conversatieboekjes om Fransch te leeren, Deel 1: Le livre des Mestiers. De Bouc vanden Ambachten* (Bruges, 1931), p. 49. The complete list

Low Countries to Santiago de Compostela surely increased its popularity among pilgrims from the North.

Not all pilgrims came to Vendôme of their own free will. Beginning
in the thirteenth century, secular and religious authorities imposed
pilgrimage as a punishment. A wrong-doer would be sentenced to
leave home and go on pilgrimage to a holy place, in hopes that he
would see the error of his ways during the journey and do penance.
The community, too, was relieved of the miscreant's presence for a
while. This is how some pilgrims found themselves in Vendôme from
the early fourteenth century on.[19] One of them was a man called
Jhan die Deckere, who had been sentenced in the abbey of Saint
Nicholas at Veurne on April 18, 1324 for tax evasion; his punishment was "to undertake a pilgrimage to the Tear of Our Lord at
Vendôme."[20] On September 26, 1355 the aldermen of Ypres passed
judgment on a Cristiaen l'Ours for insulting the town clerk, his punishment, too, was a pilgrimage to Vendôme, where he had to remain
for a whole year.[21]

Mass Production

The popular, annual procession on the Friday of Lazarus was traditionally coupled with a market, where there was a flourishing trade
in pilgrim tokens, in the form of ampullae, badges, pendants, and
medals. Most have been found in the Loire region, confirming
Vendôme's popularity as a pilgrimage destination for the surrounding areas.[22] Finds of pilgrim souvenirs in the Low Countries and

---

includes: Jerusalem, Sinai, Rome, Santiago de Compostela, Rocamadour, Vendôme,
Saint-Maur-des-Fossés, Saint-Fiacre, Saint-Denis, Noyon, Saint-Quentin, Amiens,
Saint-Josse-sur-Mer, Boulogne, and Aachen.

[19] Antoon Viaene, "Ons Heeren Trane te Vendôme. Een bedevaart uit het oude
Vlaamse strafrecht," *Biekorf* 66 (1965), 184–8; Jan van Herwaarden, *Opgelegde bedevaarten* (Assen, 1978), lists thirty-nine disciplinary pilgrimages from the Low Countries
to Vendôme in the late Middle Ages. For the complete survey see Van Herwaarden,
Opgelegde bedevaarten, pp. 410, 702.

[20] Henri Pirenne, *Le Soulèvement de la Flandre Maritime de 1323–1328: documents inédits*
(Brussels, 1900), p. 177, lines 6–9.

[21] *Registres aux sentences des échevins d'Ypres*, fol. 21v., no. 409. Published in Prosper
de Pelsmaeker, *Coutumes des Pays et Comté de Flandre. Quartier d'Ypres. Registres aux sentences des échevins d'Ypres* (Brussels, 1914), p. 258.

[22] In Orléans, fifty kilometers from Vendôme, twenty-four percent of pilgrim

England, however, indicate that Vendôme's fame had spread to these regions as well.

From the thirteenth through the sixteenth centuries, ampullae were the most popular souvenirs for Vendôme pilgrims. In 1865, Arthur Forgeais described and drew with painstaking precision five specimens which had been found in the Seine.[23] Later, more ampullae from Vendôme were found during archeological excavations in England[24] and the Netherlands.[25] Furthermore, some ampullae exist(ed) in collections in Vendôme,[26] Vienna,[27] and Utrecht.[28]

---

badges discovered there are attributed to Vendôme, the highest number of any pilgrimage site. Denis Bruna, "La diffusion des enseignes de pèlerinage," in *Pèlerinages et croisades* (Paris, 1995), pp. 201–14, here p. 205; Denis Bruna, *Enseignes de Pèlerinage et Enseignes profanes. Musée National du Moyen Age—Thermes de Cluny* (Paris, 1996), p. 46. Caution should be observed here in view of another Sacred Tear kept in the church of Saint-Pierre-le-Puellier at Orléans, raising the possibility that some of the pilgrim tokens may have come from Orléans. A remarkable aspect of this group is the absence of ampullae. François-Edmond Desnoyers, "Objets trouvés dans la Loire," *Mémoires de la Société archéologique de l'Orléanais* 12 (1873), 245–75; François-Edmond Desnoyers, "Objets trouvés dans la Loire," *Mémoires de la Société archéologique de l'Orléanais* 15 (1876), 113–96. The collection, kept in the Orléans museum, was destroyed in air-raids during World War II, and all the souvenirs were lost.

[23] Four specimens in Paris and one in Mélun. Forgeais, *Imagerie religieuse*, pp. 65–86.

[24] Two ampullae. Brian W. Spencer, *Medieval Finds from Excavations in London: 7. Pilgrim Souvenirs and Secular Badges* (London, 1998), pp. 227–30.

[25] One ampulla. H.J.E. van Beuningen and A.M. Koldeweij, *Heilig en Profaan: 1000 Laatmiddeleeuwse Insignes uit de collectie H.J.E. van Beuningen.* Rotterdam Papers VIII (Cothen, 1993), p. 139.

[26] Three pouch-shaped ampullae are in the Musée de Vendôme. A fourth, round-bellied container was once owned by this museum in 1873. De Rochambeau, "Voyage à la Sainte-Larme," pp. 171–2, figs. 18–9. The ampulla now seems to be lost. Letter of March 6, 2003 from Laurence Guilbaud, curator of the museum.

[27] There was an ampulla in the private collection of Albert Figdor at Vienna in 1919; its findspot was unknown as are its present whereabouts. Karl Berling, *Altes Zinn. Ein Handbuch für Sammler und Liebhaber* (Berlin, 1919), pp. 47, 49, fig. 30.

[28] The Museum Catharijneconvent at Utrecht owns an ampulla from Vendôme, with an unknown findspot. It comes from a private collection which was sold with a few pilgrim badges at the art store J. Polak in Amsterdam. In 1986 the badges were sold separately and the ampulla passed into the museum's collection. Henri L.M. Defoer, "Metalen reisgezelschap," *Catharijnebrief: mededelingen van de Vereniging van Vrienden van het Museum Het Catharijneconvent te Utrecht* 15 (September 1986), 3–4; Jos Koldeweij, "Te Vendôme t'Ons Heeren Tranen. Metalen reisgezelschap (2)," *Catharijnebrief: mededelingen van de Vereniging van Vrienden van het Museum Het Catharijneconvent te Utrecht* 21 (March 1988), 12–13. Since this object is identical to the round-bellied ampulla formerly kept in the collection of the Musée de Vendôme (see fn. 26), it is quite possible that it is one and the same ampulla—given the rarity of the iconography and the fact that the depictions are exactly the same.

All the recovered specimens were cast from an alloy of lead and
tin (pewter). The inexpensive materials meant that such souvenirs
were affordable for pilgrims, who might have limited spending money.
In certain combinations these metals have a very low melting-point,
making the production process easier and cheaper. The objects were
usually cast in molds made of slate or steatite, fired or dried clay,
wood, horn, or even cuttle bone. Towards the end of the Middle
Ages bronze molds also appeared.[29] It is not certain what kind of
molds were used to cast the Vendôme ampullae; as none have been
discovered.[30]

The Contents and Function of the Ampullae

Owners of a pilgrim ampulla were generally deemed protected against
all kinds of catastrophe, because the object had been blessed by its
contact with the holy place. Due to their contents—usually something tangible, found in the vicinity of that holy place—ampullae
were invested with greater value than other souvenirs such as badges,
pendants, and medals. They always contained a substance that came
directly from the venerated shrine and thus the souvenir possessed
the enhanced value of a relic, endowed with protective and healing

---

[29] Spencer, *Medieval Finds*, p. 10.

[30] Molds from various other places of pilgrimage indicate a technique, called slush
casting, might have been employed. Experiments conducted with a replica of a
medieval mold from Waltham, England, demonstrates that it would have been relatively easy to produce such ampullae. By pouring molten tin through a runner
into a cold mold and inverting it while the metal was still molten, it was possible
to produce a perfect pilgrim ampulla quickly. Fine air-vents extracted surplus air
and gases from the mold during casting. See Brian W. Spencer, "Medieval Pilgrim
Badges," in J.G.N. Renaud (ed.), *Rotterdam Papers. A Contribution to Medieval Archeology*
(Rotterdam, 1968), pp. 137–53, here pp. 141, 146, fn. 27; Spencer, *Medieval Finds*,
pp. 11–2. Another technique permitted the two halves of the ampulla to be cast
separately and joined together subsequently. This is seen in a Demetrius ampulla
from Thessalonica whose two pewter halves do not fit well, making it appear that
the neck is fitted with two pairs of loops. Charalambos Bakirtzis, "Κουτρουβια μυρου
απο τη Θεσσαλονικη [Myrrh ampullae from Thessalonica]," in *Jahrbuch der Österreichischen Byzantinistik: XVI. Internationaler Byzantinistenkongress, Wien, 4.–9. Oktober 1981. Akten
II, Part 3, 32/3* (Vienna, 1982), pp. 523–8, esp. 524–5, fig. γ. The find of a separate ampulla half in the Musée de Vendôme, indicates that the last technique
might be used at Vendôme. Molds for casting massive, tear-shaped pendants, probably from Vendôme, are discussed below.

powers. While a badge had only been in contact with the place of pilgrimage, an ampulla actually *contained* tangible material from the holy place.

No extant Vendôme ampulla retains its contents, but it was customary to fill pilgrim ampullae with liquid, such as water from a nearby well or some other form of holy water,[31] a saint's endlessly diluted blood,[32] or oil from a saint's corpse.[33] De Rochambeau suggests that the Vendôme ampullae contained water from the nearby Loir or earth from the surroundings of La Trinité.[34] He bases his hypothesis on a 1622 letter written by Saint François of Salles, who had heard of the tear relic, but did not know the tradition very well. François mentions a tear from Vendôme as a pilgrim souvenir of the *Sainte Larme*. He explains that this tear was a drop of water in which the reliquary ampulla of rock crystal had been submerged.

---

[31] At Walsingham, for instance, were two wells imputed with healing properties. In the first quarter of the sixteenth century, Erasmus described the water as surprisingly cold and an excellent remedy for headache and indigestion. Desiderius Erasmus, *Pilgrimages to Saint Mary of Walsingham and Saint Thomas of Canterbury*, translated by John Gough Nichols (London, 1875), p. 18. Pewter receptacles enabled the water to be transported to another place where it could retain its therapeutic qualities. The ampullae from Neuss are likewise thought to have held water with curative and other beneficial properties. The liquid, from the well just outside the church, was called "Quirinus water" after the saint venerated there. W. Felten, *Der hl. Martyrer und Tribun Quirinus, Patron der Stadt Neuss* (Neuss, 1900), pp. 61–2.

[32] The ampullae from Canterbury were meant to hold what was called "Canterbury Water"—Saint Thomas's blood diluted with water. It was said to perform miraculous cures when imbibed orally or rubbed on the skin. The therapeutic effect of this blood-and-water mixture is endorsed in the inscription on an early thirteenth-century ampulla in the Musée de Cluny which reads + EXILITAS OMNIS: OFFERT DOLOR EXCIDIT OMNIS: SANA[tus] BIBIT. COMEDIT., M[alum?] CU[m] MORTE RECEDIT (all weakness and pain is removed; the healed man eats and drinks, and evil and death pass away). Musée de Cluny, inv. no. Cl. 18063. English translation by Spencer, "Medieval Pilgrim Badges," p. 144. Victor Gay, *Glossaire archéologique du Moyen Age et de la Renaissance*, part 1 (Paris, 1887), p. 31; Bruna, *Enseignes de Pèlerinage*, pp. 210–1, cat. 327.

[33] In Bari, Eichstatt, York, Thessalonica, and possibly Noyon, pilgrim ampullae were filled with an oily substance (sometimes called manna) that flowed out of the body of the respectively venerated saints. The pilgrim Georges Languerant, who visited Saint Nicholas' tomb at Bari in 1485, reported that: "[. . .] là dessoubz est le corpz dud. st. Nicolas, lequel rend lad. huylle, laquelle s'appelle manne, de laquelle on en donne à cescun pélerin une ampoulette, dont, pour ma part, je trouvay la manière d'en avoir trois." (. . . there beneath is the body of St. Nicolas, which produces oil, called manna, that one gives away in an ampulla to some pilgrim; for my part, I found a way to get three of these.) Baron de la Fons-Mélicoq, "Voyage archéologique au XVe siècle. Suite de l'Italie," *Annales Archéologiques* 22 (1862), 133–41, here p. 140.

[34] De Rochambeau, "Voyage à la Sainte-Larme," p. 175.

Erroneously, François notes that this ampulla contained some earth on which tears of Christ had fallen, instead of the Holy Tear itself.[35]

Although the letter of François is a useful source regarding the contents of the ampullae, I believe De Rochambeau's interpretation is incorrect. The mention of earth is clearly a mistake and the Loire held no importance for the cult of the Sainte Larme. However, the well into which Geoffrey and Agnes had seen the three stars fall, and over which they later commissioned a church to be built, was directly linked to the cult in Vendôme itself. Pilgrims venerated the well at Vendôme because of the miraculous falling stars witnessed by Geoffrey and Agnes. In addition, the water of this well might have been used for the Baptism, the Eucharist, and the submerging of the tear relic. Excavations at Vendôme uncovered a well in the last bay of the north aisle, surrounded by four walls forming a square basin, which undoubtedly was the well mentioned in the twelfth-century chronicle.[36]

The ritual of submerging the relic was begun by transferring some water from the well into a large chalice, which then was placed on the altar—as the iconography on the ampullae of the thirteenth and the first half of the fourteenth century shows.[37] This was possibly the altar which was placed directly above the well, as the priests urged Geoffrey when he asked their advice. The abbot or a monk of La Trinité abbey held the reliquary above the chalice and subsequently blessed the water by submerging the reliquary in it.[38] Drops of this

---

[35] Dated June 7, 1622, published in De Rochambeau, "Voyage à la Sainte-Larme," p. 175.

[36] Gabriel Plat, *L'Église de la Trinité de Vendôme* (Paris, 1934), p. 10, fn. 1.

[37] The tradition of submerging relics in water or wine and distributing the blessed liquid to pilgrims, was already in use in the eleventh century and might date even earlier. Stephan Beissel, *Die Verehrung der Heiligen und ihrer Reliquien in Deutschland während der zweiten Hälfte des Mittelalter* (Freiburg im Breisgau, 1892), p. 90.

[38] A similar ritual is described for the Church of St. Servaas at Maastricht in *Ordinarius Custodum of St. Servaas*, Maastricht, Rijksarchief Limburg, archief van het kapittel van St. Servaas, BK 166, fol. 15r: After communion on Good Friday, the dean and his assistants collected the relics on the altar, for the blessing of the water. At the same time the *custos* brought the key of St. Servaas, and a chalice was cleaned so that water could be poured in there by the dean, in order to be blessed by the submerging of the key. The manuscript is an early-seventeenth-century copy of the *Ordinarius chori of St. Servaas*, dating to the fourth quarter of the thirteenth century. In the Church of Our-Dear-Lady, in Maastricht, the water in the font was blessed by submerging of relics. *Ordinarius Custodum of Our-Dear-Lady's*, Brussels, General Archives, Ms. 1945, p. 14. With thanks to Rob Dückers, who is preparing a publication regarding both *ordinarii* from Maastricht.

blessed, curative water could be taken home in ampullae, in the hope that the healing powers would be effective elsewhere. For, these drops of medicinal water in the same shape as the *Sainte Larme*— thus forming a pseudo-collection of the tear—and the iconography of the ampullae emphasized not only the sanctity of the contents of the vessel, but the whole pilgrim's experience at Vendôme. In addition, many pilgrims tried to rub the ampulla over the *Sainte Larme* reliquary, in order to establish direct contact between the souvenir and the most venerated relic and thus supply it with even greater power.

The ampulla's precious contents were preserved by sealing the opening, so that the contents became one with their container, which then itself acquired the status of a devotional object. If necessary, the contents of the ampullae thus could be used by drinking the liquid as medicine or rubbing it on the skin as a medicinal lotion. We do not know precisely how the Vendôme ampullae were closed, but examples from other shrines have been found with wooden or metal stoppers[39] while others were closed with pitch or wax. Because the pewter, from which the ampullae were made, was so soft and malleable, they could also be sealed simply by squeezing or carefully folding the rim. The frayed rims of some Vendôme examples suggest that they had been opened, closed, and re-opened in this manner.

The ampulla and its contents ensured its owner's safe return and protected him from illness and other vicissitudes he might encounter on his journey. Once safely home, the pilgrim could continue to benefit from the amulet's power to bring luck and avert disaster. The souvenir might be put in a special place in the home or stable, where it would retain its salutary properties, as suggested by a thirteenth-century pilgrim ampulla from Bromholm which was fixed to a piece of wood with an iron nail.[40] Presumably the ampulla was

---

[39] H.J.E. van Beuningen, A.M. Koldeweij, and D. Kicken, *Heilig en Profaan 2: 1200 Laatmiddeleeuwse insignes uit openbare en particuliere collecties.* Rotterdam Papers 12 (Cothen, 2001), p. 384, figs. 1617–8.

[40] Brian W. Spencer, "Pilgrim Souvenirs," in Jonathan Alexander and Paul Binski (eds.), *Age of Chivalry: Art in Plantagenet England 1200–1400* (London, 1987), pp. 218–25, esp. p. 223, cat. 77; Spencer, *Medieval Finds*, p. 163, 165, fig. 180a. The ampulla— with a clearly visible hole for the nail bored through the middle of the body—was excavated in Billingsgate and transferred to the Museum of London. The piece of wood has not survived. A few centrally pierced Canterbury ampullae found in London, may have been affixed in a similar fashion. Spencer, *Medieval Finds*, p. 39, figs. 15 (right), 16c, 17.

given a prominent position on a wall so that its beneficial forces could spread through the house and over those who lived there. Finally, an ampulla could accompany its owner posthumously, buried with its owner, whom it would continue to protect after death.

Pouch-Shaped Ampullae

The earliest Vendôme ampullae, which date from the thirteenth to the mid-fourteenth century, are shaped like a pouch or bag. Ampullae of this type have been found in Paris, Mélun, London, Dordrecht, and in collections in Vienna and Vendôme.[41] The containers are fitted at the top with a pair of semicircular loops. These loops are so fragile that they could never have borne the extra weight of relatively-heavy contents and consequently could not have been used to attach the object to the pilgrim's clothes, nor could they have been suspended around the neck on a cord if they were completely filled with the blessed water. All the pouch-shaped ampullae show, on one side, the ritual of submerging the tear relic in a large chalice and on the other an equestrian St. George or a crucified Christ. Although no two extant representations of the submerging ritual are exactly identical, the composition is roughly the same. It pictures a prominent altar with a large chalice, above which the *Sainte Larme* is held. If Geoffrey did take the priests' advice, this might be the altar which was placed above the well. On each ampulla, the altar is decorated with wrought ironwork or covered with a decorative cloth, and flanked by two standing figures. The main differences lie in the details.

Near the Pont au Change in Paris, two ampullae from Vendôme were found in 1863. The earliest, which Forgeais dated to the thirteenth century, illustrates a figure on the left, who holds the *Sainte Larme* in his hand, directly above a vertically-striped chalice.[42] (fig.

---

[41] Three ampullae in the Musée de Vendôme are all pouch-shaped and have on one side the tear relic flanked by two persons; on the other St. George on his horse—with slight differences. (All three inv. no. 760). Letter of March 6, 2003 from Laurence Guilbaud, curator of the museum. As I did not have the opportunity to study these ampullae prior to the publication of this article, I cannot describe them with more precision. However, two of these might be the same objects described briefly in De Rochambeau, "Voyage à la Sainte-Larme," pp. 166–8.

[42] Forgeais, *Imagerie religieuse*, pp. 65–74; De Rochambeau, "Voyage à la Sainte-

214a) The right-hand figure holds a lit candle in his left hand. The two figures are depicted in profile, but their heads are shown frontally. Each wears a long tunic and appears to be veiled, or hooded like monks. Their tunics have vertical pleats and are fastened round the waist by a cord. Between the two figures, the visible side of the altar is decorated with four small St. Andrew's crosses or stars, each with a dot in the center, which are separated by horizontal and vertical lines. The altar is bordered at the bottom by a narrow fringe. On the left edge of the altar stands a small Greek cross with slightly tapered arms. An two-line inscription above the scene reads +LACR // IMA DEI (God's tear). Above the inscription is a zigzag border and a narrow zigzag line runs round the belly of the ampulla from loop to loop.

On the reverse, a knight on horseback rides from left to right. (fig. 214b) Rider and steed are depicted in profile, as the rider's face is turned three-quarters towards the viewer. He wears a mail coat and his flat helmet is topped by a Greek cross with tapering arms, like that seen on the altar. His visor forms a mask where an opening is formed by seven horizontal slits. The knight brandishes a pointed sword in his right hand, as if about to charge into battle. His body is protected by a shield decorated with lines radiating from a central dot. On his right foot—the only visible one—is a spur in the form of a star. The horse raises its left foreleg and dips its head. On its back is probably a horse blanket, for its neck, belly and hindquarters are decorated with rosettes, while four small rings or bells are attached to its reins. The mane is neatly trimmed, the tail plaited. The background is filled with seven heart-shaped leaves, probably from a lime tree.[43] Some of these leaves are tied together with a long stalk. From one of these stalks, under the horse's belly, sprouts a fleur-de-lis as a symbol of French royalty.[44] Behind the horse, one can see a diagonal staff, perhaps a lance, rendered as

---

Larme," pp. 163–6, figs. 10–1. (66 × 41 mm) The present whereabouts of this ampulla are unknown. In 1865 it was still in Forgeais' collection, but was apparently not transferred to the Musée de Cluny.

[43] I am not aware of a specific lime tree tradition in Vendôme; nor of any association of St. George with this kind of tree.

[44] Arthur Forgeais, *Collection de plombs historiés trouvés dans la Seine et recueillis par Arthur Forgeais, Tome V: Numismatique populaire* (Paris, 1866), pp. 99–100.

two thin lines with diagonal hatching in between. A two-line caption above the scene identifies the horseman as S':GEO // RGIVS, St. George.

A similar ampulla was found in the Seine in 1866.[45] Only the iconography of the reverse shows a striking difference. Instead of walking in the foreground, the knight is situated behind a tree. As the neck of this container is damaged on both sides, only one of the two lines of the inscription above the scene is visible. On the front it reads: [LACRIMA] DEI, on the back: [S.GEOR]GIVS. Compared with other pouch-shaped ampullae from Vendôme, these two examples are fairly slim, and are cast in the form of a tear.

The third ampulla, like the first one found in 1863 near the Pont au Change in Paris, is dated to the beginning of the fourteenth century.[46] (fig. 215a) The submerging ritual is executed somewhat more crudely than that on the previous ampullae. Both figures are depicted entirely in profile as they look at the *Sainte Larme* hanging above the chalice. The left-hand figure does not holding the relic as in the previous examples, but rather prays to it. The figure on the right clutches a staff instead of a candle. The decorative border above the inscription also differs as a dot is placed in each angle of the zigzag line. Otherwise the representations on the three ampullae are similar in many respects: the two figures are veiled or hooded and wear the same long, vertically-pleated, corded tunics; the altar is similarly decorated, and the caption above the scene may originally have been identical, but because the ampulla had been forcibly opened, the first two characters of each line are missing.

The reverse of the ampulla was already in bad condition when Forgeais drew it. (fig. 215b) The nineteenth-century drawing shows that a piece had broken off at the top right, but the scene resembles that on the first ampulla—although the detailing is not as fine. St. George is in armor, on horseback, with his flat helmet topped by a Greek cross. He raises the sword in his right hand, and again,

---

[45] De Rochambeau, "Voyage à la Sainte-Larme," p. 166. In 1873 purchased by the Musée de Vendôme (inv. no. 760). (56 h × 43 w × 18 mm thick).

[46] Forgeais, *Imagerie religieuse*, pp. 75–6; De Rochambeau, "Voyage à la Sainte-Larme," pp. 166–7, figs. 12–3. (69 × 44 mm) The current whereabouts of this object is unknown. In 1865 it was still in Forgeais' collection, but was apparently not transferred to the Musée de Cluny.

the horse walks from left to right. A marked difference is that the animal is less richly caparisoned: there is apparently no blanket, no rings or bells on its reins, and its tail is not plaited. The top part of this ampulla shows the zigzag pattern again under which reads the two-line caption, S':GEO // RGES (the I and V on the other ampullae replaced here by an E).

In 1866 a similar ampulla was dredged from the Seine.[47] The front again depicts two figures flanking the altar with a large chalice, above which the *Sainte Larme* is shown, while the reverse illustrates St. George on his horse. The knight wears a mail coat and holds a lance in his left hand. As on the first ampulla, the horse's blanket is decorated with rosettes. The caption at the top is damaged and therefore illegible.

A fifth pouch-shaped ampulla, dated to the thirteenth century, was found prior to 1849 in the Seine at Mélun, not far from Paris.[48] (fig. 216a) The most obvious differences between this ampulla and the previous ones are the figures' hairstyles, the altar decoration, and the caption. As on the first example, the figures are shown in profile, but their faces turn toward the viewer. The figure on the left wears a somewhat shorter tunic and rubs his right hand over the *Sainte Larme* while holding up a small bowl in his left. A plausible interpretation is that the bowl is filled—probably with water from the well in the church—and that the figure desires to infuse it with some of the relic's miraculous properties by means of this direct contact, as was probably the case with the filled ampullae. Above the figure are the letters S and M. The figure on the right holds a tall, slender candle in his hand and is surrounded by the letters M, E, S and A. The small Greek cross seen on the other ampullae on the left-hand side of the altar has moved here to the right. The altar is decorated with fine lines and dots, which are probably represent precious stones, while the lower border has somewhat wider, vertical stripes. The caption at the top is fairly legible, but the letters do not appear to form existing words: OME IS // LIER S. Forgeais, however, suggests

---

[47] De Rochambeau, "Voyage à la Sainte-Larme," pp. 167–8. In 1873 purchased by the Musée de Vendôme (inv. no. 760). (83 h × 63 w × 11 mm thick).

[48] Eugène Grésy, "Reliquaire en plomb trouvé dans la Seine à Melun," *Bulletin du Comité Historique des Arts et Monuments* 2 (1849), 287–88; Forgeais, *Imagerie religieuse*, pp. 77–80; De Rochambeau, "Voyage à la Sainte-Larme," pp. 168–70; figs. 14–5. (71 × 55 mm). Present whereabouts unknown.

that they spell *Lacrima Dei*, the tear of Christ.[49] On the other hand, the captions on this ampulla might be pseudo-texts.

On the reverse, the knight and his horse are shown in profile. (fig. 216b) The execution of the scene is more stylized than before, and the zigzag line encircling the body is a little wider. The main difference, however, is that the horse walks in the opposite direction, but St. George is still outfitted for battle. His shield is decorated with diagonal lines and his pointed lance sports a banner. On top of his semicircular helmet is a Greek cross with tapering arms. The helmet is fitted with a protective mask. The horse's fancy blanket is decorated with circles, but here the mane is uneven and the tail unplaited. The background is filled with several leaves, some of which sprout from the same stalk. The two-line caption is enclosed by horizontal lines and should probably read GLIEUM // SGE-ORGI. The meaning of the first line is unclear,[50] while the second line is a contraction of *Sanctus Georgius*.

Further variations can be seen on an ampulla found in 1989 in London, which shows the ritual of submerging the tear relic in reverse.[51] (fig. 217a) Left of the altar, a figure holds a tall candle in both hands; and the other figure holds the *Sainte Larme* over the chalice with his right hand. The two are depicted in profile, with their heads turned to face the viewer. Both wear headgear and each has a pointed chin. The altar is again covered by a patterned cloth (unfringed this time) or embellished with wrought ironwork, which is decorated with four St. Andrew's crosses or stars with little dots in their centers and between the arms. The crosses are separated by lines forming a Greek cross with a dot in the center. On two corners of the altar stand small Greek crosses. The inscription on the flat border around the bottom of the ampulla is now illegible; only SIGNVM (in reverse) can be discerned. Between the scene and the text border is a zigzag pattern. The two-line caption on top reads +LACR // +IMA:DEI.

---

[49] Forgeais, *Imagerie religieuse*, p. 78.
[50] Perhaps Forgeais was unable to read the original letters due to oxidation or some other damage, or because illiterate craftsmen had botched the mold. De Rochambeau, "Voyage à la Sainte-Larme," p. 170 suggests the letters might read *Sigillum Sancti Georgii* (sign of St. George).
[51] The ampulla came from the Thames Exchange site, Upper Thames Street and is kept in the British Museum, Department of Medieval and Later Antiquities (inv. no. 1992, 1–3,1). (74 mm h). Spencer, *Medieval Finds*, p. 227, fig. 239c.

On the reverse, is St. George in profile, seated somewhat awk-wardly on his horse, riding from left to right. (fig. 217b) He wears a coat of mail and a flat-topped, cylindrical helmet with a small Greek cross on top. By the helmet's shape, the ampulla can be dated in the thirteenth century.[52] The saint carries a lance with pennon in his right hand and a shield, rounded at the top, in his left. A small Greek cross is repeated on the shield. The horse's blanket is richly ornamented with dots or rosettes. The background is again deco-rated with foliate motifs. Above the scene, between horizontal lines, the inscription reads :S:GEOR // GIVS, while a double zigzag bor-der runs round the body from loop to loop.

Another ampulla from London shows the *Sainte Larme* being held above the chalice by two figures, both of whom appear to be floating.[53] (fig. 218a) Each wears a long tunic tied round the waist with a wide band. The round line encircling each head might indicate a veil, a nimbus, or a monk's hood. The altar is decorated with narrow ver-tical bands patterned with a herringbone motif, but the Greek crosses are absent. Because the top of the neck and both loops are miss-ing—perhaps in order to extract the contents—it is not certain whether it originally had an inscription.

The iconography on the reverse differs from what we have seen on the previously discussed Vendôme ampullae. This example is unique among the pouch-shaped ampullae found thus far, in that it shows Christ on the cross instead of St. George. (fig. 218b) Christ is flanked by Mary and John, wearing long tunics. At the foot of the cross and the extremities of the transverse beam are groups of three large roundels, which might refer to the Holy Trinity—as the patrons of the church where the *Sainte Larme* was kept.[54] The ampulla dates to the thirteenth or first half of the fourteenth century.

On an ampulla found at Dordrecht, the figure to the left of the altar holds the *Sainte Larme* aloft above a chalice decorated with vertical lines; the figure on the right holds a long, lighted candle.[55]

---

[52] Spencer, *Medieval Finds*, p. 227.

[53] This ampulla came from the Billingsgate Market Lorry Park site, Lower Thames Street (1983). Present whereabouts unknown, (50 mm h). Spencer, *Medieval Finds*, pp. 227–8, fig. 239d.

[54] Spencer, *Medieval Finds*, p. 228.

[55] The container is in the Van Beuningen private collection, Cothen (inv. no. I 1891). (68 × 45 mm) Van Beuningen and Koldeweij, *Heilig en Profaan*, p. 139; Frits Scholten, "Heerlijke resten," *Kunstschrift* 6 (1999), pp. 14–7, here 16.

(fig. 219a) Both wear long tunics with vertical pleats, but erosion has made it impossible to establish whether these figures wore veils or hoods. The scene has many details in common with those on the ampulla described first. Fixed to the left-hand corner of the altar is a Greek cross with tapering arms; the altar cloth is decorated with four St. Andrew's crosses or stars with a small dot in the centers. The inscription above the scene is virtually illegible. The border running round the body from loop to loop is decorated with a zigzag pattern and an inscription, but once again the letters are illegible. On the reverse is a knight on horseback who is likely St. George.[56] (fig. 219b) The ampulla dates to the first half of the fourteenth century.

The last pouch-shaped ampulla in this group originally belonged to the private collection of Albert Figdor (1843–1927) in Vienna, but it disappeared after its sale in 1930.[57] (fig. 220) Although the front view of the ampulla has never been published, it illustrated the submerging of the *Sainte Larme* for, according to the 1930 sale catalogue, it was decorated with "figurative portrayals, chalice, and the Tear of Christ."[58] The reverse shows St. George on horseback, erroneously identified by Berling as an equestrian Geoffrey Martel.[59] Horse and rider are depicted in profile; the horse is walking from right to left. St. George is clad in armor, his flat helmet is crowned with a small Greek cross with tapering arms and his shield decorated with lines radiating from a central dot. In his right hand is a long lance with a banner. His steed's reins are decorated with straps from which hang bells. A date in the fourteenth or fifteenth century was suggested.[60] However, the thirteenth or first half of the fourteenth century seem more likely in view of this ampulla's iconographic and stylistic resemblance to those previously discussed.

---

[56] Although very worn, a few details are similar to those on other ampullae. The saint's shield is rounded at the top, like the shield on one of the London examples. The horse walks from left to right and its blanket is decorated with dots or rosettes.

[57] Berling, *Altes Zinn*, pp. 47, 49 fig. 30. (80 × 50 mm). Findspot and present whereabouts unknown. The ampulla was auctioned in June 1930 in Vienna. Otto von Falke (ed.), *Die Sammlung Dr. Albert Figdor—Wien. Erster teil* (Vienna, 1930), no. 216.

[58] Von Falke, *Die Sammlung Dr. Albert Figdor*, no. 216.

[59] Berling, *Altes Zinn*, p. 47.

[60] Berling, *Altes Zinn*, p. 49; Von Falke, *Die Sammlung Dr. Albert Figdor*, no. 216.

Pilgrim Badges from Vendôme

While many badges have been supposed to come from La Trinité in Vendôme, only a few can be securely assigned to this particular place of pilgrimage.[61] Although they bear no inscriptions, the close resemblance between the scenes on these badges and on the pouch-shaped ampullae, allow them to be attributed to Vendôme. Two of them, dating to the mid-fourteenth century, fashioned from pewter in pentagonal form, were found in Dordrecht. Similar to the ampullae, these two badges are decorated on both sides and feature scenes focusing on the Holy Tear.[62]

One badge shows the ritual of submerging the tear relic: two figures flank an altar on which there is a large chalice, above which the *Sainte Larme* is held aloft.[63] (fig. 221a) Two corners of the altar bear small crosses, while the front is decorated with four St. Andrew's crosses or stars separated by a cruciform element. The two figures, shown in profile, are attired in long tunics. The kneeling figure on the left of the altar seems to be praying to the *Sainte Larme*, which is held out above the altar by a large, horizontal arm appearing from the left. This arm is perhaps a reference to the hand of God or to the arm relic of St. George's. The standing figure on the right holds a candle. In the top section of the badge, as on the reverse of nine of the ten ampullae, St. George is shown in profile, grasping a lance and banner in his hand. The horse walks from left to right and appears to be wearing a blanket. Two stylized plants fill the background.

The reverse side shows an enthroned Virgin with the Christ Child on her left knee. (fig. 221b) Their heads are surrounded by nimbuses; Mary holds a lily-scepter in her right hand. Two pilgrims kneel, flanking these central figures, their hands folded in prayer.

---

[61] See fn. 22.

[62] This double-sided decoration is rather unique to the Vendôme badges. In other pilgrim sites, badges were usually decorated only on one side. Besides Vendôme, other exceptions include Maastricht, Waver, Diegem, and Cologne. Van Beuningen and Koldeweij, *Heilig en Profaan*, p. 196, fig. 354; p. 229, fig. 479; Van Beuningen, Koldeweij, and Kicken, *Heilig en Profaan 2*, p. 255, fig. 1084; p. 256, figs. 1087–9; pp. 260–1, fig. 1110; p. 288, fig. 1231.

[63] The badge is in the Van Beuningen private colletion, Cothen (inv. no. I 3524), and was previously in a private collection in Zwijndrecht. (43 × 38 mm). Van Beuningen, Koldeweij, and Kicken, *Heilig en Profaan 2*, p. 364, fig. 1530.

This scene—unique among the pilgrim souvenirs from Vendôme—
might refer to a fourteenth-century veneration of the Virgin at the
abbey.[64]

The front of the second Dordrecht badge also shows an altar and
a chalice above which the *Sainte Larme* relic is held.[65] (fig. 222a) An
oil-lamp hangs on its right, while small crosses decorate the two corners of the altar, which is shown with nine St. Andrew's crosses or
stars, separated by horizontal and vertical lines. This time the altar
is not flanked by two figures, but by two slim, burning candles.[66]
These objects also flank the large chalice on the reverse, which is
decorated with lines and spheres. (fig. 222b) Above the chalice is a
Greek cross with tapering arms. The two Dordrecht finds were originally fitted with at least four eyelets with which the badges could
be fastened to a pilgrim's clothes or hat.

Round, Footed Ampullae from Vendôme

In the late fourteenth or early fifteenth century a second group of
ampullae, distinguished by a round body set on a small foot, appeared
in Vendôme. This metamorphosis probably reflected alterations to
the shrine.[67] So far, only a few examples of this type have been discovered, all dating to the fifteenth or early sixteenth century. One
ampulla and one fragment were in the Musée de Vendôme, but are

---

[64] I am not aware of a cult statue of Our Lady in La Trinité abbey of Vendôme,
but in the fourteenth century the cult for Mary was widespread through the entire
Christian world, so it is conceivable that the abbey possessed a statue of the Virgin.
Additionally, the church has a twelfth-century stained-glass window of Our Lady.
Frédéric Lesueur, "Vendôme (Loir-et-Cher)," in Jacques Brosse (ed.). *Dictionnaire des
églises de France, Belgique, Luxembourg, Suisse,* part III D (Paris, 1967), pp. 169–72, here
171; Éliane Vergnolle, *L'art Roman en France. Architecture—Sculpture—Peinture* (Paris,
1994), p. 275, fig. 373.

[65] The badge is owned by the town of Dordrecht (inv. no. 9701.1078.002).
(38 × 34 mm). Van Beuningen, Koldeweij, and Kicken, *Heilig en Profaan 2,* p. 364,
fig. 1531.

[66] On later Vendôme ampullae the relic is also flanked by two candles.

[67] According to Lesueur, "Vendôme (Loir-et-Cher)" p. 171, the *Monument of the
Sainte Larme* was reconstructed at the beginning of the fourteenth century. Bruna,
Enseignes de Pèlerinage, p. 46, also states that the reliquary was "without a doubt
altered in the fourteenth century," but the exact nature of the alterations is not
known. So far, not a single ampulla dating to the second half of the fourteenth
century has been found.

now missing; two containers have surfaced in Paris; while the find spot of a fifth, now in the Catharijneconvent Museum in Utrecht, is unknown. These later ampullae are also fitted with two fragile handles. They are triangular on one of them and semicircular on all the others. Like the first group of ampullae, all the intact containers in this second group show the *Sainte Larme* relic on one side with variable iconography on the other side. St. George, a subject so popular on the early ampullae, completely disappears. Also eliminated are the two figures who flanked the altar in scenes with the *Sainte Larme* relic. Here, on the body of the round containers, the Sacred Tear takes pride of place between two lighted candles in candlesticks.

An ampulla found in 1858 near the Pont-Neuf in Paris depicts the *Sainte Larme* in a reliquary chest decorated with finely-carved Gothic pointed trefoil motifs.[68] (fig. 223a) On its doors is a jewel in the form of a tear edged with beading. The jeweled tear is surrounded by twelve smaller gems. On either side of the chest is a lighted candle and a stylized tear. Around this scene is a border with a rosary or string of beads, placed between two concentric circles. At the bottom of the neck, between the two triangular handles, is a coarse zigzag border. The tips of four stylized leaves can be seen on the straight-sided foot. On the reverse, a French coat of arms with three fleurs-de-lis dominates. (fig. 223b) There is a dot between the top two "lilies" and an openwork crown along the top of the shield. Two stylized tears flank the shield, while the other decorative motifs match those on the front. This ampulla has been dated to the fourteenth century,[69] but considering the coat of arms of the French kings, it should be re-dated after 1467—the year La Trinité came under royal protection.

The Vendôme ampulla in the Catharijneconvent at Utrecht also dates from the fifteenth century,[70] (fig. 224) as does an identical

---

[68] Forgeais, *Imagerie religieuse*, pp. 81–82; De Rochambeau, "Voyage à la Sainte-Larme," pp. 170–1, figs. 16–7; Edmond du Sommerard, *Catalogue et description des objets d'art de l'Antiquité du Moyen Age et de la Renaissance exposés au musée de Cluny* (Paris, 1883), no. 8890; Bruna, *Enseignes de Pèlerinage*, pp. 46–7, cat. 1. The ampulla is in the collection of the Musée de Cluny (inv. no. Cl. 4819), 65 h × 41 w × 7 mm thick.

[69] Forgeais, *Imagerie religieuse*, p. 81; Bruna, *Enseignes de Pèlerinage*, p. 46.

[70] Inv. no. RMCC m173 (72 h × 50 w × 11 mm thick). Defoer, "Metalen reisgezelschap," pp. 3–4; Henri L.M. Defoer, "Rijksmuseum *Het Catharijneconvent*," in

container formerly kept in the Musée de Vendôme, but now missing.[71] The round-bellied containers have short, slightly-tapered feet
and necks, a little taller than the feet. Both sides of the necks are
decorated with geometric patterns, with concentric circles between
geometric motifs placed on both sides of the body. Each inner circle contains an image. That on the front refers to the *Sainte Larme*,
here prominently displayed between two candlesticks holding twisted,
lighted candles. (fig. 224a) The relic rests on a large chalice, but
there is no altar depicted here. The text framing the image is not
entirely clear, but it does contain the word LARME, or tear. On
the reverse is a Greek cross with tapering arms between which four
small St. Andrew's crosses are placed. (fig. 224b) These five elements
might refer to Christ's five wounds (his hands, feet, and cut in his
side).[72] This motif also appeared on the side of the altars depicted
on a few early pouch-shaped ampullae. Perhaps they reflect the decoration on the altar (or altar cloth) or on the well in the church.

Another ampulla of the second type, dated to the beginning of
the sixteenth century, was found in 1863 near the Pont Notre-Dame
in Paris.[73] The base is missing, but it seems likely that the ampulla
originally stood on a foot. Above the large chalice on the main body
is a large, stylized tear, bordered by two candlesticks holding lighted
candles. (fig. 225a) Arabesques in a border formed by two concentric circles, surround the scene. There are also a few curved lines
on the neck. On the reverse is an image of the Trinity, also known
as the *Dreifaltigkeit* type or *Gnadenstuhl*. (fig. 225b) A separate ampulla
half with an identical depiction was noted in 1873 by De Rochambeau

Nederlandse Rijksmusea in 1986 ('s Gravenhage, 1987), pp. 289–300, here 293; Koldeweij,
"Te Vendôme . . .," pp. 12–3; Marike de Kroon, "Medieval Pilgrim Badges in the
Collection of the Museum for Religious Art: Het Catharijneconvent, Utrecht," in
Guy de Boe and Frans Verhaege (eds.). *Art and Symbolism in Medieval Europe. Papers
of the 'Medieval Europe Brugge 1997 Conference.'* 5 (Zellik, 1997), pp. 145–8, here 146–7.

[71] De Rochambeau, "Voyage à la Sainte-Larme," pp. 171–2, figs. 18–9. There
is a possibility the two ampullae are one and the same, see fn. 28.

[72] Koldeweij, "Te Vendôme," p. 13.

[73] Forgeais, *Imagerie religieuse*, pp. 83–4; De Rochambeau, "Voyage à la Sainte-
Larme," pp. 172–4, figs. 20–1; Koldeweij, "Te Vendôme," pp. 12–3. (54 × 42
mm). The container's present whereabouts are unknown. In 1865 it was still in
Forgeais' collection, but was apparently not transferred to the Musée de Cluny.

in the Musée de Vendôme.[74] On both objects, a bearded God the Father sits on a bench, facing forward, with his hands resting on each end of the cross to which his son is nailed. Christ's knees are bent slightly towards the right. As Christ is shown here as the savior, this image can be connected with his sacrifice. God accepts this sacrifice of his son and gives it back to the humankind as a sign of mercy. When found, the ampullae were in poor condition, which is why the Holy Ghost, usually symbolized by a dove, is not visible. On either side of God is a sacred tear. Two concentric circles containing the inscription SANTA TRNITS VNVS DEVS (Holy Trinity one God), frames the scene. The neck of the ampulla found in Paris is decorated with a few scrolls ending on the right in a wheel-like form.

The images on two more pilgrim badges of pewter, found in the Seine, share a marked resemblance to the depiction of the Trinity on these two ampulla sides. One badge was dredged up in 1864 near the Pont au Change in Paris.[75] (fig. 226) All that can still be seen today on this fifteenth-century plaquette, is a crucified Christ, but thanks to a drawing made by Arthur Forgeais (when the badge was in better condition)[76] and to a better-preserved example in Rouen,[77] we know what the badge looked like originally: a bearded God the Father, seated and facing forward, holds both ends of the cross to which Christ is nailed. The vertical portion of the cross rests between his legs; Christ's knees are bent to the right. This similarity to the image on the two ampullae justifies the badges' attribution to Vendôme. Here, the dove symbolizing the Holy Ghost can be clearly seen above Christ's head.

---

[74] The neck and the foot have broken off. De Rochambeau, "Voyage à la Sainte-Larme," p. 175. The ampulla half is now missing. Letter of March 6, 2003 from Laurence Guilbaud, curator of the museum.

[75] The badge is in the collection of the Musée de Cluny (inv. no. Cl. 23509). In its present condition it measures 25 mm maximum height (originally 51 mm) × 29 mm. Bruna, *Enseignes de Pèlerinage*, pp. 49–50, cat. no. 6.

[76] Forgeais, *Imagerie religieuse*, pp. 9–10.

[77] The badge was found in 1875 in the Seine at Rouen and is now in the collection of the Musée des Antiquités at Rouen (inv. no. 1628/1646). (30 × 26 mm). Henry Decaëns, "Les pèlerinages," in François Avril *et al.*, *Tresors des abbayes normandes* (Rouen, 1979), pp. 294–305, here 299, no. 304.

Pendants and Medals

In addition to ampullae and badges, pewter or brass tear-shaped pendants were also sold at Vendôme. All pendants of this kind found thus far date from the sixteenth century. They were worn round the neck or fastened to garments by means of an eyelet at the top of the tear. Some are simply designed, while others are decorated with some ornament, like a small rosette. One plain pewter pendant was found in the Seine[78] and another, found in the Loire at Orléans, is a brass tear hanging from a dove's beak—probably presenting the Holy Spirit.[79] In addition, several stone molds for *Sainte Larme* pendants have been found, showing the potential for casting as many as sixteen souvenirs at the same time.[80] (fig. 227) The method for producing these souvenirs was much simpler and faster than the method used for casting ampullae.

However, it is not certain whether the pendants come from Vendôme or from another place of pilgrimage where a sacred tear was venerated, because their provenance cannot be confirmed by an inscription.[81] The same applies to the sixteenth-century pewter and brass medals showing an isolated image of the *Sainte Larme*. Many souvenirs of this type were quite small, measuring twenty-six millimeters at their maximum height. Most are fitted with an eyelet at the top, though some lack this element. Their shapes range from round[82] (fig. 228) to oval[83] (fig. 227) to a crowned heart with a tear below.[84] (fig. 229)

---

[78] Musée de Cluny (inv. no. Cl. 18012). (30 × 6 mm). Bruna, *Enseignes de Pèlerinage*, p. 47, cat. no. 2.

[79] Desnoyers, "Objets trouvés," 1876, p. 185.

[80] De Rochambeau, "Voyage à la Sainte-Larme," pp. 159–62, figs. 1–5. The Musée de Vendôme owns several slate molds for producing tear-shaped pendants.

[81] At least eight other French churches claimed to house a sacred tear. See fn. 3 for a enumeration of these places and fn. 22 for comments on finds from Orléans.

[82] For instance two medals in Musée de Cluny: inv. no. Cl. 4926 (26 × 22 mm); inv. no. Cl. 4943 (23 × 22 mm). Forgeais, *Imagerie religieuse*, p. 85; De Rochambeau, "Voyage à la Sainte-Larme," pp. 162–3, fig. 8; Du Sommerard, *Catalogue et description*, nos. 8997, 9014; Bruna, *Enseignes de Pèlerinage*, pp. 48–9, cat. 3, 5.

[83] For instance in Musée de Cluny (inv. no. Cl. 23333), 26 × 18 mm. Desnoyers, "Objets trouvés," 1876, p. 185, pl. V, fig. 6; Du Sommerard, *Catalogue et description*, no. 9921; Bruna, *Enseignes de Pèlerinage*, p. 48, cat. 4. De Rochambeau, "Voyage à la Sainte-Larme," p. 162, figs. 6–7 shows a small brass medal in the Musée de Vendôme.

[84] Forgeais, *Imagerie religieuse*, p. 86; De Rochambeau, "Voyage à la Sainte-Larme," p. 163, fig. 9. 29 × 18 mm; whereabouts unknown.

Interpretations and Conclusions: Vendôme Ampullae

Although a variety of souvenirs was made at Vendôme, it appears that ampullae were by far preferred. Their popularity flourished from the thirteenth century, early in the life of the pilgrim trade in Vendôme. The vogue for badges came a century later and perhaps even later, in the early sixteenth century, tear-shaped pendants and round, oval, or heart-shaped medals came into vogue.

The sought-after ampullae must have been produced and sold on a vast scale for four hundred years; why then, have only fourteen-and-a-half examples have turned up so far? First and foremost, ampullae were cheap, mass-produced goods which catered to the large demand from pilgrims. Many medieval pilgrim souvenirs disappeared once they had lost their original function. Scant aesthetic or historical importance was attached to what, from a material point of view, were "worthless" objects. Furthermore, the pewter of which the ampullae were made is a fragile material that soon decomposes in unfavorable soil conditions.

The Vendôme souvenirs have appeared not only in the surrounding areas, such as the Loire at Orléans and in the Seine at Paris, but as far afield as London and the Low Countries. All of the ampullae were empty when found, and medieval sources fail to inform us as to their contents. Still, it is likely that the ampullae were filled with a few drops of water, that was blessed in a large chalice on the altar by submerging the tear relic in it. The water might have originated from the well into which Geoffrey and Agnes saw the three stars fall and over which they situated the altar and built their church. The submerging of the tear sanctified the water and seemed to endow it with curative powers. In addition, these drops of blessed water might also be interpreted as a pseudo-collection of the tear and imagined contact with Christ. Together with the iconography of the ampullae, these ideas emphasized the sanctity of the contents of the vessel and the whole pilgrim's experience at Vendôme.

Ten pouch-shaped ampullae dating between the thirteenth and the first half of the fourteenth century, show the ritual of submerging the tear relic. (figs. 214a, 215a, 216a, 217a, 218a, 219a) Two monks of La Trinité abbey, dressed in long tunics fastened round the waist with a cord or band, flank the altar above which the tear is held.[85]

---

[85] Until now, these two people have not been identified as monks of La Trinité

Usually one of them holds the *Sainte Larme* above the large chalice, the other bears a tall candle. The ampulla found at Melun, shows only one monk; the figure on the left wears a somewhat shorter tunic and can therefore be identified as a layman. (fig. 216a) He rubs his right hand over the *Sainte Larme* while holding up a small bowl—possibly filled with water—in his left. A plausible interpretation is that this figure (a pilgrim?) desires to establish direct contact between his bowl and the most-venerated tear to supply his souvenir with some of the relic's healing powers, as might had been the case with the ampullae too. The prominent position of the altar on all these ampullae could be a reference to the altar built above the well at Geoffrey's instigation. On both ampullae and the two pilgrim badges found at Dordrecht (figs. 221a, 222a), this altar is covered with a decorative cloth or embellished with wrought ironwork. The decorative details occasionally vary. A recurring motif consists of four St. Andrew's crosses or stars with a dot in the center, separated by horizontal and vertical lines, perhaps referring to the five wounds of Christ.

Interestingly, the *Sainte Larme* appears as a large tear-shaped element on these ampullae, while the reliquary made on Bishop Notker's instructions shortly before the middle of the eleventh century, in which the tear was kept, was apparently of little significance. The depicted object is the enlarged cut-rock crystal ampulla, which according to tradition contained the tear shed by Christ. (fig. 213) The chalice, not mentioned in descriptions of the reliquary or the relic does, however, seem to have been significant. It is depicted on almost all the ampullae in the same fashion (as two semicircles, one for the cup, the other for the base) and is decorated with vertical lines. A chalice like this is also displayed prominently on the reverse of one of the Dordrecht badges. (fig. 222b) From this iconography, it can be concluded that the chalice played an import part in the cult at Vendôme. During the ritual of submerging the tear relic, it was

abbey. Forgeais believed they were Lazarus' sisters, St. Mary Magdalene and St. Martha. Forgeais, *Imagerie religieuse*, pp. 65, 77. Mary Magdalene was involved in the cult at Vendôme, for she was there when Christ shed his tear. An angel caught it in a vial and gave it to her. Spencer on the other hand, draws attention to their pointed, beard-like chins on a London ampulla—without giving another interpretation—which denies Forgeais' identification. Spencer, *Medieval Finds*, p. 227.

placed prominently on the altar where water was poured into the chalice, to be blessed and distributed to pilgrims.[86]

This ritual of submerging the tear relic is also illustrated on the front of a badge found in Dordrecht. (fig. 221a) The top section of this badge, however, shows St. George on his steed. On the ampullae, too, these two themes are combined—one on each side.[87] Geoffrey Martel is said to have received another relic at the same time as the *Sainte Larme*: St. George's arm, explaining why this saint also appears on the pilgrim souvenirs from Vendôme. Shortly before 1050, Geoffrey's wife Agnes commissioned a church, Saint-Georges, to be built within their castle walls. Even though it is not known whether pilgrims to Vendôme had access to this collegiate church, which stood on the count's private land, the pouch-shaped ampullae (with only one exception) depicted an equestrian St. George. (figs. 214b, 215b, 216b, 217b, 219b, 220) He is invariably clad in armor, usually holding a shield and sword or lance, and is always wearing a helmet. His horse's blanket is often decorated with dots or rosettes. The inscription S GEORGIVS on the neck of the ampullae confirms his identity. The dragon, an often-featured element of his legend, is absent.

It might be concluded from discoveries of these pilgrim souvenirs that the St. George relic had an important devotional significance for Vendôme pilgrims. Perhaps the arm was kept temporarily in La Trinité in the thirteenth or early fourteenth century, or perhaps the Church of Saint-Georges was accessible to pilgrims for a time. Another possibility is that the relic was carried in the annual procession or displayed to the faithful on the saint's day, April 23. Whatever the case, representations of St. George disappear from the pilgrim ampullae after the middle of the fourteenth century. Perhaps the arm was no longer in Vendôme, or perhaps its popularity had been superseded by that of the *Sainte Larme*.

---

[86] For a comparable ritual in Maastricht, see fn. 38.

[87] The combination of two objects of veneration on a single ampulla, one on each side, is not unique to Vendôme; it is also found in other places of pilgrimage including Burton-on-Trent (St. Modwen and Mary), Bromholm (St. Andrew and a cross relic), Thessalonica (St. Demetrius in combination with Sts. Nestor, George, Theodora, or Mary), Worcester (St. Wulfstan and Mary), Westminster (St. Edward the Confessor and St. Peter), and probably Evesham (Sts. Egwin and Edwin). These ampullae are discussed in detail in my dissertation, to be published in 2005. Literature regarding these souvenirs is cited in fns. 88–99.

All of the pouch-shaped ampullae are decorated with zigzag borders from loop to loop, combined in some cases with an inscription. A similar border is found on a few (round) Demetrius ampullae from Thessalonica.[88] The decoration is different, but the phenomenon is comparable. Moreover, the pouch form in this group of Vendôme souvenirs is reminiscent of various late twelfth-century and thirteenth-century pilgrim ampullae, most from Great Britain. These include Canterbury,[89] Burton-on-Trent,[90] Worcester,[91] (perhaps) Evesham,[92] and Boulogne-sur-Mer (in France).[93] The pouch form may have been deliberately adopted in Vendôme because of the associations it evoked with the shape of the tear relic. In contrast cruciform ampullae made in Bromholm[94] and Waltham,[95] for instance, refer to the cross relics venerated in both places. The circular pilgrim ampullae from Vendôme—dating from the fifteenth to the beginning of the sixteenth century—however, appears to be fairly unique. (figs. 223–5) Round-bellied examples were of course more prevalent, notably in Jerusalem,[96] Thessalonica,[97] Noyon,[98] and Maastricht,[99] but the relatively tall, decorated foot is uncommon among other medieval pilgrim ampullae.

The four intact receptacles of this second group also display the tear relic on one side, but without the two flanking monks; on the later examples a large *Sainte Larme* occupies pride of place on the con-

---

[88] Charalambos Bakirtzis, "Byzantine Ampullae from Thessaloniki," in Robert Ousterhout (ed.), *The Blessings of Pilgrimage* (Urbana, 1990), pp. 140–9, figs. 49–54.

[89] Spencer, *Medieval Finds*, pp. 38–72, esp. figs. 2b, 5, 6b–c, 7, 7a, 9, 11–4, 17a (most surrouded by an openwork frame).

[90] Brian Spencer, "Two Leaden Ampullae from Leicestershire," *Transactions of the Leicestershire Archaeological and Historical Society* 55 (1982), 88–9.

[91] Brian Spencer, "A Thirteenth-Century Pilgrim's Ampulla from Worcester," *Transactions of the Worcestershire Archaeological Society* 9 (1984), 7–11.

[92] Brian Spencer, "An Ampulla of St. Egwin and St. Edwin," *The Antiquities Journal* 51 (1971), 316–8.

[93] Bruna, *Enseignes de Pèlerinage*, pp. 87–8, cat. 83–5; Van Beuningen, Koldeweij, and Kicken, *Heilig en Profaan 2*, pp. 331–3, figs. 1383–90.

[94] Spencer, *Medieval Finds*, pp. 161–5, figs. 178–180a.

[95] For the ampulla mold from Waltham, Spencer, "Medieval Pilgrim Badges," pp. 141, 146, fn. 27, 151; fn. 30.

[96] Lieselotte Kötzsche, "Zwei Jerusalemer Pilgerampullen aus der Kreuzfahrerzeit," *Zeitschrift für Kunstgeschichte* 51 (1988), 13–32.

[97] See fn. 88.

[98] Arthur Forgeais, *Collection de plombs historiés trouvés dans la Seine et recueillis par Arthur Forgeais, Tome II: Enseignes de pèlerinage* (Paris, 1863), p. 164.

[99] Van Beuningen, Koldeweij, and Kicken, *Heilig en Profaan 2*, p. 296, fig. 1272.

tainer's body, between two burning candles. (figs. 223a, 224a, 225a) On one ampulla, the relic is placed in a chest decorated with Gothic motifs and flanked by two stylized tears. (fig. 223a) As it depicts one of the reliquary boxes in the fifteenth century, this ampulla is valuable for its iconography; it may show one of the alterations made to the shrine in the course of the fourteenth century, which could have caused the metamorphosis of the ampullae. On one of the Dordrecht badges, too, the tear is flanked by two burning candles, under which—as on the early ampullae—the altar or the well is depicted. (fig. 222a) The stylized tear on all the ampullae from the second group also appears in the sixteenth century on medals and as pendants. (figs. 227–9) The iconography varies on the reverse sides of the later, round-bellied ampullae. One shows a coat of arms with three fleurs-de-lis, symbolizing the kings of France since the thirteenth century. (fig. 223b) As this motif refers to the royal protection of La Trinité abbey, this ampulla should be dated after 1467.

Two containers illustrate a Greek cross with tapering arms between which are four small St. Andrew's crosses. (fig. 224b) They might refer to the five wounds of Christ, as does the cross of Jerusalem. The same decorative motif appears on the side of the altar depicted on some earlier pouch-shaped ampullae, perhaps echoing the decoration on the altar (or the well), which pilgrims could see in the church. Moreover, the ampullae indicate that the Greek cross played an important part in the cult of Vendôme. It is shown not only as an independent design or standing on the altar, but also crowning St. George's helmet. These repeated images suggest that a little cross with tapered arms was venerated at Vendôme.

The last intact container and one ampulla half with a round shape both picture the Holy Trinity, under whose patronage the abbey church existed. (fig. 225b) The representation probably referred to a painting or sculpture of the *Gnadenstuhl* in the church itself, which could be connected with the sacrifice of Christ. Two fifteenth-century badges found in Paris and Rouen bear close resemblances to the scene on these two ampulla sides and are therefore assigned to Vendôme. (fig. 226)

Interestingly, the fourteen-and-a-half Vendôme ampullae show many differences as well as numerous similarities—sometimes with just subtle distinctions—but not one of them depicts an identical scene on both sides. It is remarkable that in *all cases* the scene on one side is related to the *Sainte Larme* which came into the possession

of La Trinité at Vendôme in the mid-eleventh century. The fact
that all the ampullae, from the thirteenth through the beginning of
the sixteenth century, make direct reference to the tear relic venerated so intensively at Vendôme, is a sign of the *Sainte Larme*'s continuing, devotional significance to pilgrims throughout the Middle
Ages.

CHAPTER EIGHTEEN

SEARCHING FOR SIGNS: PILGRIMS' IDENTITY AND EXPERIENCE MADE VISIBLE IN THE *MIRACULA SANCTI THOMAE CANTUARIENSIS**

Jennifer M. Lee

It is a paradox of the history of popular culture that the most ubiquitous practices can be the most obscure in historical texts.[1] The creation and use of pilgrims' signs present the historian with just such a problem. From the twelfth century on, pilgrims to European shrines commemorated their journeys by collecting souvenirs, or *signs* as contemporaries called them, in the form of wearable items cast from lead or lead-tin alloys.[2] Thousands have been recovered from archaeological sites in northern Europe, yet the texts that help us understand their function are few. The pilgrimage cult of St. Thomas Becket of Canterbury generated thousands of pilgrims' signs and an

---

* The research and writing of this article has been generously supported by the Chester Dale Fellowship at the Metropolitan Museum of Art and by the Emory University Fund for Internationalization. I am also indebted to David Bright, Ryan Fowler, and Cilla Rodgers for their assistance with my Latin translations throughout this essay.

[1] Aaron Gurevich, *Medieval Popular Culture: Problems of Belief and Perception*, trans. János M. Bak and Paul A. Hollingsworth (Cambridge, 1988).

[2] Medieval documents and inscriptions on pilgrims' signs themselves used a range of terms including *signum*, *signaculum*, and *sigillum*. This last makes explicit a connection with seals. Evidence for Canterbury ampullae being perceived as signs is given by the anonymous author of a *Vita* who wrote, "The first [pilgrims], and in fact only those returning either from the tomb of Christ or from St. James used to bring back a sign of their pilgrimage—these brought cockle shells, those the fronds of palms. Those returning from St. Thomas took up a third sign, but one far more precious, as if it were the martyr's easy yoke and his light burden, the tin ampulla hanging down from the neck clearly onto the chest, full of holy water mixed with a drop of his sacred blood . . ." (*Peregrinationis suae signum primi quidem et soli vel a Christi sepulchro vel a sancto Jacobo revertentes, hi cochleas, illi plamarum spatulas, referre consueverunt. Susceperunt et a sancto Thoma redeuntes tertium sed longe pretiosius signum, velut jugum martyris suave et onus ijus leve, ampullam videlicet staneam in pectus a collo dependentem, plenam aquae benedictae stilla sacri cruoris immixtae. . . .) Vita Sancti Thomae, Cantuariensis Archiepiscopi et Martyris, Auctore Anonymo II*, ed. James C. Robertson, *Materials for the History of Thomas Becket, Archbishop of Canterbury*, vol. 4, (London, 1879), p. 142.

unusually large collection of miracle stories that offers contemporary remarks about the objects. Taken together, these material and textual sources provide important information about the role of pilgrimage in the lives of hundreds of thousands of people who traveled to Canterbury between the late twelfth and early sixteenth centuries.[3]

The pilgrimage to the tomb and shrine of St. Thomas Becket at Canterbury began in 1171, after Becket's 1170 murder in Canterbury Cathedral by four knights, and continued until the destruction of the shrine in 1538. The resulting long, continuous sequence of pilgrims' signs is ideal for observing formal and ideological changes. From 1171 through most of the thirteenth century, all of the pilgrims' signs from Canterbury were ampullae decorated on the exterior with images and filled with "Canterbury water," a diluted mixture of the blood collected immediately after St. Thomas' martyrdom and known for its thaumaturgic properties.[4] By the end of the thirteenth century, ampullae began to be phased out in favor of badges that were worn pinned to the hat or outer clothing. This formal change reveals an underlying conceptual change: an image now takes on the role formerly reserved for relics, implying a shift in the pilgrims' expectations.

In addition to providing an excellent sequence of pilgrims' signs, the pilgrimage to St. Thomas at Canterbury is also the source of the collection of miracle stories that contains more references to pilgrims' signs than any other medieval text.[5] Indeed, the *Miracula Sancti Thomae Cantuariensis*, or *Miracles of St. Thomas of Canterbury*, is the largest collection of miracles attributed to any medieval saint. Scattered

---

[3] Patrick Geary questioned Gurevich's claim that the ideals of popular culture are implicit in elite texts, noting that this can be "asserted but not demonstrated." By observing the distribution of Canterbury pilgrims' signs, we have a second opinion, as it were, with which to compare our deductions from the texts. Patrick Geary, *Living with the Dead in the Middle Ages* (Ithaca, 1994), p. 21.

[4] On the development and use of Canterbury water, see Benedicta Ward, *Miracles and the Medieval Mind* (Philadelphia, 1982), pp. 101–4.

[5] The Canterbury miracles are published in two volumes: William of Canterbury, *Miracula Sancti Thomae Cantuariensis*, ed. James C. Robertson, *Materials for the History of Thomas Becket, Archbishop of Canterbury*, vol. 1 (London, 1875); Benedict of Peterborough, *Miracula Sancti Thomae Cantuariensis*, ed. James C. Robertson, *Materials for the History of Thomas Becket, Archbishop of Canterbury*, vol. 2 (London, 1876). Pilgrims' badges feature once in the miracles of Our Lady of Rocamadour and of Henry VI. *The Miracles of Our Lady of Rocamadour: Analysis and Translation*, ed. and trans. Marcus Bull (Woodbridge, UK, 1999), p. 125. *Henrici VI Angliae Regis Miracula Postuma*, ed. Paulus Grosjean, (Brussels, 1935), pp. 205–6.

throughout more than 700 stories are over 100 references to the metal ampullae that served as the signs of the Canterbury pilgrimage during the first century of the cult of St. Thomas.[6]

In this essay, I will reassess the evidentiary value of the *Miracles of St. Thomas of Canterbury* for understanding the significance of pilgrims' signs, and will propose an interpretive method for this rich textual source. Formal analysis of the extant pilgrims' signs from Canterbury, along with consideration of the archaeological context from which they have been retrieved, is evaluated in combination with textual evidence from the *Miracula* to suggest a normative ideology for the use of pilgrims' signs. These sources considered together allow us to ask what it meant to wear pilgrims' signs suspended around the neck or pinned prominently on the clothing.

The miracle stories collected at Canterbury share a number of characteristics with pilgrims' signs. Both were produced in quantity. Pilgrims' signs were cast in molds, so many of them are identical. Where variation occurs, its range is limited, so that even a badge or an ampulla from an unfamiliar shrine would have been recognizable as a sign of pilgrimage. The consistency of form has a textual counterpart in the near-formulaic pattern in which miracle stories were written, so while the details vary endlessly, most stories fit easily into a typological canon.[7] More importantly, their monastic authors represent the same social group as the monks who oversaw the production of pilgrims' signs. Among other uses, *miracula* could be read to pilgrims at the shrine, and were sometimes used as sources for *exempla* in sermons.[8] Thus, miracles and pilgrims' signs shared an audience in the laity who listened to the stories and wore or encountered pilgrims wearing signs.

The *Miracula Sanctae Thomae Cantuariensis* was written by two

---

[6] The approximate number 700 comes from the 712 numbered entries as published in Robertson's edition. The Lambeth Palace ms. 135, Trinity College Cambridge ms. 321 and Westminster College ms. 4 show that Robertson's divisions reflect those of the thirteenth century. Some of the entries contain multiple cures, usually related in some way, while others confirm previously-recorded miracles. An exact count would produce a similar number, but would depend on fine distinctions between events narrated together. Since the narration is more important than the miracle itself, I will consider one miracle to mean one narrative unit as presented in the text.

[7] Bull, *Rocamadour*, p. 13.

[8] Pierre-André Sigal, *L'homme et le miracle dans la France médiévale, XIe–XIIe Siècle* (Paris, 1985), p. 13.

Benedictine monks of Christ Church at Canterbury, Benedict and William, during the 1170s. The writers ostensibly recorded miracles as they were reported by pilgrims visiting the tomb, however, literary structure demonstrates that the writers carefully organized and constructed their texts rather than entering them directly into the books. The stories are often grouped by type, as in a series of rescues at sea or a cluster of cures of a single ailment such as leprosy or blindness. Several dozen letters from bishops or monks of other monasteries describing or confirming miracles are also collated into the collection. These practices, along with rhetorical flourishes and moralizing inclusions, indicate the active editorial role performed by the authors.[9] By comparison, the first author of the miracles of St. Foy of Conques, Bernard of Angers, writing in 1013, recounts making notes on bits of parchment, and then fleshing out his text from those.[10] William implies that a similar method of work was followed at Canterbury, where he "touched on things briefly," being concerned about the "truth and not the sequence" of events, and writes of his desire that these things might be written in "more polished and expressive" form.[11]

St. Thomas' miracles come to us as two separate books, one by Benedict and one by William. Most of the stories are specific to one book or the other, but enough stories are found in both that the two cannot be considered entirely separate. Based on internal evidence, it appears that Benedict began the project in 1171 and was joined by William in 1172, and the two men worked in cooperation until *c.* 1174. After a hiatus, William returned to add the final sections of his book after 1178.[12] Since the analytical method advo-

---

[9] For the Miracles of St. Foy as an authored text see Kathleen Ashley and Pamela Sheingorn, *Writing Faith: Text, Sign, and History in the Miracles of Sainte Foy* (Chicago, 1999).

[10] Bernard of Angers, *The Book of Ste. Foy*, ed. and trans. Pamela Sheingorn (Philadelphia, 1995), p. 63; Kathleen Ashley and Pamela Sheingorn, "Translations of Sainte Foy: Bodies, Texts, Places," in *The Medieval Translator*, vol. 5, ed. Roger Ellis (Turnhout, 1996), pp. 29–49.

[11] William, *Miracula* 1. prologus, pp. 138–39. *Scribens itaque pauca perstringit, veritatem non ordinem sequens eorum quae mirifice gesta sunt.... pro parvitate scribentis effigiatam, longe melius incidendam licet assumat, de qua, tanquam de novo, juxta sibi collatae gratiae beneficia, martyrem poterit elimatius et expressius exsculpere . . .* See also, William's *Vita Sancti Thomae*, ed. Robertson vol. 1, p. 2.

[12] For the dating of these texts, see Emmanuel Walberg, *La Tradition Hagiographique de Saint Thomas Becket* (Paris, 1929), pp. 55–73.

cated here depends more heavily on instances of writing about miraculous events than on miraculous occurrences themselves, it is most fruitful to study the entire collection as a single body of 712 stories authored by two monks.[13]

Of course, to use miracle stories as historical sources is to run into interpretive problems immediately, for medieval miracles reside at the intersection between solid fact and narrative fiction.[14] Ronald Finucane traced the historiography of *miracula* as source material from the mid-nineteenth century to 1975, and his book *Miracles and Pilgrims* remains an important landmark in studies based on the miracles of St. Thomas in particular.[15] Pierre-André Sigal and Benedicta Ward have also advanced our understanding of history and ideology of medieval miracles,[16] and Pierre Bonnassie, Raymond Van Dam, and André Vauchez have demonstrated the value of the miracle genre as an historical source able to illuminate various aspects of medieval society.[17] However, Kathleen Ashley and Pamela Sheingorn have warned of the dangers of mining miracle solely stories for the insights they offer on other aspects of medieval life without due regard for the hagiographer's project.[18] In the introductory essay to his translation of *The Miracles of Our Lady of Rocamadour*, Marcus Bull

---

[13] Gervase of Canterbury suggested that the two books were considered a single project: *Extant in ecclesia Christi Cantuariae duo volumina miraculourm eius, quae ut huic compendio insererem non est necesse* . . . Gervase of Canterbury, "*Opera Historica*" in *The Historical Works of Gervase of Canterbury* vol. 1, ed. William Stubbs (London, 1879), p. 230; Benedicta Ward, *Miracles and the Medieval Mind*, p. 93.

[14] Bull, *Rocamadour*, p. 11. For historiographic trends in hagiographical scholarship, see Patrick Geary, *Living with the Dead in the Middle Ages*, 9–29, esp. 15–6 for miracle collections.

[15] Ronald C. Finucane, "The Use and Abuse of Medieval Miracles," *History* 60 (1975), 1–10; Ronald C. Finucane, *Miracles and Pilgrims: Popular Beliefs in Medieval England* (London: Dent, 1977). For Marian miracles in particular, see Gabriela Signori, "The Miracle Kitchen and its Ingredients: A Methodical and Critical Approach to Marian Shrine Wonders (10th to 13th century), *Hagiographica* 3 (1996): 277–303.

[16] Sigal, *L'homme et le miracle*, p. 13; Ward, *Miracles*, pp. 89–109.

[17] Pierre Bonnassie, "Descriptions of Fortresses in the Book of Miracles of Sainte-Foy of Conques," in *From Slavery to Feudalism in South-Western Europe*, trans. Jean Birrell (Cambridge, 1991), pp. 132–48; Raymond Van Dam, *Saints and their Miracles in Late Antique Gaul* (Princeton, 1993); Andre Vauchez, *Sainthood in the Later Middle Ages*, trans. Jean Birrell (Cambridge, 1997).

[18] Ashley and Sheingorn, *Writing Faith*, p. 11; David W. Rollason, "The Miracles of St Benedict: A Window on Early Medieval France," in *Studies in Medieval History Presented to R.H.C. Davis*, eds. Henry Mayr-Harting and R.I. Moore (London, 1985), pp. 73–90.

presents a sensitive discussion of *miracula* that largely avoids the pit-
falls identified by Ashley and Sheingorn.[19] Bull seeks a balance between
retaining the literary integrity of *miracula* and locating historical data
within them, for "there are limits to how far the overtly miraculous
elements of a given *miraculum* can be detached from the story as a
coherent whole without unravelling the narrative so completely that
its value as a source is undermined."[20] His method allows us to
return to *miracula* for historical information contained within their
formulaic frames and to draw on the rich anecdotal evidence these
stories provide. This is crucial for the study of pilgrims' signs, for
which we must inevitably turn to the *Miracula Sancti Thomae Cantuariensis.*

Although the documentation for pilgrims' signs is limited, they
were commonplace objects in the late medieval world. This is attested
not only by the abundant surviving examples, but also by the contexts from which archaeologists have retrieved so many of them. The
excavations that have revealed the most Canterbury signs have been
conducted along the shore of the Thames in London. Late medieval
Londoners undertook land-reclamation projects along the banks of
the Thames during the fourteenth and fifteenth centuries when St.
Thomas' cult was at its height. The work involved the construction
of a series of wooden revetments that were back-filled with organic
debris and assorted rubbish.[21] The presence of pilgrims' signs among
this discarded material indicates the low intrinsic value ascribed to
individual pilgrims' signs once they were no longer being worn. And
yet, they played a vital role in religious practice. Although the objects
themselves may not have been exalted, their function was integral
to the pilgrimage cult. One particular miracle story in demonstrates
explicitly that the Canterbury monks considered the signs to be an
important part of St. Thomas' cult. This miracle, recorded by Benedict,
describes the invention of the first metal ampulla at Canterbury.[22]
The story is retold with similar emphasis by another cleric of Canter-

---

[19] Bull, *Rocamadour*, pp. 11–20, 32–4.
[20] Bull, *Rocamadour*, p. 15.
[21] Gustav Milne, "Medieval Riverfront Reclamation in London," in *Waterfront
Archaeology in Britain and Northern Europe*, eds. Gustav Milne and Brian Hobley (London,
1981), pp. 32–36. Brian Spencer, "Pilgrim Souvenirs from the Medieval Waterfront
Excavations at Trig Lane London, 1974–1976," *Transactions of the London Middlesex
Archaeological Society* (1982), pp. 304–23.
[22] Benedict, *Miracula*, 3.22, pp. 134–5.

bury, Herbert of Bosham, in his *Vita of St. Thomas*, written after 1186.[23] The text tells us nothing about the practical side of ampulla production, but suggests an intended function for the objects in the first years of the pilgrimage.

Benedict relates that, at the very beginning of the cult, pilgrims carried Canterbury water in pyxes made of boxwood. These were prone to leaks and breakage, events regarded as miraculous critiques of their owners. It was suggested by divine inspiration to a young man that he replace these inadequate wooden vessels with ampullae of lead and tin. Benedict writes, ". . . it fell into the heart of a youth that he should make lead and tin ampullae by casting, and the miracle stopped the breakages." The final lines of Benedict's narration are particularly telling:

> We know it was divine will that the ampullae of Canterbury's healer be carried through the whole world and that all the world should recognize his sign in his pilgrims and in his cured ones. In fact, previously they used to wear the vessels concealed beneath their clothes, however, they wore the ampullae openly, hung from the neck.[24]

This story introduces the ampulla form, which would remain standard until the introduction of badges over a century later. By attributing the idea to begin manufacture of metal ampullae to divine inspiration, and by constructing the invention of the ampullae and the failure of the wooden vessels as miracles, Benedict claims the ampullae themselves as integral parts of the cult, authorized by the saint as well as the monks. The privileged role of the ampullae is reiterated in an 1184–1220 stained glass window in the north aisle of the ambulatory of Canterbury Cathedral's Trinity Chapel, that shows two pilgrims wearing oversized ampullae suspended from cords.[25]

---

[23] Herbert of Bosham, "De pixidibus prius gestatis," in *Excerpti ex Herberti*, ed. James C. Robertson, *Materials for the History of Archbishop Thomas Becket* vol. 3 (London, 1877), p. 252; Robertson, "Introduction," pp. xvii–xxv.

[24] ". . . *et cognovimus fuisse in voluntate Divina, ut portarentur Cantuariensis medici ampullae per totum orbem terrarum, et signum ejus in peregrinis suis et in curatis suis mundus universus cognosceret. Priora enim vasa sub vestimentis suis ferebant abscondita, ampullas autem in propatulo a collo suspensas.*" Benedict, *Miracula*, 3.22, pp. 134–5.

[25] Madeline H. Caviness, *The Windows of Christ Church Cathedral, Canterbury, Corpus Vitrearum Medii Aevii, Great Britain*, vol. 2 (London, 1981), pp. 197–8, pl. 142, fig. 313. An additional window panel, in the south ambulatory, shows a wounded man drinking from a pilgrimage ampulla, Caviness, p. 202, pl. 148, fig. 331. Other

One of the purposes of recording miracles most often mentioned in the texts is that of spreading the fame of the martyr. Here we see that the more durable ampullae could share the task of spreading fame wherever they were worn. In addition to claiming the *ampullae* as an authorized aspect of a pilgrimage to Canterbury, Benedict's text indicates that the ampullae were now to have a wider audience as public markers of the cult. The pyxes had been private objects, carried under the clothes where only the owner need know about them. The new ampullae were "worn openly, hung from the neck." By authorizing the ampullae, the monks directing the cult, whose interests we can assume Benedict to represent, approved the display of Canterbury ampullae by pilgrims. A pilgrim who had been to the tomb of St. Thomas could now be visually distinguished by friends and strangers alike at first glance.

For ampullae worn openly to communicate effectively, they had to be recognizable. Benedict writes, "that all the world should recognize his sign in his pilgrims . . ." The verb *cognoscere*, translated here as "recognize," includes in its range of meanings such concepts as to understand and to identify. Thus, for an ampulla to be an effective signifier, its form must be something the viewer has seen before. The material change from wood to metal implies greater regularization of images. While wooden pyxes would have been individually constructed, metal casting allowed the replication of forms through reuse of a single mold.[26] Although Canterbury ampullae came in several shapes and with various images, the range is narrow and the objects cluster into a few clear types that demonstrate a basic regularity of form and a conservative attitude toward innovation. Too much variety would compromise recognition and undermine the efficacy of the objects as signifiers.

Changes in the form of ampullae from the late twelfth to the late thirteenth century attest to increasing concern for recognition. The earliest Canterbury ampullae are as small as one inch in height and width, rounded along the bottom edge, with a pattern of radiating

---

vessels shown in the miracle windows represent the flasks in which the monks mixed the Canterbury water at the shrine (and in one case a vessel of urine held up for uroscopic diagnosis) rather than pilgrim's ampullae *per se*.

[26] There are no extant examples of the wooden pyxes. Their characteristics must be deduced from the texts.

ridges like a scallop shell. (fig. 230) Because the miracles were written in the 1170s, it is reasonable to assume that many of the stories refer to ampullae of this small, scalloped type. The scalloped shape deliberately recalls the natural scallop shells that since the early twelfth century had been universally recognized as signs of the pilgrimage to Santiago de Compostella.[27] In fact, the scallop shells were so closely identified with the pilgrimage to Compostella that they became signs not merely of that pilgrimage, but of pilgrimage in general. The universality of the shell is echoed by Benedict's claim that St. Thomas' ampullae would be recognized "through the whole world" (*per totum orbem terrarum*).

Technically, the pilgrims' sign, whether badge or ampulla, was superfluous for identifying the wearer as a pilgrim. The official attributes of pilgrimage were the staff and scrip or bag. Liturgies for blessing these items at the beginning of a pilgrimage show how they marked their bearers as pilgrims.[28] Furthermore, medieval writers' overwhelming emphasis on the journey to the shrine implies that the homeward journey, when the pilgrim might have a badge or ampulla, was less important to the conceptual structure of pilgrimage.[29] Thus, the signs were unnecessary for identifying their wearers as pilgrims. Rather, they announced which saint the pilgrim had visited, and changes in the Canterbury ampullae reflect this function.

The progression of imagery on Canterbury ampullae developed over the course of a century from the early scallop shell to imagery more specifically associated with St. Thomas. Simultaneously, the imagery became larger, and the images of St. Thomas expanded to cover a larger portion of the ampullae's surface. The early shell-shaped ampullae generally bore an image of the saint's mitered head on the side with the scalloped ridges. The heads were very small,

---

[27] Brian Spencer, *Pilgrim Souvenirs and Secular Badges* (London, 1998), p. 43. Spencer observed that the initial purpose of the ampullae was to announce the importance of a new pilgrimage by means of a universally-recognized emblem; Christopher Hohler, "The Badge of St. James," in *The Scallop: Studies of a Shell and its Influences on Humankind*, ed. Ian Cox (London, 1957), pp. 49–70. Pilgrims' signs from Mont St. Michel also incorporated the scallop motif. See Denis , *Ensignes pélerinage et ensignes profane* (Paris, 1996), pp. 185–6.

[28] James A. Brundage, "Cruce Signari: The Rite for Taking the Cross in England," *Traditio* 22 (1966): 289–310. *Editors' note: see Anja Grebe's essay in this volume.

[29] Donald, R. Howard *Writers and Pilgrims: Medieval Pilgrimage Narratives and Their Posterity.* (Berkeley, 1980), pp. 6–10.

and occupied only the upper portion of the ampullae's surface, above the scallop-shaped area. The reverse sides showed a low-relief image of the saint at the moment of his martyrdom, with a single knight striking him on the head with a sword.

These tiny ampullae were not produced after *c.* 1200.[30] Thereafter, ampullae became larger, as did the imagery on their surfaces. (fig. 231) The tiny head of St. Thomas was replaced by a bust-length or full-body image of the saint. The full body images portrayed the saint standing frontally in his episcopal vestments, holding a crozier or cross staff. The scalloped ridges are gone, and the image occupies the entire front surface of the ampullae, sometimes with the addition of ornamental borders or mandorla-shaped framing elements surrounding the saint. Most examples show the saint with his right hand raised in a gesture of benediction. When the ampulla was worn on the chest of a pilgrim, the frontality of the archbishop positions the viewer, that is, the person encountering the pilgrim, as the recipient of the gesture of benediction. These larger ampullae have distinct fronts and backs.[31] A casting process using three-part molds allowed the archbishop's crozier or cross staff to protrude from the front surface of the ampulla.[32] The addition of flanges or frames that extended the broad surface of many examples would also have reduced the ampulla's spinning on its cord and kept the front side facing outwards.[33] These augmentations indicate concern for the way the objects were to be viewed. Both the increase in the specificity of the image and the increase in attention to the viewer foreshadow the introduction of pilgrims' badges in the second half of the thirteenth century.

The *miracula* are the most explicit source for the various ways pilgrims' signs were regarded by their contemporaries. Scholars have often turned to William and Benedict's *miracula* for the ways pilgrims'

---

[30] The early date for the tiny ampullae is determined by the position of the miter on Thomas' head, shown with the ridge line dorsal so that both peaks are visible in the frontal view. The seal of Richard, Archbishop of Canterbury (r. 1174–84) also depicts the miter with this orientation, while the seal of Archbishop Stephen Langton, who took office in 1207, pictured the miter turned in the direction familiar to this day. Spencer, *Pilgrim Souvenirs*, p. 41.

[31] Spencer, *Pilgrim Souvenirs*, p. 41.

[32] Spencer, *Pilgrim Souvenirs*, p. 9.

[33] Spencer, *Pilgrim Souvenirs*, p. 47.

signs could provoke miracles, but the these stories also inform us about more ordinary functions of these objects. Very few of the miracles of St. Thomas feature pilgrims' signs at the center of the action, and the previously cited example describing the invention is unique. Only about twelve out of the total corpus involve pilgrims' ampullae in any role that suggests the objects themselves had thaumaturgic power, although more than one hundred describe cures instigated by the Canterbury water inside the ampullae. Thus, the frequent citation of these exceptional examples by scholars writing about pilgrims' signs has resulted in an incomplete picture of how these objects were regarded.[34]

These exceptional examples show that pilgrims' signs were sometimes considered to have talismanic power or to be agents of the miraculous. Material evidence corroborates this interpretation. The condition of a few of the objects indicates that they were given ritualized attention. A small percentage of the signs have been found folded or deliberately mutilated prior to being tossed into the water, whether as refuse or as a ritual gesture in itself. Thus, both the *miracula* and the condition of the objects suggest that amuletic and talismanic uses of pilgrims' signs were known and occasionally practiced.[35]

However, we should not allow these exceptional examples to obscure the more common uses suggested by the much greater number of pilgrims' signs that have been found unharmed or showing only natural wear. Similarly, the *miracula*, when read in their entirety, indicate that the less spectacular function of simply designating St. Thomas' pilgrims was more often in the minds of the monks, who both produced the texts and oversaw the production of the signs. The vast number of signs extant today implies that the laity was not resistant to their ideas.

How, then, do we deduce the mundane from miracle stories, which by their very nature describe abnormal events? Bull addresses this

---

[34] Brian Spencer, "Medieval Pilgrim Badges: Some General Observations Illustrated Mainly from English Sources," in *Rotterdam Papers* (Rotterdam, 1968), pp. 143–4; Sarah Blick "A Canterbury Keepsake: English Medieval Pilgrim Souvenirs and Popular Culture" (Ph.D. diss., University of Kansas, 1994), pp. 267–9.

[35] For talismanic and amuletic uses of relics and of the limits of this line of interpretation, see Richard Kieckhefer, *Magic in the Middle Ages* (Cambridge, 1990), pp. 78–9; Valerie Flint, *The Rise of Magic in Early Medieval Europe* (Princeton, 1991), pp. 304–11.

question directly, citing the examples of authors including Van Dam and Bonnassie. One of the rhetorical strategies employed by the writers of medieval *miracula* was to embed the miraculous event in a setting of mundane detail. This served the dual function of throwing the miracle into high relief against the normalcy of the background, and also to lend credibility to the miracle by its association with things familiar and easily believed. Thus, if we want to discern the most conventional understanding of medieval pilgrims' signs, we should look for their appearance not at the center of the miraculous action, but in the surrounding narrative frame.[36]

Two things are revealed when we do this. First, our inventory of miracle stories pertaining to Canterbury pilgrims' signs expands from twelve miracles centered on ampullae to fifty-four explicit references to ampullae, and 124 more miracles provoked by Canterbury water administered at some distance from Canterbury, where we can assume the fluid to have been contained in ampullae. Second, the impression of how these signs were generally understood and used shifts from the realm of the miraculous into the domain of the everyday.

Let us turn to some examples, quoted here at length in order to demonstrate the position of the pilgrims' signs in relation to the rest of the tale:

> Six boys were returning from prayer wearing ampullae and water of St. Thomas, of whom one, not paying attention, was hit by the impact of an iron-clad carriage coming down the street, and fell to the ground. The wheel, together with its load and the driver seated on top, ran over the middle of the fallen boy's cheek at the place on the upper jaw where the beard gives way to smooth skin and leads up to the temples. Prior Nicholaus of the Church of Coventry of venerable memory was also returning from the same place by the same road, and moved by pity, because he thought the boy had been trampled, applied his hand and wiped the boy's face, saying, "Son, are you greatly injured?" He responded, "I think so, Lord." When his face had been cleaned, however, he appeared unhurt, not having even the slightest mark of injury. For the martyr kept his pilgrim unharmed.[37]

---

[36] Bull, *Rocamadour*, p. 11.

[37] "*Redibant ob oratione pueri sex, ferentes ampullas et aquam beati Thomae; quorum unus, vagum circumferens aspectum, impetu ferratae bigae in obviam venientis propulsus, in terram corruit. Transibat autem rota cum sarcinulis suis et insidente auriga per medium maxillae corruentis, qua superiorem partem lanuginis excedens planam cutem traducit ad tempora. Superveniens vero venerandae memoriae prior Nicholaus Conventriensis ecclesiae, qui pariter eadem via et ab eodem loco remeabat, putans quia puer contereretur, misericordia motus manum admovit, et faciem*

In this story, the boy struck by the cart was wearing an ampulla of Canterbury water. A close reading shows that it was not the object functioning as an amulet, but the pilgrim's relationship with the saint that provoked the miracle. The final line of the first story, "the martyr preserved his own pilgrim unharmed," (*conservabat enim peregrinum suum martyr illaesum*) indicates that the saint took special care of his own people. The boy, after all, was returning from pilgrimage to St. Thomas' shrine when the accident occurred, and our author indicates that the saint considered the boy "his own pilgrim."

A similar example is recorded in a letter of a monk from Reading:

> . . . I had set out for the village of Wycombe at the order of Lord William Abbot of Reading, and was to return on the same day by his order. My business done, I had withdrawn and began to return home, and at the village of Marlow I was crossing the Thames on foot with my mount preceding me. Around the middle of the bridge, the horse on which I had sat fell through a hole, from his back end to his flank, with his legs hanging down under the bridge. Bystanders ran up from all sides, and tried to raise the dangling horse with poles placed beneath him. But there were either too few people for so much weight, or so many as to endanger the fragility of the bridge. Those who had come to me in help then left off their fruitless labor, leaving me with only one choice, that I should widen the hole and cast the creature down into the torrent. But these [considerations] called me back from that decision—the dwindling daylight, the command of the Abbot, the coming night, and the long road. And so, left alone but for God, I looked around, but there was none to help. I sought, and there was no one who could help, and then, in the bitterness of my soul, with a deep breath, I began to invoke the most blessed martyr whose sacred vessel I wore suspended from my neck. A wonderful thing! Immediately, in a manner impossible to explain, without human support, at the invocation of the holy martyr, God stood the horse on its feet, and directed my steps, and put into my mouth a new song, a song to our God, who is blessed above everything in this age.[38]

---

extersit, dicens, 'Fili, laesus es multum?' Respondit, 'Puto, domine.' Facies autem extersa apparuit illaesa, ne minimam quidem habens laesionis maculam. Conservabat enim peregrinum suum martyr illaesum." William, *Miracula*, 4.29, p. 343.

[38] "*. . . Jussu domini Willelmi Radingensis abbatis ad villam Wicumbiam profectus sum, eadem die Radingiam ex mandato ejus reversurus. Actis jam eis quorum gratia secesseram, domum redire coepi, Tamisiamque apud villam Merelave pontis adminiculo pedester transibam, meo me praecedente subsellio. Circa pontis medium, equus cui insederam incidit per scissuram a parte sua posteriori usque ad ilia, cruribus subtus pontem dependentibus. Concurrerunt undique circumstantes, pendulumque equum vectibus suppositis erigere nisi sunt; sed nec tanto ponderi suffecit paucitas, nec multitudinem pontis admisit fragilitas vel dispositio. Recedunt tandem qui mihi casso labore venerant in auxilium, unicum mihi consilium relinquente[s], ut aperta pontis scissura jumentum*

In this story, rescue comes at the invocation of St. Thomas by a monk who was wearing the ampulla designating him as a pilgrim. The ampulla's only role in this story is to indicate that the monk had a prior relationship with the saint, and was therefore entitled to special protection from the saint. The rescue itself was instigated by prayer.

That relationships between humans and saints mirrored relationships between humans has been demonstrated repeatedly by Peter Brown, Sharon Farmer, Thomas Head, and André Vauchez who have described the nature of human affiliations with saints at different phases of medieval history.[39] Vauchez especially emphasized that a vow of pilgrimage and its fulfillment initiated an ongoing bond between the pilgrim and the saint. In a story that appears in both William's and Benedict's texts, a returned pilgrim who has fallen into the River Tweed invokes the saint in this capacity, crying out, "Hurry and help me, excellent Martyr Thomas, lest your servant perish—I who have recently gone to the holy threshold of your martyrdom—come and aid me, athlete of God, lest your pilgrim be lost!"[40]

The role of pilgrims' signs in these relationships can be clarified here. Whereas the ampullae had contained Canterbury water, which was powerful as a relic, the badges were merely imges.[41] As images,

---

in amnem dejicerem. Sed ab hoc me consilio revocabant lux brevis, imperium patris, cita nox, via longa. Solus itaque soli Deo relictus circumspexi, et non erat auxiliator; quaesivi, et non fuit qui adjuvaret. Unde et in amaritudine animae meae medullatis suspiriis beatissimum martyrem Thomam, cujus sacra collo suspensa gestabam, invocare coepi. Res mira. Protinus indicibili modo, sine humano adminiculo, ad invocationem sancti martyris statuit Dominus equum super pedes suos, et direxit gressus meos, et immisit in os meum canticum novum, carmen Deo nostro, qui est super omnia benedictus in saecula." William, *Miracula*, 6.7, pp. 415–6.

[39] Peter Brown, *The Cult of the Saints: Its Rise and Function in Latin Christianity* (Chicago, 1981); Sharon Farmer, *Communities of Saint Martin: Legend and Rritual in Medieval Tours* (Ithaca, 1991); Thomas Head, *Hagiography and the Cult of the Saints: The Diocese of Orlèans 800–1200* (Cambridge, 1990). Vauchez, *Sainthood in the Later Middle Ages*, pp. 444–53.

[40] "*Succurre, martyr egregie Thoma, ne pereat servus tuus, qui sacrosancta martyrii tui limina nuper adivi. Subveni, athleta Dei, ne peregrinus tuus intereat.*" William, *Miracula*, 3.41, p. 297; Benedict, *Miracula*, 4.3, p. 266. On the medieval topos of saints as God's "athletes," see Colin Eisler, "The Athlete of Virtue. The Iconography of Asceticism," in *De Artibus Opuscula XL, Essays in Honor of Erwin Panofsky*, ed., Millard Meiss (New York, 1961): Vol. 1, pp. 82–97, Vol. 2, pp. 23–6.

[41] This is corollary to the point that an ampulla was "more than a badge," made by Katja Boertjes, "Pelgrimsampullen Uit Nederlandse en Belgische Bodem," in *Heilig en Profaan 2*, eds. H.J.E. van Beuningen, A.M. Koldeweij, D. Kicken (Cothen, 2001), p. 79.

they could not claim the power of relics, although they could function very effectively as labels. Moreover, the increase in the number of surviving pilgrims' badges compared to the number of ampullae may indicate the success of the badge form.

The change from ampullae to badges, begun no earlier than 1270 and perhaps closer to 1300, suggests how both pilgrims and monks expected the signs to function.[42] Ampullae have a dual function in the *miracula*, where they serve simultaneously as portable reliquaries and as social markers that label their wearers. However, the percentage of miracles that describe the objects being used in each way strongly favors the labeling function. The signs' multivalence during the early period when the *miracula* were written was later reduced by the formal change from ampullae to badges that occurred at least a century into the cult.

Thomas Head, writing on Orléans in the period 800–1200, cautions us that, "The relics themselves, however, were not responsible for the miraculous; they did not serve as a direct conduit of some mysterious thaumaturgic radiation. Rather, personal relationships formed between the living and the dead . . . allowed the saint to exercise his *virtus* on behalf of his living servants."[43] This idea is especially important for understanding the change from ampullae to badges. Together, the contexts in which pilgrims' ampullae appear in the *miracula*, and that badges proved to be suitable replacements for ampullae, indicate that the primary function of the pilgrims' signs was to signify the wearer's relationship with the saint.

The pilgrims' signs in the Museum of London result from a series of archaeological excavations conducted between 1972 and 1989. The finds represent the years when St. Thomas' cult was at its height. This collection is as close as it is possible to come to a representative sample of the Canterbury signs in circulation at a given time. This sample shows an increase from six ampullae from contexts from the years 1170–1270 to thirteen badges dating from 1270–1350, a

---

[42] In the absence of documentation, dates can only be established by archaeological context, and thus refer not to production, but to deposition after an unknown interval of use. None of the Canterbury badges can be definitively dated before 1300, Spencer, *Pilgrim Souvenirs*, p. 78. Production of ampullae did not end abruptly with the introduction of badges, but was gradually phased out over the fourteenth century.

[43] Head, *Hagiography and the Cult of the Saints*, p. 12.

peak of sixty badges in the years 1350–1400, and twenty-two dated 1400–1450. These figures represent only those examples found in datable contexts. A fuller picture is obtained by including the many undatable finds as well, in which case the total number of Canterbury ampullae or fragments is sixty-eight, and the total number of Canterbury badges or fragments is 324.[44]

It has been argued by Spencer and others that pilgrims' badges were touch relics, pressed against the shrine to imbue them with supernatural power and render them more similar to ampullae.[45] While it would be in keeping with medieval tradition for this to have been practiced sporadically and by individual choice, the evidence for it as a widespread practice is indirect and limited.[46] However frequently pilgrims performed this act, it did not seem to be the use that determined the objects' form. There is no visual evidence of such behavior at Canterbury, such as imprints of the shrine on surviving badges or images of badges in contact with the reliquary, as we might expect if their primary function had been to serve as touch relics.

Instead of focusing on the ways Canterbury badges could have served as relics, we might more profitably follow the lead suggested by their closest formal kin, English livery badges. Livery badges in England appear from the reign of Edward III (1312–77) on.[47] Some were made of precious materials, but those that survive are cast mostly from pewter and tin. They are similar to pilgrims' badges in terms of material, general size, vocabulary of ornament, method of construction, and like pilgrims' signs, they were worn on the exterior clothing.[48] These formal parallels between pilgrims' badges and

---

[44] Identifications of objects for this count were made by the author, with the assistance of the John Clark and Geoff Eagan of the Museum of London.

[45] Spencer, *Pilgrim Souvenirs*, pp. 16–7.

[46] Some evidence for touching badges to reliquaries comes from the documents pertaining to a two-centuries long dispute at Le Puy between the hospital of St. Mary and the local merchants over the rights to manufacture and sell pilgrims' badges. A fifteenth-century document states that the hospital would allow only "legitimate" badges to be touched to the statue of St. Mary that was the object of pilgrimage. Esther Cohen, "*In haec signa*: Pilgrim-Badge Trade in Southern France, *Journal of Medieval History* 2 (1976), p. 213, fn. 29.

[47] *The Westminster Chronicle, 1381–1394*, eds. Leonard C. Hector and Barbara F. Harvey (Oxford, 1981), pp. 356–67.

[48] A.M. Koldeweij, "Lifting the Veil on Pilgrimage Badges," in *Pilgrimage Explored*, ed. Jennie Stopford (York, 1999), pp. 161–88 pointed out the need for greater inte-

livery badges suggest a shared function, that of signifying affiliations between their wearers and powerful individuals, living or sainted.[49]

Returning to the *miracula* with the similarities to livery badges in mind, we find that the representation of affiliations with the saint was an important function of pilgrims' signs even in the first decades of St. Thomas' cult, when the only signs of this affiliation were ampullae. The special privileges of those who had established relationships with the saint as pilgrims is clearly articulated in a miracle in which a girl lies approaching death from a tumor growing in her womb.

> ... There approached one unknown to her, returning from Canterbury bearing the water of the martyr. Since he had relieved his mind by his proximity to that blessed man, he was able to alleviate her. He [the pilgrim] would direct prayers to him [the saint], so that he [the saint] would raise her from the bed.
>
> She said, "He can't help me, though it would surely be delightful if he could. I have cried out to him many times, and he has not heard me."
>
> "Make a vow, " he said, "And vow that you will go to his tomb in the poorest of clothes, refusing all vehicles, and barefoot." She vowed, and as I recall, swallowed some of the martyr's water. Immediately at that moment, the tumor inside her ruptured...[50]

On one hand, this story provides another example of the miraculous healing power of the relic-water contained in the pilgrim's ampulla. However, Benedict makes it clear that it was not merely the Canterbury water, but the pilgrim's "proximity to that blessed man" that mattered more. Because the man had made a pilgrimage to St. Thomas' tomb, he was especially privileged to have his

---

gration between the study of pilgrims' signs and livery badges. The method of analyzing the miracle stories advocated in this essay, then, is in part an answer to this call.

[49] This parallel is pointed out by Brian Spencer in, *Salisbury and South Wiltshire Museum: Medieval Catalogue, Pilgrim Souvenirs and Secular Badges* (Salisbury, 1990), p. 95 and Spencer, *Pilgrims Souvenirs*, p. 278.

[50] "... *institit unus ex notis ejus, a Cantuaria revertens, aquamque martyris afferens, quatenus ad beatum illum mentem levaret, ut ille allevaret eam; ad illum preces dirigeret, ut eam ille de lecto erigeret. At illa, 'Non potest me adjuvare, juvisset quippe si posset; clamavi enim ad ipsum multoties, et non exaudivit me.' 'Insta'" inquit, 'adhuc, votumque martyri vove adituram te ad sepulchrum illius abjectis lineis, vehiculo contempto, pedibus nudis.' Vovit et, ut memini, de martyris aqua gustavit. Statim in momento ruptus est tumor ille interius...*" Benedict, *Miracula*, 4.53, pp. 221–2.

prayers answered by the saint. Although the girl does drink some of the Canterbury water, it is her vow that she would go to his tomb that instigates her cure.

Pilgrims' ampullae were able to play a double role as agents of miraculous events by virtue of the Canterbury water that they contained, and as markers of their owners' ties to the saint. However, the analysis of the collection as a whole indicates that their more consistent function is to mark their wearers as affiliates of the saint. Out of 712 miracles, only twelve involve ampullae as direct agents of the miraculous. On the other hand, 206 miracles were performed on behalf of people in exchange for a vow of devotion to the saint. In addition, forty-seven miracles were performed for people with prior relationships to the saint or for former pilgrims, of which thirteen were second cures of people who had previously benefited from miracles. A further twenty-six describe the saint's punishments of people who failed to perform their promised devotions. These figures demonstrate the importance of an ongoing relationship with the saint represented by a pilgrims' sign.[51]

While the miracles tell us about the ideas prevalent in the first decade after Becket's murder, these ideas were clarified later as the cult reached its maximum popularity in the late thirteenth and early fourteenth century. The shift at the end of the thirteenth century from ampullae, which were both portable reliquaries and insignia of affiliation, to badges, which were purely the latter, can be explained as a change from a dual-purpose object to a form that served only the more important role of insignia, but served that purpose with greater clarity.

Benedicta Ward has described the cult of St. Thomas as both a "traditional" cult focused on the site of Thomas' bodily relics, and also a more personal cult, geographically dispersed, and focused on proper fulfillment of obligations of devotion.[52] As we have seen, ampullae were well attuned to the more traditional aspects of the cult. As William and Benedict made explicit in the 1170s, they desired that the fame of St. Thomas be spread throughout the world, a

---

[51] For a more extended analysis of the *Miracula Sancti Thomae Cantuariensis* see my dissertation "Signs of Affinity: Canterbury Pilgrims' Signs Contextualized, 1171–1538" (Ph.D. diss., Emory University, 2003).

[52] Ward, *Miracles*, pp. 97, 109.

process that, by its success, necessarily drew devotional attention away from Canterbury itself. In the absence of a miracle collection from the latter years of the Canterbury pilgrimage, there is perhaps no better indication of the depth of this change than the pilgrims' signs themselves, whose formal change from ampulla to badge makes visible the ideological substance of devotion.[53]

The suggestions presented here concerning the changing form of Canterbury pilgrims' signs and the way these changes speak to the meaning of the signs for their wearers are based on a reading of the *Miracula Sancti Thomae Cantuariensis* as a complete text, rather than depending on exceptional examples. They are corroborated by the archaeological circumstances in which so many Canterbury signs have been found, as items disposed of, rather than cherished, and also by the substantial change from exclusively ampullae to mostly badges after the thirteenth century. Naturally, we should assume variety in the way individual pilgrims regarded their ampullae and badges, and both the miracles and the condition of the surviving badges indicate such latitude. However, exceptions should not be confused with the norm. Instead, exceptions should be looked at against a backdrop of norms, especially since the medieval authors of miracle collections employed this very principle.

---

[53] The *Miracula* continued to be compiled for about eleven years after Becket's canonization in 1173. Later promotions of the cult took other forms including liturgies and artistic and architectural projects.

CHAPTER NINETEEN

"SHAMELESS AND NAKED IMAGES": OBSCENE BADGES AS PARODIES OF POPULAR DEVOTION

Jos Koldeweij

Over the past few decades, thanks to the aid of the metal-detector, in the course of excavations carried out by both official and amateur archeologists, a vast quantity of small medieval metal objects has been unearthed in the Low Countries, which include a spectacular number of lead-tin pilgrim badges. (fig. 232) All of them were mass-produced and must have been widely distributed from the early thirteenth century until about 1550. A systematic inventory of these popular trinkets has resulted in the publication of more than two thousand religious and profane badges found in Dutch and Flemish soil.[1] A survey of this important historico-cultural material, a visual source of information about late-medieval popular culture, is particularly surprising in that it shows an almost equal incidence of religious and secular images. Finds of badges from outside the Netherlands show that the phenomenon of mass-produced lead-tin trinkets was known throughout Northwest Europe, but far fewer objects of an erotic nature have been found in the British Isles. This article draws attention to a specific group within this rich material: obscene badges dating from the period from *c.* 1350–*c.* 1450—objects which seem to mock pilgrims and religious processions.

---

[1] H.J.E. Van Beuningen, A.M. Koldeweij, *Heilig en profaan. 1000 laatmiddeleeuwse insignes uit de collectie H.J.E. van Beuningen, Rotterdam Papers* 8 (Cothen, 1993); A.M. Koldeweij, "The Wearing of Significative Badges, Religious and Secular: The Social Meaning of a Behavioural Pattern," in *Showing Status. Representation of Social Positions in the Late Middle Ages*, ed. W. Blockmans & A. Janse (Turnhout, 1999), pp. 307–28; H.J.E. Van Beuningen, A.M. Koldeweij & D. Kicken, *Heilig en Profaan 2. 1200 Laatmiddeleeuwse insignes uit openbare en particuliere collecties, Rotterdam Papers* 12 (Cothen, 2001).

Genuine Pilgrims and Dissemblers

In Geoffrey Chaucer's *Canterbury Tales*, the Wife of Bath (fig. 233) personifies the pleasure-seeker rather than the pious pilgrim.[2] Her moral views are clear from Chaucer's description in his General Prologue and from her own Prologue. The Wife of Bath, in the company travelling to Canterbury, symbolizes all those who regarded a "pilgrimage" as an opportunity for erotic adventure. She was certainly not lacking in experience: "And thries hadde she been at Jerusalem; She hadde passed many a straunge stem; At Rome she hadde been, and at Boloigne, In Galice at Seint Jame, and at Coloigne. She koude muchel of wandrynge by the weye. Gat-tothed was she, soothly for to seye."[3] Her travels, then, have taken her to Jerusalem three times, across many a strange river, to Rome, to Boulogne-sur-Mer, to Galicia and St. James of Compostela, and to Cologne; she knows all about life on the road. She prides herself on her wide-spaced teeth, which have unmistakably erotic connotations—as she herself points out in her Prologue: "Gat-tothed I was, and that bicam me weel; I hadde the prente of seinte Venus seel,"[4] adding that she stood under Venus' protection ...[5] There was nothing about her appearance to suggest a pilgrimage; she does not seem to have pinned to her clothing any tokens of her *Peregrinationes Maiores*, the three most important Christian pilgrimages,[6] nor from any of the other places on her itinerary, but such souvenirs would, of course, have been religious badges and hence, less suited to her purpose.

In certain passages from the *Canterbury Tales*, Chaucer mentions such badges and other devotionalia. The *Tales* are perhaps an account of the pilgrimage to the shrine of Thomas Becket in 1387. It is quite possible that Chaucer himself went there to pray for the recovery of his ailing wife, who died later that summer. In that case, the tales could be a direct report of what he heard, saw, and thought about

---

[2] The editions consulted and quoted here are Geoffrey Chaucer, *Geoffrey Chaucer, De vertellingen van de pelgrims naar Kantelberg, Prisma-boeken* 1506, trans. A.J. Barnouw (Utrecht, 1974); Geoffrey Chaucer, *The Works of Geoffrey Chaucer*, ed. F.N. Robinson (Oxford, 1983).

[3] *Canterbury Tales*, ed. Robinson, p. 21, I 463–8.

[4] *Canterbury Tales*, ed. Robinson, p. 82, III 603–4.

[5] *Canterbury Tales*, trans. Barnouw, p. 537, fn. 21; *Canterbury Tales*, ed. Robinson, p. 663, fn. 468.

[6] To Rome, Jerusalem, and Santiago de Compostela.

on the way. Yet Chaucer had temporarily fallen out of grace at royal court, and between 1386 and 1389, when the *Tales* were written, he was living in Kent, on one of the busy roads to Canterbury; perhaps the framework of his narrative was inspired by the continuous, motley procession of pilgrims on their way to Canterbury, sporting their souvenirs and particularly—on the homeward journey—Becket badges.

The first person introduced by Chaucer in his Prologue to the Tales is the knight whose story opens the framework narrative. This gentleman, Chaucer tells us, was noted for his extensive peregrinations in Christian and heathen lands.[7] His journeys had taken him from Russia and Lithuania to Granada and Turkey and, St. Christopher being the patron saint of travellers, he wore a "Christopher on his brest of silver sheen,"[8] but there is no Christopher badge in the miniature of the knight in the famous Ellesmere manuscript,[9] in which most of Chaucer's descriptions are illustrated in faithful detail.[10] Late medieval Christopher badges and pendants were made of tin-lead as well as silver,[11] such as the contemporary ring-brooch showing a knight (St. George) and St. Christopher.[12] (fig. 235)

The Pardoner or indulgence-seller is the only pilgrim wearing a badge in the Ellesmere manuscript's well-known and frequently copied illustrations. Pinned to his hat is a clearly identifiable Roman Vera Icon: a small piece of parchment with a painted face of Christ. (fig. 234) This cheap though "precious" badge makes him recognizable not so much as a pilgrim coming from Rome, but as a hawker demonstrating how to use his merchandise.

From the dignified prioress's arm hung a rosary, "and thereon heng a brooch of gold ful sheene,/On which ther was first write a

---

[7] *Canterbury Tales*, ed. Robinson, p. 17, I 49–50.
[8] *Canterbury Tales*, ed. Robinson, p. 18, I 115.
[9] San Marino, California, Huntingdon Library, Ms. 26.C.9.
[10] Theo Stemmler, *The Ellesmere Miniatures of the Canterbury Pilgrims*, Poetria Mediaevalis II (Mannheim 1977), pp. 2–3.
[11] Ronald Lightbown, *Mediaeval European Jewellery—with a Catalogue of the Collection in the Victoria and Albert Museum* (London, 1992), pp. 99, 172, 226, 382, 383, 495, 515; Van Beuningen & Koldeweij, *Heilig en profaan*, pp. 130–1, figs. 58–68; Brian Spencer, *Pilgrim Souvenirs and Secular Badges, Medieval Finds from Excavations in London* 7 (London, 1998), pp. 180–1; Van Beuningen, Koldeweij & Kicken, *Heilig en Profaan* 2, p. 251, figs. 1070–1.
[12] Lightbown, *Mediaeval Jewellery*, pp. 226, 495, cat. 17.

crowned A,/And after *Amor vincit omnia.*"[13] The interpretation assigned here to a badge with the letter A appeared on the brooch itself in the form of a Latin proverb. In this case there is no doubt that by all-conquering love the prioress' love of God is meant; in a different context the brooch could be a reference to earthly love. The parallel with the lead-tin crowned A-brooches is suggestive to say the least: these amorous trinkets can refer as well both to spiritual and earthly love.[14] On the miniature in the Ellesmere manuscript the red rosary can be clearly seen, but the letter-brooch is absent.

The portrait of the author in the famous Ellesmere manuscript of the *Canterbury Tales* shows Chaucer riding along in the procession, a pen-case round his neck identifying him as the author. He has that same attribute in the miniature painted in Thomas Hoccleve's early fifteenth-century *De Regimine Principum.*[15] (fig. 236) The pen-case was formerly mistakenly interpreted as a pilgrim ampulla worn by Chaucer to denote the Canterbury pilgrimage; ampullae containing a curative fluid—St. Thomas's blood, diluted over and over again with water—had been sold at Canterbury since the late twelfth century.[16]

Chaucer's unfinished *Canterbury Tales* were continued by an anonymous author in *The Tale of Beryn*, with a highly-detailed account of how badges were sold to pilgrims. The typical pilgrimage souvenirs were obviously much in demand, and the company of travellers broke their journey for the express purpose of purchasing them: "Then, as the usual custom is, pilgrim signs they bought/For men at home should know what saint the pilgrims here had sought./ Each man laid out his silver on the tokens he liked best . . ./They set their tokens on their heads, some on their caps did pin . . ."[17] But for the Miller and the Pardoner the temptation of these shiny badges was too strong: "And while they were all doing this, the Miller then had pressed/His bosom full of tokens of Canterbury brooches/Which the Pardoner and he at last, secretly in their pouches/Hid there with such cleverness that none of theme would

---

[13] *Canterbury Tales*, ed. Robinson, p. 18, I, 160–2.
[14] Van Beuningen & Koldeweij, *Heilig en Profaan*, p. 311 figs. 962–65; Spencer, *Pilgrim Souvenirs*, pp. 320–1; Van Beuningen, Koldeweij & Kicken, *Heilig en Profaan 2*, p. 442, figs. 1967–8.
[15] London, The British Library, Harley MS 4866, fol. 88.
[16] *Editor's note, see Katja Boertjes' article on ampullae in this volume.
[17] Spencer, *Pilgrim Souvenirs*, p. 15.

know/Except the Summoner who saw and said to both then 'ho!/ You must go halves with me,' whispering in their ears." Exactly which souvenirs they purchased is not known, but a wide range of badges could be bought at Canterbury. There is no complete survey as yet; new archeological finds continue to yield hitherto unknown badges and ampullae or variants of known examples which pilgrims wore round their necks or pinned to their clothes.[18]

All Kinds of Merchandise

A well-known Bible passage relates how Christ, at the beginning of the Passion, casts out the money-changers and tradesmen from the temple (Matthew 21,12–13; Mark 11,15–16; Luke 19,45–46, John 2,13–16), saying: "Take these things hence; make not my Father's house a house of merchandise." (John 2, 16) Yet places of pilgrimage were buzzing with commercial activity, especially on feast-days. In many towns the church had an interest in, and sometimes even a monopoly on, the production and sale of a varied assortment of devotionalia. The Onze-Lieve-Vrouwekerk (Church of Our Lady) at Bollezeele (French Flanders) for example was no exception. In 1483 the parish priest there explained his large and splendid church to a pilgrim: "All this was paid for by the offerings of pilgrims who came in large numbers and found consolation from Our Lady and purchased badges at the door."[19]

A few late-medieval representations of the sale of pilgrim tokens and other devotionalia illustrate the situation. In the *Wolfgang Missal*

---

[18] Van Beuningen & Koldeweij, *Heilig en Profaan*, pp. 198–9, figs. 361–9; Spencer, *Pilgrim Souvenirs*, pp. 37–133; A.M Koldeweij, "'Te Sente Thomas van Cantelberghe, in Inghelant . . .' Pelgrimsinsignes en pelgrimstochten naar Thomas Becket," in *Thomas Becket in Vlaanderen. Waarheid of legende?* ed. R. Bauer (Kortrijk, 2000), pp. 49–72; A.M. Koldeweij, "'Tsente Thomas te Cantelberghe.' Pelgrimstochten vanuit de Nederlanden naar Canterbury: teruggevonden insignes en berichten uit andere bron," in Van Beuningen, Koldeweij & Kicken, *Heilig en Profaan 2*, pp. 88–104; Brian Spencer, "Canterbury Pilgrim Souvenirs Found in the Low Countries," in Van Beuningen, Koldeweij & Kicken, *Heilig en Profaan 2*, pp. 105–11; Van Beuningen, Koldeweij & Kicken, *Heilig en Profaan 2*, pp. 297–303, figs. 1275–91.

[19] Jonathan Sumption, *Pilgrimage, an Image of Mediaeval Religion* (London, 1975), p. 161. No Bollezeele badges or pilgrim pennons, cited in later archive records, have been found; R. van der Linden, *Mariabedevaartvaantjes. Volksdevotie op 1175 vaantjes* (Brugge, 1988), p. 76 no. B95.

(1492/3), kept in the Cistercian monastery of Rein (Styria, Austria), the text for the Feast of the Dedication is headed by an historiated initial showing a view of the abbey complex. In the grounds, inside the abbey walls, as a procession is preparing to leave, some pilgrims approach the gates through which a single figure has just passed. Standing at the gate is a vendor with a array of attractive merchandise.[20] The 1524 *Santiago Window*, from the Minster at Freiburg in Breisgau, shows a market stall at the entrance to the church, where churchgoers could buy a variety of religious objects, including pilgrim badges in the form of a St. James' scallop shell.[21]

Around the middle of the sixteenth century, Pieter Aertsen (1507/8–75) painted his *Return from a St. Anthony Pilgrimage*.[22] A long procession of pious church-goers issues from the chapel in the background; in the foreground some of them walk past a large wooden cross. Midway between this cross and St. Anthony's chapel are two stalls which offer a large and varied selection of wares.[23] In addition to devotional objects such as crucifixes and figures of saints, there are sheathed knives, pewter plates, and all kinds of toys. Similar examples can be cited to illustrate the commercial activities related to popular devotion.[24] While such activites were deplored centuries before in the New Testament, the souvenir trade that flourished in the direct vicinity of holy places due to the large numbers of pilgrims in the later Middle Ages now attracted the criticism. The practice was censured in a text attributed to Jean Gerson (1363–1429), chancellor of the University of Paris and a scathing critic of many expressions of popular religion. Gerson focuses his critical comments on the objects frequently for sale.[25] The author expatiates on the

---

[20] Stift Rein, Codex 206, fol. 247v.

[21] Nuremberg, Germanisches Nationalmuseum, documentation Prof. Dr. Kurt Köster. *Stadtische Museen Freiburg. Augustinermuseum. Führer durch die Sammlungen* (Freiburg i. Br., 1978), p. 92.

[22] Brussels, Koninklijke Musea voor Schone Kunsten, inv. Oude Kunst 7524, oak panel, 110 × 170 cm.

[23] For the toys see A.M. Willemsen, *Kinder Delijt. Middeleeuws speelgoed in de Nederlanden* (Nijmegen, 1998), pp. 66, 115, 128, 270–2.

[24] Willemsen, *Kinder Delijt*, pp. 271–3 examines Pieter van der Borcht's print,*Guild Feast with Procession of the Marksmen, c.* 1550, where three market stalls have been set up right next to the church.

[25] Johannes Gerson, *Opera Omnia* (Antwerpen, 1706), III cols. 291–2. Cited by Jean Wirth in *Iconoclasm. Vie et mort de l'image médiévale*, ed. C. Dupeux, P. Jezler & J. Wirth (Bern, 2001), p. 256, cat. 107–8.

evil influences to which young people are exposed by lewd pictures and suchlike, making explicit mention of the "shameless and naked images displayed for sale in churches and during church festivals." The author is obviously alluding here to the various ex-votos produced as votive offerings bought and sold for feasts of dedication in churches and chapels—representations of every conceivable part of the body as well as the most bizarre scenes. Possibly the author is also referring to erotic badges: cheap, lead-tin amulets and pins of an obscene nature. Late-medieval erotica of this kind turn up in an archeological context with astonishing frequency and in mind-boggling variety among pilgrim badges, devotional and other popular ornaments.[26]

Misjudged Badges and Other Erotica

The Frenchman Arthur Forgeais, who in the 1860s, having already published his collection of pilgrim badges (later given to the Musée de Cluny in Paris),[27] was probably the first author to write about medieval erotic badges. Entitled *Priapées*, and almost forgotten today, his small, sixteen-page brochure described six erotic badges and a number of gaming chips or counters, all found in the Seine and decorated with male and female sexual organs. The booklet must have appeared around 1865/6.[28] Despite this early publication, the public—certainly a more general public—found it hard to accept the fact that this material had its place in "our" immediate past history, in the Christian, late-medieval western world. The medieval erotic badges went either unrecognised or unacknowledged, or were dubbed

---

[26] For an overview see: Van Beuningen & Koldeweij, *Heilig en Profaan*, pp. 254–64 figs. 610–68; Denis Bruna, *Enseignes de Pèlerinage et Enseignes Profanes* (Paris, 1996), pp. 317–21, cat. 607–14; Van Beuningen, Koldeweij & Kicken 2001, pp. 406–13 fig. 1724–79; Malcolm Jones, "Een andere kijk op profane insignes," in *Heilig en Profaan. Laatmiddeleeuwse insignes in cultuurhistorisch perspectief*, ed. A.M. Koldeweij & A. Willemsen (Amsterdam, 1995), pp. 64–74; Malcolm Jones, "The Sexual and the Secular Badges," in Van Beuningen, Koldeweij & Kicken, *Heilig en Profaan 2*, pp. 196–206.

[27] Bruna, *Enseignes de Pèlerinage*, pp. 20–8.

[28] Arthur Forgeais, *Priapées* (n.d., probably Paris, 1865). The earliest of the illustrated finds were made in 1865; as cited by Thomas Wright (who adopted some of the illustrations) in *The Worship of the Generative Powers During the Middle Ages of Western Europe* (1866) reprinted in *A History of Phallic Worship* (New York, 1992), II, pp. 59–65, pls. IX–X.

"antique," "Roman," and "heathen." A late-medieval wooden phallus excavated on the Norwegian coast near Bergen raised those very questions: its function is puzzling, three possibilities were suggested when it was published—a "toy"(!), an "amulet," and a "votive offering."[29] A relief on the choir-stalls in St. Peter's Church at Oirschot in North-Brabant (1508–11), destroyed by fire in World War II, showed a jester with an identical huge phallus in his hands. The carving was not illustrated in the 1941 publication on these choir-stalls; instead, it was described as the "figure of a fat jester . . . On his head is a fool's cap and in his hands an object resembling a pig's bladder or a rumbling-pot."[30] (fig. 237) In the 1976 pewter catalogue of the Kunstgewerbemuseum at Cologne two badges in the form of winged phallic creatures, one of them hung with a bell, were still described as *spätantik* (late antique), (fig. 238) and the unmistakably medieval, gigantic phallus of a man with a small dog, surrounded by an illegible text border, is described as a *nicht identifizierbarer Gegenstand* (unidentifiable object).[31] (fig. 239) In the catalogue of the exhibition *Stadtluft, Hirsebrei und Bettelmönch* (City Air, Gruel and Mendicant Friars), which even merited a reprint in 1992, the medieval erotic badge was unacknowledged. A really special find from Konstanz (fig. 240) was deemed *unklar* (unclear). The catalogue describes it as a "nude, female figure, recognisable as a smith because she is shaping a workpiece on an anvil while standing at the blazing forge . . ."[32] The description fails to do justice to the industrious craftswoman and the workpiece on the anvil, for the object being fashioned from the incandescent metal by the naked smith is a winged phallus!

Many other finds of medieval objects have shown that the erotic, titillating badges should not be regarded as isolated, late-medieval curiosities. The tradition in which we ought to see them is as old

---

[29] A.E. Herteig, *Kongers havn og handels sete. Fra de arkeologiske undersøkelser på Bryggen i Bergen 1955–68* (Oslo, 1969), fig. 18.

[30] M. Coppens & C. van Goirle, *De koorbanken van Oirschot fotografisch gezien* (Eindhoven, 1941), p. 70; M. Coppens & Pater Concordius (van Goirle), *De Sint-Petruskerk van Oirschot en haar koorgestoelte* (1941, repr. Eindhoven, 1980), p. 31, fig. 80. "Rommelpot": a noisemaker carried around on Twelfth Night, a pot covered with a pig's bladder, pierced to admit a straw which when moistened and moved up and down causes the bladder to vibrate (translator's note).

[31] H.-U. Haedeke, *Zinn* (Cologne, 1976), p. 56, cat. 9a–b, p. 74, cat. 67.

[32] M. & N. Flüeler, *Stadtluft, Hirsebrei und Bettelmönch. Die Stadt um 1300* (Zurich, 1992), pp. 434–5.

as humankind itself, and archetypal.[33] Good parallels to the medieval world of imagination as far as phalluses and phallic creatures are concerned are to be found in, for instance, Greek Antiquity, notably on painted vases dating from the sixth and fifth century B.C.: with winged phalluses, phallic biped and quadruped creatures, collections of phalluses in baskets, and "stand-alone" phalluses.[34] The Romans, too, bequeathed us a variety of phallic objects such as amulets and the phallus-tintinnabula—little bronze bells suspended from a winged phallus;[35] by comparison, incidentally, the Roman erotica exhibit a remarkably high degree of abstraction and differ markedly from the almost absurd, realistic medieval fantasies. Nevertheless, one notices a striking resemblance to the late-medieval iconographic tradition, although this much older material cannot be obviously related to it in terms of a continuous tradition. These representations do, however, prove that we are not dealing with the occasional fantasy here— not in the prehistoric, Greek and Roman material, nor in that of the late Middle Ages. The odd example shows that the line from prehistoric or antique sexual images, imagery and the concomitant— albeit if not gradually—changing customs continues into and after the Middle Ages. A good example is the Cerne Abbas Giant on a hillside in Dorset, south England. (fig. 241) Outlined by deep trenches cut into the chalk rock, the naked figure is some sixty meters tall. It was long thought to date from shortly before the beginning of the Christian era, but recent suggestions place it in a much later, per- haps even post-medieval period.[36] The giant brandishes a huge cudgel

---

[33] A. Daniélou, *Der Phallus. Metapher des Lebens, Quelle des Glücks—Symbole und Riten in Geschichte und Kunst* (Munich, 1998).

[34] Jones, "The Sexual and Secular Badges"; Eva Keuls, *The Reign of the Phallus. Sexual Politics in Ancient Athens* (Berkeley, 1985).

[35] A fine example in an early nineteenth-century sheath is in a private Danish collection: A. Dierichs, "Klingendes Kleinod. Ein unbekanntes Tintinnabulum in Dänemark," *Antike Welt* 30 (1999), pp. 145–9.

[36] Bournemouth University commissioned an enquiry in 1996, but no definitive anwers were given. The earliest written reference to the giant obviously occurs in the Churchwardens' accounts for 1694 when some money was paid "for repairing the Giant." Nigel Clarke is rather careful in his recent guide on chalk carvings and mentions several possibilities (post-medieval, Celtic or Roman). Thomas Hinde, *The Domesday Book: England's Heritage Then and Now* (London, 2002) dates the Cerne Abbas Giant to the first century A.D. as a Hercules or 150 years earlier as a Celtic figure. N. Clarke, *The Rude Man of Cerne Abbas and other Wessex Landscape Oddities* (Lyme Regis, no date), pp. 5–7; Hinde, *The Domesday Book*, p. 92; *Cerne Abbas Dorset*, leaflet of the Cerne Historical Society, *c.* 2002.

in his right hand above his head, an intimidating gesture which, as in one of the margin decorations in a Paris manuscript of the *Roman de la Rose* of c. 1350,[37] is counterpointed by an impressive erection. Formerly thought to avert evil, the Cerne Abbas Giant has been turned by popular belief into a fertility symbol. A centuries-old local tradition has it that a night spent with the virile giant will bless barren women with children, a superstition that persists to this day. The figure's nude maleness has lost none of its impact, as was demonstrated in the summer of 1993, when a copy of the giant was made on the site of a big pop music festival in the direct vicinity of the "real" one—but emasculated!

Living Phalluses

Isolated genitalia also occur as decorative motifs on medieval household utensils—sometimes even dictating the shape of such objects. A late fourteenth-century earthenware plate—a waster—found in Aardenburg, Zealand Flanders, is decorated with a phallus in white-yellow slip.[38] On view in the Stadtmuseum, Siegburg, along with numerous examples of local stoneware, is a jug dating from the second half of the fifteenth century, its body decorated with three phalluses in relief. More explicitly erotic are the drinking-glasses made in the form of phalluses during the late medieval or early modern era in Germany and, probably, the Netherlands.[39] (fig. 242) Relatively

[37] A.M. Koldeweij, "A Barefaced *Roman de la Rose* (Paris, BN MS français 25526) and some Late Medieval Mass-Produced Badges of Sexual Content," in *Flanders in a European Perspective, Manuscript Illumination around 1400 in Flanders and Abroad*, ed. M. Smeyers & B. Cardon (Leuven, 1995), pp. 499–516. On the same margin illustrations see Michael Camille, *Image on the Edge. The Margins of Medieval Art* (London, 1992), pp. 147–9; G. Bartz, A. Karnein & C. Lange, *Liebesfreude im Mittelalter* (Stuttgart, 1994), pp. 54–5; M. Müller, *Minnebilder. Französische Minnedarstellungen des 13. und 14. Jahrhunderts* (Cologne, 1996), pp. 53–6, 161.

[38] Now in the collection of the Municipal Archeological Museum at Aardenburg. J.A. Trimpe Burger, "Aardenburgse potterbakkerswaar," *Mededelingenblad Nederlandse Vereniging van Vrienden van de Ceramiek* 72 (1974), pp. 2–12, fig. 5; A. van Dongen, "Het gebruiksvoorwerp als draagteken," in Koldeweij & Willemsen, *Laatmiddeleeuwse insignes*, p. 83.

[39] E. Baumgartner, *Glas des späten Mittelalters. Die Sammlung Karl Amendt* (Dusseldorf, 1987), p. 104, cat. 126; E. Baumgartner & I. Krueger, *Phönix aus Sand und Asche. Glas des Mittelalters* (Munich, 1988), pp. 421–2, cat. 530; Koldeweij, "A Barefaced *Roman de la Rose*," pp. 18–20.

large numbers of these obscene glasses have turned up in the mean-
time, but none can be dated prior to the late fifteenth century. This
is remarkable in view of the fact that the Romans had phallus glasses.
The recent discovery of one such glass is interesting in view of its
archeological context: the drain of the abbess (!) of the convent at
Herford in northern Germany.[40] Oddly, and in marked contrast to
the abundance of phallic brooches, no examples of this type of glass
are known from the high Middle Ages.

Of course there are countless parallels, both visual and literary,
for the sexual badges, particularly in old French fabliaux, where surprising analogies are to be found.[41] Of particular interest is the frequent appearance of autonomous sexual organs in the fabliaux in
exactly the same guise as their badge counterparts. "Detached sexual organs are an integral part of the representation of the body in
the fabliaux and more the rule than the exception" R. Howard Bloch
states in *The Scandal of the Fabliaux*.[42] Mention has already been made
of the Paris *Roman de la Rose* manuscript of *c.* 1350, in which phalluses nest high up in the trees, acting quite independently. Among
hundreds of other illustrations in the manuscript are eight spectacular erotic margin decorations which clearly convey the same apotropaic
meaning which must also be attributed to the badges.[43] More than
a century later, in 1487, the Dominican monks and inquisitors Jacob
Sprenger and Heinrich Institoris gave a similar description in their
infamous *Malleus Maleficarum*. Among the many examples of witchcraft they cite are repeated reports of the greatly-feared loss of male
fertility. Sexual organs were detached from their rightful owners,
bewitched and hidden: ". . . in considerable numbers, twenty to thirty
male sexual organs . . . in a bird's nest, where they move like living

---

[40] H. Grewe & M. Wemhoff, "Die 'Frau von Herford' und ihr Hausrat," in *Ein
Land macht Geschichte. Archäologie in Nordrhein-Westfalen*, ed. H.G. Horn (Cologne, 1995),
p. 320. My thanks to Stephan Lütgert for drawing my attention to this glass and
to the Siegburg jug.

[41] J.B. Bedaux, "Profane en sacrale amuletten," in Koldeweij and Willemsen,
Laatmiddeleeuwse insignes, pp. 26–35; Jones,"Een andere kijk op profane insignes,"
1995; J. van Os, "Seks in de 13de-eeuwse fabliaux: literaire voorlopers van de erotische insignes?" in Koldeweij and Willemsen, *Laatmiddeleeuwse insignes*, pp. 36–43.

[42] R. Howard Bloch, *The Scandal of the Fabliaux* (Chicago, 1986), p. 63.

[43] Koldeweij, "A Barefaced *Roman de la Rose*," pp. 499–516; Camille, *Image on the
Edge*, pp. 147–9; Bartz, Karnein & Lange, *Liebesfreude im Mittelalter*, pp. 54–5; Müller,
Minnebilder, pp. 53–6, 161.

beings, feeding on corn and other nourishment. . . ."[44] A similar gigantic, winged phallic creature is depicted on a late-fifteenth-century
copper plate engraved on one side with an erotic scene.[45] (fig. 243)
No old prints from the presumably northern-Italian plate are known.
It shows a couple copulating on a Gothic seat, behind which a life-
size phallus with a tail and a bell rears up on its claws. A banderole curling round the couple bears the still unexplained text
PURINEGA T(EN)EDURO. Another, more allegorical, erotic print
was taken from the other side of the plate. A similar phallic animal
was drawn in the margin at the top of a page from a copy of
Johannis Andrea's *Novella in librum tertium Decretalium Gregorii IX* of
1392.[46] A bell is tied round this creature too, which has been shot
from behind by—of all things—a huntress's arrow. (fig. 244) Shooting
the phallus seems to be the wrong way round: surely it is the huntress
who is meant to be hit? Be that as it may, we are confronted here
with the same imaginary world as the one on the badges: those who
wore these sexual amulets undoubtedly wanted to hunt or be hunted.

Pietro Aretino

So far no contemporary representations of medieval men or women
wearing these erotic, amulet-like badges have been found. Nevertheless,
in view of the frequency with which they turn up among other late-
medieval finds, they were surely worn by many people, and in view
of the cheapness of these popular mass-produced souvenirs, they were

---

[44] J. Sprenger & H. Institoris, *Malleus Maleficarum* (1487), ed. J.W.R. Schmidt, *Der Hexenhammer* (Berlin, 1937/8), II p. 56 (II, Question 1, Kapitel 7).

[45] Washington, National Gallery of Art. J.A. Levenson, K. Oberhuber & J.L. Sheehan, *Early Italian Engravings from the National Gallery of Art* (Washington, 1973), pp. 526–7, Appendix A (Konrad Oberhuber). Thanks to Dr. Fritz Koreny, Wien, who drew my attention to this spectacular copper plate. Koldeweij, "A Barefaced *Roman de la Rose*," pp. 21–2.

[46] 45 Paris, Bibliothèque Nationale, Ms lat. 4014, fol. 1. J.B. Bedaux, "Functie en betekenis van randdecoratie in middeleeuwse handschriften", *Kunstlicht* 14 (1993), p. 31; Bedaux, "Profane en sacrale amuletten," pp. 28–9; Koldeweij, "The Wearing of Significative Badges," pp. 172, 186. Malcolm Jones also referred to this manuscript in a lecture in Vienna in November 1991, in which he also mentioned the Washington copper plate: Malcolm Jones, "Sex and Sexuality in Late Medieval and Early Modern Art," in *Privatisierung der Triebe. Sexualität in der frühen Neuzeit*, ed. D. Erlach, M. Reisenleitner and K. Vocelka (Frankfurt am Main, 1994), pp. 187–304; Jones, "The Secular Badges," pp. 104, 108, fn. 47.

certainly not intended for the upper classes. Therefore the lack of both visual and written sources is not surprising, since the poor leave very few traces. There is currently only one extant, relatively-late, text about the wearing of phallic amulets, coming from an Italian upper-class source. In a letter to his friend Battista Zatti from Brescia, the poet Pietro Aretino writes that when he successfully petitioned Pope Clement VII (1478–1534) to release Marcantonio Raimondi in 1524, he desired to see the prints that had landed Raimondi in prison.[47] The moment Aretino set eyes on them, he had the same flash of imagination as that which had inspired Giulio Romano to make the original drawings from which Raimondi had taken prints. Aretino subsequently wrote candid sonnets to *I Modi*, sixteen erotic prints of naked lovers. In his opinion lovemaking ought to be seen: it was better to cover the hands or the mouth than the member from which all human life stems . . .: "It seems more to me that the organ of procreation bestowed upon us by nature should be worn as a pendant around the neck or as a medal on the hat. . . ."[48] We do not know if this was actually a custom in Aretino's times, but we should certainly not rule out the possibility that he may have been familiar with ancient Roman pendants and brooches, and perhaps also with the late-medieval kind discussed here.[49] At any rate, a few scrawls, probably by Leonardo da Vinci's apprentice, servant and model, in the *Codex Atlanticus*, perhaps from around 1493, confirm that phallus creatures were known in Italy around 1500.[50] (fig. 245)

---

[47] Aretino's letter dated December 15, 1537, was probably written earlier, in 1527, as a letter of dedication for the sonnets. Aretino, *Pietro Aretino, I Modi. Stellungen. Die Sonette des göttlichen Pietro Aretino zu den Kupfern Marcantonio Raimondi*, ed. and transl. Thomas Hettche (Frankfurt am Main, 1997), p. 82, fn. 12.

[48] Aretino ed. 1997, p. 9; J.B. Bedaux, "Laatmiddeleeuwse sexuele amuletten. Een sociobiologische benadering,"in *Annus Quadriga Mundi. Opstellen over middeleeuwse kunst opgedragen aan prof. dr. Anna C. Esmeijer, Clavis Kunsthistorische Monografieën* 8 (Utrecht, 1989), pp. 26–7.

[49] Bedaux, "Laatmiddeleeuwse sexuele amuletten," pp. 26–7, interprets the text as proof that phallus-amulets were also worn "normally."

[50] C. Zammiattio, A. Marinoni & A.M. Brizio, *Leonardo der Forscher* (Stuttgart, 1987), pp. 155–65.

Erotic Parodies

The phallus brooches and other erotic badges seem a far cry from pilgrim tokens and other devotional accessories. Nevertheless, they all belong to the same large and highly varied group of late-medieval, cheap, mass-produced, popular trinkets. Brooches conveying what to us seem quite different kinds of subject-matter were worn in the same social group and perhaps simultaneously by the same or different persons in the same context. Where the archeological circumstances were favorable and the late-medieval metal was conserved, badges of all categories have been encountered close together and some-times in amazing concentrations. Evidently both profane and reli-gious badges were incredibly popular, and, as lucky charms, they all conformed with the late-medieval view of the world. The afore-mentioned text attributed to Jean Gerson would seem to confirm this: offensive to sensitive souls perhaps, but the common pilgrim was not surprised to see what we regard as two extremes—sacred and profane culture—side by side. How close those extremes could be is demonstrated by a number of erotic badges which seem to parody popular piety, pilgrims and their badges. Examples of this genre have been excavated in the Low Countries and in France.

In Rotterdam a fragment showing phallic creatures bearing a stretcher was found, in Bruges a complete example of a variant: a brooch consisting of three phalluses carrying a crowned vulva on a bier.[51] (fig. 246) The association with a religious procession will have been evident to everyone of that period who saw the brooch. About two hundred years after these objects were made, Pieter Bruegel the Younger painted his *Procession with Statues of Cornelius and Anthony*, prob-ably modelled on a work by his father, Bruegel the Elder: simple peasants shouldering statues of their saints on stretchers.[52] (fig. 247) There are plenty of representations made up to hundreds of years earlier to show how traditional this is, such as the shrine of Saint

---

[51] Van Beuningen & Koldeweij, *Heilig en Profaan*, p. 262, figs. 652–3.
[52] Brussels, Koninklijke Musea voor Schone Kunsten, Cat. 671, Inv. 3592: panel (fragment), 26.5 × 36.5 cm. A.M. Koldeweij, "Reliekentoningen, heiligdomsvaarten, reliekenprocessies en ommegangen," in: P.M.L. van Vlijmen, A.M. Koldeweij (eds.), *Schatkamers uit het Zuiden* (Utrecht, 1985), p. 70; *Pieter Brueghel der Jüngere—Jan Brueghel der Ältere. Flämische Malerei um 1600. Tradition und Fortschritt* (Lingen, 1997), pp. 416–9, cat. 143.

Dominic borne by priests in the lower margin of a page in the *Belleville Breviary*, Paris, early fifteenth century,[53] or the fourth tapestry, woven in 1517–8 at Brussels, from the series of Onze-Lieve-Vrouw van de Zavel, showing such eminent figures as the young emperor Charles V and his brother Ferdinand carrying the miraculous statue of the crowned Virgin Mary on a bier.[54] (fig. 248)

Among the obscene badges, we encounter pilgrims both male and female, overt sexual organs which have come to life as erotic travellers. (figs. 251, 252, 253) This is, of course, the very thread that is spun throughout the long, long *Roman de la Rose*: the traveller or pilgrim who gets the rose in the end. In the course of the fifteenth century, people's understanding of the text underwent a change of meaning that is quite clear in some illustrations in the various manuscripts of the *Roman de la Rose*: direct allusions to sexuality are replaced by a more courtly interpretation, physical love becomes *minne*, spiritual love.[55] There is a big difference in approach between the miniature in a Paris manuscript of about 1410 of the lover achieving his goal, (fig. 249) and the same moment illustrated by a Flemish miniaturist in *c.* 1500. The lover has penetrated the castle inside which is the rose. In the earlier illustration the pilgrim pushes his staff through an elongated embrasure between the two columns on which stands a statue of his beloved. (fig. 250) The *c.* 1500 miniature also shows a traveller with the characteristic long pilgrim's staff; having entered a walled garden he courteously draws near to a rosebush in full bloom. Another 1487–95 manuscript, by the Frenchman Robinet de Testart, shows the proceedings in two successive illustrations in a less metaphorical, but just as courtly manner. First the lover, equipped with his staff and pouch, girded with his sword and having gallantly doffed his hat, draws aside the curtain to reveal his beloved, his rose incarnate. The lovers then stretch out on the bed behind the open curtain, fully clothed, exchanging modest kisses.

[53] Paris, Bibliothèque Nationale, Ms 104484, fol. 218v. Koldeweij, *Schatkamers uit het Zuiden*, p. 69.
[54] Brussels, Koninklijke Musea voor Kunst en Geschiedenis, inv. 3153. *Brusselse wandtapijten van de pre-Renaissance* (Brussels, 1976), pp. 94–9, cat. 23.
[55] D.D.R. Owen, *Noble Lovers* (London, 1975), pp. 70–74; G. Bartz, A. Karnein & C. Lange, *Liebesfreuden im Mittelalter. Kulturgeschichte der Erotik und Sexualität in Bildern und Dokumenten* (Stuttgart, 1994), pp. 74–7; Michael Camille, *The Medieval Art of Love* (London, 1998), pp. 150–2.

It is interesting to note that the erotic badges, including the vulvas and phalluses got up as pilgrims, all date from the late fourteenth and early fifteenth century. In the course of the fifteenth century their popularity waned. This development is perfectly congruent with the change of mentality reflected in the interpretation of the thirteenth-century *Roman de la Rose* text by Guillaume de Lorris and Jean de Meung. A *c.* 1400 badge found in 's Hertogenbosch showing a phallic creature equipped with a pilgrim's staff and a traveller's pouch and being crowned by a young woman because he has evidently reached his goal, might well have been meant to represent the pilgrim in the *Roman de la Rose* being welcomed by his beloved. (fig. 251)

The female pilgrim is parodied in a distinctive group of erotic badges: the vulva-creature—the female sexual organ incarnate— dressed up as a devout pilgrim, complete with a pilgrim's hat, staff, and rosary. (fig. 252, fig. 255) There are at least ten known variants of this type.[56] In some examples the staff is crowned with a phallus, in others the vulva wears boots and in one case she walks on pattens. The visual game is taken to extremes in the variants in which the vulva-pilgrim has pinned her own "pilgrim tokens"—huge phallus badges, naturally—to her garments. Of course these badges allude to activities which could take place among the group of pilgrims and which were neither pious nor devotional. Warnings were frequently issued against "falling by the wayside" on these long journeys; despite Christian morality, pilgrims were often unable to resist the temptations of the flesh on their travels. As early as 774, the Archbishop of Canterbury was asked to ban pilgrimages to Rome for the reason that few men and women returned "uncorrupted." An English light-o'-love who had stayed behind was to be found in every French town and in Lombardy.[57] The popular Franciscan preacher Berthold of Regensburg (*c.* 1210–72) gives a graphic description of the dangers to which female pilgrims were exposed: many

---

[56] E. Poche & J. Pesina, *Stredovekeho Umeleckého Remeslo* (Prague 1986), p. 24, cat. 176; Van Beuningen & Koldeweij, *Heilig en Profaan*, p. 264, figs. 663–6; Van Beuningen, Koldeweij & Kicken, *Heilig en Profaan 2*, p. 413, fig. 1774.

[57] S. Beissel, *Die Verehrung der Heiligen und ihrer Reliquien in Deutschland bis zum Beginne des 13. Jahrhunderts, Stimmen aus Maria Laach*, Erg.-H. 47 (Darmstadt, 1976), p. 67; E. Schubert, *Fahrendes Volk im Mittelalter* (Darmstadt, 1995), p. 285.

of them took more sins back home than they had set out with![58] In many places women, girls and certainly nuns had to obtain express permission from a bishop or priest to join a pilgrimage.[59]

Immoral behavior was by no means confined to females. In 1497, a German chronicler reported that many Santiago pilgrims took home the new epidemic disease, syphilis, as a souvenir of their journey.[60] A brooch excavated in Ypres showing two obscene pilgrims, (fig. 253) and another from Flanders, with a very intimate couple (fig. 254) indeed are parodies on this aspect of pilgrimages. On the Ypres brooch the "woman" is wearing a pilgrim's hat and the "man" has a staff; the Flemish "woman" has pinned four phalluses to her clothes. The word PINTELIN on the latter badge has not yet been fully explained and recent speculations are rather unsatisfactory.[61]

Verbal and Visual Criticism

Pilgrims and pilgrimages were criticised and parodied in many ways, in words and pictures. The Middle Ages were over and done with when Erasmus, writing about fools in his *Praise of Folly*, applied the epithet to the pilgrim who set off for ". . . Jerusalem, Rome or Saint James, where he had no business to be, leaving his wife and children at home."[62] Erasmus vents his criticism of pilgrims elsewhere too, notably in his sarcastic *Peregrinatio religionis ergo*, "A Devout Pilgrimage," in the *Colloquia*, published in 1526 in Basel and in which a certain "Menedeius" and "Ogyvius" engage in conversation. These Greek names mean "stay at home" and "simple-minded." The latter, a somewhat naive soul, has returned from a pilgrimage to St. Thomas' shrine at Canterbury garlanded with scallops, bristling with

---

[58] Schubert, *Fahrendes Volk im Mittelalte*, p. 285.

[59] S. Beissel, *Die Verehrung der Heiligen und ihrer Reliquien in Deutschland während der zweiten Hälfte des Mittelalters, Stimmen aus Maria Laach, Erg.-H.* 54 (Darmstadt, 1976), p. 118.

[60] Schubert, *Fahrendes Volk im Mittelalte*, p. 285.

[61] Van Beuningen, Koldeweij & Kicken, *Heilig en Profaan 2*, pp. 411–2, figs. 1762, 1766.

[62] Erasmus, *Laus Stultitiae*, caput 48: Erasmus, *Lof der Zotheid*, Prisma-Boeken 1359, transl. A.J. Hiensch (Utrecht, 1970), p. 90.

tin and lead effigies, wreathed in straw rosaries, and wearing strings of beads round his arms.[63]

A few centuries earlier the pilgrim had been treated no less cynically in the twelfth-century fable of *Reynard the Fox*. Reynard featured in four tales as a pilgrim who pretends to be more pious than he really is. Hypocritical and egoistic, he has no scruples about posing as a "traveller in God's name" in order to outwit his fellow-animals.[64] In other stories too, some of them known from texts, others documented in illustrations but not handed down, Reynard disguises himself as a pilgrim.[65] Two badges from the middle or the second half of the fourteenth century, found in Rotterdam and Amsterdam, (figs. 256–7) belong to the latter category.[66] The fox posed as a pilgrim who carried a staff and had a pouch slung round his neck. The cunning animal is accompanied by a plump goose on a chain. We do not know which tales these badges are meant to illustrate. The Reynard fable was undoubtedly known in Holland, for the two badges indicate a wide distribution. They are each other's mirror-images, which means that a new, negative mold was made from a model and that each mold—each badge variant—could theoretically have been used to cast numerous examples, each of which would have been a reminder of how the story of the fox on a pilgrimage with a nice fat goose ended. The impressive erection of the fox on the Amsterdam badge suggests that he is up to no good.[67] The holy expedition is unlikely to end well for the tasty bird.

---

[63] Erasmus, *The Colloquies of Erasmus. A New Translation* (Chicago, 1965), transl. C.R. Thompson 1965, p. 287; Koldeweij 2001, pp. 59–60.

[64] P.W.M. Wackers, "Reynaert de Vos als pelgrim," in Koldeweij & Willemsen, *Laatmiddeleeuwse insignes*, pp. 44–52; Kenneth Varty, *Reynard, Renart, Reinaert and Other Foxes in Medieval England. The Iconographic Evidence* (Amsterdam, 1999), pp. 79, 92, 128–9, 223.

[65] Wackers, "Reynaert de Vos als pelgrim," pp. 44–6; Varty, *Reynard*, pp. 79, 80–3, 178–9.

[66] Wackers, "Reynaert de Vos als pelgrim," p. 44, fig. 18; Varty, *Reynard*, p. 84, fig. 56; Van Beuningen, Koldeweij & Kicken, *Heilig en Profaan*, p. 415, figs. 1790–1.

[67] Wackers, "Reynaert de Vos als pelgrim," pp. 45–6.

PART VI

COMMON CAUSE FOR MEDIEVAL CHRISTIANS:
POLITICS AND PRACTICALITIES OF
CULT DEVELOPMENT

CHAPTER TWENTY

DOUBT AND AUTHORITY IN THE HOST-MIRACLE SHRINES OF ORVIETO AND WILSNACK

Kristen Van Ausdall

This is a tale of two Host miracles, both of which attracted throngs of pilgrims to their shrines in the late Middle Ages and early Renaissance. Two extraordinary sites, the Chapel of the Holy Corporal at Orvieto Cathedral in Italy, and the Church of St. Nicholas with its Chapel of the Miraculous Blood, in Wilsnack in northern Germany, together represent a duality in the phenomenon of Eucharistic miracle shrines. (figs. 258–9) On one hand, some Eucharistic relics, like those in Orvieto, were sanctioned by papal authority as a legitimate didactic response to the elusive concept of transubstantiation and the grave doubts that it engendered. Conversely, tremendous theological controversy surrounded other bleeding-Host shrines. Tracing the visual, historical, and theological threads that connect these two popular pilgrimage sites, this essay will also explore the chasm that separated their ecclesiastical acceptance and ultimate survival.

One important difference between the way pilgrims experienced these two holy blood relics lies in the setting in which they were placed. The relics of the Italian miracle were translated to Orvieto Cathedral, according to legend, by Pope Urban IV in 1263, rather than kept in the Church of St. Christina in nearby Bolsena where the miracle reputedly occurred. Although pilgrims often visited the Church of St. Christina as well, the real focus of the pilgrimage was at the cathedral, where a chapel, completed in the 1350s, dedicated to the miracle had been built as a repository for the relics.[1] On the contrary, the parish church of St. Nicholas in Wilsnack kept their

---

[1] Still indispensable in the bibliography of the Orvieto shrine are Luigi Fumi's many books and articles on the subject, including: *Il Duomo di Orvieto e il Simbolismo Cristiano* (Rome, 1891) and *Il Santuario del SS. Corporale nel Duomo di Orvieto, Ricordo*

three Host relics. With the help of the bishop of Havelberg, the formerly insignificant village church became an important and popular pilgrimage site.[2] The building was expanded and its decorative program developed from the late fourteenth century until the destruction of the cult in the sixteenth century.

Doubt about the Real Presence of Christ in the Eucharist had originally provided both of these Eucharistic miracles with an impetus and a didactic framework, and the two shrines tell a complex story of dubiety and authority on the eve of the Reformation. A fever pitch of Eucharistic worship had developed by the fifteenth century, and the Church's dependence on it as a barometer of orthodoxy was a double-edged sword for the faithful.[3] On one hand, to commit to a pilgrimage to view a blood relic of a Eucharistic miracle, could garner significant spiritual benefit, including indulgences. On the other hand, theologians in some dioceses preached against certain sites as lacking in authenticity and pilgrims risked not only incurring clerical wrath for visiting them, but they also risked exposing themselves to the evil of idolatry in shrines of dubious legitimacy.[4] Despite their sometimes debatable authenticity, these shrines

---

del XV Congresso Eucaristico di Orvieto (Rome, 1896). See also Dominique N. Suhr, Corpus Christi and the Capella del Corporale at Orvieto (Ph.D. diss., University of Virginia, 2000) who provided a thorough bibliography.

[2] Ernst Breest, "Das Wunderblut von Wilsnack (1383–1552)," Märkische Forschungen, 16, Berlin (1881), pp. 131–301. Fundamental for Wilsnack and for a description of the pilgrimage by the provost of Havelberg is Hartmut Boockmann, "Der Streit um das Wilsnacker Blut, zur Situation des deutschen Klerus in der Mitte des 15. Jahrhunderts," Zeitschrift für Historische Forschung, vol. 9 (1982): 385–408, esp. pp. 391–2.

[3] For an overview of medieval eucharistic teachings and practices see Josef R. Geiselmann, Die Eucharistielehre de Vorscholastik (Paderborn, 1926); James J. Megivern, Concomitance and Communion. A Study in Eucharistic Doctrine and Practice (Fribourg, Switzerland, 1963). For a thorough study of medieval Eucharistic theology see Gary Macy, The Theologies of the Eucharist in the Early Scholastic Period. A Study of the Salvific Function of the Sacrament according to the Theologians c. 1080–c. 1220, (New York, 1984). For an exploration of Eucharistic history from the eleventh through the fourteenth centuries, emphasizing the interrelationships of social usage, see Miri Rubin, Corpus Christi. The Eucharist in Late Medieval Culture, (Cambridge, 1991).

[4] In 1405, the archbishop of Prague issued a decree prohibiting any inhabitant of his diocese from making the pilgrimage to Wilsnack. Jan Hus, De sanguine Christi. Opera Omnia, ed. W. Flajshans, vol. 1, part 3 (Prague, 1904) pp. 33–6. Wilsnack was also banned in other German diocese, like Magdeburg, based on the scholastic argument of latria, or idolatry. Only God himself could be worshipped in this way, and the blood resulting from Host miracles, as Thomas Aquinas had argued (Pt. 3, Q. 76) in his Summa Theologica (Chicago, 1947), could not be considered as

offered a unifying visual experience, and demonstrate the widespread draw of blood relics in the late Middle Ages.[5] Records of first-hand visual experience in the fourteenth and fifteenth century are rare, and although a number of pilgrims recorded their journeys, commentary on the art is skimpy at best. For example, the chronicle of the consistently-peregrinating Margery Kempe records her visit to Wilsnack, but the text devotes far more time to her trials and tribulations in getting to the site than to the shrine itself.[6] Still, viewing a shrine was firmly integrated into the larger spiritual experience of piety: touching, contemplating, and getting as close as possible to a sacred relic.[7]

---

part of the corporeal body of Christ. On this issue see also Charles Zika, "Hosts, Processions and Pilgrimages: Controlling the Sacred in Fifteenth-Century Germany," *Past and Present*, no. 118 (Feb. 1988), pp. 25–64, esp. pp. 48–59; Nicholas Vincent, *The Holy Blood. King Henry III and the Westminster Blood Relic* (Cambridge, 2001), p. 122, fn. 14.

[5] Scholarship has focused on the historical and theological context of Host miracles and pilgrimage to their sites. For Eucharistic miracles treated as relics see Gofridus J.C. Snoek, *Medieval Piety from Relics to the Eucharist. A Process of Mutual Interaction* ed. Heiko A. Oberman (Leiden, 1995); Zika, "Hosts," pp. 25–64. Questions of an art-historical nature have been slower to emerge, despite the often richly-decorated shrines dedicated to these miracles. For discussion on Eucharistic tabernacles, including some related to Holy Blood miracles, see Achim Timmermann, *Staging the Eucharist: Late Gothic Sacrament Houses of Swabia and on the Upper Rhine, Architecture and Iconography*, (Ph.D. diss., University of London, 1996), and Kristen Van Ausdall, *Tabernacles of the Sacrament: Eucharistic Imagery and Classicism in the Early Renaissance* (Ph.D. diss., Rutgers University, 1994). No comprehensive study of the type of art produced to enhance and explicate this devotional experience exists, and more particularly, there has been no comparative analysis of Northern Europe and Italy.

[6] *The Book of Margery Kempe*, ed. Lynne Staley (Kalamazoo, MI, 1996), Book I, Ch. 4, lines 272–4, states: "And sodeynly a man, comyng to hir, askyd yf sche wolde gon on pilgrimage a fer cuntré fro thens to a place clepyd Wilsnak wher is worschepyd the Precyows Blod of owr Lord Jhesu Crist whech be miracle cam of thre oostys, the sacrament of the awter, the whech three oostys and precyows blood ben ther onto this day had in gret worschip and reverens and sowt fro many a cuntré."

[7] Despite the fine line drawn between this kind of pious behavior towards images and idolatry (*latria*), Thomas Aquinas, *Summa Theologica*, II, Pt. 2, Q. 94, a. 2, asked, "Whether idolatry is a sin?" His response to this issue of idolatry acknowledges the need of imagery for the faithful, saying: "Neither in the Tabernacle or Temple of the Old Law, nor again now in the Church are images set up that the worship of latria may be paid to them, but for the purpose of signification, in order that belief in the excellence of angels and saints may be impressed and confirmed in the mind of man. It is different with the image of Christ, to which latria is due on account of His Divinity, as we shall state in the III, 25, 3."

Orvieto Cathedral's relics are housed in a chapel built and decorated in the mid-fourteenth century.[8] The shrine still exists today as a bastion of Roman Catholic orthodoxy, continuing to attract pilgrims, and preserving its processional tradition every year on the Feast of *Corpus Domini*.[9] The later shrine at Wilsnack did not fare as well. It was eradicated in 1552 during the Reformation, despite having been one of the most popular pilgrimage destinations in Europe well into the sixteenth century. Based on a Host miracle of 1383, its attraction to the pious was nearly instantaneous after Urban VI granted an indulgence in 1384.[10] Its promotion steadily increased and a new, very elaborate, chapel was dedicated to it in the early 1460s. For the art historian, studying the Wilsnack shrine is problematic because little remains of the extensive decorative program. Yet, as Cremer has shown, numerous visual aids, arranged throughout the church, focused the viewer on the Host miracle at Wilsnack.[11]

Although she did not discuss visual connections to the Orvieto shrine, Lichte noted the relevance of the Bolsena miracle story to the evolution of the Wilsnack legend.[12] Indeed, the extant visual evidence shows that the iconography of the Orvieto shrine was utilized in the effort to establish the authority of the Wilsnack miracle. The two Eucharistic-miracle shrines are thus linked, despite their geographic and chronological differences, and doubt and proof are the vital strands in this closely-woven chain of connection.

---

[8] For the history of the legend and the history of the chapel of the Sacrament devoted to the miracle see Fumi, *Il Santuario*, pp. 22, 75–6; for the inscriptions on the marble tabernacle dedicated to the Corporal, see *Il Santuario*, pp. 111–7.

[9] The feast of *Corpus Christi* (called *Corpus Domini* in Italy) was established in August 1264 by Urban IV with the bull, *Transiturus de Mundo*. It is a moveable feast, falling on the Thursday immediately following the eighth day after Pentecost (Whitsunday). Since 1977 it has been celebrated on the Sunday immediately following the Thursday. For a study of the foundations of the feast in Italy see Frédégand Callaey, *L'origine della Festa del "Corpus Domini,"* (Rovigo, 1958).

[10] Breest, "Das Wunderblut von Wilsnack," esp. pp. 137–43.

[11] For the Church of St. Nicholas and its chapel dedicated to the miraculous blood, see Folkhard Cremer, *Die St. Nikolaus-und Heiligblut-Kirche zu Wilsnack (1383–1552)*, 2 vols. (Munich, 1996). Cremer (see esp. p. 181) has shown that Christ's body and blood were pervasive in the church in the form of sculpture, painting, and stained glass, part of which is extant: a bleeding Man of Sorrows sculpted in wood, a large Crucifix, a figure of Christ resting, the head of a stone *Schmerzensman*, stained-glass windows, and the paintings on the doors of the shrine.

[12] Claudia Lichte, *Die Inszenierung einer Wallfahrt. Der Lettner im Havelberger Dom und das Wilsnacker Wunderblut* (Worms, 1990), p. 16. In her pivotal study, Lichte investigates the choirscreen of Havelberg Cathedral in relation to the pilgrimage site of St. Nicholas at Wilsnack.

Before addressing the shrines of Wilsnack and Orvieto, a brief overview of Host miracles and their foundation in Eucharistic theology, will help provide a fundamental key to these sites.

Host Miracles and Eucharistic Theology

In his late thirteenth-century, *Summa Theologica*, the Dominican priest Thomas Aquinas codified what would become the dominant view of the Eucharist.[13] His work spelled out the orthodox position on Eucharistic worship and transubstantiation, including a discussion of Host miracles.[14] Despite the eventual ascendence and authority of Dominican tenets, the intricacy of Eucharistic theology required a depth of understanding beyond the ability of most of the laity and of lesser-educated clergy.[15] Doubts about its substance continued to plague theologians and laity alike. The daily miracle of transubstantiation, the ritual transformation of the consecrated Eucharist at the Mass, had never really satisfied the need for a more accessible way of perceiving the Real Presence of Christ in the Eucharist.[16] A number of tangible visual metaphors were used to explain the concept: the wine became blood in the chalice, the Host on the altar was transformed into an Infant, or when Sacrament was stabbed or boiled, it miraculously bled.[17] (fig. 260) Variations on the theme seem

---

[13] The authoritative discussion of the Eucharist by the fifteenth century is St. Thomas Aquinas, *Summa Theologica*, Third Part. The Franciscans were also devoted to the concept of the Real Presence and engaged in a controversy over the Holy Blood which Pius II, in 1464, finally decided in favor of the Dominican point of view. *Pii secundi Pontificis Max. Commentarii rerum memorabilium, quae temporibus suis contigerunt* (Frankfurt, 1614), pp. 278–9.

[14] Aquinas, *Summa Theologica*, Question 76, article 8. Aquinas took a clear stance, separating the relics of Eucharistic miracles from the Eucharist of the Mass ritual. In his view, miraculous Host relics, should not be regarded as the body of Christ, since the Host assumes the appearance of the bread and wine and, in the theology of transubstantiation, does not take tangible form as flesh and blood. After his resurrection and ascension, Christ's physical body exists solely in Heaven, not in any form on earth.

[15] For an overview of the scholastic position on Host miracles, see Browe, "Die scholastische Theorie der eucharistischen Verwandlungswunder," *Theologische Quartalschrift*, 110 (1929), pp. 305–32, esp. p. 312.

[16] Snoek, *Medieval Piety*, p. 49 states, "The collective consciousness remained captive to the realistic notion of the Eucharist."; Miri Rubin, *Corpus Christi*, pp. 110–26, also discussed the Eucharistic *exempla* used to teach the laity.

[17] Miri Rubin, *Gentile Tales. The Narrative Assault on Late Medieval Jews* (New Haven, 1999), p. 1, discusses the many stories of Host desecration by Jews: "The enormity

unlimited.[18] These stories made the faithful aware of the reality of the humanity of Christ in a way that orthodox theology never could, and the visual arts brought this concept to life.

Increasing devotional and liturgical concentration on the Eucharist from the thirteenth through the fifteenth century helped create the spiritual environment in which Eucharistic miracles occurred evermore frequently. The miraculous tales of the transformed Sacrament left corporeal relics behind: some centered around the Eucharistic wine, but the vast majority involved Host wafers mystically infused or spotted with the Blood of Christ.[19] Promoted as an efficacious means to salvation, the popular expression of the mystery of transubstantiation in these graphic miracle tales created a new category of relic,[20] and by the early fourteenth century these miracle Hosts came to be enshrined as relics of special veneration.

Miraculous Hosts represented an alternative to saints' relics which had been the primary focus of pilgrimages earlier in the Middle Ages.[21] The limited supply of saintly bones and other relics, the intense promotion of the Eucharist as the central Sacrament of salvation, and the difficulty in understanding an intangible theological concept, combined to provide a renewable resource of Blood relics. Moreover, the phenomenon was widespread—pilgrimage sites throughout Northern and Southern Europe utilized Eucharistic blood mir-

---

of the offence which it imputed to Jews was defined by the holiness of their victim: the host—the consecrated eucharistic wafer—was believed to be Christ himself, in the generous form within which he offered himself daily and ubiquitously at the altar, consecrated by priests during the Mass."

[18] For the multitude of Eucharistic miracles, see Peter Browe, *Die Eucharistischen Wunder des Mittelalters*, Breslau, 1938.

[19] For examples of Host wafer-miracles and the frequency of their occurrence in contrast to miracles of the wine see Browe, *Eucharistischen Wunder* and Lionel Rothkrug, "Religious Practices and Collective Perceptions: Hidden Homologies in the Renaissance and Reformation," *Historical Reflections/Réflextions Historiques*, vol. 7, no. 1 (Spring, 1980): 205–41.

[20] A related type of relic was that of Christ's blood from the Crucifixion; among the most famous shrines dedicated to examples of this relic were at Bruges and Mantua. These became theologically problematic; the issue of the Holy Blood culminated in the fifteenth-century debate regarding the re-absorption of Christ's blood lost at the Crucifixion. Marita Hörster, "Mantuae Sanguis Preciosus," *Wallraf-Richartz Jahrbuch*, vol. 25 (1963): 151–81. For the failed mid-thirteenth-century Holy Blood shrine in Westminster and the Scholastic debate on the Holy Blood see Vincent, *Holy Blood*, pp. 83–117.

[21] See Snoek, *Medieval Piety*, for a study of the connections between relics and the Eucharist.

acles as foci of piety.[22] From the early fourteenth century on, the Feast of *Corpus Christi* featured processions displaying the consecrated Host and/or Eucharistic miracle relics.[23] In many ways, the relics of Eucharistic miracles and consecrated Host wafers were confused by this processional interchangeability during *Corpus Christi*, especially since they were also used for relic processions at pilgrimage churches. Emphasizing the important act of viewing the Eucharist, the processions attracted crowds of pilgrims during the octave of the Feast.[24]

The concept of doubt is fundamental to Host miracles—these supernatural stories manifest early in Christian thought as a response to questions about the Real Presence of Christ in the Eucharist.[25] Numerous stories of Host miracles arose from the general difficulty in comprehending the complex theology of transubstantiation, and doubt, on multiple levels, informed the imagery of the shrines dedicated to the miracles. In addition to elaborate reliquaries used to display the relics, visual narratives provided pilgrims, who sought grace by visiting and viewing the manifested body and blood of the Lord, with didactic explanation and visual evidence. By the fifteenth century, doubt about the veracity of the miracles themselves, rather than simple doubt about the dogma of transubstantiation, helped determine the imagery as well as the fate of these pilgrimage sites.[26]

---

[22] Eucharistic miracles were venerated in Augsburg, Paris, Florence, Amsterdam, Dijon, Walldürn, Brussels, and Siena, and many other sites. In addition to the especially beneficent indulgences granted to pilgrimages to Orvieto and Wilsnack, pilgrims also garnered indulgences for visits to the miracle shrine in Andechs. Browe, *Eucharistschen Wunder*, p. 115; Snoek, *Medieval Piety*, p. 290. Rothkrug, "Religious Practices, p. 64, fn. 214 listed more than twenty bleeding-Host pilgrimages sites in Austria, Franconia, Schwabia, and Bavaria.

[23] For *Corpus Christi* processions see Peter Browe, *Verehrung der Eucharistie im Mittelalter* (Munich, 1933); Peter Browe, "Die Entstehung der Sakramentenprozessionen," *Bonner Zeitschrft für Theologie und Seelsorge*, vol. 8 (1931): 97–117; Zika, "Hosts," pp. 25–64.

[24] Zika, "Hosts," pp. 38–47.

[25] Browe, *Eucharistischen Wunder*; Peter Browe "Die scholastische Theorie der eucharistischen Verwandlungswunder," *Theologische Quartalschrift*, vol. 110 (1929): 305–32.

[26] Although most theologians addressed the issue of Holy Blood relics in terms of the blood shed by Christ at the Crucifixion, Jan Hus's tract, *De Sanguine Christi*, stands out by his examination of all types of blood relics. He singled out Host miracle relics for scathing denunciation, with Wilsnack as its instigation. A decade after the attack on Wilsnack and other relics of the Holy blood, Jan Hus was declared a heretic and executed at the Council of Konstanz in 1415. Although Hus' *De Sanguine Christi* was essentially orthodox in its beliefs, he came to be deeply involved in another related controversy—that of Utraquism—offering the Eucharist to the faithful in both species, bread and wine. This was in opposition to the practice of reserving both the chalice and the wafer for priests, while offering only the conse-

Pilgrimages devoted to Blood relics were burgeoning, especially in Northern Europe, almost threatening to overtake the precedence of Italy with an abundance of homegrown Eucharistic relics.[27] Among all the pilgrimage shrines of Northern Europe, that of the Church of St. Nicholas in Wilsnack stands out; only Jerusalem, Aachen, Rome, and Santiago were considered more popular.[28] Although Wilsnack had captured the popular imagination, Orvieto in Italy, a town long associated with the papacy, had a shrine focused on the relics of a Host miracle which had continuing papal sanction and therefore greater authority. In Orvieto pilgrims could view a Host miracle that had reputedly sparked the liturgical feast honoring the body of the Lord—the feast of *Corpus Christi*.

The Miraculous Mass at Bolsena—the Orvieto Shrine

Perhaps the most significant thing about the Host miracle enshrined in Orvieto Cathedral is the tradition of its impact on the liturgy and calendar of the Roman Catholic Church. By the early fourteenth century, the miracle was credited with providing the final induce-ment for Urban IV's 1264 creation of the Feast of the Corpus Christi on the Church calendar,[29] and with Thomas Aquinas' writing of the

---

crated bread to the laity. See Howard Kaminsky, *A History of the Hussite Revolution* (Berkeley, 1967), pp. 97–140.

[27] For a systematic listing of the distribution of all pilgrimage shrines in Germany by region and date, see Rothkrug, "Religious Practices," pp. 205–41.

[28] Zika, "Hosts," p. 49, fns. 75–6. Zika stated that the "growing popularity of bleeding-host shrines as pilgrimage sites in the later fourteenth and fifteenth cen-turies was also related to the general expansion of regional and transregional pil-grimage—a phenomenon, it has been argued, which grew out of the increasingly precarious financial conditions of late medieval ecclesiastical institutions in the face of political conflict, agrarian crisis and economic depression."

[29] The origin of the devotion is most often attributed to the efforts of Juliana of Liège (1193–1258), a nun at the Augustinian convent of Mt. Cornillon, who reported to her confessor a vision which she interpreted to mean that the Church was in need of a feast in honor of the blessed Sacrament. The vision was communicated to the Dominicans and to the Bishop of Liège, Robert of Turotte, who in turn reported the idea of a feast to the chancellor of the University of Paris, who did not object to the idea. The bishop issued a pastoral letter, *Inter alia mira*, to estab-lish the feast in his diocese in October of 1246. The presence of Jacques Pantaleon (a long-time associate of Robert of Turotte and archdeacon of Campines in the Diocese of Liège from 1243–48) should also be noted, as Pantaleon became Pope

liturgical Office for that feast.[30] There are no contemporary records of the miraculous event in Bolsena or of the transfer of the relic to Orvieto; the papal bull, *Transiturus*, which established the Feast in 1264, does not mention the miracle.[31] The miracle was alleged to have occurred in 1263 in the small town church of St. Christina in Bolsena, under the religious jurisdiction of the episcopate of Orvieto. The legend asserts that the miracle Host and the corporal on which it bled were translated to nearby Orvieto, where Pope Urban IV then resided. The Bolsena story concerns a visiting priest, later identified in written versions as either German or Bohemian, who privately harbored doubts about the Real Presence of Christ in the Eucharist.[32] In answer to that doubt, at the moment of consecration, the Host bled in his hands and onto the corporal.[33] The earliest complete version of this story is related in images on the 1337–38 reliquary, in Orvieto Cathedral.[34] (fig. 261) The narrative, as it unfolds

---

Urban IV in 1261. For a synopsis of the origins of the feast in France and for bibliography see Rubin, *Corpus Christi*, pp. 164–85.

[30] Although a connection of the Mass of Bolsena to the Feast of *Corpus Christi*, and the attribution to Aquinas of the liturgical office for the feast is promoted in the imagery and later written versions of the miracle story, the historical evidence for the miracle is not strong (*Catholic Encyclopedia*, vol. 11, p. 331). The case for Aquinas' authorship of the liturgy is stronger, and has both adherents and dissenters; Rubin, *Corpus Christi*, pp. 185–90. In Italy the feast is generally called *Corpus Domini*. Frédégand Callaey, "Origine e sviluppo delle festa del 'Corpus Domini,'" in *Eucaristia: il mistero del'altare nel pensiero e nella vita della chiesa*, ed. Antonio Piolanti (Rome, 1957), p. 916; Vincenzo Fineschi, *Della festa e della processione del Corpus Domini di Firenze* (Florence, 1768). For a discussion of the association of Orvieto with the feast see Suhr, *Corpus Christi*, pp. 4–46.

[31] Gregory XI, in a Brief of June 25, 1337, gives a short account of the miracle, which parallels the visual narrative on the reliquary. Many references to it are found in the mid-fifteenth century, as in the sermons of the Dominican preacher Leonardo Mattei of Undine, *Festo Corp. Christi*, XIV (Venice, 1652), p. 59.

[32] I. Taurisano, "Per la festa di S. Tommaso d'Aquino," *Il Rosario Memorie Domenicane*, vol. 33 (1916), pp. 114–5. One of the most common versions of the story dubbed the priest, "Peter of Prague." The visiting priest was also identified in an inscription at the later shrine of Santa Christina in Bolsena.

[33] A corporal is the cloth on which the holy Eucharist was placed on the altar, as distinguished from the altar cloth. H. Thurston, "Corporal," in *Catholic Encyclopedia*, vol. 4, (Robert Appleton: New York, 1908) p. 386, states that it is, "A square white linen cloth ... upon which the Sacred Host and chalice are placed during the celebration of Mass. The corporal was described as palla corporalis, or velamen dominic mens, or opertorium dominici corporis, etc.; and it seems generally to have been of linen, though we hear of altar-cloths of silk ... the corporal was never to remain on the altar, but was to be put in the Missal [Sacramentorum libro] or shut up with the chalice and paten in some clean receptacle."

[34] The miracle is not supported by historical evidence, nor is the written tradi-

there, shows the miraculous Mass, with the priest standing at the altar with the bleeding Host. The next scene shows Pope Urban IV being informed of the miracle and directing the Bishop of Orvieto to go to Bolsena to validate the miracle. After the Bishop's legitimization of the miracle, the Bishop and the Pope, with their retinues in a processional arrangement, meet at the river flowing between the two towns. Significantly, the final scene of the legend shows a seated Urban IV, with Thomas Aquinas kneeling before him presenting the liturgy for the feast of Corpus Christi.[35]

Doubt and Authenticity in the Orvieto Shrine

The extravagant reliquary, (fig. 261) commissioned from Ugolino di Vieri, a Sienese goldsmith,[36] and completed in 1338, was cleverly constructed not only to hold the relic of the Host wafer, but also

---

tion altogether consistent. The oldest written document of the miracle is a *sacra rappresentazione* dated between the late 1290s–1344, known from a 1405 manuscript. For the Orvietan *Corpus Christi* play based on the Miracle of Bolsena, see V. de Bartholomaeis, *Laude drammatiche e rappresentazioni sacre*, vol. 1 (Florence, 1943, repr. 1967), pp. 368–81. The earliest complete version of the official legend is found on the 1337–38 reliquary. For the history of the legend and the chapel devoted to the miracle see Fumi, *Il Santuario*, pp. 22, 75–6. In a carefully reasoned argument, Gary Macy, "Fourteenth-Century Propaganda in Orvieto: The Case of the Miracle Corporal of Orvieto," a paper given at the second annual conference of the Arizona Center for Medieval and Renaissance Studies, Tempe, Arizona, February 16, 1996, proposed that the miracle play and reliquary narratives most likely conflates political events of the 1290s with the presence of Urban IV and Aquinas in Orvieto in the 1260s. Dating the miracle to 1264 would serve both the hagiography of the Dominicans and the political agenda of the Orvietan government in the 1330s, promoting an idealized Orvieto, where the Monaldeschi dictators were in accord with the papacy and the Dominicans in ruling over the cities of the Val di Lago. (My thanks to Dr. Macy for providing me with the text of his unpublished 1996 paper.) For further discussion of the discrepancies between the miracle play and the official legend of the miracle, see Suhr, *Corpus Christi*, pp. 28–36.

[35] Suhr, *Corpus Christi*, pp. 42–3, wrote that the subject of the scene immediately preceding this one, has been consistently identified as Pope Urban IV displaying the relic; she disagrees and suggests that it represents Urban IV instituting the Feast of Corpus Christi.

[36] The inscription around the base of the reliquary states: *Per Magistrum Ugolinum et sotios aurifices de Senis factum fuit sub anno Domini MCCCXXXVIII, tempore Domini Benedicti Pape XII.* (Made by Master Ugolino and fellow goldsmiths from Siena in the year of the Lord 1338, under sovereign Pope Benedict XII.) Fumi, *Il Duomo di Orvieto*, p. 433; Enzo Carli, *Il Reliquiario del Corporale ad Orvieto* (Milan, 1964). For documents as they relate to the Bishop of Orvieto, Tramo Mondaleschi della Cervara, his patronage of the reliquary, and the promotion of the miracle relics, see Giovanni Freni, "The Reliquary of the Holy Corporal in the Cathedral of Orvieto: Patronage

the bloody corporal which had become the main object of ostension. Made of silver with colorful cloisonné enamels, the reliquary includes narrative panels of the *Miraculous Mass of Bolsena* on one side and the *Passion of Christ* on the other.[37] On both sides of the reliquary the enameled panels could be removed and the frame remain to support the bloody corporal for ostension. (fig. 262) The linen cloth, suspended in the frame to reveal the spots of blood, is large enough to view at a distance. This reliquary has been carried in the *Corpus Domini* procession since 1338.[38] Pilgrims would not only view the shrine during the octave of the feast, but on the climactic day, the relic was held aloft for the benefit of the faithful throughout the procession, as dramatic, blood-stained evidence of the truth of the Real Presence.

After 1350, a large chapel dedicated to the *Sacro Corporale* (Holy Corporal) was added to the left transept of Orvieto Cathedral to accommodate pilgrims and to further dignify the relics of the miracle.[39] (fig. 263) A massive marble tabernacle behind the altar was built (1358–66) to hold the silver reliquary.[40] The decorative scheme also included frescos (1357–62), by Ugolino di Prete Ilario, on the ceiling and the three walls of the chapel.[41] On the altar wall, a large

---

and Politics," *Art, Politics and Civic Religion in Central Italy, 1261–1352* (Aldershot, UK, 2000), pp. 117–77. For the restoration see, Giuseppe Basile, "Il reliquiario del Corporale di Orvieto: interventi di conservazione e restauro," *Arte medievale*, 6/1 (1992), pp. 193–7.

[37] The reliquary's tripartite design resembles the facade of the Cathedral. It also has a number of small sculptures distributed around the base and the top which constitute a coherent iconographic program.

[38] The relic was protected by thin silk coverings; Suhr, *Corpus Christi*, p. 38, fn. 61.

[39] The Chapel was constructed 1350–64, under Nino di Andrea Pisano. The cathedral of Orvieto, built on the older church of St. Maria Prisca, was begun in 1290, with the cornerstone blessed by Pope Nicholas IV. It was to be "big and noble, in the style of a basilica such as Santa Maria Maggiore in Rome." Scholarship on the architecture of the Cathedral attributes the design to Arnolfo di Cambio, who was in the papal court at that time in Orvieto. The Cathedral building was completed in only eighteen years. The facade by Lorenzo Maitani was begun in 1310. Its size and magnificence are unusual and can be related to the long-standing papal presence in Orvieto. David M. Gillerman, "The Evolution of the Design of Orvieto Cathdral, *ca.* 1290–1310," *Journal of the Society of Architectural Historians*, 53/3 (1994): 300–21.

[40] Fumi, *Il Santuario*, pp. 109–10, showed that the tabernacle was constructed between 1358–66.

[41] Fumi, *Il Duomo di Orvieto*, 433. Ugolino di Prete Ilario and his workshop were also responsible for other frescoes in the Cathedral. Due to heavy damage, the fresco decoration of the chapel underwent restoration in 1855–60; Fumi, *Il Duomo*,

narrative of the *Crucifixion* provides a visual climax for the marble tabernacle on the altar, as the apex of the gable on the tabernacle converges with the Cross in the center of the fresco. On the right side of the chapel, seven scenes recount the *Miracle of Bolsena*. (fig. 263) The scenes are organized in three registers and divided into three equal fields on the top register and two unequal fields in the middle and lowest registers. The narrative follows that of the earlier scenes on the silver reliquary, but they would have been far more legible for visitors to the chapel. Narrated from left to right, the story begins in the upper left corner: the priest who has doubts about the Host as the true body of the Lord celebrates Mass on the altar of Santa Cristina in Bolsena, and as he holds the Host, he sees the miraculous transformation of the bread as it bleeds freely on the linen cloth on the altar; (fig. 264) then, an enthroned Pope Urban IV, residing in the papal palace in Orvieto, is told about the miracle; last, in the same setting, Urban IV tells the Bishop of Orvieto to retrieve the corporal from Bolsena and to bring it to him. In the middle register, the first scene is set again in Santa Cristina in Bolsena, where the Bishop of Orvieto examines the bloody corporal on the altar (fig. 265) and in the second, double scene, a procession, led by the pope, flows from the city gate of Orvieto to the bridge on the Chiaro river, where they are met by the Bishop with the corporal. The pope kneels before the blood relic, followed by his retinue—papal court, civic dignitaries, and then the townspeople—who flock out of the Orvietan city gate. (fig. 266) In the lowest register the setting moves to the town of Orvieto, where Urban IV displays the bloody corporal from the loggia of the papal palace. (fig. 267) Again, there is a strong processional arrangement in this composition.[42] The final scene shows the enthroned Pope Urban IV who, with a gesture, orders Thomas Aquinas, surrounded by Cardinals, to compose

---

p. 347. Suhr, *Corpus Christi*, Appendix II, published documents concerning the restoration, and states that there were compositional changes to the frescoes as that time.

[42] Suhr, *Corpus Christi*, pp. 144–6, argued that the scene (one of the most-heavily damaged on the wall) we see today is the result of a misinterpretation of the 1855–60 restoration of this fresco. Rather than a display of the corporal, she believes that the fresco originally deviated from the iconography of the silver reliquary to focus on the Corpus Christi procession that had been instituted in Orvieto in 1338 and carried out every June ever since that time. *Editors' note: see Rita Tekippe's essay in this volume.

the Office of the Sacrament. (fig. 268) Aquinas kneels before the Pope and presents the liturgy. The emphasis on papal authority is clear: Urban IV is placed in the center of the composition, and he is much larger than the other figures.

On the other side of the chapel, topped in the lunette by the image of St. Gregory the Great, the narratives are also organized in three registers to be read from left to right. They focus on a broad collection of Eucharistic marvels—miracles recorded and utilized to explain the Real Presence of Christ prior to the earliest treatise on Eucharistic worship.[43] In the uppermost register, the cycle begins with the *Miraculous Mass of St. Gregory the Great*, the most authoritative, widespread, and enduring of Host miracles. (fig. 269) The earliest written version is found in Paul the Deacon's eighth-century *Vita* of Gregory the Great († 604), in which Paul states that while Pope St. Gregory was officiating at Mass in Rome, a Roman woman in attendance doubted the true presence of Christ in the Eucharist.[44] As Gregory recited the words of consecration, in answer to the woman's doubt, the Eucharist was transformed into flesh and blood, in the form of a disembodied bleeding finger. In the Orvieto fresco,[45] this gruesome sign of the Eucharistic flesh and blood, is generalized, as is the account in the late thirteenth-century *Golden Legend* by Jacobus de Voragine, in which Gregory displays not a bleeding finger, but

---

[43] Paschasius Radbertus wrote the first theological treatise devoted to a doctrinal treatment of the Eucharist *c.* 831–33: *De corpore et sanguine domini.* M. Cristiani, "La Controversia eucaristica nella cultura del secolo XI," *Studi medievali*, 9 (3rd series): 269–92. For a discussion of the earlier Paschasius/Ratramnus debate see Celia Chazelle, "Figure, Character, and the Glorified Body in the Carolingian Eucharistic Controversy," *Traditio*, 47 (1992), pp. 1–36. My thanks to Dr. Gary Macy for bringing this article to my attention.

[44] Paul the Deacon's short *Vita Gregorii Magni* (770–80) account ends with a clear statement on the orthodoxy of transubstantiation, as noted by Browe, *Eucharistischen Wunder*, pp. 113–4, fn. 11. A century later, John the Deacon, at the request of John VIII (r. 872–82), produced his *Vita Gregorii*, which also included a similar account of the miraculous Mass of St. Gregory.

[45] Heavily damaged, this fresco was also repainted in the 1855–6; Suhr, *Corpus Christi*, pp. 123–6. The fourteenth-century inscription indicates that the subject was indeed the *Mass of St. Gregory*. The restorers must have had enough of the composition remaining to guide their reconstruction, because they did not depict this miracle in the version that became nearly universal from the fifteenth century on, that is, conflated with a man-of-sorrows image (see discussion of the Wilsnack cupboard below), but in the simpler fourteenth-century terms.

rather a piece of bleeding flesh the "size of the little finger of a hand," as proof of the True Presence to the unbelieving woman.[46]

The second scene in the uppermost register shows a priest, with his back turned to us, elevating the Host at the altar. Based on the numerous graphic stories of the late Middle Ages, during the elevation, the Host was transformed into a child to convince and convert heretical onlookers. The meaning of transubstantiation is again made explicit by this apparition. The last part of the top register is broken into three small scenes illustrating a complicated Host narrative regarding unworthy reception.[47] In the middle register we find an oft-told tale of a Jewish boy who receives communion, one of the many anti-Semitic Host miracles told in the late Middle Ages.[48] In the Orvieto frescoes, this scene represents the broader Eucharistic concept of radical, heretical disbelief in the Real Presence, evidence of this truth, and finally, conversion.[49]

---

[46] *The Golden Legend of Jacobus de Voragine*, trans. Granger Ryan and Helmut Ripperger, (1941, repr., New York, 1969) 3, pp. 27–31. "St. Gregory saw the holy sacrament in figure of a piece of flesh as great as the little finger of a hand, and anon after, by the prayers of St. Gregory, the flesh of the sacrament turned into semblance of bread as it had been before."

[47] First, a fisherman forces a fish to eat a consecrated Host wafer; second, the fisherman repents and is seen confessing the misdeed to a priest; third, the priest and the sinner are seen kneeling at river's edge as the fish swims toward them to return the Host wafer. The middle register is divided into two narratives, each subdivided into three scenes: In the first, a Eucharistic miracle concerning the sacrament of a last communion (the sacrament of Extreme Unction) shows St. Ugo on his deathbed. Since Ugo was too ill to swallow, the monks attending him were fearful that the Sacrament would be regurgitated or in some way lost, so an unconsecrated Eucharist is brought to him. The saint is shown rejecting the unconsecrated Host, since he intuitively recognizes the absence of the true presence. In the final scene of this narrative, mystically descending, saints bring him a consecrated Host, which then mysteriously levitates out of the priest's hands, and two angels hovering above the roof of the bedchamber hold out their hands to receive the consecrated Host.

[48] Rubin, *Gentile Tales*, pp. 7–39 discusses the evolution of this fascinating story, which had many versions. Tracing this Marian miracle from its origins to its transposition as a bleeding Host tale, Rubin states that, "early medieval tales reflected the official Christian position on the historic role of Jews. One of the cultural frames within which stories about the conversion of Jews were elaborated was the powerful world of the Marian tale." The tale of the Jewish Boy, is a tale of witness and conversion, but also one of punishment and violence. It is of Greek origin and it spread west where it attracted the attention of Gregory of Tours (d. 595), winning a place in his *De gloria martyrum* (pp. 7–8). In nearly all the versions of the story, the boy recounts his ordeal and says that he sees a Lady holding an infant, who protects him.

[49] In the first scene we see the Jewish child kneeling before the priest and receiv-

The lowest register of the left wall portrays the narrative of the Christians and Saracens, including a Eucharistic miracle episode.[50] Visually and thematically paralleling the middle scene in the top register, this one focuses on a centralized altar with a priest standing at the altar celebrating Mass, elevating the Host. Like the miracle above, at the moment of elevation, a tiny child appears in place of the Host. In the final scene during the consecration of the wine, a drop of blood falls from the side of the Child (the transubstantiated Host) and into the chalice. The Christians and Saracens kneel to either side of the altar, acknowledging the proof that both species, body and blood, are present in the Host.

All of these images speak to the concept of doubt about the true presence of Christ in the Eucharist. The Bolsena miracle is bolstered by carefully selected miracles that repeatedly grapple with different aspects of the doubt and proof of transubstantiation. It parallels St. Thomas Aquinas' dialogue in the *Summa*, which provides an objection and then is answered with authoritative proof. In fact, Aquinas addressed the question of why the Host, when consecrated, did not take the physical form of flesh in the eyes of the faithful. His three reasons were stunningly practical: because of the revulsion ordinary people would feel if they actually were compelled to eat the species in its appearance as human flesh, so that the Sacrament could not be derided by the faithless, and because the faith required to believe in transubstantiation was meritorious in itself.[51]

Pilgrims, especially those flocking to Orvieto for the *Corpus Domini* festival, would have understood these frescoes not only in terms of their size and didactic content, but because of their focus on the procession, which essentially imitates the activities of the Feast celebrated in Orvieto since 1317.[52] Pious visitors, looking across to the

---

ing communion. The second scene shows the boy at home where his father, having been told of the boy's reception of the Eucharist, throws him into the open furnace. The final scene shows the boy's mother, along with neighbors, after finding the child unharmed in the fiery furnace. The story generally concludes with the conversion of the mother and the execution of the unbelieving father. Rubin, *Gentile Tales*, p. 9.

[50] The first is a battle scene, with a medieval European walled town in the background—the Christians are shown defeated and kneeling at the left before the victors, who lean menacingly toward them with bows and arrows drawn. The King of the Saracens promises the Christians freedom if they can show him a miracle.

[51] *Summa Theologica*, III, Q. 75.

[52] See Rubin, *Corpus Christi*, pp. 181–84, on the resurgence of the feast under

opposite wall, would have found an authoritative underscoring of the legitimacy and meaning of the Bolsena miracle. Other festivities in Orvieto during the octave of *Corpus Domini* rounded out the visual experiences of pilgrimage to the shrine. By the fifteenth century, the viewing of the relic, the images in the chapel, and the *Corpus Domini* procession were enhanced by miracle plays which dramatically recounted the Bolsena miracle, reinforcing the ideas which had been brought home to the devout in the Orvieto Cathedral shrine.[53]

Although the Host miracle most bound by tradition to Catholic doctrine occurred in Italy, more Host miracles were recorded in Northern Europe in the late Middle Ages, and it was in Belgium that the impetus for the feast of Corpus Christi emanated.[54] Conversely, it was also in Northern Europe in the fifteenth century that the idea of Host miracles and their shrines were directly challenged by reforming theologians. This ironic circumstance had solid political roots, since the papal connection to Orvieto was long-standing and the Bolsena miracle had the stamp of papal approval—not just in its legendary origins with Urban IV, but with a continued connection of the popes with Orvieto and its papal palace.[55]

John XXII in 1317. Although the papal Bull *Transiturus* established the Feast on the Church calendar in 1264, its promulgation was delayed due to Urban IV's death the same year. In Italy the first documented civic celebration of the feast was in Venice in 1295. Browe, *Verehrung der Eucharistie*, pp. 70–80; Dennis Devlin, *Corpus Christi: A Study in Medieval Eucharistic Theory, Devotion and Practice* (Ph.D. diss., University of Chicago, 1975), pp. 278–92.

[53] In the fifteenth century, records also indicate that an Italian Eucharistic miracle play linked the miraculous Mass of Bolsena to an important fifteenth-century miracle—the famous Host of Dijon. The play opens with the announcement of an angel and proceeds to dramatize the Paris incident, and papal endorsement of the feast of the Eucharist. Rubin, *Gentile Tales*, pp. 169–70, 172–3. For an Orvietan play for *Corpus Christi*, based on the Miracle of Bolsena, see V. de Bartholomaeis, *Laude drammatiche e rappresentazioni sacre*, vol. 1 (1943, repr., Florence, 1967), pp. 368–81. *Editors' note: see also Mitchell Merbeck's essay in this volume.

[54] For the origin of the Feast, see fn. 31.

[55] For the papal presence in Orvieto especially as it relates to the Host relic of Bolsena, see Carol Lansing, *Power and Purity. Cathar Heresy in Medieval Italy* (Oxford, 1998), pp. 160–6. Although Orvieto was no longer an important strategic stronghold for the papacy, their special connection to Orvieto had not diminished by 1513 when Raphael created an image of the *Miraculous Mass of Bolsena* in the Vatican for his patron, Pope Julius II. In this painting, Julius mystically takes part in the spiritual/historical event. See James Beck, *Raphael* (New York, 1976).

Wilsnack, Doubt, and Authority

Despite the papal authority given to the Eucharistic shrine at Orvieto, in the fifteenth century doubt about Host miracles led to theological tracts which disparaged some of the pilgrimage sites dedicated to them. The first and most famous of these attacks by Jan Hus concerned the miracle Hosts at Wilsnack in Brandenburg, about seventy miles northwest of Berlin.[56] The Wilsnack miracle story was relatively simple. Unlike the Host stories of St. Gregory or Bolsena, the miracle did not take place while a priest was saying Mass at the altar. Instead, three consecrated Hosts were found intact after a fire had destroyed the parish church of Wilsnack in 1383.[57] Not only had they been spared destruction, but the priest of the parish found spots of blood visible in the center of each wafer.[58] The three Host relics of this miraculous event were enshrined and became the object of devout pilgrimage.[59] A number of surviving pilgrim badges, showing the three wafers attached by a thin metal armature, attest to the popularity of the site.[60] (fig. 232) The Wilsnack church of St. Nicholas, rebuilt with the money brought by pilgrims to the shrine, became the subject of serious theological doubt and great controversy from the early fifteenth century until its demise in the sixteenth century.[61]

The story of the Wilsnack miracle was eventually enhanced to include a doubting Bishop, a Mass, and papal approbation. This expanded narrative of the miracle echoes the process of acceptance

---

[56] Jan Hus, *De Sanguine Christi*, written *c.* 1405, focused on the Wilsnack relic. A number of theological attacks followed; those of Nicholas of Cusa and Heinrich Tocke of the mid-fifteenth century, were particularly important. Wilsnack was tied politically to Prignitz, but was under the jurisdiction of the bishop of Havelberg.

[57] Breest, "Wunderblut von Wilsnack," pp. 137–43, discussed the account of the provost of Havelberg, the pilgrimage, and attendant healings. The Bishop's account, as cited by Breest, is found in Matthäus Ludecus, *Historia von der erfindung, Wunderwerken und zerstörung des vermeinten heiligen Bluts zu Wilsnagk* (Wittenberg, 1586).

[58] Breest, "Wunderblut von Wilsnack," pp. 137–43; Zika, "Hosts, Processions and Pilgrimages," p. 50.

[59] In 1384 Pope Urban VI granted an indulgence for visiting the shrine. Zika, "Hosts," p. 50, noted that the indulgence was meant to support the rebuilding of the parish church.

[60] R.M. van Heeringen, A.M. Koldeweij, and A.A.G. Gaalman, *Heiligen uit de Modder in Zeeland Gevonden Pelgrimstekens* (Utrecht, 1988), pp. 54–5.

[61] Zika, "Hosts," p. 50, called the fifteenth-century written tracts on the subject a "pamphlet war" providing "rich materials for decoding the religious thought and practice."

found at the Orvieto shrine. Its utilization of the authority provided by a Host-miracle so closely connected to the papacy, was an important assertion of legitimacy, not only of a specific Eucharistic miracle, but also of the concept of Host miracles.

The shrine and the cult had been established for twenty years before the trouble began, but in 1403, after receiving reports of the possibility that some of the healing miracles credited to the Wilsnack relics might be false, Archbishop Sbinko (Zbynek) of Prague sent Jan Hus to investigate. The visit resulted in the unequivocal denunciation of the relic and the shrine. Sbinko ordered all Bohemian priests to preach against the pilgrimage to Wilsnack at least once a month.[62] Around 1405, Hus wrote *De sanguine Christi*, attacking the shrine and the concept of Host miracles,[63] and condemning the Wilsnack miracle as a fiction created by the parish priest in order to raise money for the rebuilding of the church after the fire.[64] He set up his argument by dismissing all bodily remains of Christ (such as, the foreskin of Christ and the blood shed at the circumcision), and then denied that Eucharistic relics could be true miracles.[65] He asserted that the transformations might be the work of the Devil himself, or simply of priests who wish to line their coffers by duping the unsuspicious and encouraging pilgrimage to the false shrine. Hus cited an example of

---

[62] Browe, "Eucharistischen Wunder," pp. 168–9; Zika, "Hosts," p. 50.

[63] For a comparison of the Hus treatise to the pro-Holy Blood treatise of William Sudbury (for the blood relic of Westminster), see Vincent, *Holy Blood*, pp. 118–36; Zika, "Hosts," pp. 50–1.

[64] Boockmann, "Der Streit um das Wilsnacker Blut," pp. 385–408; Breest, "Das Wunderblut von Wilsnack," 296–301.

[65] Hus, *De sanguine*, 12–30. Hus never mentioned Aquinas' commentary on the Eucharist. See Vincent, *Holy Blood*, p. 118. Although Aquinas came to the conclusion that Host miracles were simply visual signs and not truly Christ's Blood, he was tolerant of the concept of these miracles. *Summa Theologica*, III, Q. 75, art. 5 asked: "Whether the accidents of the bread and wine remain in this sacrament after the change?" Objection 4 stated: "Further, what remains after the change has taken place seems to be the subject of change. If therefore the accidents of the bread remain after the change has been effected, it seems that the accidents are the subject of the change. But this is impossible; for 'an accident cannot have an accident' (Metaph. iii). Therefore the accidents of the bread and wine ought not to remain in this sacrament." On the contrary, Augustine says in his book on the Sentences of Prosper (Lanfranc, *De Corp. et Sang. Dom.* xiii): "Under the species which we behold, of bread and wine, we honor invisible things, i.e. flesh and blood." Aquinas' explanation and understanding of the physical revulsion that would be felt by priests if the species appeared as blood and flesh also helps explain why priests did not consume the products of Host miracles, as Hus advised in his treatise condemning Wilsnack and similar miracle shrines he had deemed false.

a pilgrim from Prague, Petrus von Aich, who hoped to cure his withered hand. Unfortunately, despite his leaving a silver hand at the shrine, no cure was effected. This did not stop the priest at Wilsnack from announcing that a cure had been obtained for a withered hand, and holding up the silver votive hand as proof. According to Hus, the Prague pilgrim happened to be in attendance while the priest was preaching about this false cure and displayed his still-withered hand to the congregation.[66] Hus' attack on Wilsnack's authenticity did not have the desired impact; instead, pilgrims came to Wilsnack in ever-greater numbers during the fifteenth century.

Imagery at the Wilsnack Shrine

The extant images pertaining to the Wilsnack pilgrimage are few in comparison to the rich decoration that exists in Orvieto Cathedral. Although the Wilsnack reliquary and the three miraculous Host wafers were destroyed in the Reformation, a large wooden tabernacle, made to enshrine the reliquary, is intact. (fig. 270) Its style indicates a date no later than the mid-fifteenth century, predating the building of the chapel dedicated to the miraculous blood relics. The use of wood in Northern shrines lent itself to painted imagery, as can be seen on the Wilsnack cupboard on both its exterior and interior. The narrative of the *Miraculous Mass of St. Gregory* spans both doors on the exterior of the tabernacle. In comparison to the Orvieto fresco of the same subject, a significant difference appears in the Wilsnack narrative. In place of the original eighth-century Eucharistic tale of St. Gregory, with the disembodied bleeding finger, or the thirteenth-century *Golden Legend* account of a lump of bleeding flesh, the Wilsnack cupboard displays a new version of the story in which St. Gregory's vision of the True Presence takes the form of a full-length bleeding Christ on the altar, surrounded by the *arma Christi*.[67]

---

[66] Hus, *De sanguine*, pp. 32–3; Breest, "Wunderblut von Wilsnack," pp. 163–4. One wonders if this famous account by Hus may have stimulated the identification of the doubting priest of the Miracle of Bolsena as a German or a Bohemian (Peter of Prague).

[67] See Joseph A. Endres, "Die Darstellung der Gregoriousmesse im Mittelalter, *Zeitschrift für christliche Kunst*, 30/11/12 (1917): 145–56; Erwin Panofsky, "'Imago Pietatis,' Ein Beitrag zur Typengeschichte des 'Schmerzensmanns' und der 'Maria Mediatrix,'" in *Festschrift für Max J. Friedländer zum 60. Geburtstage* (Leipzig, 1927),

Two distinct Eucharistic types emerged in the fifteenth century as a new visual synthesis: the narrative image of St. Gregory's Mass, a Holy Blood miracle, combined with the devotional image of the Real Presence known as the Man of Sorrows.

This visual evolution depended on an altered account of the Mass of St. Gregory connecting it to the devotional *imago pietatis* (image of pity), that had been gaining popularity since the late fourteenth century. The new version was similar to the traditional one: St. Gregory still celebrates Mass in a Roman church but the image of Christ appears to him as if He were really there at the moment of consecration.[68] An alternate legend, in effect, was provided in place of the earlier Host miracle of St. Gregory, with its rather unappealing bloody finger or piece of bloody flesh.[69] This conflation of the *imago pietatis* with the Mass of St. Gregory did not have a specific relic attached to it; instead, the *Man of Sorrows* image came to hold the properties of a relic, as the authentic manifestation of Gregory's vision. More than one pilgrimage site in Rome promoted this image,[70] which lent itself readily to a pre-established pattern of competing relics.[71] Several different images of the Man of Sorrows are mentioned by pilgrims and pilgrim guidebooks to Rome in the fifteenth century.[72] Perhaps the most frequently mentioned was the Byzantine

pp. 261–308. For the Eucharistic character of the Man of Sorrows in art, see Romuauld Bauerreiss, *Pie Jesu, Das Schmerzensmann-Bild und sein einfluss auf die Mittleaterliche Frömmigkeit* (Munich, 1931); Colin Eisler, "The Golden Christ of Cortona and the Man of Sorrows in Italy," *Art Bulletin*, 51 (1969), pp. 107–18, 233–46.

[68] Flora Lewis, "Rewarding Devotion: Indulgences and the Promotion of Images," in *The Church and the Arts, Studies in Church History*, vol. 28, (Oxford, 1992), p. 186. This story was popularized around the beginning of the fifteenth century, making its first appearance in the late fourteenth century. None of the versions specify in which Roman church Gregory's miraculous Mass was celebrated.

[69] Voragine, *The Golden Legend*, vol. 3, pp. 27–31.

[70] Lewis, "Rewarding Devotion," p. 186, states that a 1375 pilgrim guidebook, *Marvels of Rome*, contained a reference to an altar in the Church of S. Prisca, where the image of the crucified Christ appeared to St. Gregory. Although the Church of S. Prisca in Rome must be the one referred to in the guidebook, it should be noted that before the present Cathedral of Orvieto was built and dedicated to S. Maria Assunta (*c.* 1290), the old church on that site was known as S. Maria Prisca.

[71] St. Veronica's veil, for example, was claimed by a number of churches in Rome, and these made competing claims for the authenticity of the relic. Flora Lewis, "The Veronica: Image, Legend and Viewer," in W. Mark Ormrod, ed., *England in the Thirteenth century: Proceedings of the 1984 Harlaxton Symposium* (Woodbridge, 1985), pp. 100–6.

[72] Carlo Bertelli, "The 'Image of Pity' in Santa Croce in Gerusalemme," in *Essays in the History of Art Presented to Rudolf Wittkower* (London, 1967), p. 50, cited Nicholas

mosaic in the church of Sta. Croce in Gerusalemme, Rome.[73] To promote the practice of visiting the Roman shrines with images of the Man of Sorrows, a fictive history for the indulgences purported to originate with Gregory the Great.[74] The manuscripts which promulgated this pilgrimage stated that Pope Gregory felt such compassion at the sight of the suffering Christ that he had granted an indulgence to all those who said five *Paternosters* and five recitations of the *Ave Maria* before the image.[75]

The iconography of the Wilsnack shrine asserted its relationship with perhaps the most fundamental and authoritative bleeding-Host miracle involving doubt and proof, the Mass of St. Gregory. The left wing shows a large altar table, prominently displaying liturgical objects in three-quarter view, with a tilted perspective. St. Gregory is seen kneeling in profile before the altar, with his back to the painted congregation. Behind him, in the right wing, are two priests, whose scale, although also kneeling, is extraordinarily large. Slightly smaller in scale, additional figures, procession-like, spread out toward

Muffel who, on a 1452 visit to Rome, went to the church of S. Gregorio al Celio and saw an image of the *Mass of St. Gregory* in which Christ appears on the altar as the Man of Sorrows, accompanied by the *arma Christi*. Lewis, "Rewarding Devotion," p. 186, fn. 22, cites a guide to the churches of Rome, written for Margaret of York in the 1470s, which stated that the vision occurred in the Basilica of S. Sebastiano. Lewis also noted examples in which an image in the Pantheon is promoted.

[73] Bertelli, "The 'Image of Pity,'" p. 54, discussed the image in Sta. Croce in Gerusalemme, Rome, as having been promoted as the original. By the late fifteenth century, this image was reproduced in a print by Israhel van Meckenem. E. "Breitenback, "Israhel van Meckenem's Man of Sorrows," *Quarterly Journal of the Library of Congress*, 31 (1974): 21–6.

[74] Pilgrims visiting in Rome were to receive an indulgence for visiting the Man of Sorrows image, but not from a particular site. Lewis, "Rewarding Devotion," pp. 183–4, fn. 15–6, related the connection of the Man of Sorrows with the St. Gregory legend to a fictive history of the indulgence dating to around 1400, which can be found "in a group of English manuscripts." These focused on the alternate version of the Mass of St. Gregory where the image of Christ as the Man of Sorrows appears on the altar as the Pope celebrates Mass. The images accompanying the manuscripts show Christ as the Man of Sorrows.

[75] Lewis, "Rewarding Devotion," p. 184, fn. 16. My thanks to Dr. Sarah Blick, who suggested that the five repetitions of these indulgence prayers might be related to the five wounds of Christ. Caroline Bynum discusses the five wounds of Christ in conjunction with the *arma Christi* in "Violent Imagery in Late Medieval Piety," *German Historical Institute Journal*, 30 (Spring, 2002): 3–36, esp. pp. 5, 18–23. In this context she showed the outer panel of the Buxheim Altar (*c.* 1500) now in the Ulm Museum (pl. 5), in which the body of Christ disappears and the five bleeding wounds appear as body parts surrounded by the *arma Christi*.

the far right of the picture plane. This procession-like arrangement recalls the *Corpus Christi* parades which were standard throughout the fifteenth century, and an important attraction for masses of pilgrims who came to the village every June for the octave of the Feast.

Although one might expect to see the Wilsnack miracle narrative depicted, the Mass of St. Gregory takes precedence on the doors, in the new fifteenth-century formula. Fourteenth-century images were inexplicit as to the form of Christ's flesh found on the altar of St. Gregory. The original bleeding finger—unpalatable, but more important, inexplicit—becomes the Risen Christ standing on the altar, bleeding into a chalice.

On days of ostension of the relics, during *Corpus Christi* and at Easter, the cupboard doors would remain open to display the reliquary, and the paintings on the interior of the doors would have been visible to further elucidate the meaning of the Eucharist and its relics. The left interior door represents the devotional image of the *Gnadenstuhl*: God the Father holding Christ on the cross, with the dove of the Holy Spirit suspended between the two.[76] (fig. 271) On the right wing is an *imago pietatis*, recalling the images in Roman churches promoted as a type of relic of the Mass of St. Gregory. One can easily connect the Wilsnack shrine to the instructions to repeat the *Paternoster* and the *Ave Maria* before the Gregorian images of the Man of Sorrows in Rome. Pilgrims in Wilsnack must have knelt in front of these images praying, the *Gnadenstuhl* aiding in the contemplation of the sacrifice of Christ and the mystery of the Trinity. The *imago pietatis*, the devotionally isolated vision of Gregory the Great's miracle, would have reinforced the meaning of the Wilsnack miracle Hosts, and clarified Christ's real presence in the Eucharist.

The Wunderblutkapelle *at Wilsnack*

With the ever-increasing popularity of the Wilsnack shrine, the revenues of the Church of St. Nicholas grew, and in 1462 a new chapel was dedicated to the Host relics. The *Wunderblutkapelle* (miracle-blood

---

[76] My thanks to Dr. Gerhard Lutz for his generosity in supplying me with his as-yet unpublished photograph of the interior of the Wilsnack cupboard.

chapel) was built in the southeastern part of the church.[77] Almost
nothing remains of the painted imagery in the chapel, but a group
of fifteen woodcuts (*c.* 1520) provide a glimpse of the iconography.
The cycle seems to have focused not just on doubt of the Real
Presence, but on a more complicated construction of the doubting
of the miracle by the Bishop of Havelburg, the ecclesiastical authority over the parish of Wilsnack.

By 1462, the Wilsnack shrine had successfully weathered the most
recent attack, by Nicholas of Cusa, along with a large group of
reformist theologian/scholars associated with the University at Erfurt,
including Heinrich Tocke.[78] In 1443, Tocke went to Wilsnack to
view the shrine. He and the Erfurt theologians took the same stand
that Hus had taken on the issue: the mystery of transubstantiation
was not a physical phenomenon, and all of Christ's corporeal blood
had been glorified with his body at the time of his Resurrection,
thus the blood of Host miracles could not be considered, in truth,
that of Christ's body.[79] In 1451, Tocke spoke to the provincial Synod
at Magdeburg condemning the relics of Wilsnack as a deception.
His speech was attended by Nicholas of Cusa, who was engaged in
an extended trip, as the reforming papal legate to the Germanies,
from January 1451–April 1452.[80] As the controversy raged on, Cusa
issued a decree attacking bleeding-Host cults, excommunicating those

---

[77] For discussion and diagrams see Folkhard Cremer, *Die St. Nikolaus-und Heiligblut-Kirche*, especially the reconstruction of the placement of altars and sculpted figures in Ground plan I, and the diagram showing the flow of pilgrims through the chapel, apse and transepts in Ground plan IX.

[78] The extended attack was initiated in 1443 by Tocke, a theologian at the University of Erfurt before becoming lector and canon at Magdeburg; he attacked other Host-miracle shrines as well as Wilsnack. Zika, "Hosts," p. 51, fn. 82. At the beginning of the fifteenth century, Jan Hus set the tone for these later attacks on the shrine, and in 1446, following Hus' line of thought, Tocke drew up "Fourteen Questions." In 1447, the Erfurt theologians responded with the tract "*Super dubiis*," answering the crucial questions asked by Tocke: whether any blood at all was to be found on the miraculous Hosts, and whether this could in any way be Christ's blood. Zika, "Hosts," p. 53, fn. 89, cites Herzo-August-Biliothek, Wolfenbüttel, Cod-Guelf. 152 Helmst., "Super dubiis circa sacrum, quod dicitur esse in Wilczenack," folios 160–4; Breest, "Wunderblut von Wilsnack," pp. 213, 221.

[79] Powerful clerics and laity who disagreed met to discuss the issue in a series of five conferences during 1446–47. Zika, "Hosts," p. 52.

[80] Morimichi Watanabe, "The German Church Shortly Before the Reformation: Nicolaus Cusanus and the Veneration of the Bleeding Hosts at Wilsnack," in *Reform and Renewal in the Middle Ages and the Renaissance: Studies in Honor of Louis Pascoe*, ed. Thomas M. Izbicki and Christopher M. Bellitto (Leiden, 2000), p. 211.

who displayed such Hosts, and threatening interdict on any territories where these practices continued.[81] The dissenters refused to comply with Cusa's decree, ignoring their archbishop's subsequent edict of excommunication and interdict. Confounding Cusa's order, Pope Eugenius IV issued a bull in 1446 which endowed lavish indulgences on the cult, and his successor, Nicholas V approved the recommendations made by Eugenius.[82] In 1453 Nicholas V put an end to the conflict by removing the censures and interdict imposed by Nicholas of Cusa.[83]

The cult of the Wilsnack miracle continued to grow in size and importance, countering the doubt expressed by many theologians. The fifteen woodcut images (*c.* 1520) demonstrate that the paintings in the Wunderblutkapelle were intentionally linked to the Orvieto legend.[84] (fig. 272) According to Tocke's 1443 description of the shrine, it appears that the paintings were part of the later program of the Wilsnack chapel dedicated in 1462.[85] These woodcut scenes

---

[81] Cusa did not name Wilsnack specifically in his decree of July 5, 1451. Watanabe, "The German Church Shortly Before the Reformation," p. 220, states that "it is quite possible that as papal legate, he did not wish to contradict directly Pope Nicholas V's approval of Wilsnack in 1447." Watanabe also considered Cusa's decisions against the background of papal indulgences granted by Pope Eugenius IV and Nicholas V, and discussed the possibility that Cusa visited Wilsnack, pp. 219–21. See also Dennis Sullivan, "Nicholas of Cusa as Reformer: the Papal Legation to the Germanies, 1451–1452," *Medieval Studies* 36 (1974), pp. 403–4; Morimichi Watanabe, *Concord and Reform: Nicholas of Cusa and Legal and Political Thought in the Fifteenth Century* (Aldershot, UK, 2001).

[82] In 1433 Eugenius granted a miracle Host to Philip the Good of Burgundy, and issued a bull describing the gift. The Host relic was placed in the Burgundian family funerary chapel in the Chartreuse de Champmol. A gold reliquary was made for this Host relic in 1454, and a full-page illumination was dedicated to the "Holy Host of Dijon" in a book of hours. Rubin, *Gentile Tales*, p. 163, fns. 90–1. See fig. 300 in this volume. To counteract one of the fears expressed by Hus and by subsequent deriders of bleeding-Host shrines, Eugenius recommended that a newly-consecrated Host be placed beside the Host relics and that they be permitted to be exposed on specific days. Zika, "Hosts," pp. 51–2.

[83] Breest, "Wunderblut von Wilsnack," pp. 209–10, 229, 241–6; Zika, "Hosts," pp. 51–2. Nicholas of Cusa turned his attention to reforms in Rome and Orvieto during the last year of his life. Erich Meuthen, *Die letzten Jahre des Nikolaus von Kues: Biographische Untersuchungen nach neurern Quellen* (Cologne, 1958), pp. 110–25, 249–300.

[84] Lichte, *Die Inszenierung einer Wallfahrt*, p. 16, noted that the narration of the Wilsnack miracle was based on the widespread fourteenth-century legend of the Mass of Bolsena. She states that the narrative of the bishop of Havelberg's doubt solidified the Wilsnack miracle blood in two ways: first, it announced the confirmation of the local ecclesiastical authorities, and second it reminded the faithful indirectly of a similar event which had received papal approval.

[85] Cremer, *Die St. Nikolaus- und Heiligblut-Kirche*, pp. 178–9.

follow the iconography of fifteen panel paintings that were installed, along with a placard recounting the legend, in the new chapel. In visual form, they connect the finding and reporting of the Wilsnack miracle directly to that at Bolsena.

The woodcuts series begins with the destruction of Wilsnack, with flames shooting out from the houses and from the parish church. A mystical typology is established in the next scene, not unlike the annunciation to the shepherds in a christological cycle, with the parish priest and villagers in the countryside, after the routing and fire, receiving a divine revelation. The fifth and sixth scenes of the series are significant and here the intersections with the Orvieto frescos become apparent: the priest finds the intact Host wafers on the altar of the ruined church and then, with the same simple folk in attendance, the priest kneels at the altar with the three blood-spotted Hosts in a monstrance. In the eighth and ninth scenes, the parish priest alerts the Bishop of Havelberg of the miracle, and the similarity to Orvieto increases through formal and iconographic means.

As the Wilsnack legend states, the Bishop had doubted the truth of the miraculous bloody Hosts, and thus the tenth scene shows him traveling on horseback, about to cross a river to Wilsnack, to investigate the miracle. In the next scene, the Bishop, celebrating Mass at the altar in Wilsnack and, like the priest at St. Christina at Bolsena in the Orvieto reliquary and frescoes, on seeing the bloody Hosts, is convinced of the authenticity of the miracle. The closing scenes again strengthen the connection to the Orvieto imagery: the Bishop, from an arched window, displays the miracle Hosts in a monstrance-reliquary for the crowd to see.

The final scene establishes once and for all the authority of the miracle: it shows the Bishop, standing before the Pope and his retinue. However, instead of Urban IV as seen in the Orvieto frescos, it is Urban VI, who granted Wilsnack its first indulgence in 1384 to help with the rebuilding of the church of St. Nicholas, the *Heiligblut Kirche*, the church of the Holy Blood.

The frescoes in Orvieto and the panel paintings in Wilsnack concentrate on doubt and subsequent authoritative proof. The Bolsena miracle was meant to illustrate the True Presence to the laity, at a time when the dogma of transubstantiation was still newly-resolved. A century later, the pilgrimage church of Wilsnack promoted its Host relics in a way that connected them to earlier authoritative miracles. Like Orvieto, its program built a foundation on the Mass of St.

Gregory, but after the controversy of the mid-fifteenth century, Wilsnack also used the iconography of the Host-miracle shrine in Orvieto to help establish its legitimacy. The intimate connection of the papacy to the Orvieto miracle protected it from clerical questions of authenticity. However, at the Wilsnack shrine the issue addressed was not just doubt about transubstantiation, but doubt about the miracle itself. In its implied connection to the Bolsena relics, with their special papal approbation, and in the explicit recollection of Urban VI's 1383 endorsement, the Wilsnack imagery was a resounding answer to those who had doubted the miracle and questioned its spiritual efficacy for the pilgrims who came to visit the shrine.

CHAPTER TWENTY-ONE

BUILDING A PRESBYTERY FOR ST. ÆTHELTHRYTH: BISHOP HUGH DE NORTHWOLD AND THE POLITICS OF CULT PRODUCTION IN THIRTEENTH-CENTURY ENGLAND*

Virginia Blanton

Over time, Hugh de Northwold, bishop of Ely (r. 1229–54), became a strong proponent of the cult of Æthelthryth, Ely's founder and patron saint, and during his administration of the diocese, he worked to develop the monastic cathedral as a significant center of pilgrimage.[1] While the monastic community had been fairly successful at cult promotion during the twelfth century, producing numerous *vitae* and a collection of miracle stories that documented pilgrimage to Æthelthryth's shrine, Hugh's position as bishop and civil servant to Henry III (1216–72) offered a pivotal opportunity to draw even more lay visitors to Ely and by extension, to enlarge the reputation of the monastic cathedral.[2] Specifically, the bishop increased episcopal revenues and land holdings, gave the Benedictine priory at Ely manors

---

* I wish to thank three research assistants, who provided invaluable help bringing this article to fruition: Gale Canale, Tara Krompinger, and Martha Johnson-Olin.

[1] Since the saint is Anglo-Saxon, I retain the use of Æthelthryth throughout this piece. Her Latin name is Etheldreda, but the Anglo-Norman derivation became Audrey. Throughout this article, feast days or translation feast days will be used for saints rather than their life dates, which are rarely certain for seventh-century saints; those given for royals and bishops will reflect their reigns, not their life dates unless otherwise noted.

[2] The monastic chronicle, *Liber Eliensis*, compiled between 1131–74, includes a collection of miracle stories associated with the shrine, as well as an extended *vita* of Æthelthryth in Latin. Based on this narrative account, several others were written or translated, including one in Anglo-Norman which has been edited as *La Vie Seinte Audree: Poème Anglo-Normand du XIIIe Siècle*, (ed.) Östen Södergard, Uppsala Universitets Årsskrift, no. 11 (Uppsala, 1955). The Anglo-Norman text has been dated as early as 1174 and as late as 1250, so it might be associated with Bishop Hugh's administration. The standard edition of the monastic chronicle is *Liber Eliensis*, (ed.) Ernest O. Blake (London, 1962). Blake discussed the source text for the Latin *vita* of Æthelthryth, pp. xxx–xxxi.

to increase the monks' income, rebuilt episcopal palaces, reorganized and refurbished the two monastic hospitals in Ely, and financed a major expansion of the cathedral's east end, which became a sanctuary for the relics of Ely's most important saints: Æthelthryth, her sisters, Sexburg († after 695) and Wihtburg († c. 743), as well as her niece, Eormenhild († c. 700).[3] Hugh's development activities indicate that he was an invested administrator of the diocese; his improvement of the cathedral fabric, which included the construction of the presbytery and the erection of a new shrine base, reveals an attention to the visual manifestations associated with Æthelthryth's shrine. In so doing, he drew upon the economic wealth of the diocese to construct the cathedral space, and he decorated it in lavish fashion to attract attention to the setting of her repose.[4]

Although Hugh de Northwold had served previously as abbot of the monastery at Bury St. Edmunds and had been a devotee of St. Edmund, the bishop embraced the cult of Æthelthryth after his appointment to Ely, and his architectural expansion of the cathedral's east end resulted in a presbytery created to showcase Ely's magnificence.[5] In effect, the space was designed to house the four

---

[3] James Bentham, *The History and Antiquities of the Cathedral and Conventual Church of Ely, from the Foundation of the Monastery, A.D. 673, To the Year 1771* (Norwich, 1812). Wihtburg's identity is in dispute, as is her date of death, but I use the date accepted by the monastic community at Ely as evidence of their active cult promotion of these women.

[4] For Bishop Hugh's systematic enlargement of the episcopal lands and revenues see Edward Miller, *The Abbey and Bishopric of Ely: The Social History of an Ecclesiastical Estate from the Tenth Century to the Early Fourteenth Century* (Cambridge, 1951).

[5] Marion Roberts, "The Effigy of Bishop Hugh de Northwold in Ely Cathedral," *Burlington Magazine* 130 (1988), pp. 77–84 discussed how the bishop's tomb slab illustrated Bishop Hugh's regard for the two saints. The martyrdom of Edmund is carved at his feet, and figures of Edmund and Æthelthryth decorate the sides of his tomb. Although the top of the effigy is missing, several architectural details beneath the bishop's head are visible, and one wonders if the building of the presbytery (or perhaps Æthelthryth's foundation of Ely) was originally represented. Adjacent to the presbytery, Bishop Hugh dedicated a chapel to Edmund, and a wall painting showing his martyrdom survives there. The presbytery, the tomb slab, and the chapel indicate that Bishop Hugh used his position to promote his two favorite saints. Given that he directed his burial at the feet of Æthelthryth in the presbytery, it is clear he identified with the saint and wanted to lie within the space he had erected for her. While this essay will demonstrate Hugh's patronage of Ely, Rodney M. Thomson, *The Chronicle of The Election of Hugh, Abbot of Bury St. Edmunds and Later Bishop of Ely* (Oxford, 1974), pp. 195–6 discussed Hugh's resources and named him a generous benefactor to Bury St. Edmunds who initiated the building of a new cloister.

shrines and to provide lay access to the saints' tombs without inter-
fering with the monastic choir, which in the medieval period was
situated at the crossing.[6] To promote the new presbytery or retro-
choir as a site of pilgrimage, the bishop devised a spectacular dedication ceremony to mark the completion of this building program;
those present included Henry III, Prince Edward (1239–1307), and
various prelates and nobles, all of whom were promised indulgences
for attending. Just prior to the event, the shrines were moved from
the original high altar east into the newly-fabricated presbytery, and
on September 17, 1252, Bishop Hugh re-dedicated the entire cathedral to the Virgin Mary, Peter, and the founder, Æthelthryth.[7]

No records indicate the numbers of pilgrims or their gifts to the
shrine following the 1252 dedication ceremony. Ben Nilson examined the surviving shrine receipts, which begin in 1291, and concluded that "the shrine of St. Etheldreda was a considerable source
of profit," with a per annum average of £40 between 1330 and
1520.[8] While the credit for the significant revenues generated at
Æthelthryth's shrine in the fourteenth and early fifteenth centuries
cannot be directly attributed to Hugh de Northwold's thirteenth-
century vision, this later evidence suggests that his administrative
foresight influenced the shape and scope of the late medieval cult;
it seems that he continued the traditions of an already-successful pilgrimage center and provided the physical space necessary to draw
pilgrims as well as to accommodate them.[9] Yet, it appears that despite
the bishop's best-laid plans, the production at Ely was hindered by
the patronage activities of Henry III, whose investment in the cult
of St. Edward the Confessor at Westminster Abbey lay in direct

---

[6] Ben Nilson, *Cathedral Shrines of Medieval England* (Woodbridge, UK, 2001), p. 74.
Following the present arrangement, many floor plans of Ely misrepresent the place
of the choir during the medieval period, which was located at the crossing. Peter
Draper wrote an excellent discussion of the medieval liturgical arrangement in
"Bishop Northwold and the Cult of Saint Etheldreda," in *Medieval Art and Architecture
at Ely Cathedral*, ed. Nicola Coldstream and Peter Draper (Leeds, 1979), p. 9.

[7] Henry Wharton, *Anglia Sacra*, part 1 (London, 1591), p. 636.

[8] Nilson, *Cathedral Shrines*, p. 154, 235.

[9] Draper, "Bishop Northwold," pp. 8–27 discussed the bishop's attention to the
cult of Æthelthryth, detailing the building campaign of the presbytery and indicating that the bishop provided the lion's share of revenues for the project. Draper
also compared the construction of the presbytery to other English building programs effected between 1190–1270, and suggested that Æthelthryth's shrine base
was a model for Edward the Confessor's.

conflict with Bishop Hugh's promotion of St. Æthelthryth. In effect, this conflict shortchanged the bishop's plans and effectively curtailed the established traditions associated with Æthelthryth's translation feast.

The confrontation between Bishop Hugh and Henry III occurred in 1248, after the king had embarked on a campaign to build a new shrine for Edward the Confessor in 1241. Drawing upon the presentation of Henry's patronage activities in Matthew Paris' *Chronica Majora*, Suzanne Lewis discussed Henry's support of this cult and his promotion of the abbey as a pilgrimage center.[10] This study indicates that Henry III was highly invested in promoting the royal cult of Edward, in part to illustrate the king's direct connection with an Anglo-Saxon predecessor who had asserted ecclesiastical prerogatives over the bishops of England.[11] Henry's patronage of Westminster Abbey extended throughout his reign, but as Lewis argued, the king initiated a program in 1245 to extend the east end of the abbey, just as his conflicts with episcopal authorities became more heated. In effect, Henry copied the models already in progress at Canterbury and Worcester, imitating and overshadowing projects like Hugh de Northwold's, begun in 1234. Certainly, cathedrals across England were competing for pilgrims, many by enlarging the space reserved for holy relics, and Ely was not a larger threat to Westminster than any of the cult centers being promoted at this time,[12] but several passages within Matthew's chronicle indicate a rift between Bishop Hugh and Henry III over their respective building programs. Their devotion to the patrons of these institutions, I argue here, lies at the heart of their discord, for each deliberately promoted the cult of an Anglo-Saxon saint; each developed a new building project and had the shrine of his patron translated into it; and each directed that he be buried in close proximity to the shrine he had promoted. These activities might simply suggest an established pattern of institutional patronage in the thirteenth century, but it is important to examine the close relationship between the bishop and the king and to consider their behavior as patrons and rivals for the considerable profits

---

[10] Suzanne Lewis, "Henry III and the Gothic Rebuilding of Westminster Abbey: The Problematics of Context," *Traditio* 50 (1995): 129–72.

[11] Lewis, "Henry III and the Gothic Rebuilding of Westminster Abbey," p. 158.

[12] Draper, "Bishop Northwold," pp. 10–2, 20–1 noted the competition among Westminster, Canterbury, and St. Paul's.

of pilgrimage. In the following discussion I examine the accord and rivalry between Bishop Hugh and King Henry III over cult-building activities and discuss these endeavors as part of a larger initiative of institutionalized patronage in thirteenth-century England. At the center of this study is a consideration of Hugh de Northwold's effect on pilgrimage at Ely. Ultimately, the shrine receipts for the cult of Æthelthryth far exceeded those for the shrine of Edward the Confessor in the fourteenth century, indicating that despite the king's efforts to minimize the influence of Westminster's competitor institutions, the cult of Æthelthryth was not diminished; indeed, lay pilgrimage at Ely remained a norm whereas Westminster became a site of royal pilgrimage but not necessarily one for laity in general.[13]

Bishop Hugh's Presbytery

Not unlike spectacles at other cathedrals in this period, the re-dedication of Ely Cathedral was designed to showcase the new presbytery, to impress outsiders with Ely's wealth and stature as a repository of relics, and to encourage pilgrims to visit this ornate space. The event was recorded in detail by Matthew Paris, who had long been an admirer of Hugh as an episcopal administrator:

> On the 17th of September in this year, which was St. Lambert's day, the noble cathedral of Ely was dedicated with great pomp and magnificence. The presbytery of this church, besides a handsome tower of wonderful and expensive workmanship, had been entirely and completely built by, and at the sole expense of, Hugh, bishop of that place, a special observer of all that was honorable and good. This same bishop had also built in his court of Ely, a handsome royal palace, with rooms and other appropriate buildings, in which those who were present at the ceremony of dedication partook of the rich delicacies of a festive banquet, as will be related in the following narrative. In performing the rites of dedication, which had been an object of his earnest desire for a long time before, the bishop of Ely was assisted by the bishops of Norwich and Llandaff, there being also present at

---

[13] Nilson, *Cathedral Shrines*, pp. 117–21. Brian Spencer, *Pilgrim Souvenirs and Secular Badges* (London, 1998), pp. 182–3, 186–9 wrote that while royalty visited shrines at Westminster, other lay pilgrims were not drawn there, despite Henry VII's gift of a shrine for St. George, a popular cult figure.

the ceremony the king himself, and a great many of the nobles of the
kingdom, besides innumerable prelates and clerks. An indulgence of
several days was granted to all those who had come to participate in
the ceremonies, and also to those who might come afterwards. After
a due observance of spiritual festivities, they directed their thoughts to
the feasting of their bodies, and the dwellings of the monks, as well
as of the bishops and of those living in the town, were filled with
guests; yet the bishop lamented the small number of the assembled
guests, declaring that the entertainment he had proposed to himself
was, in a great measure, shorn of its just dimensions. He, however,
rejoiced in spirit with the greatest exultation, that by God's favor he
had been allowed to wait for that day in which he had beheld the
happy consummation of all his long-preconceived designs and arrangements; so that in his joy and exultation the happy old bishop could
say, with the venerable Simeon, 'Now lettest thou thy servant' . . .[14]

Matthew Paris's description of the celebration activities is highly
specific, as is his account of Bishop Hugh's deflation over the limited number of gifts. Still, the passage does not recount the dedication ceremony, nor does it include architectural details about the
presbytery or the translation of the saints' relics.[15] Instead, Matthew

---

[14] *Matthew Paris's English History, from the Year 1235 to 1273*, trans. John A. Giles
(London, 1853), pp. 515–6. The original text, which is Matthew Paris, *Chronica
Majora*, vol. 5, ed. Henry Richards Luard (London, 1880), p. 322:
  *Anno quoque sub eodem, decimo quinto kalendas Octobris, die videlicet sancti Lamberti, ded-
  icata est magnifice ac sollempniter nimis nobilis ecclesia cathedralis Elyensis; cujus presbi-
  terium, præterque hoc turrim excellentissimam, opere admirabili ac sumptuoso nimis Hugo
  ejusdem loci episcopus, omnis honoris et honestatis amator magnificus, propriis sumptibus
  usque ad perfectam consummationem construxerat. Idem quoque episcopus regale palatium
  cum thalamis et aliis ædificiis ad idem pertinentibus in curia sua Elyensi gloriose ædificaverat,
  in quo festive coepulabantur et laute, qui sollempnitati dedicationis intererant, sicut dicetur
  in sequentibus. Officio igitur intererant dedicationis ipse Elyensis episcopus, quod diu ante
  sitienter desiderarat; item Norwicensis et Landavensis episcopi. Affueruntque eidem sollempnitati dominus rex et multi magnates regni, prælati quoque et clerici innumerabiles. Et con-
  cessa est multa[rum] dierum indulgentia cunctis qui ad illam sollempnitatem convenerant et
  fuerant in posterum conventuri. Et post festa spiritualia gloriose celebrata ad corporalia con-
  sequenter diverterunt. Et repleta sunt tam ipsorum monachorum quam episcopi vel in ipso
  municipio conversantium ædificia convivantibus. Et adhuc doluit episcopus de paucitate con-
  gregatorum, affirmans convivium citra propositum suum pro magna parte mutilatum. Gratulabatur
  igitur in spiritu maximæ exultationis, quod Deo propitio diem illum meruit expectasse, qua
  omnia in suo longo proposito quæ præconceperat et concepta præordinaverat, viderat jam feliciter
  consummata, ut ipse beatus senex cum sene, episcopus cum Symeone, exultans in jubilo diceret,
  Nunc dimittis servum tuum, . . .*
[15] In his 1254 eulogy of Bishop Hugh, Matthew Paris, *Chronica Majora*, vol. 5,
pp. 454–5 indicated that the presbytery was magnificent, built of marble at the
bishop's expense. The lack of architectural detail and the omission of information
about the dedication ceremony may be indicative of a type of chronicle narrative
about translation ceremonies. For instance, two poems were written about the trans-

focuses on the construction of the presbytery and the episcopal palace, the eminence of the attendees, and the abundance of food, all planned by the bishop to demonstrate the magnificence of his diocese. Matthew stresses, moreover, that attendees, as well as those who were to visit the shrine after the event, were granted indulgences.[16] This small detail speaks to the bishop's concern that people visit Ely, that they see his new presbytery, and that they pray at Æthelthryth's shrine. Despite the bishop's careful preparation, the chronicler indicates that Hugh was disappointed in the number in attendance, intimating that the spectacle did not go as planned. Undoubtedly, individual pilgrims were recorded carefully to account for their promised indulgences, but outside the king and the bishops of Norwich and Llandaff, no details survive to demonstrate who attended the ceremony. Likewise, no surviving records indicate the number or identity of visitors to the shrine after the dedication.

The presentation of events, including the disappointment of the bishop, is curiously revealing. When many narratives recount the fantastic elements of an ecclesiastical event—in part to inflate its importance—this one reads more realistically, and it seems safe to accept the presentation of the bishop's investment in the Ely cult. The description of Hugh's activities, moreover, indicates an interest in providing spaces designed to house guests during the dedication revelries, and the construction of lavish accommodations indicates the bishop's awareness of the effect of architectural munificence on visitors. His desire to increase the grandeur of the cathedral, as well as his insistence on building guest houses, speaks to his concern that attendees leave the celebration impressed by the feasting and by the new architectural spaces. Matthew Paris' account, as well as his

---

lation of Thomas Becket in 1220, and neither offers names of important laymen and only one describes the procession and the translation. More important, however, the former noted the importance of the indulgences promised to pilgrims and the latter recounts the lavish meals shared by the guests, which accords with Matthew Paris' recitation of the Ely festivities. See "Life and Translation of St. Thomas à Becket," in *The Shorter Latin Poems of Master Henry of Avranches*, ed. Josiah Cox Russell and John Paul Heironimus (1935; repr. New York: Kraus, 1970), pp. 64–78. My thanks go to Sarah Blick for bringing this reference to my attention.

[16] In response to some egregious examples, the Fourth Latern Council curtailed episcopal authority to grant indulgences, and the sixty-second canon limited a bishop to offering one hundred days to mark the dedication of a church. Diana Webb, *Pilgrimage in Medieval England* (London, 2000), p. 66.

description of the bishop's disappointment, suggests he knew about
Hugh's plans, even as it intimates a close relation to him. It is unclear
whether or not Matthew attended the dedication, but the lengthy
description of revelries suggests that he was actually present. A lack
of architectural details, on the other hand, suggests that he was not,
for he offers no details about the dedication or about the position
of the shrines. Perhaps, too, this omission indicates a lack of interest in the Ely cults or perhaps only a significant interest in Bishop
Hugh as an administrator. In any case, the record of this event offers
concrete evidence of the bishop's activities as patron, even if it does
not provide a great deal of direct information about the spectacle
itself.

While the generality of Matthew Paris' description of the architectural
program thwarts an investigation of the new presbytery as a site of
pilgrimage, and while there is no contemporary account of its details,
enough of Bishop Hugh's work remains to demonstrate the scope
and intention of the project. The fabric of the eastern extension has
been discussed in detail by Thomas D. Atkinson, who indicated that
the project comprised removing the existing Norman apse, adding
six bays and aisles to the four Romanesque ones east of the choir,
and replacing the semicircular form with a square east end.[17] Figure
273 illustrates the cathedral floor plan *c.* 1225 and figure 274 provides a reconstruction of the liturgical layout *c.* 1530, including the
presbytery and tomb placements, for comparison. The entire space,
including the elaborate vaulting, was constructed with Purbeck marble. (fig. 275) Atkinson stressed that the ornamental details in Early
English style were quite rich, "carved with the characteristic foliage
of the period."[18] Peter Draper's assessment affirmed that the rich
ornamentation of the presbytery was in accord with its use as a space
for holy relics, and he contended that "in the Early English style
Ely presbytery is unsurpassed in the degree of surface embellishment."[19] (fig. 276) This architectural space, which must have seemed
magnificent in comparison to the Norman apse, provided pilgrims
with a larger, more ornate space. The increased size alone would have

---

[17] Thomas D. Atkinson, "The Cathedral," in *The Victoria History of the County of
Cambridge and the Isle of Ely*, vol. 4, (ed.) Ralph B. Pugh (London, 1953), pp. 50–77,
esp. pp. 57–60.
[18] Atkinson, "The Cathedral," p. 59.
[19] Draper, "Bishop Northwold," pp. 8–10.

been awe-inspiring, but the decorative details indicate that Bishop
Hugh intended that the space be visually arresting, not to detract
from the shrine, but to emphasize its importance. In other words,
if the building project was completed precisely to house the shrine
of Æthelthryth, fabric ornamentation had to equal the magnificence
of the shrine, which was the crown jewel of the presbytery.

The ritual arrangement of tombs in 1252 has never been satis-
factorily presented, in part because no record, monastic or episcopal, notes the exact placement of Æthelthryth's shrine or the location
of the sororal tombs in the presbytery.[20] Draper suggested that three
roof bosses indicate the site of the central shrine, even if they do
not reveal the location of the other tombs. Featured on the vaulted
ceiling are images of Æthelthryth, the Annunciation, and St. Peter,
which accord with the bishop's re-dedication of the cathedral to these
three figures. The placement of the boss featuring Æthelthryth in
the center of the vault, five bays from the east, most likely indicates
that the shrine was placed directly under it.[21] (fig. 277) While the
destruction of the shrines at the Reformation means that the precise locations of the tombs cannot be known, surviving records indicate that Eormenhild lay at the northeast corner of the presbytery
next to a relic of St. Alban and that, upon the death of Hugh de
Northwold, the bishop's body was placed at the feet of Æthelthryth.[22]
Atkinson's conjectural plan (fig. 274) demonstrated a possible arrangement, with the sororal tombs behind the high altar, though they
may have been positioned just before the high altar and nearer to
the central shrine of Æthelthryth. The details about Eormenhild's
and Hugh's tombs indicate that an earlier liturgical arrangement was
changed significantly when the presbytery was built to highlight
Æthelthryth's tomb, and possibly, to allow Bishop Hugh to place his
own tomb in close proximity to the central shrine.

The placement of each tomb in 1106 was carefully recorded in
the monastic chronicle, known as the *Liber Eliensis*. During the twelfth-
century promotion of the cult, Ely produced a detailed record of

---

[20] Atkinson, "The Cathedral," pp. 57–9; Draper, "Bishop Northwold," pp. 13–5.

[21] Draper, "Bishop Northwold," p. 13; Charles J.P. Cave, *Roof Bosses in Medieval Churches: An Aspect of Gothic Sculpture* (Cambridge, 1948). Note that Figure 2, dated 1937, incorrectly positions the roof boss and shrine at the fourth bay, rather than at the fifth.

[22] Draper, "Bishop Northwold," pp. 13–4.

Æthelthryth's life, her foundation at Ely, and the monastery's history up until 1174. The *Liber Eliensis* records that, as part of a campaign to gain approval for an episcopal seat at the Benedictine abbey,
the abbot finished building the Norman church, and on October 17,
1106, he enshrined there the four tombs of Æthelthryth, Sexburg,
Wihtburg, and Eormenhild. The chronicle is explicit about the placement of Æthelthryth's sarcophagus in the new church, indicating that
it was positioned adjacent to the high altar with Sexburg's tomb to
the east of it, Eormenhild's to the south, and Wihtburg's to the
north.[23] (fig. 278) The monastic chronicle also offers a detailed description of the gabled shrine, which was included in an inventory list
revised after 1143. The shrine was covered in silver plate, ornamented with gems, and engraved with images on the four sides and
on the gabled ends. Bentham offers a reconstruction of the shrine,
based on this description.[24] (fig. 279) Between the 1106 translation
and the beginning of Bishop Hugh's building program, the shrine
itself was augmented by two Ely bishops, Geoffrey Ridel (r. 1174–89),
who repaired the silver on two sides, and Hugh's predecessor, Geoffrey
de Burgh (r. 1225–29), who gilded the shrine and added an ornamental piece to the top.[25]

The placement of the shrines in 1106 demonstrates the intention
of showcasing the four women together.[26] The embellishment of the
shrine on two occasions just prior to Bishop Hugh's building program illustrates an episcopal interest in honoring Ely's patron, as
well as a concern with the visual aspect of Æthelthryth's tomb. This
concern accords with the increased interest in shrine cults during
this period, when cathedrals were actively translating the shrines of

---

[23] *Liber Eliensis*, pp. 230–1, 290.

[24] *Liber Eliensis*, pp. 289–90. The editor of the chronicle indicated that the inventory is dated January 5, 1134, but it included losses that occurred after 1143 when
the bishop required the priory to help him pay a pay a penalty for supporting
Matilda over Stephen. The monks used silver from the shrine to raise the required
£200, and in exchange, the bishop gave them a manor specifically to pay for
repairs. See Nilson, *Cathedral Shrines*, p. 140.

[25] Bentham, *Church of Ely*, pp. 142, 146. Geoffrey de Burgh also arranged for a
candle to burn perpetually on Æthelthryth's altar, which must have been positioned
to the west of her shrine.

[26] For a discussion of the 1106 translation and its political terms, see my article,
"King Anna's Daughters: Genealogical Narrative and Cult Formation in the *Liber
Eliensis*," *Historical Reflections/Réflexions Historiques* 30.1 (2004): 127–49.

saints and developing new shrine bases for the tombs.[27] The re-
arrangement of the shrines at Ely is suggestive of the interest in promoting Æthelthryth individually. The chronicle indicates that in 1106,
Eormenhild lay to the south of Æthelthryth and that Sexburg was
buried at Æthelthryth's feet; after 1252, Eormenhild rested in the
northeast corner of the presbytery, and Bishop Hugh's tomb was
placed east of Æthelthryth's shrine. These details indicate that once
the presbytery was complete the tombs were not simply moved eastward into the new space in their original configuration. Instead, it
appears that the founder's shrine stood alone or at least some distance from the others in order to accommodate Bishop Hugh's burial to the east of it. As Atkinson showed (fig. 274), two of the bays
lay to the east of the high altar and the west bay was taken up by
the choir altar. With a complete length of ninety-four and a half
feet and with each bay measuring on average fifteen and three-quarters feet, the central space of the presbytery itself is just over forty-
seven feet long.[28] It seems reasonable to conclude that the tombs of
Sexburg, Wihtburg, and Eormenhild were placed in the two bays
behind the high altar. This position would downplay the importance
of the secondary tombs and, at the same time, provide greater access
to Æthelthryth's shrine.[29] While it is possible that all four tombs were
arranged within the presbytery itself, an analysis of the shrine base
suggests that forty-seven feet would not have been enough to accommodate Æthelthryth's shrine, an altar for the shrine, the tomb of
Hugh de Northwold, and the family tombs as well.

Only fragments of the stone shrine base survive, but they match
the Early English ornamentation in the presbytery and provide evidence that Hugh de Northwold was intentionally identifying the space

---

[27] Nicola Coldstream, "English Decorated Shrine Bases," *Journal of the British
Archaeological Association* 129 (1976): 15–34.

[28] These measurement are from Draper, "Bishop Northwold," p. 9 who noted
that the bay length was approximately 4.80 meters.

[29] Nilson, *Cathedral Shrines*, pp. 76–91 argued that the exhibition of the shrines
came to be a happy result of these campaigns, not the reason for them. His evidence suggests that in several cathedrals he is correct, but it does not accord with
what is known about Ely and Bishop Hugh's dedication ceremony. It is possible
that the Ely presbytery was begun in 1234 without regard to the shrine and that
the idea evolved to use the space as a presbytery. Certainly by 1252, when the
space was completed, the intention was to demonstrate the presbytery as the new
home to Æthelthryth's shrine.

with the shrine, the shrine with the space.[30] Based on these stone fragments, Atkinson offered a reconstruction of the shrine base.[31] (fig. 280) While the exact shape or scope of the monument cannot be confirmed, Atkinson's drawing shows a base roughly six feet wide and nine feet long, and as Nilson stressed, the base was larger than the standard four by eight.[32] One might account for the enlarged length and width of the base, if one were to accept Bede's description of the first translation in 695, when Sexburg placed Æthelthryth in a Roman sarcophagus found near Cambridge.[33] A painted panel from a late medieval retable provides an illustration of this event, and while it is a fifteenth-century representation, it shows Sexburg and others placing Æthelthryth's body in a rather large carved stone tomb.[34] If the representation accurately depicts the sarcophagus in use during the thirteenth century, it might account for the increased size of the shrine base, even as it might indicate the necessity of a larger presbytery. More likely is that the shrine base was made larger to dominate the space of the presbytery and to call attention directly to the shrine as the principal site of pilgrimage.

---

[30] Draper, "Bishop Northwold," p. 13.

[31] Atkinson, "The Cathedral," p. 71.

[32] Nilson, *Cathedral Shrines*, p. 48 accepted Atkinson's reconstruction of the shrine base and drew his conclusion about the unusual length and width of the Ely shrine from other English examples. See also Coldstream's discussion of shrine bases in "English Decorated Shrine Bases," p. 17, where she indicated that the standard size for English examples was eight × three feet.

[33] A cursory examination of Roman sarcophagi found in Britain indicates that tomb sizes vary widely, so it is possible that the size of the sarcophagus necessitated a larger shrine base. Two examples (in the British Museum and in the Gloucester City Museum) have lengths of approximately six and half feet. Since Æthelthryth's sarcophagus has not been found, one can only speculate why a more traditional shrine base (usually eight by four feet) would not have sufficed. For details on the sarcophagus in the British Museum, see Susan Walker, *Catalogue of Roman Sarcophagi in the British Museum* (London, 1990), p. 58. Walker included details on four sarcophagi, with the largest measuring approximately six and one half feet in length by two feet in width. I would also like to extend special thanks to members of the Gloucester City Council's division of Culture and Heritage, who provided information on the second example from Olympus Park, Quedgeley, Gloucester. Malcolm Watkins, Susan Byrne, and Rachel Atherton were extremely generous in providing materials about the Quedgeley tomb, which measures approximately six and one half feet in length × three feet in width at the head.

[34] See image in Virginia Blanton-Whetsell, "*Imagines Ætheldredae*: Mapping Hagiographic Representations of Abbatial Power and Religious Patronage," *Studies in Iconography* 23 (2002), p. 81.

Surviving evidence suggests that the shrine base was designed to accommodate pilgrims, even as the presbytery was sculpted to impress them. Atkinson's reconstruction showed three arched openings on the side, with two on the east end. This detail indicates pilgrims could approach the shrine and place their head, hands, or diseased body parts in the openings or they could kneel within niches to pray beneath the saint's body. Columns support foliated capitals, but since the survivals are fragments, it is difficult to estimate the height of the shrine base. Other survivals from this period confirm that Atkinson's reconstruction is in keeping with established architectural practice at Canterbury and elsewhere.[35] The arches provide further evidence that Bishop Hugh not only allowed greater access to Æthelthryth's shrine, but that he also wished to encourage prayer directly at the site.[36] If pilgrims had been encouraged to approach shrines at other cathedrals and to kneel within the niches, they would expect to do the same if a similar architectural base was used at Ely. Further, the distancing of Æthelthryth's tomb from those of her family members indicates an accommodation of pilgrims, for the original configuration would have restricted direct access to the central shrine.[37] Bishop Hugh's activities indicate that he intended to feature Æthelthryth's shrine as the premier attraction of the cathedral and that he constructed the presbytery and base to showcase Æthelthryth's tomb; the improvements to the shrine, the addition of a new shrine base, the removal of the sororal family to the east end, and the lavishness of the architectural ornamentation appear to have been coordinated to make a significant impact on pilgrims. Collectively, then, these details indicate that the bishop emphasized the cult of Æthelthryth by creating an extravagant visual program, one that accommodated a much larger group of visitors and one that allowed direct access to the patron's shrine. The change in arrangement, moreover, suggests

---

[35] Coldstream, "English Decorated Shrine Bases," pp. 15–34; Frederick H. Crossley, *English Church Monuments, A.D. 1150–1550* (London, 1921), pp. 42–54. Editors' note: see Sarah Blick's essay in this volume.

[36] Drawing upon evidence from the sacrist roll for 1349/50, Nilson indicates that the presbytery was surrounded on three sides by fences and on a fourth by the high altar, but that a gate on the north allowed access, *Cathedral Shrines*, p. 53, 98. What is unclear is when the fence was erected. Even if it was in place during Hugh's episcopacy, it would indicate that access was controlled, not discouraged, and it might signal a regular crowd of visitors.

[37] Nilson makes this point in *Cathedral Shrines*, p. 74.

an intentional shift to focus more attention on Æthelthryth, even as it allowed the bishop to mark the space as his own by requesting burial adjacent to the central shrine.

The majesty of the new presbytery was matched by its expense, but the bishop's ability to pay for this costly venture has not been highlighted. As an administrator, Bishop Hugh was remarkably adept at generating revenues, enlarging Ely's episcopal estates through the reclamation of forests and fenlands and raising the rents on existing and new tenancies. Edward Miller noted that assized rents rose sixty percent between 1222–51.[38] This administrative action was initiated at Ely before Hugh de Northwold's appointment to the see in 1229, but the evidence indicates that he perfected the role of landlord and generated substantial revenues during his tenure.[39] No records exist to indicate the annual income during Hugh's administration, but the episcopal income in the late thirteenth-century provides some idea of the wealth of the appointment; the bishop's net proceeds by the end of the century ranged between £2000 and £2500, with a gross income of about £3500.[40] That Hugh de Northwold had considerable resources at his disposal is undeniable. Draper argued that the costs of the presbytery exceeded £5300 and that the payments for the project were divided between the bishop (who paid three quarters of the total) and the monastery. Draper's examination of the building expenses led him to conclude that it was "an exceptionally well-ordered campaign with a meticulous balance being maintained between expenditure and income."[41] Significantly, the total outlay was more than double the annual net salary of Bishop Hugh's successor in 1291. The enormity of the costs demonstrates that Hugh de Northwold was not only able, but also willing to expend considerable monies to increase the stature of Ely Cathedral and its patron saint—and by extension, his own diocese.[42] The effectiveness of the building campaign, however, was tempered by a royal directive,

---

[38] Miller, *The Abbey and Bishopric of Ely*, pp. 107–8. Thomson discussed Hugh's resources in *The Chronicle of The Election of Hugh*, pp. 193–6. See also David A. Postles, "Heads of Religious Houses as Administrators," *England in the Thirteenth Century*, ed. William M. Ormrod (Stamford, UK, 1991), pp. 37–50.

[39] Bentham, *Church of Ely*, pp. 119–91 discussed the reign of each medieval bishop and his civic responsibilities before and during his appointment to Ely.

[40] Miller, *The Abbey and Bishopric of Ely*, pp. 81–2.

[41] Draper, "Bishop Northwold," pp. 26–7.

[42] Bentham, *Church of Ely*, p. 148.

which eliminated an important Ely fair that generated significant revenues for the bishop and curtailed Hugh de Northwold's plans to induce even more pilgrims to visit the shrine.

Competing Patrons, Competing Cults

The re-dedication of Ely Cathedral was performed on September 17, a full month before Æthelthryth's translation feast of October 17, and the timing was significant. Monastic tradition held that Æthelthryth's remains had first been exhumed in 695 by her sister and successor, Sexburg, although the feast day goes unrecorded. In Bede's *Historia Ecclesiastica Gentis Anglorum*, he indicated that Æthelthryth, a twice-married virgin and daughter of the East Anglian royal house, had died from illness, leaving her double monastery in Sexburg's care.[43] After sixteen years, Sexburg wanted to move her sister's body from the nuns' graveyard into the church, so she asked the monks to find a suitable tomb for the body. The Roman sarcophagus described above was located and when the translation ceremony was conducted, Æthelthryth's body was found to be incorrupt, which the monastic community considered as proof of her sanctity and of her perpetual virginity. Whether or not this first translation was effected on October 17 remains unclear, but as I have indicated above, the *Liber Eliensis* is explicit that the second translation took place on that day in 1106. The date of the third translation in 1252 is confusing, for Matthew Paris places Bishop Hugh's spectacle on September 17, which is St. Lambert's day, a full month before Æthelthryth's translation feast.[44] It is likely that Bishop Hugh must have intended to

---

[43] Bede, *Historia Ecclesiastica Gentis Anglorum* 4.19, ed. and trans. Bertram Colgrave and Roger A.B. Mynors (1969; repr. Oxford, 1992), pp. 390–401.

[44] It does not appear that Lambert was an important saint to the Ely community, but his narrative and his feast day were co-opted for Ely's use after the king's mandate. Lambert's feast occurred before Edward the Confessor's, which privileged Ely's feast before Westminster's. Moreover, Lambert's feast might also have recalled the story of this martyr saint, who was Bishop of Maastricht between 670–674 and again 682–c. 705, after being exiled for supporting Childeric II. Lambert was a contemporary of Æthelthryth, and his legend indicates that he challenged Pepin of Heristal about an adulterous relationship and was assassinated for his accusation. In essence, then, the association with Lambert allowed Bishop Hugh to remind Henry III of Lambert's loyalty to Childeric, as well as his fierce disdain of the abuses of kingship. See David Farmer, *Oxford Dictionary of Saints*, 4th ed. (Oxford, 1997), p. 293.

hold his dedication on October 17 in 1252; such an action would have continued established tradition and encouraged pilgrims to identify the date with Æthelthryth's translation feast. If so, this plan was effectively derailed by Henry III, who wanted to celebrate the translation feast of Edward the Confessor, which occurred four days prior to Æthelthryth's, on October 13.

As noted above, Henry's patronage of Westminster Abbey and his desire to increase the cult status of Edward the Confessor was manifested by a large and expensive building campaign. Perhaps taking a cue from Bishop Hugh's building program, initiated in 1234, Henry began building a new shrine for Edward the Confessor in 1241.[45] His efforts to support the most significant shrine in Westminster Abbey stemmed from his life-long admiration for the last Anglo-Saxon saint and a desire to be associated with him. In effect, Lewis has found that by associating himself with "an image of sacred rulership . . . and the quasi-priestly powers confirmed at [Edward the Confessor's] consecration by the rite of unction . . . Henry III could claim the right to exert royal power over the bishops."[46] The struggle between episcopal and royal authority epitomizes the problems Henry had throughout his reign. Henry's inability to court the favor of the bishops or the barons, as well as his lack of foresight when making decisions, earned him a questionable reputation as a ruler.[47] Matthew Paris' chronicle often indicates that the king made unwise decisions or imposed autocratic mandates on barons and bishops alike, including one that curtailed a major fair held at Ely on Æthelthryth's translation feast in favor of a new fair established by the king at Westminster:

> On the 13th of October in this year, in the fortnight of Michaelmas, [Henry III] proceeded to London, to keep the feast of St. Edward, that is, of the translation of that saint, and sent word to a great number of the prelates and nobles, begging them, out of their friendship and devotion to him, to make their appearance at Westminster, to

---

[45] Lewis, "Henry III and the Gothic Rebuilding of Westminster Abbey," p. 161.

[46] Lewis, "Henry III and the Gothic Rebuilding of Westminster Abbey," p. 147.

[47] Studies of Henry III's reign include Frederick M. Powicke, *The Thirteenth Century, 1216–1307* (Oxford, 1953); David A. Carpenter, *The Reign of Henry III* (London, 1996). For a larger discussion of Henry's interactions with the clergy, see Frederick M. Powicke, *King Henry III and the Lord Edward: The Community of the Realm in the Thirteenth Century* (Oxford, 1947).

join with him in solemnly and devoutly celebrating the feast of St. Edward . . . The king then declared it as his pleasure, and ordered it to be proclaimed by herald throughout the whole city of London, and elsewhere, that he instituted a new fair to be held at Westminster, to continue for a fortnight entire. He also strictly interdicted, under penalty of heavy forfeiture and loss, all fairs which usually lasted for such a length of time in England; for instance, that of Ely and other places, and all traffic usually carried on at London, both in and out of doors, in order that by these means the Westminster fair might be more attended by people and better supplied with merchandise . . . The bishop of Ely, in consequence of the loss of his fair at Ely, which was suspended by the king's warrant, made a heavy complaint to him in the matter, for introducing such novelties; but he gained nothing but words of soothing promises of future consolation.[48]

The new fair at Westminster was intended to promote the cult of Edward the Confessor and to bring substantial monies into the Westminster coffers, but Henry's decree that all other fairs in competition be suspended eliminated a revenue-generating fair in Æthelthryth's honor and caused the bishop's resentment, for this event lay in direct conflict with Bishop Hugh's patronage of the Ely presbytery and the promotion of Æthelthryth's shrine.[49]

The account appears at first glance to be a simple record of the king's patronage, yet the passage explicitly names Hugh de Northwold as being present to celebrate the feast of Edward the Confessor's translation, it identifies the Ely fair as one that lasted a fortnight, and it ends by recording the bishop's displeasure with the king's interdict. Matthew's narrative, moreover, intimates that the king's

---

[48] Giles, pp. 272–3. Matthew Paris, *Chronica Majora*, vol. 5, p. 29:

Anno quoque sub eodem, dominus rex [Henry III] cum Londoniam properaret ad festum sancti Ædwardi, quod est de translatione ejusdem sancti, in quindena scilicet Sancti Michaelis, tertio idus Octobris, quamplurimis prælatis magnatibusque sub optentu amicitaiæ et devotionis significavit, ut præsentialiter cum ipso apud Westmonasterium beati Ædwardi festum solempniter ac devote concelebrarent . . . Jussit autem dominus rex denuntiari, et voce præconia fecit per totam civitatem Londoniarum et alibi acclamari, quod constituit nundinas novas exerceri, plene apud Westmonasterium per quindenam duraturas. Omnes quoque nundinas quæ solent per tantum tempus per Angliam exerceri, utpote nundinas Elyenses et alias, et omnem mercaturam quæ solet Londoniis haberi et extra tectum vel sub tecto exerceri, sub poena magnæ forisfacturæ et jacturæ præcise interdixit, ut sic nundinæ Westmonasteriales populis et mercibus copiosius abundarent . . . Episcopus autem Elyensis, pro jactura nundinarum suarum Elyensium edicto regio suspensarum, graviter conquestus est domino regi super hoc, qui tales adinvenit in gravamen subditorum novitates. Sed nihil nisi inania verba mulcentis promissionis et futuræ consolationis reportavit.

[49] Dorothy Owen, *The Medieval Development of the Town of Ely* (Ely, 1993), p. 15.

mandate was unreasonable for the merchants who were required to travel far from home and set up shop in canvas tents during the rainy October season. Hugh de Northwold's complaints over the loss of the Ely fair apparently gained him little but conciliatory promises, which was precisely the point of Matthew's account: he wanted to emphasize the king's autocratic imposition and the effect this decision had on others. In so doing, the chronicler overtly demonstrated yet another point of dissension between episcopal power and royal power, even as he indicated subtly that patronage of saints' cults was a highly politicized economic activity during the period. A patron stood to gain if a fair drew merchants and pilgrims, even as the spiritual reputation of the saint would be increased. The subtext of Matthew's narrative was that the king deliberately curtailed the bishop's revenues to enhance Westminster Abbey's economic circumstances. By extension, it meant that the king demeaned other saints in favor of Edward the Confessor, even as he directly used the cult of Edward the Confessor to exercise his authority over the bishop, an irony that was undoubtedly clear to Hugh de Northwold, Matthew Paris, and other clergy.

Unfortunately, Matthew Paris' account is the only record of the October fair at Ely, which must have been a considerable event, lasting a fortnight. While there is no evidence from Ely or elsewhere about this festival, royal documents describe several fairs granted to Ely, and collectively, they demonstrate the monastery's concerted effort to maintain a celebration for the saint's feast. The records indicate that between 1121–29, Henry I granted a seven-day fair to the church of Ely for Æthelthryth's feast day, June 23.[50] The grant states that the fair was to begin three days before the feast, to encompass the feast day, and to continue for three days after. It appears to have been given to support the construction of the Norman church; as Dorothy Owen found, another charter to the prior and convent absolves them from paying customs and tolls on building supplies.[51]

---

[50] Ethel M. Hampson, "Fairs," in *VCH Cambridgeshire*, vol. 4, p. 50. Bentham provided a charter of this grant in his appendix to *Church of Ely*, p. 18. See also the online source for medieval English fairs, *Gazetteer of Markets and Fairs in England and Wales to 1516*, comp. Samantha Letters, Center for Metropolitan History at the Institute of Historical Research, July 12, 2002 <http://www.ihrinfo.ac.uk/cmh/gaz/gazframe.html>.

[51] Owen, *The Medieval Development of the Town of Ely*, p. 15.

This original June fair continued throughout the medieval period, but the October fair was short-lived. No record of the original grant survives, but one can speculate, given Bishop Hugh's investment in cult production at Ely, that it was made during Hugh de Northwold's administration. Evidence regarding the June fair shows that the monastic community received approval for it on three separate occasions, each after a new bishop had been elected to the see: on October 10, 1189, Richard I confirmed the monastery's ancient rights and customs, including the fair, to bishop-elect William Longchamp (r. 1189–97); the king re-confirmed this privilege on July 1, 1198 after the election of Bishop Eustace (r. 1197–1215); and specific to our purposes, Henry III confirmed this grant July 3, 1233, after Hugh de Northwold had been elected and invested as bishop of Ely in 1229.[52] Since the bishop secured support for the June fair in 1233, it is difficult to imagine that he would not have sought approval for the October fair as well. That the fair for the translation feast was not named in the confirmation charter given to Hugh de Northwold at his consecration suggests that it may have been granted by Henry near the time construction on the presbytery began in 1234.[53] While it is not certain when Hugh received a grant for the October fair, it is likely he petitioned for it early in the construction project, probably closer to 1234 than to 1248 when the fair was closed.

Henry's fear that Ely's October fair might divert people from Westminster is evident by his mandate, and this detail indicates that the event was a significant draw for merchants and buyers alike. The Ely fair lasted two weeks and seems to be one that had no

---

[52] *Gazetteer of Markets and Fairs in England and Wales to 1516* <http://www.ihrinfo.ac.uk/cmh/gaz/gazframe.html>.

[53] Hampson, "Fairs," in *VCH Cambridgeshire*, vol. 4, p. 50. Later evidence demonstrates that two additional fairs were granted by Edward I, perhaps to make up for the loss caused by his father: in 1312, the prior was granted a fair for fifteen days at the festival of St. Lambert (September 17), the day of Ely's rededication, and in 1318, the bishop was granted a fair for twenty-two days beginning on the Vigil of the Ascension. That year, Ascension Day fell on June 1, so the fair encompassed the time leading to, and including, Æthelthryth's feast day of June 23, which was a very generous gift to the bishop. In any case, the dates of these grants suggest that Edward I offered these grants as a conciliatory gesture after the insult of the 1248 mandate, if not as a direct replacement for the translation fair. After Henry's decree, no medieval fair seems to have been granted for October 17. For the dating of Ascension Day in 1318, see Christopher R. Cheney, *Handbook of Dates for Students of English History* (1945, repr. Cambridge, 1996), p. 149.

major competitors in the region. The June fair, by contrast, had to compete with a three-day fair Henry had granted to the canons of St. Giles, Barnwell (near Cambridge) in Æthelthryth's honor.[54] The conclusion is that the bishop must have counted on the October revenues as a significant source of income, and their unjust elimination must have angered him considerably.[55] One can also imagine the resulting friction between the two patrons. The king's authority to sanction or to suspend fairs positioned him to support or reject a cult overtly, even as it allowed him to maximize or minimize the revenues generated by a festival. Henry's position as king also gave him the right to penalize those who transgressed or ignored his mandates.

The bishop's displeasure over the loss in 1248 is noted by Matthew Paris, who marks it as one of two times when the bishop and king were in clear disagreement. The second point of discord occurred four years later when the king delivered a papal injunction to the English bishops. Henry convened the bishops at London on the translation feast of Edward the Confessor, October 13, 1252, to announce that he had vowed to fight in the Holy Land. In support, Innocent IV (r. 1243–54) mandated that Henry's pilgrimage be financed by the tithes of all English churches for a period of three years.[56] The bishops initially resisted the papal mandate, but finally agreed on the condition that the king

> will henceforth keep inviolate the charter of our liberties, so often granted, and so often sworn to be observed by him, and will also grant us another charter, that he may not at some other time, on the plea of our having granted him this favour, require the English church to be subjected to such an execrable contribution and extortion.[57]

The bishops' conditions stemmed from previous occasions when the king had ignored the Magna Carta, and they sought to make a firm stand. The king had ignored the bishops' claim of ecclesiastical liberty and instead given the revenues of episcopal vacancies to his

---

[54] *Gazetteer of Markets and Fairs in England and Wales to 1516* <http://www.ihrinfo.ac.uk/cmh/gaz/gazframe.html>.

[55] Owen, *The Medieval Development of the Town of Ely*, p. 15.

[56] Matthew Paris, *Chronica Majora*, vol. 5, pp. 324–5.

[57] Giles, p. 521. Matthew Paris, *Chronica Majora*, vol. 5, p. 327:
velit cartam totiens pactam, totiens debitam, libertatum nobis juratarum, inviolabiliter observare; necnon et aliam cartam conficere, ne alia vice sub prætextu hujus gratiæ talia exigat, ut ecclesia tam execrabili tributo supponatur.

favored French in-laws.[58] Henry then shifted his strategy, summoning only Hugh de Northwold to meet with him privately.

Thinking to sway the bishop and gain support for his pilgrimage, Henry called on a man who had always backed him, one who had suspended a revenue-generating fair at the king's mandate, and one who had enjoyed the king's presence at the re-dedication of Ely Cathedral only a month prior. Perhaps, too, it is not so remarkable that the king chose to single out the Ely bishop. Hugh de Northwold's appointment to the diocese of Ely followed sixteen years as abbot of Bury St. Edmunds, where his election had been contested among the monks. One contingent of Bury monks wanted to continue a tradition of royal endorsement of elections and another wished to elect Hugh without first gaining the approval of King John (r. 1199–1216). While there is some evidence that Hugh was a baronial sympathizer, he does not appear to have ever directly refused a royal demand.[59] In addition, Bury St. Edmunds had been favored by Henry because Edward the Confessor was its founder. As abbot of Bury, it appears that Hugh was well-regarded by Henry III, if not by the king's father. Henry had appointed Hugh an itinerant justice in Norfolk and had endorsed Hugh's election to the see of Ely in 1229.[60] Henry's letter of recommendation to the pope calls Hugh "a wise and provident man, one who is loyal to us and useful to our reign."[61] This regard for the bishop is documented by the king's use of Hugh in civic matters. In 1236, Hugh went to Provence to escort Henry's bride to England, and during this period, it appears the bishop had some political influence with the king.[62] Further,

---

[58] Matthew Paris, *Chronica Majora*, vol. 5, pp. 328–30.

[59] Thomson, *The Chronicle of The Election of Hugh*, pp. 193–6 offered a brief overview of Hugh's life and political leanings. Unfortunately, few records of Hugh's reign as abbot survive and little is known about the charges included in the chronicle that he sympathized with the barons' complaints and that he would betray royal liberties. Certainly these charges were leveled by those who opposed his election, so they cannot be taken at face value. More is known about Hugh's nephew, Nicholas, who was first an archdeacon at Ely before being elected Bishop of Worcester and then Bishop of Winchester and chancellor to Henry III. As Thomson indicated, "Nicholas's later political attitudes, notably his sympathy with the baronial cause under Henry III, bear the stamp of his uncle's influence."

[60] *Patent Rolls of the Reign of Henry III, A.D. 1225–1232* (London, 1903), pp. 249–50. The king's letter of confirmation to Hugh de Northwold appears on p. 271; Bentham, *Church of Ely*, p. 146.

[61] *Patent Rolls of the Reign of Henry III, A.D. 1225–1232*, p. 238.

[62] Matthew Paris, *Chronica Majora*, vol. 3, p. 335. Thomson, *The Chronicle of the*

documentary evidence reflects Henry's support: he visited Ely several times; between 1243–48 he gave gifts of lumber from the royal forests to Ely for church building (which may have directly contributed to the presbytery); he was present to celebrate Æthelthryth's feast day of June 23, 1244; and he offered a garland to Æthelthryth's shrine on July 5 of that same year.[63]

The king's regard appears to have been reciprocated, for Hugh endowed a chantry college at Ely with four chaplains to pray for the souls of Henry and Eleanor and their children, for the bishops and monks of Ely and their benefactors, and for himself.[64] After the baronial revolt of 1237, with which Hugh sympathized, historical accounts do not record his continued participation in political events. Given that Hugh remained bishop of Ely for close to twenty-five years and was not promoted to a more important bishopric, one wonders if his support of the barons changed Henry's desire to consult the bishop in political matters. By contrast, it appears that Henry continued to call upon Hugh regarding church matters, and in 1252 the king requested that Hugh hold the feast of Edward the Confessor (January 5) during his absence from England. This request might be read as an attempt to ameliorate the rift caused by the suspension of the Ely fair in 1248; likewise, it might be understood as an insult, one that would underscore Henry's identification with, and support of, a king who had successfully exercised authority over his bishops.[65]

Election of Hugh, indicated that Hugh served as one of the royal ambassadors to the emperor's conference at Vaucouleurs and helped put down disorder at Cambridge on Henry's behalf, p. 195. On those who influenced Henry between 1236–39, see Robert C. Stacey, *Politics, Policy, and Finance Under Henry III, 1216–1245* (Oxford, 1987), pp. 93–131 who indicated that Hugh de Northwold was regularly at court, contending that the bishop of Ely was one of a few "influential figures" including the Bishops of Bath, Carlisle, and Chichester. Still, these events seem limited to the period before the breach over the fair at Ely, which occurred in 1248.

[63] For these various notices, *Close Rolls of the Reign of Henry III* (London, 1911–27). Henry visited Ely at least three times between 1238–251, including the feast day June 23, 1277; vol. 2, p. 203. His gave swans to the abbot (vol. 4, p. 223), and deer to the bishop (vol. 2, p. 208), and lumber which came primarily from Kygeswode and Woodstock for building the cathedral; vol. 1, p. 62; vol. 2, pp. 131, 452, 508 (this last citation specifically states that the wood is for building in the church); and vol. 3, pp. 34, 193. The king also reconfirmed the liberties of Ely several times between 1248–51, vol. 4, pp. 103, 128. The record of Henry's gift of a garland to Æthelthryth's shrine is recorded in vol. 2, p. 208.

[64] Bentham, *Church of Ely*, pp. 147–8.

[65] Matthew Paris, *Chronica Majora*, vol. 5, p. 270.

Faced with the bishops' refusal to finance his pilgrimage, Henry chose to call upon Hugh to disrupt the bishops' collective stand, though it seems unclear why. There were other more powerful bishops, but Henry may have seen Hugh as more malleable. Hugh had once been a close advisor, and Henry may have thought he could easily gain the bishop's endorsement. According to Matthew Paris, the king tried to flatter the bishop when they met, thinking to coerce Hugh by reminding him of previous loyalty. As Matthew Paris recorded the discussion, he used the opportunity to recount the suspended fair at Ely and to demonstrate the bishop's steadfastness in the face of coercion. Specifically, Matthew Paris explains that while Hugh "observ[ed] silence concerning the injury done to him by the institution of the fair of St. Ethelred in lieu of that [of] St. Edward, at Westminster,"[66] the bishop reprimanded the king by invoking two archiepiscopal figures who had resisted royal authority:

> "You should, if it so please you, recall to your memory how many saints have with joy submitted to banishment, and perished gloriously as martyrs for the liberty of the holy Church. Why need I mention that glorious martyr, the blessed Thomas? or his blessed successor St. Edmund, our contemporary? An abundance of examples shine forth, all of which evidently tend to reproach and rebuke you."[67]

Thomas Becket's refusal to bend to the will of Henry II is well known; less well known is Edmund of Abingdon's contempt for royal interference and mismanagement. Between 1234–36, Edmund used his position as archbishop of Canterbury to galvanize episcopal unity and to mediate between Henry III and his barons.[68] The invocation

---

[66] Giles, p. 524. Matthew Paris, *Chronica Majora*, vol. 5, p. 331:
subticens moderate dampnum sibi illatum de nundinis sanctæ Etheldredæ pro nundinis sancti Edwardi apud Westmonasterium innovatis . . .

[67] Giles, p. 524. Matthew Paris, *Chronica Majora*, vol. 5, p. 331:
"Ad memoriam si placet revocandum est, qualiter sancti multi pro sanctæ ecclesiæ libertate feliciter exularunt, et gloriose occubuerunt interempti. Quid beatum Thomam commemorem martirem gloriosum? quid beatum successorem suum beatum Edmundum nobis contemporaneum?"
Bishop Hugh's allusion to episcopal saints is significant. Only two saints were canonized in the second half of the twelfth century: Edward the Confessor and Thomas Becket. This fact indicates that Hugh was not only reminding the king of the well-known conflict between Henry II and Archbishop, Thomas Becket, but he also indicated that all canonizations of English saints during the early thirteenth century were given to ecclesiastical figures: Wulfstan of Worcester in 1203, Hugh of Lincoln in 1220, William of York in 1226, and Edmund Rich in 1247. Webb, *Pilgrimage in Medieval England*, p. 63.

[68] Farmer, *Oxford Dictionary of Saints*, p. 152; Powicke, *The Thirteenth Century*, pp. 55–9.

of these two archbishops provided a stinging rebuke, and according to Matthew Paris, Henry blasted back, turning the bishop out and declaring that he would never again receive Hugh de Northwold in his presence.[69] Following this outburst, the king approached other bishops, and, when he remained unsuccessful at convincing them to aid his cause, he turned his anger on London, requiring merchants to maintain their stalls at the Westminster fair, despite the terrible weather, and requiring London shop owners to close their shops and attend.

At this point in Matthew Paris' history, the loss of the Ely fair is mentioned a third time, indicating the chronicler's great sympathy with Hugh de Northwold.[70] Matthew makes it clear that the rift between the bishop and king is a direct result of the king's mandate regarding the October fair at Ely. While the narrative describing the tension between Henry III and Bishop Hugh is clearly a one-sided account, written by a monk who routinely represented the bishops as victims of Henry's ineffective management, it obliquely reveals how cults were being used to manifest power, revenues, and status. Providing a context for Matthew's narrative, Nicola Coldstream commented on a number of English building programs and relic translations between 1091 and 1350.[71] Principally, she argued that pilgrimage in England became important because Henry made it a fashionable activity which he embraced in high style, visiting shrines at St. Albans, Bury St. Edmunds, and Walsingham, among others. Notably, Henry attended the major relic ceremonies during his lifetime, including the 1220 translation of Thomas Becket at Canterbury (when he was 13), the 1252 translation of Æthelthryth into the presbytery; the translation of Alban and Amphibalus in 1257; and of course, Westminster's translation of Edward the Confessor in 1269.[72] Between his many pilgrimages, his attendance at translations, and his gifts to shrines (including those at Bury St. Edmunds, Hailes, and Walsingham), it seems that Henry supported cults generally and modeled pilgrimage specifically as a lay activity. Yet, when his most favored house,

---

[69] Matthew Paris, *Chronica Majora*, vol. 5, p. 332.
[70] Matthew Paris, *Chronica Majora*, vol. 5, p. 332.
[71] Coldstream, "English Decorated Shrine Bases," pp. 15–34.
[72] Coldstream, "English Decorated Shrine Bases," pp. 30–3. For Henry's itinerary to various pilgrimage sites, see Powicke, *The Thirteenth Century*, p. 516; Powicke, *King Henry III and the Lord Edward*, p. 731.

that of Westminster Abbey, needed more revenues, he was perfectly willing to suspend grants already given to other institutions.

The composite narrative provided by Matthew Paris situates the conflict between king and bishop in light of larger political debates of the thirteenth century that would have most certainly have been clear to Matthew's audience. The record shows that Matthew and others recognized that the patronage activities of the period were not just sacred affairs but ones embroiled in social and economic politics. Still, Matthew is more sympathetic to Hugh de Northwold, portraying him as an effective and honorable administrator of the Ely Diocese and contrasting his behavior with Henry's. He presents the bishop's patronage of the presbytery as a spiritual gesture, not an economic one.[73] Hugh's financial support of church building confirmed, in Matthew's view, the bishop as God's servant on earth. The chronicler's description of the dedication ceremony and of the suspended fair, therefore, serves as a means to mark Hugh's largesse in spite of a financial shortfall. The well-known eulogy at Bishop Hugh's death in 1254, moreover, confirms Matthew's regard for the administrator's abilities and sense of purpose:

> [Hugh de Northwold] died at his manor on the 9th of August, and his body was carried with much and well-deserved reverence to Ely, where it was buried in his own church, in a magnificent presbytery, which he had founded and built of marble at his own expense . . . At his death perished the flower of masters and of monks; for as he was the abbat of abbats [*sic*] in England, so he shone forth as the bishop of bishops.[74]

---

[73] Matthew compared Hugh to Simeon, the devout man who thanks God for the salvation of Israel when the infant Jesus is brought into the Temple. This suggests that the completion of the cathedral is akin to Jesus as the salvation of God's creation and that Bishop Hugh is as devout and faithful a servant as Simeon, who had long awaited the "consolation of Israel"; Luke 2.25–34.

[74] Giles, p. 87. Matthew Paris, *Chronica Majora*, vol. 5, pp. 454–5:
Obiit autem apud manerium suum, quinto idus Augusti. Et transportatum est corpus cum magna merito veneratione, et sepultum apud Ely in sua ecclesia, scilicet in presbiterio nobilissimo, quod a fundamentis propriis sumptibus magnifice nimis opere indissolubili et marmoreo construxerat . . . In cujus obitu flos Nigrorum obiit monachorum; quia sicut abbas abbatum in Anglia extiterat, ita et episcopus episcoporum choruscavit.

Residual Effects on Pilgrimage at Ely

Without firm data to illustrate the numbers of pilgrims who visited
Æthelthryth's shrine before and after the construction of the presbytery, it is difficult to reconstruct the immediate influence of Hugh
de Northwold's building program at Ely. The erection of an elaborate marble presbytery and the construction of a base for the newly-
gilded shrine indicate the bishop's intent to provide a more impressive
and more accommodating space for Æthelthryth's shrine. In offering
indulgences for attendance at the re-dedication, the bishop demonstrated that the building program was designed to bring more visitors. The revenues put forward by the bishop to build the presbytery
and to stage the event indicate further that this was an important
enterprise for the bishop, not just a ritual endorsement of a local
saint. Hugh used the episcopal ceremony to remind his royal guests,
Henry III and Prince Edward, that despite Henry's best efforts to
promote Edward the Confessor before all saints, the Diocese of Ely
would use its considerable resources to promote its patron and her
cathedral.[75] One can easily conceive of this spectacle as a performance of Hugh de Northwold's episcopal authority and as a way to
make a public statement about Ely's significance, both as a cathedral and as a pilgrimage center. In light of his plans, Hugh's anger
and disappointment over the loss of the October fair is understandable.

Undoubtedly, the bishop lost significant revenues when the fair
was supplanted, but overall, the king's mandate does not seem to
have negatively affected the bishop's support for the building program or for the cult itself.[76] Indeed, it may have galvanized Hugh's
resolve to showcase the shrine of Æthelthryth before such an important audience. One can easily imagine that the bishop would have
held Henry accountable to his promise of a consolation by requir-

---

[75] Matthew Paris does not name Edward as one of the attendees, but his presence is recorded in Lambeth Palace MS 448, from which Wharton, *Anglia Sacra*,
p. 636 draws his information on the Ely bishops.

[76] In the last few years of the building project, the bishop contributed all but
thirty pounds to pay for the presbytery expenditures. In 1248, he was within fifty
pounds, which might indicate that subscriptions were good enough that he was able
to give slightly less. It might also suggest that he was affected by the loss of the
fair. Certainly, the largest contributions came between 1246–50, and among them,
the smallest contribution came the year after the fair was suspended, 1249–50;
Draper, "Bishop Northwold," p. 27.

ing the king's presence at the re-dedication. It is not difficult to suppose that when Hugh hoped to draw an even larger audience by having the king in attendance, that his expectations were not met. With the bishop's death two years later, one might easily conclude that the importance of cult promotion faded, and it may well have been that Hugh de Northwold's grand vision was completely supplanted by Henry III's patronage of Westminster's main shrine, especially when one considers that by the time the presbytery was finished in 1251, "the style of the building was outdated, having none of the fashionable motifs like bar tracery being introduced at Westminster."[77] As a result, one might conclude that the presbytery did little to promote the saint. While it might appear that Bishop Hugh's presbytery was a thirteenth-century folly that could not compete with larger, more expansive programs, it is more than fair to say that had the conflict over royal and episcopal power not been so heated in this period, that had the relation between the king and Bishop Hugh not have become so strained, the bishop may have been able to enlist Henry's support for Ely in a more significant way. It is clear, at the very least, that Hugh de Northwold sustained an ideology of episcopal patronage that encouraged later Ely bishops to take up the challenge of promoting their patron saint, for it is clear that the space was used to good effect in the fourteenth century, bringing significant revenues to the monastic community.[78]

---

[77] Draper, "Bishop Northwold," p. 8.

[78] The feretrar's records in the fourteenth century indicate that pilgrimage exploded in popularity. This may be because the bishop and prior cultivated Edward III (1327–77) and Philippa (1311–69), who frequently visited Ely and supported the cult. It did not hurt that while John Hotham was bishop of Ely (r. 1316–37), he was also chancellor and, later, treasurer under Edward II (r. 1307–27) and keeper of the seal under Edward III. The prior was also a devotee of the queen, who had her own apartments within the monastic close and her own pew overlooking the choir. For the feretrar's accounts, see Nilson, *Cathedral Shrines*, pp. 216–8; for a discussion of Bishop Hotham, see Bentham, *Church of Ely*, pp. 156–8; for the connection between Prior Crauden and Queen Philippa, see Thomas D. Atkinson, "Queen Philippa's Pews in Ely Cathedral," *Proceedings of the Cambridge Antiquarian Society* 41 (1948), pp. 60–6; Thomas D. Atkinson, "Monastic Buildings and Palace" in *VCH Cambridgeshire*, vol. 4, pp. 77–82.

CHAPTER TWENTY-TWO

'*Y ME TARDE*': THE VALOIS, PILGRIMAGE, AND THE CHARTREUSE DE CHAMPMOL

Laura D. Gelfand

The Chartreuse de Champmol is an example of a pilgrimage site where the semiotics of salvation were appropriated to bolster aspirations which were as much secular as spiritual. While this is hardly a unique example of such a practice, it was expressed very visibly and stated quite clearly at Champmol. However, the significance of pilgrimage at Champmol has not been subject to critical examination by previous scholars. Because Champmol had no major relics, other means were needed to encourage pilgrims. The promise of indulgences was one enticement, but there were other forces at work as well. In this essay we will take a virtual tour through the major monuments located within the monastery and describe the experience of a late fifteenth-century pilgrim. Champmol housed a programmatic display of images that vividly promoted the dynastic significance and piety of the Valois dukes of Burgundy, and its visitors were expected to take notice of, and react to, this imagery.

The Valois dukes had numerous reasons for founding Champmol, but two were of primary importance. Philip the Bold wished to create an institution that would provide for him and his heirs in this world and the next. Ducal display at the foundation validated the legitimacy of his rule and confirmed its legacy, and the imagery at Champmol helped stimulate prayer by the monastic residents and visitors. Such prayer was essential for the salvation of Philip's soul and the souls of his family.

Philip the Bold (1342–1404) was the first of the Valois dukes. The youngest of the four sons of King John II of France (1319–64), he was named First Peer of France and duke of Burgundy in 1363.[1]

---

[1] Wim Blockmans and Walter Prevenier, *The Low Countries Under Burgundian Rule, 1369–1530*, trans. Elizabeth Fackelman (Philadelphia, 1988), p. xi.

(fig. 281) Philip's heirs to the duchy of Burgundy, John the Fearless (1371–1491), Philip the Good (1396–1467), and Charles the Bold (1433–77) benefited from his expansionist policies and streamlined governmental systems that he instituted in the areas under his control. Through his marriage to Margaret of Flanders (1350–1405) in 1369, he extended his holdings far beyond Burgundy and became an important player on the European political stage. Upon the death of Margaret's father Louis of Mâle in 1384, the territories of Franche-Comté, Rethel, Mechelen, Artois, and Nevers were added to his already-sizable Burgundian lands.[2] (fig. 282) His arrangement, in 1385, of an important double-marriage cemented his growing power. This wedding, which took place in Cambrai, united the male heirs of Burgundy-Flanders-Artois and Hainault-Holland-Zeeland with each other's sisters. Blockmans and Prevenier wrote that, "With the wedding there emerged a peaceful alliance between the two most powerful ruling dynasties in the Low Countries, and through them it united spheres of influence in the German Empire and France."[3] These important political events were concurrent with the founding of Champmol. In fact, Philip signed the founding charter for the monastery while he was in Paris making preparations for the wedding.[4]

Clearly Philip's political aspirations affected his plans for the monastery.[5] As the ambitious founder of a new ducal dynasty, Philip had a sizable task before him; he needed to argue for the legitimization of his expanding territorial rule and to create the percep-

---

[2] Blockmans and Prevenier, *Low Countries*, p. 24.

[3] Blockmans and Prevenier, *Low Countries*, p. 29. The French king Charles VI (1380–1422) attended the wedding of Philip the Bold and Margaret's daughter, Margaret of Burgundy, to William of Bavaria while their son, John of Burgundy, married Margaret of Bavaria.

[4] Kathleen Morand, *Claus Sluter, Artist at the Court of Burgundy* (Austin, TX, 1991), p. 58.

[5] Several authors have discussed the political aspects of the founding of Champmol and although it lies outside the confines of the present study it is naturally of great significance. This is examined at length in Sherry Lindquist's *Patronage, Piety and Politics in the Art and Architectural Programs at the Chartreuse de Champmol in Dijon* (Ph.D. diss., Northwestern University, 1995). Using extensive archival work, Lindquist reconstructs the monastery more completely than any previous scholar. See also Jean-Philippe Lecat, "La Chartreuse de Champmol dans la vie politique de Philippe le Hardi," in *Actes des Journées Internationales Claus Sluter* (Dijon, 1990), pp. 9–11; Christian de Mérindol, "Art, spritualité et politique: Philippe le Hardi et la Chartreuse de Champmol, nouvel aperçu," *Les Chartreux et l'Art, XIVe–XVIIIe siècle* (Paris, 1989), pp. 93–116.

tion of power and longevity for his heirs. Like most of his royal peers, Philip capitalized upon the use of visual propaganda to establish himself and his family as the equal of other noble families. To this end he began the construction of a monument, one that he may have hoped would rival St. Denis in Paris or other well-known centers of dynastic power. Philip recognized the need to construct such a monument as early as 1377, when he began to acquire lands near Dijon for the planned mausoleum and monastic foundation.[6]

Margaret's important hereditary role in the construction of the Burgundian territories has been noted,[7] but her significance in the planning and design of Champmol is less-widely recognized.[8] In 1383, she laid the first stone for the new monument, and also acted as the family representative at Champmol's May 24, 1388 dedication ceremony,[9] which she attended with her son, John the Fearless, while Philip was otherwise occupied. Her coats of arms are featured prominently throughout the monastic complex and on its seal. Margaret's impact on the foundation extended well beyond that of simply providing the financial means for its construction and her role is worthy of further study.[10]

The monument founded by Margaret and Philip, the Chartreuse de Champmol, is a complex site in which housing for twenty-four Carthusian monks co-existed with areas carved out for the duke and duchess, the lay people who served as support staff (*conversi*), and the pilgrims who visited. As was typical for Carthusian architecture, each monk was housed in a separate two-story, house-like cell where they could pray in complete isolation.[11] Here they were provided with all the materials thought necessary for their devout lifestyle including

---

[6] Morand, *Claus Sluter*, p. 58.

[7] Blockmans and Prevenier, *Low Countries*, p. 19.

[8] Sherry C.M. Lindquist, "Women in the Charterhouse: the Liminality and Legibility of Cloistered Spaces at the Chartreuse de Champmol in Dijon," in *Architecture and the Politics of Gender in Early Modern Europe*, ed. Helen Hills (Aldershot, UK, 2003).

[9] Whitney S. Stoddard, *Art and Architecture in Medieval France* (New York, 1972), p. 336.

[10] Étienne Picard, "La Dévotion de Philippe le Hardi et de Marguerite de Flandres, d'apres des documents inedits." *Mémoires de l'Académie des sciences, arts et belles letters de Dijon* 12/4 (1910–13), pp. 1–71.

[11] Guiges Ier, Prieur de Chartreuse, *Coutumes de Chartreuse: Introduction, texte critique, critique, traduction et notes par un Chartreux* (Lyon, 1984). Guiges described Carthusian life and its architectural setting.

furniture, running water (of a sort), and even paintings. Each cell included a painted crucifixion by Jean de Beaumetz (d. 1396) in which a model Carthusian monk prostrates himself at the foot of the cross. Two of the original twenty-six paintings commissioned survive.[12] (fig. 283) These images provided a focus for the daily devotions practiced by the Carthusians. In the founding documents for the monastery the monks were charged with the duty of praying night and day for the souls of the duke and duchess, as well as their patron's ancestors and their descendants.[13]

In addition to the accommodations made for the lay brothers who facilitated the monks' eremitic lifestyles, the foundation included accommodations for visitors to the monastery. A parlor where monks could greet visitors and a hostel for overnight guests reveal that providing access for visitors was an important aspect of the foundation's design.[14] Despite the cloistered nature of the lives of the monks, it is clear from its architectural plan that the foundation had an intended audience greater than those in residence and the Valois dukes who founded it.[15]

Many of the artists and architects selected to design and complete this project came from the duke's newly acquired territories in Flanders, including Jacques de Baerze (act. 1384–99) who in 1399, with Melchior Broederlam (act. 1381–1409), completed the remarkable altarpiece still in Dijon. Claus Sluter (1350–1406) of Haarlem was responsible for the portal sculptures and the large sculpted crucifixion group of which only the base, known as the Well of Moses, survives.[16] The crucifixion group figures were painted and

---

[12] One is in the Louvre and the other in the Cleveland Museum of Art. Henry S. Francis, "Jean de Beaumetz, Calvary with a Carthusian Monk," *Bulletin of the Cleveland Museum of Art* 53 (1966), pp. 329–38.

[13] Cyprien Monget, *La Chartreuse de Dijon* (Tournai, 1898–1905), I, p. xxi.

[14] Additional elements that indicate planning for access to outside visitors are discussed below.

[15] It is possible that pilgrim souvenirs were created for visitors to the monastery. H.J.E. van Beuningen, *et al.*, *Heilig en Profaan 2: 1200 Laatmiddeleeuwse Insignes uit openbare en particuliere collectives* (Cothen, 2001), pp. 381–6. Thanks to Sarah Blick for bringing this to my attention.

[16] For the chronology of construction of the portal and the Moses Well, together with a listing of all the artists named in the accounts, see David Henri and Aenne Leibrech, "Le calvaire de Champmol et l'art de Sluter," *Bulletin Monumental* 92 (1933), pp. 419–67; and by the same authors, "Le portail de l'Eglise de Champmol; Chronologie de la constuction," *Bulletin Monumental* 94 (1935), pp. 329–52.

gilded by the Nijmegen artist Jean Malouel (act. 1396–1419) from whom five other canvases were commissioned to decorate the monastery at Champmol. It should be noted that Champmol was built and furnished quite rapidly. Many of the paintings and decorations were painted on canvas because they could be finished more quickly than those on panel.[17] The urgency with which this project was approached is matched by its extraordinary richness. Champmol was so costly that at the time of Philip's death, in 1404, his sons had to pawn silver in order to pay for the elaborate funeral so memorably evoked in Claus de Werve's (1380–1439) tomb, completed in 1410.[18]

The location of the monastery provides some clues about Philip and Margaret's intentions. Champmol is located very near the city of Dijon, an important economic center for Philip the Bold and his descendants. Dijon was the largest of the Burgundian cities at the time of the founding of the monastery, with about 10,000 inhabitants, although it was relatively small compared to the wealth and power of numerous Flemish towns that made up the northern territories of the duke. The highest noble rank held by Philip and Margaret was that of duke and duchess of Burgundy, so the founding of a monastic mausoleum in the center of Burgundy was politically appropriate. Additionally, relations between the Valois dukes and the Flemish residents of Ghent, Bruges, and Ypres were always problematic, but Philip's rule over the southern territories was secure. The placement of a monument in the economic center of his lands was a decisive statement about his power, but it also located him and his descendants in a particular geographic area where they were acknowledged as rulers with a minimum of potential friction.

Champmol quickly became a place of pilgrimage. In 1390 and 1399 Philip reimbursed the Carthusians for expenses incurred in hosting visitors to the monastery,[19] demonstrating his approval of the guests' presence at the monastery. Such recompense may also have

---

[17] References to the purchase of materials by Malouel are found in Monget, *Chartreuse de Dijon*, I, pp. 312–4. I wish to thank Sherry Lindquist for her generosity in sharing her research on the foundation at Champmol. Her work is seminal to understanding the monument and I eagerly await publication of her forthcoming book on the monastery. For further information on the relationship between the patrons and the craftsmen at Champmol see her essay, "Accounting for the Status of Artists at the Chartreuse de Champmol," *Gesta* 41/1 (Spring, 2002), pp. 15–28.

[18] Stoddard, *Art and Architecture*, p. 336.

[19] Monget, *Chartreuse de Dijon*, I, p. 215.

encouraged the monks to host future pilgrims. These early records predate the first of the indulgences granted to Champmol's visitors, so the motivation behind their visits must lie elsewhere. Perhaps they wished to honor the Valois dukes or to make a gesture acknowledging their political significance. Surely, political reasons motivated numerous visitors, but a great number of pilgrims visited Champmol in the following decades in order to satisfy a different set of desires. These later pilgrims came primarily to earn the indulgences that were promised to those who prayed before Claus Sluter's Great Cross, which included the Well of Moses, in the large cloister.

Indulgences were frequently the incentive for pilgrimage and alms-giving in the later Middle Ages. Although not providing the actual forgiveness for sin, indulgences were attractive for their potential to reduce the associated punishment due for transgressions.[20] Thus, they allow those who earn them to avoid time that would otherwise be spent enduring purgatorial torment to atone for their sins. This highly-influential system was developed shortly after the formulation of the doctrine of Purgatory in the late twelfth century,[21] whereby definitions for movement through Purgatory were established. The creation and promotion of an "economy of death" had profound effects on pilgrimage practices and on medieval church construction.

It was imperative to be remembered by the living in order to expedite one's progress through Purgatory. Prayer for the dead had been practiced since the early days of Christianity, but it was taken up with a new fervor during the later medieval period in response to the doctrine of Purgatory.[22] Prayer for the souls in Purgatory was the only way to speed their period of purgation and, as it became increasingly apparent to many that they were likely to spend time in Purgatory, the wish for an expedited release became urgent.

At the same time stimulants to memory of those suffering began to appear in far greater numbers and in new places. It has long been acknowledged that the number of portraits, including those of

---

[20] Among the many sources on indulgences one of the most informative is Nikolaus Paulus, *Indulgences as a Social Factor in the Middle Ages* (New York, 1922).

[21] Jacques Le Goff, *The Birth of Purgatory*, trans. A. Goldhammer (Chicago, 1984).

[22] Clive Burgess, "'Longing to be prayed for': Death and Commemoration in an English Parish in the Later Middle Ages," in *The Place of the Dead: Death and Remembrance in Late Medieval and Early Modern Europe*, ed. Bruce Gordon and Peter Marshall (Cambridge, 2000), pp. 44–65.

donors and owners, increased throughout the Middle Ages and this has frequently been seen as a reflection of the wish for personal recognition and glory.[23] While such prosaic motives may have played a role, the donor or owner's portrait on a work of art should also be recognized as a stimulus for prayer. In funerary art, the desire for prayer is often explicit and inscriptions that beseech the viewer to pray are frequently included.[24] This new system of salvation involved reciprocity between the living and the dead, as those who were freed from Purgatory could then intercede on behalf those who had prayed for them. This system benefited both laity and the clergy, but its rapid association with financial benefits for the churches meant that it was also ripe for abuse.[25]

The dramatic growth in the number of donor and owner portraits created during this period and their greater naturalism, provides clear evidence for the effect that the doctrine of Purgatory had on artistic modes of production. The belief that an image which closely resembled its sitter was more effective in stimulating memory and prayer than a generic depiction may also be linked to the "new naturalism" of northern art. Naturalistic donor portraits may also have served as surrogate selves.[26] They had roles in achieving salvation not only as passive inducements for the prayer of others, but also as stimulants to provide perpetual prayer for the souls of those represented. Certainly, the portraits of the Valois dukes found in the sculpture and painting at Champmol give ample evidence of their wish to have their actual appearance recorded and to amass as much prayer as possible, as seen in the entrance to the church and atop their large tombs in the center of the nave. They were

---

[23] Craig Harbison, *Jan van Eyck: The Play of Realism* (London, 1991), pp. 100–11. Harbison refered to others who have seen Chancellor Nicolas Rolin's depiction in Jan van Eyck's painting (Louvre, Paris) of him with the Virgin as an example of hubris. There are countless other examples of donors being viewed in this way.

[24] For example, in Chancellor Rolin's family chapel in Autun, his tomb, which was placed beneath Jan van Eyck's painting, bore an inscription listing his numerous donations and requesting prayer. Harold de Fontenay, "Notre-Dame: Église paroisiale et collégiale," *Mémoires de la Société Eduenne* 8 (1879), pp. 396–432. For a list of Rolin's donations, many intended to provide prayer for him after his death see Hermann Kamp, *Memoria und Selbstdarstellung: Die Stiftungen des burgundischen kanzler Rolin* (Sigmaringen, 1993).

[25] Patrick Geary, *Living with the Dead in the Middle Ages* (Ithaca, 1994).

[26] Laura D. Gelfand and Walter S. Gibson, "Surrogate Selves: the *Rolin Madonna* and the Late-Medieval Devotional Portrait," *Simiolus* 29 (3/4, 2002): pp. 119–38.

also depicted in paintings that decorated the walls of the church while their coats of arms and other symbolic devices decorated nearly every available surface.[27] Pilgrims were encouraged to visit Champmol where it was expected that the dynastically-charged symbols they saw there would have prompted their prayers while promoting the idea of a powerful dynastic family.

Papal bulls were issued in 1418, 1432, and 1445. Each granted 100 days indulgence to those who prayed before the Great Cross in the large cloister at Champmol every Saturday, on Good Friday, and on several other feast days.[28] It was promised that their prayers, like most to which indulgences were attached, would be effective if those praying were suitably contrite and pious. The wish to earn indulgences proved to be a powerful incentive for pilgrims in the late Middle Ages and their wishes translated into considerable financial resources for the Church. At Champmol, as at other places, pilgrims' donations provided important income for the upkeep of the monastic community. Interestingly, both men and women were able to visit Champmol until 1506 when Julius II withdrew this privilege for women.[29] It should be noted that women could still obtain the promised indulgences if they sent others in their place to make the required contribution.

While it is not known how numerous pilgrims were at Champmol, Sherry Lindquist discovered archival material that enables us to posit that these numbers could be sizable.[30] Twenty-one rings were installed before the porter's house to act as hitching posts. Although it is not clear if more than one horse at a time could be tied to each of these rings, their number is nearly equal to that of the monks housed at Champmol. Visiting equestrian parties probably consisted primarily of nobles, each with an entourage that accompanied them on foot. The installation of more than twenty hitching rings at Champmol shows that the monks were expecting, and prepared for, sizable crowds.

---

[27] Jeffrey Chipps Smith, "The Chartreuse de Champmol in 1486: The earliest visitors account," *Gazette des Beaux-Arts* 106 (July, 1985), p. 3. Records of portraits in the church appear in the financial accounts for the monastery. Philip the Good is recorded as having paid Jean de Maisoncelles for a portrait that would be placed next to those of his father and grandfather in the church. Monget, *Chartreuse de Dijon*, II, p. 111.

[28] Monget, *Chartreuse de Dijon*, I, pp. 54–5; and Morand, *Claus Sluter*, pp. 341–2.

[29] Monget, *Chartreuse de Dijon*, I, p. 204.

[30] Lindquist, "Patronage, Piety and Politics," pp. 29–30, 242.

Pilgrims would have entered the monastery complex through a large gate on the northern border of the monastery's lands closest to Dijon. (fig. 284, no. 1) The gatehouse included a parlor where monks and lay brothers could visit with their guests.[31] Despite Carthusian regulations against such socializing, space for guests was created during the planning and construction phases of the foundation.[32] One assumes that proscriptions against social interactions were obeyed within the confines of the individual monk's cells, but there seems to have been a good deal of communication between monks and visitors within designated areas of the monastic complex. The gatehouse featured a sculpture of the Virgin and Child, protected by a small roof, and the arms of Philip the Bold and Margaret of Flanders were displayed here, together with those of their estates.[33] Beginning with the entrance, and distributed liberally throughout the complex, were visual reminders of the Valois appearing in the form of portraits, arms, and symbols. The frequency with which the symbols were repeated makes it apparent that it was very important to the founders that they be remembered and acknowledged by those in residence at the Charterhouse and by those who visited.

From the gatehouse it is not clear which of two paths visitors might have taken. (fig. 284, no. 1, fig. 285) Surely they would have visited the Great Cross to earn the promised indulgences, but whether this would have been done before, after, or even without, visiting the monastery's sizable church is not certain. In 1486, Georges Lengherand, the mayor of Mons in Hainaut, visited Champmol as his first stop on a two-year pilgrimage to Rome and the Holy Lands.[34] From this account, it seems that he visited the church before going on to the large cloister and he describes some of the foundation's splendid decoration with admiration. Although it is not certain that

---

[31] Lindquist, "Patronage, Piety and Politics," p. 243.

[32] In just one of the numerous places in the *Coutumes* in which silence and isolation are emphasized, Guiges writes, "Il faut savoir qu'ici nous chantons rarement la Messe, car notre principale application et notre vocation sont de vaquer au silence et à la solitude de la cellule." Guiges, *Coutumes*, p. 197.

[33] Lindquist, "Patronage, Piety and Politics," p. 29.

[34] Lengherand was born in Mons and acted as Receveur général of Hainaut from 1477–88. A description of his visit to Champmol is found in Smith, "The earliest visitors account," pp. 1–6. For more on Lengherand see *Voyages de Georges Lengherand . . . à Venise, Rome, Jérusalem, Mont Sinai and Le Kayre—1485–1486*, ed. Marquis de Godefroy Menilglaise (Mons, 1861).

all pilgrims would have moved through the complex in this way, we will follow Lengherand's itinerary in describing some of what a pilgrim might have seen at Champmol at the end of the fifteenth century. The numbers in figure 284 follow Lengherand's route through the monastery.

When one approaches Claus Sluter's portal today it is difficult to imagine its appearance when first completed. (fig. 284, no. 2, fig. 287) In addition to having been heavily restored, the grim little church to which it is now attached bears no resemblance to the magnificent edifice financed by Philip the Bold. The entire façade has been altered and the level of the ground has been dropped several feet so we are not nearly as close to the sculpted figures as was once intended. The entire portal is now situated within a drab modern enclosure and surrounded, somewhat disconcertingly, by a vast structure housing a mental health facility. This said, the dramatic impact of the sculptures on the portal remains.[35] The ensemble testifies to Sluter's tremendous talent and provides evidence about the original intentions of Philip the Bold.

Philip and Margaret of Flanders kneel on the doorjambs in prayer and focus on the Virgin who stands with her Child on the trumeau. Sts. John the Baptist, the patron saint of Burgundy and of the Carthusians, and Margaret, name saint of the duchess, stand behind the noble founders acting as intercessors on their behalf. Visitors to the foundation would probably have passed through the doors that separate Philip and Margaret from the Virgin on the trumeau. The physical act of crossing the threshold around which these naturalistic figures project the idea of devout, salvific prayer may have encouraged viewers to become engaged performers. While emulating Margaret and Philip in prayer, visitors might have read a visual confirmation of their prayer's efficacy in the immediacy of the figural grouping. In addition to acknowledging the duke and duchess as the foundation's donors and encouraging memory of them and prayer, Sluter's figures would have served as paradigmatic images of devotion. A simulacrum of efficacious prayer was created through the portal's formal arrangement. As we shall see, similar theatrical techniques were employed

---

[35] David Henri and Aenne Liebrech, "Le portail de l'Église de Champmol," *Bulletin Monumental* 94 (1935), pp. 329–52, provide a detailed description of the construction of this portal.

in a number of places at Champmol including the tombs and the Great Cross.

Philip and Margaret's insignia were found on the portal in several different places.[36] The figures carved beneath the consoles that support the sculpted portraits of Philip and Margaret once held their coats of arms which would have confronted the viewer as they made their way toward the doors and, because of their prominent placement, would have been one of the last things seen before moving into the church. Reinforcing this imagery, the doors to the church were also decorated with the arms of the ducal couple and those of their son, John the Fearless.[37] The initials of the founders were placed throughout the foundation. One of the few extant examples is beneath the feet of the Virgin and Child on the trumeau where the Ms and Ps seem to dance around the sculpted pedestal. (fig. 288) Margaret of Austria (1480–1530), daughter of Mary of Burgundy and Maximilian I of Austria, and Philip the Bold's great, great, great granddaughter, seems to have been struck but the fact that she would share these initials with her new husband, Philibert le Beau of Savoy (1480–1504). Champmol's decoration may have inspired Margaret, who visited the foundation on her way to Savoy in 1501. When she founded her own monastery and church at Brou in 1506, she included Ms and Ps throughout the foundation.[38]

The interior of the original church had a large single aisle, a three-sided chevet, and wooden vaults. The choir of the *conversi* was placed closest to the entrance with the monk's choir further to the east and the chevet with its lancet windows completing the plan. (fig. 284, no. 3, fig. 286) The three chapels that radiated from the building include the two-story ducal oratory and the chapels of Sts. Peter and Agnes.[39] The configuration with the sacristy across the nave from the duke's oratory gave the building the appearance of having a transept. Suspended from the wooden ceiling were sixty-one canvas hangings

---

[36] For a discussion of the placement of coats of arms and other symbols of Margaret and Philip see Mérindol, "Art, spritualité et politique," pp. 93–115.

[37] Lindquist, "Patronage, Piety and Politics," p. 40.

[38] Laura D. Gelfand, "The Iconography of Style: Margaret of Austria and the Church of St. Nicolas of Tolentino at Brou." in *Widowhood and Visual Culture in Early Modern Europe*, ed. Allison Levy (Aldershot, UK, 2003), pp. 145–59.

[39] Morand, *Claus Sluter*, pp. 321–3, Morand focused primarily on the ducal oratory, but mentioned these other chapels. Lindquist, "Patronage, Piety and Politics," pp. 44–52.

painted with the duke's coats of arms, while a canvas band decorated with ducal arms hung on the upper walls of the church.[40] Each
of the chapels, especially the ducal oratory, included coats of arms
and other symbols to remind monks and visitors of the founding
couple.[41]

Upon entering the church, the visitor might, like Lengherand, been
struck first by the tombs of the dukes that were elevated on platforms and lined end to end down the center of the wooden-vaulted
nave. (fig. 289) Lengherand also described seeing a third (temporary)
tomb for Philip the Good and Isabelle of Portugal († 1473) that is
no longer extant. These tombs occupied the monk's choir where seventy-two choir stalls, carved by Jean de Liège (act. 1381–62), surrounded them, where the tombs formed the visual focus for liturgical
participants. The design of these tombs, each with a *gisant* figure
placed on a black marble slab on top and an arcade through which
mourning figures process, became associated with the Valois dukes.[42]
Because they were placed on raised platforms in the nave, the funerary procession with its Carthusian participants would have been
clearly visible to the monks and others in the choir. The effigy on
top would only have been seen from an elevated viewpoint and the
two-story ducal oratory offered just such a vantage point. Privileged,
undoubtedly noble, viewers could have seen the figure of Philip in
his royal robes, which part slightly to reveal armor beneath. But for
the majority of viewers, who would have seen the tombs at ground
level, the duke's death and the role of the Carthusians and others
in the funeral cortège would have been most prominently featured.

Philip's tomb included an inscription with his motto, *Y me Tarde*,
his genealogical history, and the following plea: "Please pray devoutly
to God for his soul."[43] This motto has been interpreted variously. It

---

[40] Monget, *Chartreuse de Dijon*, I, p. 130.
[41] Lindquist, "Piety, Patronage and Politics," pp. 41–85.
[42] Anne M. Morganstern, "Le tombeau de Philippe le Hardi et ses antecedents,"
Actes des Journées Internationales Claus Sluter (Dijon, 1992), pp. 175–92.
[43] *Cy gist tres haut et tres puissant Prince et fondeur de l'eglise de ceans—Philippe fils de tres
haut et tres excellent et puissant Prince Jehan par la grace de Dieu Roy de France et de Dame
Bonne fille du bon Roy de Boaigne sa compaigne—Duc de Bourgoigne—et de Lembour—Conte
de Flandres d'Artois et de Bourgoigne—Palatin—Sire de Salins—Conte de Nevers de Rethel et
de Charolois—et Seigneur de Malines—qui trespassa a Halles en Brabant le XXVII jour d'Avril—
l'an de grace Mil quatre cent et quatre—Si vous plaise prier Dieu devotement pour son ame.*
Monget, *Chartreuse de Dijon*, I, p. 376.

translates directly as "I cannot wait" and is seen as a counterpart to his older brother, Jean of Berry's motto, "The time will come."[44] Such mottos are often multivalent and Philip's is no different. While it could describe his impatient nature and ducal prerogative,[45] it might also express his wish to move forward into the future and the promise of salvation.

Evidence of planning in anticipation of visitors is found in the choir. Champmol housed only twenty-four monks and two priors so the thirty-four extra seats in the monk's choir must have been for ecclesiastical visitors, and indicate that the monks were prepared for their guests to outnumber them. In 1469, railings (resembling those seen around the tombs today) were probably installed to protect them.[46] These were perhaps necessitated by the traffic of pilgrims moving though the choir. It may also have been important to keep people away from the delicate tombs because some of the sculpted ornaments were not actually attached and could easily have been spirited away. Finally, three entrances to the crypt were accessible from the monk's choir. While this was probably related to liturgical services, it may also have facilitated visits through the choir to the crypt to see the tombs of those buried there including Philip the Bold, John the Fearless, and Philip the Good.[47]

The interior of the church, including the monk's choir, was decorated with numerous paintings; among them altarpieces, a line of dynastic portraits, and at least one large devotional portrait diptych.[48] A number of well-known painters worked at Champmol including Jan Malouel, Melchior Broederlam, Jean de Maisoncelles, and Henri Bellechose. Some of the works installed in the church included the Broederlam and Baerze altarpiece, which was placed in Jean de Berry's chapel behind the high altar.[49] Malouel's *Life of St. Denis*

---

[44] Joseph Calmette, *The Golden Age of Burgundy*, trans. Doris Weightman, (New York, 1963), p. 56.

[45] Lindquist, "Patronage, Piety and Politics," p. 52.

[46] Monget, *Chartreuse de Dijon*, II, p. 149.

[47] Philip the Good's body was transferred from Bruges, together with those of his wives and children. Lindquist, "Patronage, Piety and Politics," p. 58. Margaret of Flanders was buried with her family in Lille; Morand, *Claus Sluter*, p. 57.

[48] Laura D. Gelfand, "Regency, Power and Dynastic Visual Memory: Margaret of Austria as Patron and Propagandist," in *The Texture of Society: Women in Medieval Flanders*, ed. Ellen Kittell and Mary Suydam (New York, 2003), pp. 203–25.

[49] Mérindol, "Art, spritualité et politique," p. 98.

Altarpiece (1416) and his *Pieta* were originally at Champmol.[50] The presence of a major altarpiece featuring the life of St. Denis, the patron saint of France and the French Royal family, emphasized connections between the Valois dukes of Burgundy and the French nobility. These heavily-gilded paintings would have amplified the effect of richness in the church interior that was also embellished with azure paint and gold.[51]

Both painted portraits and devotional portrait diptychs were featured in the church's decoration which added to its dynastically-charged iconography. A 1426 document noted that a portrait of Philip the Good was to be placed next to those of Philip the Bold and John the Fearless already hanging in the monk's choir at Champmol.[52] This is an early example of display of dynastic lineage through portraits in an ecclesiastical setting. The first devotional portrait diptychs created for the Valois dukes were quite large, nearly life-size, and were also probably first found at the Chartreuse, hung on the walls of the church, acting as a dynastic portrait gallery illustrating the royal lineage of the dukes. Only one painting survives that may have been part of this series, a *c.* 1400 *Virgin and Child* attributed to Jean Malouel. [53] This large tempera on cloth painting pictures theVirgin holding her Child who reaches toward a now-missing donor portrait that would have hung to the viewer's left. Millard Meiss and Colin Eisler both posited that this would have been a portrait of Philip the Bold or his son John the Fearless,[54] thus forming the first known Valois devotional portrait-diptych.[55] These scholars' suggestion that a portrait of John the Fearless, now known only through an eighteenth-century copy, might have been

---

[50] Both are now in the Louvre. Lindquist, "Patronage, Piety and Politics," p. 77 wrote that five altarpieces were originally commissioned from Malouel for the Chartreuse and suggests that the St. Denis panel may have been one of these. She proposes that its original location was over the altar in the chapterhouse.

[51] Monget, *Chartreuse de Dijon*, I, p. 130.

[52] Mérindol, "Art, spritu19alité et politique," p. 109.

[53] Now in the Berlin Dahlem Museum. Colin Eisler, *Masterworks in Berlin; A City's Paintings Reunited* (Boston, 1996), p. 95.

[54] The work measured "4 pieds 6 pouces de large sur 5 pieds 6 pouces de haut." This suggests a fairly large work. Patrick M. De Winter, *The Patronage of Philippe le Hardi, Duke of Burgundy (1364–1404)*, (Ph.D. diss., New York University, 1976), pp. 826-7.

[55] Millard Meiss and Colin Eisler, "A New French Primitive," *Burlington Magazine* 102 (1960), p. 238.

the pendant to the Berlin *Virgin and Child*, can be supported by visual analysis.[56] Another type of diptych at Champmol is the now-lost variant with Philip the Bold and Louis of Mâle praying to the Virgin and Child, a work that indicated the concern with dynastic linkages.[57] These diptychs at Champmol, featuring portraits of the Valois dukes, encoded dreams of dynastic power that would continue to resonate for their heirs.[58]

A complete list of the coats of arms and emblems in the church at Champmol lies outside the scope of the present study; they are simply too numerous to detail here. Arms and emblems seem to have literally covered nearly every available surface. They were on the floor tiles and the roof beams, the chairs of the officiants and the ducal oratory, the windows and doors; angels carried them above the entrance to the small cloister, and a bronze angel near the high altar carried Philip's arms.[59] The duchess's arms were located in the ducal oratory, in the Chapel of St. Pierre, on the *Saints and Martyrs Retable* by Jacques de Baerze and Melchoir Broederlam, and on the seal of the Chartreuse. Both of their coats of arms appeared with those of their son on the walls of the hostel, the doors of the church, and the portal to the parlor of the large cloister. The Ms and Ps that are seen on the base of the Virgin's trumeau statue were also found on the retable of the saints and martyrs, in the borders of the chapel windows, and on the well in the large cloister.[60] Philip's motto, *Y me tarde* is still visible on a band on his tomb, and his emblem, a golden sun, appears on the floor tiles together with Ms and Ps, and the lion of Flanders. Stained glass portraits of Philip the Bold and John the Fearless decorated the windows.[61] Coats of arms and other symbols decorated every location accessible to visitors as well as spaces reserved for the monks.

With its profusion of symbolic imagery, only the densest of visitors

---

[56] De Winter, *Philippe le Hardi*, pp. 826–7. Perhaps this portrait may have been the one taken by the German Carthusian, Dom Étienne, when he visited Champmol in 1791.

[57] De Winter, *Philippe le Hardi*, p. 756.

[58] Laura D. Gelfand, *Fifteenth-century Netherlandish Portrait Diptychs: Origins and Function* (Ph.D. diss., Case Western Reserve University, 1994).

[59] Mérindol, "Art, spritualité et politique," pp. 103–4.

[60] Mérindol, "Art, spritualité et politique," p. 105.

[61] Jeffrey Chipps Smith, "Jean de Maisoncelles' Portrait of Philippe le Bon for the Chartreuse de Champmol," *Gazette de Beaux-Arts* 99 (January, 1982), p. 9.

to Champmol could have left the foundation's church wondering who had paid for the monument. But the Valois dukes also made their identities known to those who may only have visited the Great Cross in the large cloister and by-passed the church itself. It is apparent from the plan of the monastery that it was possible to visit the large cloister without having to pass through any other areas of the complex and this arrangement may have enabled female pilgrims to visit the monastery and receive the promised indulgences.[62] Surrounding the large cloister, a wall isolated the monks from the public. At the center of this cloister was the Great Cross, which measured about four meters in height,[63] and it also included the monks' cemetery, which was separated from the rest of the cloister by a low wall decorated with statues of the Virgin and saints and a painted skeleton which warned viewers, *Hodi Mihi, Cras tibi*, (today me, tomorrow you).[64] The location of this *memento mori* in the cemetery presumably aided in promoting an appropriately earnest and contrite state of mind for those praying within the cloister.

The Well of Moses is a fragment of the Great Cross sculptural group that adorned the large cloister and served as a goal of pilgrims to the foundation. (fig. 290) Situated within a fully-functioning well was a large hexagonal base encircled by over life-size figures of prophets. This entire pedestal, with its figures, was originally elevated so that the viewer's head would have been at the level of the prophet's feet. Above this elaborate base was a life-size crucifixion, with Mary Magdalen at Christ's feet and the Virgin and John the Baptist in mourning.[65] Jean Malouel was responsible for polychroming Sluter's masterwork, installed around the beginning of the fifteenth century.[66] To amplify their verisimilitude, the sculpted figures included

---

[62] Lindquist, "Women in the Charterhouse" described the architectural systems at work at Champmol that allowed women to enter the space and earn indulgences without violating monastic codes.

[63] The scale and construction of the Great Cross are described in detail in Henri David and Aenne Liebrech, "Calvaire de Champmol," pp. 419–67.

[64] Monget, *Chartreuse de Dijon*, III, p. 92, fn. 2.

[65] A few fragments of this upper group were found in a well in the nineteenth century, including the bust of Christ, his legs, and part of his halo. The titulus, a set of crossed female arms, a fragment of the Magdalen's shoulder, part of St. John's hand, pieces of the cross, drapery, and architectural ornament were also found. Morand, *Claus Sluter*, pp. 343–4.

[66] Morand, *Claus Sluter*, p. 340.

detailed features of copper such as spectacles for Jeremiah, strings for David's harp and a diadem for the Magdalen.[67]

Pilgrims would have moved through a narrow passage decorated with the arms of Philip and Margaret to the eastern end of the cloister,[68] where they would have faced the Great Cross, [69] which was protected by a domed wooden covering (by 1411).[70] The body of Christ on the cross was compositionally aligned with the figure of David (his ancestor) on the lower level, and together they faced the entering visitors. David was a model Christian king and the paradigmatic redeemed sinner, thus it was appropriate that he was featured prominently and would make the initial intercessory gesture toward newly-arrived penitent pilgrims. Approaching the sculpture they would also see the arms of Philip the Bold placed on the upper portion of the pedestal base, at eye level with the viewer.[71] Ms and Ps were also carved near the figure of David.[72] As in the church, the identities of the founders marked every part of their donation including the devotional centerpiece of the pilgrim's goal.

While there is a political valence to the indulgences granted for prayers said before the Great Cross, other factors would have inspired the ecclesiastics who visited Champmol and furnished it with these incentives for pilgrimage. The mode of participatory devotion encouraged by the arrangement of figures at Champmol could have been thought to provoke more efficacious prayer by those who visited. Claus Sluter's naturalistic figures and their compositions, which arguably relate to contemporary theatrical productions, would have been visually compelling. The Great Cross has often been associated with contemporary Passion plays and its theatrical qualities are

---

[67] Monget, *Chartreuse de Dijon*, I, p. 347.

[68] Monget, *Chartreuse de Dijon*, I, p. 347.

[69] Pierre Quarré, "L'implantation du Calvaire du 'Puits de Moise,' à la Chartreuse de Champmol," *Mémoires de la Commission des Antiquites du Département de la Côte d'Or* 29 (1974/5), pp. 161–6.

[70] Morand, *Claus Sluter*, p. 241. The structure that protects the Moses Well was erected in 1638. It is not clear when the upper portion of this monument was destroyed and some have suggested that this may have been as early as the sixteenth century during the siege of Dijon by the Swiss, Laurence Blondaux, "Regards sur le Puits de Moise," *Claus Sluter en Bourgogne, Mythe et representations* (Dijon, 1990), pp. 30–3.

[71] Lindquist, "Patronage, Piety and Politics," p. 115.

[72] Mérindol, "Art, spritualité et politique," p. 105.

undeniable.[73] This almost-Baroque emphasis on dynamism was explored throughout the monastery and is also found in the portal sculptures and the lively recreation of his funerary scene on Philip's tomb. Champmol differed from other contemporary pilgrimage centers, in part, because of the dramatic experience it provided on a grand scale. Perhaps provoking an empathic response in the viewer through such dynamic figural groupings was one way of encouraging pilgrimage. Champmol may have acted as a devotional thrill ride, amazing in its verisimilitude and compelling in its ability to stimulate prayer.

Pilgrims were clearly important in the design and furnishing of the Chartreuse de Champmol. Accommodations for visitors appear in a number of different places within the monastic complex at Champmol, but one of the more intriguing ways in which pilgrimage affected the monastery was in its need for locking devices. Lindquist found that locks and bars constituted an annual expense at the monastery, and that nearly every window, door, box or cupboard was locked in some way.[74] While it is possible that the monks did not trust one another, it is more likely that such security measures were taken because the presence of outsiders necessitated them. The monks' practice of securing their own belongings, together with the parlors, hostel, hitching posts, protective railings around the tombs, and the size of the church indicated that from the time of its initial conception Champmol was intended to function as a place of pilgrimage. Its success as a pilgrimage destination may be seen in the monks' ongoing need to protect their space and their belongings from those who visited.

Like all medieval foundations, Champmol was founded and furnished to facilitate numerous goals and to present devotional programs for a variety of audiences. Those who founded it and those who visited benefited from the monastery. Pilgrims came to Champmol to earn the promised indulgences, and this was one of the driving forces behind pilgrimage in the Middle Ages. The threat of purgatorial torment was a powerful one and it set in motion a tremendous number of individuals eager to participate in affecting their own salvation.

---

[73] Emile Roy, *Le Mystère de la Passion en France du XIVe au XVIe siècle* (Dijon, 1903–4; repr. Geneva, 1974), p. 437.

[74] Lindquist, "Patronage, Piety and Politics," p. 224.

Pilgrims visiting Champmol may have had a single goal in mind, to see and pray before the Great Cross. However, it is also possible that an early form of tourism based on curiosity or reputation may have played a role in encouraging pilgrims to visit the monastery.

Once pilgrims walked through the gates at Champmol they were inundated with imagery intended to create a vivid impression of the political importance of the monastery's founders. Philip the Bold, with his architects, sculptors, and painters, created an environment in which his wealth and power, together with his dynastic legacy in the form of his descendants, were systematically displayed. It was expected that visitors would read the signs and symbols that proliferated on every available surface and would recognize the importance of the Valois dukes, acknowledging and validating their dynastic hegemony. It may also have been hoped that these pilgrims would take this dynamic impression away from the foundation, much like a pilgrim souvenir, and share it with others, thus encouraging them to visit. Additionally, the monies that pilgrims furnished for the upkeep of the monastery provided a somewhat baser motivation for the promotion of pilgrimage, but a vital one nonetheless.

Perhaps more significant is the desire for prayer that is clearly intrinsic to the decorative program at Champmol. Pilgrims were promised the benefits of indulgences and release from the punishment due for sin, but the Valois received similar benefits through the prayer that their foundation required from its monastic residents and encouraged from visitors. It was hoped that the naturalistic images of the Valois at the entrance to the church and within it on tombs and in paintings would prompt visitors to remember them with prayer. Should these prove insufficient, covering every available surface with Valois coats of arms, mottos, and emblems reinforced their presence. The pilgrims, in turn, were grateful to the patrons for establishing the foundation and for providing them a way to earn indulgences.

The motives that prompted Philip the Bold to found Champmol were multivalent and those who visited Champmol did so for a number of different reasons. The shared interests of both the patrons and the pilgrims intersect in the desire to obtain an expedient release from Purgatory. Most of the late medieval European population was unified in wishing for just such a positive outcome to their devotions, but the effects of Purgatory, and the "economy of death" associated with its doctrine, on the art and architecture of the time have yet to be fully understood. Previous studies have focused on particular by-products of the phenomenon, such as donor portraits or tomb sculptures, but perhaps taking a more global approach will allow us to shed further light on this important aspect of medieval spirituality. Champmol offers an unusual opportunity to study a well-documented foundation in terms of how it functioned as a place of pilgrimage, further study will undoubtedly reveal parallels to Philip the Bold's magnificent foundation in other pilgrimage sites.

CHAPTER TWENTY-THREE

CHANNELS OF GRACE: PILGRIMAGE ARCHITECTURE, EUCHARISTIC IMAGERY, AND VISIONS OF PURGATORY AT THE HOST-MIRACLE CHURCHES OF LATE MEDIEVAL GERMANY[1]

Mitchell B. Merback

Counterposed to the ecclesiastical ideal of a mystical body of all believers (*corpus mysticum*), a community of saints unified in their sacramental faith in the resurrected Christ, religious identities in the later Middle Ages were often differentiated along the lines created by regionally distinct cultic and devotional practices, religious folklore, ideals of sanctity, and evolving patterns of kin and non-kin loyalties. Religious uniformity was ever only a dream of canonists and inquisitors. Practical forms of piety emerged out of a process of interaction between the "top-down" mandates of theology, the "bottom up" impulses of folk custom and belief, and the mediating roles played by territorial church politics. In the later Middle Ages, when religious dissent movements proliferated and the schism of the institutional church rendered questionable religious authority as such, control of popular religion became increasingly desirable for elites, notably in the fragmented lands of the German empire. Princes held a strong stake in the forms of associational worship that developed in their territories, since these could become lightning rods of insurrection just as they might become sources of popular acclaim, or instruments of consensus-building, for a ruler's policies. Both tendencies reveal something of the nature of religious identities among the majority at a given moment. Of the religious practices that could become lodestones of collective identity—and collective perceptions—in the two and a half centuries before the Reformation, pilgrimage was arguably the most important.

[1] Research for this article was funded by Leo Baeck Institute, Deutscher Akademischer Austauschdienst, National Endowment for the Humanities, DePauw University, Norman and Irma Braman, Robert Weingarten, and Joseph and Tema Merback.

What the study of pilgrimage may tell us about the formation of collective identities and perceptions cannot be fully grasped until we acknowledge the limitations of our prevailing assumptions about late medieval pilgrims and the shrines they visited. Historians of religion, especially those inclined to a pious view of Christian devotional culture, tend to see "the pilgrim" as an individual undertaking a personalized journey of faith, venturing across long distances in a kind of ascetic detachment from daily life, hoping to fulfill a penitential obligation, or to find release from sin, or seek healing, or protection, or deliverance from misfortune. Coming into a perceptible, even tangible contact with divine power, experiencing a vision, or healing, becomes a personal reward. Along the way to the sacred destination the pilgrim is joined in spontaneous fellowship by other individuals on similarly personalized journeys, everyone seeking and likewise "dedicated" to God.[2] The individual's cause is his own, chosen freely or accepted humbly, as is necessary to an unfolding, spiritual biography. In their influential study of Christian pilgrimage, anthropologists Victor and Edith Turner developed a theory of pilgrimage's power to forge extended interpersonal bonds that could exist outside normal social structures. But despite its name, the *communitas* model of pilgrimage depends upon a monadic conception of religious subjectivity; moral individualism is asserted *a priori*. "In the pilgrimages of the historical religions the moral unit is the individual, and his goal is salvation or release from the sins and evils of the structural world, in preparation for participation in an afterlife of pure bliss."[3] A similar ideal is often tacitly assumed by art historians when we try to account for the role images played in "the [individual] pilgrim's" experience of a particular shrine and its visual attractions.[4]

---

[2] The ideal is captured by the phrase "ascetic homelessness" (*asketische Heimatlosigkeit*); Jan van Herwaarden, "Pilgrimages and Social Prestige. Some Reflections on a Theme," in *Wallfahrt und Alltag in Mittelalter und früher Neuzeit. Internationales Round-Table-Gespräch, Krems an der Donau 8. Oktober 1990*, ed. Gerhard Jaritz and Barbara Shuh (Vienna, 1992), pp. 27–79, with references on p. 27.

[3] Victor Turner and Edith L.B. Turner, *Image and Pilgrimage in Christian Culture: Anthropological Perspectives* (New York, 1978), p. 8; for the different forms of *communitas*, p. 135.

[4] This is the approach I took in my earlier writings on pilgrimage and visuality in *The Thief, the Cross and the Wheel: Pain and the Spectacle of Punishment in Medieval and Renaissance Europe* (London, 1999), esp. pp. 41–8; Matthew Botvinick, "The Painting

"Ascetic homelessness," solitary peregrination, visual meditation, contact with the holy, confession and penance, deliverance from affliction and misfortune—this constellation of ideals, perceptions and practices did form a historically specific model, a "horizon of expectations" for those pilgrims whose experiences we find recorded in Christendom's literary sources. It is a model geared to the mostly elite, western European culture of religious tourism: journeys taken to shrines of high prestige, at high cost, across long distances—internationally to Jerusalem, Rome, and Santiago de Compostela, and supra-regionally to a number of well-known destinations such as Bari, Einsiedeln, Wilsnack, Aachen, Canterbury, and others.[5] But to project this model, in which *private* experience takes center stage, onto the entire pilgrimage process is often to miss the forest for the trees. Obscured is the fact that, outside the cities, among rural communities, pilgrimage was very often, at certain times of the year exclusively, a *corporate* undertaking, and the efficacy of the rites it encompassed was, in a sense, vouchsafed by a thoroughgoing and often obligatory communal participation. The story of late medieval pilgrimage is often told as a gradual shift away from inaccessible international shrines and toward their European surrogates; one corollary development was a growing communal reliance on a network of local shrines. Cult centers became "regional identification points" in countries where political authority was most fragmented, the German empire especially;[6] this allows scholars to speak of a "sociological framework that develops between shrine and community."[7]

---

as Pilgrimage: Traces of a Subtext in the Work of Campin and His Contemporaries," *Art History* 15/1 (March 1992), 1–18; for the ancient world, Jas Elsner, "Between Mimesis and Divine Power: Visuality in the Greco-Roman World," in *Visuality Before and Beyond the Renaissance: Seeing as Others Saw*, ed. Robert Nelson (Cambridge, 2000), pp. 45–69, esp. 60–3. Another kind of critique of these assumptions might begin with the recognition of the class distinctions encoded by this model.

[5] Herwaarden, "Pilgrimages and Social Prestige," pp. 31–2, whose geographical classification of pilgrimages into international, supra-regional and local comes from Ludwig Schmugge, "Die Pilger," in *Unterwegssein im Spätmittelalter*, ed. Peter Moraw (Berlin, 1985), pp. 17–47, esp. 18.

[6] Herwaarden, "Pilgrimage and Social Prestige," p. 56. Another significant reason for the shift was the growing disrepute of the culture of solitary peregrinations as a result of the continued practice of "expiatory" pilgrimage, that is, pilgrimage imposed by secular justice or as part of the ecclesiastical system of penance, pp. 59–60.

[7] Johannes Heuser, "'Heilig-Blut'. In Kult und Brauchtum des deutschen Kulturraumes. Ein Beitrag zur religiösen Volkskunde" (Ph.D. dissertation, Rheinischen Friedrich Wilhelms-Universität, Bonn, 1948), p. 105.

All the more reason to follow the lead of German folklorists who routinely distinguish *Pilgerfahrten* (denoting long-distance journeys, undertaken without specific obligation by individuals) from *Wallfahrten* (communal peregrinations, usually over shorter distances, sometimes obligatory, typically involving processions and other forms of associational worship).[8]

As local shrines proliferated in response to population growth, enhanced geographical mobility, emerging political loyalties, and new cultic phenomena, territorial pilgrimage grew increasingly central to the evolution of corporate piety among the majority. Lionel Rothkrug has offered a trenchant analysis of the impact that these changes had on collective ideals of sanctity in the two centuries before the Reformation:

> Shifting patterns of peregrination reveal that interpersonal loyalties expanded in space and time as people advanced from simple to more complex levels of devotion. Slow, successive increments in the geographical and temporal range of social bonds caused the faithful to enhance the dignity of the supernatural personages to whose powers of protection they accorded continuous territorial extensions. A persistent expansion in the geography of social, political, and religious obligation contributed to a progressive differentiation of people's concept of the sacred.[9]

One decisive outgrowth of this "progressive differentiation in people's concept of the sacred" was an expanding understanding of the salvific properties attributable to certain types of shrines and the perceived efficaciousness of rites staged in one sacred locale or another. In its broadest sense, the present paper seeks to illustrate this notion by examining the salient aspects of a *visual culture* specific to the "host-miracle" (*Hostienwunder*) shrines and their related cultic types in the lands of imperial south Germany before the Reformation. First are the "host-profanation" (*Hostienfrevel*) shrines, pilgrimage locales

---

[8] These terms are broken down further in the taxonomy by Wolfgang Brückner, "Zur Phänomenologie und Nomenklatur des Wallfahrtswesens und seiner Erforschung," in *Volkskultur und Geschichte. Festgabe für Josef Dünninger zum 65. Geburtstag*, ed. Dieter Harmening, *et al.* (Berlin, 1970), pp. 384–424.

[9] Lionel Rothkrug, "Preface and Overview," *A Theory and Practice of Cultural Mapping*, ed. Lionel Rothkrug and Lewis Lancaster (in preparation), p. 50; I thank the author for sharing this work-in-progress with me, and for permission to cite it here. A similar argument is presented in Lionel Rothkrug, "Holy Shrines, Religious Dissonance and Satan in the Origins of the German Reformation," *Historical Reflections* 14 (1987), 143–286, here p. 189.

associated with sacrileges committed against the sacramental body of Christ in the eucharist, which in certain cases produced transformational blood miracles (*Blutwunder*); second are those shrines built as evocations or imitations of the Tomb of Christ in Jerusalem, popularly known as the Holy Sepulcher (called *Heilig Grab* in Germany). Within the broader development of German pilgrimage piety the symbols associated with these two types of shrines cross-fertilized to such a degree that it is possible to speak of a synthesis, one whose center of gravity is the already-hybridized cult of the Holy Blood (*Heilig-Blut*).[10]

As a basis for understanding the differing forms of supernatural power found at certain shrines, we can distinguish two broad categories of pilgrimage rites (while acknowledging that there are indissoluble links between them). Foremost in most accounts of medieval pilgrimage are rites of individual prayer, supplication, healing, and offering. Throughout Christendom, the desire for access to healing reserves associated with a local or national saint long provided the impetus for self-imposed transregional journeys. Saints who, working wonders through their fragmentary remains, healed, protected against misfortune or rescued those in need enjoyed great popular acclaim.[11] At saints' shrines, clerics kept meticulous records of miracles to reflect and confirm the continuously unfolding thaumaturgic power of the saint; and these later became the basis for propagandistic miracle books.[12]

---

[10] Heuser, "Heilig-Blut," pp. 33, 38, who affirms the idea of a fundamental "alliance" within the diversity of external forms taken by Holy Blood shrines, even as he provides a taxonomy that includes several "mixed types." In Bavaria, bleeding host pilgrimages are regarded as a bridge phenomenon, connecting earlier shrines centered on other christological relics (fragments of the True Cross or the Crown of Thorns) to the later flowering of Marian pilgrimage, the first phase of which centered on the *Pietà*; see articles "Bluthostien," cols. 545–6, "Blut Christi" cols. 544–5, and "Blutwunder" cols. 548–9 in *Lexikon für Theologie und Kirche* (Freiburg: Herder, 1958), 2.

[11] For the earlier Middle Ages, Ronald Finucane, *Miracles and Pilgrims: Popular Belief in Medieval England* (London, 1977); Benedicta Ward, *Miracles and the Medieval Mind: Theory, Record and Event* (Philadelphia, 1987). For the later period, Michael Goodich, *Violence and Miracle in the Fourteenth Century: Private Grief and Public Salvation* (Chicago, 1995). Not surprisingly, our picture of the medieval pilgrimage shrine as a place of daily miracles, as a center of "faith healing," is the one that best accords with the monadic conception of pilgrimage piety I sketched above.

[12] Phillip M. Soergel, *Wondrous in His Saints: Counter-Reformation Propaganda in Bavaria* (Berkeley, 1993); Steven D. Sargent, "Miracle Books and Pilgrimage Shrines in Late Medieval Bavaria," *Historical Reflections/Réflexions Historique* 13/2 & 3 (1986), 455–71, which concentrates on saints and Marian shrines to the virtual neglect of blood relics and wonderhosts. On the clerical production of written testimony, see Goodich, *Violence and Miracle*, pp. 4–14.

At south German host-miracle sites and specifically those linked to blood apparitions, which formed a class of shrines acknowledged as "the most widespread type of christological pilgrimage" in the later Middle Ages,[13] the picture is quite different. Scholars have noted an absence of recorded miracles at German sites before the Reformation. Printed miracle books for important shrines like those at Augsburg, Weingarten, Deggendorf, and Andechs do survive, but all come from a later period.[14] Dieter Harmening's study of Franconian miracle books includes only one compilation for a late medieval Holy Blood shrine, and this is for the blood relic (*Blutreliquien*) cult at Rothenburg on the Tauber, not a host-miracle shrine.[15] Philip Soergel concluded that "Bavaria's clerics do not appear to have associated miracles with the Bleeding Host."[16] What accounts for the apparent lack of documented miracles for the later Middle Ages? How were these shrines perceived or promoted, if traditional faith healing had not been the primary mobilizing force or source of popular acclaim?

An answer emerges when we consider a second broad category of pilgrimage rite, one that benefited strongly from the new differentiations in "people's concept of the sacred," and one that shows how salvific power could be extended to meet different levels of human need: the institutional Church's mandate for the laity to aid the "poor souls" (*Armeseelen*) passing through Purgatory. It is my con-

---

[13] Alois Döring, "St. Salvator in Bettbrunn. Historisch-volkskundliche Untersuchung zur Eucharistischen Wallfahrt," *Beiträge zur Geschichte des Bistums Regensburg* 13, ed. Georg Schwaiger and Paul Mai (1979), 35–234, esp. p. 55. The fundamental source of information for shrines of this type is the survey by Romuald Bauerreiss, *Pie Jesu. Das Schmerzensmannbild und sein Einfluss auf die mittelalterliche Frömmigkeit* (Munich, 1931), with a listing of individual shrines by region, pp. 22–79; Heuser, "Heilig-Blut," pp. 2–33. The most important examples in Germany are Augsburg, Röttingen an der Tauber, Lauda, Iphofen, Erding, Andechs, Deggendorf, Pulkau, Landshut, Heiligenstatt bei Altötting, and Passau; key northern examples include Wilsnack, Güstrow, and Sternberg. Post-medieval examples are even more numerous.

[14] Heuser, "Heilig-Blut," p. 37. Steven D. Sargent, "A Critique of Lionel Rothkrug's List of Bavarian Pilgrimage Shrines," *Archive for Reformation History*, 78 (1987), p. 357.

[15] Dieter Harmening, "Fränkische Mirakelbücher. Quellen und Untersuchung zur historischen Volkskunde und Geschichte der Volksfrömmigkeit," *Würzburger Diözesangeschichtsblätter* 28 (1966), 25–144, esp. p. 28; Heuser, "Heilig-Blut," pp. 14–15. On the Rothenburg pilgrimage, Ludwig Schnurrer, "Kapelle und Wallfahrt zum Heiligen Blut in Rothenburg," in *Rothenburg im Mittelalter. Studien zur Geschichte einer fränkischen Reichsstadt* (Rothenburg, 1997), pp. 389–400.

[16] Soergel, *Wondrous in His Saints*, p. 37. The author is referring to healing miracles which occurred once a shrine had become established.

tention that individual and collective prayers to help liberate the purgatorial dead played an important, although hitherto unacknowledged,
role in the cultic functioning of host-miracle shrines, bleeding host
shrines in particular. Within a century after Purgatory's doctrinal
consolidation in the thirteenth century, a dramatically expanded conception of Christ and Mary as the primary celestial intercessors for
humanity before God's judgment took root. Dedication of shrines to
these two celestial patrons proliferated in the Bavarian south, a process
driven also by the Eucharist's rise to universal cultic preeminence in
the fourteenth century. In regions where eucharistic shrines multi-
plied, they tended to displace cult sites where local thaumaturges
had worked miracles through their relics.[17] With popular enthusiasm
for saints' relics thus partly displaced, there developed a corresponding
loss of impetus to seek favors *from* the sanctified dead at particular
places (even while major relic collections were being amassed and
promoted by princes and emperors alike). "A long-term desacralization of relics . . . slowly diminished the protection offered by the dead;
conversely, the dead gradually assumed the role of grateful supplicants for the prayers of the living."[18] Reciprocal exchanges remained
in force—the blessed dead still joined the community of saints in
heaven where they henceforth served as intercessors *for the living*—
but the emphasis fell increasingly on the collective penitential obligation of the living to aid the dead, to endow masses, or to perform
suffrages for these "poor souls" in Purgatory.

Framing my investigation is the hypothesis that German host-
miracle shrines in the later Middle Ages enjoyed widespread popular acclaim because they functioned as "efficacious sites" for the
performance of rites of post-mortem liberation, prayers that were
concentrated in the month of November, and formalized liturgically
in the "Poor Souls' Mass."[19] These rites were crucial for generating
local and territorial sodalities, since they emphasized networks of loyalty that connected ordinary people with one another and sometimes

---

[17] Soergel, *Wondrous in His Saints*, p. 22.
[18] Rothkrug, "Preface and Overview," p. 51.
[19] This time of the year is traditionally designated in Bavaria as the "time for
[the care of] souls" or *Seelenzeit*. Yet, it should be acknowledged that Corpus Christi
(*Fronleichnamsfest*) and its octave formed the traditional high-point in the liturgical
calendar for northern and southern German shrines like Walldürn, Zehdenick,
Wilsnack, Iphofen, Büren, Posen, and Belitz; Heuser, "Heilig-Blut," p. 125.

also with elites. "The obligation of remembering extended well beyond the immediate kin group."[20] So along with the heavier penitential burden we can see new opportunities for urban and village communities to forge and reinforce kin and certain kinds of non-kin loyalties. A good deal of this pentitential labor was annexed by lay confraternities (*Bruderschaften*) that placed intercessionary prayers for the dead among their primary charitable activities. A number of these brotherhoods were directly affiliated with specific holy blood pilgrimages from the late fifteenth century onward, and scholars assume the existence of older ones whose activities were not recorded.[21] Through such institutions the qualified power to redeem souls by engaging in Christian "works," although in theory dependent on the pope's authority to transfer merits in the form of indulgences, became a durable mark of communal autonomy. Although Purgatory-cult first emerged as a social institution geared to the spiritual needs of the urban bourgeoisie, it spread readily to village communities, where it seems to have fostered the kinds of regionally-specific, collective identities that later proved capable of articulating their criticisms of society.

A conclusive test of this hypothesis would strain the limits of this essay, as well as the evidence. Relatively little information about the particular kinds of prayers medieval pilgrims recited when visiting holy blood shrines has come down to us, although prayers from later periods routinely describe release from purgatorial suffering and the promise of resurrection as among the salvific virtues of Christ's blood.[22] It is therefore material culture, rather than textual sources, that will furnish the bulk of the evidence presented. My principal aim here is to describe how the cultic environments at several impor-

---

[20] Bruce Gordon and Peter Marshall, "Introduction: Placing the Dead in Late Medieval and Early Modern Europe," in *The Place of the Dead: Death and Remembrance in Late Medieval and Early Modern Europe*, eds. Bruce Gordon and Peter Marshall (Cambridge, 2000), pp. 1–16, quote on p. 5.

[21] On the historical development of these "Bruderschaften zum hl. Blut," see Heuser, "Heilig-Blut," pp. 119–20. While some types of confraternities placed their emphasis on cultic veneration of wonderhosts or blood relics (for example, that in Sternberg in 1503), others, like the one formed in Stams in 1718, devoted themselves to harnessing the salvific powers of their affiliated shrine for individualized needs, among them the release of souls from Purgatory.

[22] Heuser, "Heilig-Blut," pp. 89–98, with transcribed prayers, litanies and songs from Weingarten, Walldürn, Jettingen, Stams, Schwenningen, and Andechs.

tant host-miracle shrines were articulated, architecturally *and* through
a changing constellation of eucharistic objects, symbols and images,
redolent of the place's founding miracle. I will look at evidence from
five cults in southern Germany: Erding (Upper Bavaria), Iphofen
(Middle Franconia), Creglingen (Middle Franconia), Pulkau (Lower
Austria) and Passau (Lower Bavaria). My emphasis is on shrines and
pilgrimages associated with *host-profanation* legends, a sub-species within
the host-miracle tradition. Throughout an attempt will be made to
recuperate the organizing symbolic principle that allowed architecture, sacra and cult imagery, as symbols, to become "operational"
in relation to certain liturgical and para-liturgical rituals associated
with pilgrimage, in particular, purgatorial prayer.[23] Sites where the
host had undergone a symbolic death, burial, and resurrection, as I
will attempt to show, display a range of attributes that allowed them
to be perceived as "efficacious sites." All of this happened at the
church's topographic and symbolic center, its channel of grace:[24] the
findspot of the profaned host's miraculous discovery.

The Host Profaned

A great miracle occurred at Easter time in the year 1125, in the diocese of Regensburg. A God-fearing shepherd went with many other
Christian folk to take communion, according to the customs of the
church. But after receiving the precious body of Our Lord, the shepherd left the church with the Blessed Sacrament still in his mouth
(because of his calling he could visit church only rarely). Walking across
a field he removed it and laid it in a clean cloth. For he desired to
have the host with him everyday out upon the pasturage lands. Eventually
he carved a hollow in his staff and inserted the host into it, so he
might elevate it over the field, and kneel before it in adoration. One
day the shepherd's flock suddenly divided, and several of the animals

---

[23] I borrow the term "operational" from Turner; for his distinctions between the
"exegetical," "positional," and "operational" meanings of symbols, *Image and Pilgrimage*,
pp. 146–7, 247–8.

[24] Another debt to Lionel Rothkrug must be acknowledged: an unconscious bor-
rowing of the phrase "channel of grace." In remarking on the process by which
relics entered into a new "intimacy" with the Eucharist, as they began to be routinely dismembered, and their fragments placed on the altars of churches throughout Europe, Rothkrug concludes: "Together with the Eucharist, relics constituted
the supreme channels of grace"; in Rothkrug, "Holy Shrines," p. 223.

became caught in a hedgerow. Forgetting the presence of the host, the shepherd hurled his staff at the dumb beasts, and there it fell to the ground. Horrified at his misdeed, he tried to lift the injured host from the ground, but he was unable; it remained fixed in its place. Even the parish priest to whom the man confessed was unable to dislodge it. And so it was that the hand of God was holding the Sacrament fast to the ground. Whereupon the bishop was called to the scene, and after pledging to build a chapel for the veneration of Our Lord's body, he elevated the miraculous host from its resting place. All those who had assembled there kneeled in veneration, and the host was carried away in festive procession. Soon after, in atonement for this sin, a small chapel, in honor of Christ, Holy Savior, was erected in that very place, and the miraculous host was set out for pious veneration. A great many pilgrims arrived with offerings and prayers, and many wonders occurred through God's power.[25]

Miracle legends played vital, multi-dimensional roles in the cultural processes that shaped the production, promotion, and perception of pilgrimage shrines and their native locales. Victor and Edith Turner referred to such legends as "charter narratives," while recognizing, contrary to the wishful thinking of clerical apologists and pious historians, that "[legends] and myths to account for a pilgrimage sometimes arise quite late in its history."[26] Many "medieval" pilgrimage legends are known only through Baroque redactions and must be read cautiously. But while their outer layers, and some peculiar motifs, may reflect post-Tridentine doctrines or pastoral concerns, all of the surviving legends for host-miracle shrines harken back unmistakably (in their primary motifs, in their structures, or both) to the corpus of eucharistic legends found in the great *exempla* collections of the thirteenth century.[27] These works, designed as sourcebooks for mendicant preachers, drew upon twelfth-century collections circulating in Clunaic and Cistercian communities, as well as older works such as

---

[25] See footnote 38 for source of legend.

[26] Turner and Turner, *Image and Pilgrimage*, p. 18, for the phrase "charter narrative," and p. 24 for quote.

[27] See Caesarius of Heisterbach's *Dialogus miraculorum* (c. 1223–4), which contains an entire section on the "Sacrament of Christ's Body and Blood"), Thomas of Cantimpré's *Bonum universale de apibus* (1256–61), Stephen of Bourbon's *De septem donis spiritus sancti*, James of Vitry's *exempla* collection (1227–40), and Jacobus de Voragine's *Legenda Aurea* (c. 1255). See Miri Rubin, *Corpus Christi: The Eucharist in Late Medieval Culture* (Cambridge, 1991), pp. 108–29. The prominence of the *Dialogus miraculorum* is a good indicator of the active role played by the Cistercian order in the spread of Eucharistic piety; Heuser, "Heilig-Blut," p. 61.

Bede's *Ecclesiastical History*, Gregory the Great's *Dialogues*, and the tract *De corpore et sanguine Christi* (*c.* 831) by Paschasius Radbertus, who grounded his physical interpretation of the eucharist in miracles tales.[28] As instruments of pastoral instruction, part of what Miri Rubin calls "eucharistic discourse,"[29] *exempla* were designed to mediate folkloric perceptions of the holy and guide popular understanding of novel, often difficult points of doctrine; at the same time they served to guard against misconduct, counter heretical challenges to dogma, and thus reinforce clerical control over the church's salvific institutions, especially confession and penance. In sum, eucharistic miracle tales were deeply embedded in the "theological controversies, cultic developments, popular conceptions, and customs and contemporary events" of the high and late Middle Ages.[30]

Host-miracle tales proliferated amidst escalating institutional and popular acclaim for the doctrine of transubstantiation from the mid-thirteenth century onward, with their heyday in the fourteenth and early fifteenth centuries. During this time we see the emergence of novel forms of ritual use and exposure of the host; a new-found penitential fervor in mystics and laypeople devoted to communion; new iconographic formulas and allegories; popular veneration on a mass scale; and new beliefs about the benefits of accessing the host's powers through vision (sometimes called "spiritual communion" or *Augen-kommunion*). All of these expressions of awe in the face of the Eucharist's salvific and amuletic powers yielded a kind of overweening sensitivity to the host's vulnerability. The species was seen as the living image of Christ in his *suffering* humanity; and miraculous visions of the host, which unveiled the real substance behind the sacrament's external appearance, often revealed Christ in his most vulnerable form: as a child or as the bleeding "Man of Sorrows."[31] Everywhere the consecrated bread was exposed or transported outside the zone of the church, or carried in procession, anxieties about its misuse

---

[28] Rubin, *Corpus Christi*, p. 110.

[29] Miri Rubin, "Imagining the Jew: The Late Medieval Eucharistic Discourse," in *In and Out of the Ghetto: Jewish-Gentile Relations in Late Medieval and Early Modern Germany*, eds. Ronny Po-chia Hsia and Hartmut Lehmann (Cambridge, 1995), pp. 177–208; Miri Rubin, *Gentile Tales: The Narrative Assault on Late Medieval Jews* (New Haven, 1999).

[30] Heuser, "Heilig-Blut," pp. 59–84, quote on p. 84.

[31] Rubin, *Corpus Christi*, p. 118.

prompted the introduction of novel safeguards, practical and sym-
bolical, though these may have fanned the embers of eucharistic
insecurity even hotter.[32]

Legends detailing mishandlings by hapless priests or misuses by
feckless laypeople—what Rubin calls "breaches of the eucharistic
code"[33]—not only enjoined Christians to greater propriety, but generated fresh suspicions about the potential for willful abuse by non-
believers, Jews in particular. While in certain tales, Jews are merely
inserted into an antagonist's role that could be played by an impious Christian or some other unbeliever, in the thirteenth century
host-desecration came to be viewed, alongside ritual murder and
iconoclasm, as characteristically "meaningful" expressions of Jewish
enmity and violence toward the sacred. Informed and enervated by
the legendary tradition, accusations of host-crimes were leveled against
contemporary Jews with often murderous consequences between the
late thirteenth and the mid-sixteenth century, and were especially
prevalent in Germany. Peter Browe counted forty-eight charges
between *c.* 1220 and 1566, with thirty-five occurring in German-
speaking regions. Nearly half of all charges appear to have led to
the foundation of a bleeding host shrine and many were implicated
in popular form of crusading violence that merged with rural insur-
gency.[34] In 1298, and, again, between 1336–39, dozens of Jewish
communities in southern Germany and Austria were decimated—
purportedly in revenge for atrocities committed against the body of
Christ in response to rumors and legends to that effect.[35]

---

[32] As Miri Rubin explained, "every area of injunction, restriction and practice,
and every custom, ritual and demand which could be mistaken, neglected, misun-
derstood or manipulated, was countered by an appropriate tale"; *Corpus Christi*,
p. 128. Various kinds of "host magic" were believed possible; Peter Browe, "Die
Eucharistie als Zaubermittel im Mittelalter," *Archiv für Kulturgeschichte* 20 (1930):
134–54.

[33] Rubin, *Corpus Christi*, p. 125.

[34] Peter Browe, "Die Hostienschändungen der Juden im Mittelalter," *Römisches
Quartalschift für christliche Altertumskunde und Kirchengeschichte* 34 (1926), 167–97.

[35] Friedrich Lotter, "Die Judenverfolgung des 'König Rindfleish' in Franken um
1298," *Zeitschrift für historische Forschung*, 15/4 (1988), 385–422; Friedrich Lotter,
"Hostienfrevelvorwurf und Blutwunderfälschung bei den Judenverfolgungen von 1298
('Rindfleisch') und 1336–1338 ('Armleder')," in *Falschungen im Mittelalter* (Hannover:
Hahnsche Buchhandlung, 1988), 533–83; Klaus Arnold, "Die Armledererhebung in
Franken 1336," *Mainfränkisches Jahrbuch für Geschichte und Kunst* 26 (1974), 35–62;
Manfred Eder, *Die "Deggendorfer Gnad": Entstehung und Entwicklung einer Hostienwallfahrt
im Kontext von Theologie und Geschichte* (Deggendorf, 1992), pp. 84–90, 158–70; Gavin

As integral as the myth of "host desecration" was to collective perceptions of eucharistic miracles, and as pivotal as these persecutory episodes were in the development of Bavarian pilgrimage culture—two key aspects of a phenomenon I call *cultic anti-Judaism*[36]—we must recognize that they are one sub-species of host-miracle legend, and not the dominant one. Less spectacular, more widespread and not overtly anti-Judaic were the stereotyped "host profanation" legends (*Hostienfrevellegende*).[37] Typically their protagonists are characters of simple, undogmatic faith, like our shepherd, who misuse the host only inadvertently; another common type is the hapless priest who fumbles the consecrated wafer on a pastoral mission through the landscape; elsewhere we encounter maids, peasants, soldiers, a traveling teacher, robbers, and knights. The *Hostienfrevel* tale furnished the late medieval imagination with a flexible set of symbols with potential operational meanings capable of driving the processes of shrine-foundation and cult-formation.

The "poor shepherd's" tale presented above is a well-intended counterfeit. I cobbled it together, with little embellishment, on the basis of two closely related Bavarian legends, that of St. Salvator at Bettbrunn, near Regensburg, and its counterpart from Einsbach, near Dachau; both are dateable to the fifteenth century.[38] Like the eucharis-

---

Langmuir, "The Tortures of the Body of Christ," in *Christendom and its Discontents: Exclusion, Persecution, and Rebellion, 1000–1500*, ed. Scott L. Waugh and Peter D. Diehl (Cambridge, 1996), pp. 287–309; Rubin, "Imagining the Jew," pp. 177–208; Rubin, *Gentile Tales*, pp. 48–57.

[36] The term was coined by Denise Despres in "Immaculate Flesh and the Social Body: Mary and the Jews," *Jewish History* 12/1 (Spring 1998), 47–69. I use the term differently, to describe the interlocking phenomena of anti-Judaic persecutions and Christian cult-formation. A book focused on four of the holy blood shrines considered here—Iphofen, Pulkau, Deggendorf and Passau—is in preparation.

[37] I translate *Hostienfrevel* as "host-profanation" to maintain some distance from the anti-Jewish legends concerned with "desecration" (*Hostienschändung*). See Browe, "Die Eucharistische Verwandlungswunder;" Manfred Eder, "Eucharistische Kirchen und Wallfahrten im Bistum Regensburg," *Beiträge zur Geschichte des Bistums Regensburg* 28 (1994): 97–172. On shepherds in foundation tales, Leopold Schmidt, "Hirtenmotive in Wallfahrtsgründungslegenden," in *Festschrift Nikolaus Grass. Zum 60. Geburtstag dargebracht von Fachgenossen, Freunden und Schulern*, vol. 2, ed. Louis Carlen and Fritz Steinegger (Innsbruck, 1975), pp. 199–215.

[38] Both have survived as rhymed poems. For the Bettbrunn legend (diocese of Regensburg), Döring, "St. Salvator in Bettbrunn," pp. 59–61; for Einsbach (diocese of Freising), Anton Bauer, "Eucharistische Wallfahrten zu 'Unserrm Herrn', zum 'Hl. Blut', und zum 'St. Salvator,' im alten Bistum Freising," *Beiträge zur altbayerischen Kirchengeschichte* 21/3 (1960): 37–71. Related examples can be found in Eder, "Eucharistische Kirchen und Wallfahrten," pp. 130–5.

tic *exempla* that fed its roots, the standard host-profanation tale uses the figure of the pious but misguided rustic to raise questions about worthy reception of the Eucharist. Like all charter narratives, the main organizing motif is the miracle itself: having tumbled to the ground, the endangered host sets nature on an impossible course; the bread becomes impossibly heavy; it can no longer be moved by human hands. In christological terms, the downward movement of the host, its physical degradation, evokes metaphorically the death and entombment of Christ during the Passion. That several hands attempt to retrieve and elevate it, and only the third, those of the bishop, succeed,[39] may recall the three days Jesus remained in the tomb, but it also functions to explain the necessity of episcopal authority in the rescue of the endangered sacrum. Performed before a crowd of onlookers, with the suggestion of great liturgical solemnity, the miracle of the host's raising by the bishop replicates the Easter-morning elevation ceremony (*elevatio*), in which the late medieval obsession with salvific display and "spiritual communion" received its strongest affirmation.[40] In short, the structure of these legends refracts the key liturgical sequences of Holy Week, from Good Friday to Easter, from the Crucifixion to the Resurrection.[41] A 1632 broadsheet published in Ingolstadt, based on a drawing of *c.* 1600, cele-

---

[39] Bauerreiss, *Pie Jesu*, p. 86. The confluence of this motif with other expressions of episcopal control deserves to be studied in particular cases, and more thoroughly as a broader phenomenon; in the case of Passau's Salvatorkirche, episcopal dignity found articulation in both the choice of patron-title and the sacra on display; the shrine as *Bischofskirche* is discussed by Vera Viertelböck, "St. Salvator in Passau. Historische und baugeschichtliche Untersuchung," *Ostbairische Grenzmarken. Passauer Jahrbuch für Geschichte, Kunst und Volkskunde* 26 (1984), 98–125, esp. p. 111.

[40] Josef A. Jungmann, *The Mass: An Historical, Theological and Pastoral Survey*, trans. Julian Fernandes, ed. Mary Ellen Evansa (Collegeville, MN, 1976), pp. 80–1; Anton L. Mayer, "Die heilbringende Schau in Sitte und Kult," in *Heilige Überlieferung: Ausschnitte aus der Geschichte des Mönchtums und des heiligen Kultes für Ildefons Herwegen* (Münster, 1938), pp. 234–62; Hans Bernhard Meyer, "Die Elevation im deutschen Mittelalter und bei Luther," *Zeitschrift für katholische Theologie* 85 (1963): 162–217. That these scenes encode a ritual consonance with the staged raising of relics (*elevatio*) is clear enough; the parallel is best understood with G.J.C. Snoek's concept of a "transposition of forms of reverence and similarity [*sic*] of miraculous power"; *Medieval Piety from Relics to the Eucharist: A Process of Mutual Interaction* (Leiden, 1995), p. 353.

[41] Hubert Faensen, "Zur Synthese von Bluthostien- und Heiliggrab-Kult. Überlegungen zu dem Vorgängerbau der Gnadenkapelle des märkischen Klosters Heiligengrabe," *Sachsen und Anhalt. Jahrbuch der Historischen Kommission für Sachsen-Anhalt. Festschrift für Ernst Schubert*, 19 (Weimar, 1997), pp. 237–55, here p. 249.

brates the Bettbrunn miracle in ten woodcuts and reproduces the legend below.[42] (fig. 291)

Within the legend, the narrative progression from accidental profanation, miraculous immobility, attempted recovery, and clerical exaltation not only underscored the authenticity of the miracle, since it was accomplished through high-level ecclesiastical intervention; it also furnished the miracle with a precise *locus*. The tale's evocation of the host's "find-spot" (*Fundort*) carries an importance that is difficult to overstate. Everything else in the pilgrimage process finds its physical and symbolic center here. It becomes a new channel of exchange between celestial patrons and earthly clients. Every symbol eventually annexed to the shrine gains a "positional" meaning with respect to this invisible vertical axis. Time and space, past and present, legend and event, coalesced around the *Fundort* of the profaned host; precisely fixed and marked, it epitomized sacred space as "the site of a past miracle which could recur at any moment."[43]

Not all host-miracle tales portray the sanctification of place in the same manner. Some touch on the issue of place lightly, as in narratives where a fugitive wafer is discovered, inexplicably, somewhere mundane—in a field, on a tree stump, inside a tree, etc.. Others call attention to the find-spot in more complex and spectacular ways. When a profaned host lies hidden from its rescuers or when it is deliberately concealed by Jewish persecutors, supernatural signs (*Wunderzeichen*) such as lights or voices above a house, or beasts kneeling in veneration, trumpet the location of the host's resting place. In desecration tales spawned by the Paris Legend of 1290, the discovery of a bleeding host is preceded by its miraculous transformation into a child or crucifix, both images of vulnerability.[44] At Röttingen an der Tauber, the embarkation point of the regional massacres of 1298, the legend tells of how the martyred Corpus

---

[42] *Wahrhafftige Abbildung deß großen vnnd fürtrefflichen Wunderwercks / welches sich hat nach der Menschwerdung Christi / als man gezaehlt / 1125. Mit dem hochwuerdigisten Sacrament deß Altars / vnd einem Viechhirten zu Bettbrunn / anjetzo zu S. Saluator gennant / im Regenspurger Bistumb gelegen / zugetragen. Ingolstadt 1632*; broadsheet published by Wilhelm Eder, 1632 (Nuremburg, Germanisches Nationalmuseum, Inv. HB 13564).

[43] Richard Wunderli, *Peasant Fires: The Drummer of Niklaushausen* (Bloomington, IN, 1992), p. 60.

[44] Lotter, "Hostienfrevelvorwurf und Blutwunderfälschung," p. 537; Rubin, *Gentile Tales*, p. 45.

Christi was discovered only after a neighbor heard child-like shrieks coming from the Jewish quarter.[45]

The logic of the desecration narratives demands that the miracle sequence involve some transformation of the host itself; this motif is indispensable. Yet something else changes as well. In these and other host-profanation tales, *the site itself* undergoes a significant transformation. There is no motif which better reveals this principle than the one describing the spontaneous eruption of a spring at the miracle's locus, found in pilgrimage narratives from Einsbach, Erding, Rosenheim, Pulkau, and others where cults of springs (*Brunnenkult* or *Quellenkult*) are attested in later centuries. Pilgrimage stations associated with springs and wells were plentiful in Catholic Bavaria in the early modern period. Some of these date to the Middle Ages; and in a few cases associations carry back to pre-Christian water cults. While it appears that the majority were sacred to Mary, like the ancient well at Chartres,[46] a significant number were associated with Christ and the saints.[47] Springs were said to have appeared upon the places where martyrs shed their blood, where, for example, a severed body part had struck the ground. Of the many pilgrimage churches that share some variant of the name *Heiligenstatt*, the majority are eucharistic sites associated with springs (St. Salvator appears as the most frequent patron of these shrines).[48] In the Einsbach legend, a spring forms in the precise spot where the shepherd's fumbled host strikes the earth; under the gaze of the onlookers, God swims in the sanctified waters.[49] The bubbling up of the sacred water

---

[45] Summarized in Lotter, "Hostienfrevelvorwurf und Blutwunderfälschung," pp. 552–3.

[46] At Chartres cathedral an ancient well in the crypt not only served as the locus of a healing cult for those suffering from *mal des ardents* (ergot poisoning, or St. Anthony's Fire) since the eleventh century, but was an especially popular site for women seeking the Virgin's intercession to resuscitate or save an afflicted child. Laura Spitzer, "The Cult of the Virgin and Gothic Sculpture: Evaluating Opposition in the Chartres West Facade Capital Frieze," *Gesta* 33/2 (1994), 132–50, esp. p. 142. Editors' note: See James Bugslag's essay in this volume.

[47] Rudolf Kriss, *Die Volkskunde der altbayerischen Gnadenstätten* (Munich, 1956), 3, pp. 58–61, here p. 60, noted that in only a few German cases can it be established that water cults (*Quellenkult*) predated their churches. Heidemarie and Peter Strauss, *Heilige Quellen zwischen Donau, Lech and Salzach* (Munich, 1987).

[48] For discussion and list of sites, see Bauerreiss, *Pie Jesu*, p. 105; all places with this name are pilgrimage churches and there are no Marian churches among them. Bauerreiss believed this type of sacred place dates from the tenth century, p. 106.

[49] Heuser, "Heilig-Blut," p. 11; Bauer, "Eucharistische Wallfahrten," p. 54.

resonates with baptismal and resurrection symbolism; for this reason central-plan structures are often chosen to house chapels built over wells. Eventually the waters become *sacra* in their own right, their powers integrated into the salvific economy of the shrine and its cult paraphernalia. As holy waters flow, the site itself is cleansed and made salvific in its turn.

Miraculous appearances of sacred springs are but one in a spectrum of legend-motifs which thematize the sanctification of place through *metaphors of elevation*. Movement along an invisible vertical axis is upward, reversing the profaned host's descent, its accidental contact with the unconsecrated earth, its miraculous immobility, or its burial by blasphemers. All of these images also point to a range of sepulchral connotations for the *Fundort* as well. Romauld Bauerreiss, the great Benedictine church historian, found sepulchral motifs to be nearly ubiquitous in the mythology of the host-crime; in his view they provide an illuminating key to the structural logic of the whole genus.[50] And this lends the sepulchral metaphors a fuller operational meaning in later orchestrations of architecture, cult objects, and symbols at the site.

Up to this point I have drawn upon motifs found in legends to apprehend the topographic and symbolic centrality of the *Fundort*. These legends often speak of church-building "over the findspot" (*über dem Fundort*).[51] Given the way medieval clerical planners marked altars with images, could we not reasonably expect to find cult-specific objects and symbols visibly deployed around it? In the following three sections, I hope to show that this was the case at the host-miracle shrines in south Germany.[52] Clerical planners conceived the space over the *Fundort* as a kind of sacred axis facilitating upward and downward movements between heaven and earth at a fixed location. Given its invisibility, pious perception had to rely, on the one hand, on the spatial orientations and symbolic connotations architecture

---

[50] Bauerreiss, *Pie Jesu*, pp. 88–9. Because the evil antagonist in these tales is never content to abuse the Host and then abandon it, symbolic burial becomes a major motif.

[51] Bauerreiss, *Pie Jesu*, p. 91.

[52] I am not arguing here for the historical veracity of these legends. On the contrary, I take it as axiomatic that the legends, even those roughly contemporary with a shrine's early career, were written to accord with already-established pilgrimages and sometimes with already-existing cult environments. Fully developed legends rarely, if ever, served as blueprints for shrines to be.

provided and, on the other, on the indexical-metaphorical cues altars, sacra and cult-imagery provided. Only through the close coordination of these elements could the sacred axis defined by the *Fundort* become a focus for ritual and visionary experience.

Holy Blood, Holy Sepulcher, Holy Earth

Standing inside the pilgrimage church of the Holy Blood at Erding, on the outskirts of Munich, one must strain to imagine the first chapel, built no later than 1360 on what was once a meadow between Altenerding and Erding proper.[53] (fig. 292) Hung with grand festoonery typical of the Bavarian neo-Baroque, the present edifice, with its abbreviated nave and open half-crypt beneath the choir, was consecrated on September 19, 1677 by the bishop of Freising, and became the most important eucharistic pilgrimage site in this important diocese.[54] Before this Baroque renewal, a single-nave Gothic church stood here for about two centuries, home to a pilgrimage which reached its height in the years around 1500.[55] In the absence of an archaeological survey, the details of this fifteenth-century edifice remain obscure.

Spontaneously-created eucharistic chapels often began as makeshift wooden structures, planned with an eye toward their eventual recognition by church officials as legitimate places of pilgrimage, deserving of indulgences. Some indication of the life-span of these temporary chapels is provided by the legend attached to the forest chapel of St. Salvator at Bogenberg (Lower Bavaria). From a 1679 source we learn that, after a profanation of the Host on Good Friday in 1413, "a wooden chapel was built upon the same place, but because so many wonders and God's mercy were imparted through the presence of the Blessed Sacrament, Abbott Benedictus Böhm built a vaulted stone chapel [to replace it] in 1463."[56] Here we see the tran-

---

[53] The sources speak of a "Chappellen dez heyligen pluetz"; Bauer, "Eucharistische Wallfahrten," p. 44; Strauss and Strauss, *Heilige Quellen*, p. 140.

[54] Bauer, "Eucharistische Wallfahrten," p. 46 for more on the Baroque additions up to 1704. For the church overall, Georg Brenninger, *Wallfahrtskirche Heilig Blut in Erding* (Ottobeuren, 1987).

[55] Bauer, "Eucharistische Wallfahrten," p. 45.

[56] *"auch auf selbe Statt ein hilzene Capellan erbauet / weil aber allda vil Wunder vnd Gnaden*

sition from wooden chapel to a stone church is represented as taking place within fifty years of the shrine's foundation. Even if it is not literally true, a norm or ideal is conveyed. At Erding, an indulgence bestowed upon the church in 1417 by Martin V signaled the first attempt to convert a wooden shrine to a stone edifice. A second indulgence was granted to help finance an enlargement on May 12, 1475.[57]

The catalyzing events that led to the shrine's foundation are not known; veneration at the earliest chapel was almost certainly directed toward a miraculous host, not a blood relic, as Bauerreiss supposed.[58] In all likelihood it was the shrine's clerical promoters who attached a stereotyped profanation legend to an existing shrine, reconstructing its foundation as an act of "atonement" (*Sühne*) on the part of the community for the dishonor paid to the body of Christ. What is clear is that veneration of a miraculous host was eventually eclipsed

durch den Segen des Allerheiligsten Sacraments erthailet wurden / hat Abbt Benedictus Böhm Anno 1463. ein schöne Steinine vnd Gewelbe Capellen bauen...," from a Baroque pilgrimage book, quoted in Bauer, "Eucharistische Wallfahrten," p. 40. For the "Katholische Kirche S. Salvator und schmerzhaffte Mutter" at Bogenberg, see Bauerreiss, *Pie Jesu*, p. 36; Georg Dehio, *Bayern II: Niederbayern*, ed. Michael Brix (Munich, 1988), pp. 72–3; *Die Kunstdenkmäler von Niederbayern XX: Bezirksamt Bogen*, ed. Bernhard Hermann Röttger (Munich, 1929), pp. 81–3. The same pattern is found in the documentation surrounding the pilgrimage church of Ettiswil, in Switzerland, where a stone church replaced a wooden structure in 1450–2; Adolf Reinle, *Zeichensprache der Architektur: Symbol, Darstellung und Brauch in der Baukunst Mittelalters und der Neuzeit* (Zurich, 1976), p. 97. Ettiswil's legend contains the "host-occultation" motif found at Erding.

[57] Issued "von Fünff Cardinaln nach ausweisung Ihrer Pullen"; Heuser, "Heilig-Blut," p. 115; Bauer, "Eucharistische Wallfahrten," pp. 44–5. The date of 1417, erroneously linked to the foundation miracle, appears in the oldest surviving version of the legend, a text painted on a wooden panel (*c.* 1600) that now hangs above the inner south door; text reproduced on pp. 41–3. For summaries of the legend with some variations, see Strauss and Strauss, *Heilige Quellen*, p. 140; Peter Steiner and Georg Brenninger, *Gnadenstätten im Erdinger Land* (Munich, 1986), p. 27.

[58] The description of the shrine in the fourteenth-century documents as a "chapel of the holy blood" (*Chappellen dez heyligen pluetz*) led Bauerreiss, *Pie Jesu*, p. 101, to conclude that early veneration at Erding was directed toward a blood relic of Christ, paving the way for the host-miracle narrative. The chronology is precisely the opposite. According to Heuser, "Heilig Blut," pp. 8–9, the parish priest Peter Fleissenderl acquired a blood relic for the church in 1738; the author lists it among shrines with blood relics, including "mixed types" sites where wonderhosts were venerated earlier. Bauer noted that, until recently, elderly Bavarian Catholics still referred to the Feast of Corpus Christi as "Holy Blood day" (*Heiligbluttag*); "Eucharistische Wallfahrten," p. 41. In Berlin, the consecrated host was designated as "Holy Blood"; Faensen, "Zur Synthese von Bluthostien- und Heiliggrab-Kult," p. 248.

by a cult focused on a wonder-working image, (fig. 299) ensuring
the pilgrimages' survival after the sixteenth century. This should be
considered normative. Baroque revivals in Bavaria, where wonder-
working images (*Gnadenbilder*) characteristically took precedence over
tomb and relic cults, seem to have occurred *only* at those places
where the "abstract" host-cults were supplanted by the more sensu-
ous and theatrical cult of images.[59]

The foundation legend of Erding tells of a poor peasant who, having heard a wealthier fellow ascribe his good fortune to the unorthodox
practice of preserving a consecrated host in his home, decided to
leave communion on Maundy Thursday[60] with a host concealed in
his mouth. On his way home, "the host escaped from his mouth,
hovered in the air above this place, lowered itself toward the ground
and finally disappeared into the earth."[61] Eventually, after the miracle
was discovered, a chapel was dedicated over the spot, "in honor of
our beloved Lord, Holy Savior, and his rose-colored blood."[62] Here
is a twist on the standard host-profanation narrative, in which contact with unconsecrated ground is reversed and undone by *elevatio*.
Unrecoverable through priestly or episcopal intervention, the Blessed
Sacrament of Erding remained hidden, metaphorically entombed in
the ground it sanctified.

In this unexpected conclusion we find an indication of the profound cross-fertilization of eucharistic legend with the imagery and
cult practices associated with older "Holy Sepulcher" cults. Sepulchral
terms and titles were routinely employed in the articulation of host-
miracle legends and the resulting cult environments, as Bauerreiss's

---

[59] Döring, "St. Salvator in Bettbrunn," p. 58. The historical timing of such transpositions is discussed below.

[60] The reference to Maundy Thursday fixes the generalized Eucharistic insecurity of these tales upon an established church rite, namely the *Missa Praesanctificatorum*,
the consecration of one extra host on the Thursday of Holy Week for communion
on Good Friday, the one non-liturgical day in the western Church when no host
is consecrated. In this association the term *sepulchrum*, for which the shepherd's
mouth stands in, is applied to the "place of repose" (*reposoir*) in which the host is
reserved; Neil C. Brooks, *The Sepulchre of Christ in Art and Liturgy with Special Reference
to the Liturgic Drama* (Urbana, IL, 1921), p. 30.

[61] *"Ist ihme die Hostia aus seinen Mund entwichen vnd sichtiglich ob disen orth in der Höhe
geschwebt, [hat] sich bald nider zur Erden gelassen vnd [ist] vnsichtbar worden. . . ."*; Bauer,
"Eucharistische Wallfahrten," p. 42.

[62] *"zu Ehren vnsers Lieben H: Salvatoris vnd seines Rosen farben Bluets"*; Bauer,
"Eucharistische Wallfahrten," p. 42.

survey showed. Some speak of a "crypt" (*Gruft*) or "cave" (*Grube*) nearby the altar, closely associated with the findspot, or they describe the host's resting place as "subterranean."[63] Did the distinctive cult practices that had evolved around the Jerusalem pilgrimage to Christ's empty tomb transfer to eucharistic sites, where the *Fundort* acquires salvific potency from its contact with the fallen host?[64] Like the oil used to anoint the True Cross or water from the Jordan River, holy earth from the area around revered tombs counted among the "blessings"(as cult souvenirs were called) pilgrims brought back from the Holy Land since early Christian times.[65] In the medieval practice most clearly attesting to this transference, pilgrims collected dust and dirt from "host-caves," sometimes located below the altar; widespread in southern Germany, the practice is reported for Heiligenstatt near Altötting, Erding, Iphofen, Bamberg, Einsbach, Zlading, and others.[66] Cult environments were set up to accommodate and acclaim the practice. At Erding a set of loose paving stones in the geometric center of the crypt chapel, where the cult-image is presently displayed, are inscribed with God's reproach to Moses: *locus, in quo stas, terra sancta est* (Exodus 3:5); apparently the pavers conceal a subterranean trap or passage, out of which sacred matter was collected in earlier centuries. The healing powers of Erding's holy earth were so highly prized that small, press-molded relief images of the shrine's patron, as well as small Sacred Hearts, were made from it and sold to pilgrims.[67] Whether these sepulchral associations and practices

---

[63] Bauerreiss, *Pie Jesu*, pp. 83–4, 90.

[64] As the "supreme relic" of the body of Christ, the consecrated host charged anything it touched with salvific power—whether that contact was sustained, as with the corporal, the cloth upon which the host lies during the Mass, or fleeting in the case of leftover *aqua ablutionis*, eagerly sought after for its curative powers; Eder, *Die "Deggendorfer Gnad,"* pp. 138–9.

[65] Simon Coleman and John Elsner, *Pilgrimage: Past and Present in the World Religions* (Cambridge, 1995), p. 85.

[66] A chapel is recorded at Heiligenstatt near Altötting from 1373 onward; Bauerreiss, *Pie Jesu*, p. 30; *Die Kunstdenkmaler Oberbayern III Bezirksämter Mühldorf, Alötting, Laufen, Berechtesgaden* (Munich, 1905), pp. 2526–2529; Georg Dehio, *München und Oberbayern* (Munich), pp. 414–15; Karl Kolb, *Heilig Blut. Eine Bilddokumentation der Wallfahrt und Verehrung* (Würzburg, 1980), p. 131. Bamberg and Zlading are listed in Faensen, "Zur Synthese von Bluthostien- und Heiliggrab-Kult," p. 242.

[67] Several of these are preserved in the Rudolf Kriss Collection of the Bavarian National Museum, Munich, though the earth-molded Holy Savior relief survives only in a wax copy (BNM, Inv. KrK 746). My thanks to Dr. Nina Gockerell for kindly allowing me to examine the Sacred Hearts.

attended the earliest cultic activity at Erding, as the Strausses suggested,[68] remains unclear. But knowing the legend's strong intimation of the transformation of *Fundort* into *terra sancta*, there can be little doubt that this zone of the church formed the fulcrum for the important transpositions between eucharistic and sepulchral symbols and images. At Erding we find a synthesis that was characteristic of this entire family of shrines.

Just how complete a synthesis was possible was revealed in the mid-1980s, when archaeological excavations at the former Cistercian convent and pilgrimage Church of Heiligengrab, near Techow in Brandenburg, found a small vaulted brick and stone "crypt" at the geometric center of the earliest chapel on the site. Arrayed around it archaeologists found eight interred skeletons.[69] First documented in 1317 with the name *claustrum Sancti Sepulchri*, the chapel at Heiligengrab became associated with a medieval host-profanation legend in which a Jewish merchant from Freiburg steals a consecrated host, finds that it becomes heavier and heavier, buries it in desperation *under a gallows*, but is then betrayed and condemned by blood traces on his hands. The extraordinary impulse that forged this legend—synthesizing blood miracle and "heft" miracle, evocations of Golgotha and Holy Sepulcher—cannot detain us here,[70] but it clearly arose in retrospective allusion to the specially-constructed "tomb," likely an Easter sepulcher, and its adjacent burials (six of which are monastic and two, beneath and therefore predating the foundations of the first chapel, may actually be executed criminals interred under the gallows!). At Heiligengrab, then, the sanctification of earth through the temporary presence of a transformed host, dishonorably buried then vindicated through a blood miracle, prepares the way for a novel, and indeed elite, variation on the practice of *ad sanctos* burial while making new salvific reserves available for ordinary pilgrims. At the site of the tomb the body is vindicated, blood reproaches its

---

[68] Strauss and Strauss, *Heilige Quellen*, p. 141.

[69] Faensen, "Zur Synthese von Bluthostien- und Heiliggrab-Kult," p. 242.

[70] Faensen, "Zur Synthese von Bluthostien- und Heiliggrab-Kult," p. 237; on the legend, Gerlinde Strohmaier-Wiederanders, "Untersuchungen zur Grundungslegende von Kloster Heiligengrabe," *Jahrbuch für Berlin-Brandenburgische Kirchengeschichte* 57 (1989), 259–75; Gerlinde Wiederanders, "Die Hostienfrevellegende von Kloster Heiligengrabe. Ausdruck des mittelalterlichen Antijudaismus in der Mark Brandenburg," *Kairos. Zeitschrift für Religionswissenschaft und Theologie*, NF 29 (1987), 99–103.

enemies and divine substance fructifies the ground, in preparation for the future assumption.

Transfigurations of Cultic Space: From Iphofen to Passau

Erding and Heiligengrab together reveal something of the capacity of host-miracle legends to direct sanctity outward, through an evolving transposition of symbols, images and spaces, and to pull it back to a gravitational center: the *Fundort*. A more detailed consideration of the architectural planning that typified this family of shrines will allow the *spatial* logic of these transpositions to come into better focus.

In the case of Iphofen, a small walled town at the foot of the Schwanberges in Middle Franconia, we are again without reliable facts concerning the character or appearance of the earliest chapel built on the site, now occupied by the Church of the Holy Blood. Beyond its modest portal one finds today a conventional assembly-hall church, consisting of a short rectangular nave covered over by a flat ceiling. (fig. 293) Although the visible features of the present building are the result of renovations carried out under Würzburg bishop Julius Echter von Mespelbrunn (1573–1617), the basic fabric of the nave, along with the chapel adjoining the choir on the north side, almost certainly dates to the fifteenth century, when these structures replaced an earlier building. In all likelihood this began, like Erding, as a modest wood "atonement chapel," erected as a temporary *locus* for the cult. By 1329, there was a structure sufficiently permanent for Bishop Wolfram von Grumbach to endow the first prebend.[71]

Even though it is nothing more than a small hole in the paving stones, the *Fundort* at Iphofen, occupying the topographical center of the church, is impossible to miss, marked as it is by a 1984 sandstone

---

[71] Andreas Brombierstäudl, *Dies und Das aus Iphofens Vergangenheit* (Iphofen, 1992), p. 192. A rhymed inscription above the northern portal praises Mespelbrunn as a donor and re-builder. Harald Schwillus, "Hostienfrevellegende und Judenverfolgung in Iphofen. Ein Beitrag zur Entstehungsgeschichte der Kirche zum Hl. Blut im Gräbenviertel," *Würzburger Diözesan- Geschichtsblätter* 58 (1996): 87–107; Josef Endres, *Iphofen. Entwicklung einer würzburgischen Landstadt von ihren Anfängen bis in die Echterzeit* (Dettelbach, 2000), pp. 115–21. My appreciation to Dr. Endres for sending me a copy of his work prior to its publication.

altar by the sculptor Friedrich Koller. When exactly the cavity came, like the crypt at Erding, to denote a kind of "holy sepulcher" within the space is a matter of conjecture. Remarkably, the modern altar marks the legendary site not only physically but "iconographically": over the hole the sculptor has fitted a bronze spider's web, emblazoned with the *chi-rho* monogram, a reference to a folkloric motif in Iphofen's host-desecration legend. A local version of the 1290 Paris tale, the narrative, preserved in the 1741 testimonies of two Iphofen parish priests,[72] describes the martyrdom of the host by two Jews, who stabbed and pierced it until it bled. In horror and desperation the two cast the transformed bread into a privy chamber inside their house, but a miraculous beacon of light above the house alerted the town. The house was then surrounded and stormed, with the Jews brought to stand trial, where they were condemned and beheaded. Discovered inside the Jew's house, safely suspended in a spider's web above the privy, the bleeding host was rescued from its makeshift tomb, and carried off to a nearby church with great ceremony.

The actual events were more complex than this narrative template suggests. On June 24, 1298 a small Jewish community of about twenty-five persons were murdered in Iphofen,[73] part of a series of regional massacres carried out by a popular army of anti-Jewish marauders, led by an obscure nobleman known to us only through his grisly moniker, King Rindfleisch.[74] Not long after the group's first

---

[72] Ignatius Gropp, *Collectio novissima scriptorum et rerum Wirciburgensium* (Würzburg, 1741), with accounts of the priests, Lorenz Helbig (1693–1700) and Dr. Johann Reß (1704–54); Brombierstäudl, *Dies und Das*, pp. 189–91, reproduces the texts. Schwillus, "Hostienfrevellegende und Judenverfolgung in Iphofen," p. 94 distinguishes motifs belonging to the accounts of Reß (R), Helbig (H) and a third document in the Stadtarchiv (S); Endres, *Iphofen*, pp. 194–5.

[73] *Germania Judaica*, ed. Zvi Avineri (Tübingen, 1968), 2, pt. 1, p. 377; Endres, *Iphofen*, p. 198; Schwillus, "Hostienfrevellegende und Judenverfolgung in Iphofen," p. 90 points out that the Hebrew authors of the *Nürnberger Memorbuch* place the number of deaths much higher.

[74] Collusion with local populations, the *de facto* authorization of the territorial ruler, Kraft I von Hohenlohe-Weikersheim, who was deeply indebted to the Jews, and political instability in the empire are now widely-accepted among scholars as factors contributing to the particular virulence of this, the second great persecution of Ashkenazic Jewry in the Middle Ages. Lotter, "Judenverfolgung"; Lotter, "Hostienfrevelvorwurf und Blutwunderfälschung," p. 402; Schwillus, "Hostienfrevellegende und Judenverfolgung in Iphofen," p. 98; Rubin, *Gentile Tales,* p. 51. By the time the movement exhausted itself later that year, at least 3,440 Jews had perished in forty-four locales across Franconia. Lotter, "Hostienfrevelvorwurf und Blutwunderfälschung," p. 551, puts the number of victims at 5,000, from no less than 130 different towns and villages in Franconia.

actions in Röttingen an der Tauber earlier that year, rumors began circulating that tortured hosts had been uncovered in Jewish homes in the wake of the violence. In his *Historiae memorabiles*, the fourteenth-century Dominican chronicler, Rudolf of Schlettstadt, tells of four places, beside Röttingen, where Jewish host-crimes had been "discovered" after pogroms: Würzburg, Weikersheim, Möckmuhl, and Iphofen.[75] Legends arose as *post facto* justifications for persecutions and the subsequent expropriation and adaptive re-use of Jewish real estate for Christian purposes. Between the normative processes of shrine-foundation and cult-formation, and the non-normative processes of accusation and persecution, a synergy was created. From its late medieval prototype the Iphofen legend carries forward, and then projects backward, a cult history scripted as a progressive transformation of a site from Jewish dwelling to symbolic sepulcher to commemorative chapel and station of grace. The constant element throughout is the *Fundort*, which clerical planners marked as a visible presence in the center of the nave.

A similar composition to Iphofen was used in the late fourteenth-century design of the Herrgottskapelle, just outside the town of Creglingen an der Tauber, in Franconia. Here, according to legend, a host was found by a plowman in his field. To commemorate the occurrence, the chapel, sited around the legendary *Fundort*, was begun in 1384 with funds from brothers Konrad and Gottfried von Hohenlohe-Brauneck. A 1389 stone altar, datable to the consecration of the church by Bishop Gerhard von Würzburg, was placed directly over it. In 1505–10, Tilman Riemenschneider was commissioned to carve a magnificent altar for the central altar. Its shrine encloses a sumptuous depiction of the *Assumption of the Virgin*, flanked by Infancy scenes on the wings; the Man of Sorrows appears in the place of honor high atop the sinewy *Gesprenge*, the altar's architectural superstructure.[76]

---

[75] *Rudolf von Schlettstadt. Historiae memorabiles. Zur Domikanerliteratur und Kulturgeschichte des 13. Jahrhunderts*, ed. Erich Kleinschmidt (Cologne, 1974), pp. 51–3. These same places were designated by the Jewish authors of the *Nuremberg Martyrlogium* as "cities of blood" (*Blustädte*); Lotter, "Hostienfrevelvorwurf und Blutwunderfälschung," p. 553.

[76] Creglingen is located about twenty kilometers northwest of Rothenburg ob der Tauber. On the Herrgottskirche, see Richard Schmidt, *Die Herrgottskirche bei Creglingen* (Augsburg, 1929); Hanswernfried Muth, *Die Herrgottskirche in Creglingen* (Regensburg, 1996). On the Riemenschneider altar, Justus Bier, *Tilmann Riemenschneider. Die reifen Werke*, 2 vols. (Augsburg, 1930), 2, pp. 56–61; Walter Paatz, *Süddeutsche Schnitzaltäre*

Without archaeological data to aid in reconstructing the original compositions at Iphofen and Creglingen, it would be hasty to discard more mundane explanations of the *Fundort*'s location at the center of the nave (for example, at Creglingen, it has been argued, the sloping site made it impossible to orient the church so as to set the eastern choir precisely over the find-spot).[77] Such explanations, however, vitiate the symbolic force of these modified "centralizing" plans, and undercut the likelihood that they express a positive intention. It is notable how the siting of the *Fundort* in these churches parallels the conventional location of temporary Easter sepulchers—around which the extra-liturgical ceremonies of the *Depositio, Elevatio,* and *Visitatio Sepulchri* were enacted—in German churches specifically. Whereas in England sepulchers were almost always set up in the north side of the chancel and in France in the choir, German planners typically sited them in the nave, on or near a Holy Cross Altar.[78] The excavations of the earliest chapel at Heiligengrab likewise revealed an Easter sepulcher sited centrally in the nave.

Sepulchral symbolism stemming from the *Fundort* acquired bolder architectural expression in two former "host-desecration churches" dating from near the beginning and end of the phenomenon's history. In both central-planning is the key to this symbolism. The earlier is the former Chapel of the Sacrament in Büren (Westphalia), consecrated as early as 1301 and planned as an octagonal center room. (fig. 294) Unfortunately, the shape of Büren's first chapel was forever obscured by 1720 construction, although a contemporary document which describes the "newly erected chapel" as being built "upon the foundations" of the old indicates a Gothic precursor that was also centrally-planned.[79] In the surviving structure, the altar is placed axially in the south quadrant, directly over a crypt that also

---

der Spätgotik (Heidelberg, 1963), 86–9; Michael Baxandall, *The Limewood Sculptors of Renaissance Germany* (New Haven, 1980), p. 263; Holger Simon, *Der Creglinger Marienaltar von Tilman Riemenschneider* (Berlin, 1998).

[77] Muth, *Die Hergottskirche*, p. 5.

[78] Brooks, *The Sepulchre of Christ*, pp. 55–6. From his study of south German liturgical rubrics, Brooks found three places where the "middle of the church is expressly mentioned as the location of the [easter] sepulchre": Freising, Moosburg, and Speyer; texts reproduced and discussed on p. 57, fn. 28.

[79] Undated document from the Paderborn archive, quoted in Alfred Cohausz, "Vier ehemalige Sakramentswallfahrten: Gottsbüren, Hillentrup, Blomberg and Büren," *Westfälische Zeitschrift* 112 (1962), p. 283; Heuser, "Heilig-Blut," p. 20.

houses a well. Whether the anti-Judaic legend would have accompanied the foundation and early development of the chapel is uncertain, but Büren carries significant marks of a shrine founded upon the ruins of an expropriated synagogue. The masonry-lined depression with a staircase under the altar appears to preserve the contours of a ritual purification bath (*mikveh*), a type of installation frequently found below medieval synagogues, sometimes at the base of deep shafts, where they made use of available running groundwater.[80]

The second example is the former diocesan and pilgrimage Church of St. Salvator (*Salvatorkirche*) in Passau. (fig. 295) This host-shrine was built almost contemporaneously with the first appearance of its legend, published in a late 1490s' broadsheet.[81] On August 16, 1479 the powerful prince-bishop Ulrich III von Nußdorf laid the foundation stone.[82] One year before this, in the spring of 1478, Ulrich had overseen the expulsion of the Jews from the city following the trial and execution of several men and their Christian accomplice, all implicated in a host desecration conspiracy. While the precise scope and timing of the site's transformation needs further study, undoubtedly the new church was erected directly over or close by a building that served the Jewish community as a synagogue (*Schul*). A certain degree of historical veracity therefore informs the narrative trope which, throughout the Passau tradition, imagined the new church

---

[80] Medieval *mikvot* were retrofitted in several cases where synagogues were converted into chapels in the wake of an expulsion or other forced expropriation. In Munich, a Marian chapel was founded in the cellar level of townhouse which served as a synagogue until 1442, when the community was expelled by the Wittelsbach Duke Albrecht III (the Pious). The layout of the building strongly suggests the former presence of a *mikveh*; see Helmuth Stahleder, "Die Münchener Juden im Mittelalter und ihre Kultstätten," in *Synagogen und jüdische Friedhöfe in München* (Munich, 1988), pp. 11–33, esp. p. 23. According to Cohausz, "Vier ehemalige Sakraments-wallfahrten," p. 285, the *Grube* at Büren is presently waterless.

[81] Single-leaf woodcut, 377 × 263 mm; Munich, Staatliche Graphische Sammlung, Inv. 118307. Entitled "A gruesome story which happened in Passau, about the Jews, as follows" (*Ein grawsamlich geschicht Geschehen zu passaw Von den Juden als hernach volgt*), the broadsheet was first printed in Nürnberg by Kaspar Hochfeder in 1497 or 1498, and then reprinted *c.* 1500 by Johann Froschauer in Augsburg.

[82] Anton Mayer-Pfannholz, "St. Salvator," in *Alte Klöster in Passau und Umgebung. Geschichtliche und kunstgeschichtliche Aufsätze*, ed. Josef Oswald (Passau, 1954), pp. 47–66; Anton L. Mayer, "Die Grundung von St. Salvator in Passau—Geschichte und Legende," *Zeitschrift für bayerische Landesgeschichte* 18 (1955), 256–78; Viertelböck, "St. Salvator in Passau," p. 98; and Herbert Wurster, "Die jüdische Bevölkerung," in *Geschichte der Stadt Passau*, eds. Egon Boshof, *et al.* (Regensburg, 1999), pp. 385–92, esp. p. 388.

built "in the place [of]" (*an der Stelle*) or, in the words of the broadsheet, "from the Jewish synagogue" (*auß der juden synagog*). This trope
was eventually refracted in the relics and cultic paraphernalia pilgrims encountered there.[83]

More to the point is the legend's *architectural* refraction; from virtually every approach, the Salvatorkirche appears as a polygonal,
central-plan building, but it is not a central-plan structure in the
strict sense, as the groundplan reveals. (fig. 296) An abruptly termi-
nated west end (very nearly abutting the rock face outside) looms up
over an aisle-less, three-bay nave that merges into a 3/8-polygonal
choir. Sharing this "centralizing tendency," as Wolfgang Götz has
termed it,[84] is the crypt chapel, (fig. 297) which closely resembles
those at Lienz (St. Andreas) and Neuenburg (Franciscan Priory
Church), in addition to being loosely affiliated with many others of
this type. Circumscribed by a stone bench typical of this kind of
Gothic central crypt, the space served as a mortuary chapel before
the early nineteenth century, when the tombs were torn up and
looted as part of the church's forced desacralization by the royal
government;[85] it may have also housed an Easter sepulcher. With its
great domed canopy traced out by a stellar rib vault, the crypt must
have been seen by its medieval visitors—and later traditions are
explicit in identifying it—as the remains of the former synagogue.

Central-plan structures hold a critical place in the development of
Christian architecture and in the history of the pilgrimage shrine in
particular. In early Christianity, the domed center-room became the
characteristic form for the tombs of martyrs and, after the fourth
century, baptistries as well.[86] Within such spaces, the binary pairs

---

[83] As part of their circuit through the church, pilgrims venerated a red-marble
stone upon which, it was claimed, the host had been martyred in the former synagogue. This *Hostienstein* resided on or nearby a Holy Cross Altar in the church's
crypt chapel; the "Jew's knife" (*Judenmesser*), allegedly used in the attack, is also
attested in the early history of the shrine. I dissect this phenomenon in *Pierced with
a Knife: Christians, Jews, and Passion Relic Pilgrimage in Late Medieval Germany*, a book in
preparation.

[84] Wolfgang Götz, *Zentralbau und Zentralbau Tendenz in der gotischen Architektur* (Berlin,
1968), p. 42.

[85] Mayer-Pfannholz, "St. Salvator," p. 64; Raymund Maier, *Bischof Heinrich von
Hofstätter (1839–1875) und seine Kunstschöpfungen* (Winzer, 2001), p. 151.

[86] Constantine and his planners deployed this symbolic form strategically at the
site of Christ's Tomb after its (re)discovery. The imperial biographer Eusebius
referred to it as "the venerable and most holy *martyrion* of the Savior's Resurrection";

death/rebirth and burial/resurrection could be conceived spatially, as if impelled along a vertical axis connecting earth and heaven. Such formal arrangements as evolved for these building types encouraged the perception of a symbolic homology between mortuary and baptismal rites of passage, which were coded in terms of Easter ceremonial. Assuming the form of a richly canopied enclosure, central-plan sanctuaries bestowed a kind of celestial dignity upon the martyr's remains, or configured the space of baptism into a channel of spiritual elevation. Round or octagonal chapels were also used to enshrine relics brought to Europe from the Holy Land.[87] Supreme among these was the Holy Blood.[88] Where central crypts such as that in Passau are associated with mortuary functions, they also closely parallel the form and function of the German charnel house (*Karner*). Over 100 examples of circular or polygonal charnel houses, sited in cemeteries, survive in Austria, Bavaria, and Bohemia.[89] An important early thirteenth-century example is in Pulkau,[90] in Lower Austria, the site of a 1338 pogrom, host-crime accusation, and bleeding host

---

Robert Ousterhout, "The Temple, the Sepulchre, and the *Martyrion* of the Savior," *Gesta* 29/1 (1990), 44–53, here p. 51.

[87] Veronica Sekules, "Easter Sepulchre," in *The Dictionary of Art* (New York, 1996), 9, p. 680.

[88] At the Weingarten monastery in Bavaria cultic veneration of a famous blood relic (*Blutreliquie*), donated by Duke Welf IV and his wife Judith of Flanders (who inherited it from her father, Count Balduin V of Flanders), found berth in a *Rundkapelle* (c. 1124, dedicated to St. Leonard) in the north tower of the monastery church. On Weingarten, *900 Jahre Heilig-Blut-Verehrung in Weingarten 1094–1994. Festschrift zum Heilig-Blut-Jubiläum am 12. Marz 1994*, 2 vols., eds. Norbert Kruse and Hans Ulrich Rudolf (Sigmaringen, 1994); Kolb, *Heilig Blut*, pp. 20–7.

[89] Justin E.A. Kroesen, *The Sepulchrum Domini through the Ages: Its Form and Function*, trans. Margaret Kofod (Leuven, 2000), p. 43. Other examples include Mödling, Tulln, Deutsche-Altenberg (Austria), and Doberan (Germany). At the Church of St. Stephen in Kourim (Bohemia), the oldest example of a regular polygonal crypt with central column and star-vaults (begun c. 1270–80), we find not only a crypt but an even deeper chamber, or sub-crypt, beneath it, recalling the two-tiered design of charnel houses in which the upper level, furnished with an altar for requiems, served as a memorial chapel (*Gedächtniskapelle*); Götz, *Zentralbau*, pp. 237–8. There is evidence that some central-plan Gothic crypts carried the popular designation *Karner* (from the Latin *carnarium*).

[90] Built 1219–21, the Pulkau charnel house first appears in documents in 1430 as *Kapelle zum Heiligen Grab; Geschichte der bildenden Kunst in Österreich, Bd. I: Früh- und Hochmittelalters*, ed. Hermann Fillitz (Munich, 1997), no. 64, pp. 293–4. It is south of the parish church of St. Michaels, just a few hundred meters away from the Holy Blood Church, founded in 1339. I owe this reference, and much kind assistance with the case of Pulkau, to Drs. Herbert and Herta Puschnik.

pilgrimage. Many of these independent, central-plan mortuary chapels, known as *Herrgottsruhkapellen* (the resting place of the Lord), were dedicated *sub voce sancti sepulchri* (under the name Holy Sepulcher) indicating their symbolic affiliation with the Tomb of Christ in Jerusalem.[91] Formal, symbolic, and functional homologies linked the charnel house and the central-plan crypt. Both were perceived as representations of the *Heilig Grab* in Jerusalem and could have functioned ritually, if not magically, as its local surrogate.[92]

We are therefore obliged to think in terms of what Richard Krautheimer called "a network of reciprocal half-distinct connotations," in which symbolic meaning shadows the application and development of particular architectural forms, culturally and historically, without relying on simple *denotation* or direct copying.[93] According to Krautheimer, connotations may arise from a building's "material" forms, features that visibly signal the allegiance of a copy to its prototype (the center-room, ambulatory, gallery, niche chapels, the number of supports or various canonical measurements). Or they may be the result of "immaterial" affiliations such as ecclesiological designations and patron-titles (such as *zum Heiligen Grab*, *Santo Sepulcro*, *S. Sepulchrum*, and a range of titles associated with "St. Salvator"). Material and immaterial connotations were capable of bestowing episcopal, royal, or even imperial dignity on a fledgling shrine, affiliating it with others of the same title, past and present.[94]

We have seen how two very different Gothic building types, the rectangular hall-church (Iphofen and Creglingen), and the central-plan church (Büren and Passau), spatialized and thematized the leg-

---

[91] Kroesen, *The Sepulchrum Domini*, p. 43. Altars could also be dedicated this way. D.Gustaf Dalman, *Das Grab Christi in Deutschland* (Leipzig, 1922), p. 18.

[92] Götz, *Zentralbau und Zentralbautendenz*, p. 246. On the magical function of holy sepulcher simulations, Dalman, *Das Grab Christi*, p. 16, 30.

[93] Richard Krautheimer, "Introduction to an 'Iconography of Medieval Architecture'," *Journal of the Warburg and Courtauld Institutes* 5 (1942), 1–33, esp. p. 9.

[94] St. Salvator titles not only fostered a pervasive cultic focus on the resurrected Christ, a triumphal image, but linked new Eucharistic shrines back to Constantinian and Carolingian imperial prototypes. From the documentation assembled by Adolf Ostendorf for the thirteenth to fifteenth centuries, I count twenty-seven Eucharistic shrines in ten different diocese (Regensburg, Eichstätt, München-Freising, Salzburg, Passau, Bamberg, Rottenburg, Halberstadt, Ermland, Cologne) with some connection to the St. Salvator title; Adolf Ostendorf, "Das Salvator-Patrocinium, seine Anfänge und seine Ausbreitung im mittelalterlichen Deutschland," *Westfälische Zeitschrift*, 100 (1950), 357–76, esp. pp. 373–4.

endary *Fundort*, the shrine's invisible axis of resurrection, in order to invoke the magical efficacy of the prototype, the Holy Sepulcher in Jerusalem. Remembered in legend as a sacred space transfigured from dishonor to vindication, pollution to purity, synagogue to church, the *Fundort* in practical terms organized the entire architectural composition by marking out the ground zero of sanctification. The next section will explore how the visible objects of pilgrimage and cult were coordinated around this vibrating, supra-visible center.

Fountains of Blood

To find Erding's eucharistic cult-image today, one must descend a flight of stairs below the choir and move through a small vaulted corridor to the cruciform crypt-chapel, now protected by an iron gate. Beneath a canopy-like ceiling adorned with floral stucco reliefs stands a sumptuous neo-Baroque altar. A lithe figure depicting the shrine's patron, crowned with thorns, vested with a crimson robe and proclaimed as *SALVATOR MUNDI* by a bronze plaque is ensconced within a marble and gilt niche above the altar. (fig. 298) Over the figure's chest hovers the Sacred Heart, radiating divine light. Streams of crimson blood—thick, corpuscular drops made rope-like by the sculptor—issue from the wounds in hand, feet and chest, arc downward and collect in a gilded mussel-shell. Eternally supplying this basin with its life-giving liquids, the patron-image at Erding appears to its devotees as a "fountain of grace" (*fons pietatis*). Baroque and modern writers refer to this same type of Christ as the "blood-shedding Savior" or, alternately, as "Christ, Source of [Life-Giving] Blood" (a separate type from the medieval "Man of Sorrows" and the resurrected, enthroned Salvator Mundi).[95] As the iconographic type is post-medieval, so too is the wooden figure beneath the props. Only a glance is needed to render dubious the "late-medieval" provenance suggested by some authors.[96]

---

[95] The German terms, traditional Catholic designations enshrined by early twentieth-century folklorists, have a specificity that can not be translated; relevant here are *blutvergießende Heiland*, and *Christus als Blutquell*.

[96] Strauss and Strauss, *Heilige Quellen*, p. 141; Bauer, "Eucharistischen Wallfahrten," p. 46; according to Johann Nepomuk Kißlinger, *Die Wallfahrt Hl. Blut in Erding* (Erding, 1975), p. 18, the sculpture is "doubtless to be ascribed to the gothic and

Yet the object's importance as a reference point in the history of the shrine, which spanned the late Middle Ages and the early modern period, is not diminished. Like many of the relics and cult-paraphernalia associated with host-miracle shrines, the cult-image of Erding marks the location of the *Fundort*, channels its salvific power and vouchsafes its authenticity.[97] It was not always the sole conduit of sanctity. Erding's profanation legend encodes in its narrative a dispersion of healing reserves from the host into a limited number of "secondary eucharistic relics" whose common locus was the *Fundort*: "holy earth" below the altar, a cult-image above and, since at least 1700, a sacred spring or *Brunnen*, enclosed in its own chapel north of the choir.[98] In commemoration of the founding miracle, the first two are still vertically aligned in the physical space of the lower chapel. A pictorial reflection of this arrangement appears in an 1705 ex-voto, which shows a female devotee kneeling in prayer before an apparition of the wounded St. Salvator, his blood drizzling over clouds and into the basin.[99] (fig. 299) Below the figure we see a square stone altar set in a mountain landscape; open on two sides, the structure shelters a mound of earth in which the occulted host is embedded. A staircase with an iron hand-rail, descending into the rocky substrate below the altar, offers itself to the woman's vision.

Art historians are naturally curious about the roles images played

---

baroque era." Brenninger, *Wallfahrtskirche Heilig Blut in Erding*, believed the figure replaced an older cult-statue, lost prior to the seventeenth-century renovations; though it is unclear to what he may be referring. Heuser, "Heilig-Blut," p. 9 correctly assigned the St. Salvator figure at Erding (my fig. 298) to the "sixteenth or early seventeenth century." Another St. Salvator figure associated with the pilgrimage is in Karin Hösch, *Erding: Die Kirchen der Pfarrei St. Johann* (Passau, 1997), p. 28; I have not been able to locate this. A third figure in stone, representing the Resurrected Christ, is reproduced in Hösch, p. 6; Kißlinger, p. 21. Belonging to the parish church of St. John, it is associated with the traditional consecration date of 1464.

[97] Heuser, "Heilig-Blut," p. 114 confirmed the importance of the findspot (using the term *Fundgrube*) as an organizing visual center of host-profanation shrines generally, a highly ornate focus which "still vibrated in the pious perception of the pilgrim with the dreadfulness of the former sacrilege." The author noted that shrines associated with alleged desecrations by Jews were especially likely to become magnets for bizarre cult paraphernalia.

[98] The term "secondary Eucharistic relics" comes from Snoek, *Medieval Piety from Relics to the Eucharist*, p. 385.

[99] Painted panel, 262 × 211 mm, signed "A. C. B. Ex Voto 1705." Kriss Collection, Bavarian National Museum, Munich (Inv. Kr V 345). Maj-Brit Wadell, *Fons Pietatis. Eine ikonographische Studie* (Göteborg, 1969); Lenz Kriss-Rettenbeck, *Bilder und Zeichen religiösen Volksglauben* (Munich, 1963), fig. 252.

when they became the dominant symbol in a cult environment. For the shrines under consideration here, one brake on this curiosity is the available evidence. That is, for the majority of south German host-miracle shrines whose histories span the later Middle Ages, Reformation, and Baroque eras, there is disappointingly-little evidence to suggest that cult-images were installed *in conjunction with the founding of medieval shrines*. Eucharistic images with wonder-working powers, such as Erding's St. Salvator (labeled *Gnadenbilder* in traditional German Catholic culture)[100] appear on the cultic scene at a number of important shrines, but *only* at a later stage in their development. With one or two exceptions, surviving Eucharistic *Gnadenbilder* post-date the Reformation.[101] In cultural-historical terms this is not unexpected. In late medieval Bavaria, the attribution of sanctity to images and statues was associated mostly with Marian pilgrimage,[102] and during the Counter-Reformation, the broad drive toward re-catholicization coalesced around Marian image-cults. This paradigm eventually encompassed christological cults, as individual shrines underwent renewal. Erding and its wonder-working eucharistic image is a textbook case of this process. But what came before the images? What did pilgrims venerate, through what kinds of objects did they access salvific power when they peregrinated to Germany's host-miracle shrines before the Reformation?

Late medieval German pilgrimage culture knew two principle types

---

[100] Much has been written on Marian *Gnadenbilder*. For fundamental perspectives and types, Hans Dünninger, *Wallfahrt und Bilderkult. Gesammelte Schriften*, ed. Wolfgang Brückner, Jürgen Leussen and Klaus Wittstadt (Würzburg, 1995); Nina Gockerell, "'*Sie durchstachen mich mit mannigfaltigen Waffen . . .*' Neuerworbene Bildwerke zum Themenkreis der 'Geheimen Leiden' als Ergänzung der Sammlung Kriss in Bayerischen Nationalmuseum," in *Frömmigkeit. Formen, Geschichte, Verhalten, Zeugnisse. Lenz Kriss-Rettenbeck zum 70. Geburtstag*, ed. Ingolf Bauer (Munich, 1993), pp. 161–94; on Marian themes, Torsten Gebhard, "Die Marianischen Gnadenbilder in Bayern. Beobachtungen zur Chronologie und Typologie," in *Kultur und Volk. Beiträge zur Volkskunde aus Österreich, Bayern und der Schweiz (Festschrift für Gustav Gugitz)*, Veröffentlichungen des Österreichen Museum für Volkskunde, V, ed. Leopold Schmidt (Vienna, 1954), pp. 93–116.

[101] Determining presence of *Gnadenbilder* at shrines is part of a larger problem of documentation, and a debate over scholarly criteria in making the case for the existence of medieval pilgrimages; for a skeptical view, see Sargent, "A Critique of Lionel Rothkrug's List," pp. 351–8. Heuser, "Heilig-Blut," p. 14, offered a short list of shrines where the Eucharistic *Gnadenbilder* formed the primary goal of pilgrimage; of the six he listed, four are from the Counter-Reformation and a fifth concerns a Marian statue in a *species sui generis* (at Neukirchen bei Heiligenblut).

[102] Soergel, *Wondrous in His Saints*, 26.

of *primary* Eucharistic cult-objects.[103] At host-miracle shrines that did
not involve blood miracles (Bettbrunn, Einsbach, Creglingen, Mainburg,
Bogenberg, and Heiligenstatt) the primary cult object would have
been the preserved and incorrupt host, elevated to a place of honor
after the ordeal of its mishandling or misplacement. These hosts,
pampered and promoted as "the most worthy" of relics, were exposed
in monstrances and carried in processions.[104] Meanwhile, at bleeding host shrines like Wilsnack, Iphofen, Pulkau, Deggendorf, Passau,
and Sternberg, the reddened or pock-marked wonderhost (*Bluthostie*)
played this role, also exposed in monstrances and processed. Several
fifteenth-century Books of Hours associated with the Burgundian
court provide a glimpse of what the pious gaze found when it looked
inside the gilt monstrance—a large wafer impressed with an image
of Christ, flecked with ersatz blood stains.[105] (fig. 300) In both instances,
the miraculous host appeared to pilgrims as *relic and image* of the
suffering, historical body of Christ, supremely worthy of adoration
(*latria*), thus differentiated from the relics of saints and other kinds
of sacred objects.[106]

Medieval wonderhosts rarely survived the vicissitudes of their
shrine's history; they usually gave way to "secondary eucharistic
objects," especially images, serving as the shrine's dominant symbol.
The question is, at what point in a shrine's career, how and why
did this happen? For lack of an explanatory model, scholars tend to
generalize.[107] Consider Bettbrunn, Bavaria's oldest host-miracle shrine,

---

[103] A third type of Eucharistic pilgrimage may be found in the cult of the "three
holy hosts" of Andechs, famed for their association with the visionary blood miracle of Pope Gregory the Great; Alois Schütz, "Legende und Wahrheit. Der Andechser
Heiltumsschatz," *Charivari* 7/8 (July–Aug. 1993), pp. 12–16.

[104] On the conception of the host as a unique, if not the supreme relic, Snoek,
Medieval Piety from Relics to the Eucharist, pp. 353–80. For the exposition of the host,
Charles Zika, "Hosts, Processions and Pilgrimages: Controlling the Sacred in Fifteenth
Century Germany," *Past and Present* 118 (1988): 25–64, esp. pp. 32, 46, 52.

[105] *Hours of Mary of Burgundy* of *c.* 1465 (Vienna, Österreichische Nationalbibliothek,
Cod. 1857, fol. 1v. A similar image of a blood-pocked host appears in the *Hours
of Ogier Benigne, c.* 1500 (Baltimore, Walters Art Gallery, MS W291, fol. 17); Rubin,
Gentile Tales, fig. 24.

[106] Indicating this new status, from the twelfth century onward, was the practice
of stamping hosts with *images* of Christ rather than aniconic symbols like crosses or
monograms; Caroline Walker Bynum, *Fragmentation and Redemption: Essays on Gender
and the Human Body in Medieval Religion* (New York, 1992), p. 127.

[107] Bauerreiss, *Pie Jesu*, p. 93, who argued that the Man of Sorrows often took
the place of the host as the "the primary object of cult and the goal of pilgrimage."

which claimed a medieval provenance for its conspicuously-primitive wooden cult-statue of St. Salvator; by "surviving" a fire (dated either 1300 or 1350) that consumed the church and the original wonder-host, the gnarled little figure rose to cultic pre-eminence and came to stand unequivocally "in the middle point of the baroque pilgrimage cult."[108] Alois Döring considered the completed transference from host-relic to eucharistic cult-image something of a precondition for a shrine's successful Baroque renewal.[109] But when in the shrine's career these transferences actually took place, Döring, noting the connection between christological images and Passion piety, answered only "late Middle Ages,"[110] yet the cult of *Gnadenbild* at Bettbrunn has no attestation until the sixteenth century.[111]

As a model for this process of transference, Bettbrunn therefore begs more questions than it answers, but its complexity is typical. Relic to image transfers did take place at most of the host-shrines that have endured, but we need a better theory to explain the evidence. Such a theory is possible, in my view, but it entails a number of explanatory steps that can be presented here only in outline.

The first step is the most important: we must apprehend the lines of affiliation connecting Baroque *Gnadenbilder* to their sources in late medieval eucharistic imagery. To do so, let us return to the Holy Blood Church at Iphofen. From 1892 until the installation of the Koller altar in 1984, a *Heilig Grab* altar stood over the *Fundort*. Around the base of this altar one still sees today four painted panels, set into quatrefoil frames, retelling in telescoped form the anti-Jewish desecration myth and its cultic outcome; while crowning the ensemble is a Gothic-revival *Ecce Homo* figure. Before this, this place of cultic preeminence was occupied by another figure, an early eighteenth-century votive statue of Christ (still preserved, though now relocated) portrayed as the muscular "blood-spouting Savior." (fig. 301) Ejaculating blood in powerful streams, heroic images of this type resonated strongly in German folk-piety, especially in wine-making regions like

---

[108] Döring, "St. Salvator in Bettbrunn," p. 121; Rudolf Kriss and Lenz Kriss-Rettenbeck, *Wallfahrtorte Europas* (Munich, 1950), pp. 38–9; Bauerreiss, *Pie Jesu*, p. 43.

[109] Döring, "St. Salvator in Bettbrunn," p. 120.

[110] Döring, "St. Salvator in Bettbrunn," p. 58.

[111] Bettbrunn sheds its character as a Eucharistic pilgrimage only in the early seventeenth century; Eder, "Eucharistische Kirchen und Wallfahrten im Bistum Regensburg," pp. 130–5, esp. 133, fn. 84.

Franconia. It is descended from the mystical image of "Christ in the Winepress," the most popular of several related eucharistic allegories of God's self-offering that emerged in the twelfth century.[112] A closer iconographic affiliation is found in the late medieval iconography of the "Fountain of Life" (*fons vitae* or *Lebensbrunnen*), which shows blood spouting from all five wounds into a basin or bowl. One major variant, seen in a *c.* 1500 colored woodcut, depicts five crimson streams cascading down from the Crucified into a large basin, almost a vintner's barrel, labeled "fountain of mercy."[113] (fig. 302) Sinners stand erect and rejoice, waist-deep in the blood of forgiveness, with clasped hands stretching upward in the manner of the "poor souls" striving upward through Purgatory. A second variant presents the bleeding St. Salvator unencumbered by the apparatus of the Cross or winepress. This type, predominant in south Germany's host-miracle shrines, is the visual schema used for the bleeding St. Salvator images of Erding (fig. 298) and Iphofen. (fig. 301)

With the exception of the Herrgottskirche in Creglingen, where the Assumption of the Virgin rose over the *Fundort*,[114] all iconographic traces at the host-miracle shrines themselves, before and after the Reformation, lead back to the dense eucharistic symbolism of the *imago pietatis*, the devotional portrait of the dead Christ, paradoxically suffering and rising from the tomb, known as the Man of Sorrows (*Schmerzensmann*).[115] Romuald Bauerreiss noted the pervasive connections between the Man of Sorrows and German cult-stations where the host was abused, concealed, preserved, and rediscovered. Against the grain of later authors who would see the image only for

---

[112] Leopold Kretzenbacher, *Bild-Gedanken der spätmittelalterlichen Hl. Blut-Mystik und ihr Fortleben in mittel- und südosteuropäischen Volksüberlieferung* (Munich, 1997).

[113] *"Fons misericordie"*; 118 × 74 mm, Netherlandish or German (The British Museum).

[114] Although this is not the place to dissect the iconography of Riemenschneider's altar (*c.* 1505–10), it should be noted that the central Marian theme, with its theological reference to the Immaculate Conception, is vertically framed by two zones of Eucharistic imagery: a relief scene of *Two Angels Holding the Sudarium* set within the central compartment of the predella (*Sarg*), which served as a receptacle for monstrance (perhaps once displaying the miraculous host) and a Man of Sorrows figure in the superstructure (*Gesprenge*).

[115] The literature on the Man of Sorrows topic is large and diverse because it overlaps with studies devoted to other iconographic types (the *Mass of St. Gregory*, the *arma christi*, *Wundbilder*, the *Pietà*, *Christ in the Winepress*, the *fons pietatis* and its variants, etc.), it defies summary. See fn. 142–3, for selected references.

its affective power as a devotional icon, Bauerreiss explored a triad of *eucharistic*, *mortuary*, and *intercessionary* meanings for which the image was enlisted. He highlighted its appearance not only on sacrament-houses, tabernacles, and in the predella niches of countless Gothic sanctuaries, but also in the cemetery, where the theme found frequent use in epitaphs.[116] With regret, Bauerreiss also linked the Man of Sorrows to the sites of destroyed synagogues and places associated with massacres and executions, which carried names like *Judenberg*, *Judenbüchel*, *Judenstein*, and *Judengrube*.[117] This trail likewise led back to the Holy Blood and host-miracle shrines, where he believed the Man of Sorrows received intensive veneration as a *Gnadenbild*. As to when eucharistic cult-images appeared in the development of a these shrines, Bauerreiss did not say. Nevertheless, his analysis reveals the embeddedness of the *imago pietatis* within a broad matrix of institutional, cultic, penitential, and affective contexts, all suggestive of a promethean influence over Passion piety and eucharistic pilgrimage after 1300.

Notwithstanding the force of this argument, unambiguous evidence confirming the presence of a Man of Sorrows cult-image, at any single shrine in the immediate pre-Reformation period, is difficult to come by. One tantalizing reflection appears in a set of drawings (*c.* 1611–14) depicting the presbytery of the Holy Sepulcher Church (*Hl. Grabkirche*) at Deggendorf, site of a massacre of Jews in the autumn of 1338.[118] One drawing shows an over-life-sized Man of Sorrows figure perched atop a stone column before a ciborium-shaped sacrament house; a second drawing shows the same area after the statue had been removed.[119] Although the sculpture has left

---

[116] Bauerreiss, *Pie Jesu*, p. 7, 103. This attack long, although incorrectly, was presumed to have led to the construction of the church and launched a pilgrimage

[117] It was removed through the reform efforts of the city's new parish priest, Johann Riepl (served 1610–13/4); Bauerreiss, *Pie Jesu*, p. 62. Tracing these toponymns back to medieval events is a highly problematic and contentious undertaking, the merits of which must be judged case by case.

[118] See the detailed reconstruction by Manfred Eder, *Die "Deggendorfer Gnad"*. Long permeated by anti-Semitism, the pilgrimage was abolished by the bishop of Regensburg in 1992.

[119] For reproductions, see Eder, *Die "Deggendorfer Gnad"*, pp. 370–1. The pen and ink drawings, now in the Staatsarchiv in Landshut, are part of an illustrated "Aktenvorgang" which Riepl, a former canon at SS. Martin and Kastalus in Landshut, sent to his superiors in Straubing as part of a reform proposal for his parish.

no material trace, a number of surviving wooden figures approximate its general features; a *c.* 1430 Bavarian work is similar in size and format to the lost figure from Deggendorf.[120] Also notable is a late fifteenth-century Franconian figure;[121] displaying his wounds in a gesture of pathetic vulnerability, the figure presages the more dynamic gestures of its Baroque counterparts. The figure's removable arms also suggest that it could have been employed as a "living" effigy of Christ, used in para-liturgical performances of the Deposition from the Cross and the Entombment. (fig. 303)

How long before 1611 the Man of Sorrows figure seen in Riepl's drawing stood in the Deggendorf Grabkirche is a question the foremost scholar of the pilgrimage does not attempt to answer.[122] I have confirmed only one other affiliation between a Man of Sorrows cult-image and a host-profanation church, a sandstone St. Salvator figure in Mainburg, but the figure dates from the early sixteenth century.[123] What, then, are we to do with Bauerreiss's tandem insistence that a species of eucharistic *Gnadenbild*, stemming from the medieval Man of Sorrows, attended the early careers of many south German host-shrines, and that they played a pivotal role in the articulation of their foundation legends?[124]

One thing we should not do is discard the theory for lack of a smoking gun. To apprehend the early "presence" of the Man of Sorrows image at host-miracle churches, especially those connected

---

[120] 1430s, limewood with post-medieval polychromy, 143 cm h (Munich, Bavarian National Museum, Inv. MA 1450); catalogue information and reproduction in Theodor Müller, *Die Bildwerke in Holz, Ton und Stein von der Mittel des XV. bis gegen Mitte XVI. Jahrhunderts* (Munich, 1959), no. 9.

[121] 167.5 × 52 cm (Veste Coburg Museum, Inv. Nr. Pl. 41); *Kunstsammlungen der Veste Coburg. Die Skulpturen des 14. bis 17. Jahrhunderts*, ed. Ulrike Heinrichs-Schreiber (Coburg, 1998), no. 7, p. 60. Had the latter figure once served as cult-image, it would have featured a hollow compartment in its backside, fitted with wooden doors, into which relics or a consecrated host could be inserted.

[122] Eder, *Die "Deggendorfer Gnad"*, pp. 370–8.

[123] Bauerreiss, *Pie Jesu*, p. 41; I have not been able to examine the object here. Although Bauerreiss listed ten places where the *imago pietatis* was associated with host-shrines, p. 83, fn. 176, most would appear to involve post-medieval figures (e.g. Erding), while at least one, the Gregorymass at Wilsnack, is not a figure at all, but a painted scene on a reliquary cabinet!

[124] Host-miracle legends do not place apparitions of the Man of Sorrows at the sites of violations (more often it is the Christ Child or a crucifix which appears); rather than coalescing as a response to motifs in the legend, pervasive popular devotion to the *imago pietatis* after 1300 may have itself been the catalyst for abuse-narratives and anti-Jewish accusations in certain places. On this point Bauerreiss, p. 94, is adamant.

with blood miracles, we need not look simply for objects in stone, wood, or paint. For there is, astride the world of things, a parallel sphere of the visual well-known to historians of medieval religion: images produced in the mind in the course of affective devotions to the Passion, and their more rarified counterparts in the sphere of mystical-visionary experience. Cultivating and applying one's powers of interior visualization was an ongoing preoccupation for lay spirituality and the pastoral efforts to guide it in the later Middle Ages; its parameters and impact have attracted much sustained scholarly attention.[125] An appeal to this vital nexus of pious aspiration within medieval religion is necessary, I believe, if we are to understand the function of *images*, broadly speaking, at pilgrimage sites founded for eucharistic *relics*. One force that brought visionary images into special relevance and prominence at the Holy Blood shrines were the great tensions aroused, notably in Germany, within popular religion by the condemnation of wonderhosts by reform intellectuals, and by the charged-milieu of public controversy in the fifteenth century. How did the terms of eucharistic sanctity, and visuality, shift in the wake of these controversies?

Because of the immense popularity bleeding host cults attained, suspicions of pious fraud were rampant between the early fourteenth and mid-fifteenth century, when the debate over the pilgrimage to

---

[125] Sixten Ringbom, "Devotional Images and Imaginative Devotions: Notes on the Place of Art in Late Medieval Private Piety," *Gazette des Beaux-Arts* 73 (1969), 159–170; Craig Harbison, "Visions and Meditation in Early Flemish Painting," *Simiolus* 15/2 (1985), 87–118; Margaret Miles, *Image as Insight: Visual Understanding in Western Christianity and Secular Culture* (Boston, 1985); Jeffrey F. Hamburger, "The Visual and the Visionary: The Image in Late Medieval Monastic Devotions," *Viator* 20 (1989), 161–182; Eugène Honée, "Image and Imagination in the Medieval Culture of Prayer: A Historical Perspective," in *The Art of Devotion in the Late Middle Ages in Europe, 1300–1500*, ed. Henk van Os (Princeton, 1994), pp. 157–74; Cynthia Hahn, "*Visio Dei*: Changes in Medieval Visuality," in *Visuality Before and Beyond the Renaissance: Seeing as Others Saw*, ed. Robert Nelson (Cambridge, 2000), pp. 169–96. For visualization and pilgrimage, see William Loerke, "'Real Presence' in Early Christian Art," in *Monasticism and the Arts*, ed. Timothy G. Verdon (Syracuse, 1984), pp. 29–51; Merback, *The Thief, the Cross and the Wheel*, pp. 41–54; Botvinick, "The Painting as Pilgrimage." Equally important was the role played by physical sight (*visio*) in accessing the salvific powers of the holy things, particularly the Eucharist; see Anton L. Mayer, "Die heilbringende Schau in Sitte und Kult"; Robert Scribner, "Popular Piety and Modes of Visual Perception in Late-Medieval and Reformation Germany," *The Journal of Religious History* 15/4 (December 1989), 448–69.

Wilsnack crested. Clerical opponents such as Heinrich Tocke and Nicholas of Cusa, like the Bohemian reformer Jan Hus earlier in the century, saw in reports of transformed hosts the products of either human or demonic deception. Blood stains such as those pock-marking the "Holy Host of Dijon," (fig. 300) could easily be painted in; or hosts could be rigged to ooze blood before crowds of pilgrims, like the tear-drizzling Madonnas of later centuries.[126] Yet outright censure of spurious wonderhosts was potentially more damaging to the lay piety than allowing pilgrimages to proceed. Concealing or removing them entirely opened the door to "the threat of adoration (*latria*) when the appearance of bread—and thus the *praesentia realis* (Real Presence)—had disappeared."[127] For these reasons, church officials tended to avoid unequivocal pronouncements on any onto-logical changes that occurred in hosts where apparitions were reported; the Dominicans, for example, admitted that a spiritual change took place in the beholder, even while they denied substantial change.[128] A number of compromise solutions, designed to allow lay venera-tion of blood relics and wonderhosts, were tried. During the con-troversies at Wilsnack in 1446–53 and Pulkau in 1338, papal and diocesan authorities ordered consecrated hosts placed behind or along-side spurious hosts to offset the risk that well-meaning adoration had descended into idolatry.[129] The solution allowed the spurious hosts, on whose fame the future enlargments of their shrines still depended, to remain exposed to pilgrims despite the ongoing debate. Other

---

[126] For a summary of these debates see Caroline Walker Bynum, "The Blood of Christ in the Later Middle Ages", *Church History* 71/4 (December 2002), 685–714, esp. 693–9, to whose author I am grateful for furnishing me with a copy of this article. On Eucharistic frauds see, Lotter, "Hostienfrevelvorwurf und Blutwunder-fälschung"; on Wilsnack and the response of reformers, Zika, "Hosts, Processions and Pilgrimages," esp. pp. 49–59. The earlier theological opinions are discussed in Rubin, *Corpus Christi*, pp. 113–14.

[127] Snoek, *Medieval Piety from Relics to the Eucharist*, p. 378.

[128] This was based on the Thomistic view, confirmed by a 1446 reform synod in Würzburg, on which Wolfgang Brückner, "Liturgie und Legende: Zur theolo-gischen Theorienbildung und zum historischen Verständnis von Eucharistie-Mirakeln," *Jahrbuch für Volkskunde* NF 19 (1996): 139–68, here 151; Bynum, "The Blood of Christ," p. 696. A defense of the full bodily presence of Christ in the miraculous host was mounted by Duns Scotus and his followers; Snoek, *Medieval Piety from Relics to the Eucharist*, p. 379.

[129] For Pulkau, Manfred Anselgruber and Herbert Puschnik, *Dies trug sich zu anno 1338. Pulkau zur Zeit der Glaubenswirren* (Pulkau, 1992), p. 45; Rubin, *Gentile Tales*, p. 66. For Wilsnack, Zika, "Host, Processions and Pilgrimages," p. 52; Bynum, "The Blood of Christ," p. 699.

solutions required that a disputed or decayed host be consumed by a priest and then replaced, or walled up in a depository with altar linens, or be limited in its exposure to the octave of Corpus Christi.[130]

In April 1338, a host-crime accusation in Pulkau led to a pogrom (or vice-versa, as often happened). In the aftermath of the affair, Archduke Albrecht II (r. 1330–58), anxious about unrest in his territories, turned to the Avignon Pope Benedict XII (r. 1334–42) for advice; the pontiff commissioned the bishop of Passau, Albert of Saxony, in whose diocese Pulkau belonged, to set up an inquiry into the authenticity of the bleeding host.[131] Although the final outcome of the investigation is not recorded, Albert ordered that a consecrated host be installed somewhere behind the wonderhost in the event the host proved fraudulent.[132] By 1407, less than twenty years after the new Holy Blood church in Pulkau first appears in documents,[133] the miraculous host was conspicuously absent from an account of a public exhibition of the church's *res sacrae* ("holy things" on which oaths are sworn),[134] but whether we can infer from this absence the replacement of the spurious host by a cult-image sometime in the fifteenth

---

[130] Brückner, "Liturgie und Legende," p. 152; Caroline Walker Bynum, "The Matter of Memorial," p. 13, which the author kindly allowed me to read in manuscript.

[131] Letter from Avignon August 29, 1338 reproduced in *The Apostolic See and the Jews. Documents: 492–1404*, ed. Shlomo Simonsohn (Toronto, 1988), pp. 371–4 (doc. no. 354). A letter of the same date confirms for Albrecht II that, following his appeal, the Bishop of Saxony had been ordered to investigate the matter (p. 374, no. 355). Despite the disappearance of the duke's original letter of appeal, much of its contents may be inferred from the two papal documents. Such suspicions were well-justified in light of the Korneuburg case of 1302–5, the investigation of which might have served as a model for that ordered at Pulkau. In his commission letter of 1338, Benedict refers explicitly to the Korneuburg case and others where doubts had been raised (Linz, Wernhatsdorf), entreating Albert of Saxony to be vigilant; Rubin, *Gentile Tales*, pp. 57–65; Lotter, "Hostienfrevelvorwurf und Blutwunderfälschung," p. 559.

[132] Rubin, *Gentile Tales*, p. 66; Lotter, "Hostienfrevelvorwurf und Blutwunderfälschung," pp. 576–7.

[133] In 1339 Count Johann of Hardegg provided an endowment for a church and adjoining Fransiscan cloister, though the edifice is not documented until 1396; Anselgruber and Puschnik, *Dies trug sich zu anno 1338*, p. 70; Rubin, *Gentile Tales*, p. 68. According to Herbert and Herta Puschnik, *Pulkau. Stadtgeschichte, Kunst, Kultur* (Pulkau, 1998), p. 110, construction did not begin for several decades after 1338. For the church itself, see Georg Dehio, *Die Kunstdenkmäler Österreichs: Niederösterreich nördlich der Donau*, ed. Evelyn Benesch, *et al.* (Vienna, 1990), pp. 914–15; Anton Reich, *Pulkau. Seine Kirchen und seine Geschichte* (Vienna, 1963), to be used with caution.

[134] In 1407 Johann Stendorfer swore an oath on the church's most important

century is doubtful; no trace of such an image remains.[135] It was not until 1520 that the Holy Blood Church received its public cult-image as part of a resplendent Passion altarpiece with shrine figures carved by the Viennese master Michael Tichter and painted wing panels in the Danube School style.[136] (fig. 304) Our attention must focus here on the central standing figure: a "blood-shedding Savior", crowned with thorns and cloaked with a gilded royal mantle. Below his proffered hands, pierced and engorged, two angels with chalices collect the virtual streams of blood. Despite its conventional place-ment in the choir, the altarpiece (which displays a predella cycle depicting the guilty Jews casting the host into a forest spring) con-nects to a whole cult topography extending beyond the church and the town itself. Its symbolic center was the legendary *Fundort*, a site traceable back in time, via one version of the legend, to the "rabbi's house," where the host was allegedly found in a well,[137] and forward to the miraculous eruption of a sacred spring near the present transept crossing. An installation that may have once included a subterranean passage or cave (*Grube*), later covered over with a red marble slab and now concealed by wooden pews, apparently marked the site of this spring—and the *Fundort*—within the church.[138]

Might it have been in those places where suspicions of fraud led to investigations that the need to substitute images for relics was most important? That is, might the introduction of a cult-image in Pulkau have served a legitimizing purpose analogous to the juxta-position of consecrated hosts with dubious wonderhosts, allowing for the eventual eclipse and disappearance of the wonderhost itself? *Latria*

---

relics in the presence of a sizable assembly; in the document only two reliquaries, together with two valuable candle holders (*Kerzenständern*) are mentioned; Anselgruber and Puschnik, *Dies trug sich zu anno 1338*, p. 71.

[135] Miri Rubin could not confirm the whereabouts of what she described as "the much loved and age-old cult image [of Pulkau]," apparently removed by the author-ities of the Scottish Monastery in Vienna, *Gentile Tales*, p. 134; nor have I been able to learn anything about it.

[136] The altarpiece was donated by the Abbot of the Scottish Monastery in Vienna, Benedict Cheldonius, close advisor to Emperor Maximilian I. Margit Stadlober, "Der Hochaltar der Heiligenblutkirche zu Pulkau," *Das Münster* 37/3 (1984), 235–8.

[137] Rubin, *Gentile Tales*, p. 65. Research on the church has not progressed sufficiently to throw light on whether this motif may be an allusion to a *mikveh*.

[138] Bauerreiss, *Pie Jesu*, p. 70.

could then be redirected to another kind of "secondary eucharistic relic": an authorized cult-image based on a venerable prototype. Whatever questions persisted about the authenticity of the founding miracle and its material residue could have been diffused into the network of positional symbols: the *Fundort*, the spring, the cave and the eucharistic icon combining the mystical theology of atonement found in the *fons pietatis* with the psychological realism of the Man of Sorrows. After all, such figural representations were already something like the host's mimetic doubles, literalizing surrogates for the Corpus Christi, which was itself, in a profound sense, already relic *and* image of the suffering, historical body of Christ. Locating such a surrogate on the altar, over the findspot, would certainly have sealed this impression for the ordinary pilgrim.

Unfortunately, such a theory is largely insupportable with the available evidence. Churchmen may have struggled over the legitimacy of certain eucharistic relics and fretted over the deviant devotions they inspired, but the negotiated stopgap solutions we know of were relic-based and not image-based. This would seem to be an important distinction.[139] Nevertheless, I would contend that the fifteenth-century controversies and the restrictive measures imposed on pilgrimage piety connected with them did have an impact on the visual culture of the host-miracle shrines prior to the Reformation. This impact was twofold. On the one hand, cultic veneration becomes directed toward images, but only toward the very end of the fifteenth century and only in a few exceptional cases; the period between 1490 and 1520 saw major altarpieces commissioned and installed at Creglingen, Pulkau, and possibly Iphofen.[140] On the other hand, prior to the appearance of a concrete image, the removal or veiling of wonderhosts may have provoked a different kind of response, one that registered at the level of collective perceptions and popular

---

[139] This seems to reflect the competitive relationship among shrines claiming miraculous hosts as much as it does any particular theological prescription. I am grateful to Caroline Walker Bynum for discussing these critical points with me, although the implications I draw are my own.

[140] In 1481, along with architectural modifications, the Holy Blood Church in Iphofen received a new altar, although its theme and placement in the church are not known; Endres, *Iphofen*, p. 119.

devotional practices. From an increasing inaccessibility to the "cult-unleashing" object, the transformed host, I suggest, came a compensatory emphasis on visual meditation, one that came pre-committed, as it were, to a specific object whose legendary origins placed it within the realm of visionary experience.[141]

I am thinking of the fifteenth century's programmatic image of eucharistic theology, visuality and miracle, the *Mass of St. Gregory*, and its legendary background. It was in the aftermath of Rome's *Anno Santo*, or Jubilee Year, proclaimed by Clement VI in 1350, that the "Passion portrait" of Christ, already familiar to Italian artists from Byzantine sources, burst upon the public scene as a venerable icon known as the *imago pietatis*. In a well-timed bid for institutional prestige, the Carthusians of S. Croce in Gerusaleme, in Rome, mounted a campaign to promote indulgences around a small mosaic icon in their possession. Purportedly commissioned by Pope Gregory the Great himself, the icon was to have commemorated a miraculous apparition of a bleeding Christ during the Mass, God's reproach to doubts about Real Presence.[142] Fueled by an indulgence attached to the original and its authorized copies, which were carried away, *en masse*, by pilgrims in the form of engraved sheets, the *visionary* image of the Man of Sorrows was soon joined by a *legendary* image depicting the miracle in full narrative detail. (fig. 306) Both were widespread in fifteenth-century German lands.[143]

---

[141] A third consequence of the progressive veiling or removal of wonderhosts by church officials occurred to me very late in the course of writing of this essay: its translation into legend. Is it not possible to read the related motifs of the profaned host's miraculous ponderousness, and that of its complete disappearance into the ground—both found in the Erding legend—as coded references to a moment in the cult's history when the primary Eucharistic object, the controversial wonderhost, was hidden or withdrawn?

[142] Romuald Bauerreiss, "Der 'gregorianische' Schmerzensmann und das 'Sacramentum S. Gregorii' in Andechs," *Studien und Mitteilungen zur Geschichte des Benediktiner-Ordens und seiner Zweige* 44 (1926): 57–78; Romuald Bauerreiss, "*Basileus tes doxes*: Ein frühes Eucharistisches Bild und seine Auswirkung," in *Pro mundi vita. Festschrift zum Eucharistischen Weltkongress 1960*, ed. Theologischen Fakultät der Ludwig-Maximilian-Universität München (Munich, 1960), pp. 49–67. Han Belting's located the origins of the western *imago pietatis* in the tradition of Byzantine "Passion portraits" of Christ, developed in conjunction with the Good Friday liturgy, "An Image and Its Function in the Liturgy: The Man of Sorrows in Byzantium," *Dumbarton Oaks Papers* 34–35 (1980–81): 1–16; Hans Belting, *The Image and its Public in the Middle Ages: Form and Function of Early Paintings of the Passion*, trans. M. Bartusis and R. Meyer (New Rochelle, NY, 1990).

[143] Like the Man of Sorrows, the *Gregoriusmesse* image found widespread applica-

Like their "close-up" devotional counterparts, Gregorymass images capture in emblematic pictorial form the salvific rewards of a eucharistic vision authorized by Rome. We could say that the authenticity of eucharistic miracles in the rest of Europe hinged on the ability of their clerical promoters to show a connection to St. Gregory,[144] that is, to papal authority as such, and its monopoly on remissionary powers. For successful host-miracle shrines, the stamp of Rome's authorization was the indulgence; for "contested" shrines, where no such authorization was forthcoming, popular awareness of the apparitional presence of the *imago pietatis* at the site might have provided a sort of grassroots substitute for official acclaim. This makes sense in light of the competition for papal indulgences that often flared up between Holy Blood churches, especially those struggling to survive in times of heated controversy.[145] It makes sense given the prominent role that visions of the Man of Sorrows played at sites where transformation miracles, *especially blood miracles*, were reported in the legendary tradition. In a number of recorded eucharistic visions, abuse prompts the host to change into Christ in his most vulnerable states: a child, the Crucified, and the "living Christ" of the Eucharist, the Man of Sorrows.[146]

By depicting Christ surrounded by the *arma christi* on the altar,[147] the legend of St. Gregory's Mass stood as the paradigm, indeed the

---

tion in mortuary contexts. Uwe Westfehling, ed., *Die Messe Gregors des Grossen: Vision, Kunst, Realität* (Cologne, 1982); J.A. Endres, "Die Darstellung der Gregoriusmesse im Mittelalter," *Zeitschrift für christliche Kunst* 30/11–12 (1917): 146–56.

[144] The point is made in a somewhat different form by Gertrud Schiller, *Iconography of Christian Art*, trans. Janet Seligman (London, 1972), 2, p. 226.

[145] Heuser, "Heilig-Blut," p. 116.

[146] Peter Browe, *Die Eucharistischen Wunder des Mittelalters* (Breslau, 1938), p. 93; cited in Langmuir, "The Tortures of the Body of Christ," p. 294. Hans Belting reproduced the frontispiece from a French manuscript (*c.* 1300; London, British Library, MS Add. 39843, fol. 28) containing guidelines for nuns in attaining penitential virtue; in one of two visions of the Passion vouchsafed to the nun in the miniature, the Man of Sorrows appears in a cloud with the words, "Behold what I took on myself to save the people"; in *Likeness and Presence: A History of the Image in the Era Before Art*, trans. Edmund Jephcott (Chicago, 1994), fig. 247.

[147] An earlier version of the legend, first recorded in the eighth-century *Vita* of Gregory by Paul the Deacon, then transmitted through the *Legenda Aurea*, told of the doubt expressed over God's presence in the host by the woman who baked the bread the pope had just consecrated; Gregory prayed for a sign and a bleeding finger appeared on the altar; Jacobus de Voragine, *The Golden Legend of Jacobus de Voragine*, trans. Granger Ryan and Helmut Ripperger (New York, 1941), pp. 185–6.

prototype, for localized apparitions. If the *imago pietatis* could be said
to supplement the primary eucharistic relic at the scene of dishonor
and rescue, we must admit that it "occurred" only in the sense that
supplicants were enjoined to visualize the figural counterpart of the
miraculous host at a precise visual center in the shrine, the *Fundort.*
It is precisely such a scene of devotion to the *imago pietatis* (presented
as the abused host's visionary substitute) that the princely donors of
the fifteenth-century Sacrament Chapel in Blomberg (Westphalia)
had carved in relief on their tomb monument inside the church.
Kneeling in prayer and accompanied by their patron saints in a formula derived from Franco-Flemish painting, the donor pair collectively conjure up an over-sized Man of Sorrows, arms crossed, holding
the *arma christi.* Just like Gregory's vision of Christ rising from the
tomb upon an altar, the Blomberg apparition rises up through the
shaft of an octagonal well, alleged site of the host's criminal con-
cealment according to the host-profanation legend.[148] But unlike St.
Gregory, the donors in the relief are granted a vision of a miracle
that had occurred, and now recurs, *outside the Mass.* Legitimation
flows from a pictorial formula linking the scene of local devotion to
its authorized prototype.

I suggest that fifteenth-century controversies surrounding eucharistic relics, and the corresponding refusal to grant popular perception
unlimited access to wonderhosts, drove eucharistic piety to resort to
visionary means in realizing the "Real Presence" of the Man of
Sorrows at the *Fundort.* The Blomberg relief offers a rare illustration
of this phenomenon. It suggests how the pictorial formulas late
medieval artists developed to capture, and further prompt, visionary
experiences at the host-miracle shrines may have anticipated the axial
coordination of holy image, altar, sepulcher and earth that Baroque
planners, harkening back to the "venerable" origins of these shrines,
translated into wood, stone, and paint at a time of cultic renewal.
Reading the post-medieval evidence backwards proves useful, but
this is not because it provides us a glimpse of some "lost" medieval
configuration at a shrine, rather because it opens a window onto the
visual culture of pilgrimage in the broadest sense—a constellation of

---

[148] Fig. 2 in Cohausz, "Vier ehemalige Sakramentswallfahrten," p. 281. The legend concerns an Eastertide sacrilege committed by a Christian woman from Blomberg.

shared sights, spaces, images, visual experiences and corresponding modes of visuality—actualized in the rites of veneration, commemoration and visualization, rites whose overlaps and cross-fertilizations have earned these shrines the reputation among scholars as cultic hybrids of such protean influence on religious life.

Dead Souls, Real Presence

In southern Germany the multiplication of shrines during the later Middle Ages amounted to a progressive sanctification of the territory, although the process did not attain any degree of ideological coherence until 1490, when the assimilation of Burgundian (Valois) clerico-chivalric ideals by Bavarian aristocrats inflated the piety of this region into an "official cult of the Empire."[149] Pilgrims of the rural south visited a growing network of eucharistic pilgrimage locales in their own territories, associated in legend with the martyrdom, entombment and resurrection of the Corpus Christi. Whereas existing parish churches served as settings for the annual cycle of feasts and rites of passage like baptisms and funerals, pilgrimage churches served as alternative or expanded venues for special liturgies, rites, and devotions in the life of communities.[150] Among these communal rites, Masses for the "poor souls" in Purgatory, especially those held on All Soul's Day, and during the traditional time for the care of dead souls (October 30–November 8), featured prominently in the Austro-Bavarian regions.[151] From the early fourteenth century on,

---

[149] Lionel Rothkrug, *Religious Practices and Collective Perceptions: Hidden Homologies in the Renaissance and Reformation* (Waterloo, Ontario, 1980); *Historical Reflections/Réflexions Historiques* 7/1 (Spring 1980), pp. 69–72.

[150] None of the shrines analyzed here were originally founded with parish status, but several German Holy Blood shrines were, or had these rights transferred to them (Walldürn, Wilsnack, Arnsheim, Rothenburg, Röttingen, Sternberg, Breslau, Bischofsstein, Volmarstein, Gottsbüren); Heuser, "Heilig-Blut," p. 38. In each, the physical proximity of the new pilgrimage church to an existing parish varied. At Iphofen the erection of the Holy Blood Church in the central district known as the "Gräbenviertel," under the secular jurisdiction of the Counts of Hohenlohe-Weikersheim, competed with an older parish church, St. Martin's (traceable to *c.* 1150), controlled by the Bishop of Würzburg. Once the Hohenlohe sold their rights in the Gräbenviertel, St. Martin's parish rights were transferred to the Holy Blood Church; Schwillus, "Hostienfrevellegende und Judenverfolgung in Iphofen," p. 100.

[151] On *Armeseelen* beliefs and practices, see Mengis, "Arme Seelen," in *Handwörterbuch*

prayers for the forlorn dead became a collective responsibility—and aspiration—of the first order. Building on the "fraternalization" of purgatorial prayer that began as early as the later ninth century in the great Benedictine monastery of Cluny, where intercession "was a weapon with which to fight the devil" for "rights over the souls of men,"[152] lay people without the financial means to pay monks or friars for professional otherworldly assistance formed brotherhoods and prayed for one another.[153] Although lay penitential confraternities, some direct extensions of guilds, formed for a variety of purposes, some seem to have made prayer and the procurement of indulgences on behalf of the dead a central fixture of their charitable mission. Some of these groups were affiliated with particular Holy Blood shrines and were instrumental in the dynamism the shrine was able to achieve locally and regionally.[154] Communal bonds were strengthened, not only through the penitential identification of living and dead members that such rites demanded and generated; the collective power to redeem the souls of one's relations and friends also provided these communities new modalities in the pursuit of self-regulation and political autonomy.

Perhaps because of the dearth of textual evidence, scholars have not drawn any specific connections between the performance of pur-

des deutschen Aberglaubens (Berlin, 2000), 1, pp. 584–97; Walter Hartinger, "Erde, Himmel, Hölle, Fegfeuer: Die Sorge um das Seelenheil und das irdische Leben," in Apocalypse. Zwischen Himmel und Hölle, eds. Herbert W. Wurster and Richard Loibl (Passau, 2000), pp. 177–200. On "All Soul's Day" (Commemoratio omnium fidelium defunctorium), see the article "Allerseelentag" in Lexikon für Theologie und Kirche, 2nd edn. (Freiburg, 1957), 1, pp. 349–50; "Allerseelen," in Handworterbuch des deutschen Aberglaubens I, pp. 267–73. On the visual traditions, Philipp Maria Halm, "Armeseelen," in Reallexiikon zur deutschen Kunstgeschichte (Stuttgart, 1937–), 2, col. 1084–8. For an overview of the broader contexts in which the dead were cared for, Bruce Gordon and Peter Marshall, "Introduction," pp. 1–16. Jacques Le Goff, The Birth of Purgatory, trans. Arthur Goldhammer (Chicago, 1981).

[152] Barbara H. Rosenwein, "Feudal War and Monastic Peace: Clunaic Liturgy as Ritual Aggression," Viator 2 (1971), 129–57, quotes on p. 145.

[153] Walter Hartinger, '. . . . denen Gott genad!' Totenbrauchtum und Armen-Seelen-Glauben in der Oberpfalz (Regensburg, 1979), p. 139.

[154] Heuser, "Heilig-Blut," pp. 118–22, with a list of affiliated groups on p. 120. Although the list only includes two groups with demonstrable late medieval credentials, Heuser assumed the existence of similar confraternities in locales where documentation is lacking, pp. 119–20; Rothkrug, "Holy Shrines," p. 191. Heuser described the Cologne, Mainz, and Fulda chapters of the Walldürn Holy Blood confraternity (Blutsbruderschaft) as "die steten Kultanreger, Kultträger und Kulterhalter des Gnadenortes," p. 37.

gatorial rites and christological pilgrimage. Yet Johannes Heuser, the foremost authority on Holy Blood cults and pilgrimage practices in Germany, stated unequivocally that, "testimonies for the connection between veneration of the Holy Blood (*Heiligblutverehrung*) and the cult of the dead (*Totenkult*) are numerous."[155] Part of this connection was the desire among certain aristocrats to be buried in close proximity to the area of the host-sepulcher, or to an altar where a blood relic was exposed. This practice, a variation on *ad sanctos* burial, strengthened the popular perception of these shrines as "efficacious sites" for the care of souls. In this section, I want to explore the connections between eucharistic cult, shrines and imagery on the one hand, and beliefs in the "presence" of the *Armeseelen* (poor souls) in ritual life and in everyday life on the other, by consulting the *iconographic* evidence, and by conjuring up the visionary dimensions of late medieval *Totenkult* that ran parallel to it.

Earlier I described how legend-motifs acquired "operational" meanings as factors in the outfitting of cult environments; the emphasis given to the *Fundort* played upon the expectation that, as the locus of past miracles, it was also the potential place of future ones. For the shrine to become a new channel of salvific power, for it to be perceived as holy, entailed a kind of supra-visible ontological transformation of matter and an external, visible corollary in the organization of the shrine's cult apparatus and paraphernalia. The transference of healing powers to the earth surrounding the *Fundort*, and the eruption of sacred springs (*heilige Brunnen*), were the clearest indicators that contact with the supreme relic of Christ, the Eucharist, had resulted in a sanctification of place. We also saw that this expectation of sanctity, rooted in ancient beliefs about the salvific potency of the martyr's tomb, applied equally to Holy Sepulcher replicas, or buildings with other sorts of sepulchral signs. Among an extended family of eucharistic *loca sancta* there developed a "network of half-distinct reciprocal connotations" that connected them, symbolically and magically, to the Jerusalem prototype. Anywhere the Eucharist was prompted to change, whether through human error or infidel attack, new intercessionary channels were opened, visualized as vertical axes extending upward to heaven from the earth around the

---

[155] Heuser, "Heilig-Blut," p. 131.

Fundort. How those axes may have been perceived to extend *downward* as well must now be considered. Did the sanctification of site—a sequence leading from profanation to burial, discovery to resurrection—establish a new channel of exchange between the dead below, the intercessors above, and the living between? And how was this visualized?

A hand-colored woodcut, now in Basel, provides a good starting point.[156] (fig. 305) Dating from the second half of the fifteenth century, it features a Man of Sorrows captured in the same gesture of vulnerability, and twisting in roughly the same manner, as the shrine figure carved for the Pulkau altar. In the upper left, God the Father appears in a cloud and signals his acceptance of Christ's intercession by a gesture of blessing. Below him is the Dove of the Holy Spirit and, below it, a chalice with a host. This compact and static symbol of the eucharistic wine contrasts with the cascade of hosts—symbols of the body—pouring from the wound in Christ's side into an open, T-shaped, stone basin coursing with blood. Simultaneously fountain, sepulcher, and vintner's trough, the vessel funnels its contents out through an arched opening and down into a subterranean cavity where the poor souls struggle through the purifying flames, praying to and praising the *fons pietatis*, the source of their refreshment. Along the left edge of the print a wide scroll contains the intercessionary prayer:

> You, good Jesus, are the true font of mercy, you who rule the entire world, intoxicate it and redeem us with your blood.[157]

The bounty of hosts released from Christ's side-wound (resembling coins clattering into a collection box) liquifies in the tomb and washes over the *Armeseelen* like the "well of water springing up into everlasting life" promised by Jesus in Samaria (John 4:14). Through his self-offering, Christ stands before God the Father as solicitor for humankind—a role he shares in numerous other images with the Virgin, whose expressed milk also serves to quench the blistering

---

[156] 180 × 120 mm; Öffentliche Kunstsammlung Basel, of south German, perhaps Upper Rhenish provenance.

[157] "*O bone ih(es)u qui es verus / fons mi(sericodia)e qui reg(n)avit tota(m) / terra(m) et inebriavit ea(m) et / redemit nos suo sa(n)g(ui)ne.*"

purgatorial fires. The woodcut expresses the wish for intercession and its fulfillment in the sacrament.

The placement of Christ's bleeding body directly over the vessel-like altar in the woodcut has a close parallel in the iconography of the *Mass of St. Gregory*. Having already established the historical connections between the legend, its image, the cult of the *imago pietatis* and eucharistic pilgrimage, we are ready to magnify an often-overlooked motif, found in numerous late medieval German renditions of the theme: the eruption of a small party of flame-licked *Armeseelen*, rising upward through the pavement directly beside the altar and carried toward heaven by angels. Although my example here, a wing panel painted for the Lübeck Corpus Christi Brotherhood's resplendent carved altarpiece (*c.* 1496), with shrine carvings by Henning van der Heide, is from northern Germany,[158] (fig. 306) Bavarian artists also set the supra-visible drama of post-mortem release in close proximity to the indulgenced papal altar. In the west tympanum relief of St. Martins in Landshut, where a scene of consecration takes the place of *Ecclesia* in the allegorical schema known as the "Living Cross," hammer blows from the lowest "arm" of the Crucifix crack open a rocky knoll to reveal the purgatorial prison below.[159] All of these images, like the Basel *fons pietatis* woodcut, are strong evidence of a *spatialized* concept of atonement and post-mortem liberation as processes that take place along a vertical axis extending upward into heaven and downward, so to speak, into Purgatory, a prison of fire revealed to the visionary beholder through a hole in the earth's crust.

---

[158] St.-Annen-Museum, Lübeck; *Kirchliche Kunst des Mittelalters und der Reformationszeit*, ed. Jürgen Wittstock (Lübeck, 1981), cat. 87 (pp. 134–44). A second work associated with Lübeck workshops incorporates the motif: the "Schultuper Altar" of *c.* 1500; Wittstock, *Kirchliche Kunst*, no. 94 and a Westphalian altar relief carving from Vinnenberg (Münster Diözesansmuseu), in Gert von der Osten, *Der Schmerzensmann. Typengeschichte eines deutschen Andachtsbildwerkes* (Berlin, 1935), no. 154. The motif appears on a fifteenth-century Netherlandish woodcut (Schreiber 2650) which contains the text of an indulgence written in reverse, to be read before a mirror; Hans Dünninger, "Ablaßbilder. Zur Klarung der Begriffe 'Gnadenbild' und 'Gnadenstätte,'" in Dünninger, *Wallfahrt und Bilderkult*, p. 363.

[159] For a powerful analysis of the "Living Cross" iconography, see Achim Timmermann, "The Avenging Crucifix: Some Observations on the Iconography of the Living Cross," *Gesta* 40/2 (2001): 141–60.

These visionary compositions anticipated the coordination of eucharistic images with the *Fundort*, a form of cultic display realized only
in the era of the *Gnadenbild*, during the Counter-Reformation. They
are pictorial analogues of what will later become a precise "positional" grouping of symbols above the *Fundort*. At the small rural
chapel of St. Salvator in Bogenberg, the decoration of the altar
includes the eucharistic-visionary allegory, *Christ in the Winepress*, aligned
vertically with the grateful *Armeseelen* below. To complete the intercessionary program, planners placed a *Pietà* (*c.* 1460s) upon the altar
console, directly above the winepress image.[160] Although the painting and the arrangement of the altar are post-medieval, the iconography and the spatial coordination of the iconography with the
chapel's altar and findspot, are rooted in fourteenth-century innovations.

In what sense did medieval pilgrims find it compelling, and useful, to visualize the *Armeseelen* arrayed beneath the "blood-dispens-
ing" Savior? How did those offering prayers—as well as specially
prepared breads and wine—during the post-harvest "time of souls"
in November experience the presence of the grateful dead at the
altars, in graveyards, in mortuary zones such as those the sepulcher
at Heiligengrab or in the lower chapel in Passau's Salvatorkirche,
where commemoration of the dead overlapped with veneration of
the bleeding host? Artists explored a diverse range of possibilities for
evoking the presence of the dead in relation to the living. An image
of pilgrims processing through a town square, part of a devotional
miscellany produced in south Germany *c.* 1480, now in Nuremburg,
uses a two-tiered composition (carried over from eschatological imagery
in earlier manuscripts) to create a vision of the forlorn dead shad-
owing the living in their every pious pursuit; the result is a sense of
Purgatory's spatial non-specificity.[161] Contrast this with the treatment
of altar painters such as Wilm Dedeke, who shows the *Armeseelen*

---

[160] *Die Kunstdenkmäler von Niederbayern XX: Bezirksamt Bogen*, ed. Bernhard Hermann
Röttger (Munich, 1929), p. 82. In 2000, I was able to inspect and photograph the
altar only from a considerable distance.
[161] Nuremberg, Stadtbibliothek, Handschrift Cent. IV, App. 34ª, fol. 129v. Leonie
von Wilckens,"'o mensch gedenk an mich . . .' Werke der Barmherzigkeit für die
Armen Seelen. Zur einer spätmittelalterlichen Handschrift in der Nürnberger
Stadtbibliothek," in *Frömmigkeit. Formen, Geschichte, Verhalten, Zeugnisse. Lenz Kriss-Rettenbeck
zum 70. Geburtstag*, ed. Ingolf Bauer (Munich, 1993), pp. 73–80. The drawing is one
of thirteen pen and ink miniatures depicting the "Works of Mercy."

breaking through fissures in the paving stones, suggestive of an almost-threatening closeness. (fig. 306) Within the space of the church, the dead are invested with a compelling "real presence."

With still greater specificity, other artists depicted the dead rising up from crypts near, or virtually under the altar mensa, or climbing up through floor traps that correspond to the passages, stairs, crypts, and caves attested at eucharistic sites like Passau, Büren, Erding, Heiligenstatt bei Altötting, Pulkau, Donaustauf and others.[162] A mid-fifteenth century engraving by Israhel van Meckenem (c. 1445–1503) portrays the dead soul of Duke Adalric of Alsace, father to the beloved St. Odilia, climbing up through a trap in the paving stones before an altar set with crucifix and chalice.[163] (fig. 307) Odilia († c. 720), a royal abbess who became patroness of Alsace and Strasbourg. Disinherited by her father because of her congenital blindness, but later reconciled with him through the intervention of Bishop Erhard of Regensburg, who baptized and helped her regain her sight,[164] Odilia emerged as a popular patron and protectoress against eye ailments in Bavarian south Germany.[165] In the image, the saint appears as an exemplar of efficacious prayer; her pious mien, the meditative concentration she exhibits, bear immediate results when an angel comes to liberate Adalric from his subterranean prison. We see the open passage under the cult stage, as it were, but Odilia, with eyes blinkered shut, does not. This disjuncture between carnal and spiritual vision is of fundamental importance for grasping the role of visualization techniques in *Armeseelen* rites, as it is for late medieval devotional culture in general. As a German heir to the Netherlandish tradition of visionary naturalism, Israhel van Meckenem asks us to see as concrete and literal an event

---

[162] Bauerreiss, *Pie Jesu*, pp. 83–4, fn. 182–3. In some cases Bauerrreiss found evidence of a red marble or stone slab (*Steinplatte*), laid over the gangway, although I have not been able to confirm this at the churches I have examined personally.

[163] 155 × 127 mm; Washington DC, National Gallery of Art, Rosenwald Collection.

[164] J.C.J. Metford, *Dictionary of Christian Lore and Legend* (London, 1983), p. 184. On Erhard of Regensburg, Romuald Bauerreiss, *Kirchengeschichte Bayerns*, vol. I (St. Ottilien, 1958), pp. 52–3.

[165] Other works depicting her include a 1476 painting by Gabriel Mäleskircher in Munich showing her surrounded with votive eyes, deposited by pilgrims eager or grateful for her help. For St. Odilia, her cult and votive associations (especially the tradition of depositing *Augenvotive*), Nina Gockerell, *Bilder und Zeichen der Frömmigkeit. Sammlung Rudolf Kriss* (Munich, 1995), pp. 112–4.

that exists only in the mind's eye of the pious visionary, whose penitential virtue is rewarded with a heaven-sent vision; we are entreated
to emulate her.

Not until the fifteenth century did artists venture visual descriptions of Purgatory, but long before that a tradition of monastic literature grounded the very idea of this "in between" place in visionary
experience.[166] In his account of Purgatory's theological and social triumph Jacques Le Goff placed special emphasis on changing spatial
conceptions of the afterworld. Up until the mid-twelfth century the
image of a cleansing and rejuvenating fire furnished the dominant
metaphor for thinking about purgatorial space; it was "the spatial
embodiment of the purgative phase through which certain souls
passed after death."[167] But this conception soon "proved insufficient"
as *purgatorium* became entrenched within the church's penitential
system. As a mark of its newfound reality, in the twelfth century
Purgatory was increasingly imagined as a place, one of three regions
of the afterworld, with its own geography and topography. Long
before Dante, visionaries traveled these subterranean landscapes and
returned with chastening impressions of the terrible tortures they witnessed there. The most renowned of these visions belonged to St.
Patrick (387?–493). During his mission among the Irish, Patrick was
visited by Jesus who showed him a dark, round cave, promising:

> Whoever in true repentence and constancy of faith enters this cave
> for one day and night will be purified there from all the sins they
> have committed against God during all their lives and will also not
> only see there the torments of the wicked, but, if they perservere stead-
> fastly in the love of God, they will also witness the joys of the blessed.[168]

According to legend, Patrick founded a church near the hole, which
become known as St. Patrick's Purgatory. Eventually an island cave
on Lough Derg in northwestern Ireland was associated with the legend, and pilgrims from about the twelfth century onward came to
regard it not simply as a privileged site for visions of the afterworld,
but as the very gate to Purgatory itself.[169] Accordingly, the perfor-

---

[166] Eileen Gardner, ed., *Visions of Heaven and Hell before Dante* (New York, 1989),
with the best-known version of "St. Patrick's Purgatory" on pp. 135–48.

[167] Le Goff, *The Birth of Purgatory*, p. 154.

[168] "St. Patrick's Purgatory," in Gardner, *Visions*, p. 136; Le Goff, *The Birth of
Purgatory*, p. 194.

[169] Turner and Turner, *Image and Pilgrimage*, p. 112. Visions of heaven and hell

mance of various penitential rites, most of them undertaken on behalf of the dead, became central to the flourishing pilgrimage culture there. At this liminoid zone between worlds, a sodality is formed among the living who pray and the dead who are redeemed—an inter-generational penitential identification that encapsulates the entire medieval "economy of salvation."[170]

The example of St. Patrick's Purgatory illuminates the crucial role visualization techniques played in rites of postmortem purification. Visions of redeemed souls are vouchsafed to the penitent as quasi-miraculous "proof" that his or her prayers have been efficacious. With this understanding, we can view the half-length *Armeseelen* figures still found in multi-media tableaux across Bavaria in a subtler light. For relatives, friends, and the members of charitable brotherhoods devoted to prayers for the dead, these otherworldly simulacra served as a point of departure for visualizations that accompanied masses for the dead.[171] Even at cult-stations where the *Armeseelen* were not represented in sculpted or painted form, their presence was palpable. Just as the cave of St. Patrick's Purgatory served pilgrims as a visionary node, a special-access channel for interaction with the souls of family and friends, sites of legendary host-miracles furnished German pilgrims with opportunities to visualize the pouring down of merit upon the grateful dead like so much atoning blood. Transformed through the founding miracle into a local surrogate for the Holy Sepulcher, replenished perpetually by the Savior's life-giving blood, the area around the *Fundort* came to be seen as the place

---

were supposedly vouchsafed to repentant pilgrims who held day and night vigils at the bottom of the well; Herwaarden, "Pilgrimage and Social Prestige," p. 39. Those who dared enter unrepentant and un-confessed could themselves expect to be subjected to demonic tortures and even death; Henry Charles Lea, *A History of Auricular Confession and Indulgences in the Latin Church* (Philadelphia, 1896), 3, pp. 311–2, fn. 1.

[170] Turner and Turner, *Image and Pilgrimage*, p. 113. On Station Island, where pilgrims to St. Patrick's Purgatory sought indulgences for departed family and friends, many believed "that the more they suffer deprivation . . . the more they are easing the torment of their beloved dead in purgatory," p. 121.

[171] My favorite example is the diorama made *c.* 1694 for the "Arme-Seelen-Gruft," part of a Mt. Calvary ensemble at Hohenburg near Lenggries; Paul Werner and Richilde Werner, *Vom Marterl bis zum Gipfelkreuz. Flurdenkmal im Oberbayern* (Berechtesgaden, 1991), fig. 5.4T. Comparative evidence from Chinese religion suggests that the impulse toward visualization in rites for the dead may be part of a general accommodation to popular perceptions. As Rothkrug, "Preface and Overview," p. 29, shows, such techniques proliferated in ninth-century Tang China in the wake of a nation-wide persecution of Buddhists.

where prayers for the dead would be most efficacious. Visual meditation supplied the imagery of the souls' upward movement as it followed the vertical path blazed by the "resurrected" host of legend.[172]

Conclusion

When, in 1300, the embattled Pope Boniface VIII issued his unprecedented invitation to pilgrims to visit Rome and receive a plenary indulgence, a total pardon of all sins, the promoters of the ensuing Jubilee Year asserted, in effect, "not only that it was a year of absolution, but also that it marked the beginning of a new century."[173] The medieval economy of salvation was opening onto a new era, one which entailed an expansion in the system of spiritual bookkeeping for every Christian subject, living and dead. On Christmas day, the pope made a bold display of his own power to redeem souls from Purgatory by extending the same indulgence, until then granted only to crusaders, to "all pilgrims who had died while on pilgrimage, either en route or in Rome, as well as to those who, having had the firm intention to embark on a pilgrimage, were prevented from doing so."[174] This unprecedented transfer of merits brought widespread popular acclaim to the church's penitential regime in the fourteenth century, and pilgrims carried their enthusiasm back with them to northern countries. Hitherto the laity's powers of redemption had been limited to the transfer of merits acquired through good works; after 1300, pilgrims were offered new ways to tap into Rome's remissionary reserves on their own behalf and on behalf of the dead.

At the same time the system of indulgences theoretically tied all Christian penance to the Treasury of Merits, the novel demands of the penitential system sparked innovations among town dwellers and

---

[172] Paul Binski, *Medieval Death: Ritual and Representation* (Ithaca, 1996), p. 199, arrived at a similar conclusion in his analysis of "the representational silence" surrounding Purgatory in medieval art. Religious culture consigned Purgatory to "the subjective religious imagination rather than the external visualization of artists. Purgatory left the field of everyday perception and entered the realm of the abstract, interiorized, consciousness: it was the final pilgrimage of the mind."

[173] Le Goff, *Birth of Purgatory*, p. 330.

[174] Le Goff, *Birth of Purgatory*, pp. 330–1; Binski, *Medieval Death*, p. 187.

rural folk. Expanded opportunities for commerce with the dead translated into new modes of social distinction and political self-regulation. Urban corporations (guilds, universities, and confraternities) and prominent patrician families took control of the postmortem purification of their dead through, for example, the financing of endowed chantries for the saying of perpetual masses, an institution of enormous social consequence.[175] Meanwhile, in village communities, confraternities that peregrinated to local shrines expanded their own system of "access to remissions" by allowing deceased relatives to be inscribed in the brotherhood, so the "merits earned by good works and by the indulgences granted to the confraternity" while on pilgrimage could be shared among all the generations, young and old, the dead included.[176] At the same time, communities sought for opportunities to expand obligatory collective rites beyond the confines of their parish churches. Territorial pilgrimage churches became just such alternative venues. In contrast to the local parish altar, where the salvific power of the consecrated host was accessible only under the controlled conditions of the Mass, host-miracle shrines commemorated a miracle that had occurred outside the Mass, therefore offering something more adaptable, a constellation of symbols that was more responsive to the cultic creativity of late medieval religion. Not surprisingly, reformers were deeply troubled by just this possibility—that pilgrimages to famous bleeding hosts could overwhelm the laity's regard for the benefits that were, in theory, available everywhere the host was legitimately consecrated and elevated.[177]

Communities had their own problems. In rural areas, efforts to assist departed souls evolved alongside deeply-embedded popular fears concerning the power of the malevolent dead, unpropiated souls whose presence posed a threat to village life.[178] As Rothkrug explains,

---

[175] Binski, *Medieval Death*, pp. 115–22; Rothkrug, *Religious Practices*, p. 72. On the role of testaments for the construction of post-mortem identity and piety among the patrician class, see Walter Hartinger, "Patrizische Frömmigkeit. Aufgrund von Testamenten der Reichsstadt Regensburg im 14. Jahrhundert," in *Frömmigkeit. Formen, Geschichte, Verhalten, Zeugnisse. Lenz Kriss-Rettenbeck zum 70. Geburtstag*, ed. Ingolf Bauer (Munich, 1993), pp. 45–72. My gratitude to the author for an offprint of this article and the chance to discuss the themes of this essay during my last visit to Passau.

[176] Rothkrug, *Religious Practices*, p. 72.

[177] Zika, "Hosts, Processions and Pilgrimages," pp. 61–2.

[178] *Handwörterbuch des deutschen Aberglaubens*, 1, pp. 586–9. See also Paul Barber, *Vampires, Burial and Death* (New Haven, 1988).

because villages often had no government agency "to regulate intercourse with the dead . . . they entered unimpeded into village life, sometimes in the form of unusual apparitions."[179] Dead souls were believed to be condemned to go on their own long pilgrimages to shrines like Altötting in the form of giant toads to seek their own salvation; and nighttime visions of the *Armeseelen* performing their own special Masses, led by priests who had died without fulfilling their duties in life, added to this menagerie of animal and human apparitions.[180] Elsewhere in Europe, especially in France, the poetry and imagery of the Dance of Death was understood metaphorically, as a macabre allegory, but "Only in Bavarian-South Germany did people think that the *Armeseelen* actually danced and performed purgatorial rites in the graveyards."[181]

The intensity of these popular beliefs forces us to reconsider whether the purgatorial visions found in late medieval art might not have to be taken more literally after all. An intimate, lived, and sometimes-neurotic relationship of interdependence with the *Armeseelen* seems to have obtained in the broadest stratum of religious culture. It may not have been extraordinary for people to take their presence as somehow real, their location as somehow very close—to imagine the dead souls imprisoned beneath the paving stones (a traditional place of burial), or in the same sepulchral space where the body of Christ had once fallen, or to see them rising up, liberated, moving toward heaven along the same vertical axis the Lord's resurrection had followed. Eucharistic shrines were not the only places where pilgrims had purgatorial visions. According to a later source for the Regensburg pilgrimage to the *Schöne Maria*, founded in the wake of that city's expulsion of its Jewish community (1519), the Virgin "descended and, making herself visible, talked with them [the sobbing pilgrims]. During her conversation she showed them [visually] their fathers, mothers, brothers, and other souls being delivered from Purgatory."[182] By 1520

---

[179] Rothkrug, *Religious Practices*, p. 73.
[180] *Handwörterbuch des deutschen Aberglaubens*, 1, p. 587, 590; Hermann Kirchhoff, *Christliches Brauchtum. Feste und Bräuche im Jahreskreis* (Munich, 1995), p. 199.
[181] Rothkrug, *Religious Practices*, p. 74.
[182] From *Die regensburgische Chronik*, ed. Carl Theodor Gemeiner, (Regensburg, 1824), 4, pp. 393–4; quoted in Rothkrug, "Holy Shrines," p. 250. The fundamental work on the *Schöne Maria* pilgrimage of 1519 is Gerlinde Stahl, "Die Wallfahrt zur Schönen Maria in Regensburg," *Beiträge zur Geschichte des Bistums Regensburg* 2 (1968), 35–281.

the Virgin's centrality in the politics of the afterlife was already long-established. The vision of Mary's Assumption, prelude to her reign as Queen and Heavenly Intercessor and forecast of the universal resurrection, could even be deployed around the *Fundort* as assuredly as eucharistic images of Christ's self-oblation. This partially explains the apparent situational anomaly posed by Tilman Riemenschneider's *Assumption of the Virgin* altarpiece in Creglingen.[183]

Although a coherent program for transforming Bavaria into a true "territory of faith" had to wait until the sweeping program of Catholic reform under Elector Maximilian I (r. 1623–51), who sought to emphasize the special role of Bavaria's ducal house in this providential process, territorial religious identities in the southern empire were already galvanizing in the fourteenth and fifteenth centuries through the interlocking phenomena of mass mobilizations of pilgrims, the interconnection of shrines within expanding political boundaries, the development of new sodalities around purgatorial rites, and a crusade-like fervor among elites and the popular classes alike. If the rallying cries for pogroms and bleeding host shrines were the twin expressions of this crusading piety in the early fourteenth century, the struggle against heresies and the Turk characterized the fifteenth and early sixteenth. Not only did "heretics" like the Czech reformer Jan Hus (?1369–1415) attack the core eucharistic doctrines of the Roman church, they also expressed a mordant hostility toward the existence of Purgatory, refusing the notion that there can be redemption between death and judgment.[184] Against the assertions that prayers to the dead were in vain, pious Christians in the empire clung all the more tenaciously to the rites of purification—generating, in essence, a bold new alliance of the living and the dead in the service of the Church militant. Fortifying their Catholic rulers' ambitions with grassroots support for church territorialization, "south German rural populations portrayed their cosmic, or, more precisely, their purgatorial visions in motley mosaics of churchyard cemeteries,

---

[183] As J. Michael Shin explained, in the late fifteenth century the Assumption was understood as a prolepsis of the universal Resurrection, since the Virgin's heavenly ascent was seen as a bodily resurrection. Professor Shin explores the theological parellels and their cultic implications for the Herrgottkirche in a forthcoming article "Presenting Corpus Virginis: Tilmann Riemenschneider's *Assumption Altar* (1505–10) in Creglingen," and I thank him for sharing his work in manuscript with me.

[184] Le Goff, *The Birth of Purgatory*, pp. 169, 366.

ornate ossuaries and holy shrines."[185] If these shrines, their *sacra*, their cult-images, and even the fabric of the buildings themselves once "vibrated," as anthropologists imagine, with "the never-obliterated power of the first event,"[186] then Bauerreiss was doubly justified in calling the supra-visible patron of Germany's host-profanation shrines, the bleeding Man of Sorrows, a *"Denkmal der Freveltat"*—a monument to sacrilege.[187]

[185] Rothkrug, *Religious Practices and Collective Perceptions*, p. 75.

[186] The phrase is Edith Turner's in "Preface to the Paperback Edition," *Image and Pilgrimage*, p. xv.

[187] Bauerreiss, *Pie Jesu*, p. 93. In light of the far-reaching connections between anti-Jewish persecutions and host-profanation legends, Israel Schwierz could use the same phrase, tinged with irony, to describe a cult monument like the modern center-altar at Iphofen as a "Denkmal der Freveltat"; in his remarkable survey, *Steinerne Zeugnisse jüdischen Lebens in Bayern. Eine Dokumentation*, 2nd edn. (Munich, 1992), p. 77.

PART VII

CULTS AND CULT PRACTISES:
EVOLUTION AND EXPRESSION

CHAPTER TWENTY-FOUR

THE ICONOGRAPHY OF THE RHENO-MOSAN CHÂSSES OF THE THIRTEENTH CENTURY

Benoît Van den Bossche

At the heart of the pilgrimage lies the reliquary, often a châsse. In many cases, the central iconography of the pilgrimage cult is developed there. Was this iconography conventional or original? Was it distinguished by strict theological qualities, or did it arise purely from popular faith? Did the châsses feature true iconographic programs, or were they merely images juxtaposed without much care for meaningful coherence? These are the questions that will be considered in this essay examining the Rheno-Mosan châsses of the thirteenth century.

The triple châsse of the Magi in Cologne, (fig. 308a) the châsses at the Cathedral at Aachen, (figs. 342, 344) those of the Cathedral of Tournai, (figs. 308b, 312) the châsse of St. Remaclus in Stavelot, (fig. 314) and the largely-disappeared châsse from Nivelles, (fig. 315) all are Rheno-Mosan châsses well-known to art historians who are particularly interested in the western Middle Ages. These reliquaries are imposing, indeed, they are the largest reliquaries that survive from the Middle Ages.[1] Comparison with the attractive Limousin châsses or with the beautiful Saxon châsses of the same epoch allows us to evaluate the scope of these Rheno-Mosan projects.

But despite the celebrity of the Rheno-Mosan works, much more study is required to understand them individually and as a group. Some have been the subject of thorough studies,[2] but others have

---

[1] For the dimensions, see Daniel Thurre, *L'atelier roman d'orfèvrerie de l'abbaye de St.-Maurice* (Sierre, 1992), pp. 378–9.

[2] Such as the châsse of St. Servatius at Maastricht; Renate Kroos, *Der Schrein des heiligen Servatius und die vier zugehörigen Reliquiare in Brüssel* (München, 1985) or, despite it nearly total destruction, the châsse of St. Gertrude at Nivelles; *Schatz aus den Trümmern. Der Silberschrein von Nivelles und die europäische Hochgotik*, ed. Hiltrud Westermann-Angerhausen (Cologne, 1995–6).

been generally overlooked.[3] Since the mid-twentieth century, scholarly literature has considered them individually through monographic books or articles rather than focusing on the general lines of production. Therefore, the researcher who seeks a general understanding of the issues must revisit older studies, which have retained their relevance.[4]

In Joseph Braun's study of the reliquaries of the Christian cult and their development,[5] he devotes a large section to the iconography of these reliquaries.[6] While he does not deal exclusively with Rheno-Mosan châsses, these are the reliquaries which cites he most often. Generally, Braun clearly distinguishes "ornamental"[7] iconography from "religious" iconography.[8] Within the "religious" iconography, he differentiates the purely "symbolic" images from the "real representations."[9] The "symbolic" illustrate the Son, the Father, and the Holy Spirit (the Lamb of God, the divine law, or the dove, for example).[10] The "symbolic" also include personifications, such as the Synagogue and the Church, the Sun and the Moon, and the Rivers of Paradise.[11] Among the "real representations," isolated characters are distinguished from scenes, whether they come from the Old Testament, the New Testament, or from hagiographic material.[12]

Today, these distinctions suggested by Braun appear somewhat artificial, because the iconography of a reliquary must always be regarded as a whole. The images constituting the iconography of a châsse cannot be separated from one another. While each one has an intrinsic sense, this sense is modified and enriched in response to the other images. It is the tension between the meaning that an image intrinsically bears and that which is conferred on it by the others that needs to be examined.

---

[3] Such as the châsse of St. Ermelinde at Amiens, that of Notre-Dame at Huy, or that of St. Suitbert at Kaiserwerth near Düsseldorf.

[4] For the late châsses, see Margarete Fugmann, *Frühgotische Reliquiare. Ein Beitrag zur rheinisch-belgischen Goldschmiedekunst des 13. Jahrhunderts* (Bonn: Dissertation zur Erlangung der Doktorwürde, 1931).

[5] Joseph Braun, Die Reliquiare des christlichen Kultes und ihre Entwicklung (Freiburg im Breisgau, 1940).

[6] Braun, *Die Reliquiare*, pp. 587–685.

[7] Braun, *Die Reliquiare*, pp. 589–97.

[8] Braun, *Die Reliquiare*, pp. 597–685.

[9] "Religiöses, symbolisches Bildwerk" and "Religiöse, reale Darstellungen."

[10] Braun, *Die Reliquiare*, pp. 603–14.

[11] Braun, *Die Reliquiare*, pp. 615–8.

[12] Braun, *Die Reliquiare*, pp. 623–75.

The field of this investigation is limited in a somewhat arbitrary manner, for reasons more practical than scientific. The limits are typological, spatial, and chronological. It is dealing only with "châsses," which come from the Rheno-Mosan area, created in the thirteenth century. But exclusive consideration of these châsses can be justified by the fact that, among all the reliquaries, they are the bearers of iconography *par excellence*. In other words, no other type of reliquary has demonstrated iconographic developments of a comparable scope. Among the medieval châsses of the West, those which were created in the Rheno-Mosan area are especially remarkable.

The chronological distinction is less easily justified: the Rheno-Mosan châsses of the thirteenth century are inscribed directly in the tradition of the châsses of the twelfth century, therefore, to be strictly accurate, there is no break in continuity, but the study of the large châsses of the "century of the cathedrals" makes it possible to determine an evolution within the same time frame. From an iconographic point of view, a châsse of Nicolas of Verdun (end of the twelfth/beginning of the thirteenth century) has few points in common with the châsse of St. Gertrude of Nivelles (1272–98). (figs. 315a, 315b) An evolution has taken place. It is this upon which I wish to focus.

There are two modes for studying iconography. One utilizes the image as the starting point of the study, while the other begins with the text. If the image is used as the point of departure, it is necessary for the art historian to determine the message conveyed by the images themselves; if it is the text from which the study originates, the images are by contrast a sort of illustration, thus conditioning their interpretation. The point of departure is here of primary importance. I choose to let the châsses speak for themselves—by their statuettes and their reliefs. The epigraphic inscriptions will not be explored here, although they could be very interesting theologically. It is in the conviction that a focus on the images is a necessary step and that, for a first approach, it is as justified as any other step.

Rheno-Mosan Châsses in the Thirteenth Century

The first of the great Rheno-Mosan feretories which I will consider was begun at the end of the twelfth century; and was finished only in the third decade of the thirteenth century, but not without various modifications which affected the original project. It is largest

golden reliquary which the Middles Ages produced: the châsse of
the Magi, a masterpiece attributed to Nicolas of Verdun, now displayed in the choir of Cologne Cathedral.[13] (fig. 308a) It must be
taken into account that this is a triple châsse, because it houses the
relics of the Three Kings, brought back from Milan by Bishop
Rainald von Dassel in 1164. The richness of the iconography equals
the abundance of decorative elements there. I will not describe in
detail (for others have already done that) the modifications which
the ensemble has known during the course of its creation and its
ensuing history.[14] It will suffice to relate its essentials: on the principal pinion, the Virgin and Child are represented in the center of
the lower part as part of the Adoration of the Magi scene in which
the kings are shown to the left, presented by the emperor Otto IV
himself; to the right, one sees the Baptism of Christ; and in the
upper part, Christ is shown as Judge, flanked by two angels who
probably once held the *arma Christi*. On the secondary pinion, the
Scourging and the Crucifixion are shown at the bottom, where
between the two scenes, the presence of Isaiah reminds us that the
drama of the Passion evoked by these two episodes had been foretold by this prophet. Above Isaiah at the center of the composition
is a bust of Archbishop Rainald von Dassel. The upper part of this
end also shows the crowning of Sts. Felix and Nabor by Christ—
fittingly, for the relics of these two saints were also preserved in the
châsse. On the long sides, Old Testament personalities are illustrated
on the lower level of the structure, with apostles enthroned on the
upper story. On the sides of the roofs, the original reliefs (removed
in 1781) represented twelve episodes from the life of Christ on the
lower roofs, and twelve moments from the Apocalypse on the nave
roof.

Thus the iconography of the châsse of the Magi is primarily
Christocentric. The life, the legend of the Magi are evoked only by
the means of the Adoration for which the *raison d'être* rests much
more on its Christologic meaning than in its hagiographic value.

---

[13] On the châsse of the Three Kings, see Rolf Lauer "Dreikönigenschrein", in
Ornamenta Ecclesiae 2, ed. Anton Legner (Cologne, 1985), pp. 216–23.
[14] See notably Herbert Rode, "Der verschollene Christuszyklus am Dreikönigenschrein. Versuch einer Rekonstruktion und einer Analyse", *Kölner Domblatt* 30 (1969),
pp. 27–48; Peter Diemer, "Zum Darstellungsprogramm des Dreikönigenschreins,"
Kölner Domblatt 41 (1976), pp. 231–6 (with a review of prior literature).

True, Christ is not represented enthroned on the principal pinion, but all the other scenes bespeak Him. More precisely, on the main pinion are recounted the epiphanic moments of his natural and supernatural existence, i.e. moments during which the dignity of the Son of God were particularly emphasized. The Adoration is the moment of his revelation to the pagans, the Baptism that of his revelation to the Jews, and the Last Judgment that of his revelation to the whole of humanity. On the long sides, other episodes of the life of Christ and those of the Apocalypse must also be understood in their epiphanic dimension. The secondary pinion shows the other side of the coin: the Son of God is presented in his martyrdom (the Scourging, the Crucifixion), and the saints who were led to imitate his sacrifice (in this case, the Milanese Felix and Nabor, whose relics were brought from Lombardy at the same time as those of the Magi). This brief presentation of the iconography of the châsse of the Magi concludes with stress on the importance placed upon the Virtues there—theological and others, not only are they represented, they are also mentioned in the inscriptions.

The iconography of the châsse of Notre Dame of Tournai (completed in 1205)[15] is more elementary than that of the Cologne châsse. It is characterized by an exclusive description of narrative scenes, beginning on the long side with the Annunciation, followed by the Visitation and the Nativity. The Adoration is depicted on the pinion (fig. 308b) and on the other long side are images of the Baptism of Christ, the Presentation, and the Flight into Egypt. On the roof panels, one sees the Scourging, the Crucifixion, the Holy Women at the Empty Tomb, the *Noli me tangere*, the Descent into Limbo, and the Incredulity of Thomas. Finally on the second pinion, an enthroned Christ is surrounded by angels carrying the *arma Christi*. All of the iconography is shown in a narrative sequence and therefore the appearance of the Christ of the Parousia can be regarded as the goal of the history that began with the Annunciation, rather than as in a singular vision. The Last Judgment closes the history of Revelation.

The iconography of the châsse of Charlemagne, preserved in

---

[15] Rebecca Price Gowen, "Shrine of the Virgin in Tournai, I: Its Restorations and State of Conservation," *Aachener Kunstblätter* 47 (1976/7), pp. 111–76.

[16] *Karl der Große und sein Schrein in Aachen*. Eine Festschrift, ed. Hans Müllejans (Aachen, 1988); *Der Schrein Karls des Großen. Bestand und Sicherung*. 1982–1988 (Aachen,

Aachen (1195–1215),[16] (figs. 342, 346) evokes the "saint" contained there by his representation in the center of the principal pinion and through episodes of his life on the roof panels. On the principal pinion, Charles is flanked by Pope Leo III and Archbishop Turpin of Reims; with the blessing Christ represented in bust just above. On the sides of the roof, one is present at the vocation by the appeal of St. James, at the capture of Pamplona, the blessing of the knights, the miracle of the lances, at the battle against the Saracens, at the confession of Charles, and the miracle of the glove. The series of reliefs ends in Charles' dedication of the Aachen chapel to the Virgin. On the long sides, the German emperors reputed to have succeeded Charles are illustrated enthroned alongside one another, following the example of the apostles, the Old Testament prophets, and the kings on the châsse of the Magi. It was understood: the iconography completely conflates the political and the religious spheres. Only the iconography of the secondary pinion takes another tone, depicting the Virgin and Child enthroned, surrounded by the archangels Michael and Gabriel, and surmounted by the three theological virtues.

The châsse of St. Maur of Florennes, preserved today in Becov ned Teplou (c. 1220),[17] introduces in parallel Christ and St. Maur, enthroned on its pinions. On the long sides, one sees the apostles, some with attributes which allow us to identify them. In the spandrels are figurative enamels which present Old Testament scenes (well-known to historians of Rheno-Mosan art because of their typological aspects), including the worship of the golden calf, the sacrifice of Abraham, the burning bush, (fig. 310) the application of the *tau* sign, the brazen serpent, the blessing of the sons of Jacob, and the striking of the rock. On the sides of the roof, the reliefs show, in contrast, New Testament scenes on one side and hagiographic scenes on the other. They include episodes from the life of John the Baptist (the meeting with Herod, the imprisonment, the dance of Salome, the meeting of Herodius and Salome, Salome bringing the head of

---

1998); Rita Lejeune and Jacques Stiennon, La Légende de Roland dans l'art du moyen âge (Brussels, 1967), 1, pp. 169–77. Editors' note: See Lisa Victoria Ciresi's essay in this volume.

[17] Robert Didier, "La châsse de St. Maur de l'ancienne abbaye de Florennes," *Annales de la Société archéologique de Namur*, 66 (1990), pp. 201–47; French version augmented by Robert Didier, "The Shrine of St. Maurus Rediscovered," *Apollo* CXXVII/314 (April 1988), pp. 227–43.

John, his burial) and of the life of St. Maur (the blessing by St. Paul, preaching, baptism of St. Apollinaire, the blessing by St. Peter, the judgment, and decapitation). The alignment of the apostles, and the parallel between Christ and the saint. whose relics are housed in the châsse are two conventional iconographic formulas. Yet, the spandrels and sides of the roofs present a quite different narrative iconography where, for the first time on a châsse, a cycle of Old Testament images is related to a New Testament cycle and to a cycle of the life of a local saint, with martyrdom being the unifying feature.

The iconography of the *c.* 1230 châsse of St. Potentin from Steinfeld, on the contrary, does not share this narrative richness. On its pinions one finds a conventional parallel set up between Christ and the saint whose relics the châsse honors, St. Potentin. The former is flanked by the Virgin and St. Augustine because Steinfeld was founded by the order of the Premonstratensians, whose way of life was inspired by the rule of Augustine. (fig. 311) The image of the latter is flanked by those his sons Felicius and Simplicius. On the long sides, St. Peter, St. Paul, and other apostles are shown standing rather than the more typical enthronement, after the example of the apostles on the lost châsse of St. Vincent (second quarter of the thirteenth century), formerly the glory of the collegiate church at Soignies.[18] On the sides of the roofs there are prophets in bust and angels. These latter replaced other prophets, now lost. Originally one saw not only Osee, Baruch, Jonas, Daniel, Jeremiah, Isaiah, Ezekial and Malachi, but also David, Jacob, Isaac, and Abraham.

The châsse of St. Elisabeth of Marburg (1235–49)[19] is framed in the shape of a church with a transept. Two additional pinions provide two additional places of honor, allowing the presentation of two supplementary subjects, people or iconographic scenes. In fact, the usual pinions are occupied—as would be expected—by Christ and Elisabeth of Thuringia, the saint for whom the châsse served as the sarcophagus. (fig. 309a) The two other pinions introduce the Virgin and Child, and, in an innovative change, a Crucifixion (Christ on

---

[18] Albert Lemeunier, "La châsse et le reliquaire du chef de St. Vincent de Soignies. Deux monuments d'orfèvrerie médiévale disparus," in *Reliques et châsses de la collégiale de Soignies. Objets, cultes et traditions,* ed. Jacques Deveseleer (Soignies, 2001), pp. 129–43.

[19] Erika Dinkler-von Schubert, *Der Schrein der heiligen Elisabeth zu Marburg. Studien zur Schrein-Ikonographie* (Marburg an der Lahn, 1964).

the cross, flanked by the Virgin and St. John). (fig. 309b) Of course, the subject had already been used on the châsse of the Magi; but it was integrated there, in an ensemble of scenes, whereas here, it is of a different nature from images on the other three pinions. For the remainder, one finds once more the conventional apostles on the long sides, and the scenes of the life of the saint venerated in Marburg on the panels of the roof.

The châsse of Notre Dame in Aachen (finished in 1239)[20] reflects the same type of miniature building as that of Marburg, with its added transept, expanding the possibilities of the iconography. One would have expected Christ and Notre Dame, more precisely, the Virgin and Child, to occupy two of the pinions, but on the pinion opposite that of Christ, Pope Leo III, already seen on the châsse of Charlemagne, is shown enthroned. Similarly, we once again see Charlemagne, (figs. 344, 345) on the pinion opposite that of the Virgin. The iconography of the châsse of Notre Dame, however, is less unified than that of the first feretory from Aachen, which I described as politico-religious. On the long sides, the emperors gave their places to the apostles, and on the sides of the roofs, New Testament scenes were represented, rather than the more typical hagiographic scenes.[21] Here is depicted a cycle of the Infancy of Christ and a Passion, with the latter not rendered in a particularly meaningful fashion, including some of the less significant episodes of the economy of salvation and some inspired by the apocryphal literature, while other episodes, much richer in meaning, are cruelly omitted. One sees the bath of the Christ child, but none of the events suggesting Resurrection (such as the meeting of the holy women and the angel at the empty tomb, the *Noli me tangere*, the Ascension) is evoked. On the whole, the iconography of this châsse of Notre Dame is disparate and not very convincing theologically.[22]

---

[20] Jürgen Fitschen, Die Goldschmiedeplastik des Marienschreins im Aachener Dom. Eine stilgeschichtliche Untersuchung (Frankfurt am Main: Peter Lang, 1998) and *Der Aachener Marienschrein. Eine Festschrift*, ed. Dieter P.J. Wynands (Aachen, 2000).

[21] Ernst Günther Grimme, "Die Ikonographie des Aachener Marienschreins," *Der Aachener Marienschrein* 2000, pp. 101–13.

[22] Benoît Van den Bossche, "Anmerkungen zu einer theologischen Betrachtungsweise des Marienschreines zu Aachen," *Der Aachener Marienschrein* 2000, pp. 101–13.

[23] Benoît Van den Bossche, "La châsse de St. Remacle à Stavelot: étude iconographique et stylistique des bas-reliefs et des statuettes," *Aachener Kunstblätter* 58 (1989/90), pp. 47–73; Benoît Van den Bossche, "La châsse de St. Remacle à

The châsse of St. Remaclus in Stavelot (*c.* 1240–65)[23] is more orthodox. (fig. 314) Curiously, there is no transept here, although it would have suited the iconography on the long sides. At the center of each side, there is a depiction of a local saint, who could have been featured on the transept pinions, but who is seen in the midst of the apostles. On one side is shown St. Remaclus, the main portion of whose relics is preserved in the feretory, and on the other is St. Lambert, his contemporary from Liège. Thus is conferred upon the local saints the status of apostles of the Ardennes and the lands along the Meuse and the Rhine Rivers. On the pinions, Christ and the Virgin and Child are presented, respectively, as the Creator and Master of the Universe, and the Daughter and Mother of God— interpretations reflected in the inscriptions.[24] To decorate the sides of the roofs, eight essential scenes of Revelation were selected: Annunciation, Nativity, Adoration, Presentation, Last Supper, Crucifixion, Holy Women at the empty tomb, and the Ascension.

It is necessary to return to Tournai to describe a new reliquary of grand dimensions, and of uncommon decorative richness, even more lavish than that of the Stavelotan feretory: the châsse of St. Eleutherius (completed in 1247).[25] Christ, accompanied by an angel holding the instruments of the Passion, is illustrated on the one of the pinions, while on the other is St. Eleutherius, holding in one hand a model of Tournai Cathedral, while trampling a hybrid beast underfoot. (fig. 312) He is accompanied by two angels who present him with a crown and the palm of the victory. On the long sides, eight apostles, flanked by angels represented in bust, occupy the niches. On the roof panels, three more apostles are shown—Philip, Matthew, and Thomas, while on one side is a personification of Synagoga, on the other Ecclesia, along with the archangel Gabriel,

---

Stavelot: étude des éléments décoratifs," *Bulletin de la Classe des Beaux-Arts de de l'Académie Royale de Belgique* V/1–6 (1994), pp. 109–49.

[24] SOLVS AB ETERNO CREO CVNCTA CREATA GVBERNO and TV MICHI NATE PATER ET TV MICHI FILIA MATER. Benoît Van den Bossche, " Réflexions sur l'iconologie de la châsse de St. Remacle," *Bulletin de la Société d'Art et d'Histoire du Diocèse de Liège* LXII (1997), pp. 1–12.

[25] Anton von Euw, "Châsse de St. Eleuthère," in *Rhin-Meuse: Art et civilisation. 800–1400*, ed. Anton Legner (Brussels, 1972), p. 315; Jean-Marie Lequeux ed., "La châsse de St. Eleuthère Chef-d'œuvre original malgré les restaurations des XIXᵉ et XXᵉ siècles?" in *Mémoires de la Société royale d'Histoire et d'Archéologie de Tournai* I (1980), pp. 181–201.

the Virgin Mary, and the Baptist. As imposing and rich as the châsse of St. Eleutherius is, its iconography is still conventional (with the parallel between Christ and the venerated saint, the presence of the apostles, and the Virgin), but it is curiously arranged with (the apostles partly presented in the niches on the long sides, and partly on the roof).

The iconography of the châsse of Sts. Ode and George from Amay (*c.* 1235)[26] is intriguing in another way. While the reliquary is of modest size, its iconography is quite innovative. Of course, one finds the requisite apostles on the long sides, but each of the two pinions is occupied by a standing saint: Ode and George. Thus Christ and the Virgin do not appear on the reliquary of the collegiate church of Amay, instead its iconography is dominated by the hagiographic discourse, with scenes of the life of St. Ode on one side of the roof,[27] scenes of the life of St. George on the other.[28] (fig. 313)

Another châsse of modest size which deserves to be considered here, because of its remarkable iconography, is the châsse of St. Symmetrus in Lierneux (*c.* 1250–70).[29] (fig. 317) This intriguing iconography is all the more remarkable since, from a technical point of view, the reliquary is far from perfect; one could even say that it was created by mediocre goldsmiths. On the pinions one sees the Virgin and Child and the Crucifixion—thus fitting the spirit of the times. (fig. 316) On the long sides are the standing apostles. To be honest, it is only the iconography of the roof panels which is distinctive. In spite of certain difficulties in reading the panels due to their poor condition, one can recognize three scenes directly relating to the worship of St. Symmetrus and three scenes summarizing the "Triumph of St. Remaclus."[30] (fig. 339) The first show (or showed)

---

[26] Albert Lemeunier, "La châsse de sainte Ode à Amay," in *Trésors de la collégiale d'Amay*, ed. Thomas Delarue (Amay, 1989), pp. 49–79.

[27] The charity of St. Ode, the piety of St. Ode, her death, and her funeral.

[28] St. George charging the dragon, the martyrdom on the cross, and the martyrdom by beheading.

[29] Benoît Van den Bossche, " La châsse de St. Symètre," in *Patrimoine religieux du pays de Lierneux*, ed. Benoît Van den Bossche (Stavelot, 1992), pp. 28–43.

[30] The "Triumph of St. Remaclus" refers to an episode from the history of the Principality of Stavelot-Malmedy. This was put into play by the monks of Stavelot returning to Liège with the relics of Remaclus, their founding saint, in order to convince the emperor of their supremacy while he was on sojourn in the Mosan city.

the martyrdom of Symmetrus, the exhumation of his relics, and the deposit of those relics in Lierneux.[31] As for the "Triumph of St. Remaclus," it is pictured by the voyage of the monks of Stavelot to Liege with his relics, the ultimate petition to the emperor whereby a miracle is achieved, and the veneration of the relics of Remaclus. The tone is thus, as on the châsse of Amay, hagiographic, but a displacement was carried out: the narration is concerned, beyond the saint himself, with his cult and that of St. Remaclus.

It is necessary to finish this too-brief survey with the châsse of St. Gertrude of Nivelles (1272–98).[32] Following the architectural examples of the Aachen châsse of Notre Dame and châsse of St. Elisabeth, this building is provided with a transept, thus creating four pinions. Christ and the Virgin and Child are represented on the pinions of the nave, while St. Gertrude and a Crucifixion scene are depicted on the pinions of the transept. (fig. 315) The Marburg formula is thus reprised, with slight modifications: the inversion between the Virgin and the local saint on one of the pinions of the nave and one of the pinions of the transept, that the Virgin is standing, following the example of Gothic Madonnas, and that the local saint is crowned by angels. The iconography of the roof panels of the châsse of Nivelles can also be compared with the châsse of Marburg as the subject matter is, on both sides, hagiographic. However, the history of the Nivelles abbess is characterized on her châsse by a multiplication of miracle scenes,[33] while the history of Elisabeth is depicted on her reliquary as dominated by testimony to her charity, piety, and morality. At Marburg, one witnesses, for example, the meal given by Elisabeth to the hungry, or her taking the habit; at Nivelles, one sees, on the other hand, "the miracle of the ball of fire," or the hanging of the devil by Gertrude herself.

---

[31] The relief of the deposit of the relics at Lierneux has unfortunately disappeared.

[32] *Schatz aus den Trümmern. Der Silberschrein von Nivelles und die europäische Hochgotik,* ed. Hiltrud Westermann-Angerhausen (Cologne, 1995/6).

[33] Christina Ceulemans, Robert Didier, Christiane Raynaud, "Die Ikonographie des Schreins der hl. Gertrud," in *Schatz aus den Trümmern. Der Silberschrein von Nivelles,* pp. 208–24; Bruno Boerner, "Zur Interpretation des ikonographischen Programms am Schrein der hl. Gertrud von Nivelles," *Schatz aus den Trümmern. Der Silberschrein von Nivelles,* pp. 225–33.

Recurrences and Originalities

As succint as my presentation of certain Rheno-Mosan châsses of the thirteenth century has been, the recurrences and the iconographic originalities can be highlighted. Christ, the Virgin and the apostles are represented in an almost systematic way—and amongst them, the saints whose relics the châsses honor. The angels and the archangels, as well as the prophets, are less-frequently illustrated. As for the narrative scenes, they represent various types, and the importance assigned to them is variable. In this light, we should reconsider all these figures, and revisit their subjects.

First, let us examine the isolated representations of Christ in Glory. Almost all the châsses considered reserve a central place for Him. In general, the niche contained on one of the two pinions shelters Christ, who sits on a throne whose architectural character is more or less elaborate. Even when, late in the century, the majority of the characters are illustrated standing (on the châsse of Nivelles, in particular), the iconographer still wanted Christ enthroned. One notes that, depending on the details chosen, this or that quality of the Christ in Glory was highlighted. On the principal pinions of the châsse of the Magi and of the châsse of St. Eleutherius, Christ is enthroned as a "Judge," furnished with the instruments of the Passion,[34] whereas the Christ of the châsse of St. Remaclus is represented as the "Master of the Universe," following the example of the Aachen châsse of the Virgin.[35] Once the recurrence of the representations of the glorious Christ is underlined in the iconography of the Rheno-Mosan châsses of the thirteenth century, it is necessary to point out an evolution of nuance, related to the appearance of Christ on the cross. On the pinions of the châsse of Marburg, one sees, a Crucifixion made pendant to an enthroned Christ. This formula will is reprised on the châsse of Nivelles while, later, on the feretory of Lierneux,

---

[34] Christ as "Judge" as appears on the tympana of the great Gothic cathedrals where his function as judge is rooted in his experience of the Passion.

[35] On the châsse of St. Remaclus at Stavelot as on the châsse of the Virgin at Aachen, Christ holds the universe in his hand, symbolized by a globe. In both cases, the beautiful epigraphic strips also affirm that "He governs all things." Van den Bossche, "Réflexions sur l'iconologie de la châsse de St. Remacle," pp. 10–12. Editors' note: for discussion of the imagery associated with the Virgin, see Lisa Victoria Ciresi's essay in this volume.

Christ on the Cross replaces the Christ in Glory. Finally, on the châsse of Amay, Christ is represented neither enthroned nor suffering, to the extent that one wonders about the theological relevance of the ensemble.

Like Christ, the Virgin and Child is practically omnipresent in the iconography of the Rheno-Mosan châsses of the thirteenth century. Its absence among the statuettes of the châsses of Florennes and Amay is surprising. One will remember here that, on the châsse of Charlemagne, the Virgin and Child occupy the entire niche of one of the two pinions, whereas in the opposite one, Christ is only illustrated in bust, above Charlemagne. The thirteenth century is often indicated as the "Marian century" *par excellence*; the place which Notre Dame occupies on the Rheno-Mosan châsses of the era confirms the assertion.

It is interesting to note that Our Lady is initially represented as the *Sedes Sapientiae*, according to the iconographic canon of the Romanesque epoch. Thus it appears on the pinion of the châsse of Charlemagne, where the Virgin becomes "the throne of Christ" and the physiognomic features of the Child are clearly those of an adult. Gradually, however, the *Sedes Sapientiae* is transformed into the Gothic Madonna, where, on the pinion of the châsse of St. Gertrude, she stands (as she does henceforward), holding the Child as a mother would hold her baby—like the statues of the Virgin and Child who welcome the faithful at the entry of large cathedrals. In this context, the originality of Nicolas of Verdun, who, at the dawn of the epoch taken into account here, was reluctant to isolate the Virgin from a narrative context. On the châsse of Cologne as on that of Tournai, she is an actress in the Adoration of the Magi.

As with the Virgin, the apostles are also, initially, sitting (on the châsse of the Magi and the châsse of Stavelot, in particular), before being shown standing (on the châsse of Steinfeld or the châsse of Lierneux). They are seated on the long sides as Christ and the Virgin are enthroned on the pinions, acting as celestial court for the King and Queen. Thus they surround the saint whose relics are preserved in the châsse, adopting him, so to speak and the saint is regarded as a new apostle. The iconography of the châsse of St. Remaclus shows it particularly well: a statuette of St. Remaclus and another of St. Lambert were inserted among those of the apostles. A little later, on the long sides of the châsse of St. Gertrude, several saints who lived after the time of the apostles are numbered among them, constituting an even broader assembly, with the majority of these apostles provided with attributes evoking their martyrdom. (fig. 315) Again, in this context, the originality of Nicolas of Verdun should be stressed, as he spurns the display of the apostles on the Tournai châsse of the Virgin, whereas he put the apostles and the prophets in parallel on the châsse of the Magi. The originality of the iconographers of the châsse of Charlemagne is at least equal to this, since the emperors replace the apostles there (fig. 342)—it is at once startling, directly comprehensible, and audacious.

The angels and the archangels are sometimes pointedly present, on the châsses of Aachen, for example, or on that of St. Gertrude, and sometimes astonishingly absent, such as on the châsse of Marburg or that of Stavelot, among others. In certain cases, their functions are clearly specified, such as when they hold the luminaries in their hands on the châsse of Nivelles. In other cases, their presence is not justified in such a way. Generally, the presence of the angels and archangels confer on the iconography a super-terrestrial dimension, as with the archangels Michael and Gabriel flanking the *Sedes Sapientiae* on the Marian pinion of the châsse of Charlemagne, where they situate the apparition in the beyond.

When the prophets are illustrated on the Rheno-Mosan châsses of the thirteenth century, it is not only a question of showing the authors of the prophetic books, but also of illustrating the other great Old Testament figures: Abraham, Moses, or David, to cite only a few. This very broad interpretation of the term "prophet" echoes its contemporary meaning in the thirteenth century. Like the angels and the archangels, these prophets in the broad sense of the term are missing on certain feretories (on the châsses of St. Elisabeth, St. Eleutherius, and of Stavelot), but they enrich other iconographic ensembles. There they are represented standing (on the long sides of the châsse of the Magi) or in bust (as on the sides of the roof of the châsse of Steinfeld). On the châsse of Florennes, they are the protagonists of well-known narrative scenes, but this is exceptional. There it is surprising, when one knows the succession of scenes like the sacrifice of Abraham, Moses in front of the burning bush, or the blessing of Jacob on other Rheno-Mosan metalwork.[36] Whatever

---

[36] One thinks notably, of the Portable Altar of Stavelot (Bruxelles, Musées Royaux d'Art et d'Histoire) or the foot of the Cross of St. Omer (Saint-Omer, Musée de l'Hôtel Sandelin).

way the prophets are illustrated on the châsses of the thirteenth century, they are represented because, by their acts and their words,
they announced Christ—his life, his Passion, and his Resurrection.

There is very little space given to personifications[37] on the Rheno-
Mosan châsses of the thirteenth century, which is surprising, especially when one considers that allegorical figures are frequently depicted
on other Rheno-Mosan metalwork, such as the female busts enamelled on the Pope Alexander head reliquary. One sees Patientia and
the theological virtues on the châsse of the Magi; these last are also
illustrated on the feretory of Charlemagne. But there are exceptions
which prove the rule, such as Sol and Luna represented on the
châsse of the Magi, on that of Charlemagne, and on that of Marburg.
Let us recall finally that Synagoga and Ecclesia flank the Crucifixion
on the châsse of St. Remaclus, and that they are represented as isolated figures on the roof of the châsse from St. Eleutherius. Yet, on
the whole, they do not recur.

With regard to the iconography of the saints whose relics are preserved in the châsses, we notice first of all that the place reserved
for them varies. In certain cases, the saint is represented on one of
the pinions as well as on the roof (on the châsse of Charlemagne),
while in other cases, it is almost absent (on the châsse of St. Remaclus,
where he is evoked by means of only one statuette on one of the
long sides, without ever being highlighted). Two types of images must
be distinguished: either the saint is isolated or is an actor in a narrative scene. If the saint is isolated, he is illustrated standing or
enthroned, in a niche where he is the main occupant of the space
(such as Eleutherius on one of the pinions of his châsse). (fig. 312)
Within the framework of a narrative scene, one sees an episode of
the vita (on the châsse of Marburg) or of the *miracula* (on the châsse
of Nivelles). (fig. 315) With time, the necessity for, and the effects of,
the worship rendered to the saint are highlighted (on the châsse of
St. Symmetrus). (figs. 317, 339)

When hagiographic scenes are not present on Rheno-Mosan châsse
of the thirteenth century, one might see some New Testament scenes
represented, but true cycles are rare. Only the châsse of the Magi,

---

[37] By the term "personification," I mean here, as well, the personifications properly designated, that is to say, the human figures embodying intangible realities,
that these figures hold before them a medallion on which an inscription or a motif
is engraved, designating an exemplar of this type.

those of Notre Dame of Tournai (fig. 308) and of Aachen, (fig. 344) and that of Stavelot (fig. 314) features such a cycle. The cycle of the Cologne feretory, (fig. 308) only partly preserved, is without doubt the most interesting, with its description of epiphanic scenes and episodes recalling the Passion. These scenes are enriched by their setting into an eschatological perspective by indirect reference to the images from the Apocalypse. Compared to this ensemble of New Testament scenes, that of the Aachen châsse of Notre Dame, which oscillates between a conventional account (curiously incomplete) and a penchant for anecdote, is mediocre, while the iconography of the châsse of Stavelot displays an almost tedious orthodoxy.

It is astonishing that the iconographers of the Rheno-Mosan châsses of the thirteenth century had renounced the typological vein which, in the previous century, inspired rich and stimulating ensembles of images; the images evoking the Old Testament episodes were compared with images that foretold the New Testament stories, the Old and the New Testament were thus made to echo one another.[38] On the châsses reviewed here, the Old Testament and the New Testament are simply not connected. On the subject of the New Testament iconography of the châsses of the thirteenth century, it is important to note the emergent focus on a very specific subject, which is thus isolated: the Crucifixion. This interesting phenomenon reveals a transition is effected from an iconography of the glorious Christ to an iconography of Christ suffering.

Programs

After reviewing the various subjects, characters, and scenes which constitute the iconography of the Rheno-Mosan châsses of the thirteenth century, it is appropriate to remember that the iconography of each must also be considered as a whole. Thus certain châsses present remarkable iconographic programs, while others appear to be merely unreasoned accumulations of images. An ensemble of images should be described as "program" only if those selected were juxtaposed according to a regulating idea, which confers a true coher-

---

[38] Again, one thinks of the Portable Altar of Stavelot and of the foot of the Cross of St. Omer.

ence on the whole. Thus the group of images offered on the châsse of Notre Dame in Aachen appears incoherent, so much so that it is difficult to articulate in the same discourse the glorious Christ, the *Sedes Sapientiae*, the apostles, a narrative cycle, the Emperor Charlemagne, (fig. 345) and Pope Leo III. By contrast, the iconography of the châsse of St. Remaclus is homogeneous, as is the châsse of Notre Dame of Tournai.

Among the programs, some are particularly elaborate, while others are much simpler. The program of the châsse of the Magi is particularly rich, where the scenes obey not only the chronology of the account, but also display an interpretative will. The choice and juxtaposition of the scenes and the subjects of the principal pinion originate in the idea of the Epiphany, the revelation of glorious Christ. The secondary pinion, on the other hand, focuses on the Passion and the revelation of the suffering Christ, which dominates the message. These New Testament scenes are put in perspective within the framework that evokes the Apocalypse on the long sides. Other particularly complex programs include the anomalous châsse of Charlemagne and the châsse of St. Maur, for which the unifying idea is martyrdom. Some very simple programs are constituted by the ensemble of the statuettes and reliefs as on châsse of Steinfeld or that of Stavelot.

Among the programs, one can distinguish some rather theological approaches (such that of the châsse of the Magi), from the rather hagiographic themes (the châsse of Sts. Ode and George), (fig. 313) and a rather politico-religious program (the châsse of Charlemagne). (figs. 342, 346) Certain groups are concerned with different genres: an iconographic ensemble like that of the châsse of Notre Dame of Aachen consists of a rather theological cycle (the narrative sequence of the roof, Christ, the Virgin and Child, and the apostles) to which a political tenor was conferred (with the presence of Charlemagne and Leo III), (fig. 346) while the iconographic matter of the châsse of St. Gertrude vacillates between the theological presentation of things (Christ enthroned opposed to Christ suffering, the testimony of the apostles and the saints, Gertrude put in parallel with the Virgin) and their hagiographic presentation (scenes of miracles on the roof). (fig. 315)

Conclusion

Let us consider that, in a general way, any iconography consists on one hand of vocabulary—the subjects, figures, scenes represented—and on the other hand of syntax—the way according to which these subjects, these figures, these scenes are articulated, the ones with the others. At the end of this work, the iconographic vocabulary used on the Rheno-Mosan châsses of the thirteenth century initially seems composed of a conventional vocabulary, anchored in tradition. Indeed, the Christ in Majesty, the Virgin and Child, the college of the apostles are illustrated in a quasi-systematic way, and when New Testament scenes are represented, they are almost always the same episodes. However, this assertion should be refined by two remarks. First, if the vocabulary is largely anchored in tradition, it does not mean that all the subjects employed by previous Rheno-Mosan metal-workers were reprised—far from it. On the châsses reviewed here, one sees a limited number of biblical scenes and the rare use of personifications. Second, gradually, the conventional subjects presented underwent an evolution. With time, the image of Christ enthroned was supplanted by Christ on the cross, and finally, on the châsse of St. Symmetrus, the Crucifixion omits any representation of the glorious Christ. With time, the Virgin as *Sedes Sapientiae* becomes a Madonna. With time, the enthroned apostles of the celestial court become martyr-witnesses of the same cast as the saints whose relics are preserved in the châsses. Let me emphasize here that the vocabulary of the châsse of Charlemagne in Aachen is largely atypical; the work has the effect of a meteorite.

The hagiographic vocabulary used on the châsses studied was also evolving. Admittedly, it goes without saying the scenes represented vary from one saint to another as the stories are varied. But some viewpoints taken can be ascertained. If, on certain "hagiographic" châsses, the choices of the iconographers were determined by the choice of the episodes echoing the *vitae*, other châsses present episodes pointing out the *miracula*. Lastly, the latest "hagiographic" châsses also evoke the cultic practices for which the relics were the object; the iconography of the châsse no longer relates only to its contents, but also to the châsse itself, the container.

Now let us consider the syntax of the Rheno-Mosan châsses of the thirteenth century. It was understood that it was dominated by a basic recurrent structure: Christ, the Virgin and Child, and apostles. But beyond this recurring structure, which is almost invariably used, the variety of the formulas suggested is very significant. From this point of view, there are no two identical châsses. The châsse of the Magi, that of Notre Dame of Tournai, that of St. Eleutherius, or that of St. Symmetrus are isolated works. It should be recognized however that re-groupings because of certain common points can be carried out between certain feretories: the châsses of Elisabeth and Gertrude, for example, each present four pinions occupied by Christ enthroned, a Virgin and Child, a Crucifixion, and the holy one whose relics are in the reliquary; while on the roof panels of the two châsses, narrative cycles evoke, on both sides, the acts and deeds of the saint.

In posing the question of the syntax implemented in the iconographic discourses contained on the Rheno-Mosan châsses of the thirteenth century, one returns to the determination already made above: the differences in quality between the iconographic ensembles that the châsses carry are considerable. Certain sets are elaborate and intelligent programs, others are very simple, others are nothing more than re-groupings of incoherent and superficial images, and others, while they may not have very convincing programs on the intellectual level, are still attractive.

Certain iconographic sets have a universal import while others are entirely impregnated with local history and tradition. If it is necessary to conclude, it is perhaps by stressing that the first châsses considered relate to the first type, whereas the last châsses are of the second type. I thus observe that, over time, the pilgrimage to which the châsse gives rise—its saint and the cult developed around him—has an increasingly larger impact on the iconography. This iconography loses its intellectual force, but it becomes more stirring.

CHAPTER TWENTY-FIVE

RELICS AND PILGRIMAGE IN THE XYLOGRAPHIC BOOK OF ST. SERVATIUS OF MAASTRICHT*

Scott B. Montgomery

The xylographic book of St. Servatius of Maastricht, *c.* 1461, is comprised of twenty-four pages recounting the saint's *vita* and the display of his relics at his titular church in Maastricht.[1] Each page consists of a colored woodcut and an accompanying text in French.[2]

---

* This material was originally presented at the Thirty-fifth International Congress on Medieval Studies at Kalamazoo, MI in May 2000 and the Sixteenth Century Studies Conferences in San Antonio, TX in October 2002. I offer my thanks to those colleagues in attendance whose questions and comments caused me to further scrutinize the material and refine my ideas. For their gracious help and invaluable insight during the preparation of this article, I extend my heartfelt thanks to Alice A. Bauer, Sarah Blick, Rita Tekippe, Sally J. Cornelison, Jerry Nash, Kelly Donahue-Wallace, and Elizabeth McLachlan. For putting it all into perspective in her inimitable way, I dedicate this to my darling daughter, Francesca Isabella Montgomery, who began her pilgrimage of life as this manuscript was taking shape.

[1] Though the only extant copy is in the Bibliothèque Royale Albert Ier in Brussels (Cabinet des Estamps, ms. 18.972), we must assume that other copies originally existed due to the use of the printed medium. The manuscript has been published in a facsimile edition, with commentary, by Adrianus Maria Koldeweij and Pierre N.G. Pesch, *Het Blokboek van Sint Servaas. Facsimile met commentaar op het vijftende-eeuwse blokboek, de Servaas-legende en de Maastrichtse reliekentoning. Le Livre Xylographique de Saint Servais. Fac-similé avec commentaire sur le livre xylographique du quinzième siècle, sur la légende de S. Servais et sur l'ostension des reliques à Maestricht* (Zutphen: De Walburg Pers, 1984). An earlier facsimile was published by Henri Heymans, ed., *Die Servatius-legende. Ein niederländisches Blokbuch* (Berlin, 1911). The *c.* 1461 date and the provenance of Maastricht is suggested not only by the conjunction with the septennial pilgrimage, but also by several water-marks on the pages of the book. Regarding the various attributions, dates and locations of origin that have been posited, see: Koldeweij and Pesch, *Het Blokboek*, pp. 32–41; eds. Adrianus Maria Koldeweij and P.M.L. van Vlijmen, *Schatkamers uit het Zuiden* (Utrecht, 1985), Cat. 66, pp. 179–80.

[2] Xylography, the art of printing texts and/or illustrations from wood blocks, was relatively common in the fifteenth century. The xylographic book of St. Servatius is technically a chiro-xylographic book, as the accompanying text was hand-written after the stamping of the woodblock printed image. Koldeweij and Pesch, *Het Blokboek*, pp. 16–7. The chiro-xylographic format would allow each copy of the book to be tailor-made for a linguistically-diverse audience. This linguistic flexibility supports the idea that the book was intended to serve as a program for pilgrims attending the septennial ostension of the relics.

While the first twenty pages detail the saint's life and miracles, the final four pages illustrate and describe the ostension of relics from the dwarf gallery of the apse of the Church of St. Servatius in Maastricht.[3] (figs. 318–21) The relic display portrayed consisted principally of relics associated with St. Servatius, namely, three celestial funerary cloths, his pilgrimage staff, his episcopal crozier, his chalice and paten, and finally his head, ensconced within its sumptuous early fifteenth-century reliquary bust.[4] The right arm of St. Thomas the Apostle and a cross, made by St. Luke to be worn by the Virgin Mary, accompany the head of St. Servatius in the final image. While the first three ostension scenes portray the display of important secondary relics of St. Servatius, the final image reveals the culmination of this display, wherein the reliquary bust, containing the most significant primary relics of the saint, is revealed in the company of two important additional relics. The right arm of St. Thomas, while a noteworthy primary relic of the apostle, would also be understood as a contact relic of Christ—the arm having tested the wound in Christ's side. The cross, itself a secondary relic of St. Luke, is also clearly presented and described as a secondary relic of the Virgin Mary, having graced her bosom in life. Thus, the head of St. Servatius is presented in the illustrious company of these important relics of Christ, the Virgin, and the apostles, elevating the status of the local saint. The xylographic book, in both its *vita* and ostension components, was designed to raise the reputation of St. Servatius and his relics, thereby augmenting the viewer/reader's understanding of the magnitude of the ostension.[5]

---

[3] The *vita* cycle contained in the xylographic book constitutes the most extensive illustrated life of St. Servatius. Koldeweij and Pesch, *Het Blokboek*, pp. 57–8. Regarding narrative cycles of the vita of St. Servatius, see Adrianus Maria Koldeweij, "Beeldcycli van de Servatiuslegende en het Blokboek van Sint Servaas als voorbeeld een laatgotisch retabel," in eds. Jos M.M. Hermans and Klaas van der Hoek, *Boeken in de late Middeleeuwen. Verslag van Groningse Codicologendagen 1992* (Groningen, 1994), pp. 65–76.

[4] The relics displayed are among the most important relics in the treasury of the Church of St. Servatius in Maastricht. Koldeweij and Pesch, *Het Blokboek*, pp. 86–103. Regarding the relics associated with St. Servatius in the treasury, see Adrianus Maria Koldeweij, *Der gude Sente Servas. Der Servatiuslegende en de Servatiana: een onderzoek naar de beeldvorming rond een heilige in de middeleeuwen* (Assen-Maastricht, 1985); Adrianus Maria Koldeweij and Aart J.J. Mekking, "De kerkschat van de Sint-Servaaskerk te Maastricht," *Spiegel Historiael* 17 (1982), pp. 140–2; Adrie Cense and Saskia Werner, *De schatkamer van de Sint-Servaaskerk te Maastrict:een keuze van de voorwerpen uit de schatkamer en hun functie* (Zutphen, 1984).

[5] The ostension, or display of relics, provides the visual focus and culmination of the pilgrimage and its attendant relic veneration.

The display of relics at Maastricht was part of a regular ostension and pilgrimage that occurred every seven years during the month
of July.[6] The display of relics from the dwarf gallery of the Church
of St. Servatius in Maastricht to large groups of pilgrims gathered
below in the square known as the Vrijthof, appears to have begun
in the late fourteenth century and is first documented in 1391, when
the city passed a resolution to hold the ostensions to coincide with
those at Aachen.[7] (fig. 323) The oldest description of the relic display, from July 1433, is remarkably similar to the depiction of the
event on pages twenty-one through twenty-four of the xylographic
book. With great solemnity, the crowd was shown "three celestial
drapes . . . the crozier of St. Servatius . . . his pilgrimage staff . . . the
head of St. Servatius . . . his chalice and paten . . . the right arm of
St. Thomas . . . a cross of silver and gold in a crystal, made by St.
Luke the Evangelist."[8] A.M. Koldeweij convincingly suggested that
the commentary which accompanied the ostension was given first in
fixed Latin formulae, then followed by translations in Dutch and
French.[9] The French text, provided in the xylographic book, presumably echoes or closely resembles the text of the announcements
that accompanied the ostension. While the twenty pages constituting the saint's *vita* contain prose text, the four ostension pages each
bear six lines divided into two triple-rhymes. It would appear as
though the verse text was designed for greater effectiveness in oral

[6] On the septennial pilgrimage, see H.P.H. Everson, "De Heiligdomsvaart van
Maastricht," *Publications de la Société Historique et Archéologique dans le Limbourg* 7 (1870):
398–411; Pierre Marie Hubert Doppler, "Beknopte geschiedenis der zeverjarige
Heiligdomsvaart te Maastricht," *De Maasgouw* 43 (1923), pp. 37–48; Petrus Henricus
Albers, "De Heiligdomsvaart in de middeleeuwen te Maastricht," *Publications de la
Société Historique et Archéologique dans le Limbourg* 66 (1930): 53–67; Petrus Cornelius
Boeren, *Heilogdomsvaart Maastrich: schets v. d. geschiedenis der heiligdomsvaarten en andere
jubelvaarten* (Maastricht, 1962); Adrianus Maria Koldeweij, "Sint-Servaas te Maastricht
als debevaartplaats," *De Maasgouw* 100 (1981), pp. 3–29; Koldeweij and Pesch, *Het
Blokboek*, pp. 86–103; Koldeweij, *Der gude Sente Servas*, pp. 5–22.
[7] Koldeweij and Pesch, *Het Blokboek*, pp. 10–1, 98–9; Boeren, *Heiligdomsvaart*, pp.
116–8, 181, 183; Adrianus Maria Koldeweij, "Reliekentoningen, heiligdomsvaarten,
reliekenprocessies en ommegangen," in Koldeweij and van Vlijmen, *Schatkamers*, pp.
57–71, esp. p. 63. The book containing directives for the liturgical practices in the
church, written before 1618, noted that the relics were to be displayed from the
dwarf gallery during the septennial pilgrimage. It also discussed the similar display
at Aachen. *Ordinarius custodum*, fols. 38v–39r, (Maastricht, Rijksarchief in Limburg,
Archief van het Kapittel van Sint-Servaas, no. 166); Koldeweij and Pesch, *Het
Blokboek*, p. 93.
[8] Koldeweij and Pesch, *Het Blokboek*, pp. 90–3.
[9] Koldeweij and Pesch, *Het Blokboek*, p. 93.

recitation as well as for the stimulation of memory—both practices being informed by performance.[10] The inclusion of this text in the book is intended to clarify the ostension, as well as to facilitate the repetition of the experience through reading. The images, occupying more than half of each page, accentuate the visual nature of the relic display as well as its personal, visionary re-enactment.

A fifteenth-century woodcut, made in conjunction with this septennial ostension in 1468 or 1475, illustrates the principal relics to be shown at Aachen, Maastricht, and Cornelimünster.[11] (fig. 323) Those included in the column relating to Maastricht are the same relics portrayed in the final four pages of the xylographic book. This single-sheet *pilgerblatt* woodcut illustrates the relics and provides text descriptions, thus serving as an advertisement of what a pilgrim participating in the event would hope to see. The comparison of this woodcut with the xylographic book is illustrative in elucidating how these two contemporary examples of pilgrimage-related prints address their audiences in different manners and invite different forms of engagement and use. While the single-sheet woodcut invites the would-be pilgrim to participate in the upcoming ostension of relics, the xylographic book goes beyond cataloguing the relics to be seen; it illustrates the manner in which they were displayed. The accurate portrayal of the architectural setting of the display, as seen from the pilgrim's perspective in the Vrijthof, and the inclusion of the text that accompanied the relic ostension, situate the four scenes of the relic display within a very specific time and place—the pilgrim's experience of the performance of the relic ostension in Maastricht. The specificity of this performative evocation situates the meaning of the book in a recurring present moment of relic revelation. The book could act as both a program, or guide, to accompany the relic display as well as to allow the reader to relive the moment of ostension through reading and seeing. In this commemorative guise, the xylographic book would serve as a lavish form of pilgrimage souvenir, akin to

---

[10] Mary Carruthers, *The Book of Memory. A Study of Memory in Medieval Culture* (Cambridge, 1990). *Editors' note, see Anne Harris' essay in this volume.

[11] Munich, Staatliche Graphische Sammlung, no. 118308. ed. Anton Legner, *Rhein und Maas. Kunst und Kultur 800–1400* (Cologne, 1972), cat. VIIIg, p. 139; W. Schmidt, "Die älteste Holzschnittdarstellungen der Heiligthümer von Maastricht, Aachen und Kornelimünster," *Zeitschrift des Aachener Geschichtsvereins* 7 (1885), pp. 125–6; Koldeweij and van Vlijmen, *Schatkamers*, cat. 67, pp. 180–2.

pilgrimage badges and prints.[12] But, the elaborate visual and narrative nature of the book allowed the reader to engage in a more
dynamic form of re-enactment of the culmination of the pilgrimage.
More than a token of remembrance, the xylographic book is a care-
fully-constructed tool for the continued visualization and recreation
of the pilgrimage process. The book's audience appears to have been
pilgrims, and as such, the book's users became pilgrims through the
act of reading and seeing.

The xylographic book actually fleshes out the significance of the
relics, providing a narrative setting into which the relics are inserted.[13]
Upon careful examination of the scenes chosen for inclusion and the
manner of their depiction in the xylographic book, it becomes apparent that the entire *vita* is presented as a prologue to the key event,
namely the display of the relics. The relics that are shown in the
final four scenes play important roles in the episodes of the saint's
life as depicted. The *vita* of the saint is thus orchestrated and presented so as to validate and explain the relics, the ostension of which
constitutes the finale of the book. Rather than being appendices,
added to the end of the saint's *vita*, these four scenes are the principal *raison d'etre* of the book.[14]

The cycle opens with the parents of Servatius praying for a child.
An angel appears to tell them that their prayers have been heard
and they will have a boy, who will be saintly and do great service

---

[12] On pilgrims' souvenirs: Adrianus Maria Koldeweij, "Lifting the Veil on Pilgrim
Badges," in: ed. Jennie Stopford, *Pilgrimage Explored* (York, 1999), pp. 161–88; Kurt
Köster, "Mittelalterliche Pilgerzeichen," in eds. Lenz Kriss-Rettenbeck and Gerda
Möhler, *Wallfahrt kennt keine Grenzen* (Munich, 1984), pp. 203–23; Brian Spencer,
Pilgrim Souvenirs and Secular Badges (London, 1998); Denis Bruna, *Enseignes de Pèlerinage
et Enseignes Profanes* (Paris, 1996); eds. H.J.E. van Beuningen and Adrianus Maria
Koldeweij, *Heilig en Profaan. 1000 Laatmiddeleeuwse Insignes uit de collectie H.J.E. van
Beuningen* (Cothen, 1993); eds. H.J.E. van Beuningen, Adrianus Maria Koldeweij,
and Dory Kicken, *Heilig en Profaan 2. 1200 Laatmiddeleeuwse Insignes uit openbare en particuliere collecties* (Cothen, 2001).

[13] For the most authoritative examination of the legend of St. Servatius and associated relics, see Koldeweij, *Der gude Sente Servas*.

[14] Though Koldeweij, *Der gude Sente Servas* provides the most exhaustive scholarly
examination of the relationship between the relics and their depiction in the *vita*
cycle, he implies that the four ostension scenes are additions to the *vita*, which he
believes was the principal focus of the book: "*quattre gravures . . . qui ont été ajoutées à
une série d'illustrations de la Légende de S. Servais . . .*" (. . . four prints . . . that were added
to a series of illustrations of the Legend of St. Servatius . . .) Koldeweij and Pesch,
Het Blokboek, pp. 12–3. I believe that the equation should be inverted, following the
evidence argued below that the book's purpose is the explanation of the relics.

to God and his is name will be Servatius.[15] Koldeweij notes that the prophecy of the birth of Servatius is based on Luke's account of the angel's revelation to Elizabeth and Zaccharias of the birth of John the Baptist.[16] Servatius is fashioned as a new John the Baptist, as his birth story conforms to the hagiographic trope of the Baptist's birth. This foreshadows page thirteen, when this parallel is augmented as Servatius baptizes and converts Attila the Saracen (*sic*), a topical re-naming of Servatius' contemporary, Attila the Hun (*c*. 406–53). Furthermore, the allusion to Luke's Gospel on the first page connects the birth scene to the final page, where the relic of the cross made by Luke is depicted.[17] With allusions to Luke resounding at the alpha and the omega of the book, Servatius' life is connected to that of Christ via this Gospel parallel, in a manner similar to the association that is drawn between the relics of Servatius and of Christ.

The prominent placement of the angel at the beginning of the cycle, holding a banner with an inscription proclaiming Servatius as a gift from heaven, foreshadows the active role that angelic figures play in the pictorial and textual cycle.[18] Throughout the book angels are shown and described as heavenly messengers who deliver to St. Servatius the items that become venerated as his secondary relics. As the elucidation of the origin and miraculous powers of these relics is a leitmotif running through the cycle, the angelic overture alerts the reader to the role of angels as indicators of heavenly provenance. Furthermore, given that the relics were displayed from the dwarf

---

[15] The text reads: "Icy sont priant a Dieu pour avoir ung enfant le pere et mere de Saint Servais. Vint tantost ung angele desaint leur priere estre ouye et quils auroient ung enfant saint le quel multiplieroit lonneur de Dieu et sera appelle Servais et est icelle la adjucte dudit enfant." Koldeweij and Pesch, *Het Blokboek*, facsimile p. 1, p. 61. [Note: italics indicate letters that are implied, but not actually written]. (Here the father and mother of St. Servatius are praying to God for a child. An angel suddenly appeared to declare that their prayer had been heard and that they would have a holy child who would increase the honor to God and would be named Servatius and this is the destiny of the said child.) All translations are mine, with the generous assistance of Jerry Nash.

[16] Koldeweij and Pesch, *Het Blokboek*, p. 61; Luke 1.11–17.

[17] In addition to linking the relics of Servatius and Luke, there may be additional significance to the reference to Luke. As the Evangelist who describes the Annunciation, Luke 1.26–38, such an allusion to Luke's Gospel may also have been intended to underscore the *imitatio Christi* of Servatius.

[18] The text on the banner reads: "Nascitur vobis filius/Cuius nomen Servacius/Servavit fidem prospere/Magnus erat in opere." Koldeweij and Pesch, *Het Blokboek*, facsimile p. 1, p. 61. (Unto you will be born a son named Servatius, maintaining prosperous faith. He will be great in his works.)

gallery of the apse, they would have appeared to be presented from an elevated, heavenly source by clerics who would appear as surrogate angels. This connection is made explicit in the subsequent illustrations of the book in which angels both serve as deacons to Servatius and are garbed in the same style alb as the clerics displaying the relics in the final four scenes.

The second page encapsulates many years, beginning with Servatius' journey to Jerusalem at the age of twelve,[19] there he is appointed guardian of the Holy Sepulcher. A hundred years later, an angel appears and commands the long-lived Servatius to travel to Tongres. The prominent angelic presence and guidance, depicted in the image, reiterates the theme of Servatius' life as divinely ordained and directed, as stated in the book's overture. The emphasis on travel to and from the Holy Land might also be understood as an allusion to pilgrimage. Given that the context for the book's production and use was the septennial pilgrimage and relic ostension at Maastricht, this scene of sacred travel allows the reader to connect his or her own experience with that of the saint.

The theme of divine ordination is continued in the third scene, where we see an angel appointing Servatius bishop of Tongres, placing the episcopal miter on his head and giving him the crozier.[20] (fig. 324) The angel's hands touching both items—the two principal signifiers of episcopal authority—visually calls attention to the heavenly origin of Servatius' office. Divine approval of Servatius' episcopacy is thereby established—a key theme that is further developed and reiterated in the book, with the intention of asserting the primacy of Maastricht over Tongres in both episcopal authority and

---

[19] The text reads: "Quant Saint Servais fut eage de xii ans laissa pere et mere et vint en Jherusalem et la par le patriarch fut fait prester et gardeur du Saint Sepulchre et fut la cent ans. Adoncq vint ung angele et luy commanda quil allast a Tongre comme evesque estre la de par Dieu envoye." Koldeweij and Pesch, *Het Blokboek*, facsimile p. 2, p. 63. (When St. Servatius was twelve years old, he left his father and mother and went to Jerusalem where the patriarch ordained him as priest and guardian of the Holy Sepulcher, which he did for a hundred years. Then an angel came and commanded him to go to Tongres to be bishop, as sent by God.)

[20] The text reads: "Cy donne ly angele a Saint Servais le sceptre en sa main la ville de Tongre pour la estre evesque estant envoye de par Dieu nostre Seigneur en presence de tous le peuple estans en leglise." Koldeweij and Pesch, *Het Blokboek*, facsimile p. 3, p. 63. (Here, in the presence of all the people in the church, the angel placed the crozier of the city of Tongres in the hands of St. Servatius, signifying that he should be bishop as sent by Our Lord God.)

the claim to relics.[21] This angelic gift underscores the numinous nature of the crozier, one of the principal relics displayed at Maastricht. Its importance is accentuated by Servatius' gaze and gesture, which are fixed upon it, thereby directing the viewer's attention toward the relic. The group of witnesses to the left authenticates the relic's origin and draws further attention to the act of viewing the relics. It is noteworthy that a gathering of witnesses appears in other scenes that introduce important relics into the narrative.[22]

The fourth scene portrays the saint preaching to his flock in Tongres, urging them to be good.[23] This episode is important in setting up the eventual transfer of relics from Tongres to Maastricht, a move that is justified in the *vita* because the people of Tongres did not heed the saint's admonition to piety. The appearance of Servatius, elevated in the pulpit and visible from the chest up, might also be understood as a visual precursor to the final page in which the reliquary bust of the saint is elevated above the crowds gathered in the Vrijthof in Maastricht. Noteworthy here is the angelic figure behind the saint who holds his crozier, both stressing the heavenly approval of Servatius' episcopal duties and the importance of his secondary relics.

This stress on the importance of secondary relics is elaborated upon in the fifth scene where numerous people possessed by demons gather before the bishop's palace.[24] When they are given food from the saint's table, they are cured. This not only emphasizes the bishop's

---

[21] This assertion of the legitimacy of Maastricht over Tongres appears to be a principal message of the book, and may be understood as a secondary political motive for the book's production, in addition to its primary pilgrimage function. This also further supports the assertion that the book was produced in Maastricht.

[22] On page eight the chalice is introduced into the cycle. On page eleven the key is presented to Servatius; and on page nineteen the celestial cloth is draped upon the recumbent body of Servatius. In each of these scenes a crowd gathers on the left, acting as witnesses.

[23] The text reads: "Icy fait Saint Servais ung sermon au peuple de Tongre; et pour ce quil estoit de Armenie entendoient bien leur et laultre." Koldeweij and Pesch, *Het Blokboek*, facsimile p. 4, p. 63. (Here St. Servatius delivers a sermon to the people of Tongres, and because he was from Armenia they listened attentively.)

[24] The text reads: "Icy vindrent devant le palais Saint Servais boiteux aveugles et demoniacles attendant lamonne venant de sa table, car toulz megnans diceux relieffs furrent sains et garis de leur mal." Koldeweij and Pesch, *Het Blokboek*, facsimile p. 5, p. 67. (Here a crowd of the sick and possessed gathered in front of the palace of St. Servatius, awaiting food from his table because all who had eaten his food were made healthy and cured of their ailments.)

charity, it also reveals his sanctity as expressed in contact relics. As the first miracle in the *vita*, this mass exorcism is effected by relics which had contact with the saint. The woodcut elaborates on the text by clearly portraying some of the figures as pilgrims, identifiable by their distinctive hats and pilgrimage staffs. The inclusion of pilgrims in this scene, not mentioned in the text, is intended to link this image with the book's function as a pilgrimage program. This scene sets up a holy precedent for the display of the saint's relics to a great crowd, as would be gathered in the Vrijthof in Maastricht during the septennial pilgrimage. Considering that many of the relics displayed were actually secondary relics, having had contact with the saint during his lifetime, the nature of the relics in this fifth scene would be cogent to the periodic ostension.

The next two scenes depict how the devil tempted the people of Tongres to turn against their bishop,[25] by performing false miracles, here contrasted with the true miracles effected by the victual contact relics from the saint's table in the previous image. Led astray by their diabolical leader, the people of Tongres chase Servatius from the city, whereupon he travels to Maastricht to pray for his misguided flock. As the impiety of the people of Tongres leads them to turn against the saint, the piety of the people of Maastricht guides them to welcome him. This episode provides a rationale for the eventual transferal of the bishopric (and relics) from Tongres to Maastricht. Here the people of Tongres are depicted as bringing this fate on themselves by expelling their holy bishop. The divine approval of the ensuing episcopal transfer is suggested by the angelic figure who, guiding the saint, holds the prominent crozier.

Servatius is next portrayed celebrating Mass in Maastricht, where he learns that the people of Tongres will be massacred by the Huns.[26]

---

[25] The text on page six reads: "Cy fut ly peuple de Tongre infourme du deable alencontre de Saint Servais pour ce quil convertoit le peuple par ses miracles telement quil fut enchasse." Koldeweij and Pesch, *Het Blokboek*, facsimile p. 6, p. 67. (Here the people of Tongres were incited against St. Servatius by the devil because he [the devil] was so successful in converting through miracles that St. Servatius was chased away.) The text on page seven reads: "Cy est Saint Servais par grand indignacion enchasse et est venu devotement en la ville de Trect et at la prins son repos, ayant le peuple de ce piettie." Koldeweij and Pesch, *Het Blokboek*, facsimile p. 7, p. 67. (Here, with great indignity, St. Servatius is chased away. He devoutly traveled to the city of Maastricht where he rested, through the piety of its people.)

[26] The text reads: "Cy est comment Saint Servais fut moult honorablement receu a Trecht et, ly celebrant en la chapelle Saint Materns ly fut revele comment le pays

(fig. 325) He decides to travel to Rome to pray that his people be spared as a forgiving shepherd for his flock.[27] Again, the practice of pilgrimage is emphasized, as is the saint's adherence to proper ecclesiastic hierarchy. Also noteworthy here are the angel holding the crozier and the prominent chalice on the altar table. The chalice, accentuated by its gold coloration, is thereby introduced into the cycle. While establishing the liturgical context of the saint's revelation, this chalice is also significant as one of the principal relics displayed at Maastricht. The text reinforces this by noting how Servatius was honorably received at Maastricht, as opposed to the disgraceful behavior of the people of Tongres. The pious veneration of the saint and his relics at Maastricht is further highlighted by the devout group of exemplary witnesses on the left who provide the antithesis to the violent and impious actions of the populace of Tongres shown on the previous page. The implication is clear—Maastricht is elevated as the *locus* of proper veneration of the saint and his relics.

The following two images emphasize Servatius' role as bishop and restorer of the church. First he is shown as the most prominent of the group of bishops gathered in Cologne to appoint Severinus bishop.[28] We then see him in Metz, fixing an altar table, thereby expelling the demonic vandal who had broken it.[29] It is surely not

---

de Tongre seroit destruit des Huyns, leur fist savoir pour volloir aller impretrer pardons a Rome de leurs pechies." Koldeweij and Pesch, *Het Blokboek*, facsimile p. 8, p. 69. (Here is shown how St. Servatius was very honorably received in Maastricht, and there he celebrated [Mass] in the chapel of the Holy Mother, and there was revealed how the city of Tongres would be destroyed by the Huns, and he advised them of his intention of seeking forgiveness of their sins in Rome.)

[27] In forgiving his persecutors, Servatius is modeled after Christ who begged for the forgiveness of those who crucified him. This *imitatio Christi* is suggested in the woodcut by the image of the crucifixion portrayed on the altarpiece before which Servatius prays.

[28] The text on page nine reads: "Cy vint Saint Servais en la cite de Collogne ou fut le concille de Rome pour demettre levesque Effrata le quel estoit tiran; le quel fut commis a Saint Servais et mist en lieu d'Effrata Saint Severin pour estre evesque de Collogne." Koldeweij and Pesch, *Het Blokboek*, facsimile p. 9, p. 69. (Here St. Servatius went to the city of Cologne where the bishop Effrata had been deposed by the council of Rome for being a tyrant. St. Servatius is sent to appoint St. Severinus as bishop of Cologne, in place of Effrata.) Servatius' act of installing the proper bishop in Cologne is akin to the act of transferring his own episcopal seat to its new, proper location at Maastricht.

[29] The text on page ten reads: "Cy est commant Saint Servais est venu a Metz en leglise Saint Estienne ou estoit derompu du deable le pierre del outel. Il fist une croix dessus et tantost soy joinderent touttes le pieches ensemble comme estoit paravant et celebra dessus." Koldeweij and Pesch, *Het Blokboek*, facsimile p. 10, p. 69.

accidental that the location of these two episodes emphasizes the southern direction of this leg of the pilgrimage, as though walking the reader step-by-step through the saint's journey.

The eleventh scene details the culmination of Servatius' Roman pilgrimage, where he visits St. Peter's basilica and is given a key of episcopal authority by Peter himself, while an angel holds his crozier.[30] This key, a contact relic of both Christ and Peter, was among the principal relics kept in the treasury of the Church of St. Servatius in Maastricht.[31] Yet this particular relic is not portrayed as shown from the dwarf gallery of the church in the final four ostension scenes, because the relic of the key was on display inside the church.[32] The xylographic book therefore not only details the significance of those relics displayed outside the church, above the Vrijthof, but also those that could be seen by pilgrims inside, thereby providing a complete dossier of relics seen during the septennial pilgrimage. Indeed the key and crozier are common iconographic attributes of St. Servatius, as evidenced by numerous late medieval pilgrimage badges.[33] If Koldeweij's compelling proposal for the iconographic program of the late Gothic jubé is accurate, these two important mid-fifteenth-century cycles—the xylographic book and the jubé—echoed one another.[34] More importantly, they would both underscore the importance of the relics on display during the septennial ostension. Given

---

(Here is shown how St. Servatius went to the Church of St. Stephen in Metz, where the altar table had been broken by the devil. He made the sign of the cross over it and suddenly all the pieces were rejoined as it had been before. And then he celebrated [Mass] on it.)

[30] The text reads: "Cy vint Saint Servais a Rome en leglise Saint Pierre priant Dieu pour ceux de Tongre quilz ne cheent en maledicion et la ly donna Saint Pierre le cleff de par Nostre Seigneur quil ait le puissance de ('le'— crossed out) lier et deslier en ciel et en terre." Koldeweij and Pesch, *Het Blokboek*, facsimile p. 11, p. 71. (Here St. Servatius went to the Church of St. Peter in Rome to pray to God on behalf of the people of Tongres that they not remain under malediction. And there St. Peter gave him the key from Our Lord so that he would have the power to bind and unbind in Heaven and on earth.) The image's inclusion of St. Paul, the Virgin Mary and Christ, accompanying St. Peter, further reinforces the legitimacy of this symbolic investment of authority.

[31] Regarding the key and its iconographic and cultic significance, see Koldeweij, *Der gude Sente Servas*, pp. 61–131.

[32] Koldeweij and Pesch, *Het Blokboek*, pp. 10–1.

[33] Koldeweij and van Vlijmen, *Schatkamers*, Cat. 61g,h, pp. 170–4.

[34] Koldeweij and Pesch, *Het Blokboek*, pp. 52–9. The jubé was demolished in 1731; Aart J.J. Mekking, "Bijdragen tot de Bouwgeschiedenis van de Sint-Servaaskerk te Maastricht, deel II, Het Schip," *Publications de la Société Historique et Archéologique dans le Limbourg* 116–7 (1980–81), pp. 156–65.

the striking similarities between the surviving fragments of the jubé and the same scenes as portrayed in the xylographic book, it appears that these two cycles worked in concert, linking the two principal *loci* of relic display.[35]

The following two scenes depict Servatius as a savior of Rome and converter of infidels. While *en route* from Rome to Maastricht, the saint, key in hand, rests while an eagle hovers overhead, shading him from the hot Mediterranean sun.[36] His crozier is situated prominently next to his recumbent form. Up comes Attila, King of the Saracens, who wishes to kill the saint before continuing on to sack Rome. Seeing the saint's aquiline parasol, Attila asks to be baptized and vows not to destroy Rome. In the baptismal scene, Servatius' angelic deacon is again shown holding the saint's crozier.[37] By baptizing Attila, Servatius not only saves the city of Rome, but also Tongres. Thus, the reason for the saint's Roman pilgrimage is accomplished.

The succeeding two pages catalogue important miracles effected with another of the saint's secondary relics—his pilgrimage staff. Both occur during the return leg of the saint's Roman pilgrimage. On page fourteen, we see the saint striking the ground near Worms, causing a spring to issue forth.[38] It is noteworthy that the text makes

---

[35] Koldeweij noted the strong correlation between the two depictions of the Baptism of Attila by Servatius. Koldeweij and Pesch, *Het Blokboek*, pp. 58–9.

[36] The text on page twelve reads: "Icy vint Saint Servais hors de Rome en ung fores ou il reposa. Vint illec le roy Attille Sarazin et le prist et le fist loyer a ung arbre pour le faire morir; tantost vint sur luy en lar ung egle qui le covroit pour le soleil; quant le roy ce vit pria merchy et demanda estre baptizie." Koldeweij and Pesch, *Het Blokboek*, facsimile p. 12, p. 71. (Here St. Servatius went to a forest outside Rome where he rested. There came Attila, King of the Saracens, who took him and had him tied to a tree to be killed. Upon seeing that an eagle hovered above him, shading him from the sun, the king begged for mercy and asked to be baptized.)

[37] The text on page thirteen reads: "Icy est baptizie le roy Attille et tous ses gens de saint Servais par miracles quil avoit veu de Dieu. Apres se party de la et laissa le pays de Rome en pays et ne fut point destruit." Koldeweij and Pesch, *Het Blokboek*, facsimile p. 13, p. 73. (Here the king Attilla and all his people were baptized by St. Servatius through miracles that he effected through God. Afterwards they departed from there and left Rome in peace and it was not at all destroyed.)

[38] The text reads: "Cy vint Saint Servais au pays de Warm tout affably de soiff et fist une croix sur la terre et tantost vint la unge fontaine et vint ly angele qui ly donna ung tres riche beuvoir pour le quel garist quant on boiet hors dicellui de tous fievres." Koldeweij and Pesch, *Het Blokboek*, facsimile p. 14, p. 73. (Here, in the vicinity of Worms, St. Servatius, in order to quench his thirst, made the sign of the cross on the ground, from which suddenly sprang a fountain. And an angel appeared and gave him a very fine cup, drinking from which will cure all fever.)

no specific mention of the pilgrimage staff being used, though the image clearly portrays it as the agent of the miraculous spring, which appears while an angel hands Servatius a cup with which to partake of the water.[39] That cup, described as healing the fever of those who drink from it, is introduced as yet another secondary relic.[40] By specifying the thaumaturgic qualities of this relic, the text recalls the curative victuals from the saint's table detailed on page five, thereby relating this relic to the pilgrim's desire for contact and cure. While the text underscores the miraculous potency of the cup, the image gives primacy to the saint's pilgrimage staff. The presence of the angel in this scene, which introduces the power of these additional important relics, recalls the third page on which the angel delivers the crozier to the saint. These angelic figures underscore the heavenly power of the relics, the miraculous potency of which the book is intended to elucidate.

Continuing north, the saint arrives in Elsueten, where a venomous dragon has been destroying people and property. On page fifteen, we see Servatius killing the dragon with his pilgrimage staff, while the angelic companion directs the reader's attention to the action, pointing out the power of the relic.[41] (fig. 326) The importance of this relic to pilgrims to Maastricht is evidenced by a fragmentary fourteenth-century tin pilgrim's badge which portrays Servatius killing the dragon with his pilgrimage staff.[42]

---

[39] The legend of the miraculous fountain, based upon the tale of Moses striking the rock, Exodus 17.1–7, occurs in other hagiographic legends, such as Chapter VII.12 of Bonaventura's *Legenda Maior* of St. Francis. *The Little Flowers of St. Francis. The Mirror of Perfection by Leo of Assisi. The Life of St. Francis by St. Bonaventura* (London, 1938), p. 349.

[40] The cup, venerated as the cup of St. Servatius, was kept in the treasury of St. Servatius in Maastricht from at least the late fourteenth or early fifteenth century. Koldeweij and Pesch, *Het Blokboek*, pp. 72–3; Koldeweij, *Der gude Sente Servas*, pp. 220–39.

[41] The text reads: "Cy est commant Saint Servais vint en Elsueten ou y avoit ung dragon en une vigne jectant fu et venin le quel destruoit tous gens et bestes et nuls ne le oiso(it) tues; et le tua Saint Servais de sa croche." Koldeweij and Pesch, *Het Blokboek*, facsimile p. 15, p. 77. (Here is shown how St. Servatius went to Elsueten where a dragon, spitting fire and poison, was destroying all men and beasts, and no one was able to kill it. And St. Servatius killed it with his crozier.) The text states that the saint uses his crozier to slay the dragon, while the image depicts him using his pilgrimage staff. However, the text and image of the ostension of this relic, on page twenty-one, clearly states that the saint kills the dragon with the pilgrimage staff. See fn. 53.

[42] Koldeweij and van Vlijmen, *Schazkamers*, Cat. 61f., p. 170.

Returning to Cologne, Servatius inspires Severinus to found a chapel.[43] In the left half of the woodcut, the saint is shown sleeping, receiving somnolent stimulus to build, as evidenced by the light emanating from him. On the right, Severinus is portrayed, crozier in hand, directing the construction of *une belle chapelle*, in honor of Servatius. The return to Cologne underscores the movement through time and space in the saint's pilgrimage to Rome.[44] In scene nine he is shown passing through Cologne on the way to Rome. By accentuating the saint's visit to Cologne on his return voyage in scene sixteen, the *vita* constructs a sense of the impending completion of this story-within-a-story. The pilgrimage is nearly complete.

In the seventeenth scene, the saint is shown arriving in Tongres, displaying to the people the key given to him by St. Peter in Rome.[45]

---

[43] The text reads: "Icy est commant Saint Servais est venu devant la cite de Collogne prendant son repos de nuit en une povre mainsochelle. Saint Severyn estant sur sa chambre vit sur ladite maison grand claerte. Du matin illecques alla et le receut moult devotement et fist la fondre en lameur de Saint Servais une belle chapelle." Koldeweij and Pesch, *Het Blokboek*, facsimile p. 16, p. 77. (Here is shown how St. Servatius came before the city of Cologne and rested the night in a humble little house. St. Severinus remained in his room in the house, which was filled with bright light. In the morning he [Severinus] went and received him [Servatius] very devoutly and founded a beautiful chapel in honor of St. Servatius.)

[44] This construction of spatial and temporal narrative flow through recurrent visits/depictions of the same location recalls the legend of St. Ursula and her Eleven Thousand Virgin Companions, who similarly traveled to Rome via Cologne. This parallel is particularly compelling given the similar scene of Ursula's dream in Cologne. This is portrayed in the eighteen scenes of the nearly contemporary panel of the *vita* of St. Ursula, painted in 1456 for the Church of the Eleven Thousand Virgins in Cologne. Frank Günther Zehnder, *Sankt Ursula. Legend-Verehrung-Bilderwelt* (Cologne, 1985), pp. 157–68, esp. p. 163. Regarding the cult of the Eleven Thousand Virgins of Cologne and their relics, see Scott B. Montgomery, *The Use and Perception of Reliquary Busts in the Late Middle Ages* (Ph.D. diss., Rutgers University, 1996), pp. 307–62; Joan A. Holladay, "Relics, Reliquaries, and Religious Women: Visualizing the Holy Virgins of Cologne," *Studies in Iconography* 18 (1997), pp. 67–118. I am currently preparing a book on relics, figural reliquaries and the visual culture associated with the cult of the Eleven Thousand Virgins of Cologne. Editors' note see Jeanne Neuchterlein's and Vida J. Hull's essays in this volume.

[45] The text reads: "Cy vint Saint Servais a Tongre et diest au peuple quil at a Rome vers Dieu impetre. Amendes vous en penichenc(e). Vechy la clef que saint Pierre de par Nostre Seigneur mat donne que jay la puissance de vous deslier de voz pechies." Koldeweij and Pesch, *Het Blokboek*, facsimile p. 17, p. 79. (Here St. Servatius arrives in Tongres and tells the people that, while in Rome, he interceded with God on their behalf. Correct yourselves in penitence. Behold the key that St. Peter gave me, from Our Lord, so that I have the power to free you from your sins.) The change in tone, from the initial narrative form to the command to penance, might be read as a direct address to the pilgrims/readers who are thus encouraged by the saint himself. The efficacy of such penitential acts of pilgrimage is elucidated

Servatius asserts his episcopal authority by the crozier and key; the latter presented as an emblem of authority and a token of the completed pilgrimage to Rome.[46] The emphasis on this pilgrimage memento would be cogent to the reader of the xylographic book, since relating the key to pilgrimage would connect the experience of the pilgrim to Maastricht with that of the saint. As noted, the relic of the key would be among the objects venerated by pilgrims within the church. The angel behind Servatius draws attention to the crozier by pointing directly to this prominent relic.

It is noteworthy that scenes eight through seventeen literally follow Servatius' pilgrimage to and from Rome, both spatially and temporally. The reader is thereby invited to virtually recreate the experience of the pilgrimage and its attendant miracles. Given that the book itself was created essentially as a textual and visual companion to the culmination of the pilgrimage to Maastricht, this emphasis on the process of pilgrimage is intriguing. Taken as a group, these images form the exact middle of the book, preceded by and followed by seven scenes. That this careful explication of the movement through time and space in the pilgrimage process forms the very heart of the book suggests that this notion of the recreation and re-enactment of pilgrimage is central to the way in which the book was intended to function. It is also significant that several of the principal relics on view at Maastricht feature prominently in this central pilgrimage sequence—namely the crozier, the pilgrimage staff, and the key. If reading the book was intended to walk one through a virtual pilgrimage, following in the footsteps of St. Servatius, the emphasis on the relics insures that the reader does not lose sight of the principal conduits of holy power in Maastricht. One is invited to embark upon a pilgrimage of reading and seeing, and the *locus sanctus* is clearly established at Maastricht.

Page eighteen shows the translation of all the relics (*tous les relicques*) from Tongres to Maastricht.[47] (fig. 327) Servatius is depicted holding

---

by the saint, as he relates his power to absolve sins, signified by the relic that he reveals.

[46] For pilgrim badges from Rome showing the keys of St. Peter: Spencer, *Pilgrim Souvenirs*, pp. 248–51; Bruna, *Enseignes de Pèlerinage*, pp. 197–200; van Beuningen and Koldeweij, *Heilig en Profaan*, pp. 184–7; van Beuningen, Koldeweij, and Kicken, *Heilig en Profaan 2*, pp. 282–3.

[47] The text reads: "Vechy comment Saint Servais fait avecq luy porter de Tongre a Trect tout les relicques qui la estoint ainsi luy estoit il commande a Rome de

the key and crozier, symbolizing the authority with which he effects
the relocation of the relics. The text states that this *translatio* was
commanded by St. Peter himself—a provenance underscored by the
key in Servatius' hand. The divine approval of this action is accentuated by the angel behind Servatius, pointing to the crozier, drawing attention to the translation of this relic. Because of their wicked
ways, the people of Tongres lose not only their episcopal seat, but
also all the holy relics in their possession. The relics that are transferred to Maastricht are some of the ones displayed during the septennial ostension. This scene is presented as the culminating act of the
saint's career. That the translation of the relics is depicted as the
finale to the saint's life emphasizes that the entire *vita* of the saint
depicted is constructed as a grand and detailed prelude to the ostension of relics that forms both the end of the book and the very reason for its creation.

The cycle of the saint's life closes with his death in Maastricht.[48]
(fig. 328) Although the text relates that he died while saying Mass,
the image portrays Servatius lying on a bed, still clutching his crozier.
Rather than depicting the actual moment of his death, the woodcut
concentrates attention on the veneration of his bodily relics. The
juxtaposition of the saint's recumbent body and the golden reliquary
shrine being carried to Maastricht in the previous scene suggests that
the reliquary might be understood as a visual allusion to the splendid shrine in which St. Servatius himself would later be placed.[49]
Like the key, the shrine of St. Servatius was on display inside the

---

Saint Pie*rr*e lapostel; en*de* chantere*nt* les angels en lar dess*us* les relicques jusques a
Trect." Koldeweij and Pesch, *Het Blokboek*, facsimile p. 18, p. 79. (Here is shown
how St. Servatius took all the relics from Tongres with him to Maastricht as was
commanded by the apostle St. Peter in Rome. Angels chanted, accompanying the
relics to Maastricht.)

[48] The text on page nineteen reads: "Cy est signifie le jour du trespasseme*nt* de
Saint Se*r*vais tantost alla celebrer messe et qua*nt* il eut prins le corps N*os*tre Seign*eur*
morut. Puis vindr*ent* les angels aportant sur son corps ij draps du ciel pour le en
ce encevelir." Koldeweij and Pesch, *Het Blokboek*, facsimile p. 19, p. 81. (Here is
indicated the day of passage of St. Servatius when he died while celebrating Mass,
at the moment he took the body of Our Lord. Then angels came and placed over
his body celestial cloths to enshroud him.)

[49] On the shrine of St. Servatius, see Renate Kroos, *Der Schrein des Heiligen Servatius
in Maastricht und die vier zugehörigen Reliquiare in Brüssel* (Munich, 1985); Rita W. Tekippe,
*Procession, Piety, and Politics: Three Medieval Rheno-Mosan Reliquary Shrines and the Cult of
Communities for Bishop-Saints Servatius of Maastricht, Eleutherius of Tournai, and Remaclus of
Stavelot* (Ph.D. diss., The Ohio State University, 1999).

Church of St. Servatius during the septennial ostension.[50] The prominent golden shrine in the translation scene, read in conjunction with the scene of the saint's death, therefore appears to be intended to evoke the image of the saint's shrine in the pilgrim's mind. As such, Servatius is presented as instituting the cult of his own relics, as well as all other relics, at Maastricht. His life ends with the institution of his relic cult in Maastricht, thereby setting up the ensuing pilgrimage, ostension, and veneration.

The scene of the death of Servatius includes the arrival of additional significant contact relics. Two angels appear bearing "celestial cloths" with which they cover the saint's body.[51] As with the first appearance of the crozier and the pilgrimage staff in the narrative, the introduction of important relics is marked by the dramatic appearance of angelic beings. This recalls the opening scene in which the angel, bearing the cloth-like inscription banner, announces the arrival of Servatius. Thus, angelic gifts serve as the bookends for his life—setting up a framework for understanding the heavenly source of the numinous potency of his relics.

The miraculous power of cloths associated with the saint is elucidated in the twentieth scene.[52] The text relates how two women in a village in France were weaving cloths on the feast of St. Servatius (May 13), with the intention of selling them in honor of the saint. During Mass, one of the cloths began to bleed, revealing the divine approval of the women's endeavor, and underscoring the saint's approval of the honor given him, echoing the founding of a chapel in his honor by St. Serverinus, as seen on page sixteen. While the women hold the bloody cloth, numerous witnesses are included, both verifying the miraculous event and acting as exemplars to the reader

---

[50] Koldeweij and Pesch, *Het Blokboek*, pp. 10–1.

[51] Mechtild Flury-Lemberg, "Le vêtement funéraire de saint Servais de Maastricht," *Bulletin du Centre International d'études des Textiles* 70 (1992), pp. 37–44.

[52] The text reads: "Cy est comment deux femmes tisoient des draps sur ung jour Saint Servais en ung village au France et pour ce quilz ne vindrent pour ale messe la dehors en une chapelle en on faisoit le service de Saint Servais, commencha ledit drap a sangner. Pour icelle miracle fut la faite et fondee une eglise et pent illecques encore cedit drap." Koldeweij and Pesch, *Het Blokboek*, facsimile p. 20, p. 81. (Here is shown how two women were weaving cloths in a village in France on the feast of St. Servatius, so that they could be sold in order to have masses outside a chapel, and to give service to St. Servatius. The cloth began to bleed. Because of this miracle, a church was founded, which still keeps this cloth.)

who is thus encouraged to serve as an additional witness to the prodigious capabilities of the relic of the saint. This episode shows the relics as having *living*, miraculous powers. Of particular interest here is the mention that a church was built to house the relic of the miraculous cloth, where it is still kept. The implication is that the relics remain on the site because they are properly venerated there. This contrasts dramatically with the sanctioned translation of the relics from Tongres to Maastricht, which occurred because the people of Tongres were not suitably pious and appreciative of the saint's presence. Thus, this scene not only sets up the miraculous postmortem continuity of the saint via his relics, it also serves to support the transfer of relics to Maastricht by establishing that the relics were relocated so as to foster and maintain their proper veneration. This reinforces the claim that the relics are in Maastricht because they choose to remain there, underscoring their active agency in establishing and fostering the septennial pilgrimage and ostension.

The final four scenes illustrate the display of the relics from the dwarf gallery of the Church of St. Servatius during the septennial ostension at Maastricht. They are arranged as four consecutive showings. The first of these images, contained on page twenty-one, exhibits one of the celestial cloths that the angels placed over St. Servatius' body at his death, as depicted in scene nineteen.[53] (fig. 318) The saint's pilgrimage staff is also held aloft.[54] The accompanying text notes not only the heavenly origin of the cloth, but also the two miracles effected through the pilgrimage staff—bringing forth the

---

[53] The text reads: "La pre̱mire mo̱nstre que en sera/ chest un drappe que Dieu e̱nvoia/ par ses angles qua̱nt Saint Se̱rvais trepassa/ et un bordon du quel il allat en pilgrimage/ une fontaine en fist en alla̱nt a Rome son viage/ du mimes bordo̱n un drago̱n tuwat de fort courage." Koldeweij and Pesch, *Het Blokboek*, facsimile p. 21, p. 83. (The first showing that will be/ is a cloth which God sent/ by angels when St. Servatius died/ and a staff with which he went on pilgrimage/ a fountain was made on his voyage to Rome/ with the same staff he killed a dragon with great courage.") Regarding the three cloths, see Annemarie Stauffer, *Die mittelalterlichen Textilien von St. Servatius in Maastricht* (Riggisberg, 1991), pp. 16–8; Koldeweij, *Der gude Sente Servas*, pp. 197–207.

[54] The staff, made of wood with an ivory handle and iron tip, which dates to the middle of the ninth century, was most likely made in Trier. From at least the fourteenth century it was venerated in Maastricht as the pilgrimage staff of St. Servatius. It is kept in the treasury of the Church of St. Servatius, Maastricht. Koldeweij and Pesch, *Het Blokboek*, p. 87. Regarding the iconographic and cultic significance of the relic of the pilgrimage staff, see Koldeweij, *Der gude Sente Servas*, pp. 145–61. *Editors' note see Anja Grebe's essay in this volume.

fountain and slaying the dragon—as depicted in scenes fourteen and fifteen respectively. The text changes from prose to verse for these last four scenes of relic display, suggesting that they are to be read and understood in a different manner from the rest of the book. There is a more formal air to both the images and text in these final four scenes. The use of the future tense to describe the impending display of the relics suggests that the book is to be understood as a program to the relic display. One is intended to read (or hear) the text and then look to see the relics displayed. This appears to set up a clear order of interface between text and image in the reading of the book. One is first directed to read the text and then look to the image for visual revelation, as though recreating the pilgrim's experience of the relic ostension with every reading.

In the second display scene, on page twenty-two, another celestial cloth (this one red), is draped from the dwarf gallery, while St. Servatius' episcopal crozier is elevated.[55] (fig. 319) The angelic gift of the crozier is noted in the text, as illustrated in scene three. (fig. 329) This reminder, in concert with the display of these relics from high above the viewer, and the similar garb worn by clerics and angels, would encourage the viewer to equate the clerics holding the relics with the angels who initially delivered them. The display of one of the cloth relics is also portrayed on a capital (*c.* 1485) in the cloister of St. Servatius in Maastricht, where two angels hold the cloth aloft in a manner analogous to the way in which the clerics hold the cloths in the xylographic book.[56] Thus, the relic ostension is fashioned as an evocation of the heavenly presentation of the relics. Like the miraculous pilgrimage staff in the previous display, the

---

[55] The text reads: "Apres un drappe rouge aporteis du chieul/ e j bordon que leveche Saint Valentyn/ commanda quant il trepassa an la fyn/ nullui nelle prist del lauteil Nostre Damme/ si tres digne ne venist par revelacion del ange/ li quell a Saint Servais fit mys en commande." Koldeweij and Pesch, *Het Blokboek*, facsimile p. 22, p. 83. (Afterwards, a red cloth delivered from heaven/ and the staff that St. Valentine/ held when he reached his end/ through the prayers of Our Lady/ it was returned by angelic revelation/ as that which St. Servatius held.) The crozier, now kept in the treasury of the Church of St. Servatius, Maastricht, is constructed of wood with an ivory volute and gilt bronze ornaments, and appears to have been made in Cologne *c.* 1180–85. Koldeweij and Pesch, *Het Blokboek*, pp. 86–7. Regarding the iconographic and cultic significance of the crozier, consult Koldeweij, *Der gude Sente Servas*, pp. 132–44.

[56] Stauffer, *Die mittelalterlichen Textilien*, p. 20, fig. 8.

crozier is accentuated through its central placement within the composition of the display. The prominence of the crozier, depicted in nearly half of the scenes in the *vita*, prepares the viewer to realize the importance of this secondary relic.[57]

In the third display, portrayed on page twenty-three, yet another celestial cloth is shown.[58] (fig. 320) This one, white with fine decorations, is said to have been placed by angels on the tomb of St. Servatius. The saint's chalice and paten are also revealed.[59] The saint's association with the chalice, and by implication the paten, is made in scene eight when he is depicted celebrating Mass at Maastricht. It hardly appears accidental that the chalice is portrayed in an episode that took place in Maastricht, thus accentuating its long-standing presence and use at the *locus* of its ostension.

The last scene, which provides the finale to both the book and the ostension, is centered on the display of the reliquary bust of St. Servatius (*c.* 1403).[60] (fig. 321) Additional relics are shown, such as the right arm of St. Thomas and the cross pendant made by St.

---

[57] The crozier appears in nine of the twenty images from the *vita* cycle: Servatius receives the crozier from the angel, p. 3; an angel holds the crozier while the saint speaks, p. 4; the saint holds his crozier while being chased from Tongres, p. 7; an angel holds the crozier while the saint says Mass, p. 8; an angel holds the crozier while the saint receives the key, p. 11; the saint holds his crozier while sleeping, p. 12; an angel holds the crozier while the saint baptizes Attila, p. 13; the saint holds his crozier while translating the relics from Tongres to Maastricht, p. 18; Servatius holds the crozier on his death bed, p. 19.

[58] The text reads: "Ossy on monstre du chieul venut j blanc suere/ au quel en voiet mainte belle figure/ les angles par grand solempniteit la porterent/ et sur la tombe de Saint Servais le laisserent/ sa kalice on monstre et la pataine fyne/ par grand devotion a lanoer de ses pelryn." Koldeweij and Pesch, *Het Blokboek*, facsimile p. 23, p. 83. (Then is shown how a white shroud which came from heaven/ upon which are many fine decorations/ the angels brought with great solemnity/ and laid it on the tomb of St. Servatius/ his chalice is shown and his fine paten/ with great devotion to his pilgrims.)

[59] The chalice and paten, kept in the treasury in the Church of St. Servatius, Maastricht, are of Mosan workmanship done in partial gilt silver. They date from the middle of the thirteenth century and were associated with St. Servatius from at least the fifteenth century. Koldeweij and Pesch, *Het Blokboek*, pp. 90–91; Koldeweij, *Der gude Sente Servas*, pp. 207–19.

[60] The text reads: "Le chieuff de Saint Servais reverendement/ on le monstre la a toutte gent/ une crois in cristalle ovreyt et mys/ et est la crois que Saint Lucas fist/ la Virgne le porta entre ses mammelles/ le droit bras Saint Thomas et autre reliques belles." Koldeweij and Pesch, *Het Blokboek*, facsimile p. 24, p. 85. (The head of St. Servatius reverently/ is shown to all the people/ a cross in crystal in which is placed/ the cross which St. Luke made/ the Virgin wore it between her breasts/ the right arm of St. Thomas and other fine relics.)

Luke for the Virgin Mary.[61] According to legend, this cross was given to Servatius by the patriarch of Jerusalem, a gift perhaps alluded to in the second scene when the patriarch appoints the young Servatius guardian of the Holy Sepulcher. Most dramatic however, is the display of the splendid reliquary bust, described here as the head of St. Servatius itself (*le chieuff de Saint Servais*),[62] (fig. 330) by which he literally appears to his people, bestowing upon them the grace of seeing this saintly vision. The woodcut shows the reliquary held aloft by two clerics. Through this image we know the original form of the reliquary bust, prior to its augmentation in the last quarter of the sixteenth century. This majestic image serves as the culmination of the ostension as portrayed in the xylographic book of St. Servatius.

In closing with this dramatic visual experience of a face-to-face encounter with the saint, the xylographic book stresses the visual nature of the relic display. When we consider the first page of the book, in which Servatius first appears in the form of the text of the angel's banner, this visual development is underscored. From this initial, intangible, textual introduction, the book develops the saint's life, fleshing it out in the expanded narrative of his *vita*. Like Christ, the word of Servatius is made flesh. This builds to the final, dramatic revelation of the saint himself, manifest in the here and now through his reliquary bust. His true presence is understood through direct visual stimulus. Seeing is believing. The entire *vita* is constructed so as to build to this moment of the revelation of the presence of the saint.

---

[61] The silver arm reliquary, kept in the treasury of the Church of St. Servatius, Maastricht, appears to have been made in Maastricht in the first half of the fifteenth century. Koldeweij and Pesch, *Het Blokboek*, pp. 90–91; Koldeweij and van Vlijmen, *Schatkamers*, Cat. 44, pp. 147–9; Franz Bock and Michel Antoine Hubert Willemsen, *Antiquités sacrées conservées dans les anciennes collégiales de S. Servais et de Notre-Dame à Maestricht* (Maastricht, 1873), pp. 207–11. For the cross pendant, see Koldeweij, *Der gude Sente Servas*, pp. 161–73.

[62] The *c.* 1403 reliquary bust, kept in the treasury of the Church of St. Servatius, Maastricht, was significantly remodeled in the last quarter of the sixteenth century. Fashioned of partially-gilded silver and precious and semi-precious stones, it was probably made in Maastricht. Koldeweij and Pesch, *Het Blokboek*, pp. 90–1; Koldeweij and van Vlijmen, *Schatkamers*, Cat. 39, pp. 138–40; Bock and Willemsen, *Antiquités sacrées*, pp. 215–20; Jos Koldeweij, "Das Servatius-Büstenreliquair in der Maastrichter Servatiuskirche und seine liturgische Nutzung", Römisches Jahrbuch der Bibliotheca Herziana 33 (1999–2000): 217–33. A cycle of eight silver reliefs (all of whose scenes were included in the xylographic book) ornamented the original socle of the bust. The reliefs are in the Museum für Kunst und Gewerbe, Hamburg (Inv. Nr. 1885.1195).

Given that the book appears to have been created for the celebration of the septennial pilgrimage at Maastricht, it is no surprise that its focus is on the presentation of the relics. Through text and image the xylographic book made manifest to the pilgrims the significance of each relic shown. The book could serve two related purposes, the most obvious being a veritable program or guidebook to the relic display. However, examination of the book would also serve to guide the reader through a virtual pilgrimage—a private reenactment of the public ostension. This recreative pilgrimage process is suggested by the narrative of the saint's pilgrimage to Rome as developed in the central pages of the book. Reading through the book, one embarks upon an *ersatz* pilgrimage, a process that is encouraged by the pilgrimage within the pilgrimage, as Servatius' journey to Rome provides a model for the reader's pilgrimage to Maastricht. Thus, while the book concentrates attention on the localization of the ostension in Maastricht, its portability allows for this showing to enjoy an extension beyond the specific locale of the display. This gives the relic display the possibility of expansion in both space and time. Furthermore, while the book appears to have been created in conjunction with the 1461 ostension, the use of the technique of chiro-xylography would allow the book to be reprinted for subsequent ostensions at which time its contents would again be topical.[63] Considering that some of the relics, the three celestial cloths in particular, were only displayed once every seven years, seeing them would be an opportunity rarely afforded to the faithful.[64] In the intervening years, with the aid of the book, one could recreate the act of seeing the relics beyond the actual display in Maastricht, and at a greater frequency than the institutionalized seven-year cycle of display allowed.

It is significant that the images are larger and more prominent than the text. Furthermore, the images augment and clarify the salient features of the text in terms of their relevance to the relic ostension. This visual emphasis reinforces the concentration on the act of see-

---

[63] Pesch noted this advantage of xylography, which allowed the book to be easily reprinted without excessive labor. Koldeweij and Pesch, *Het Blokboek*, pp. 22–3. As discussed in fn. 2, the chiro-xylographic format would allow the text of the book to be translated, allowing for the book to be produced in numerous languages without necessitating any alterations to the wood-block template.

[64] Koldeweij and Pesch, *Het Blokboek*, pp. 86–7.

ing that is the book's primary focus. In this it echoes the ostension itself, with its primarily visual experience. The arrangement of the xylographic book of St. Servatius reveals that the principal devotional stimulus of its audience, composed of pilgrims, was overwhelmingly visual. The text serves an explanatory function, analogous to that of the announcements that accompanied the actual showing of the relics. The book is arranged like a relic display, preceded by a recitation of the saint's *vita*. It is important to consider how the sacral performance of the relic ostension appears to have determined the organization of the book. Text is not primary here, but is part of a larger, more intricately linked web of vision and performance. In order to fully understand the manner in which pilgrimage art functions, we must consider such issues of performance and audience. Rather than focusing our attention solely on the textual or visual narratives, we ought to strive to comprehend the ways in which text and image helped form, and functioned within, a complex nexus of performed pilgrimage. Only by acknowledging this experiential engagement of the audience of pilgrims viewing the book can we more fully comprehend the language and meaning of the xylographic book of St. Servatius. Here the textual *vita*, the images, and the dynamics of reading and display work in concert to serve the interests of the cultic veneration of the saint, via the validation and display of the relics associated with St. Servatius.

CHAPTER TWENTY-SIX

PILGRIMAGE AND PROCESSION: CORRELATIONS OF MEANING, PRACTICE, AND EFFECTS

Rita Tekippe

That art associated with pilgrimage is often the same as that asso-ciated with procession is no mere coincidence. These two cultic activ-ities, although distinctive in respects, share many commonalities as Christian signifiers and frequently merged into a singular festal expres-sion. The visual effects of each ritual signified similarly, in complex reference to ultimate Christian goals. If pilgrimage to innumerable sites throughout Europe has in the past been underestimated, the study of procession has been even more woefully disregarded. For both activities, the dearth of records seems to derive from the fact that they were such frequently-performed rites,[1] and therefore did not warrant extensive commentary.[2] In this essay, I will survey their similarities and their differences, with a focus on the visual and the-oretical implications for medieval processions with relics, and more specifically, for elaborate reliquary shrines, as part of a visual display of individual and communal assertion of myriad tenets of parochial, civic, and diocesan ecclesiasticism. While I have found examples from many places, I will concentrate on the Rheno-Mosan area, where a great number of large reliquary shrines were created during the twelfth and thirteenth centuries.

---

[1] Procession was the most frequent manifestation of religious sentiment in Flanders in the Middle Ages, while pilgrimage was second most frequent. Jacques Toussaert, *Le Sentiment Réligieux en Flandre à la Fin du Moyen-Age* (Paris, 1963), p. 267.

[2] Clifford Flanigan opined that such a "... display of power (archpriest, garb, scepter,) ... belongs to the most basic conventions of medieval ritual ... so taken for granted that it is unlikely to have elicited the conscious attention of the medieval participants. But this is just the point. The display of power relationships encoded ... serves to authenticate and authorize the prevailing order in ways that seem 'nat-ural', beyond comment, and virtually beyond conscious observation." C. Clifford Flanigan, "The Moving Subject: Medieval Liturgical Processions in Semiotic and Cultural Perspective," in *Moving Subjects: Processional Performance in the Middle Ages and Renaissance*, (eds.) Kathleen Ashley and Wim Hüsken (Atlanta, 2001), p. 147.

From its inception in use for congregational Christian rites, the basilica form embodied the processional sense of movement from entry to altar, from profane to sacred, and provided a sense of the Christian life journey through the rhythmic passage down the nave.[3] The metaphor for movement toward the heavenly realms was a persistent theme in architecture and in rites. Pilgrim experience was closely aligned with pervasive imaging of celestial teleology, and it permeated the development of both pilgrimage and procession, and all of the associated art.

The distinctions between pilgrimage and procession are often blurred, as medieval Christians regularly formed processional groups to journey to cult centers, and made pilgrimages to join into processional celebrations. Many established processions regularly drew crowds of pilgrims, as did singular processional events.[4] Seeing the differences between the two activities is not always possible because often such distinctions did not exist. The consistent and insistent multivalency in the Middle Ages poses challenges in understanding and interpretation. Stepping beyond formalism and connoisseurship,[5] we encounter an intricate web which defies complete disentanglement, but we can pick out certain threads and find insights into the elusive interconnections.[6]

Many agree on the importance of trying to discern the visual experience of medieval people, and of utilizing the visual as textual contribution,[7] but while semeiotic analysis can yield a broader under-

---

[3] Richard Krautheimer, *Early Christian and Byzantine Architecture*, 1989 reprint ed., *Penguin Books* (London, 1965), pp. 39–41.

[4] Alan E. Knight, *Les Mystères de la Procession*, vol. 1 (Geneva, 2001), p. 3, such as that at Tournai, beginning in 1090 and at Lille, beginning in 1270.

[5] Frequent repairs, restorations and changes to original objects made them less desirable subjects for study by formalists and connoisseurs of art history until recently when scholars became more interested in reconstructing the context of medieval life, ritual, and associated objects of art. For an excellent account of the vicissitudes which objects might undergo, see the essay in this volume by Albert Lemeunier.

[6] Ilene Forsyth laid important groundwork for the investigation of medieval use of, and attitudes toward, images and reliquaries, as well as of their frequent transportation in Ilene H. Forsyth, *The Throne of Wisdom—Wood Sculptures of the Madonna in Romanesque France* (Princeton, 1972). See Rita W. Tekippe, *Procession, Piety, and Politics: Three Medieval Rheno-Mosan Reliquary Shrines and the Cult Communities for Bishop-Saints Servatius of Maastricht, Eleutherius of Tournai, and Remaclus of Stavelot* (Ph.D. diss., Ohio State University, 1999), esp. pp. 4–5; Sabine Felbecker, *Die Prozession: Historische und Systematische Untersuchungen zu Einer Liturgischen Ausdruckshandlung* (Altenberg, 1995).

[7] Margaret Ruth Miles, *Image as Insight: Visual Understanding in Western Christianity and Secular Culture* (Boston, 1985), pp. 9–10.

standing of both pilgrimage and procession, it also spotlights "the ambiguity and polysemity of ritual messages."[8] Both cult practices were prone to variegated forms, in myriad times and places, and even to shifting points of presentation across the duration of a single ritual occasion, so the range of implications remains elusive, to some extent. Their visuality was astounding and complicated, while connotations of display often encompassed the whole of Christian mysteries when considered in sum. Like the understanding and expression of the Christian faith, they evolved over time and revealed tendencies to emphasize particular and current aspects, with many timely nuances unlikely to be recovered.

In the later Middle Ages, many images of these rites appeared, although there are fewer representations from the eras when processions first became customary,[9] but there is verbal documentation of the transportation of relics, and of the more formalized rite of procession as a frequent and familiar one. Walcaud of Liège (r. 809–831) stated that among the necessary objects for each church was a reliquary, adding to the previous directive that the relics of each parish be accorded great care both day and night.[10] Theology regarding the touching of relics by the faithful evolved, ultimately resulting in their encasement in appropriate containers, to fend off inappropriate gestures of devotees. The number of extant reliquaries is telling,

---

[8] Thomas A. II Boogaart, "Our Saviour's Blood: Procession and Community in Late Medieval Bruges," in *Moving Subjects*, (eds.) Ashley and Hüsken, p. 70, warned that "conceiving rituals as 'texts' or as producing 'images' tends to endow them implicitly with a sense of universality which can obscure the distinctive aspects of the medieval 'style of reading.'" Each event may have had a current meaning, distinctive iconography, and certain general implications, so that each generated its own meaning, but I maintain that the over-arching significance as a Christian signifier of certain commonly-held beliefs would be present in each. See also Donald Preziosi, *Rethinking Art History: Meditations on a Coy Science* (New Haven, 1989); Mieke Bal, and Norman Bryson, "Semiotics and Art History," *The Art Bulletin* 73/2 (1991): 174–208.

[9] Felbecker, *Die Prozession . . .* p. 30. She focused primarily on processions for Corpus Christi and Palm Sunday, avoiding a fuller treatment of reliquary processions, which she deemed sufficiently-treated elsewhere, although unfortunately she did not point the reader to any such treatments.

[10] Alain Dierkens, "Réliques et Reliquaires, Sources de l'Histoire Du Moyen Age?," in *Sainteté et Martyre Dans Les Religions Du Livre*, ed. Jacques Marx, *Problèmes D'histoire du Christianisme* (Bruxelles: Université de Bruxelles, 1989), p. 316. The capitulary on liturgy and sacraments treated issues of religious feasts, divine cults and cult objects, and directed that parish tithes were to be divided so that 1/3 went for *ornamentum ecclesiae*, (church decoration) 1/3 to pilgrims and paupers, 1/3 to the priests.

as is their complex hierarchy of size, quality, and type, bespeaking profuse ceremonial interests, beyond mere protective concerns.[11] Their uses in cult centers and their transportation out from those centers were at play in their proliferation and in their designs.

Visual drama in the liturgy[12] and the ritual address of spaces outside of the church building reflect passion for pageantry as a means of community expression of desire for, and belief in, the miraculous powers of relics—powers which were evidently enhanced by their ritual transport and display. This surge in spectacle is paralleled by the design of reliquary shrines and other cult objects, which became increasingly large and lavish, from the eleventh century on. (e.g. figs. 308, 312, 314, 315, 342) Earlier châsses, such as the ninth-century Enger Reliquary[13] were also richly decorated, but were much smaller, and demanded less visual attention. It would appear that the act of transporting relics dictated a more demonstrative emphasis on the shrine which housed the sacred companion of the community. A picture of a cohesive spiritual community emerges, in which groups traveled frequently, for homage, petition, or reunion, transporting the relics of their churches on their journeys. The items now treasured as objects of art were familiar liturgical equipment, which saw regular ritual use, especially for deployment in procession.

The concepts and practices of procession and of pilgrimage became increasingly intertwined, as both were concrete expressions of the same basic life-journey metaphor, albeit with sometimes different physical forms and goals. Often, the two practices were thoroughly associated, and even interchangeable. Group pilgrimages were regular, customary rites, often carried out in processional form, and processions expanded to emulate longer pilgrimages, and they also accrued pilgrimage-site goals, especially other churches or monasteries, as stations or as end-points. In the medieval era when urbanism burgeoned and a desire for spiritual expression by the individual in community flourished, procession was available as concept and as practice, amenable to modification and re-interpretation, for meaningful assim-

---

[11] Heinrich Denzinger et al., *Enchiridion Symbolorum, definitionum et declarationum de Rebus Fidei et Morum* (Freiburg-im-Breisgow, Herder & Co., Edition 21–23, 1937). Fourth Lateran Council, 1215, Cap. 62: "de *reliquiis sanctorum*."

[12] See Miri Rubin, *Corpus Christi: The Eucharist in Late Medieval Culture* (Cambridge: University Press, 1991) and Tekippe, "*Procession, Piety, and Politics*".

[13] In the Berlin-Dahlem Kunstgewerbemuseum. See in Peter Lasko, *Ars Sacra 800–1200* (New Haven: Yale University Press, 1994), figs. 10, 11.

ilation into the corpus of devotional practice. In both rites, the movement through space and time was a symbol of the transformation of the pilgrim/marcher, seeking transcendence, and physical or spiritual healing/miracles.[14] Physical accoutrements intensified and augmented the experience, both during and after the event.[15] The anagogical and allegorical experience of celestial kinship and harmony was the ultimate processional and pilgrimage goal.[16] In this spiritual climate, procession with reliquary shrines became more common and shrines representing the presence of the saints in their communities became larger, more elaborate, and more visually prominent in the ritual.

Several levels of analysis of the processions with reliquaries are possible, and the rites and shrines functioned on more than one level at a time—providing a rich mix of impetus and effect. While some scholars[17] have differentiated processions as festal and penitential types, or by their purposes as expressing something or in making something happen,[18] the complexity of the marches is lacking in such categories. Sabine Felbecker described those which are "expressions of something" as components of celebration, while those held to make something happen were aimed at influencing the future in either apotropaic or soothing ways. While procession may be further seen as evidence of an active cult in a particular locale, we must seek more definition and explore its history to appreciate its significance.

---

[14] Simon Coleman, and Elsner, John, *Pilgrimage Past and Present: Sacred Travel and Sacred Space in the World Religions* (Cambridge: Harvard University Press, 1995), p. 6.

[15] Coleman and Elsner *Pilgrimage Past and Present*... (p. 6) noted that pilgrimage is, in some measure, "... as much about returning home with the souvenirs and narratives of the pilgrim's adventure ..." as it is about the trip and its physical goal. Interrelationship of holy objects, architecture, and rituals in the experience, and such tokens extend the influence of the sacred site, by stimulating memory and desire for repeated experiences.

[16] Paul Rorem, *Biblical and Liturgical Symbols within the Pseudo-Dionysian Synthesis*, vol. 71, *Medieval Studies and Texts* (Toronto: Pontifical Institute of Medieval Studies, 1984).

[17] F.L. and E.A. Livingstone Cross, ed., *The Oxford Dictionary of the Christian Church* (Oxford: Oxford University Press, 1997), "Procession."

[18] Felbecker, *Die Prozession*, p. 33.

Terminology and Accoutrements

One reason for scant data on the practices is their largely extra-liturgical character as rites. There are rubrics for processions performed as part of the Mass, but those which featured relics were not dictated by canonical forms. While "extra-liturgical" rites were extensions of the liturgy, in the sense that they served the same beliefs and hopes, they were less rigorously delineated and often more localized. Some records indicate concerns with filial obligations to parish or diocese or with abuses and excess in non-standard devotions. Following the widespread reforms of the high Middle Ages, there were frequent inclusions of relics/reliquaries in the regular liturgy—signifying the participation of the enshrined saint in community events. In Germany, from at least the twelfth century, reliquaries were featured in various liturgical processions, both within and outside the churches, on the feasts of Good Friday,[19] Christmas, Epiphany,[20] and Palm Sunday.[21] In later periods, processional embellishment of the liturgy became increasingly frequent, as at St. Servatius Church in Siegburg where, by 1789, an *ordo* prescribed processions for twenty-five different feasts—many of them including stations, or visitations to neighboring communities.[22]

The roots of these observances[23] bear further exploration, as does verbal description, since accounts of customary practices of ceremonial conveyance of relics are illuminating with regard to terminology. In many documents, the standard relic containers were called *fiertes*, a French adaptation of the Latin *feretrum*—a litter or bier used in ceremonies, especially religious rites,[24] and related to Anglo Saxon

---

[19] Xaver Haimerl, *Das Prozessionswesen des Bistums Bamberg im Mittelalter* (Hildesheim: H.A. Gerstenberg, 1973), p. 22.

[20] Mauritius OSB Mittler, *Betrachtungen Studien und Untersuchungen zum Siegburger Kirchenschatz*, vol. XXIII, *Siegburger Studien* (Siegburg: Respublica-Verlag, 1991), (p. 56), noted reliquaries in liturgical processions at Siegburg and other Benedictine houses, included arm reliquaries, Staurotheques, *capsa*, etc.

[21] Stephan Beissel, *Die Verehrung der Heiligen und Ihrer Reliquien in Deutschland im Mittelalter*, Unverand. reprograf. Nachdr. der im Verl. Herder erschienenen, Original-ausg., 1890 u. 1892/mit e. Vorw. zum Nachdr. von Horst Appuhn. Darmstadt: Wissenschaftliche Buchgesellschaft, [Abt. Verl] ed. (Freiburg im Breisgau: Herder, 1892), p. 2.

[22] P. Gabriel Busch, *St. Servatius und der Michaelsberg: das Ehemalige dekanat Siegburg* (Siegburg: Verlag Abtei Michaelsberg, 1987), pp. 57–69.

[23] Tekippe, "*Procession, Piety, and Politics*". Appendix A.

[24] Sometimes fiètre or fiertre. *Dictionnaire d'ancien français—Moyen Age et Renaissance*. Paris: Librairie Larousse, 1947. Also used is the Latin *scrinium*: chest, box.

ferian—to convey and *faran*—to travel[25] or as châsse, or capsa—the feretory, chest, or box for carrying a body, more specifically, the relics of a saint, in procession.[26] Feretory is also described as an ornate bier or shrine for relics and, by extension, as the chapel in which it was kept.[27]

The records in which these terms appear flesh out our knowledge of processions. Ninth-century councils issued documents[28] encouraging commemoration of saints' feastdays (without clearly specifying processions), and it became customary from the Carolingian era on, to divide relics and put the greater portion into an easily-transportable chest, as when Hincmar of Reims had a châsse made, specifying that it be easy to carry.[29] It is reasonable to infer that the raising of the relics from the tomb was performed so that they could be moved about. The tenth-century *Continuator Regionis* speaks to the availability of containers with greater transportability, specifically for the relics of Servatius.[30] Conversely, the *Book of Sainte Foy* relates obstacles to carrying the treasured relics out of their protected environment, and subjecting them to claim by a more powerful institution and thus loss: moreover the monks would have less control in recording miracles and fewer opportunities to ask reciprocation for favors, but for processions they did relinquish a measure of control,[31] as St. Foy was brought out on numerous occasions.

---

[25] Webster's *New Collegiate Dictionary*. Springfield, 1961.

[26] Domino Du Cange, ed., *Glossarium Mediae et Infimae Latinitatis* (Paris: Léopold Favre, 1954 (originally c. 1680)). *feretrum* which he defines as *capsa* or *arca*, rather than litter.

[27] *Webster's New Collegiate Dictionary*. This usage seems more common in England than on the continent, as far as I can determine.

[28] Nicole Herrmann-Mascard, *Les Reliques des Saints: Formation Coutumière d'un Droit*, vol. 6, *Société D'histoire du Droit: Collection D'histoire Institutionelle et Sociale* (Paris: Éditions Klincksieck, 1975), pp. 173, 198–9. The custom of ceremonial transportation of relics is traced to at least the seventh century, to a decree from the Council of Braga (675), which condemned bishops who allowed carrying relics around the necks of levites during the solemnities of the feasts of martyrs (showing that relic processions were normal for such occasions). See also Martin Heinzelmann, *Translationsbericht und Andere Quellen des Reliquienkults* (Turnhout: Brepols, 1979), p. 39.

[29] Herrmann-Mascard, *Les Reliques des Saints:* . . . . p. 197.

[30] Renate Kroos, *Der Schrein des Heiligen Servatius in Maastricht und die Vier Zugehörigen Reliquiare in Brüssel* (München: Zentralinstitut für Kunstgeschichte, 1985), p. 342.

[31] Kathleen Ashley and Pamela Sheingorn, "'Sainte Foy on the Loose', or the Possibilites of Procession," in *Moving Subjects*, ed. Kathleen Ashley and Wim Hüsken (Atlanta: Rodopi, 2001), pp. 54–5.

A tenth-century shrine consecration formula from a Cologne Cathedral customary specifies the deployment of portable reliquaries against a variety of evils: "the vessel . . . made ready . . . against the devil and his angels, against lightning and storms, against hail and various plagues . . . evil beasts . . . against evil men plotting evil deeds."[32] Many shrines had separate bases, litters, or biers[33] to facilitate transport, as shown in a panel from a 1580 bust reliquary of St. Servatius, showing the translation of St. Valentinus. (fig. 331) The relics of Servatius were paraded through the streets of Maastricht, in both celebration and petition, earning the twelfth-century châsse[34] the nickname *Noodkist* or need chest, because to the citizens of Maastricht, it represented their hope for help from above, and was frequently brought out in the face of danger. The reliquary shrines were apparently never carried about without the accompaniment of certain liturgical accoutrements, including the cross and candles, and various other objects, so the display was always somewhat elaborate.

Liturgical processions used ordinary liturgical equipment, such as the processional cross, candleholders, censers, and the aspergillum, but the accoutrements proliferated in the context of extra-liturgical rites, both in the number of accessories employed and in the addition of types, such as the châsses, canopies, statues, pluvials, and group garb and insignia, which then found their way back into the standard collections of liturgical equipment. The origins of both the expanded processional form and the profusion of apparati are obscured, but that they evolved in concomitance is apparent. That they were believed to cooperate for ritual efficacy and for devotional expression is also patent.

Felbecker posited a processional purpose of sanctification of an outer space, by means of externalization from the sanctified inner space, accomplished in part by taking along items and effects which serve sacred purposes in the sanctuary, and provide means for sanctification.[35] The transmission of the sacred into the profane space

---

[32] Kroos, *Der Schrein des Heiligen Servatius in Maastricht*, p. 344. From Köln, Dombibliothek cod. 141, fol. 109rf. "*vasculum . . . praeparatum . . . contra diabolum et angelos eius, contra fulmina et tempestates, contra grandines et varias pestes . . . malas bestias . . . contra malorum hominum adinventiones pessimas.*"

[33] See Albert Lemeunier in this volume for mention of provision of litters in the Huy records.

[34] For the image, see Kroos, *Der Schrein des Heiligen Servatius . . .* fig. 44.

[35] Felbecker, *Die Prozession*, p. 470. There is no single or absolute sacred space

may blur distinctions which limit the experience of the divine in the terrestrial realms, with the somewhat artificial boundaries between "holy" and "other than holy" precincts. Pilgrimage and processions with relics aimed to overcome these differences, both by changing space and by altering mentalities. The Church understands itself as being in a state of pilgrimage, as a people on the way to God, interpreting itself as in motion. This gives insight into the symbolism and corporeality of the liturgy, including the elements of movement, display, and play. In these aspects, procession—liturgical or extra-liturgical—is a means of expression by the people on the way and in view.[36]

Cumulative Visual Effects; Shrine Gestalt; Dynamic Presence of the Saint

The processions in which large and lavish late medieval châsses were featured must have been remarkable events, although they went largely unrecorded. All of the equipment, like procession itself, was intended to be impressive, attractive, and to pictorially convey messages about the saint whose remains were housed in the *fierte*, in relationship to the community who transported them. There were decidedly political connotations in many shrine programs and in the ways they were used. And each accoutrement had particular ritual connotations,[37] with the cross ubiquitous, and candles having the most universal meaning. But even these often took singular forms, expressive of specific communites as distinct from others—some were favored gifts commemorative of giver or occasion, while others were reliquaries themselves.[38] Perhaps most richly-varied were relic containers for a

---

in the earthly realm, but the sanctification can be extended beyond the church precincts, into the city, and diffused, although, ultimately, it lay beyond the world, so the participant remains restless until reaching the final goal outside this realm. This is surely based on Augustine.

[36] Felbecker, *Die Prozession*, p. 27. This characterization is not restricted to this one author, though.

[37] Tekippe, "*Procession, Piety, and Politics*," Appendix B.

[38] Exemplary is the Byzantine cross at Tournai, Paul Rolland, *Histoire* de *Tournai* (Tournai, 1956), p. 76. This richly-jeweled piece (eighth or ninth century) was a gift of Emperor Baudouin IX of Constantinople. Rolland reports that, as Count of Flanders, Baudouin, and his wife, Marie de Champagne, had attended the 1095 procession in Tournai, and credits him as possible donor of the funds for the châsse of Notre Dame.

saint favored by a given community—each so distinctive that they conveyed the very individual ongoing presence of that saint amidst their devotees, with pronounced messages to communicate.[39]

If the head reliquary was intended to convey a sense of a portrait-like presence, and the arm signified the ongoing power of greeting and blessing by the saint,[40] the coffin size châsses would suggest the continuing presence of the saints in their corporeal entirety, and this implied custody of the complete saint[41] is significant for the community, providing a gestalt of group identity and a palladium for many purposes. While some were designed to emulate the funerary coffin, they also have architectonic emphasis—and the thirteenth-century works of this genre resemble church architecture specifically, approaching Gothic architectural form. In both the casket and the church building emulation are implications of the Heavenly Jerusalem, where the saint has joined the celestial court in divine adoration, and can serve as intercessor for the living, both in mundane matters, and, more importantly, at the Last Judgment. These works also have certain qualities and imagery by which they call attention to themselves and their own significance,[42] and I would contend that the same observation should be made about procession itself as an art form. Yet there are few medieval accounts of the experience of these shrines *in situ*, and fewer still of the visual impact they had as they were moved through different environments, so this is a matter for extrapolation. But, since this impact was surely among the paramount concerns in creation of the works, it is worthy of careful hypothesis.

Most frequently, processional or group pilgrimage events are recounted as being led by the clergy, who went with their cross, banner, and candles, and often, with their relics. The Verviers procession to Liège (on Pentecost Tuesday) was headed by three men: one car-

---

[39] There are details of many shrine programs discussed elsewhere in this volume, in essays by Van den Bossche, Cerisi, Abend-David, Lemeunier, and Neuchterlein.

[40] Cynthia Hahn, "The Voices of Saints: Speaking Reliquaries," *Gesta* XXXVI/1 (1997); Barbara Drake Boehm, "Body-Part Reliquaries: The State of the Research," *Gesta* XXXVI/1 (1997), Barbara Drake Boehm, "Medieval Head Reliquaries of the Massif Central" (Ph.D. diss., New York University, 1990).

[41] Although there is often an inconsistency between container and contents.

[42] See Jeanne Neuchterlein's comment on this, elsewhere in this volume, and her tale about the abbot who was chastised for not providing a suitable container for relics he had been given.

rying the cross, from which a bourse was suspended, and two with banners—one with an image of their city patron, St. Remaclus, the other, the arms of the city. Front ranks also often included city officials and the newly-married of the parish. The green silk bourse contained the offering during the excursion to Liège, while, on the return trip an exchange gift (incense).[43]

The banner, whether or not it bore the cross emblem, was a traditional insignia for the Church, particularly in processional rites.[44] By the late Middle Ages, customary banners with images of the saints seem to have also given rise to the use of small *drapelets*, which perhaps eventually supplanted badges awarded to pilgrims in some areas,[45] and identified march participants. With ancient roots in the vexillum, or battle standard, the banner served as rallying point—a fitting symbol for community members processing together, underscoring the profoundly traditional nature of these rites.[46]

Many accounts create an impression that the transportation of relics/reliquaries was part of overall custom for these events, an expected and routine part of the ritual. Narratives indicate there was nothing unusual about the inclusion of the relics, nor any special instructions for their deployment—listing them along with the cross and banners was sufficient. The foremost arena for innovation was

---

[43] Aug. Neyen, "De l'Origine et du But Véritable de la Procession Dansante d'Echternach," *Bulletin de l'Institut Archéologique Liégeois* XV (1880), p. 230. This discourse on the practice describes a late form of the custom, which may not reflect earlier medieval practice, but since the event is traced back to the thirteenth century, it is considered to have its origins in the custom of *bancroix*.

[44] R. Naz, *et al.* (eds.), *Dictionnaire de Droit Canonique, Contenant Tous les Termes du Droit Canonique, Avec un Sommaire de L'histoire et des Institutions et de L'état Actuel de la Discipline*, 7 vols. (Paris, 1935–65): *Banniere*. He noted cross-currents between civil and ecclesiastical connotations so common in medieval use in the oriflamme of France, kept in St. Denis, and carried into battle. Some descriptions imply that the image of the cross appears on the banner, or that both cross and banner were mounted on the same standard, rather than being separate liturgical objects. This is documented in the sixth century by Venantius Fortunatus, and in the seventh century in Rome, becoming customary in the feudal era for both civil and ecclesiastical purposes.

[45] These two inexpensive types of souvenirs co-existed for a long time, and the drapelets, while popular on the continent, were not in evidence in England. Personal communication, Sarah Blick.

[46] R. Naz, *Dictionnaire de Droit Canonique.... banniere, ban*, refer to the *drapeaux* for marching or stationary troops—their standard or vexillum. See also Emile Henri van Heurck, *Les Drapelets de Pèlerinage en Belgique et dans les Pays Voisins: Contribution à l'Iconographie et à l'Histoire des Pèlerinages* (Anvers, 1922).

the design of reliquary containers and the replaceable decorative covers for châsses or biers. Some accounts of relic quests to raise funds comment on the inclusion of châsses as containers and on their visual aspects. While sometimes moved on harnessed carts,[47] reliquaries were generally carried on decorated litters, often with embroidered covers for the shrines, and there were costumes for the shrine-carriers—all increasing the ceremonious atmosphere of these events.[48] In Corbeny in 1102, the châsse of St. Marculf was carried on an elegantly-decorated litter,[49] while for a 1364 foray out of Tournai, the châsse of Notre Dame (fig. 308) was specified as the main inspirational feature.[50]

The use of fragrant and beautiful flowers, smoking incense, instrumental music, hymns, and Psalms—all associated with procession from antiquity—was expanded, enhancing physical and emotional excitement. The rhythmic movement of the cortège, a sort of ritual march or dance, perhaps joined to music or song, provided another very dynamic outlet. A generalized impression of lavish magnificence, ceremony, and festive celebration was sought, at least when the processional event was commemorative, as opposed to a supplicatory occasion. Even then, a solemn atmosphere of amplified dignity was joined to the petition to honor God and the saints.[51]

There were also means to control the displays, including the careful arrangements and ordering of groups and objects, and using such devices as veils and canopies, as means of disclosure, or emphatic framing. The restriction of rites to certain days and times also

---

[47] Pierre and Marie-Laure Chastang Héliot, "Quêtes et Voyages de Reliques au Profit des Églises Françaises du Moyen Âge," *Révue d'histoire écclesiastique* LIX, LX (1964–65), p. 819. He reported cases in 1333 of Notre Dame of Amiens and the College of St. Quentin in 1451 and 1484. In 1463, three horses were used at Noyon to pull coffers with the châsses.

[48] Héliot, *Quêtes et Voyages*, pp. 77–8, 814. The number of personnel in the quest cortège was not as great as in feastday processions, but a fair-size company usually was involved—twelve to twenty, generally—for porters, guards, etc. Preachers were often included so that they could extol the virtues of the saint, in the interest of encouraging generosity.

[49] Héliot, *Quêtes et Voyages*, pp. 811–3.

[50] J. Warichez, *La Cathédrale de Tournai et Son Chapitre* (Wetteren, 1934), p. 82. Héliot, *Quêtes et Voyages* also cited this quest for Tournai.

[51] Felbecker, *Die Prozession*, pp. 608–9, discussed these effects, noting that, for all possible goals of the occasion, there was a perceptible generosity and a readiness for lavishness.

enhanced the experience, lending a sense of value and rarity and, in its own way, functioned as veiling and disclosure.[52]

Although visual reflections of the rites are not numerous until later centuries, imagery in various media across the centuries gives a general impression of means, customs, effects, and expectations. A panel from the sixteenth-century bust reliquary of St. Lambert, (fig. 332) may be taken to reflect long-standing practice, where some imagery of ritual events may be based on the visual effects of co-eval procession, such as the depiction of the translation of relics in the thirteenth-century portal sculpture at St. Benoît-sur-Loire, Fleury, (fig. 333) the twelfth-century representation of the Entry of Christ into Jerusalem at St. Gilles du Gard, (fig. 334) and the thirteenth-century funeral of the Virgin at Strasbourg.[53] In addition, some images of cultic processions seem to record current practice with shrines, such as that of St. Firmin at Amiens. (fig. 116) One of the most important visual records of the practice in Tournai is the frieze on the west façade of the cathedral.[54] (fig. 335) Whether these sculptures represent the Grand Procession or some other event in Tournai, they furnish valuable information, confirming the importance of the processional rite in this community, with the reliquaries from the cathedral.

Along with all the art objects, the moving aesthetic is a signifier in itself—a gestalt of the life journey, as is pilgrimage itself. In each

---

[52] Felbecker, *Die Prozession*, pp. 553–6. The action of the ritual revelation of interior, hidden elements, seen in such articles as the winged altarpieces and the *vierge ouvrante* statues, as well as in the post-Lenten unveiling of interior church decorations, had its counterpart in the bringing out of the reliquaries, statues, and other liturgical objects, for procession from the church through the city streets.

[53] Anton Legner, *Deutsche Kunst der Romanik* (Munich, 1982), fig. 14.

[54] Elizabeth Schwartzbaum, *The Romanesque Sculpture of the Cathedral of Tournai* (Ph.D. diss., New York, 1977), Appendix II, maintained that the sculptural reliefs were created in 1300 and restored in a late-sixteenth/early-seventeenth-century style, after they were viciously damaged by the Protestants in 1566. Nathalie Vermaut, "La Grande Procession sur les Sculptures du Porche," in *La Grande Procession de Tournai (1092–1992) Une Realite Religieuse, Urbaine, Diocesane, Sociale, Economique et Artistique* (ed.), Jean Dumoulin; Jacques Pycke, *Tournai—Art et Histoire* (Tournai, 1992), pp. 61–2 proposed dates ranging from 1400 (based on stylistic and iconographic similarities to *Les Tres Riches Heures du Duc de Berry*) to *c.* 1600 ("romanizing, antiquizing" approach to garments and heads), while seeing differences among various panels. Vermaut, "La Grande Procession Sur Les Sculptures Du Porche," believed that it is a generalized or specific depiction of the annual Grand Procession. I agree with Schwartzbaum's dating. See also Cecelia Gaposchkin in this volume for the portal sculpture at Amiens. For further analysis of these reliefs, see Tekippe, "*Procession, Piety, and Politics*," pp. 274–6.

instance, the accumulated works and aspects had complicated and dynamic messages to convey, far surpassing the effects which accrued to groupings of objects, of clergy, rulers, citizen/pilgrims, united in physical movement. In the process, the aesthetic elements are subordinated to the whole, and the aesthetic qualities of the whole may be uneven, and not of primary value. The occasion of procession was always a remarkable event in some regard. Whether the rite was conducted for joyful or serious purpose might have affected the perception of any associated aesthetic values, as well.

In the centuries prior to the Reformation, an ever-increasing number of extra-liturgical processions fed the appetite for visual demonstration (*Schaubedürfnis*),[55] while also providing a variety of other stimuli—both sensual and spiritual. A primary instance of ostentation was the elevation of the host during the Mass, elaborated in the medieval period,[56] but many practices associated with display and use of reliquaries were also predicated on a desire by the faithful to have a visual experience and a physical proximity to the recipients of their veneration. This expansion included not only the emergent variety of reliquary types and sizes, but also many other sensual stimuli—all of which worked together to produce an insistent, aggregated embellishment of the ritual expression. Growth of the populace, and consequent divisions and subdivisions, led to adoption of costumes, banners, placards, and equipment, as means of group identification, and additional sensual stimulation. The extension of the decoration into the processional space expanded the ambience of festivity.[57]

Occasions and their Meanings

Processional transportation of relics was performed for regular and special occasions, with differences in form and implications. Examination of regular rites—liturgical or extra-liturgical—helped to define

---

[55] Christopher S. Wood, "Ritual and the Virgin on the Column: The Cult of the Schöne Maria in Regensberg," *Journal of Ritual Studies* 6/1, Winter (1992), pp. 100–1.

[56] Rubin, *Corpus Christi*, p. 78, Felbecker, *Die Prozession*, 175, Tekippe *Procession, Piety, and Politics*, Ch. 6.

[57] Many accounts relate the cleaning and decoration of streets and houses along the march routes.

meaning and purpose. As a festal expression, procession was known from the early centuries of the Church, with roots in pre-Christian antiquity.[58] There was a definitive change in liturgical emphasis in the West during the ninth century, whereby the participation of the laity in ritual decreased, while the roles of the clergy were more strongly emphasized, and the forms showed a tendency to become increasingly fixed. As van Tongeren noted ". . . the form and content disagreed with the religious experience of the community. After all, the liturgy did not come from the faithful, and, moreover, the religious experience of the community developed, in contrast to the liturgy, which did not respond greatly to popular sentiment."[59] These circumstances created a matrix in which the expression of faith by the laity through procession became increasingly prolific, and expansive.

Translations as Models

The promotion of regional saints in the face of papal intervention in sanction of cults also influenced relic processions. The primary means of canonization throughout the early and central Middle Ages had been the elevation of the relics from the grave, instigated by the most immediate community of veneration. From the seventh century on, the bishop's role and dominion increased, as they emphasized the value of their recognition of a cult, as an authorization and endorsement. Translation of the relics to a devotional site was part of the essential recognition of that person as a saint, and often constituted the second phase of the *elevatio*, up to the twelfth and thirteenth centuries, when these rites were gradually supplanted by control of the process by the papacy,[60] but not without considerable resistance from bishops. The battle for control was definitively settled with the decree *De reliquiis et veneratione sanctorum* by Boniface VIII in

---

[58] Tekippe, "*Procession, Piety, and Politics*," Appendix A.

[59] Louis van Tongeren, "A Sign of Resurrection on Good Friday. The Role of the People in the Good Friday Liturgy until C. 1000 A.D. and the Meaning of the Cross," in *Omnes Circumadstantes: Contributions Towards a History of the Role of the People in the Liturgy* (eds.) Charles Caspers and Marc Schneiders (Kampen, 1990), p. 101.

[60] Pierre André Sigal, "Le Voyage de Reliques au XIe et XIIe Siècles," in *Voyage, Quete Pelerinage Dans La Litterature et La Civilisation Médiévales* (Paris, 1976), p. 75.

1298, that established clear, systematic processes for canonization—standardized for all dioceses, with ultimate control in Rome.[61] There is no evidence of papal canonization before the tenth century,[62] and there was considerable theological controversy when Rome inserted itself into the process. By the eleventh century, the bishop's role weakened, as Rome asserted its right of jurisdiction.[63]

Many early reports of procession were associated with the translation of relics from the grave site to a cult center, or with ensuing re-locations. (The 1074 transfer of some relics of St. Quentin from Vermandois to Beauvais was decreed a processional occasion and one in which they were received by Bishop Guy of Beauvais, and by all of the châsses of the city.)[64] It is important to consider translation separately as a seminal type, and as a model, which was often commemorated through later processional rituals. The translations were extremely influential, not only for the form of transportation of relics for other purposes, but also for the encapsulation of conceptual significance which they present. This point of solemn, ceremonial acknowledgement of the relics as signifier of the saint in the community was crucial in the establishment of the cult. The relics of

---

[61] Eric Waldram Kemp, *Canonization and Authority in the Western Church* (London, 1948), pp. 109–10.

[62] Kemp, *Canonization and Authority*, p. 147.

[63] Herrmann-Mascard, *Les Reliques des Saints*, pp. 73–4, 91, noted that and, at one stage, at the 1120 Synod of Beauvais, a number of bishops demanded that the elevation, under their control and supervision, remain the definitive act for recognition of sanctity, but the statement was one of protest, accentuating their increasing loss of control. In many locales, an intermediate phase in the shift of power included the requirement of approval by a metropolitan or by a diocesan synod for recognition of a cult. Also at stake, although perhaps to a lesser degree, was the "power of the keys"—which was interpreted by some to give the bishop the full and ultimate authority of administration within his own diocese, as well as the final say in the matter of judgment and remission of sins. This issue seems pointed in the program of the Servatius shrine, where the power of the keys is definitively attributed to the saint as bishop, and additional emphasis is linked to the distinctions between secular, ecclesiastical and priestly powers. It may also be at play, generally, in all the shrines whose bishop/saints are depicted in the court of the apostles, with implications of participation with the apostles in the Last Judgment. Benson wrote that the twelfth-century *Summa* of the theologian Rufinus was concerned with these same quarrels, especially as they affected the contest for temporal power which was interwoven here—and which erupted in the strife with secular rulers, as well. Robert L. Benson, *The Bishop-Elect: A Study in Medieval Ecclesiastical Office* (Princeton:, 1968), pp. 74–5, noted because many bishops also wielded great temporal power, the questions were quite complex. See also Tekippe, *"Procession, Piety, and Politics,"* ch. 5.

[64] Herrmann-Mascard, *Les Reliques*, p. 196.

Juste had been translated, with great ceremony, to Malmedy 940–80,[65] and were soon included in the litanies at Stavelot.[66] The cult of Quirinus has accounts relating the solemn cortège for a translation of the relics of this saint and of several others in a châsse, from Condé, near Paris, to Malmedy, in 808, with stops along the way and a great many miracles. Upon arrival at Malmedy, a pilgrimage was organized,[67] and a *scrinium novum Rogationem* was created so that the relics of Quirinus could be easily carried for the Rogation Days processions, for blessing of the field work and the crops.[68]

Relocation of the relics of St. Eleutherius, in their châsse, from his resting place at Blandain to the city of Tournai in 1064 included a grand cortège of clergy and faithful, led by Bishop Baudouin, to the great exultation of the whole city, and affirmed by the occurrence of many miracles. Such surge in display and spectacle is often paralleled by elaboration of the designs of the shrines themselves, with newer, larger containers replacing existing ones. The relics of Remaclus at Stavelot drew pilgrims from near and far.[69] The first transportation of his relics, according to Heriger's *vita*, and the *Miracula*, was at the time of the *elevatio*, June 25, 685, when Abbot Goduin disinterred the body, and placed it in a gold and silver châsse "of great price,"[70] which was then transported from the oratory of St. Martin to the new abbey church and placed behind the altar of Peter and Paul. While this is not described as a procession *per se*, it seems unlikely to have been accomplished without ceremony.

---

[65] Sylvan Balau, *Les Sources de l'Histoire de Liège au Moyen Age: Étude Critique* (Brussels, 1982), p. 95.

[66] Philippe George, *Les Routes de la Foi en Pays Mosans IVᵉ–XVᵉ Siècles* (Liège, 1995). p. 4.

[67] Philippe George, "Stavelot & Malmedy: Monachisme & Hagiographie en Ardenne (VIIᵉ–XIIᵉ Siecles)" (Ph.D. diss., Université de Liège, 1993), p. 227. The other relics were of Nicaise, Scuvicule, Mellance, and Ouen, all verified by the clergy at Rouen. Organized with the help of Archbishop Hildebald of Cologne and King Charles, the chief account was in the *Translatio Malmundarium et Miracula sancti Quirini et aliorum*, c. 1062.

[68] Philippe George, "Documents Inédits sur le Trésor des Reliques de l'Abbaye de Stavelot-Malmedy et dependances (IXᵉ–XVIIᵉ Siècles)" (1987), p. 71.

[69] (ed.) B. Krusch, "Vita Remacli Episcopi et Abbatis," in *MGH SS Rer. Merov T.V.*, V. p. 92; Tekippe, *"Procession, Piety, and Politics,"* Benoît Van den Bossche, "La Châsse de Saint Remacle À Stavelot (Étude Iconographique de Bas-Reliefs et Statuettes)" *Aachener Kunstblatter*, no. 58 (1989–90) for discussion of possible successive châsses for Remaclus.

[70] François Baix, *Étude sur l'Abbaye et Principauté de Stavelot-Malmedy*, vol. 6 (Brussels, 1981), p. 50.

The translation was, to some extent, commemorated with each subsequent procession, as signifier of the patronal relationship of saint to devotees, reiterating that the local community kept the memory of the saint alive, for all practical purposes. When some saints were favored with universal recognition through the support of Rome, while others were not, the local community and its devotion were crucial. This was also the key to the preservation of reliquaries, which, in most instances, only survived the French Revolution and other such vicissitudes because they were cherished as the houses for the saints by the specific communities who took pains to protect them from assault and destruction. The many celebratory processions are also evidence of this same esteem and care. Moreover, those communities were linked in many other aspects of the sustenance of the cult. The management of the precious treasures, including liturgical and cult objects, was an important responsibility which fell to those who administered the church's assets. In 852, the Council of Reims ordained that churches carefully conserve the resources of altar decorations, books, relics encased in precious containers, crosses, sacred vessels, and priestly vestments—all the accoutrements of cult.[71]

Regular Processions:
Liturgical Feasts: Sunday, Pentecost, Palm Sunday, Rogations

Regular types of liturgical procession embedded in the Mass were part of Sunday observance in most churches, although not always with equal regularity, but they were indicated in the statutes of the Synods of Cambrai and Tournai of 1277 and 1301.[72] There were also smaller marches to carry the viaticum and to perform Extreme Unction, to carry the body of the deceased from home, for stages of funeral rites, for many annual feasts (fixed and moveable), marches for kermesses and fair openings, the feastdays of patron saints, and for the *ommegangen* (walking the bounds) of the village territory, which became the model for Corpus Christi observances.[73]

---

[71] M. (Chanoine) Dehaisnes, *Histoire de l'Art dans la Flandre, l'Artois & le Hainaut Avant le XVe Siècle* (Lille, 1886), p. 17. This sense of duty is reflected in the article by Albert Lemeunier in this volume.

[72] Toussaert, *Le Sentiment Réligieux en Flandre*, p. 245.

[73] Toussaert, *Le Sentiment Réligieux en Flandre*, p. 245.

Numerous processions accentuated the Easter season, during Holy Week and the extended Paschal celebration, beginning in Lent.[74] Palm Sunday marches, rooted in Christ's Entry into Jerusalem, accrued the display of relics and other features over the centuries. From the Merovingian era in France and Germany, several churches were accustomed to carry the Gospels and phylacteries with relics on this occasion.[75] The time around Pentecost accrued perhaps the greatest number of processional and pilgrimage rites—appropriately for a feast which marks the birth of *Ecclesia* as a solemn occasion, commemorating the consecration of the Church under the invocation of the Holy Ghost[76] as well as the mission of the Church in evangelization. Medieval theologian Johannes Beleth described this as a fitting period for procession and pilgrimage, since it falls within Eastertide, with its symbolism of Resurrection and the movement toward the eternal celestial life.[77] Moreover, many processions were customary at Pentecost, coinciding with the synods which were often held at this season and because the fair weather was favorable.[78]

Rogation Days were processional occasions, in customs traced to 474, when Bishop Mamertus of Vienne (Gaul) instituted the practice as a plea for divine help in agricultural concerns, after an earthquake

---

[74] Sylv Balau, *Chroniques Liégeoises* (Brussels, 1913), I, p. 479, citing Jean d'Outremeuse' 1307 chronicle for Liège.

[75] Herrmann-Mascard, *Les Reliques des Saints*, p. 197. According to Beissel, *Die Verehrung der Heiligen*, p. 2, they were included in a Palm Sunday procession in Augsburg by 973 and in Rogation Days processions in Marburg, noting the participation of St. Elizabeth, so occurring in the early thirteenth century.

[76] Auguste Neyen, "De l'Origine et du But," pp. 236–7. According to Ursmer Berlière, "Les Processions des Croix Banales," *Bulletin de la Classe des Lettres de l'Académie royale de Belgique* VIII, 5e série (1922), p. 438, the feast of Pentecost was pivotal in the practice of *bancroix* and related processions. Jean Paquay, "Les Antiques Processions des Croix Banales À Tongres," *Bulletin de la Société Scientifique et Litteraire du Limbourg* XXI (1903), p. 156, projected the celebration of Pentecost as integral to the custom, providing a core feast.

[77] Kroos, de*r Schrein des Heiligen*, p. 177. Paquay, "Les Antiques Processions," p. 134 also noted the Pentecost offering customs among French parishes.

[78] Berlière, "Les Processions," pp. 426, 432–3, 438. Gaposchkin, elsewhere in this volume, also noted the processions at Pentecost in Amiens. Pentecost was featured in some writings as a time for the commemoration of the dead, as by Benedict of Aniane (745–821), Isadore of Seville († 636), Alcuin († 804), and Amalaire († 853), according to Michel Lauwers, *La Mémoire des Ancêtres, Le Souci des Morts, Rites et Société au Moyen Age (Diocèse de Liège XIe–XIIIe Siècles)* (Paris, 1997), p. 99, in concert with the performance of processional rites.

and the destruction of the palace by lightning.[79] To seek divine mercy, Mamertus imposed a fast and called for three days of procession and chanting just before the Feast of Ascension.[80] For the Diocese of Tongres/Maastricht/Liège, the custom of Rogations procession through the fields by the bishop, clerics, crowds of the faithful, and the relics of the saints, is recounted as early as the eighth century in the *vita* of St. Hubert[81] In the thirteenth century in Bamberg Diocese, the observances were expanded into three-day, multi-part pilgrim marches, with several stations, which acknowledged the larger, interconnected community.[82] Rites at Strasbourg, lasted several days and involved several saints, with similar customs for Ascension, with a tour going around the city.[83] In the tenth century at Corbie, an anonymous sermon on Rogations referred to processional rites as integral to the observance of all these feasts.[84]

Promotion of such practices was echoed in many concilar decrees,[85]

---

[79] Terence Bailey, "Processions, Liturgical," in *Dictionary of the Middle Ages*, (ed.) Joseph R. Strayer (New York, 1982). Jean Leclercq, "Rogations," in *DACL*, (ed.) Henri Leclercq Fernand Cabrol (Paris, 1948), also recounted this event.

[80] Leclercq, "Rogations."

[81] Herrmann-Mascard, *Les Reliques des Saints*, p. 198. This probably represents a later interpolation, perhaps from—the late tenth–early eleventh century, so may represent custom from that era. See *Vita S. Huberti* in *MGH SRM* vol. VI, p. 486.

[82] Haimerl, *Das Prozessionswesen*, pp. 9–10.

[83] Herrmann-Mascard, *Les Reliques des Saints*, p. 198.

[84] D. de Bruyne, "L'origine des Processions de la Chandeleur et des Rogations— a Propos d'un Sermon Inédit," *Revue Bénédictine* 34 (1922), p. 23. This general type of procession, called a lustration in Roman times, a purification rite, involved contact with the area to be purified. Various authors make ths connection. de Bruyne tells of the connection between pagan and Christian forms being treated by various early- and high-medieval writers, including Bede, 725, Rhabanus Maurus, 819, Jean Beleth, *c.* 1160, Innocent III, late 12th century, and Durandus de Mende, 1286, but cites those who say that probably all later ones were based on Bede's writings (which may themselves be conjectural), so do not represent separate evidence or opinions, in effect. De Bruyne's general argument revolves around an anonymous sermon for Rogations, from the 10th century from Corbie, (which he cites only as # 18296, f. 81, Bibl. Nat. Paris). This sort of contact was adapted in the Candlemas procession and Rogation Days processions (re-fashioned from the Ambarvalia), aimed at seeking blessings for the fields and the crops. According to D.R. Dendy, *The Use of Lights in Christian Worship*, vol. 41, *Alcuin Collections* (London: 1959), p. 180 (from PL: LXXXVII, 602) a sermon attributed to St. Eligius († 660) tells us that "Each period of five years was called a lustrum because . . . the Roman people assembled for a sacrifice and purified the city of Rome with candles and religion of faith. Once the city of Rome was purified (*lustratur*) every five years, towards the end of February . . . now every year at the beginning of the month the whole city of God, that is the Holy Church, is lit up (*illustratur*)."

[85] Leclercq, "Rogations. in *DACL*; Cross, *Rogations*. Orleans 511, Gerone 517, Tours and Lyons 567, Braga 572, Toledo 636, and Clovesho, 747.

and for Rogations Days, the faithful were to refrain from work, creating the sense of a feast day, which later became the standard for days of procession. The march was accompanied by recitation of litanies—lists of petitions and invocations of the saints' names—and although other types of songs and chants were voiced, the association of procession and litany is very strong. Such invocation of the saints might have furthered the impetus to carry along the relics in processions, especially when coupled with antique practices of carrying along trophies and symbols of favor or power. This valuation also showed in cult centers and pilgrimage to them. Related customs accrued to Ascension season: tours of Angers featured relics of several saints, as at Hirsau, while at Chartres, the thirteenth-century feast's procession included the Gospel book, borne on a litter.[86]

Trinity Sunday, Corpus Christi

The processional feast of Corpus Christi emerged in the thirteenth century in the Diocese of Liège, as had that of Trinity Sunday in the tenth century[87]—in a region where large reliquary shrines were created and widely seen. A penchant for local devotional tenor was manifest in such cult display and visual spectacle. This apparent saturation provided a fertile seedbed for evolution of the processional celebration of the Body of Christ as the consummate relic—which clearly arose in the framework of existing practices.[88] The Eucharist was also increasingly included in reliquary processions, perhaps inspired by the Corpus Christi rites, but also by the widespread elaboration of this ritual genre.[89]

---

[86] Herrmann-Mascard, *Les Reliques des Saints*, p. 198. See also James Bugslag's essay in this volume.

[87] Stephanus Axters, *The Spirituality of the Old Low Countries*, trans. Donald Attwater (London, 1954), p. 12. The feast was instituted by Stephen of Liège († 920) for his diocese and he wrote an office for its celebration.

[88] Boogaart, "Our Saviour's Blood," pp. 73–4, cited the incorporation of elements of various customs, arising from a matrix of local processional practices, including Holy Cross rites customary at Bruges, and other elements from the Gallican rites. See also Rubin, *Corpus Christi*; Carole Heitz, "Architecture et Liturgie Processionale À L'époque Pré-Romane," *Révue de l'art* 24 (1974); Haimerl, *Das Prozessionswesen*; Felbecker, *Die Prozession*; Dendy, *The Use of Lights*; Tekippe, "*Procession, Piety, and Politics*," pp. 240–5.

[89] Busch, *St. Servatius und der Michaelsberg*, p. 19.

At Tournai, a separate Corpus Christi feastday procession, documented in 1566, was referred to as a customary observance, including the transportation of the *fiertes*. By the same token, the inclusion
of various devotional objects in the Corpus Christi processions, such
as relics, chalices, statues, and other images, became the norm in
many locales. Corpus Christi celebrations demonstrated the desire
for ritual address of spaces outside the church building, making a
circuit which began in the church and returned to it, as opposed to
an elaborated entry which began outside and used the church as an
endpoint. This distinction is important—describing the difference
between many relic processions and regular liturgical ones. In these
more elaborate shrine processions was not only the apparent desire
for pageantry but also community expression of desire for the miraculous powers of the Host and of relics (especially in ritual). That
Christ as signified by the cross which led the procession was not as
potent a symbol as his Real Presence in the Eucharist is also implied
by the embrace of the Corpus Christi as a separate feast.

Extraliturgical/Regular Types: Annual Events: Rationale and Purpose

Perhaps the most predominant way procession was used was for
commemoration of some event significant in salvation history, with
its earliest example in Exodus.[90] This memorial function made the
performance of the rite self-referential and created a constant reminder
of all other Christian processional events and the journey of every
Christian soul. Carrying relics in processional rites increased in the
Rhine-Meuse Valleys, and neighboring regions, in the latter half of
the tenth century.[91] They evolved into singular rites for re-enactments,
thanksgiving, feasts and offerings, as more or less direct reflections
of liturgical aspects, while affirming relationships among ecclesiastical and civic subgroups. These extra-liturgical processions were more
fluid and subject to a greater range of expression and interpretation
than was possible in the more canonical forms associated with the
Mass. While there are specifications given for personnel, equipment,

---

[90] Flanigan, "The Moving Subject," p. 36.
[91] Herrmann-Mascard, *Les Reliques des Saints*, pp. 197–9.

and order of various liturgical processions, these matters were locally and individually determined for extra-liturgical events.[92]

Anniversary / Commemorative / Thanksgiving

Contemporary visual experience may have influenced the representation of past historical events such as the translation of St. Stephen in the eleventh century *Echternach Pericopes*. (fig. 334) In depicting such translations, often for claiming or repatriation of a favored patron, the artists could draw on what they commonly saw, although present events *per se* were rarely recorded visually (until they became legendary). The ceremonial re-location of relics often produced miracles along the way, as when the monks of St. Benoît brought the relics of Sts. Benedict and Scholastica from Italy to Fleury, inducing the sick to rise from their beds as the relics passed by, as commemorated on the eleventh century portal of the abbey church. (fig. 335) Processions were also performed to announce fealty and for thanksgiving for favors granted, and to fulfill associated pledges, illustrated by the commemorative rites at Tournai, Stavelot, Lierneux and elsewhere.[93]

The châsses of the Virgin Mary (fig. 308) and of St. Eleutherius (fig. 314), and other ritual objects at Tournai, were kept in the choir and visited by the faithful for prayers of joy, sorrow, petition, and thanksgiving—and carried out of the cathedral precincts on many occasions each year, marked by the sounding of the great bell, a profusion of lights, and solemn chants, etc.[94] These rites were not

---

[92] Colin Dunlop, *Processions—a Dissertation Together with Practical Suggestions, Alcuin Club Tracts* (London, 1932), p. 20, described such customaries as that in use at Salisbury (Use of Sarum), which include diagrams for the different events, as local adaptations of the Roman Rite.

[93] Busch, *St. Servatius und der Michaelsberg*, pp. 17–8. The 1183 *Mirakelbuch* of Siegburg reported a procession instigated in response to the miraculous revival of five citizens who were struck by lightning, wrought by the touching of St. Anno's relics to their lifeless bodies. Simultaneously, the house fire that injured them, ignited by the lightning, was extinguished, and the weather calmed, as were the hysterical crowds which witnessed the calamities. A procession of thanksgiving was organized, featuring the five revived people, the Blessed Sacrament, and the relics of Anno, and was repeated again by all the citizens on the next feastday of the Assumption, with the added feature that the five each carried a five-pound candle, decorated with Anno's name and flowers, and made donations.

[94] J. Warichez, *S. Eleuthère, Premiere Évêque de Tournai* (Wetteren, 1931), p. 64.

simply religious, for the saints were invoked for diverse civic, political, and social events.[95] The early history of procession in Tournai
apparently began during Eleutherius' life (455–531), according to the
vitae, when he returned from Rome with relics of St. Stephen and
St. Mary of Egypt, greeted by a solemn cortège of clerics in festive
garb.[96] The 531 funeral cortège of Eleutherius, led from the martyrdom site at the cathedral to the burial site at St. Peter's in
Blandain.[97] The ninth-century elevation and translation were followed
in the eleventh century by a re-location procession of the relics to
the cathedral and in 1092 by a dramatic processional plea for relief
from the plague. Reported efficacious against the epidemic, it was
re-enacted in gratitude annually thereafter, as well as in other times
of need, distress, and celebration.[98] Featured in the first procession
were the "precious chests from the cathedral, which had contained,
for some thirty years already, the relics of Eleutherius and other
saints,"[99] indicating the fabrication of reliquaries about the time of
the translation.[100]

Like many processions, the event at Tournai centered around a
number of distinctive medieval works of art including the Shrine of
Eleutherius. Typically, over time, the body of works accrued notable
additions which became integral to the fabric of visual spectacle of
the event, while certain items fell into disuse. The oldest processional
object is probably the richly-jeweled Byzantine cross reliquary which
was carried by a priest, sometimes under a baldacchino.[101]

Croix Banals

A particular group of processional customs known as *croix banals* or
as *bancroix* is the most closely linked to pilgrimage, because these

[95] Warichez, *S. Eleuthère*, p. 64. As Alfred Cauchie, *La Grande Procession de Tournai*
(Louvain, 1892), p. 5, observed, to study the history of the procession is to study
the history of all Tournai's institutions, and of its social, political, and religious life.

[96] Joseph Warichez, *Les Origines de l'Église de Tournai* (Louvain, 1902), p. 113.

[97] (ed.) Guiberto, *S. Eleutherius Tornacensis Episcopatus*, vol. 65, *Patrologia Cursus
Completus. Series Latina* (Paris, 1801), p. 74.

[98] There is dispute as to whether the first procession was in 1090 or 1092, since
plague is known to have been a problem in this region from 1089 on, but the 1092
date has gained general acceptance by tradition.

[99] Dumoulin, *La Grande Procession*, p. 16.

[100] Both châsses were replaced in the thirteenth century.

[101] Dumoulin, *La Grande Procession* for this object and others at Tournai.

group rites were performed with the goal of visitation to an esteemed center at some distance from the point of origination.[102] These gave a specific processional form to bringing obligatory annual offerings of filial churches to their mother church. Accounts and directives for these now-obscure practices often mentioned the carrying of relics as part of the observance, thus they are persuasive as evidence of frequent reliquary transportation. These rites not only formalized the gesture of offering, but also emphasized the relationship between a parish and its bishop or its mother church.[103]

The required offerings (generally bread, cheese, and money),[104] subject to episcopal ordinance, were due from each household in a parish. Related processional customs,[105] involved a census tax of

---

[102] Manfred Van Rey, "Les Divisions Politiques et Ecclésiastiques de l'Ancien Diocèse de Liège au Haut Moyen Age," *Le Moyen Age* LXXXVII (1981), pp. 194–6. They are also referred to as *droit banal, bancruces, vulgo cruces, sinodali banno, cruces bannales,* and *bancroix*. See also Manfred Van Rey, "Die Lütticher Gaue Condroz und Ardennen im Frühmittelalter: Untersuchungen zur Pfarrorganisation," *Rheinisches Archiv* 102 (1977); A. Vanrie, "Les Croix Banales aux Abbayes en Belgique au Moyen Age," *Contributions à l'histoire économique et sociale* II (1963). J.P. Migne, *Lexicon Manuale ad Scriptores Medie et Infime Latinitatis* (1866). (ed.) Du Cange, *Glossarium Mediae et Infimae Latinitatis.* and *Medieval Latin Wordlist,* among others. These imply a variety of underpinnings. The *croix* refers to the Christian character of the rite, to churches from which processions emanate, to ecclesiastical rights or properties, to the cross-symbol carried at the head of the procession. The cross was apparently, sometimes,on a pastoral banner or a banner hung from the cross—which may supply the *banal* element of the title. However, this term *banal* is interpreted by some to be rooted in the legal geographic designation of *bannum* for an ecclesiastical or civil district—hence, also the terms *Pflichtprozession* and *Bannfahrten,* emphasizing the legalistic, obligatory aspects of the rites. *Banal* also may be interpreted as "common," signifying an ordinary duty incumbent upon parishes each year. It does seem that medieval accounts play upon the potential for ambiguity in the appellation. The linguistic terminology is unclear, as are the roots of the custom, although they may have begun in Belgian lands. Nikolaus Kyll, *Pflichtprozessionen und Bannfahrten Im Westlichen Teil des Alten Erzbistums Trier,* vol. 57, *Rheinisches Archiv* (Bonn, 1962), p. 16 cited two meanings for the term *bann* or *bannum,* the first referring to an inscribed geographic area, the second to the rights associated with the area so inscribed. Léopold Genicot, *Rural Communities in the Medieval West* (Baltimore, 1990), p. 62 described it as founded on the German legal notion of *bannum,* the right of ordering and prohibiting under penalty of sanction. Vanrie, "Les Croix Banales," p. 24 pointed out that not all parishes had such filial connections with abbeys, and not all filial churches made the *croix banal* processions. It might also be true that not all abbeys or collegial churches had filials. For full discussion of terms, see Tekippe, *Procession, Piety, and Politics,* pp. 215–39.

[103] Kyll, *Pflichtprozessionen und Bannfahrten,* p. 76.

[104] George, *Stavelot & Malmedy,* p. 123; Van Rey, "Les Divisions Politiques," p. 192.

[105] Associated with *obole de feu (obolus ignis, vuurgeld, Kreuzpfennige).* Paquay, "Les Antiques Processions," pp. 127–96.

money incumbent upon serfs, or the bringing of rents by tenants.[106] All of these duties customarily involved the annual ceremonial transportation of the offerings, with the parish relics, on a prescribed day.[107]

The concept of the relationship of the bishop to his diocese in the early Church was that of a pastor to his parish, and this model was maintained as numbers of the faithful increased and the see was subdivided, for it remained the ultimate parish for all, with the bishop as overall pastor.[108] The ideal of unity of the people and clergy, especially the bishop, was clear, as priests were obliged to celebrate the main feasts with the bishop,[109] perhaps in the interest of continuing the parochial sense of the larger community. Although the original charge was incumbent upon the clergy[110] rather than the laity,[111] over time, it evolved to require a more active role for all the faithful. In the *Decretals*, Gratian discussed the importance of the relationship of the individual to his parish church, especially the one in which he was baptized,[112] so the matrix in which the *bancroix* evolved

---

[106] Paquay, "Les Antiques Processions," cited a 1139 charter at St. Trond which described the *obole de feu* as income from serfs of the abbey, who came from the parish of St. Marie at Tongres, while a 1202 charter with a seal of Gui de Palestrine (Limbourg Diocese) distinguished the *obole banale* from annual offerings by parishes, which they carried, along with *croix banal* offerings to their conventual churches.

[107] Berlière, "Les Processions," p. 424.

[108] Traced to a decree of the Council of Clermont in 535, by Bishop Domitian of Tongres, who was reputed to have ruled in the sixth century the Diocese of Tongres/Maastricht/Liège. His shrine, another of the large châsse-type reliquaries, was created *c.* 1172, and is conserved at Huy. See the article by Albert Lemeunier in this volume.

[109] Berlière, "Les processions," p. 428, Kyll, *Pflichtprozessionen und Bannfahrten*, pp. 19–21. Similar decrees were issued at the Councils of Agle in 506, Auvergne 535, Epion 517, and Orleans 511, and the obligatory visitation custom was also known in Trier Diocese as early as the sixth century. According to Berlière, p. 425, in the thirteenth century, a Picard *curé* preached a sermon which encouraged his parishioners to join in the annual pilgrimage to the cathedral, to go in procession there. Jean Leclercq, "Paroisses Rurales," in *DACL* (ed.) Henri Leclercq (1948), pp. 22–32, noted that some rural parishes disappeared because they refused to pay required imposts to their bishop, monastery, or collegial church, losing their rights to continue in service despite their apparent prosperity and wealth.

[110] The ancient requirement to make pilgrimages *ad limina (apostolorum)*. Paquay, "Les Antiques Processions," p. 167.

[111] Leclercq, "Paroisses Rurales," p. 2218.

[112] Anthony Melnikas, *The Corpus of Miniatures in the Manuscripts of decretum Gratiani*, 3 vols., *Corpus Picturarum Minutarum Quae in Codicibus Manu Scriptis Iuris Continentur* (Rome, 1975), vol. II, p. 433.

was apparently an extension of the sense of the familial models of early Christianity. So, too, evangelizing abbeys and collegial churches responsible for fostering new parishes, had filial bonds and associated duties of reciprocal homage and material support.[113]

Some such processions also expressed gratitude for concessions, privileges, and exemptions from the sovereign, such as St. Willibrord at Echternach, who abolished the degrading tasks of the plebs, replacing them with "pious works and gentle offerings"—thus, the annual pilgrimage derived from the benevolent disposition engendered in subject communities and parishes toward the saint who had released them from feudal exactions.[114] Willibrord, founder of many parishes, was viewed as both spiritual and temporal lord, with the right to receive fealty and use duties.[115] Such generosity was descriptive of other patron saints at the mother churches—notably, Remaclus at Stavelot—known to have freed slaves, and Servatius at Maastricht—during whose processions, prisoners were released.[116] The beginning of the *bancroix* custom in Maastricht was linked to the annual pilgrimages by the faithful to Servatius' gravesite, by 726.[117]

The earliest firm documentation of this *bancroix* custom appears in the early ninth century.[118] It was believed to have been a widespread

---

[113] Paquay, "Les Antiques Processions," pp. 157, 160. It is not clear that reasons for choices were spiritual at core, as some scholars posit a civil basis, in the beginning, for fealty, under a feudal system,—a type of regalian or seigneurial right (according to Kyll, *Pflichtprozessionen und Bannfahrten*, p. 78, with the bishop as landed overlord) which lingered into the later Middle Ages. The offering pilgrimage from Verviers to Liège was hypothesized as rooted in the exemption from *tonlieu*, due as a market fee, as much as loyalty to the mother church,—while those at Lobbes, Hachez, and Bormans might have supplanted such antique customs as the old Roman processions. See Vanrie, "Les Croix Banales," p. 19; Neyen, "de l'Origine," p. 242; Van Rey, "Les Divisions Politiques," p. 194; Tekippe *Procession, Piety, and Politics*, pp. 215–39.

[114] Neyen, "de L'origine," pp. 239–40.

[115] Neyen, "de L'origine," p. 236. The pilgrimage to Echternach included the peculiar custom of jumping/dancing. While some believe that the procession goes back to the seventh-eighth centuries, I find this dubious, in light of the other discussion here.

[116] Tekippe *Procession, Piety, and Politics*, pp. 308–9. This was customary at other locations, as well, and was known as the "the privilege of the fierte" at Rouen.

[117] Beissel, *Die Verehrung der Heiligen*, p. 122.

[118] Neyen, "de L'origine," p. 240, stated that the Echternacht procession began in the seventh or eighth century. In the eighth and ninth centuries the original parishes into which the dioceses had been divided were further subdivided, making it a logical period for the institution of the *croix banal* districts and consequent incipience of offering customs. Charters from the tenth and eleventh centuries

practice by the tenth century in France, England, Belgium, and
Germany, requiring parishioners to return to the mother church,
with their parish standard (*croix banal*) and relics and offerings.[119] An
1139 Bull of Innocent II stipulated that the procession include a representative from each household in the parish,[120] and several documents refer to the event as taking place in Pentecost week.[121] Pilgrims
were expected to take part in worship and listen to a sermon at the
mother church, as expression of their filial duty and unity.[122]

Not surprisingly there were a great many *bancroix* processions in
the Diocese of Liège, (heart of the Rheno-Mosan country)—the most
extensive see in the Middle Ages, with the greatest number of ecclesiastical institutions,[123] including many parishes located at considerable distance from the bishop's church, a circumstance which would
create greater affinity between the parish and an institution of authority which lay closer to home.[124] The practice of celebrating feasts
differently with the bishop is also mentioned in Tournai Diocese
records for the annual exposition of the *fiertes* and the cross reliquary
in the town market during the 1226 Pentecost offering period. They
were carried in solemn procession from the cathedral to the marketplace, accompanied by candlebearers and the communal magistrate.[125] An adjunct to practices at Tournai, by the fourteenth century,

---

describe the associated processions as being instituted by the bishop in an earlier
epoch, going back to a *"date immemoriale."* Van Rey, "Les Divisions Politiques,"
p. 201; Tekippe, *Procession, Piety, and Politics*, pp. 229–30.

[119] VDB, "des Processions Banales," *Collection de précis historiques—Mélanges litteraires
et scientifiques* XVII (1868), pp. 326–7; Kyll, *Pflichtprozessionen und Bannfahrten*, p. 15.
This offering ritual was ordinarily a processional occasion, perhaps in remembrance
of the practice known at Jerusalem at Pentecost, where the faithful returned to the
temple to the sound of trumpets, with the fruits from their fields.

[120] Vanrie, "Les Croix Banales," p. 15.

[121] Paquay, "Les Antiques Processions," pp. 158–9.

[122] Haimerl, *Das Prozessionswesen*, pp. 16–17. Paquay, "Les Antiques Processions,"
p. 161, fn. 3. From the *Ordonnances de la Dame de Dalhem*, 1345, 1353. The accounts
noted that the relics were then exposed for veneration in the middle of the church
at Aachen and at Tongres, also pp. 131, 161, fn. 1. This may describe the type
of outing which this author would describe as *obole banal* rather than *croix banal*, but
for my purposes here in establishing the practice of processing with relics, such distinctions are not crucial. Tekippe, *Procession, Piety, and Politics*, p. 235.

[123] Vanrie, "Les Croix Banales," p. 22.

[124] Vanrie, "Les Croix Banales," p. 20. There was a great number of large
Benedictine houses there of very ancient foundation—viewed as divine instruments
in the *premiers foyers d'evangelisation*, according to Van Rey, "Les Divisions Politiques,"
p. 193.

[125] (eds.) J Dumoulin, T. Hackens, J. Pycke, *La Croix Byzantine du Trésor de la*

involved the placement, alongside the reliquaries in the market place, of an oath book, brought along for pilgrims coming to make their offerings. The book also accompanied the relics when encouragement to participate in the procession was preached in diocesan churches, and was lent to parishes when the châsse of Notre Dame was carried there for visits.[126] The full implications are unclear, but there is an association of oath and obligatory offerings.[127]

Income from these offerings led to competition among monasteries and colleges of canons for the offerings from parishes, as well as for attention and prestige.[128] Some records which give definition to *bancroix* customs result from settlement of disputes among houses vying for the right to be processional goals, such as Tongres. There are also tales of bribes and gifts made to parish priests in hopes of luring them to a particular abbey.[129] Such competition is related to the known rivalries between such establishments as cult center pilgrimage goals.

By the tenth century, the faithful from Famenne made processional pilgrimages, to bring offerings to Remaclus at Stavelot.[130] Often the crowds included many of the ill, who were placed before the altar of the saint, in hopes of miraculous healings, as was also their custom when they came for the feasts of John the Baptist, June 24[131] or that of the church dedication June 25.[132] The *Miracula* account infers that these processions were a long-standing custom by the eleventh century.[133] The serfs of Stavelot also came annually with

---

Cathédrale de Tournai, Publications d'Histoire de l'Art et d'Archéologie de l'Université Catholique de Louvain (Tournai, 1987), p. 16.

[126] (ed.) Jean Dumoulin, *Trésors Sacrés* (Tournai, 1971), p. 43, cat. no. 7.

[127] Dumoulin, *La Croix Byzantine*, p. 15. In 1226 offerings (apparently were of food) were so numerous that some were resold to raise funds for construction costs at the cathedral. Tekippe, *Procession, Piety, and Politics*, p. 220.

[128] Vanrie, "Les Croix Banales," p. 16.

[129] Vanrie, "Les Croix Banales," p. 16.

[130] Berlière, "Les Processions," p. 436.

[131] Berlière, "Les Processions," p. 438.

[132] François Baix, "L'Hagiographie à Stavelot-Malmedy" *Revue Bénédictine* LX (1950), p. 140.

[133] George, *Stavelot & Malmedy*; anonymous, "de S. Remaclo Conf. et Episc. Trajectensi Ac dein Abbate Stabulensi," in *Acta Sanctorum Quotquot Toto Orbe Coluntur* (1863), *Miracula* I:123. George took exception to Berlière's description of this occasion as fitting the category of *croix banal*, but that is not crucial here. If anything, it would indicate that there were other types of frequent and customary processions to Stavelot, in addition to those under consideration.

offerings on the feast of Remaclus,[134] and they joined the pilgrims on that saint's feast and on other occasions, with numbers increasing over time, as its fame spread, with visitors from as far away as Lombardy.[135] It was a center of a *croix banal* district, with parishioners visiting from all over Belgium and Luxembourg (from Famennes, Theux, Sart, Glain, Verviers, and Lierneux.)[136] Stavelot had a great number of rural parishes for which it held the rights to bestow benefices and to receive tithes, because they had been founded during past eras by the monastery, and continued under its jurisdiction.[137]

The frequent accompaniment of the parish relics for these processions/pilgrimages is of the greatest interest, but the accounts of the events lack sufficient detail to reconstruct an accurate visual description of the events. Moreover, not all accounts relate the inclusion of relics or their containers. It seems reasonable to assume, however, from the number and variety of extant reliquaries from many centuries, and from records in other circumstances, as well as the rubrics for handling the relics, that in most cases they were part of the rite. A great number of records do mention the relics prominently, including the earliest account of the *bancroix*, in the *Miracula Huberti, c.* 850, which recorded a procession of parishioners from Andage, to bring oblations to St. Hubert, led by their clergy, cross, and relics.[138] The *Annals* of Trier Diocese reveal that Archbishop Egbert, in 983, prescribed carrying the local relics as co-leader, with the pastor, for those processions, reiterated in an early twelfth century account, in the same record.[139] A description of procession from

---

[134] *Miracula* I:106; George, *Stavelot & Malmedy.*

[135] *Miracula* I:103, 117.

[136] Van Rey, "Les Divisions Politiques," p. 197, citing the *Miracula* and (eds.) Joseph Halkin and C.G. Roland, *Recueil des Chartes de L'abbaye de Stavelot-Malmedy*, 2 vols. (Brussels, 1909, 1930), #154:310.

[137] George, *Stavelot & Malmedy*, I, pp. 118–9.

[138] Dierkens, "Réliques et Reliquaires," pp. 326–7. A number of other authors cite this instance, as well.

[139] Similar descriptions are noted for Luxembourg in 1284, by Archbishop Bruno. A 1619 document lists twenty-six parishes which went to Munster. Kyll, *Pflichtprozessionen und Bannfahrten*, pp. 40, 125–6 Others are cited by him p. 84. "... *rogationes cruciumque et sanctorum reliquiarum gestaciones per circuitum vallis Treberica ab omnibus, qui sunt in sua parochia.*" (MGH SS VIII:S170) An 1128 document from Pope Honorius II confirms a privilege to Munster Abbey for parishioners who visit on the Friday after Misericordia Sunday, with their relics and oblations. Alberon II, Bishop of Liège, at an 1139 synod, decreed that residents of Diest (one per family) must return to St. Trond each Pentecost, with their relics, to make offerings at the main altar,

St. Matthias to Trier Cathedral June 29, 1150 (feast of the cathedral patron) notes that it was performed with relics and litanies.[140] An 1170 charter by Pope Alexander III grants a concession for parishes to go to the monastery at Andennes, specifying that the oblations of the faithful be taken in procession, with cross and relics.[141]

Cologne records from 1190 disclose that parishioners from Kirchherten and Bergheim were to process to the cathedral with their relics, which they placed upon the altar of St. Peter, when they brought a money oblation.[142] A 1391 document specified that the Chapter of Tongres be the goal of annual *bancroix* processions of a notable person from each family in the parishes of Freeren, Nederrhein, Wihogne, Paifve, and Heure-le-Tiexhe, who would come on Pentecost Friday to offer the *obole*, with their cross and relics. It further relates that they would process to the stone gate, where the clergy would meet them with a cross and holy water,[143] the customary ceremonial greeting afforded to visiting relics, as to visiting dignitaries.

Accounts generally refer to priests, banners, relics, and other insignia.[144] The cross was the most important and eloquent symbol for all.[145] Yet, the predominant visual effect was that of the procession itself, both as an event and as a signifier. Still, the relics of a saint would have particular import for parishioners with whom he traveled. Kyll posited that the saint was a legal entity, in a sense—a leading representative of the parish, integrally involved in the obligatory

---

by filial obligation. This decree specified that the faithful were paying alms which St. Trond had promised, and that they proceeded into the church, to the altar of St. Trond, to place there money offerings (*oboles*) for their hearth (*foco*). The *gesta Treverorum* (before 1132–52), described the *Bannfreitag* procession of all parishioners, including the cross and saints' relics.

[140] Kyll, *Pflichtprozessionen und Bannfahrten*, pp. 74–5. "... *cum reliquis et letaniis* ..."

[141] (eds.) Jean-Patrick Duchesne, Dominique Allart, Pierre-Yves Kairis, *Mélanges Pierre Colman, Revue des Historiens de l'Art, des Archéologues, des Musicologues et des Orientalistes de l'Université de Liège* (Liège, 1996): *cruces*.

[142] Kyll, *Pflichtprozessionen und Bannfahrten*, p. 124.

[143] Paquay "Les Antiques Processions," p. 134.

[144] Paquay "Les Antiques Processions," pp. 135–40. A 1401 ordinance in Liège officials required parishioners of Lens-sur-Geer, as a mother church, to go in procession, along with members of its filial churches, to Tongres on Pentecost Tuesday, as reported in the oldest archives of Notre Dame of Tongres, while various other churches and their filials were specified for each day of Pentecost octave—Monday through Sunday. Seventeenth-century accounts report transport of statues by some groups.

[145] Kyll, *Pflichtprozessionen und Bannfahrten*, pp. 126–7.

aspects of the pilgrimage. This saint participated, in the form of relics/sacred vessel or image, along with the priest and nobility, honored as leader of the ritual visitation, as described as a traditional solemn custom of the Gallic people in the *Miracula* of St. Matthias of Trier (1150).[146]

However, in relation to the *bancroix* processions as part of the familial structure of the diocese, it is necessary to also consider the regular obligation of the bishop to go out for visitation of his parishes, with a two-fold patriarchal duty: the *visitatio hominum*, whereby the shepherd looked after his sheep, and the *visitatio rerum*, which was concerned with proper stewardship.[147] In this latter capacity, the bishop would inspect the revenues and administration of the parish, and (more to the point here) the physical goods—buildings, furniture, decorations, and liturgical equipment, including reliquaries. Such episcopal visits were similar to the filial pilgrimages in their ceremonial form, with the accompaniment of cross and relics. The *bancroix* processions with parishioners paying filial visits with certain of the physical goods may also represent inverted episcopal visitation, in much the same way that processions out of the church can be seen as inverted pilgrimages.[148] Often, these were not actual trips to the parishes, but set up at deaneries or other "overseer" churches, where the prelates would receive representatives from regional parishes. Parish delegations included cures or vicars, and often, important parishioners.[149] This is significant in that the theoretical framework of medieval religious sojourns obviously included variegated processional forms reflecting filial interconnections within the dioceses and may not always fit into clear categories.

Reinforcing Relationships

Other processions and pilgrimages had the primary or subsidiary aim of showing fraternity or mutual regard or common goals for

---

[146] Kyll, *Pflichtprozessionen und Bannfahrten*, p. 124 (MGH SS VIII:s.231). The *bancroix* procession fell into disuse in the late Middle Ages in most areas, according to Vanrie, "Les Croix Banales," pp. 16, 27.

[147] Noël Coulet, *Les Visites Pastorales* (Turnhout, 1977), p. 31.

[148] Discussed by Cecelia Gaposchkin elsewhere in this volume and by me in *Procession, Piety, Politics*.

[149] Coulet, *Les Visites Pastorales*, p. 32.

groups traveling with their relics to meet one another, sometimes at places far away from home for each. The Reims episcopal chronicles of Dadon of Verdun (880–923) describe a ceremony in which the relics of St. Boudri were carried from the monastery of Montfaucon to meet with those of St. Jovin.[150] The meeting of two important saints, in their relic forms, became one of the customary reasons for transportation and it was not uncommon to see the reconciliation of enemies induced by such solemn processions.[151]

Since practices associated with relics and reliquaries generally simulated the thaumaturgic methods available when the saint had been in life,[152] the faithful sought to be in the proximity of the châsse as it passed by, or to touch it, much as they sought contact when they visited the relics at the cult center.[153] The physical presence was not simply symbolized—rather physical activities and contact of all sorts were sought and prized—another reason why the bodily performance of procession and pilgrimage were valued.

Among the pronounced effects of both rites was the statement and reiteration of relationships, articulated by address of routes and goals, and by interactions among participants, explicating connections of religious groups, guilds, confraternities, and monasteries, and self-proclaimed Christian cities, as well as showing allegiance and the connections between sacred and profane spaces. This performative means of drawing lines could be a profoundly expressive statement of spiritual or ideological links.

The offering processions functioned on one level as a sort of courtly or neighborly gesture between churches, with the co-leadership of the cortège by the saints' relics as appropriate and symbolic.[154] As the saint was often considered the true owner of a church, its goods, and its lands, his authority was fittingly in evidence, especially when

---

[150] Pierre-André Sigal, *L'Homme et le Miracle* (Paris, 1985), p. 156; *Hist. Remensis Eccl.*, *MGH SS* XIII: 592–3.

[151] É. deMoreau, *Histoire de L'église en Belgique des Origines aux Débuts Du XIIe Siècle* (Brussels), vol. II, p. 405.

[152] Sigal, *L'Homme et le Miracle*, p. 42.

[153] (ed.) Pamela Sheingorn, *The Book of Sainte Foy* (Philadelphia, 1995), p. 124.

[154] Vanrie, "Les Croix Banales," pp. 17, 27, reported that the income from these offerings may have been a fairly insignificant portion of overall revenues for some of the abbeys, especially in the later Middle Ages.

carried in procession in a church-shaped shrine.[155] The character of relationships was at play in many processional occasions.

St. Roch, whose cult was centered in the Ardennes, near Stavelot, was an important goal for pilgrims seeking alleviation of illness. The citizens of Malmedy processed there annually with the monks from their monastery, praying for good health, while demonstrating their common affection for a distant saint and his cult center.[156] Such petition for protection was a common purpose for collective journeys, both on occasional and regular bases in this region. Some ritual pleadings were more specific,[157] like those for relief from particular illness or adverse weather. In Liège Diocese, there were more than 800 cult loci and at least twenty-six large reliquary shrines in the twelfth and thirteenth centuries,[158] many of which were carried on these journeys, or were goals for them, creating a network of inter-filial links.

There were times when several processional congregations joined together, each accompanied by their own relics, for elaborate communal celebration of feastdays, such as Palm Sunday or Rogation days; or members of smaller parishes would transport their saint to a larger cult center, or attend the consecration of a new church or cloister, as in 1070, when people from many cities and monasteries along the borders of Flanders came to Hagenau, with their relics, for the dedication of new living quarters.[159] Processional gestures of acknowledgement frequently provided sub-text for other types and purposes. The Pentecost Monday procession at Soignies (reported for 1262) was described as a "prayer march"—the Tour of St. Vincent (Magdelaire) pilgrimage, with a circuit through the town to the mill at Beaumont, across the river and pond, and fording the river.[160] Such address of local landmarks showed the blessing of temporal aspects of human life for the community.

---

[155] Joseph Milz, *Studien Zur Mittelalterlichen Wirtschafts- und Verfassungsgeschichte der Abtei deutz*, vol. 30 (Cologne, 1970), p. 67, proposed the Abbey at Deutz as probably also a *bancroix* goal, since it had so many dependancies and possessions on outlying properties, although documentation is lacking.

[156] Arsène de Noüe, *Études Historiques sur l'Ancien Pays de Stavelot et Malmédy* (Liège, 1848), p. 286.

[157] de Noüe, *Études Historiques*, p. 277.

[158] George, *Les Routes de la Foi*, p. 10.

[159] Beissel, *Die Verehrung der Heiligen*, p. 3.

[160] Paul Hazebroucq, *La Procession Historique du Lundi de Pentecôte* (Soignies, 1996), p. 3.

The choice of route could serve to acknowledge certain quarters, parishes, monasteries, and secular establishments as part of the community fabric. In Picardy, processions with St. Quentin traced circuits throughout the town, with stations which symbolized unification of disparate parts of the community, emphasizing their dependency on the Church and on the canons of the collegiate church.[161] While, theoretically, the processional route and the endpoint played no particular role in the physical sense,[162] it is clear that the choice of streets and roads, and the sites along the path were very important. These might recognize or affirm relationships between certain churches, businesses, guild halls, civic structures, and residential neighborhoods. This effect was noted for the connection between parishioners of St. Servatius and St. Michael's Monastery in Siegburg, to which they marched regularly, and in their annual ritual processions to Trier during Pentecost. The rubrics for this latter pilgrimage are found in the confraternity prayerbook, the *Matthias-Wallfahrer* (whose name hints at the ritual), as well as in other prayer- and song-books for the parish. The trip began with a four-day walk on foot, from Siegburg to Trier, with the return mostly by water, visiting specific stations along the way.[163]

Records at Tournai reveal considerations in choice of routes, at times, to accommodate the great numbers of participants and observers, and to control traffic flow and provide for safety. The route varied year to year, according to taste, needs, and politics. During war, the circuit was confined inside the walls, and in really harsh conditions, was limited to cathedral precincts, or the cathedral building. In times of peace, it was possible to process outside the walls, and even to extend the routes.[164] There were many participants from throughout the diocese, re-inforcing the sense of the cathedral church as

---

[161] Ellen M. Shortell, "Dismembering Saint Quentin: Gothic Architecture and the Display of Relics," *Gesta* 36/1 (1997), p. 38

[162] Felbecker, *Die Prozession*, p. 32.

[163] Busch, *St. Servatius und der Michaelsberg*, p. 164.

[164] Cauchie, *La Grande Procession de Tournai*, pp. 46–8, noted that the procession went, as a rule, around the city and its exterior, whenever possible, and went out the second valley gate and through the St. Martin Gate (p. 15). At the earliest period, according to Rolland, *Histoire de Tournai*, p. 48, the right bank of the Escaut was part of old Brabant, a region of Lotharingia, and was not considered part of Tournai, rather part of the Germanic Empire, while the left bank was within the realm of the French Empire. At that time, the river also separated the ecclesiastical domains of Tournai and Cambrai.

mother for all Christians within the diocese, who returned "home" for these events.[165] In some years, there were distinguished visitors from other cities, such as the shrines of St. Amand, St. Piat, and St. Steven, in 1626, and the addition of new types of participating groups over time,[166] as well as other processions in and to the city. In 1659, the parishioners from St. Niçaise celebrated the Peace of the Pyrenees by making a processional pilgrimage, with great pomp and enthusiasm, in costumes, with banners, standards, and images of the Seven Dolors of the Virgin.[167]

St. Piat, in his primary reliquary was carried in procession from Séclin to Tournai on two notable occasions, with great pomp. In a 1457 quest to raise funds for a new châsse, they were ceremoniously met by the shrine of Eleutherius. In 1626 they were brought to Tournai, to process through the city in petition for succor from a tenacious epidemic which afflicted Séclin.[168] It is clear that the atmosphere in Tournai was conducive to processional rites, encouraging the citizens, and their neighbors, to employ this means of communal expression for many purposes, and to create an outlet for spiritual, social, cultural, political aspects of life in the city, while creating significant opportunities for artistic endeavor, as well.

---

[165] Dumoulin, *La Grande Procession de Tournai*, pp. 74–6. The annual event at Tournai included three separate processions, by the fourteenth century, as the directives in the *Liber fabricae ecclesiae Tornacensis* indicate. Each of these events had a separate starting time, a different goal, and a distinct purpose.

[166] Rolland, *Histoire de Tournai*, pp. 89–90. In 1315, Louis X attended, and in 1353, a German doctor, Jean de Mayence. Artists and artisans of every type worked on the procession providing decorations and equipment and marching with their guilds. One of the chief industries was that of the cloth-makers, and the clerics drew upon their talents frequently for vestments and liturgical décor, as did the civil and political figures for their garb and paraphernalia, including fabricators and workers in metalwork, fabric, stone, arms & armor, porcelain, pottery, painting, tapestry, embroidery, damask, bells, cannons, sculpture, musical instruments, etc. Rolland credited the cloth trade with making Tournai a significant center for ceremonial events. Stoneworkers supplied the local ecclesiastical establishments with monuments and buildings. In the processions were such notables as André Beauneveu, who helped in the Grand Procession in 1392. Rogier Van der Weyden (known locally as Rogier de le Pasture), born in Tournai in 1399, was a noted visitor at the 1441 event, where he was praised as the official painter of Brussels. Van der Weyden's teacher was Robert Campin, *peintre ordinaire* of the city from 1410 credited as decorator of the *"châsse de la ville"* (*Damoiseaux*), creating the covering, and the banners for the group. The artists' Guild of St. Luke marched in the annual procession under the banner of their patron saint.

[167] Dumoulin, *La Grande Procession de Tournai*. The next day there was a pontifical Mass, a sermon, and various other ceremonies, after which they returned to Tournai.

[168] Warichez, *S. Eleuthère*, p. 19.

In 1509, a solemn procession at Stavelot was organized by Count Guillaume de Manderscheid, Abbot of Stavelot-Malmedy, to induce the recalcitrant county of Logne to submit to his authority. Despite the enmity of counter-claimants and heightened tensions, a contemporary account credits the count with pious intentions to soothe tribulations, by having the Stavelot monks go out of their abbey with the shrines of Remaclus, Babolene, and several other precious reliquaries, while the monks from Malmedy came there, with reliquaries of Quirinus, Just, Peter, and Philip, and, from Lierneux, parishioners with the relics of Symmetrus. The cortège was headed by the crucifer with the vexillis, candlebearers, other luminaria, an image of the Virgin, other images, the head reliquary of Pope Alexander, and followed by the several châsses, with the place of honor, at the end of the ranks, given to that of Remaclus.[169] They marched, chanting, around the village and church, then celebrated Mass and listened to a sermon. The three-day observance also included a popular procession through the countryside,[170] to articulate the wish for peace.

A dramatic march in Cologne was the twelfth-century funeral procession of Archbishop Anno II. The body of this controversial archbishop, renowned as a prolific builder and remodeller of church buildings, was carried in procession to each of the major churches in Cologne, over a period of several days, and finally buried in St. Michael's Abbey in Siegburg, in a monastery church which he had established. (fig. 337) This tour reaffirmed the bishop's accomplishments, and bonds he forged among the faithful.[171]

The reiteration of communal meaning and impact is also suggested through repetition of thematic elements, seen in the structure of medieval Rogation Days rites in Bamberg. On the first day, a theophorish procession led from the cathedral through the fields to the parish of St. Erhard, where Masses were offered, and those parishioners were joined by those from other churches, went on to St. Lorenz, for another Mass and sermon, and a circuit of the courtyard was

---

[169] A. Delescluse, "Une Procession à Stavelot en 1509," *Bulletin de la Société d'Art et d'Histoire du Diocèse de Liège* VIII (1894), pp. 367–70. Also discussed by Van den Bossche and others.

[170] A. Delescluse, "Une Procession a Stavelot en 1509," pp. 367–70.

[171] Günther Binding, *Städtebau und Heilsordnung—Künstlerische Gestaltung Fder Stadt Köln in Ottonischer Zeit* (Düsselforf, 1986), Anton Legner, *Monumenta Annonis: Köln und Siegburg Weltbild und Kunst Im Hohen Mittelalter* (Cologne, 1975). The route is shown in a diagram and the procession shown in an eighteenth-century version of his *vita*.

followed by a blessing by aspersion. On the second day, the procession with cross and relics went to St. Lorenz for Mass and then a procession led by the chaplain to neighboring villages, where the cross was handed over, and then they returned home in procession. The third day, they gathered to process to all of the nearby parishes, ending at St. Michael's. There was a very strong expression of belonging to the community for each member of the parishes and the collegiate churches, as these were stations of the march, and their members participated.[172] Potential for display of unity and fellowship was often exploited in both routine and extraordinary circumstances. The repetition of the links and bonds was effected in part by a sense of the sketching of lines by the processional route, designating and affirming space and boundaries. Processional rites repeatedly traced the routes between various churches in Bamberg and the cathedral, bespeaking their ties.

One of the aims of the regular processions at Tournai was the sanctification of secular space, a dissemination of holiness outward from the sanctuary, facilitated by images, relics, and candles. The processional routes as the lines of communication between the sacred and secular realms were reinforced by the transportation of these sacred objects and by the performance of sacred activities in the spaces outside the church precincts, exemplified at Tournai by the reading of the Gospels and benediction with the Holy Eucharist at stational churches, or at the city gates, to purify and sanctify public spaces, and the book was used for blessing the sick. From 1293—1964, a nocturnal penitential march included this chanting of the beginnings of the four Gospels at the four corners of the city. The fourteenth century *Liber fabricae* explained that this custom publicly affirmed the faith by drawing these four points as a Christian mark on the city—a cross which would protect its citizens with the Gospels and the Eucharist, a missionary gesture and a witness by the Christian community to their belief.[173] The intention apparent in the custom

---

[172] Haimerl, *Das Prozessionswesen*, p. 16.

[173] Dumoulin, *La Grande Procession de Tournai*, pp. 29–31. The elaborate gesture was relinquished in 1964 to speed up the procession. In conception, this practice may be related to an ancient observance in the pre-baptismal rite—the *Expositio evangeliorum*, a part of the *Apertio aurium*, known from the seventh century. It helped initiate the catechumens, and it was customary on the last Wednesday of Lent. Although it largely disappeared in the West by the ninth century, the vestiges lin-

was emphatic symbolic delineation of the Christian character of the community of Tournai. The cult of the Virgin, paramount in Tournai, was evident through a variety of images, including Notre Dame des Malades and Notre Dame de la Brune, which were traditionally supplied with special robes for the occasion and were accompanied by pilgrims from parishes all over the diocese, who processed with images of their local Marian cults or of their patron saints, or with reliquaries.[174]

Special Singular Occasions

At Fosses, there were longstanding distinctions between two basic types of extra-liturgical processional rites: *ordinary* processions, on fixed dates, which were led around the immediate environs of the church building; and *grand* processions through the city and neighboring countryside. The latter type were held as needed for petitions for rain, good harvest, against contagious disease, or in thanksgiving for favors received.[175] Toussaert distinguished three types for Flanders as a whole: the regular (or liturgical); the general, ordained by religious or civil authorities; or those in honor of special occasions. The general type was called for important reasons and dire emergencies—such as drought, flood, plague, military victories, and reconciliation. Although each was singular, they were an habitual response, with customs accumulated around their performance, such as chants, litanies, and Psalms. The special type was in honor of saints, the Virgin,

---

gered in certain localities until the seventeenth century, including Tournai, and the Diocese of Liège. It appeared in seventh and eighth century sacramentaries with directives for presenting the gospels at the corners of the altar, and then reading them from the pulpit. Felbecker, *Prozession*, p. 455 cited the importance in the Corpus Christi processions of the idea of four altars oriented to the four directions of the Heavens, where the initia of the gospels were read—in each direction of the field or city, so that the totality was thus blessed. Similarly, the author of the *Translatio Sancti Justi*, before relating his tale, turns solemnly towards the four cardinal points, thus addressing himself to all of Christianity.

[174] Ludovic Nys (ed.), *Gloria Mariae—Statues et Reliquaires Portés À La Grande Procession de Tournai* (Tournai, 1992). Another separate category of processional custom, popular in the late Middle Ages, is called the seven-year, or septennial, feast. See Scott Montgomery elsewhere in this volume.

[175] Joes Noel, *Processions et la Marche Militaire de saint Feuillen à Fosses, Folklore Wallon d'entre Sambre et Meuse* (Fosses, 1956), p. 20. There were customarily four per year of the first type—ordinary processions: on fixed dates (January 16, September 3, October 24, and October 31).

or commemorative events, and may be more purely a "community
expression."[176]

The Grand Procession at Tournai was initiated in dire need, as
were many others in the region.[177] Also at play was the custom of
visitation by groups of pilgrims from throughout Flanders to the
Virgin at Tournai, in homage and petition.[178] In these singular occasions, we see that procession arises as a response to circumstances
that affected a group which shared an identity in some respect. They
might have sought a common purpose to show solidarity, perhaps
in association with a group authority or to demonstrate shared devotion or need. Also implied was a claim on the affections of the saint,
the Virgin, or God, which should elicit response.

Legal Actions, Synods, Meetings, Fairs

Among events for which transportation of the relics evolved were
those where the accompaniment or leadership of the patron was valued, including their assent to whatever activities were involved and
when the presence of the saint enhanced the power of the clergy,
particularly if they were seen as the true landholder. In the *Book of
Sainte Foy* are accounts of processions to places where Foy held pro-
prietary rights, either to assert a claim over disputed property or to
formally take possession of regained or donated land,[179] and she was
taken to councils "where the disruptive and violent armed horsemen
were required to take the oaths of peace on relics."[180] In 1060, St.
Ursmer's relics were carried from Lobbes through Brabant and
Flanders to regain lost properties.[181] In 1073, the Corbie monks
sought their rights against the Count of Flanders, assisted by the
relics of St. Adalhard.[182]

---

[176] Toussaert, *Le Sentiment Réligieux*, pp. 24–48.
[177] Dumoulin, *La Grande Procession*, p. 24.
[178] Dumoulin, *"Trésors Sacrés,"* p. 19; Sigal, *L'Homme et le Miracle*, pp. 157–60.
[179] Sheingorn, *Book of Sainte Foy*, pp. 120–4; p. 80 she noted a similar use of the
image of Mary, which was carried to a place where a conflict over landholding
was at issue: ". . . effigy should go to that farm, as is the custom, carried in a procession of the people, so that through divine intervention, they might recover. . . .
what was rightfully theirs."
[180] Ashley, "Sainte Foy on the Loose," p. 59.
[181] Beissel, *Die Verehrung der Heiligen*, p. 6.
[182] Kroos, *Der Schrein des Heiligen*, p. 67.

A parish saint would often accompany the faithful on a visit to another venerable saint, in gatherings of two or more reliquaries for some specific occasion. Assemblies of saints were not uncommon at such events where numerous living dignitaries convened. This would indicate the honor or approval by the saints, especially important when they had authority in the community,[183] much as the presence of provincial bishops at a church consecration implied their consent.[184] Relics of saints also attended synods, councils, and secular meetings.[185] In the tenth century, Bishop Arnold of Rodez called a diocesan meeting, requiring that various saints from all over the diocese be brought there to give more authority to the council.[186] And the Maastricht Servatius shrine was one of many transported to the winter court held at Aachen by Henry II, in 1003.[187]

For monastic visits of the thirteenth to fifteenth centuries by important dignitaries, the general practice was to receive the visitors with solemnity and to lead them in procession to the altar, for celebration of the office.[188] On episcopal visits, scribes would note the sense of ceremony observed in receiving and announcing the legates, and record the quantity, quality, and condition of parish goods.[189] When Bourges archbishop Simon de Beaulieu visited Paris in the seventeenth century, the accounts described the reception ceremony for the prelate in detail.[190]

The annual fairs at Tournai, as elsewhere, were originally religious in nature, even before the advent of the annual procession, and the two became closely associated. The first commemoration of the original Grand Procession (1093) was linked to an established occasion of fair and feast, at the May anniversary of the cathedral dedication (the season of Ascension and Pentecost thus linked to the offering period.) The fair was a period of safe-conduct, and temporary reopening of the city to the banished, the temporary exemption of

---

[183] Kroos, *Der Schrein des Heiligen*, pp. 73–4.
[184] Benson, *The Bishop-Elect*, p. 37.
[185] Beissel, *Die Verehrung der Heiligen*, p. 5 wrote they were seen in attendance as landlords of their respective foundations.
[186] Ashley, "Sainte Foy on the Loose," p. 59.
[187] Kroos, *Der Schrein des Heiligen*, p. 45.
[188] Coulet, *Les Visites Pastorales*, p. 29.
[189] Coulet, *Les Visites Pastorales*, p. 38.
[190] Coulet, *Les Visites Pastorales*, p. 65.

debtors—with greater liberality overall.[191] During the twelfth and thirteenth centuries, the fairs became increasingly commercial and secular and an increasingly inappropriate adjunct to the procession.[192] So, a separate season was chosen for the procession but, ironically, a second great annual fair soon began, with a *kermesse*, in September, the time to which the procession had been shifted.[193] This era, upon which Abbot Herman commented disparagingly, witnessed changes in the religious feast, when the marchers no longer went barefoot, the devotional tenor was dissipated, and horsemen and young people held games and races.[194]

Consecration and Canonization

The day of a church consecration was often occasion for a ceremonial translation, with the attendance of various saints' relics adding a sense of visitation by esteemed dignitaries. By the 1039 consecration of the Cathedral at Cambrai, the practice was a usual part of the repertoire of reliquary customs.[195] The transportation of many relics is mentioned in connection with the 1040 consecration of the new monastery church at Stavelot by Abbot Poppon, an occasion of great pomp and celebration, including the ceremonial translation of the relics of St. Remaclus. Present were King Henry III, his courtiers, Archbishop Erimann of Cologne, Bishops Nithard of Liège, Hermann of Munster, Richard of Verdun, Gerard of Cambrai, and others. The service was begun with a blessing, after which the relics of Remaclus, Juste, and other saints were carried around the walls, as they were blessed with holy water. A multitude assisted in this procession, with the cortège leading out to the gates of the monastery. The king and his ministers helped to carry the relics of Remaclus in procession, with great devotion, across the crowd, to place them in the position where they were displayed for veneration.[196]

---

[191] Rolland, *Histoire de Tournai*, pp. 86–7; Dumoulin, *La Grande Procession*, p. 19.
[192] Rolland, *Histoire de Tournai*, p. 59. The number of villages in the diocese increased to twelve by the mid-twelfth century, and the number of churches doubled in only one generation at the same period.
[193] Cauchie, *La Grande Procession*, p. 15.
[194] Cauchie, *La Grande Procession*, pp. 26–9.
[195] Kroos, *Der Schrein des Heiligen*, p. 23.
[196] de Noüe, *Études Historiques*, p. 184. The consecration was celebrated annually thereafter, with a fair, for which Henry of Bavaria granted rights.

In 1151, the celebration for the election of Arnold von Wied as Archbishop of Cologne included a procession led by the shrines of the city's patron saints, including previous archbishops.[197] The 1624 canonization of Abbot Poppon at Stavelot featured a grand procession of his relics, in their new shrine, led by deacons, monks, priors, and laypeople, and numerous reliquaries and the Blessed Sacrament in a monstrance, which was exposed, along with the relics, for veneration in the abbey church.[198] Ceremonial transportation of relics from one church to another signified confraternity among congregations—an important indication of the concept of overall unity of the Christian community, encompassing those near and far, living and deceased—adherents of the faith, with special emphasis on legendary leaders, represented by their enshrined relics.

Petitions

Such rituals were often ordained in response to bad circumstances, as petition for protection or relief, prescribed for danger, both present and potential,[199] including famine, drought, and flood,[200] epidemic

---

[197] Kroos, *Der Schrein des Heiligen*, p. 50.

[198] "Ordre de L'office et Procession . . . Poppon," in *AEL Stavelot Malmedy 376 #s4–11 (c.* 1620). Indulgences were granted for participation in this event, as they were for support of the confraternities which were founded to sustain their work, in the ensuing years. "Ferdinandus dei Gra.," in *AEL Stavelot Malmedy 376 #39* (1624), "Ferdinandus dei Gratia &C," in *Ael Stavelot Malmedy 376 #31* (1624), "Forma dell'indulgenze," in *AEL Stavelot Malmedy 375 #43* (1631 or 1657), "Mass Readings for Feasts of Sigisbert, Remaclus, Poppon, Hadelin," in *AEL Stavelot Malmedy 377 Stablo-Malmedy Acten MR4* (1634), "Qua Ratione Suffragandus Noster Leodiens Consecrationum Sancti Popponis," in *AEL Stavelot Malmedy 376 #32* (1624), "Sommaire des Indulgences," in *AEL Stavelot-Malmedy 375 #21* (1626), "Suffraganeus Leodien Scribit Se Examin Naturum Utrum Veneration Reliquiarum Sti Popponis a Solo Episcopo decerni Possit an Forte Aliunde Peti," in *AEL Stavelot Malmedy 376 #36r* (1634).

[199] Perhaps rooted in the Old Testament Psalm 67 concerning God's Triumphal Procession, which may be taken up "to scatter enemies." (verse 3)

[200] The Severinus shrine was taken in procession against drought in Cologne in both 1021 and 1036. Friedrich Wilhelm Oediger, *Die Regesten der Erzbischöfe Von Köln Im Mittelalter—Erster Band 313–1099,* vol. 21 (Bonn, 1954–61), 1, p. 763. The shrine of St. Edmund at Bury, 1095, for the same purpose; the St. Alban shrine at St. Albans in 1257 against rain and flood, 1257. Kroos, *der Schrein des Heiligen*, p. 344 noted a 1639 march at Maastricht for crops; in 1651, for rain.

and plague,[201] devastation from fires,[202] military invasions, riots, and
civil disturbances,[203] heresy, and other spiritual malaise. That this
was a customary response to calamities[204] is borne out by the *Book
of Sainte Foy* which reported that ". . . one day the sacred image had
to be carried to another place for some necessary reason . . ."[205] The
images or reliquaries were transported in the belief that the faithful
could convince the saint to intervene with God, and that his presence and participation would facilitate relief from the problem,[206]
while the processional demarcation of the affected space and surrounding area helped to create a spiritual barrier against the men-
ace.[207] It was believed possible to achieve sanctification through the
ritual, with associated prayer, fasting and alms.[208] While these rites
were extraordinary in many senses, especially in singular specific circumstances, the formation of a procession in such conditions had
become a customary and significant expression in the face of oppo-

---

[201] Remission of a plague through the intercession of St. Remigius at Reims in
the sixth century, after a procession with a mock bier, fashioned from the shroud
of the saint, is recounted by Gregory of Tours, *Glory of the Confessors*, trans. Raymond
Van Dam (Liverpool, 1988), pp. 82–3. The *archa lignea* of St. Mansuetus was taken
in procession in the mid-tenth century against pestilence (AASS Sept. 1: 629, 656);
the relics of Benedict and Maur in Fleury, against a plague-like illness. Kroos, de*r
Schrein des Heiligen*, p. 344. The relics of Servatius were carried for relief from plague
in 1720, and the model procession at Tournai in 1092, was in response to epidemic. In 1130, a procession of St. Geneviève was taken up in the face of epidemic, and upon its success, an annual commemorative procession was inaugurated
in 1131, as in Tournai.

[202] Kroos, de*r Schrein des Heiligen*, p. 344, cited a 1027 procession at Cambrai for
relief from fire.

[203] Guibert of Nogent, de *vita Sua: Self and Society in Medieval France: The Memoirs
of Abbot Guibert of Nogent († 1125)*, (ed.) John F. Benton (New York, 1970), p. 217.
Herrmann-Mascard, *Les Reliques des Saints*, pp. 221–2, noted that after the thirteenth
century, public calamity processions required the permission of the bishop, and were
generally of a penitential character, including fasts and prayer, with stations and
sermons.

[204] Sigal, *L'Homme et Le Miracle*, p. 157 noted that relic processions were firmly
established by the eleventh–twelfth centuries, were more frequent in the cases of
weather problems, especially in agricultural societies.

[205] Sheingorn, *Book of Sainte Foy*, p. 78. The purpose here was to raise money.

[206] Kroos, *Der Schrein des Heiligen*, p. 344.

[207] Dumoulin, *La Grande Procession*, p. 22. Other authors cite this function as well.

[208] When the Archdeacon of Tyre, in 518, sought to quell a civil disturbance,
he announced a procession, designating that the faithful process on the following
Sunday to the Church of St. Mary, with Psalms, tapers, and incense, for the purpose of offering supplication and synaxis. de Bruyne, "L'origine des Processions,"
p. 14.

sition, as, for instance, in war, or against schismatics and heretics. The unification was believed to be not just an outward display, but also to result in an inner, spiritual effect for community members. At Fosses, civil registers note that the time after the processions with St. Feuillen were periods of great serenity for the citizens.[209]

Travels with relics were often undertaken when calamity threatened, as when the priests of Amiens joined the monks of Corbie, both marching with crosses and relics in the face of a plague in 1021; or the 1053 epidemic which led fifteen Benedictine monks from Fontanelles to carry St. Wulfram's relics to Ouen, where they were joined by the canons with the relics of St. Romanus.[210] The use of processional rites to propitiate a patron saint, with or without their relics, as an apotropaic against various types of threatening evil was widespread, and the evidence of efficacy is seen in such images as the 1220 *Universal Chronicle* depiction of a procession with an image of the Virgin that stopped the plague.[211] (fig. 338) In 959, according to the *Gesta abbatum Sancti Bertini*, Bishop Guifred of Therouanne ordered a day of fasting and processions with Sts. Omer, Bertin, Riquier, and Valéry to prevent the plague; in 964 the relics of St. Epiphanus were carried out processionally from the Church of Hildesheim; in 962–70 the relics of St. Toul were carried in petition for rain; in 974 the relics of St. Ursmer were carried across the Sambre River from Lobbes and placed on a hill, in petition for rain; in 974 St. Mansuy against epidemic.[212] As noted, it was customary for the Malmedy monks and villagers to go in procession to see St. Roch.[213]

In Tournai the relics of Eleutherius were believed to have special powers of "meteoric order,"[214] so the community was accustomed to

---

[209] Noël, *Les Processions*, p. 32.

[210] Beissel, *Die Verehrung der Heiligen*, p. 3.

[211] Dendy, *The Use of Lights in Christian Worship*, p. 111. Since the account comes from the *Gloria Confessorum*, by Gregory of Tours, it must be early, prior to the late sixth century.

[212] Sigal, *L'Homme et Le Miracle*, pp. 156–7.

[213] de Noüe, *Études Historiques*, p. 286. There were confraternities of St. Roch all over Europe in the late Middle Ages, including two at Tournai. Jean Cassart, *Saints Populaires dans le Diocese de Tournai—Iconographie—Attributs—Devotion* (Tournai, 1975). p. 154. Known for protection against epidemic, this saint's shrine was one of the most frequently visited pilgrimage sites throughout the Middle Ages.

[214] Warichez, *S. Eleuthère*, p. 64.

taking them in procession for special intercession in times of trouble, such as drought and flood,[215] and their patron was always included in every type of great political event,[216] sometimes with the other reliquaries and statues, and sometimes by himself.[217] A 1509 Maastricht march included the magistrates, citizens, and *domini servatiani* (lords of Servatius), pleading for relief from a virulent pestilence which had troubled the city for two years. It was held on the feast of Mary's birthday, September 8, so more people could participate.[218] For a 1475 Maastricht event, one notes four types of detail: the need for petition, the preparations, implementation of the plans, and the associated rescue of prisoners. The occasion was the Siege of Neuss, during the war between Charles le Tèmèraire and Frederick III. The procession took place on the Monday after Corpus Christi and was, as usual, accompanied by miracles.[219] Instigated by the citizens, the march went out from the city to visit all the churches and chapels.

From its inception, the Grand Procession at Tournai was dedicated to the Virgin and Child, to worship of the Cross, and to the

---

[215] Dumoulin, *Trésors Sacrés*, p. 101.

[216] Warichez, *S. Eleuthère*, p. 64.

[217] Rolland, *Histoire de Tournai*, pp. 117–8; M. Adolphe Hocquet, Maurice Houtart, Walther Ravez, E.-J. Soil de Moriamé, "Tournai dans l'Art et dans l'Histoire," *Wallonia* 21/5–6 (1913), p. 324; Warichez, *La Cathédrale de Tournai*, pp. 64–5. In 1214, there was a spontaneous procession of solemn thanksgiving by the French chevaliers and the communal magistrate, followed by feasting and celebration, when Philip Augustus, with the aid of Tournai, conquered the Count of Flanders. The clocks were sounded for three days, and there were eight days of jousts, carousels, and tournaments. Perhaps the most poignant and intense use of the reliquary was in other times of siege by plague. In addition to the 1090 event, there were epidemics in 1349 (with 2500 victims in the city), in 1514 (30,000–40,000 victims), and in 1579, 1627, 1650, and 1668. In each of these assaults, the people were moved to traverse the streets with their patron saint, pleading for relief. Warichez, *S. Eleuthère*, p. 66.

[218] Kroos, de*r Schrein des Heiligen*, pp. 344–8. Ernst Günther Grimme, *Goldschmiedekunst im Mittelalter: Form und Bedeutung des Reliquiars Von 800 Bis 1500* (Cologne, 1972). The first documented procession with the later Servatius shrine appears in 1409, but the *Chronick* of the parishioners of Beek indicates that it was not unprecedented, and that it was for a very specific current need. There is an account of a bridge collapse during a procession in 1275 ". . . with the feretory of St. Servatius" (". . . *cum feretro sancti Servatii*,") that does not find correspondence in other accounts of the event. The reason for the petitionary procession is not known. From the late fifteenth to the mid seventeenth century, there were a number of processions reported, involving epidemic, plague, war, and weather problems. Perhaps best documented procession associated with this shrine was in 1475—known from the Maastricht chronicler Mathew Herbenus. Tekippe, *Procession, Piety, Politics*, Ch. 7.

[219] Kroos, der *Schrein des Heiligen*, pp. 345–6.

celestial court, because these three cults were emphasized within the cathedral itself.[220] In later centuries, the veneration of the Holy Sacrament was added, in enthusiasm for the Corpus Christi feast.[221] It was conceived as an entreaty for assistance from all possible sources, but since the Virgin was the dedicatrix of the cathedral and chief patroness of Tournai, her cult dominated.[222]

Flight

When communities were put to flight, they often took their relics along, and this may have been instrumental in origination of the practice of removal of relics from their burial sites. While there were "strict prohibitions against disturbing their tombs" such events as the Norman invasions of the ninth century seem to have led to processions to petition help from the saints[223] as well as their removal for safekeeping, when groups were routed from their quarters. There are many reports of the accompaniment of the saint's relics when a community fled under various threats, such as when the monks from Stavelot fled, as they sought safety from maurauders' attacks, and their saint, Remaclus, was transported both as member of the community, and as a primary treasure, to several successive safe havens.[224] And from Tournai, according to legend, the relics of Eleutherius were taken along as canons fled the Normans.[225] In general, the relics were listed among the most highly-prized treasures, along with sacred vessels, maps, and other treasures. The monks from Séclin were reputed to have gone to Chartres, with the sarcophagus of Piat on their shoulders, while the monks from Elnone carried the châsse of

---

[220] Lys, *Gloria Mariae*, p. 10.

[221] Dumoulin, *La Grande Procession*, p. 79.

[222] Dumoulin, *La Grande Procession*, p. 19 stated the reason for a shift from May to September as competition with secular feasts and fairs in the Spring and the decline of the Pentecost offering pilgrimages.

[223] Ashley, "Sainte Foy on the Loose," p. 56, citing Claire Wheeler Solt.

[224] "de S. Remaclo Conf. et Episc. Trajectensi Ac *dein* Abbate Stabulensi.," *Miracula II:* I:1,2.

[225] Warichez, *Les Origines de L'église de Tournai*, p. 205, although historical accounts do not reveal the elevation of relics until after that invasion, the tales indicate a belief in the saints' protection during such events.

St. Amand to a series of French cities, seeking refuge and protection.[226] Similar responses prevailed during religious wars, civil wars,
and during the French Revolution. In 1376, the Heribert shrine was
taken to Siegburg, when the cloister at Deutz was threatened during the 30 Years War in Cologne—as the patron/founder, he was
the protector of the community in all difficulties.[227] The relics were
described as the "palladium" of the monastery,[228] the guardian apparently inspiring a passionate desire to protect him in return. A rich
housing for the relics might also have inspired them to take along
that which would surely be prey to looters.

Politics and the Triumphus

Protest against injustice also induced devotees to transport relics in
expression of supplication for righteousness. The canons of Maastricht
brought the Servatius relics in a portable shrine to Duisberg in 944,
in an effort to prevail upon Otto I to grant them protection against
Landgrave Immo, who was ravaging their lands. Similar situations
led them to petition Henry IV for protection in 1087and 1088.[229]
At the death of Otto III, in 1002, and again in 1088, the chapter
found occasion to seek justice, with the help of Servatius, the first
time with great pomp and flourish, the second, in a more sober procession. When the chapter at Coblenz, also under the patronage of
Servatius, sought to mollify a situation of their alienation by the
nobility of their city, in the mid-eleventh century, they walked with
their patron saint, along with the laity, to visit several cities in the
region, and when they returned to Coblenz, the door to the cathedral miraculously sprang open to allow entry.[230] Sometimes, repeated
processional entreaties were necessary to elicit the saint's help.

---

[226] Warichez, *Les Origines de L'église de Tournai*, p. 205.

[227] Monica Sinderhauf, *Die Abtei Deutz und Ihre Innere Erneuerung: Klostergeschicht im Spiegel des Verloren Codex Theodorici*, ed. Wolfgang Schmitz, vol. 39 (Cologne, 1996), p. 154, fn. 454.

[228] Héliot, "Quêtes et voyages," p. 765.

[229] Kroos, *Der Schrein des Heiligen*, pp. 47–8; Herrmann-Mascard, *Les Reliques des Saints*, pp. 228–9; George, *Les Routes de la Fo*, p. 21, fn. 63; Beissel, *Die Verehrung der Heiligen*, p. 6. In the Jocudus *vita*, they apparently derive from the Continuatio Reginonis (MGH SS 1:619).

[230] Kroos, *Der Schrein des Heiligen*, pp. 47–8. Sheingorn, *Book of Sainte Foy*, p. 80, described a similar use of the image of Mary, which was carried to a place where

In one of the most fascinating relic sagas of the Middle Ages, the monks of Stavelot protested the takeover of Malmedy by Archbishop Anno II, of Cologne who, with dubious pretext, named Tegernon of Brauweiler to the post of abbot of Malmedy in 1065. An age-old arrangement had placed that monastery under the care of the abbot of Stavelot, and consequently, within the purview of the Bishop of Liège, even though Malmedy lay within the geographic limits of the Diocese of Cologne.[231] The Stavelotan monks undertook a series of counter-attacks, including the humiliation of their patron's relics, and a procession to Malmedy with Remaclus' pastoral staff—to remind the rebellious monks of the traditional order and authority which their founder had instituted; the transportation of Remaclus' relics and staff to protest before an imperial diet Henry IV held in Goslar. In 1066, they went, again in procession with Remaclus to Aachen and to Fritzlar; the following year to Bitburg and to Bamberg. These plaintive pleadings expressed their misery and were fraught with the fear that the relics had lost their potency, or that the monks were being punished by their patron. Abbot Thierry even went to Rome in 1067, and 1068, to appeal to Pope Alexander II. The Pope issued orders for restitution, which were ignored. The affair lingered for another three years, until Henry held court at Liège, Eastertime of 1071. With great ceremony, the monks transported Remaclus to meet with his legendary fellow bishop, Lambert. En route to Liège, they were joined at Louveigné by the faithful of Lierneux, with the relics of St. Symmetrus, in support of their demonstration. Bishop Theoduin of Liège feared to anger his metropolitan, Anno, but tradition convinced him to receive the legendary bishop saint, his predecessor Remaclus with customary pomp and formality.[232]

---

a conflict over landholding was at issue: "... effigy should go to that farm, as is the custom, carried in a procession of the people, so that through divine intervention, they might recover. . . . what was rightfully theirs," p. 72.

[231] Baix, "L'Hagiographie à Stavelot-Malmedy," pp. 154–5. This literary construction, called the *Passio S. Agilolfi*, implied that there was past time when Malmedy was independent of Stavelot. Tekippe *Procession, Piety, Procession*, Ch. 7.

[232] Beissel, *Die Verehrung der Heiligen*, p. 8. Once in the episcopal city, they went in procession to the cathedral, singing Psalms and litanies, placing the relics, in succession, on the altars of the Holy Trinity, of St. Lambert (in the crypt), of the Virgin, and back to that of the Holy Trinity, where they left the reliquary while they went in supplication to the emperor. The châsse was reported to miraculously rise, with a great noise, from the altar table, taken as a sign of divine support. Later the monks brought the shrine to Henry at his dinner table, demanding justice,

When numerous miracles finally convinced the emperor to recognize the union of the two monasteries and the superiority of
Stavelot, Anno was forced to capitulate. Rejoicing in their success,
Abbot Thierry, the Stavelot monks and St. Remaclus left Liège in
procession to return home, stopping en route to celebrate Mass on
the banks of the Meuse, where a great crowd gathered, and additional miracles were reported. In a final march, the monks and abbot
of Stavelot transported their patron to Malmedy, in a symbolic gesture of reclamation of his and their authority.

This series of episodes is recounted in the heroic narrative of the
Triumph of St. Remaclus,[233] a title with rich resonance in the context
of the saga,[234] and strong symbolic associations for processional events.
As a type of literary epic, it arose in the Diocese of Liège, during
this era, to describe a series of events in a sustained campaign, join-
ing nationalistic sentiments to spiritual ones, eventually resulting in
political success ascribed to the power of the relics,[235] with miracles

---

and when the emperor balked at the affront, the table collapsed. Many miracles
accompanied all of these episodes, and huge crowds flooded the cathedral precincts—
all taken as portents. Henry, with the fearful prodding of his wife, became convinced that divine vengeance was at work, so he pled with Anno to reverse his
stance. Still firm, the Cologne archbishop ordered the monks to return the shrine
of Remaclus to the cathedral, but when they tried to comply, the châsse could not
be lifted, even after Anno sent reinforcements. Only after he agreed to reconsider
the matter on the following day, were the monks able to carry the relics back to
the church, but by this time, they were fearful that Remaclus had only succeeded
in irritating both emperor and archbishop. While Henry spent the night in penitence and prayer, more spectacular events took place and continued the next day.
A white dove, taken as premonition of eventual triumph, arose from the reliquary,
flew around, and returned to alight on the châsse. The shrine again levitated from
the altar where it had been placed. A thick cloud, followed by light more brilliant
than the sun, filled the crypt below, where St. Lambert lay, and in it appeared
Lambert and Remaclus, murmuring to one another, as though in discussion about
the state of affairs—in a vision seen by Bishop Lietbert, of Cambrai. The bells,
spontaneously ringing each time a miracle happened, drew more and more pilgrims
to the site. The Stavelot monks, in a vigil of prayer and chanting, were joined by
recipients of miracles, reportedly effected by Remaclus in the church, and by Lambert
in the crypt below.

[233] Stabulensis monachus Godefredus, "Triumphus Sancti Remacli de Malmundariensi Coenobio," in *Patrologiae Latina Cursus Completus*, (ed.) J.P. Migne (Paris,
1085). This saga is confirmed by a number of contemporary sources. See also Baix,
"L'hagiographie À Stavelot-Malmedy," George, *Les Routes de la Foi*, and Otto Dietrich,
der *Triumphus St. Remacli: Eine Quelle Für Die Geschichte des 11. Jahrhunderts* (Halle,
1887). Written soon after the spectacular drama, it was then commemorated annually at Stavelot, May 9.
[234] George, "Stavelot & Malmedy," pp. 241–2.
[235] George, "Stavelot & Malmedy," p. 241.

along the way, and the unification of the people as part of its effect.[236] This first tale, about Remaclus, was followed by those of Lambert and Hubert. The conquest also resulted in the political victory of Liège over Cologne, and that of the emperor over Cologne—long struggles in both instances—and was instrumental in stemming the aggrandizement of the ecclesiastical empire of Anno and Cologne.[237] The flowing rhythms of the beautifully-told tales are vitally linked to rhythms of the solemn rites which constitute its episodes.[238]

The parishioners and St. *Symmetrus* of Lierneux, a filial of Stavelot,[239] who joined the procession to Liège, were inspired to commemorate that event in a roof panel of the châsse created in 1260–70.[240] (fig. 339) In deference to this link, and in commemoration of their part in the *Triumphus*, they went to Stavelot each May, in a procession consisting of their chaplains, and at least one person from each family in their parish and the parish of Ottré, with the relics of St. *Symmetrus*, chanting.[241] As they entered the abbey church, each stopped to kiss the relics, and then pass beneath the châsse. Their offerings were put in a common bourse with those of the parishioners of Amblève, who also processed there the same day.[242]

Relic Quests

Customs arose, by the tenth-eleventh centuries, to use relics and reliquaries for purposes of raising revenues. These quests were important

---

[236] George, *Les Routes de la Foi*, pp. 8–9.

[237] George, "Stavelot & Malmedy," p. 257.

[238] George, "Stavelot & Malmedy," pp. 241–2. Moreover, the potency of inferences which relate to the triumphal entry ceremonies of antiquity should not be lost. While this is not really his thought with regard to the genre of *Triumphus*, it was in reading his treatment of this as a local literary type that these ideas occurred to me.

[239] George, "Documents Inédits sur le Trésor des Reliques," p. 69. It was shown in a list of collations of the abbot, established 1130–1.

[240] MGH SS v.XI:433. The connection with Stavelot and Remaclus was revered by Lierneux parishioners, who obtained Symètre's relics when the Stavelot Abbot St. Babolene († 670–78), brought them back from Rome, and had built the church at Lierneux in his honor.

[241] George, *Les Routes de la Foi*, pp. 227–30. See also Benoit Van den Bossche, "La Châsse de Saint Symètre," in *Patrimoine Religieux Du Pays de Lierneux* (ed.) Benoit Van den Bossche (Lierneux, 1992). Their song was one they had sung with the monks in Liège.

[242] de Noüe, *Études Historiques*, p. 81.

occasions for transportation of relics, with related practices, such as ceremonial reception of the questing party, exposition of the relics, preaching, benediction, and indulgences and miracles.[243] That funds were raised and miracles wrought as combined outcome explains the frequently-warm reception of those who processed with the saint's relics for the purpose of raising funds. In the *Liber miraculorum*, Bernard of Angers wrote that the processional ritual with St. Foy was good for raising funds because it inspired so much enthusiasm and generosity.[244]

A fourteenth-century quest undertaken for repairs to the Cathedral of Notre Dame of Tournai illuminates the practice.[245] Bishop Philippe d'Arbois sent a pastoral letter to the clergy in the diocese, appealing to them, as devoted sons of the Church of Tournai, to honor the clerics and deputies who would henceforth visit them once each year with the châsse of Notre Dame. They were to assemble the faithful, and go out, with lit candles and standards, to the sound of bells, to receive the holy relics.[246] The bishop specified that the day should be made solemn, like a Sunday, with the church open for deposit of the reliquary, and there would be a Mass, sermon, and Divine Office.[247] The deployment of the reliquary became part of a

---

[243] Héliot, *Quêtes et Voyages*, pp. 799–800. It was initially most common in northern France, between the Loire and the Escaut (later in the Midi), and it was undertaken most often by cathedrals and monasteries, which sought to draw on resources from outside their immediate environs.

[244] Forsyth, *Throne of Wisdom*, pp. 40–1. Often the expectations of miracles or favors from the saint were based in medieval notions of exchange—the customs of reciprocal gift exchange—including the offering of vows, votives, money, gold, or jewels. Sigal, *L'Homme et le Miracle*, p. 79.

[245] Warichez, *La Cathédrale de Tournai*, p. 81, described the church fabric as incurably needy.

[246] Warichez, *La Cathédrale de Tournai*, p. 82, cited the Manuscript du Fief, Bibliothèque royale de Bruxelles, 14, 762–8.

[247] Warichez, *La Cathédrale de Tournai*, p. 82. Héliot, *Quêtes et Voyages*, p. 819. One questions if châsses taken on quest were the simple wooden coffers, at the core of the elaborate shrines, or the entire luxuriously decorated containers, with gold, silver, jewels, and enamels. The account from Tournai, of the quest with the Notre-Dame châsse, and other reports of the careful decoration of litters, would not indicate any debasement of the containers for fear of robbery, or to appear less extravagant or more needy. Héliot and Chastang hypothesize, that, in general, despite their opulence, the lavish works were considered safe due to their status as church treasures and, besides, the retribution of the saint would have been a cause for fear by thieves. Since there were restrictions on the opening of reliquaries to exceptional circumstances, Héliot, *Quêtes et Voyages*, p. 819. It does not seem likely that the inner containers would have been separated from the exterior decorative

community event in each destination, and a significant episode in the fabric of their visual experience. Typically this included a greeting in processional ceremony, when people in the destination town, responding to pealing bells, joined their *curé*, took up their cross, banners, candles and censers, to go and welcome the visiting saint, observing a day of celebration of their common faith. The requisite sermon included injunctions against stinginess, promoted available indulgences, and recounted the life and miracles of the saint.[248]

coverings for these quests. (See Lemeunier essay this volume.) Plus, there seems to have been a spirit of generosity proportionate to the beauty and elegance of the shrines, with those most treasured, as evidenced by their decoration, exciting the most devotion and generosity, wherever they were shown. Tekippe, *Procession, Piety, Politics*, Ch. 1. These quests were rather long journeys, in duration. While they were understandably slow paced, with the companies covering an average of 10–13 kilometers a day, they often stayed for extended periods in a locale, being away from home two weeks to six months, usually.

[248] Héliot, *Quêtes et Voyages*, p. 12. Sometimes, the visitation would apparently draw upon existing ties, such as the later 1457 quest from Séclin to Tournai, with the relics of St. Piat, presumably not in a lavish châsse, since the purpose was to raise funds for a new reliquary. This saint, long linked to Tournai as the city's first missionary and founder of its first church, had also been martyred there, and subsequently honored as namesake for a parish church. When his remains were brought on quest to Tournai, they were ceremonially and cordially greeted by clergy and faithful, and by the reliquary of St. Eleutherius. The magnificent shrine which housed the relics of Eleutherius might have been exploited to encourage generosity so that St. Piat could have equally appropriate splendor. But quests were frequent sources of conflict in host communities. Local clergy and civic officials were sometimes resistant to requirements imposed upon them for safe-conduct, and the competition for limited resources of both spiritual attention and material donations was often unwelcome. Héliot, *Quêtes et Voyages*, pp. 10–11. Perhaps the most violent opposition was encountered in the Diocese of Reims, where the Archbishop and his Cathedral Chapter skirmished with suffragens after a 1210 fire left damages which motivated fund-raising quests, for which the Pope granted indulgences. Rebellious prelates refused to call upon communities to gather for the requisite welcoming processions. Subsequent threat of excommunication led to appeal to Rome, resulting in curtailment, but not cessation of the quests. That these were profitable ventures, with indulgences as popular features, is widely reported. In a 1501–02 ledger for Troyes Cathedral, are payments for fourteen monasteries and other institutions for rights to offer indulgences in their diocese when they were traveling with the relics to raise funds. A.N. Galpern, "Late Medieval Piety in Sixteenth-Century Champagne," in *The Pursuit of Holiness in Late Medieval and Renaissance Religion* (ed.) Charles Trinkaus & Heiko A. Oberman (Leiden, 1974), p. 148.

Penitentials

As a singular strain of late medieval Christian piety, penitentialism was expressed within the framework of processional custom.[249] A striking type of intermittent asceticism came with the appearance of the flagellants in the mid-fourteenth century. Characterized as a fanatic reaction against generalized public depravity, especially indecency of dress and public immorality,[250] the movement expressed a penchant for self-mortification and self-punishment, with a pointedly public and visual demonstration, meant to counter perceived evils and to incite widespread participation—a fitting component of such events as the Grand Procession at Tournai. In 1349, the flagellants created a conspicuous visual display, through their garb and their actions. (fig. 340) They wore sleeveless camisoles, slit on either side for access of their metal-pointed scourges to their skin. Their heads were covered with cowls and hats. Crosses adorned the hats and the fronts and backs of their camisoles. Each carried the penitent's baton and walked barefoot. Entering the city in ranks, led by crucifer, banner, and candlebearers, they chanted, each in his own language. In the cathedral, before the image of the Virgin, they disrobed their upper bodies, and, forming a circle, scourged themselves, while pleading for divine mercy. Each also thrice prostrated himself, in cruciform posture on the ground. Then, kneeling and chanting, they again lashed themselves. Then the leader preached and led a prayer for all the community. They left the church in ranks, bleeding and chanting to the Virgin,[251] stimulating devotion and drawing many to join or follow their pilgrimages. In the Grand Procession, they marched without cross, banners, or candles, and their leader had to restrain them from too much bloodletting.[252] There is little question of their strong visual impact.

---

[249] André Vauchez, *The Laity in the Middle Ages: Religious Beliefs and Devotional Practices*, trans. Margery J. Schneider (Notre Dame, 1993), pp. 49–50.

[250] Rolland, *Histoire de Tournai*, p. 129.

[251] Rolland, *Histoire de Tournai*, pp. 129–30.

[252] Henri Lemaître (ed.), *Chronique et Annales de Gilles le Muisit, Abbé de Saint-Martin de Tournai* (Paris, 1906), pp. 227–52; Cauchie, *La Grande Procession*, p. 32. According to the coeval chronicle of Abbot Gillis li Muisis, of St. Martin, viewing these demonstrations lent a great sense of tranquility and devotion to the people of the commune, and more than 250 local men formed a similar penitential group, led by Brother Robert, who promenaded around the city for nine days, barefoot, barechested, in cowls, and with whips. Some reported seeing visions of an angel, who

Both pilgrimage and procession were prescribed to rectify conditions of sinfulness. Medieval clergy often sent sinners on pilgrimage, and when communities were judged as having given themselves over to temptation, purificatory processions were ordained to rectify the general sinfulness. For the initial Grand Procession in 1092 in Tournai, the bishop had decreed that the youth of the city had lapsed into too great a love of frivolity, and prescribed the remedy of barefoot procession, preceded by fast and vigil, considered altogether as appropriate antidote for the works of the devil. When Bishop Hugh of Lincoln († 1200) complained of the lapse of processional customs in his diocese, he pointed to their continued use in other locales as an effective means to offer oblations and to effect the remission of sins. The belief in the value of their penitential character is reinforced by the customary processions as appropriate rituals for Good Friday observations.[253] Ironically, the large annual processions which attracted pilgrims also became occasions of festivity deemed so excessive that prelates were inclined to prescribe penitential measures to counteract them.[254]

Drama/ Tableaux

Late medieval processions elaborated with tableaux, strongly linked to the development of drama,[255] could be means of catechizing with scenes from the Old Testament, the Gospels, and Church history, but at the same time, they could do the opposite,[256] making superficial and shallow that which ought to be profound in both understanding and expression. Many pilgrimages and processions of the later period were subject to this effect, and the dramatic tableaux were one of the features of later events which give evidence of the attempts to dissect and to humanize religious ideas in a way that serve also

---

advised them that their display of penitence had earned them absolution from their sins. Dumoulin, *La Grande Procession*, pp. 32–3. Also Jean Cousin, *Histoire de Tournay*, 4 vols. (Douay, 1619).

[253] Cross and Livingston, *Dictionary*, *"Procession."*

[254] Johan Huizinga, *The Waning of the Middle Ages*, 1984 reprint (New York, 1924), p. 142.

[255] Herman Braet, Johan Nowe, Gilbert Tournoy, *The Theatre in the Middle Ages* (Louvain, 1985).

[256] Toussaert, *Le Sentiment Réligieux*, p. 262.

to degrade them. At Furnes in 1459, the long-standing procession was re-vamped and prizes were offered for designs for new tableaux which represented biblical or Holy Cross scenes. Six silver cups were offered for the grand prize.[257]

Conclusion

Exploring the arts of procession and pilgrimage, including the rites themselves, as performative arts, can help us to understand the visceral and spiritual responses evoked by structures, shrines, and accoutrements, and, consequently, how religion was "danced, not believed"—to borrow a phrase from Patrick Geary.[258] But, as he noted, there are difficulties because these portions of medieval religion/ spirituality were not usually recorded and they were not officially sanctioned. Moreover, medieval faith was a living, growing, changing entity, bringing additional challenges of interpretation. In the second half of the Middle Ages, the mobility of relics (*umhertragen*) increased notably, perhaps so that the treasures of the great abbeys and churches could have wider influence, by travelling to other churches, and by participating in diverse events.[259] While many collective expressions of the relic cult fell into disuse in the later Middle Ages, this was not generally the case for relic processions,[260] and many of them continue today, even some as group pilgrimage. But elaboration of the rites entailed diverse abuses. In 1549, a Cologne synod issued a reform decretal, condemning excesses of vanity, spectacle, and a taste for the ostentatious and calling for greater modesty and restraint, with a return to propriety and solemnity.[261] The

---

[257] Toussaert, *Le Sentiment Réligieux*, pp. 256–8.

[258] Patrick J. Geary, *Living with the Dead in the Middle Ages* (Ithaca, N.Y., 1994), p. 178.

[259] Beissel, *Die Verehrung*, p. 5.

[260] Herrmann-Mascard, *Les Reliques*, p. 194.

[261] Haimerl, *Das Prozessionswesen*, pp. 36–7, 42. Haimerl and Felbecker make this same observation regarding the Corpus Christi procession at Bamberg. It seems to me that this is too simplistic considering the relative organization of the other processional elements. Kathleen and Pamela Sheingorn Ashley, "*Discordia et Lis*: Negotiating Power, Property, and Performance in Medieval Sélestat," *Journal of Medieval and Early Modern Studies* 26/3 (Fall, 1996). Some scholars describe the basis for evolution of the Feast of Corpus Christi as essentially a financial interest, and this same charge could be laid to the motivation for the concurrent elaboration of other processional

general embellishment, and consequent profanation of processional rites, was central to the Protestant revolt of the sixteenth century. Post-Tridentine customs dictated that, whatever the purpose of a procession, the place of highest honor in the ranks was to be given to the Eucharist,[262] seeking to re-focus the Church on its central message.[263] This was generally deemed to be at the end of the procession, with the preceding foci serving as prelude to it.[264]

In addition to the use of procession as a vehicle for the expression of power for ritual participants, the practice also created or reinforced a sense of the power of the officiating clergy and the civil authorities who were increasingly involved. The associated rights were jealously guarded by the bishops authorized to control them. In 1191, the Bishop of York pronounced the excommunication of the Bishop of Durham for usurping the rights of the processions of Pentecost week.[265] In the fifteenth century, the Abbot at Lobbes, to revive the lagging processional customs and concomitant revenues from filial churches, sent out a notice in which he likened the practice to pilgrimages by early Christians to Rome despite the invasions of the Goths and the Huns.[266]

When the rights to receive filial processions and the associated offerings were conceded, it was done in a formal manner, by decree that the powers and rights had been transferred by the bishop to a subject church, warranted, for a specific reason.[267] In Siegburg, an 1818 document refers to the celebration of St. Servatius' Day, which had been held since time immemorial, as a church feast, for the worship of God and the veneration of the relics, including many processions, which drew clergy and the trading public into the neighborhood, and, therefore, that the city should support it financially, as did neighboring communities. There was also papal support, in

---

rituals. Since the Mass and the Office did not have the same potential for generating the type of interest which processions aroused in the public, processions were more attractive commercially.

[262] Kroos, der *Schrein des Heiligen*, pp. 350–1.

[263] I would contend that the Corpus Christi feast itself was embraced as a remedy for undue dissipation of devotion, with too much unrestrained focus on the saints' cults.

[264] Haimerl, *Das Prozessionswesen*. The reliquaries were customarily positioned most immediately before the Holy Sacrament in the processional ranks.

[265] Berlière, "Les Processions," p. 425.

[266] Berlière, "Les Processions," pp. 422–3.

[267] Berlière, "Les Processions," p. 420.

the form of indulgences granted for specific years, to draw in pilgrims.[268]

The increases in population of the late Middle Ages, especially in urban communities which used procession as expression were often interpreted in Old Testament terms, such as those in Chapter 3 of Jeremiah:

> *16* When you multiply and become fruitful in the land, says the Lord, they will in those days no longer say, 'The ark of the covenant of the Lord.'; *17* At that time they will call Jerusalem the Lord's throne; there all nations will be gathered together to honor the name of the Lord at Jerusalem, and they will walk no longer in their hard-hearted wickedness. *18* In those days the house of Juda will join the house of Israel; together they will come from the land of the north to the land which I gave your fathers as a heritage.

Such grounding in scripture draws the metaphorical links in which the earthly community presages the reunion of its members in heaven. This restoration was anticipated in Tournai procession and pilgrimage, where the various civic groups who were regularly contentious could participate in a temporary harmony, through the rites, in a way which would both presage the celestial dissolution of their dissension and also echo the Old Testament reunion of the scattered tribes of Israel.[269]

The reliquary shrines of saints and artistic accoutrements were functional tools in this process. Their visual aspects signified the other realm, as the abode of the divine, and the place where the saints dwelled, while they also continued to accompany the faithful in their realm. Particularly, the art, like the pilgrim in procession, explicated the eschatological potential of earthly life, which is encapsulated and heightened in the processional ritual. The visual experience co-operates in the attainment of comprehension of symbolic import, and of transportative, anagogical experience. The assertion of local identity and claim to power was mediated through devotion to a locally-venerated saint, and procession was an emphatic expression of membership in the discreet group on the march, while there were clearly reflections of all Christian marches. The elements which conveyed the localized sentiment were equally clear, to the extent that signs

---

[268] Busch, *St. Servatius*, p. 20. The indulgences were noted for 1739, 1764, 1801.
[269] Warichez, *La Cathédrale*, p. 293; Tekippe *Procession, Piety, Politics*, Ch. 5, Appendix A.

of individuality (within the local community) could at once be compliant and defiant. There were such strong relationships between pilgrimage and procession in the Middle Ages that many instances of each involved implications of the other, both in their co-incidence in time and in place, and in their significance and symbolism. The involvement of art and architecture in these rites was crucial in conveying their ultimate implications in medieval Christian life.

CHAPTER TWENTY-SEVEN

THE AACHEN KARLSSCHREIN AND MARIENSCHREIN

Lisa Victoria Ciresi

In 799 Charlemagne obtained a collection of precious relics affiliated with the "Holy Site of the Resurrection of Our Lord."[1] These included objects associated with the Virgin Mary, to whom his chapel at the center of his palace complex in Aachen was dedicated and consecrated *c.* 801.[2] (fig. 341) In 814, fourteen years after he was crowned Emperor of the Romans by Pope Leo III in Rome, Charlemagne died and was entombed in his chapel.[3] With this Charlemagne's

---

[1] At least two sources mention the acquisition of the relics, *Annales regni Francorum DCCXCVIIII*, in *MGH SS* 1:146, "Eodem anno monachus quidam de Hierosolimis veniens benedictionem et reliquias de sepulchro Domini, quas patriarcha Hierosolimitanus domno regi miserat, detulit," (A certain monk came from Jerusalem and brought benediction and relics from the Holy Land, which the patriarch had sent to the emperor.); as cited by Walter Kaemmerer, ed., *Aachener Quellentexte* Veröffentlichungen des Stadtarchivs Aachen 1 (Aachen, 1980), p. 22. According to Vincent Sablon, *Histoire de l'auguste et vénérable église de Chartres* 2nd ed. (Chartres, 1683), chapter 12, "How the holy tunic of Our Lady came to Chartres and how it miraculously saved the town several times;" as reproduced in *Chartres Cathedral*, ed. Robert Branner (New York, 1969), pp. 110–4, "Charlemagne, while returning from Jerusalem, passed through Constantinople, . . . where [he] found the Emperor Nicephoras and his wife, Irene. These magnificent princes opened their treasury to Charlemagne and offered him several rare and inestimable things, among which was the holy tunic [a shift purportedly worn by the Virgin Mary while nursing the infant Jesus]; he refused them all except for the tunic and some other reliquaries and had them taken to Aachen in Germany." Unfortunately, Sablon did not describe the "other reliquaries."

[2] The earliest account of the alleged consecration of the chapel by Leo III appears in an 1157 letter by Hadrian IV. According to the *Annales Iuvavenses maiores*, in *MGH SS* 1:87, the dubious event occurred on the Feast of the Epiphany in 805; Kaemmerer, *Quellentexte*, pp. 32–4.

[3] Presumably Charlemagne was buried in a second-century Roman sarcophagus, the so-called Proserpina sarcophagus, believed to be interred beneath the pavement of the west narthex; Helmut Beumann, "Grabe und Thron Karls des Grossen zu Aachen," in *Karl der Grosse, Lebenswerk und Nachleben*, IV: *Das Nachleben*, eds. Wolfgang Braunfels, Percy E. Schramm (Düsseldorf, 1967), pp. 9–38. Excavations in 1910 of the chapel revealed that beneath the narthex was a subterranean chamber large enough for the Proserpina sarcophagus (2.5 m l, 64 cm w, 58 cm h); Walter Maas

chapel became an imperial mausoleum, but beginning in 936 with Otto I, it became the official coronation church for the Roman-German Kings.[4] From the time of the consecration of the chapel, the relics acquired by Charlemagne were enshrined and preserved somewhere within the high altar room, itself dedicated to the Virgin.[5] The relics, including the *camisia* or shift of the Virgin, defined the visual and spiritual focal point—the *locus sanctus*—of the Carolingian chapel.[6] In 1165 Charlemagne was canonized[7] and in 1215 his

---

and Herbert Woopen, *Der Aachener Dom* (Cologne, 1984), p. 15. The sarcophagus is located today in Aachen Cathedral's Treasury.

[4] This was the first in a series of thirty coronations in the chapel; the last to be crowned king here was Ferdinand I, 1531. Previous coronations there are noted as well. On September 11, 813, in the Palace Chapel, Charlemagne crowned his son Louis the Pious co-emperor and "Augustus." Similarly, Louis the Pious crowned his son Lothar I in 817.

[5] Commonly referred to as the "Altarraum," the altar room refers to the high altar complex—the Carolingian rectangular apse that extended from the east end of the original Carolingian octagon.

[6] The sacred character of the Carolingian rectangular apse, or altar room, was defined by the efficacy of the relics preserved there. The altar room housed the original Carolingian mensa, an altar table with a cavity that held relics. The exact location of the mensa in the rectangular apse is not known, nor is the nature of the relics that were kept in its cavity. It is possible that this mensa was connected with at least one other known reliquary thought to be Carolingian, the "original" Marienschrein, or Shrine of Mary. According to a 1239 translation document, the original Aachen shrine of Mary preserved various relics, including the shift of the Virgin, which on the occasion of the 1238–9 exposition and translation, were allegedly removed from the old shrine for the first time since the days of Charlemagne; Erich Meuthen, ed. *Aachener Urkunden 1101–1250*, Publikationen der Gesellschaft für Rheinische Geschichtskunde 58 (Bonn, 1972), pp. 349–52, no. 124. This was corroborated by a *c.* 1200 document, which confirmed that at least three of the four main relics that were later sealed in the new Marienschrein were placed in the old Marienschrein; Stephan Beissel, *Die Aachenfahrt: Verehrung der Aachener Heiligtümer seit den Tagen Karls des Großen bis unsere Zeit* (Freiburg im Breisgau, 1902), pp. 54–5, fn. 2. Unfortunately, these documents are compromised by the chronicler Alberich von Troisfontaines, *Chronica Albrici*, in *MGH SS* 23:943, who, in 1238, wrote that after the fires which devastated the city of Aachen in 1224 and 1236, the relics, the swaddling cloth of the Christ child, the crucifixion cloth of Christ, and the shift of the Virgin, were revealed—some three to fourteen years sooner than testified to by the translation document. Klaus Herbers, "Die Aachener Marienschrein-Reliquien und ihre karolingische Tradition," in *Der Aachener Marienschrein: Eine Festschrift*, ed. Dieter P.J. Wynands (Aachen, 2000), pp. 129–34. For a reconstruction of both the Carolingian rectangular apse and its mensa, see Joseph Buchkremer, "Zur Baugeschichte des Aachener Münsters," *Zeitschrift des Aachener Geschichtsvereins* 22 (1900), pp. 198–271; Joseph Buchkremer, "Das Grab Karls des Großen," *Zeitschrift des Aachener Geschichtsvereins* 29 (1907), pp. 68–210; Eduard Teichmann, "Zur Lage und Geschichte des Grabes Karls des Grossen," *Zeitschrift des Aachener Geschichtsvereins* 39 (1917), pp. 155–217.

[7] The canonization ceremony was conducted by Frederick I, Rainald von Dassel,

exhumed bones were translated into the Karlsschrein, or Shrine of St. Charlemagne, the great sarcophagus-shaped reliquary, (fig. 342) which was then given a place of honor *in medio chori* and *sub corona*, in the middle of the Carolingian octagon, or choir,[8] beneath the Barbarossa chandelier[9] at an altar on the main axis west of the high

and Bishop Alexander of Liège. Although Pascal III was not present for the ceremony, he sanctioned the act, which, according to recent scholarship, was legitimate; Odilo Engels, "Karl der Große und Aachen im 12. Jahrhundert," in *Krönungen: Königen in Aachen—Geschichte und Mythos*, ed. Mario Kramp (Mainz, 2000), 1, p. 348. The legitimacy of Charlemagne's canonization is not covered by this study, but suffice to say Charlemagne's sainthood was never declared invalid by Rome and was thus silently approved. It should be noted that the liturgical celebrations in honor of St. Charlemagne were largely regional, though eventually recognized and adopted beyond the Aachen sphere, including Capetian France. For the liturgical cult of St. Charlemagne, see August Brecher, "Die kirchliche Verehrung Karls des Großen," in *Karl der Große und sein Schrein in Aachen: Eine Festschrift*, ed. Hans Müllejans (Aachen, 1988), pp. 151–66. For the canonization and liturgical cult of Charlemagne note Robert Folz, "Le chancellerie de Frédéric Ier et la canonisation de Charlemagne," *Le moyen âge* 70 (1964), pp. 13–31; Robert Folz, *Le Souvenir et la Légende de Charlemagne dans l'Empire germanique médiéval*, 2nd ed. (Geneva, 1973); Robert Folz, *Études sur le Culte Liturgique de Charlemagne dans les Églises de l'Empire*, 2nd ed. (Geneva, 1973); Robert Folz, "Aspects du Culte Liturgique de Saint Charlemagne en France," in *Karl der Grosse Lebenswerk und Nachleben*, IV, pp. 79–99; Jürgen Petersohn, "Kaisertum und Kultakt in der Stauferzeit," in *Politik und Heiligenverehrung im Hochmittelalter*, ed. Jürgen Petersohn, Vorträge und Forschungen 42 (Sigmaringen, 1994), pp. 101–46; Jürgen Petersohn, "Saint-Denis-Westminster—Aachen: Die Karls-Translatio von 1165 und ihre Vorbilder," *Deutsches Archiv für Erforschung des Mittelalters* 31 (1975), pp. 420–54; Emil Pauls, "Die Heiligsprechung Karls des Großen und seine kirchliche Verehrung in Aachen bis zum Schluß des 13. Jahrhunderts," *Zeitschrift des Aachener Geschichtsvereins* 25 (1903), pp. 335–60.

   [8] During the twentieth-century restoration of the Carolingian portions of the chapel, Joseph Buchkremer, "Das Grab Karls des Grossen," p. 92, fn. 1, identified slits in the piers as indications that choir stalls must have been installed in the octagon.

   [9] The Barbarossa chandelier is an octagonal architectural corona whose shape and iconographic program evoke the Heavenly Jerusalem. Although the original arrangement of the text on the "walls" of the chandelier is not known for certain, the inscription nevertheless makes clear that Frederick I and Empress Beatrix were the donors. It is possible that the chandelier was created in conjunction with plans for the Karlsschrein, however, as Georg Minkenberg has suggested, the chandelier must have been completed sometime between 1156, the date of Frederick's marriage to Beatrix, and 1184, the year of Beatrix's death. Georg Minkenberg, "Der Barbarossaleuchter im Dom zu Aachen," *Zeitschrift des Aachener Geschichtsvereins* 96 (1989), pp. 69–102, esp. p. 91. For a reconstitution of the inscription, see Clemens Bayer, "Die beiden großen Inschriften des Barbarossa-Leuchters," in *Celica Iherusalem: Festschrift für Erich Stephany*, ed. Clemens Bayer (Cologne, 1986), pp. 213–40; Helga Giersiepen, *Die Inschriften des Aachener Doms*, Die Deutschen Inschriften 31 (Wiesbaden, 1992), pp. 24–7. With a circumference of 4.16 m, the curved golden walls of the octagonal corona are articulated with sixteen miniature square and round towers intended to evoke John's Apocalyptic vision of the Heavenly Jerusalem, Rev. 21,

altar.[10] (fig. 343) Immediately following the installation of the Karls-chrein, in an effort to promulgate the sainthood of Charlemagne and to unite his relic-cult to that of the Virgin at the high altar, a new shrine, the Aachen Marienschrein (1220–38), or Shrine of Mary, was commissioned not only to replace the existing Marian reliquary at the high altar,[11] but also to encode into its iconographic program the revival of the cult of Charlemagne. (figs. 344–5) In 1238, the relics once preserved in the older reliquary were removed and exposed for adoration until 1239 when they were translated into the new Marienschrein, which was then sealed and given its place of honor at the high Marian altar.

Together, the holy presence of the Virgin and that of Charlemagne presided over the principal altars in the Carolingian octagon and demarcated sacred cult spaces reserved for specific liturgies exclusive to the chapel. Beginning in 1349 and every seven years since, the Marienschrein has been opened and its four so-called Great Relics—

---

as explained by the inscription on the segments between the towers. Additionally, forty-eight candle holders crown the rims of the walls of the celestial corona. Although most of the eighty-four silver relief figures that once adorned the towers were destroyed in the eighteenth century, the engraved bronze-gilt base-plates of the six-teen towers still survive. The base-plates of the larger, square towers depict the Eight Beatitudes, while the circular plates of the smaller towers are reserved for Christological events: Annunciation, Nativity, Adoration of the Magi, Crucifixion, Three Marys at the Tomb, Ascension, Pentecost, and Christ in Majesty. The "key-stone" was reserved for an image of Saint Michael. On the chandelier's relief plates, see Bernhard Andermahr, "Zwischen Himmel und Erde. Die Bodenplatten des Barbarossa-Leuchters im Aachener Dom: Ein Beitrag zur staufischen Goldschmiede-kunst im Rhein-Maas-Gebiet" (Ph.D. diss. Aachen Technische Hochschule, 1994). From 1990–98 the chandelier underwent conservation and was returned to its place in the octagon where it continues to function in liturgical ritual. On the conserva-tion of the Barbarossa chandelier, see Herta Lepie and Lothar Schmitt, *Der Barba-rossaleuchter im Dom zu Aachen* (Aachen, 1998). See also fn. 36.

[10] Most scholars agree that the Karlsschrein was originally installed beneath the Barbarossa chandelier and in the center of the Carolingian octagon until it was relocated to the Gothic choir in 1414, the year of its consecration. Contrary to this view, Joseph Buchkremer, "Rezension der Kunstdenkmäler der Rheinprovinz," *Zeitschrift des Aachener Geschichtsvereins* 38 (1916), p. 303; "Zur Geschichte des Grabes Karls des Großen," *Zeitschrift des Aachener Geschichtsvereins* 38 (1916), pp. 257–8, sug-gested that the Karlsschrein was connected to the altar table of St. Peter located in the bay west of the high altar.

[11] With the exception of Jürgen Fitschen, *Die Goldschmiedeplastik des Marienschreins im Aachener Dom: Eine stilgeschichtliche Untersuchung* Europäische Hochschulschriften Reihe 27, vol. 312 (Frankfurt am Main, 1998), pp. 55–7, most scholars agree that the new Marienschrein was installed at the high altar table in the Carolingian rectan-gular apse.

the shift of the Virgin, the swaddling cloth of the Christ child, the crucifixion loincloth of Christ, and the decollation cloth, or cloth that preserved the decapitated head of St. John the Baptist—were exposed in a ceremony known as the *Heiligtumsfahrt*.[12] The copious liturgy written for this ceremony,[13] along with the liturgy for the Feast of St. Charlemagne, reaffirmed and further defined the sacred union between the Virgin and Charlemagne, ultimately increasing the prestige of Aachen as one of the most sacred centers of royal cult and pilgrimage in northern Europe proclaiming the "City of Aachen" as "the principal seat of the kingdom and the first court of kings."[14]

---

[12] The translation document recorded all the relics removed from the old shrine and translated into the Marienschrein in 1239. At some later time, the chapter decided that the Marienschrein should preserve only the four Great Relics. The oldest report of a *Heiligtumsfahrt*, or pilgrimage to Aachen to venerate the chapel's principal relics, dates from 1312, but the tradition of showing the relics every seven years did not begin until 1349; Dieter P.J. Wynands, *Die Aachener Heiligtumsfahrt. Kontinuität und Wandel eines mittelalterlichen Reliquienfestes* (Siegburg, 1996), pp. 7–14. Heinrich Schiffers, *Karls des Großen Reliquienschatz und die Anfänge der Aachenfahrt* (Aachen, 1951), pp. 63–6, proposed that the year-long exposition of the relics (1238–9) prior to their tranlsation into the new Marienschrein could conceivably be considered the first *Heiligtumsfahrt*. During this time, pilgrims who reached the city to adore the exposed relics one week before or after the Feast of the Dedication of the chapel (July 17) were awarded indulgences tantamount to the ones granted by Pope Leo III and the 365 bishops who allegedly consecrated the chapel *c.* 802. Schiffers also proposed that the completion of the new Marienschrein and the translation document were closely connected to the introduction of the septennial rotation of the exposition of the relics and that the translation document and the promise of indulgences served, in part, as an advertisement to lure pilgrims to Aachen. For a transcription of the relics that were exposed and translated into the new Marienschrein, see Meuthen, *Aachener Urkunden*, pp. 349–52, No. 124. On the indulgences granted, see Meuthen, *Aachener Urkunden*, p. 269, No. 74, p. 352, No. 125, p. 369, No. 154. On the pilgrimage in general, see Johann Hubert Kessel, *Geschichtliche Mitteilungen über die Heiligtümer der Stiftskirche zu Aachen nebst Abbildung und Beschreibung der sie bergenden Behälter und Einfassungen* (Cologne, 1874); Beissel, *Aachenfahrt*.

[13] Studies on the pilgrimage liturgy include, Michael McGrade, "Affirmations of Royalty: Liturgical Music in the Collegiate Church of Mary in Aachen, 1050–1350" (Ph.D. diss., University of Chicago, 1998); Eric Rice, "Music and Ritual in the Collegiate Church of Saint Mary in Aachen, 1300–1600" (Ph.D. diss., Columbia University, 2002).

[14] "Urbs Aquensis, urbs regalis Regni sedes principalis Prima regum curia," "City of Aachen, royal city, principal seat of the kingdom and first court of kings." The complete text appears in a late twelfth-century gradual, Aachen Domarchiv, HS G13 fol. 149v–150r. As a sequence, *Urbs aquensis* comprised part of the liturgy of the Mass for the Feast of St. Charlemagne (January 28) and was performed immediately before the gospel was read. Its place in the Mass can be found in an Aachen Missal, Aachen Domarchiv HS G18 fol. 180r. On the identity and significance of

The two Aachen shrines belong clearly to the tradition of gold-smithing in the Rhine and Meuse regions during the Middle Ages. As golden architectural structures encrusted with glistening gemstones, ancient cameos, and opulent enamel, the shrines radiate a majestic aura reminiscent of the Heavenly Jerusalem envisioned by John in Rev. 21.[15] Art historians have long discussed the political significance of the Karlsschrein as a manifestation of the sacred empire revived by Frederick I Barbarossa (1155–90).[16] Additionally, they have addressed the anomalous program of rulers that has displaced the more tra-ditional apostles and prophets who typically appear on the lateral sides. Most notably, Ursula Nilgen identified and discussed the significance of an extended genealogy of kings and emperors;[17] and more recently, Renate Kroos has noted anew that several of the rulers comprising the so-called genealogy on the Karlsschrein share a unique bond as benefactors or donors,[18] each ruler has offered, in the tradition of Charlemagne, a considerable donation to the chapel of St. Mary.

the city of Aachen and its Palace Chapel, see Erich Stephany, "Aachen im Land zwischen Rhein und Maas," in *Rhein und Maas: Kunst und Kultur 800–1400*, ed. Anton Legner (Cologne, 1973), 2, pp. 123–8. For the promotion of Barbarossa's political interests manifested in the text of *Urbs Aquensis*, see Michael McGrade, "O Rex Mundi Triumphator: Hohenstaufen Politics in a Sequence for Saint Charlemagne," *Early Music History* 17 (1998), pp. 183–219; McGrade, "Affirmations of Royalty," pp. 121–67; Birgit J. Lermen, "'Urbs Aquensis, urbs regalis . . .'—Versuch einer Deutung der Karlssequenz," in *Karl der Große und sein Schrein in Aachen: Eine Festschrift*, ed. Hans Müllejans (Aachen, 1988), pp. 167–86.

[15] The Karlsschrein measures 94 cm h, 204 cm l, 57 cm w and its conservation project was completed in 1988. The Marienschrein measures 95 cm h, 184 cm l, and 54 cm w and its conservation project was completed in 2000.

[16] Hans Peter Hilger, "Sacrum Imperium Insignien und Denkmale," in *Ornamenta Ecclesiae: Kunst und Künstler Romanik*, ed. Anton Legner (Cologne, 1982), 3, pp. 185–92; Ernst Günther Grimme, "Das Bildprogramm des Aachener Karlsschreins," in *Karl der Große und sein Schrein in Aachen*, ed. Hans Müllejans (Aachen, 1988), p. 126, sug-gested that the representation of a row of kings transforms the Karlsschrein into a "radiating apotheosis of the legitimization of Staufen lordship;" but this interpreta-tion is compromised by the fact that rulers other than Staufens are depicted. See fn. 39.

[17] Ursula Nilgen, "Amtsgenealogie und Amtsheiligkeit, Königs-und Bischofsreihen in der Kunstpropaganda des Hochmittelalters," in *Studien zur mittelalterlichen Kunst 800–1250: Festschrift für Florentine Mütherich zum 70. Geburtstag*, ed. Katharina Bierbrauer (Munich, 1985), pp. 217–34. Editors' note: see also Benoit van den Bossche's essay in this volume.

[18] Renate Kroos, "Zum Aachener Karlsschrein 'Abbild staufischen Kaisertums' oder 'fundatores ac dotatores,'" in *Karl der Große als vielberuferer Vorfahr: Sein Bild in der Kunst der Fürsten, Kirchen und Städt*, ed. Lieselotte E. Saurma-Jeltsch (Sigmaringen, 1994), pp. 49–61.

Often overlooked, however, is the function of the Karlsschrein as a reliquary—that is, as a manifestation of the holy—and its iconographic and liturgical relationship with the Marienschrein. As manifestations of the holy, both the Karlsschrein and Marienschrein reflect the visual narratives of sacred history that defined the cults of Charlemagne and the Virgin in Aachen, and more significantly, reinforced the metaphysical union between the two patron saints of the chapel. In the following paper I will focus on the extent to which the shrines were brought into "communion" with one another, that is, how, as vessels of divine intervention, the shrines were joined in the same liturgical dialogues of prayer that summoned the efficacies of their relics.

From the manuscripts in the Aachen Cathedral archives it is possible to glean information regarding the rituals performed in and around the altars where the shrines were installed and in many cases, the liturgy written exclusively for the Carolingian chapel concords with the imagery on the two shrines.[19] Before I begin my liturgical study of these reliquaries, I will first present a brief overview of the art-historical significance of the Karlsschrein and its iconographic relationship to the Marienschrein.

The Karlsschrein: Background and Description

"On Monday, July 27, 1215, after celebrating the feast of St. James, Frederick II, grandson of Frederick I Barbarossa, laid down his mantle, and with hammer in hand and accompanied by the master goldsmith, climbed the scaffold, and drove in the last nail that sealed shut the Karlsschrein."[20] With this dramatic gesture, Frederick II

---

[19] Fortunately Aachen's primary source material is abundant, albeit not complete. The exhibition, "Federstrich: Liturgische Handschriften der ehemaligen Stiftsbibliothek" (2000–2001) showcased the Cathedral archive in Aachen as home to one of the most complete collections of extant liturgical manuscripts written for a single church. *Federstrich: Liturgische Handschriften der ehemaligen Stifsbibliothek* (Eupen, 2000); Odilo Gatzweiler, "Die liturgischen Handschriften des Aachener Münsterstiftes," *Zeitschrift des Aachener Geschichtsvereins* 46 (1924), pp. 1–222.

[20] *Reineri Annales S. Iacobi Leodiensis*, in *MGH SS*, 16:673, cited by Kaemmerer, *Quellentexte*, pp. 126–9:

> *Feria secunda missa sollemniter celebrata, idem rex corpus beati Carlomanni, quod avus suus Fredericus imperator de terra levaverat, in sarcofagum nobilissimum, quod Aquenses fecerant,*

sealed not only the great sarcophagus-shaped reliquary of Charlemagne, but the fate of all later medieval German rulers who claimed descent from their newly-sainted Carolingian forefather.[21] It is not known precisely when work began on the Karlsschrein; the 1215 eyewitness account of Reiner of Liège is the only extant dated document to mention the "sealed" work. Recent dendrochronological examinations conducted on the wooden core of the Karlsschrein during the 1980s conservation prove 1182 as a *terminus post quem*[22]—fifteen years after the canonization of Charlemagne. Nevertheless, it is highly probable that plans for the Karlsschrein were well underway when, on December 29, 1165, Frederick I Barbarossa ceremoniously raised the body of Charlemagne from its tomb in the chapel, and with the help of Rainald von Dassel chancellor and archbishop of Cologne († 1167), personally canonized Charles as an episcopal act with the consent of the imperial anti-pope Paschal III (1164–68).[23] The solemn event occurred thirteen years after Frederick I was crowned (March 9, 1152) and instituted his new polity between his self-acclaimed Holy Roman Empire and the papacy in Rome.[24]

---

auro argento contextum reponi fecit et accepto martello depositoque pallio, cum artifice machinam ascendit, et videntibus cunctis, cum magistro clavos infixos vasi firmiter clausit; reliquum diei predicationie cessit.

[21] No doubt Frederick II was aware of the political and religious implications of his act; Petersohn, "Kaisertum und Kultakt," pp. 101–46.

[22] The results of this examination revealed that the oak tree used for the wooden core was felled, at the earliest in 1182, and that it was worked immediately afterwards; Mechtild Neyes, "Dendrochronologische Untersuchungen," in *Der Schrein des Karls des Großen, Bestand und Sicherung 1982–1988* (Aachen, 1998), pp. 111–3; Dietrich Kötzsche, "Der Holzschrein des Karlsschreins in Aachen," *Kunstchronik* 38/2 (1985), p. 41. Nilgen, "Amtsgenealogie," p. 232, fn. 10, points out that 1182 could also mark the *terminus ante quem* for the conceived program of the shrine.

[23] See fn. 7.

[24] According to Heinrich Appelt, "Die Kaiseridee Friedrich Barbarossas," in *Friedrich Barbarossa*, ed. Günther Wolf (Darmstadt, 1975), pp. 218–9, the earliest evidence of the term *sacrum imperium* or sacred empire, appeared in a March 1157 letter written by Barbarossa to Bishop Otto von Freising; *MGH Diplomata regum et imperatorum Germaniae*, 10, *Friderici I Diplomata*, ed. Heinrich Appelt, pt. 1, No. 163, p. 280. For the foundations of Barbarossa's "holy empire," see Rainer Maria Herkenrath, "Regnum und Imperium in den Diplomen der ersten Regierungsjahre Friedrichs I.," (1969; repr. in *Friedrich Barbarossa*, pp. 323–359); Bernhard Töpfer, "Kaiser Friedrich Barbarossa—Grundlinien seiner Politik," in *Kaiser Friedrich Barbarossa: Landesausbau—Aspekte seiner Politik—Wirkung*, eds. Evamarie Engel, Bernhard Töpfer (Wiemar, 1994), pp. 9–30; Engels, "Karl der Große und Aachen," pp. 348–56; Ursula Nilgen, "Herrscherbild und Herrschergenealogie der Stauferzeit," in *Krönungen:*

Scholars have speculated on the extent of Barbarossa's involvement with the program of the Karlsschrein, as well as the circumstances regarding the preservation of Charlemagne's remains before,
during, and immediately after the 1165 canonization ceremony.
Unfortunately, no documentary sources survive that reveal the original
location of Charlemagne's tomb within the Palatine Chapel, or the
placement of his remains before Frederick I canonized him. Apparently,
sometime before his death in 814, Charlemagne had expressed his
wish to be buried near the grave of his father Pepin in the Abbey
Church of Saint-Denis.[25] According to Einhard (c. 770–840), Charlemagne was entombed in his beloved chapel on the day of his death
and a gilded arch with his statue and an inscription were raised
above the tomb.[26] After the late ninth-century Norman invasion of
Aachen, the chapel was looted and the location of Charlemagne's
grave fell into oblivion. Determined to align himself with the legacy
of his grandfather, Otto III (r. 996–1002) set out to uncover the lost
tomb of Charlemagne. Various accounts record how Otto III uncovered the grave; however, as Helmut Beumann suggested, these were
likely to have been embellished and redacted in response to the 1165
canonization.[27]

Könige in Aachen, 1, pp. 357–67; Karl Leyser, "Frederick Barbarossa and the
Hohenstaufen Polity," in *Communications and Power in Medieval Europe: The Gregorian
Revolution and Beyond*, ed. Timothy Reuter (London, 1994), pp. 115–42; Günther
Wolf, "Imperator und Caesar—zu den Anfängen des staufischen Erbreichsgedankens,"
in *Friedrich Barbarossa*, pp. 360–74; Erich Meuthen, "Karl der Grosse—Barbarossa—
Aachen: Zur Interpretation des Karlsprivilegs für Aachen," in *Karl der Große Lebenswerk
und Nachleben*, IV, pp. 54–76. See also Benjamin Arnold, *Medieval Germany, 500–1300:
A Political Interpretation* (Toronto, 1997).

[25] *MGH Diplomata regum Germaniae ex stirpe Karolinorum*, ed. Engelbert Mühlbacher,
No. 55, p. 81.

[26] Einhard, *Vita Caroli* 4.30, *Einhard and Notker the Stammerer, Two Lives of Charlemagne*,
ed. and trans. Lewis Thorpe (Baltimore, 1969), p. 31. Einhard did not specify the
exact location.

[27] The *Chronicon Novaliciense* (1027–1050) 3.32 in *MGH SS* 7:106, which reports
how, on Pentecost of 1000, Otto III—led by Divine Providence—uncovered the
tomb and found the body of Charlemagne seated upright in his throne and in good
condition, and that he (Charlemagne) was crowned and held [a] scepter in [his]
hand; Beumann, "Grabe und Thron," pp. 24–9. According to Stephen Nichols,
Romanesque Signs: Early Medieval Narrative and Iconography (New Haven, 1983), p. 66,
the most reliable account seems to be that of Thietmar, bishop of Merseburg
(975–1018) who recorded that the emperor

> was in doubt as to the exact spot where the remains of the emperor Charles
> reposed. He ordered the stone floor to be secretly excavated at the place where
> he thought them to be; at last they were discovered in a royal throne. Taking

After Otto III's death in 1002, his body was also laid to rest in the chapel. Several medieval chronicles record that his grave was located in the middle of the Carolingian choir;[28] and according to Aachen's oldest extant necrology (thirteenth century) Otto III was buried "beneath the reliquary of St. Charlemagne."[29] It is not entirely clear if Otto III was responsible for relocating Charlemagne's remains to the middle of the choir.

According to the *Annales Cameracenses* (*c.* 1170), Frederick I "raised the relics of Charlemagne from a sarcophagus and carefully and deferentially placed them in a golden vessel."[30] The *Continuatio Sigiberti Aquicinctina* (1182–92) reports that the body of Charlemagne "was raised out of its marble grave [and] was held *in locello ligneo*—in a wooden casket—in the middle of the chapel."[31] From the former

---

the golden cross which hung from Charlemagne's neck, as well as the unrotted parts of his clothing, Otto replaced the rest with great reverence. See also Nichols, *Romanesque Signs*, pp. 217–8, esp. fn. 5–7.

[28] Joseph Buchkremer, "Zur Baugeschichte des Aachener Münsters," p. 228, fn. 1; "Das Grab Karls des Großen," p. 178, gathered evidence from the *Chronicle of Thietmar of Merseburg*, which recorded Otto III's remains as "*in medio sepelitur chori,*" (being buried in the middle of the choir). Chronicles written by Lantbertus, Thangmar, and Agidius von Orval similarly document the grave as "*in choro sancte marie*" (in the choir of St. Mary's); "*sepultus est in medio chori*" (in the middle of the choir); and "*ante altare sanctae mariae in choro*" (before the altar of St. Mary in the choir), respectively.

[29] "*sub feretro sancti Karoli,*" (written in a later hand, *c.* 1280–1331); Eduard Teichmann, "Das älteste Aachener Totenbuch," *Zeitschrift des Aachener Geschichtsvereins* 38 (1916), p. 53. Otto was buried in this place of honor, until his remains were relocated to the center of the Gothic choir after its consecration in 1414.

[30] *Annales Cameracenses* (1170), in *MGH SS* 16:538, cited by Meuthen, *Aachener Urkunden*, p. 107, "*Dominus Fredericus semper augustus domni Caroli Magni corpus de sarcophago sustulit et in vaso aureo diligenter et honorifice restituit 4. Kal. Ianuarii*" (referring to the year 1165).

[31] *Sigiberti Continuatio Aquicinctina*, in *MGH SS,* 6:411; cited in Meuthen, *Aachener Urkunden*, p. 107

Fredericus imperator natale Domini in palacio suo celebravit Aquis, ad cuius curiam omnes optimates tocius regni, sive ecclesiastici seu seculares, ab ipso submoniti convenerunt, et corpus domini Karoli Magni imperatoris, qui in basilica beate Marie semper virginis quiescebat, de tumulo marmoreo levantes, in locello ligneo in medio eiusdem basilice reposuerunt.

For additional documents regarding the twelfth-century elevation and preservation of Charlemagne's relics, see *Gaufredi de Bruil prioris Vosiensis Chronica* (1183), in *MGH SS* 26:202; *Gotifredi Viterbiensis Memoria seculorum* (1175/85), in *MGH SS* 22:159; cited by Meuthen, *Aachener Urkunden*, p. 107. On the basis of these reports, Nilgen, "Amtsgenealogie," p. 218, argues that a greater reliquary was originally planned for all the relics, but since the canonization was rather sudden, there was no time to complete a larger and more appropriate shrine befitting the saint.

document, Ursula Nilgen has interpreted "golden vessel" (*in vaso aureo*) to mean the Louvre Arm Reliquary, donated by Frederick I and most likely completed for the canonization ceremony in 1165.[32] The word *corpus* as the arm relics—a powerful symbol of Charlemagne's imperial and ecclesiastical might—further represented all the relics of Charlemagne. Nilgen deduced that the remaining relics of Charlemagne (minus the arm) were held in a wooden casket in the middle of the chapel until the sealing of the Karlsschrein in 1215, and further proposed that even before the 1165 canonization ceremony a reliquary shrine, grander than the present Louvre casket, was intended for the remains of Charlemagne, and that Frederick I provided for some of its expenditures, because the final conception and iconographic program of the Karlsschrein was consistent with the Staufen ideology of sacred empire.[33] Also linking Frederick I to the Karlsschrein, Ernst Günther Grimme has suggested that the image of Charlemagne on the narrow end of the shrine was intended to be a dual portrait of Charlemagne and Frederick as the "Novus Carolus Fridericus."[34]

---

[32] The Arm Reliquary donated by Barbarossa to the chapel is a rectangular wooden casket with a hinged lid. On the inside of the lid, an inscription identifies the relics as "the arm of the glorious and holy emperor Charles," (BRACHIUM SANCTI ET GLORIOSISSIMI IMPERATORIS KAROLI). Resembling a portable altar, the casket is covered with gilt silver, copper-embossed reliefs, and champlevé enamel. Slender colonnettes support an arcade that wraps around the sides of the reliquary. In the spandrels are champlevé enamel plaques and beneath the arches are half-length figures. Central on the front is the crowned Virgin holding the Christ Child flanked by the archangels Gabriel and Michael. In parenthetical fashion, the donor, identified by the inscription FREDERICUS ROMANORUM IMPERATOR AUGUSTUS appears beneath the outer left arch, and beneath the outer right is Empress Beatrix. On the back, Christ is flanked by Peter and Paul. Beneath the outer two arches are Conrad III (Barbarossa's uncle) and Duke Frederick of Swabia (possibly Frederick I's father). On one narrow end Louis the Pious is shown, while on the opposite is Otto III. Both figures are identified by inscriptions. In 1794 Napoleon removed the Arm Reliquary from the Aachen Treasury and brought it to Paris where it was later acquired by the Louvre. *Krönungen Könige in Aachen*, vol. 1, pp. 72–3, 387–88; *Rhein und Maas*, 2, p. 244; Dietrich Kötzsche, "Zum Stand der Forschung der Goldschmiedekunst des 12. Jahrhunderts im Rhein-Maas-Gebiet," in *Rhein und Maas*, 2, pp. 191–236, *Die Zeit der Staufer. Geschichte, Kunst, Kultur*, ed. Reiner Haussherr (Stuttgart, 1977–9), 1, Cat. No. 538.

[33] Nilgen, "Amtsgenealogie," pp. 218–20.

[34] Ernst Grimme, "Der Aachener Domschatz," *Aachener Kunstblätter* 42 (1972), p. 66; *Goldschmiedekunst des Mittelalters, Form und Bedeutung des Reliquiars* (Cologne, 1972), pp. 66, 70; "Bildprogramm," 126–7, based his interpretation on the similarity between the figure of Charlemagne on the Karlsschrein and the Cappenberg Head of Frederick I. Even before Grimme, Erich Stephany, *Der Karlsschrein* (Mönchengladbach, 1965), p. 15, drew attention to the similarities between the two works. Kroos, "Zum

Frequently criticized, Grimme's interpretation should not be dismissed too quickly: Frederick I's association with the Karlsschrein must be reassessed, especially in connection with the elaborate chandelier he commissioned. Like a monumental halo suspended from the cupola directly above the octagonal space of the Carolingian choir, the chandelier encircled the remains of Charlemagne before and after their translation into the Karlsschrein.[35] As mentioned, the *Continuatio Sigiberti Aquicinctina* suggests that the middle of the choir was already associated with Charlemagne's relics before their elevation and translation into the Karlsschrein in 1215.[36] As a result, the Barbarossa-chandelier emphatically punctuated the Carolingian octagon, transforming the middle of the choir into a sacred space reserved for "Saint" Charlemagne, while simultaneously glorifying the munificence of Frederick I. The result was a carefully calculated manipulation of objects in space and their visual effect from above. From "God's" view from above the cupola, and from the Imperial Throne in the gallery, the chandelier encircling the Karlsschrein echoed an image of Frederick I on his golden Imperial Bull, *c.* 1168.[37] Such a visual parallel is compelling and warrants further investigation. Overlooked, but nevertheless pertinent to this study, is the prominence of this space, a new *locus sanctus* that was now a major focal point

---

Aachener Karlsschrein . . .," esp. pp. 49–57, on the other hand, argued against Frederick I's involvement with the program of the Karlsschrein.

[35] Grimme,"Bildprogramm," p. 133, also makes this observation.

[36] That the middle of the choir was reserved as a sacred "Charlemagne" space seems to have originated here.

[37] On the bull, a bust portrait of Frederick I is surrounded by an architectural corona intended to represent the City of Rome, the *Aurea Roma*. Grimme, "Bildprogramm," pp. 33–4, has suggested that the overall architectural profile of the city represented here echoes that of the Barbarossa chandelier, and that the chandelier was perhaps also intended to evoke the City of Rome itself. In my opinion, more important is the similarity between the golden bull and the visual effect of the chandelier encircling the Karlsschrein. Such a comparison strengthens the argument that Frederick I was involved in the initial plans for the Karlsschrein to be installed beneath the chandelier, particularly if we consider Grimme's suggestion that Frederick I was represented in the figure of Charlemagne on the Karlsschrein. For an in-depth analysis of the imagery, inscriptions, and iconography of Barbarossa's chandelier and their liturgical relationships to the Karlsschrein in the middle of the choir, see my doctoral dissertation, "Manifestations of the Holy as Instruments of Propaganda: the Cologne Dreikönigenschrein and the Aachen Karlsschrein and Marienschrein in Late Medieval Ritual," (Ph.D. diss. Rutgers University, 2003), pp. 120–6.

of the chapel, perhaps second only to the high altar itself.[38] Indeed, a unique liturgy was written for this new sacred space demarcated by the presence of "Saint" Charlemagne *sub corona* and *in medio chori*.

Description of the Karlsschrein

The Karlsschrein is raised on a socle, the architectural/sarcophagus-shaped reliquary is topped by a saddle roof. The lateral walls are articulated by an arcade, eight round arches to a side, framing sixteen enthroned figures of rulers, of which fifteen are identified by inscriptions running along the bands of the framing arcade.[39] In the spandrels of the arcade are three-quarter length figures of (counseling?) angels, some of whom hold books. A lengthy inscription around the base of the shrine reaffirms the chapel in Aachen as the site of the royal coronation and as seat of the imperial throne. Moreover, it states unequivocally that the heirs to Charlemagne's realm have the right to seek the imperial title in Rome.[40]

---

[38] Prior to the elevation of Charlemagne's relics, the altar in the middle of the octagon, also referred to as the *Altare omnium sanctorum*, or Altar of All Saints, was dedicated in 1076 by Henry, Bishop of Liège; *MGH SS* 30: 780 (no. 11). It is also possible that as early as 1230, the altar was associated with Charlemagne; Buchkremer, "Das Grab Karls des Grossen," p. 92.

[39] For a transcription of the inscriptions, see Giersiepen, *Die Inschriften des Aachener Doms*, p. 29; Helga Giersiepen, "Die Inschriften," in *Der Schreins Karl des Großen, Bestand und Sicherung 1982–1988* (Aachen: Einhard, 1998), pp. 28–31. The arrangement is as follows: (to the right of the Charlemagne side, left to right) Henry III, Zwentibold, Henry V, Henry IV, Otto IV, Henry I, Lothar (I), and Louis the Pious. To the left: Henry II, Otto III, Otto I, Otto II, Charles (the Fat?), an unidentified king, Henry VI, and Frederick II. Whether or not these inscriptions, as well as those along the base of the shrine, have been rearranged is a frequently posed question. The corresponding nail holes suggest that the current arrangement, after the restoration/conservation work, is original. Chronologically the rulers reigned: the Carolingians Louis the Pious, Lothar, Charles the Fat, Zwentibold of Lotharingia; the Saxons Henry I, Otto I, II, III, Henry II; the Salians Henry II, IV, V; the Staufer Henry VI; the Guelph Otto IV, and the Staufer Frederich II. The genealogy on the Karlsschrein does not however represent a complete line of rulers; the west Frankish lines are absent: Conrad II, Lothar von Dupplinburg, and Conrad III. Nilgen, "Amtsgenealogie," pp. 218–20, has suggested that Frederick I Barbarossa, who is not represented on the shrine, was perhaps the "unknown" king, and that the gap in the lineage suggests that the "original" composition may have included two additional rows of rulers. Morever, Kroos, "Zum Aachener Karlsschrein . . .," p. 60; *Der Schrein des heiligen Servatius in Maastricht und die vier zugehörigen Reliquiare in Brüssels* (Munich, 1985), p. 123, has posed the question as to whether or not Otto IV would have been represented beneath the missing inscription.

[40] +DECRETV(M)· ET · SANCITV(M) · E(ST) · A · DO(MI)NO ·

As was customary for this genre of reliquary shrines, the roof was reserved for a hagiographic cycle. On the Karlsschrein's roof, eight rectangular fields are filled with reliefs that show scenes from the *Vita Sancti Karoli*[41] that emphasize the twelfth-century Crusader ethos.

AP(OSTO)LICO • LEONE • ET • A • ME • KAROLO• ROM(ANORVM) • I(M)P(ER)ATORE • AVGVSTO • EX • ASSENSV • ET • BENIVOLENTIA • O(M)NIV(M) • P(RI)NCIPV(M) • I(M)P(ER)II • V(T) • AQ(V)ISG(RA)NI • IN • TE(M)PLO • BEATE • MARIE • MATRIS • D(OMI)M [sic!] I IH(ES)V (CHRISTI) • REGIA • SEDES • LOCARETVR • ET • LOC(VS) • REGAL(IS) • ET • CAPVT • O(M)NIV(M) • CIVITATV(M) ET • P(RO)VINCIARV(M) • GALLIE • T(RA)NS • ALPES • HABERETVR • AC • IN • IPSA • SEDE • REGES • SVCCESSORES • ET • HEREDES • REGNI • INIETARENTVR • ET • SIC • INICIATI /+IVRE • DEHINC • I(M)P(ER)ATORIA(M) • MAIEST(AT)E(M)• ROME • SINE • VLLA • INTERDICTIONE • PLANIVS • ASSEQVENTVR • ET • VT • EVNDE(M) • LOC(VM) • ET • SEDE(M) • REGIA(M) • CONT(RA) • O(M)NES • TVRBINES • TVRBINES(!)• VNIVERSI • PRINCIPES • ET • FIDELES • REGNI •·TVERENTVR • SE(M)P(ER) • H(VN)C • LOC(VM) • VENERANTES • ET • HONORANTES • IBI • STATVS • LEGIS • RESVRGAT • INIVRIA • CONDE(M)PNETVR • IVSTICIA • REFORMETVR • AC • O(M)NECS(!)• PARITER • EX • AVIS • ET • A[TTAVIS AD] /HA(N)C • SEDE(M) • P(ER)TINENTES • LICT(!) • ALIBI • MORA(M) • FACIENTES • NV(M)QVA(M) • DE • MANV • REGIS • V(E)L • I(M)P(ER)ATORIS • ALCVI(!) • P(ER)SONE • NOBILI • V(E)L• IGNOBILI • IN • BENEFICIO • TRADANTVR • DECRETV(M) • E(ST) • ETIA(M) • VT • NON • SOLV(M) • CLERICI + ET • LAICI • LOCI • HVIVS • INDIGENE • SED • ET • OM(NE)S • INCOLE • ET • ADVENE • HIC • INHABITARE • VOLENTES • P(RE)SENTES • ET • FVTVRI • SVB • ·TVTA • ET • LIBERA • LEGE • AB • O(M)NI • SERVILI • CONDITIONE • VI[TAM • AGANT].

Giersiepen, "Die Inschriften," p. 31. (It was decreed and ratified by the apostolic reverend Leo [Pope Leo III] and by me, Charles, emperor and augustus of the Romans . . . that the royal seat be located in Aachen, in the temple of blessed Mary, mother of the Lord Jesus Christ, and [that] the city be held as capital of all cities and provinces in Gallia North of the Alps. And succeeding kings and heirs to the realm should be appointed in this place [*sedes*], and those so appointed by right should then attain the imperial majesty in Rome without further resistance or difficulties . . . Let the condition of the law rise again [in Aachen], let injustice be judged, and justice be restored.) English translation in McGrade, "Affirmations of Royalty," p. 222. Hermann Fillitz, "Die Kunsthistorische Stellung des Karlsschreins," in *Der Schrein Karls des Großen*, p. 13, has demonstrated that the language of the inscription harks back to a forged document issued by Frederick I to promulgate the canonization of Charlemagne. On the forged document, see Meuthen, "Karl der Gross . . ." pp. 54–76.

[41] Scenes include: The Dream of Charlemagne (on the left, an apparition of St. James the Apostle appears to the emperor in his sleep; on the right, Charlemagne stares at the Milky Way); The Conquest of Pamplona; The Miracle of the Cross; The Miracle of the Blooming Lances; The Cavalry Battle; The Confession of Charlemagne; Charlemagne receiving the Crown of Thorns; and the so-called Widmungs Relief, or Dedication of the Palace Chapel to the Virgin. Written in c. 1180, the *Vita Sancti Karoli*, or *Karlsvita*, inspired, along with the *Kaiser Chronik*, the themes of the roof reliefs. On the *Vita Sancti Karoli*, see Gerhard Rauschen, ed., *Die Legende Karls des Großen im 11. und 12. Jahrhundert* (Leipzig, 1890). On the concor-

On one narrow end a figure of Charlemagne is enthroned., flanked by diminutive figures of Pope Leo III and Bishop Turpin of Reims (748/9–94).[42] (fig. 346) Charlemagne is directly beneath the Pantocrator who extends his hand in a benediction over the head of the newly-sainted Carolingian, perhaps to confer the imperial title and to approve his sainthood. The inscription in the clipeat around the Pantocrator reads, "Guide of the World, you who rule eternally, be protector of Creation."[43] The inscription following the rise and fall of the gable refers to Charlemagne, "You are the light, who has been the precious stone of the church of Christ, Charles, flower of the kings, ornament of the globe, and Guarantor of the law.[44] The latter inscription identifies Charlemagne as co-ruler with Christ, a sentiment which harks back to the sequence *Urbs Aquensis*.[45] Empty today, the two outer roundels were likely filled with bust-length figures.[46] They have been replaced with modern gilded copperplates decorated with lozenge patterns. On the narrow side opposite Charlemagne are the enthroned Virgin and Child flanked by archangels Gabriel and Michael. (fig. 347) An inscription on the arch framing the Virgin identifies her as "Holy Mary, Mother of Mercy,"[47] while

---

dances between the *Vita* and the themes of the roof reliefs, see Folz, *Le souvenir*, pp. 281–2; Eduard Arens, "Die Inschriften am Karlsschrein," *Zeitschrift des Aachener Geschichtsvereins* 34 (1921), pp. 159–94. On the extent to which the legends of Charlemagne and Roland are depicted in the roof reliefs, see Grimme, "Bildpro-gramm," pp. 129–32; Rita Lejeune and Jacques Stiennon, *La Légende de Roland dan's l'art du moyen âge* (Brussels, 1967), 1, pp. 169–77. On the themes of the reliefs and their liturgical concordances with the Office of St. Charlemagne, see McGrade, "Affirmations of Royalty," For the significance of these scenes as propaganda to establish Aachen as a major pilgrimage site, see Engels, "Karl der Große und Aachen," pp. 353–4.

[42] In the twelfth century, Bishop Turpin was erroneously believed to have been the author of the *Pseudo-Turpin Chronicle*, which was consulted by the writers of the twelfth-century *Vita Sancti Karoli*.

[43] +CVNCTA • REGENS STABILIS • Q(VE) MANENS DO CVNTA(!) • MOVERI. My English translation was aided by Stephany's German translation, *Der Karlsschrein*, p. 13.

[44] ECCLESIE CRISTI TV • LVX • TU GEMMA • FVISTI + KAROLE FLOS • REGVM DEC(VS) • ORBIS (ET) ORBITA • LEGVM.

[45] Stephany, *Der Karlsschrein*, p. 13.

[46] Hans Peter Hilger, "Zum Karlsschrein in Aachen," *Jahrbuch der rheinischen Denkmalpflege* 30/31 (1985), pp. 69–70, argues that personifications of "Sol" and "Luna" once filled the roundels; whereas Erich Stephany, *Der Karlsschrein*, pp. 13–4, suggested figures of SS. Peter and Paul, and Hermann Schnitzler, *Rheinische Schatzkammer* (Düsseldorf, 1959), 2, *Die Romanik*, pp. 19–20, proposed angels.

[47] S(ANCTA) • MARIA • MATER • MISERICORDIE + Giersiepen, "Die In-schriften," p. 28.

the inscription on the gable is a petition for her intercession as "Mary, Star of the Sea."[48] In roundels above are personifications of the three theological virtues: Fides (Faith), Spes (Hope), and Caritas (Divine Love); around the central clipeat is the inscription, "This is the heavenly love, which includes all the virtues."[49] After the Karlsschrein was sealed in 1215, plans were launched for a new Marienschrein, and the Karlsschrein's imagery and inscriptions contributed to the iconographic program designed for the new Marienschrein.

The Marienschrein: Background, Description, and its Iconographic Connection to the Karlsschrein

When the decision was made to create a new shrine dedicated to the Virgin, one truly suitable to worthily house the relics preserved in the older container, it was not surprising to find the cult of Charlemagne revived and incorporated into its program, and Frederick II, like his illustrious grandfather Frederick I, responsible for part of the expenditures of such a costly and precious project.[50] The new Marienschrein was commissioned not only to replace the older reliquary at the high altar,[51] but also to reaffirm and to further define the revived cult of Charlemagne: his relic-cult was inextricably woven into the Virgin's, and their union was visually reinforced in the program of the new Marienschrein.

---

[48] +STELLA MARIS • PARERE • QVE • SOLA • DEVM • MERVISTI • VIRGO • MANENS • PLACA • NOBIS • PRECE • QVEM • GENVISTI; Giersiepen, "Die Inschriften," p. 28.

[49] +HEC • EST • VIRTVTES • KARITAS • QVE • CONTINET • OMNES; Giersiepen, "Die Inschriften," p. 28.

[50] The earliest mention of the new Marienschrein is in the April 19, 1220 document recording Frederick II's decision to give a quarter of the revenues of an offering to the chapter for repairs of damaged church furnishings, with the stipulation that work be executed on the Marienschrein; Meuthen, *Aachener Urkunden*, pp. 261–2, no. 67. It is not entirely clear in the document whether work on the shrine had already begun by this time; however, it is generally believed that Frederick II's offer was substantial and funded part of its expenses.

[51] According to the translation document, the older reliquary was described as being "demolished from old age and very scarcely decorated with gold, silver or precious stones and appeared not so worthy to hold such a significant collection of relics." (*et idem feretrum non apertum fuisset, vetustate demolitum minimoque decore auri vel argento seu preciosorum lapidum decoratum, ut comprehensione tantarum reliquiarum, sicut in eo fuisse legimus, minus dignum videretur.*)

Begun by some of the same goldsmiths who worked on the Karls-schrein, the Marienschrein innovatively points to a new direction in the evolution of micro-architecture.[52] Constructed in the shape of a single-aisled church with a sloping roof, the Marienschrein is bisected in the middle at right angles by a shorter cross-aisle. The overall impression is that of a miniature church with a central transept.[53] Unlike the rounded arches on the Karlsschrein, the pointed gables on the Marienschrein form right angles, consisting of decorative strips of alternating enamel and filigree work set with gemstones. The outer edges of the gables are decorated with combs and crowned with the traditional knobs. The gables rest upon clusters of slender colon-nettes and frame seated figures. Another striking feature of the Marienschrein is its stylistic dichotomy, an issue discussed by art historians for more than two centuries.[54]

[52] The Master of the Dedication relief on the Karlsschrein has been identified as the first supervisor of the workshop where the Marienschrein was constructed and the roof reliefs on the Charlemagne side of the Marienschrein are stylistically similar to the Dedication relief on the Karlsschrein; Schnitzler, *Rheinische Schatzkammer*, 2, p. 23; Ernst Günther Grimme, *Aachener Goldschmiedekunst im Mittelalter von Karl dem Grossen bis zu Karl V* (Cologne, 1957), p. 72.

[53] Scholars have longed discussed the architectural nature of the Marienschrein and its innovative form. While there was no specific prototype for its "transept," the Marienschrein is not entirely without a forerunner. For example, the Aetheriusschrein subtly suggests a transept, but its form is more dependent on Roman and Late Antique sarcophagi than it is on monumental architecture; *Ornamenta Ecclesiae*, 2, p. 350. Other examples include the early thirteenth-century Honoratusschrein in Siegburg. It is possible that its "transept"—which is closer to a dormer in appearance—was a later addition and worked into a pre-existing sarcophagus-shaped shrine. In addition to shrines produced in the Rhineland, there were a number of Limoges enameled architectural reliquaries with "transepts"; Marie-Madeleine Gauthier, *Émaux du moyen âge occidental*, 2nd ed. (Fribourg, 1972), pp. 335–6; Joseph Braun, *Die Reliquiare des christlichen Kultes und ihre Entwicklung* (Freiburg im Breisgau, 1940); these, too, lack the architectural vocabulary and integration of components that set the Marienschrein apart from the others. Schnitzler, *Rheinische Schatzkammer*, 2, p. 23, noted that the architectonic nature of the Marienschrein's "transepts" dominate the otherwise broad and symmetrical lateral sides of the shrine. The emphatic middle axis, which Schnitzler suggested reflects the influence of "centrally planned" reliquaries, draws attention away from the narrow ends of the shrine and creates its own display side.

[54] Two distinct styles are apparent: the lateral side with the main figure of Charlemagne, the six apostles, and the roof reliefs, as well as the narrow end with Pope Leo III, belong to one stylistic group and exhibit the characteristic *Rillenfaltenstil*, sharp drapery folds that fall without any reflection of an underlying anatomy. On the opposite lateral side, the Virgin and Child and corresponding apostle figures and roof reliefs, as well as the narrow end with Christ in Majesty, reflect the introduction of a new Gothic style, fully developed, plastic figures charged with movements accentuated by the drapery. See Fitschen, *Goldschmiedeplastik des Marienschreins*.

Four large-scale figures are placed on the narrow ends and on the transept sides. Under pointed trefoil arches on one lateral side and in the central transept-portal the Virgin and Child are enthroned. On the opposite lateral side, in an analogous arrangement, is an enthroned figure of Charlemagne. Garbed in the contemporary dress of a king, he once held an orb in his left hand and the scepter in his right.[55] Beneath a gable on one narrow end is Christ in Majesty; on the opposite is Pope Leo III.

Unlike the Karlsschrein, the Marienschrein adheres closely to the traditional program of architectural reliquaries. Figures of the apostles appear beneath the pointed gables on the lateral walls, while above, the sloping roof is divided into framed fields that are enclosed under trefoil arches and separated by paired colonnettes. Bust-length angels, five to a segment, fill the spandrels. On the Charlemagne side the scenes from the infancy of Christ are shown,[56] and on the Virgin side the scenes from the Passion are shown.[57] The cycles begin and end with the figure of Christ in Majesty on the narrow end.[58]

---

[55] According to Arthur Martin, "La châsse de Notre Dame," *Mélanges d'archéologie, d'histoire et de littérature* 1, ed. C. Cahier and Arthur Martin (1847), pp. 5–20, esp. plate III, Charlemagne held an orb in his left hand and a scepter in his right. In addition, Charlemagne's crown was missing. Kessel, *Geschichtliche Mittheilungen über die Heiligthümer*, p. 11, shows the Marienschrein with Charlemagne holding a model of the church in his left hand. C.G. Schervier, *Die Münsterkirche zu Aachen und deren Reliquien* (Aachen, 1853), p. 33, recorded that the figure of Charlemagne on the Marienschrein held the scepter in one hand and the orb in the other. The left arm of Charlemagne, the orb, and the model of the chapel are now lost. A decision was made not to replace them during the 1989–2000 conservation project. There is no way of knowing whether Charlemagne originally held an orb or a model of the chapel, these could have been replacements for an earlier model of the chapel, but it is likely that the orb came first.

[56] From left to right they are the Annunciation, Visitation, Birth, Dream of Joseph, Bath of Christ, Annunciating Angels (two reliefs), Shepherds, Adoration of the Magi, and Presentation in the Temple.

[57] From left to right they are the Baptism, Temptation of Christ, Last Supper, Arrest, High Priest Caiphas, Pilate, Flagellation, Crucifixion, Deposition, Embalming/Entombment.

[58] Erich Stephany, "Der Marienschrein im Aachener Dom, Ein Zeugnis für die Marienverehrung im Hohen Mittelalter," in *Die Gottesmutter. Marienbild in Rheinland und in Westfalen*, ed. Leonhard Küppers (Recklinghausen, 1974), pp. 111–2, demonstrated that the roof reliefs on the Marienschrein form a crescendo as they unfold the "beginning and end" of the sacred history of Christ's Nativity (on the Charlemagne side) and Passion (on the Virgin side), ultimately culminating in the triumphal image of Christ in Majesty on the narrow end. Ernst Grimme, "Die Ikonographie des Aachener Marienschreins," in *Der Aachener Marienschrein*, pp. 91–9, suggested that the roof relief depicting the Entombment conflated with the Anointing of Christ's dead

When the Marienschrein was sealed in 1239, its original plan provided no means for making the relics visible, nor did it permit the
easy removal of its relics from the cavity. Herta Lepie proposed that
the addition of the little door on the wooden core behind the figure
of the Virgin was made at some uncertain date after the 1239 translation.[59] Around the same time of the alterations, a decision was
reached that the Marienschrein would preserve only four relics, the
so-called "Great Relics," and that the rest be placed in smaller reliquaries, which were soon incorporated into liturgies and became
focal point of pilgrimage as well.[60] As a result of this alteration, the
transept façade of the Marienschrein now had a unique and innovative function: the little door behind the transept, with its figure of
the *Dei Genetrix* or Mother of God, on its portal, was transformed
into a gateway that gave access to the inner sanctuary of the reliquary, the "womb" of *Maria Ecclesia* or Mary as the Church.[61]

Like the Karlsschrein, the Marienschrein includes in its program
the same individuals who helped shape the history and identity of
Aachen as a sacred and royal city. On the Marienschrein, their
emphatic presence is crucial to the overall program and function of

body, is an unusual subject with which to conclude a Passion cycle. In my dissertation, I have suggested that perhaps this was an allusion to the anointing of the
king at the Marienschrein during his Coronation Mass. Lisa Victoria Ciresi,
"Manifestations of the Holy as Instruments of Propaganda: the Cologne
Dreikönigenschrein and the Aachen Karlsschrein and Marienschrein in Late Medieval
Ritual" (Ph.D. diss. Rutgers University, 2003), p. 175. Gertrud Schiller, *Iconography
of Christian Art*, trans. Janet Seligman (Greenwich, CN, 1972), 2, p. 172, pl. 590,
discussed this relief as an example of the early thirteenth-century practice of conflating
the Anointing and Entombment of Christ.

[59] Herta Lepie, "Die Aachenfahrt," in *Wallfahrt im Rheinland*, ed. Amt für Rheinische
Landeskunde (Cologne, 1981), pp. 79–84; Herta Lepie, "Der Aachen Marienschrein,"
in *Rheinische Heimatpflege* 24 (1987), p. 193.

[60] Many of these reliquaries are kept in the Aachen Cathedral Treasury, including the Reliquary of Charlemagne or *Karlsreliquiar* (*c.* mid-fourteenth century); the
Three Tower Reliquary or *Dreiturmreliquiar* (*c.* 1370–90); the Reliquary of St. Simeon
or *Simeonsreliquiar* (*c.* 1330–40); *Drei kleinen Heiligtümer* (*c.* 1370–80) or reliquary for
Christ's belt, reliquary for Mary's belt (*c.* 1360), and the reliquary for the cord used
to scourge Christ (*c.* 1380). Grimme, "Der Aachener Domschatz."

[61] Only one Rhenish architectural shrine allowed viewing of relics, the Cologne
Shrine of the Three Kings or *Dreikönigenschrein* (*c.* 1180–*c.* 1220, possibly later) by a
trapezoid plate, which, when removed, allowed the relics of the Three Kings pre-
served within to be seen. The trapezoid was removed during Masses on Sundays,
Mondays, Wednesdays, and on the feast of the Epiphany (January 6), among others;
Walter Schulten, "Der Ort der Verehrung der Heiligen Drei Könige," in *Die Heiligen
Dreikönige—Darstellung und Verehrung*, ed. Rainer Budde (Cologne, 1982), pp. 61–72.

the shrine and to understanding its relationship to the Karlsschrein. The inscriptions and figural imagery on both shrines resonated with one another as they united the two relic-cults of the patron saints and tied the late medieval cult of kingship to the legacy of a newly-"sainted" Charlemagne.

E.G. Grimme was among the first to discuss the twelfth-century Staufen revival of Charlemagne's cult and its connection to the "Heiligtum," the principal relics preserved in the chapel.[62] Like Grimme, I believe the significance of this connection was politically motivated. Although the liturgy for the Feast of Charlemagne had already established the spiritual bond between the two patron saints of the chapel, a relationship reaffirmed each time the Mass and Office of St. Charlemagne were celebrated, the visible manifestations of their metaphysical union were further encoded into the programs of Aachen's two principal shrines. The repetition of the characters on the new Marienschrein reflected the chapter's effort to promulgate Charlemagne's canonization and to weave his legendary deeds—including his acquisition of the Marian relic as recorded anew in the twelfth-century *Vita Sancti Karoli*,[63] and the spurious papal consecration of the chapel, into the cult of the Virgin Mary, thereby rendering their newly sainted Carolingian forefather inseparable from the Mother of God. While the legitimacy of Charlemagne's canonization ceremony was questionable, the chapters' attempts to update his legendary associations with the Virgin's cult in Aachen would have helped to validate his sainthood.

Oddly enough, the program of the Marienschrein reveals little, if anything, about the relics which it held—those allegedly acquired by Charlemagne. The canons of the chapel had some idea of the nature of the relics they possessed, as noted in an inventory dating *c.* 1200, the list includes a "tunic (*velamine*) of the Virgin," "the loincloth worn by Christ while he was being crucified," and a "tattered swaddling cloth within which he was wrapped while in his crib."[64] Nevertheless, there seems to have been no attempt to reflect the nature of these relics in the program of the new Marienschrein. What is certain is

---

[62] Ernst Günther Grimme, "Karl der Große in seiner Stadt," in *Karl der Große, Lebenswerk und Nachleben*, IV, pp. 229–73.

[63] Rauschen, *Legende Karls des Großen*, p. 62.

[64] "*de velamine . . .*," "*de vestimentis Domini cum quibus crucifixus est*," "*de pannis Domini quibus in presepio fuit involutus*;" Beissel, *Aachenfahrt*, pp. 54–5, fn. 2.

the intent to repeat on the Marienschrein the same principal figures on the Karlsschrein: the Virgin and Christ child, an image of Christ making a gesture of benediction, Charlemagne enthroned and adorned with his insignia, and Pope Leo III. These four figures are crucial to the programs of both the Karlsschrein and the Marienschrein, and to understanding the unique and dynamic relationships between the two shrines, their relics, and their surrounding spaces within the chapel.

On the Marienschrein, the significance of the Virgin is clear: as the *Regina Coeli* or Queen of Heaven, Mary wears the crown, as the *Sedes Sapientiae*, or Throne of Wisdom, she supports the princely Christ child on her lap; and as the apocalyptic woman, she crushes the dragon beneath her feet—a reference to her triumph over evil in Rev. 12.1–18. Here, the golden cult-figure of the Virgin becomes the representative image of the Virgin's presence, the divine instrument of intercession.[65] Like the image of Charlemagne on the Karlsschrein, the figure of Charlemagne on the Marienschrein held the orb in one hand and the scepter in the other.[66] Jürgen Fitschen noted that Charlemagne's presence on the Marienschrein also represents the great Carolingian as Christ's co-ruler, and further signifies the source and symbol of the Roman-German empire.[67] The accompanying inscriptions reaffirm this sentiment,[68] but more significantly, they resonate with the inscriptions on the Karlsschrein that declare Charlemagne as Christ's co-ruler, whose kingdom should be lawfully inherited by all his rightful successors.[69] As a result, the shrines were conceived of as legal documents translated into precious materials, validating the king's right to inherit the holy office founded upon Charlemagne's

---

[65] This is reinforced by the inscription, [. . . . .] E NATO PRECE CUNCTA REGENTEM UT REGAT ET SALVET NOS O [P]IA PO[. . .]; Gierseipen, *Die Inschriften*, p. 37. Loosely translated, "through your prayers to the all Governing, may he guide and protects us." For the effectiveness of an image as a representative proxy for a saint, see Ilene Forsyth, *The Throne of Wisdom: Wood Sculptures of the Madonna in Romanesque France* (Princeton, 1972), p. 49. The same may be said for the golden cult-figures of the Virgin and Child on the Karlsschrein, another reference to the Throne of Wisdom.

[66] See fn. 55.

[67] Fitschen, *Goldschmiedeplastik des Marienschreins*, p. 73.

[68] [. . .] MAGNIQ[V]I REGVA GVBERNA[N]S MVNDI REX NERVIT SVP[ER] OM[NE]S MAGN[VS] HABERI[. . .]; Giersiepen, *Inschriften des Aachener Doms*, p. 37. Loosely translated, ". . . who, governing empire, to be rightfully earned above all great kings of the world."

[69] See fn. 40.

kingdom. This was significant for the king during his coronation ritual and Mass, which as mentioned above, occurred in the chapel in
the presence of both the Karlsschrein and Marienschrein.[70]

One narrow end of the Marienschrein was reserved for the figure
of Christ in Majesty. Crowned, Christ is shown as the King of kings.
In his left hand he holds the orb, while his right arm is raised in a
gesture of benediction. As the inscription suggests, the figure of Christ
is understood as both the Creator and the *Iudex*, or Judge, who sits
in judgment at the altar on high during the Second Coming.[71] On
both shrines, the figure of Pope Leo III confirms the legendary papal
consecration of the chapel—as suggested by the accompanying inscription on the Marienschrein,[72] and by the aspergillum with which he
is shown on the Karlsschrein. In addition, Leo III's presence also
reaffirms Charlemagne's imperial title and right to govern above all
other kings, as implied in the inscription around the figure of
Charlemagne on the Marienschrein.[73]

More significantly, I believe that the figure of Charlemagne on
the Marienschrein should be understood in connection with the
figures of the Virgin and Child (on the opposite end of the shrine),
as he is symbolically aligned along the same axis, a spatial relationship between the two patron saints analogous to that on the
Karlsschrein. On the Karlsschrein, Charlemagne is enthroned, and
with his earthly representatives at his side,[74] he gazes towards the

---

[70] See final fn.

[71] Fitschen, *Goldschmiedeplastik des Marienschreins*, pp. 58–9, 77, fn. 76, discussed the
significance of the inscriptions around Christ, +SOLUS AB ETERNO CREO
CUNCTA CREATA GUBERNO PONTUS TERRA POLUS MIHI SUBDITUR
HEC REGO SOLUS and beneath Christ's feet, +SPES EGO LAPSORUM PAX
IUSTIS PENA REORUM, suggesting that the latter had a unique significance for
the coronation ceremony, referring to the king's conferral of title by Christ himself. Fitschen cites what he believes to be a literary prototype for the inscriptions
used on the shrine, claiming that the Marienschrein's deviation from this source
results from its unique role in coronation ritual.

[72] In the trefoil arch above and around the head of Pope Leo III the inscription
reminds one that Leo III's blessing consecrated the church that Charlemagne built,
"ECCE LEO PAPA CVI(VS) BENEDICTIO SACPA TEMPLVM SACRAVIT
QVOD KAROL(US) EDIFICAVIT."

[73] See fn. 68.

[74] Enthroned on the Karlsschrein, the figure of Charlemange sits half-way between
heaven (emphasized by his relatively-large size and his alignment directly beneath
the Pantocrator's blessing) and earth (represented by Bishop Turpin and Pope Leo
III); another visual evocation of the analogous iconographic arrangement of the
Imperial Throne in the gallery. From his throne in the gallery, Charlemagne could

Virgin and Child who await him on the opposite end—a heavenly realm that could be likened to the high altar itself. This interpretation is supported by the host of angels surrounding the Virgin and Child on the Karlsschrein, and Charlemagne's dedication—his offering of the chapel to the Virgin—is to be understood in this alignment. (The symbolic offertory gesture is also reinforced in the Dedication roof relief.) In such a reading, the donation of each ruler represented on the lateral walls of the shrine is likewise commemorated.[75] The axial relationship between Charlemagne and the Virgin on the shrines is also found in the interior space of the octagon. Turned inside out, both shrines share a program that echoes the spatial dispositions in the chapel. To the west and aligned on the same axis as the high Marian altar (in the east) are the Imperial Throne—itself a reliquary[76]—in the gallery and the "Charlemagne" space in the middle of the Carolingian octagon and beneath the Barbarossa chandelier. (fig. 348) In my opinion, such an evocation of this macrocosmic alignment on the main axes of Aachen's two principal shrines could hardly be coincidental or without significance.

The four main figures not only occupy prominent positions on both shrines, reaffirming their roles in the sacred history of Aachen, but they imply in their alignments to one another on the shrines, a series of dynamic interactions among the figures themselves and to their surrounding spaces within the Carolingian octagon. The significance of these spatial relationships depended, in part, on the iconographic relationships between the shrines, as well as to their

---

gaze directly into the cupola at an image of a triumphal Christ, underscoring the Christomimetic nature of the emperor's kingship. Forsyth, *Throne of Wisdom*, pp. 88–9, suggested that this visual metaphor was made explicit by its axial relationship to the Altar of the Savior in the east-end of the gallery and directly above the high Marian altar. For literature concerning the cupola's original Carolingian programs and twelfth-century decorations, see Ernst Günther Grimme, *Der Dom zu Aachen: Architectur und Ausstattung*, (Aachen, 1994), pp. 42–6; Ulrike Wehling, *Die Mosaiken im Aachener Münster und ihre Vorstufen* (Cologne, 1995), pp. 12–50.

[75] My dissertation, "Manifestations of the Holy," pp. 66–106, presents the significance of this interpretation within the context of the coronation ritual that was performed in the chapel. See fn. 101.

[76] Frequently associated with the Throne of Solomon, the Imperial Throne—the seat of secular and sacerdotal rule—was not only one of the single most significant symbols of the German dynastic heritage, but it also functioned as a reliquary. According to recent dendrochronological tests, the throne dates from around the year 800, during Charlemagne's reign; Sven Schütte, "Der Aachener Thron," in *Krönungen: Königen in Aachen*, 1, (Mainz, 2000), pp. 213–22.

connections to their respective altars, including the orientations of
the shrines, facing west or east.

Most art historians agree that both the old and new Marienschreins
were closely connected to the high altar table,[77] however, the precise locations of both Marian shrines and their altar table in the
sacred space of the Carolingian rectangular apse remain obscure.
Moreover, the original orientation of the Karlsschrein in the middle
of the choir and the new Marienschrein at the high altar table have
also been lost.[78] Fortunately, the oldest extant ordinale (c. 1339–51),
written exclusively for the Carolingian chapel, lists all the altars before
the consecration of the Gothic choir in 1414.[79] One of the most
revealing ordos in the manuscript was written for Maundy Thursday
for the Procession of the Washing of the Altars. Beginning with the
three most significant altars, the high Marian altar, the altar of St.
Peter, and the altar dedicated to All Saints in the middle of the
choir—also later referred to as the altar of St. Charlemagne—the ordo
lists, in sequence all the altar tables that were included in the procession, and provides the appropriate prayers and ablutions performed at each. From the entry it is possible to understand the spatial
dispositions of the altars and their relationships throughout the ground
floor and gallery of the Carolingian octagon. Interestingly, the first
three altars shared a unique relationship: they were, along with the
Karlsschrein and Marienschrein, on the same axis and aligned with
the Eucharist at the high altar. The axial relationships among these
principal altars and their shrines were strengthened during the celebration of a liturgy written specifically for these spatial demarcations.

The Karlsschrein and its Significance in Aachen's Liturgy

Recently, scholars have broadened the definition of liturgy to include
social conduct such as the traditional lay rituals enacted in and
around sacred cult sites.[80] Such a definition is indeed applicable to

---

[77] While most art historians agree that the new Marienschrein was connected to
a mensa, they do not agree on which one; Fitschen, *Goldschmiedeplastik des Marienschreins*,
pp. 55–7.

[78] See fn. 87.

[79] Aachen, Aachen Domarchiv, HS G1, fol. 23v.

[80] C. Clifford Flanigan, Kathleen Ashley, and Pamela Sheingorn, "Liturgy as

the Heiligtumsfahrt ceremonies;[81] however, to discuss the function of medieval instruments that aided in the service of the Office and Mass, I shall consider a more traditional definition. In this context, I define liturgy as a dialogue of speech, chant and gesture, which opens the gateway to the cosmic realm and allows the temporal world to embark upon its processional journey into sacred time and space; where the infinite intersects with the finite and the two realms momentarily co-exist.[82] With this definition, I shall examine the function of the Karlsschrein in one of the most significant liturgies written for the chapel, the Feast of the Purification.

Among the highest feasts in the Carolingian octagon during the Middle Ages was the Marian feast of the Purification, celebrated on February 2.[83] The ceremony commemorates the symbolic cleansing (or purification) of Mary in the temple, forty days after she gave birth to Christ, as stipulated by Jewish Law. For Aachen, this was a particularly significant celebration because the Marian feast of the Purification fell within the octave, the eight-day cycle, of the Feast of Charlemagne, whose own high feast was on January 28. According to an ordinale written after the late canonization of Charlemagne and particularly for the Carolingian octagon, the following are directions for second Vespers for the Office of Purification

---

Social Performance: Expanding the Definitions," in *The Liturgy of the Medieval Church*, eds. Thomas J. Heffernan and E. Ann Matter (Kalamazoo, MI, 2001), pp. 695–714.

[81] An important eye-witness account of the various lay rituals enacted during the *Heiligtumsfahrt* ceremonies in Aachen is that of Phillip de Vigneulles in 1510. How these rituals enhanced the pilgrimage experience for the supplicants deserves to be examined in its own right; but such an investigation is beyond the scope of this study. For the Memoirs of Phillipe de Vigneulles, *Das Gedenkbuch des Metzer Bürgers Phillipe von Vigneulles aus den Jahren 1471 bis 1522 nach der Handschrift des Verfassers*, ed. Heinrich Michelant (Stuttgart, 1852), pp. 170–84; Wynands, *Die Aachener Heiligtumsfahrt*.

[82] My use of liturgy in this context is based upon the Catholic theology of liturgy as presenting in "new reality" the events of the Gospel in Anamnesis (a prayer in the context of a Eucharistic service that calls to mind the Passion, Resurrection, and Ascension of Christ) as a perpetual sign not of a past history, but as a present reality of life in Christ; Robert Taft, *The Liturgy of the Hours in East and West* (Collegeville, MN, 1986), pp. 331–64.

[83] Referred to today as Candlemas, the feast commemorating the purification of the Virgin in the temple and the presentation of Christ in the temple forty days after his birth, as required by Jewish law (Luke 2:21–39). To conclude the purification ritual, the mother was required to offer a lamb or doves; Frederick G. Holweckt, "Candlemas," *The Catholic Encyclopedia*, vol. 3, Online ed., (Accessed March 2, 2003) http://www.newadvent.org.

Then two boys [*scholares*] wearing albs, [and] standing behind [*retro*] the shrine of blessed Charles, sing the antiphon *Ecce completa sunt omnia*. Then [they sing the same antiphon] in polyphony [*in organis*], [then it is sung] the same way after this by the choir. The verse *Speciosus forma* and the collect *Deus qui salutis*. The *Benedicamus domino* [is sung by] the aforementioned two boys.[84]

That the *scholares* are instructed to approach the Karlsschrein—to enter literally into the sacred space of Charlemagne—and to chant a Marian antiphon during a high Marian feast—demonstrates a conscious attempt to bring into communion the two patron saints of the chapel during the overlap in their liturgical cycles. More importantly, the commingling of liturgies strengthens the mystical bond between the relic-cult of Charlemagne and that of the Virgin, a relationship manifested in the imagery on both shrines.

As specified in the ordinal, the Marian chant *Ecce completa sunt*[85] was recited during second vespers, the hour that signified the culmination of the feast.[86] While the text itself was universal, its performance behind the Karlsschrein is exclusive to the Carolingian octagon. My examination of this text vis-à-vis the imagery on the Karlsschrein and its spatial relationship to the Marienschrein, offers a possible solution to an otherwise unresolved issue regarding the orientation of the Karlsschrein, which end of the shrine faced east and thus towards the high Marian altar where the Marienschrein was installed. For both shrines, the question of orientation has received attention;[87] however none of the proposed suggestions have convincingly

---

[84] Aachen, Aachen Domarchiv, HS G1 fol. 61v, "*Deinde duo scholares induti albis sta(n)tes retro capsam beati karoli cantent an(tiphona) Ecce completa sunt omnia, deinde in organis ide(m) post hec a choro. V(ersus) Specios(us) forma coll(ecta) Deus qui salutis. A predictus duob(us) scolaribus Benedicamus d(omino).*" Teichmann, "Zur Lage und Geschichte des Grabes Karls des Großen," p. 168; McGrade, "Affirmations of Royalty," p. 235; Rice, "Music and Ritual," p. 259. The English translation from Rice, "Music and Ritual," p. 258.

[85] "*Ecce completa sunt omnia quae dicta sunt per angelum de virgine maria,*" comes from the thirteenth-century antiphonal, Aachen, Aachen Domarchiv, HS G20 fol. 244v.

[86] Often specific acts and miracles of the saint were symbolically dedicated to a specific hour of the Divine Office. Moreover, some hours were associated with certain mysteries or events in the life of Christ; Dom Baudot, *The Breviary: Its History and Contents* (London, 1929), pp. 124–38. For additional literature on the liturgy of the office, see Taft, *Liturgy of the Hours*; Pierre Salmon, *The Breviary Through the Centuries*, trans. Sister David Mary (Collegeville, MN, 1962).

[87] Based on the function of the Marienschrein during the Coronation Mass of the Roman-German king, which occurred at the Marian altar, Joseph Buchkremer,

demonstrated the relationship between the liturgy and imagery on these multifaceted reliquaries.[88]

On one narrow end of the Karlsschrein is an image of the enthroned Virgin and Child. According to the ordo quoted above, two *scholares* stand *retro capsam beati karoli*, behind the shrine of blessed Charles. Thus, the most appropriate façade for the *scholares* to address on the Karlsschrein while reciting a Marian antiphon would be the Virgin side. The image not only reaffirms the historical and spiritual bond between the Virgin and Charlemagne, but it is transformed into a mediating device as the text *Ecce completa sunt*, is recited and recalls, "all things have been completed as said by the angel of Mary." On the Karlsschrein, the archangels Gabriel and Michael, identified by their inscriptions, flank the image of the Virgin and Child, as they further signify the beginning and culmination of Mary's role in salvation through Christ, the Annunciation and Last Judgment, and thus

---

"Rezension der Kunstdenkmäler der Rheinprovinz," *Zeitschrift des Aachener Geschichtsvereins* 38 (1916), p. 303, suggested that the most appropriate side of the Marienschrein to face west would be the narrow end with Christ in Majesty "greeting" the Virgin side of the Karlsschrein, which he argued was at the altar dedicated to St. Peter beneath the east bay (before it was moved to the Gothic choir in 1414). He also suggested that the Virgin side of the Marienschrein faced the north, or "female side" of the chapel, while the Charlemagne side faced the south, or towards the "male side." This would have left Pope Leo III facing east. Scholarship supports this reconstruction including Fitschen, *Goldschmiedeplastik des Marienschreins*, p. 57, fn. 112, who has dismissed the markings found on the underside of the bottom board of the wooden core of the Marienschrein during its restoration. Regina Urbanek, "Bericht zur Untersuchung und Konservierung der Fassungen am Holzkern des Aachener Marienschreines," (Aachen: unpublished report, June 1997), p. 3, suggested that the shrine was attached to a rotation mechanism (date unknown); an observation made earlier by Stephany, "Der Marienschrein im Aachener Dom," p. 106. In my doctoral dissertation, "Manifestations of the Holy," I examine anew the function of the Marienschrein's imagery during the Coronation liturgy and consider all the possible "appropriate sides to face west" that would have been facilitated by a rotation device.

[88] The significance of the passage from Aachen Domarchiv HS G1 fol. 61v, with the full text of the chants performed by the shrine has not been considered. Teichmann, "Zur Lage und Geschichte des Grabes Karls des Großen," p. 168, focused on the meaning and significance of *retro* and *ante* in an attempt to establish the locations of the altars and shrines in the Carolingian octagon. McGrade, "Affirmations of Royalty," p. 235, cites the passage to demonstrate the relationship between Charlemagne and the Virgin during such an "extraordinary digression" of ritual in the chapel. Rice, "Music and Ritual," pp. 259–62, focused on the aspect of performance, chant, polyphony, and the significance of the phrase *in organis*, as well as the fifteenth-century alterations of the performance to conform to the new space offered by the Gothic choir.

Ecce completa sunt, all things are completed. Together, the *scholares'* gesture towards the shrine and their recitation of the Marian text emphasize the overlap in the two feast cycles, strengthen the bond between the relic-cult of St. Charlemagne and the Virgin, and literally join Charlemagne and the Virgin in a common dialogue of gesture and chant as the liturgies intersect—a metaphysical mystery perpetually recounted in the imagery on both the Karlsschrein and Marienschrein. Apart from the concordance with the liturgical text, the figural programs on the shrines echo the macrocosmic relationship between the *loca sancta* of Charlemagne and the Virgin in the chapel. On both shrines Mary and Charlemagne are aligned along the same axis, a spatial and dynamic connection first established between Charlemagne's Imperial Throne and the Marian altar. (fig. 348)

Originally, the Carolingian chapel was a centrally-planned structure with two focal points. The middle of the choir was emphasized by its octagonal shape crowned with a cupola from which was suspended the Barbarossa chandelier; to the east was the little Carolingian rectangular apse, which gave the otherwise centrally-planned building its longitudinal focus. Uniting these two focal points, or sacred spaces, was an east-west axial relationship reinforced by the Marian liturgy. With the Virgin side of the Karlsschrein facing east and towards the Marienschrein, a unique "Marian" space was partitioned. (fig. 343). This provided the stage for the temporal world to journey into sacred space and time as the efficacies of the relics of the Virgin and Charlemagne were summoned as transmitters of power. Moreover, the axial relationship between the Karlsschrein and the Marienschrein reinforced the symbolic link between the relics of Charlemagne, the Virgin, and the Eucharist at the high altar.[89] As a result, the interior space of the Carolingian chapel was defined by a complex network of vertical and horizontal axial relationships that united the various focal points as the liturgy was being performed.[90]

---

[89] Thomas Dale, *Relics, Prayer and Politics in Medieval Venetia: Romanesque Painting in the Crypt of Aquileia Cathedral* (Princeton, 1997), p. 16 reached a similar conclusion concerning the relationships among the altars and relics. For the relationship between relics and Eucharist, see Godefridus J.C. Snoek, *Medieval Piety from Relics to the Eucharist: A Process of Mutual Interaction* (Leiden, 1995).

[90] On the same axis as Charlemagne's throne, the altar of the Savior was originally installed in the gallery directly above the high Marian altar. Forsyth, *Throne of Wisdom*, pp. 88–90, suggested that the spatial relationship between Mary's pres-

The liturgical union of the two relic-cults of the patron saints of the Aachen chapel is not limited to the feast of Purification. Written for the Mass of St. Charlemagne, the twelfth-century sequence *Urbs Aquensis* [91] consists of three parts. The first celebrates the "presence" of King Charlemagne,[92] the second recounts his deeds, and the final part summons Mary as the *Stella Maris*,[93] or Star of the Sea, and concludes with an invocation to Christ, the Virgin, and to Charlemagne.[94] With regard to the Karlsschrein, the penultimate versicle[95] is significant, because it invokes Mary as the *Stella Maris*. From the hymn, *Ave Maris Stella*[96] comes the association with Mary as the Star of the Sea. Inspired by this Marian appellation, the composer of the inscription on the gable of the Virgin side of the Karlsschrein invokes the Stella Maris, and the inscription reads, "Mary, Star of the sea, who alone earned to give birth to God and remained Virgin, reconcile us through your intercession with the one to whom this one has given birth."[97] Additionally, the inscription in the arch above the Virgin refers to her as the Mother of Mercy, a reminder that through

---

ence at the Marian altar and the manifestation of Christ at the Altar of the Savior was not unlike the relationship between the Virgin and Child in the Throne of Wisdom imagery.

[91] See fn. 14.

[92] "*Regi regum pange laudes quae de magni regis gaudes Karoli praesentia.*" Aachen, Aachen Domarchiv, HS G13 fol. 149v–150r. (Sing to the King of Kings the praises with which you celebrate the presence of King Charlemagne.) The use of the present tense here re-affirms the medieval perception of relics in which the saint was indeed alive and the efficacy of his deeds and miracles were "present." Translations from McGrade, "Affirmations of Royalty," pp. 131–4.

[93] "*Stella maris O Maria Mundi salus vitae via Vacillantum rege gressus Et ad regem des accessus In perhenni gloria*" Aachen, Aachen Domarchiv, HS G13 fol. 149v–150r. (Star of the sea, O Mary, salvation of the earth, way of life, guide the unsteady step and grant access to the king in perennial glory.)

[94] "*Christe splendor dei patris Incorrupte fili matris Per hunc santum cuius festa Celebramus nobis presta sempiterna gaudia,*" Aachen, Aachen Domarchiv, HS G13 fol. 149v–150r. (Christ, splendor of God the Father, Son of the incorrupt mother, offer us everlasting joy through this saint whose feast we celebrate.)

[95] In Christian liturgies, a versicle is any short text (often said by celebrant or deacon) followed by an answer or response from the congregation or choir; Peter Le Huray, "Versicle," *The New Grove Dictionary of Music*, Online edition, ed. L. Macy (Accessed February 5, 2003) http://www.grovemusic.com.

[96] The hymn *Ave Maris Stella* (ninth-century) Codex Sangallensis 95 has been attributed to various authors including Paul the Deacon (*c.* 720–*c.* 800), "Ave Maris Stella," in *The Oxford Dictionary of the Christian Church*, eds. F.L. Cross, E.A. Livingstone, 2nd ed. (New York, 1974), p. 115.

[97] See fn. 48.

her divine mercy and virtues, personified above in the roundels, she intercedes for the supplicant. Similarly, this theme is manifested in the last two versicles of *Urbs Aquensis*, the passage invoking Mary as the *Stella Maris*, and one that concludes, "Christ, splendor of the Father, Son of the incorrupt Mother, grant us eternal joy through the saint (Charlemagne) whose feast we now celebrate."[98] The liturgical union of the two cults is therefore recounted in the sequence for the Mass of St. Charlemagne, and indelibly inscribed on the Karlsschrein as well.

Reference to the *Stella Maris* on the Karlsschrein may also have additional significance in the context of a reliquary. According to the text of the *Ave Maris Stella*, "Mary the Mother of God and Gate of Heaven appears as the loving helper who frees prisoners from their fetters, brings light to the blind, drives away ills and asks for all good things."[99] Significantly, she helps sinners in her position of mother. The composer of the prayer asks her to show herself a mother by using her influence with her son, Christ. Moreover, the

---

[98] See fn. 94.

[99] Hilda Graef, *Mary A History of Doctrine and Devotion*, 4th ed. (London, 1994), pp. 174–5. Associated with the attributes of her Assumption, Mary as Star of the Sea in the hymn, *Ave Maris Stella*, is not the queen of heaven celebrated on the Assumption, but the maternal intercessor who shows herself a mother by using her influence with her son,

Ave, maris stella, Dei Mater alma, Atque semper Virgo, Felix caeli porta. Sumens illud Ave Gabrielis ore, Funda nos in pace, Mutans Hevae nomen. Solve vincla reis, Profer lumen caecis, Mala nostra pelle, Bona cuncta posce. Monstra te esse matrem, Sumat per te preces, Qui pro nobis natus Tulit esse tuus. Virgo singularis, Inter omnes mitis, Nos culpis solutos, Mites fac et castos. Vitam praesta puram, Iter para tutum, Ut, videntes Iesum, Semper collaetemur. Sit laus Deo Patri, summo Christo decus, Spiritui Sancto, Tribus honor unus. Amen.

Breviarium Romanum (Rome, 1961).

Hail, Star of the Sea. Blessed Mother of God, yet ever a Virgin. Thou that didst receive the Ave from Gabriel's lips, confirm us in peace, and so let Eva be changed into an Ave of blessing for us. Loose the sinner's chains, bring light to the blind, drive from us our evils, and ask all good things for us. Show thyself a mother, and offer our prayers to him, who would be born of thee, when born for us. O incomparable Virgin, and meekest of the meek, obtain us the forgiveness of our sins, and make us meek and chaste. Obtain us purity of life, and a safe pilgrimage; that we may be united with thee in the blissful vision of Jesus.

Trans. 1997 EWTN Online Services (Accessed February 15, 2003) http://www.EWTN.com.

composer prays that she, gentle above all others, should make us gentle and chaste, giving us a pure life and a safe journey.[100] The *Stella Maris* was a favorite theme of Marian devotion frequently interpreted and commented upon by exegetes throughout the centuries;[101] however, by the time of Franciscan theologian Bonaventure (1217–74) the association of the *Stella Maris* with the Feast of Purification was firmly established, for as Star of the Sea Mary purifies, illuminates and perfects those in this world.[102] Bonaventure also stressed the need for sinners to bid her intercession and to imitate her virtues. This dogma is echoed in both the imagery and inscription on the Virgin side of the Karlsschrein.[103] The inscription on the gable is a petition

---

[100] Graef, *Mary*, pp. 174–5.

[101] It was favored by the barbaric Germanic tribes who found comfort in and were "tamed" by the gentle maternal nature of Mary as the Guiding Star of the Sea. In his sermon on the beginning of the Gospel of St. Matthew, Walafrid Stabro († 849) a monk from the abbey of Fulda, and later abbot of Reichenau, referred to Mary as the Star of the Sea, and interpreted the light of this star as "Christ whom we must follow." Graef, *Mary*, p. 175. It is possible that the figure of Mary on the Karlsschrein was also understood as the Guiding Star or star of Bethlehem, and the light of this star as Christ whom led the Magi to the new-born king. Such an interpretation is reinforced by the rock-crystal mounted in the peak of the gable above the figure of Mary on the Virgin side of the Karlsschrein. As the new Magi, the Roman-German kings were required to offer gifts to the Virgin and Child on the occasion of their coronation. See fn. 104.

[102] In his first sermon on the Purification, the Franciscan theologian Bonaventure interpreted Mary's name as "bitter sea," "mistress," and as "Star of the Sea." This is based on the assumption that M*iryam* (Hebrew for Mary) is composed of the words *mar* (bitter) and *yam* (sea). At times *Miryam* is considered as a compound word consisting of two nouns, *mari* and *yam*, meaning mistress of the sea and Star of the Sea. *Stella Maris* is the most popular interpretation of *Miryam*, dating to St. Jerome (*c.* 342–420). See A.J. Maas, "The name of Mary," *The Catholic Encyclopedia* vol. 15, On-line ed. (Accessed February 11, 2003) www.newadvent.org; Graef, *Mary*, pp. 285–6. Although the Karlsschrein was completed before Bonaventure's time, the *Stella Maris* as the maternal intercessor was firmly associated with purification and reconciliation. The hymn, *Ave Maris Stella*, was incorporated into the Office for the feast of the Purification (first Vespers), but when this occurred is unclear.

[103] Mary, Star of the Sea, was invoked in the personal plea of Frederick I which appeared on the chandelier he donated: "Stella Maris shining forth bright in heaven, take into your devoted prayers the munificent Frederick. Unite him to his co-ruler Beatrix." (ERGO STELLA MARIS ASTRIS PREFVLGIDA CLARIS SVSCIPE MVNIFICVM PRECE DEVOTA FRIDERICUM CONREGNATRICEM SIBI IVNGE SVAM BEATRICEM.) Transcription by Clemens Bayer; reproduced in Lepie and Schmitt, *Der Barbarossaleuchter*, p. 8. Barbarossa's personal plea to the Stella Maris resonates with the inscription around the Virgin on the Karlsschrein and should be understood in connection with the shrine and its iconographic program.

of reconciliation, or purification of the sinner who prays for the miraculous intercession of the saint and Virgin mother. Undoubtedly the theologians who designed the Karlsschrein's Marian program were fully aware that the Marian feast of the Purification fell within the octave of the Feast of Charlemagne; the invocation of the *Stella Maris* on the Karlsschrein reflect another conscious attempt to unite the two relic-cults during the overlap in their liturgical cycles.

In sum, the unique bond between Charlemagne and the Virgin began immediately after the eponymous Carolingian acquired the relics of Mary and consecrated his Palace Chapel to her. After Charlemagne's canonization and the subsequent elevation of his remains to the altar *sub corona*, the relic-cults of the Virgin and Charlemagne became inseparable here and virtually synonymous with *Urbs Aquensis*, establishing the "City of Aachen" not only as a crossroads of sacred and royal devotion, but as one of the most prestigious pilgrimage sites in the North.

The holy manifestations of the Virgin and Charlemagne were nowhere more conspicuous than in the programs of the two great Aachen shrines and in their spatial relationships to one another in the Carolingian octagon. With regard to the Karlsschrein, it is tempting to suggest that Frederick I was indeed associated with the program, nevertheless, a program designed for the reliquary shrine of one of Aachen's most significant patron saints and certainly its single most significant emperor, would have involved consultation of highly-trained theologians, perhaps the scholastics among the canons. As mentioned, the theologians responsible were aware that the Marian Feast of the Purification fell within the octave of the Feast of Charlemagne. Perhaps in an effort to emphasize the liturgical overlap, they chose to manifest the Marian attributes of purification in the imagery on the Virgin side on the Karlsschrein, while simultaneously capturing the sentiments of the sequence for the Mass of Charlemagne, *Urbs Aquensis*—the prayer that invoked the intercession of both patron saints.

Moreover, in the larger iconographic program of the Karlsschrein, which included a genealogy of royal donors, it is conceivable that the maternal intercessor would have been summoned to purify and reconcile the souls of the future heirs of Charlemagne's throne. According to a fourteenth-century coronation ritual, the king was to meditate upon the *Te Deum* beneath the Barbarossa chandelier and near the Karlsschrein where he would have invoked Mary, Star of the Sea to make him worthy and pure to be anointed and to receive the crown that awaited him at the high altar and Marienschrein, the Coronation site of the Roman-German king.[104]

---

[104] Erich Stephany, "Über den Empfang des römischen Königs vor seiner Krönung in der Kirche der Hl. Maria zu Aachen—nach der Handschrift ADD. 6335 im Britischen Museum, London," in *Miscellanea pro Arte; Herrmann Schnitzler zur Vollendung des 60. Lebensjahre am 13. Januar 1965*, V, 1 (Düsseldorf, 1965), pp. 274–5. Stephany commented on this passage, probably written in the fourteenth-century, but later appended to a twelfth-century manuscript of diplomas issued under Frederick I Barbarossa (British Library Add. Ms. 6335). The passage describes the rituals for the king on the eve of his Coronation Mass in the Carolingian chapel.

BIBLIOGRAPHY

Abbreviations

MGH   *Monumenta Germaniae historica*
PG   *Patrologia cursus completus, series graeca.* Edited by Jacques-Paul Migne. Paris: Garnier fratres, 1857–1903.
PL   *Patrologia cursus completus, series latina.* Edited by Jacques-Paul Migne. Paris: Garnier fratres, 1844–1903.
SS   *Scriptores*

Primary Sources

Aachen, Aachen Domarchiv:
  – HS G 1.
  – HS G 13.
  – HS G 18.
Acta sanctorum, eds. Jean Bolland, Jean Carnandet, *et al.* Paris and Rome, 1863, Reprint, 1965.
Acta sanctorum, eds. Johannes Bollandus, Godefridus Henschenius. Antwerp: ex officina Plantiniana Balthasaris Moreti, 1643.
Adamnanus. *De locis sanctis*, ed. Denis Meehan. Scriptores Latini Hiberniae, vol. III. Dublin: School of Celtic Studies, 1983.
Ambrose. *De obitu Theodosii*, ed. Otto Faller. Corpus scriptorum ecclesiasticorum latinorum, ed. Karl Schenkl, vol. 73. Leipzig: G. Freytag, 1866.
Anonymous. "De S. Remaclo Conf. Et Episc. Trajectensi Ac Dein Abbate Stabulensi." In *Acta Sanctorum Quotquot Toto Orbe Coluntur* (1863): 669–728.
Augustine. *Sermones de tempore.* In *PL* 39:1973–2096.
De Beauvillé, Victor. *Recueil de Documents Inédits concernant la Picardie.* Vol. 3. Paris: L'Imperimerie Nationale, 1877.
———, ed. *Ordinaire de l'église Notre-Dame, Cathédrale d'Amiens, Mémoires: Documents inédits concernant la province 22.* Amiens: Société des antiquaires de Picardie; A. Picard, 1934.
Bede. *Historia Ecclesiastica Gentis Anglorum*, ed. and trans. Bertram Colgrave and Roger A.B. Mynors. Oxford Medieval Texts. 1969. Reprint, Oxford: Clarendon Press, 1992.
Benedict of Peterborough. *Miracula Sancti Thomae Cantuariensi*, ed. James C. Robertson. *Materials for the History of Thomas Becket, Archbishop of Canterbury.* Vol. 2. Longman and Co., 1876.
Bernard of Angers. *The Book of Sainte Foy*, ed. and trans. Pamela Sheingorn. Philadelphia: University of Pennsylvania Press, 1995.
———. *Liber miraculorum sancte Fidis*, 2 vols., ed. A. Bouillet. Paris: A. Picard, 1897.
Bernard of Clairvaux. *Epistolae.* In *PL* 182.
———. *Sermones de tempore.* In *PL* 183:35–360.
Biblia Sacra iuxta Vulgatam Clementinam: nova editio, logicis partitionibus aliisque subsidiis ornata a Alberto Colunga et Laurentio Turrado. 4th ed. Madrid: Editorial Católica, 1965.

The Book of Margery Kempe, ed. Lynne Staley. Kalamazoo, Michigan: Western Michigan University, 1996.

Bridget of Sweden, Saint. *Revelation of St. Bridget on the Life and Passion of Our Lord and his Blessed Mother*. Fresno: Academy Library Guild, 1957.

Burchard of Mount Sion. "*Descriptio Terrae Sanctae*." in *Palestine Pilgrims' Text Society* 12, 1896, repr., NY: AMS Press, 1971.

Canterbury Cathedral Archives:
- DCc/DE 163 (Miscellanous Accounts and Registers).
- Treasurers' Accounts, DCc/MA 1, f. 1.
- DCc/Prior 9.
- Reg. E, f. 143.
- DCc/MS Reg. K, f. 220; List of Works of Henry Eastry (*Nova Opera in Ecclesia et in Curia Tempore Henrici Prioris*).

Capes, William W., ed. *Charters and Records of Hereford Cathedral*. Hereford: Wilson and Philips, Printers, 1908.

Cassiodorus Senator. *Historia Ecclesiastica*. In *PL* 69.

Chapman, J.B.W., ed. and trans. *Calendar of the Liberate Rolls Preserved in the Public Record Office, Henry III (A.D. 1240–1245)*. 3 vols. London: Stationery Office, 1930.

The Chronicle of The Election of Hugh, Abbot of Bury St Edmunds and Later Bishop of Ely, ed. Rodney M. Thomson. Oxford: Clarendon Press, 1974.

Chrysostom, John. *In Ioannem. Homiliae*, ed. Bernard de Monfauçon. In *PG* 59.

Close Rolls of the Reign of Henry III, 4 vols. London: H.M.S.O., 1911–27.

Cyril of Jerusalem. *Epistolae ad Constantium piissimum imperatorum*, ed. Antonii Augustini Touttée. In *PG* 33:1165–76.

Daniel the Abbot. "The Life and Journey of Daniel, Abbot of the Russian Land" in *Jerusalem Pilgrimage, 1099–1185*, ed. John Wilkinson with Joyce Hill and W.F. Ryan. London: Hakluyt Society, 1988: 120–71.

——. *The Pilgrimage of the Russian Abbot Daniel in the Holy Land*, ed. and annot. Sir Charles W. Wilson. *The Library of the Palestine Pilgrims' Text Society*, vol. 3. London: The Palestine Pilgrims' Text Society, 1895: iii–82.

Dinter, Peter. *Rupert von Deutz, Vita Heriberti: Kritische Edition mit Kommentar und Untersuchungen*. Bonn: Rohrscheid, 1976.

Dossier: Neuvy-Saint-Sépulcre, Archives départementales de l'Indre, Châteauroux.

Dossier: Neuvy-Saint-Sépulcre, Bibliothèque et Archives du Patrimoine, Paris.

Dugdale, William. *Monasticon Anglicanum, sive Pandectae Coenobiorum Benedictinorum, Cluniacensium, Cisterciensium, Carthusianorum, à primordiis ad eorum usque dissolutionem, ex MSS. Codd.ad Monasteria olim pertinentia; archivis Turrium Londinensis, Eboracensis, Curiarum Scaccarii, Augmentationum; Bibliothecis Bodleianâ, Coll. Reg. Coll. Bened., Arundellianâ, Cottonianâ, Seldenianâ, Hattonianâ, aliisque digesti per Rogerum Dodsworth Eborac., Gulielum Dugdale Warwic, Monasticon Anglicanum: A History of the Abbies and other Monasteries, Hospitals, Frieries [sic.], and Cathedral and Collegiate Churches, with their Dependencies, in England and Wales. Also of all such Scotch, Irish, and French Monasteries, as were in any manner connected with Religious Houses in England. Together with a Particular Account of their Respective Foundations, Grants, and Donations, and a Full Statement of their Possessions, as well Temporal as Spiritual. Originally published in Latin*. London: James Bohn, 1846, reprint of 1655.

——. *Book of Monuments*, n.d. British Library Loan MS. 38, f. 105v.

——. *The History of Saint Paul's Cathedral in London, from its Foundation: Extracted out of Original Charters, Records, Ledger-Books, and other Manuscripts*. London: Longman, 1818.

Durandus, William. *The Symbolism of Churches and Church Ornaments: A Translation of the First Book of the Rationale Divinorum Officiorum*, trans. John Mason Neale and Benjamin Webb. London: Gibbings, 1893.

Durham: Dean and Chapter Archive, Feretrars' Rolls for 1397.

Egeria. *Itinerarium seu peregrinatio ad loca sancta*, ed. by Hélène Pétré. Sources chrétiennes, vol. 21. Paris: Éditions du Cerf, 1948.

Ellis, Henry, ed. *Chronica Johannis de Oxenedes*. London: Rolls Series, 1859.

Erasmus Desiderius. *Lof der Zotheid*, transl. A.J. Hiensch. Utrecht-Antwerpen: Uitgeverij Het Spectrum, 1970 (*Prisma-Boeken* 1359).

———. *Pilgrimages to Saint Mary of Walsingham and Saint Thomas of Canterbury*, ed. and trans. John Gough Nichols. Westminster: John Bowyer Nichols and Son, 1849 and 1875.

———. *The Colloquies of Erasmus. A new Translation*, ed. Craig R. Thompson. Chicago-London: The University of Chicago Press, 1965.

Eucherius of Lyon. *Instructionum ad Salonium*. In *PL* 50.

Eugenius III. *Epistolae et privilegia*. In *PL* 180:1013–1614.

Eusebius of Caesarea. *De Vita beatissimi Imperatores Constantini*, ed. Friedhelm Winkelmann, Die Griechischen Christlichen Shriftsteller, vol. 1. Reprint, Berlin: Akademie Verlag, 1975.

De Expugnatione Lyxbonensi: The Conquest of Lisbon, ed. Charles Wendell David. New York: Columbia University Press, 1936.

Fowler, Joseph Thomas, ed. *Rites of Durham Being a Description or Brief Declaration of all the Ancient Monuments, Rites, & Customs belonging or being within the Monastical Church of Durham before the Suppression, Written 1593*. Durham: Surtees Society, 1963 reprint of 1903 edition.

Fulcher of Chartres. *Historia Hierosolymitana* 3.6. Edited by Heinrich Hagenmeyer, in Fulcheri Carnotensis: Historia Hierosolymitana (1095–1127). Heidelberg: Carl Winters, 1913.

Furnivall, F.J. and W.G. Stone, eds. *The Tale of Beryn, with A Prologue of the Merry Adventure of the Pardoner with a Tapster at Canterbury*. London: Kegan Paul, French, Trubner & Co., Ltd., 1909.

Gairdner, James, ed. *Letters and Papers. Foreign and Domestic. Calendar of Henry VIII*. London: Longman, 1862–1932, vol. XIII.

Gelasius I. *Appendix Tertia: Consiliorum sub Gelasio habitorum relatio*. In *PL* 59:157–90.

Gelasius of Caesarea. *Historia ecclesiastica*, eds. Gerhard Loeschcke and Margret Heinemann, Die Griechischen Christlichen Shriftsteller, vol. 28. Leipzig: J.C. Hinrichs, 1918.

Gerson, Johannes. *Opera Omnia*, Antwerpen 1706.

Gervase of Canterbury. "Tract on the Burning and Repair of the Church of Canterbury," trans. R. Willis, *The Architectural History of Canterbury Cathedral*, London: Longman 1845.

———. *Opera Historica*, in *The Historical Works of Gervase of Canterbury*, Vol. 1, ed. William Stubbs. London: H.M.S.O., 1879.

Gessler, Jan, ed. *Het Brugsche Livre des Mestiers en zijn navolgingen: vier aloude conversatieboekjes om Fransch te leeren, Deel 1: Le livre des Mestiers. De Bouc vanden Ambachten*. Bruges: Consortium der Brugsche meesters boekdrukkers, 1931.

Gesta abbatum Lobbiensium. In *MGH*, Scriptores, ed. Georg Heinrich Pertz, vol. 21. Hannover, Hahnsche Buchhandlung, 1826 ff.

Gesta Francorum et aliorum Hierosolimitanorum. The Deeds of the Franks and Other Pilgrims to Jerusalem, ed. and trans. by Rosalind Hill. London: T. Nelson, 1962.

Gesta Francorum et aliorum Hierosolimitanorum, ed. and trans. Louis Brehier. Paris: H. Champion, 1924.

La geste des Francs: chronique anonyme de la première Croisade, trans. André Matignon. Paris: Arléa, 1992.

Godefredus, Stabulensis monachus. "Triumphus Sancti Remacli de Malmundariensi Coenobio." In *PL* 1085: 287–334.

The Golden Legend of Jacobus de Voragine, volume 3, trans. Granger Ryan and Helmut Ripperger. New York: Arno Press, 1969, repr. 1941.

Goronne, J.B. *Incunabula Ecclesiae Hoyensis*, ed. J. Alexandre. Liège: 1685 repr. 1880: 47.

Gragg, Florence, ed. and trans. *The Commentaries of Pius II. Smith College Studies in History*, 22, Nos. 1–2 (Oct. 1936–Jan. 1937).

Gregory of Tours. *Glory of the Confessors*, trans. Raymond Van Dam. Liverpool: Liverpool University Press, 1988.

Gropp, Ignatius. *Collectio novissima scriptorum et rerum Wirciburgensium*. Würzburg: [n.p.]., 1741.

Guérard, Benjamin, ed. *Cartulaire de l'abbaye de Saint-Père de Chartres*, 2 vols. Paris: Imprimerie de Crapelet, 1840.

Guiberto, ed. *S. Eleutherius Tornacensis Episcopatus*. In *PL* 65:801.

Guibert of Nogent. *Gesta Dei per Francos*, ed. Lucas d'Achery. In *PL* 156:679–838.

——. *De Pignoribus sanctorum*, ed. Lucas D'Achery. In *PL* 156:607–79.

Guiges Ier, Prieur de Chartreuse. *Coutumes de Chartreuse; Introduction, texte critique, critique, traduction et notes par un Chartreux*. Lyon: Les Éditions du Cerf, 1984.

Henrice VI Angliae Regis Miracula Postuma, ed. Paulus Grosjean. Brussels: Société des Bollandistes, 1935.

Henry of Avranches. *The Shorter Latin Poems of Master Henry of Avranches Relating to England*, eds. Josiah Cox Russell and John Paul Hieronimus. Cambridge, MA: The Medieval Academy of America, 1935.

Henry of Huntingdon. *Henry, Archdeacon of Huntingdon: Historia Anglorum, The History of the English People*, ed. and trans. by Diana Greenway. Oxford: Clarendon Press, 1996.

Herbert of Bosham. *Excerpti ex Herberti*, ed. James Craigie Robertson. *Materials for the History of Thomas Becket, Archbishop of Canterbury*, Vol. 3. London: Longman and Co., 1877.

Honorius of Autun. *Gemma animae, sive de divinis officiis*. In *PL* 172:541–738.

——. *Liturgica: Speculum ecclesiae*. In *PL* 172:1004–6.

Hughes, Andrew. *Late Medieval Liturgical Offices: Texts. Subsidia Mediaevali 23*. Toronto: Pontifical Institute for Medieval Studies, 1994.

Huy, *Archives de l'Etat*:
 – Cures de Huy-Paroisse Notre-Dame, Registres ou dossiers 9, 36, 116
 – Fonds Collégiale Notre-Dame de Huy, Registres ou dossiers 20, 20ter, 23, 24, 25, 29, 37, 215, 216, 227, 229 bis, 237
 – Fonds Cour de Huy, Registre 11
 – Fonds Ville de Huy, Registre ou dossiers 14, 40, 43, 49, 179, 180, 238

Inventio Sanctae Crucis, Actorum Cyriaci pars I: Latine et graece ymnus antiqus de Sancta Cruce, ed. Alfred Holder. Leipzig: B.G. Teubneri, 1889.

Jan Hus. *De sanguine Christi. Opera Omnia*, ed. W. Flajshans. Prague: Jar. Busík and J.R. Vilímek, 1904.

Jerome. *Commentariorum in Ezechielem prophetam*. In *PL* vol. 25.

——. *The Pilgrimage of the Holy Paula*, trans. Aubrey Stewart, *The Library of the Palestine Pilgrims' Text Society*, vol. 1. London: The Palestine Pilgrims' Text Society, 1896.

John of Winterthur. *Die Chronik Johanns von Winterthur*, ed. Friedrich Baethgen. In *MG*, Scriptores, vol. 3. Berlin: Weidmannsche Buchhandlung, 1924.

Krusch, B. ed. "Vita Remacli Episcopi et Abbatis." In *MGH Scriptores* 88–111.

Lambert von Deutz. *Vita Heriberti. Miracula Heriberti. Gedichte. Liturgische Texte*, ed. Bernhard Vogel, *MGH. Scriptores*, LXXIII. Hanover: Hahnsche Buchhandlung, 2001.

Langton, Stephen. "Tractatus de Translatione Beati Thomae." In *PL*. 190:407–424.

Liber Eliensis, ed. Ernest O. Blake. Camden 3rd s., no. 92. London: Royal Historical Society, 1962.

Liber Pontificalis, ed. Louis Duchesne. Paris: E. Thorin, 1886–92.

Liège, *Musée Archéologique liègeois (Musée Curtius)*: Manuscrit dit Obituaire ou Nécrologe de l'abbaye du Neufmoustier (legs Grandgagnage).

Luard, Henry Richards, ed. *Annales Monastici: Annales Monasterii de Waverleia (A.D. 1–1291)*, II. London: Rolls Series, 1865.

———, ed. *Chronicon Vulgo Dictum Chronicon Thomae Wykes* in *Annales Monastici*, 4. London: Rolls Series, 1869.

Ludolph the Saxon. *The Hours of the Passion taken from The Life of Christ by Ludolph the Saxon*, ed. and trans. Henry James Coleridge. London: Burns and Oates, 1887.

Magnússon, Eirikr, ed. and trans. *Thómas Saga Erkibyskups*, II. London: Rolls Series, 1875–83.

Malbrancq, Jacques. *De Morinis et Morinorum rebus*, vol. 2. Tournai: Adrien Quinqué, 1636–1639.

Manchester, John Rylands University Library, MS lat. 235, f. 10.

Marracci, Hippolytus. *Polyanthea Mariana*. In *Summa Aurea de Laudibus Beatissme Virginis Mariae*. Vols. 9–10. Ed. Joannes Jacobus Bourassé. Paris: J.P. Migne, 1862.

Martin, Père Simon. *La Vie de Saint Vulphly, confesseur, patron, prestre et curé de la ville de Rue, en Ponthieu, au diocèse d'Amiens. Avec l'histoire du crucifix miraculeux de la mesme ville*. Paris: F. Dehors, 1636.

Matthew Paris's English History, from the Year 1235 to 1273, trans. John A. Giles. London: Henry G. Bohn, 1853.

Matthew Paris. *Chronica Majora*. 5 Vols., ed. Henry Richards Luard. London: Longman, 1880.

———. *The Lives of Saints Alban and Amphibalus*, Trinity College, Dublin MS 177, fol. 61a.

———. *Matthaei Parisiensis, Monachi Sancti Albani, Historia Anglorum, Sive, ut Vulgo Dicitur, Historia Minor. Abbreviatio Chronicorum Angliae*, 2, ed. Frederic Madden. London: Rolls Series, 1875–83.

Métais, Charles, ed. *Cartulaire de l'abbaye cardinale de la Trinité de Vendôme*. Part 1–2. Paris: Alphonse Picard et fils, 1893–94.

Mombritius, Boninus. *Prologus in vitam Sancti Sylvestri, papae et confessoris*. In *Sanctuarium seu Vitae Sanctorum (1480)*, ed. Adrien M. Brunet. Paris: Albert Fontemoing, 1910.

Odo of Deuil. *De profectione Ludovici in Orientem*, ed. Virginia Gingerick Berry. New York: Columbia University Press, 1948.

Ordinarius Custodum of St. Servaas, Maastricht, Rijksarchief Limburg (Public Record Office Limburg), Archief van het kapittel van St. Servaas (Archive of the Chapter of St. Servatius), Bk. 166.

Ordinarius Custodum of Our-Dear-Lady's, Brussels, General Archives, MS. 1945.

Otto of Freising. *Gesta Friderici I. Imperatoris*. In *MGH*, Scriptores rerum Merovingicarum, ed. Georg Waitz, vol. 14. Berlin: Apud Weidmannos, 1920.

Peel, Robert, ed. *State Papers of King Henry the Eighth*, I, Part II. London: Great Britain Record Commission, 1831.

Petrus Venerabilis. *In laudem sepulcri Domini*, in Jacques-Paul Migne, *Patriologiae cursus completus. Series secunda (Latina)*. Paris: J.-P. Migne, 1854, vol. 189, cols. 973–92.

Pii secundi Pontificis Max. Commentarii rerum memorabilium, quae temporibus suis contigerunt. Frankfurt: In Officina Aubriana, 1614.

Praun, Stephan. "Was sich auf meiner Reise zugetragen . . ." [Diary of his journey to Constantinople in 1569], ed. Friedrich von Praun. *Mitteilungen aus dem Germanischen Nationalmuseum* 1916–17: 45–62, 49–58.

Rabanus Maurus. *De laudibus Sanctae Crucis*. In *PL* 107:133–294.

Raymond of Aguilers. *Historia Francorum qui ceperunt Jerusalem*. In *PL* 155:591–668.

Riley, Henry T., ed. *Gesta Abbatum Monaterii S. Albani A Thoma Walsingham (A.D. 793–1401)*. London: Rolls Series, 1867–69, vol. 2.

Robert of Reims. *Historia Hierosolymitana*. In *PL* 155:667–758.

Roulliard, Sébastien. *Parthenie, ou Histoire de la très-auguste et très-dévote église de Chartres; dédiée par les vieux druides, en l'honneur de la Vierge qui enfanteroit: Avec ce qui s'est passé de plus memorable, au faict de la Seigneurie, tant Spirituelle que Temporelle, de ladicte Église, ville, & Païs chartrain*. Paris: Rolin Thierry and Pierre Chevalier, 1609.

Roux, Joseph and Edmond Soyez. *Cartulaire du chapitre de la cathédrale d'Amiens, Mémoires de la société des antiquaires de Picardie*. Amiens: Yvert et Tellier, 1897–1912.

Royal Office Exchequer Augmentation Official Treasury Roll, i, m. 110.

Rozière, Eugene de, ed. *Cartulaire de l'église du Saint-Sépulcre de Jérusalem*. Paris: Imprimerie nationale, 1849.

Rudolf of Schlettstadt. *Rudolf von Schlettstadt. Historiae memorabiles. Zur Domikanerliteratur und Kulturgeschichte des 13. Jahrhunderts*, ed. Erich Kleinschmidt. Cologne, 1974.

Rufinus of Aquileia. *Historia ecclesiastica*, ed. by Domenico Vallarsi. In *PL* 21:461–540.

Rupert of Deutz. *De incendio Tiutiensis*, ed. P. Jaffe, *MGH. Scriptores* 12. 1856.

Sablon, Vincent. *Histoire de l'auguste et vénérable église de Chartres* 2nd ed. Chartres: Chez R. Bocquet, 1683.

——. *Histoire et description de l'église cathédrale de Chartres, dédiée par les druides à une vierge qui devait enfanter, Revue et augmentée D'une description de l'Église de Sous-Terre et d'un récit de l'incendie de 1836*, ed. Lucien Merlet, 1671; Chartres: Petrot-Garnier, 1860.

Sacrorum conciliorum nova et amplissima collection, ed. John Mansi. Graz: Akademische Druck- und Verlaganstalt, 1960–61.

Sanson, Père Ignace. *L'histoire ecclésiastique de la ville d'Abbeville et de l'archiodiaconé de Ponthieu, au diocèse d'Amiens*. Paris: François Pélican, 1646.

Schedel, Hartmann. *Chronicle of the World: The Complete and Annotated Nuremberg Chronicle of 1493*. Cologne: Taschen, 2001.

Sharpe, Reginald R., ed. *Calendar of Wills Proved and Enrolled in the Court of Husting, London, A.D. 1258–A.D. 1688*. London: John C. Francis, Took's Court, 1890. 2 vols.

Sheppard, J.B., ed. *Christ Church Letters: A Volume of Medieval Letters Relating to the Priory of Christ Church Canterbury*, Westminster: Camden Society, 1877.

Smith, Lucy Toulmin, ed. *The Itinerary of John Leland in or about the Years 1535–1543*. Carbondale, Illinois: Southern Illinois University Press, 1964.

Sprenger, Jakob and Heinrich Institoris. *Der Hexenhammer* [1487], ed. J.W.R. Schmidt. Leipzig: 1937–38, reprint.

Stavelot-Malmedy, *Archives de l'Etat*, Liège.
  - Ordre De L'office Et Procession . . . Poppon. *376 #s4–11*, 1620s.
  - Ferdinandus Dei Gra. *376 #39*, 1624.
  - Qua Ratione Suffragandus Noster Leodiens Consecrationum Sancti Popponis. *376 #32*, 1624.
  - Sommaire Des Indulgences. *375 #21*, 1626.
  - Mass Readings for Feasts of Sigisbert, Remaclus, Poppon, Hadelin. *377 (Stablo-Malmedy Acten MR4)*, 1634.
  - Suffraganeus Leodien Scribit Se Examin Naturum Utrum Veneration Reliquiarum Sti Popponis a Solo Episcopo Decerni Possit an Forte Aliunde Peti. *376 #36r*, 1634.
  - Forma Dell'indulgenze. *375 #43*, 1657.

Stone, John. *The Chronicle of John Stone*, ed. W.G. Searle. Cambridge: Cambridge Antiquarian Society, 1902, vol. 34.

Stow, John. *The Annales of England faithfully collected out of the most authenticall Authors, Records, and other Monuments of Antiquitie from the first inhabitation untill . . . 1592*. London: Ralph Newbery, 1592.

Stubbs, William, ed. *Memoriale Fratis Walteri de Coventria*. London: Stationery Office, 1873, Kraus Reprint, Ltd. 1965, II.

Suger, Abbot of St. Denis. *Abbot Suger on the Abbey Church of St.-Denis and Its Art Treasures*, ed. Erwin Panofsky, 2nd ed. Princeton: Princeton University Press, 1979.

Thangmar. *Vita Bernwardi, Episcopi Hildesheimensis*. In *MGH*, Scriptores. Georg Heinrich Pertz, ed. Hannover: Hahnsche Buchhandlung, 1826.

Theoderich. *Guide to the Holy Land*. trans. Aubrey Stewart. 2nd ed. New York: Italica Press, 1986.

Theoderic. "The Booklet on the Holy Places as Told by Theoderic," in *Jerusalem Pilgrimage, 1099–1185*, ed. John Wilkinson with Joyce Hill and W.F. Ryan. London: Hakluyt Society, 1988: 274–314.

Theoderich of Würzburg. *Guide to the Holy Land*, trans. Aubrey Stewart, 2nd ed., with a new Introduction by Ronald G. Musto. New York: Italica Press, 1986.

Theodericus Aedituus. *Thioderici Aeditui Tuitiensis Opuscula*, ed. Oswald Holder-Egger, *MGH. Scriptores* 14. 1883.

Thietmar. *Thietmari Merseburgensis Episcopi Chronicon*, ed. Robert Holtzman, *MGH. Scriptores* 9. 1955.

Thomas Aquinas. *Summa Theologica*, 2nd and rev. ed., trans. Fathers of the English Dominican Province. Chicago: Benziger Bros. Press, 1947.

Thomas of Burton. *Chronica Monasterii de Melsa*, 3 vols. London: Longmans, 1866–8.

Thomas à Kempis. *The Imitation of Christ*, trans, Richard Whitford. New York: Pocket Books, 1953.

Thompson, Craig R. *The Colloquies of Erasmus*. Chicago: University of Chicago Press, 1967.

V. de Bartholomaeis. *Laude drammatiche e rappresentazioni sacre*, vol. 1. Florence: Felice le Monnier, 1943, repr. Florence, 1967.

Vasari, Giorgio. *Le Vite de' Piú Eccellenti Pittori, Scultori, e Architettori*. 9 vols. Milan: Edizione per il Club del Libro, 1962.

La Vie Seinte Audree: Poème Anglo-Normand du XIIIe Siècle. Ed. Östen Södergard. Uppsala Universitets Årsskrift, no. 11. Uppsala: Almquist and Wiksells, 1955.

Vincenzo Fineschi. *Della festa e della processione del Corpus Domini di Firenze*. Florence: Pietro Gaetano Viviani, 1768.

Vita Sancti Thomae, Cantuariensis Archiepiscopi et Martyris, Auctore Anonymo II, ed. James Craigie Robertson. *Materials for the History of Thomas Becket, Archbishop of Canterbury*, London: Longman and Co., 1879, vol. 4: 80–144.

Von Breydenbach, Bernhard. *Die Reise ins Heilige Land, Ein Reisebericht aus dem Jahre 1483*. Wiesbaden: Guido Pressler, 1977.

The Vyel and Kyngydton Customary of the Shrine of St. Thomas Becket (1428) British Library (Add. MS 59616).

The Westminster Chronicle, 1381–1394, ed. and trans. Leonard Charles Hector and Barbara F. Harvey. Oxford: The Clarendon Press, 1981.

Wharton, Henry. *Anglia Sacra*. London: Richard Chiswel, 1691.

Wilkinson, John J. *Egeria's Travels to the Holy Land*, rev. ed. Warminster: Aris and Phillips, 1981.

William of Canterbury. *Miracula Sancti Thomae Cantuariensis*, ed. James Craigie Robertson. *Materials for the History of Thomas Becket, Archbishop of Canterbury*, vol. 1. London: Longman and Co., 1875.

———. *Vita Sancti Thomae*, ed. James Craigie Robertson. *Materials for the History of Thomas Becket, Archbishop of Canterbury*, vol. 1. London: Longman and Co., 1875.

Wisplinghoff, Erich, ed. *Rheinisches Urkundenbuch: Ältere Urkunden bis 1100*. Bonn: P. Hanston, 1972.

Woodruff, C.E., ed. *Sede Vacante Wills: A Calendar of Wills Proved before the Commissary of the Prior and Chapter of Christ Church Canterbury, during Vacancies in the Primacy*. Kent: Kent Archaeological Society Records Branch, vol. 3.

Secondary Sources

Abbot, Edwin A. *St. Thomas of Canterbury; His Death and Miracles*. London: Adam and Charles Black, 1898.

Abou-El-Haj, Barbara. "The Urban Setting for Late Medieval Church Building: Reims and its Cathedral between 1210 and 1240." *Art History* 11/1 (1988): 17–41.

———. *The Medieval Cult of Saints: Formations and Transformations*. New York: Cambridge University Press, 1994.

Achilles-Syndram, Katrin and Rainer Schoch, eds. *Die Kunst des Sammelns: Das Praunsche Kabinett. Meisterwerke von Dürer bis Carracci*. Nuremberg: Verlag des Germanischen Nationalmuseums, 1994.

Ainsworth, Maryam W. and Maximilian P.J. Martens. *Petrus Christus. Renaissance Master of Bruges*. New York: The Metropolitan Museum of Art, 1994.

Ainsworth, Maryan W. *Gerard David: Purity of Vision in an Age of Transition*. New York: Metropolitan Museum of Art, 1998.

Albers, Petrus Henricus. "De Heiligdomsvaart in de middeleeuwen te Maastricht." *Publications de la Société Historique et Archéologique dans le Limbourg* 66 (1930): 53–67.

Alexander, James W. "The Becket Controversy in Recent Historiography." *The Journal of British Studies* 9:2 (May 1970): 1–26.

Alexander, Jonathan and Paul Binski, eds. *Age of Chivalry: Art in Plantagenet England*. London: Royal Academy of the Arts, 1987.

Algermissen, Konrad, ed. *Lexikon für Marienkunde*, I: *Aachen bis Elisabeth*. Regensburg: Friedrich Pustete, 1967.

Altet, Xavier Barral I. "Les Mosaïques de Pavement Médiévales de la Ville de Reims." *Congrès Archéologique de France, 135th session, 1977*. Paris: Société Française d'Archéologique, 1980: 79–108.

Altman, Charles. F. "The Medieval Marquee—Church Portal Sculpture as Publicity." *Journal of Popular Culture* 14/1 (1980): 37–46.

Amé, Émile. *Les Carrelages Émaillés du Moyen-Age et de la Renaissance précédés de l'histoire des anciens pavages: mosaique, labyrinths, Dalles Incrustées*. Paris: Morel and Co., 1859.

Andermahr, Bernhard. "Zwischen Himmel und Erde. Die Bodenplatten des Barbarossa-Leuchters im Aachener Dom: Ein Beitrag zur staufischen Goldschmiedekunst im Rhein-Maas-Gebiet." Ph.D. diss., Aachen Technische Hochschule, 1994.

Andrea, Alfred J. *Contemporary Sources for the Fourth Crusade*. Leiden: E.J. Brill Press, 2000.

Andrews, Lew. "Ordering Space in Renaissance Times: Position and Meaning in Continuous Narration." *Word & Image* vol. 10 (1994): 84–94.

Anselgruber, Manfred and Herbert Puschnik. *Dies trug sich zu anno 1338. Pulkau zur Zeit der Glaubenswirren*. Pulkau: Fremdensverkehrsverein der Stadt Pulkau und Umgebung, 1992.

Appelt, Heinrich. "Die Kaiseridee Friedrich Barbarossas," in Wolf., 1975: 208–44.

Arens, Eduard."Die Inschriften am Karlsschrein." *Zeitschrift des Aachener Geschichtsvereins* 34 (1921): 159–94.

Arnold, Klaus. "Die Armledererhebung in Franken 1336," *Mainfränkisches Jahrbuch für Geschichte und Kunst* 26 (1974): 35–62.

L'art au temps des rois maudits: Philippe le Bel et ses fils, 1285–1328. Paris: Réunion des Musées Nationaux, 1998.

Aru, Carlo and Étienne de Geradon. *La Galerie Sabauda de Turin, Les Primitifs Flamands, I. Corpus de la peinture des anciens Pays-Bas méridionaux au quinzième siècle*, 5. Antwerp: De Sikkel, 1952.

Ashley, Kathleen and Pamela Sheingorn. *Writing Faith: Text, Sign, and History in the Miracles of Sainte Foy*. Chicago: University of Chicago Press, 1999.

———. "Translations of Sainte Foy: Bodies, Texts, Places," in *The Medieval Translator*, Roger Ellis and René Tixier, ed. Turnhout: Brepols, 1996: 29–49.

—— and Wim Hüsken, eds. *Moving Subjects: Processional Performance in the Middle Ages and Renaissance*. Atlanta: Rodopi, 2001.

—— and Pamela Sheingorn. "'Sainte Foy on the Loose,' or the Possibilites of Procession," in Ashley & Hüsken, 2001: 53–67.

——. "*Discordia Et Lis*: Negotiating Power, Property, and Performance in Medieval Sélestat." *Journal of Medieval and Early Modern Studies* 26:3 (Fall 1996): 419–46.

Atkinson, Thomas D. "The Cathedral" and "Monastic Buildings and Palace." In *The Victoria History of the County of Cambridge and the Isle of Ely*. Vol. 4, ed. Ralph B. Pugh. London: Institute of Historical Research, 1953: 50–77; 77–82.

——, "Queen Philippa's Pews in Ely Cathedral." *Proceedings of the Cambridge Antiquarian Society* 41 (1948): 60–66.

Aufrère, Léon. "Essai sur l'église Saint-Wulphy et la chapelle du Saint-Esprit de Rue." *Bulletin de la Société d'Émulation d'Abbeville* (1924–25): 434–534.

Augenti, Andrea, ed. *Art and Archaeology of Rome: From Ancient Times to the Baroque*. Florence: Scala Group S.P.A., 2000.

Avineri, Zvi, ed. *Germania Judaica*, vol. 2, pt. 1. Tübingen: J.C.B. Mohr, 1968.

Axters, Stephanus. *The Spirituality of the Old Low Countries*, trans. Donald Attwater. London: Aquin Press, 1954.

Bächtold-Staubli, Hanns, ed. *Handworterbuch des deutschen Aberglaubens*. 9 vols. Berlin/Leipzig, 1927–39.

Backman, E. Louis. *Religious Dances in the Christian Church and in Popular Medicine*. Westport, CT: Greenwood Press, 1977.

Bailey, Terence. "L'hagiographie À Stavelot-Malmedy." *Revue Bénédictine* LX (1950): 120–62.

Bakirtzis, Charalambos. "Κουτρουβια μυρου απο τη Θεσσαλονικη [Myrrh ampullae from Thessaloniki]," in *Jahrbuch der Österreichischen Byzantinistik: XVI*. Vienna: Verlag der Österreichischen Akademie der Wissenschaften, 1982: 523–28.

——. "Byzantine Ampullae from Thessaloniki," in Ousterhout, 1990: 140–49.

Bal, Mieke and Norman Bryson. "Semiotics and Art History." *The Art Bulletin* 73/2 (1991): 174–208.

Balau, Sylv. *Les Sources De L'histoire De Liège Au Moyen Age: Étude Critique*. Brussels: Éditions Culture et Civilisation, 1982.

——. *Chroniques Liégeoises*. Brussels: Kiessling, 1913.

Baldass, Ludwig von. *Hans Memling*. Vienna: Anton Schroll & Co., 1942.

Ball, W.E. "The Stained-Glass Windows of Nettlestead Church," *Archaeologia Cantiana*, 28 (1909): 157–249.

Barasch, Moshe. *Crusader Figural Sculpture in the Holy Land*. New Brunswick, NJ: Rutgers University Press, 1971.

Barb, A.A. "*Mensa Sacra*: The Round Table and the Holy Grail." *Journal of the Warburg and Courtauld Institute*, 19 (1956): 40–67.

Barbeau, Marius. *Trésor des anciens Jésuites*. Ottawa: Musée National du Canada, 1957.

Barber, Malcolm. *The New Knighthood. A History of the Order of the Temple*. Cambridge: Cambridge University Press, 1994.

Barber, Paul. *Vampires, Burial and Death*. New Haven: Yale University Press, 1988.

Barlow, Frank. *Thomas Becket*. Berkeley: University of California Press, 1986.

Barnes, Carl F. "Cross-Media Design Motifs in XIIIth-century France: Architectural Motifs in the Psalter and Hours of Yolande de Soissons and in the Cathedral of Notre-Dame at Amiens." *Gesta* 17/2 (1978): 37–40.

Barnes, Timothy. "Constantine, Athanasius and the Christian Church" in eds Lieu & Montserrat, 1998: 7–20.

——. *Constantine and Eusebius*. Cambridge, MA: Harvard University Press, 1981.

Barnouw, A.J., transl. *Geoffrey Chaucer, De vertellingen van de pelgrims naar Kantelberg*, Utrecht/Antwerpen, 1974 repr. of 1506.

Baron, Françoise. "Mort et résurrection du jubé de la cathédrale d'Amiens." *Revue de l'Art* 87 (1990): 29–41.

———. "Le cavalier royal de Notre-Dame de Paris et le problème de la statue équestre au moyen âge," *Bulletin monumental* 127 (1968): 141–54.

———, et al., *Les fastes du gothique. Le siècle de Charles V*, exh. cat. Paris: Éditions de la Réunion des musées nationaux, 1981.

Bartz, Gabriele, Alfred Karnein, Claudio Lange. *Liebesfreuden im Mittelalter. Kulturgeschichte der Erotik und Sexualität in Bildern und Dokumenten*, Stuttgart – Zürich: Belser Verlag, 1994.

Basile, Giuseppe. "Il reliquiario del Corporale di Orvieto: interventi di conservazione e restauro." *Arte medievale* 6/1 (1992): 193–97.

Baudot, Dom. *The Breviary: Its History and Contents.* Trans. Benedictines of Stanbrook. London: Sands & Co., 1929.

Bauer, Anton. "Eucharistische Wallfahrten zu 'Unserrm Herrn', zum 'Hl. Blut', und zum 'St. Salvator', im alten Bistum Freising." *Beiträge zur altbayerischen Kirchengeschichte* 21/3 (1960): 37–71.

Bauer, Ingolf, ed. *Frömmigkeit. Formen, Geschichte, Verhalten, Zeugnisse. Lenz Kriss-Rettenbeck zum 70. Geburtstag.* Munich/Berlin: Deutscher Kunstverlag, 1993.

Bauerreiss, Romauld. *Pie Jesu. Das Schmerzensmannbild und sein Einfluss auf die mittelalterliche Frömmigkeit.* Munich: Widmann, 1931.

———. "*Basileus tes doxes:* Ein frühes eucharistisches Bild und seine Auswirkung," in *Pro mundi vita. Festschrift zum eucharistischen Weltkongress 1960*, ed. Theologischen Fakultät der Ludwig-Maximilian-Universität München. Munich: Max Hueber, 1960: 49–67.

———. *Kirchengeschichte Bayerns.* 7 vols. St. Ottilien: EOS Verlag der Erzabtei, 1958–70.

Baumgartner, E. *Glas des späten Mittelalters. Die Sammlung Karl Amendt.* Düsseldorf: Kunstmuseum, 1987.

——— and I. Krueger. *Phönix aus Sand und Asche. Glas des Mittelalters.* Munich: Klinkhardt und Biermann, 1988.

Bautier, G. "Le Saint Sépulcre de Jérusalem et l'occident médiévale." Ecole de Chartes, Paris, 1971.

Baxandall, Michael. *The Limewood Sculpture of Renaissance Germany.* New Haven: Yale University Press, 1980.

Bayer, Clemens. "Die beiden großen Inschriften des Barbarossa-Leuchters," in *Celica Iherusalem: Festschrift für Erich Stephany*, ed. Clemens Bayer. Cologne-Siegburg: Respublica-Verlag Schmitt, 1986: 213–40.

Beaven, Marilyn. "A Medieval Procession: Sacred Rites Commemorated in a Stained Glass Panel from Soissons Cathedral." *Bulletin of the Detroit Institute of Arts* 67/1 (1992): 30–37.

Beauvillé, Victor de. *Recueil de documents inédits concernant la Picardie*, vol. 3–4. Paris: Imprimerie impériale, 1860–82.

Beck, James. *Raphael.* New York: Abrams Publishers, 1976.

Bedaux, J.B. "Laatmiddeleeuwse sexuele amuletten," in eds J.B. Bedaux, A.M. Koldeweij, *Annus Quadriga Mundi. Opstellen over Middeleeuwse Kunst opgedragen aan Prof. dr. Anna C. Esmeijer.* Zutphen: De Walburg Pers-Utrecht: Stichting Clavis, 1989: 16–30.

———. "Profane en sacrale amuletten," in Koldeweij & Willemsen, 1995: 26–35.

———. "Functie en Betekenis van randdecoratie in middeleeuwse handschriften," *Kunstlicht*, 14 (1993): 28–33.

Beissel, Stephan. *Die Aachenfahrt: Verehrung der Aachener Heiligtümer seit den Tagen Karls des Großen bis unsere Zeit.* Freiburg im Breisgau: Herdersche Verlagshandlung, 1902.

———. *Die Verehrung der Heiligen und ihrer Reliquien in Deutschland bis zum Beginne des 13. Jahrhunderts*, Freiburg im Breisgau: Herder Verlag, 1890; repr. Darmstadt: Wissenschaftliche Buchgesellschaft, 1976.

——. *Die Verehrung der Heiligen und ihrer Reliquien in Deutschland während der zweiten Hälfte des Mittelalters*, Freiburg im Breisgau: Herder Verlag, *1892*; repr. Darmstadt: Wissenschaftliche Buchgesellschaft, 1976.

Belting, Hans. "An Image and Its Function in the Liturgy: The Man of Sorrows in Byzantium." *Dumbarton Oaks Papers* 34–35 (1980–81): 1–16

——. *The Image and its Public in the Middle Ages: Form and Function of Early Paintings of the Passion*, trans. M. Bartusis and R. Meyer. New Rochelle, NY: Aristotle D. Caratzas, 1990.

——. *Likeness and Presence: A History of the Image before the Era of Art*, trans. Edmund Jephcott. Chicago: University of Chiacgo Press, 1994.

Bénézet, Jean-Pierre. *Pharmacie et médicament en Méditerranée occidentale (XIIIᵉ–XVIᵉ siècles)* Paris: Honoré Champion, 1999.

Benjamin, Arnold. *Medieval Germany, 500–1300: A Political Interpretation*. Toronto: University of Toronto Press, 1997.

Benson, E.G. "The Lost Brass of the Cantilupe Shrine." *Transactions of the Woolhope Field Club*, 33 (1949–51): 68–76.

Benson, Robert L. *The Bishop-Elect: A Study in Medieval Ecclesiastical Office*. Princeton: Princeton University Press, 1968.

Bentham, James. *The History and Antiquities of the Cathedral and Conventual Church of Ely, from the Foundation of the Monastery, A.D. 673, T o the Year 1771*. Norwich: Stevenson, Matchett, and Stevenson, 1812.

Benton, John F., ed. and trans. *Self and Society in Medieval France: The Memoirs of Abbot Guibert of Nogent (1064–c. 1125)*. Toronto: University of Toronto Press, 1984.

Bercé, Françoise. *Les premiers travaux de la commission des monuments historiques 1837–48: procès-verbaux et relevés d'architectes*. Paris: Picard, 1979.

Berger, Blandine. *Le drame liturgique de Pâques*. Paris: Beauchesne, 1976.

Berlière, Ursmer. "Les Processions Des Croix Banales." *Bulletin de la Clesse des Lettres de l'Académie royale de Belgique* VIII, 5e série (1922): 419–47.

Berling, Karl. *Altes Zinn. Ein Handbuch für Sammler und Liebhaber*. Berlin: Schmidt, 1919.

Berne. *Iconoclasme. Vie et mort de l'image médiévale*. Zürich: Verlag Neuer Zürcher Zeitung/Éditions d'art Somogy.

Bertelli, Carlo. "The 'Image of Pity' in Santa Croce in Gerusalemme." *Essays in the History of Art Presented to Rudolf Wittkower*. London: Phaidon, 1967.

Beumann, Helmut. "Grab und Thron Karls des Grossen zu Aachen," in Braunfels & Schramm , 1967: 9–38.

Beuningen, H.J.E. van and A.M. Koldeweij. *Heilig en Profaan. 1000 Laatmiddeleeuwse Insignes uit de collectie H.J.E. van Beuningen*. Rotterdam Papers 8. Cothen: Stichting Middeleeuwse Religieuze en Profane Insignes, 1993.

——, A.M. Koldeweij and D. Kicken. *Heilig en Profaan 2. 1200 Laatmiddeleeuwse Insignes uit openbare en particuliere collecties*. Rotterdam Papers 12. Cothen: Stichting Middeleeuwse Religieuze en Profane Insignes, 2001.

Biddle, Martin. The *Tomb of Christ*. Stroud, Gloucestershire: Sutton Publishing, 1999.

Biervliet, Lori Van. *Ursula in Bruges: An Approach to the Memling Shrine*. Bruges: Van Damme Beke, 1984.

Binding, Günther. *Städtebau Und Heilsordnung—Künstlerische Gestaltung der Stadt Köln in Ottonischer Zeit*. Düsselforf: Droste, 1986.

Binski, Paul. *Westminster Abbey and the Plantagenets: Kingship and the Representation of Power 1200–1400*. New Haven: Yale University Press, 1995.

——. *Medieval Death: Ritual and Representation*. Ithaca: Cornell University Press, 1996.

Birkmeyer, Karl M. "The Arch Motif in Netherlandish Painting of the Fifteenth Century." *The Art Bulletin* 43 (1961): 1–20.

Bischoff, Franz. "Les maquettes d'architecture," in *Les bâtisseurs des cathédrales*, ed. Roland Recht, Strasbourg: Musées de la ville de Strasbourg (1989): 287–95.

Bismanis, Maija. "The Necessity of Discovery." *Gesta* 28/2 (1989): 115–20.

Biver, Paul. "Tombs of the School of London at the Beginning of the Fourteenth Century." *Archaeological Journal* 67 (1910): 51–65.

Blaettler, James R. *Through Emmaus Eyes: Art, Liturgy, and Monastic Ideology at Santo Domingo de Silos*, vol. 1, Ph.D. diss., University of Chicago, 1989.

Blake, Ernest Oscar. "The Formation of the 'Crusade' Idea." *Journal of Ecclesiastical History* 21 (1970): 11–31.

Blanton, Virginia. "King Anna's Daughters: Genealogical Narrative and Cult Formation in the *Liber Eliensis*." *Historical Reflections/Réflexions Historiques*, 30/2 (Summer 2004): 127–49.

Blanton-Whetsell, Virginia. "*Imagines Ætheldredae*: Mapping Hagiographic Representations of Abbatial Power and Religious Patronage." *Studies in Iconography* 23 (2002): 55–107.

Blick, Sarah. "A Canterbury Keepsake: English Medieval Pilgrim Souvenirs and Popular Culture." Ph.D. diss., University of Kansas, 1994.

———. "Comparing Pilgrim Souvenirs and Trinity Chapel Windows at Canterbury Cathedral," *Mirator* (September 2001): 1–27.

Blier, Louis-Adrien. *Histoire du Crucifix miraculeux honoré dans la chapelle du Saint-Esprit de la ville de Rue, en Picardie, Diocèse d'Amiens*. Amiens: 1778, repr. Lenoel-Herouart, 1855.

Bloch, R. Howard. *The Scandal of the Fabliaux*, Chicago: The University of Chicago Press, 1986.

Blockmans, Wim and Walter Prevenier. *The Low Countries under Burgundian Rule, 1369–1530*. trans. Elizabeth Fackelman. Philadelphia: University of Pennsylvania Press, 1988.

Blondaux, Laurence. "Regards sur le Puits de Moise." *Claus Sluter en Bourgogne, Mythe et representations*. Dijon: Musée des Beaux-Arts de Dijon, 1990: 30–33.

Blum, Shirley Nielsen. *Early Netherlandish Triptychs*. Berkeley: University of California Press, 1969.

Bock, Franz and Michel Antoine Hubert Willemsen. *Antiquités sacrées conservées dans les anciennes collégiales de S. Servais et de Notre-Dame à Maestricht*. Maastricht: J. Russel, 1873.

Bodenschaft, Sister Mary Immaculate. *The* Vita Christi *of Ludolphus the Carthusian*. Washington, D.C.: The Catholic University of America Press, 1944.

Boeckler, Albert. *Das Stuttgarter Passionale*. Augsburg: Filser, 1923.

Boehm, Barbara Drake. "Body-Part Reliquaries: The State of Research." *Gesta* 36/1 (1997): 8–19.

———. "Medieval Head Reliquaries of the Massif Central." PhD diss., New York University, Institute of Fine Arts, 1990.

Boëll, Charles. "Le huitième centenaire de la consécration de la cathédrale." *Semaine religieuse d'Autun, Chalon et Mâcon* 58/18 (April 30, 1932), unpaginated.

Boeren, Petrus Cornelius. *Heilogdomsvaart Maastrich: schets v. d. geschiedenis der heiligdomsvaarten en andere jubelvaarten*. Maastricht: U.M. Ernest van Aelst, 1962.

Boerner, Bruno. "Zur Interpretation des ikonographischen Programms am Schrein der hl. Gertrud von Nivelles" in Westermann-Angerhausen, 1995–96: 225–33.

Boertjes, Katja. "Pelgrimsampullen uit Nederlandse en Belgische Bodem," in H.J.E. van Beunigen, A.M. Koldeweij, D. Kicken, 2001: 79–87.

Boëthius, Axel and John Ward Perkins. *Etruscan and Roman Architecture*. Harmondsworth: Penguin, 1970.

Bonnassie, Pierre. "From One Servitude to Another: The Peasantry of the Frankish Kingdom at the Time of Hugh Capet and Robert the Pious (987–1031)" and "Descriptions of Fortresses in the Book of Miracles of Sainte-Foy of Conques," in *From Slavery to Feudalism in South-Western Europe*. Trans. Jean Birrell Cambridge: Cambridge University Press, 1991.

Bony, Jean. "La collégiale de Mantes." *Congrès archéologique de France* 104th session (1946): 163–220.

——. *The English Decorated Style: Gothic Architecture Transformed 1250–1350*. Ithaca, NY: Cornell University Press, 1979.

——. *French Gothic Architecture of the 12th and 13th Centuries*. Berkeley: University of California Press, 1983.

Boockmann, Hartmut. "Der Streit um das Wilsnacker Blut, zur Situation des deutschen Klerus in der Mitte des 15. Jahrhunderts." *Zeitschrift für Historische Forschung* 9 (1982): 385–408.

Boogaart, Thomas A. II. "Our Saviour's Blood: Procession and Community in Late Medieval Bruges" in Ashley & Hüsken, 2001: 68–116.

Borchert, Till-Holger, ed. *The Age of Van Eyck: The Mediterranean World and Early Netherlandish Painting 1430–1530*. New York: Thames & Hudson, 2002.

Borchgrave d'Altena, Joseph de. "Le Triptyque reliquaire de la Vraie Croix de Notre-Dame à Tongres." *Chronique archéologique du Pays de Liège* (1925): 43–49.

——. "La châsse de Saint Firmin." Bulletin Monumental 85 (1926): 153–58.

——. *Art mosan*. Paris: C. Dessart, 1951.

——. "Les châsses de saint Domitien et de saint Mengold." *Bulletin de la Société d'Art et d'Histoire du Diocèse de Liège* XLII (1961): 25–42.

Bordonove, Georges. *Les croisades et le Royaume de Jérusalem*. Paris: Pygmalion, 1992.

Borenius, Tancred. *St. Thomas Becket in Art*. London: Methuen & Co., 1932.

——. "Some Further Aspects of the Iconography of St. Thomas of Canterbury" *Archaeologia* 83 (1933): 171–86.

Borgehammar, Stephan. *How the Holy Cross Was Found: From Event to Medieval Legend*. Stockholm: Almqvist & Wiksell Intl., 1991.

Bornert, René. "La Célébration de la Sainte Croix dans le rite byzantin." *La Maison-Dieu* 75 (1963): 92–108.

Borst, Arno. "Die Sebaldus-Legenden in der mittelalterlichen Geschichte Nürnbergs." *Jahrbuch für fränkische Landesforschung* 26 (1966): 19–177.

Botvinick, Matthew. "The Painting as Pilgrimage: Traces of a Subtext in the Work of Campin and His Contemporaries." *Art History* 15/1 (March 1992): 1–18.

Bouchon, Chantal, Catherine Brisac, Claudine Lautier and Yolanta Zaluska, "La 'Belle-Verrière' de Chartres." *Revue de l'art* 46 (1979): 16–24.

Braet, Herman, Johan Nowe, Gilbert Tournoy. *The Theatre in the Middle Ages*. Belgium: Leuven University Press, 1985.

Brandt de Galametz, Comte de. "Analyse d'une charte de Charles le Téméraire en faveur de l'église du Saint-Esprit de Rue." *Bulletin de la société d'émulation d'Abbeville* (1890): 309–11.

Branner, Robert. *Burgundian Gothic Architecture*. London: A. Zimmer, 1960.

——. "The Labyrinth of Reims Cathedral." *Journal of the Society of Architectural Historians*, 21 (1961): 18–25.

——, ed. *Chartres Cathedral*. New York: W.W. Norton & Co., 1969.

Braun, Joseph, S.J. *Der Christliche Altar in Seinter Geschichtlichen Entwcklung*, vol. 1. Munich: Guenther Koch, 1924.

——. *Die Reliquiare des christlichen Kultes und ihre Entwicklung*. Freiburg im Breisgau: Herder and Co., 1940.

Braunfels, Wolfgang and Percy E. Schramm, eds. *Karl der Große, Lebenswerk und Nachleben*, IV: *Das Nachleben*. Düsseldorf: L. Schwann, 1967.

Brecher, August. "Die kirchliche Verehrung Karls des Großen," in ed. Hans Müllejans, *Karl der Große und sein Schrein in Aachen: Eine Festschrift*. Aachen: Einhard, 1988: 151–66.

Bredero, Adriaan H. "Studien zu den Kreuzzugsbriefen Bernhards von Clairvaux und seiner Reise nach Deutschland im Jahre 1146." *Mitteilungen des Instituts für Österreichische Geschichtsforschung* 66 (1958): 331–43.

——. "Jerusalem in the West," in *Christendom and Christianity in the Middle Ages: the*

Relations between Religion, Church and Society, trans. R. Bruinsma. Grand Rapids, MI: Eerdmans, 1994.

Breest, Ernst. "Das Wunderblut von Wilsnack (1383–1552)." *Märkische Forschungen*, 16 (1881), 131–301.

Breitenback, E. "Israhel van Meckenem's Man of Sorrows." *Quarterly Journal of the Library of Congress* 31 (1974): 21–26.

Brenninger, Georg. *Wallfahrtskirche Heilig Blut in Erding*, 2nd edn. Ottobeuren: Hannes Oefele, 1987.

Bresc-Bautier, Geneviève. "Les imitations du Saint-Sépulcre de Jérusalem (IXᵉ–XVᵉ siècles)—archéologie d'une devotion." *Revue d'histoire de la spiritualité* 50 (1974): 319–42.

Brodsky, Joyce. "The Stavelot Triptych: Notes on a Mosan Work." *Gesta* 11 (1972): 19–33.

Brombierstäudl, Andreas. *Dies und Das aus Iphofens Vergangenheit.* Iphofen: Stadt Iphofen, 1992.

Brooks, Neil C. *The Sepulchre of Christ in Art and Liturgy with Special Reference to the Liturgical Drama.* Urbana: University of Illinois, 1921.

Brouillette, Diane. *Early Gothic Sculpture of Senlis.* Ph.D. diss., University of California at Berkeley, 1981.

Browe, Peter. "Die Hostienschändungen der Juden im Mittelalter." *Römisches Quartalschrift für christliche Altertumskunde und Kirchengeschichte* 34 (1926): 167–97.

———. "Die eucharistische Verwandlungswunder des Mittelalters." *Römische Quartalschrift* 37 (1929): 137–64.

———. "Die scholastische Theorie der eucharistischen Verwandlungswunder." *Theologische Quartalschrift* 110 (1929): 305–32.

———. "Die Eucharistie als Zaubermittel im Mittelalter." *Archiv für Kulturgeschichte* 20, Heft 20 (1930): 134–54.

———. "Die Entstehung der Sakramentenprozessionen." *Bonner Zeitschrift für Theologie und Seelsorge* 8 (1931): 97–117.

———. *Verehrung der Eucharistie im Mittelalter.* Munich: M. Heuber, 1933.

———. *Die eucharistischen Wunder des Mittelalters.* Breslau: Verlag Müller & Seiffert, 1938.

Brown, Elizabeth A.R. and Michael W. Cothren. "The Twelfth-Century Crusading Window of the Abbey of Saint-Denis." *Journal of the Warburg and Courtauld Institutes* 49 (1986): 1–40.

Brown, Peter. *The Cult of the Saints: Its Rise and Function in Latin Christianity.* Chicago: University of Chicago Press, 1981.

Brückner, Wolfgang. "Zur Phänomenologie und Nomenklatur des Wallfahrtswesens und seiner Erforschung," in *Volkskultur und Geschichte. Festgabe für Josef Dünninger zum 65. Geburtstag*, ed. Dieter Harmening, *et al.* Berlin: Erich Schmidt, 1970: 384–424.

———. "Liturgie und Legende: Zur theologischen Theorienbildung und zum historischen Verständnis von Eucharistie-Mirakeln." *Jahrbuch für Volkskunde* NF 19 (1996): 139–68.

Brun, Robert. *Avignon au Temps des Papes.* Brionne: Monfort, 1983.

Bruna, Denis. "La diffusion des enseignes de pèlerinage" in *Pèlerinages et croisades.* Paris: Comité des travaux historiques et scientifiques, 1995: 201–14.

———. *Enseignes de Pèlerinage et Enseignes profanes. Musée National du Moyen Age—Thermes de Cluny.* Paris: Réunion des Musées Nationaux, 1996.

———. "Enseignes de pèlerinage et identité du pèlerin" in *Les pèlerinages à travers l'art et la société à l'époque préromane et romane: actes du XXXIIᵉ journées romanes de Cuxa, Les Cahiers de Saint-Michel de Cuxa* 31 (2000): 59–63.

———. "Quelques Images de Chefs-Reliquaires à Travers les Enseignes de Pèlerinage" in Kicken *et al.*, 2000: 73–79.

Brundage, James A. *The Crusades: A Documentary Survey.* Milwaukee: Marquette University Press, 1962.

——. "Cruce Signari: The Rite for Taking the Cross in England." *Traditio* 22 (1966): 289–310.

Brussels. *Brusselse wandtapijten van de pre-Renaissance*. Brussels: Koninklijke Musea voor Kunst en Geschiedenis, 1976.

Bucher, François. "Micro-architecture as the 'Idea' of Gothic Theory and Style." *Gesta* 15 (1976): 71–89.

Buchkremer, Joseph. "Zur Geschichte des Grabes Karls des Großen." *Zeitschrift des Aachener Geschichtsvereins* 38 (1916): 257–8.

——. "Rezension der Kunstdenkmäler der Rheinprovinz." *Zeitschrift des Aachener Geschichtsvereins* 38 (1916): 293–310.

——. "Zur Baugeschichte des Aachener Münsters." *Zeitschrift des Aachener Geschichtsvereins* 22 (1900): 198–271.

——. "Das Grab Karls des Grossen." *Zeitschrift des Aachener Geschichtsvereins* 29 (1907): 68–210.

Buchner, Ernst. "Die Werke Friedrich Herlins." *Münchner Jahrbuch der bildenden Kunst* 13 (1923): 1–51.

Budde, Rainer. *Köln unde seine Maler 1300–1500*. Cologne: DuMont Buchverlag, 1986.

—— and Roland Krischel. *Das Wallraf-Richartz-Museum Hundert Meisterwerk*. Cologne: DuMont Buchverlag, 2000.

Bugslag, James. "The Shrine of St. Gertrude of Nivelles and the Process of Gothic Design." *Revue d'art canadienne/Canadian Art Review* 20/1–2 (1993): 16–28.

——. "Entre espace pictural et architectural. La fenêtre est de la chapelle Saint-Piat à la cathédrale de Chartres." *Représentations architecturales dans les vitraux*. Liège: Commission royale des Monuments, Sites et Fouilles de la Région wallonne, 2002: 85–94

——. "St Eustace and St George: Crusading Saints in the Sculpture and Stained Glass of Chartres Cathedral." *Zeitschrift für Kunstgeschichte* 66/4 (2003): 441–64.

Bull, Marcus. *The Miracles of Our Lady of Rocamadour: Analysis and Translation*. Woodbridge, Suffolk: The Boydell Press, 1999.

Bulteau, Marcel. *Description de la cathédrale de Chartres*. Chartres: Garnier, and Paris, 1850.

——. *Monographie de la cathédrale de Chartres*, I. Chartres: Librairie R. Selleret, 1887.

——. *Monographie de la cathédrale de Chartres*, III. Chartres: Société Archéologique d'Eure-et-Loir, 1892 and Librairie R. Selleret, 1901.

Burgess, Clive. "'Longing to be Prayed for': Death and Commemoration in an English Parish in the Later Middle Ages," in Gordon & Marshall, 2000: 44–65.

Burnet, Gilbert. *The History of the Reformation of the Church of England*. Oxford: Clarendon Press, 1865.

Busch, P. Gabriel. *St. Servatius Und Der Michaelsberg: Das Ehemalige Dekanat Siegburg*. Siegburg: Verlag Abtei Michaelsberg, 1987.

Buyle, Marjan and Christine Vanthillo. *Retables flamands et Brabançons dans les monuments belges*. Brussels: M&L, no. 4, 2000.

Bynum, Caroline Walker. *Fragmentation and Redemption: Essays on Gender and the Human Body in Medieval Religion*. New York: Zone, 1992.

——. "The Blood of Christ in the Later Middle Ages." *Church History* 71/4 (December 2002): 685–714.

——. "Violent Imagery in Late Medieval Piety." *German Historical Institute Bulletin* 30 (Spring 2002): 3–36.

—— and Paula Gerson. "Body-Part Reliquaries and Body Parts in the Middle Ages." *Gesta* 36/1 (1997): 3–7.

Cahn, Walter and Linda Seidel. *Romanesque Sculpture in American Collections*, vol. 1. New York: Franklin, 1979.

Caillaud, Abbé. *Notice sur le Précieux Sang de Neuvy-Saint-Sépulcre*. Bourges: Pigelet, 1865.

Cali, François. *L'ordre flamboyant et son temps. Essai sur le style gothique du XIVe au XVIe siècle*. Paris: Arthaud, 1967.

Callaey, Frédégand. *L'origine della Festa del "Corpus Domini."* Rovigo: Istituto padano di arti grafiche, 1958.

——. "Origine e sviluppo delle festa del 'Corpus Domini'." *Eucaristia: il mistero del'altare nel pensiero e nella vita della chiesa*, ed. Antonio Piolanti. Rome: Desclée, 1957.

Calmette, Joseph. *The Golden Age of Burgundy*. trans. Doris Weightman. New York: W.W. Norton and Co., 1963.

Cameron, Averil. "The Early Cult of the Virgin," in Vassilaki, 2000: 3–15.

Camille, Michael. *Image on the Edge. The Margins of Medieval Art*. London: Reaktion Books, 1992.

——. *The Medieval Art of Love*, London: Laurence King, 1998.

Campbell, Lorne. *Renaissance Portraits*. New Haven: Yale University Press, 1990.

——. *National Gallery Catalogues: The Fifteenth-Century Netherlandish Schools*. London: National Gallery, 1998.

Canard, Marius. "La destruction de l'église de la Résurrection par le Calife Hakim et l'histoire de la descente du feu sacré." *Byzantion* 35 (1965): 16–43.

Cantigas de Santa Maria de Don Alfonso el Sabio, 2 vols. Madrid: Real Academia Española, 1889.

Carlen, Louis. *Wallfahrt und Recht im Abendland*. Freiburg: Universitätsverlag Freiburg Schweiz, 1987.

Carpenter, David A. *The Reign of Henry III*. London: Hambledon Press, 1996.

Carr, Annemarie Weyl. "The Mother of God in Public," in Vassilaki, 2000: 325–37.

Carru, Dominique and Sylvain Gagnière. "Notes sur quelques objets de dévotion populaire. Ampoules et enseignes de pèlerinage du Moyen Age tardif provenant d'Avignon." *Mémoire de l'Académie de Vaucluse*, 8th s., I (1992): 55–92.

Carruthers, Mary. *The Book of Memory. A Study of Memory in Medieval Culture*. Cambridge Studies in Medieval Literature, 10. Cambridge: Cambridge University Press, 1990.

——. *The Craft of Thought: Meditation, Rhetoric, and the Making of Images, 400–1200*. Cambridge: Cambridge University Press, 1998.

Caspar, Erich. "Die Kreuzigungsbullen Eugens III." *Neues Archiv* 45 (1924): 285–305.

Cassagnes-Brouquet, Sophie. *Vierges noires*. Rodez: Éditions du Rouergue, 2000.

Cassart, Jean. *Saints Populaires Dans Le Diocese De Tournai—Iconographie—Attributs—Devotion*. Tournai: Cathédrale Notre-Dame de Tournai, 1975.

Cauchie, Alfred. *La Grande Procession De Tournai*. Louvain: Ch. Peeters, Libriare-Éditeur, 1892.

Caumont, D. "Le Labyrinthe de Chartres." *Bulletin Monumental* 13 (1847): 202–03.

Cave, Charles J.P. *Roof Bosses in Medieval Churches: An Aspect of Gothic Sculpture*. Cambridge: Cambridge University Press, 1948.

Caviness, Madeline. "A Lost Cycle of Canterbury Paintings of 1220." *Antiquaries Journal* 54 (1974): 66–74.

——. *The Early Stained Glass of Canterbury Cathedral, circa 1175–1220*. Princeton, NJ: Princeton University Press, 1977.

——. *The Windows of Christ Church Cathedral, Canterbury*. Corpus Vitrearum Medii Aevii, Great Britain, Volume 2. London: Oxford University Press, 1981.

——. "Canterbury Cathedral Clerestory: the Glazing Program in Relation to the Campaigns of Construction," in *Medieval Art and Architecture at Canterbury before 1220*. London: British Archaeological Association with Kent Archaeological Society, 1982: 46–55.

Cense, Adrie and Saskia Werner. *De schatkamer van de Sint-Servaaskerk te Maastrict:een keuze van de voorwerpen uit de schatkamer en hun functie*. Zutphen: De Walburg Pers, 1984.

Ceulemans Christina, Didier Robert, Raynaud Christiane. "Die Ikonographie des Schreins der hl. Gertrud," in Westermann-Angerhausen, 1995–96: 208–24.

Challine, Charles. *Recherches sur Chartres, transcrites et annotées par un arrière-neveu de l'auteur.* Chartres: Société archéologique d'Eure-et-Loir, 1918.

Charlier, Chr. and Ph. George. "Ouverture des châsses des saints Domitien et Mengold au Trésor de Notre-Dame de Huy." *Annales du Cercle hutois des Sciences et Beaux-Arts* 36 (1982): 31–75.

Chauveau, Abbé. "Origine de la Métropole de Sens." *Congrès Archéologiques de France,* 14 (1847–48): 170–218.

Chazelle, Celia. "Figure, Character, and the Glorified Body in the Carolingian Eucharistic Controversy." *Traditio* 47 (1992), 1–36.

Chédeville, André. *Chartres et ses campagnes (XIe–XIIIe s.)* Paris: C. Klincksieck, 1973.

Cheney, Charles R. *Handbook of Dates for Students of English History.* 1945. Repr., Cambridge: Cambridge University Press, 1996.

Ciresi, Lisa Victoria. "Manifestations of the Holy as Instruments of Propaganda: the Cologne Dreikönigenschrein and the Aachen Karlsschrein and Marienschrein in Late Medieval Ritual." Ph.D. diss. Rutgers University, 2003.

Clark, William W. "Sens (architecture)." in *The Grove Dictionary of Art* 28, 1996: 413–16.

Clarke, Nigel. *The Rude Man of Cerne Abbas and Other Wessex Landscape Oddities.* Lyme Regis: Nigel J. Clarke Publications, n.d.

Clarke, William. "Reading Reims, I. The Sculptures on the Chapel Buttresses." *Gesta* 39/2 (2000): 135–45.

Claussen, Peter Cornelius. *Chartres-Studien zu Vorgeschichte, Funktion und Skulptur der Vorhallen.* Wiesbaden: Franz Steiner Verlag, 1975.

Coales, John, ed. *The Earliest English Brasses: Patronage, Style and Workshops 1270–1350.* London: Monumental Brass Society, 1987.

Cohausz, Alfred. "Vier ehemalige Sakramentswallfahrten: Gottsbüren, Hillentrup, Blomberg and Büren." *Westfälische Zeitschrift* 112 (1962): 275–304.

Cohen, Esther. "*In haec signa*: Pilgrim-badge Trade in Southern France." *Journal of Medieval History* 2 (1976): 193–214.

Cohen, Gustave. "La Scène des Pèlerins d'Emmaüs: Contribution à l'étude des origines du théâtre comique" in *Mélanges de philologie romane et d'histoire littéraire offerts à M. Maurice Wilmotte,* vol. 1. Paris: Champion, 1910.

Coldstream, Nicola. "English Decorated Shrine Bases." *Journal of the British Archaeological Association* 129 (1976): 15–34.

———. "Base of the Shrine of St. Alban, St. Albans Cathedral" in Alexander & Binski, 1987: 207–8.

———. *The Decorated Style: Architecture and Ornament, 1240–1360.* Toronto: University of Toronto Press, 1994.

Coldwells, Alan. *St. George's Chapel Windsor Castle.* Norwich: Jarrold Publishing, 1993.

Coleman, Simon and John Elsener. *Pilgrimage Past and Present in the World Religions.* Cambridge: University of Harvard Press, 1995.

Collinson, Patrick, Nigel Ramsay, and Margaret Sparks, eds. *A History of Canterbury Cathedral.* Oxford: Oxford University Press, 1995.

Collon-Gevaert, Suzanne. *Histoire des arts du métal en Belgique.* Brussels: Palais des académies, 1951.

Comblen-Sonkes, Micheline and Philippe Lorentz. *Les Primitifs Flamands, Corpus de la peinture des anciens Pays-Bas méridionaux et de la principauté de Liège au quinzième siècle 17.* 2 vols. Brussels: Centre international d'étude de la peinture médiévale des bassins se L'Escaut et de la Meuse, 1995.

Conant, Kenneth J. *Carolingian and Romanesque Architecture 800–1200.* New York: Penguin Books, 1979.

Connolly, Daniel K. "Imagined Pilgrimage in Gothic Art: Maps, Manuscripts and Labyrinths." Ph.D. diss., University of Chicago, 1998.

———. "Imagined Pilgrimage in the Itinerary Maps of Matthew Paris." *Art Bulletin* 81/4 (1999): 598–622.

Constable, Giles. "Opposition to Pilgrimage in the Middle Ages." *Studia Gratiana* 19 (1976): 125–46.

——. "The Second Crusade as Seen by Contemporaries." *Traditio* 9 (1953): 223–37.

Coppens, Martien and Concordius van Goirle. *De koorbanken van Oirschot, fotografisch gezien*, Eindhoven: Uitgeversmaatschappij 'De Pelgrim', 1941.

——. *De Sint-Martinuskerk van Oirschot en haar koorgestoelte*. Eindhoven: Lecturis bv, 1980.

Corblet, Abbé Jules. *Hagiographie du diocèse d'Amiens*. 5 vols. Paris and Amiens: J.-B. Dumoulin, 1868–75.

Corbo, Virgilio. *Il Santo Sepolcro di Gerusalemme. Aspetti archaeologici dalle origini al periodo Crociato*. 3 vols. Jerusalem: Franciscan Printing Press, 1981–82.

Corley, Birgitte. *Painting and Patronage in Cologne 1300–1500*. Turnout, Belgium: Harvey Miller/Brepols, 2000.

Corpus vitrearum, France. Les vitraux de Paris, de la région parisienne, de la Picardie et du Nord-Pas-de-Calais. Paris: Éditions du Centre national de la recherche scientifique, 1978.

Corti, Maria and Giorgio T. Faggin. *L'opera Completa di Memling*. Milan: Rizzoli, 1969.

Coulet, Noël. *Les Visites Pastorales*. Turnhout: Brepols, 1977.

Coulombeau, Maurice. *La cathédrale de Chartres*. Paris: Librairie Bloud & Gay, 1927.

Cousin, Jean. *Histoire De Tournay*. 4 vols. Douay: Marc Wyon, 1619.

Le Couteur, J.D. and J.H.M. Carter. "Notes on the Shrine of St. Swithun formerly in Winchester Cathedral." *Antiquaries Journal* 4 (1924): 360–70.

Cowdrey, Herbert E.J. "Pope Urban II's Preaching of the First Crusade." *History: Journal of the Historical Association* 55 (1970): 177–88.

Cremer, Folkhard. *Die St. Nikolaus- und Heiligblut-Kirche zu Wilsnack (1383–1552)*, 2 vols. Munich: Scaneg, 1996.

Creswell, Keppel A.C. *Early Muslim Architecture*. 2 vols. Oxford: Clarendon Press, 1969.

Crook, John. "The Thirteenth Century Shrine and Screen at St. Swithun at Winchester." *Journal of the British Archaeological Association* 138 (1985): 125–31.

——. "The Typology of Early Medieval Shrines—A Previously Misidentified 'Tomb-Shrine' Panel from Winchester Cathedral." *The Antiquaries Journal*, 70, Pt. 1 (1990): 49–64.

——. *The Architectural Setting of the Cult of Saints in the Early Christian West, c. 300– c. 1200*. Oxford: Oxford University Press, 2000.

Cross, Frank L. and Elizabeth A. Livingstone, eds. *Oxford Dictionary of the Christian Church*. 2nd ed. Oxford: Oxford University Press, 1958, rev. repr. 1990.

Crossley, Fredrick. *English Church Monuments A.D. 1150–1550: An Introduction to the Study of Tombs & Effigies of the Medieval Period*. London: B.T. Batsford, 1921.

Crozet, René. "Le Monument de la Sainte Larme à la Trinité de Vendôme." *Bulletin monumental* 121 (1963): 171–80.

——. "A propos des chapiteaux de la façade occidentale de Chartres." *Cahiers de la civilisation médiévale* 14 (1971): 159–65.

Cuttler, Charles D. *Northern Painting from Pucelle to Bruegel*. New York: Holt, Rinehart and Winston, 1968.

Dale, Thomas. *Relics, Prayer and Politics in Medieval Venetia: Romanesque Painting in the Crypt of Aquileia Cathedral*. Princeton: Princeton University Press, 1997.

Dalmann, Gustaf. *Das Grab Christi in Deutschland*. Leipzig: Dieterich, 1922.

Daniélou, Alain. *Der Phallus. Methapher des Lebens, Guelle des Glücks. Symbole und Riten in Geschichte und Kunst*. München: Eugen Diederichs Verlag, 1998, repr. Puiseaux: Pardes, 1993.

Dantinne, E. *Les Anciennes Fêtes Hutoises*, Gembloux, 1937.

Darsy, François-Irénée. "Notes historiques sur la ville de Rue," in *La Picardie*, Amiens: Delattre-Lenoël, 1877.

David, Henri and Aenne Leibrech. "Le calvaire de Champmol et l'art de Sluter." *Bulletin Monumental* 92 (1933): 419–67.

——. "Le portail de l'Eglise de Champmol; Chronologie de la construction." *Bulletin Monumental* 94 (1935): 329–52.

Davidson, Linda Kay and Maryjane Dunn-Wood. *Pilgrimage in the Middle Ages: A Research Guide.* New York: Garland, 1993.

De Bruyne, D. "L'origine Des Processions De La Chandeleur Et Des Rogations— a Propos D'un Sermon Inédit." *Revue Bénédictine* 34 (1922): 14–26.

Decaëns, Henry. "Les pèlerinages," in François Avril *et al. Tresors des abbayes normandes.* Rouen: Musée des Antiquités, 1979: 294–305.

Deér, Josef. "Die Siegel Kaiser Friedrichs I. Barbarossa und Heinrichs VI. in der Kunst und Politik ihrer Zeit" in *Festschrift Hans R. Hahnloser, zum 60. Geburtstag,* ed. Ellen J. Beer. Basel: Birkhauser, 1961.

Defoer, Henri L.M. "Metalen reisgezelschap." *Catharijnebrief: mededelingen van de Vereniging van Vrienden van het Museum Het Catharijneconvent te Utrecht* 15 (September 1986): 3–4.

——, "Rijksmuseum *Het Catharijneconvent," Nederlandse Rijksmuseum in 1986.* 's Gravenhage: Staatsuitgeverij, 1987: 289–300.

Dehaisnes, M. (Chanoine). *Histoire De L'art Dans La Flandre, L'artois & Le Hainaut Avant Le XVe Siècle.* Lille: L. Quarré, Libraire-Éditeur, 1886.

Deichmann, Friedrich Wilhelm. *Ravenna Hauptstadt des spätantiken Abendlandes,* vols. 1–2. Wiesbaden: Steiner, 1969–1974.

De Kroon, Marike. "Medieval pilgrim badges in the collection of the Museum for Religious Art: Het Catharijneconvent, Utrecht," in eds Guy de Boe and Frans Verhaege. *Art and Symbolism in Medieval Europe. Medieval Europe Brugge 1997 Conference.* Zellik: Institute for the Archaeological Heritage, 1997: 145–48.

De la Fons-Mélicoq, Baron. "Voyage archéologique au XVe siècle. Suite de l'Italie." *Annales Archéologiques* 22 (1862): 133–41.

Delaporte, Yves. *Le voile de Notre Dame.* Chartres: Maison des clercs, 1927.

——. "Les druides et les traditions chartraines," *La voix de Notre-Dame de Chartres* (Sept. 1936): 245–55.

——. *L'Ordinaire chartrain du XIIIe siècle publié d'après le manuscript original.* Chartres: Société archéologique d'Eure-et-Loir, 1953.

——. *Les Trois Notre-Dame de la cathédrale de Chartres,* 2nd ed. Chartres: Houvet, 1955.

—— and Étienne Houvet. *Les vitraux de la cathédrale de Chartres. Histoire et description.* Chartres: É. Houvet, 1926.

Delescluse, A. "Une Procession a Stavelot En 1509." *Bulletin de la Société d'Art et d'Histoire du Diocèse de Liège* VIII (1894): 367–70.

Delforge, J. "Le Bréviaire de saint-Adrien de Grammont." *Scriptorium* 12 (1958): 102–04.

Delignières, Émile. "Abbeville: église Saint-Wulfran," in *La Picardie historique et monumentale* vol. 3. Amiens: Impr. de Yvert et Tellier, 1904–06: 3–44.

Demaret, H. *La collégiale Notre-Dame à Huy, troisième partie (ameublement artistique, trésor et archives).* Huy, 1924.

DeMoreau, É. "Histoire De L'église En Belgique Des Origines aux Débuts du XIIe Siècle." I:30–39; II:401–10; III:100–13; III:23–29. Brussels: L'édition universelle, n.d.

Dendy, D.R. *The Use of Lights in Christian Worship.* Vol. 41, *Alcuin Collections.* London: SPCK, 1959.

Denzinger, Heinrich, Clemens Bannwart, eds. *Enchiridion Symbolorum, Definitionum et Declarationum de Rebus Fidei et Morum.* Fribourg: Herder & Co., 1937.

De Pelsmaeker, Prosper. *Coutumes des Pays et Comté de Flandre. Quartier d'Ypres. Registres aux sentences des échevins d'Ypres.* Brussels: Goemaere, 1914.

De Rochambeau, Achille. "Voyage à la Sainte-Larme de Vendôme, étude historique et critique sur cet antique pèlerinage." *Bulletin de la Société archéologique scientifique et littéraire du Vendômois* 12 (1873): 157–212.

De Roover, Raymond. *The Rise and Decline of the Medici Bank 1397–1494.* Cambridge: Harvard University Press, 1963.

Deshoulières, François. "Les églises romanes du Berri." *Bulletin Monumental* 73 (1909): 469–92.

—— and Emile Chénon in *Bulletin de la Société nationale des antiquaires de France* (1916): 190–96, 214–29.

Desnoyers, François-Edmond. "Objets trouvés dans la Loire." *Mémoires de la Société archéologique de l'Orléanais* 12 (1873): 245–75.

——. "Objets trouvés dans la Loire." *Mémoires de la Société archéologique de l'Orléanais* 15 (1876): 113–96.

Despres, Denise. "Immaculate Flesh and the Social Body: Mary and the Jews." *Jewish History* 12/1 (Spring 1998): 47–69.

Deuchler, Florens. *Der Ingeborgpsalter.* Berlin: de Gruyter, 1967.

Devlin, Dennis *"Corpus Christi: A Study in Medieval Eucharistic Theory, Devotion and Practice."* Ph.D. diss., University of Chicago, 1975.

De Vos, Dirk. *Bruges Musées Communaux, Catalogue des Tableaux du 15ᵉ et du 16ᵉ siécle,* trans. J. Lebbe. Bruges: Stadt Brugge, 1982.

——, *Hans Memling, the Complete Works,* trans. Ted Alkins. Antwerp: Fonds Mercator; Ghent: Ludion Press, 1994.

Devoucoux, Abbé, *Description de l'église cathédrale d'Autun.* Autun: Dejussieu, 1845.

Dhanens, Elisabeth. *Hugo van der Goes,* trans. Catherine Warnant and Marnix Vincent. Antwerp: Fonds Mercator, 1998.

Dictionnaire d'Histoire et de Géographie. Paris: Letouzey, 1914, s.v. "Arras".

Didier, Robert. "The Shrine of St Maurus Rediscovered." *Apollo. International Magazine of the Arts* CXXVII/3–4 (April 1988): 227–43.

——. "La chasse de saint Maur de l'ancienne abbaye de Florennes." *Annales de la Société archéologique de Namur* 66 (1990): 201–47.

—— et al. "La châsse de Notre-Dame à Huy et sa restauration." *Histoire-Etude archéologique, Bulletin de l'Institut royal du Patrimoine artistique* 12 (1970): 8–54.

Diemer, Peter. "Zum Darstellungsprogramm of Dreikönigenschreins." *Kölner Domblatt* 41 (1976): 231–36.

Dierichs, Angelika. "Klingendes Kleinod. Ein unbekanntes Tintinnabulum in Dänemark." *Antike Welt. Zeitschrift für Ärcäologie und Kulturgeschichte,* 30 (1999): 145–49.

Dierkens, Alain. "Réliques Et Reliquaires, Sources De L'histoire Du Moyen Age?" in *Sainteté et Martyre Dans Les Religions Du Livre,* ed. Jacques Marx. Brussels: Université de Bruxelles, 1989: 47–56.

Dietrich, Otto. *Der Triumphus St. Remacli: Eine Quelle Für Die Geschichte Des 11. Jahrhunderts.* Halle: Buchdruckerei des Waisenhauses, 1887.

Dinkler-von Schubert, Erika. *Der Schrein der heiligen Elisabeth zu Marburg. Studien zur Schrein-Ikonographie. Marburg.* Marburg an der Lahn, 1964.

Dobson, Barrie. "The Monks of Canterbury in the Later Middle Ages, 1220–1540" in Collinson, Ramsay, & Sparks, 1995: 69–153.

Doob, Penelope Reed. *The Idea of the Labyrinth: from Classical Antiquity through the Middle Ages.* Ithaca: Cornell University Press, 1990.

Doppler, Pierre Marie Hubert. "Beknopte geschiedenis der zeverjarige Heiligdomsvaart te Maastricht." *De Maasgouw* 43 (1923): 37–48.

Döring, Alois. "St. Salvator in Bettbrunn. Historisch-volkskundliche Untersuchung zur eucharistischen Wallfahrt" in eds. Georg Schwaiger and Paul Mai. *Beiträge zur Geschichte des Bistums Regensburg* 13 (1979): 35–234.

Douais, Celestin. "Deux Reliquaires de l'église Saint-Sernin à Toulouse." *Revue de l'Art chrétien* 38 (1888): 154–69.

Draper, Peter. "Bishop Northwold and the Cult of Saint Etheldreda," in *Medieval*

Art and Architecture at Ely Cathedral, eds. Nicola Coldstream and Peter Draper. Leeds: BAR, 1979.

Dressler, Rachel. "Medieval Narrative: The Capital Frieze on the Royal Portal, Chartres Cathedral." Ph.D. diss. Columbia University, 1992.

Drijvers, Jan Willem. *Helena Augusta: The Mother of Constantine the Great and the Legend of Her Finding of the True Cross.* Leiden: E.J. Brill Press, 1992.

Dubois, Pierre. *Rue (Somme). Notice historique et guide du visiteur. La chapelle du Saint-Esprit, l'église, l'hôpital, l'hôtel de ville.* Amiens: T. Jeunet, 1909.

Du Cange, Charles Du Fresne. *Glossarium mediae et infimae latinitatis*, vol. 13, Pierre Carpentier, ed. Paris: Didot, 1845.

Du Cange, Domino, ed. *Glossarium Mediae Et Infimae Latinitatis.* Paris: Léopold Favre, 1680, repr. 1954.

Duchesne, Jean-Patrick, Dominique Allart, Pierre-Yves Kairis, eds. *Mélanges Pierre Colman, Revue Des Historiens De L'art, Des Archéologues, Des Musicologues Et Des Orientalistes De L'université De Liège.* Liège, 1996.

Duffy, Eamon. *The Stripping of the Altars: Traditional Religion in England c. 1400–c. 1580.* New Haven: Yale University Press, 1992.

Duggan, Anne. "The Cult of St. Thomas Becket in the Thirteenth Century," in *St. Thomas Cantilupe Bishop of Hereford*, ed. Meryl Jancey. Hereford: Friends of Hereford Cathedral, 1982: 21–44.

——. "John of Salisbury and Thomas Becket," in ed. Michael Wilks, *The World of John of Salisbury.* London: Blackwell Publishers, 1994: 427–38.

Duggan, Lawrence. "Was Art really the 'Book of the Illiterate'?" *Word and Image* 5 (1989): 227–51.

Dulong, M. "Etienne Langton, versificateur." *Mélanges Mandonnet.* Paris: J. Vrin, 1930, II: 183–90.

Dumoulin, J., T. Hackens and J. Pycke, eds. *La Croix Byzantine Du Trésor De La Cathédrale De Tournai.* Tournai: Archives du Chapître Cathédrale, 1987.

—— and Jacques Pycke. *La Grande Procession De Tournai (1092–1992) Une Réalité Religieuse, Urbaine, Diocesane, Sociale, Économique Et Artistique.* Tournai: Fabrique de l'Église Cathédrale de Tournai, 1992.

——, ed. *"Trésors Sacrés."* 173. Tournai: Cathédrale Notre-Dame de Tournai, 1971.

Dunlop, Colin. *Processions—a Dissertation Together with Practical Suggestions, Alcuin Club Tracts.* London: Oxford University Press, 1932.

Dünninger, Hans. *Wallfahrt und Bilderkult. Gesammelte Schrifte.* Wolfgang Brückner, Jürgen Leussen and Klaus Wittstadt, ed. Würzburg: Echter, 1995.

Dupertuis Bangs, Jeremy. *Church Art and Architecture in the Low Countries before 1566.* vol. 37, *Sixteenth Century Essays & Studies.* Kirksville, MO, 1997.

Dupont, Jacques. "Les disciples d'Emmaüs (Lc 24, 13–35)" in *La Pâque du Christ: Mystère et salut, Lectio Divina* 112. Paris: Cerf, 1982: 167–95.

Dupront, Alphonse. *Du sacré. Croisades et pèlerinages. Images et langages.* Paris: Gallimard, 1987.

Durand, Georges. *Monographie de l'église Notre-Dame, cathédrale d'Amiens.* Mémoires de la Société des antiquaires de Picardie. Paris: A. Picard et fils, 1901.

——. "Notices sur le Canton d'Acheux. Mailly" in *La Picardie historique et monumentale* vol. 5. Paris-Amiens: De Yvert et Tellier, 1912–14: 85–97.

Durand, Jannic. *The Louvre: Objets d'Art.* London: Zwemmer, 1995.

Durliat, Marcel. *Saint-Sernin de Toulouse.* Toulouse: Eché, 1986.

Durrieu, Paul. *Les Très Belles Heures de Notre-Dame du duc Jean de Berry.* Paris: Société français de reproductions de manucrits à peintures, 1922.

Du Sommerard, Edmond. *Catalogue et description des objets d'art de l'Antiquité du Moyen Age et de la Renaissance exposés au musée de Cluny.* Paris: Hôtel de Cluny, 1883.

Dussaut, Louis. "Le triptyche des apparitions en Luc 24 (analyse structurelle)." *Revue biblique* 94 (1987): 161–213.

Dyas, Dee. *Pilgrimage in Medieval English Literature, 700–1500.* Woodbridge, UK: Boydell & Brewer, 2001.

Dynes, Wayne. "Medieval Cloister as Portico of Solomon." *Gesta,* 12 (1973): 61–69.

Eade, John and Michael J. Sallnow, eds. *Contesting the Sacred: The Anthropology of Christian Pilgrimage.* London: Routledge, 1991.

Eames, Elizabeth. "Notes on the Decorated Stone Roundels in the Corona and Trinity Chapel in Canterbury Cathedral," in *Medieval Art and Architecture at Canterbury before 1220.* London: British Archaeological Association, 1982: 67–70.

Eder, Manfred. *Die "Deggendorfer Gnad":Entstehung und Entwicklung einer Hostienwallfahrt im Kontext von Theologie und Geschichte.* Deggendorf: Stadt Deggendorf, 1992.

——. "Eucharistische Kirchen und Wallfahrten im Bistum Regensburg" in Scwaig & Mai, 1994: 97–172.

Edler, Josef. *Die Liebfrauen-Kirche zu Frankfurt am Main und ihre Kunstwerke.* Düren: Danielwsky, 1938.

Edson, Evelyn. *Mapping Time and Space: How Medieval Mapmakers Viewed Their World.* London: The British Library, 1997.

Ehrenberg, Richard. *Capital & Finance in the Age of the Renaissance: A Study of the Fuggers and Their Connections,* trans. H.M. Lucas. London: Jonathan Cape, 1928.

Ehresmann, Donald L. "The Frankfurt Three Kings Portal, Madern Gerthener, and the International Gothic Style on the Middle Rhine." *Art Bulletin* 50 (December 1968): 301–08.

Eisler, Colin. "The Athlete of Virtue. The Iconography of Asceticism" in ed. Millard Miess, *De Artibus Opuscula XL, Essays in Honor of Erwin Panofsky.* New York: New York University Press, 1961, Vol. 1: 82–97; Vol. 2, 23–26.

——. "The Golden Christ of Cortona and the Man of Sorrows in Italy." *Art Bulletin* 51 (1969): 107–18, 233–46.

——. *Masterworks in Berlin: A City's Paintings Reunited.* Boston: Little Brown and Co., 1996.

Elbern, Victor Heinrich. *Dom und Domschatz in Hildesheim.* Königstein im Taunus: Karl Robert Langewiesche, 1979.

——. *Die Goldschmiedekunst im frühen Mittelalter.* Darmstadt: Wissenschaftliche Buchgesellschaft, 1988.

——. "Vier karolingische Elfenbeinkästen." *Deutscher Verein für Kunstwissenschaft* 20/1–2 (1966): 8–11.

Elisabeth of Schönau. *Elisabeth of Schönau: The Complete Works,* trans. Anne L. Clark. Mahwah: Paulist Press, 2000.

Falkenburg, Reindert Leonard. *Joachim Patinir: Landscape as an Image of the Pilgrimage of Life.* Amsterdam: J. Benjamins Pub. Co., 1988.

Elliot, Thomas George. *The Christianity of Constantine the Great.* Scranton: University of Scranton Press, 1996.

Elsner, Jas. "Between Mimesis and Divine Power: Visuality in the Greco-Roman World," in ed. Robert Nelson, *Visuality Before and Beyond the Renaissance: Seeing as Others Saw.* Cambridge: University Press, 2000: 45–69.

Endres, Joseph. "Die Darstellung der Gregoriousmesse im Mittelalter." *Zeitschrift für christliche Kunst,* 30/11/12 (1917): 146–56.

——. *Iphofen. Entwicklung einer würzburgischen Landstadt von ihren Anfängen bis in der Echterzeit.* Dettelbach: Verlag Dr. J.H. Röll, 2000.

Engels, Odilo. "Karl der Große und Aachen im 12. Jahrhundert," in Kramp, 2000, 1: 348–56.

Enlart, Camille. "Notices sur le canton de Ham," in *La Picardie historique et monumentale* vol. 6. Paris-Amiens: Impr. De Yvert et Tellier, 1923–31: 147.

Enzo Carli. *Il Reliquiario del Corporale ad Orvieto.* Milan: Martello, 1964.

Erdmann, Carl. "Kaiserliche und päpstliche Fahnen im hohen Mittelalter." *Quellen und Forschungen aus italienischen Archiven und Bibliotheken* 25 (1933/34): 1–48

Erens, A. "De Eeredienst van Sint Job te Wezemaal." *Eigen Schoon en De Brabander* 22 (1939): 1–12.

Erlande-Brandenburg, Alain. *The Cathedral: The Social and Architectural Dynamics of Construction*. trans. Martin Thom. Cambridge: Cambridge University Press, 1994.

———. "La cathédrale de Fulbert," in *Enseigner le moyen âge à partir d'un monument, la cathédrale de Chartres. Le temps* de Fulbert. Chartres: Société archéologique d'Eure-et-Loir, 1996: 121–28.

Esmeijer, Anna C. *Divina Quaternitas: A Preliminary Study in the Method and Application of Visual Exegesis*, Amsterdam, 1978.

Essen, Luca. *Pieter Brueghel der Jüngere—Jan Brueghel der Ältere. Flämische Malerei um 1600. Tradition und Fortschritt*. Lingen: Lucca Verlag, 1997.

Evans, Helen C. and William D. Wixom, eds. *The Glory of Byzantium Art and Culture of the Middle Byzantine Era, A.D. 843–1261*. New York: The Metropolitan Museum of Art, 1997.

Evans, Joan. *Pattern: A Study of Ornament in Western Europe from 1180–1900*. New York: Hacker Art Books, 1975 repr. Oxford, Clarendon Press, 1931.

Everson, H.P.H. "De Heiligdomsvaart van Maastricht." *Publications de la Société Historique et Archéologique dans le Limbourg* 7 (1870): 398–411.

EWTN Online Services (Accessed 15 February, 2003) http://www.EWTN.com

Faensen, Hubert. "Zur Synthese von Bluthostien- und Heiliggrab-Kult. Überlegungen zu dem Vorgängerbau der Gnadenkapelle des märkischen Klosters Heiligengrabe." *Sachsen und Anhalt. Jahrbuch der Historischen Kommission fuur Sachsen-Anhalt. Festschrift für Ernst Schubert* 19. Weimar: Böhlaus Nachfolger, 1997: 237–55.

Falke, Otto von and Heinrich Frauberger. *Deutsche Schmelzarbeiten des Mittelalters und andere Kunstwerke der Kunsthistorischen Ausstellung zu Düsseldorf, 1902*. Frankfurt: Joseph Baer & Heinrich Keller, 1904.

Falkenburg, Reindert. *Joachim Patinir: Landscape as an Image of the Pilgrimage of Life*. Amsterdam: John Benjamins, 1988.

Farmer, David. *Oxford Dictionary of Saints*. 4th ed. Oxford: Oxford University Press, 1997.

Farmer, Sharon. *Communities of Saint Martin: Legend and Ritual in Medieval Tours*. Ithaca: Cornell University Press, 1991.

Fassler, Margot. "Liturgy and Sacred History in the Twelfth-Century Tympana at Chartres." *Art Bulletin* 75/3 (Sept. 1993): 499–520.

———. "Mary's Nativity, Fulbert of Chartres, and the Stirps Jesse: Liturgical Innovation circa 1000 and Its Afterlife," *Speculum* 75 (2000), 389–434.

———. *Making History: The Liturgical Framework of Time and Cult of the Virgin at Chartres* (forthcoming).

Faussett, T.G. "On a Fragment of Glass in Nettlestead Church." *Archaeologia Cantiana* 6 (1864–1865): 129–34.

Favière, Jean. *Berry Roman*. La nuit des temps 32, La Pierre-qui-Vire: Zodiaque, 1970.

Federstrich: Liturgische Handschriften der ehemaligen Stifsbibliothek. Eupen: Grenz-Echo, 2000.

Felbecker, Sabine. *Die Prozession: Historische Und Systematische Untersuchungen Zu Einer Liturgischen Ausdruckshandlung*. Vol. 39, *Münsteraner Theologische Abhandlungen*. Altenberg: Oros Verlag, 1995.

Feldbusch, Hans. "Emmaus," in *Lexikon der christlichen Ikonographie*, vol. 1. Rome: Herder, 1968: cols. 622–26.

Felten, W. *Der hl. Martyrer und Tribun Quirinus, Patron der Stadt Neuss*. Neuss: [n.p.], 1900.

Ferber, Stanley. "The Armorial Device in Memling's *Christ on the Cross*." *North Carolina Museum of Art Bulletin* 6 (1966): 17–20.

Fillitz, Hermann. "Die Kunsthistorische Stellung des Karlsschreins," in *Der Schrein Karls des Großen: Bestand und Sicherung 1982–1988*. Aachen: Einhard, 1998: 11–27.

——. *Die Insignien und Kleinodien des Heiligen Römischen Reiches*. Vienna: Anton Schroll, 1954.

——. "Das Kreuzreliquiar Heinrichs II. in der Schatzkammer der Münchner Residenz." *Münchner Jahrbuch* 9/10 (1958/59): 15–31.

——. *Die Schatzkammer in Wien: Symbole Abendländischen Kaisertums*. Salzburg: Residenz Verlag, 1986.

——. ed. *Geschichte der bildenden Kunst in Österreich, Bd. I: Früh- und Hochmittelalters*. Munich: Prestel, 1997.

Finucane, Ronald C. "The Use and Abuse of Medieval Miracles." *History* 60 (1975): 1–10.

——. *Miracles and Pilgrims: Popular Beliefs in Medieval England*. London: Dent & Sons, 1977, repr. New York: St. Martin's Press, 1995.

Fitschen, Jürgen. *Die Goldschmiedeplastik des Marienschreins im Aachener Dom. Eine stilgeschichtliche Untersuchung* Europäische Hochschulschriften Reihe 27, vol. 312. Frankfurt am Main: Peter Lang, 1998.

Fitzmyer, Joseph A. *The Gospel According to Luke (X–XXIV)*, Anchor Bible, vol. 28A. Garden City, NY: Doubleday, 1985.

Flanigan, C. Clifford. "The Moving Subject: Medieval Liturgical Processions in Semiotic and Cultural Perspective" in Ashley & Hüsken, 2001: 35–51.

——, Kathleen Ashley and Pamela Sheingorn. "Liturgy as Social Performance: Expanding the Definitions," in eds. Thomas J. Heffernan and E. Ann Matter, *The Liturgy of the Medieval Church*. Kalamazoo: Medieval Institute Publications, 2001: 695–714.

Flint, Valerie. *The Rise of Magic in Early Medieval Europe*. Princeton: Princeton University Press, 1991.

——. "The Hereford Map: Its Author(s), Two Scenes and a Border." *Transactions of the Royal Historical Society* 8 (1998): 19–44.

Fluck, Hanns. "Der risus paschalis: Ein Beitrag zur religiösen Volkskunde." *Archiv für Religionswissenschaft* 31 (1934): 188–212.

Flury-Lemberg, Mechtild. "Le vêtement funéraire de saint Servais de Maastricht." *Bulletin du Centre International d'études des Textiles* 70 (1992): 37–44.

Folda, Jaroslav. *Crusader Manuscript Illumination at St.-Jean d'Acre, 1275–1291*. Princeton: Princeton University Press, 1976.

——. "Reflections on Art in Crusader Jerusalem about the Time of the Second Crusade," in ed. Michael Gervers, *The Second Crusade*. New York: St. Martins' Press, 1992: 171–182.

——. *The Art of the Crusaders in the Holy Land, 1098–1187*. Cambridge: Cambridge University Press, 1995.

Folz, Robert. "Le chancellerie de Frédéric Ier et la canonisation de Charlemagne," *Le moyen âge* 70 (1964), pp. 13–31.

——. "Aspects du Culte Liturgique de Saint Charlemagne en France," in Braunfels & Schramm, Schwann, 1967: 79–99.

——. *Études sur le Culte Liturgique de Charlemagne dans les Églises de l'Empire*, 2nd ed. Geneva: Slatkine Reprints, 1973.

——. *Le souvenir et la légende de Charlemagne dans l'Empire germanique médiéval*, 2nd ed. Geneva: Slatkine Reprints, 1973.

Fontenay, Harold de. "Notre-Dame: Eglise paroisiale et collégiale." *Mémoires de la Société Eduenne* 8 (1879): 396–432.

Foreville, Raymonde. *Le Jubilé de Saint Thomas Becket du XIIIe au XVe siècle (1220–1470); études et documents*. Paris: S.E.V.P.E.N, 1958.

——. "Mort and Suivie de saint Thomas Becket." *Cahiers de Civilization Médiévale* 15 (1971): 21–38.

Forgeais, Arthur. *Collection de plombs historiés trouvés dans la Seine: Enseignes de pèlerinages.* Paris: Arthur Forgeais, vol. 2, 1863; vol. 4, 1865; vol. 5, 1866.

——. *Priapées.* Paris: [n.p.] 1865/1866.

Forsyth, Ilene H. *The Throne of Wisdom: Wood Sculptures of the Madonna in Romanesque France.* Princeton: Princeton University Press, 1972.

——. "The Vita Apostolica and Romanesque Sculpture: Some Preliminary Observations." *Gesta* 25/1 (1986): 75–82.

Foucart, Jacques. "L'église Saint-Wulphy de Rue édifiée par l'enfant du pays Charles Sordi (1771–1857)." *Dossiers archéologiques, historiques et culturels du Nord et du Pas-de-Calais* 34 (1992): 1–29.

Fournier, Bertrand. "Abbeville. Collégiale Saint-Vulfran" in *Picardie gothique*, eds Jean-Charles Capronnier *et al.* Tournai: Casterman, 1995: 68–69.

France, John and William G. Zajac. *The Crusades and Their Sources: Essays Presented to Bernard Hamilton.* Aldershot: Ashgate Publishing Limited, 1998.

Francis, Henry S. "Jean de Beaumetz, Calvary with a Carthusian Monk." *Bulletin of the Cleveland Museum of Art* 53 (1966): 329–338.

Franz, Adolph. *Die kirchlichen Benediktionen im Mittelalter*, vol. 2. Freiburg im Breisgau: Herder, 1909.

Franz, Gunther. *Codex Egberti der Stadtbibliothek Trier.* Wiesbaden: L. Reichert, 1984.

Freedberg, David. *The Power of Images: Studies in the History and Theory of Response.* Chicago: University of Chicago Press, 1989.

French, Thomas. *York Minster: The St. William Window.* Oxford: Oxford University Press, 1999.

Freni, Giovanni. "The Reliquary of the Holy Corporal in the Cathedral of Orvieto: Patronage and Politics" in *Art, Politics and Civic Religion in Central Italy, 1261–1352.* Aldershot, UK: Ashgate, 2000: 117–77.

Friedländer, Max J. *Early Netherlandish Painting.* 14 vol., trans. Heinz Norden. New York: Praeger, 1967–76.

Fries, Walter. "Die Kostümsammlung des Germanischen Nationalmuseums zu Nürnberg." *Anzeiger des Germanischen Nationalmuseums* 1924/25 (1926): 3–14.

Frolow, Anton. "La Vraie Croix et les expéditions d'Héraclius en Perse." *Revue des Études byzantines* 11 (1953): 88–105.

——. *La Relique de la Vraie Croix: recherches sur le développement d'un culte.* Paris: Institut français d'études byzantines, 1961.

——. *Les Reliquaires de la Vraie Croix.* Paris: Institut français d'études byzantines, 1965.

Fugmann, Margarete. *Frügotische Reliquiare. Ein Beitrag zur rheinisch-belgischen Goldschmiedekunst des 13. Jahrhunderts.* Bonn-Leipzig: Dissertation zur Erlangung der Doktorwürde, 1931.

Fuhrmann, Horst. *Germany in the High Middle Ages c. 1050–1200.* Cambridge: Cambridge University Press, 1986.

Fumi, Luigi. *Il Duomo di Orvieto e il Simbolismo Cristiano.* Rome: Studi e documenti di storia e diretto, vol. 17, 1891.

——, *Il Santuario del SS. Corporale nel Duomo di Orvieto, Ricordo del XV Congresso Eucaristico di Orvieto.* Rome: Danesi, 1896.

Gaalman, A.A.G., R.M. van Heeringen, A.M. Koldeweij. *Heiligen uit de Modder in Zeeland Gevonden Pelgrimstekens.* Utrecht: De Walburg Pers, 1988.

Gaborit-Chopin, Danielle. *La décoration des manuscrits à Saint-Martial de Limoges et en Limousin du XIe au XIIe siècle.* Paris: Droz, 1969.

——. *Ivoires du moyen âge.* Fribourg: Office du Livre, 1978.

Gaier, Cl. "Contribution à la chronologie des châsses de saint Domitien et de saint Mengold à Huy." *Annales du Cercle hutois des Sciences et Beaux-Arts* (1994): 181–200.

Galpern, A.N. "Late Medieval Piety in Sixteenth-Century Champagne" in eds. Charles Trinkaus & Heiko A. Oberman, *The Pursuit of Holiness in Late Medieval and Renaissance Religion.* Leiden: Brill, 1974: 145–76.

Gardiner, Ellen, ed. *Visions of Heaven and Hell*. New York: Italica Press, 1989.
Gardiner, F.C. *The Pilgrimage of Desire: A Study of Theme and Genre in Medieval Literature*. Leiden: Brill, 1971.
Gardner, Arthur. *English Medieval Sculpture*. New York: Hacker Art Books, 1973.
Gargiolli, C. *Viaggi in Terra Santa*. Florence, n.p., 1862.
Gasquet, Francis Aidan. *Henry VIII and the English Monasteries: An Attempt to Illustrate the History of Their Suppression*. London: John Hodges, 1889.
Gatzweiler, Odilo. "Die liturgischen Handschriften des Aachener Münsterstiftes." *Zeitschrift des Aachener Geschichtsvereins* 46 (1924): 1–222.
Gauthier, Marie-Madeleine. *Émaux du moyen âge occidental*. Fribourg: Office du Livre, 1972.
———. *Les Routes de la foi: reliques et reliquaires de Jérusalem à Compostelle*. Fribourg: Office du Livre, 1983.
Gay, Victor. *Glossaire archéologique du Moyen Age et de la Renaissance*. Part 1. Paris: Librairie de la Société bibliographique, Éditions Picard, 1887.
Geary, Patrick. *Living with the Dead in the Middle Ages*. Ithaca, NY: Cornell University Press, 1994.
Gebhard, Torsten. "Die Marianischen Gnadenbilder in Bayern. Beobachtungen zur Chronologie und Typologie," in *Kultur und Volk. Beiträge zur Volkskunde aus Österreich, Bayern und der Schweiz (Festschrift für Gustav Gugitz)*, ed. Leopold Schmidt. Vienna, 1954: 93–116.
Gechter, Marianne. "Das Kastell Deutz im Mittelalter." *Kölner Jahrbuch für Vor- und Frühgeschichte* 22 (1989): 373–416.
Gee, Loveday Lewes. "'Ciborium' Tombs in England 1290–1330." *Journal of the British Archaeological Association*, 132 (1979): 29–41.
Geirnaert, Noël. "Bruges and the Northern Netherlands." *Bruges and Europe*, ed. Valentin Vermeersch. Antwerp: Fonds Mercator, 1992: 72–97.
Geiselmann, Josef R. *Die Eucharistielehre de Vorscholastik*. Paderborn: F. Schöning, 1926.
Gelfand, Laura D. "The Iconography of Style: Margaret of Austria and the Church of St. Nicolas of Tolentino at Brou," in *Widowhood and Visual Culture in Early Modern Europe*, ed. Allison Levy. Aldershot, UK, Ashgate Press, 2003: 145–59.
———. "Regency, Power and Dynastic Visual Memory: Margaret of Austria as Patron and Propagandist" in *The Texture of Society: Women in Medieval Flanders*, eds. Ellen Kittell and Mary Suydam, New York: Palgrave Press, 2003: 203–25.
———. "Fifteenth-century Netherlandish Devotional Portrait Diptychs: Origins and Functions." Ph.D. diss., Case Western Reserve University, 1994.
——— and Walter S. Gibson. "Surrogate Selves: the *Rolin Madonna* and the Late-medieval Devotional Portrait." *Simiolus* 29 (3/4, 2002): 119–38.
Genicot, Léopold. *Rural Communities in the Medieval West*. Baltimore: Johns Hopkins University Press, 1990.
George, Philippe. "Noble, chevalier, pénitent, martyr. L'idéal de sainteté d'après une *Vita* mosane du XIIᵉ siècle." *Le Moyen Age* 3–4 (1983): 357–80.
———. "Vie et Miracles de S. Domitien." *Analecta Bollandiana* 103/3–4 (1985).
———. "Les Miracles de saint Mengold de Huy. Témoignage privilégié d'un culte à la fin du XIIᵉ siècle." *Bulletin de la Commission Royale d'Histoire* 152 (1986): 25–48.
———. "Documents Inédits Sur Le Trésor Des Reliques De L'abbaye De Stavelot-Malmedy Et Dependances (IXᵉ–XVIIᵉ Siècles)" *Bullétin de la Commission Royale d'Histoire* CLIII (1987): 65–108.
———. "Stavelot & Malmedy: Monachisme & Hagiographie En Ardenne (VIIᵉ–XIIᵉ Siecles)." Ph.D. diss., Université de Liège, 1993–1994.
———. *Les Routes De La Foi En Pays Mosans IVᵉ–XVᵉ Siècles*. Liège: Trésors de la Cathédrale de Liège, 1995.
Géro, Jules. *Bibliographie du vitrail français*. Paris: Porte étroite, 1983.

Gervers, Michael, ed. *The Second Crusade and the Cistercians*. New York: St. Martins' Press, 1992.

Greet Ghyslen. "The Passion Tapestries of the Saragossa Cathedral and Pre-Eyckian Realism," *Flanders in a European Perspective, Manuscript Illumination around 1400 in Flanders and Aboard*, eds. Maurits Smeyers and Bert Cardon. Louvain: Uitgeverij Peeters, 1995: 401–416.

Gibson, Margaret. "Normans and Angevins, 1070–1220" in Collinson, Ramsay, & Sparks, 1995: 38–68.

Gibson, Shimon and Joan E. Taylor. *Beneath the Church of the Holy Sepulchre Jerusalem. The Archaeology and Early History of Traditional Golgotha*. London: Committee of the Palestine Exploration Fund, 1994.

Giersiepen, Helga. *Die Inschriften des Aachener Doms*. Wiesbaden: L. Reichert, 1992.

——. "Die Inschriften" in *Der Schreins Karl des Großen, Bestand und Sicherung 1982–1988*. Aachen: Einhard, 1998: 28–31.

Gillerman, David M. "The evolution of the design of Orvieto Cathdral, *ca.* 1290–1310." *Journal of the Society of Architectural Historians* 53/3 (1994): 300–21.

Gockerell, Nina. *Bilder und Zeichen der Frömmigkeit. Sammlung Rudolf Kriss*. Munich: Bayerische National Museum, 1995.

——. "'*Sie durchstachen mich mit mannigfaltigen Waffen . . .*' Neuerworbene Bildwerke zum Themenkreis der 'Geheimen Leiden' als Ergänzung der Sammlung Kriss in Bayerischen Nationalmuseum," in Bauer, 1993: 161–94.

Godfrey, John. *1204: The Unholy Crusade*. Oxford: Oxford University Press, 1980.

Goodich, Michael. *Violence and Miracle in the Fourteenth Century: Private Grief and Public Salvation*. Chicago: University of Chicago Press, 1995.

Gordon, Beverly. "The Souvenir: Messenger of the Extraordinary." *Journal of Popular Culture* 20/3 (Winter 1986): 135–46.

Gordon, Bruce and Peter Marshall. "Introduction: Placing the Dead in Late Medieval and Early Modern Europe," in *The Place of the Dead: Death and Remembrance in Late Medieval and Early Modern Europe*, eds. B. Gordon and P. Marshall. Cambridge: University Press, 2000: 1–16.

Gosselin, Abbé Jules. *Rue et le pèlerinage du Saint-Esprit*. Abbeville: C. Paillart, 1894.

Gothic and Renaissance Art in Nuremberg 1300–1550. New York: Prestel-Verlag, 1986.

Götz, Wolfgang. *Zentralbau und Zentralbau Tendenz in der gotischen Architektur*. Berlin: Gebr. Mann, 1968.

Gould, Karen. "Illumination and Sculpture in Thirteenth-Century Amiens: The Invention of the Body of Saint Firmin in the Psalter and hours of Yolande of Soissons." *The Art Bulletin* 59/2 (1977): 161–66.

Grabar, André. *Ampoules de Terre Sainte*. Paris: C. Klincksieck, 1958.

Grabar, Oleg. *The Shape of the Holy. Early Islamic Jerusalem*. Princeton: Princeton University Press, 1996.

Graboïs, Aryeh. *Le pèlerin occidental en Terre Sainte au moyen âge*. Brussels: de Boeck Université, 1998.

Graef, Hilda. *Mary: A History of Doctrine and Devotion*, 4th ed. London: Sheed & Ward, 1994.

Graves, Robert. *The Greek Myths*. New York: Penguin Books, 1992.

Grésy, Eugène. "Reliquaire en plomb trouvé dans la Seine à Melun." *Bulletin du Comité Historique des Arts et Monuments* 2 (1849): 287–88.

Grewe, H. and M. Wemhoff, "Die 'Frau von Herford' und ihr Hausrat," in ed. H.G. Horn, *Ein Land macht Geschichte. Archäologie in Nordrhein-Westfalen*. Cologne: 1995: 316–20.

Grimme, Ernst Günther. *Aachener Goldschmiedekunst im Mittelalter von Karl dem Grossen bis zu Karl V*. Cologne: E.A. Seeman Verlag, 1957.

——. "Karl der Große in seiner Stadt," in Braunfels & Schramm, 1967: 229–73.

——. "Der Aachener Domschatz." *Aachener Kunstblätter* 42 (1972).

——. *Goldschmiedekunst des Mittelalters, Form und Bedeutung des Reliquiars*. Cologne: M. DuMont Schauberg, 1972.

——. "Das Bildprogramm des Aachener Karlsschreins," in *Karl der Große und sein Schrein in Aachen*, ed. Hans Müllejans. Aachen: Einhard, 1988: 124–35.

——. *Der Dom Zu Aachen: Architectur und Ausstattung*. Aachen: Einhard, 1994.

——. "Die Ikonographie of Aachener Marienschreins." Wynands, 2000: 91–99; 101–13.

Grivot, Denis. *Le monde d'Autun*, 2nd ed. La Pierre-qui-Vire: Zodiaque, 1965.

—— and George Zarnecki. *Gislebertus: Sculptor of Autun*. New York: Orion, 1961.

Grodecki, Louis, Françoise Perrot, *et al. Les vitraux du Centre et des pays de la Loire*, Inventaire général des monuments et richesses artistiques de France, Corpus Vitrearum France. Paris: CNRS, 1981.

—— and Catherine Brisac. *Gothic Stained Glass, 1200–1300*. trans. Barbara Drake Boehm. Ithaca, NY: Cornell University Press, 1985.

Gugitz, Gustav. *Österreichisches Gnadenstätten in Kult und Brauch. Ein topographisches Handbuch zur religiösen* Volkskunde. Vienna: Hollinek, 1955.

Guizot, François-Pierre-Guillaume, ed. *La Philippide, poëme, par Guillaume le Breton*. Paris: J.-L.-J. Brière, 1825.

Gurevich, Aaron. *Medieval Popular Culture: Problems of Belief and Perception*, trans. János M. Bak and Paul A. Hollingsworth. Cambridge: Cambridge University Press, 1988.

Guth, Klaus. *Guibert von Nogent und die hochmittelalterliche Kritik an der Reliquienverehrung*. Ottobeuren: Winfried-Werk GmbH, 1970.

Hadermann-Misguich, Lydie. "Conceptual and Formal Relationships Between the Paintings of Van der Weyden and the Sculpture of his Time" in *Rogier van der Weyden,*1979.

Haedeke, Hans-Ulrich. *Zinn. Kunstgewerbemuseum der Stadt Köln*. Cologne: Kunstgewerbemuseum, 1976.

Hahn, Cynthia. "Loca Sancta Souvenirs: Sealing the Pilgrims' Experience," in Ousterhout, 1990: 85–96.

——. "The Voices of Saints: Speaking Reliquaries." *Gesta* 29/1 (1997) 20–31.

——. "*Visio Dei*: Changes in Medieval Visuality," in *Visuality Before and Beyond the Renaissance: Seeing as Others Saw*, ed. Robert Nelson. Cambridge: University Press, 2000: 169–96.

Hahnloser, Hans R. *Villard de Honnecourt: Kritische Gesamtausgabe des Bauhüttenbuches ms. Fr. 19093 der Pariser Nationalbibliothek*. 2nd ed. Graz: Akademische Druck- und Verlagsanstalt, 1972.

Haimerl, Xaver. *Das Prozessionswesen des Bistums Bamberg im Mittelalter*. Hildesheim: H.A. Gerstenberg, 1973.

Halkin, Joseph and C.G. Roland, eds. *Recueil des Chartes de L'abbaye de Stavelot-Malmedy*. 2 vols. Brussels: Librairie Kiessling et Cie., P. Imbrechts, Successeur, 1909, 1930.

Hallier, Amédée. *The Monastic Theology of Aelred of Rievaulx: an Experiential Theology*. trans. Columban Heaney. Shannon, Ireland: Irish University Press, 1969.

Halm, Philipp Maria. "Armeseelen," *Reallexiikon zur deutschen Kunstgeschichte* (Munich), 2, 2, cols. 1084–88.

Halphen, Louis and Poupardin, René. *Chroniques des comtes d'Anjou et des seigneurs d'Amboise*. Paris: [n.p.], 1913.

Hamburger, Jeffrey. "The Visual and the Visionary: The Image in Late Medieval Monastic Devotions." *Viator* 20 (1989): 161–182.

——. *The Visual and the Visionary: Art and Female Spirituality in Late Medieval Germany*. New York: Zone Books, 1998.

Hampson, Ethel M. "Fairs" in *The Victoria History of the County of Cambridge and the Isle of Ely*, ed. Ralph B. Pugh, Vol. 4. London: Institute of Historical Research, 1953: 50.

Harbison, Craig. "Visions and Meditations in Early Flemish Painting." *Simiolus* 15 (1985): 87–118.

——. "The Northern Altarpiece as a Cultural Document," in Humphrey & Kemp, 1990: 49–75.

——. *Jan van Eyck: The Play of Realism*. London: Reaktion Books, 1991.

——. "Miracles Happen: Image and Experience in Jan Van Eyck's *Madonna in a Church*," in ed. Brendan Cassidy, *Iconography at the Crossroads*. Princeton: Princeton University Press, 1993: 157–66.

——. "Fact, Symbol, Ideal: Roles for Realism in Early Netherlandish Painting." *Petrus Christus in Renaissance Bruges: An Interdisciplinary Approach*, ed. Maryan W. Ainsworth. New York: Metropolitan Museum of Art, 1995: 21–34.

Hardison, O.B. *Christian Rite and Christian Drama in the Middle Ages*. Baltimore: Johns Hopkins University Press, 1965.

Harley, J.B. and D. Woodward, eds. *The History of Cartography in Ancient and Medieval Europe and the Mediterranean*. Chicago: University of Chicago Press, 1987.

Harmening, Dieter. "Fränkische Mirakelbücher. Quellen und Untersuchung zur historischen Volkskunde und Geschichte der Volksfrömmigkeit." *Würzburger Diözesange-schichtsblätter*, 28 (1966): 25–144.

Harris, Anne F. "The Spectacle of Stained Glass in Modern France and Medieval Chartres: A History of Practices and Perceptions." Ph.D. diss., University of Chicago, 1999.

Harris, John Wesley. *Medieval Theatre in Context: An Introduction*. London: Routledge, 1992.

Hartinger, Walter. '. . . *denen Gott genad!' Totenbrauchtum und Armen-Seelen-Glauben in der Oberpfalz*. Regensburg: Pustet, 1979.

——, "Patrizische Frömmigkeit. Aufgrund von Testamenten der Reichsstadt Regensburg im 14. Jahrhundert," in Bauer, 1993: 45–72.

——, "Erde, Himmel, Hölle, Fegfeuer: Die Sorge um das Seelenheil und das irdische Leben," in *Apocalypse. Zwischen Himmel und Hölle*, eds Herbert W. Wurster and Richard Loibl. Passau: 177–200.

Harvey, John. *English Medieval Architects. A Biographical Dictionary*. Boston: Boston Book and Art Shop, 1954.

Harvey, P.D.A. *Mappa Mundi: The Hereford World Map*. Toronto: University of Toronto Press, 1996.

Haseloff, Gunter. *Email in Fruhen Mittelaltar: Frühchristliche Kunst von der Spätantike bis zum den Karolingern*. Marburg: Hitzeroth, 1990.

Hastings, Maurice. *St. Stephen's Chapel and its Place in the Development of the Perpendicular Style in England*. Cambridge: Cambridge University Press, 1955.

Haubrichs, Wolfgang. "*Error Inextricabilis*: form und funktion der labyrinthabbildung in mittelaltern handschriften" in *Text und Bild: Aspekte des Zusammenwirkens zweier Künste in Mittelalter und früher Neuzeit*. eds C. Meier and U. Ruberg. Wiesbaden: L. Reichert, 1980.

Haussherr, Reiner. "Das Imervardkreuz und der Volto-Santo-Typ." *Zeitschrift für Kunstwissenschaft* 16 (1962): 129–70.

——. *Die Zeit der Staufer: Geschichte, Kunst, Kultur*, ed., 5 vols. Stuttgart: Württembergisches Landesmuseum, 1977–79.

Hayes, Dawn Marie. "Body and Sacred Place in Medieval Europe, 1100–1389: Interpreting the Case of Chartres Cathedral." Ph.D. diss., New York University. 1998.

Hazebroucq, Paul. *La Procession Historique Du Lundi De Pentecôte*. Soignies: Le Cahiers du Chapitre, 1996.

Head, Thomas. *Hagiography and the Cult of the Saints, The Diocese of Orlèans 800–1200*. Cambridge: Cambridge University Press, 1990.

Hearn, M.F. "Canterbury Cathedral and the Cult of Becket." *Art Bulletin*, 76/1 (March, 1994): 19–52.

Heimann, Adelheid. "The Capital Frieze and Pilasters of the Portail Royal, Chartres." *Journal of the Warburg and Courtauld Institutes* 31 (1968): 73–102.

Heinrichs-Schreiber, Ulrike, ed. *Kunstsammlungen der Veste Coburg. Die Skulpturen des 14. bis 17. Jahrhunderts.* Coburg: Kunstsammlung der Veste Coburg, 1998.

Heinzelmann, Martin. *Translationsbericht und Andere Quellen des Reliquienkults.* Turnhout: Brepols, 1979.

Heitz, Carole. "Architecture et Liturgie Processionale À L'époque Pré-Romane." *Révue de l'art* 24 (1974): 30–47.

———. "Quête et voyages de reliques au profit des église française du moyen âge." *Révue d'histoire écclesiastique* 59/4 (1964): 759–822; 60/1 (1965): 5–32.

Henriet, Jacques. "La Cathédrale Saint-Étienne de Sens: Le Parti du Premier Maître et les Campagnes du XIIᵉ Siècle." *Bulletin Monumental* 140 (1982): 81–174.

Henry, Avril. *Biblia Pauperum: A Facsimile and Edition.* Aldershot: Scholars Press, 1987.

Hens, H., H. van Bavel, G.C.M. van Dijck and J.H.M. Frantzen, *Mirakelen van Onze Lieve Vrouw te 's-Hertogenbosch 1381–1603.* Tilburg: Stichting Zuidelijk Historisch Contact, 1978.

Herbers, Klaus. *Der Jakobsweg. Mit einem mittelalterlichen Pilgerführer unterwegs nach Santiago de Compostela.* Tübingen: Gunter Narr Verlag, 1986.

———. "Die Aachener Marienschrein-Reliquien und ihre karolingische Tradition," in Wynands, 2000: 129–34.

Herkenrath, Rainer Maria. "Regnum und Imperium in den Diplomen der ersten Regierungsjahre Friedrichs I" in Wolf., 1975: 323–59.

Herrmann-Mascard. *Les Reliques Des Saints: Formation Coutumière D'un Droit.* Vol. 6, *Société D'histoire Du Droit: Collection D'histoire Institutionelle Et Sociale.* Paris: Éditions Klincksieck, 1975.

Herteig, A.E. *Kongers havn og handels sete: Fra de arkeologiske undersøkelser pao Bryggen i Bergen 1955–68,* Oslo, 1969.

Heurck, Emile Henri van. *Les Drapelets de Pèlerinage en Belgique et dans les Pays Voisins: Contribution à L'iconographie et À l'histoire des Pèlerinages.* Anvers: Buschmann, 1922.

Herwaarden, Jan van, "Pilgrimages and Social Prestige. Some Reflections on a Theme," in *Wallfahrt und Alltag in Mittelalter und früher Neuzeit. Internationales Round-Table-Gespräch, Krems an der Donau 8. Oktober 1990,* eds Gerhard Jaritz and Barbara Shuh. Vienna: Verlag der Österreichischen Akademie der Wissenschaften, 1992: 27–79.

Heslop, T.A. "The Conventual Seals of Canterbury Cathedral 1066–1232," in *Medieval Art and Architecture at Canterbury before 1220.* London: British Archaeological Association, 1982: 94–100.

Hettche, Th. *Pietro Aretino, I Modi. Stellungen. die Sonette des göttlichen Pietro Aretino zu den Kupfern Marcantonio Raimondis.* Frankfurt am Main: Eichborn Verlag, 1997.

Heuser, Johannes. "'Heilig-Blut.' In Kult und Brauchtum des deutschen Kulturraumes. Ein Beitrag zur religiösen Volkskunde." Ph.D. diss., Rheinischen Friedrich Wilhelms-Universität, Bonn, 1948.

Heymans, Henri ed. *Die Servatius-legende. Ein niederländisches Blokbuch.* Berlin: B. Cassirer, 1911.

Hilberry, Harry H. "The Cathedral at Chartres in 1030," *Speculum* 34 (1959): 561–72.

Hilger, Hans Peter. "Sacrum Imperium Insignien und Denkmale," in *Ornamenta Ecclesiae* 1985, vol. 3: 185–92.

———. "Zum Karlsschrein in Aachen." *Jahrbuch der rheinischen Denkmalpflege* 30/31 (1985): 55–74.

Hilpert, Hans-Eberhard. "Geistliche Bildung und Laienbildung: Zur Überlieferung der Schulschrift *Compendium historiae in genealogia Christi* (Compendium veteris testamenti) des Petrus von Poitiers (d. 1205) in England." *Journal of Medieval History* 11/4 (1985): 315–32.

Hinde, Thomas, ed. *The Domesday Book. England' Heritage, Then and Now.* London: Greenwich Editions, 2002.

Hoade, Eugene. *Western Pilgrims.* Jerusalem: Franciscan Printing Press, 1952, repr. 1970.

Hoc, M. "Médailles de S. Job vénéré à Wesemaal." *Revue Belge de Numismatique et de Sigillographie* 89 (1937): 39–48.

Hocquet, M. Adolphe, Maurice Houtart, Walther Ravez, E.-J. Soil de Moriamé. "Tournai Dans L'art Et Dans L'histoire." *Wallonia* 21/5–6 (1913): 315–428.

Hohler, Christopher. "The Badge of St. James," in *The Scallop: Studies of a Shell and its Influences on Humankind*, ed. Ian Cox. London: The "Shell" Transport and Trading Company, Ltd., 1957: 49–70.

Holladay, Joan A. "Relics, Reliquaries, and Religious Women: Visualizing the Holy Virgins of Cologne." *Studies in Iconography* 18 (1997): 67–118.

Holt, Peter M. *The Age of the Crusades: The Near East from the Eleventh Century to 1517.* London: Longman, 1986.

Holweckt, Frederick G. "Candlemas." *The Catholic Encyclopedia*, vol. 3, Online ed. (Accessed 2 March, 2003) http://www.newadvent.org

The Holy Bible (Douay 1609 A.D.–Rheims 1582 A.D. translation from the Vulgate). London: Catholic Truth Society, 1963.

Honée, Eugène. "Image and Imagination in the Medieval Culture of Prayer: A Historical Perspective," in *The Art of Devotion in the Late Middle Ages in Europe, 1300–1500*, ed. Henk van Os. Princeton: University Press, 1994: 157–74.

Hook, Walter Farquhar. *Lives of the Archbishops of Canterbury.* Vol. II. London: Richard Bentley, 1862.

Horn, Walter and Ernst Born. *The Plan of St. Gall: A Study of the Architecture and Economy of and Life in a Paradigmatic Carolingian Monastery.* Berkeley: University of California Press, 1979.

Hörster, Marita. "Mantuae Sanguis Preciosus." *Wallraf-Richartz Jahrbuch* 25 (1963): 151–81.

Hösch, Karin. *Erding: Die Kirchen der Pfarrei St. Johann.* Passau: PEDA Kunstverlag, 1997.

Houvet, Étienne. *Cathédrale de Chartres. Architecture.* Chelles: A. Faucheux, 1919–21.

——. *Monographie de la cathédrale de Chartres. Extrait d'un ouvrage couronné par l'Académie des Beaux-Arts.* Chartres: Étienne Houvet, 1927.

Howard, Donald R. *Writers and Pilgrims: Medieval Pilgrimage Narratives and Their Posterity.* Berkeley: University of California Press, 1980.

Hübener, Susanne. "Das Kreuzreliquiar aus Mariengraden im Kölner Domschatz." *Kölner Domblatt* (1983): 231–74.

Hubert, Eugène. *Recueil des chartes intéressant, le département de l'Indre.* Paris, 1899.

Hubert, Jean. "Le Saint-Sépulcre de Neuvy et les pèlerinages de Terre-Sainte au XIème siècle." *Bulletin Monumental* 90–91 (1931–32): 91–100.

Hughes, Andrew. "Chants in the Rhymed Office of St Thomas of Canterbury." *Early Music* 16 (1988): 185–201.

Hughes, Christopher G. "Visual Typology in Early Gothic Art, 1140–1240." Ph.D. diss., University of California at Berkeley, 2000.

Huizinga, Johan. *Herfsttij der Middeleeuwen*, Haarlem: Uitgeverij Contact, 1997, repr. Haarlem, 1919.

——. *The Waning of the Middle Ages.* New York: St. Martin's Press, 1984 repr. 1924.

Hull, Vida Joyce. *Hans Memlinc's Paintings for the Hospital of Saint John in Bruges.* Outstanding Dissertations in the Fine Arts. New York: Garland Press, 1981.

——. "Devotional Aspects of Hans Memlinc's Paintings." *Southeastern College Art Conference Review* 11 (1988): 207–13.

Humphrey, Peter and Martin Kemp, eds. *The Altarpiece in the Renaissance.* Cambridge: Cambridge University Press, 1990.

Hunt, E.D. *Holy Land Pilgrimage in the Later Roman Empire, AD 312–460.* Oxford: Oxford University Press, 1982.

Hurwit, Jeffrey M. *The Athenian Acropolis: History, Mythology, and Archaeology from the Neolithic Era to the Present*. Cambridge: Cambridge University Press, 1999.

Hyde, Kenneth J. "Italian Pilgrim Literature in the Late Middle Ages." *Bulletin of the John Rylands Library* 72 (1990): 13–33.

Iogna-Prat, Dominique. "La Croix, le moine et l'empereur: dévotion à la croix et théologie politique à Cluny autour de l'an mil," in *Haut Moyen-Age: Culture, education et société. Études offertes à Pierre Riché*, ed. Michel Sot. La Garenne-Colombes: Erasme, 1990.

——. "Le culte de la Vierge sous le règne de Charles le Chauve," in Iogna-Prat, et al., 1996: 65–98.

——, Éric Palazzo and Daniel Russo, eds. *Marie. Le culte de la Vierge dans la société médiévale*, Paris: Beauchesne, 1996.

Jacobowitz, Ellen S. et al. *The Prints of Lucas van Leyden and his Contemporaries*. Washington: National Gallery of Art, 1983.

Jacobs, Lynn F. *Early Netherlandish Carved Altarpieces, 1380–1550: Medieval Tastes and Mass Marketing*. Cambridge: Cambridge University Press, 1998.

Johnson, Penelope D. *Prayer, Patronage, and Power: The Abbey of La Trinité, Vendôme, 1032–1187*. New York: New York University Press, 1981.

Joly, Roger. *La cathédrale de Chartres avant Fulbert*. Chartres: Éditions Houvet, 1999.

Jones, Malcolm. "The Secular Badges," in Van Beuningen & Koldeweij 1993: 99–109.

——. "Sex and Sexuality in Late Medieval and Early Modern Art, in ed. Daniela Erlach, *Privatisierung der Triebe? Sexualität in der frühen Neuzeit*. Wien: Institut für die Erforschung der Frühen Neuzeit/Peter Lang, 1994 187–304.

——. "Een andere kijk op profane insignes," in Koldeweij & Willemsen, 1995: 64–74.

——. "The Sexual and the Secular Badges," in Van Beuningen, Koldeweij & Kicken 2001: 196–206.

Josse, Hector. *La légende de S. Honore, eveque d'Amiens*. Amiens: A. Douillet, 1879.

Jouanneaux, Françoise, *Le tour du choeur de la cathédrale de Chartres, Eure-et-Loir*. Orléans: AREP-Centre Éditions et la Société Archéologique et Historique de l'Orléanais, 2000.

Joubert, Fabienne. "Les peintures de la chapelle Saint-Léger" in *La splendeur des Rolin. Un mécénat privé à la cour de Bourgogne*, ed. Brigitte Maurice-Chabard. Paris: Picard, 1999: 280–81.

Jounel, P. "Le Culte de la Croix dans la liturgie romaine." *La Maison Dieu* 75 (1963): 68–91.

Jourdain, Louis and Antoine Théophile Duval. "Le grand portail de la cathédrale d'Amiens." *Bulletin Monumental* 11 (1845): 145–176; 12 (1846): 96–105.

——. *Le portail Saint-Honoré, dit de la Vierge Dorée de la cathédrale d'Amiens*. Amiens: Duval et Herment, 1844.

Jung, Jacqueline. "Beyond the Barrier: The Unifying Rôle of the Choir Screen in Gothic Churches." *Art Bulletin* 82/4 (2000): 622–57.

Jungmann, Josef A. *The Mass: An Historical, Theological and Pastoral Survey*, trans. Julian Fernandes, S.J., ed. Mary Ellen Evans. Collegeville, MN: The Liturgical Press, 1976.

Jusselin, Maurice. "Dernières recherches sur les traditions de l'église de Chartres." *Mémoires de la Société archéologique d'Eure-et-Loir* 15 (1915–22): 100–16.

——. "Les traditions de l'église de Chartres, à propos d'une bulle du pape Léon X concernant la construction de la cloture du choeur." *Mémoires de la Société archéologique d'Eure-et-Loir* 15 (1915–22): 1–26.

——. *Imagiers et cartiers chartrains*, 2nd ed. Paris: Librairie d'Argences, 1957.

——. "Introduction à l'étude du tour du choeur de la cathédrale de Chartres." *Mémoires de la Société archéologique d'Eure-et-Loire* 20–21 (1957–61): 81–172.

Just, Arthur A., Jr. *The Ongoing Feast: Table Fellowship and Eschatology at Emmaus.*
Collegeville, MN: The Liturgical Press, 1993.
Kaemmerer, Walter, ed. *Aachener Quellentexte.* Aachen: Verlag der Mayer'schen Buch-
handlung, 1980.
Kagan, Judith. "La restauration de la grande scène du calvaire à Notre-Dame de
Dijon." *Bulletin monumental* 148/2 (1990): 191–93.
Kahl, Hans-Dietrich. "Crusade Eschatology as Seen by St. Bernard in the Years
1146 to 1148" in ed. Michael Gervers, *The Second Crusade.* New York: St. Martins'
Press, 1992: 35–47.
Kaminsky, Howard. *A History of the Hussite Revolution.* Berkeley: University of California
Press, 1967: 97–140.
Kamp, Hermann. *Memoria und Selbstdarstellung: Die Stiftungen des burgundischen kanzler
Rolin.* Sigmaringen: Thorbecke, 1993.
Katzenellenbogen, Adolf. "The Central Tympanum at Vézelay: Its Encyclopedic
Meaning and Its Relation to the First Crusade." *The Art Bulletin* 26 (1944): 141–51.
———. "The Prophets on the West Façade: Cathedral at Amiens." *Gazette des Beaux-
Arts,* ser. 6, 40 (1952): 241–60.
———. "Tympanum and Archivolts on the Portal of St. Honoré at Amiens" in *De
artibus Opuscula XL: Essays in Honor of Erwin Panofsky,* ed. Millard Meiss. New York:
New York University Press, 1961: 280–91.
———. *Allegories of the Virtues and Vices in Medieval Art from the Early Christian Times to
the Thirteenth Century.* New York: W.W. Norton, 1964.
Kaufmann, Thomas DaCosta. *The Mastery of Nature: Aspects of Art, Science, and Humanism
in the Renaissance.* Princeton: Princeton University Press, 1993.
Kelke, W.H. "Master John Schorne." *Records of Buckinghamshire* vol. 2 (1869): 60–74.
Kemp, E. Waldram. *Canonization and Authority in the Western Church.* London: Geoffrey
Cumberlege, 1948.
Kendall, Alan. *Medieval Pilgrims.* London: Wayland, 1970.
Kern, Hermann. *Through the Labyrinth: Designs and Meanings over 5,000 Years.* Munich:
Prestel, 2000.
Kessel, Johann Hubert. *Geschichtliche Mitteilungen über die Heiligtümer der Stiftskirche zu
Aachen nebst Abbildung und Beschreibung der sie bergenden Behälter und Einfassungen.* Cologne:
L. Schwann'schen Verlagshandlung, 1874.
Kessler, Herbert L. *The Illustrated Bibles from Tours.* Princeton: Princeton University
Press, 1977.
———. and Johanna Zacharias. *Rome 1300: On the Path of the Pilgrim.* New Haven:
Yale University Press, 2000.
Keuls, Eva C. *The Reign of the Phallus. Sexual Politics in Ancient Athens.* Berkeley:
University of California Press, 1985.
Kicken, D., A.M. Koldeweij and J.R. ter Molen, eds. *Gevonden Voorwerpen. Opstellen
over middeleeuwse archeologie voor H.J.E. van Beuningen.* Rotterdam Papers 11. Rotterdam:
BOOR, 2000.
Kieckhefer, Richard. *Magic in the Middle Ages.* Cambridge: Cambridge University
Press, 1990.
Kier, Hiltrud. *Der Mittelalterliche Schmuckfussboden.* Düsseldorf: Rhineland Verlag, 1970.
——— and Ulrich Krings, ed. *Stadtspuren—Denkmaler in Köln. Köln: Die Romanischen
Kirchen im Bild.* Cologne: Verlag J.P. Bachem, 1984.
Kimpel, Dieter. "Die Skulpturenwerkstatt der Vierge Dorée am Honoratusportal
der Kathedrale von Amiens." *Zeitschrift für Kunstgeschichte* 36/4 (1973): 217–65.
Kirchhoff, Hermann. *Christliches Brauchtum. Feste und Bräuche im Jahreskreis.* Munich:
Kösel, 1995.
Kitzinger, Ernst. "Mosaic Pavements in the Greek East and the Question of a
'Renaissance' under Justinian." *Actes de VIe Congrès International d'Études Byzantines,*
2 (1951): 209–223.

——. "Studies on Late Antique and Early Byzantine Floor Mosaics, I. Mosaics at Nikopolis." *Dumbarton Oaks Papers* 6 (1951): 81–122.

——. "World Map and Fortune's Wheel: A Medieval Mosaic Floor in Turin." *Proceedings of the American Philosophical Society*, 117 (1973): 344–73.

Kjellberg, Pierre. "Week-end flamboyant en Picardie." *Connaissance des arts* 279 (1975): 84–87.

Klapheck, Richard. *Der Dom zu Xanten und seine Kunstschätz.* Berlin: Deutscher Kunstverlag, 1930.

Kline, Naomi Reed. *Maps of Medieval Thought: The Hereford Paradigm.* Woodbridge, England: Boydell Press, 2001.

Knight, Alan E. *Les Mystères De La Procession De Lille. 1 Le Pentateuque.* Vol. 1. Geneva: Librairie Drooz, 2001.

Knippenberg, W.H.Th. *Kultuurhistorische verkenningen in de Kempen. III Oude pelgrimages vanuit Noord-Brabant.* Oisterwijk: Stichting Brabants Heem, 1968.

Knowles, David, ed. *The Works of Aelred of Rievaulx, I: Treatises, The Pastoral Prayer.* Spencer, MA.: Cistercian Publications, 1971.

——. *The Religious Orders in England.* Cambridge: Cambridge University Press, 1979.

Koenigsmarkova, Helena. "Prace z Pra prostych kovu," *Remeslo umelècke stredoveke: ze sbirek Umelecko Prumsylového Musea v Praze.* Prague: 1980: 54–71.

Kolb, Karl. *Heilig Blut. Eine Bilddokumentation der Wallfahrt und Verehrung.* Würzburg: Echter, 1980.

Koldeweij, A.M. "Sint-Servaas te Maastricht als debevaartplaats." *De Maasgouw* 100 (1981): 3–29.

——. *Der gude Sente Servas. Der Servatiuslegende en de Servatiana: een onderzoek naar de beeldvorming rond een heilige in de middeleeuwen.* Assen: Van Gorcum, 1985.

——. "Reliekentoningen, heiligdomsvaarten, reliekenprocessies en ommegangen," in Koldeweij & van Vlijmen, 1985: 57–71.

——. "Te Vendôme t'Ons Heeren Tranen. Metalen reisgezelschap (2)." *Catharijnebrief: mededelingen van de Vereniging van Vrienden van het Museum Het Catharijneconvent te Utrecht* 21 (March 1988): 12–13.

——. "Onder een Sint-Jan met drie torens. Pelgrimstekens uit 's-Hertogenbosch," in ed. Wim Denslagen, *Studies in vriendschap voor Kees Peeters.* Amsterdam: Architectura & Natura Pers, 1993: 304–15.

——. "Beeldcycli van de Servatiuslegende en het Blokboek van Sint Servaas als voorbeeld een laatgotisch retabel," in eds. Jos M.M. Hermans and Klaas van der Hoek, *Boeken in de late Middeleeuwen. Verslag van Groningse Codicologendagen 1992.* Groningen: Egbert Forsten, 1994.

——."A barefaced *Roman de la Rose* (Paris, B.N., ms. Fr. 25526) and some late medieval mass-produced badges of a sexual nature," in Maurits Smeijers & Bert Cardon, *Flanders in a European Perspective. Manuscript Illumination around 1400 in Flanders and Abroad.* Leuven: Uitgeverij Peeters, 1995: 499–516.

——. "Laatmiddeleeuwse insignes. Verzamelgeschiedenis en stand van onderzoek, cultuurhistorische aspecten" in Koldeweij & Willemsen, 1995: 13–22.

——. "Vroomheid in tin en lood. Bossche pelgrimsinsignes als historische bron." *Brabants Heem* 50/2 (1998): 52–61.

——. "Lifting the veil on pilgrim badges" in ed. Jennie Stopford, *Pilgrimage Explored.* Woodbridge: The Boydell Press, 1999: 161–88.

——. "The Wearing of Significative Badges, Religious and Secular: The Social Meaning of a Behavioural Pattern" in W. Blockmans & A. Janse, *Showing Status. Representation of Social Positions in the Late Middle Ages.* Turnhout, 1999: 307–28.

——. "'Tsante Thomaes te Cantelberghe.' Pelgrimstochten vanuit de Nederlanden naar Canterbury: teruggevonden insignes en berichten uit andere bron" in Van Beuningen, Koldeweij & Kicken 2000: 88–104.

——. "'Te Sente Thomas van Cantelberghe, in Inghelant . . .' Pelgrimsinsignes en pelgrimstochten naar Thomas Becket," in *Thomas Becket in Vlaanderen. Waarheid of legende?* Kortrijk: Stedelijke Musea, 2000: 49–72.

—— and Aart J.J. Mekking. "De kerkschat van de Sint-Servaaskerk te Maastricht." *Spiegel Historiael* 17 (1982): 140–42.

—— and Pierre N.G. Pesch. *Het Blokboek van Sint Servaas. Facsimile met commentaar op het vijftende-eeuwse blokboek, de Servaas-legende en de Maastrichtse reliekentoning. Le Livre Xylographique de Saint Servais. Facsimilé avec commentaire sur le livre xylographique du quinz-ième siècle, sur la légende de S. Servais et sur l'ostension des reliques à Maestrich.* Zutphen: De Walburg Pers, 1984.

—— and P.M.L. van Vlijmen, eds. *Schatkamers uit het Zuiden.* Utrecht: Rijksmuseum het Catharijneconvent, 1985.

—— and A. Willemsen. *Heilig en Profaan. Laatmiddeleeuwse insignes in cultuurhistorisch perspectief.* Amsterdam: Van Soeren & Co., 1995.

Köster, Kurt. "Pilgerzeichen und Wallfahrtsplaketten von St. Adrian in Geraardsbergen. Zu einer Darstellung auf einer flämischen Altartafel des 15. Jahrhunderts im Historischen Museum zu Frankfurt am Main." *Städel-Jahrbuch* 4 (1973): 102–30.

——. "Die Pilgerzeichen der Neusser Quirinus-Wallfahrt im Spätmittelalter." *Neusser Jahrbuch* 1984: 11–29.

——. "Mittelalterliche Pilgerzeichen," in Kriss-Rettenbeck & Möhler, 1984: 203–23.

Kostof, Spiro. *The City Shaped.* London: Thames and Hudson, 1991.

Kötzsche, Dietrich. "Der Holzschrein des Karlsschreins in Aachen." *Kunstchronik* 38/2 (1985): 41.

——. "Zum Stand der Forschung der Goldschmiedekunst des 12. Jahrhunderts im Rhein-Maas-Gebiet," in *Rhein und Maas*, 1972, 2: 191–236.

——. "Zum Stand der Forschung der Goldschmiedekunst im Rhein-Maas-Gebiet," in, *Rhein und Maas*, 1972, vol. 2.

Kötzsche, Lieselotte. "Zwei Jerusalemer Pilgerampullen aus der Kreuzfahrerzeit." *Zeitschrift für Kunstgeschichte* 51 (1988): 13–32.

Kramp, Mario, ed. *Krönungen: Könige in Aachen—Geschichte und Mythos.* 2 vols. Mainz: Philip von Zabern, 2000.

Krautheimer, Richard. "Introduction to an 'Iconography of Medieval Architecture.'" *Journal of the Warburg and Courtauld Institutes* 5 (1942): 1–33. Reprinted in R. Krautheimer. *Studies in Early Christian, Medieval, and Renaissance Art.* New York: University Press, 1969: 115–150.

——. *Rome. Profile of a City, 312–1308.* Princeton, NJ: Princeton University Press, 1980.

——. *Early Christian and Byzantine Architecture.* London: Penguin Group, 1965, repr. 1989.

Kretzenbacher, Leopold. *Bild-Gedanken der spätmittelalterlichen Hl. Blut-Mystik und ihr Fortleben in mittel- und südosteuropäischen Volksüberlieferung.* Munich: Verlag der Bayerischen Akademie der Wissenschaften, 1997.

Kriss, Rudolf. *Die Volkskunde der altbayerischen Gnadenstätten.* 3 vols. Munich: Filser, 1953–6.

Kriss-Rettenbeck, Lenz. *Bildern und Zeichen religiösen Volksglauben.* Munich: Callwey, 1963.

——. *Ex Voto: Zeichen, Bild und Abbild im christlichen Votivbrauchtum.* Zurich: Atlantis, 1972.

—— and Gerda Möhler, eds. *Wallfahrt kennt keine Grenzen.* Munich: Bayerisches Nationalmuseum, 1984.

Kroesen, Justin E.A. *The Sepulchrum Domini through the Ages: Its Form and Function*, trans. Margaret Kofod. Leuven: Peeters, 2000.

Kroos, Renate. *Der Schrein des heiligen Servatius und die vier zugehörigen Reliquiare in Brüssel.* Munich: Deutscher Kunstverlag, 1985.

——. "Vom Umgang mit Reliquien" in *Ornamenta* Ecclesiae, vol. 3, 1985.

——. "Zum Aachener Karlsschrein 'Abbild staufischen Kaisertums' oder 'fundatores ac dotatores,'" in ed. Lieselotte E. Saurma-Jeltsch, *Karl der Große als vielberuferer Vorfahr: Sein Bild in der Kunst der Fürsten, Kirchen und Städt.* Sigmaringen: Thorbecke, 1994: 49–61.

Kroyanker, David. *Jerusalem Architecture.* London: Tauris Parks, 1994.

Kruse, Norbert and Hans Ulrich Rudolf, eds. *900 Jahre Heilig-Blut-Verehrung in Weingarten 1094–1994.* 2 vols. Sigmaringen: Thorbecke, 1994.

Kubach, Hans Erich and Albert Verbeek. *Romanische Baukunst an Rhein und Maas.* Berlin: Deutscher Verlag für Kunstwissenschaft, 1976–89.

Kühnel, Bianca. *From the Earthly to the Heavenly Jerusalem: Representations of the Holy City in Christian Art of the First Millennium.* Freiburg: Herder, 1987.

Kunsthistorisches Museum Vienna. *The Secular and Ecclesiastical Treasuries: Illustrated Guide.* Vienna: Residenz Verlag, 1991.

Kunstmann, Pierre ed., Jean le Marchant, *Miracles de Notre-Dame de Chartres.* Ottawa: Éditions de l'Université d'Ottawa, 1973.

Kupfer, Marcia. "Medieval World Maps: Embedded Images, Interpretive Frames." *Word & Image* 10 (1994): 262–88.

Kurmann-Schwarz, Brigitte and Peter Kurmann. *Chartres. La cathédrale,* trans. Thomas de Kayser. La Pierre-qui-vire: Zodiaque, 2001.

Kyll, Nikolaus. *Pflichtprozessionen und Bannfahrten im Westlichen Teil des Alten Erzbistums Trier.* Vol. 57, *Rheinisches Archiv.* Bonn: L. Rohrscheid, 1962.

Labande, Edmond-René. "'Ad limina': le pèlerin médiéval au terme de sa démarche," in eds. Pierre Gallais and Yves-Jean Riou, *Mélanges offerts à René Crozet à l'occasion de son soixante-dixième anniversaire.* 2 vols. Poitiers: Société d'Etudes Médiévales, 1966, I: 283–91.

Labande, L.H. "Notes sur deux médailles du bienheureux Pierre de Luxembourg et sur son portrait conservé au Musée Calvet," *Mémoires de l'Académie de Vaucluse* 18 (1899): 409–13.

Lafontaine-Dosogne, Jacqueline. "L'Art byzantin en Belgique en relation avec les Croisades." *Revue Belge d'archéologie et d'histoire de l'art* 56 (1987): 13–47.

Lambert, Elie. *L'Architecture des Templiers.* Paris: Picard, 1955.

Lamia, Stephen. *Sepulcrum Domini: The Iconography of the Holed Tomb of Christ in Romanesque and Gothic Art.* Ph.D. diss., University of Toronto, 1982.

——. "Souvenir, synaesthesia, and the *sepulcrum Domini*: sensory stimuli as memory stratagems." in eds. Elizabeth Valdez del Álamo and Carol Stamatis Pendergast *Memory and the Medieval Tomb.* Aldershot: Ashgate, 2000: 19–41.

Langmuir, Gavin. "The Tortures of the Body of Christ," in eds. Scott L. Waugh and Peter D. Diehl *Christendom and its Discontents: Exclusion, Persection, and Rebellion, 1000–1500.* Cambridge: University Press, 1996: 287–309.

Lansing, Carol. *Power and Purity. Cathar Heresy in Medieval Italy.* Oxford: Oxford University Press, 1998.

Lasko, Peter. *Ars Sacra: 800–1200.* 2nd ed. New Haven: Yale University Press, 1994.

Lauer, Rolf. "Dreikönigenschrein" in *Ornamenta Ecclesiae,* vol. 2, 1985: 216–23.

Lautier, Claudine. "Les vitraux de la cathédrale de Chartres à la lumière des restaurations anciennes," in ed. Thomas W. Gaehtgens, *Künstlerischer Austausch/Artistic Exchange,* vol. 3. Berlin: Akademie Verlag, 1993: 413–24.

——. "Les restaurations des vitraux de la cathédrale de Chartres du Moyen Age à nos jours." *La Sauvegarde de l'art français* 12 (1999): 6–19.

——. "Les vitraux de la cathédrale de Chartres. Reliques et images." *Bulletin Monumental* 161/1 (2003): 3–97.

Lauwers, Michel. *La Mémoire des Ancêtres, Le Souci des Morts, Rites et Société au Moyen Age (Diocèse de Liège XIᵉ–XIIIᵉ Siècles).* Paris: Beauchesne, 1997.

Lavalleye, Jacques, ed. *Primitifs Flamands Anonymes.* Bruges: City of Bruges, 1969.

Lea, Henry Charles. *A History of Auricular Confession and Indulgences in the Latin Church,* vol. 3, Philadelphia: Lea Brothers & Co., 1896.

Leach, Arthur, ed. *Memorials of Beverly Minster: The Beverly Chapter Act Book of the Collegiate Church of S. John of Beverley A.D. 1286–1347.* Durham: Surtees Society by Andrews & Co., 1903.

Leach, Edmund R. *Culture and Communication: The Logic by Which Symbols are Connected.* Cambridge: Cambridge University Press, 1976.

Lecat, Jean-Philippe. "La Chartreuse de Champmol dans la vie politique de Philippe le Hardi." *Actes des Journées Internationales Claus Sluter.* Dijon: Association Claus Sluter, 1990: 9–11.

Lecat, Lucien. *Deux siècles d'histoire en Picardie: 1300–1498.* Amiens: C.R.D.P d'Amiens, 1982.

Leclercq, Jean. "Paroisses Rurales" and "Rogations" in ed. Henri Leclercq, *Dictionnaire D'archéologie Chrétienne.* Paris: Librairie Letouzey at Ane, 1948.

——. "Monachisme et Pérégrination du IXᵉ au XIIᵉ Siècle." *Studia Monastica,* 3 (1961): 33–52.

Lecocq, Adolphe. "La cathédrale de Chartres et ses Maîtres de l'Oeuvre." *Mémoires de la Société archéologique d'Eure-et-Loir* 6 (1876): 396–479.

——. "Recherches sur les enseignes de pèlerinages et les chemisettes de Notre-Dame-de-Chartres." *Mémoires de la Société archéologique d'Eure-et-Loir* 6 (1876): 194–242.

Lefévre-Pontalis, Eugène. *Le puits des Saints Forts et les cryptes de la cathédrale de Chartres.* Caen: Henri Delesques, 1904.

Legner, Anton, ed. *Rhein und Maas. Kunst und Kultur, 800–1400.* 2 vols. Cologne: Schnütgen-Museum der Stadt Köln, 1972.

——. *Monumenta Annonis: Köln und Siegburg Weltbild und Kunst im Hohen Mittelalter.* Cologne: Schnütgen-Museums in der Stadt Köln, 1975.

——, ed. *Die Parler und die Schöne Stil, 1350–1400.* Cologne: Schnütgen-Museum der Stadt Köln, 1978.

——, ed. *Ornamenta Ecclesiae: Kunst und Künstler Romanik.* 3 vols. Cologne: Schnütgen-Museum, 1985.

——. *Reliquien in Kunst und Kult: zwischen Antike und Aufklärung.* Darmstadt: Wissenschaftliche Buchgesellschaft, 1995.

Le Goff, Jacques. *The Birth of Purgatory,* trans. Arthur Goldhammer. Chicago: University of Chicago Press, 1984.

Legrand, Lucien. "Deux voyages: Lc 2, 41–50; 24, 13–33" in *À cause de l'Evangile: Etudes sur les Synoptiques et les Actes.* Paris: Cerf, 1985: 409–29.

Le Huray, Peter. "Versicle," *The New Grove Dictionary of Music,* Online edition, ed. L. Macy (Accessed 5 February 2003) http://www.grovemusic.com.

Lejeune, Rita and Jacques Stiennon. *La Légende de Roland dan's l'art du moyen âge,* 2 vols. Brussels: Arcade, 1967, 1: 169–77.

Lemeunier, Albert, *et al.,* eds. *Trésors du Musée d'Arts réligieux et mosan de Liège.* Paris: Musée du Petit Palais, 1985.

——. "Der Schrein des hl. Mangold in Huy" in eds K. Schmid and H. Schadek, *Die Zähringer. Anstass und Wirkung, Fribourg-en-Brisgau.* Sigmaringen, 1986: 206–08.

——. "L'ancienne châsse de sainte Ode (XIIᵉ s.)" and "La châsse de sainte Ode à Amay" *Trésors de la collégiale d'Amay,* ed. Delarue, Thomas. Amay, 1989: 49–79; 81–89.

——. *Le Trésor, dans Musée et Trésor de Huy, Musea Nostra.* Huy: Crédit Communal, 1992: 82–91.

——. "La châsse et le reliquaire du chef de saint Vincent de Soignies. Deux monuments d'orfèvrerie médiévales disparus" in ed. Jacques Deveseleer, *Reliques et châsses de la collégiale de Soignies. Objets, cultes et traditions.* Soignies, 2001: 129–143.

—— and G. Dewanckel. *La châsse de saint Mengold et sa restauration.* Huy, 1998.

Lepie, Herta. "Der Aachen Marienschrein." *Rheinische Heimatpflege* 24 (1987): 189–96.

——. "Die Aachenfahrt," in *Wallfahrt im Rheinland.* Cologne: Rheinland-Verlag, 1981: 79–84.

—— and Lothar Schmitt. *Der Barbarossaleuchter im Dom zu Aachen*. Aachen: Einhard, 1998.

Lépinois, Eugène de. *Histoire de Chartres*. I–II, Chartres: Garnier, 1854, 1858.

—— and Lucien Merlet, eds. *Cartulaire de Notre-Dame de Chartres*, I–III, Chartres: Garnier, 1862, 1863, 1865.

Lequeux, Jean-Marie. "La châsse de saint Eleuthère. Chef-d'œuvre original malgré les restaurations des XIXe et XXe siècles?" *Mémoires de la Société royale d'Histoire et d'Archéologie de Tournai* I (1980): 181–201.

Lermen, Birgit J. "'Urbs Aquensis, urbs regalis . . .'—Versuch einer Deutung der Karlssequenz," in ed. Hans Müllejans, *Karl der Große und sein Schrein in Aachen: Eine Festschrift*. Einhard: Aachen, 1988: 167–86.

Leroquais, Victor. *Les sacramentaires et les missels manuscrits des bibliothèques publiques de France*. 3 vols. Paris: [n.p.], 1924.

—— *Les bréviaires manuscrits des bibliothèques publiques de France*. 5 vols. Paris: Macon Protat frères imprimeurs, 1934.

Le Sueur, Abbé A. "Le Crucifix de Rue et le St Vou de Lucques." *Bulletin de la Société d'Émulation d'Abbeville* 2 (1922): 254–66.

Lesueur, Frédéric. "Vendôme (Loir-et-Cher)," in ed. Jacques Brosse, *Dictionnaire des églises de France, Belgique, Luxembourg, Suisse*. Part III D. Paris: Laffont, 1967: 169–172.

Letters, Samantha, comp. *Gazetteer of Markets and Fairs in England and Wales to 1516*. Center for Metropolitan History at the Institute of Historical Research. July 12, 2002. <http://www.ihrinfo.ac.uk/cmh/gaz/gazframe.html>.

Letts, Malcolm. *The Travels of Leo of Rozmital through Germany, Flanders, England, France, Spain, Portugal, and Italy 1465–1467*. Cambridge: Cambridge University Press, 1957.

Levenson, J.A., K. Oberhuber, and J.L. Sheehan. *Early Italian Engravings from the National Gallery of Art*, Washington, 1973.

Levison, Wilhelm. "Konstantinische Schenkung und Silvester-Legende" in *Miscellanea Francesco Ehrle: Scritti di Storia e Paleografia*, vol. 2. Rome: Bibliotheca Apostolica Vaticana, 1924.

Lewis, Flora. "The Veronica: Image, Legend and Viewer," in ed. W. Mark Ormrod, *England in the Thirteenth Century: Proceedings of the 1984 Harlaxton Symposium*. Woodbridge: Boydell Press, 1985: 100–6.

——. "Rewarding Devotion: Indulgences and the Promotion of Images" in *The Church and the Arts, Studies in Church History* 28. Oxford: Blackwell Publishers, 1992.

Lewis, Suzanne. "Henry III and the Gothic Rebuilding of Westminster Abbey: The Problematics of Context." *Traditio* 50 (1995): 129–172.

Leyser, Karl. "Frederick Barbarossa and the Hohenstaufen Polity," in ed. Timothy Reuter ,*Communications and Power in Medieval Europe: The Gregorian Revolution and Beyond*. London: Hambledon Press, 1994: 115–42.

Lichte, Claudia. *Die Inszenierung einer Wallfahrt. Der Lettner im Havelberger Dom und das Wilsnacker Wunderblut*. Worms: Wernersche Verlagsgesellschaft, 1990.

Lidov, Alexei. "Miracle-Working Icons of the Mother of God," in Vassilaki, 2000: 47–57.

Lieu, Samuel N.C. "From History to Legend and Legend to History: The Medieval and Byzantine Transformation of Constantine's *Vita*" in Lieu & Montserrat, 1998: 136–76.

—— and Dominic Montserrat, eds. *Constantine: History, Historiography and Legend*. London: Routledge, 1998.

Lightbown, Ronald W. *Mediaeval European Jewellery (with a Catalogue of the Collection in the Victoria & Albert Museum)*. London: Victoria & Albert Museum, 1992.

Linden, Renaat van der. *Mariabedevaartvaantjes. Volksdevotie op 1175 vaantjes*. Bruges: Uitgeverij Tabor, 1988.

Lindquist, Sherry C.M. *Patronage, Piety and Politics in the Art and Architectural Programs at the Chartreuse de Champmol in Dijon*. Ph.D diss., Northwestern University, 1995.

———. "Accounting for the Status of Artists at the Chartreuse de Champmol." *Gesta* 41/1 (Spring 2002): 15–28.

———. "Women in the Charterhouse: the Liminality and Legibility of Cloistered Spaces at the Chartreuse de Champmol in Dijon," in ed. Helen Hills, *Architecture and the Politics of Gender in Early Modern Europe*. Aldershot, UK: Ashgate, 2002: 177–92.

Little, Charles T. "Pilgrim's Badge Depicting the Shrine of Saint Thomas Becket at Canterbury Cathedral" in *Recent Acquisitions, A Selection: 2000–2001, Bulletin of the Metropolitan Museum of Art* (Fall, 2001): 19.

Livett, Rev. G.M. "Nettlestead Church: Architectural Notes." *Archaeologia Cantiana*, 28 (1909): 250–82.

Llompart, Gabriel. "El sombrero de peregrinación compostelana de Stephan Praun III (1544–1591). " *Revista de Dialectología y Tradiciones Populares* 17 (1961): 321–29.

Lloyd, Simon. *English Society and the Crusades, 1216–1307*. Oxford: Clarendon Press, 1988.

Löcher, Kurt. *Die Gemälde des 16. Jahrhunderts*. Stuttgart: Verlag Gerd Hatje, 1997.

Loerke, William "'Real Presence' in Early Christian Art," in ed. Timothy G. Verdon, *Monasticism and the* Arts. Syracuse: University Press, 1984: 29–51.

Longnon, Jean and Raymond Cazelles. *The Trés Riches Heures of Jean, Duke of Berry, Musée Condé, Chantilly*. New York: George Braziller, 1969.

Loomis, Laura Hibbard. "The Oriflamme of France and the War-Cry 'Monjoie' in the Twelfth Century" in ed. Dorothy Miner, *Studies in Art and Literature for Belle da Costa Greene*. Princeton: Princeton University Press, 1954.

Lotter, Friedrich. "Die Judenverfolgung des 'König Rintfleisch' in Franken um 1298." *Zeitschrift für historische Forschung* 15:4 (1988): 385–422.

———. "Hostienfrevelvorwurf und Blutwunderfälschung bei den Judenverfolgungen von 1298 ('Rindfleisch') und 1336–1338 ('Armleder')," in *Falschungen im Mittelalter. Internationaler Kongreß der Monumenta Germaniae Historica München, 16.–19. September 1986*. Hannover: Hahnsche Buchhandlung, 1988: 533–83.

Loxton, Howard. *Pilgrimage to Canterbury*. London: David and Charles, 1978.

Lubin, Helen. *The Worcester Pilgrim*. Worcester: Worcester Cathedral Publications, 1990.

Lutze, Eberhard and Eberhard Wiegand. *Die Gemälde des 13. bis 16. Jahrhunderts*. Leipzig: K.F. Koehler, 1936–37.

Maas, A.J. "The name of Mary," in *The Catholic Encyclopedia* vol. 15, Online ed. (Accessed February 11, 2003) http://www.newadvent.org

Maas, Walter and Herbert Woopen. *Der Aachener Dom*. Cologne: Greven Verlag, 1984.

Mabillon, Jean. "Mémoires pour servir d'éclaircissement à l'histoire de la sainte Larme de Vendôme," in Jean Mabillon and Thierri Ruinart. *Ouvrages posthumes de D. Jean Mabillon et de D. Thierri Ruinart, bénédictins de la congregation de saint Maur*. Part 2. Paris: François Babuty, Jean-François Josse, and Jombert le Jeune, 1724: 383–94.

MacCormack, Sabine. "Loca Sancta: The Organization of Sacred Topography in Late Antiquity" in ed. Ousterhout, 1990: 7–40.

Macy, Gary. *The Theologies of the Eucharist in the Early Scholastic Period. A Study of the Salvific Function of the Sacrament according to the Theologians c. 1080–c. 1220*. New York: Oxford University Press, 1984.

Madden, Thomas F. *A Concise History of the Crusades*. Lanham, MD: Rowman and Littlefield, 1999.

Maguire, Henry. *Earth and Ocean: The Terrestrial World in Early Byzantine Art*. University Park, PA: Pennsylvania State University Press, 1987.

Maier, Raymund. *Bischof Heinrich von Hofstätter (1839–1875) und seine Kunstschöpfungen*. Winzer: Duschl, 2001.

Mâle, Emile. *Religious Art in France: the Twelfth Century*, ed. Harry Bober, trans. Martiel Mathews. Princeton: Princeton University Press, 1978 repr. 1922.

Mallion, Jean. *Le jubé de la cathédrale de Chartres*. Chartres: Société archéologique d'Eure-et-Loir, 1964.

Mango, Cyril. "Constantinople as Theotokoupolis" in Vassilaki, 2000: 16–25.

Marshall, George. "The Shrine of St. Thomas de Cantilupe, in Hereford Cathedral." *Transactions of the Woolhope Naturalists' Field Club*, 27 (1930–32): 34–50.

Marin, Louis. *Des pouvoirs del'image: gloses*. Paris: Editions du Seuil, 1993.

Marlier, Georges. *Ambrosius Benson et la peinture à Bruges au temps de Charles-Quint*. Damme: Editions du Musée van Maerlant, 1957.

Martens, Didier. "Observations sur la châsse de Sainte Ursule de Hans Memling: sa structure, ses commanditaires et ses sources." *Annales d'histoire de l'art et d'archéologie* 16 (1994): 79–98.

Martens, Maximiliaan P.J. "New Information on Petrus Christus's Biography and the Patronage of His Brussels Lamentation." *Simiolus* 20/1 (1990–91): 5–23.

———. "Patronage and Politics: Hans Memling's *St. John Altarpiece* and 'The Process of Burgundization.'" in ed. Hélène Verougstraete and Roger van Schoute, *Le dessin sous-jacent dans le processus de création*. Louvain-la-Neuve: Collège Érasme, 1995: 169–76.

Martin, Arthur. "La châsse de Notre Dame" in eds. C. Cahier and Arthur Martin *Mélanges d'archéologie, d'histoire et de littérature* 1, (1847): 5–20.

Martiny, Victor-G. "Architecture in Brussels in Van der Weyden's Time" in *Rogier van der Weyden*, 1979.

Mas Latrie, Léon de. "Les patriarchs latins de Jérusalem." *Revue de l'Orient latin* 1 (1893): 16–41.

Mason, Arthur. *What Became of the Bones of St. Thomas?* Cambridge: Cambridge University Press, 1920.

Matthews, W.H. *Mazes and Labyrinths: A General Account of their History and Developments*. Detroit, MI: Singing Tree, 1969 repr. 1922.

Maxe-Werly, L. "Médaille du bienheureux Pierre de Luxembourg du XVe siècle." *Mémoires de la Société des Lettres, Sciences et Arts de Bar-le-Duc*, 3rd series, 7 (1898): 49–56.

Mayer, Anton L. "Die heilbringende Schau in Sitte und Kult," in *Heilige Überlieferung: Ausschnitte aus der Geschichte des Mönchtums und des heiligen Kultes für Ildefons Herwegen*. Münster, 1938: 234–62.

———. "Die Grundung von St. Salvator in Passau—Geschichte und Legende." *Zeitschrift für bayerische Landesgeschichte* 18 (1955): 256–78.

Mayer, Hans Eberhard. *The Crusades*, 2nd ed., trans. John Gillingham. Oxford: Oxford University Press, 1988.

Mayer-Pfannholz, Anton. "St. Salvator," in ed. Josef Oswald, *Alte Klöster in Passau und Umgebung. Geschichtliche und kunstgeschichtliche* Aufsätze. Passau: Passavia, 1954: 47–66.

Mayr-Harting, Henry. *Ottonian Book Illumination: An Historical Study*. London: Oxford University Press, 1991.

McFarlane, Kenneth B. *Hans Memling*. Oxford: Clarendon Press, 1971.

McGrade, Michael. "Affirmations of Royalty: Liturgical Music in the Collegiate Church of St. Mary in Aachen, 1050–1350." Ph.D. diss., University of Chicago, 1998.

———."O Rex Mundi Triumphator: Hohenstaufen Politics in a Sequence for Saint Charlemagne." *Early Music History* 17 (1998): 183–219.

Medding, Wolfgang. *Die Westportale der Kathedrale von Amiens und ihre Meister*. Augsburg: B. Filser, 1930.

Megivern, James J. *Concomitance and Communion. A Study in Eucharistic Doctrine and Practice*. Studia Friburgensia 33, n.s. Fribourg, Switzerland: University Press, 1963.

Meiss, Millard. *French Painters in the Time of Jean de Berry: The Limbourgs and Their Contemporaries.* 2 vols. New York: George Braziller, 1974.

—— and Colin Eisler. "A New French Primitive." *Burlington Magazine* 102 (1960): 233–40.

Mekking, Aart J.J. "Bijdragen tot de Bouwgeschiedenis van de Sint-Servaaskerk te Maastricht, deel II, Het Schip." *Publications de la Société Historique et Archéologique dans le Limbourg* 116–17 (1980–1981): 156–65.

Melczer, William. *The Pilgrim's Guide to Santiago de Compostela.* New York: Italica Press, 1993.

Melnikas, Anthony. *The Corpus of Miniatures in the Manuscripts of Decretum Gratiani.* 3 vols., *Corpus Picturarum Minutarum Quae in Codicibus Manu Scriptis Iuris Continentur.* Rome: The Index of Juridical and Civic Iconography, 1975.

Mely, Fernand de. *Le trésor de Chartres 1310–1793.* Paris: Alphonse Picard, 1886.

——. "L'image du Christ du Sancta Sanctorum et les reliques chrétiennes apportées par les flots." *Mémoires de la Société des Antiquaires de France* 58 (1902): 113–44.

——. "Notes et études archéologiques. La Croix des premiers croisés." *Exuviae sacrae constantinopolitanae,* edited by Fernand de Mély, vol. 3. Paris: E. Leroux, 1904.

Memling Tentoonstelling, ingericht door het stadtsbestuur in het Stedelijk Museum te Brugge (22 Juni–1 October 1939) Catalogus. 2nd edition. Bruges: Desclée, De Brouwer, 1939.

Merback, Mitchell B. *The Thief, the Cross and the Wheel: Pain and the Spectacle of Punishment in Medieval and Renaissance Europe.* Chicago: University of Chicago Press, 1999.

Mérindol, Christian de. "Art, spritualité et politique: Philippe le Hardi et la Chartreuse de Champmol, nouvel apercu." *Les Chartreux et l'Art, XIVᵉ–XVIIIᵉ siècle.* Paris: Cerf, 1989: 93–116

Merlet, Lucien. *Catalogue des reliques et joyaux de Notre-Dame de Chartres.* Chartres: Garnier, 1885.

——. *Histoire des relations des Hurons et des Abnaquis du Canada avec Notre-Dame de Chartres, suivi de documents inédits sur la Sainte Chemise.* Chartres: Petrot-Garnier, 1858.

—— and Alexandre Clerval. *Un manuscrit chartrain du XIᵉ siècle.* Chartres: Garnier for the Société archéologique d'Eure-et-Loir, 1893.

Merlet, René. "Les architectes de la cathédrale de Chartres et de la construction de la chapelle Saint-Piat au XIVᵉ siècle." *Bulletin monumental,* 7th s., 10 (1906): 218–34.

——. *The Cathedral of Chartres.* Paris: Henri Laurens, 1913.

——. "Le puits des Saints-Forts et l'ancienne chapelle de Notre-Dame-sous-Terre." *Congrès archéologique de France, Chartres 1900.* Paris: 1901: 226–55.

Metford, J.C.J. *Dictionary of Christian Lore and Legend.* London: Thames and Hudson, 1983.

Meuthen, Erich, ed. "Karl der Grosse-Barbarossa-Aachen: Zur Interpretation des Karlsprivilegs für Aachen," in Braunfels, & Schramm, 1967: 54–76.

——. *Aachener Urkunden 1101–1250.* Bonn: Peter Hanstein-Verlag, 1972.

Meyer, Hans Bernhard. "Die Elevation im deutschen Mittelalter und bei Luther." *Zeitschrift für katholische Theologie,* 85 (1963): 162–217.

Michelant, Heinrich, ed. *Das Gedenkbuch des Metzer Bürgers Phillipe von Vigneulles aus den Jahren 1471 bis 1522 nach der Handschrift des Verfassers.* Stuttgart: Bibliothek des literarischen Vereins in Stuttgart, 1852.

Michel-Dansac, R. "Neuvy-Saint-Sépulcre." *Congrès archéologique de France* 94 (1931): 523–55.

Michelli, Pippin. "A Gordian Knot: Notes on Chartres Pilgrim Badges." *Peregrinations* 1/2 (July 2002): 2–4.

Migne, J.P. *Dictionnaire de numismatique et de sigillographie religieuses.* Paris: Chez l'editeur, 1852.

——. *Lexicon Manuale Ad Scriptores Medie Et Infime Latinitatis,* 1866.

Miles, Margaret Ruth. *Image as Insight: Visual Understanding in Western Christianity and Secular Culture.* Boston: Beacon Press, 1985.

Miller, Edward. *The Abbey and Bishopric of Ely: The Social History of an Ecclesiastical Estate from the Tenth Century to the Early Fourteenth Century.* Cambridge: Cambridge University Press, 1951.

Milne, Gustav. "Medieval Riverfront Reclamation in London" in eds Gustav Milne and Brian Hobley, *Waterfront Archaeology in Britain and Northern Europe.* London: Council for British Archaeology, 1981: 32–36.

Milz, Joseph. *Studien zur mittelalterlichen Wirtschaft- und Verfassungsgeschichte der Abtei Deutz.* Cologne: Wamper, 1970.

Minkenberg, Georg. "Der Barbarossaleuchter im Dom zu Aachen." *Zeitschrift des Aachener Geschichtsvereins* 96 (1989): 69–102.

Mitchiner, Michael. *Medieval Pilgrim Badges.* London: Hawkins Publications, 1986.

Mittler, Mauritius OSB. *Betrachtungen Studien Und Untersuchungen Zum Siegburger Kirchenschatz.* Vol. XXIII, *Siegburger Studien.* Siegburg: Respublica-Verlag, 1991.

Molinier, Auguste. *Obituaires de la province de Sens,* vol. II: *Diocèse de Chartres.* Paris: G. Klincksieck, 1906.

Monget, Cyprien. *La Chartreuse de Dijon.* 3 vols., Tournai: Montreuil-sur-Mer, 1898–1905.

Monroe, William S. "The Guennol Triptych and the Twelfth-Century Revival of Jurisprudence" in ed. Elizabeth C. Parker, *The Cloisters: Studies in Honor of the Fiftieth Anniversary.* New York: The Metropolitan Museum of Art, 1992.

Montfauçon, Bernard de. *Les Monuments de la monarchie française.* Paris: J.M. Gandouin, 1729.

Montgomery, Scott B. "The Use and Perception of Reliquary Busts in the Late Middle Ages." Ph.D. diss., Rutgers University, 1996.

Moore, Marie Dolores. "The Visitatio Sepulchri of the Medieval Church." Ph.D. diss., University of Rochester, Eastman School of Music, 1971.

Morand, Kathleen. *Claus Sluter, Artist at the Court of Burgundy.* Austin: University of Texas, 1991.

Morgan, Nigel. "Life of St. Edward the Confessor" in Alexander & Binski, 1987: 216–17.

——. "The Iconography of Twelfth-Century Mosan Enamels" in *Rhein und Maas,* 1972.

——. *Early Gothic Manuscripts: 1250–1285,* vol. II, *A Survey of Manuscripts Illuminated in the British Isles,* ed. J.J.G. Alexander. Oxford: Oxford University Press, 1988.

Morgan, P. "The Effect of the Pilgrim Cult of St. Thomas Cantilupe on Hereford Cathedral," in ed. Meryl Jancey, *St. Thomas Cantilupe, Bishop of Hereford: Essays in his Honour.* Hereford: Friends of Hereford Cathedral, 1982: 145–52.

Morganstern, Anne M. "Le tombeau de Philippe le Hardi et ses antecedents." *Actes des Journées Internationales Claus Sluter.* Dijon: Association Claus Sluter, 1992: 175–92.

Morris, Colin. "Picturing the Crusades: The Uses of Visual Propaganda, *c.* 1095–1250" in J. France and W. Zajac, 1998: 195–216.

—— and Peter Roberts, eds. *Pilgrimage: The English Experience from Becket to Bunyan.* Cambridge: Cambridge University Press, 2002.

Morris, John. *The Relics of St. Thomas of Canterbury.* Canterbury: Hal Drury, 1888.

Morris, Richard. "The Remodelling of the Hereford Aisles." *Journal of the British Archaeological Association,* 3rd s., 37 (1974): 21–39.

Müllejans, Hans, ed. *Karl der Grosse und sein Schrein in Aachen. Eine Festschrift.* Aachen: einhard/Mönchengladbach: B. Kühlen, 1988.

Müller, Chrisian, *et al. From Schongauer to Holbein: Master Drawings from Basel and Berlin.* Washington: National Gallery of Art, 1999.

Müller, Heribert. *Heribert Kanzler Ottos III. Und Erzbischof von Köln.* Cologne: Verlag der Buchhandlung, 1977.

Müller, Markus. *Minnebilder. Französische Minnedarstellungen des 13. und 14. Jahrhunderts.* Cologne:Verlag, 1996.

Müller, Theodor. *Die Bildwerke in Holz, Ton und Stein von der Mittel des XV. bis gegen Mitte XVI. Jahrhunderts.* Munich: Bruckmann, 1959.

Munz, Peter. "Frederick Barbarossa and the 'Holy Empire'." *Journal of Religious History* 3 (1964–5): 20–37.

———. *Frederick Barbarossa: a Study in Medieval Politics.* Ithaca: Cornell University Press, 1969.

Murray, Alan V. "'Mighty Against the Enemies of Christ': The Relic of the True Cross in the Armies of the Kingdom of Jerusalem" in J. France & W. Zajac, 1998: 217–38.

Murray, Stephen. "Looking for Robert de Luzarches: The Early Work at Amiens Cathedral." *Gesta* 19/1 (1990): 111–31.

———. *Notre-Dame, Cathedral of Amiens: The Power of Change in Gothic.* Cambridge: Cambridge University Press, 1996.

Musée des arts décoratifs (France). *Les tresors des églises de France.* 2nd ed., Paris: Caisse nationale des monuments historiques, 1965.

Musée des Beaux-Arts de Dijon. *Claus Sluter en Bourgogne: mythe et representations.* Dijon: Musée des Beaux-Arts de Dijon, 1990.

Muth, Hanswernfried. *Die Herrgottskirche in Creglingen.* Regensburg: Schnell & Steiner, 1996.

Naz, R., *et al.*, ed. *Dictionnaire De Droit Canonique, Contenant Tous Les Termes Du Droit Canonique, Avec Un Sommaire De L'histoire Et Des Institutions Et De L'état Actuel De La Discipline.* 7 vols. Paris: Letouzey and Ane, 1935–65.

Nebenzahl, Kenneth. *Maps of the Holy Land: Images of Terra Sancta through Two Millennia.* NY: Abbeville, 1968.

Nees, Lawrence. "On Carolingian Book Painters: The Ottoboni Gospels and Its Transfiguration Master." *The Art Bulletin* 83 (2001): 209–39.

Nevison, J.L. and J.A. Hudson. "Sir John Schorne and his Boot." *Country Life* vol. 131/3391 (March 1, 1962): 467–8.

Neyen, Aug. "De l'origine et du But Véritable de la Procession Dansante d'Echternach." *Bulletin de l'Institut Archéologique Liégeois* XV (1880): 223–97.

Neyes, Mechtild. "Dendrochronologische Untersuchungen," in *Der Schrein des Karls des Großen, Bestand und Sicherung 1982–1988.* Aachen: Einhard, 1998: 111–13.

Nichols, Stephen. *Romanesque Signs: Early Medieval Narrative and Iconography.* New Haven: Yale University Press, 1983.

Nicholson, Helen. *The Knights Templar: A New History.* Stroud: Sutton, 2001.

Niehoff, Franz. "Umbilicus mundi—der Nabel der Welt. Jerusalem und das Heilige Grab im Spiegel von Pilgerberichten und- Karten, Kreuzzügen und Reliquien" in *Ornamenta Ecclesiae*, 1985.

Nilgen, Ursula. "The Epiphany and the Eucharist." *Art Bulletin* 49 (1967): 311–16

———. "Amtsgenealogie und Amtsheiligkeit, Königs- und Bischofsreihen in der Kunstpropaganda des Hochmittelalters," in ed. Katharina Bierbrauer, *Studien zur mittelalterlichen Kunst 800–1250: Festschrift für Florentine Mütherich zum 70. Geburtstag.* Munich: Prestel, 1985: 217–34.

———. "Manipulated Memory: Thomas Becket in Legend and Art," in eds. Wessel Reinik and Jeroen Stumpel, *Memory and Oblivion; Proceedings of the XXIXth International Congress of the History of Art.* Dordrecht: Kluwer Academic Publishers, 1999: 765–72.

———. "Herrscherbild und Herrschergenealogie der Stauferzeit," in Kramp, 2000, vol. 1: 357–67.

Nilson, Ben. *Cathedral Shrines of Medieval England.* Woodbridge: Boydell Press, 1998.

Nolan, Kathleen. "Narrative in the Capital Frieze of Notre Dame at Étampes." *The Art Bulletin* 71 (1989): 166–84.

———. "Ritual and Visual Experience in the Capital Frieze at Chartres." *Gazette des Beaux-Arts*, ser. 6, 123 (1994): 53–72.

Noroff, Avraam de. *Pèlerinage en Terre Sainte de l'igoumène russe Daniel au commencement du XIIème siècle.* St. Pétersbourg: Académie impériale des sciences, 1864.

Norton, E.E. and M.C. Horton. "A Parisian Workshop at Canterbury. A Late Thirteenth-Century Tile Pavement in the Corona Chapel, and the Origins of Tyler Hill." *Journal of the British Archaeological Association,* 134 (1981): 58–80.

Novum glossarium mediae Latinitatis, vol. 30, Copenhagen: Munksgaard, 1998.

Oakley, Francis. *The Western Church in the Later Middle Ages.* Ithaca: Cornell University Press, 1979.

Oediger, Friedrich Wilhelm. *Die Regesten der Erzbischöfe von Köln im Mittelalter—Erster Band 313–1099.* Bonn: P. Hanstein, 1954–61.

Oman, Charles. *English Church Plate: 597–1830.* London: Oxford University Press, 1957.

O'Neill, John P., ed. *The Art of Medieval Spain, A.D. 500–1200.* New York: The Metropolitan Museum of Art, 1993.

——, ed. *Enamels of Limoges: 1100–1350.* New York: The Metropolitan Museum of Art, 1996.

O'Reilly, Jennifer. "'Candidus et Rubicundus'—an Image of Martyrdom in the 'Lives' of Thomas Becket." *Analecta Bollandiana* 99 (1981): 303–14.

Orme, Margaret. "A Reconstruction of Robert of Crickdale's *Vita et Miracula S. Thomae Cantuariensis.*" *Analecta Bollandiana* 84 (1966): 379–98.

Os, Henk van. *The Art of Devotion in the Late Middle Ages in Europe, 1300–1500.* Princeton: Princeton University Press, 1994.

Os, Jaap van. "Seks in de 13de-eeuwse fabliaux: literaire voorlopers van de erotische insignes?" in Koldeweij & Willemsen, 1995: 36–43.

Osten, Gert von der. *Der Schmerzensmann. Typengeschichte eines deutschen Andachtsbildwerkes.* Berlin: Deutscher Verein für Kunstwissenschaft, 1935.

Ostendorf, Adolf. "Das Salvator-Patrocinium, seine Anfänge und seine Ausbreitung im mittelalterlichen Deutschland." *Westfälische Zeitschrift* 100 (1950): 357–76.

Ousterhout, Robert. "Rebuilding the Temple: Constantine Monomachus and the Holy Sepulchre." *Journal of the Society of Architectural Historians* 48 (March 1989): 66–78.

——, ed. *The Blessings of Pilgrimage.* Urbana, IL: University of Illinois Press, 1990.

——. "Loca Sancta and the Architectural Response to Pilgrimage" in Ousterhout, 1990: 108–24.

——. "The Temple, the Sepulchre, and the *Martyrion* of the Savior." *Gesta* 29/1 (1990): 44–53.

——. "Flexible Geography and Transportable Topography," in ed. Bianca Kühnel, *Jewish Art* 23–24 (1997–98): 393–404.

——. "Architecture as Relic and the Construction of Sanctity, The Stones of the Holy Sepulchre." *Journal of the Society of Archiectural Historians* 62 (March 2003): 4–23.

Owen, D.D.R. *Noble Lovers.* London: Phaidon Press, 1975.

Owen, Dorothy. *The Medieval Development of the Town of Ely.* Ely: The Ely Society, 1993.

Paatz, Walter. *Süddeutsche Schnitzaltäre der Spätgotik.* Heidelberg: Carl Winter/Universitätsverlag, 1963.

Pächt, Otto. *The Master of Mary of Burgundy.* London: Faber and Faber, 1948.

——. *The Rise of Pictorial Narrative in Twelfth-Century England.* Oxford: Clarendon, 1962.

——, C.R. Dodwell, and Francis Wormald. *The St. Albans Psalter (Albani Psalter).* London: Warburg Institute, 1960.

Panofsky, Erwin. "'Imago Pietatis,' Ein Beitrag zur Typengeschichte des 'Schmerzensmanns' und der 'Maria Mediatrix,'" in *Festschrift für Max J. Friedländer zum 60. Geburtstage.* Leipzig: E.A. Seemann, 192, 261–308.

——. "Über die Reihenfolge der Vier Meister von Reims." *Jahrbuch Für Kunstwissenschaft* (1925): 55–82.

——. *Tomb Sculpture*. New York: Harry N. Abrams, 1964.

——. *Abbot Suger on the Abbey Church of St.-Denis and its Art Treasures*. 2nd ed. Princeton: Princeton University Press, 1979.

——. *Early Netherlandish Painting, Its Origin and Character*. 2 vols. Cambridge: Harvard University Press, 1953, repr. New York: Harper & Row, Icon Editions, 1971.

Paravicini, Werner. "Bruges and Germany" in ed. Valentin Vermeersch, *Bruges and Europe*. Antwerp: Fonds Mercator, 1992: 98–127.

Parshall, Peter. "Imago Contrafacta: Images and Facts in the Northern Renaissance." *Art History* 16/4 (1993): 554–79.

Paquay, Jean. "Les Antiques Processions Des Croix Banales À Tongres." *Bulletin de la Société Scientifique et Litteraire du Limbourg* 21 (1903): 127–96.

Paul, Georges, and Pierre Paul. *Notre-Dame du Puy. Essai historique et archéologique*. Le Puy: Cazes-Bonneton, 1926.

Pauls, Emil. "Die Heiligsprechung Karls des Großen und seine kirchliche Verehrung in Aachen bis zum Schluß des 13. Jahrhunderts." *Zeitschrift des Aachener Geschichtsvereins* 25 (1903): 335–60.

Paulus, Nikolaus. *Indulgences as a Social Factor in the Middle Ages*. New York: The Devin-Adain Company, 1922.

Paxson, James. "A Theory of Biblical Typology in the Middle Ages." *Exemplaria* 3/2 (1991): 359–83.

Pedica, Don Stephano. "Il Volto Santo. Nei documenti della Chiesa." Ph.D. diss.,Pontificia Universita S. Tomaso d'Aquino, 1958.

Penninck, Jozef. *De Jeruzalemkerk te Brugge*. Bruges: Koninklijke Gidsenbond van Brugge en West-Vlaanderen, 1986.

Perier-d'Ieteren, Catheline. "Rogier Van der Weyden, His Artistic Personality and His Influence on Painting in the XVth Century" in *Rogier van der Weyden*, 1979.

Perkins, Jocelyn. *Westminster Abbey: Its Worship and Its Ornaments*. London: Oxford University Press, 1938, 2 vols.

Perrault-Desaix, Henri. *Recherches sur Neuvy-Saint-Sépulcre et les monuments de plan ramassé*. Paris: Ernest Leroux, 1931.

Perrot, Françoise. "Le vitrail, la croisade et la Champagne: réflexion sur les fenêtres hautes du choeur à la cathédrale de Chartres," in eds Y. Bellenger and D. Quéruel, *Les Champenois et la croisade*. Paris: 1989: 109–30.

Peters, Edward. *Christian Society and the Crusades, 1198–1229: Sources in Translation Including the Capture of Damietta by Oliver of Paderborn*. Philadelphia: University of Pennsylvania Press, 1971.

Peters, Francis E. *Jerusalem. The Holy City in the Eyes of Chroniclers, Visitors, Pilgrims, and Prophets from the Days of Abraham to the Beginnings of Modern Times*. Princeton: Princeton University Press, 1985.

Petersohn, Jürgen. "Saint-Denis—Westminster—Aachen: Die Karls-Translatio von 1165 und ihre Vorbilder." *Deutsches Archiv für Erforschung des Mittelalters* 31 (1975): 420–54.

——. "Kaisertum und Kultakt in der Stauferzeit," in ed. Jürgen Petersohn, *Politik und Heiligenverehrung im Hochmittelalter*. Sigmaringen: Thorbecke, 1994: 101–46.

Petricioli, Ivo. *St. Simeon's Shrine in Zadar*. Zagreb: JAZU, 1983.

Philippart, Guy. "Le récit miraculaire marial dans l'Occident médiéval," in Iogna-Prat, *et al.*, 1996: 563–90.

Phillips, Jonathan. *Defenders of the Holy Land: Relations between the Latin East and the West, 1119–1187*. Oxford: Clarendon Press, 1996.

Picard, Étienne. "La Dévotion de Philippe le Hardi et de Marguerite de Flandres, d'apres des documents inedits." *Mémoires de l'Académie des sciences, arts et belles letters de Dijon* 12/4 (1910–13): 1–71.

Pickering, Frederick P. *Literature and Art in the Middle Ages*. Coral Gables: University of Miami Press, 1970.

Pirenne, Henri. *Le Soulèvement de la Flandre Maritime de 1323–1328: documents inédits.* Brussels: Librairie Kiessling, 1900.

Plat, Gabriel. *L'Église de la Trinité de Vendôme.* Paris: Laurens, 1934.

Plötz, Robert. "Imago Beati Iacobi. Beiträge zur Ikonographie des Hl. Jacobus Maior im Hochmittelalter" in Kriss-Rettenbeck, 1984: 248–64.

Poche, Emanuel and Jaroslav Pesina. *Stredovekeho Umeleckého Remeslo.* Prosinec, 1986–87.

Pohlkamp, Wilhelm. "Kaiser Konstantin, der heidnische und der christliche Kult in den Actus Silvestri." *Frühmittelalterliche Studien* 18 (1984): 357–400.

Postles, David A. "Heads of Religious Houses as Administrators" in ed. William M. Ormrod, *England in the Thirteenth Century.* Stamford: Paul Watkins, 1991: 37–50.

Powicke, Frederick M. *King Henry III and the Lord Edward: The Community of the Realm in the Thirteenth Century.* 2 vols. Oxford: Clarendon Press, 1947.

——. *The Thirteenth Century, 1216–1307.* Oxford: Clarendon Press, 1953.

Prache, Anne. "La chapelle de Vendôme à la cathédrale de Chartres et l'art flamboyant en Île-de-France." *Jahrbuch für Kunstgeschichte* 47–48 (1993–94): 569–75.

——. "L'influence de la cathédrale de Fulbert sur l'art roman," in *Enseigner le moyen âge à partir d'un monument, la cathédrale de Chartres. Le temps de Fulbert.* Chartres: Société archéologique d'Eure-et-Loir, 1996: 129–33.

Pradalier, Henri. "Saint-Sernin médiéval" in *Saint-Sernin de Toulouse: trésors et méta-morphoses. Deus siècles de restaurations 1802–1989.* Toulouse: Musée Saint-Raymon, 1989.

Preziosi, Donald. *Rethinking Art History: Meditations on a Coy Science.* New Haven: Yale University Press, 1989.

Price Gowen, Rebecca. "The Shrine of the Virgin in Tournai, I: Its Restorations and State of Conservation." *Aachener Kunstblätter* 47 (1976–77): 111–76.

Pugh, Ralph B., ed. *The Victoria History of the County of Cambridgeshire and the Isle of Ely.* Vol. 4. Oxford: Institute of Historical Research, 1953.

Puschnik, Herbert and Herta. *Pulkau. Stadtgeschichte, Kunst, Kultur.* Pulkau: Fremden-verkehrsverein der Stadt Pulkau und Umgebung, 1998.

Quarré, Pierre. "L'implantation du Calvaire du 'Puits de Moise' a la Chartreuse de Champmol." *Memoires de la Commission des Antiquités du Departement de la Cote d'Or* 29 (1974–5): 161–66.

Queller, Donald E. *The Fourth Crusade: The Conquest of Constantinople.* Philadelphia: University of Pennsylvania Press, 1997.

Rackham, Bernard. "The Early Stained Glass of Canterbury Cathedral," *Burlington Magazine* 52 (1928): 33–41.

——. *The Ancient Glass of Canterbury Cathedral.* London: Lund Humphries & Co., Ltd., 1949.

Radford, Ursula M., "Wax Images Found in Exeter Cathedral." *Antiquaries Journal,* 29 (1949): 164–68.

Raguenet de Saint-Albin, O. "Chemises de Chartres." *Revue de l'art chrétien* (1887): 95.

Ragusa, Isa and Rosalie Green, eds. *Meditations on the Life of Christ,* trans. Isa Ragusa. Princeton: Princeton University Press, 1961.

Raine, James. *St. Cuthbert: With an Account of the State in Which his Remains were Found Upon the Opening of his Tomb in Durham Cathedral, in the Year MDCCCXXVII.* Durham: George Andrews, 1828.

Ramsay, Nigel. "Artists, Craftsmen and Design in England, 1200–1400" in Alexander & Binski, 1987: 49–54.

Randall, Lillian M.C. *Medieval and Renaissance Manuscripts in the Walters Art Gallery, vol. I–III France 875–1530.* Baltimore: Johns Hopkins University Press, 1989, 1992, 1997.

Rash-Fabbri, Nancy. "A Drawing in the Bibliothèque Nationale and the Romanesque Mosaic Floor in Brindisi." *Gesta* 13 (1974): 5–14.

Rauschen, Gerhard, ed. *Die Legende Karls des Großen im 11. und 12. Jahrhundert.* Leipzig: Verlag von Duncker & Humblot, 1890.

Reader-Moore, Anthony. "The Liturgical Chancel of Canterbury Cathedral," *Canterbury Cathedral Chronicle* 73 (1979): 25–44.

Réau, Louis. "Emmaüs,"in Louis Réau, *Iconographie de l'art chrétien*, vol. 2, part 2. Paris: Presses universitaires de France, 1957: 561–67.

Recht, Roland *et al. Architecture gothique*. Paris: Berger-Levrault, 1979.

Regteren Altena, I.Q. van. "Hidden Records of the Holy Sepulchre" in *Essays in the History of Architecture Presented to Rudolph Wittkower*. Douglas Fraser, Howard Hibbard, and Milton J. Lewine, eds. London: Phaidon, 1967: 17–21.

Reich, Anton. *Pulkau. Seine Kirchen und seine Geschichte*. Vienna: Bergland, 1963.

Reinle, Adolf. *Zeichensprache der Architektur: Symbol, Darstellung und Brauch in der Baukunst Mittelalters und der Neuzeit*. Zurich: Verlag für Architektur Artemis, 1976.

Reynaud, Nicole. "Reconstruction d'un triptyque de Memling." *La Revue du Louvre* 24 (1974): 79–90.

Rice, Eric. "Music and Ritual in the Collegiate Church of Saint Mary in Aachen, 1300–1600." Ph.D. diss., Columbia University, 2002.

Richard, Jean. *Les Récits de Voyages et de Pèlerinages*. Tournhout: Brepols, 1985.

———. *The Crusades, c. 1071–c. 1291*, trans. Jean Birrell. Cambridge: Cambridge University Press, 1999.

Rickard, Marcia R. "The iconography of the Virgin Portal at Amiens." *Gesta* 22/2, (1983): 147–57.

Riley-Smith, Jonathan. "Family Traditions and Participation in the Second Crusade" in ed. Michael Gervers, *The Second Crusade and the Cistercians*. New York: St. Martin's Press, 1992.

———. *The Knights of Saint John in Jerusalem and Cyprus*. London: Macmillan, 1967.

Riley-Smith, Louise and Jonathan. *The Crusades: Idea and Reality, 1095–1274*. London: E. Arnold, 1981.

Ring, Greta. *A Century of French Painting, 1400–1500*. London: Phaidon, 1949.

Ringbom, Sixten. "Devotional Images and Imaginative Devotions: Notes on the Place of Art in Late Medieval Private Piety." *Gazette des Beaux-Arts* 73 (1969): 159–70.

Rishel, Joseph J. "The Philadelphia and Turin Paintings: The Literature and Controversy over Attribution" in *Jan van Eyck's Two Paintings of Saint Francis Receiving the Stigmata*. Philadelphia: Philadelphia Museum of Art, 1997.

Roberts, Eileen. *The Hill of the Martyr: An Architectural History of St. Albans Abbey*. Dunstable, Bedfordshire: The Book Castle, 1993.

Roberts, Marion. "The Tomb of Giles de Bridport in Salisbury Cathedral." *Art Bulletin*, 65/4 (Dec. 1983): 559–86.

———. "The Effigy of Bishop Hugh de Northwold in Ely Cathedral." *Burlington Magazine* 130 (1988): 77–84.

Roberts, Phyllis B. "Langton on Becket: A New Look and a New Text." *Mediaeval Studies* 35 (1973): 38–48.

———. "Archbishop Stephen Langton and his Preaching on Thomas Becket in 1220," in ed. Thomas L. Amos, Eugene A. Green, Beverly Mayne Kienzle, *De Ore Domini: Preacher and Word in the Middle Ages*. Kalamazoo, MI: Medieval Institute Publications, 1989: 75–92.

———. *Thomas Becket in the Medieval Latin Preaching Tradition*. The Hague: Martinus Nijhoff International, 1992.

Robinson, Bernard P. "The Place of the Emmaus Story in Luke-Acts." *New Testament Studies* 30/4 (1984): 481–97.

Robinson, F.N., ed. *The Works of Geoffrey Chaucer*, Oxford: Oxford University Press, 1983 repr. 1933.

Rode, Herbert. "Der verschollene Christuszyklus am Dreikönigenschrein. Versuch einer Rekonstruktion und einer Analyse." *Kölner Domblatt* 30 (1969): 27–48.

Rodière, Roger. "Rue" in *Congrès archéologique de France* (session tenue à Amiens). Paris: A. Picard (1937): 268–92.

Rogers, Nicholas J. "English Episcopal Monuments, 1270–1350" in ed. John Coales, *The Earliest English Brasses: Patronage, Style and Workshops 1270–1350*. London: Monumental Brass Society, 1987: 8–68.

Rogier van der Weyden, Rogier de le Pasture. Official Painter to the City of Brussels. Portrait Painter of the Burgundian Court. Brussels: Maison du roi, 1979.

Rolland, Paul. *Histoire De Tournai*. Tournai: Casterman, 1956.

Rollason, David W. "The Miracles of St Benedict: A Window on Early Medieval France" in eds Henry Mayr-Harting and R.I. Moore, *Studies in Medieval History Presented to R.H.C. Davis*. London and Ronceverte: The Hambledon Press, 1985: 73–90.

Rorem, Paul. *Biblical and Liturgical Symbols within the Pseudo-Dionysian Synthesis*. Toronto: Pontifical Institute of Medieval Studies, 1984.

Rosenau, Helen. *The Ideal City: Its Architectural Evolution in Europe*. London: Methuen, 1983.

Rosenwein, Barbara H. "Feudal War and Monastic Peace: Clunaic Liturgy as Ritual Aggression." *Viator* 2 (1971): 129–57.

Rothkrug, Lionel. *Religious Practices and Collective Perceptions: Hidden Homologies in the Renaissance and Reformation*. Waterloo, Ontario: University of Waterloo, 1980.

——. "Holy Shrines, Religious Dissonance and Satan in the Origins of the German Reformation." *Historical Reflections* 14 (1987): 143–286.

Rowe, John Gordon. "The Origins of the Second Crusade: Pope Eugenius III, Bernard of Clairvaux and Louis VII of France." In *The Second Crusade and the Cistercians*, edited by Michael Gervers. New York: St. Martin's Press, 1992.

Roy, Emile. *Le Mystère de la Passion en France du XIVᵉ au XVIᵉ siécle*. Dijon, 1903–04, Repr. Geneva; Slatkine, 1974.

Rubin, Miri. *Corpus Christi: The Eucharist in Late Medieval Culture*. Cambridge: Cambridge University Press, 1991.

——. "Imagining the Jew: The Late Medieval Eucharistic Discourse," in eds. R. Po-chia Hsia and H. Lehmann, *In and Out of the Ghetto: Jewish-Gentile Relations in Late Medieval and Early Modern Germany*. Cambridge: Cambridge University Press, 1995: 177–208.

——. *Gentile Tales: The Narrative Assault on Late Medieval Jews*. New Haven: Yale University Press, 1999.

Rudy, Kathryn M. "A Guide to Mental Pilgrimage: Paris, Bibliothèque de l'Arsenal MS. 212." *Zeitschrift für Kunstgeschichte* 63 (2000): 494–515.

Runciman, Steven. *A History of the Crusades*. 3 vols. Cambridge: Cambridge University Press, 1951–54.

Rupin, Ernest. *Roc-Amadour*. Paris: G. Baranger Fils, 1904.

Saguez, Abbé. "La paroisse Saint-Wulphy de Rue." *Bulletin de la Société d'Émulation d'Abbeville* 7 (1908): 345–54.

Salet, Francis. "La sculpture romane en Bourgogne: à propos d'un livre récent." *Bulletin Monumental* 119 (1961): 325–43.

—— and Jean Adhémar. *La Madeleine de Vézelay*. Melun: d'Argences, 1948.

Salmon, Charles. *Histoire de Saint Firmin: martyr, premier évêque d'Amiens: patron de la Navarre et des Diocèses d'Amiens et de Pampelune*. Arras and Amiens: Rousseau-Leroy, A. Caron, 1861.

——. "Iconographie du portail de Saint-Firmin." *Revue de l'Art Chrétien* 4 (1860): 617–26.

Salmon, Pierre. *The Breviary Through the Centuries*, trans. by Sister David Mary. Collegeville, MN: Liturgical Press, 1962.

Sandron, Danny. *Picardie gothique. Autour de Laon et Soissons: L'Architecture religieuse*. Paris: Picard, 2001.

Sanfaçon, André. "Événement, mémoire et mythe: le siège de Chartres de 1568," in ed. Claire Dolan, *Événement, identité et histoire*. Sillery, Québec: Les éditions du Septentrion, 1991: 187–204.

Sanfaçon, Roland. *L'architecture flamboyante en France*. Québec: Presses de l'Université Laval, 1971.

Sargent, Steven D. "Miracle Books and Pilgrimage Shrines in Late Medieval Bavaria." *Historical Reflections/Reflexions Historique*. 13: 2 & 3 (1986): 455–71.

——. "A Critique of Lionel Rothkrug's List of Bavarian Pilgrimage Shrines." *Archive for Reformation History* 78 (1987): 351–8.

Sauerländer, Willibald. "Gislebertus von Autun: Ein Beitrag zur Entstehung seines künstlerischen Stils," in ed. Kurt Martin, *Studien zur Geschichte der europäischen Plastik: Festschrift Theodor Müller*. Munich: Hirmer, 1965: 17–29.

——. *Gothic Sculpture in France, 1140–1270*. London: Thames and Hudson, 1972.

Scherer, Annette. "Mehr als nur Andenken. Spätmittelalterliche Pilgerzeichen und ihre private Verwendung" in ed. Frank Matthias Kammel, *Spiegel der Seligkeit. Privates Bild und Frömmigkeit im Spätmittelalter*. Nuremberg: Verlag des Germanischen Nationalmuseums, 2000: 131–36.

Schervier, C.G. *Die Münsterkirche zu Aachen und deren Reliquien*. Aachen: Im Selbstverlage des Karls-Vereins, 1853.

Schiel, Hubert. *Codex Egberti der Stadtbibliothek Trier*. Basel: Alkuin-Verlag, 1960.

Schiffers, Heinrich. *Karls des Großen Reliquienschatz und die Anfänge der Aachenfahrt*. Aachen: Verlag Johannes Volk, 1951.

Schiller, Gertrud. "Die Emmausjünger," in Gertrud Schiller, *Ikonographie der christlichen Kunst*, vol. 3. Gütersloh: Mohn, 1971: 99–104.

——. *Iconography of Christian Art*, trans. Janet Seligman. London: Lund Humphries, 1972.

Schlumberger, Gustav. *Sigillographie de l'Orient latin*. Paris: P. Guenther, 1943.

Schlunk, Helmut. "The Crosses of Oviedo: A Contribution to the History of Jewelry in Northern Spain in the Ninth and Tenth Centuries." *Art Bulletin* 32 (1950): 91–114.

Schmidt, Leopold. "Hirtenmotive in Wallfahrtsgründungslegenden," in ed. Louis Carlen and Fritz Steinegger, *Festschrift Nikolaus Grass. Zum 60. Geburtstag dargebracht von Fachgenossen, Freunden und Schulern*, 2. Innsbruck: Universitätsverlag Wagner, 1975: 199–215.

Schmidt, Richard. *Die Herrgottskirche bei Creglingen*. Augsburg: Benno Filser, 1929.

Schmidt, W. "Die älteste Holzschnittdarstellungen der Heiligthümer von Maastricht, Aachen und Kornelimünster." *Zeitschrift des Aachener Geschichtsvereins* 7 (1885): 125–26.

Schmit, J.P. "le labyrinthe" in *Nouveau Manuel Complet de L'Architecture des Monuments Religieux*. Paris: Librarie Encyclopédique de Roret, 1859 repr.

Schmitt, Jean-Claude. "Cendrillon crucifiée. À propos du Volto Santo de Lucques" in *Miracles, prodiges et merveilles au Moyen Âge*. Paris: La Sorbonne Publications, 1995: 241–69.

Schmitt, Marilyn Low. "Traveling Carvers in the Romanesque: The Case History of St.-Benoît-sur-Loire, Selles-sur-Cher, Méobecq." *The Art Bulletin* 63 (March, 1981): 6–31.

Schmugge, Ludwig, "Die Pilger," in ed. Peter Moraw, *Unterwegssein im Spätmittelalter*. Berlin: Duncker & Humblot, 1985: 17–47.

Schnitzler, Hermann. *Rheinische Schatzkammer*, 2 vols. Düsseldorf: L. Schwann, 1957–59.

——. "Eine Metzer Emmaustafel." *Wallraf-Richartz-Jahrbuch* 20 (1958): 41–54.

——. *Der Schrein des Heiligen Heribert*. Munich: B. Kuhlen Verlag, 1962.

Schnurrer, Ludwig. "Kapelle und Wallfahrt zum Heiligen Blut in Rothenburg," in *Rothenburg im Mittelalter. Studien zur Geschichte einer fränkischen Reichsstadt*. Rothenburg: Verlag des Vereins Alt-Rothenburg, 1997: 389–400.

Scholten, Frits. "Heerlijke resten." *Kunstschrift* 6 (1999): 14–17.

Schramm, Percy Ernst and Florentine Mütherich. *Denkmale der deutschen Könige und Kaiser*. 2 vols. Munich: Prestel Verlag, 1962–78.

Der Schrein Karls des Grossen. Bestand und Sicherung. 1982–1988. Aachen: Einhard, 1998.

Schrenk, Klaus, ed. *Die Karlsruhe Passion: Ein Hauptwerk Straßburger Malerei der Spätgotik, Die.* Karlsruhe: Staatliche Kunsthalle 1996.

Schuler, Ernst. *Die Musik der Osterfeiern, Osterspiele und Passionen des Mittelalters.* Basel: Bärenreiter, 1951.

——. *Fahrendes Volk im Mittelalter.* Darmstadt: Wissenschaftliches Buchgesellschaft, 1995.

Schulten, Walter. "Der Ort der Verehrung der Heiligen Drei Könige," in ed. Rainer Budde, *Die Heiligen Dreikönige—Darstellung und Verehrung.* Cologne: Locher, 1982: 61–72.

——. "Kölner Reliquien" in *Ornamenta Ecclesiae,* vol. 2, 1985: 61–78.

Schütte, Sven. "Der Aachener Thron," Kramp, 2000, 1: 213–22.

Schütz, Alois. "Legende und Wahrheit. Der Andechser Heiltumsschatz." *Charivari* 7/8 (July-Aug. 1993): 12–16.

Schwaiger, Georg and Paul Mai, eds. *Wallfahrt im Bistum Regensburg. Beiträge zur Geschichte des Bistums Regensburg,* vol. 28. Regensburg, 1994.

Schwartzbaum, Elizabeth. "The Romanesque Sculpture of the Cathedral of Tournai." Ph.D. diss., New York, 1977.

Schwarzweber, Annemarie. *Das Heilige Grab in der deutschen Bildnerei des Mittelalters.* Freiburg im Breisgau: Eberhard Albert Universitätsbuchhandlung, 1940.

Schwierz, Israel. *Steinerne Zeugnisse jüdischen Lebens in Bayern. Eine Dokumentation,* 2nd edn. Munich: Bayerische Landeszentrale für politische Bildungsarbeit, 1992.

Schwillus, Harald. "Hostienfrevellegende und Judenverfolgung in Iphofen. Ein Beitrag zur Entstehungsgeschichte der Kirche zum Hl. Blut im Gräbenviertel." *Würzburger Diozesan- Geschichtsblätter* 58 (1996): 87–107.

Schwineköper, Berent. "Christus-Reliquien-Verehrung und Politik. Studien über die Mentalität der Menschen des früheren Mittelalters, insbesondere über die religiöse Haltung und sakrale Stellung der früh- und hochmittelalterlichen deutschen Kaiser und Könige." *Blätter für deutsche Landesgeschichte* 117 (1981): 183–281.

Scott, Mary Ann. *Dutch, Flemish, and German Paintings in the Cincinnati Art Museum, Fifteenth through Eighteenth Centuries.* Cincinnati: Cincinnati Art Museum, 1987.

Scribner, Robert. "Popular Piety and Modes of Visual Perception in Late-Medieval and Reformation Germany." *The Journal of Religious History* 15/4 (December 1989): 448–69.

Seidel, Linda. "Installation as Inspiration: The Passion Cycle from La Daurade." *Gesta* 25 (1986): 83–92.

Sekules, Veronica. "Easter Sepulchre," in *The Dictionary of Art.* New York: Grove, 1996, vol. 9: 680–82.

Setlak-Garrison, Hélène Sylvie. "The Capitals of St.-Lazare at Autun: Their Relationship to the Last Judgment Portal." Ph.D. diss., UCLA, 1984.

Setton, Kenneth M., ed. *A History of the Crusades.* 6 vols. Madison: University of Wisconsin Press, 1969–89.

Shaver-Crandell, Annie, Paula Gerson and Alison Stones. *The Pilgrim's Guide to Santiago de Compostela: A Gazetteer.* London: Harvey Miller Publishers, 1995.

Sheingorn, Pamela, ed. *The Book of Sainte Foy.* Philadelphia: University of Pennsylvania Press, 1995.

Shortell, Ellen M. "Dismembering Saint Quentin: Gothic Architecture and the Display of Relics." *Gesta* XXXVI/1 (1997): 32–47.

Sigal, Pierre André. "Le Voyage De Reliques Au XIᵉ Et XIIᵉ Siècles" in *Voyage, Quete Pelerinage Dans La Litterature Et La Civilisation Médiévales.* Paris: Édition CUER MA, diffusion H. Champion, 1976: 73–104.

——. *L'homme et le miracle dans la France médiévale (XIᵉ–XIIᵉ Siècle).* Paris: Les Éditions du Cerf, 1985.

——. "Reliques, pèlerinage et miracles dans l'église médiévale (XIᵉ–XIIIᵉ siècles)." *Revue d'histoire de l'église de France* 76/197 (1990): 193–211.

Signori, Gabriela. "Marienbilder im Vergleich: Marianische Wunderbücher zwischen Weltklerus, städtische Ständvielfalt und ländlichen Subsistenzproblemen (10.–13. Jahrhundert)," in *Maria. Abbild oder Vorbild? Zur Sozialgeschichte mittelalterlicher Marienverehrung*, ed. Hedwig Röcklein, Claudia Opitz and Dieter R. Bauer. Tübingen: edition diskord, 1990: 58–90.

——. *Maria zwischen Kathedrale, Kloster und Welt. Hagiographische und historiographische Annäherungen an eine hochmittelalterliche Wunderpredigt.* Sigmaringen: Jan Thorbecke Verlag, 1995.

——. "La bienheureuse polysémie. Miracles et pèlerinages à la Vierge: pouvoir thaumaturgique et modèles pastoraux (X^e–XIIe siècles)" in Iogna-Prat, *et al.*, 1996: 591–617.

——. "The Miracle Kitchen and its Ingredients: A Methodical and Critical Approach to Marian Shrine Wonders (10th to 13th century)." *Hagiographica* 3 (1996): 277–303.

Simon, Holger. *Der Creglinger Marienaltar von Tilman Riemenschneider.* Berlin: Verlag für Wissenschaft und forschung, 1998.

Simonsohn, Shlomo, ed. *The Apostolic See and the Jews. Documents: 492–1404.* Toronto: Pontifical Institute of Medieval Studies, 1988.

Simpson, W. Sparrow. "Master John Schorne." *Records of Buckinghamshire* vol. 3 (1870): 354–69.

——, ed. "Two Inventories of the Cathedral Church of St. Paul, London, dated Respectively 1245 and 1402." *Archaeologia*, vol. 50 (1888): 439–524.

Sinderhauf, Monica. *Die Abtei Deutz ihre innere Erneuerung: Klostergeschichte im Spiegel des verschollenen Codex Thioderici.* Cologne: SH-Vrlag, 1996.

Singleton, Barrie. "Köln-Deutz and Romanesque Architecture." *Journal of the British Archaeological Association* 143 (1990): 49–76.

Sint-Janshospitaal Brugge 1188–1976. 2 vols. Bruges: Commissie van Openbare Onderstand van Brugge, 1976.

Smeyers, Maurits. *Flemish Miniatures from the 8th to the Mid-16th Century: The Medieval World on Parchment.* Turnhout: Brepols, 1999.

Smith, Jeffrey Chipps. "Jean de Maisoncelles' Portrait of Philippe le Bon for the Chartreuse de Champmol." *Gazette de Beaux-Arts* 99 (January, 1982): 7–12.

——. "The Chartreuse de Champmol in 1486: The Earliest Visitors Account." *Gazette des Beaux-Arts* 106 (July, 1985): 1–6.

Smith, Jonathon Z. *To Take Place: Toward Theory in Ritual.* Chicago: University of Chicago Press, 1987.

Sneyd, Charlotte Augusta, ed. *A Relation, or Rather a True Account, of the Island of England; with Sundry Particulars of the Customs of these People and of the Royal Revenues under the King Henry the Seventh, about the Year 1500.* London: Camden Society, 1847, vol. 37.

Snoek, Godefridus J.C. *Medieval Piety from Relics to the Eucharist. A Process of Mutual Interaction.* Leiden: E.J. Brill, 1995.

Snyder, James. "Jan van Eyck and the Madonna of Chancellor Nicolas Rolin." *Oud-Holland* 82 (1967): 163–170.

——. "Observations on the Iconography of Jan van Eyck's "Saint Francis Receiving the Stigmata." In *Jan van Eyck's Two Paintings of Saint Francis Receiving the Stigmata.* Philadelphia: Philadelphia Museum of Art, 1997.

Soergel, Philip M. *Wondrous in His Saints: Counter-Reformation Propaganda in Bavaria.* Berkeley: University of California Press, 1993.

Souchet, Jean-Baptiste. *Histoire du diocèse et de la ville de Chartres*, II–IV. Chartres: Garnier for the Société archéologique d'Eure-et-Loir, 1868, 1869, 1873.

Soyez, Edmond. *La Procession du Saint-Sacrement et les Procession Générales à Amiens.* Amiens, Yvert & Tellier, 1896.

Spaemann, Cordelia. "Wallfahrtslieder" in Kriss-Rettenbeck, 1984: 181–92.

Spencer, Brian. "Medieval Pilgrim Badges: Some General Observations Illustrated
    Mainly from English Sources" in ed. J.G.N. Renaud, *Rotterdam Papers: A Contribution
    to Medieval Archaeology*. Rotterdam: Coördinatie Commissie van Advies inzake
    Archeologisch Onderzoek binnen het ressort Rotterdam, 1968: 135–53.
———. "An ampulla of St. Egwin and St. Edwin." *The Antiquities Journal* 51 (1971):
    316–18.
———. "The Ampullae from Cuckoo Lane in eds. Colin Platt & Richard Coleman-
    Smith, *Excavations in Medieval Southampton 1953–1969*. Leicester University Press,
    1975, 2: 242–49.
———. "King Henry of Windsor and the London Pilgrim." *Collectanea Londiniensia:
    Studies in London Archaeology and History Presented to Ralph Merrifield*, London and
    Middlesex Archaeological Society, Special Paper No. 2 (1978): 235–64.
———. "Pilgrim Souvenirs from the Medieval Waterfront Excavations at Trig Lane
    London, 1974–6." *Transactions of the London and Middlesex Archaeological Society*, 33
    (1982): 304–23.
———. "Two Leaden Ampullae from Leicestershire." *Transactions of the Leicestershire
    Archaeological and Historical Society* 55 (1982): 88–89
———. "A thirteenth-century pilgrim's ampulla from Worcester." *Transactions of the
    Worcestershire Archaeological Society* 9 (1984): 7–11.
———. "Pilgrim souvenirs" in Alexander & Binski, 1987: 218–25.
———. "Pilgrim Souvenirs" in ed. P.F. Wallace, *Medieval Dublin Excavations 1962–91:
    Miscellanea I*, Fascicule 5, 1988: 33–48.
———. *Pilgrim Souvenirs and Secular Badges: Salisbury Museum Medieval Catalogue*. Salisbury:
    Salisbury Museum, 1990.
———. *Pilgrim Souvenirs and Secular Badges: Medieval Finds from Excavations in London*.
    London: The Stationery Office, 1998.
———. "Medieval pilgrim badges found at Canterbury, England" in D. Kicken, A.M.
    Koldeweij & J.R. ter Molen, 2000: 316–26.
———. "Canterbury pilgrim souvenirs found in the Low Countries" in: van Beuningen,
    Koldeweij & Kicken, 2001: 105–11.
Spencer, Eleanor P. *The Sobieski Hours, a Manuscript in the Royal Library at Windsor
    Castle*. London and New York: Academic Press, 1977.
Spiegel, Gabrielle. "Political Utility in Medieval Historiography: A Sketch." *History
    and Theory* 14 (1975): 314–25.
Spitzer, Laura. "The Cult of the Virgin and Gothic Sculpture: Evaluating Opposition
    in the Chartres West Façade Capital Frieze." *Gesta* 33/2 (1994): 132–50.
Sprusansky, Svetozar, ed. *Der Heilige Sebald, seine Kirche, seine Stadt*. Nuremberg:
    Selbstverlag St. Sebald, 1979.
Spufford, Peter. *Money and Its Use in Medieval Europe*. Cambridge: Cambridge University
    Press, 1988.
Stacey, Robert C. *Politics, Policy, and Finance Under Henry III, 1216–1245*. Oxford:
    Clarendon Press, 1987.
Stadlober, Margit. "Der Hochaltar der Heiligenblutkirche zu Pulkau." *Das Münster*
    37/3 (1984): 235–8.
Stadtische Museen Freiburg. Augustinermuseum. Führer durch die Sammlungen, Freiburg i. Br.:
    Augustinermuseum, 1978.
Stahl, Gerlinde. "Die Wallfahrt zur Schönen Maria in Regensburg." *Beiträge zur
    Geschichte des Bistums Regensburg* 2 (1968): 35–281.
Stahleder, Helmuth. "Die Münchener Juden im Mittelalter und ihre Kultstätten"
    in *Synagogen und jüdische Friedhöfe in* München. Munich: Aries Verlag, 1988.
Stange, Alfred. *Deutsche Malerei der Gotik*, VI: *Nordwestdeutschland in der Zeit von 1450
    bis 1515*. Munich: Deutscher Kunstverlag, 1954.
Stanley, Arthur. *Historical Memorials of Canterbury*. New York: Anson D.F. Randolph
    & Co., n.d.

Stauffer, Annemarie. *Die mittelalterlichen Textilien von St. Servatius in Maastricht.* Riggisberg: Abegg-Stiftung, 1991.

Staunton, Michael. *The Lives of Thomas Becket.* Manchester: Manchester University Press, 2001.

Stechow, Wolfgang. "Emmaus," in *Reallexikon zur deutschen Kunstgeschichte*, vol. 5. Stuttgart: Metzler, 1959: 228–42.

——. *Northern Renaissance Art, 1400–1600; Sources and Documents.* Englewood Cliffs: Prentice-Hall, 1966.

Stegeman, Charles. *Les cryptes de la cathédrale de Chartres et les cathédrales depuis l'époque gallo-romaine.* Chartres: Société archéologique d'Eure-et-Loir, n.d.

Steiner, Peter and Georg Brenninger. *Gnadenstätten im Erdinger Land.* Munich: Schnell & Steiner, 1986.

Stemmler, Theo, ed. *The Ellesmere Miniatures of the Canterbury Pilgrims.* Mannheim: Poetria medievalis, 2, 1977.

Stephany, Erich. *Der Karlsschrein.* Mönchengladbach: B. Kühlen Verlag, 1965.

——. "Über den Empfang des römischen Königs vor seiner Krönung in der Kirche der Hl. Maria zu Aachen—nach der Handschrift ADD. 6335 im Britischen Museum, London," in *Miscellanea pro Arte; Hermann Schnitzler zur Vollendung des 60. Lebensjahre am 13. Januar 1965.* Düsseldorf: L. Schwann, 1965: 272–78.

——. "Aachen im Land zwischen Rhein und Maas," in *Rhein und Maas* 1973, vol. 2: 123–28.

——. Der Marienschrein im Aachener Dom, Ein Zeugnis für die Marienverehrung im Hohen Mittelalter," in ed. Leonhard Küppers, *Die Gottesmutter: Marienbild in Rheinland und in Westfalen,.* 2 vols. Recklinghausen: Bongers, 1974, 1: 101–12.

Stevens, Denis. "Music in Honor of St. Thomas of Canterbury." *Music Quarterly* 56:3 (July, 1970): 311–48.

Stiennon, Jacques. "La Personalité de Wibald de Stavelot et de Corvey: une problematique" in ed. Jacques Stiennon. *Wibald, Abbé de Stavelot-Malmedy et de Corvey, 1130–1158.* Stavelot: Musée de l'ancienne abbaye, 1982.

St. John Hope, William Henry. *Windsor Castle: An Architectural History.* 2 vols. London: Offices of Country Life, 1913.

Stocker, David. "The Mystery of the Shrines of St. Hugh" in ed. Henry Mayr-Harting, *St. Hugh of Lincoln: Lectures Delivered at Oxford and Lincoln to Celebrate the Eighth Centenary of St. Hugh's Consecration as Bishop of Lincoln.* Oxford: Clarendon Press, 1987: 89–124.

Stoddard, Whitney S. *Art and Architecture in Medieval France.* New York: Harper and Row Publishers, 1972.

Stopford, Jennie, ed. *Pilgrimage Explored.* York: University of York, 1999.

Strait, Paul. *Cologne in the Twelfth Century.* Gainsville, FL: University Press of Florida, 1974.

Stratford, Neil. "La sculpture médiévale de Moutiers-Saint-Jean (Saint-Jean-de-Réome)." *Congrès Archéologique de France* 144 (1986): 167–69.

——. *Catalogue of Medieval Enamels in the British Museum.* London: British Museum Press, 1993.

——, Pamela Tudor-Craig and Anna Maria Mathesius. "Archbishop Hubert Walter's Tomb and its Furnishings" in *Medieval Art and Architecture at Canterbury before 1220.* London: British Archaeological Association, 1982: 71–93.

Strauss, Heidemarie and Peter Strauss. *Heilige Quellen zwischen Donau, Lech and Salzach.* Munich: Hugendubel, 1987.

Strieder, Peter, ed. *Meister um Albrecht Dürer.* Nuremberg: Verlag des Germanischen Nationalmuseums, 1961.

Strohm, Reinhard. *Music in Late Medieval Bruges*, rev. ed. Oxford: Clarendon Press, 1990.

Strohmaier-Wiederanders, Gerlinde. "Untersuchungen zur Grundungslegende von

Kloster Heiligengrabe." *Jahrbuch für Berlin-Brandenburgische Kirchengeschichte* 57 (1989): 259–75.

Sullivan, Donald. "Nicholas of Cusa as Reformer: The Papal Legation to the Germanies, 1451–1452." *Medieval Studies* 36 (1974): 403–04.

Sumption, Jonathan. *Pilgrimage: An Image of Medieval Religion.* Totowa, NJ: Rowman and Littlefield, 1975.

Swanson, R.N. *Catholic England: Faith, Religion and Observance Before the Reformation.* Manchester: Manchester University Press, 1993.

———. *Religion and Devotion in Europe, c. 1215–c. 1515.* Cambridge: Cambridge University Press, 1995.

Swarzenski, Hans. *Monuments of Romanesque Art.* 2nd ed. Chicago: University of Chicago Press, 1974.

Sweeting, Walter D. *The Cathedral Church of Ely: A History and Description of the Building with a Short Account of the Former Monastery and of the See.* London: George Bell & Sons, 1902.

Taft, Robert. *The Liturgy of the Hours in East and West.* Collegeville, MN: Liturgical Press, 1986.

Tait, Hugh. "Pilgrim-Signs and Thomas, Earl of Lancaster." *British Museum Quarterly* 20 (1955): 39–47.

———. *Jewellery Through 7000 Years.* London: British Museum, 1976.

Tanner, Norman P., ed. *Decrees of the Ecumenical Councils,* 2 vols. London: Sheed & Ward, 1990.

Taurisano, I. "Per la festa di S. Tommaso d'Aquino." *Il Rosario Memorie Domenicane* 33 (1916): 114–15.

Taylor, A.J. "Edward I and the Shrine of St. Thomas of Canterbury." *Journal of the British Archaeological Association,* 132 (1979): 22–27.

Taylor, Baron, Charles Nodier and Alphonse Cailleux. *Voyages pittoresques et romantiques dans l'ancienne France,* vol. 1: La Picardie. Paris: Firmin Didot Frères, 1835–45.

Taylor, Michael D. "The Pentecost at Vézelay." *Gesta* 19 (1980): 9–15.

Teichmann, Eduard. "Zur Heiligtumsfahrt des Philipp von Vigneulles im Jahre 1510." *Zeitschrift des Aachener Geschichtsvereins* 22 (1900): 121–34.

———. "Das älteste Aachener Totenbuch." *Zeitschrift des Aachener Geschichtsvereins* 38 (1916): 1–213.

———. "Zur Lage und Geschichte des Grabes Karls des Grossen." *Zeitschrift des Aachener Geschichtsvereins* 39 (1917): 155–217.

Tekippe, Rita. *Procession, Piety and Politics: The Evolution of Form and Custom for Rheno-Mosan Reliqaury Shrines in Three Medieval Cult Communities, Associated with the Bishop-Saints Servatius of Maastricht, Eleutherius of Tournai, and Remaclus of Stavelot.* Ph.D. diss., The Ohio State University, 1999.

Tellier, Ed. "Travaux de la collégiale de Huy au XVIIIe s." *Leodium* LIX, n.s. 1–6 (January-June 1972): 54–76.

Le Temps des Croisades. Brussels: Credit Communal, 1996.

Terret, Victor. *La sculpture bourguignonne aux XIIe et XIIIe siècles: ses origines et ses sources d'inspiration: Autun.* vol. 2. Autun: Victor Terret, 1925.

Thiébaut, Dominique and Michel Laclotte. *l'Ecole d'Avignon.* Paris: Flammarion, 1983.

Thiebaut, Jacques. "Arras (cathedral)" in *The Grove Dictionary of Art.* v. 2. New York: Grove Dictionaries Inc., 1996.

Thier, Ludwig. "Christus Peregrinus: Christus als Pilger in der Sicht von Theologen, Predigern und Mystikern des Mittelalters," in eds. Karl Amon *et al., Ecclesia Peregrinans: Josef Lenzenweger zum 70. Geburtstag.* Vienna: Verband der wissenschaftlichen Gesellschaften Österreichs, 1986: 29–41.

Thiers, Ottie. *Bedevaart en kerkeraad. De Amersfoortse vrouwevaart van 1444 tot 1720.* Hilversum: Verloren, 1994.

Thomas, A., ed. "Les Miracles de Notre Dame de Chartres. Texte latin inédit." *Bibliothèque de l'école des chartes* 42 (1881): 505–50.

Thompson, A. Hamilton. "Master Elias of Dereham and the King's Works." *Archaeological Journal*, 48 (1941): 1–35.

Thorpe, Lewis, ed. and trans., *Einhard and Notker the Stammerer, Two Lives of Charlemagne*. Baltimore: Penguin Books, 1969.

Thoss, Dagmar. *Flämische Buchmalerei. Handschriftenschätze aus dem Burgunderreich*. Graz: Akademische Druck- und Verlagsanstalt, 1987.

Thurre, Daniel. *L'atelier roman d'orfèvrerie de l'abbaye de Saint-Maurice*. Sierre: Monographic, 1992.

Thurston, H. "Corporal" *Catholic Encyclopedia* 4, Robert Appleton Press: New York, 1908.

Thurston, Herbert. *The Stations of the Cross: An Account of Their History and Devotional Purpose*. London: Burnes and Oates, 1906.

Timmermann, Achim. "Staging the Eucharist: Late Gothic Sacrament Houses of Swabia and on the Upper Rhine, Architecture and Iconography." Ph.D. diss., University of London, 1996.

——. "The Avenging Crucifix: Some Observations on the Iconography of the Living Cross." *Gesta* 40/2 (2001): 141–60.

Le Tombeau de Saint Lazare et la sculpture romane à Autun après Gislebertus. Autun: Musée Rolin, 1985.

Töpfer, Bernhard. "Kaiser Friedrich Barbarossa—Grundlinien seiner Politik," in eds. Evamarie Engel, Bernhard Töpfer, *Kaiser Friedrich Barbarossa: Landesausbau—Aspekte seiner Politik—Wirkung*. Wiemar: Böhlau, 1994: 9–30.

Torra de Arana, Eduardo, Antero Hombría Tortajada and Tomás Domingo Pérez. *Los Tapices de La Seo de Zaragoza*. Aragon: La Caja de Ahorros de la Immaculada, 1985.

Toussaert, Jacques. *Le Sentiment Réligieux En Flandre À La Fin Du Moyen-Age*. Paris: Librairie Plon, 1963.

Trapp, Oswald Graf. *Churburg, Kleiner Kunstführer* 779. Munich: Schnell & Steiner, 1963.

Travis, William J. "The Iconography of the Choir Capitals at Saint-Lazare of Autun and the Anagogical Way in Romanesque Sculpture." *Konsthistorisk Tidskrift*, 68/4 (1999): 220–49.

Trésors de la Cathédrale de Chartres. Chartres: Musée des beaux-arts de Chartres, 2002.

Trexler, Richard C. *The Journey of the Magi: Meaning in History of a Christian Story*. Princeton: Princeton University Press, 1997.

Trimpe Burger, J.A. "Aardenburgse pottebakkerswaar." *Mededelingenblad Nederlandse Vereniging van Vrienden van de Ceramiek*, 72 (1974): 2–12.

Tronzo, William L. "Moral Hieroglyphs: Chess and Dice at San Savino in Piacenza." *Gesta* 16 (1977): 15–26.

Tudor, V. "The Misogyny of St. Cuthbert." *Archaeologia Aeliana*, 5th s., 12 (1984): 158–64.

Tudor-Craig, Pamela and Laurence Keen. "A Recently Discovered Purbeck Marble Sculpted Screen of the Thirteenth Century and the Shrine of St. Swithun" in *Medieval Art and Architecture at Winchester Cathedral*. London: British Archaeological Association, 1983: 63–72.

Turner, D.H. "The Customary of the Shrine of St. Thomas Becket." *Canterbury Cathedral Chronicles*, 30 (1976): 16–22.

Turner, Victor. *The Ritual Process: Structure and Anti-Structure*. Chicago: Aldine Publishing Co., 1969.

——. *Image and Pilgrimage in Christian Culture: Anthropological Perspectives*. New York: Columbia University Press, 1978.

Tuve, Rosamond. *Allegorical Imagery: Some Mediaeval Books and Their Posterity*. Princeton: Princeton University Press, 1966.

Urbanek, Regina. "Bericht zur Untersuchung und Konservierung der Fassungen am Holzkern des Aachener Marienschreines." Aachen: unpublished report, June 1997.

Urry, William. "Some Notes on the Two Resting Places of St. Thomas Becket at Canterbury" in ed. Raymond Foreville, *Thomas Becket: Actes du Colloque International de Sédières, 19–24 août 1973*. Paris: Beauchesner, 1975: 195–209.

Valentiner, Wilheim R. *Catalogue of Paintings*. Raleigh: North Carolina Museum of Art, 1956.

Van Ausdall, Kristen. "Tabernacles of the Sacrament: Eucharistic Imagery and Classicism in the Early Renaissance." Ph.D. diss., Rutgers University, 1994.

Van Bastelaer, M.D.A. "Étude sur un reliquaire-phylactère du XIIᵉ siècle." *Annales de l'Académie royale d'Archaéologie* 6 (1880): 32–52.

Van Dam, Raymond. *Saints and their Miracles in Late Antique Gaul*. Princeton: Princeton University Press, 1993.

Van den Bossche, Benoît. "La châsse de saint Remacle à Stavelot: étude iconographique et stylistique des bas-reliefs et des statuettes." *Aachener Kunstblätter* 58 (1989–90): 47–73.

———. "La châsse de Saint Symètre" in *Patrimoine religieux du Pays de Lierneux*, edited by Benoit Van den Bossche. Lierneux: La Commune de Lierneux, 1992: 28–43.

———. "La châsse de saint Remacle à Stavelot: étude des éléments décoratifs." *Bulletin de la Classe des Beaux-Arts de de l'Académie Royale de Belgique* 5/1–6 (1994): 109–149.

———. "Réflexions sur l'iconologie de la châsse de saint Remacle." *Bulletin de la Société d'Art et d'Histoire du Diocèse de Liège* LXII (1997): pp. 1–12.

———. "Anmerkungen zu einer theologischen Betrachtungsweise des Marienschreines zu Aachen." in Wynands, 2000: 101–13.

Van der Meulen, Jan. *Notre-Dame de Chartres: Die vorromanische Ostanlage*. Berlin: Gebr. Mann Verlag, 1975.

——— and Jürgen Hohmeyer. *Chartres. Biographie der Kathedrale*. Cologne: DuMont Buchverlag, 1984.

———, Rüdiger Hoyer and Deborah Cole. *Chartres. Sources and Literary Interpretation: A Critical Bibliography*. Boston: G.K. Hall, 1989.

Vandewalle, André. *Adornes en Jeruzalem: International Levens in het 15de- en 16de-eeuwse Brugges*. Bruges, 1983.

———, ed. *Les marchands de la Hanse et la banque des Médicis: Bruges, marché d'échanges culturels en Europe*. Oostkamp: Stichting Kunstboek, 2002.

Van Dongen, Alexandra. "Het gebruiksvoorwerp als draagteken en beeldteken" in Koldeweij & Willemsen, 1995: 75–87.

Van Engen, John H. *Rupert of Deutz*. Los Angeles: University of California Press, 1983.

Van Herwaarden, Jan. *Opgelegde bedevaarten*. Assen: Van Gorcum, 1978.

Van Rey, Manfred. "Die Lütticher Gaue Condroz Und Ardennen Im Frühmittelalter: Untersuchungen Zur Pfarrorganisation." *Rheinisches Archiv* 102 (1977): 7–51; 136–79; 96–241.

———. "Les Divisions Politiques Et Ecclésiastiques De L'ancien Diocèse De Liège Au Haut Moyen Age." *Le Moyen Age* LXXXVII (1981): 165–206.

Vanrie, A. "Les Croix Banales Aux Abbayes En Belgique Au Moyen Age." *Contributions à l'histoire économique et sociale* II, 1963: 8–28.

Van Tongeren, Louis. "A Sign of Resurrection on Good Friday. The Role of the People in the Good Friday Liturgy until *c.* 1000 A.D. and the Meaning of the Cross" in ed. Charles Caspers and Marc Schneiders, *Omnes Circumdastantes: Contributions Towards a History of the Role of the People in the Liturgy*. Kampen: Uitgeversmaatschaappij J.H. Kok, 1990: 101–19.

Varty, Kenneth. *Reynard, Renart, Reinaert and Other Foxes in Medieval England. The Iconographic Evidence*, Amsterdam: Amsterdam University Press 1999.

Vassilaki, Maria, ed. *The Mother of God: Representations of the Virgin in Byzantine Art*. Milan: Skira, 2000.

Vauchez, André. *The Laity in the Middle Ages: Religious Beliefs and Devotional Practices.* Trans. Margery J. Schneider. Notre Dame: Notre Dame University Press, 1993.

———. *Sainthood in the Later Middle Ages.* trans. Jean Birrell. Cambridge: Cambridge University Press, 1997.

VDB. "Des Processions Banales." *Collection de précis historiques—Mélanges litteraires et scientifiques* XVII (1868): 525–27.

Velden, Hugo T. van der. "Gerard Loyet en Karel de Stoute: het votiefportret in de Bourgondische Nederlanden." Ph.D. diss., Universiteit van Utrecht, 1997.

———. *The Donor's Image. Gerard Loyet and the VotiveImages of Charles the Bold.* Turnhout: Brepols, 2000.

Verdier, Philippe. "Un Monument inédit de l'art mosan du XIIᵉ siècle: la crucifixion symbolique de Walters Art Gallery." *Revue belge d'archéologie et d'histoire de l'art* 30 (1961): 115–75.

———. "Le Reliquaire de la Sainte Epine de Jean de Streda." In *Intuition und Kunstwissenschaft. Festschrift für Hanns Swarzenski,* edited by Peter Bloch *et al.* Berlin: Gebr. Mann Verlag, 1973.

———. "Les Staurothèques mosanes et leur iconographie du Jugement dernier." *Cahiers de civilisation médiévale, Xᵉ–XIIIᵉ siècles* 16/2 (1973): 97–121, and 16/3 (1973): 199–213.

———. "Émaux mosans et rheno-mosans dans les collections des Étas-Unis." *Revue Belge d'archéologie et d'histoire de l'art* 44 (1975): 3–107.

Vergnolle, Eliane. "Les chapiteaux de la Berthenoux et le chantier de Saint-Benoît-su-Loire au XIᵉ siècle." *Gazette des beaux-arts* 80 (November, 1972): 249–60.

———. *Saint-Benoît-sur-Loire et la sculpture du XIᵉ siècle.* Paris: Picard, 1985.

———. *L'art roman en France: architecture, sculpture, peinture* (Paris: Flammarion, 1994).

Vermaut, Nathalie. "La Grande Procession Sur Les Sculptures Du Porche" in ed. Jean Dumoulin, and Jacques Pycke, *La Grande Procession De Tournai (1092–1992) Une Realite Religieuse, Urbaine, Diocesane, Sociale, Economique Et Artistique.* Tournai: Fabrique de l'Église Cathédrale de Tournai, 1992: 61–65.

Vermeersch, Valentin, ed. *Bruges and Europe.* Antwerp: Fonds Mercator, 1992.

Viaene, Antoon. "Ons Heeren Trane te Vendôme. Een bedevaart uit het oude Vlaamse strafrecht." *Biekorf* 66 (1965): 184–88.

Vidal, Jaime R. "The Infancy Narrative in Pseudo-Bonaventure's 'Meditationes Vitae Christi:' A Study in Medieval Franciscan Christ-Piety (*c.* 1300)." Ph.D. diss., Fordham University, 1984.

Viertelböck, Vera. "St. Salvator in Passau. Historische und baugeschichtliche Unter-suchung," *Ostbairische Grenzmarken. Passauer Jahrbuch für Geschichte, Kunst und Volkskunde* 26 (1984): 98–125.

Villete, Jean. "Quand Thésée et le Minotaure ont-ils disparu du Labyrinthe de la Cathédral de Chartres." *Mémoires de la Société archéologique* 25 (1969–72): 265–70.

———. "L'énigme du labyrinth de la cathédrale." *Notre-Dame de Chartres* (March, 1984): 4–12.

Vincent, L.-Hugues and F.M. Abel. *Jérusalem nouvelle, Jérusalem: Recherches de topogra-phie, d'archéologie et d'histoire,* II. Paris: Gabalda, 1914.

Vincent, Nicholas. *The Holy Blood. King Henry III and the Westminster Blood Relic.* Cambridge: Cambridge University Press, 2001.

Viollet-le-Duc, Eugène Emmanuel. *Dictionnaire raisonné de l'architecture française.* VIII, Paris: A. Morel, 1859.

———. *Dessins inédits.* Paris: A. Guerinet, 1894–1902.

Voelkle, William. *The Stavelot Triptych: Mosan Art and the Legend of the True Cross.* New York: The Pierpont Morgan Library, 1980.

Volbach, Wolfgang Fritz. *Elfenbeinarbeiten der Spätantike und des frühen Mittelalters.* 3rd ed. Mainz: Philipp von Zabern, 1976.

Von Euw, Anton. "Châsse de saint Eleuthère" in *Rhein-Meuse* 1972: 315.

Von Falke, Otto, ed. *Die Sammlung Dr. Albert Figdor—Wien. Erster teil.* Vienna: Artaria and Berlin: Cassirer, 1930.

Von Simson, Otto. *The Gothic Cathedral: Origins of Gothic Architecture and the Medieval Concept of Order.* Princeton: Princeton University Press, 1988.

Voronowa, Tamara and Andrej Sterligov. *Westeuropäische Buchmalerei des 8. bis 16. Jahrhunderts in der Russischen Nationalbibliothek, Sankt Petersburg.* Augsburg: Bechtermünz Verlag, 2000.

De Vos, Dirk. *Hans Memling: Bruges, Groeningemuseum 12 August–15 September 1994.* Antwerp: Fonds Mercator Paribas, 1994.

——. *Hans Memling: The Complete Works.* London: Thames and Hudson, 1994.

——. *Rogier Van Der Weyden: The Complete Works.* New York: Harry N. Abrams, 1999.

"Voyage héraldique dans quelques églises du Ponthieu en 1697," ed. and annotated Roger Rodière in *Mémoires de la Société d'Émulation d'Abbeville.* Abbeville: Imprimerie F. Paillart, 1905: 18–23.

Wackers, P.W.M. "Reynaert de Vos als pelgrim" in Koldeweij & Willemsen, 1995: 44–52.

Wadell, Maj-Brit. *Fons Pietatis. Eine ikonographische* Studie. Göteborg: Gratia, 1969.

Walberg, Emmanuel. *La Tradition Hagiographique de Saint Thomas Becket.* Paris: Librarie E. Droz, 1929.

Walker, Susan. *Catalogue of Roman Sarcophagi in the British Museum.* Corpus Signorum Impreii Romani. Great Britain vol. 2, fascicule 2. London: British Museum Publications, 1990.

Wallet, E. "Labyrinthe de Saint-Bertin." *Bulletin Monumental* 13 (1847): 199–202.

Warburg, Aby. "Flemish Art and the Florentine Early Renaissance (1902)" in *The Renewal of Pagan Antiquity: Contributions to the Cultural History of the European Renaissance.* Trans. David Britt. Los Angeles: Getty Research Institute for the History of Art and the Humanities, 1999.

Ward, Benedicta, *Miracles and the Medieval Mind: Theory, Record and Event 1000–1215,* rev. ed. (Philadelphia: University of Pennsylvania Press, 1987).

——. "Two Letters Relating to Relics of St. Thomas of Canterbury" in ed. Lesley Smith and Benedicta Ward, *Intellectual Life in the Middle Ages; Essays Presented to Margaret Gibson.* London: Hambledon Press, 1992: 175–78.

Warichez, Joseph. *S. Eleuthère, Premiere Évêque De Tournai.* Wetteren, 1931.

——. (Chanoine). *La Cathédrale De Tournai Et Son Chapitre.* Wetteren: De Meester, 1934.

——. *Les Origines De L'église De Tournai.* Louvain: Typographie Charles Peeters, 1902.

Warner, G., ed. *The Guthlac Roll.* Oxford: Oxford University Press, 1928.

Warning, Rainer. *The Ambivalences of Medieval Religious Drama,* trans. Steven Rendall (1974; reprint: Stanford: Stanford University Press, 2001).

Morimichi Watanabe. "The German Church Shortly Before the Reformation: Nicolaus Cusanus and the Veneration of the Bleeding Hosts at Wilsnack" in eds Thomas M. Izbicki and Christopher M. Bellitto, *Reform and Renewal in the Middle Ages and the Renaissance: Studies in Honor of Louis Pascoe.* Leiden: E.J. Brill Press, 2000.

——, *Concord and Reform: Nicholas of Cusa and Legal and Political Thought in the Fifteenth Century.* Aldershot: Ashgate, 2001.

Weale, William Henry James. *Hans Memlinc.* London: George Bell & Sons, 1907.

Webb, Diana. *Pilgrims and Pilgrimage in Medieval Europe.* London: J.B. Tauris, 1999.

——. *Pilgrimage in Medieval England.* London: Hambledon and London, 2000.

——. *Pilgrims and Pilgrimage in the Medieval West.* London: I.B. Taurus, 2001.

Wehling, Ulrike. *Die Mosaiken im Aachener Münster und ihre Vorstufen.* Cologne: Rheinland-Verlag, 1995.

Weiss, Daniel H. *Art and Crusade in the Age of Saint Louis.* Cambridge: Cambridge University Press, 1998.

Wemaëre, J. "Les armures royales du Trésor de Chartres," *Monuments historiques de la France* (1974): 57–62.

Wenzel, Siegfried. "The Pilgrimage of Life as a Late Medieval Genre." *Mediaeval Studies* 35 (1973): 370–88.

Werckmeister, Otto K. *Der Deckel des Codex Aureus von St. Emmeran.* Baden-Baden: Verlag Heitz GMBH, 1962.

———. "The Emmaus and Thomas Pillar of the Cloister of Silos," in *El románico en Silos.* Burgos: Abadía de Silos, 1990: 149–71.

Werner, Paul and Richilde Werner. *Vom Marterl bis zum Gipfelkreuz. Flurdenkmal im Oberbayern.* Berechtesgaden: Plenk, 1991.

Westermann-Angerhausen, Hiltrud. "Das ottonische Kreuzreliquiar im Reliquientriptychon von Ste. Croix in Lüttich." *Wallraf-Richartz-Jahrbuch* 36 (1974): 7–22.

———. *Schatz aus den Trümmern. Der Silberschrein von Nivelles und die europäische Hochgotik.* Cologne: Locher, 1995–96.

Westfehling, Uwe, ed. *Die Messe Gregors des Grossen: Vision, Kunst, Realität.* Cologne: Schnütgen-Museum, 1982.

Westrem, Scott D. *The Hereford Map.* Turnhout: Brepols, 2001.

Wharton, Annabel Jane. *Refiguring the Post Classical City: Dura Europos, Jerash, Jerusalem and Ravenna.* Cambridge: Cambridge University Press, 1995.

Wieck, Roger S. *Painted Prayers: The Book of Hours in Medieval and Renaissance Art.* New York: George Braziller, Inc., 1997.

Wiederanders, Gerlinde. "Die Hostienfrevellegende von Kloster Heiligengrabe. Ausdruck des mittelalterlichen Antijudaismus in der Mark Brandenburg." *Kairos. Zeitschrift für Religionswissenschaft und Theologie,* NF 29 (1987): 99–103.

Wilckens, Leonie von. "'o mensch gedenk an mich . . .'—Werke der Barmherzigkeit für die Armen Seelen. Zur einer spätmittelalterlichen Handschrift in der Nürnberger Stadtbibliothek," in Bauer, 1993: 73–80.

———. "Die Kleidung der Pilger" in Kriss-Rettenbeck, 1984: 174–80

Wilkinson, John. "The Tomb of Christ: An Outline of its Structural History." *Levant* 4 (1972): 83–97.

———. *Jerusalem Pilgrims Before the Crusades.* Warminster: Aris and Phillips, Ltd., 1977.

———. *Egeria's Travels.* 3rd ed. Warminster: Aris and Phillips, Ltd., 1999.

———, et al., eds. *Jerusalem Pilgrimage, 1099–1185.* London: Hakluyt Society, 1988.

Willemsen, Annemarieke. *Kinderdelijt. Middeleeuws speelgoed in de Nederlanden.* Nijmegen: Nijmegen University Press, 1998.

Willis, Robert. *Architectural History of Some English Cathedrals: A Collection in two parts of Papers delivered during the years 1842–1863,* I. Chicheley: Paul P.B. Minet, 1972.

———. *The Architectural History of Canterbury Cathedral,* London: Longman, 1845.

Wilpert, Joseph. *Die Römischen Mosaiken und Malereien der kirchlichen Bauten vom IV. bis XIII. Jahrhundert.* 2nd ed. Freiburg im Breisgau: Herder, 1917.

Wilson, Anna. "Biographical Models: The Constantinian Period and Beyond" in Lieu & Montserrat, 1998: 107–35.

Wilson, Christopher. *The Shrines of St. William of York.* York: York Minster, 1977.

———. "The Medieval Monuments," in Collinson, Ramsey, & Sparks, 1995: 451–510.

Wilson, Jean C. "Reflections on St. Luke's Hand: Icons and the Nature of Aura in the Burgundian Low Countries During the Fifteenth Century" in eds Robert Ousterhout and Leslie Brubaker, *The Sacred Image East and West.* Urbana: University of Illinois Press, 1995: 132–46.

Winkelmann, Friedhelm. "Die älteste erhaltene griechische hagiographische *Vita* Konstantins und Helenas (BHG Nr. 365z, 366, 366a)" in ed. Jürgen Drummer, *Texte und Textkritik: eine Aufsatzsammlung.* Berlin: Akademie-Verlag, 1987.

Winter, Patrick M. de. "The Patronage of Philippe le Hardi, Duke of Burgundy, (1364–1404)." Ph.D. diss., New York University, 1976.

Winton, Ivor. "Labyrinths: Chapters Towards an Historical Geography." Ph.D. diss., University of Minnesota, 1987.

Wittstock, Jürgen, ed. *Kirchliche Kunst des Mittelalters und der Reformationszeit.* Lübeck: Museum für Kunst und Kulturgeschichte der Hansestadt Lübeck, 1981.

Wojcik, Jan. *The Road to Emmaus: Reading Luke's Gospel*. West Lafayette, IN: Purdue University Press, 1989.

Wolf, Günther, ed. *Friedrich Barbarossa*. Darmstadt: Wissenschaftliche Buchgesellschaft, 1975.

——. "Imperator und Caesar—zu den Anfängen des staufischen Erbreichsgedankens," in Wolf, 1975: 360–74.

Wood, Christopher S. "Ritual and the Virgin on the Column: The Cult of the Schöne Maria in Regensberg." *Journal of Ritual Studies* 6/1 (Winter 1992): 87–107.

Woodman, Francis. *The Architectural History of Canterbury Cathedral*. London: Routledge & Kegan Paul, 1981.

Woodruff, C. Eveleigh. "The Financial Aspect of the Cult of St. Thomas of Canterbury as Revealed by a Study of the Monastic Records." *Archaeologia Cantiana*, 44 (1932): 12–32.

Woods, Kim. "The Netherlandish Carved Altarpiece *c.* 1500: Type and Function" in eds. Humphrey & Kemp, 1990: 76–89.

Woodward, Kathryn Christi. "*Error Labyrinthi*: An Iconographic Study of Labyrinths as Symbolic of Submission and Deliverance in Manuscripts and on Pavements" Ph.D. diss., Bryn Mawr College, 1981.

Wright, Craig. "The Palm Sunday Procession in Medieval Chartres," in eds. Margot E. Fassler and Rebecca A. Baltzer, *The Divine Office in the Latin Middle Ages: Methodology and Source Studies, Regional Developments, Hagiography*. New York: Oxford University Press, 2000: 344–71.

——. *The Maze and the Warrior: Symbols in Architecture, Theology and Music*. Cambridge: Harvard University Press, 2001.

Wright, Thomas. *The Worship of the Generative Powers during the Middle Ages of Western Europe*, 1866; repr in *A History of Phallic Worship*, New York: Dorset Press 1992.

Wunderli, Richard. *Peasant Fires: The Drummer of Niklaushausen*. Bloomington: Indiana University Press, 1992.

Wurster, Herbert. "Die jüdische Bevolkerung," in eds. Egon Boshof, *et al. Geschichte der Stadt Passau*. Regensburg: Pustet, 1999: 385–92.

Wynands, Dieter P.J. *Die Aachener Heiligtumsfahrt: Kontinuität und Wandel eines mittelalterlichen Reliquienfestes*. Siegburg: Rheinlandia Verlag, 1996.

——. *Der Aachener Marienschrein. Eine Festschrift*. Aachen: Einhard, 2000.

Young, Brian. *The Villein's Bible: Stories in Romanesque Carving*. London: Barrie and Jenkins, 1990.

Young, Karl. *The Drama of the Medieval Church*. 2 vols. Oxford: Clarendon Press, 1933.

Zammattio, Carlo, Augusto Marinoni & Anna Maria Brizio. *Leonardo der Forscher*. Stuttgart: Belser Verlag, 1987.

Zehnder, Frank Günther. *Sankt Ursula. Legend- Verehrung- Bilderwelt*. Cologne: Wienand, 1985.

——. *Katalog der altkölner Malerei*. Cologne: Wallraf-Richartz Museum, 1990.

Zijlstra-Zweens, H.M. "Heiligen in het harnas" in van Beuningen, Koldeweij, & Kicken, 2001: 161–72.

Zika, Charles. "Hosts, Processions and Pilgrimages: Controlling the Sacred in Fifteenth-Century Germany." *Past and Present* 118 (Feb. 1988): 25–64.

Zülch, Walter K. *Frankfurter Künstler, 1223–1700*. Frankfurt am Main: Diestereg, 1935.

Zürich, *Stadtluft, Hirsebrei und Bettelmönch. Die Stadt um* 1300. Stuttgart: Thesis, 1992.

INDEX OF NAMES AND PLACES

Note: This index also includes titles of works of art (such as books and paintings), themes, personifications, and (religious) buildings and festive days. Persons living before the 17th Century have been alphabetized based on their first name.

Abbreviations: Du.=Dutch, Eng.=English, Fr.=French, Germ.=German, Heb.=Hebrew, Lat.=Latin.

SUBJECT INDEX

STUDIES IN MEDIEVAL AND REFORMATION TRADITIONS

(Formerly Studies in Medieval and Reformation Thought)

Founded by Heiko A. Oberman†
Edited by Andrew Colin Gow

1. DOUGLASS, E.J.D. *Justification in Late Medieval Preaching*. 2nd ed. 1989
2. WILLIS, E.D. *Calvin's Catholic Christology*. 1966 *out of print*
3. POST, R.R. *The Modern Devotion*. 1968 *out of print*
4. STEINMETZ, D.C. *Misericordia Dei*. The Theology of Johannes von Staupitz. 1968 *out of print*
5. O'MALLEY, J.W. *Giles of Viterbo on Church and Reform*. 1968 *out of print*
6. OZMENT, S.E. *Homo Spiritualis*. The Anthropology of Tauler, Gerson and Luther. 1969
7. PASCOE, L.B. *Jean Gerson: Principles of Church Reform*. 1973 *out of print*
8. HENDRIX, S.H. *Ecclesia in Via*. Medieval Psalms Exegesis and the *Dictata super Psalterium* (1513-1515) of Martin Luther. 1974
9. TREXLER, R.C. *The Spiritual Power*. Republican Florence under Interdict. 1974
10. TRINKAUS, Ch. with OBERMAN, H.A. (eds.). *The Pursuit of Holiness*. 1974 *out of print*
11. SIDER, R.J. *Andreas Bodenstein von Karlstadt*. 1974
12. HAGEN, K. *A Theology of Testament in the Young Luther*. 1974
13. MOORE, Jr., W.L. *Annotatiunculae D. Iohanne Eckio Praelectore*. 1976
14. OBERMAN, H.A. with BRADY, Jr., Th.A. (eds.). *Itinerarium Italicum*. Dedicated to Paul Oskar Kristeller. 1975
15. KEMPFF, D. *A Bibliography of Calviniana*. 1959-1974. 1975 *out of print*
16. WINDHORST, C. *Täuferisches Taufverständnis*. 1976
17. KITTELSON, J.M. *Wolfgang Capito*. 1975
18. DONNELLY, J.P. *Calvinism and Scholasticism in Vermigli's Doctrine of Man and Grace*. 1976
19. LAMPING, A.J. *Ulrichus Velenus (Oldřich Velenský) and his Treatise against the Papacy*. 1976
20. BAYLOR, M.G. *Action and Person*. Conscience in Late Scholasticism and the Young Luther. 1977
21. COURTENAY, W.J. *Adam Wodeham*. 1978
22. BRADY, Jr., Th.A. *Ruling Class, Regime and Reformation at Strasbourg, 1520-1555*. 1978
23. KLAASSEN, W. *Michael Gaismair*. 1978
24. BERNSTEIN, A.E. *Pierre d'Ailly and the Blanchard Affair*. 1978
25. BUCER, M. *Correspondance*. Tome I (Jusqu'en 1524). Publié par J. Rott. 1979
26. POSTHUMUS MEYJES, G.H.M. *Jean Gerson et l'Assemblée de Vincennes (1329)*. 1978
27. VIVES, J.L. *In Pseudodialecticos*. Ed. by Ch. Fantazzi. 1979
28. BORNERT, R. *La Réforme Protestante du Culte à Strasbourg au XVIᵉ siècle (1523-1598)*. 1981
29. CASTELLIO, S. *De Arte Dubitandi*. Ed. by E. Feist Hirsch. 1981
30. BUCER, M. *Opera Latina*. Vol I. Publié par C. Augustijn, P. Fraenkel, M. Lienhard. 1982
31. BÜSSER, F. *Wurzeln der Reformation in Zürich*. 1985 *out of print*
32. FARGE, J.K. *Orthodoxy and Reform in Early Reformation France*. 1985
33. 34. BUCER, M. *Etudes sur les relations de Bucer avec les Pays-Bas*. I. Etudes; II. Documents. Par J.V. Pollet. 1985
35. HELLER, H. *The Conquest of Poverty*. The Calvinist Revolt in Sixteenth Century France. 1986

36. MEERHOFF, K. *Rhétorique et poétique au XVIe siècle en France.* 1986
37. GERRITS, G.H. *Inter timorem et spem.* Gerard Zerbolt of Zutphen. 1986
38. POLIZIANO, A. *Lamia.* Ed. by A. Wesseling. 1986
39. BRAW, C. *Bücher im Staube.* Die Theologie Johann Arndts in ihrem Verhältnis zur Mystik. 1986
40. BUCER, M. *Opera Latina.* Vol. II. Enarratio in Evangelion Iohannis (1528, 1530, 1536). Publié par I. Backus. 1988
41. BUCER, M. *Opera Latina.* Vol. III. Martin Bucer and Matthew Parker: Flori-legium Patristicum. Edition critique. Publié par P. Fraenkel. 1988
42. BUCER, M. *Opera Latina.* Vol. IV. Consilium Theologicum Privatim Conscriptum. Publié par P. Fraenkel. 1988
43. BUCER, M. *Correspondance.* Tome II (1524-1526). Publié par J. Rott. 1989
44. RASMUSSEN, T. *Inimici Ecclesiae.* Das ekklesiologische Feindbild in Luthers "Dictata super Psalterium" (1513-1515) im Horizont der theologischen Tradition. 1989
45. POLLET, J. *Julius Pflug et la crise religieuse dans l'Allemagne du XVIe siècle.* Essai de synthèse biographique et théologique. 1990
46. BUBENHEIMER, U. *Thomas Müntzer.* Herkunft und Bildung. 1989
47. BAUMAN, C. *The Spiritual Legacy of Hans Denck.* Interpretation and Translation of Key Texts. 1991
48. OBERMAN, H.A. and JAMES, F.A., III (eds.). in cooperation with SAAK, E.L. *Via Augustini.* Augustine in the Later Middle Ages, Renaissance and Reformation: Essays in Honor of Damasus Trapp. 1991 *out of print*
49. SEIDEL MENCHI, S. *Erasmus als Ketzer.* Reformation und Inquisition im Italien des 16. Jahrhunderts. 1993
50. SCHILLING, H. *Religion, Political Culture, and the Emergence of Early Modern Society.* Essays in German and Dutch History. 1992
51. DYKEMA, P.A. and OBERMAN, H.A. (eds.). *Anticlericalism in Late Medieval and Early Modern Europe.* 2nd ed. 1994
52. 53. KRIEGER, Chr. and LIENHARD, M. (eds.). *Martin Bucer and Sixteenth Century Europe.* Actes du colloque de Strasbourg (28-31 août 1991). 1993
54. SCREECH, M.A. *Clément Marot: A Renaissance Poet discovers the World.* Lutheranism, Fabrism and Calvinism in the Royal Courts of France and of Navarre and in the Ducal Court of Ferrara. 1994
55. GOW, A.C. *The Red Jews: Antisemitism in an Apocalyptic Age, 1200-1600.* 1995
56. BUCER, M. *Correspondance.* Tome III (1527-1529). Publié par Chr. Krieger et J. Rott. 1989
57. SPIJKER, W. VAN 'T. *The Ecclesiastical Offices in the Thought of Martin Bucer.* Translated by J. Vriend (text) and L.D. Bierma (notes). 1996
58. GRAHAM, M.F. *The Uses of Reform.* 'Godly Discipline' and Popular Behavior in Scotland and Beyond, 1560-1610. 1996
59. AUGUSTIJN, C. *Erasmus. Der Humanist als Theologe und Kirchenreformer.* 1996
60. McCOOG S J, T.M. *The Society of Jesus in Ireland, Scotland, and England 1541-1588.* 'Our Way of Proceeding?' 1996
61. FISCHER, N. und KOBELT-GROCH, M. (Hrsg.). *Außenseiter zwischen Mittelalter und Neuzeit.* Festschrift für Hans-Jürgen Goertz zum 60. Geburtstag. 1997
62. NIEDEN, M. *Organum Deitatis.* Die Christologie des Thomas de Vio Cajetan. 1997
63. BAST, R.J. *Honor Your Fathers.* Catechisms and the Emergence of a Patriarchal Ideology in Germany, 1400-1600. 1997
64. ROBBINS, K.C. *City on the Ocean Sea: La Rochelle, 1530-1650.* Urban Society, Religion, and Politics on the French Atlantic Frontier. 1997
65. BLICKLE, P. *From the Communal Reformation to the Revolution of the Common Man.* 1998
66. FELMBERG, B.A.R. *Die Ablaßtheorie Kardinal Cajetans (1469-1534).* 1998

67. CUNEO, P.F. *Art and Politics in Early Modern Germany*. Jörg Breu the Elder and the Fashioning of Political Identity, ca. 1475-1536. 1998

68. BRADY, Jr., Th.A. *Communities, Politics, and Reformation in Early Modern Europe*. 1998

69. McKEE, E.A. *The Writings of Katharina Schütz Zell*. 1. The Life and Thought of a Sixteenth-Century Reformer. 2. A Critical Edition. 1998

70. BOSTICK, C.V. *The Antichrist and the Lollards*. Apocalyticism in Late Medieval and Reformation England. 1998

71. BOYLE, M. O'ROURKE. *Senses of Touch*. Human Dignity and Deformity from Michelangelo to Calvin. 1998

72. TYLER, J.J. *Lord of the Sacred City*. The *Episcopus Exclusus* in Late Medieval and Early Modern Germany. 1999

74. WITT, R.G. *'In the Footsteps of the Ancients'*. The Origins of Humanism from Lovato to Bruni. 2000

77. TAYLOR, L.J. *Heresy and Orthodoxy in Sixteenth-Century Paris*. François le Picart and the Beginnings of the Catholic Reformation. 1999

78. BUCER, M. *Briefwechsel/Correspondance*. Band IV (Januar-September 1530). Herausgegeben und bearbeitet von R. Friedrich, B. Hamm und A. Puchta. 2000

79. MANETSCH, S.M. *Theodore Beza and the Quest for Peace in France, 1572-1598*. 2000

80. GODMAN, P. *The Saint as Censor*. Robert Bellarmine between Inquisition and Index. 2000

81. SCRIBNER, R.W. *Religion and Culture in Germany (1400-1800)*. Ed. L. Roper. 2001

82. KOOI, C. *Liberty and Religion*. Church and State in Leiden's Reformation, 1572-1620. 2000

83. BUCER, M. *Opera Latina*. Vol. V. Defensio adversus axioma catholicum id est criminationem R.P. Roberti Episcopi Abrincensis (1534). Ed. W.I.P. Hazlett. 2000

84. BOER, W. DE. *The Conquest of the Soul*. Confession, Discipline, and Public Order in Counter-Reformation Milan. 2001

85. EHRSTINE, G. *Theater, culture, and community in Reformation Bern, 1523-1555*. 2001

86. CATTERALL, D. *Community Without Borders*. Scot Migrants and the Changing Face of Power in the Dutch Republic, c. 1600-1700. 2002

87. BOWD, S.D. *Reform Before the Reformation*. Vincenzo Querini and the Religious Renaissance in Italy. 2002

88. PELC, M. *Illustrium Imagines*. Das Porträtbuch der Renaissance. 2002

89. SAAK, E.L. *High Way to Heaven*. The Augustinian Platform between Reform and Reformation, 1292-1524. 2002

90. WITTNEBEN, E.L. *Bonagratia von Bergamo*, Franziskanerjurist und Wortführer seines Ordens im Streit mit Papst Johannes XXII. 2003

91. ZIKA, C. *Exorcising our Demons*, Magic, Witchcraft and Visual Culture in Early Modern Europe. 2002

92. MATTOX, M.L. *"Defender of the Most Holy Matriarchs"*, Martin Luther's Interpretation of the Women of Genesis in the *Enarrationes in Genesin*, 1535-45. 2003

93. LANGHOLM, O. *The Merchant in the Confessional*, Trade and Price in the Pre-Reformation Penitential Handbooks. 2003

94. BACKUS, I. *Historical Method and Confessional Identity in the Era of the Reformation (1378-1615)*. 2003

95. FOGGIE, J.P. *Renaissance Religion in Urban Scotland*. The Dominican Order, 1450-1560. 2003

96. LÖWE, J.A. *Richard Smyth and the Language of Orthodoxy*. Re-imagining Tudor Catholic Polemicism. 2003

97. HERWAARDEN, J. VAN. *Between Saint James and Erasmus*. Studies in Late-Medieval Religious Life: Devotion and Pilgrimage in The Netherlands. 2003

98. PETRY, Y. *Gender, Kabbalah and the Reformation*. The Mystical Theology of Guillaume Postel (1510–1581). 2004

99. EISERMANN, F., SCHLOTHEUBER, E. und HONEMANN, V. *Studien und Texte zur literarischen und materiellen Kultur der Frauenklöster im späten Mittelalter.* Ergebnisse eines Arbeitsgesprächs in der Herzog August Bibliothek Wolfenbüttel, 24.-26. Febr. 1999. 2004

100. WITCOMBE, C.L.C.E. *Copyright in the Renaissance.* Prints and the *Privilegio* in Sixteenth-Century Venice and Rome. 2004

101. BUCER, M. *Briefwechsel/Correspondance.* Band V (September 1530-Mai 1531). Herausgegeben und bearbeitet von R. Friedrich, B. Hamm, A. Puchta und R. Liebenberg. 2004

102. MALONE, C.M. *Façade as Spectacle: Ritual and Ideology at Wells Cathedral.* 2004

103. KAUFHOLD, M. (ed.) *Politische Reflexion in der Welt des späten Mittelalters / Political Thought in the Age of Scholasticism.* Essays in Honour of Jürgen Miethke. 2004

104. BLICK, S. and TEKIPPE, R. (eds.). *Art and Architecture of Late Medieval Pilgrimage in Northern Europe and the British Isles.* 2004

105. PASCOE, L.B., S.J. *Church and Reform: Bishops, Theologians, and Canon Lawyers in the Thought of Pierre d'Ailly (1351-1420).* 2005

106. SCOTT, T. *Town, Country, and Regions in Reformation Germany.* 2005